"*Paul and the Gift* is one of the more i
many years. It reopens the question of
of Paul's time and carefully redescribes
in Jesus Christ."

"The importance of this book to Pauline scholarship cannot be overestimated, for it forges new trajectories in thinking, teaching, and 'theologizing' about grace."

— *Theology Today*

"What else can possibly be said about 'grace' in the letters of Paul? Quite a lot, as it turns out. John Barclay reveals just how little we have grasped the multitude of ways in which grace — 'the gift' — was parsed among Paul's contemporaries, including questions of reciprocity and the worth of recipients. The resulting bold proposal for reorienting Pauline theology is a landmark in New Testament scholarship. A must-have, must-read, must-ponder book!"

— **Beverly Roberts Gaventa**
Baylor University

"In this exceptional book, John Barclay places Paul in the context of Jewish and Greco-Roman ideas about divine and human giving, arguing that — contrary to popular belief — Paul does *not* teach that grace is 'free' or 'unconditional.' Rather, divine grace is *incongruous*, given without regard for conventional criteria of status and worth, thereby questioning the legitimacy of those criteria. This hermeneutically sophisticated work opens up a range of new perspectives on key themes of Pauline theology, beyond the entrenched positions that so often characterize the debate in this area."

— **Francis Watson**
Durham University

"Barclay has provided New Testament scholarship with a gift whose impact can hardly be overestimated. . . . You need not be a prophet to predict that this study will serve the efforts of understanding Paul's theology as a bright and far-shining lighthouse for many years."

— **Michael Wolter**
University of Bonn

"This brilliant book is a substantial and methodological tour de force. Barclay's fascinating study complicates the notion of 'grace' in Paul's thinking in terms of 'gift' primarily by threading together insights drawn from anthropological, ancient Jewish and Greco-Roman, and exegetical realms of analysis. . . . A deeply impressive study by a superb scholar from whom all will learn a great deal. Indeed, future Pauline scholars are now significantly indebted to Barclay for this superabundant scholarly gift."

— **Douglas A. Campbell**
Duke Divinity School

"We have come to expect superb work from John Barclay, but that should not lessen our appreciation when it appears! . . . Barclay's magisterial analysis results in a powerful and compelling new understanding of Paul's theology of grace that cuts across traditional debates and disciplinary categorizations, remaps Paul's location among his fellow Jews, and manages to be both historically sensitive and theologically rich."

— **David G. Horrell**
University of Exeter

"John Barclay's *Paul and the Gift* has the singular virtue of making seem self-evident a point missed in the extensive literature spawned by Sanders's *Paul and Palestinian Judaism*: modern understandings of grace — shaped by Paul — have prevented us from seeing aright the real but diverse ways in which grace functioned in Jewish literature of the Second Temple period. . . . This book as a whole represents a watershed in Pauline studies."

— **Stephen Westerholm**
McMaster University

"Reading Barclay's *Paul and the Gift* is a gripping and humbling experience. Gripping because it has a clear, original thesis that is pursued lucidly and tenaciously. Humbling because Barclay shows such a remarkable range of expertise across anthropology, Jewish literature, and the Pauline epistles, and exudes here both theoretical sophistication and sound exegetical good sense. If you are at all interested in Paul, block out two days, switch off your electronic devices, and digest this book."

— **Simon Gathercole**
University of Cambridge

Paul and the Gift

John M. G. Barclay

William B. Eerdmans Publishing Company
Grand Rapids, Michigan

Wm. B. Eerdmans Publishing Co.
2140 Oak Industrial Drive N.E., Grand Rapids, Michigan 49505
www.eerdmans.com

Hardcover edition 2015
Paperback edition 2017
Printed in the United States of America

26 25 24 23 22 21 20 19 18 17 2 3 4 5 6 7 8 9 10 11

Library of Congress Cataloging-in-Publication Data

Barclay, John M. G.
Paul and the gift / John M.G. Barclay.
pages cm
Includes bibliographical references and index.
ISBN 978-0-8028-7532-7 (pbk.: alk. paper)
1. Bible. Epistles of Paul — Theology.
2. Grace (Theology) — Biblical teaching. I. Title.

BS2655.G65B37 2015
227'.06 — dc23

2015018062

For John Riches

Contents

Preface

This book has been at least ten years in the making, the last four devoted to writing. Since I have learned a lot about gifts, I am acutely aware of the thanks I owe to the many people who have encouraged, clarified, and supported this project in numerous ways. My Durham colleagues — especially Francis Watson, Lutz Doering, Jane Heath, Dorothee Bertschmann, Stephen Barton, Bill Telford, Walter Moberly, and Robert Hayward — have each given encouragement and support, and the Department of Theology and Religion at Durham University generously urged me not to rush a book that took longer than expected. Several doctoral students at Durham have been to varying degrees co-workers in this exploration, and have given friendship, advice, and research support, including Gary Griffith, Debbie Watson, Dean Pinter, Ben Blackwell, Kyle Wells, John Goodrich, Susan Mathew, Wesley Hill, Jeanette Hagen, and David Briones. Three others — Matthew Scott, Jonathan Linebaugh, and Orrey McFarland — have made particularly significant contributions, both to me personally and to the analysis of texts and ideas: I could not count the times we have chewed over this project, in person and by email, both during their doctoral research and afterwards, and their input has always been of immense value. The research foundations were laid during a period of leave in Dunedin, New Zealand, in 2009-10, and I remain ever grateful for the hospitality of Paul Trebilco and of the Department of Theology and Religion at the University of Otago, where I also had the privilege of offering the De Carle Lectures in 2010. Since then I have been fortunate to receive feedback and constructive criticism on many elements of this book in lectures, seminars, and conference papers in Melbourne, Sydney, Vancouver, Chicago, Singapore, Copenhagen, Berne, Heidelberg, Groningen, and several universities in the UK. Highlights have included the Hooker Lectures at McMaster University (Hamilton, Ontario), the annual lecture for the International Centre for Biblical Interpretation (University of Gloucestershire), the inaugural lecture at the Centre for the Social-Scientific Study of the Bible (St. Mary's University, London), the Nils Dahl Lecture (Oslo University), and the Ethel Wood Lecture (King's College, London). In each case, the audience has been kind enough to pose challenging questions and to point me in fruitful directions, only some of which I have so far been able to pursue. As this project grew, I realized that there are dimensions of gift-giving in Paul that I would not be able to cover in this book, at the human level of gift-reciprocity. I hope to return to these in a subsequent volume.

I record my gratitude to the British Academy, who funded a year of research leave (2010-11, on the BARDA scheme), without which this project would not have got beyond its initial stage. Many friends around the world have offered wisdom and support along this lengthy journey, among whom I am especially grateful to Susan Eastman, Beverly Gaventa, Barry Matlock, Stephen Chester, Lou Martyn, Stephen Westerholm, Troels Engberg-Pedersen (who suggested my title), and Tom Wright (whose *Paul and the Faithfulness of God* appeared too late for interaction here). Diana, my wife, has put up with my preoccupation with this book well beyond what was reasonable, and for this, as for so much else, I offer my deep and heartfelt thanks.

Michael Thomson and his colleagues at Eerdmans have waited patiently for a long-delayed book, and I am very grateful for their commitment to this project from the start. At the final stages I have been extremely fortunate to have Orrey McFarland as editor of my manuscript. He has saved me from many errors (all that remain are, of course, my responsibility), while his extensive knowledge of the subject has made him a superb dialogue partner over many years. His editorial labor on the text and the bibliography has been immense, and I am greatly indebted to him for his care and attention to detail. Finally, Tavis Bohlinger was enormously helpful in the labor of proofreading and indexing, for which I am hugely grateful.

I dedicate this book to John Riches, who for nearly two decades was my colleague in New Testament at Glasgow University and, more than that, became a mentor and friend, one who inspired me to explore the history of reception of Paul and to tease out what it was that made Paul's letters so fertile for the Christian tradition.

EASTER 2015

Abbreviations

Abbreviations of primary and secondary sources follow the *SBL Handbook of Style,* with the addition of the following:

CO	*Ioannis Calvini Opera quae supersunt omnia* (Brunsvigae: C. A. Schwetschke, 1863-1900)
DK	*Die Fragmenta der Vorsokratiker,* ed. H. Diels and W. Kranz (Berlin: Weidmann, 1951-52)
LW	*Luther's Works,* 55 vols., ed. J. Pelikan and H. L. Lehmann (St. Louis: Concordia; Philadelphia: Fortress Press, 1955-1986)
WA	*Dr. Martin Luthers Werke,* 69 vols. (Weimar: Böhlau, 1883-1993)

Prologue

Paul is famous for speaking of Christ with the language of gift. "Thanks be to God for his inexpressible gift" (2 Cor 9:15), he exclaims, referring to the life, death, and resurrection of Christ. The giver of the gift can equally be figured as Christ himself, who "gave himself for our sins to deliver us from the present evil age" (Gal 1:4). A rich variety of gift-terms pepper Paul's discourse; among them χάρις — a common Greek word for gift or favor — is traditionally translated (via the Latin *gratia*) as "grace." "You know the grace (χάρις) of our Lord Jesus Christ," Paul reminds the Corinthians (2 Cor 8:9); "I do not reject the grace of God" (Gal 2:21). Paul's converts have experienced being "called in grace" (Gal 1:6), and so has he himself (Gal 1:15; cf. 1 Cor 15:9-10). Under the influence of Paul, the language of gift and grace has become central to the Christian theological tradition. Radical readings of this Pauline motif — by Augustine, Luther, Calvin, and Barth, to name some of the most famous — have caused significant shifts in the history of Christian theology. Within Christian piety, the language of grace has become embedded in prayers and hymns, as a means of recognizing God's gratuitous initiative toward inadequate or worthless human recipients. Many individual believers connect most deeply with Paul's theology in their personal celebration of "amazing grace."

Paul is also well known as an apostle to the Gentiles, the missionary theologian who preached the "good news" to Gentiles in the cities of the Roman world and developed a controversial policy whereby Gentile converts were not required to adopt Jewish customs such as male circumcision or kosher food-laws. Scholars now commonly note that Paul's theology — including his theology of justification and his famous antithesis between "faith in Christ" and "works of the law" — is best understood as articulated in and for this Gentile mission. The creation of new communities of Jews and Gentiles in Christ was central to Paul's purpose and to his understanding of history, since he identified here the fulfillment of God's promises to Abraham and a sign of hope for Israel.

Do these two aspects of Paul — his theology of grace and his establishment of churches that bridged the division between Jews and non-Jews — belong together? Does his theology of grace accompany his social practice in the formation of innovative communities? Is Paul's theology, in its original context, as much about social as individual transformation, and does the gift of God in Christ ground the creation of communities capable of challenging taken-for-granted norms?

In the Christian tradition, Paul's theology of grace has often been interpreted as the antithesis of Judaism, as if by Paul's day Judaism had corrupted its biblical theology of grace with a soteriology of "works-righteousness" and reward. Paul's language, laden with nuances derived from internal Christian disputes, has been conscripted to differentiate Christianity from Judaism on these terms, and to diminish the latter. On this reading, Paul was the premier theologian of grace who resisted the "legalism" of "late" Judaism, a works-based religion that amounted to auto-salvation. In recent decades this negative image of Judaism has been challenged with a counter-image, presenting Judaism as a "religion of grace." Students of Judaism have traced grace everywhere in Second Temple literature, as the foundation of Israel's covenant relationship with God and the frame within which the Torah was observed. Thus, for many, Paul says nothing remarkable about grace, and if his theology departs in any respect from his Jewish tradition, this has little if anything to do with grace.

But if "grace" is everywhere in Second Temple Judaism — in the celebration of divine beneficence, goodness, and mercy — is it everywhere the same? Are Jewish configurations of this topic uniform, or is the map of Jewish theology over-simplified if labelled "a religion of grace"? Might there be various construals of divine mercy and goodness, and of their relationship to justice? Is there evidence for diversity, even debate, regarding the generosity of God, its expressions, its beneficiaries, and its patterns of distribution? If so, where should Paul be placed within this Jewish diversity?

More fundamentally, what do we mean by "grace"? In the Christian tradition, the nature of "grace" has been the subject of intense controversy and polemical redefinition; the term comes to us already over-determined by particular connotations. It is the strategy of this book to place the relevant terms and concepts, both those of Paul and those of his fellow Jews, within the category of "gift." This is not to say that all the vocabulary we take into our purview is best *translated* as "gift": in some cases, even for χάρις, that is manifestly not the case. It is rather to claim that the conceptual field we are studying, with its varied terminology, is best captured by the anthropological category of gift. This category is broad, but covers a sphere of voluntary, personal relations that are characterized by goodwill in the giving of some benefit or favor and that elicit some form of reciprocal return that is both voluntary and necessary for the continuation of the relationship. Hence, our study is confined to no single term (and certainly not to χάρις); its focus is on concepts, not words. Among other things, by approaching this topic through the category of gift we hope to gain some analytical distance from the specific theological meanings of "grace," even where we continue to use that term.

Ever since Mauss's anthropological classic "Essai sur le Don," the notion of gift as a form of reciprocity that is basic to society has fascinated anthropologists and historians, who have used this category to analyze social structures and their changes over time.[1] The deployment of the concept by Derrida has occasioned a flurry of philosophical treatments of this topic, ranging from phenomenology to economics, while theologians have embraced "gift" as a framework for exploring a large range of theological topics.[2] Concepts of "gift" have been used to chart intellectual and social trends over the centuries down to the present peculiarities of Western, postmodern capitalism.[3] It is important to be conscious of this history, not least so as to free ourselves from modern assumptions regarding the "free" gift, but the focus of attention here will be the historical meanings of gift at the time of Paul and his Jewish contemporaries. A number of recent books have made valuable contributions to this enterprise, placing Paul's theology and practice of "grace" in the context of gifts and benefactions in the Greco-Roman world.[4] A contextual approach such as this

1. M. Mauss, "Essai sur le Don: Forme et Raison de l'Échange dans les Sociétés Archaïques," in *Sociologie et Anthropologie* (Paris: Presses Universitaires de France, 1950), 145-279 (first published in 1925). Translated into English as M. Mauss, *The Gift*, trans. W. D. Hall (London: Routledge, 1990). Famous historical studies of the gift include N. Zemon Davis, *The Gift in Sixteenth-Century France* (Oxford: Oxford University Press, 2000). For detail on the anthropology and history of gift, see chapter 1, below.

2. J. Derrida, *Given Time*, vol. 1: *Counterfeit Money*, trans. P. Kamuf (Chicago: University of Chicago Press, 1992). Cf. J.-L. Marion, *Being Given: Towards a Phenomenology of Givenness*, trans. J. L. Kosky (Stanford: Stanford University Press, 1997); K. Tanner, *Economy of Grace* (Minneapolis: Fortress Press, 2005). The theology of Milbank has recently been centered on this theme; see, e.g., J. Milbank, *Being Reconciled: Ontology and Pardon* (London: Routledge, 2003).

3. A recent overview, broad but well informed, is provided by P. J. Leithart, *Gratitude: An Intellectual History* (Waco: Baylor University Press, 2014).

4. E.g., S. Joubert, *Paul as Benefactor: Reciprocity, Strategy, and Theological Reflection in Paul's Collection* (Tübingen: Mohr Siebeck, 2000); J. R. Harrison, *Paul's Language of Grace in Its Graeco-Roman Context* (Tübingen: Mohr Siebeck, 2003). See further below, 3.7.3.

seems the most promising addition to the long history of the scholarly study of "grace" in Paul and his contemporaries.[5]

An anthropological approach reveals how complex and multi-faceted is the business of gift-giving and helps to separate facets of "grace" that are traditionally run together. Studies of grace have directed their attention sometimes to the character of the giver, sometimes to the nature of the gift, and sometimes to the relationship between the giver and the recipient. Is God "gracious" in being purely generous, to the exclusion of judgment or wrath? Is grace a power, a decision, a gift, or some combination of these three? Is it to be found in creation, or in historical events, or in divine predestination before all time? Is grace "free" in its abundance, or in its application to worthy and unworthy alike, or in not requiring a return? The more we probe, the greater the complexity of the topic.

The book before you is large, but even so has limits. The title, *Paul and the Gift,* has a double nuance. It gestures toward Mauss and thus toward the framing of our discussion within the anthropology of gift. But it indicates also that our primary focus will be on *divine* gift-giving, which for Paul is focused and fulfilled in the gift of Christ (*the* gift). There are many aspects of gift-giving on the human level that are significant for Paul but not investigated here: the formation of community through reciprocity, the Jerusalem collection, the gifts of the Spirit, and the mutuality of gift and need in the body of Christ. All of these were intended to be part of this project, but will have to wait for a subsequent book. What lies before you is a reconsideration of "grace" within the anthropology and history of gift, a study of Jewish construals of divine beneficence in the Second Temple period, and, within that context, a new appraisal of Paul's theology of the Christ-event as gift, as it comes to expression in Galatians and Romans.

The first part of this book sets the foundation for the rest, and those inclined to skim through other parts of the volume are encouraged to read at least chapters 1 and 2. The first chapter frames our topic in the anthropology of gift and in the historical realities of gift-reciprocity in the Greco-Roman (including the Jewish) world. Chapter 2 then provides some crucial analytical tools, introducing the notion of a "perfection" (the drawing out of a concept to an end-of-the-line extreme) and suggesting *six* ways in which gift-giving has

5. Classics in this field include G. P. Wetter, *Charis: Ein Beitrag zur Geschichte des ältesten Christentums* (Leipzig: Hinrichs, 1913); J. Moffatt, *Grace in the New Testament* (London: Hodder and Stoughton, 1931); and J. Wobbe, *Der Charis-Gedanke bei Paulus* (Münster: Aschendorff, 1932). More recent treatments include D. Zeller, *Charis bei Philon und Paulus* (Stuttgart: Katholisches Bibelwerk, 1990), and B. Eastman, *The Significance of Grace in the Letters of Paul* (New York: Peter Lang, 1999).

been "perfected," particularly with reference to God. (Ideally, of course, there should have been seven.) The long chapter 3 is also foundational. It charts a number of points in the history of reception of Paul that continue to shape our understanding of the topic of grace. It is crucial to attempt to understand these figures, not least at a time when dismissive and poorly informed comments on Augustine and Luther have gained currency in New Testament scholarship.[6] Disaggregating the six perfections of grace proves to be helpful in understanding the history of reception of Paul, explaining why interpreters who equally emphasize grace interpret it in different and even contradictory ways.

The second part of this volume, on divine gift in Second Temple Judaism, provides an alternative to a central thesis of Sanders's famous *Paul and Palestinian Judaism.*[7] It selects five Jewish texts in which divine beneficence is a central theme and analyzes their theologies in depth. What emerges is not uniformity but diversity, of a type very different from Sanders's image of "covenantal nomism," a diversity again made visible by disaggregating the differing perfections of grace. Readers primarily interested in Paul may want to go first to the concluding chapter of this part (chapter 10), but I hope that they will be sufficiently intrigued to read at least some of these studies of Jewish texts that are important in their own right. I also hope that scholars of Second Temple Judaism will find here readings that further the scholarly analysis of some fascinating texts.

Part III (chapters 11-14) offers a reading of Galatians from the perspective of Paul's theology of grace. Of course, not every part of this letter can be discussed in detail, but I offer an integrated reading of its theological logic in a fashion that goes beyond both the Augustinian-Reformation tradition of interpretation and the "new perspective on Paul." In comparison with my earlier work on Galatians,[8] I here advance a fuller and perhaps more convincing interpretation of a letter that through the work of Martyn, Dunn, and others has become a storm-center of Pauline scholarship.

The final part of the book (chapters 15-17) consists of a reading of Romans, necessarily also selective but intended to establish the coherence of a letter that is often reduced to its parts; it deliberately climaxes in a discussion of Romans 9–11, which the majority of scholars now consider central to the letter, but many have judged to be self-contradictory. A number of similarities

6. My intent is similar to that of S. Westerholm, *Perspectives Old and New on Paul: The "Lutheran" Paul and His Critics* (Grand Rapids: Eerdmans, 2004), though my focus is primarily on the topic of grace.

7. E. P. Sanders, *Paul and Palestinian Judaism* (London: SCM Press, 1977).

8. J. M. G. Barclay, *Obeying the Truth: A Study of Paul's Ethics in Galatians* (Edinburgh: T&T Clark, 1988).

and differences between Romans and Galatians appear in this reading. Readers are encouraged to read the whole of this part as a single entity, even if their primary interest is in one or another segment of the letter.

The conclusions draw the threads of this volume together by identifying its key contributions in a number of areas. Readers who wish to know where this lengthy journey is heading are welcome to start there and to work backwards into the meat of the book. Alternatively, its theses can be summarized in shortened form as follows:

1. "Grace" is a multi-faceted concept best approached through the category of gift. It is susceptible to "perfection" (conceptual extension) in a number of different ways, which do not constitute a unified package. Some who discuss this theme will maximize the superabundance, the priority, or the efficacy of grace, and others its incongruity with the worth of the recipients (as gift to the unworthy). Others again will urge the singularity of grace (that God is nothing but gracious), and some that God's gifts are given "with no strings attached." These are not better or worse interpretations of grace, just different, and it is perfectly possible to speak of grace without defining it, for instance, as gift to the unworthy. These perfections have been variously deployed in the history of reception of Paul, though some are better supported than others by the Pauline texts themselves. Much in Jewish interpretations of grace, and in the history of interpretation of Paul, can be clarified by distinguishing between these six perfections.
2. Grace is everywhere in Second Temple Judaism but not everywhere the same. Instead of uniformity, a careful examination of the texts indicates diversity in their representations of divine beneficence; they differ, for instance, on whether God's mercy is properly applied without regard to worth. Paul stands in the midst of this diversity. His theology of grace does not stand in antithesis to Judaism, but neither is there a common Jewish view with which it wholly coincides.
3. Paul's theology of grace characteristically perfects the *incongruity* of the Christ-gift, given without regard to worth. This theology is articulated within and for Paul's Gentile mission, and grounds the formation of innovative communities that crossed ethnic and other boundaries. This incongruous gift bypasses and thus subverts pre-constituted systems of worth. It disregards previous forms of symbolic capital and thus enables the creation of new communities whose norms are reset by the Christ-gift itself. Grace took its meaning in and from Paul's experience and social practice: the nature of the gift was embodied and clarified in novel social

> experiments. In the subsequent interpretation of Paul, within an established Christian tradition, this motif has played a number of other roles, but has generally shifted from undermining the believers' previous criteria of worth to undercutting their self-reliance in attaining to Christian norms or their understanding of this effort as necessary for salvation.

I hope that the reading of Paul offered here will prove to be historically plausible, exegetically responsible, theologically informed, and (as had better be declared up front) hermeneutically useful. No one reads from nowhere, and this reading of the evidence, like every other, has its own context and interests. It springs from the conviction that a respectful, though not uncritical, reading of Paul contains resources that are theologically important today, though in ways that stretch beyond the usual interpretative frameworks. Paul has the capacity to think about communities and their social identities, and the ability to reset their norms around the Christ-event by a theology of grace that suspends other criteria of worth; such tools may prove valuable for churches that are required to rethink their identity and social location in a pluralist or secularizing context. By a strange paradox, Paul may be most significant today when he is most carefully re-situated in his own original context.

PART I

The Multiple Meanings of Gift and Grace

CHAPTER 1

The Anthropology and History of the Gift

"Gift" is neither a single phenomenon nor a stable category. A great variety of objects, acts, and relationships have been regarded as "gifts" in different cultures and at different times. Likewise, in many cultures, the definition of "gift" (in distinction from other forms of exchange) has altered over time. If Paul and his contemporaries spoke about divine and human benevolence using the language of "gift," we need to be sure that we know what is implied in the evocation of such terms, and what is not. A modern Western dictionary tells us that "gift" means something handed over "gratuitously, for nothing."[1] But even the slightest knowledge of antiquity would inform us that gifts were given with strong expectations of return — indeed, precisely in order to elicit a return and thus to create or enhance social solidarity. Those of us brought up in the modern West are likely to be surprised (even shocked) by the gift practices of non-Western cultures today. We should expect a similar or even greater surprise when we encounter ancient practices and opinions.

In this chapter I hope to achieve three ends: first, to use the rich discussion of "the gift" in the field of anthropology in order to raise appropriate questions about the operation of gifts in contexts outside and before modern Western culture (1.1); second, to outline the role of gifts or benefactions in the Greco-Roman world contemporary to Paul (1.2); and third, to trace what has happened to notions of "gift" in Western modernity, in order to alert us to unconscious assumptions liable to distort our reading of first-century practices and texts (1.3). (When in a subsequent chapter [3] we examine significant moments in the interpretation of Paul on "grace," it may prove possible to

1. *Oxford English Dictionary,* s.v. gift. Cf. A. Rey et al., eds., *Dictionnaire historique de la langue française,* 2 vols. (Paris: Dictionnaire Le Robert, 1992), s.v. don: "l'action d'abandonner gratuitement qqch. à qqn."

identify correlations between shifts in the reception of Pauline theology and changes in conceptions of the gift.) By pursuing these three ends, we begin to interrogate what is meant by "gift" and "grace" and to lay both conceptual and historical foundations for the investigations to follow in the rest of this book.

1.1. The Gift in Anthropological Perspective

1.1.1. Mauss and "the Gift"

Marcel Mauss's famous "Essai sur le Don" (1925) is justly regarded as the seminal treatment of our topic, spawning a vast array of anthropological research and academic debate in subsequent decades.[2] In this uneven but immensely suggestive essay, Mauss harvested the research of ethnographers working at various points around the Pacific Rim (on the western seaboard of America and Canada; in Melanesia; and in the Polynesian islands, including the Maori population of Aotearoa/New Zealand), supplementing this with his own encyclopedic knowledge of ancient languages and texts in the Indo-European tradition. Reconfiguring the sociological tradition of Durkheim (his uncle), Mauss took care to use detailed and historically specific ethnographic evidence, but constructed from it a synthetic hypothesis about a core characteristic of archaic societies, which he called "le régime du don" or "le système des dons échangés."[3] His analysis was innovative in interpreting society as a "totality," in all its interconnected and correlative parts; it was also powerful in suggesting how, in archaic societies, the gift-system was basic to, and the glue between, all the realms which modernity has distinguished — economics, law, kinship, religion, aesthetics, ritual, and politics.[4] Although the essay title speaks of "le Don," the term Mauss preferred was the old-fashioned French "prestations" (with a meaning something like "obligatory community services"): the "gift"

2. The essay was originally published in *Année Sociologique* (marked 1923-24, but published in 1925); it is best accessed in the 1950 collection of Mauss's works: M. Mauss, "Essai sur le Don: Forme et Raison de l'Échange dans les sociétés Archaïques," in *Sociologie et Anthropologie* (Paris: Presses Universitaires de France, 1950), pp. 145-279. The best complete English translation is by W. D. Halls: M. Mauss, *The Gift* (London: Routledge, 1990).

3. Mauss, "Essai sur le Don," pp. 194, 197. For Mauss's intellectual context and a reappraisal of his work, see W. James and N. J. Allen, eds., *Marcel Mauss: A Centenary Tribute* (New York: Berghahn Books, 1998); K. Hart, "Marcel Mauss: In Pursuit of the Whole. A Review Essay," *Comparative Studies in Society and History* 49 (2007): 473-85.

4. Mauss, *The Gift*, pp. 49, 101-2. On Mauss's notion of "total social facts," see A. Gofman, "A Vague but Suggestive Concept: The 'Total Social Fact,'" in James and Allen, eds., *Marcel Mauss*, pp. 63-70.

being discussed is not confined to objects (or people) passed from one hand to another, but includes a large range of favors and services, symbolic and material, performed by one party for another. Mauss's thesis is that in such societies the exchange of such "prestations" constitutes a unifying social choreography "under different forms and for reasons different from those with which we are familiar."[5]

Mauss identified three key elements in "l'institution de la prestation totale": the obligation to give, the obligation to receive, and the obligation to return.[6] Each of these interdependent moves carries the force of social necessity, since they constitute the most important bonds of society (and of relations between humans and gods). Families and groups (tribes) are tied together internally and externally by the offering and receiving of gifts — an unwillingness to receive is a sign of hostility or mistrust. Since "things are never completely detached from those carrying out the exchange," "the mutual ties and alliance that they establish are comparatively indissoluble."[7] Such bonds may be the chief source of cohesion in a gift-centered culture, although their very significance is also often the occasion for rivalry and competition. Mauss was fascinated by the extremes of "agonistic" gift-giving in the "potlatch," the enormous disposal (even destruction) of wealth that had been reported (and perhaps misunderstood) by ethnographers among the First Nations of the North American western seaboard.[8] As he rightly noted, generosity in such contexts is a form of power — a display of wealth that challenges the honor of others by requiring them to reciprocate with an even greater return. He noted how in many contexts gift-giving operates as a substitute for war — soothing or sublimating hostility with gifts that constitute either challenge or riposte.[9] In such a system, how and to whom one gives matters greatly. A gift given inappropriately or received in the wrong spirit can create resentment, even hostility (as Mauss noted, the word *Gift* in German can mean "poison").[10] And, given the importance of the tie created by gifts, the choice of recipient is strategic. Commenting on the *kula* gifts circulated around the Trobriand Islands, Mauss

5. Mauss, *The Gift*, p. 42.

6. Mauss, *The Gift*, pp. 16-17, 50-55.

7. Mauss, *The Gift*, p. 42. Tracing a survival of this principle in Brahmin society, Mauss notes that "the gift is therefore at one and the same time what should be done, what should be received, and yet what is dangerous to take. This is because the thing that is given itself forges a bilateral, irrevocable bond, above all when it consists of food" (*The Gift*, p. 76).

8. Mauss, *The Gift*, pp. 6-9.

9. Mauss, *The Gift*, pp. 47-48, 52-53, 95-96.

10. His essay on this topic is translated in A. D. Schrift, ed., *The Logic of the Gift: Toward an Ethic of Generosity* (London: Routledge, 1997), pp. 28-32.

notes: "They seek out the best possible partner in the opposing tribe. The affair is a serious matter, for the association one attempts to create establishes a kind of clan link between the partners."[11] If there is a danger in omitting (and therefore offending) powerful people from the circle of recipients of one's gift,[12] there is also a danger in including unfitting recipients, who would be unable to make a return, or from whom one would not wish to receive it.[13]

Mauss's essay specifically sets out to explain the obligation to *return* a gift. Whence comes the pressure (real even if not enforceable in law) for the gift to be reciprocated to an equal if not greater value?[14] Why is it that a gift is received "with a burden attached"?[15] His answer is that the thing or service given is not detachable from the person who gives it, and that the tie with the donor can only be acknowledged by a counter-gift. In this connection, he famously (and controversially) made appeal to a report from a Maori informant, who spoke of the *hau* of the gift that had to return to the giver.[16] Taking this to refer to the "spirit" inhabiting the gift, Mauss concluded that

> one must give back to another person what is really part and parcel of his nature and substance, because to accept something from someone is to accept some part of his spiritual essence, his soul. . . . The thing given is not inactive. Invested with life, often possessing individuality, it seeks to return to what Hertz called its "place of origin" or to produce, on behalf of the clan and the native soil from which it sprang, an equivalent to replace it.[17]

Elsewhere, Mauss speaks of the social forces obliging a return — the loss of honor that would result from failure to reciprocate[18] or the general need to maintain a profitable alliance with the donor.[19] But he is generally concerned to emphasize the fact that the gifts themselves were not simply objects, that is,

11. Mauss, *The Gift*, pp. 35-36.

12. Mauss, *The Gift*, pp. 50-51.

13. Mauss, *The Gift*, p. 149 n. 175.

14. In the archaic societies Mauss was examining, there is no distinguishable sphere of "law," and so no possible distinction between what is morally and legally obliged. Testart's criticism of Mauss for failing to distinguish between what is legally and socially obligatory illustrates well the misunderstanding of gift that arises from adopting the assumptions of modernity: A. Testart, "Uncertainties of the 'Obligation to Reciprocate': A Critique of Mauss," in James and Allen, eds., *Marcel Mauss*, pp. 97-110.

15. Mauss, *The Gift*, p. 53.

16. Mauss, *The Gift*, pp. 13-16.

17. Mauss, *The Gift*, p. 16; "Essai sur le Don," p. 161.

18. Mauss, *The Gift*, p. 54.

19. Mauss, *The Gift*, p. 94.

the passive, depersonalized things that are passed from one person to another; rather, they "had a personality and an inherent power."[20] The very distinction between property and persons, which is basic to Western legal systems at least since Roman times, is, he insists, absent from the archaic societies he is analyzing:[21] the gifts not only belong to people, they are invested with the personality of the donor.

Mauss thus observed that his analysis requires a mixing, or scrambling, of the categories and values that have become associated with "gifts" and their opposites in modern, Western culture. At the beginning of the essay, he speaks of gifts that are "apparently free and disinterested but nevertheless constrained and self-interested," as if they were part of a "polite fiction" and "social deceit."[22] But by the end, he suggests that, more fundamentally, our polarized categories need to be reassessed:

> These concepts of law and economics that it pleases us to contrast: liberty and obligation; liberality, generosity, and luxury, as against savings, interest, and utility — it would be good to put them into the melting pot once more. . . . This [Trobriand] notion is neither that of the free, purely gratuitous rendering of total services ["prestation"] nor that of production and exchange purely interested in what is useful. It is a sort of hybrid which flourished.[23]

In this connection, Mauss criticizes the representation of the Trobriand gift-system offered by Malinowski (his chief informant on the *kula* exchange). Malinowski had distinguished between various kinds of gifts, placing at one end of the spectrum what he considered "free" or "pure" gifts — gifts given "willingly" and "free of any counter-gift" — which he found operative between husbands and wives, and fathers and children.[24] As Mauss insists, this moral gradation of gifts is inapplicable and loaded with inappropriate assumptions: if, as Malinowski himself reported, husbands' gifts to wives are regarded in their culture as "a kind of salary for sexual services rendered," then that is what they were, an obligatory counter-gift that is not at all "free" or "pure" in a modern

20. Mauss, *The Gift*, p. 63.

21. Mauss, *The Gift*, pp. 61, 69.

22. Mauss, *The Gift*, p. 4.

23. Mauss, *The Gift*, p. 93; "Essai sur le Don," p. 267.

24. B. Malinowski, *Argonauts of the Western Pacific* (London: Routledge, 1922), pp. 177-80. He notes — but then discounts — the fact that "the natives" have a "very coarse" way of thinking of such gifts, as in fact not "free," but the repayment by the husband for the sexual favors of his wife, and for her production of sons.

sense.[25] In effect, Mauss insists that gifts can be both "voluntary" and "obliged," both "disinterested" and "self-interested," both "free" and "compulsory": if we find this confusing or nonsensical, the problem may lie with the categories that we have invented.

The boldness and fertility of Mauss's essay includes his suggestion that "the economy of gift-exchange" that he identified in archaic societies also lies at the root of Indo-European society, and can be traced in shadowy outline in the early texts and customs of Indian, German, and Roman cultures.[26] He thus suggests not an absolute contrast between different cultures of gift, but a *trajectory*, by which Western culture has evolved out of a common "total" system of gift into the differentiated domains and practices of today. In this regard, he suggests that "it is precisely the Romans and Greeks, who, perhaps following upon the Semites of the north and west, invented the distinction between personal and property law, separated sale from gift and exchange, isolated the moral obligation and contract, and in particular, conceived the difference that exists between rites, laws, and interests."[27] He does not altogether bemoan this "great revolution," but he notes the way it has led to a conceptual distinction between "free" gifts and obligatory exchange (in sales or contracts), as also between "disinterested" generosity and "utilitarian" or "interested" procedures of *quid pro quo*. The final chapter of the essay celebrates co-operative gift-relations as against the "cold" and "calculating" ethos of utilitarian individualism, contributing to political debates of the 1920s by showing that alternative systems of social relation have left traces even in twentieth-century Europe, and can be created anew.[28] In this way, Mauss indicated that the analysis of gift-relations could play a crucial role in revealing the structural relations operative within any society; he thus placed "gift" at the centre of subsequent anthropological analysis and debate.

There is much in Mauss's essay that is (as he acknowledged) incomplete and ambiguous, but also (and partly for that reason) much that has proved

25. Mauss, *The Gift*, pp. 93-94. Malinowski accordingly retracted his category of "pure gift" in a subsequent book (B. Malinowski, *Crime and Custom in Savage Society* [London: Kegan Paul, 1926], pp. 40-41). Nonetheless, some anthropologists have continued to speak as if "a gift is not a gift unless it is a free gift, i.e., involving no obligation on the part of the receiver," J. Pitt-Rivers, "Postscript: The Place of Grace in Anthropology," in J. G. Peristiany and J. Pitt-Rivers, eds., *Honor and Grace in Anthropology* (Cambridge: Cambridge University Press, 1992), pp. 215-46, at p. 233.

26. Mauss, *The Gift*, pp. 60-82.

27. Mauss, *The Gift*, p. 69, translation adapted.

28. On Mauss's political context and commitments, see M. Fournier, *Marcel Mauss* (Paris: Fayard, 1994).

fertile for future thought and research. It would be a mistake to use Mauss's analysis of archaic societies as a kind of "model," applicable to every relation of gift: as we have seen, he was acutely aware of cultural developments that have changed the role and even the understanding of "gifts" over time.[29] But his work generates fruitful questions for the analysis of gift-relations, their functions within society, their relation to other domains (if their reach is not comprehensive), and the values and power-dynamics with which they are loaded. By highlighting the role of gifts in the creation of social solidarity, and the patterns of obligation which they represent and induce, Mauss alerts us to aspects of gifts/benefactions in antiquity that will be important to explore. He simultaneously draws attention to the cultural relativity of modern assumptions about "gifts," which are liable to distort our perspective on the past.

1.1.2. The Anthropology of "Gift" Post-Mauss

The iconic status of Mauss's "Essai sur le Don" ensured that, in the extensive subsequent debates, it was both co-opted and criticized in the service of various agendas.[30] This fate was evident already in the way Lévi-Strauss presented Mauss as the forerunner of a structuralist analysis of culture: he took Mauss's three movements of gift (giving, receiving, and returning) to constitute a single structure of exchange, a system of reciprocal relations lying deep in the universal, but unconscious structures of the human mind.[31] Lévi-Strauss criticized the role Mauss had given to the Maori notion of *hau* (the spirit in the gift): such "native mystification" was not necessary to explain the obligation to return the gift, which was built into the very structure of gift-reciprocity.[32] However, Mauss's question about the obligation to return has continued to haunt debates about "the gift" for many decades. His interpretation of the Maori *hau* has been strongly disputed, and his appeal to the notion of a non-material presence of

29. Mauss specifically denies that he is offering a model: he sees his work as "really posing questions to historians and ethnographers, and putting forward subjects for enquiry rather than resolving a problem and giving a definitive answer" (*The Gift*, p. 100).

30. For the reception of Mauss's "Essai sur le Don," see L. Sigaud, "The Vicissitudes of *The Gift*," *Social Anthropology* 10 (2002): 335-58.

31. Lévi-Strauss's introduction to Mauss's work (for the 1950 collection of Mauss's essays) is available in translation (C. Lévi-Strauss, *Introduction to the Work of Marcel Mauss*, trans. F. Baker [London: Routledge & Kegan Paul, 1987]); the section on "Le Don" is reprinted in Schrift, *Logic of the Gift*, pp. 45-69.

32. Lévi-Strauss, *Work of Marcel Mauss*, pp. 45-60. Mauss's interpretation of the Maori statement on this matter had already come under criticism in R. Firth, *Primitive Economics of the New Zealand Maori* (Wellington: A. R. Shearer, 1929), pp. 393-432 (esp. pp. 420-21).

the giver in the gift has proved distasteful to those who would banish such ideas as the naïve objectification of social forces.[33]

Everyone is agreed that recipients of gifts *are* under a strong (though non-legal) obligation to make some return for a gift — even if only in gratitude. Is this in order to preserve honor, or out of ambition for some further gift (i.e., out of the self-interest of the recipient)? Does it represent the power of the donor, in some sense present in the gift, laying on the recipient the requirement to return?[34] It seems impossible to decide absolutely between these forms of explanation, and it may be best to conclude more generally that the return of the gift represents the desire to reproduce social relations: each party to the gift-relation is in some sense "produced" by the exchange between them, and social relations can only be maintained or reproduced in the continual motion of exchange.[35] In this sense, the counter-gift is rarely the end of the relationship, replacing an inequality with a stable equilibrium: it is liable to constitute, rather, a form of "giving-again," adding to the gift-relationship a continuing forward momentum.

Since Mauss, the analysis of such exchange relations has been further refined, as research has probed more deeply into a variety of traditional societies. Weiner brought to the fore the gender-dimension of gifts, and the vital but often unnoticed role of women in gift-relations, though her analysis of male exploitation was challenged by Strathern, who questioned her use of Western notions of identity and ownership.[36] The importance of honor or prestige has also been emphasized by a variety of researchers: if material gifts are returned in the form of honor, such "symbolic capital" should not be downplayed as

33. Sahlins contested the meaning of *hau* (M. Sahlins, *Stone Age Economics,* 2nd ed. [London: Routledge, 2004], pp. 149-84), which he took to be not the spirit in the gift, but the interest earned by it. The debate has continued to rumble, without clear resolution; see A. Weiner, *Inalienable Possessions: The Paradox of Keeping-while-Giving* (Berkeley: University of California Press, 1992), pp. 44-65; J. Parry, "*The Gift,* the Indian Gift and the 'Indian Gift,'" *Man* 21 (1986): 453-73, at pp. 464-66; M. Godelier, *The Enigma of the Gift,* trans. N. Scott (Chicago: University of Chicago Press, 1999), pp. 49-56.

34. For discussion, see, e.g., Sahlins, *Stone Age Economics,* and Godelier, *Enigma of the Gift* (who returns to something close to Mauss's notion of the presence of the giver in the gift).

35. For the reproduction of social relations, see Weiner, *Inalienable Possessions,* and M. Strathern, *The Gender of the Gift* (Berkeley: University of California Press, 1998).

36. See Strathern, *Gender of the Gift,* based on her own field research in Papua New Guinea, in reaction to A. Weiner, *Women of Value, Men of Renown: New Perspectives in Trobriand Exchange* (Austin: University of Texas Press, 1976). Strathern's sophisticated analysis suggests that in such societies a person does not possess a stable individual identity, but is composed of social relations (on an ongoing basis), such that identity does not inhere in a person or thing, but is the *outcome* of social interaction.

an insubstantial return, since the power that is entailed by the possession of honor may be precisely the purpose of the gift-giving. The power-dynamics of gift-giving, already recognized by Mauss, have indeed drawn much attention. Sahlins, for instance, noted the importance of the time delay between the gift and the return, and of the imprecision in the value of the gift: both keep the obligations of the recipient open-ended, and cement the power of the original donor.[37] Gift-giving is thus by no means always an innocent or even a friendly enterprise, but is easily manipulated by those in a position of power: as Sahlins cynically remarks, "everywhere in the world the indigenous category for exploitation is 'reciprocity.'"[38]

As Mauss had noted, there are some forms of exchange which are not "gift": he learned from Malinowski, for instance, that even in the Trobriand Islands there are forms of trade *(gimwali)* that are very different from the personalized and enduring relationships formed by *kula*-gifts.[39] Even gift exchange can take extremely diverse forms, and gifts can vary greatly in their value, in the personality they bear, their productivity, and the time gap between gift and return. In this connection, Sahlins helpfully charted the correlation between different kinds of exchange and the different types of people with whom that exchange is carried out. For immediate kin, or those in a closest relationship, he mapped forms of "generalized" (or "indefinite") reciprocity, where "the counter is not stipulated by time, quantity, or quality: the expectation of reciprocity is indefinite."[40] At a midpoint, there is "balanced reciprocity" or "transactions which stipulate returns of commensurate worth or utility within a finite and narrow period":[41] such, he suggests, are liable to occur between individuals or groups on friendly but less intimate terms. At the "unsociable extreme" he places "negative reciprocity," where, in a contest of opposed interests, each looks "to maximize utility at the other's expense."[42] The mapping is necessarily simplified, drawing from a wide range of ethnographic material, but the essential point is valid: different forms of exchange reflect, and create, different degrees of social proximity and thus different kinds of social relation. Not every gift-relation is the same, and not everyone is a desirable partner. Even a lavish giver is not indiscriminate: gifts are carefully placed, or refused, according to prior and desired relations, and even in societies strongly deter-

37. Sahlins, *Stone Age Economics*, pp. 206-8.

38. Sahlins, *Stone Age Economics*, p. 134.

39. See Mauss, *The Gift*, p. 28, on the "mere economic exchange of useful goods." Cf. Malinowski's spectrum of exchange relations (*Argonauts*, pp. 177-91).

40. Sahlins, *Stone Age Economics*, p. 194.

41. Sahlins, *Stone Age Economics*, pp. 194-95.

42. Sahlins, *Stone Age Economics*, p. 195.

mined by gift-relations there are limits to gift-distribution where the ties which gifts produce would be unprofitable or unfit.[43]

Gift-research also shows that not everything is exchangeable; some things simply cannot be given away. Mauss had noticed that even in the "potlatch," some family possessions are *sacra* and therefore cannot be given, and this notion of "inalienable" goods has been the subject of much further research.[44] One might distinguish here between different kinds of "inalienability." There are some possessions that simply cannot be alienated (given away) at all, without loss of individual or group identity. There are others that are in one sense given, but in another sense still belong to the giver: a sister remains a sibling even when a family gives her in marriage, and a group may retain a strong attachment to, and interest in, property or possessions even after they are "given away." Other gifts again are given on the expectation that they, or something closely equivalent, will be returned: like a ball on an elastic string, they remain ever liable to be retracted into the hands of the original giver. The relationship between objects that can and that cannot be given may vary greatly in traditional cultures, but "inalienable" goods serve to remind us of the strong investment of the giver in the gift.

As we saw, Mauss's interpretation of gift-giving advocated a conceptual scrambling of contemporary polarities between exchanges that are "free" *or* "obliged," "pure" *or* "interested." But it is striking how often these modern moral polarities have crept back into the anthropology of gift. Sahlins persisted in regarding certain types of gift (at the "generalized" end of his spectrum) as "pure" and "altruistic," labeling contrasting forms of exchange "selfish" or "interested."[45] In the preface to the second edition of his work (2004), he recognized that there is something wrong with assessing economic life as "a contest between self-satisfaction and social constraint": too much here suggests "the thoroughly bourgeois standpoint of how individuals go about acquiring and disposing of the material means of their personal existence."[46] But the main text of his work is still beset with antithesis between "sacrifice in favor of another" and "self-

43. For examples of the refusal of gift (e.g., hospitality) to distant kinsmen, outsiders, or well-known "spongers," see, e.g., Sahlins, *Stone Age Economics,* p. 246; J. P. Johansen, *The Maori and His Religion in Its Non-Ritualistic Aspects* (Copenhagen: Munksgaard, 1954), p. 54.

44. See esp. Weiner, *Inalienable Possessions,* and Godelier, *Enigma of the Gift,* pp. 108-210.

45. Sahlins, *Stone Age Economics,* pp. 191-94. "At one end of the spectrum stands the assistance freely given, the small currency of everyday kinship, friendship and neighbourly relations, the 'pure gift' Malinowski called it . . . At the other pole, self-interested seizure" (p. 191). "Put another way, the spirit of exchange swings from disinterested concern for the other party through mutuality to self-interest" (p. 193).

46. Sahlins, *Stone Age Economics,* p. xi.

interested gain," or between "obligations" and "altruistic assistance," as if the categories were unproblematic.[47] The same categories dominate the analyses of Weiner,[48] and reappear in a subtle form in the famous analysis of Kabyle gift-giving by Bourdieu. Acutely sensitized to the power-dynamics of gift-giving, Bourdieu argued that there is a deliberate ambiguity, a "double reality," in the exchange of gift. The "official reality" is of generosity, with the delayed return imagined as an independent act of disinterested giving; but the "objective reality" is of power, domination, and "the law of self-interest," cloaked by relations of gift. In his view, it is important to regard both aspects as socially "real," and not merely to discount one in favor of the other. But he concludes that the objective reality requires for its working a careful, even conscious policy of self-deception. When domination cannot take place overtly, it "must be disguised under the veil of enchanted relationships, the official model of which is presented by relations between kinsmen; in order to be socially recognized it must get itself misrecognized."[49] Thus, "the whole society pays itself in the false coin of its dream";[50] everyone plays their part in the fiction. It is hard to avoid the impression that Bourdieu's Marxian analysis requires the subtle reimposition of exactly those polarities (between "interested" and "disinterested," "obligated" and "free") that Mauss suggested were liable to skew our perception of gifts. If, as Mauss insists, gifts in traditional societies exhibit *both things at once* (and not just one at one level, and one at another), it is important precisely *not* to play off against one another characteristics that are not contradictory in their cultural context.

One further trend in the anthropology of gift should also be noted here. If traditional gift-societies still preserve a place for ordinary trade, that space has grown greatly in importance where the Western market for commodities has penetrated cultures traditionally built around gift.[51] In the analysis of

47. E.g., Sahlins, *Stone Age Economics*, pp. 196, 231.

48. E.g., Weiner, *Women of Value*, pp. 212-23, interpreting gift-giving as a disguised form of control: "The Trobriand informants who say they exchange for 'love' or 'generosity' are following a myth that serves in their society to hide a reality of self-interest. The anthropologist who then insists on labelling this act as a 'gift' seems to be perpetuating the Trobriand natives' myth" (p. 221). Cf. L. Marshall, "Sharing, Talking, and Giving: Relief of Social Tensions among !Kung Bushmen," *Africa* 31 (1961): 231-49, who finds few if any unilateral gifts among the !Kung Bushmen and concludes that there is little evidence for "genuine generosity" ("Altruism, kindness, sympathy, or genuine generosity were not qualities which I observed often in their behaviour," p. 231).

49. Bourdieu, *Outline of a Theory of Practice*, trans. R. Nice (Cambridge: Cambridge University Press, 1977), p. 191.

50. Bourdieu, *Outline of a Theory of Practice*, p. 195.

51. See, for instance, the analysis of Papua New Guinea in C. A. Gregory, *Gifts and Commodities* (London: Academic Press, 1982).

this phenomenon, there has arisen a tendency to "essentialize" a distinction between a Western "commodity-economy" and a traditional "gift-economy," the one characterized by the alienation of goods, in a "cold" and "calculated" exchange, the other by the personal relations in which people and property are closely interlinked.[52] There is value in this distinction if it can be used to question our assumptions about exchange; but there is a danger of making "gift" *in every sense* the opposite of "commodity" and thus forgetting that in traditional or archaic societies gifts too are exchanged and carry heavy loads of obligation. What has happened to "gifts" in the modern West is a subject we will explore below (1.3), but for now we must note the danger of retrojecting a modern conceptualization of the polarity "commodity vs. gift" onto the relations between gifts and commodities in a pre-modern context.

The anthropology of traditional gift-giving offers no simple "model" of gift-relations, and is not straightforwardly transferable to the world of Paul and his contemporaries, who are the main subject of this book. It cannot be used to "essentialize" the gift, or to provide a defined and clearly delimited concept. But it does generate some valuable angles of perception, raising salient questions and sensitivities that alert us to possibilities we might miss (or misconstrue) from a modern perspective. Thus, for our further study we should note:

1. It may be helpful to work with a broad definition of "gifts," including favors, benefactions, and services of many kinds. Such services may include important forms of "symbolic capital" such as prestige or honor, which may be precisely the kind of "return" that more material gifts expect, especially in asymmetrical relationships. Gifts and counter-gifts may be presumed to function as important media of power.
2. It is important to map the role and the significance of "gifts" within the larger social matrix of relations: how significant are they beside other modes of transaction and forms of exchange? What spheres of social life are affected by gift relations (or kept separate from them)? And how do gifts relate to trade and commodity exchange?
3. It is equally important to map what kinds of relationship are created, ce-

52. Strathern, *Gender of the Gift*, self-consciously adopts this oppositional fiction in order to expose inappropriate Western categories. See the summary of this polarity by Gregory: "Commodity exchange is an exchange of alienable objects between people who are in a state of reciprocal independence that establishes a quantitative relationship between the objects exchanged. . . . Gift exchange is an exchange of inalienable objects between people who are in a state of reciprocal dependence that establishes a qualitative relationship between the transactors" (*Gifts and Commodities*, pp. 100-101).

mented, and reproduced by gift-relations, and by what kinds of gift.[53] For instance, one should trace, where possible, the correlation between the depth of gift-relations and the intimacy or importance of the connection thus formed. It is important also to observe where gift-giving does *not* take place, and where discrimination is exercised in the distribution of the gift.

4. We should assume, unless there is strong evidence to the contrary, that gifts carry expectations of a return. The strength and nature of the obligation to return is worth observing closely, as is also the sense in which the gifts themselves are (or are not) "alienated" from the giver. Some form of reciprocity is likely to be present, since gifts have generally functioned to create social bonds, which can only be recognized and reproduced through return.[54] But the form this takes, and the weight of obligation entailed, may vary greatly from case to case.
5. We should beware the use of value labels such as "free" and "pure" in relation to gifts, lest they carry the connotations of modern ideologies of gift, and lest they imply polarities that are not applicable to other cultures and contexts. Thus, we should be open to the possibility that gifts could be, at the same time, both "voluntary" and "obliged," both "disinterested" and "interested," both "generous" and "constrained" by the social connections they represent. In any case, as Panoff notes, "productive research will not be aided by the elaboration of formal typologies based on moral evaluation."[55] At the same time, ancient sources themselves may weigh the value of gifts by emotive or moral terminology in ways that signify their symbolic significance relative to other forms of exchange.

53. As Algazi puts it: "gifts are not given, fixed, entities, but contested constructions of social transactions. The meanings and implications of such transactions are neither evident nor inherent in the acts themselves. Such meanings are 'negotiated' between social actors." G. Algazi, "Introduction: Doing Things with Gifts," in G. Algazi, V. Groebner, and B. Jussen, eds., *Negotiating the Gift: Pre-Modern Figurations of Exchange* (Göttingen: Vandenhoeck & Ruprecht, 2003), pp. 9-27, at p. 10.

54. Cf. Mary Douglas's comment in the preface to the latest translation of Mauss's essay: "Even the idea of a pure gift is a contradiction. By ignoring the universal custom of compulsory gifts we make our own record incomprehensible to ourselves: right across the globe and as far back as we can go in the history of human civilization, the major transfer of goods has been by cycles of obligatory returns of gifts" (Douglas, Introduction to Mauss, *The Gift*, p. x). See further, H. van Wees, "The Law of Gratitude: Reciprocity in Anthropological Theory," in C. Gill, N. Postlethwaite, and R. Seaford, eds., *Reciprocity in Ancient Greece* (Oxford: Oxford University Press, 1998), pp. 12-49.

55. M. Panoff, "Marcel Mauss's *The Gift* Revisited," *Man* 5 (1970): 60-70, at p. 63.

As Mauss indicated, the nature of "gifts" and their relation to other forms of exchange have developed significantly over time.[56] In order to position our research more precisely, it is therefore necessary to outline the role of "gifts" or "benefactions" in the context of the Greco-Roman world contemporary to Paul (1.2) before noting the changes that have taken place in Western culture since that time (1.3). Such changes have inevitably affected the way in which interpreters of Paul (including ourselves) have heard what he has to say about gifts and "grace."

1.2. Gift and Reciprocity in the Greco-Roman World

The hybrid adjective "Greco-Roman" in the title of this section gestures to the complexity of the Mediterranean world in the first century, where the overlay of Roman political power onto "Greek" traditions created a complex and socially layered interaction of cultural traditions, changing over time and varying from East to West. It will be well to begin by surveying the assumptions of Greek gift-reciprocity and some of its institutional forms, before introducing distinctively Roman systems of "patronage" and outlining the problematics surrounding gifts or benefactions in the early Roman Empire.[57]

1.2.1. Greek Reciprocity and the Limits of the Gift

It is widely recognized that one of the fundamental principles of Greek social relations, both among humans and in the relationship between humans and gods, was the expectation of reciprocity in gifts, favors and "good turns."[58] Hesiod's advice on this matter seems well tuned to the everyday lives of farmers:

56. The simple transfer of anthropological analysis derived from archaic societies (e.g., Sahlins) to the interpretation of the Roman world is justifiably criticized by Z. A. Crook, "Reflections on Culture and Social-Scientific Models," *JBL* 124 (2005): 515-32.

57. For the importance of historical context in understanding gifts in the ancient world, see the essays in M. L. Satlow, ed., *The Gift in Antiquity* (Chichester: Wiley-Blackwell, 2013).

58. The literature on this topic is enormous; recent important contributions include S. von Reden, *Exchange in Ancient Greece* (London: Routledge, 1995), and the essays in C. Gill et al., eds., *Reciprocity in Ancient Greece*. The discussion was opened by Finley's analysis of the social world of the Homeric epics (M. Finley, *The World of Odysseus* [London: Chatto & Windus, 1956]), influenced by Mauss's analysis of the gift.

> Invite your friend, but not your enemy,
> to dine; especially be cordial to
> your neighbour, for if trouble comes at home,
> a neighbour's there, at hand. . . . Measure carefully
> when you must borrow from your neighbour, then,
> pay back the same, or more, if possible,
> and you will have a friend in time of need.
> Shun evil profit, for dishonest gain
> is just the same as failure. Love your friends,
> visit those who visit you, and give
> to him who gives, but not, if he does not.
> We give to a generous person (δώτης), but no-one gives
> to someone who is stingy (ἀδώτης). . . .
> The man who gives ungrudgingly is glad
> at heart, rejoicing in his gift, but if
> a man forgets his shame and takes something,
> however small, his heart grows stiff and cold. (*Works and Days* 342-59)[59]

In its commonsense ordinariness, this advice shows acute awareness of the vulnerability of everyday existence: taking care in reciprocal relations not only makes life pleasant; it makes it more secure. It is important to be generous, and glad-heartedly so, but also discriminating and cautious: to give to the stingy, to those who cannot or will not give back, would be as useless as "sowing seeds in the sea" (Ps.-Phocylides 152). A reputation for "grasping" is dangerous: when you are the recipient of the gift, it is crucial to give a well-measured return, if possible with sufficient increment to place your friend under obligation (for when you need his aid). Such ordinary reciprocal favor excludes exact calculation, but requires a rough awareness of who is under obligation to whom. Nonetheless, these are gifts — the exchange of services

59. Translation by D. Wender in *Hesiod and Theognis* (London: Penguin, 1973), pp. 69-70, slightly adapted. Hesiod's date is unknown (c. 700 BCE?), his social level somewhere between the peasant farmer and the aristocrat. For commentary on this passage, drawing out its similarities with Mauss's analysis of reciprocal gift-giving, see P. Millett, *Lending and Borrowing in Ancient Athens* (Cambridge: Cambridge University Press, 1991), pp. 30-34. There is every reason to think that the social norms outlined here were constant and pervasive in the Mediterranean world for centuries; Cicero cites this passage as still highly relevant in his day (*De Off.* 1.48). A millennium after Hesiod, the rabbis considered it grounds for divorce when a man prevented his wife from lending kitchen implements to a neighbor or from mourning with a bereaved friend (*y. Ketubbot* 7.5, 31b — a reference I owe to S. Schwartz, *Were the Jews a Mediterranean Society?* [Princeton: Princeton University Press, 2010], p. 14 n. 26). By this inability to give she will be deprived of the social credit necessary for her own flourishing in the future.

not a trade in goods — and it is crucial that they are suffused with the warm sentiments of "friendship."

While every social situation has its specific nuance, these norms of reciprocity could be illustrated a thousand times over from Greek sources of many different kinds. Never specified in legislation (they were too deeply embedded, too obvious, and too incalculable for legal purposes), such norms are the stuff of popular maxims and high literature, the everyday etiquette of social communication as well as the formulaic language of civic proclamation. As everyone knows, "one hand washes another" (the Greek equivalent of "you scratch my back, I'll scratch yours"); "give something and get something" (Epicharmus, DK 30). Plenty of popular maxims encourage people to "favor a friend" while being sure to "return a favor."[60] The rules of gift-reciprocity — the willing exchange of valued items or services, the obligation to return in some form and at some time — are fundamental also to the dynamics of Greek literature, from Homeric epic to tragedy, comedy, and novel: as Sophocles pithily puts it, "one favor always begets another" (χάρις χάριν γάρ ἐστιν ἡ τικτουσ' ἀεί, *Ajax* 522). The semantic field for gifts and counter-gifts embraces a broad array of terms, but prominent are nouns from the δωρ-root (δῶρον, δωρεά, etc.), with their associated verbs (δίδωμι and its counterpart, ἀποδίδωμι), interwoven with nouns and verbs from the χαρ-stem.[61] These latter (among nouns, most commonly χάρις and its plural, χάριτες) typically convey the ethos of the gift as voluntary benevolence, but are also used often for specific acts of beneficence, favor expressed in a particular object or action.[62] As Sophocles' line makes clear, the fact that the same term could be used for a favor given and a favor returned made the reciprocity of gift-giving all the more obvious: when χάρις is returned, it is often hard to distinguish between the meaning "favor" and

60. See the Delphic maxims cited by J. R. Harrison, *Paul's Language of Grace in Its Graeco-Roman Context* (Tübingen: Mohr Siebeck, 2003), pp. 44-45 (φίλῳ χαρίζου; χάριν ἐκτέλει, etc.) and the school model-sentence from the third to fourth century CE: λαβὼν πάλιν δὸς ἵνα λάβῃς ὅταν θέλῃς (cited in G. W. Peterman, *Paul's Gift from Philippi: Conventions of Gift Exchange and Christian Giving* [Cambridge: Cambridge University Press, 2005], p. 61). Morgan observes the prominence of proverbs and *gnomai* regarding friendly generosity, while noting a common wariness about whom one could trust to reciprocate a gift: T. Morgan, *Popular Morality in the Early Roman Empire* (Cambridge: Cambridge University Press, 2007), pp. 41, 93-94, 142, 167.

61. See below, Appendix: The Lexicon of Gift.

62. See R. Parker, "Pleasing Thighs: Reciprocity in Greek Religion," in Gill et al., eds., *Reciprocity in Ancient Greece*, pp. 105-25, at 108-14. Of course, authors could deploy and develop the sense of such a significant term in a variety of ways. For a subtle analysis of Pindar in this connection, see L. Kurke, *The Traffic in Praise: Pindar and the Poetics of Social Economy* (Ithaca: Cornell University Press, 1991); her analysis starts from the assumption that "*Charis*, as always, designates a willing and precious reciprocal exchange" (p. 67).

"thanks" (cf. χαριστήριον; εὐχαριστία), since gratitude is always expressed in, and at least part of, the counter-gift. By at least the fourth century BCE, the image of the Three Graces (Χάριτες) dancing in a ring had become a trope for the perpetual cycle of gift-and-return, both graceful and tightly bound (Aristotle, *Eth. Nic.* 1133a2-4).[63]

The sense of obligation arising from the gift is particularly clear in papyrus letters, where individuals, across the social range, call on favors from those they have helped and express their gratitude in what seem to us tactlessly explicit and extreme terms. Authors routinely indicate their obligation to return some favor to their beneficiary, and according to Ps.-Demetrius's template of a letter of gratitude, one should put oneself under practically limitless obligation: "if you wish anything that is mine, do not write requesting it, but demand a return favor (ἀπαιτῶν χάριν). For I am in your debt" (ὀφείλω γάρ).[64] The use of the language of debt indicates the common roots of the financial sphere of loan-and-debt and the gift sphere of gift-and-return. As we shall see, it was the proximity, yet distinction, between these two transactional realms that was to become one of the problematics of the gift.[65]

Relations between humans and the gods are closely modeled on the expectations of gift-reciprocity at the human level, even where the relationship is acknowledged to be grossly asymmetrical. Fundamental to the structure of Greek religion is, in fact, the acknowledgement of the gods as benefactors (to nations, cities, and individuals), distributing their favors (χάριτες) with appropriate discrimination, while humans, in prayer, in dedicatory gifts, and, above all, in sacrifice, participate in the reciprocatory cycle of gifts.[66] As in

63. Cf. Ps.-Aristotle's Letter 4 on the social bond created by the exchange of gifts, detailing the three Maussian "moments" of gift, receipt, and return: χάριτος ἀμοιβὴ καὶ δόσις συνέχει τοὺς τῶν ἀνθρώπων βίους, τῶν μὲν διδόντων, τῶν δὲ λαμβανόντων, τῶν δ' αὖ πάλιν ἀνταποδιδόντων (M. Plezia, *Aristotelis Privatorum Scriptorum Fragmenta* [Leipzig: Teubner, 1977], pp. 42-43).

64. See A. J. Malherbe, *Ancient Epistolary Theorists* (Atlanta: Scholars Press, 1988), pp. 40-41. For the use of χάρις in the papyri, see Harrison, *Paul's Language of Grace*, pp. 64-96.

65. Cf. Pericles' observation that recipients of a gift are slow to make a return when it feels less like making a gift (χάρις) and more like paying a debt (ὀφείλημα), Thucydides 2.40.4. Aristotle notes that most people think of the return of a gift as akin to the repayment of a loan (*Eth. Nic.* 1167b16-24).

66. See especially Parker, "Pleasing Thighs." Cf. J. Gould, "On Making Sense of Greek Religion," in P. E. Easterling, ed., *Greek Religion and Society* (Cambridge: Cambridge University Press, 1985), pp. 15-16, on the assumption of reciprocity with the gods, expressed in the use of χάρις. S. C. Mott, "The Power of Giving and Receiving: Reciprocity in Hellenistic Benevolence," in G. F. Hawthorne, ed., *Current Issues in Biblical and Patristic Interpretation: Studies in Honor of Merrill C. Tenney* (Grand Rapids: Eerdmans, 1975), pp. 64-67, rightly mixes Greek, Roman,

the normal cycle of human reciprocities, it is not always clear, or necessary to be clear, about where the cycle began: sacrifices can be figured as return-gifts (for benefits already given), or as gifts of inducement (for benefits to be given in the future), or both at once.[67] The common representation of Greek (and Roman) religion as *do ut des* ("I give that you may give") is right to recognize the reciprocity ethos of ancient religious practice, but is wrong in putting one-sided stress on the human giver as the initiator of the gift-cycle, and in suggesting a crude commercialism in the transaction. Just as friends are engaged in continuous cycles of benefit exchange, without calculating who started the process or totting up precisely what each benefit is worth, so Greek (and Roman) worshipers gave honor, gratitude, and gifts to the gods to recognize and continue the bonds of benevolence between them, always with the potential that the relationship may go sour.[68] Among other things, such gifts made clear who were fitting recipients of the favors that the gods would distribute to worthy (e.g., pious and grateful) partners in such an exchange.[69]

Ever since Homeric times, friendship has been the paradigm relationship of gift-reciprocity.[70] The common tag that "friends have things in common" (κοινὰ τὰ φίλων) usually meant in practice that friends could call on one another for benefits or good turns whenever they needed them ("pooling" in this case is a higher order description of reciprocal exchange).[71] Already by the

---

and Jewish sources on "benefactor relationships with the gods," since the same dynamic of gift-and-return pervades them all.

67. For examples of all three, see Parker, "Pleasing Thighs." Cf. J.-M. Bremmer, "The Reciprocity of Giving and Thanksgiving in Greek Worship," in Gill et al., eds., *Reciprocity in Ancient Greece,* pp. 127-37; Harrison, *Paul's Language of Grace,* pp. 53-57.

68. See esp. A. J. Festugière, "ἈΝΘ' ὯΝ: La Formule 'en échange de quoi' dans la Prière Grecque Hellénistique," *Revue des Sciences Philosophiques et Théologiques* 60 (1976): 369-418, mirrored in Bremmer, "Reciprocity of Giving." On the air of unpredictability around the behavior of the gods in the Greek tradition, see Gould, "On Making Sense." Apuleius suggests that it is characteristic of "blind Fortuna" to give to "the wicked and unworthy, never favoring anyone by discerning choice" (*Metamorphoses* 7.2), while Isis properly gives to those whose purity and faith are worthy of her sovereign protection (11.6, 16).

69. On the worth of the recipients, see, e.g., *SEG* 8:550 and *SIG*[3] 708 (cited in Harrison, *Paul's Language of Grace,* pp. 55-56).

70. Finley, *World of Odysseus,* pp. 61-66; for an analysis of the shift in gift-relations between the Homeric era and the fifth century BCE, see R. Seaford, *Reciprocity and Ritual: Homer and Tragedy in the Developing City-State* (Oxford: Oxford University Press, 1994). S. D. Goldhill rightly insists that "the appellation or characterization *philos* is used to mark not just affection but overridingly a series of complex obligations, duties, and claims" (*Reading Greek Tragedy* [Cambridge: Cambridge University Press, 1986], p. 82).

71. See Sahlins, *Stone Age Economics,* p. 188, on pooling as "an organisation of reciprocities, a system of reciprocities." The closer the relationship, the more a friend could be sure that

fourth century BCE, the term "friend" had been stretched to cover a wide range of reciprocal relations, some extremely unequal. Aristotle notes that the term becomes less meaningful the more asymmetrical the relationship it describes, but he finds the principle of reciprocal benefit everywhere present (*Eth. Nic.* 1158b13ff.). Though children can never fully pay back the benefits (of life and upbringing) received from their parents, they are beholden to them to give service and honor in any way they can; honor is indeed the main form of return that the socially inferior can give to superiors (*Eth. Nic.* 1163b1-4). With elite and philosophical refinement, Aristotle can distinguish between friendships founded on pleasure, those founded on utility, and those (the best) founded on the quality of friends, in themselves. But even (in fact, especially) here, the friendship is figured as reciprocal, not unilateral: friends can be called such only if they love *each other*, "if they derive pleasure from and confer benefits on each other" (*Eth. Nic.* 1157b7-8).[72]

The reciprocity, and therefore the sense of obligation, inherent in gift-giving is vividly illustrated by a particular kind of friendship that was to become problematic with the rise of the Greek city-states. The friendship (ξενία) that tied aristocrats to one another across geographical and ethnic divides was an important tool in international "diplomacy" in the Greek world: pledges to support the interest of a foreign party in your home environment were reciprocal, and the elaborate exchange of gifts (both presents and costly grants or favors) placed their recipients under strong and lasting obligations.[73] Such alliances could be greatly beneficial to the emerging Greek city-states, but there could also arise a clash of obligations, highly significant in the history of the gift. In fifth- and fourth-century Athens, we find a number of accusations

---

"he would never fail to win any favor he asked of me" (Ps.-Demosthenes, *Nicostratus* 53.4). On the domain and connotations of Greek φιλία, see Millett, *Lending and Borrowing*, pp. 109-26; L. Mitchell, *Greeks Bearing Gifts: The Public Use of Private Relationships in the Greek World, 435-323 BC* (Cambridge: Cambridge University Press, 1997), pp. 1-21; D. Konstan, "Reciprocity and Friendship," in Gill et al., eds., *Reciprocity in Ancient Greece*, pp. 279-301; D. Konstan, *Friendship in the Classical World* (Cambridge: Cambridge University Press, 1997).

72. Aristotle's distancing of friendship from factors of utility made him insist that one does not give to a friend *in order to* get something back (*Eth. Nic.* 1163a1-2); but he is unabashed in claiming that doing good to a good person is inseparable from doing good to oneself, and that self-love is no bad thing (*Eth. Nic.* Book 9 passim). For a subtle analysis, see C. Gill, "Altruism or Reciprocity in Greek Ethical Philosophy?" in Gill et al., eds., *Reciprocity in Ancient Greece*, pp. 303-28, who rightly insists that the modern polarity between "egoism" and "altruism" serves us very badly in assessing Aristotle's ethic (and Greek thought in general): "other-benefiting" is part of a total structure of mutual benefit, governed by solidarity and reciprocity.

73. See esp. G. Herman, *Ritualised Friendship and the Greek City* (Cambridge: Cambridge University Press, 1987), and Mitchell, *Greeks Bearing Gifts*.

against leading figures in the city that their acceptance of gifts from foreign kings or cities had caused harm to the city, compromising or weakening civic interests because of the obligations arising from their friendships with external powers. Their receipt of such gifts (δωροδοκία) was entirely in accord with the rules of friendship, but this term gained a negative nuance by the fact that it clashed with an alternative regime of obligation, that owed to the home city. It is important to observe here that the gift takes on this negative coloring not because it was in itself irregular or underhand — only because it stands in conflict with an alternative, communal interest. Critics of such gifts (which we would term "bribes") insist on the superior authority of the local political community (or, in Athens, "the people"). Precisely because the gift is so powerful, they insist on its limitation in a context where a centralized and depersonalized power ("the city") makes a higher claim on the individuals concerned. To abstain from gift exchange (to be ἀδωροδόκητος) became a mark of good citizenship, a virtue acclaimed in speeches and in civic decrees.[74] As Herman remarks, "to turn this negation of heroic virtue into a term of praise and offer communal interest as a new standard of individual morality was probably one of the most significant victories of the community over the hero."[75]

A parallel restriction of the power of gift-reciprocity is evident in laws concerning the administration of justice. Because gifts expect, and oblige, a return, those invested with judicial roles who are also embedded in gift relationships, and therefore have obligations to their benefactors, are liable to skew their assessment of legal disputes. Hence Pericles' innovation, in fifth-century Athens, that citizens who took part in judicial hearings should receive payment from the state (a source that commits them to the interests of the city) — and this to counter the power of Cimon, whose gifts to his demesmen kept them beholden to him.[76] Wherever we find civic officials swearing to conduct their roles without regard to favors, and judges required to refuse gifts, we find the clash between two transactional regimes, the regime of the gift, with its strong personal ties of loyalty and reciprocation, and the regime of civic-legal power, which claims a higher authority within its own domain.[77] Gifts are no longer

74. Herman, *Ritualised Friendship*, pp. 75-80.

75. Herman, *Ritualised Friendship*, p. 78; for further analysis of gifts that shade into "bribes" (without changing their name: there is no Greek word for "bribe"), see D. M. MacDowell, "Athenian Laws about Bribery," *RIDA* 30 (1983): 57-78; Mitchell, *Greeks Bearing Gifts*, pp. 181-86; von Reden, *Exchange in Ancient Greece*, pp. 94-97.

76. Aristotle (?), *Ath. Pol.* 27.3 (with commentary by P. J. Rhodes, *A Commentary on the Aristotelian* Athenaion Politeia [Oxford: Oxford University Press, 1993]).

77. A gymnasiarch binds people to judge without regard to χάρις, *SEG* 28:261 (second century BCE; cited in Harrison, *Paul's Language of Grace*, p. 37); punishment for judges who

"total social facts" (Mauss): a centralized and partly depersonalized civic power is claiming some spheres of life as being beyond the influence of the gift.

The *Athenian Constitution* figures the city's reward of citizen-jurors not as gift but "pay" (μισθοφορά, 27.2), and thus evokes another limitation to the sphere of the gift: its distinction from "pay" and trade. In the economy of the Greek world, trade transactions became increasingly important, with many kinds of goods transported and exchanged in markets using the impersonal medium of coins.[78] Parties involved in gift relations at all social levels might continue to exchange material goods: the difference between these two spheres of exchange is not the goods themselves but the ethos of the exchange and its social connotations. For instance, Strabo, commenting on the Arab spice trade, concedes that a merchant may get "some sort of wealth" by this trade, "whereas Menelaus [of Homeric fame] needed booty or presents from kings or dynasts who did not only have something to give, but also had the goodwill to make him presents because of his distinction and fame" (*Geogr.* 1.2.32). This comment reflects the snobbery of the self-sufficient (land-owning) elite all through the Greek and Roman eras: they typically disdain those who are vulnerable to the vicissitudes of trade, and who are suspected of gaining profit ("money for its own sake") by underhanded means. But Strabo's remarks also reflect something of the difference in ethos felt to distinguish gifts from trade: for gifts, it matters greatly whom you receive them from (in Menelaus's case, from those of his own social class), why they are given (as a mark of social worth), and in what spirit they are given (with "goodwill," εὐνοία). As we have seen, gifts, like trade or pay, involve *reciprocity:* in all these spheres, there is a common structure of *quid pro quo.* What distinguishes the sphere of gift is not that it is "unilateral," but that it expresses a social bond, a mutual recognition of the value of the *person.* It is filled with sentiment because it invites a personal, enduring, and reciprocal relationship — an ethos very often signaled by the use of the term χάρις.[79] In this connection, a subtle change comes over the

---

accept gifts, *Ath. Pol.* 54.2 (fourth century BCE); parallel rules in the Jewish tradition, Exod 23:6; Deut 16:19; 27:25 (historical origins uncertain). Josephus emphasizes the conflict between "money" and "justice" (*Ant.* 4.196), but elsewhere recognizes that this is about "gifts" not just "money" (*Apion* 2.207); his strictness in this matter mirrors Plato, *Leg.* 955c-d.

78. For recent discussion of the ancient economy, see W. Scheidel and S. von Reden, eds., *The Ancient Economy* (Edinburgh: Edinburgh University Press, 2002), and W. Scheidel, I. Harris, and R. Saller, eds., *The Cambridge Economic History of the Greco-Roman World* (Cambridge: Cambridge University Press, 2007); for an overview of trade in the Roman era, see W. V. Harris, "Trade," in A. Bowman et al., eds., *The Cambridge Ancient History,* vol. 10: *The High Empire,* 2nd ed. (Cambridge: Cambridge University Press, 2000), pp. 710-40.

79. For the use of this term for expressing what is given and owed over and above a merely financial relationship, see Millett, *Lending and Borrowing,* pp. 123-26.

meaning of such words as μισθός. Its traditional meaning (and its continuing meaning in the sphere of gifts) may be conveyed by such English terms as "prize" and "reward," the recognition of worth that is part of a benefit or gift. But within the domain of commodity exchange or work-for-pay, it gains the meaning of "wage" or "hire," with a commercial sense outside of (and morally inferior to) the domain of gift. It was a devastating rhetorical jibe for Demosthenes to suggest that Aeschines, who enjoyed a noble ξενία-friendship with Alexander, was nothing more than Alexander's μισθωτός (*De Cor.* 51-52).[80]

1.2.2. Civic Euergetism

In recent years, particular attention has been given to a form of public gift relation, "euergetism," that is prominent in the inscriptional record of Greek cities deep into the Roman era.[81] With roots in the royal gifts made by kings to their subjects, a form of civic benefaction arose in the Greek city-states where members of elite families were expected to perform "voluntary" services (λειτουργίαι) for their fellow citizens while exercising a variety of civic roles, including magistracies. In time, a large array of public benefits might be fulfilled in this way: the construction and refurbishment of public buildings, the provision of military equipment and defences, the dedication and enhancement of temples (together with the public sacrifices, feasts, and banquets associated with the worship of the gods), the funding of games and choral competitions, the equipment of gymnasia, and the performance of embassies, priesthoods, and civic administration — all, or chiefly, at their own expense. In most cities, where taxation was inadequate for "extraordinary" expenses, these burdens were shouldered by a small number of wealthy families, whose unequal status was tolerated by their fulfilment of such services.[82]

80. "Like harvesters and those who do something for μισθός" (51). The word thus forms a paradigm case of the change in the meanings of words effected by large-scale transformations in social structures (with resulting alteration, or disaggregation, of modes of relation). On the changing meanings of this term, see E. Benveniste, *Le vocabulaire des institutions indo-européens,* vol. 1: *Économie, Parenté, Société* (Paris: Minuit, 1969), pp. 163-70, with further discussion in von Reden, *Exchange in Ancient Greece,* pp. 89-92.

81. The label was made popular by the seminal work of P. Veyne, *Bread and Circuses,* abr. and trans. B. Pearce from the French original, 1976 (London: Penguin, 1990); the benefactors are commonly described in inscriptions as εὐεργέται.

82. For all its quirkiness, Veyne, *Bread and Circuses,* pp. 70-200, remains a classic treatment of this phenomenon. For a selection of relevant inscriptions, see F. W. Danker, *Benefactor: Epigraphic Study of a Graeco-Roman and New Testament Semantic Field* (St. Louis: Clayton, 1982), and Harrison, *Paul's Language of Grace,* pp. 26-63. Aristotle spells out the implicit social

Such services were generally figured not as duties but as gifts; even where the city paid part of the expenses, it was incumbent on the magistrate to add his contribution. The social pressure bearing on elite families in this regard was enormous; in the Roman era, when it became increasingly difficult to find people able and willing to undertake such expenses, many forms of "persuasion" were required.[83] Nonetheless, the ethos remained that of gift — a voluntary investment into a significant social relationship — which therefore presumed a reciprocating return.[84] The key element of the return was public honor: public announcements and decrees, front seats at public events, wreaths, statues, and, crucially, all of this inscribed on stone or metal to be a permanent, public record of the gratitude of the city. These inscriptions, of which we have hundreds from all across the Mediterranean world, eloquently proclaim the generosity of the benefactor, while making clear that the purpose of their public display is both to reward donors with appropriate honor and to incite them to continue their good work. At the same time, they unapologetically encourage others to emulate them in an enterprise where the competitive love of honor (φιλοτιμία) is powerfully at work at an elite social level.[85] Public honor, exceeding that of one's peers, and as permanent as possible, was indeed the chief return sought by benefactors in this highly asymmetrical form of exchange. As Aristotle notes, people of high social status seek honor above all, just as honor is the highest human tribute to the gods: any material benefits accrued are of *symbolic* significance, since superior status is demonstrated precisely by the fact that the elite are given not financial but social rewards (*Eth. Nic.* 1123b16-24).

It is in this connection that Aristotle speaks of "worth" (ἡ ἀξία), a concept frequently applied to prestigious gifts and their return. Like Aristotle, the inscriptions often speak of "fitting" honors, to those who are "worthy" or "deserving" of such public recognition. It is honor above all of which "great men" are worthy (ἀξιόω, *Eth. Nic.* 1123b24), while recipients are careful to show "fitting gratitude" (ἀξία χάρις) to those who have benefited the community

contract: "the people . . . will take no offence at the privileges of their rulers when they see that they pay a heavy fine for their dignity" (*Pol.* 1321a30).

83. Veyne, *Bread and Circuses*, pp. 134-42, citing a fine example of the difficulty faced by a wealthy individual in Hermoupolis (second century CE) trying to wriggle out of public demands (*Rylands Papyrus* 2:77).

84. As we saw in relation to Mauss, that a gift is both obligatory and voluntary is not a self-contradiction. As Veyne insists, euergetism was "both spontaneous and forced, voluntary and constrained" (*Bread and Circuses*, p. 103); for examples of inscriptions making much of the "willing" participation of the donor, see Veyne, *Bread and Circuses*, pp. 158 n. 14 and 187 n. 214.

85. For convenient access to examples, see Harrison, *Paul's Language of Grace*, pp. 37-63, pointing out that the term χάρις is, as we would expect, used both for the favor/gift of the benefactor and for the favor/gratitude of the city in return.

(e.g., *SIG*³ 834). At the same time, donors are careful to seek out "worthy" recipients of their benefaction: as Aristotle sees it, a generous person will give lavishly but certainly not indiscriminately (τοῖς τυχοῦσι), "so he can give to the right people at the right time, and where it is noble to do so" (*Eth. Nic.* 1120b3-4). Of course, what counts as "noble" (καλόν) will be variously defined according to the donor's system of values, and not all would share Aristotle's definition of worthy recipients as people of "respectable character" (οἱ μέτριοι τὰ ἤθη, 1121b7). But it is clear that the status of the recipient was important in cementing and enhancing the worth of the giver. The civic benefactions we are discussing here were given to the city — that is, to its citizens — whose effusive response did much to prove that they were a "most worthy home city."[86] Sometimes the benefactions reach a wider circle — not just male citizens, but also visiting foreigners (e.g., at festivals or games) and women.[87] Where the benefaction was designed to meet an economic crisis (e.g., a shortage of grain, relieved by subsidizing the price), the beneficiaries would certainly include "the poor" (citizens) — sometimes expressly so — but it is clear that they are receiving this benefaction *qua* citizens and not *qua* the poor. There was a widespread presumption in the Greco-Roman world that the poor were morally as well as economically at the bottom of the scale: in a revealing mix of categories, Theognis warns that it would be futile to do favors (χάριτες) to the despicable poor (δειλοί) since, unlike the good (ἀγαθοί), they will never repay (Theognis, 105-12). Indeed, giving specifically or only to the poor would be a gift-without-return, since even their gratitude would be worth nothing. Aristotle clearly spoke from a great height when he said that the person who wants to be "magnificent" (μεγαλοπρεπής) will not waste money on objects of small importance, like Odysseus who claimed to give alms often to the homeless (*Eth. Nic.* 1122a26-27, citing Homer, *Odys.* 17.420). But, as we saw in Hesiod, even for those of modest means, there was every reason not to give to those who could only be "stingy" in return.[88]

The implicit social contract operative in Greek civic euergetism was easily applied to new institutions as they arose. Thus, we find identical language used in the numerous honorific inscriptions to benefactors of "clubs" and "associations," whose proliferation in the cities of the Greek and Roman worlds gave new opportunities for wealthy individuals to gain honor by constructing or

86. See Veyne, *Bread and Circuses*, p. 132, citing a Laodicean inscription.

87. For examples, see Veyne, *Bread and Circuses*, pp. 106-7, 144-47.

88. In friendship-relations, the same considerations apply: "In choosing friends, primary considerations were willingness and ability to repay services in full" (Millett, *Lending and Borrowing*, p. 118). Millett cites Democritus in support: "When you do a favor, study a recipient first, in case he prove a scoundrel and repay evil for good" (DK 93).

equipping club premises, funding sacrifices, and subsidizing meals.[89] Such decrees give plenty of scope for the clubs to parade their worth — their ethnicity, their trade, their local identity, or whatever else was the ground of their association — while praising their donors in terms that will make it worth their while to continue their generosity. With the arrival of the power and presence of Roman sponsors, the same rules of gift-reciprocation were readily applied, since they made as immediate sense to Romans as to Greeks. By the first century, the ultimate prize was to attract the emperor as the supreme benefactor, with provinces, cities, institutions, and individuals going to extraordinary lengths to win, and then to publicize, his superior gifts. Given the magnitude of his extraordinary power, and the tendency towards obsequious exaggeration in the grateful response, it is no surprise that emperors were soon given honors equal to the gods, whether they wanted them or not.[90]

1.2.3. Roman Patronage

The term "patronage" can be used in a wider or a narrower sense, as a broad label for unequal but enduring personal relations involving an exchange of services and favors, or in specific reference to the "patron-client" relations that were integral to Roman systems of social transaction. Given the confusions that this variability has created among classicists and historians of early Christianity, it seems best, in discussing antiquity, to restrict the label to distinctively Roman phenomena.[91] Drawing on cross-cultural anthropology,

89. The literature on this topic is now immense. For a recent selection of inscriptions, see R. S. Ascough, P. A. Harland, and J. S. Kloppenborg, *Associations in the Greco-Roman World: A Sourcebook* (Waco: Baylor, 2012); J. S. Kloppenborg and R. S. Ascough, *Greco-Roman Associations: Texts, Translations, and Commentaries*, vol. 1: *Attica, Central Greece, Macedonia, Thrace* (Berlin: de Gruyter, 2011).

90. For the range of honors (loosely bundled together by scholars as "the imperial cult"), and the logic of exchange that underlay them, see esp. S. R. F. Price, *Rituals and Power: The Roman Imperial Cult in Asia Minor* (Cambridge: Cambridge University Press, 1984). Veyne, *Bread and Circuses*, pp. 292-482, also traces this development in detail.

91. For the discussion among classicists, following R. P. Saller, *Personal Patronage under the Early Empire* (Cambridge: Cambridge University Press, 1982), see A. Wallace-Hadrill, ed., *Patronage in Ancient Society* (London: Routledge, 1989), and C. Eilers, *Roman Patrons of Greek Cities* (Oxford: Oxford University Press, 2002). New Testament scholars rightly note that "patronage," broadly defined, overlaps with some forms of "benefaction," leading to an often confusing debate over whether the two are, or are not, distinct; see, e.g., S. Joubert, *Paul as Benefactor: Reciprocity, Strategy, and Theological Reflection in Paul's Collection* (Tübingen: Mohr Siebeck, 2000), pp. 58-69; Z. A. Crook, *Reconceptualising Conversion: Patronage, Loyalty, and Conversion in the Religions of the Ancient Mediterranean* (Berlin: de Gruyter, 2004), pp.

Saller described a patronage relationship as a *reciprocal* exchange of goods and services, which is *personal, enduring,* and *asymmetrical* (thus involving the exchange of different kinds of service).[92] He also rightly insisted that such a relationship could be traced even when the terms *patronus* and *cliens* were not employed, social etiquette often requiring the ambiguous and less demeaning language of "friendship."[93] But, as we have seen, many forms of unequal gift relations could fit into this broad description (e.g., between the gods and humans, or between parents and children), such that the term is in danger of losing analytical precision. In this context, I speak of "patronage" only in reference to the unequal but personalized relationships of reciprocal gifts and services operated by Roman senatorial families (and, in due course, by the emperor), offering access to the resources of the Roman state.[94]

The social and political life of the Roman Republic was dominated by a cluster of elite families whose privileged access to the Senate and to the skills necessary for legal and political influence made them indispensable channels to all the key resources of a rapidly growing and increasingly wealthy "state." Their rivalries set up competing, and often heritable, networks of political connection in which less powerful figures desired relations of loyalty *(fides)* and dependence as a means of social, financial, or political advancement. A

59-67; A. Batten, "God in the Letter of James: Patron or Benefactor?" *NTS* 50 (2004): 257-72. Cf. J. K. Chow, *Patronage and Power: A Study of Social Networks in Corinth* (Sheffield: JSOT Press, 1992), admirably focused on local specifics. A timeless, structural definition is apt to miss the precise nuances of specific social institutions. Roman systems of patronage played very specific roles within Roman culture and underwent change over time; they should not be deduced from idealized accounts such as Dionysius's unreliable report of early Roman law (*Ant. rom.* 2.9-11). I focus here on the late Republic and early Empire.

92. Saller, *Personal Patronage,* p. 1. Some authors in Wallace-Hadrill, ed., *Patronage in Ancient Society,* would add the characteristic of "voluntariness," although this would not apply to the relationship of a *libertus* to his former owner (his *patronus*). Saller's *description* of the chief characteristics of patronage is not best used as a *definition* of Roman patronage, since it would include many kinds of relation that the Romans would not have recognized to be similar in character.

93. Saller, *Personal Patronage,* pp. 8-22, defended in R. P. Saller, "Patronage and Friendship in Early Imperial Rome: Drawing the Distinction," in Wallace-Hadrill, ed., *Patronage in Ancient Society,* pp. 49-62.

94. I leave to one side the relationship between freedmen and their *patroni,* as a special form of patronage imposing legal obligations on *liberti* (who were not called *clientes*). For the social and political functions of senatorial and imperial patronage, see esp. A. Wallace-Hadrill, "Patronage in Roman Society: From Republic to Empire," in Wallace-Hadrill, ed., *Patronage in Ancient Society,* pp. 63-87. Of course, many forms of gift exchange existed in the Roman era apart from "patronage"; for resistance to applying this label too broadly, see M. Griffin, "*De Beneficiis* and Roman Society," *JRS* 93 (2003): 92-113.

magistrate or powerful senatorial figure in Rome thus acquired protégés of many different social levels — and, as Cicero remarks, those closest in status would hate to be dubbed explicitly "clients" (*De Off.* 2.69). The guiding principle in all cases was a reciprocity in services *(officia* or *operae)* or benefits *(beneficia* or *merita),* bringing advantage to both parties. "Patrons" provided legal advocacy, financial aid, political influence, and, in general, access to the levers of power, while "clients" extended the power network of the patron, ensured political support (e.g., in voting), and, as an entourage about town, enhanced the prestige of their patron.[95] Roman observers noted in particular the most visible aspects of this patronage (the crowds at the door for the morning *salutatio;* the dinner invitations to the houses of patrons; the sponsorship of public entertainment, such as spectacular games), but its webs of power ran right through the political system of Rome, based on the reciprocity ethic of service and grateful return. In a city without a strong, independent, or impartial bureaucracy, whom one was connected to, and what favors one could ask or call upon, were the crucial mechanisms for success: from a modern perspective, it could be described as one huge system of corruption and graft.

As Roman power spread throughout the Mediterranean, the same system of power was extended to embrace foreign "clients." Roman generals and provincial officials quickly became part of the Greek system of euergetism, whose rules of reciprocity they understood well; but in the late Republic, where these power networks ran back to the core senatorial families in Rome, ancient sources speak of Roman "patronage" of individuals, cities, and even larger units.[96] These networks of gift and obligation served to integrate Rome's foreign interests into a single system of power, but they also threw up clashes between public and private interest that were present, but less noticed, in the internal affairs of Rome. When a provincial governor favored his friends in a legal or financial dispute, and when he took powerful locals or whole cities into his patronage (accepting their gifts of gratitude in exchange), the potential damage to the reputation and interests of the Roman *res publica* was immense.[97]

95. In this context, literary patronage, while understandably prominent in our literary sources, is only a fragment of a wider socio-political phenomenon, with special expectations of its own; see B. K. Gold, ed., *Literary and Artistic Patronage in Ancient Rome* (Austin, TX: University of Texas Press, 1982).

96. See E. Badian, *Foreign Clientelae (264-70 BC)* (Oxford: Oxford University Press, 1958) modified by E. S. Gruen, *The Hellenistic World and the Coming of Rome,* 2 vols. (Berkeley: University of California Press, 1984), vol. 1, pp. 158-200. For the language of patronage in such contexts, see J. Rich, "Patronage and International Relations in the Roman Republic," in Wallace-Hadrill, ed., *Patronage in Ancient Society,* pp. 117-35.

97. See the analysis by D. Braund, "Function and Dysfunction: Personal Patronage in

The Roman extortion laws *(de repetundis)* represent an attempt to limit the public harm caused by the patronage of powerful Romans abroad, but these were notoriously ineffective, not least because competing patronal interests in Rome could manipulate such laws or blunt their force. What Cicero called *corruptela* was pervasive, not least in his own behavior in Cilicia; it is striking that his definition of "corruption" is not that it damages the state, but that it demeans people who should be looking for honor not in financial kickbacks but in the rewards of virtue (*De Off.* 2.52-53).

The Roman Republic collapsed as powerful individuals sacrificed the common interests of the state to their quest for political supremacy, and in place of this dysfunctional pluralism Augustus eventually emerged as the supreme patron of the Roman state. Although Augustus and his successors certainly curtailed the exercise of senatorial patronage in Rome, and developed their own direct patronage of the Roman *plebs,* it would be a mistake to regard the emperor's universal patronage as entailing a monopoly of patronal power.[98] Rather, by making the senatorial families, together with his "friends" and *familia,* the brokers of his own power, the emperor enhanced their patronal networks in extension of his interests. The same provincial governors who extol emperors as universal benefactors (mirroring the precedent of Augustus's *Res Gestae*) can be found promoting their friends and cultivating local clients through the influence they acquired as friends of the emperor: Pliny's *Panegyricus* of Trajan and his letters of recommendation, dispensing and calling in favors, are good examples of this duality. In this sense, as Saller has shown, the establishment of the Empire was not the end of Roman patronage, but simply its realignment; now state power was operative through imperial benefactions (directly granted or mediated through brokers), which were reciprocated in deference, loyalty, and "voluntary" contributions, in legacies or donations, to the imperial purse.[99]

Evident in both senatorial and imperial patronage is the common system of reciprocal exchange pervasive in Roman culture, in this case adjusted to

---

Roman Imperialism," in Wallace-Hadrill, ed., *Patronage in Ancient Society,* pp. 137-52. Sallust's *Bellum Iugurthinum* offers a paradigm example from North Africa.

98. See Saller, *Personal Patronage* and Wallace-Hadrill, "Patronage in Roman Society"; the latter rightly insists that the emperor was the *universal* but not the *sole* patron of the Empire.

99. Saller, *Personal Patronage,* pp. 41-78, building on F. Millar, *The Emperor in the Roman World, 31 BC–AD 337* (London: Duckworth, 1977); on the High Empire, see R. P. Saller, "Status and Patronage," in A. Bowman et al., eds., *The Cambridge Ancient History,* vol. 11: *The High Empire,* 2nd ed. (Cambridge: Cambridge University Press, 2000), pp. 817-54. As Wallace-Hadrill comments, "conflict between the interests of the state and the interests of the patron became more difficult where the emperor became at once both state and patron. Symptomatic of the change is the fact that, in contrast to the republic, bribery by kings is simply not an issue under the principate" ("Patronage in Roman Society," p. 151).

the unequal status of the parties involved and their varying needs. In every manifestation of this system of "duties" *(officia)*, it was taken for granted that a benefit expected a return — not immediately, and not necessarily in kind, but as a powerfully pressing, if extra-legal, requirement.[100] Romans were explicit and completely unapologetic about the fact that gifts create ties of obligation: the language of "binding" *(obstringere; obligare)* is ubiquitous in such contexts.[101] For this reason, they also insist that the donor must judge the *worth* of the recipient: one does not want to tie oneself to a disreputable, ungrateful, or otherwise worthless beneficiary. Cicero's discussion of this matter makes it clear that different benefactors will use different criteria of worth. Most will judge on the utility of the connection formed by benefactions, and thus by the financial or other benefits to be reaped in return. As a philosopher, he advocates a moral criterion: people might be suitable *(idoneus)* beneficiaries if they are good, even if they are poor (*De Off.* 2.54, 69-71). But it is clear to him that indiscriminate gifts are disreputable: among his three rules of generosity is the rule that benefits should be given *pro dignitate* ("on the basis of worth," *De Off.* 1.42-45). Thus, in the complex etiquette involved in the giving and receiving of favors, where each party strives to make clear its open-ended commitment of gratitude, it is common to insist that the recipient of the benefit is in some sense worthy *(dignus; meritus)* of the gift.[102] Naturally so: nobody wants to think that they have voluntarily tied themselves to people who degrade their social capital.

1.2.4. Were the Jews Different?

It has recently been argued by Seth Schwartz that, in contrast to the "Mediterranean" culture of reciprocity and exchange, the Jews preserved a quite differ-

100. Cicero is probably representative in insisting that no obligation is more pressing *(magis necessarium)* than the return of gratitude (*referenda gratia, De Off.* 1.47). For the ubiquity of this assumption in Seneca, see below, 1.2.5. For the accompanying virtues as noted in inscriptions, see E. Forbis, *Municipal Virtues in the Roman Empire* (Stuttgart: B. G. Teubner, 1996). J. Michel, *Gratuité en droit romain* (Brussels: Université Libre de Bruxelles, 1962), has clarified the distinction in Roman law between contracts, with legal obligations, and gifts, where a return is desired and expected but not legally enforceable.

101. E.g., Pliny, *Ep.* 2.13; 6.18; 10.6; Cicero speaks of a patron obligating/tying others to himself by his benefactions (*beneficiis suis obligare, Ad Fam.* 13.65). In all these cases, obligations are not resented or concealed, but positively advertised as the reason for giving or requesting favors. As Saller notes, "The Roman ethic of exchange was precise and powerful: a man who accepted a *beneficium* was considered to be indebted to his benefactor and obliged to display gratitude" ("Status and Patronage," p. 839).

102. E.g., Cicero, *Ad Fam.* 2.6.1-2 *(meritus)*; Pliny, *Ep.* 10.51 *(non indignus)*.

ent tradition, founded on the "rejection of reciprocity" and harboring "profound reservations about the gift itself."[103] Schwartz associates reciprocity (or at least "institutionalized reciprocity," like "friendship" and "patronage") with inequality, dependency, and oppression, and finds in the Torah, and to some extent also in later Jewish literature, an ideology of solidarity and equality constituting "mediterraneanism's nearly perfect antithesis": here concern for the poor fosters "charitable donation" not "gift," rejecting personal dependency in favor of dependency only on God, within a community bound together by "unconditional love."[104] Schwartz recognizes that he has created a contrast between "ideal types" in the Weberian sense, and also that the Torah's vision is to some degree "utopian." In practice (and in the texts he surveys, from Ben Sira, Josephus, and the rabbis), these two systems of thought are intertwined and mutually dependent. Nonetheless, he thinks that their combination causes acute tensions, because Jews had a "core religious ideology" that idealized the "pure, unreciprocated gift."[105]

There are many features of this construction of Jewish difference that are immediately open to question. It is not clear why "solidarity" and "equality" are in principle opposed to "reciprocity" since, as we have seen, the normal give-and-take among kin, and the friendship of equals extolled by Aristotle, both operated in expectation of reciprocal exchange.[106] Given that the narratives of the Hebrew Bible depict both Jews and non-Jews engaging in the reciprocal exchange of gifts, one may question whether the Torah is plausibly read as instilling a quite opposite ideology of social relations.[107] At the same time, Schwartz's use of the language of "pure" gift should make us wonder whether

103. Schwartz, *Mediterranean Society,* pp. 5, 75; Schwartz describes this tradition as "antireciprocal" (p. 10) and "non-reciprocal" (p. 17).

104. Schwartz, *Mediterranean Society,* pp. 18-19, 26.

105. Schwartz, *Mediterranean Society,* pp. 15-16, 30-31, 41, 134.

106. Schwartz claims inspiration from Sahlins on the notion of "pooling" as the basis for non-reciprocal solidarity (Schwartz, *Mediterranean Society,* pp. 14, 18 n. 33). However, Sahlins does not *contrast* pooling with reciprocity, but describes it as "an organisation of reciprocities," which is also typically not egalitarian but governed by an extreme hierarchy of power (*Stone Age Economics,* pp. 188-91).

107. Where he recognizes the presence of gift exchange in narratives, Schwartz considers these marginal phenomena subject to criticism by the authors (e.g., Schwartz, *Mediterranean Society,* pp. 27-28, 58 n. 27). But there are plenty of examples of ordinary exchange that are integral to Hebrew Bible narratives (e.g., Gen 33:1-14; Exod 2:16-22; 1 Sam 22–24). The self-sacrificing conduct of heroes in battle is by no means a rejection of reciprocity (*pace* Schwartz, *Mediterranean Society,* pp. 94-95, on Saul) but central to the honor culture of antiquity, where glory is the *chief* form of return for the noble gift; see C. Barton, *Roman Honor: The Fire in the Bones* (Berkeley: University of California Press, 2001).

a specifically modern construction of gift is here being retrojected onto the past (see below, 1.3). Nonetheless, Schwartz is right that there is something distinctive about the Torah's legislation regarding care for the poor, yet this is best seen not as a rejection of ancient assumptions regarding gifts, but as a Jewish *modulation* of those assumptions, wholly dependent on the expectation of reciprocity — in a different form.

It is often and rightly noted that the Torah's legislation regarding the poor, the widow, and the orphan (e.g., Exod 22:25-27; Deut 24:10-15, 19-22) created a Jewish ethic of "almsgiving" that was distinctive in the ancient world both in its focus on the poor *qua poor* and in the profile that it gave to almsgiving as a virtue (e.g., *Tobit* passim).[108] The best explanations of this phenomenon would appeal to both structural and ideological differences between Jews and others, but not in the terms that Schwartz suggests. In the Greek and early Roman traditions, "the poor" were rarely identified as a distinct social category, since social categorization depended more on political than on economic status.[109] Thus, as we have seen, most acts of "euergetism," including economic relief, were given to the city and (for the most part) to citizens: subsidization of food prices or free food handouts would certainly benefit poor citizens but were not specifically targeted on, or restricted to, the poor, since the city elite were bound in ties of reciprocal exchange with citizens, above all (see above, 1.2.2). We may guess that most relief for the impoverished came from kin and neighbors, in the sorts of low-level support we have seen advocated by Hesiod. Where such support was absent or inadequate, beggars could hope for small coins from strangers, but because these gifts were random and impersonal, and because beggars were generally considered morally reprehensible (e.g., lazy and importunate), this form of almsgiving could never be given the moral dignity of a meaningful reciprocal exchange.[110] By contrast, since the structure

108. The classic discussion remains H. Bolkestein, *Wohltätigkeit und Armenpflege im vorchristlichen Altertum* (Utrecht: A. Oosthoek, 1939); Veyne's description of the distinctive Christian ethos gives minimal recognition to its Jewish roots (*Bread and Circuses*, pp. 19-34). See the nuanced discussion of the matter in B. W. Longenecker, *Remember the Poor: Paul, Poverty, and the Greco-Roman World* (Grand Rapids: Eerdmans, 2010), pp. 60-107, though his attention to a criterion of motivation in the definition of charity is apt to skew the analysis; as he himself points out, the modern polarity of "altruism" versus "self-interest" is unhelpful in analyzing ancient gift-ethics (*Remember the Poor*, p. 95).

109. See, in broad outline, R. Osborne, "Roman Poverty in Context," in M. Atkins and R. Osborne, eds., *Poverty in the Roman World* (Cambridge: Cambridge University Press, 2006), pp. 1-20, suggesting that the size and significance of the Roman *plebs* in the first century BCE began to change perceptions in this regard.

110. For begging and attitudes to beggars in the Roman world, see A. Parkin, "'You Do Him No Service': An Exploration of Pagan Almsgiving," in Atkins and Osborne, eds., *Poverty*

of Israelite/Jewish society was based on ethnicity, internal divisions were apt to be based not on political status (which was the same for all Jews) but on levels of wealth, such that "the poor" could be recognized as a distinguishable (if only loosely definable) social entity.[111] Again, most relief for the destitute would come from affective bonds with their immediate kin and neighbors,[112] but there are indications that efforts were made toward communal redistribution of wealth, in which the wealthier felt responsible for all their ethnic "kin," and thus for "the poor," even in the absence of more personal ties of kinship or patronage.[113] In the Hellenistic and Roman eras, we find examples of benefaction to Jewish communities both in the Diaspora and in the homeland parallel to non-Jewish phenomena, but since Jewish communities combined the power of individual benefactors with an obligation on the wealthy to assist the whole community, there was a better chance that all of the Jewish poor would receive some benefits from their social superiors.[114]

---

in the Roman World, pp. 60-82, and Longenecker, *Remember the Poor,* pp. 74-80. Aristotle considers giving to beggars (a distribution of money to objects of only small or moderate importance) outside the category of "magnificent" giving (*Eth. Nic.* 1122a26-28), while Seneca refuses to classify tossing a coin to a beggar *(stips aeris abiecti)* as a *beneficium* (*De Beneficiis* 4.29.2-3). In his view, such acts are too trifling, too indiscriminate, and too impersonal to be considered a genuine "benefit"; if the language of gift is to be used, one gives here *non homini, sed humanitati.*

111. The Jewish social context is thus structurally parallel to that of the later Roman Empire, when citizenship distinctions became increasingly insignificant, and the *humiliores* began to emerge as a distinct social category; see Osborne, "Roman Poverty in Context."

112. Philo presumes that the poor are generally reliant on the equally poor (*Spec. Leg.* 2.107); cf. Sirach 40:24. The blinded Tobit is cared for by relatives (Tobit 2:10).

113. For the "third tithe," see Tobit 1:8 (based on Deut 14:28-29); whether the periodic redistribution of land and cancellation of debts commanded in the Torah (e.g., Lev 25; Deut 15) was ever practiced is uncertain. For communal meals in Diaspora communities, see Josephus, *Ant.* 14.215-16; for the common (charitable?) fund set up by Jews in Aphrodisias (third century CE?), see J. M. Reynolds and R. Tannenbaum, *Jews and Godfearers at Aphrodisias* (Cambridge: Cambridge Philological Society, 1987).

114. For benefactors in the Diaspora (e.g., sponsoring synagogue buildings), see T. Rajak, *The Jewish Dialogue with Greece and Rome: Studies in Cultural and Social Interaction* (Leiden: Brill, 2001), pp. 373-91. Schwartz has noted how Josephus portrays himself as a local patron in Galilee: S. Schwartz, "Josephus in Galilee: Rural Patronage and Social Breakdown," in F. Parente and J. Sievers. eds., *Josephus and the History of the Greco-Roman Period* (Leiden: Brill, 2004), pp. 290-308. The benefactions of Helena of Adiabene to the Jewish people in the homeland are well documented and honored by Josephus (e.g., *Ant.* 20.49-53). Tacitus notes that Jews support one another (*apud ipsos . . . misericordia in promptu, Hist.* 5.5.1), and Josephus takes some pride in this matter (*Apion* 2.207, 211-14, 283). Tobit makes clear that this is generally a matter of intercommunal support to fellow Jews ("brothers from my people," 1:3, 16; 2:2-3, etc.). The solidarity here is by no means a matter of equality, as is made clear by indications of

With regard to the ideology of benefaction, both Greek and Roman cultures encouraged a general ethos of benevolence (φιλανθρωπία; *benevolentia*), one of whose manifestations was donating the basic requirements of existence to those who needed help.[115] The fact that it was worth begging in Greek and Roman cities indicates that it was common to exercise some pity on the destitute, and the prevalence of beggars around temples might suggest that this pity was evoked in the context of religious ritual.[116] However, the fact that the practice of ritual was in general not integrated in either Greek or Roman tradition with philosophical (and thus ethical) discourse on religion meant that benevolence to the needy was connected to the motif of divine benevolence only in philosophical circles.[117] And since the destitute could give nothing worthwhile back to the donor (except the limited good of ceasing to "hassle" them), the motivation for giving to the poorest members of society was comparatively weak. By contrast, within the Jewish tradition, the domains of law, ethics, and ritual practice were more closely integrated, such that giving to the poor was both (unusually) a matter of legislation and integral to a religious piety that pervaded all spheres of life. Within this context, all Jews were expected to live out their allegiance to God, and their commitment to "righteousness," in giving to the poor; and since this expectation was flexibly adjustable to the resources of the giver (see Tobit 4.8), everyone could perform this religious duty, however great or little were their financial resources. Moreover, since such giving to the poor was closely connected to religious piety, both giver and recipient could figure benefaction as receiving its most important return not from the human recipient but from *God*.[118]

Tobit's wealth (e.g., 1:14) and the references to fellow Jews who are malnourished and poorly clad (1:16-17; 4:16-17). See further, G. Hamel, *Poverty and Charity in Roman Palestine: First Three Centuries* C.E. (Berkeley: University of California Press, 1990).

115. For the widely known rules on giving fire, water, and food to those who need them, known as "the curses of Bouzyges," see T. Williams, "The Curses of Bouzyges: New Evidence," *Mnemosyne* 15 (1962): 396-98; they are known by Cicero (*De Off.* 1.52; 3.54-55) and enter into the ethic of Josephus (*Apion* 2.211). On poverty in the Roman world and reactions to it, see Atkins and Osborne, eds., *Poverty in the Roman World.*

116. See Longenecker, *Remember the Poor,* pp. 96-104, also noting the traditional label of Zeus as the god of hospitality.

117. On the different discourses of ancient religion (a "tripartite theology") and the largely distinct modes of conceptualization and practice, see D. C. Feeney, *Literature and Religion at Rome: Cultures, Contexts and Beliefs* (Cambridge: Cambridge University Press, 1998), pp. 11-14, 92-97, and M. Beard, J. North, and S. Price, eds., *Religions of Rome,* 2 vols. (Cambridge: Cambridge University Press, 1998), vol. 1, pp. 30-41, 211-44.

118. This motif is not wholly absent from Greek and Roman traditions: see, e.g., Plutarch, *Nicias* 3.7; Seneca, *Ben.* 4.11.3: when there is no possibility of a human return, a beneficiary deputes the gods to return the favor. Sorek is right to emphasize the Jewish motif of recompense

This emphasis on the return of the gift as both human *and divine* is clear already in the Torah and is prominent in later Jewish texts, such as Tobit. In the Torah, it is anticipated that the beneficiary of a favor will "bless you" (Deut 24:13; that is, invoke God's blessing on the giver), or at least not "cry to the Lord against you" (24:15; cf. 15:9), so that the gift will be "to your credit before the Lord your God" (Deut 24:13); indeed, throughout this legislation, it is repeatedly stressed that doing good to the poor will result in blessings from God (Deut 14:29; 15:4-5, 10; 24:19, etc.). Thus, even if the poor are unable to return anything matching the gift, the transaction is by no means without return, but is undergirded and justified by the expectation of a return *from God.*[119] Similarly, in Tobit, instructions on giving to the poor are routinely supported by a promise of return. Giving "will lay up a good treasure for yourself against the day of necessity" (4:9; probably an expectation of some human return) and will certainly be rewarded by God. Those who do not turn their face from the poor will not have God turn his face from them (4:6); if you serve God (through just treatment of your workers) you will be paid back (4:14); almsgiving rescues from death and cleanses from all sin (12:9; 14:10-11).[120] In other words, contrary to Schwartz, Jewish giving to the poor is fully enmeshed in the expectation of reciprocity, and its distinctive elements are justified not by an "anti-reciprocal" ethos but by the modulation of the reciprocity-ethos into the expectation of reciprocity from God. The Jewish ideology is undergirded not by the ethos of a "pure," unreciprocated gift, but by an emphasis on the certainty of reciprocation from God.[121] Jews were perhaps more likely than

by God (in the afterlife) in the motivation of Jewish benefactions in Palestine, but overplays the contrast with this-worldly recognition as found in Roman euergetism: S. Sorek, *Remembered for Good: A Jewish Benefaction System in Ancient Palestine* (Sheffield: Sheffield Phoenix, 2010).

119. For recent discussion of charity and divine reward in the Jewish tradition, see G. A. Anderson, *Charity: The Place of the Poor in the Biblical Tradition* (New Haven: Yale University Press, 2013). The divine participation in the "infinite circle" of gift giving in the Jewish tradition is emphasized by P. J. Leithart, *Gratitude: An Intellectual History* (Waco: Baylor University Press, 2014); as he writes, "the promise of divine reward underwrites Israel's economy of generosity to those who cannot pay" (p. 61).

120. Cf. Sirach 12:2: "Do good to the devout, and you will be repaid — if not by them, certainly by the Most High." The author also urges care in the distribution of the gift: "Give to the devout, but do not help the sinner; do good to the humble but do not give to the ungodly" (12:4-5).

121. For this figuring of God as the ultimate source of reward, greater than crowns, money, or public proclamations, see Josephus, *Apion* 2.217-18. This makes clear that although Jewish forms of honor may not be identical to those common in Greco-Roman culture (e.g., in declining to make statues of benefactors), this by no means signals a renunciation of honor or reciprocity *tout court.* The expectation of divine reward could even make philanthropy less humiliating for the poor, who cannot reciprocate in kind; as Barton notes, the unreciprocated

non-Jews to give to beggars, not because they did not care about a return, but because they had stronger ideological grounds for expecting one — not of course from the beggar, but from God.

1.2.5. Stoic Solutions to the Problems of the Gift

Among the ancient philosophical discussions of the gift, the fullest extant example is Seneca's seven-book *De Beneficiis,* written in the mid-first century CE.[122] Writing from an elite position among the imperial "friends," Seneca analyzes the gift, the receipt, and the return of "benefits" *(beneficia, munera, officia, dona),* drawing examples largely from his own social level.[123] Nonetheless, the favors and services he depicts are intentionally varied, since his object of study is not any single social institution, but the whole system of voluntary reciprocal exchange that "is the chief factor in tying human society together" (*quae maxime humanam societatem alligat,* 1.4.2).[124] Seneca's perspective on this system is distinctly Stoic, and it would be a mistake to take his recommendations as representative of his contemporaries' opinions. Rather, his treatise should be read as a combination of three elements: (i) a selective restatement of largely common assumptions about gift-reciprocity; (ii) an intelligent analysis of the problems of gift exchange; and (iii) the provision of distinctively Stoic solutions to those problems, aimed at keeping the system

gift is generally unwelcome in antiquity, because it places the recipient in a position of permanent inferiority (Barton, *Roman Honor,* p. 225). If the recipients can at least "bless" the giver, they can look to God to provide the necessary return.

122. For a survey of its literary predecessors, most of which we know only by title, see B. Inwood, "Politics and Paradox in Seneca's *De Beneficiis,*" in A. Laks and M. Schofield, eds., *Justice and Generosity: Studies in Hellenistic Social and Political Philosophy* (Cambridge: Cambridge University Press, 1995), pp. 242-43. The relevant treatises by Aristotle and Cicero have been touched on above. For the date of *De Beneficiis* (between 56 and 64 CE), see M. Griffin, *Seneca: A Philosopher in Politics,* 2nd ed. (Oxford: Clarendon Press, 1991), pp. 399-400. For an introduction and new translation, see *Seneca: On Benefits,* trans. M. Griffin and B. Inwood (Chicago: University of Chicago Press, 2011).

123. Thus, we hear most frequently of the favors circulating among Roman aristocrats, such as legal assistance, parcels of land, honors, legacies, political advancement, and sizeable financial subventions. For Seneca's social and political location, see M. Griffin, "*Imago Suae Vitae,*" in C. D. N. Costa, ed., *Seneca* (London: Routledge & Kegan Paul, 1974), pp. 1-38, and eadem, *Seneca.* In what follows, I shall give only a few illustrative references on each point: the treatise is full of repetition and overlapping arguments.

124. Griffin, "*De Beneficiis,*" rightly insists that Seneca's scope includes but is not confined to relations of patronage.

of benefit exchange operational for the good of all.[125] We will consider each of these elements in turn.

Both from what Seneca himself claims, and from parallels in other texts (both literary and non-literary), we know that *De Beneficiis* restates a host of common assumptions about the reciprocal exchange of gifts. Thus, Seneca here takes for granted that gift giving is a matter not of individual ethics but of sociality (*res socialis,* 5.11.5), tying people together in bonds of debt or obligation (the verbs *debeo* and *obligo* are ubiquitous). The strength of this bond arises from the strong (though extra-legal, 3.6-17) expectation that a gift must be returned in one form or another: "the whole world" regards ingratitude as among the worst social vices (3.1.1; 3.6.1-2). In one of his favorite images (borrowed from Chrysippus), Seneca describes the gift-exchange system as a ball-catching game, whose point is to keep the ball (the gift) continually circulating back and forth (2.17.3-5; 2.32.1; 7.18.1); although he will offer a particular Stoic definition of what constitutes a return (see below), Seneca shares with all his contemporaries the assumption that gifts are meant to be reciprocal, not unilateral.[126] Seneca also stresses, in common with others, that gifts or favors can only be recognized as such if they are in some sense voluntary, given "freely" *(libenter; sponte sua)* and from friendly goodwill (*a bona voluntate,* 6.9.3). At the same time, he presumes, with others, that gifts are best given discriminately, to "worthy" recipients. Although he will give some Stoic nuance to this notion, it is a foundational assumption that we should choose those worthy *(digni)* of benefits (1.1.2); it is the combination of freedom and personal selection in the giving of gifts that endows them with their strongly obliging character (1.7.1-3; 2.18.7–19.2). Seneca also presumes a common awareness of the power in gifts: those who give benefits are in a superior position, and are apt to humiliate or aggravate those to whom they give (1.1.4-8; 2.4-5; 3.34.1).[127]

125. Drawing on parallel comments among the Roman elite, Griffin is largely right to insist that "Seneca is not misdescribing reality: he is urging his readers to realize an ideal they already share" (*"De Beneficiis,"* p. 106). Inwood, "Politics and Paradox," stresses that Seneca's Stoic perspective on the subject (e.g., his use of distinctively Stoic paradoxes) is propounded not in order to set an impossibly high ideal but to offer a framework for the amelioration of ordinary social practice. See further, M. Griffin, "Seneca's Pedagogic Strategy: *Letters* and *De Beneficiis,*" in R. Sorabji and R. W. Sharples, eds., *Greek and Roman Philosophy 100 B.C.–200 A.D.* (London: Institute of Classical Studies, University of London, 2007), pp. 89-113.

126. Cf. Seneca's use of the image of the three Graces, which he identifies with the giving, the receiving, and the returning of the gift (1.3.2); as T. Engberg-Pederson notes ("Gift-Giving and God's Charis: Bourdieu, Seneca, and Paul in Romans 1–8," in U. Schnelle, ed., *The Letter to the Romans* [Leuven: Peeters, 2009], pp. 95-111, at p. 98), it is interesting that these are exactly the same three "moments" of the gift identified by Mauss.

127. For this as a common perception in Roman society, see Griffin, *"De Beneficiis,"* pp. 102-4.

Because of this power differential, the recipient often tries not just to match but to outdo the initial favor, in the spirit of competition basic to Greek and Roman culture (1.4.3-5; 3.36-38). Finally, Seneca presumes (and develops) the commonly felt proximity *and* difference between gift-exchange and commercial exchange, as operative in loans or sales. The language of debt and reciprocity makes the two spheres easily comparable, but it is also felt inappropriate to "reduce" gift-exchange to trade *(negotiatio)* or loans (*feneratio*, 1.1.9; 2.31.2 and passim). As we shall see, Seneca can use this distinction to give gift-return a peculiarly Stoic twist, but he continues here an old elite distinction between friendly gift-exchange and the impersonal calculation of "sordid" monetary transactions (1.2.3; 3.15.4; 4.1).

But Seneca's treatise is designed to do more than describe common practice and belief: it is specifically targeted at a number of interrelated dysfunctions in the system of gift-exchange. In his perception, the motor in the system, the benefactors' willingness to give, is being disabled by the failure or reluctance of the recipients to reciprocate with an appropriate return; when giving becomes unfruitful, its motivation will simply collapse.[128] There are a number of ways in which he thinks that benefactions, as currently practiced, fail to create — indeed even destroy — healthy reciprocal relations. Part of the blame rests on the benefactors themselves, who give unwisely (to the wrong people), indiscriminately (creating no personal goodwill), or grudgingly (causing not gratitude but resentment; 1.1.2-8; 1.7.3; 2.1-17). Benefactors who use their gifts for self-publicity or similar selfish purposes, and those who follow up their gifts with insistent reminders, are also at fault for degrading the ethos and thus the fruitfulness of gift exchange (1.1.4; 2.11-13). On the other hand, the recipients of favors are also often at fault. They are reluctant or tardy in expressing gratitude, and frequently forget the benefits they have received (2.26-28; 3.1-5). Sometimes they decline even to acknowledge a benefit and, where there are significant disparities in power or wealth, they despair of their ability to give an adequate return (2.35.3). Precisely because gifts are everywhere obliging, the recipients may be unwilling to accept their social indebtedness; in the attempt to escape this condition, they may give an over-hasty return, fearful of a reputation for ingratitude but also of the social disgrace in being an indebted beneficiary (4.40.3-5; 6.41-43). In lauding benefactions, Seneca is acutely aware

128. This problem is immediately highlighted in 1.1-3, forms the basic problematic addressed through the early, core books (books 1-4), and is reiterated at the end of book 7; as Inwood remarks, "from the opening lines to the conclusion of book VII Seneca is persistently concerned with ingratitude and with the discouraging effect it has on the giving of benefits" ("Politics and Paradox," p. 263).

of their potential to dry up or to go sour; his treatise is perhaps the fullest and most acute analysis of the problematics of gift exchange from any age.

In addressing these problems, Seneca does not advocate the one-way, unilateral gift: since humans are social animals (7.1.7) and society is constituted by the interchange of benefits (*beneficiorum commercio,* 4.18.1-4), Seneca's ideal is neither individual isolation nor unreciprocated gift, but a better reciprocity for the sake of friendship between the parties involved (2.18.5; 6.16) and for the "public good" (7.16.2). What he brings to the discussion is a distinctively Stoic value theory, according to which the only true "good" is what is virtuous (*honestum,* 5.12.5), while every other phenomenon normally considered "good" is redescribed as merely preferable (1.7.2). Thus, for Seneca, the essence of a benefaction is not its *content,* the favor or gift contributed by one party to another, but the *goodwill* in which it is given: as a Stoic, his primary focus is on the *animus,* not the *res* (2.34-35; 6.2.1). What matters about a benefaction is not *what* is given or how much it is worth (which may be determined by fortune, good or bad), but *how* it is given (1.5.3); it is at this, the deepest, level that human relationships are most powerfully formed. At the same time, and for the same reasons, what matters about the return is not the thing reciprocated but the grateful attitude of the beneficiary: since Stoics refer all things to the *animus* (2.31.1), what a benefit aims to achieve is not an external counter-gift, but an internal virtue, gratitude.

This Stoic reevaluation of "goods" does not *wholly* discount the material, social, or political favors constituting the benefaction-as-thing; it does not operate at a level completely unrelated to the benefactions exchanged, but is offered as a way of alleviating the problems of a system in which such things continue to be exchanged.[129] Thus, donors should be concerned first and foremost with eliciting *gratitude:* this element of the "return" is certainly necessary (anonymous giving is contemplated only as a rare exception, and is not ideal, 2.10.1-4). This means, among other things, that in giving generously they should give judiciously; there is no point scattering goods at random (where they are scarcely unnoticed) or to people known to be ungrateful, but one should choose instead "the worthy" — not the rich who can give back handsomely, but the morally worthy who are likely to show fidelity and gratitude (1.2.1; 1.15.3; 3.14.1-2). Seneca advocates a careful balance here (every virtue

129. On the relationship between the level of virtue (benefaction as *animus*) and the objects exchanged (benefaction as *res*), see Inwood, "Politics and Paradox," with close analysis of two key passages, 5.12-17 and 2.31-35: although the material exchange, required by social norms, is not strictly speaking part of the *beneficium* (which can be complete without it), it is an additional factor that should accompany the goodwill of the *animus,* so far as this is possible for the actors involved.

is a mean, 2.16.2). One should not be over-scrupulous (he wants to encourage, not limit, benefactions); like the gods, one should give generously even to the ungrateful and even after disappointment (1.1.9-10). On the other hand, one should use judgment *(iudicium)* to place goods with those likely to be grateful (or at least give only less valuable goods to the unworthy, 1.10.4-5; 4.9-11). If the gods give widely, it is only because some blessings (e.g., sun and rain) can be given to the good *only* if they are also given at the same time to everyone (4.28). A well-placed gift will also be a visible gift (1.3.5), meant to be seen and to endure: in that way, the recipient will be constantly reminded to be grateful, which is what the gift is really about (1.12.1-2; 2.11.5).

To preclude the giver from always looking for a return-as-*res*, Seneca employs a famous paradox: the benefactor should immediately forget the gift; the beneficiary should always remember it (2.10.4). At the end of the treatise, Seneca admits that this is somewhat hyperbolic language (7.22-25): what he is really targeting is the tendency of donors to keep harping on about their gifts and their desire to enhance their honor, to humiliate the recipient, or to prompt some material return. In the same vein, he criticizes any benefaction that is performed for the sake of *utilitas:* one should give for the goodness of giving alone (1.2.3), and for the benefit of the beneficiary, not for one's own profit (4.1-15).[130] This argument is replete with the language of commerce, strongly contrasting benefactions with loans, sales, and other such "sordid" transactions (4.1; 4.13.3). But the renunciation of *utilitas* does not entail the renunciation of a return *tout court,* since a return *is* sought — in gratitude. In a less stringent mode, Seneca can allow that a benefaction should be recognized with gratitude if it benefits *both* the giver *and* the recipient (2.15.1; 6.12-24); the essential point is that it is performed from a genuine desire *(voluntas)* to bring benefit to another (2.35.1). The donor should be perfectly happy to receive a material return (2.17.7); it does not "sully" the gift. But one should not demand it, or give with such a return primarily in mind; what matters is the *animus,* the *benevolentia* toward the recipient.[131]

130. Although *utilitas* is often translated "self-interest" (e.g., by Basore in the Loeb translation), the term has the particular resonance of material benefit; Seneca is not renouncing, for instance, the satisfaction in giving or any other benefits that arise from the exercise of this virtue. The chief target throughout this section (4.1-15) is the Epicurean assertion that pleasure is the goal of all human activity.

131. See the fine analysis by T. Engberg-Pedersen, "Gift-Giving and Friendship: Seneca and Paul in Romans 1–8 on the Logic of God's χάρις and Its Human Response," *HTR* 101 (2008): 15-44, at pp. 18-22. He notes that Seneca combines interest in the other (in goodwill) with an interest in the good operation of the system of gift exchange, which allows for a certain "self-interest in the system as a whole" (p. 21). He thus rightly distinguishes Seneca's renunciation of *utilitas* from the modern concept of the "pure gift" (on which see 1.3, below).

By the same token, the most essential task for the recipient is gratitude: those who are grateful have already made a return (2.31-35). The purpose of this consciously paradoxical statement is to insist that there is no excuse for failing to acknowledge benefits (*everyone* can be grateful, even if they can't make a material return, 7.16.1-4) and also no need to feel crushed by one's inability to make a sufficient counter-gift (2.35.3-4). Where a counter-gift is possible, it should be made (2.31.4-5), and in this sense, gratitude is only the first installment on a debt (2.22.1). But it is the only *essential* part of the debt, Seneca insists, so that even if one feels one still owes something, one is not weighed down or rendered anxious by a sense of indebtedness (2.35.5). Seneca's Stoic advice is subtle but realistic, sophisticated but designed for practice.[132] It is a fine example of the Stoic ambition both to understand and to *solve* the problems that threaten both the individual psyche and the welfare of society.

Seneca's philosophical concern to refine the meaning of a *beneficium* offers a number of examples of a tendency that we will trace throughout this book, the tendency to "perfect" the notion of gift (or grace) in a variety of forms.[133] Several factors contribute to this tendency to paint the motif of gift in a refined or exaggerated form. As a philosopher, Seneca seeks to distinguish between the meanings of sometimes ambiguous words (e.g., 5.12-17) and will thus delight in distinguishing the "real" sense of a term from its common, unreflected usage: thus "gift" for him is more the *animus* than the *res* in an act of giving. Secondly, Seneca is well trained in exploiting the power of rhetorical polarities; his constant efforts to distinguish gifts from financial exchanges lead him to stretch the distance between these transactional spheres, "purifying" gifts from the connotations attached to "sordid" trade. Thirdly, Seneca often uses analogies regarding the gods, who are held up as models for imitation; and in speaking of the beneficence of the gods, whose giving is unrestrained in scope and requires no material return, the conceptualization of the perfect gift will tend towards an extreme. Seneca thus provides some good examples of ancient "perfections" of the gift, which we will categorize in the following chapter. But one thing is striking: for all the extremes in his conceptualization of the gift, Seneca *never* idealizes the one-way, unreciprocated gift. While he figures the return in unusual ways (primarily as gratitude itself), he retains the

132. Thus, Inwood rightly claims that "Seneca begins from an apparently paradoxical and rigorously ethical thesis and concludes with a position which makes a serious contribution to social thought while still maintaining a consistency with the technical Stoic position" ("Politics and Paradox," p. 258).

133. For the notion of "perfection," see chapter 2 below, where we will return to some examples from *De Beneficiis*.

unanimous ancient assumption that the point of gifts is to create social ties; thus, *the proper expression of gift is reciprocal exchange.*

1.3. The Emergence of the Western "Pure" Gift

As we noted above (1.1.1), Mauss initiated interest in the way that gifts have changed in meaning over the course of time, in association with changes in the economy (e.g., the invention of money) and in the social location of gifts vis-à-vis other transactional modes (market exchange, contracts, taxation, etc.). In his wake, it has been common to narrate an oversimplified evolutionary narrative, according to which the growth of markets has caused gifts to shrink into insignificance, or to retreat to the sentimentalized margins of modern societies. Since Mauss, such a narrative has commonly adopted a heavily moral tone, bemoaning the loss of solidarity and traditional generosity in the wake of the "cold" and "calculating" search for profit, driven only by utilitarian self-interest.[134] Historians could then argue as to when this "turn" from gift to market took place in the history of Western civilization, with answers ranging from the eleventh to the nineteenth centuries.[135]

Recent scholarship has rightly insisted that "gifts" and "commodities" are not mutually exclusive: the two modes of interaction can overlap or interpenetrate (e.g., payments with additional "gratuities"), and the same items can move from one form of transaction to another.[136] Philanthropic gifts and mutual services among family and friends have not withered away, even in advanced capitalist societies. Nonetheless, it is clear that gifts play different and more limited roles in modern Western societies than in earlier eras, a change accompanied by a significant shift in their ideological configuration.

134. See, e.g., Mauss, *The Gift,* pp. 83-91. The tone is continued in Godelier, *Enigma of the Gift,* pp. 204-10.

135. For examples, see G. Duby, *The Chivalrous Society,* trans. C. Posten (Berkeley: University of California Press, 1977), on the medieval period and K. Polanyi, *The Great Transformation: The Political and Economic Origins of Our Time* (Boston: Beacon Press, 1944), on the nineteenth century. For historians' disputes over shifts in early modernity, see I. K. Ben-Amos, *The Culture of Giving: Informal Support and Gift-Exchange in Early Modern England* (Cambridge: Cambridge University Press, 2008), pp. 1-4.

136. The absolute contrast between "gifts" and "commodities" was encouraged by the ideal-type definitions offered by Gregory (*Gift and Commodities,* pp. 100-101; see above, n. 52). But he himself noted the ways in which items move from one mode to the other; for their mixing and the gray areas between them in the medieval period, see, e.g., W. Davies and P. Fouracre, eds., *The Languages of Gift in the Early Middle Ages* (Cambridge: Cambridge University Press, 2010).

For our purposes, it is especially important to trace the emergence of the "pure" gift — the notion of the gift as ideally "free" from obligation, and unreciprocated, given *without a return.* As we have seen, in antiquity it was taken for granted that gifts are accompanied by obligations and should elicit some form of return; even philosophers who disavowed a material return (Aristotle) or scorned *utilitas* (Seneca) considered gifts/benefactions to be necessarily embedded in reciprocal relations. They did not share the modern idealization of the unilateral gift, which has such a powerful hold on contemporary notions of "altruism," especially in religious discourse. Given the tendency of this ideology to color our reading of the ancient evidence, it is important to trace its origins. Once we understand the "pure" gift as a cultural product, we can resist the modern tendency to take it as a natural or necessary configuration of the paradigmatic gift.

1.3.1. Persisting Modes of Gift Exchange

A recent flurry of research on gift exchange in medieval Europe has emphasized the persistence and importance of gifts at all social levels (and across social strata), while giving nuanced attention to different gift-repertoires in varying social and cultural contexts.[137] It is clear that gifts "normally implied both a social relationship and some form of reciprocity,"[138] varying in kind and size according to the relationship sought or expressed. While the boundary between gifts and market sales was not watertight, a distinction between the two modes of transaction was normally clear: remuneration for sales was immediate, certain, and calculable, while gifts fostered enduring relations in which the return was uncertain and often not commensurable with the gift. Gifts could cause conflict as well as harmony, and in awkward social situations the exchange of goods might be negotiated as one form of transaction rather than another, deploying a range of gift and non-gift terminology. But there was no specialized vocabulary for "bribes," since "gifts" influenced political decision-making and appointments, whatever efforts might be made to limit their operation in courts. Donations to the church (or to God) constituted in this period an important domain of gift giving, but these too operated with an implicit (and often explicit) expectation of return: while the difference in status, and God's self-sufficiency, ensured that God could never be put under

137. See, e.g., Algazi, Groebner, and Jussen, eds., *Negotiating the Gift;* Davies and Fouracre, *Languages of Gift.*

138. Wickham in Davies and Fouracre, *Languages of Gift,* p. 246.

obligation by human gifts, it was clear that one could "deal with God," hoping for reward (for one's self or for others) either in this life or, more significantly, in the next.[139]

Early modern Europe was similarly characterized by formal and informal exchanges of gift, as Zemon Davis demonstrated in her famous book *The Gift in Sixteenth-Century France* (2000). While distinguished from sale and from taxation, gifts (of many different kinds) continued to be both voluntary and obliged/obliging — just the combination that Mauss had noted in earlier contexts. As Zemon Davis notes, it was important to insist that gifts were given "freely," as a matter of choice outside the regularities and calculations of the market, but it was also obvious to all concerned that they laid the recipient under obligation, requiring at least gratitude if not a counter-gift: "one favor begets another" and "a thing well given is never lost."[140] Zemon Davis traces an increasing anxiety in the sixteenth century about the power of gifts to pervert politics — at least, *the king*'s anxiety about controlling his judicial and political officers, whose loyalty could be diluted by gifts received from local sources of influence. She also notes that the king's right to give as he pleased became the subject of discussion in this century: in some views, the king's absolute sovereignty was demonstrated precisely in his right to give gifts *without regard to merit* — a notion of "sovereign grace" that we will find paralleled in the theology of Calvin (see below, 3.4).[141]

Tracing the pattern of gifts in early modern England reveals a similar story: gifts were ubiquitous at all social levels, charitable giving was not diminished but if anything invigorated by civic systems for the care of the poor, and ties of friendship and patronage continued to infiltrate mechanisms for social advancement, in commerce, politics, and church (from our perspective, all heavily "corrupt"). Although giving to the poor received no material return, it was generally paraded as a matter of virtue and honor, and even "anonymous" gifts were carefully recalled in funerary addresses in memory of the deceased.[142]

139. See Wickham's conclusions in Davies and Fouracre, *Languages of Gift*, pp. 244-45: "Whatever theologians thought, people wanted to feel safe, and thought that one could deal with God; and influential parts of the church hierarchy must have in part agreed, if the eighth-century Gregorian Sacramentary could include the phrase 'receive, Lord, the host which we offer you, and by this holy commerce *(sancta commercio)* absolve the chains of our sins.'"

140. N. Zemon Davis, *The Gift in Sixteenth-Century France* (Oxford: Oxford University Press, 2000), p. 20 (French proverbs); "both volition and obligation were expected to inspire the charitable gift" (p. 24).

141. Zemon Davis discusses Calvin in another context (*The Gift*, pp. 190-203), which we will note below; on the king's power, and the influence of "bribes," see pp. 142-66.

142. See Ben-Amos, *Culture of Giving*, pp. 242-76, with discussion of the tension between

Giving continued to be characterized as voluntary and personal, expressive of an enduring relationship and attended by "high coding" in social etiquette. Although the return was not defined, and was never certain, it was strongly expected, since gifts continued to function as vital social ties, providing exchanges necessary for welfare and social success.[143]

1.3.2. Modern Social and Ideological Transformations

Although gifts continue to flourish in many modes in modern Western culture, it would be hard to deny that their operation and their conceptuality have significantly changed in the course of the last few centuries. A large number of social, political, and economic factors have combined in effecting this change, which cannot be analyzed here in depth.[144] In outline, one may point to the effects of urbanization, migration, and mass production, which have diminished the number and range of social bonds among increasingly "alienated" individuals, or at least reduced reliance on familial and neighborhood ties for the everyday necessities of existence. At the same time, the rise in the power and scope of centralized states has limited the range of relations in which gifts are necessary or legitimate (though not their intensity outside those boundaries). The use of local rates, and then national taxes, to support the poorest members of society has shifted the pattern of "charity" away from local institutions towards large-scale national or international aid-organizations; a "return" in the form of public reputation is now rarely possible in forms of giving that are, from the recipients' perspective, anonymous and without personal ties. To the extent that impersonal state bureaucracies have assumed essential public services (protection from violence, health services, education, etc.), they have reduced the range of life spheres in which gifts are necessary for survival or advance. Moreover, as democracy has accorded centralizing states authority to control

---

the publicity and anonymity of gifts; Matthew 5:16 could legitimate the one, and Matthew 6:1-4 the other (with the return, however, not renounced but anticipated from God). Ben-Amos also charts the continuing importance of honor and public deference as the return for philanthropy, alongside the internalization of honor as self-esteem (pp. 195-241).

143. On "high coding in terms of etiquette and appropriateness," see A. Appadurai, ed., *The Social Life of Things: Commodities in Cultural Perspective* (Cambridge: Cambridge University Press, 1986), p. 25.

144. For attempts to trace this development, see, e.g., J. G. Carrier, *Gifts and Commodities: Exchange and Western Capitalism since 1700* (London/New York: Routledge, 1995); J. T. Godbout with A. Caillé, *The World of the Gift*, trans. D. Winkler (Montreal: McGill-Queen's University Press, 1998). On the divergence between "interest" and "disinterest" in modern notions of gift, see A. Caillé, *Don, intérêt et désintéressement* (Paris: La Découverte, 1994).

"objectively" regulated and merit-based domains of public service, the power of gifts (as "bribes") to sway political decisions has been increasingly policed (with varying degrees of success).[145] The potential for a "conflict of interests," which we noted already in fifth-century Athens (see above, 1.2.1), is here made a central issue in the tussle between state power and gift obligations to family or friends. Advancement in the now enlarged public domain is no longer (meant to be) dependent on ties of friendship or patronage; even businesses are subject to legislation in the gray area of "gifts" and "inducements."

The effect of these deep social changes is not only to restrict the range of gifts, but to change their identity. In the process of disaggregation between modes of social transaction, gifts in advanced capitalist societies now more rarely provide essential social or financial support. More often, they serve merely symbolic roles (preserving friendships and sweetening personal relations) in which a return is no longer necessary; and where charity operates to supply essential needs, this is often through impersonal channels where no return is possible, even if it were desired. Far from "total systems" (Mauss), modern societies have become differentiated in a way that distinguishes the private gift from the public domain, and the personal gift from the impersonal operations of the market. A distinction between sale and gift is no modern phenomenon (we noted it already in the Greco-Roman period), but the distance between these two transactional modes has arguably increased to the extent that they have become not just differentiated but ideologically polarized. The market is viewed (and analyzed) in terms of individualism, rational choice, and utilitarian considerations of profit; the "economy of gift" is associated with the opposite qualities of solidarity, sentiment, and disinterest. Thus, as Parry has argued, "the ideology of a disinterested gift emerges in parallel with an ideology of a purely interested exchange," and both are, in an important sense, "*our* invention."[146] Crucially, the market is here associated with reciprocal exchange (a process of *quid pro quo*), while gifts are associated with the *absence of reciprocation,* or *non-exchange.* This is a major development beyond the ancient antitheses between noble gifts and "sordid" trade, because in those antitheses, as we saw, it was presumed that both gifts and trade were systems of reciprocity. It is only in modernity that there emerges the ideal of the unreciprocated gift.[147]

145. For analysis of the role of the modern state in centralizing, monopolizing, and depersonalizing power, see M. Weber, *Economy and Society: An Outline of Interpretative Sociology,* trans. E. Fischoff et al. (Berkeley: University of California Press, 1978). On the history of "bribery," see J. T. Noonan, *Bribes* (New York: Macmillan Press, 1984).

146. Parry, "*The Gift,*" p. 458 (italics original); this essay has had a seminal influence on the modern discussion of the gift.

147. Leithart, *Gratitude,* p. 143, sums up the matter: "By erecting a market economy as a

Alongside the social changes outlined above, we may trace the development of a new ideology of the gift, distinctively Protestant in origin, which has contributed greatly to the antithesis Parry has articulated. The Christian tradition inherited from Judaism the effort to enmesh ethics within religious piety, and thus to view gift giving within a specifically religious frame of reference. It also inherited (from the same biblical roots, with New Testament elaborations) the Jewish perception that in giving to those who do not (or cannot) return, one is giving to God, or at least will receive from God a reward, in one form or another.[148] Thus, the exhortations and motivations for giving expressed from early Christianity onward through the Middle Ages include the hope of a return from God. Gifts to the church, and to the poor, could be expected to reap some reward, whether in earthly blessings or in the redemption of the soul: in the words of an old French proverb, "Who gives, God gives to him."[149]

Zemon Davis has traced in Calvin an attempt to break with this ideology of reciprocity with God (and by extension reciprocity with fellow humans), contrasting Catholic "reciprocity" with Reformed "gratuitousness."[150] In one important respect, this antithesis seems incorrect. Calvin, in fact, put great emphasis on the return of gratitude to God, characterizing a life of obedience and holiness as what is owed to God in return for the immeasurable gift of Christ.[151] Nonetheless, it is right to say that the Protestant Reformers put great effort into figuring a return to God as always only a response to the one completed and all-sufficient gift, and *not* as the means toward earning a future gift or favor from God. In that sense, human praise and obedience are never *instrumental* in Protestant theology, never part of a *repeatable* pattern of gift and return.

In fact the architect and in many respects the "purest" exponent of this ideological break was Martin Luther (1483-1546). As we shall analyze in greater depth below (3.3), Luther challenged the construction of human relations with

zone of pure self-interest, the political and economic theorists of the seventeenth and eighteenth centuries conversely freed the realm of social relations for pure altruistic generosity."

148. See above, 1.2.4. New Testament expressions of this theme include Matthew 6:1-4; 25:31-46; Luke 6:27-36.

149. "Qui donne Dieu luy donne" (cited by Zemon Davis, *The Gift*, pp. 18 and 228 n. 2); for the reciprocity from God expected from charity to the poor ("with no hope of recompense except from God") and from payment for masses and various *pro anima* donations to the church, see Davis, *The Gift*, pp. 83, 167-82. For early Christian expectations of a "return" from God for giving to others, see, e.g., 2 Clement *passim*.

150. Zemon Davis, *The Gift*, pp. 190-203.

151. See below, 3.4, and, on this point especially, B. A. Gerrish, *Grace and Gratitude: The Eucharistic Theology of John Calvin* (Minneapolis: Fortress Press, 1993) and J. T. Billings, *Calvin, Participation, and the Gift: The Activity of Believers in Union with Christ* (Oxford: Oxford University Press, 2007).

God as a repeated cycle of gift-and-return, and thereby countered notions of human merit as eliciting benefits from God. Luther's theology is centrally about *gift* — the gift (grace) of God expressed definitively and once-for-all in the life, death, and resurrection of Christ, and the gift/generosity of Christ passed on to others in free Christian service. Against a long-established tradition, Luther reconfigured the Mass as the reception of grace in Word and sacrament, not as a sacrifice offered to God in the hope of obtaining benefits (for oneself or for others) from God. God, in other words, gives freely and without strings attached, and believers are to do likewise. Luther places much emphasis on imitation of Christ or, better, participation in the dynamic of the Christ-event: believers are to be (as he puts it) "Christs" to one another, passing on the unconditional love of Christ to others (see below, 3.3.2). It is essential for him that this love is practiced for no reward or calculation of return: it is not an interested or instrumental love. The believer "lives only for others and not for himself . . . considering nothing except the need and advantage of the neighbor."[152] The spirit of this self-giving is also crucial: service must not be grudging or obliged, but given cheerfully, willingly, and freely. Gift-giving is, in other words, a pure, gratuitous act, liberated from the need to gain anything by the fact that Christ has given all things already, and freed from a self-seeking attitude by pure concern for the other.[153]

This tradition is lifted to the position of a universal ethical ideal in the moral philosophy of Immanuel Kant (1724-1804). On Kant's definition, the duties of virtue (ethics) are not externally imposed but constitute a *freely chosen* constraint, founded on pure reason alone. Such duties should be performed solely for their own sake, not from any prudential considerations: "the thought of duty for its own sake is the sufficient incentive of every action conforming

152. *Freedom of the Christian, LW* 31, pp. 364-65.

153. Melanchthon (1497-1560) offers a fine example of this principle of unilateral giving in his commentary on Colossians 1:4: "The Colossians do not do good to the saints as if they were money-lenders, buying big profits by small favors. The world, on the other hand, is generous in the hope of getting more back. All gifts are greedy, as the saying goes. In Martial's felicitous expression, 'Presents are like fish-hooks.' But the saints do good because they know this is what God wants, and because they value his will above the promised rewards. Their action is not prompted by the desire to earn something in return. For they know that all things have already been freely given, and that they cannot be won by any human merits, nor given their due value by them. . . . Thus the magnitude of the reward stirs the Colossians into doing good works, not to obtain fuller blessings, but because they believe themselves to have obtained so much already, that they long to show God their gratitude." (P. Melanchthon, *Paul's Letter to the Colossians,* trans. D. C. Parker [Sheffield: Almond Press, 1989], p. 34; I am grateful to Stephen Chester for drawing this citation to my attention).

to duty" (*Die Metaphysik der Sitten* 6.393).[154] The key duties are one's own perfection *(eigene Vollkommenheit)* and the other's happiness *(fremde Glückseligkeit)* — crucially, not one's own happiness, except in a purely moral sense. Thus, one should never serve another's happiness as a means to one's own; duty should be performed without hope of return: "To be beneficent, that is, to promote according to one's means the happiness of others in need, without hoping for something in return, is everyone's duty" (6.453). Any resulting benefits to oneself are an accidental product, falling outside the moral compass of the duty (they have prudential but not moral value). Kant is acutely aware of the fact that gifts are liable to put the recipient under obligation, and in a position inferior to the donor, but he is morally uneasy with this fact: "since the favor we do implies that his well-being depends on our generosity, and this humbles him, it is our duty to behave as if our help is either merely what is due him or but a slight service of love, and to spare him humiliation and maintain his respect for himself" (6.448-49). It is apparent here that individual self-respect is more important than the ties of obligation that bind persons together. The rich person "must carefully avoid any appearance of intending to bind the other," otherwise "it would not be a true benefit that he rendered him." He must try every means to avoid obliging the other; indeed, it would be "better" if possible to "practice his beneficence in complete secrecy" (6.453).

Kant thus provides a powerful ideological (and easily secularized) sanction for the one-way, non-obliging, and preferably anonymous gift. There are clearly motifs here in common with Seneca (whose works were highly influential on European thought from the Renaissance onward): among others, the notion of virtue for virtue's sake is closely parallel. But the discrepancies indicate how the gift now operates within a significantly different context. Whereas Seneca's concern, as we saw (above, 1.2.5), was to foster the social ties of friendship that were enabled by the circulating, reciprocal gift, such that obligation and return were recognized as essential elements of social cohesion, Kant prioritizes the moral integrity and self-respect of the autonomous individual. Although society is still characterized by Kant as a community of mutual help (6.453), it is morally desirable to minimize or even remove the obligation that arises from the gift; indeed, the gift can be considered morally valuable without reference to its construction or consolidation of social ties. Kant thus legitimates the unilateral gift, which is given universalizable definition as a moral ideal. When this ideology becomes influential within the

154. I cite from the translation of M. Gregor: E. Kant, *The Metaphysics of Morals* (Cambridge: Cambridge University Press, 1996 [original: 1797-98]). The following citations are from "Part Two: On Duties of Virtue to Others," with page references to the AK (German) edition.

social-structural developments outlined above, the conditions are set for the celebration of the "gratuitous" gift — "gratuitous" not only in the sense that it is freely willed, but in the novel sense that it expects and even desires no return.[155]

1.3.3. The Modern Notion of the "Pure" Gift

The argument outlined above suggests that the modern ideology of the "pure" gift is the construct of a specific historical and cultural configuration — an invention of the modern West. As Parry argues, "those who make free and unconstrained contracts in the market also make free and unconstrained gifts outside it. But these gifts are defined as what market relations are not — altruistic, moral, and loaded with emotion." In this ideological polarization, "*Gift-exchange* — in which persons and things, interest and disinterest are merged — has been fractured, leaving gifts *opposed* to exchange, persons *opposed* to things, and interest to disinterest."[156] As we saw from the anthropology of the gift and from the Greco-Roman evidence, the traditional role of the gift in creating and reproducing social ties entails that gifts create obligations and expect returns, mixing disinterest and self-interest in ways that confound modern categories. But the ideal of a pure "altruism" (a term created in nineteenth-century France) necessitates the suppression of these traditional elements.[157] Thus, Noonan presents as the "ideal case" a gift on which "no obligation is imposed which the donee must fulfill. The donee's thanks are but the ghost of a reciprocal bond. That the gift should operate coercively is indeed repugnant and painful to the donor, destructive of the liberality that is intended. Freely given, the gift leaves the donee free."[158] In a similar vein, Hyde polarizes the gift and the market economy, relating to each other as the emotional to the impersonal, the dynamic to the static, the generous to the accumulative, and the excessive to the scarce. Pervading these polarities is another, that between freedom and obligation — and if the gift cannot be completely unobliging, it is best if it "disappears" by moving among more than two parties, preventing any direct return.[159]

It is easy to see how this ideology fits the social context in which many

155. For a fuller reading of Kant on this topic, see Leithart, *Gratitude*, pp. 154-60.

156. Parry, "*The Gift*," pp. 466 and 458 (italics original).

157. "Altruism" (French: *altruisme*) was coined by A. Comte (1798-1857), whose motto was "*vivre pour altrui*"; see *Oxford English Dictionary, s.v.*

158. Noonan, *Bribes*, p. 695.

159. L. Hyde, *The Gift: Imagination and the Erotic Life of Property* (New York: Vintage Books, 1979) (on the gift "passing out of sight," see p. 16).

kinds of "gift" take place in the modern West.[160] Charitable giving, generally mediated through large nonprofit organizations, leaves donors and recipients unknown to one another and receives no recipient-return. Where gifts are reciprocated (at Christmas, in the workplace, etc.), they are typically of merely symbolic significance; a return is rarely essential for economic or social survival and therefore easily trivialized. In modern forms of "euergetism," where charitable foundations or wealthy individuals support "good causes," the return (generally in the form of honor) is hardly recognized as a form of return, so the gift can still be conceptualized as a unilateral transaction. What is idealized is the anonymous, unreciprocated and disinterested gift, where no return is possible or expected: Titmuss's famous analysis of blood donation elevated this particular form of gift to the level of a modern paradigm.[161]

Of course not all gifts are, or can be, this detached, and alongside the theory of the "pure" gift ("the bearer of a utopia"),[162] there is also a deep recognition that gifts do oblige their recipients and do look for a return.[163] Gifts of patronage, favor, and friendship continue to create relationships of obligation and reciprocity, and it is the recognition of this dynamic that, in some countries, severely restricts their operation in business and politics. Such gifts are treated with suspicion precisely because of their power to oblige; everyone knows that "there is no such thing as a free lunch." In some cases, the reciprocity can be masked by the fact that the return is delayed in time, or radically different in kind; or where the reciprocity is simultaneous (e.g., Christmas presents), it can be figured as the presentation of matching unilateral gifts. As always, the development or manipulation of language can also shift the same transaction into or out of the "gift" domain. In general, as Carrier comments, "At the level of articulated cultural values the perfect present may be free. At the level of

160. For the analysis of modern philanthropy and its relation to the anthropology of the gift, see, e.g., D. J. Cheal, *The Gift Economy* (London: Routledge, 1988), and I. Silber, "Modern Philanthropy: Reassessing the Viability of a Maussian Perspective," in W. James and N. J. Allen, eds., *Marcel Mauss: A Centenary Tribute* (New York: Berghahn Books, 1998), pp. 134-50.

161. R. M. Titmuss, *The Gift Relationship; From Human Blood to Social Policy* (London: George Allen & Unwin, 1970). His conclusion that voluntary donations (in the UK) were in fact medically safer than payment for blood (in the USA) has had a wide influence on the discussion of altruism in medical ethics. As he notes, even blood donation may be motivated by a hope for a return if and when required (in a form of generalized reciprocity, as defined by Lévi-Strauss). But in the "free gift" of blood to unknown strangers, there is "no formal contract . . . no situation of power, domination, constraint or compulsion . . . no gratitude imperative . . . and no explicit guarantee of or wish for a reward or a return gift" (p. 89).

162. Godelier, *Enigma of the Gift*, p. 208.

163. For sociological analysis of gifts in contemporary forms of solidarity, see A. E. Komter, *Social Solidarity and the Gift* (Cambridge: Cambridge University Press, 2005).

structural cultural expectation and everyday behavior the obligation that giving generates can be strong."[164] Although the etiquette of gift-giving has always been delicate, this mismatch between (modern) ideal and persistent reality appears to be the product of a particular Western development.

Two theoretical attempts to analyze this mismatch indicate the modern allure of the wholly disinterested gift. As we noted above (1.1.2), Pierre Bourdieu assumes a polarity between "interest" and "disinterest" in his analysis of the structural "self-deception" entailed in all gift-giving. Taking the gift to be ambiguous, the site of a "dual truth," he suggests:

> On the one hand, it is experienced (or intended) as a refusal of self-interest and egoistic calculation, and an exaltation of generosity — a gratuitous, unrequited gift. On the other hand, it never entirely excludes awareness of the logic of exchange or even confession of the repressed impulses or, intermittently, the denunciation of another, denied, truth of generous exchange — its constraining and costly character.[165]

This doubleness, he suggests, is created by the time delay between the gift and its return, so that each appears, independently, as an act of pure disinterest. The "misrecognition" here involved is not necessarily conscious, but it operates at a deep level of individual or collective self-deception that is part of the labor of gift-giving itself. On this view, the "purely disinterested" gift is actually, at an "objective" level, an interested act of power, but society needs to think otherwise for its own good.

At a philosophical level, this tension between ideal and reality became central to the highly influential analysis of the gift offered by Jacques Derrida. Derrida considers that the gift, on the one hand, necessarily operates within a circular "economy," characterized by return and obligation. But on the other hand, in his view, what makes it *gift* (as opposed to economic exchange) is that *it does not come back:* "it must not circulate, it must not be exchanged."[166]

> For there to be a gift, there must be no reciprocity, return, exchange, countergift, or debt. If the other *gives* me *back* or *owes* me or has to give me back

164. Carrier, *Gifts and Commodities,* p. 157.

165. P. Bourdieu, "Marginalia — Some Additional Notes on the Gift," in A. D. Schrift, ed., *The Logic of the Gift,* trans. R. Nice (London: Routledge, 1997), p. 231. This essay summarizes and develops themes explored in Bourdieu, *Outline of a Theory,* pp. 171-97, and P. Bourdieu, *The Logic of Practice,* trans. R. Nice (Stanford: Stanford University Press, 1990), pp. 98-121.

166. J. Derrida, *Given Time,* vol. 1: *Counterfeit Money,* trans. P. Kamuf (Chicago: University of Chicago Press, 1992), p. 7.

> what I give him or her, there will not have been a gift, whether this restitution is immediate or whether it is programmed by a complex calculation of a long-term deferral or differance.[167]

Pushing this thought to its logical limits, Derrida insists that any kind of return will destroy or annul the gift. If the recipient *recognizes* the gift as a gift (let alone expresses gratitude for it), if the gift *appears as a gift* to either donor or recipient, if the donor *knows* or *intends* it as such (and thus pays himself back with self-congratulation), if the gift is *remembered* by either party, either consciously or subconsciously — in all these ways, it is annulled and ceases to be a gift.[168] Since the gift is both necessarily engaged in circularity *and* destroyed by it, this makes the gift "the impossible" (not just impossible, but "the very figure of the impossible"),[169] and thus an essential tool with which to clarify the indeterminate openness characteristic of deconstruction. With the gift thus defined, Derrida claims that Mauss's "monumental work" "speaks of everything but the gift: It deals with economy, exchange, contract *(do ut des),* it speaks of raising the stakes, sacrifice, gift *and* countergift — in short, everything that in the thing itself impels the gift *and* the annulment of the gift."[170]

Theological reactions to Derrida have ranged from rejection of his insistence on the impossibility of the gift to delight in its openness and excess (identified with God).[171] Derrida's provocative analysis of this central religious theme has certainly catalyzed an outpouring of contemporary Christian theology on gift, which cannot be surveyed here.[172] For our present purposes, what

167. Derrida, *Given Time,* vol. 1, p. 12 (italics original).

168. Derrida, *Given Time,* vol. 1, pp. 13-18. For the continuation of these reflections in relation to "the gift of death," see J. Derrida, *The Gift of Death,* trans. D. Wills (Chicago: University of Chicago Press, 1995).

169. Derrida, *Given Time,* vol. 1, p. 7.

170. Derrida, *Given Time,* vol. 1, p. 24.

171. For the first, see J.-L. Marion, *Étant donné: Essai d'une phénoménologie de la donation,* 2nd ed. (Paris: Presses Universitaires de France, 1997), and the dialogue between Derrida and Marion in J. D. Caputo and M. J. Scanlon, *God, the Gift, and Postmodernism* (Bloomington: Indiana University Press, 1999), pp. 54-78; on the philosophical issues at stake between them, see R. Horner, *Rethinking God as Gift: Marion, Derrida, and the Limits of Phenomenology* (New York: Fordham University Press, 2001); Leithart, *Gratitude,* pp. 196-214. For the second, see J. D. Caputo, ed., *Deconstruction in a Nutshell: A Conversation with Jacques Derrida* (New York: Fordham University Press, 1997), and his essay "Apostles of the Impossible: Of God and Gift in Derrida and Marion," in Caputo and Scanlon, *God, the Gift, and Postmodernism,* pp. 185-222.

172. The theme is central to the work of Milbank and others associated with "radical orthodoxy"; see, e.g., J. Milbank, "Can a Gift Be Given? Prolegomenon to a Future Trinitarian Metaphysic," *Modern Theology* 11 (1995): 119-61, and Milbank, *Being Reconciled: Ontology and Pardon* (London: Routledge, 2003). For a very different theological perspective, refiguring

is important to note is that Derrida's construction of the impossibility of the gift is based on the premise that the gift *by definition* should be free of reciprocity or return. But this definition, I have argued, is a modern construction, not a natural or necessary construal of the gift. The pure gift, free of interest and unsullied by return, is an extreme "perfection" of the gift, reflecting a modern ideological polarization between freedom and obligation, interest and disinterest. From an anthropological point of view, "even the idea of a pure gift is a contradiction," since such a gift, anonymous and unreturned, does nothing to enhance solidarity.[173] Taking a long historical and anthropological perspective, one might even retort that Derrida's treatment of the aporia of the gift "speaks of everything but the gift." In any case, we should be conscious that, despite the enormous influence of Bourdieu and Derrida, it would be arbitrary to make the absence of reciprocity and "self-interest" the very essence of the gift.

1.4. Conclusions

Our journey through the anthropology and history of the gift has clarified a number of issues of foundational importance for this volume. We have found that the broad anthropological field of "gift" may be valuable in encompassing many kinds of service, favor, and donation in a common field of social relations, which tend to be characterized as voluntary, personal, and enduring. The relation between such "gifts" and other modes of transaction has varied over time and between cultures (and may be open to complex forms of negotiation), but we should be alert to the possibility that their sphere of significance is more extensive than in modern Western cultures. Anthropology does not provide any single "model" or "essence" of the gift, but it suggests that gifts may have important roles in creating or reproducing social ties. It further suggests a presumption (well-founded in relation to the Greco-Roman world) that gifts operate in reciprocal relations, and entail the expectation and obligation of return, whether the parties are equal or unequal in status. In the latter case, the return of honor is often found in pre-modern societies to be an essential element of the gift-relationship, expressing differentials in social and political power. We have noted the possibility that gifts may scramble and combine

gift-giving as the pooling of resources, see K. Tanner, *Economy of Grace* (Minneapolis: Fortress Press, 2005). I hope to return to this matter in a subsequent volume focusing not (as in this volume) on the divine gift, but on the social configurations of gift in Pauline and Christian ethics.

173. Douglas, introduction to Mauss, *The Gift*, p. x. From her perspective, "the whole idea of a free gift is based on a misunderstanding" since "refusing requital puts the act of giving outside any mutual ties" (p. ix).

what we are accustomed to regard as polar opposities: freedom and debt, choice and obligation, interest and disinterest. On this basis, we have learned to beware the use of epithets such as "pure" and "free" in relation to the gift, or at least to require a clear definition of their meaning. In particular, the anthropology of the gift has raised the possibility that the notion of the "pure" gift, a gift without return, is a historically and culturally specific Western invention.

A historical perspective is, therefore, necessary for contextualizing every discourse on gift/grace, including those we will study in the remainder of this book. In our survey of Paul's cultural context in the Greco-Roman world, we have noted the universal significance of gift-reciprocity, despite large variations in the types and contexts of gifts between human partners, and between humans and gods. The importance of the ties established by gifts, and the expectations of return, explain why it is important for donors to be selective in their distribution of gifts, using some criterion of "worth" to give discriminately and well. Everywhere in the Greco-Roman world we have traced the power of the gift to put recipients under obligation, resulting in predictable clashes between competing obligations, private and public. Judaism, we have suggested, was not structurally distinct in its understanding of gift-relations, even if the notion of a return *from God* (in this life or the next) could justify the extension of gift-giving to those generally regarded as too poor or too insignificant to be worthy of a gift. Seneca's Stoic analysis of the social problems and potential of benefaction displayed a refined Stoic concentration on the *spirit* in which the gift is given and received, at least partly disregarding the materiality of the gift and the benefit one might hope to gain from a counter-gift. But even Seneca is not interested in promoting a unilateral, unreciprocated gift, since the whole point of benefaction is to create (or continue) mutual social relations.

At the end of this chapter, we have sketched some explanations for the rise of the modern, Western concept of the "pure" gift, with its roots both in social, economic, and political changes and in an ideological reconfiguration of the gift. This renders it necessary to be highly self-conscious of the categories and assumptions that modern, Western interpreters are apt to bring to the discussion of gift and grace; they represent not timeless but culturally relative configurations of our topic.

As a complex but central form of social interaction, gifts have been the subject of reflection and experimentation in many different ways. Although we will focus primarily in this book on divine benefaction, it is clear that assumptions about gifts operative on the human plane are apt to shape expectations of the gifts of God. We have noted at a number of points, especially in relation to Seneca and Derrida (very different as they are), the possibility of "thinking" the gift to an extreme, drawing one or another motif associated with gift to a point of radical expression. The possibility of a gift that is completely indiscriminate, that is wholly distinct from sale or loan, that is utterly without return — these are some of the historical and cultural forms that we have noticed in this regard. Before our analysis proceeds, we need to clarify what is happening in such "perfections" of the gift, and the various forms that this phenomenon can take. If we can establish a clear taxonomy in this regard, that could help us understand why different texts (and different interpreters of the same text) can all insist that they are speaking about gift or grace, but differ widely in how they understand the concept.

CHAPTER 2

The Perfections of Gift/Grace

What is a gift? What makes it a gift, rather than a loan, a sale, a tax, or a salary? Is there a quintessential or perfect gift — perfect not just in content but in form? If God gives perfect gifts, what makes divine giving perfect? Or, in related terms, what makes divine "grace" gracious? Indeed, what do we mean by "grace," and what do we mean when we speak of "free grace," "sheer grace," or "pure grace"? What do we intend by drawing the notion of grace toward some such perfected form?

As we saw in the previous chapter, Derrida identified a paradox in the fact that gifts always circulate in patterns of gift-and-return, while (in his view) the gift is, in its purest essence, *without return* and unrecompensed (see above, 1.3.3). Logically extending this "pure gift" to its extreme, Derrida wanted to strip it of *every* possible element of return, even gratitude and self-congratulation, even the consciousness of having been given. Derrida was well aware that this "perfect gift" is an impossibility; it is also, arguably, a problematic notion, since such a gift does nothing to create or cement social bonds. Derrida's "perfection" of gift is thus both intellectually alluring and conceptually questionable, fulfilling one possible criterion for what constitutes a "gift" while apparently flouting another.

Seneca's discussion of benefits (see above, 1.2.5) threw up a different kind of "perfection," which was also both attractive and problematic. Unlike Derrida, Seneca does not "perfect" the gift as, in principle, unreciprocated: while he disregards the material return, he wants the gift to create reciprocal relationships of (at least) goodwill and gratitude. But he presses the question whether the gift would be most perfect if *given to everyone,* that is, whether the supreme benefaction would know no boundaries and no pre-conditions. One should expect the gods, from their infinite resources, to give unstintingly to everyone all the time: it is surely the essence of their generosity that it is completely indiscriminate (*Ben.* 1.1.9-11). Seneca affirms this truth, since the gods (as Nature) give their good gifts to everyone, good and bad. However, since this indiscriminate giving makes the gods appear morally indifferent, he also argues that they give certain gifts to all (wind, rain, sun, etc.) only because, in wanting to benefit the worthy, they can do so only by making their gifts universal (*Ben.* 4.28). Seneca thus considers a different "perfection" from that explored by Derrida (the perfect gift not as unreciprocated, but as universal and unmerited), although he is aware that this perfection also creates problems of another kind.

On occasion, Paul appears to offer some defining, or at least limiting, description of χάρις: if something is by χάρις, it is not "from works," "otherwise χάρις would not be χάρις" (Rom 11:6; cf. 4:4-5; 1 Cor 15:9-10). In these cases, χάρις is χάρις because it is *not* something else. This definitional gesture has encouraged Paul's interpreters to seek the essence of "grace," to define its core or proper characteristics. But not everyone agrees on that essence, and, as we shall illustrate below (chapter 3), some of the greatest disputes in the history of Christian theology have revolved around the meaning of "grace" in the Pauline letters. In order to gain some clarity, we need to analyze first this tendency to "perfect" a concept, and why it comes about (2.1). Then we must consider the different ways (I will suggest six) in which "grace" can be, or at least has been, "perfected" (2.2). This classification provides a taxonomy for much of the analytical work that follows in this book, and we will conclude this chapter by suggesting how recognition of the polyvalence of "grace" might clarify ambiguities that surround this subject and still bedevil analyses of Judaism and of Paul (2.3).

2.1. Perfecting a Concept

The term "perfection" is borrowed from the work of Kenneth Burke, and refers to the tendency to draw out a concept to its endpoint or extreme, whether for definitional clarity or for rhetorical or ideological advantage.[1] We speak of a "perfect storm" (where all that makes a storm "stormy" is combined in an extreme form), or a "perfect nuisance" (where the obstacle is the most tenacious and aggravating of nuisances). But even where we do not use the adjective "perfect," we are often inclined to "draw out" a concept to its "logical conclusion" or "ultimate reduction." As Burke argues, this tendency is implicit within the very act of definition: "As soon as some act is brought within the realm of

1. See K. Burke, *Permanence and Change: An Anatomy of Purpose* (Berkeley: University of California Press, 1954), pp. 292-94; idem, *Language as Symbolic Action: Essays on Life, Literature, and Method* (Berkeley: University of California Press, 1966), pp. 16-20.

symbols, there is such an end-of-the-line speculation vibrant within the terms for it. The logic of symbolic resources drives towards its fullness in a universal definition."[2] Thus, although concepts are generally employed alongside other balancing and limiting concepts, which inhibit their extreme expression, any definitional project is likely to use reductions, generalizations, or polarities in order to express some "true" sense: "the mere desire to name something by its 'proper' name, or to speak a language in its distinctive ways, is intrinsically 'perfectionist.'"[3] To ask what something is "by definition" invites its expression in an absolute or "pure" form.

This tendency is all the more pronounced when rhetoric requires some extreme or antithetical construction. Scholars like to think of themselves as usefully engaged in the world, but a hostile observer might dismiss their academic contributions as "purely academic," drawing the adjective "academic" to one end-of-the-line extreme, with the sense "having no relation to ordinary reality." Rhetoric often tends towards extremes, absolutes, and disjunctions, employing polarity or paradox to set potentially compatible notions into conceptual opposition. In some Christian quarters, those who *really* live "by faith" live without predictable material support (such as salaried employment): interpreting "faith" in this way, and drawing it to an extreme, forges a polarity that other Christians would neither recognize nor welcome. As this example shows, perfections can serve an ideological function. One way to legitimate oneself as the bearer of a tradition, and to disqualify others, is to appropriate to oneself the "true" and "proper" meaning of a traditional concept, such that others are not simply limited in understanding but are fundamentally in error: what *they* mean by X is non-X, once it has been defined in a particular, "perfect" form.

This perfecting tendency is always possible, but not everywhere performed. In normal usage, terms or concepts are modified by a web of links with other terms or concepts, and do not appear in any perfected form. Where perfections occur, they tend to serve the purposes of definitional clarity or polarizing rhetoric. They are also likely to arise in relation to God: since God is *ens perfectissimum* ("the most perfect entity"), concepts used with reference to God are likely to appear in their most complete, extreme, or absolute form. Thus, in connection with gift, God's gift, favor, or grace will be imagined as the ultimate "gift," the complete expression or very definition of "grace."[4] For this reason, we are likely to find clustered around divine gift/grace a variety

2. Burke, *Permanence and Change,* p. 292.

3. Burke, *Language as Symbolic Action,* p. 16.

4. Cf. James 1:17: "Every good act of giving and every perfect gift is from above, coming down from the Father of lights, in whom there is no variation or shadow due to change."

of linguistic signs marking the perfection of this concept. God operates in "pure grace" or by "sheer grace": his gifts are "utterly free," "totally gratuitous," or "by grace alone." Since perfections thrive on polarities, divine grace is also frequently defined in negative terms: it is unmerited, unalloyed, indiscriminate, unstinting, or unconditional.

Such claims about God are rarely theological niceties: they serve the interests (polemical or material) of those who deploy them. This is to say nothing, either positive or negative, about the truth of such claims, but it alerts us to the possibility that, in perfecting divine grace in one form or another, a struggle for superiority may be at work. Perfecting a theological motif may constitute an implicit or explicit claim to theological correctness, discrediting those who understand (and even perfect) the concept in a different way. Where such conceptual perfection is matched by social practice, it becomes the ideology of a distinctive pattern of life, and can prove enormously powerful in legitimating a religious tradition.[5]

Since gift-giving is a multifaceted phenomenon, gift or grace can be perfected in multiple ways. The attitude or character of the giver is one thing; the form and scale of the gift another; the relationship between the giver and the recipient another again. To speak of the perfect gift may be to speak about the "sheer" benevolence and "disinterest" of the giver, about the quantity or quality of the gift, or about the manner of its giving, or its effects. Because of this complexity, there is no single form in which gift/grace is perfected, and no necessity that a perfection of one facet will entail a perfection of others. In fact, one may distinguish at least *six* common perfections of the gift. In relation to the gift, one may perfect its *superabundance* in scale or permanence. In relation to the giver, one might perfect the *singularity* of benevolence (that the giver is characterized by this, and this alone). Concerning the manner of giving, the *priority* of the gift may be perfected, where its timing signals its freedom and generosity. Regarding the choice of recipient, a perfect gift may be said to bear no relation to the worthiness of its recipient; it is therefore celebrated in its unconditionality or *incongruity*. In terms of its effect, one may speak of the *efficacy* of the gift, its perfect achievement of its ends. And finally, as Derrida shows, the gift may be considered most "pure" in its *non-circularity*, its escape from recompense or reciprocation. These six forms of perfection are

5. Burke suggests that "a given terminology contains various *implications*, and there is a corresponding 'perfectionist' tendency for men to attempt carrying out those implications" (*Language as Symbolic Action*, p. 19). Because this can have unfortunate as well as beneficial effects, his "definition of man" finishes with the "wry codicil" that man is "rotten with perfection" (*Language as Symbolic Action*, p. 16). I use his term, however, without any such negative connotations.

sufficiently different to require individual analysis; and as their individuality emerges it will become clear that they by no means constitute a "package deal." One may perfect one or several facets of gift-giving without perfecting them all. Rival claims to maintain or defend the principle of "grace" may turn out to constitute *not different degrees of emphasis, but different kinds of perfection.*

2.2. Six Perfections of Grace

1. *Superabundance.* The first possible perfection of grace concerns the size, significance, or permanence of the gift, aspects which we may group under the heading "superabundance." We are not concerned here with the content of the gift, which, in relation to God, may take many different forms. What is emphasized here is scale: the more excessive and more all-encompassing the gift, the more perfect it may appear. The first anthropologists were fascinated by the extravagance of gift-giving in traditional societies, with "big men" proving their superior status by the overwhelming scale of their giving.[6] The same phenomenon can be traced elsewhere, not least in the extravagant largesse of rulers in the Greco-Roman era.[7] It was natural that the gods/God should be considered supreme in this respect, giving all things always from the complete abundance of divine satiety. Thus, Seneca speaks of the "lavish and unceasing" benevolence of the gods (*Ben.* 1.1.9) and lists the enormous benefits they pour out day by day in the gifts of nature (*Ben.* 4.25.1-2). Similarly, Philo speaks of the grace of God as a treasure-store of "boundless and illimitable wealth" (*Leg.* 3.163-64; *Sacr.* 124) that God "pours forth from a continuous and inexhaustible spring" (*Post.* 32, 127-28). The language of excess and superabundance is ubiquitous in Philo's depictions of divine grace, and is also to be found in the letters of Paul (Rom 5:12-21; 2 Cor 9:8, 11).[8]

It would be difficult to imagine any depiction of divine gift-giving that did not include this perfection. But to perfect this facet of grace is not to express what is usually meant by "pure grace" or "free gift." For that, we need to consider other possible perfections of this motif.

2. *Singularity.* In this perfection, attention shifts from the gift to the giver, and specifically to the *spirit* in which the gift is given. By "singularity," I mean the

6. On the potlatch (probably misrepresented by early anthropologists) see Mauss, *The Gift*, pp. 6-9.

7. See Seneca's critical comments on Alexander's enormous donations (*Ben.* 2.16; 5.6.1).

8. For Philo, see below, chapter 6; for Paul, see Part III and Part IV.

notion that the giver's *sole and exclusive* mode of operation is benevolence or goodness. In antiquity, the motivation of the giver was carefully scrutinized by philosophers such as Seneca (see 1.2.5), who were also likely to stress the character of the gods/God as singularly and purely benevolent. Reacting against the ambiguous representation of the gods in Greek mythology, Plato insisted that God, as the highest form of being, was also morally the most perfect; and because he is purely good, God does only what is good and beautiful (*Tim.* 29b-d; *Resp.* 379b-d). On this assumption, and against the popular conception, the divine could not be considered the cause of suffering or harm: God causes nothing except (as far as possible) what is purely and entirely good.[9] On this basis, Seneca speaks of the gods' benevolence as derived from their nature and the necessity of their being (*Ben.* 1.1.9; 4.25.1); their gifts are perfectly good because, by definition, they can do nothing else.

One can trace the impress of this assumption on Jews who were trained in the Greek philosophical tradition. Despite biblical stories of God's anger in the destruction of evildoers, *The Wisdom of Solomon* does everything possible to emphasize the benevolence of God's ways: God by no means hates, but loves everything that he has made (*Wis* 11:23–12:1; see below, chapter 5). Similarly, Philo is careful to insist that God is the cause only of what is good. While God could do anything, what he wills is what is morally excellent (*Abr.* 268; *Spec.* 4.187). Indeed, Philo's philosophy is governed by the rule that "the fountains of God's eternal gifts (χάριτες) should be kept free from not only what is, but also from what is thought to be, evil" (*Conf.* 182).

Such emphasis on the singularity of God's benevolence is not unproblematic in the Judeo-Christian tradition. Quite apart from biblical evidence to the contrary, and the human experience of suffering and evil, "pure benevolence" is not easily reconciled with standard understandings of justice, which require the upholding of the right by the punishment of evil. For this reason, this perfection of "grace" will not be satisfactory to all, but it has exercised a powerful attraction from antiquity to today. Marcion has not been alone in thinking that it is only when God's grace is made absolute in the singularity of nothing-but-benevolence that it appears in its "purest" form as "grace" (see below, 3.1).

3. *Priority.* Here the focus lies on the timing of the gift, which is perfect in taking place always prior to the initiative of the recipient. This chronological factor has many connotations. As the initiating move, the prior gift is not a

9. On these assumptions, which correlate a hierarchy of being with a scale of moral worth, see D. Martin, *Inventing Superstition: From the Hippocratics to the Christians* (Cambridge, MA: Harvard University Press, 2004), pp. 51-78.

reaction to a demand or request, and thus is spontaneous in its generosity; it is not obliged by a previous gift, and thus is absolutely "free"; and it signals the superiority of the giver, who is not in the subordinate position of returning a gift. Parents were often figured in this way as the benefactors of their children: their absolute priority made it doubtful whether children could ever "get even" in return (e.g., Seneca, *Ben.* 3.29-38). By extension, God, as the source of life, was considered the first giver, and this priority was perfected as a supreme expression of gift.[10]

Philo is once again a good representative of this particular perfection. It is fundamental to his religious philosophy that God is the source, the beginning, and the cause of every good thing: God is the sole, the primal (πρῶτον), and the most original (πρεσβύτατον) cause of the world (*Conf.* 123; *Ebr.* 73, 75). This is an essential counterweight to human pride, with its insidious tendency to take credit to itself. The core of piety, for Philo, is the recognition of divine causation, expressed in gratitude and thanksgiving to God; the whole of life should be characterized by recognition of divine priority in grace (*Her.* 102-24). Thus, even where he stresses human agency, Philo is apt to insist that God anticipates (προαπαντάω) those who come to him in worship (e.g., *Virt.* 185): it is characteristic of the divine to be always already on the scene. As we shall see, priority will play a significant role in the history of interpretation of grace, sometimes expressed as "prevenience," or (with additional connotations) "predestination." In certain forms, this perfection can appear problematic in reducing or excluding the responsibility of human agents. But it often occurs in one form or another as an expression of God's superiority and freedom in grace.

4. *Incongruity.* As we have seen, because gifts form social connections, in which discrimination is necessary, it is normally emphasized in antiquity that gifts should be given generously but selectively; care should be taken that the gift is given to suitable, worthy, or appropriate recipients (see above, 1.2). Such discrimination is not a diminishment of the gift, but ensures that it is, in fact, a *good* gift. Gifts given indiscriminately could appear random or trivial; if disbursed arbitrarily, they could not satisfy the criterion of just distribution; and if given without regard to the capacity of the recipient, they appeared thoughtless or cruel.

It was always possible to argue, however, that such a limitation of the gift was less than fully generous: a perfect gift could be figured as one given

10. For God as the source of life, see, e.g., Seneca, *Ben.* 4.4.3. On the superiority of the first gift in a history of gift exchange (e.g., the first, free gift of the ancestors), see J. Parry, "*The Gift*, the Indian Gift and the 'Indian Gift,'" *Man* 21 (1986): 453-73, at p. 466.

without condition, that is, *without regard to the worth of the recipient.* Thus, a hyper-generous benefactor might advertise the fact that he distributed food and wine "to all the citizens, and to the resident foreigners and to all who held property in the country," since "he wanted there to be no-one who did not share in his philanthropy."[11] Seneca emphasizes that a benefactor should not be overly choosy regarding the recipients of his gift, but should take a risk on those considered unworthy; and he cites in support the indiscriminate giving of the gods (*Ben.* 1.1.9). Even here, he introduces some qualifications. Lesser gifts (such as the grain-dole) could be given to all, but more significant gifts should be carefully placed; and although the gods give benefits even to the ungrateful, they intend them only for the good (4.28).[12] But it is clearly possible to perfect the incongruity of a gift as supremely excellent precisely because it does *not* take account of prior conditions of worth.

5. *Efficacy.* Turning to the effect of the gift, a perfect gift may also be figured as that which fully achieves what it was designed to do. Seneca portrays how a beneficiary can feel totally beholden to his benefactor, owing everything to him (*Ben.* 2.11), and certain kinds of benefit (giving birth to children, or rescuing a person from death) amount to the gift of life itself, and thus of the very capacity to give in return (*Ben.* 3.29.3). Once again, this perfection is common in relation to God, since divine agency can be taken to ground, encompass, and even cause the activity of the human recipient of grace. Thus, Seneca discourages boasts regarding human inventions, since "God draws forth from the secret depths of our being our various talents" (*Ben.* 4.6.4-5). Philo is often anxious to trace virtue to the agency of God: the soul's capacity to conceive of God is "inbreathed" by God in creation (*Det.* 86 on Gen 2:7), and human virtue (represented by the patriarchs' wives) is "sown" by divine grace (*Leg.* 2.46-48). In this connection, Philo is normally content to speak also of the vigorous activity of the human agent, but in one famous text he extends the efficacy of grace to the point of human passivity and inactivity, attributing all to the sovereignty of God.[13]

11. So Epaminondas in Ptoia (Boeotia) in the first century CE (*IG* 7.2712), cited in P. Veyne, *Bread and Circuses,* abr. and trans. B. Pearce (London: Penguin, 1990), pp. 145-46.

12. Cf. the parallel discussion in Philo: as the Sodom story shows (Gen 18–19), God is prepared to be benevolent to the unworthy, but only on account of the worthy (*Sacr.* 121–25). Since the gifts of creation are universal, they go to the imperfect as well as the perfect (*Leg.* 1.33-34), and in one sense nothing could ever be considered worthy of God (*Deus* 106). But Philo still normally insists on the worth of the recipients even (indeed, especially) of divine benefits; see below, 6.3.

13. The fragment, from the lost *Legum Allegoriae,* book 4, can be found in J. R. Harris,

The development of this perfection is associated most famously with Augustine, whose theology of grace we will study below (3.2). In one extreme form (for every perfection of grace is capable of extra refinement), claiming complete efficacy for divine grace may reduce human responsibility to a vanishing point; the development of this perfection is correspondingly controversial. In some form or another, everyone can agree that God's gifts are effective: the extent to which they are the sole and sufficient cause of the human response is the degree to which this facet of grace has been perfected.

6. *Non-Circularity.* Is a gift defined as gift by the fact that it escapes reciprocity, the system of exchange or *quid pro quo* that characterizes sale, reward, or loan? As we have seen, such is the modern notion of the "pure gift" (see above, 1.3.3). This was not a common conception of perfect gifts in antiquity. Gifts were distinguishable from loans or market transactions by the fact that no return could be demanded or enforced, but they were not detached from every notion of exchange or return; indeed, they could fulfill their function as gifts only if they were *not* unilateral (see above, 1.2). Philosophers might argue that one should give for the sake of giving, and for the sake of the other, not out of expectation of a return, while they could characterize the essential element in the return as non-material, that is, the gift of honor or the display of gratitude. But it was rare to find the gift perfected as a one-way, unilateral donation.

This is not to say that this perfection of gift was unimaginable in antiquity. Because the gift could never guarantee a return, a gift might always remain unreciprocated or fruitless: the use of the adverb δωρεάν in the sense "in vain" or "to nil effect" (e.g., by Paul in Gal 2:21) testifies to that possibility. As we have noted, anonymous gifts were rare, but were not unheard of, and could be justified if the alternative was humiliating for the recipient (Seneca, *Ben.* 2.10). There is even evidence for attempts to disparage honor as a return, with some rabbis arguing that the true reward is not to be blessed by the poor, but to be cursed.[14] Once again, this form of perfection was most likely to apply to the gods, since they need no return and could therefore give without its expectation. Thus, Seneca can portray the gods as benefactors giving without pay and without advantage to themselves: a benefit should carry no price tag *(ullum pretium)*; we have the gods for free (*gratuitos habemus deos, Ben.* 4.25.3). Even here, however, "for free" means "for no material benefit," rather than "without

Fragments from Philo Judaeus (Cambridge: Cambridge University Press, 1886), p. 8, and is discussed in J. M. G. Barclay, "'By the Grace of God I Am What I Am': Grace and Agency in Paul and Philo," in J. M. G. Barclay and S. J. Gathercole, eds., *Divine and Human Agency in Paul and His Cultural Environment* (London: T&T Clark, 2006), pp. 140-57, at pp. 145-46.

14. *Y. Pe'ah* 8.7, 21a, cited by Schwartz, *Mediterranean Society,* pp. 131-32.

any form of return," since Seneca is otherwise clear that the gods both deserve and desire human gratitude (1.6.3; 2.30.2). In this connection, Philo offers the strongest expression of the non-reciprocated gift in his discussion of the difference between sale and gift (*Cher.* 122–24). Here he criticizes benefactors for "selling" rather than "giving" benefactions, since they seek praise or honor as their return (ἀμοιβή), a repayment of their gift (χάριτος ἀντίδοσις). But God, Philo insists, "is no salesman (πωλητήρ) but a giver of everything (δωρητικὸς δὲ τῶν ἁπάντων), pouring out eternal fountains of gifts and seeking no return. For he needs nothing and no created being is capable of giving him back a gift" (*Cher.* 124).

One could point out that elsewhere Philo's God most certainly wishes a return, in the form of gratitude and praise; although that is not strictly speaking a gift, Philo can play on the double meaning of χάρις, and figure εὐχαριστία as the return of χάρις for χάρις (e.g., *Her.* 104). Philo thus witnesses both to the ancient possibility of imagining a gift as completely "without return" and to the difficulty of identifying any relationship in which this ideal could or should be practiced. The one-way gift establishes no relation, creates a permanent and potentially humiliating dependency, and frees the recipient of all responsibility. Nonetheless, its emergence in the modern era as a powerfully alluring perfection of grace, identified with "pure" altruism or disinterest, makes this an important facet of the perfected gift to place alongside the others we have outlined.

2.3. Grace as a Polyvalent Symbol

As noted above, it is not necessary to perfect either human or divine gift-giving. It makes good sense to speak of God or human agents exercising benevolent generosity without extending or absolutizing the notion of gift/grace in any of the directions sketched above. Indeed, since almost every perfection makes problematic some principle of justice, mutuality, or responsibility, the normal discourse of gift does not contain any perfecting momentum. However, the concept of gift-giving is certainly susceptible to one or more of these perfections, especially when this serves rhetorical or definitional ends, or when the discourse concerns God, the ultimate Giver.

But as our classification has shown, there is more than one way in which gift/grace can be perfected, and each of the six forms of perfection outlined above can stand on its own. *To perfect one facet of gift-giving does not imply the perfection of any or all of the others.* Thus, one could speak of divine gifts as superabundant or absolutely prior without implying that they are also incongruous with the worth of the recipient. Alternatively, God's grace may be figured as wholly and completely incongruous, without at the same time being "pure" in the sense of seeking no return. As we shall see in the following chapter, it is not uncommon for certain perfections to cluster together: the priority of divine grace is regularly paired with its efficacy, or its superabundance with its incongruity. The Protestant slogan *sola gratia* groups a number of these perfections, although even here we will note significant differences between Luther and Calvin (see below, 3.3 and 3.4). The important point is that these six perfections do not constitute a "package": to adopt one is not to commit to any or all of the rest. Therefore, two authors may each perfect the motif of grace, but still disagree strongly in their interpretation of this motif, because each is drawing a different facet to its end-of-the-line extreme.

Since the concept of grace is polyvalent, even in its perfected forms, common perfecting terms can mask deep differences in meaning. To speak of "pure grace" may mean its singularity (God is nothing but benevolent) or its non-circularity (God's grace seeks no return) — or some other of its six perfections. To describe God's grace as "free" could mean many things: that it is unconstrained by previous circumstances (in our terms, prior), that it is given irrespective of the recipients' worth (in our terms, incongruous), or that it is given without subsequent expectations (in our terms, non-circular) — or, indeed, some combination of these three. Similarly, the epithet "unconditional" could mean at least two things: without prior conditions (thus, incongruous) or without resulting obligations (thus, non-circular), or both.

Considering the centrality of this matter for the comprehension of Paul and of other Second Temple Jews, it is surprising how rarely the definition of "grace" has been subject to careful analysis. Westerholm has noted this as a significant problem in Sanders's analysis of Judaism,[15] but it often passes unnoticed when one or another perfection is presupposed as the essential meaning of grace. We may take just two examples from recent discussions of Paul and Judaism. VanLandingham works from a (modern) dictionary definition of "grace" as "the free and unmerited favor of God as manifested in the salvation of sinners and the bestowing of blessings," and concludes that "God can never confer 'grace' as a recompense; for, indeed, the opposite of grace is the reward for good behavior."[16] This polarity would have astounded Seneca, who considers that God gives his benefits, wherever possible, to those worthy of

15. S. Westerholm, *Perspectives Old and New on Paul: The "Lutheran" Paul and His Critics* (Grand Rapids: Eerdmans, 2004), pp. 341-51; we will analyze Sanders's reading of Judaism below, in 3.6.1.

16. C. VanLandingham, *Judgment and Justification in Early Judaism and the Apostle Paul* (Peabody, MA: Hendrickson, 2006), p. 20, citing the *Oxford English Dictionary*.

them. It is only if grace has already been defined as *necessarily incongruous* that Seneca's (or Philo's) superabundant divine gifts to the worthy would be disqualified from the category "grace." In a similar vein, Campbell uses a specific definition of "grace" to promote one reading of Paul against another. Declaring that "the language of 'grace' commonly refers to *unconditional* actions by God that deliver salvation to a given constituency with no strings attached as pure gift," Campbell presumes both the incongruity of grace ("unconditional") and its non-circularity ("no strings attached").[17] On this basis, Campbell denies that what Sanders identified as "grace" in Second Temple Judaism is truly such, because it includes elements of "conditionality" and necessary response; he also insists that some interpretations of Paul (including the mainstream reading of Rom 1–4) introduce elements into Pauline theology that are simply incompatible with the proper Pauline doctrine of "grace."[18]

It is clear from such examples that there is much at stake in the definition of "grace," which is subject to strong and interested acts of interpretation. It is essential to disaggregate the various perfections of "grace," and to warn against two matching assumptions: that any one perfection (or even a small cluster of them) is self-evidently *the* definition of grace, and that a perfection of one facet of grace will necessarily entail the perfection of others. When two different authors speak of divine benevolence or grace, but disagree on its meaning and its implications, this may be not because one *emphasizes* grace more than the other, or grasps its "true" meaning while the other does not, but simply because they are *perfecting different facets of grace.* As we shall see, Pelagius held firmly to the superabundance of divine grace, which was prior to all human activity; but (for theological reasons) he could not accept Augustine's perfection of the incongruity of grace (see below, 3.2.3). Augustine did not believe in grace *more* than Pelagius; he simply believed in it *differently.*

This taxonomy and disaggregation of the perfections of gift/grace is an analytical tool that will be put to work in the rest of this book. Paul's emphatic discourse on divine grace, with its antithetical formulations, has encouraged his interpreters to perfect this motif, but in varied and often contradictory ways; they accordingly read Paul as perfecting grace in precisely *their* way, and are apt to dismiss others as failing to capture the essence of "grace." As we have just seen, these same perfections also subtly control the ways in which scholars

17. D. A. Campbell, *The Deliverance of God* (Grand Rapids: Eerdmans, 2009), p. 100 (italics original). The footnote clarifies that "unconditional" is the essential term here, and that it includes the sense that "reciprocity in response to this gift is appropriate but not necessary" (pp. 955-56 n. 14).

18. For further discussion of these and other readers of "grace" in contemporary debates on Paul and Judaism, see below, 3.7.1.

may approach the analysis of divine mercy/grace in Second Temple Judaism. Thus, before we turn to the discourse on this theme in Second Temple Judaism (Part II) and in Paul (Parts III and IV), we need to analyze critical moments in the perfection of this Pauline motif (chapter 3). The purpose of this exercise is not merely to trace formative moments in the history of reception (though they are important enough, and sometimes insufficiently understood), but also to raise awareness of the deep, underlying presuppositions that continue to shape the interpretation of Second Temple Judaism and of Paul. The aim is not ground-clearing (as if one could then discuss the topic of grace without any influence at all from the history of interpretation) but consciousness-raising. Equipped with the taxonomy developed here, we aim to identify *how* and *why* different interpreters of Paul have read his theology of grace in strikingly different ways. By examining the shifting pattern of perfections over time, we will attempt to locate such differences *as historical constructs* within their original contexts, while tracing their impact on recent readings of Paul and of Judaism. We will thereby also become more self-conscious regarding our own reading of Paul and of his ancient Jewish context.

CHAPTER 3

Interpreting Paul on Grace: Shifting Patterns of Perfection

"I do not reject the grace of God; for if righteousness were by the law, Christ died in vain" (Gal 2:21). Thus Paul concludes the first stage of his polemical argument in Galatians, with the stakes raised high. *He* does not reject the grace of God; the implication is that others do. This grace is associated with the death of Christ, the central symbol of the Christian faith. To read that death rightly, with Paul, is to grasp the grace of God; the alternative is to misconstrue both Christ and grace (cf. Gal 5:4). Interpreters of Paul will want to ensure that they get him right. Proper understanding of Christ and of salvation is inseparable from proper comprehension of the grace of God.

In this chapter, we will examine a number of attempts to interpret grace "rightly" in the history of the reception of Paul. Due to the polemical and antithetical rhetoric of the Pauline text, the theme of grace has often been "perfected" (drawn to an end-of-the-line extreme) over nearly two millennia of interpretation, though in many different ways. The following examples are inevitably selective, but it would be hard to deny the significance and influence of each of the authors here discussed, from Marcion in the second century to Martyn in the twentieth. Our aim is twofold: first, to observe *how* these interpreters construe Paul's theology of grace, and in what dimensions they perfect this motif; secondly, to understand *why* they adopt these particular perfections of grace, by placing their reading in its historical, social, or ideological context. Due to the constraints of space, many points can be developed only in outline, but the goal is to say enough to trace how different perfections of grace have become significant in the history of reception of Paul, why they are so varied and contradictory, and how they reflect their own historical conjunctures and theological interests.[1]

1. The closest recent parallel to the survey in this chapter is that by S. Westerholm, *Per-*

To understand our past is to understand ourselves. No contemporary interpreter of Paul can afford to remain ignorant of the history of interpretation, which influences us at levels deeper than we tend to recognize. Hence the detailed studies here of Augustine, Luther, and Calvin, who have shaped the modern reception of Paul, not least in the case of those who reject their readings.[2] The last three sections of this chapter (3.5–3.7) analyze twentieth-century readings, in which former patterns of perfection are renewed, adapted, or developed, sometimes under the influence of a modern ideology of the gift (1.3). These readings form our immediate context for the reception of Paul, but also for the ways we figure Paul's relationship to his Jewish traditions. I will trace here also how particular perfections of grace have shaped the current discussion of "Paul and Judaism," in an attempt to clarify a deeply confusing debate. By such means I hope to provide a clearer framework for a new analysis of this topic, which we will pursue in Part Two (on Second Temple Judaism) and in Parts Three and Four (on Paul's theology in Galatians and Romans).

3.1. Marcion

Marcion will forever remain an elusive figure, whose texts, theology, and hermeneutical principles have been distorted by the selective and polemical forms in which his work has been represented and transmitted. We are fortunate to have Tertullian's extensive refutation of Marcion's work (*Adversus Marcionem,* books 1-5), although the object of attack may be as much the Marcionites of Tertullian's time and place of writing (c. 210 CE in Carthage) as the Marcion who established his alternative church in the 140s to 160s in Rome.[3] Modern

---

spectives Old and New on Paul: The "Lutheran" Paul and His Critics (Grand Rapids: Eerdmans, 2004), pp. 3-87 (on Augustine, Luther, Calvin, and Wesley) and pp. 101-258 (on twentieth-century readings of Paul). My focus here is on fewer figures, and specifically on their reading of "grace."

2. Other seminal figures in the history of reception of Paul on grace could have been added to this survey, e.g., Aquinas, Melanchthon, the Jansenists, Baur.

3. The problems in reconstruction are strongly featured in a new book by Judith Lieu, *Marcion and the Making of a Heretic: God and Scripture in the Second Century* (Cambridge: Cambridge University Press, 2014); see also J. M. Lieu "'As Much My Apostle as Christ Is Mine': The Dispute over Paul between Tertullian and Marcion," *EC* 1 (2010): 41-59, with cautious suggestions about the historical Marcion. For our purposes, the possible differences between Marcion and his immediate successors are not of major import, since the interpretation of Paul's language of grace seems consistent with and characteristic of them all. On the dating of Marcion's life, see S. Moll, *The Arch-Heretic Marcion* (Tübingen: Mohr Siebeck, 2010), pp. 25-46. For the text of Tertullian, *Adversus Marcionem,* with English translation, see E. Evans, ed. and trans., *Tertullian: Adversus Marcionem,* 2 vols. (Oxford: Clarendon Press, 1972).

caution regarding the "mirror-reading" of polemical texts has contributed to increasing criticism of Harnack's classic reconstruction of Marcion's theology (which is also imbued with distinctively Lutheran and liberal characteristics).[4] Nonetheless, the quantity of indirect evidence for Marcion's theology is sufficient to illuminate its central elements; we will focus here on his reading of Paul.

Marcion's Christian canon consisted of (an edited version of what we call) the Gospel of Luke and ten letters of Paul, beginning with the letter to the Galatians.[5] Both were important to Marcion: the gospel for depicting the life and teaching of Jesus, with its notable emphasis on generosity and love (e.g., Luke 6:27-38), the Pauline letters for placing this Jesus within the drama of redemption with its sharply polarized conceptual framework.[6] The opening chapters of Galatians (Marcion's only history of the church) were evidence for early attempts to corrupt the gospel (Gal 1:6-9; 2:5-6), and for the unreliability of the other apostles (Gal 2:11-14). Paul, however, stood uncompromisingly for "the truth of the gospel," which came not through human mediation, nor via the traditions of Judaism, but through a revelation of Jesus Christ (1:10-16).[7] The antithetical structures of this letter laid bare for Marcion the character of the gospel as the in-breaking of a new reality into "the present evil age" (Gal 1:4; 6:15). The "God and Father of Jesus Christ" is here placed in opposition to human tradition and the traditions of Judaism (Gal 1:1, 10, 13-14); the gospel stands in utter antithesis to such phenomena, as blessing to curse (3:10-14), freedom to slavery (2:4; 4:21–5:1), faith to (works of) the law (2:16; 3:2, 5), the new creation to "the world" (6:14-15). This starkly polarized picture was confirmed by the parallel antitheses that run through Romans (e.g., Rom 7:4-6; 8:1-11), 1 Corinthians (e.g., 1 Cor 1:18-31; 2:6-16), and 2 Corinthians (e.g., 2 Cor

4. A. von Harnack, *Marcion: Das Evangelium von Fremden Gott,* 2nd ed. (Leipzig: J. C. Hinrichs, 1924); for recent treatments see, e.g., May's essays collected in G. May and K. Greschat, eds., *Marcion and seine kirchengeschichtliche Wirkung* (Berlin: de Gruyter, 2002) and the rebuttal of Harnack in Moll, *Arch-Heretic.* Many of the essays in May and Greschat, *Marcion,* offer new evaluations of the evidence.

5. On Marcion's collection of the Pauline letters and their text, see U. Schmid, *Marcion und sein Apostolos* (Berlin: de Gruyter, 1995), who argues that the collection was already established before Marcion. The pastoral letters are ignored (either unknown or rejected).

6. Marcion's famous *Antitheses* seem to have drawn their positive material primarily from the gospel (the work is not cited in Tertullian's rebuttal of Marcion on Paul, *Adv. Marc.* 5), but the larger antithetical structure of Marcion's theology appears to owe more to Paul. In this respect, Moll overreacts to Harnack by downplaying the significance of Paul for Marcion (*Arch-Heretic,* pp. 70-71, 84-86); cf. B. Aland, "Marcion/Marcioniten," *TRE* 22 (1992): 93-94.

7. It is likely that Marcion interpreted Luke 10:22 as referring to Paul, the one to whom the Son was pleased to reveal the Father; the language is strikingly similar to Galatians 1:15-16.

3:6-18; 4:3-6). It is within this antithetical structure that Marcion places Paul's striking emphasis on God's "favor" or "grace" (Gal 1:3, 6, 15; 2:21, etc.), whereby "the Father of all mercies" (2 Cor 1:3) has revealed his love in the death of Christ on behalf of the ungodly and the weak (Rom 5:6-11). This deity, revealed in Christ, stands opposed to "the world" (Gal 4:8; 6:14) and "this age" (1 Cor 2:6) or, more precisely, "the God of this age" (2 Cor 4:4).

Marcion's notion of two Gods — the supreme God (Luke 6:35: ὕψιστος) and the Creator God — has been the subject of renewed study in recent years, which questions aspects of its representation both by Tertullian and by Harnack.[8] For our purposes, it is Marcion's portrayal of the supreme God as *purely and totally good* that is most important, and this is fortunately the least uncertain of Marcion's purported claims. As becomes clear through Tertullian's awkward response, Marcion insisted that the God newly revealed in Jesus Christ is a God of perfect and pure goodness: in Tertullian's Latin, he is not only *bonus* but *optimus* (supremely good; *Adv. Marc.* 1.6.1; 5.5.6, etc.), indeed *tantummodo* or *solummodo bonus* (good and nothing else; *Adv. Marc.* 1.24.7; 1.27.2; 2.11.3). In his supreme and especial goodness *(summa et praecipua bonitate sua)* he has set humankind free from its entrapment (1.17.1), manifesting his primary and perfect goodness (*principalis et perfecta bonitas,* 1.23.3; cf. 1.24.6), a sole and unadulterated benevolence (*sola et pura benignitas,* 1.2.3; *solitaria bonitas,* 1.26.2), consisting of fullness of grace and undivided mercy (*plena gratia et solida misericordia,* 1.24.6; cf. 5.5.6). This God, who is mild, forgiving, and merciful (1.26.3; 5.12.9, etc.; cf. Luke 6:36; 2 Cor 1:3; Rom 12:1) is an object of love, not fear (1.27.3; 5.12.9; cf. Rom 8:15).

Juxtaposed with (and in some senses opposed to) this God, revealed in Jesus, is the Creator God of the Jewish Scriptures, which were treated by the majority church as an authoritative testimony to the same God. The crucial function of this God is not so much that he is creator of the material world, although his character and power are certainly compromised by its manifest flaws. More important for Marcion is that he acts as a judge *(iudex),* and in this judicial role (expressly refused by Jesus, Luke 6:37; 12:14), he causes harm in the punishments he necessarily inflicts. Although Tertullian likes to describe this God as "just" (*iustus;* e.g. *Adv. Marc.* 2.12; the epithet serves his argumentative purpose), it seems that Marcion highlighted first and foremost his judicial role as judge *(iudex);* in accordance with this role, laws were laid down and

8. See, e.g., E. Norelli, "Marcion: Ein Philosoph oder ein Christ gegen Philosophie?" in May and Greschat, *Marcion,* pp. 113-30; W. Löhr, "Did Marcion Distinguish between a Just God and a Good God?" in May and Greschat, *Marcion,* pp. 131-46; Moll, *Arch-Heretic,* pp. 47-76. The question most disputed is the characterization of the creator God (as "just," "judge," and/or "evil").

humans inevitably punished, since the Creator's law exposes the weakness of the flesh and even incites sin (Rom 7:5-13).[9] Marcion associates the judicial functions of this God with a set of negative emotions and effects: anger, fear, offence, severity, vengeance, cruelty, punishment, condemnation, destruction, and death (*Adv. Marc.* 2.13, 18, 27, 29). For Marcion, none of these are compatible with the goodness of God, whose purpose in Christ is to save and not to destroy, to bless and not to condemn. It only makes matters worse that the God of the Jewish Scriptures is often inconsistent, jealous, petty, warlike, and ignorant (2.18-26). If, as Tertullian reports (1.2.1), Marcion made much of the dominical saying about the tree and its fruits (Luke 6:43-44: "no good tree bears bad fruit"), it was impossible to associate the good God with these negative products: whatever else may be said of the legislating and judging God, he is clearly not good.[10]

Marcion's reading of Paul thus not only *emphasizes* Paul's association of the Christ-event with the grace and mercy of God, but *perfects* this association in the direction of *singularity* (see above, 2.2), distancing the God who is purely and entirely good from any hint of the exercise of judgment. It served Marcion well that Paul is sometimes unclear about how God will deal with evil; and if the Pauline texts represented him in a judicial role, they had clearly been corrupted by the conspiracy that perverted the gospel from the very beginning (Gal 1:6).[11] In fact, Marcion represents a paradigm case of the rhetoric and ideology of perfection: a single notion (here the benevolence of God) is radicalized, purified, and made internally consistent, forming a polar opposite to its negative foil. It is likely that this perfection of singularity was influenced

9. For the primary importance of this judicial role, see, e.g., Irenaeus, *Haer.* 3.25.2; Tertullian, *Adv. Marc.* 1.6.1; 1.26; see also Löhr, "Did Marcion Distinguish."

10. The inferior God may be the cause of evil things (*malorum factor,* Irenaeus, *Haer.* 1.27.2), though it is not clear that Marcion thought him unambiguously or essentially evil, still less the root of all evil (*pace* Moll, *Arch-Heretic,* pp. 47-76). If he called the creator God "just," Marcion thereby exposed the moral difficulties in the common-sense notion of justice, which both upholds the good and punishes wrongdoers, and is necessarily resistant, at some point, to appeals for mercy. For ancient awareness of these problematics, see *4 Ezra* 7–8 (discussed below, chapter 9).

11. In Galatians, God/Jesus is not directly associated with judgment: 5:10 does not indicate who will exercise judgment, nor 5:21 how those who do the works of the flesh will fail to enter the kingdom; 6:8 suggests that the flesh itself will be the cause of destruction. Texts in Romans required textual surgery, to "restore" the uncontaminated original (e.g., the removal of τὰ κρίματα from the otherwise excellent celebration of God in Romans 11:33-35; Tertullian, *Adv. Marc.* 5.14.9). If we may trust Tertullian, Marcion's purely good God dealt with evil by prohibiting it, and removing himself from it, but not by punishment or destruction (*Adv. Marc.* 1.26-27).

by the widespread concern in the Greek intellectual tradition to ensure that God/the gods were depicted in ways truly "worthy" of deity (θεοπρεπές), and by the common philosophical notion that the divine is, by definition, perfectly and completely *good.*[12] While this axiom is especially associated with the Platonic tradition (cf. Plato, *Resp.* 376e-392c: ἀγαθὸς ὅ γε θεὸς τῷ ὄντι, 379b), it was shared by all philosophical schools who strove to justify God's apparently heartless treatment of humanity, or to distance God wholly from the travails of human existence. Tertullian unfairly associates Marcion with this latter, Epicurean, option (*Adv. Marc.* 1.25.3), but it is clear that Marcion's purely good God has intervened in human history, in the life and death of Christ. Indeed, Marcion's adoption of the philosophical axiom that deity must be entirely good serves, paradoxically, an anti-philosophical stance: his God cannot be associated with nature, or with the ordering purposes of "reason," but has emerged from hiddenness, inexplicably, in the event of Christ. It is Tertullian who insists that God's goodness must accord with reason, and thus with the ordered punishment of evil. Marcion, not beholden to that philosophical demand, insists on the extremity and irrationality of God's grace, given in profusion to those not even his own.[13] Coming in Christ to strangers *(alieni),* the God of Jesus Christ is, from a human perspective, a wholly other *(alienus)* God. The *singularity* of God's grace is thus here supplemented by aspects of *incongruity,* as God gives gifts to those he neither created nor owned, unlimited by pre-formed ties of obligation.

The simplicity of Marcion's solution to the moral problems of the Jewish Scriptures, and the ethical purity of his concept of goodness (both human and divine), may account for the enormous popularity of the Marcionite gospel. If the churches in Rome were by his day largely Gentile, and socially separate from the Jewish synagogues, it was easy to interpret Paul's statements on freedom from the law as implying that the Jewish Scriptures did not belong within the church, except as the negative foil to the gospel.[14] If Christians were victims

12. For Jewish appropriation of this tradition, see, e.g., Josephus, *Ant.* 4.180; *Apion* 2.166, 238-54; for *The Wisdom of Solomon,* wisdom is the image of the "goodness of God" (7:26); for Philo, God is τὸ πρῶτον ἀγαθὸν καὶ καλόν (*Legat.* 5). Other early Christian writers were also well attuned to the need to "purify" the image of God: cf. Tertullian, *Apol.* 14; Origen, *Cels.* 5.14, 23-24.

13. For discussion, see Norelli, "Marcion." Marcion's high level of education would have exposed him to the philosophical critique of "mythology," even if he adopted no particular philosophical school of thought and, under Pauline influence (1 Cor 1–2), reacted against the philosophical commitment to reason (see Aland, "Marcion/Marcioniten," pp. 94, 98).

14. Marcion emended Galatians 4:24-25 to create a supplementary antithesis between the "synagogue of the Jews" and "the holy church" (Schmid, *Marcion und sein Apostolos,* pp. 317-18; Tertullian, *Adv. Marc.* 5.4.8).

of social prejudice and harassment, this was explicable in Pauline terms as representing the intrinsic opposition to the gospel by "the god of this age." Moreover, Marcion's churches were able to embed their opposition to the Creator and his world in a definitive token of resistance that affected their *habitus* at a centrally significant point: opposing the sexual drive, and thus both marriage and child-bearing, they were enlisted in the Pauline struggle between the spirit and the flesh in a daily and life-changing manner. This freedom from sex and marriage was the physical token of liberation, the sign that God's supreme and unqualified goodness had rescued them from the ambiguous, and often pernicious, conditions of the created world. The singularity of God's grace is thus put to powerful ideological effect. It separates Marcionites from the transient creation (1 Cor 7:29-31), but also from compromised Christians who mistakenly dilute their faith with homage to the inferior God — the one who created the desires of the flesh and is honored, with fear, in the Scriptures of Judaism.

3.2. Augustine

No interpreter of Paul — indeed, no Christian theologian — has given greater or more profound attention to the theme of "grace" than Augustine of Hippo (354-430 CE). Among his scriptural sources, the letters of Paul feature prominently in this connection, and not just in isolated tags. As Augustine reads Romans, grace is almost the only theme in the letter (*Spir. et litt.* 12), and it is here that he finds Pauline precedent not only to urge this theme but to press for a clear definition: grace would not be grace if it were owed (Rom 4:4) or were given on the basis of works (Rom 11:6).[15] Pauline antitheses encourage Augustine, like Marcion, to "perfect" grace into a set of articulated polarities, but the nature of his perfections could hardly be more different. Far from "purifying" God's grace from all taints of judgment, Augustine's notion of grace shines all the more brilliantly against the dark backcloth of divine justice. The punishment for sin to which all are liable, since all share in Adam's guilt, is the debt that God is justly entitled to demand: if for inscrutable reasons he chooses to exercise on some his "un-owed" favor *(indebita gratia),* he supersedes but does not contradict his justice.[16] This *incongruous gift to the undeserving* forms the bedrock of Augustine's theology of grace, though in its exposition he will

15. For the significance of these two verses as summarizing the message of Romans and defining the nature of grace, see *Spir. et litt.* 13, 16, 40, etc.; cf. *Ad Simpl.* 1.2.2: *eo ipso quo gratia est evangelica operibus non debetur, alioquin gratia iam non est gratia.*

16. This line of thought is illustrated by a commercial analogy in *Ad Simpl.* 1.16; thereafter it is often repeated.

add further perfections in combinations that have influenced the interpretation of Paul to this day.

Augustine's theology of grace is best understood as a momentum that develops in changing historical and polemical contexts.[17] We can trace this development from his earliest engagements with Romans through a significant development in 396 (his *Ad Simplicianum*) and on into the Pelagian and subsequent controversies. In some cases, our knowledge of his opponents (Pelagius; John Cassian), who had their own theologies of grace, helps to sharpen the profile of the distinctively Augustinian perfections. Where we can also trace correlations between Augustine's theology and his personal experience or social practice, these will give depth to the analysis of a phenomenon that was always for Augustine a reality he inhabited, not just a doctrine he believed.

3.2.1. Early Works on Romans

Augustine's very incomplete commentary on Romans *(Epistolae ad Romanos inchoata expositio)* and his *Expositio quarundam propositionum ex epistula ad Romanos* on the same letter (both 394-395 CE) represent some of his first attempts to rethink the interpretation of Paul after his departure from the Manichaean brand of Paulinism.[18] Many central elements in his reading of Paul are already in place. Paul's polemic against "works of the law" is taken to be directed not against particular Jewish "ceremonies" but against Jewish believers who took pride in their works, through which they thought they had merited the grace of the gospel (*ex. prop. Rm.* 60.13). The law and its works are thus associated with pride, which was always for Augustine the foundational human sin: Paul attacks those who presume to boast in their works as

17. For the early stages see W. S. Babcock, "Augustine's Interpretation of Romans (A.D. 394-396)," *AugStud* 10 (1979): 55-74 and C. Harrison, *Rethinking Augustine's Early Theology: An Argument for Continuity* (Oxford: Oxford University Press, 2006) (the latter insisting, against Brown, Fredriksen et al., that little actually changes in the *Ad Simpl.* of 396). For the whole span of Augustine's works, see J. Patout Burns, *The Development of Augustine's Doctrine of Operative Grace* (Paris: Études Augustiniennes, 1980) and P.-M. Hombert, *Gloria Gratiae: Se glorifier en Dieu, principe et fin de la théologie augustinienne de la grâce* (Paris: Études Augustiniennes, 1996).

18. For texts and translation, see P. Fredriksen Landes, *Augustine on Romans* (Chico: Scholars Press, 1982); and for Augustine's early engagements with Paul, see Harrison, *Augustine's Early Theology,* pp. 115-63. The commentary on the letter to the Galatians *(Expositio Epistolae ad Galatas)* comes from this same period (for text and translation, see E. Plumer, *Augustine's Commentary on Galatians: Introduction, Text, Translation, and Notes* [Oxford: Oxford University Press, 2003]).

if performed in their own strength, thus establishing "their own merit" rather than attributing credit to God (*ex. prop. Rm.* 64).[19] Against the common and reasonable appreciation of virtue as a product of human effort that elicits the favor of God, Augustine advances a theology of grace that *precedes* all merit, enabling moral virtue but not in any sense dependent on it. The key Romans text, to which he will return again and again in the years to come, is Romans 5:5: "the love of God [read as: love for God] has been poured into our hearts by the Holy Spirit which has been given to us" (*ex. prop. Rm.* 26; 60.6-7, 10; 61.5, etc.).[20] Here is the gift — the infusion of the Spirit — which is necessary for believers if they are not just to obey but to love God, instilling in them that desire or longing by which they are drawn into the purpose and being of God. As in the motif to be articulated in his *Confessions* (397-401 CE), but already implicit here, Augustine suggests that for humanity to fulfill God's will, God himself must give what he commands: *da quod iubes et iube quod vis* ("give what you command and command what you will," *Conf.* 10.29.40; cf. 10.31.45; 10.37.60). The language of gift thus serves to make clear the attribution of source: *non ex nobis sed dei donum* ("this is not from ourselves, but the gift of God," Eph 2:8; cf. *Ad Simpl.* 1.2.3, 6). Augustine takes Paul as striking at the root of human pride, self-assertion, and self-congratulation; even in their virtues, believers are to acknowledge their dependence on what is not their own, but God's.

But it is another matter to decide if or how this applies to faith. In the *Expositio Propositionum* Augustine famously, and to his later regret, argued that whatever may be said of subsequent good works, "faith is ours" (60.12); in order to counter Manichaean determinism, he endeavored to preserve at least here a space for free will. Defending this thesis against the flow of Romans 9, he insists that God's choice of Jacob over Esau must have some basis, else it would be arbitrary: since Paul rules out works as the grounds for this choice, God's pre-birth calling must have arisen from his foreknowledge that Jacob would believe (62.15). Summing up his reading, Augustine writes: "It is the nature of grace that the calling is made in advance to the sinner, when he

19. For pride as the quintessential human sin, countered by Christ's own humility in becoming human, see Harrison, *Augustine's Early Theology*, pp. 173-77. She elsewhere quotes Augustine's insistence that to follow Christ is "first humility, second humility, third humility . . . pride will wrest from our hand any good work we do while we are in the very act of taking pleasure in it" (*Ep.* 118). Augustine is able to turn this principle against all his varied opponents (Manichees, Donatists, and Pelagians), just as he takes Paul to employ it against his (both Jewish and Christian).

20. According to Harrison (*Augustine: Christian Truth and Fractured Humanity* [Oxford: Oxford University Press, 2000], p. 96 n. 33), there are more than 200 citations of this verse in the Augustinian corpus; readers will find countless more allusions.

had no merits except such as would issue in damnation. But if the one who was called followed the calling — now by his free will — he will merit also the Holy Spirit through whom he can do good works; and remaining in the Spirit — no less by his free will — he will merit eternal life" (*ex. prop. Rm.* 60.14-15, my translation).

We see here already Augustine's concern to define "grace" ("it is the nature of grace . . ."). By definition, it *precedes* merit and is given to the *sinner:* this accent on *priority* and *incongruity* is indeed the hallmark of grace throughout Augustine's life.[21] At this point, since he holds to God's foreknowledge of faith, Augustine allows the temporal, but not the logical, priority of grace. Knowing that the believer will believe, and thus gain the gift of the Spirit as the *meritum fidei,* God calls in advance, in accordance with the faith that is yet to be. The essential point, however, is that the grace of God precedes the merit of virtue, and since he justifies the ungodly, not those already godly, God's grace is in origin and at its initial point of impact an incongruous gift. But the purpose of this gift is, for Augustine, different from its origin: God justifies the ungodly *in order to make them godly,* and their subsequent good life, enabled by the gift of the Spirit, will render them fitting and deserving heirs of eternal life (*ex prop. Rm.* 21–22). This move from incongruity to congruity is effected by the Spirit, whose work in believers' hearts is transformative. God does not cause unbelievers to sin (he merely abandons them to it), but he does both aid and (in some sense) "make" *(facio)* the good working of the believer *(ex prop. Rm.* 61.12: *facit eum bene operari).* With his already strong sense that love for God can arise only from the effectual operation of God himself, Augustine looks beneath and within human agency to find that, at the deepest level, the primary agent is God.

Priority, incongruity, and efficacy are the three perfections around which Augustine's theology of grace will hereafter revolve, in ever closer integration. The efficacy of grace will shortly be retrojected before works to the initial act of faith itself, and then before the act of faith to the believer's predestination. In addition, the efficacy of grace will be extended forward, throughout life, as the gift of perseverance, drawing the free human agent into a nexus of effective action attributable only to God. This grace will thus become prior both in time

21. The central issue in Romans is defined by Paul's term "grace," which means that "no one dare say that he has been led to the Gospel because of the merits of his previous life" *(vitae prioris merita):* grace "cleanses and justifies sinners" (*peccatores sanet et justificat, ep. Rm. inch.* 6). God "loved us first before all merit" (*prior dilexit nos ante omnia merita, ep. Rm. inch.* 7.6). "The nature of grace is that the call reaches the sinner in advance, when he had no merits except what would lead to damnation" (*Est autem gratia, ut vocatio peccatori praerogetur, cum eius merita nulla, nisi ad damnationem praecesserint, ex. prop. Rm.* 60.14).

and in logic, enabling human merit but never proceeding from it. Augustine will retain to the end his dual emphasis on the incongruity of grace (given to sinners before they were worthy) and the congruity of its result (creating humans fit for God). He strongly repudiates the language of debt or merit as grounds for grace, but speaks freely of merit or reward as the product of the believer's life, since in the latter case believers' "merits" are nothing other than the gifts of God.[22] Luther will find this duality in Augustine's treatment of "merit" unhelpful, since incongruity is for Luther the abiding essence of grace. But Augustine's own melding of perfections renders possible and appropriate the language of human merit — though only so long as it is founded securely on the prior efficacy of grace.

3.2.2. Further Wrestling with Romans 9: *Ad Simplicianum*

Augustine recognized that a shift in his thinking took place while answering questions posed by Simplicianus (396 CE), when he tried to make sense of Paul's apparently outrageous statements in Rom 9:6-23.[23] He insists again on

22. See, e.g., *Spir. et litt.* 40; *Grat. et Lib. Arb.* 13-20; *C. Jul.* 6.12.39 *(ipsa bona merita nostra nonnisi dei dona esse fateamur); Ep.* 194.5.19 *(cum Deus coronat merita nostra, nihil aliud coronat quam munera sua).* Augustine sometimes displays anxiety about the Pauline language of reward, the "crown of righteousness" that God will render *(reddo)* to him on the last day (2 Tim 4:7-8), since this appears to clash with the repudiation of "debt" *(debitum)* in the realm of grace (Rom 4:4). His solution is to insist that Christ does not render but gives gifts (*non reddidit sed dedit,* alluding to Ephesians 4:8): no "debt" can be spoken of unless it is prefaced by reference to the fact that Paul had "first received grace that was *not* due to him." He obtained mercy as a blasphemer and persecutor from the God who justifies not the godly but the ungodly, though with the purpose, of course, that "by justifying him he may make him godly" (*ut justificando pium faciat, Ad Simpl.* 1.2.3)

23. For reference to this development, see *Retr.* 1.22.2-4: "I indeed labored in defense of the free choice of the human will, but the grace of God triumphed" (*Retr.* 2.27.1). For close analysis, see Babcock, "Augustine's Interpretation"; Burns, *Development,* pp. 2-51; Harrison, *Augustine's Early Theology,* pp. 142-54, 265-80. Babcock rightly insists that it is the press of Romans 9 itself on Augustine's mind that is the chief factor in this change ("Augustine's Interpretation," pp. 67-74; cf. Babcock, "Comment: Augustine, Paul, and the Question of Moral Evil," in idem, ed., *Paul and the Legacies of Paul* [Dallas: Southern Methodist University Press, 1990], pp. 251-61 in dialogue with P. Fredriksen, "Beyond the Body/Soul Dichotomy: Augustine's Answer to Mani, Plotinus, and Julian," in Babcock, *Paul and the Legacies of Paul,* pp. 227-51). On the match with Augustine's interpretation of his own conversion, see J. Wetzel, *Augustine and the Limits of Virtue* (Cambridge: Cambridge University Press, 1992), pp. 150-60 and Wetzel, "Snares of Truth: Augustine on Free Will and Predestination," in R. Dodaro and G. Lawless, eds., *Augustine and His Critics: Essays in Honour of Gerald Bonner* (London: Routledge, 2000), pp. 130-32.

the priority of grace before the merit of works: "good works do not produce grace but are produced by grace"; "grace comes before all merits: Christ died for the ungodly" (*Ad Simpl.* 1.2.3; 1.2.7). But he finds it no longer sustainable to hold that "faith is ours," since "faith itself is to be numbered among the gifts of grace": if it is ours (exercised by free will) it is also God's, since it is the product of God's calling (1.2.7). In particular, when he considers what is involved in faith — the willing assent to God's call — Augustine is impressed by the Pauline statement that "it is not of the one who wills, or the one who runs, but of the mercy of God" (Rom 9:16). This is combined with a text which (in its Latin form) becomes pivotal in Augustine's thinking from this point onwards: "God is at work in you both to will and to work for a good will" (*deus est qui operatur in vobis et velle et operari pro bona voluntate,* Phil 2:13; cited in *Ad Simpl.* 1.2.12 and elsewhere). If the will itself, the necessary means of assent to God, is itself in some sense produced by God, Augustine can no more isolate the freedom to believe as "up to us," nor hold to God's foreknowledge of this choice as the grounds for his call. The *bona voluntas* necessary for all good action, even and especially the willing receipt of God's call, is itself a gift of God (*dei donum, Ad Simpl.* 1.2.12). One can observe Augustine's logic in a chain of rhetorical questions toward the end of this pivotal work:

> We are commanded to believe that we may receive the gift of the Holy Spirit and become able to do good works by love [cf. Rom 5:5]. But who can believe unless he is touched *(tangatur)* by some calling, by some testimony borne to the truth? [cf. Rom 10:14] Who has it in his power that his mind is struck by such a vision *(tali viso attingi mentem suam)* by which his will is moved *(moveatur)* to faith? Who can welcome in his mind something which does not give him delight *(delectat)*? But who has it in his power to ensure that something that will delight him will turn up, or that he will take delight in what turns up? If those things delight us which serve our advancement towards God, that is due not to our assent or industry or meritorious works, but to the inspiration and provision of the grace of God *(inspiratur hoc et praebetur gratia dei).* That there is the assent of our will *(nutus voluntatis),* that there is industrious effort, that there are fervent works of charity, God provides, God gives *(ille tribuit, ille largitur).*[24]

This line of reasoning is the product of Augustine's deep reflection on the inner operation of the will, its divisions and wounds, and the perversity with which it delights in what is sinful and harmful, unless touched by the grace of God.

24. *Ad Simpl.* 1.2.21, trans. Burnaby, altered.

Such introspection is the glory of his *Confessions,* which ranks as perhaps the most acute (and certainly the most influential) of all ancient reflections on the motivations and dispositions of the human will. From the depth of his experience and the breadth of his reflection, Augustine here reconstructs the chain of causes necessary for delight in the truth, and finds this impossible but for the grace of God. Matching this logic is the Pauline tag that here and henceforth resounds through all of Augustine's treatments of grace: "For what aspect of the good do you have that you have not received?" (*quid enim boni habes quod non accepisti?,* 1 Cor 4.7; *Ad Simpl.* 1.2.9; cf. *Conf.* 7.21.27). Drilling down into the depths of the human psyche, Augustine finds nothing that falls outside the reach of this Pauline question.[25]

Ad Simplicianum thus advances the notion that God's call is congruent *(congrua)* to those who believe, the effective cause of their good will (*effitrex bonae voluntatis,* 1.2.13). Augustine uses various terms for the nature of this effect ("help," "touch," "inspire," and "move" are some of the most common), but the crucial step is to trace the efficacy of grace deep into the motivating forces of the human mind. At the same time, Augustine notes the impossibility of frustrating the will of God, for "God has mercy on no one in vain" (*Ad Simpl.* 1.2.13). We see here the logical extension of a particular perfection of grace, the perfection of *efficacy,* once it is ascribed to a God whose will cannot be thwarted. While Augustine will continue to insist that the human mind is active and willing (indeed, becomes most truly "free") in being moved by God, the combination of agencies will always give priority, in time and potency, to the divine agent. He justifies the selectivity in God's effective calling by the notion that (following Romans 9:21-23) God can make from the same lump vessels of honor and vessels of destruction — the "lump" being henceforth dubbed the *massa peccati* or *massa perditionis,* which God justly condemns to destruction. The more Augustine stresses God's prior, incongruous, and *effective* choice in grace, the more he is driven to appeal to the inscrutability of God's decision (*Ad Simpl.* 1.2.16, appealing to Romans 11:33). But once the perfection of efficacy has reached deep into the human mind, there can be no limit to the impact of this grace, which operates with divine power.[26]

25. As Westerholm comments (*Perspectives Old and New,* p. 16), "Augustine elevated Paul's query to an axiom in the light of which all Scripture is to be read, all doctrine tested, and all life lived" (cf. *Praed. Sanct.* 8-9; *Retr.* 2.27.1).

26. Harrison insists that Augustine has done no more than work through with full "clarity" his earlier theology of grace (*Augustine's Early Theology,* pp. 142-63, 238-87, echoing Augustine's own language in *Retr.* 2.27.1). But as we have seen, appeal to God's grace can mean many different things, and here our analysis of the various possible "perfections" of grace becomes particularly useful. Augustine moves no further than before in stressing the priority

3.2.3. The Pelagian Controversy

Augustine's controversies with Caelestius, Pelagius, and Julian of Eclanum (from 412 to his death in 430) developed his conviction that the incongruity of grace is the hallmark of salvation, without fundamentally altering his views. What they also reveal, however, is the significance of the correlation between theologies of grace and the theologians' social context. What made sense to Pelagius, who strove to awaken elite Christian friends from moral laziness and half-hearted commitment, looked unconvincing to the bishop of Hippo, whose congregation of ordinary Christians prayed daily for forgiveness and protection as they struggled with the pressures and temptations of everyday life.[27]

Pelagius and Augustine, both careful exegetes of Paul, agreed in their emphasis on the priority of grace, and this agreement led many contemporaries to think that there was no essential difference between them. Pelagius identified as the prime gift of grace the ability *(posse)* to do the good, an ability given by God in human nature, subsequently informed by the instruction of revelation, and strengthened by the example of good people, supremely Christ. This knowledge assists believers to do more easily what they are instructed to do, but the choice or will *(velle)* to do the good is ours, as is the action itself *(facere)*, for which we rightly applaud the human agent. God acts upon the will by revealing the truth (e.g., about rewards and punishments) and by moral exhortations, but Pelagius was convinced that to make God responsible for human willing and doing in any more direct sense would undermine the freedom of the human agent and make God himself responsible for evil as well as good.[28]

---

of grace, but he here removes the last possible vestige of correlation between human worth (in believing) and divine grace, while pressing its efficacy into even the *initium* of the act of faith. Once the efficacy of grace is thus comprehensively applied, questions of God's justice and selectivity have to be faced, or expressly relegated to the sphere of the incomprehensible (as in *Ad Simpl.* 1.2). Harrison is right to insist that this text does not signal a complete change in Augustine's theology, but neither is it simply a return to an original theology of grace "with new clarity and confidence" (*Augustine's Early Theology,* pp. 153-54). It is an extension of the efficacy of grace into the last remaining bastion of human initiative and, as with many such extensions, the final step has momentous consequences.

27. For Pelagius's patrons and social environment, see P. Brown, *Religion and Society in the Age of Saint Augustine* (London: Faber and Faber, 1972), pp. 183-226; for Augustine's context in Hippo, see S. Lancel, *Saint Augustine,* trans. A. Neville (London: SCM Press, 2002), pp. 246-70.

28. For Pelagius's views, sometimes quoted at length, see especially Augustine, *De natura et gratia* and *De gratia Christi, et de peccato originali.* For Pelagius's commentary on Romans, see T. de Bruyn, *Pelagius' Commentary on St. Paul's Epistle to the Romans* (Oxford: Clarendon Press, 1993). For detailed descriptions of the Pelagian controversies, with abundant secondary

Pelagius's aim was "to arouse and kindle cold and sluggish souls by Christian exhortation to lead good lives" (Augustine, *Nat. et Grat.* 68), and his message had considerable impact on elite but morally compromised Christians whose education and social power encouraged them to think that self-mastery and moral control were within their grasp. Divine grace provides the conditions in which human beings could resist evil, but the responsibility for choosing and doing remains our own; for this task the Christian tradition provides all the necessary inducements and external aids (together with forgiveness for past sins). As Augustine quotes Pelagius: "Though we have in ourselves a free choice which is so strong and so resolute for avoiding sin, a free choice which the Creator implanted generally in human nature, we are also defended by his daily help in accord with his incalculable kindness" (*Grat. Christi* 1.29). Pelagius clearly believed in the *priority* and *superabundance* of grace — but those perfections were not nearly sufficient for Augustine.

The question that Augustine immediately fires back to Pelagius is revealing: "Why do we need this help if our free choice is strong and so resolute for avoiding sin?" (*Grat. Christi* 1.29). For Augustine, grace is necessarily operative not only in our (natural) capacities but also in our willing and acting, for the latter require not just knowledge and freedom of will, but a delight or love for God that only God himself can provide (*Spir. et litt.* 4-5). Augustine continues to speak of the freedom of the will (at least in the sense that it is freed by God, *Spir. et litt.* 52), and he is anxious to avoid overly blunt language of divine causation (*Pecc. merit.* 1.31). But it is crucial for him that the divine aid given to human willing and acting is not just external but internal, God's working *in our very will* to do the good (with frequent citations of Philippians 2:12-13; cf. *Spir. et litt.* 52-53, 58-60). For, in Augustine's view, the free choice is not "strong" and not "resolute." It is wounded, weak, and sick, requiring not just instruction but healing. In a telling phrase, he laments that "there are wretched shadows in the human soul" (*Nat. et Grat.* 40), deep flaws that render us incapable of responding to God. In effect, he insists on the *incongruity* of grace not just in the initial gift of forgiveness, but in repeated gifts of healing and aid to the wounded believer. Grace is not just assistance that helps believers do more easily what they could do with difficulty themselves; its incongruity with their capacities and desires is a structurally integral component of salvation, from start to finish. In a carefully nuanced debate over the possibility of human sinlessness, Augustine's concern is not primarily to declare human sinlessness impossible, but to insist that it could

literature, see G. Bonner, *St Augustine of Hippo: Life and Controversies* (Norwich: Canterbury Press, 1963), pp. 312-93; P. Brown, *Augustine of Hippo* (New York: Dorset Press), pp. 340-75; Lancel, *Saint Augustine*, pp. 325-67.

be realized only with the infusion of the Holy Spirit, "who helps in our weaknesses and co-operates with our strengths" (*Nat. et Grat.* 69). In fact, because he understands "sinlessness" not just as the absence of sin, but more positively as a full and perfect love for God, Augustine is skeptical about this possibility within the conditions of this life (*Spir. et litt.* 64); some shadows within the soul are bound to remain throughout believers' earthly lives.

The sickness and insufficiency of the condition even of believers are corroborated for Augustine by two phenomena of Christian practice. In the first place, he presses Pelagius and his associates to explain infant baptism, a practice that had become traditional in the North African church and was conducted very soon after birth.[29] For Augustine, this made sense only as the corollary of belief in original sin, an inherited guilt through which even "innocent" babies shared in the sin of Adam (see *Pecc. Mer.*, passim). Baptism made concupiscence (the perverted desire of the soul) non-fatal, but it did not remove its power. Infant baptism thus demonstrated our entanglement in a flawed existence that was neither caused nor solved by the exercise of our own free will. But the logic of this position was made salient and convincing by appeal to a second and more pervasive practice: daily prayers of confession, gratitude, and petition. Augustine's arguments during these later years of his life make notable and persistent reference to the fact of prayer: if believers recite the Lord's Prayer with integrity, they repeatedly ask for forgiveness, requesting help for deliverance from temptation.[30] Why would they do this, if they did not really depend on God for his powerful intervention in their lives? In integrating the logic of prayer with the logic of doctrine, Augustine insists that the foundational prayers of Christian piety demonstrate Christian dependence on grace. To pray, "Lead us not into temptation, but deliver us from evil," is to pray that future offenses be avoided *by the aid of God.* "Indeed, this cannot be accomplished without the co-operation of our will; nevertheless, our will alone is not enough. Hence the prayer which is offered up to the Lord for this purpose is neither superfluous nor offensive. For what can be more foolish than to pray to do what you already have it in your power to do?" (*Nat. et Grat.* 18).

By associating his theology of grace with the daily prayers of an ordinary Christian, Augustine manages to depict Pelagius's doctrine as not just erroneous but impious: "they attribute so much power to the will that they would exclude prayer from our religious duties" (*Nat. et Grat.* 58). Confession of sin, gratitude for divine aid, and prayer for divine assistance are indeed the staple

29. For the significance of infant baptism in Augustine's anti-Pelagian theology, see Bonner, *St. Augustine,* pp. 320-23, 381-84; Brown, *Augustine of Hippo,* pp. 344, 350, 368-69.

30. See, e.g., *Pecc. Mer.* 2.3, 6, 28, 33; *Nat. et Grat.* 18, 58, 60, 68.

diet of Christian piety, but few have pressed their logic into the doctrinal definition of grace with as much force and skill as Augustine. Indeed, since this piety is an expression of Christian humility, Augustine will continually raise the suspicion of pride against any doctrine that rejoices in the doing of good without also acknowledging profound dependence on God (*Nat. et Grat.* 27). In churches of believers entangled in the passions and temptations of everyday existence, Augustine spoke of grace in ways that resonated with lived experience, even if Christian ascetics and monks found his language dangerously demeaning of the Christian capacity to fight evil and to choose the good.[31] But for a man such as Augustine, who inhabited the psalms and conducted his life to the accompaniment of prolonged and soul-searching intercession, the piety of prayer was the strongest possible argument for the efficacy and incongruity of grace.

3.2.4. Against the Massillians

The final developments of Augustine's theology of grace took place in argument with a set of admirers associated with John Cassian and the monastery at Marseilles. These misnamed "semi-Pelagians" shared most of Augustine's convictions, but in the wake of the Pelagian disputes Augustine found it natural to extend his own views into ever more comprehensive forms, which the "Massillians" found extreme. For Augustine, the truth of a doctrine was now proved if dissenting from it led to "Pelagian error" (*Praed. Sanct.* 29), and this final stage in Augustine's development exemplifies a tendency in the Christian theme of grace, a polarizing momentum that develops its own perfections into ever more perfect forms. John Cassian could speak in fulsome terms of the abundance of grace, but he and his fellow monks were dissatisfied with Augustine's demotion of human initiative and his relentless emphasis on the incongruity of grace. For Cassian, there may indeed be cases in which God's grace acts unbidden on a wayward sinner, but it is also quite proper to imagine that God responds to a human appeal for aid. For Augustine, this throws into doubt the *essential* incongruity of efficacious grace.[32] He is now more than ever

31. Augustine's sermons and letters illustrate more clearly than his doctrinal treatises the ecclesial realities of the continuous, and often unsuccessful, Christian struggle against sin. What he finds notable as much as sexual transgressions are outbursts of anger among the honor-obsessed members of his congregation (*Ep. Rm. Inch.* 18.11).

32. As Wetzel puts it ("Snares of Truth," p. 127), "In place of overwhelming grace, Cassian praises grace abounding." For analysis of Cassian and his relationship to Augustine, see O. Chadwick, *John Cassian*, 2nd ed. (Cambridge: Cambridge University Press, 1968).

convinced that even faith is a gift of God, included with everything else in the logic of 1 Corinthians 4:7 ("what have you that you did not receive?"); one can hardly think otherwise if Paul prays and gives thanks for faith (*Praed. Sanct.* 1-8). Thus, salvation is from beginning to end the gift of God, worked into (and not produced by) the human will; even our thoughts are attributable to God (2 Cor 3:5). In a crucial move, Augustine now reconsiders his earlier assumption that God has willed all to be saved (1 Tim 2:4). If faith is effected by God's grace alone, it is more logical to think that God has predestined to faith and to salvation only the elect, since no human can either effect or frustrate God's will.[33] By an inscrutable choice, God has thus given to some, not all, the gift of faith, preparing their wills by his mercy, and accomplishing his promises by his power, not ours. There is now a notably stronger use of causative language (based on Ezek 36:27), while the Pauline motif of the irrevocable call (Rom 11:29) is deployed to support the notion of a divine plan whose fulfillment cannot fail. From here it is but a short step to the conviction that even the perseverance of the saints is not dependent on human choice, since it too is a gift of God, for which we habitually pray *(Dono Pers.).*

Throughout these final treatises, Augustine insists again that God's grace is not grace unless it is "gratuitous" (e.g., *Praed. Sanct.* 43: *non nisi gratuita*), and by this he means his distinctive constellation of gift-perfections: *prior, incongruous,* and *efficacious.* At no point (after *Ad Simplicianum*) must grace be envisaged as secondary or reactive to human initiative: just as grace precedes our merits, and is not God's response to them, so it is antecedent also to our faith. But this insistence on the *priority* of grace is a principle shared with Pelagius and John Cassian, and is by no means sufficient on its own, not even with additional emphasis on its incalculable superabundance. In the development of Augustine's thought, *priority* becomes ever more closely affiliated with *efficacy* (God's bringing about our response to his prior grace), such that grace remains in all respects *incongruous,* and never a reward for human effort. As Augustine's opponents insisted, there is no *a priori* reason why grace should be perfected in these three dimensions at once, and serious theological objections could be raised to this configuration of grace. Not only did it challenge ordinary notions of equity and human responsibility; it was also not unambiguously supported, still less necessitated, by Scripture itself. But Augustine had integrated his theology of grace with the virtue of humility and with the common-sense piety of daily prayer, and had wielded this integrated doctrine-cum-practice as a powerful weapon against "Pelagian error." Henceforth it would prove difficult to unpick Augustine's tightly wo-

33. See further Burns, *Development,* pp. 159-81.

ven bundle of grace-perfections without appearing "Pelagian," while its close connection with the routines of prayer made this definition of grace seem "obvious" and proper to the Christian faith. Such is Augustine's influence that "grace" has come to mean for many theologians precisely that set of perfections with which he endows it (priority, incongruity, and efficacy). It takes a clear-eyed perspective to see that a strong theology of grace does not require to be perfected in this fashion. Whether this constellation of perfections is integral to Pauline theology, and whether the priority and incongruity of grace can be more fruitfully interpreted in other terms today, are questions that should remain open.

3.3. Luther

Martin Luther's (1483-1546) profound engagement with Paul's letters has left an indelible mark on all subsequent interpreters of Paul, whether admirers or critics of the Reformer. His distinctive construal of grace constituted a significant break with the Augustinian and medieval theological tradition, and contributed to the emergence of a new perfection of gift — as "pure altruism" — that has become widely influential in the modern era. Such is the volume of Luther's works, with their ever-developing dynamic and their varied genres and concerns, that it is almost always possible to find a statement from Luther apparently or actually at odds with whatever one cites as a characteristic idea. Despite this fluidity, the following analysis adopts readings common among Luther scholars in order to expose, in new ways, the characteristically Lutheran perfections of grace.

3.3.1. The Context

Luther's theological context is complex and multi-layered but, drawing from his own comments, recent scholarship places him in three interrelated theological traditions: the nominalism *(via moderna)* of his own training, the broader scholastic tradition associated with Aristotle and Aquinas, and the Augustinian tradition that underlay much of Western theology but was particularly influential on Luther's early theological development. In each case, we may trace in Luther a point of difference that highlights what is distinctive in the Lutheran theological turn.

Luther's teachers (Truttfetter and von Usingen) trained him in the nominalist tradition systematized by Gabriel Biel (d. 1495), which attempted to give weight both to God's prevenient grace and to human responsibility in meriting the final grace of eternal life.[34] By a gracious and unconstrained decision, God has established a covenant wherein human acts are respected and rewarded with far more than they deserve. Because the first, baptismal infusion of grace is generally lost through mortal sin, God has established the possibility for the reacquisition of grace when, from our weakened but still capable natural strength *(ex puris naturalibus),* we do what is in us *(facere quod in se est)* to accomplish God's will, at least as an external requirement. That effort is rewarded by an infusion of grace as a congruent reward *(meritum de congruo).* Subsequently, with the cooperation of the Spirit, we can act in harmony with God, so that as a matter of justice we are finally rewarded (by a *meritum de condigno*) with eternal life. The covenant thus operates by an ordered justice: God's grace, which establishes the covenant, is neither arbitrary nor unfair, since it culminates in a final judgment in which God's law is vindicated and responsible humanity is justly rewarded. At the same time, the whole system is created and suffused by a grace that is both prevenient (with Augustinian accents on divine priority in election) and superabundant.

Luther reacts strongly against this system of "merit" and, reading nominalism from within its covenantal system, castigates it as blatantly "Pelagian."[35] The nominalist system operates on the widely accepted assumption that good gifts are justly distributed to those worthy of them, by a principle of *quid pro quo* that is certainly not "pay" but entails the fittingness of reward.[36] God's grace is given to those who have done at least the minimum of attrition or contrition, and once infused, it enables them to perform the works that will make them worthy of eternal life. As we shall see, Luther's theology constitutes a breach with this and every other form of *instrumental reciprocity* — that is, any placement of grace within a system of gift or return *that is given with a view to a counter gift.*[37] For Luther, God's grace has been given in Christ once

34. See H. A. Oberman, *The Harvest of Medieval Theology: Gabriel Biel and Late Medieval Nominalism* (Cambridge, MA: Harvard University Press, 1963) and *The Dawn of the Reformation: Essays in Late Medieval and Early Reformation Thought* (Edinburgh: T&T Clark, 1986), pp. 1-103.

35. See, e.g., the 1535 lectures on Galatians 2:16 (*LW* 26.124-26; *WA* 40.1 220.4–223.28).

36. Luther can, however, caricature this system as making God a "huckster," a cheap salesman of his goods, *Treatise on Good Works* (1520), *LW* 44.31; *WA* 6 210.

37. As we shall see, Luther scholars are right to insist that there is a form of *simple reciprocity* within the God-human relationship in Luther's theology, in that believers make a return of thanks and trust for God's gift in Christ (see B. K. Holm, *Gabe und Geben bei Luther: Das Verhältnis zwischen Reziprozität und reformatorischer Rechtfertigungslehre* [Berlin: de Gruyter, 2006]). What is important is that this human move is only ever the *response* to God's gift, and is not offered *with a view to* any further gift. In this sense, the reciprocity is never *instrumental.*

and for all, and there is nothing that humans can or should do to *elicit* grace either now or at the future judgment. To condition grace in this way would be to make it, in Luther's eyes, not a *gift* but a form of *exaction,*[38] and that would be the deepest form of sin and unbelief.[39]

On a wider front, Luther also reacts against central features of the scholastic tradition, which he considers to have corrupted theology with Aristotelian anthropology and ethics.[40] To what extent he knew or understood the authentic Thomist tradition (e.g., Aquinas's treatise on grace, *Summa* II.1) has been disputed: his accusations that "the scholastics" were peddling a false assumption that human free will is able to desire the good in its own capacity do not fit many medieval theologies outside the nominalist tradition. But Luther did depart from a widespread medieval configuration of soteriology that spoke of the infusion of grace into the human soul. Augustine's understanding of divine grace as an effective power that enters and empowers the believer was easily interpreted in Aristotelian terms as a quality infused into the soul, transforming it into a condition of righteousness and rendering it thereby worthy of salvation.[41] Receiving the gift of grace as an internally formative infusion *(gratia habitualis),* and assisted by it to become progressively more righteous, the believer is effectually rendered "acceptable" to God *(gratia gratum faciens).* This is a gradual process working from initial justification (the forgiveness of sins) along a journey of sanctification, which is necessary to render the believer fit for the final and still threatening day of judgment. Faith certainly has a part to play in this process, but, following one Latin translation of Galatians 5:6 (*fides charitate formata,* "faith formed by love"), faith alone is

38. *Against Latomus* (1522), *LW* 32.153.

39. Commenting on Galatians 3:2, Luther writes: "The human heart neither understands nor believes that such a great prize as the Holy Spirit can be granted solely through hearing with faith; but it thinks this way: 'The forgiveness of sins, deliverance from sin and death, the granting of the Holy Spirit, of righteousness, and of eternal life — this is all something important: therefore you must do something great to obtain these inestimable gifts' *(ideo oportet te aliquid magni praestare, ut ista inenarrabilia dona consequaris).* The devil approves of this opinion and magnifies it in the heart" (*LW* 26.213; *WA* 40.1 343.22-27).

40. Luther's polemics on this point stretch all the way from his early treatise *Against Scholastic Theology* (1517) (*WA* 1 221-28) to his 1535 lectures on Galatians (on 2.16: *LW* 26.126-31; *WA* 40.1 225.25–231.19).

41. Aquinas's views on grace are themselves variously interpreted; among major treatments see B. Lonergan, *Grace and Freedom: Operative Grace in the Thought of Thomas Aquinas* (London: Darton, Longman and Todd, 1971) and J. P. Wawrykow, *God's Grace and Human Action: "Merit" in the Theology of Thomas Aquinas* (Notre Dame: University of Notre Dame, 1995). For Luther's relation to this tradition, see B. Gerrish, *Grace and Reason: A Study in the Theology of Luther* (Oxford: Oxford University Press, 1962), pp. 114-36.

insufficient (*informis*, "unformed"); it must be completed and formed by the works of love *(informata per charitatem).*

At one level, Luther's reaction to this tradition revolves around the definition of "faith" and the interpretation of Galatians 5:6 — which he read, following the Greek, as "faith operating through [not formed by] love."[42] Since faith is, for Luther, not intellectual assent to propositions about God but trust that abandons itself utterly to God's promises and benefits in Christ, he will insist that in faith (and by faith alone) we have everything necessary for justification and for salvation (near synonyms in Lutheran discourse). To talk of supplementing faith by works would render God's work in Christ insufficient or incomplete. In this respect, Luther will challenge the dominant image of the Christian life as a journey toward an uncertain future. As we shall see, in his distinctively dialectical fashion he will consider believers, inasmuch as they are *in Christ,* as having already arrived (though *in themselves* certainly not so). At a deeper level, Luther questioned the whole medieval construal of grace as a quality (or "medicine") infused into the soul. Drawing on Erasmus's philological observations on the meaning of χάρις, mediated via Melanchthon, Luther insisted that Paul meant by this term God's favor, his inclination to accept or welcome, not a transformative power that operates in the human soul.[43] Paul was announcing therefore not the means by which God works within humans to make them worthy of ultimate salvation but God's decision in Christ to accept them just as they are. Luther, in fact, backs away from the Augustinian emphasis on the efficacy of grace inasmuch as it issued, via Aristotelian ethics, in the notion of a substance or quality "poured into the soul." Because he takes grace in Paul (and in the Bible) to be a *relation,* not a *substance,* he will

42. In Greek: πίστις δι' ἀγάπης ἐνεργουμένη (the participle probably in the middle voice); see the discussion of this matter in the 1535 lectures on Galatians (*LW* 27.28-31; *WA* 40.2 34.10–39.15).

43. For Melanchthon's indebtedness to Erasmus (and to Reuchlin on the Hebrew *ḥen*), and for his influence on Luther, see R. Schäfer, "Melanchthon's Interpretation of Romans 5:15: His Departure from the Augustinian Concept of Grace Compared to Luther's," in T. J. Wengert and M. P. Graham, eds., *Philip Melanchthon (1497-1560) and the Commentary* (Sheffield: Sheffield Academic Press, 1997), pp. 79-104. Although Luther, like Melanchthon, could thus distinguish "grace"/"favor" from "gift" (following Romans 5:15), he did not always do so; where he did, he took the "gift" to be faith (or Christ), whereby God shows "grace"/"favor" toward those joined to Christ (e.g., *Against Latomus, LW* 32.227-29). As Schäfer comments, "when grace is defined in this way as divine favor alone, then it cannot accord with the Thomistic understanding of it as a quality in the human being" ("Melanchthon's Interpretation," p. 95). For a close analysis of *gratia* and *donum* in *Against Latomus,* see R. Skottene, *Grace and Gift: An Analysis of a Central Motif in Martin Luther's* Rationis Latomianae Confutatio (Frankfurt am Main: P. Lang, 2007).

depart radically from centuries of theological thought that used categories of anthropological ontology at odds with scriptural discourse.

In many respects, of course, Luther was heavily indebted to Augustine, whose theology had an appreciable effect on his thought in the years after 1513. His instruction by Staupitz in a tradition shaped by Gregory of Rimini, and his own close reading of Augustinian texts, exercised a deep influence upon him.[44] The incapacity of the human will in its slavery to sin, and the deep corruption of the self in arrogant rebellion against God, are core convictions derived from Augustine. Luther's early works are peppered with references to "Paul and Saint Augustine," and to some degree he saw himself as reviving Augustine's battle against a now regnant "Pelagianism." But in at least one important respect Luther knew himself to be going against (or beyond) a central element in Augustinian thought. As we have seen, Augustine's emphasis on the incongruity of grace (God gives to the ungodly and the undeserving) was integrated into a system of divinely ordered justice by which grace was designed to make the ungodly godly, instilling within them a genuine love of God and thus rendering them ultimately (if in this life incompletely) worthy of eternal life. If at the beginning of the process believers start off worthy of nothing, by the end one may speak freely of their merits, provided that these merits are understood to be themselves, through the effective operation of grace, the gifts of God *(bona merita dei dona).*

Luther will refuse all reference to merit in the context of soteriology — or, if the language is used, it is applied only to Christ and not to believers themselves.[45] And this is not merely a linguistic peculiarity. It represents the distinctively Lutheran insistence that God's grace is not only initially incongruous with the worth of its recipients, but remains perpetually so, as a structural characteristic of the Christian life. For Luther, as we shall see, the righteousness of believers (at least such righteousness as counts before God) is never precisely their own, but remains the righteousness of Christ; it is fundamentally

44. For the relation between Luther and Augustine, see E. L. Saak, *High Way to Heaven: The Augustinian Platform between Reform and Reformation 1292-1524* (Leiden: Brill, 2002); the role of Staupitz in this regard is disputed (see D. C. Steinmetz, *Luther and Staupitz: An Essay in the Intellectual Origins of the Protestant Reformation* [Durham, NC: Duke University Press, 1980]; H. A. Oberman, *Luther: Man between God and the Devil* [New Haven: Yale University Press, 1986], pp. 179-85). *De Spiritu et Littera* is among the works of Augustine most influential on Luther's interpretation of Paul.

45. On Christ meriting for believers the gift and grace of God, see, e.g., *Against Latomus, LW* 32.228. As far as humans are concerned, "there is no such thing as merit" (*nullum esse meritum prorsus, WA* 18 769.33). For medieval developments in the notion of merit, see A. E. McGrath, *Iustitia Dei: A History of the Christian Doctrine of Justification,* 2 vols. (Cambridge: Cambridge University Press, 1986), vol. 1, pp. 109-19.

another's *(alienus)* even when they possess it in Christ. This dialectic of "having yet not owning" makes Luther averse to even the Augustinian language of merit. In this, as in many of his characteristic paradoxes, Luther seeks to preserve the incongruity of grace as its quintessential characteristic, applicable to every dimension of the believer's life. It is this perfection of grace as a *permanent incongruity* that makes the Lutheran theology of grace stand out from its context, and so difficult for non-Lutherans to comprehend.[46] At the same time, whereas Augustine's theology of grace had matched and reinforced traditional church practices, Luther's undermined the deep assumptions supporting many ecclesial practices of his day, and was itself increasingly radicalized as his relations with the Catholic Church worsened to the point of rupture. In this sense, Luther's theology of grace was never purely abstract: it was embodied in, and in turn supported by, new configurations of church that have had a lasting impact on the history of Western Christianity.

Luther indicates that his reading of Paul underwent a decisive change in his reevaluation of "the righteousness of God" (Rom 1:17) as "that by which the righteous lives by a gift of God, namely by faith."[47] But it has proven impossible to establish the date of this shift, and close analysis of his early works suggests rather a gradually developing momentum in which his study of Scripture (especially the Psalms and Romans) drove, and was itself driven by, growing disenchantment with the practices of the church and the authority of the Pope.[48] In this polemical context, several Pauline antitheses shaped Luther's sense of the alternatives facing his contemporaries, and none more so than the antithesis between "works of the law" and "faith in Christ" (Gal 2:16; 3:2, 5; Rom 3:28, etc.). His analysis of this polarity takes us to the heart of his theology.

3.3.2. Not by Works of the Law

Like Augustine, Luther identifies the problematic of "works of the law" to lie not in their content, nor in the human capacity to perform them in an exter-

46. For the common misperceptions of Luther by Catholic theologians, see D. Hampson, *Christian Contradictions: The Structures of Lutheran and Catholic Thought* (Cambridge: Cambridge University Press, 2001).

47. Luther speaks of this moment only from long hindsight (1545) in the preface to the first volume of his collected works (*LW* 34.336-37; *WA* 54 185.12–186.20).

48. For discussion of this "Reformation breakthrough," see Oberman, *Luther,* pp. 151-74; B. Lohse, *Martin Luther's Theology: Its Historical and Systematic Development* (Minneapolis: Fortress, 2006), pp. 85-95; O. Bayer, *Promissio: Geschichte der reformatorischen Wende in Luthers Theologie,* 2nd ed. (Darmstadt: Wissenschaftliche Buchgesellschaft, 1989).

nally observable performance, but in the deep corruption of the human heart. Unlike Augustine, however, the stress lies less on the waywardness of human desires than on the existential relation of humans toward themselves, their works, and God. In Luther's view, and in his experience as a monk, perfect outward observance of God's commands can mask an inner resentment of the law, a rebellion (even hatred) directed against God. Worse, humans harbor a deep desire to *be God,* wishing to substitute human achievement for the solely sufficient gift of God in Christ. At the root of sin, for Luther, is this arrogant self-reliance, a self-interestedness whereby humans "turn in" on themselves, and thereby turn away from God. This, for Luther, is a form of "idolatry" that refuses to acknowledge, in gratitude, the work of God, and is presumptuous enough to regard our own work as a form of saving righteousness that deserves (and even demands) a reward from God.

It is important to note that the critical target of this analysis is not the *content* of the "works of the law" (which includes the whole law of God and therefore law in its highest form), nor the *agent* performing these works. The issue is not *who* is acting (God or humans; believer or unbeliever): the same critique can apply to Christians as to non-Christians, and thus to law-observance performed "by natural powers or by human strength or by free will or by the gift and power of God."[49] What matters is the *self-understanding* operative in the performance of "good works," a hermeneutic composed of three conjoined elements: the *faulty understanding* of these works by the one who performs them, the *corrupt motivation* for performing them, and the *arrogant or anxious attitude* in which they are performed. Firstly, they are understood (by a "false opinion") as the *necessary means* to salvation, the cause (rather than the result) of justification. Secondly and accordingly, they are performed with an irreligious and self-regarding motivation, in order to obtain salvation and thus to gain benefit for oneself (rather than purely to please God, to discipline the body, or to benefit one's neighbor).[50] Thirdly, they are performed in a spirit of presumption or trust in our own righteousnesss — or, as the correlative characteristic of this bipolar condition, in anxiety, fear, or doubt.[51] The language

49. *LW* 26.123; *WA* 40.1 219.18-21.

50. Luther takes the performance of works within this hermeneutic as a quest for one's own advantage, and thus as a symptom of the fundamental human sickness as *homo incurvatus in se ipsum* (*Lectures on Romans* [1515-16], *LW* 25.291; *WA* 56 304); cf. *Treatise on Good Works* (1520) *LW* 44.71, 73; *WA* 6 242, 244.

51. This construal of the problem of "works of the law" and "works" is ubiquitous in Luther from 1518 onward. See, for instance, *The Heidelberg Disputation* (1518), 7 on the sin of pride as self-worship rather than worship of the Creator, and *Freedom of a Christian* (1520) (*LW* 31.350-51; *WA* 7 24-25) on the meta-sin of unbelief in those who do not trust God's promises

of "trust" or "doubt" reflects Luther's fascination with the Pauline theme of faith. Everyone trusts in *something:* the only question is whether we trust in ourselves or in the benefits incongruously gifted to us in Christ.

Luther knows very well that when Paul writes of the "works of the law" he is referring to the Mosaic Torah. With Augustine he insists, against Jerome (and in his own day, Erasmus), that Paul does not mean only the "ceremonies" of the Old Testament law, which might be considered simply outdated after the coming of Christ. He means the whole law, including the Decalogue and the moral law of God; and if Paul attacks justification by this, the most perfect law, he would surely include the pursuit of justification by the works of *any* law, including the rules instituted by the church itself.[52] Paul's letters to the Galatians and Romans thus become instantly applicable to Luther's own context: the *Papistae,* who insist that we are justified not by faith alone but by faith "informed by charity," are "our Jews" *(nostri Iudaei).*[53] Indeed, Paul's letters are on this point universally relevant, because humans fall into the very same error in every age and context. Whatever the difference between the *content* of the works, what matters is their *meaning,* the irreligious understanding, motivation, and attitude outlined above: "the works vary only in appearance and in name. For they are still works. And those who do them are not Christians, but hirelings (lit. 'workmen,' *operarii*), whether they are called Jews, Mohammedans, papists, or sectarians."[54] Indeed, in Luther's eyes (in a motif influential on later Lutheran construals of Judaism), those who are especially pious are liable to a kind of supersized sin, because they are all the more confident that their excellent works of righteousness will obtain the favor of God.[55]

---

but imagine they can fulfill the law through works of charity. Luther's 1535 Galatians lectures amplify but do not alter this analysis (e.g., *LW* 26.122-39). For "trust in the law" *(fiducia legis),* see *LW* 27.17; *WA* 40.2 19.27.

52. For this generalizing interpretation of "law" (following Augustine), see, e.g., *The Heidelberg Disputation* (1518), 1; *LW* 26.251; *WA* 40.1 395.15-23.

53. *LW* 26.207; *WA* 40.1 336.13.

54. *LW* 26.10; *WA* 40.1 49.20-23; cf. *LW* 26.396 (*WA* 40.1 603.25-29): "Therefore there is no difference at all between a papist, a Jew, a Turk, or a sectarian. Their persons, locations, rituals, religions, works, and forms of worship are, of course, diverse; but they all have the same reason, the same heart, the same opinion and idea. . . . 'If I do this or that, I have a God who is favorably disposed towards me; if I do not, I have a God who is wrathful.' "

55. *Heidelberg Disputation* 16: "The person who believes that he can obtain grace by doing what is in him adds sin to sin and he becomes doubly guilty" (adding "haughty arrogance" to his ingrained sin). Elsewhere Luther speaks of this illusion as a kind of "white devil": "The world is at its best in men who are religious *(religiosi),* wise, and learned; yet in them it is actually evil twice over *(dupliciter malus)*" (*LW* 26.40; *WA* 40.1 95.19–96.11).

This interpretation of Paul's theology was formed in the crucible of Luther's own experience and of the increasingly bitter controversies surrounding the validity of church practices that carried not only traditional but papal authority. Luther's personal torments as a monk — his inner resentments, doubts, and fears — have sometimes been given an exaggerated role in this matter, but they certainly strengthened his conviction that the essential religious question was the means by which an individual could obtain the grace rather than the wrath of God. As Oberman has stressed, Luther took his own conflicts (both psychological and social) to be manifestations of an apocalyptic war breaking out in the last days of the church, a conviction that gave the Pauline antitheses enormous weight as the end-time alternatives, fiendishly masked by the wiles of the devil.[56] Moreover, Luther's critique of the works-hermeneutic outlined above gained clarity and urgency in his burgeoning assault on a range of church practices. The early critique of indulgences soon expanded to a number of activities (pilgrimages, fasts, endowments of churches, subscriptions for masses, monastic vows, etc.) whose performance and motivation he suspected of enthrallment to a theology of "works." For all his stress on the "conscience" and the "inner man," Luther was acutely aware that the theological distinction between "law" and "grace" must be evidenced in practice and not just in words.[57] His outspoken attack on the conduct of the Mass (e.g., in *The Babylonian Captivity of the Church,* 1520) reconfigured this central rite as the reception of grace in word and sacrament, rather than a performance offered to God in order to obtain a divine benefit (for oneself or for others). Here and elsewhere Luther's theology began to erode the power wielded by the church in its demand for particular works, as well as its graded notions of piety, where in chastity or poverty elite believers offered to God what could only be rewarded in the life to come. Although he soon became anxious lest insistence on church reform turn into another form of necessary "work," Luther's critique of works as an instrumental means of salvation was bound to relativize, if not abolish, many features of church practice whose rationale lay in their capacity to merit grace. When on December 10, 1520, Luther burned not only the papal bull decreeing his excommunication but also the *Decretales,* containing centuries of canon law, it became clear that in Luther's hands Paul's theology of grace had the capacity to subvert every form of ecclesial authority. Once embedded within the Protestant tradition, that subversive power would prove difficult to contain.

56. See esp. Oberman, *Luther,* pp. 82-110.
57. *LW* 26.144; *WA* 40.1 251.27-28.

3.3.3. But by Faith in Jesus Christ

For Luther, the essential truth of the gospel is that Jesus is our sole and sufficient Savior, who has already effected all that is necessary for justification/salvation. He is unequivocally Savior (and Mediator or Intercessor), not Legislator or Judge: he does not *demand* from us, but *gives* us salvation, so long as we grasp it in faith. Luther here broke decisively with the prevalent impression of Christ (in word and image) as the stern Cosmocrator, author of a new law and final judge. Echoing Paul (Rom 8:32-34), he insists that Christ is always "for us," and does not stand against us as Judge.[58] What is more, the "righteousness of God" *(iustitia dei)* is not to be understood as the divine act of justice that punishes sinners and rewards the righteous, but as the gift given in Christ and received in faith; this gift, already given once for all *(einmal)* and completely sufficient, leaves no room for uncertainty or fear.[59] With this simple, easily communicable, and deeply attractive message, Luther attempted to sever completely the pattern of interested circularity by which human works, offered to God, were understood and intended to elicit future benefit or reward. A single gift has already been given and has only to be received in faith; the works that result from that faith possess no instrumental value in the sphere of salvation. Faith is indeed pleasing to God, as it properly honors God in gratitude for his gift. But this "return" is neither able nor intended to obtain a future benefit.[60] Faith operates, by definition, not in self-reliance but in reliance only and wholly on Christ. In this sense, although faith is exercised by human agents, it is not a "work" but rather the polar opposite of the self-understanding represented by "works."

When Luther controversially insisted that believers are justified "by faith alone" *(sola fide)*, he intended to exclude the notion that faith needed to be

58. E.g., *LW* 26.8, 11, 37-38 *et passim*. In his introduction to the Gospels, Luther is careful to insist that Christ's teaching and example must be understood in the light of Christ as gift. Christ is not a new Moses who "horribly forces us and drives us": we follow Christ's example only in the works that *follow from* Christ as gift (*A Brief Instruction on What to Look For and Expect in the Gospels, LW* 35.117-24).

59. See Oberman, *Luther*, p. 153: "What is completely new about Luther's discovery is that he sees God's righteousness as inseparably united and merged with the righteousness of Christ: already *now* it is received through faith" (italics original); cf. Oberman, *Dawn of the Reformation*, pp. 104-25.

60. For this element of "reciprocity" in Luther, see Holm, *Gabe und Geben*. However, Holm's analysis suffers from a static structural representation of reciprocal relations, and does not take into account the diachronic movement of gift-and-return over time. What is important for Luther is that the human "return" (of trust and praise) does not enter into an ongoing momentum designed to elicit further gifts from God.

"formed" or supplemented by charity (or any other work). This was possible only because he understood faith not as intellectual assent to historical information or to creedal formulae but as complete self-abandonment to the mercy of God in Christ. Since *fides* for Luther means *trust* in the promises of God and in the work of Christ, it constitutes a personal "grasping" of Christ: it is important not in itself, as if it were some superior mental or emotional disposition, but in its relationship to Christ. "If it is true faith, it is a sure trust and firm acceptance of the heart *(certa fiducia cordis et firmus assensus).* It takes hold of Christ *(quo Christus apprehenditur)* in such a way that Christ is the object of faith, or rather not the object but, so to speak, the One who is present in the faith itself *(in ipsa fide Christus adest).*"[61]

This emphasis on the presence of Christ, and union with Christ in faith, is central to Luther's theology from the very beginning. In a favorite metaphor, he refers to Christian existence as a marriage with Christ (drawing on Ephesians 5 and the Song of Songs): in this union, of which faith is "the wedding ring," all that is Christ's belongs to the believer and all that is the believer's is taken by Christ.[62] Through this "happy exchange," the believer already possesses the righteousness, holiness, and goodness of Christ (who takes the believer's sin, guilt and impurity) — "possesses" but does not "own," since these gifts remain Christ's own and are not "infused" into the believer.[63] For this reason, Luther can insist that Christ's righteousness remains *alienus,* extrinsic to ourselves *(extra nos);* at the same time, it is truly "ours" inasmuch as we are united to Christ by faith. As recent analysis has rightly shown, Luther thereby melds the Pauline themes of justification by faith and participation in Christ without the polarity that has often arisen in later readings of Paul. Where Luther uses the language of "imputation," this is never a bare "forensic" metaphor, and certainly involves no "fiction," since Christ's righteousness is real and really shared by the believer.[64] Believers are justified by union with

61. From the 1535 Lectures on Galatians: *LW* 26.129; *WA* 40.1 228.33–229.15. On the Christo-centrism of faith in Luther, see J. A. Linebaugh, "The Christo-Centrism of Faith in Christ: Martin Luther's Reading of Galatians 2:16, 19-20," *NTS* 59 (2013): 535-44.

62. For the marriage metaphor, see, e.g., *Two Kinds of Righteousness* (1518/1519) and *Freedom of the Christian* (1520).

63. Oberman, *Dawn of the Reformation*, pp. 120-25 draws attention to the distinction between "possession" (*possessio,* i.e., the right of use) and "ownership" *(proprietas)* in the Roman law of marriage known to Luther: a wife may "possess" items that remain *de iure* not her own.

64. Emphasis on participation in Christ and the presence of Christ in justification has been the hallmark of the recent Finnish school of interpretation of Luther: see, e.g., T. Mannermaa, *Christ Present in Faith: Luther's View of Justification,* trans. and ed. K. Stjerna (Minneapolis: Fortress Press, 2005); C. E. Braaten and R. W. Jenson, eds., *Union with Christ: The New Finnish Interpretation of Luther* (Grand Rapids: Eerdmans, 1998). S. Chester, "It is No Longer

Christ, inasmuch as they continue, in faith, to grasp hold of Christ. In that sense, faith for Luther is both an "active" and a "passive" phenomenon, with all the active passivity of receiving someone else's gift.

The paradox of "having yet not having," in fact, "having [in Christ] precisely because one does not have [in oneself]," is inscribed across many features of Luther's theology, and is skillfully joined to Paul's theology of the cross. From early on, Luther took Paul's depiction of "the scandal of the cross" (Gal 5:11; cf. 1 Cor 1:18-25) to represent the essential dynamic of the Christian life. In the midst of weakness and foolishness, and out of unrighteousness and suffering, God creates the opposite, entering into our emptiness to fill it with his, and only his, gift. This juxtaposition of opposites remains a permanent feature of the believer's existence: in fact, this remains a life of faith only inasmuch as it does not attribute to itself the power, the wisdom, or the righteousness of Christ, even as gifts. Any "theology of glory" is at the same time, for Luther, a theology of self-righteousness, and *vice versa:* to the very end of our lives we remain "beggars," transformed in our connection to Christ but not by some inner progress toward holiness.[65] Luther's famous formulation of this paradox — that the believer is *simul justus et peccator* — has been endlessly misunderstood, by both friend and foe.[66] He is speaking not of partial degrees of righteousness and sin, but of the simultaneous and permanent juxtaposition of polar opposites. Before God, we are "righteous" inasmuch as we belong to Christ; in our own right (at the deepest level of the corruption of our hearts), we remain "sinners." By insisting on this dialectic, Luther intends to preserve the incongruity of grace in a totalized form. To claim that believers become (through grace) anything other than still, in and of themselves, "sinners" would be to diminish that incongruity, and thus, in Luther's eyes, to cancel out grace.

We find an important expression of this dynamic in Luther's understanding of baptism. Against a tradition that had tended to relegate baptism to the

---

I Who Live: Justification by Faith and Participation in Christ in Martin Luther's Exegesis of Galatians," *NTS* 55 (2009): 315-37, rightly criticizes those who blame Luther for the subsequent tendency to take "justification" and "participation" as separable or even incompatible structures of thought (for this antithesis, see most recently D. Campbell, *The Deliverance of God: An Apocalyptic Rereading of Justification in Paul* [Grand Rapids: Eerdmans, 2009]).

65. It was no accident that friends found a scribbled note on Luther's desk after his death: "Wir sind Bettler: hoc est verum" ("We are beggars: this is true," *WA TR* 5 318.2-3). For a recent discussion of Luther's theology of the cross, and his critique of a theology of glory, see T. Mannermaa, *Two Kinds of Love: Martin Luther's Religious World,* trans. K. Stjerna (Minneapolis: Fortress Press, 2010).

66. For the phrase, see, e.g., *LW* 26.332; *WA* 40.1 336.26. For discussion, see Hampson, *Christian Contradictions,* with emphasis on Luther's dialectical and nonlinear construal of this concept (pp. 24-35).

status of the "first grace" with little further significance for the believer's journey in holiness, Luther attempted to place baptism at the center of Christian experience. For him, the dividing line of baptism runs not between the past and present of believers' lives, but through the center of their present existence, which is lived continually on the boundary between sin and grace, the flesh and the Spirit, the devil and God. In this sense, the Christian life is, for Luther, a continuous return to baptism: "a Christian life is nothing else than a daily Baptism, once begun and ever continued. For we must keep at it incessantly, always purging out whatever pertains to the old Adam, so that whatever belongs to the new man may come forth."[67] Although Luther can speak of progress in faith, he remains nervous about any sense of achievement or satisfaction in which Christian progress could be considered self-wrought or secure. Since baptism refers to the promises of God and the finished work of Christ, it remains the touchstone of faith, to which the believer returns ever anew: to progress is to enter deeper into faith in Christ, not to grow in virtue.[68] This has an important application in Christian experience, offering strength and comfort to the soul when oppressed by sin or doubt. In such circumstances (which he experienced frequently himself), Luther recommends: "we must retort, 'But I am baptized *(baptisatus sum),* and if I am baptized I have the promise that I shall be saved and have eternal life, both in soul and in body.'"[69] Baptism thus makes a deep daily impact on the interior life of the individual believer. But it was characteristic of Luther that he declined to find here also a marker of change in the social or political content of Christian behavior. When such was urged by "enthusiasts" as the necessary outcome of the Reformation, he was strongly critical of what he interpreted as confusion between the "two kingdoms" and the reintroduction of "works" into the sphere of salvation.[70]

3.3.4. The Lutheran Perfections of Grace

In his introduction to the Gospels, Luther insists that "gospel" means not a new or higher standard of righteousness, but gift. "The chief article and foundation of the gospel is that before you take Christ as an example, you accept

67. *Large Catechism,* Holy Baptism 65; *WA* 30.1 218-20.

68. See the discussion in J. D. Trigg, *Baptism in the Theology of Martin Luther* (Leiden: Brill, 1994), pp. 151-73, suggesting the image of the spiral, which combines the linear sense of progress with a circular return to an equivalent point of beginning.

69. *Large Catechism,* Holy Baptism 44; *WA* 30.1 217.26-29.

70. On Luther's dialectical understanding of the "two kingdoms," see G. Ebeling, *Luther: An Introduction to His Thought,* trans. R. A. Wilson (London: Collins, 1970), pp. 175-91.

and recognize him as a gift, as a present that God has given you and that is your own."[71] The gospel presents the deeds of Christ in the first instance not so we can copy them, but so we can depend on them, since they express "the overwhelming goodness of God . . . the great fire of the love of God for us, whereby the heart and conscience become happy, secure and content." Citing Isaiah 9:6 ("for to us a son *is given*") and Romans 8:32 ("how will God not *give us* all things with his Son?"), Luther exclaims: "See, when you lay hold of Christ as a gift which is given you for your very own and have no doubt about it, you are a Christian." On the basis of this gift, everything else follows — but crucially *follows,* and does not precede, enable, or elicit the gift:

> Now when you have Christ as the foundation and chief blessing of your salvation, then the other part follows: that you take him as your example, giving yourself in service to your neighbor just as you see that Christ has given himself for you. See, there faith and love move forward, God's commandment is fulfilled, and a person is happy and fearless to do and to suffer all things. Therefore, make note of this, that Christ as a gift nourishes your faith and makes you a Christian. But Christ as an example exercises your works. These do not make you a Christian. Actually they come forth from you because you have already been made a Christian. As widely as a gift differs from an example, so widely does faith differ from works, for faith possesses nothing of its own, only the deeds and life of Christ. Works have something of our own in them, yet they should not belong to you but to your neighbor.[72]

In this pithy paragraph we find summed up most of the essential ingredients of Luther's theology of grace: that God's relationship to us in Christ is *gift* (and purely such); that this is the foundation of everything in the Christian life, not only prior but basic to everything else that might be said about the Christian; that this gift is in one sense made "our own," but only in faith that "possesses nothing of its own, only the deeds and life of Christ"; that the Christ-gift issues in "works," undertaken out of joy and fearlessness, but is not infused into or identical to them ("works have something of your own in them"); and that it enables a parallel self-giving for the neighbor, which is in fact the only purpose of "works" ("they belong not to you but to your neighbor"). We may thus draw out in conclusion the distinctively Lutheran perfections of grace.

The *superabundance* of divine grace ("the overwhelming goodness of

71. *A Brief Instruction, LW* 35.119.
72. *A Brief Instruction, LW* 35.120.

God") is identified by Luther first and foremost with the *Christ-event,* not with the gifts of creation or nature. As we have seen, the Pauline terminology of "grace" is taken to signify a *relationship* of favor, not a quality in the character of God nor, by infusion, a human quality or capacity. God's favorable relation to humanity is embodied in the gift of Christ, who comes to us *only* as the Savior who gives, *not* as a Legislator or Judge who demands.[73] In this respect, Luther's theology tends toward perfecting the *singularity* of grace, though (unlike Marcion) only in dialectical relationship to the law of the same God, who is "hidden" behind apparent contradictions, and with his "other hand" threatens us with judgment. The *priority* of grace is also fundamental for Luther: his Augustinian tradition equips him to make strong statements about the predestination of the elect, but he is wary to enter this perplexing terrain since the essence of the gospel is its address to individual lives, not the eternal disposition of God toward the world.[74] At the heart of the gospel is the gift of Christ, "the foundation and chief blessing of salvation." In Aristotelian terms, it is not the works that make the person, but the person who makes the works; in Lutheran terms, persons are reconstituted when they receive the all-sufficient gift of God in Christ.[75] *Sola gratia* thus preserves the sense that all that is essential to salvation has not just been started but has already been achieved by Christ *(solus Christus).*

As we have seen, a hallmark of Luther's theology of grace is its emphasis on *incongruity;* it never loses this character even in the "progress" of the life of faith. In the words of the final thesis in the Heidelberg Disputation (28), "the love of God does not find, but creates that which is pleasing to it."[76] Since he generally equates "justification" with "salvation," Luther understands the salvific dynamic from start to finish to consist of "the justification of the ungodly."[77] In this context, to speak of the grace of God as "pure" and "free"

73. *LW* 26.178; *WA* 40.1 298.19-20: *Itaque Christus non est Moses, non exactor aut legislator, sed largitor gratiae, Salvator, et miserator* ("Thus, Christ is not Moses, not an exactor or legislator, but the distributor of grace, the Savior and the One who has mercy"). For the contrast between gift and demand, see *LW* 26.208-9; *WA* 40.1 336.33–337.22.

74. The contrast with Calvin is significant; see below, 3.4.

75. For Luther's polemic against the notion that a person is made righteous by doing righteous works, see, e.g., *Freedom of a Christian, LW* 31.360-61; *WA* 7 31-32. Here, as frequently elsewhere, appeal is made to the parable of the tree and the fruits (Matt 7:18). Luther believes that the *persona* is made "good" by faith in Christ, but not in any straightforwardly moral sense; see Ebeling, *Luther,* pp. 150-58.

76. *LW* 31.57; *WA* 1 365 *(Amor dei non inventit sed creat suum diligibile).*

77. "It is of the nature of God that he makes something out of nothing. . . . Thus God accepts no one except the abandoned, makes no one healthy except the sick . . . makes no one pious except sinners, makes no one wise except the foolish, and, in short, has mercy on

is essentially to clear it of all traces of human "merit," which can never be acquired even by a life of strenuous good works. The life of the Christian remains *simul justus et peccator.* In this coexistence of opposites, Luther insists that whatever Christians may be said to "possess" of salvation is possessed only inasmuch as they live *in* and *out of* Christ; he is wary of the presumption that anything of salvific value inheres in believers themselves. This sense of living not in oneself but in another (cf. Gal 2:19-20) gives to the Christian life an indelibly "eccentric" character, and stations believers permanently at the point of conversion. Whatever may be said about their "maturity" or "progress," they are forever dependent on an undeserved grace.

For these reasons, Luther has no desire to stress the *efficacy* of grace in the heart of the believer. He can certainly speak of the agency of God, the Spirit, or Christ within the believer, and of faith as a gift created, exercised, and increased by God.[78] But he has no hesitation in speaking also of human agency, both in faith and in the good works that result from it. The language of "passive righteousness" is complemented by a set of verbs expressing the vigorous activity of faith, which "grasps," "holds," and "seizes" as much as it "receives."[79] This discourse of active faith is no anomaly in Luther, because what faith grasps is precisely not its own but Christ's ("faith possesses nothing of its own"). Luther's theology does not turn on the simple attribution of agency ("who is acting, we or God?"), but on a deeper hermeneutic concerning the meaning and motivation of human activity: when we act, what are we looking to as the ground of our salvation? The essential question for Luther is not whether the believer acts or the Spirit (or whether there might be some form of synergy between the two), but whether a person acts *as a believer* (grounded in Christ alone) or *as an unbeliever* (looking to secure his/her own salvation). Thus, Luther departs from the Augustinian scrutiny of the inner inclination of the heart toward the good (or God), just as he repudiates the medieval notion that grace constitutes a habit-forming infusion. The believer is reconstituted *relationally* by becoming, we might say, "re-centered" in Christ.[80] Whatever

---

no one except the wretched, and gives no one grace except those who have not grace" (*WA* 1 183.39–184.7).

78. E.g., *LW* 26.44; *WA* 40.1 130.14-15.

79. On the righteousness of faith as a "purely passive righteousness" *(mere passiva iustitia)* as opposed to any number of forms of "active righteousness," see the preface to the Galatians lectures in *WA* 40.1 40.15–51.34. On faith as "laying hold of" *(apprehendo)* and "embracing" *(involvo)* Christ, see, e.g., *LW* 26.177; *WA* 40.1 297.30.

80. The new center is thus for Luther not an internal point of gravity, but lies "outside" of the believer: the gospel "snatches us away from ourselves *(rapit nos a nobis)* and places us outside ourselves *(extra nos),* so that we do not depend on our own strength, conscience,

refashioning may then take place in interior judgments and desires — and Luther takes Romans 7 (as Christian experience) to indicate that in this life this will never be complete — cannot be the heart of the matter. Salvation depends not on degrees of moral or spiritual improvement but on whether believers participate in an "alien righteousness," the righteousness of Christ.[81]

Finally, we should note the emergence in Luther of a striking additional perfection of grace, which has exercised a long-term influence on the Protestant West. If the grace of God is given *gratis,* it is given not in order to elicit a return or benefit for God, but for our sake alone: this non-selfish love is both in intent and motive *non-circular.*[82] In the same way, Luther insists, our good works of love for our neighbors (in which we become "Christs" to them) should be entirely free of self-interest.[83] We do such works in Christ neither in order to gain some return from God (God's grace does not enter into any such instrumental reciprocity), nor in order to gain some benefit from others, but purely for the sake of those others. The whole pattern of gift, both divine and human, is thus freed from the snare and the burden of instrumentality. This is significant — and delicate — enough to require some further elaboration.

Although we receive from God in gratitude, and desire to please him in our works, we do not thereby seek to gain any benefit.[84] If there is reciprocity in this relationship, it is for Luther entirely free of instrumental ends: we love and obey God only *because,* not *in order that.*[85] Putting all the stress on the single, once-for-all, completed gift of God, Luther seeks to take the gift-relationship with God out of a pattern of repeated circularity. Although the believers' subsequent relation to God can be couched in the language of

---

experience, person, or works, but depend on that which is outside ourselves *(extra nos),* that is, on the promise and truth of God, which cannot deceive" (*LW* 26:387; *WA* 40.1 589.25-28).

81. For Luther's pessimism (or realism) on the continuance of sin in the life of a believer, see esp. *Against Latomus.*

82. On God's giving and taking nothing in return, see *Treatise on Good Works, LW* 44.64; *WA* 6 237.

83. The notion of being "Christs" to one another, giving aid to our neighbor that is as *gratis* as God's aid in Christ, is central to Luther's *Freedom of the Christian;* see *LW* 31.367-68; *WA* 7 35-36.

84. The believer "seeks to gain neither benefit nor salvation *(nihil quaerens aut commodi aut salutis),* since he already abounds in all things and is saved through the grace of God, because in his faith he now seeks only to please God," *Freedom of the Christian, LW* 31.361-62; *WA* 7 32.

85. On this innovative and important move, see Oberman, *Luther,* p. 154: "Luther's discovery was not only new, it was unheard-of; it rent the very fabric of Christian ethics. Reward and merit, so long undisputed as the basic motivation for all human action, were robbed of their efficacy."

"obedience" *(obsequium)*, he is extremely cautious lest God's gift be turned into a new type of "law" or demand. In this new obedience, all the emphasis lies on believers' "willing," "cheerful," and "free" performance of the works of love, which issue, like fruit, "naturally" and spontaneously from their new centeredness in Christ.[86] Against possible misunderstandings, Luther insists again and again that these works *will* result from faith and are a natural result of the life of a Christian, but he refuses to allow that they are integral to faith or to justification, lest they become again a necessary means to salvation.[87] The structure of moral obligation is thus significantly changed: works arise only from the prior gift and have no role to play in making God look favorably on the Christian. Stripped of this conditionality, believers act out of love for God, not from self-concern.[88] In distancing Christian ethics from the legal language of demand, Luther tries to re-found Christian obligation in the personalized language of gratitude, freedom, and love.[89]

Since Christians' love for others is derived from and modeled on Christ's, this same dynamic will apply to their service for the neighbor. This

86. See, e.g., *Freedom of the Christian, LW* 31.359; *WA* 30: "The inner man, who by faith is created in the image of God, is both joyful and happy because of Christ in whom so many benefits are conferred upon him; and therefore it is his one occupation to serve God joyfully and without thought of gain in love that is not constrained" *(ut cum gaudio et gratis deo servat in libera charitate)*. The adverbs *sponte* and *hilariter* recur frequently in this connection.

87. For careful articulation of this matter, see, e.g., *LW* 26.136-37; 27.28-31; *WA* 40.1 239.14–241.16; 40.2 34.10–39.15. Here as elsewhere Luther tends to distinguish faith as the "inner" life of the Christian from works as the "outer" dimension; for justification, only the "inner" counts. If works can be called "necessary" at all, this is at most because they "*show evidence* that we are righteous and that there is faith in a man which saves inwardly" (*The Disputation Concerning Righteousness* (1535), *LW* 34.165; *WA* 39.1 96a). As we shall see, this notion of evidential necessity will play a far larger role in Calvin's theology (see below, 3.4.3).

88. See Mannermaa, *Two Kinds of Love*, pp. 77-87, citing Luther's contrast between the person who loves and praises God for God's own sake, and the parasite who fawns on God for his or her own advantage (*LW* 21.309; *WA* 7 556.18-29).

89. In the *Small Catechism*, Luther prefaces each of the Ten Commandments with the phrase "We should fear and love God, and so. . . ." The effect of God's gift is that "I am bound to thank, praise, serve, and obey him," but the emphasis lies on the manner in which this is done: "We should therefore love him, trust in him, and cheerfully do what he has commanded" (*Book of Concord*, 344-45). Thus, if we may speak of the believer's "counter-gift" to God, enabled by God, this looks backwards (as response to the divine gift), never forwards (as means to a future grace). For excellent clarifications of this topic, see Bayer, *Martin Luther's Theology*, pp. 282-308, and Bayer, "The Ethics of Gift," *LQ* 24 (2010): 447-68. Bayer rightly insists that "God's categorical giving does not exclude the counter-gift of the creature, but rather empowers the creature to this counter-gift as a response." Even so, "this orientation and expectation of the gift cannot and need not be understood as a condition attaching to it: it need not be understood as its *causa finalis*" ("Ethics of Gift," p. 458).

service is no longer instrumental, motivated by the desire for a benefit or reward in return. It is thus, in Luther's terms, truly "free": it can spend itself entirely for others, as Christ humbled and spent himself fully for us, since it "needs" nothing now (from God or neighbor), having all things already in Christ. A believer "lives only for others and not for himself . . . considering nothing except the need and advantage of the neighbor."[90] Although Luther still speaks of this service in reciprocal terms (in Pauline terms, being slaves to one another, Gal 5:13), the reciprocity is no longer of structural significance to the service. If all such giving should be shorn of self-interest and self-concern, it is ideally conceived as a kenotic and *non-circular* gift. In thus figuring service to others as self-giving, in seeking to purify it from any taint of self-interest, and in idealizing the gift that gains no reward, Luther articulates a notion of "altruistic" gift-giving that contributes toward the modern ideal of the "pure" gift, the gift which neither desires nor welcomes a return (see above, 1.3.3).[91]

As Oberman has emphasized, this shift in the conception of "good works" has radical effects.[92] If Luther "horizontalizes" good works (making them no longer part of an ongoing transaction with God), he also renders them all, in principle, of equal worth. If chastity and poverty accrue no divine benefit, now or in the afterlife, they are reduced to personal vocations, on a par with the vocation of a nobleman or a married believer. All believers are required to use their differing stations in life to benefit others, no longer to benefit themselves. The extraordinary revolution in attitudes to marriage and everyday work effected by the Protestant Reformation here draws its inspiration from

90. *Freedom of the Christian, LW* 31.364-65; *WA* 7 34. In the same context: "I will therefore give myself as a Christ to my neighbor, just as Christ offered himself for me . . . since through faith I have an abundance of all good things in Christ. Behold, from faith thus flow forth love and joy in the Lord, and from love a joyful, willing, and free mind that serves one's neighbor willingly and takes no account of gratitude or ingratitude, of praise or blame, of gain or loss. For a man does not serve that he may put men under obligation . . . he most freely and willingly spends himself and all that he has, whether he wastes all on the thankless or whether he gains a reward" (*LW* 31.367; *WA* 7 36).

91. Although P. Malysz ("Exchange and Ecstasy: Luther's Eucharistic Theology in Light of Radical Orthodoxy's Critique of Gift and Sacrifice," *SJT* 60 [2007]: 294-308) rightly insists that Luther's theology of the Mass involves a non-instrumental reciprocity of human thanksgiving to God, he does not successfully distance Luther's "gift for the neighbor" from the tendency to non-reciprocal altruism identified here. For Luther's ethic of gift without return, see B. Wannenwetsch, "Luther's Moral Theology," in D. K. McKim, ed., *The Cambridge Companion to Martin Luther* (Cambridge: Cambridge University Press, 2003), p. 124.

92. Oberman, *Luther,* p. 192: "Good works have not been repudiated, but their aim and direction have been radically 'horizontalized': they have moved from Heaven to earth; they are no longer done to please God but to serve the world" (cf. pp. 80, 179).

Luther's theological reconfiguration of gift and work, taking ordinary life into the realm of service to others, freed from the burden of "merit," and dignified with its own rationale in love.[93] It is not accidental that Luther inspired new attempts to institutionalize charity for the poor.[94] Taken out of the realm of salvation, and thus removed from the special or spectacular duties of religion, almsgiving can be rethought from the perspective of the poor themselves. For Luther, charitable initiatives should thus be the responsibility of civic society, not the special concern of the church — a move that simultaneously broadens and deepens the Christian concern for the poor while cutting the sinew of the benefactors' own benefit, which had long given almsgiving the force of a Christian necessity.

At the heart of the Lutheran Reformation was the reconfiguration of Paul's theology of grace, with a set of perfections not entirely identical to those developed by Calvin. Luther did not "rediscover" grace (which was near the center of practically every form of medieval theology), nor did he simply reinvigorate the Augustinian tradition. As an isolated slogan, *sola gratia* tells us far too little about its precise Lutheran configuration. What is distinctive in Luther is not only the relentlessly Christological reference of grace, but also its permanent state of incongruity. On these grounds, believers live perpetually from a reality outside of themselves, a status of divine favor enjoyed only in and from Christ. Their agency does not need to be re-attributed to the agency of grace, because their works are non-instrumental, and are performed in faith, that is, from the security of a salvation already granted. On the same grounds, gift-giving is stripped of the instrumental reciprocity that had been basic to its rationale since time immemorial. In this sense, Luther did not just reform the church. He offered a new theological definition of gift whose ramifications continue to be felt today.

3.4. Calvin

The theology of John Calvin (1509-1564) was self-consciously drawn from the whole of Scripture, but Paul's letters indisputably played a dominant role. Introducing Romans, the subject of his first biblical commentary, Calvin makes a strong claim for its hermeneutical priority: "if we have gained a true un-

93. For this "doxology of the ordinary," the new value placed on ordinary good works (in trade, labor, and the normal routines of life), see, e.g., *Treatise on Good Works* (1520), *LW* 44.39; *WA* 6 217.

94. See C. Lindberg, *Beyond Charity: Reformation Initiatives for the Poor* (Minneapolis: Fortress Press, 1993), esp. pp. 95-127.

derstanding of this Epistle, we have an open door to all the most profound treasures of Scripture."[95] During his stay in Strasbourg (1538-41), theologically the most formative period of his career, Calvin not only completed his Romans commentary but also radically reshaped his first edition of the *Institutes* (1536); its second (1539) and all subsequent editions (1543, 1550, 1559) bore the impress of Melanchthon's *Loci Communes* and thus acquired a specifically Pauline structure of thought.[96] After Romans (1540), Calvin published commentaries on the entire Pauline corpus (complete by 1551) before turning to the rest of the Bible, eventually covering almost the whole by the time of his death. As the accompaniment to those commentaries, the revamped *Institutes* structured and colored all of the biblical material with Pauline themes. The Calvinist tradition would require no Pauline "canon within the canon," because the entire canon is viewed through a subtly Pauline lens.[97]

As a "second generation" Reformer, Calvin was indebted to both Luther and Melanchthon for his emphasis on the "free," unmerited grace of God in Christ. Like Luther, he also drew extensively on Augustine's theology of grace; particularly influential on Calvin were Augustine's "anti-Pelagian" treatises, which traced the efficacy of grace in the predestination and perseverance of the elect (see above, 3.2). Although Calvin could occasionally distance himself from Augustine, no reader of the *Institutes* could fail to note the strong Augustinian accents in Calvin's theology.[98] Like Augustine, Calvin paints this grace on the widest possible canvas, but in his reflections on the goodness of God he is influenced also by his humanist training in classical philosophy. While Calvin frequently criticizes ancient philosophers, his deep engagement with Stoic thought continued well beyond his early commentary on Seneca's *De Clementia* (1532). In later years, he still devoted considerable time to studying the classics, and one can readily trace their influence in Calvin's biblically

95. *Comm. Rom.* 5.

96. See R. A. Muller, *The Unaccommodated Calvin: Studies in the Foundation of a Theological Tradition* (Oxford: Oxford University Press, 2000), pp. 101-39. On the "Pauline logic" accompanying the shift from a catechetical (1536) to a topically ordered structure for the *Institutes*, cf. J. T. Billings, *Calvin, Participation, and the Gift: The Activity of Believers in Union with Christ* (Oxford: Oxford University Press, 2007), pp. 76-84.

97. On Calvin as a "Pauline theologian," see A. Ganoczy, "Calvin als paulinischer Theologe," in W. H. Neuser, ed., *Calvinus Theologus* (Neukirchen-Vluyn: Neukirchener, 1976), pp. 39-69.

98. Of the 800 direct patristic references in the final edition of the *Institutes* (1559), almost half are to Augustine, who is often quoted at length. In the works of Calvin as a whole, it is reported that 1700 out of the 3200 explicit references to the Fathers are to Augustine. Calvin is himself aware of quoting Augustine often "as the best and most reliable witness of all antiquity" (*Inst.* IV.15.26).

inflected theology of providence and divine benevolence.[99] At the same time, Calvin's efforts to shape Geneva into a model of reformed church life (1541-64) required him to reflect on the operation of grace in the developments and struggles of faith. As we shall see, both his classical hinterland and his success in constructing a durable church piety gave to Calvin's theology of grace a range of accents rather different from those we have traced in Luther.

3.4.1. Grace in Creation, Providence, and History

The first two books of Calvin's *Institutes* are organized around the two-fold knowledge of God: "The Knowledge of God the Creator" and "The Knowledge of God the Redeemer in Christ." These twin poles of theology are bound together by Calvin's insistence on the overflowing goodness of God: the term "grace" *(gratia)* is part of a rich pool of synonyms, depicting the "mercy," "benevolence," "blessings," "goodness," and "benefits" of God. These benefits abound in creation, the theater of God's glory, although, since Adam, humanity has lost the capacity to recognize that generosity, and to respond to it with gratitude, except through faith in Christ: "the truth is that God has given himself from the beginning: now he gives himself again, to be beheld more clearly in the face of his Christ."[100] Calvin draws from his classical heritage the philosophical presumption that God is the Author of all things, and specifically the Source of all goodness: the theme goes back at least as far as Plato, and was mediated by the Stoics.[101] Thus, Calvin freely employs the term "grace" to refer to all the benefits of nature, both external and internal to the human frame. This "general *(generalis)* grace of God" ("common grace") has continued to flood and uphold the world despite the Fall (*Inst.* II.2.12-17), while particular individuals have received "special graces" — extraordinary talents and aptitudes — even as fallen human beings (II.3.4). What was lost through the Fall was the recognition of this goodness, and thus the proper response of submission, obedience, and gratitude (I.14.20-22). Natural gifts were corrupted in humanity (but not wholly lost), while "spiritual gifts" such as faith, love of God, dedication to his glory, and "zeal for holiness and righteousness" were taken away (II.2.12). It is these spiritual gifts that are restored when God's grace is manifested more clearly, and

99. Rightly highlighted by B. A. Gerrish, *Grace and Gratitude: The Eucharistic Theology of John Calvin* (Minneapolis: Fortress Press, 1993), pp. 31-41.

100. From the 1535 preface to Olivétan's translation of the New Testament (*CO* 9.815). On creation as a theater of glory, see *Inst.* I.14.20; everyone feels internally the heavenly grace that gives life (I.5.3). Adam's sin was to spurn God's bounty, which was lavished upon him (II.1.4).

101. For Calvin's proximity to this tradition, see Gerrish, *Grace and Gratitude*, pp. 31-37.

undeservedly, to humanity in Christ, evoking faith and the proper alignment of believers to God, that is, their regeneration in the image of God as grateful beneficiaries of God's overflowing goodness (I.18.3).

Because God's goodness is integral to his creation and governance of the cosmos, it does not stand alone. After defining God as "the fountain of every good," Calvin adds:

> This I take to mean that not only does he sustain the universe (as he once founded it) by his boundless might, regulate it by his wisdom, preserve it by his goodness, and especially rule mankind by his righteousness and judgement, bear with it in his mercy, watch over it by his protection; but also that no drop will be found either of wisdom or light, or of righteousness or power or rectitude, or of genuine truth, which does not flow from him and of which he is not the cause. (*Inst.* I.2.1)

There are at least two features of this statement, which is characteristic of Calvin, that are worthy of note. First, God's goodness is integrated with God's power and God's justice. As for his classical forebears, it would be inconceivable for Calvin that God's benefits would contradict or circumvent the requirements of justice, and he will not allow the grace of the Christ-event to be any less than (by God's marvelous goodness) a satisfaction of perfect righteousness. Secondly, there is a strong drive to attribute *every* virtue, and *every "drop"* of it, to God, and God alone, in pious recognition of God's omnicausality. It is the pressure of this total attribution of cause that makes Calvin insist that God's providence rules every circumstance of life — both good and "bad" — and that leads him to adopt Augustine's theology of predestination. This latter, which until the final edition of the *Institutes* was located within the discussion of providence, is a matter on which Calvin warns against excessive exploration, but which he also robustly defends, taking his stand on Pauline texts (Rom 9:6-23; Eph 1:4-5; *Inst.* III.21-24). He gives full play to Augustine's logic on the omnipotence, free choice, and inscrutable justice of God, uninhibited by Augustine's fear of sounding Manichaean. The fact that Calvin risks further controversy over this "scandalous" doctrine indicates how much his theology is invested in pitting the nullity of human achievement against the omnicompetence of God. That inscrutable but all-pervasive power of God also undergirds Calvin's concern to provide "comfort" and "assurance" in chaotic conditions of change.[102]

102. On Calvin's fascination with power, see W. J. Bouwsma, *John Calvin: A Sixteenth Century Portrait* (Oxford: Oxford University Press, 1988), pp. 162-76.

Calvin's synthetic view of the Scriptures encourages him to place the election of Israel within the eternal election of believers in Christ (Eph 1:4). There is one covenant of grace, in two administrations: Abraham and the Old Testament saints believed in the promise, which was Christ (*Inst.* II.6.1-4). Here again, Calvin's theology of grace is both all-embracing and Christological — the latter inasmuch as Christ constitutes the climax of Israel's (and of all human) history. What was present but obscure becomes fully clear in the coming of Christ (II.9.4), and faith, which is assurance and trust in the benevolence of God, is given a definitive object in the undeserved grace of the Christ-event.[103] By the same token, "the gospel did not so supplant the entire law as to bring forward a different way of salvation. Rather, it confirmed and satisfied whatever the law had promised, and gave substance to the shadows" (*Inst.* II.9.4). This is not just a matter of the unity of Scripture; it is also a sign that God's justice and God's goodness are inextricably entwined. God's mercy cannot be enacted without some "satisfaction" of his law. Its purpose is precisely that his will, expressed in the law, is brought to fulfillment in the perfect righteousness of Christ and the stumbling but slowly increasing righteousness of believers.

3.4.2. Grace in Justification

Calvin's theology of justification by faith *alone,* without works, takes its inspiration from Luther, but is articulated in distinctive patterns that would shape the Calvinist tradition. Although his fullest statement is found in the *Institutes* (III.11-18), we may trace its essential contours in his commentary on Galatians 2:15-21.[104] Here his skills as a commentator — in nuanced analysis of Pauline rhetoric, in linguistic precision, and in pithy comment — are combined with a sharp polemical tone, aligning the "papist" opinions of his day with Paul's opponents in Galatia. Calvin is acutely aware that the Protestants' issue with their opponents is *not* whether justification is by grace through faith: Calvin's opponents, like Paul's in Galatia, "did not entirely exclude the grace of Christ but ascribed the half of salvation to works" (45). The issue is hardly, then, a straightforward choice between faith and works, but whether justification is obtained *by faith alone* (39) or whether, to the contrary, God's grace provides

103. "Now we shall possess a right definition of faith if we call it a firm and certain knowledge of God's benevolence towards us, founded upon the truth of the freely given promise in Christ, both revealed to our minds and sealed upon our hearts through the Holy Spirit" (*Inst.* III.2.7).

104. *Comm. Gal.*, pp. 37-45; numbers in parentheses in the following paragraphs represent pages from this section of the Galatians commentary.

the opportunity for works to merit salvation in conjunction with the forgiveness provided in the death of Christ (45).[105] On contextual grounds, Calvin insists (like Luther, and against Origen and Jerome) that by "works of the law" Paul means not just "ceremonies" but all the law's works, including "moral works" (38-39). But the nub of the issue is the principle that in Pauline theology there is no such thing as "semi-righteousness" (39). In the matter of salvation it is, and absolutely has to be, all or nothing. Either *all* of our righteousness is attributed to Christ and *none* to ourselves, or we have not grasped the gospel at all: "we have to ascribe either nothing or everything to faith or to works" (40).

In this zero-sum calculation, "the foundation of free righteousness is when we are stripped of our own righteousness" (40): Paul "does not allow one drop of righteousness to works" (45). Calvin echoes the Lutheran critique of human confidence in ourselves, but the essential problematic with what he calls "works-righteousness" is not the self-reliant hope of gaining salvation (as in Luther's analysis of "works"; see 3.3.2) so much as the self-deluding opinion that human righteousness can count for anything before God. The characteristic Calvinist claim is that "to be reckoned righteous in the sight of God is not what we men imagine, but what is absolutely perfect" (45). With ruthless perfectionism, Calvin will insist time and again that all human virtue is "stained," "polluted," "defiled," and "corrupt." We only have to think for one moment about the terrifyingly absolute perfection of God's justice to realize that even our highest achievements are hopelessly "impure," and even the most virtuous acts vitiated by improper motives.[106] The righteousness of the law requires nothing less than this perfection: the problem with "works" is not so much the improper attempt to gain righteousness outside of Christ, but the sheer impossibility of achieving God's standard. It is on this basis that Paul categorically rules out justification by works in Galatians 2:16, echoing the depiction of universal sinfulness spelled out in Romans 1–3 (and Rom 7:7-25). "All mortals are excluded from the righteousness of the law," for the simple reason that "none can possibly reach it" (40). Although the Jews were privileged

105. Cf. *Inst.* III.14.11: there is no quarrel on "the beginning of justification," but because the "schoolmen" include "regeneration" under the heading of "justification," they "so describe the righteousness of the regenerated man that a man once for all reconciled to God through faith in Christ might be reckoned righteous before God by good works and be accepted by the merit of them." For Calvin's insistence on a categorical distinction between the (nonetheless inseparable) categories of "sanctification" and "righteousness," see III.11.14 and further below.

106. *Inst.* III.12.1: God's justice is "so perfect that nothing can be admitted except what is in every part whole and complete and undefiled by any corruption. Such was never found in any man, and never will be." In the light of this we should not be deceived by "empty confidence" but should "learn how to tremble" (III.12.2).

with a certain "holiness" through their election, such that "the corruption of nature" was met by "the remedy of sanctifying grace" (37), they "were mistaken in claiming any holiness outside Christ, for there was none" (41). Calvin reads Galatians 2:15-17 to show that Jewish believers now realize that, like the "polluted" Gentiles, their natures are deeply corrupted by sin. "The grace of Christ places them on a level with Gentiles" (40-41), for Christ unveils their common condition, destitute of righteousness in themselves. Their confidence is false because it is empty (*Inst.* 3.19.9), their error not so much existential misalignment (turning to themselves, not God) but the failure to recognize the objective truth that no human righteousness can stand for one second before the judgment seat of God.

When Calvin insists that God's grace is "free," he means above all that this gift contains no element of "return" (or payment of "debt") on the part of God, because there is nothing in the corrupt human condition that gives humans "worth" or "merit" in God's sight. But this does not mean that God, in his grace, simply ignores their sinfulness or opts to accept them despite their unrighteousness: that would compromise the justice that is integral to the goodness of God. Rather, he accepts them inasmuch as they are "clothed" with, or "engrafted into" the righteousness of Christ. Justification requires the "imputation" of Christ's righteousness: "since we can do nothing of ourselves, we are accepted in him by God" (43). As with Luther, Calvin's theology of justification depends on a strong doctrine of "union" with Christ (*vera et substantialis communicatio*, 42-43), but it is characteristic of Calvin to put stress on the legal logic of this salvific mechanism. It is because of Christ's "satisfaction" of God's justice on the cross that sins can be forgiven, and because of his "perfect obedience" (Rom 5:19) that believers, who are covered by this righteousness in faith, can be accepted by God. Only the perfect can stand before God. Believers, as "partakers in Christ," are considered perfectly righteous, since "the obedience of Christ is reckoned to us as if it were our own" (*Inst.* III.9.23).[107]

It is important to insist that this redemptive grace derives entirely and wholly from God's unmerited benevolence, and not from any obligation on God, legal or otherwise. Commenting on Galatians 2:20, Calvin notes, "Paul ascribes the whole to love; it is therefore free" (44). But this free grace is not law-less: through the "merits" and "perfect obedience" of Christ, believers are placed in a position where God can justly accept them with favor. God's justice and holiness are thus by no means set aside: it would make no sense

107. In Calvin's pithy definition: justification is "the acceptance with which God accepts us into his favor as righteous men. And we say that it consists in the remission of sins and the imputation of Christ's righteousness" (*Inst.* III.11.2).

to Calvin to contrast God's just governance of the universe with his fatherly benevolence to those adopted in Christ.[108] Calvin will not allow his emphasis on the grace of God to come to rest in Lutheran paradox, or to slide an inch towards Marcionite unease with the "justice" of God, or to open a door to antinomian temptations. The purpose of the Christ-event, in its unmerited grace, is to bring about God's just benevolence toward people who are remade in Christ to be righteous, sanctified creatures. In dispute with Osiander, Calvin admits that the "righteousness of God" can mean the righteousness that God bestows upon us, but he insists that its primary meaning is "that righteousness which is approved by God," such that "we stand, supported by the sacrifice of Christ's death, before the judgment seat of God" (*Inst.* III.11.9). For Luther, the judgment seat of God is precisely the wrong image to invoke in this regard. For Calvin, it stands for the fact that the unmerited love of God is directed toward the ordering of the cosmos by a good and just Ruler.[109]

3.4.3. Grace in Sanctification

Although Calvin insists that justification is effected through faith without works, he is equally insistent that it is not devoid of good works, and he devotes considerable attention to the process of sanctification. In this connection, he famously speaks of a "double grace" *(duplex gratia):*

> Christ was given to us by God's generosity, to be grasped and possessed by us in faith. By partaking of him we principally receive a double grace: namely, that being reconciled to God through Christ's blamelessness, we may have in heaven instead of a Judge a gracious Father; and secondly, that sanctified by Christ's Spirit, we may cultivate blamelessness and purity of life. (*Inst.* III.11.1)

It is important for Calvin that these two operations are distinct but inseparable, like the heat and light of the sun (III.11.6). The combination of motifs in

108. For this reason, Gerrish's suggestion that in insisting on the fatherly love of God, Calvin's legal language of justification by faith "self-destructs" (*Grace and Gratitude,* p. 60) is wide of the mark. Calvin will hardly permit God's paternal love to compromise his justice.

109. In his version of the Aristotelian categories of causation, Calvin identifies the efficient cause of salvation as God's mercy and freely given love; the material cause as Christ's obedience, "through which he acquired righteousness for us"; the formal or instrumental cause as faith; and the final cause as "the proof of divine justice and the praise of God's goodness" (*Inst.* III.14.17; cf. III.11.7).

1 Corinthians 1:30 is significant: citing this verse, Calvin insists, "Christ justifies no one whom he does not at the same time sanctify" (III.16.1).[110] Calvin is unwilling to follow the Lutheran distinction between *inner* saving faith and *outer* works of service, because the believer's good works are integral to participation in Christ, whose purpose is to conform believers into his image (Rom 8:29) and thus to transform them into some approximation of the holiness of God (*Inst.* III.8.1).[111] Calvin's task — and considerable achievement — is to position a life of good works within the scheme of salvation, without making these works instrumental in obtaining or "meriting" grace, that is, without compromising the priority and incongruity of grace. To the extent that he succeeded, he laid the foundation for a Protestant theology of grace that envisaged an extended narrative of moral progress as an integral element of the life of faith.[112]

The deep structures of Calvin's theology help explain the prominence that he gives to this matter. If the purpose of salvation is regeneration — the restoration of the divine image in humanity — then the grace of justification can hardly rest content without also "manifest[ing] in the life of believers a harmony and agreement between God's righteousness and their obedience" (*Inst.* III.6.1). Taking "repentance" to be a lifelong reformation into accord with the will of God, Calvin insists that "no one can embrace the grace of the gospel without betaking himself from the errors of his past life into the right way, and applying his whole effort to the practice of repentance" (*Inst.* III.3.1). Pauline texts such as Titus 2:11-14 and Ephesians 2:8-10 are frequently cited in this connection. The former makes a direct connection between grace and "godly lives," relating that "the grace of God has appeared . . . training us to renounce impiety and worldly passions, and in the present age to live lives that are self-controlled, upright, and godly." The latter identifies good works as the purpose of grace: "by grace you are saved through faith . . . for we are his creatures, since we have been reborn in Christ Jesus for good works, which God prepared beforehand that we should walk in them."[113] Since such works

110. For the significance of 1 Corinthians 1:30 (Christ "became for us wisdom from God, and righteousness and sanctification and redemption"), see M. A. Garcia, *Life in Christ: Union with Christ and Twofold Grace in Calvin's Theology* (Milton Keynes: Paternoster Press, 2008), pp. 219-26.

111. Commenting on Romans 6:2, Calvin writes: "Believers are never reconciled to God without the gift of regeneration. Indeed, we are justified for this very purpose, that we may afterwards worship God in purity of life" (*Comm. Rom.*, p. 122).

112. On both graces as resulting from union with Christ, see the full discussion in Garcia, *Life in Christ*.

113. For representative citations of these texts, see *Inst.* III.7.3; III.15.7. Both texts associate grace with the kind of double effect that leads Calvin to coin the expression "double grace."

are the goal of the Christian life, and God's will does not change over time, Calvin can insist that "the law" is essentially at one with the purpose of grace in Christian obedience. While the law sets an impossibly high standard for those unconnected to Christ, its promised blessings are not empty, but are granted to "the works of believers" (*Inst.* III.17.3). Indeed, the law's "third use," in instruction for Christian believers, can be considered its principal function (*Inst.* II.7.12).[114] This forges a harmony between "law" and "gospel" in a fashion quite alien to Lutheran discourse. *Obedience* to God emerges as the hallmark of the Christian life, even if this is carefully glossed as the voluntary submission of sons to a benevolent Father (*Inst.* III.19.5).

With such emphasis on good works as the purpose of salvation, Calvin also hopes to rebuff powerful contemporary accusations against the Protestant movement, which alleged that justification by faith *alone* was morally unserious and prone to antinomian license. It also enables him to deal with those biblical texts, often cited by Catholic opponents, which promise reward for good works, and where good works are seemingly integral to, even the condition for, salvation. Unlike Luther, Calvin will not dismiss such passages as "law." He accepts that God rewards the grace-induced works of believers with further graces (the blessings and gifts of the Spirit, *Inst.* II.3.11); it is natural that God should reward "what is pleasing and acceptable to him," counting it "worthy" of honor (*Inst.* III.15.4). But this recognition must be carefully qualified. These works are only ever the *result* of God's grace, not the primary *means* toward it; if they are placed first, this expresses *sequence* more than *causation* (*Inst.* III.14.21). And there is still a categorical distinction between *reward* (freely determined by an unobliged donor) and *merit* (which constitutes a claim on the giver, III.15.1-7).[115]

Equally importantly, Calvin is careful to trace the grace of God even in the good works that believers perform. He draws heavily on Augustine, who, as we saw above (3.2), emphasized the *efficacy* of grace, as a power that incites and enables the believer's will: thus, when God "crowns" the works of the believer, he is simply rewarding his own gifts (*Inst.* II.3.11-14; 4.2; III.15.7). But Calvin is well aware that the Augustinian tradition used the language of "merit" and

114. One of the key marks of spiritual insight is "knowing how to frame our life according to the rule of [God's] law" (*Inst.* II.2.18). "Where the whole law is concerned, the gospel differs from it only in clarity of manifestation" (II.9.4).

115. Calvin knows he is turning against a long tradition of "merit" language. He attempts to shift the biblical language of "reward" away from the domain of "pay" or "desert" into the domain of "prize." This preserves the freedom of God as giver, so that even the reward for perfect obedience is determined by God (*Comm. Gal.*, p. 38). The modern distinction between a "prize" and a "right" expresses something of the difference that Calvin was striving to maintain.

was apt to attribute credit to the graced believer in a way that could threaten the *complete* attribution of honor to God, and thus the absolute incongruity of grace. He therefore takes care to distance himself from Augustine at key points (e.g., *Inst.* III.11.15) and characteristically insists that the believer's works, however good, remain "stained" by the pollution of sin.[116] Where Luther insisted that any "righteousness" attributed to believers was not their own, but only Christ's (see above, 3.3.3), Calvin maintained that the believers' works, even if "righteous," will always be "spattered" with sin and impurity (*Inst.* III.14.5). Once again, the definition of righteousness as *perfect* righteousness is crucial to Calvin's theology: "When the Spirit of God forms us to such love, why is it not for us a cause of righteousness, except that even in the saints it is imperfect, and for that reason merits no reward of itself" (*Inst.* III.11.17).[117]

It is because of this imperfection that God's grace is again the crucial factor in the acceptability of believers' works. Like a benevolent father, he graciously accepts works that are "incomplete, half-done, and even defective" (*Inst.* III.19.5), "covering" them in Christ's perfection (*Inst.* III.17.8). Moreover, at a deeper level, whatever is *truly good* in what we do is the product of God, not us. "Whatever is praiseworthy in works is God's grace; there is not a drop that we ought by rights to ascribe to ourselves. . . . To man we assign only this: that he pollutes and contaminates by his impurity those very things which were good" (*Inst.* III.15.3). In this schema, it is important that believer-agency is *not* entirely absorbed into the agency of God, even if the *value* of what is done is entirely attributed to God. It is precisely the inadequacies of believers as agents that preserve the incongruity of grace, at the same time as God's effective grace is accorded one hundred percent of the credit for the goodness in human good works. If agency itself is not a zero-sum game in Calvin's construal of believers' relation to God, any goodness (i.e., perfection) that results from their doubled agency most certainly is.

It is because he does not reduce believers to mere passivity (while attribut-

116. For Calvin's criticisms of Augustine, see P. Helm, *Calvin at the Centre* (Oxford: Oxford University Press, 2010), pp. 202-7. *Pace* Helm, the issue is not just Augustine's failure to distinguish between (in Calvin's terms) "justification" and "sanctification," but his inclination to merge the agency of God with that of the believer, thus attributing (some measure of) true "righteousness" to the grace-infused believer. For Calvin, Paul means to exclude even the works of the regenerate believer from justification, not just because those works belong in the category of sanctification, rather than justification, but because they do not, and cannot, exhibit that *perfection* that alone can count for justification before God (*Comm. Rom.*, pp. 71-72).

117. Cf. *Inst.* III.14.11: "There never existed any work of a godly man which, if examined by God's stern judgement, would not deserve condemnation." Thus, "the best work that can be brought forward from them [believers] is still always spotted and corrupted with some impurity of the flesh, and has, so to speak, some dregs mixed with it" (III.14.9).

ing the *value* of their work to God) that Calvin can encourage them to consider their good works as "signs" and "proofs" of their status in Christ, the visible demonstration of their election, and thus a source of comfort and strength (*Inst.* III.14.18). Indeed, he injects into the Protestant way of life a strong prospect of progress. In contrast to Luther, Calvin makes much of the believer's "journey" as a life of "advancement," "growth," and "struggle," a lifelong "race" (e.g., *Inst.* III.3.9; 6.5; 9.5). Progress may be slow, but because it is continual (III.3.8) the Christian life has a meaningful linear shape; it does not consist only of a perpetual return to the beginning.[118] This emphasis matches the social context of Calvin's theological endeavors, his establishment of the church in Geneva as a school for lifelong instruction and discipline (*Inst.* IV.1.4). In reordering church ministry (in the fourfold pattern of teacher, pastor, elder, and deacon) and in the institutionalization of Christian education and pastoral oversight, Calvin took pains to ensure that every believer could advance in piety, and could observe that advance, ideally on a daily basis. Teachers took care of catechetical instruction (based on Calvin's new *Catechism* of 1541), together with teaching in school and (eventually) the higher "Academy," while the pastors' regular preaching (informed by weekly Bible study meetings) was designed to instruct the whole body of believers in the whole truth of Scripture.[119] Pastors and elders formed the "Consistory," whose moral oversight imposed discipline on the daily lives of the congregation; exclusion from the Lord's Supper constituted an effective sanction.[120] Indeed, mutual reproof and counseling were expected within the whole body of believers, whose piety was shaped both by song (the Genevan Psalter) and by daily prayer.[121] Through

118. Cf. Calvin's commentary on Romans 6:7: "This work of God is not completed on the day when it is begun in us, but gradually increases, and by daily advancement is brought by degrees to its completion . . . you are continually to study to increase your communion in the death of Christ until you arrive at the goal" (*Comm. Rom.*, pp. 125-26). For similar comments elsewhere, cf. Bouwsma, *John Calvin*, pp. 185-87.

119. See T. H. L. Parker, *Calvin's Preaching* (Edinburgh: T&T Clark, 1992). On Calvin's church order and its influence, see D. Wright, "Calvin's Role in Church History," in D. K. McKim, ed., *The Cambridge Companion to John Calvin* (Cambridge: Cambridge University Press, 2004), pp. 277-88. Regarding the catechism, see N. Watanabe, "Calvin's Second Catechism: Its Predecessors and Its Environment," in W. H. Neuser, ed., *Sacrae Scripturae Professor: Calvin as Confessor of Holy Scripture* (Grand Rapids: Eerdmans, 1994), pp. 224-32.

120. See R. S. Wallace, *Calvin, Geneva, and the Reformation* (Edinburgh: Scottish Academic Press, 1988), pp. 46-52; cf. J. E. Olson, "Calvin on Social-ethical Issues," in McKim, ed., *Cambridge Companion to John Calvin*, pp. 153-72.

121. On the psalms and the practice of piety in prayer, see J. R. Beeke, "Calvin on Piety," in McKim, ed., *Cambridge Companion to John Calvin*, pp. 125-52. The latter is given extended discussion in *Inst.* III.20.

all such means, Calvin expected the believer's faith and obedience to grow on an incremental basis, struggling daily against temptation, not least the temptation to "indolence," "coldness," and "sloth." Like a tightly strung bow, Calvin himself was poised to make good use of every moment of time: he expected every Christian to be similarly committed to a journey of increasing holiness, right up to the moment of death.

3.4.4. Calvin's Perfections of Grace

Like Augustine, Calvin took the difference between him and his opponents to be the way in which they used the term "grace," and in the wake of Augustine, it was convenient to label all who used it differently "Pelagian" (*Inst.* III.11.15). Also like Augustine, Calvin made the grace of God the flipside of God's judgment and wrath, his hatred of sinners and of sin. Following the dualities of Romans 1:17-18 and Romans 9:6-23, Calvin shows no tendency to perfect grace as *singular,* that is, as exclusive of judgment: God's predestination is double, following an equal (if inscrutable) distribution of justice, with a deliberately discriminate dispersal of grace.[122] As we have seen, Calvin puts heavy stress on the *priority* of God's grace, as God is the Author of all reality and the Source of election from before the foundation of the world (Eph 1:4). In this connection, Calvin is particularly keen to emphasize the *freedom* of God's will and power (*Inst.* III.22.1-2). In freely choosing whom he elects, God is not bound by any prior condition of worth. In fact, his free choice is established by the fact that he owes no one anything, pays no reward, and is never debtor or second giver (III.21.1). In his unequal distribution of grace, without regard to worth, Calvin's God in fact resembles nothing so much as the contemporary sovereign king, who was keen to prove his liberality and greatness precisely by *disregarding* the normal expectation that gifts are given to those who deserve them.[123] If some thought that royal power should be tempered by the principle of desert, it was of the essence of God's omnipotence, for Calvin, that his "secret good pleasure" should operate in absolute freedom from any such constraint. It is

122. For Calvin, our understanding of God's "free mercy" is safeguarded only if we recognize that "he does not indiscriminately adopt all into the hope of salvation, but gives to some what he denies to others" (*Inst.* III.21.1). In other words, the *freedom* of God's mercy is more important to Calvin than its universality, and is established precisely by the fact that it is *not* universal: "the very inequality of his grace proves that he is free" (III.21.6).

123. For the disputes on this matter in contemporary sixteenth-century France, see N. Zemon Davis, *The Gift in Sixteenth-Century France* (Oxford: Oxford University Press, 2000), pp. 159-65.

no accident that the Calvinist tradition would come to emphasize the "sovereignty" of grace.

As we have just seen, the priority and freedom of grace is closely tied to its *incongruity.* All of God's grace since the Fall has been necessarily incongruous, but the grace of God in Christ is its clearest and climactic expression. In justification, grace is undeserved and therefore all the more clearly God's, and God's alone. But even in relation to sanctification, given believers' "fouling" of every good work, the value of their works continues to be incongruous with their actual performance. It is not clear whether the incongruity of God's grace is an accidental quality — necessary since the Fall — or of its very essence; if God's benefits were bestowed on Adam before the Fall (I.15.3) and even on Christ (III.11.10), divine gifts can apparently be congruous with the worth of their recipients. Calvin will not explore this point, but it is noticeable that the incongruity in sinners' receipt of grace is effected by the *worth* of Christ's righteousness, with which they are "clothed." It is clear for Calvin that a just God can have no commerce with a sinner: "he cannot receive him into grace or join him to himself unless he turns him from a sinner into a righteous man" (III.11.21). As we have seen, this can take place only through the free pardon of sins, and the imputation of the righteousness of Christ — and thus only through the "worth" that God accords to sinners in Christ. It is characteristic of Calvin that he will not allow God's mercy and grace to suggest any diminution in God's just demand for perfect righteousness.

Calvin thus stresses the necessity of believers' obedience, so long as it is clear that this is the *result* not the *cause* of grace (we must not "invert Paul's order," *Inst.* III.22.3). As we have seen, there are strong Augustinian strands in Calvin's emphasis on the *efficacy* of grace: not only is faith itself a gift, but every valuable feature of the believers' new life arises from the gift of the Spirit. This ensures that the *value* of believers' work is attributed wholly to God, but Calvin does not advocate a *monergism,* reducing the believers' agency to zero. Avoiding also synergistic notions of the cooperation of two independent wills, Calvin conceives of the believers' actions as *both* wholly God's *and* wholly their own.[124] If a label is required for this construction of agency, *energism* might be the best available. Believers are energized by the Spirit to work, actively and strenuously, recognizing that whatever real "good" ensues can be credited only to God.

Calvin has no hesitation in describing this strenuous activity as the believers' return for the divine gift, and in this respect he does *not* perfect the

124. On this non-competitive, but also non-partitive, relationship between divine and human agency, see Billings, *Calvin, Participation, and the Gift,* pp. 47-49, 141-42.

non-circularity of gift; such a perfection, which we have traced in Luther (see above, 3.3.4), has been wrongly attributed to Calvin.[125] "In all covenants of his mercy the Lord requires of his servants in return uprightness and sanctity of life" (III.17.5). Calvin can figure praise and obedience directed to God, and love directed to the neighbor, as forms of this return, fulfilling the creaturely *telos* of humble gratitude for divine gifts. In this context, Calvin is careful to insist that "the covenant is at the outset drawn up as a free agreement, and perpetually remains so" (III.17.5): believers' return to God, which arises from God's grace, is never *instrumental* in acquiring initial or subsequent grace from God. Nonetheless, believers' active commitment to holiness is a necessary sign of the grace that activates their work, for it is in such return that this grace fulfills its purpose. In the same way, Calvin advocates a reciprocity in human relations, as each person is encouraged to give the other his or her due; in this connection, he combines Pauline motifs of mutuality in the body with Senecan advice on the proper distribution of alms (III.7.7). Although he reorganized the relief of poverty in the city of Geneva, we do not find in Calvin that impulse toward the modern "pure" gift that we have traced in Luther.[126] Calvin's theology of the superabundant and incongruous grace of God results not in the idealization of unilateral giving, but in the circulation of human gifts in the bonds of social due, and this as part of the human return to God of the obedience and righteousness that echo God's good-and-just governance of the cosmos.

3.5. From Barth to Martyn

3.5.1. Karl Barth

The history of theological engagement with the Pauline theme of grace took a new turn with the publication of Barth's *Römerbrief,* whose second edition (1922) influenced leading Pauline scholars throughout the twentieth century.[127]

125. Zemon Davis's reading of Calvin on this point (*The Gift,* pp. 189-203) has been corrected by Billings, *Calvin, Participation, and the Gift;* cf. Gerrish, *Grace and Gratitude,* on the "return" of gratitude.

126. For Calvin's theology of poverty and the practice of poor-relief, see B. L. Pattison, *Poverty in the Theology of John Calvin* (Eugene, OR: Pickwick Publications, 2006) and E. A. McKee, *John Calvin on the Diaconate and Liturgical Almsgiving* (Geneva: Librairie Droz, 1984).

127. K. Barth, *Der Römerbrief,* 2nd ed. (1922; reprinted, Zürich: Theologischer Verlag, 1954), and available online in the *Digital Karl Barth Library,* from which all German citations are here taken; English translation: *The Epistle to the Romans,* trans. E. C. Hoskyns, 6th ed. (London: Oxford University Press, 1933).

Not only Bultmann and Käsemann, but also, through the latter's influence, Martyn, were indebted to the radical turn in theology instigated by Barth through his scintillating reading of Romans.[128] Barth's interpretation of the *incongruity* of grace was clearly indebted to Luther,[129] but his relentless deployment of this theme to bring dominant modes of theology into crisis reactivated its subversive potential in a form still powerful today.

Barth read Romans as a radical critique of the human tendency to speak and think about God in ways that *start* from human conceptions of history, religion, and experience. In speaking of "the righteousness of God" (Rom 1:17; 3:21) against the backdrop of human sin and ignorance, Paul is speaking of the radically Other (not just a relatively Greater entity or an Other within a human system of differentiation). Stressing the "infinite qualitative distinction" between time and eternity, that is, between God and the human, Barth found in Romans the depiction of a boundary, a limit or chasm, which could not be crossed from the human side.[130] On this side of the line lie all human knowledge, history, and achievement, and it is the greatest human error to imagine "God" in terms that are extended, developed, or projected from within these human capacities.[131] Barth here challenged at the deepest level the whole edifice of "liberal" theology in which he had been reared, with its tendency to speak of "God" from the standpoint of human consciousness, as the deepest reality of human history and experience.[132] In contrast, he insisted that God is unknown and unintuitable, not the fulfillment of human possibility, but the humanly impossible, who can be known only if God speaks and acts from the *other* side of the barrier. God *has* acted and spoken *in* history, specifically in the (death and) resurrection of Jesus Christ, but this is not an event *of* history, causally explicable in human terms, but "pure miracle," a word and act

128. Barth's reading of 1 Corinthians (*Die Auferstehung der Toten* [Munich: Chr. Kaiser Verlag, 1924]; trans. H. J. Stenning, *The Resurrection of the Dead* [New York: Hodder and Revell, 1933]) is also important but less immediately relevant to our theme.

129. Note the substantial citations from Luther in *Epistle to the Romans,* pp. 39, 42, 93, 106, 155, 185, etc. For Barth's debt to Luther, see G. Hunsinger, *Disruptive Grace: Studies in the Theology of Karl Barth* (Grand Rapids: Eerdmans, 2000), pp. 279-304.

130. The preface to the second edition draws attention to this principle as the only "system" in Barth's reading of the letter, and draws out its negative as well as its positive significance: "God is in heaven, and thou art on earth" (*Epistle to the Romans,* p. 10).

131. "To suppose that a direct road leads from art, or morals, or science, or even from religion, to God is sentimental, liberal self-deception" (*Epistle to the Romans,* p. 337).

132. As is well known, Barth's break with Herrmann and others began with his horror at their uncritical support for the Kaiser at the outbreak of World War I. For detailed analysis of Barth's theological development, see B. L. McCormack, *Karl Barth's Critically Realistic Dialectical Theology: Its Genesis and Development 1909-1936* (Oxford: Clarendon Press, 1995).

intersecting with the human plane "vertically, from above."[133] In this radical transcendence, God is not the extension or enhancement of human capacity, but the contradiction of human possibility, the critical "No" which contains at the same time the liberating "Yes" of divine revelation and salvation. The "new man" created by this divine act is not an enhanced version of the human but a miraculous creation founded on the resurrection and living from the future Kingdom of God. Faith is no inner piety or refined sensibility, but the mark of a human void, a "bomb-crater" or "empty space" that bears witness to the hiddenness and otherness of God.[134]

To speak of "grace" in this context is to speak of an event (not a divine quality, still less a human *habitus*), an absolutely free and unconditioned act of God. In line with his dialectical mode of theology, Barth speaks of grace as "the gift of Christ, who exposes the gulf which separates God and man, and, by exposing it, bridges it."[135] This exposure is also God's judgment on all human achievement, not least the arrogant illusion that we can bridge the gulf ourselves. In this sense, grace always also contains God's "No." The wrath and the mercy of God do not cancel each other out, but can be understood only in relation to each other: we are forgiven only where we are also condemned.[136] Where the gulf is bridged (*only* from the side of God) it is therefore always *despite* and not *because of* the human condition. Countering every thought that grace might be the recognition or result of human worth, Barth stresses that God's action is never "Consequently" but always "Nevertheless": it is life *from the dead* and the justification *of the ungodly* (cf. Rom 4:5, 17), not the enhancement of life nor the reward of the righteous.[137] In the Pauline pattern

133. See, e.g., *Epistle to the Romans*, pp. 30, 50, 62. By translating Paul's eschatology into the terms of "eternity" and "time," Barth spoke of the resurrection, the new world, touching the old "as a tangent touching a circle, that is, without touching it" (p. 30). For the problems in this conception of the relation between God and time, later abandoned by Barth, see McCormack, *Dialectical Theology*, pp. 241-90.

134. For the metaphors, see, e.g., *Epistle to the Romans*, p. 29.

135. *Epistle to the Romans*, p. 31; *Römerbrief*, p. 7: "als Geschenk des Christus, der die Distanz zwischen Gott und Mensch überbrückt, indem er sie aufreißt."

136. "Men are forgiven by God only when He condemns them; life rises only from death; the beginning stands at the end, and 'Yes' proceeds from 'No'" (*Epistle to the Romans*, p. 112; cf. p. 187). "In manifesting the utmost limit of the wrath of God, [the death of Christ] exposes his unfathomable mercy" (p. 162). We are clearly far from Marcion's undialectical construal of these motifs (see above, 3.1).

137. "The righteousness of God is that 'nevertheless!' by which He associates us with Himself and declares Himself to be our God. This 'nevertheless' contradicts every human logical 'consequently,' and is itself incomprehensible and without cause or occasion, because it is the 'nevertheless!' of God" (*Epistle to the Romans*, p. 93) ("Gerechtigkeit Gottes ist das Trotzdem! mit dem Gott sich erklärt als unser Gott und uns zu sich rechnet, und unbegreif-

of grace, God rejects what we are and elects what we are not: "only when grace is recognized to be incomprehensible is it grace."[138] By this relentless emphasis on the incongruity of grace, Barth seeks to cut off all attempts to match God's grace with the conditions of human possibility. Like Luther, he applies this dynamic also to the life of believers, who live in the paradox of faith, from a reality not their own, by a grace that is not once received and then forever owned, but continually received in each new moment.[139] To live from grace is to live from the "impossible possibility," created *ex nihilo* by the unconditioned fiat of God.

Besides being a broad critique of the liberal confidence that had (in Barth's view) seduced European culture into self-affirming arrogance, the particular target of Barth's *Römerbrief* is the pretentious claim of "religion."[140] Paul's statements about "the Jew," "Israel," and "the Law" are taken to refer to "the religious man" and "religion," and this not in distinction from the church or Christianity, but precisely as religion comes to expression in the church.[141] In Barth's discourse, "religion" — the subject of intense analysis and high evaluation in his contemporary context — sat squarely on the human side of the line that divides humanity from God. It may be the highest of human achievements, but precisely as such it fosters the ultimate illusion that it constitutes a direct

---

lich, grundlos, nur in sich selbst, nur in Gott begründet, von allem 'Darum' rein ist dieses Trotzdem!", *Römerbrief*, p. 68).

138. *Epistle to the Romans*, p. 31 (*Römerbrief*, p. 7: "Nur wenn sie als unbegreiflich erkannt wird, ist Gnade Gnade"). On the relationship between grace and Barth's early theology of "*Krisis*," see M. Beintker, "Krisis und Gnade: Zur theologischen Deutung der Dialektik beim frühen Barth," *EvTh* 46 (1986): 442-56.

139. We "have been lifted up into the air, so that we have no standing-place except the protection of God . . . the new man has no existence except non-existence: for the pre-eminence of his origin lies in the miracle of God" (*Epistle to the Romans*, p. 163).

140. For critical remarks on western European culture, see *Epistle to the Romans*, p. 68. The historical context of this commentary suggests parallels with the general crisis of confidence following the Great War, but Barth's target was specifically false ways of speaking, thinking, and acting in relation to God.

141. For "the Jew" as "the religious and ecclesiastical man" ("der religiös-kirchliche Mensch"), see *Epistle to the Romans*, p. 40 (*Römerbrief*, p. 15). In his *Römerbrief* (unlike in his later *Kirchliche Dogmatik* II/2), Barth takes Paul's discussion of Israel in Romans 9–11 to concern, primarily, the church; see W. Hill, "The Church as Israel and Israel as the Church: An Examination of Karl Barth's Exegesis of Romans 9:1-5 in *The Epistle to the Romans* and *Church Dogmatics* 2/2," *JTI* 6 (2012): 139-58. Although Barth occasionally makes comments about non-Christian religions, it would be a mistake to read his comments about "religion" as focused on world religions in the modern sense; see J. A. di Noia, "Religion and the Religions," in J. Webster, ed., *The Cambridge Companion to Karl Barth* (Cambridge: Cambridge University Press, 2000), pp. 243-57.

route to God. Like Luther's analysis of "works of the law" as tempting humanity into the ultimate sin of self-justification (see above, 3.3.2), Barth could make the most withering comments about the arrogance of "religion," celebrating its dissolution by the gospel.[142] In fact, he does identify a positive function for religion, but only in a paradoxical role, as a parable of, or sign-post to, the hiddenness of God. He is clear that to take a human stance outside or against religion is no better than standing within and for it. Humanly speaking, there is no other place for the believer to stand. But precisely here the grace of God may make its impact, enabling a witness to the gospel that is not identical to the church, but remains always beyond it, even its deadliest critic.[143] Here again Barth wished to preserve a critical distance between revelation and all its human media. He detects in "religion" the greatest danger of turning God into an idol, that is, a projection of human experiences or desires.

Looking back on his *Römerbrief*, Barth would later judge it one-sided in its negativity, though necessarily so, as a rubble-clearing exercise.[144] Subsequently, he would find appropriate ways to articulate the positive impress of revelation *onto* human history, in the history of Israel, in the incarnation of the Word, and in the life of believers. But the Christological focus of Barth's theology of grace would become, if anything, even more intense, while he would subtract nothing from the absolute *incongruity* between divine grace and inherent human possibility. Barth sees no need to perfect the *singularity* of grace: God's grace is at the same time the revelation of God's judgment, even if the resurrection demonstrates God's irrevocable resolve that grace will triumph over human sin and unbelief.[145] Because he resists placing divine agency on the same plane as human agency, and thus in competition with it, Barth will wrestle long and hard with ways to speak of the *efficacy* of grace in the life of the believer.[146] But for the early Barth, the most important feature of

142. In this connection, the translation of the term *"Aufhebung"* has become a matter of intense dispute: "abolition" (as in *Church Dogmatics* I/2, §17) may be a misleading rendition.

143. "The opposition between the Church and the Gospel is final and all-embracing; the Gospel dissolves the Church, and the Church dissolves the Gospel," *Epistle to the Romans*, p. 333 ("Es ist klar, daß der Gegensatz von Evangelium und Kirche grundsätzlich und auf der ganzen Linie unendlich ist. . . . Das Evangelium ist die Aufhebung der Kirche, wie die Kirche die Aufhebung des Evangeliums ist," *Römerbrief*, p. 317).

144. *Kirchliche Dogmatik* II/1, pp. 715-16; cf. McCormack, *Dialectical Theology*, pp. 288-90.

145. Hence the subsequent development in Barth's theology of a kind of "universalism," which arises from his doctrine of election in Christ and moves decisively beyond Calvin's double predestination; see B. L. McCormack, "Grace and Being: The Role of God's Gracious Election in Karl Barth's Ontology," in Webster, ed., *Cambridge Companion to Karl Barth*, pp. 92-110.

146. In his later theology, Barth will speak of a grace that founds or creates the freedom, the integrity, and even (within limits) the "autonomy" of the believer, in covenant partnership

grace, drawn to its extreme in a classic case of "perfection," is its incongruity with the capacity and worth of the human. It is this emphasis, with strong Lutheran overtones but reapplied in such a way as to require a reappraisal of the nature of theology, that resonates with striking clarity in Barth's early work, and that created the trajectory of Pauline scholarship surveyed in this section.

3.5.2. Rudolf Bultmann

Barth's *Römerbrief* had a major impact on Bultmann's reading of Paul, which was later given definitive expression at the heart of his *Theologie des Neuen Testaments.*[147] Bultmann reacted warmly to Barth's emphasis on the Christ-event as the eschatological (and thus ultimate) contradiction of human norms and achievements, an emphasis that expressed, in his view, "the simple — Pauline — radicalism, which is clear about what faith means and what grace means."[148] However, already in the 1920s Bultmann was signaling his discomfort with Barth's "overdrawn" paradox of the "impossible possibility": if revelation is sheer miracle and beyond human consciousness, can it relate to the human condition at all? And does Barth sufficiently recognize (and distance himself from) Paul's occasional and unfortunate tendencies to treat God or the events of salvation as matters of "objective" or speculative knowledge?[149] Drawing on

---

with God; see J. Webster, *Barth's Ethics of Reconciliation* (Cambridge: Cambridge University Press, 1995), and G. Hunsinger, *How to Read Karl Barth: The Shape of His Theology* (Oxford: Oxford University Press, 1991), pp. 185-224.

147. R. Bultmann, *Theologie des Neuen Testaments,* vol. 1 (Tübingen: Mohr Siebeck, 1948); translated as *Theology of the New Testament,* trans. K. Grobel (London: SCM Press, 1952). Bultmann's review of Pauline scholarship ("Zur Geschichte der Paulus-Forschung," *Theologische Rundschau* n.f. 1 [1929]: 26-59), several key entries in *ThWNT* (e.g., on πιστεύω, καυχάομαι, and γινώσκω), and a major dictionary article ("Paulus," in *Religion in Geschichte und Gegenwart* 4 [1930], pp. 1019-45; translated as "Paul" in S. M. Ogden, ed., *Existence and Faith: Shorter Writings of Rudolf Bultmann* [London: Hodder and Stoughton, 1961], pp. 111-46) laid the foundations for the later work. For Bultmann's reading of Paul, see C. Landmesser, "Rudolf Bultmann als Paulusinterpret," *ZThK* 110 (2013): 1-21. I have given a detailed analysis of one part of the *Theologie* in "Humanity under Faith," in B. W. Longenecker and M. C. Parsons, eds., *Beyond Bultmann* (Waco: Baylor University Press, 2014), pp. 79-99.

148. See his 1922 review of the second edition of Barth's *Römerbrief,* reprinted in J. Moltmann, ed., *Anfänge der Dialektischen Theologie,* vol. 1 (Munich: C. Kaiser, 1962), pp. 119-42, translated as "Karl Barth's *Epistle to the Romans* in Its Second Edition," in J. M. Robinson, ed., *The Beginnings of Dialectical Theology* (Richmond: John Knox Press, 1968), pp. 100-120 (citation from p. 104).

149. See the review of Barth's *Römerbrief* (previous note) and, in particular, the 1926 review of Barth's theological commentary on 1 Corinthians *(Die Auferstehung der Toten),* re-

his Lutheran heritage, already radicalized by W. Herrmann, Bultmann insisted that "to know Christ is to know his benefits" (Melanchthon).[150] Paul had no investment in a theoretical system of thought or a merely factual, external account of salvation-history, only in what addresses the human condition and elicits faith. "Every assertion about God is simultaneously an assertion about man and vice versa. For this reason and in this sense Paul's theology is at the same time anthropology."[151] Bultmann accordingly melds a Lutheran focus on the individual believer with existentialist concepts developed in dialogue with Heidegger; his aim is to clarify how faith's understanding and appropriation of salvation is also, indeed primarily, a new understanding of oneself.[152]

Bultmann's famous analysis of Pauline theology in his *Theology of the New Testament* thus begins with what faith reveals of the human condition.[153] Paul's anthropological terms are taken to reveal both the "ontological" structures of human existence (what belongs essentially to humankind) and its "ontic" condition (what is actually, in fact, the case). The bodiliness of existence (i.e., that a person can have a relation to him/herself) and a person's capacity for desire, aim, and choice reveal an ontological "double possibility": "to be at one

---

printed in *Glaube und Verstehen. Gesammelte Aufsätze*, vol. 1 (Tübingen: Mohr Siebeck, 1933), pp. 38-64 (translated in *Faith and Understanding*, ed. R. W. Funk, trans. L. Pettibone Smith [London: SCM, 1969], pp. 66-94). This brought to the fore Bultmann's (Luther-inspired) commitment to *Sachkritik* (critical analysis of a text by reference to its subject matter), and signaled the growing divide between Barth and Bultmann. For their relationship, see K. Hammann, *Rudolf Bultmann: Eine Biographie* (Tübingen: Mohr Siebeck, 2009), pp. 131-45 *et passim*.

150. The tag is quoted in, e.g., "Glaube und Geschichte" (1948), translated as "Grace and Freedom," in R. Bultmann, *Essays Philosophical and Theological*, trans. J. C. Greig (London: SCM, 1955), pp. 168-81, at p. 173. The verb "objektivieren" and the adjective "spekulativ" are commonly used to define what Pauline theology is *not* (e.g., *Theologie*, pp. 186-88).

151. *Theology*, p. 191; *Theologie*, p. 187. Here and unless otherwise indicated I cite Grobel's translation.

152. Bultmann is conscious of needing to go beyond Paul's own statements in order to clarify Paul's "real intention" (e.g., *Theology*, pp. 300-301; *Theologie*, pp. 295-96). He explicitly follows Luther's step *beyond Paul* in internalizing and individualizing the understanding of faith: "Luther's progress over Paul consists . . . in the question: How do *I* get a gracious God? Paul demands obedience for the message of faith, and the question of how I can be obedient does not come into view for him. Obedience consists in the acknowledgement of the proclaimed facts of salvation and the new saving ordinance of God. For Luther, as a true son of the church, this acknowledgement was self-evident, but he saw that obedience did not really consist in *that*, and that such obedience was dead if it were not at the same time the personal appropriation of the message, the inner submission to revelation" ("Barth's *Epistle*," p. 115).

153. Bultmann is quite clear that this analysis is derived from faith (*Theology*, pp. 191, 270; *Theologie*, pp. 188, 266). E. P. Sanders voices a persistent misreading when he identifies as Bultmann's "principal fault" that "he proceeded from plight to solution and supposed that Paul proceeded in the same way" (*Paul and Palestinian Judaism* [London: SCM, 1977], p. 474).

with himself, or to be at odds, estranged from himself."[154] From Paul's faith perspective, ontically the human self has in fact already forfeited its authentic life, because it has failed to recognize that life can be had only in dependence on God the Creator. It is from God alone, and not from himself or from anything at his own disposal, that a person who is estranged from himself can be "brought back to himself." In fact, Paul's discussion of "flesh" and "sin" indicates that the essence of sin is not transgression of divine commands, nor sensual desires, but the rebellious idea that a human being can secure his/her own "life" on the basis of natural, creaturely resources, that is, on the basis of his/her own power and achievements *(Leistungen)*.[155] "The *real sin* reveals itself therefore to be the illusion that life, rather than being received as the gift of the Creator, is to be procured by one's own power, that one may live from one's own self rather than from God."[156]

This self-reliant *(eigenmächtige)* attitude results in human "boasting," both Gentile boasting in wisdom and Jewish boasting in the law; and it is from this understanding of sin that Bultmann interprets Paul's critique of "the works of the law."[157] The problem is not the content of these works, nor the human incapacity to do them, but the fact that in doing them the Jew is already attempting to secure "life" (salvation) by his own efforts; in relying on his own resources and privileges, he sinfully promotes his "own righteousness" (Rom 10:3; Phil 3:9).[158] Bultmann here develops Luther's understanding of "works" as Pauline shorthand for a perverse self-understanding, expressed in the sinful desire to gain salvation by self-sufficient achievement (see above, 3.3.2). According to Bultmann, it is precisely in zealous observance of the Law that Paul finds the greatest potential for the (conscious or unconscious) rejection of grace. Through its demand for works, the Law offers not a counterweight to sin but "the uttermost possibility of living as a sinner."[159] He is well aware

154. *Theology*, p. 196; *Theologie*, p. 192. The male pronouns were standard in a day before gender sensitivity in such matters.

155. Elsewhere, Bultmann speaks of the universal "need for recognition," and our desperate attempts to establish this from our own resources; see, e.g., "Grace and Freedom," and "Christ the End of the Law," in Bultmann, *Essays*, pp. 36-66.

156. My own translation: "Als die *eigentliche Sünde* offenbart sich also der Wahn, das Leben nicht als Geschenk des Schöpfers zu empfangen, sondern es aus eigener Kraft zu beschaffen, aus sich selbst statt aus Gott zu leben" (*Theologie*, p. 228; emphasis original).

157. "It is the insight which Paul has achieved into the nature of sin that determines his teaching on the Law" (*Theology*, p. 264; *Theologie*, p. 260).

158. Cf. Bultmann's essay on the plight of humanity as articulated in Romans 7: "Römer 7 und die Anthropologie des Paulus," in W. Schneemelcher, ed., *Imago Dei* (Giessen, 1932), pp. 53-62, translated in *Existence and Faith*, pp. 147-57.

159. *Theology*, p. 267; *Theologie*, p. 263.

that this is Paul's view of Judaism, not Judaism's view of itself. In fact, Judaism knows much about the grace of God, as indulgence toward erring Israel and as gracious guidance to the pious person who aims to fulfill the law.[160] The Jew would thus "contradict [Paul's] proposition that justification by works of the Law and justification by divine grace appropriated in man's faith exclude one another." "But that," Bultmann adds, "is the decisive thesis of Paul."[161]

What is "decisive" here is Paul's understanding of grace. Grace, for Paul, is not divine indulgence, nor divine assistance. The gospel does not present a kindly God in place of a deity of wrath and judgment (*pace* Marcion): in fact, God's grace is only comprehensible as the grace of a judge, who paradoxically acts to justify sinners. Grace is, in the Pauline perspective, a deed, an event — and specifically the eschatological (and therefore decisive) event of the death and resurrection of Jesus, which is present in the preaching of the gospel to encounter, accost, and "strike" the hearer. What is announced is the divine gift of righteousness (that is, a positive relation to God, not a moral quality), and because this is "absolutely free" and "pure gift," not at all dependent on "works," it poses the critical question "whether a man is willing to give up his old understanding of himself and henceforth understand himself only from the grace of God."[162] Bultmann does not use the Barthian language of "crisis," but the effect is the same. Precisely because this grace is wholly incongruous to the condition of the human (God justifies the *sinner*), it cuts the ground from under all human achievement and every human boast: grace, so understood, is the polar opposite of "works."

The announcement of God's gift calls for the decision of "faith" — which is a human act *(Tat)* but certainly not a work *(Werk)* in the sense of an achievement on which one relies.[163] Faith is, in fact, the surrender of one's former illusion of self-sufficiency and former efforts at self-reliance: it is the radical renunciation of achievement.

> In his "confession" of faith, the believer turns away from himself, confessing that all that he is and has, he is and has through that which God has done. Faith does not appeal to whatever it itself may be as act or attitude, but to God's prevenient deed of grace, which preceded faith.[164]

160. See "Christ the End of the Law," p. 46. Elsewhere, Bultmann's disparaging comments about Second Temple Judaism suggest that his Lutheran theology has skewed his historiography; see his *Primitive Christianity in Its Contemporary Setting*, trans. R. H. Fuller (London: Thames and Hudson, 1956), pp. 59-71.

161. *Theology*, p. 263; *Theologie*, pp. 259-60.

162. *Theology*, p. 301; *Theologie*, p. 296.

163. See *Theology*, pp. 283-84, 315-16; *Theologie*, pp. 278-79, 311-12.

164. *Theology*, p. 319; *Theologie*, p. 314. Against recent misunderstandings of Bultmann

Faith is made possible only by the grace of God, experienced in the preaching of the Word, and it entails not the assertion but the renunciation of human capacity. Nonetheless, it *is* a decision, what Paul calls "the obedience of faith" (Rom 1:5). Because grace-as-gift *(Gabe)* strikes at sin as self-reliance, it issues the demand *(Aufgabe)* of the surrender of the self, an obedience expressed not in special Christian practices but in self-surrender to God (faith) and in self-giving to others (love).

In this sense Bultmann may speak of grace as a "power" *(Macht)* that "determines" *(bestimmen)* the life of the believer, but this does not take the form of compulsion: if it did, one could hardly speak of obedience. Although Paul can use mythological language for the powers and for the leading of the Spirit, he can hardly mean this in the sense that human agency is either compelled or replaced.[165] What the grace-act of God has done is, rather, to open the possibility of genuine decision. Paul's predestinarian language (e.g., in Romans 9) is intended to indicate that God's grace operates both "without us" and "before us," but to take it literally would be to attribute to Paul complete self-contradiction.[166] Grace creates a new situation for the believer, the possibility of a new understanding of one's self, but this is "no magical or mysterious transformation of man in relation to his substance, the basis of his nature."[167] Although Paul uses participatory language when he speaks of the believer sharing in Christ's body and in his death and new life, Bultmann insists that such language (derived from Gnosticism or from the mystery religions) was not intended to mean that believers share in some "supernatural substance."[168] Neither here nor in relation to the resurrection of Christ is it appropriate to use objectifying concepts.[169]

---

and objections to the "objective genitive" reading of πίστις Χριστοῦ (e.g., by Martyn; see below, 3.5.4), it is important to make this point clear. While faith is for Bultmann the "condition" of salvation, in the sense that the divine gift is not forced upon believers but has to be received, it is not some special human capacity or a spiritual or cognitive achievement.

165. *Theology,* pp. 257-59, 336-37; *Theologie,* pp. 253-55, 332-33. "To be led by the Spirit does not mean to be dragged along willy-nilly *(ein entscheidungsloses Hingerissenwerden)* . . . but directly presupposes decision in the alternatives: 'flesh' or 'Spirit'" (*Theology,* p. 336; *Theologie,* p. 333).

166. *Theology,* pp. 329-30; *Theologie,* pp. 325-26. Cf. *Theology,* pp. 285-87; *Theologie,* pp. 281-83 on the "priority" of grace expressed by the divine initiative in reconciliation.

167. *Theology,* pp. 268-69; *Theologie,* p. 265: "es findet keine magische oder mysteriöse Verwandling des Menschen hinsichtlich seiner Substanz als seiner Naturgrundlage statt." Bultmann is at pains to stress that though the new situation opened by grace is not some development from the old, the believer's "new existence stands in historical continuity with the old" (*Theology,* p. 269; *Theologie,* p. 265).

168. *Theology,* p. 302; *Theologie,* p. 297: "übernatürliche Substanz."

169. In interpreting Paul, Bultmann's greatest awkwardness concerns Paul's language of the resurrection — both Paul's attempt to provide evidence for the resurrection as a historical

Grace does not convey some "thing"; it changes the conditions of possibility, such that humans can fulfill their authentic existence, living no longer from themselves but from the gift of God, who in the preaching of the Christ-event freely releases them from the powerful illusions of sin.

Influenced by both Luther and Barth, Bultmann makes the *incongruity* of grace the center of Pauline theology: this grace exposes, judges, and overcomes the perverted human desire to seek recognition and reward from our own resources. He likewise emphasizes the *priority* of grace, though distancing himself from the Augustinian understanding of predestination: God's grace is prevenient *(vorkommende)* in opening up the possibility of a new self-understanding, not in determining how one will respond. Bultmann's cautious treatment of Paul's language of powers, and his emphasis on freedom, decision, and obedience, signal his reluctance to perfect the *efficacy* of grace, at least as found in the Augustinian and Calvinist traditions. Unlike Marcion and modern liberalism (but here like Augustine and Calvin), for Bultmann, grace is not *singular* in the sense that it is incompatible with notions of divine judgment and wrath: it is, rather, the paradoxical act of the righteous judge. Nor is it *non-circular* in the sense that it carries no demands: Bultmann's emphasis on the *demand* of grace and the *obedience* of faith is markedly different from Luther's, at least in tone. For Bultmann, to speak of "pure gift" or "radical grace" means above all one thing: there are no grounds for boasting before God, whose grace operates not in accordance with human effort but precisely to undercut the self-destructive human desire to establish our own righteousness and worth.

3.5.3. Ernst Käsemann

Strongly influenced by his teacher, Bultmann, and drawing from the same revival of the Lutheran tradition, Käsemann also makes the *incongruity* of grace the hallmark of Pauline theology. Insisting on the centrality of "the justification of the ungodly" (Rom 4:5), Käsemann frequently foregrounds Paul's definition of God as the one "who gives life to the dead and calls into existence the things that do not exist" (Rom 4:17). This reading of Paul, combined with a Lutheran "theology of the cross," highlights the mismatch between God and humanity that is expressed in grace: God does not reward or supplement human achieve-

event (1 Cor 15:1-11), and his apparent conception of the life of the risen Christ as something objectively existent and accessible to be shared by the believer. See, especially, Bultmann's review of Barth's *Die Auferstehung der Toten* (above, note 149) and his famous essay, "The New Testament and Mythology," in *The New Testament and Mythology and Other Basic Writings*, trans. and ed. S. Ogden (London: SCM, 1985), pp. 1-43.

ment, but reduces human pretensions to dust in order to prove powerful among the weak and to create something "out of nothing."[170] In addition, one may trace the influence on Käsemann of Karl Barth and Adolf Schlatter, whose emphasis on the "Godness" *(Gottheit)* of God, in sovereign otherness from humanity, inclined Käsemann to resist the tendency of Bultmann to reduce salvation to the possibility of a new self-understanding.[171] Käsemann sometimes describes the target of Paul's polemics in Barth's language of "religion," though more often it is labeled "piety" *(Frömmigkeit),* reflecting his persistent tension with forms of privatized, conservative spirituality in German Protestantism. Indeed, the church controversies in which Käsemann was engaged, first with "German Christians" in the 1930s and then on numerous fronts after the Second World War, had a significant impact on his readings of Paul, which, even in academic form, were always intended to serve the church.[172]

Käsemann's interpretation of Paul was shaped by his lifelong dialogue with Bultmann's widely influential existentialist reading. While acknowledging that Paul's theology has unparalleled anthropological depth, Käsemann contested the way Bultmann made anthropology its starting point and center.

170. On this *redigi ad nihilum* and subsequent *creatio ex nihilo,* see E. Käsemann, "Der Glaube Abrahams in Röm 4," *Paulinische Perspektiven,* 2nd ed. (Tübingen: Mohr Siebeck, 1972), pp. 140-77 (at pp. 149-54); translated as "The Faith of Abraham in Romans 4," in *Pauline Perspectives,* trans. M. Kohl (Philadelphia: Fortress Press, 1971), pp. 79-101 (at pp. 90-93). Thus, "God creates only where from the earthly standpoint nothing exists" (*Commentary on Romans,* trans. G. W. Bromiley [London: SCM, 1980], p. 124; *An die Römer,* 4th ed. [Tübingen: Mohr Siebeck, 1980], p. 117). For this reason, God's grace is also a judgment on human illusions, "Zur Thema der urchristlichen Apokalyptik," in *Exegetische Versuche und Besinnungen,* vol. 2 (Göttingen: Vandenhoeck & Ruprecht, 1965), pp. 105-31 (at p. 119); translated as "On the Subject of Primitive Christian Apocalyptic," in *New Testament Questions of Today,* trans. W. J. Montague (Philadelphia: Fortress Press, 1969), pp. 108-37 (at p. 123). "Grace is granted only from the Judge's hand," *Romans,* p. 83 (*An die Römer,* p. 78).

171. "Only the godless are ever justified. So long as this lesson has not been learned at the foot of the Cross of Jesus, the godhead of God *(Gottes Gottheit)* is not truly acknowledged and honoured: and in consequence man has not yet become human *(zur wirklichen Menschwerdung des Menschen),*" "Paul and Israel," in *New Testament Questions,* pp. 183-87 (at p. 186); "Paulus und Israel," *Exegetische Versuche,* vol. 2, pp. 194-97 (at p. 196). On the influence of Barth, see D. W. Way, *The Lordship of Christ: Ernst Käsemann's Interpretation of Paul's Theology* (Oxford: Clarendon Press, 1991), pp. 37-42. Käsemann said he "ravenously devoured" Barth's early publications, "A Theological Review," in *On Being a Disciple of the Crucified Nazarene: Unpublished Lectures and Sermons,* ed. R. Landau, trans. R. A. Harrisville (Grand Rapids: Eerdmans, 2010), pp. xii-xxi (at p. xv). For Käsemann's relationship to Schlatter, see P. Zahl, *Die Rechtfertigungslehre Ernst Käsemanns* (Stuttgart: Calver Verlag, 1996), pp. 135-47.

172. For his own account of his experiences in the 1930s, see "A Theological Review," pp. xvii-xxi. For the ecclesial conflicts, see *Kirchliche Konflikte* (Göttingen: Vandenhoeck & Ruprecht, 1982) and numerous essays in *On Being a Disciple.*

If "every assertion about God is simultaneously an assertion about man and vice versa" (Bultmann, see above), Käsemann stressed the "vice versa." For him, it is constitutive of human existence that a person is "a challengeable and a continually challenged being": "He is a created being in that he experiences the divine address, which compels him to earthly pilgrimage."[173] Thus, the key question about humans is not *how they relate to themselves* and to their own inner goal, but *to whom they are answerable* and to whom they belong: the change effected in salvation concerns first and foremost not a change in self-understanding but a change in "Lordship" *(Herrschaftswechsel)*.[174] Käsemann reacted strongly against the individualism inherent in existentialist interpretation of Paul, under the conviction that Paul works as much in collective as in individual categories, and places the drama of salvation on a large historical, indeed cosmic, stage.[175] This conviction emerged from Käsemann's early work on Paul's ecclesiology and participatory theology, read against a background of "Gnostic" notions of spheres of power. But it also arose from a disagreement with Bultmann on the meaning of Paul's term "body" (σῶμα), which Käsemann took to represent not the individual's relation to him/herself (Bultmann) but the embeddedness of the self in a larger physical and social environment. The body, on this reading, is that "bit of the world" to which God lays claim, as sovereign Creator.[176] The scope of Paul's theology is nothing less than cosmic.

From the late 1940s onward, Käsemann identified the history-of-religions "background" of Paul's thought not as Gnosticism but as Jewish apocalyptic.[177] Although in his hands the term "apocalyptic" was sometimes only loosely related to Jewish apocalyptic literature, Käsemann's thesis that "apocalyptic is the mother of Christian theology" was intended to emphasize that, however "mythical" it may sound, God's anticipated victory over the powers that

173. "On Paul's Anthropology," *Pauline Perspectives*, pp. 1-31 (at p. 5); "Zur paulinischen Anthropologie," *Paulinische Perspektiven*, pp. 9-60 (at p. 15).

174. "'The Righteousness of God' in Paul," *New Testament Questions*, pp. 168-82 (at p. 176); "Gottesgerechtigkeit bei Paulus," *Exegetische Versuche*, vol. 2, pp. 181-93 (at p. 188).

175. As the essay "On Paul's Anthropology" makes clear, Käsemann was here responsive to shifts in the intellectual horizons of European thought, which interpreted the human condition in social, economic, and biological terms, far removed from existentialist forms of analysis.

176. The phrase *(das Stück der Welt)* recurs often; see, e.g., "Amt und Gemeinde im Neuen Testament," *Exegetische Versuche*, vol. 1, pp. 109-34 (at p. 111); "Ministry and Community in the New Testament," in *Essays on New Testament Themes*, trans. W. J. Montague (London: SCM Press, 1964), pp. 63-134 (at p. 65); *An die Römer*, p. 169.

177. On this shift, see Way, *Lordship*, pp. 53-176, citing a significant letter to Bultmann in 1949 that signals this change (perhaps stimulated by the discovery of the Dead Sea Scrolls).

govern and oppress the world was the originating dynamic of early Christian, including Pauline, theology.[178] Early Christian "apocalyptic" looked to the Parousia as an imminent event, but the theological substance of this belief was the enthronement of Jesus over the powers that threaten and enslave the cosmos. The critical question of apocalyptic is "to whom does the world belong?"[179] Its horizon stretches beyond the covenant community to the cosmos in its entirety, to which God as Creator is faithfully committed. Its central drama is the divine claim of sovereignty expressed in the Pauline notions of "the righteousness of God" and the "Lordship" of Christ. Paul's apocalyptic narrative in 1 Cor 15:20-28 is central to this reading of Paul, locating believers in the midst of the power struggle between the flesh and the Spirit (Gal 5:16-23). "Apocalyptic" here stands opposed to "existentialist" and "individualizing" interpretations of Paul, but not necessarily to readings that trace in Paul a form of "salvation-history." In fact, apocalyptic, with its successive aeons, is taken to be the origin of early Christian narratives, and Käsemann cautiously embraced a "salvation-historical" reading which could account for Paul's interest in the past, present, and future of Israel (Romans 9–11) in a way that Bultmann could not. Only it must be clear that salvation-history runs not by immanent processes of development or through human continuity: the divine "salvation-plan" *(Heilsplan)* operates through disjuncture and disaster *(Unheil),* and thus only by the miracle of grace. In other words, the pervasive pattern of salvation-history is the justification of the *ungodly* (not of the privileged, the righteous, or the pious).[180]

Käsemann's reading of grace fits within this "apocalyptic" frame. In his pivotal and controversial essay "On 'The Righteousness of God' in Paul," he insisted that the interpretation of "God's righteousness" as "gift" (central to the Lutheran tradition, including its Bultmannian version) must be complemented by its reading as "power" *(Macht):* when God gives, he "comes into the arena" in his salvation-forming power, his "righteousness" representing also his right

178. For the controversial thesis that apocalyptic was the "mother" of early Christian theology, see "The Beginnings of Christian Theology," *New Testament Questions,* pp. 82-107 (at p. 102); "Die Anfänge christlicher Theologie," *Exegetische Versuche,* vol. 2, pp. 82-104 (at p. 100). The term "apocalyptic" was chosen to mark a departure from previous theological uses of "eschatology," which in dialectical theology could signify not a future expectation so much as the ultimacy that confronts every individual and requires a daily decision of faith (see Way, *Lordship,* p. 174).

179. "Primitive Christian Apocalyptic," p. 135.

180. See "Justification and Salvation History in the Epistle to the Romans," *Perspectives on Paul,* pp. 60-78 ("Rechtfertigung und Heilsgeschichte im Römerbrief," *Paulinische Perspektiven,* pp. 108-39), a somewhat confused but nonetheless revealing response to K. Stendahl (on whom see below, 3.6.2).

as Creator over his creation.[181] Thus, grace must also be understood as power *(Gnadenmacht,* or *Gnadenherrschaft);* it is not something handed to recipients (and then in their possession), but is inseparable from the Giver.[182] With the gift comes the Giver, the Lord who through the gift exercises not only his benevolence but also his authority, such that the gift *itself* becomes the call to obedience, as well as the capacity to serve.[183] Thus:

> Salvation never consists in our being given something, however wonderful. Salvation, always, is simply God himself in his presence for us. . . . But where he appears, he also meets us as our lord and judge; we experience his gifts, but also the power which lays claim to us, the sovereign rights of the creator to his whole creation.[184]

Käsemann perceived and countered several potential problems in a theology of grace. His reading was directed against "cheap grace" (that God gives, expecting nothing in return), but also against the reduction of God to a gracious source of a new self-understanding. He was also wary lest God's gifts become viewed, over time, as human privileges or secure possessions: God's righteousness is a presently active saving power *(heilsetzende Macht),* a continuous source of grace and demand.[185] Judaism, too, was the recipient of divine gifts (Rom 9:1-5), but the Pauline perspective has to be clearly differentiated. Like Bultmann, Käsemann took Paul to polemicize against "works" as "achievements" *(Leistungen)* and "self-righteousness," but the perversion of gifts into privileges and presumptions was an equally significant aspect of this target.[186] For Käsemann, the "root sin" *(Grundsünde)* is the human attempt to gain independence over against God, which constitutes both a challenge to God's sovereignty and a false claim to authority or power.[187] What Paul crit-

181. "The Righteousness of God," pp. 168-76. The argument that the phrase δικαιοσύνη θεοῦ was a fixed formula in the apocalyptic tradition was less convincing than the claim that God's own agency is evoked in this phrase, which is not only (although it also includes) "the righteousness given by God."

182. *Gnadenmacht* ("grace-power"): "Gottesgerechtigkeit," p. 187; *Gnadenherrschaft* ("grace-sovereignty"): *An die Römer,* p. 175. "Die hier mitgeteilte Gabe ist nicht and nie von ihrem Geber ablösbar": "Gottesgerechtigkeit," p. 186.

183. As our study of the anthropology of gift has shown (see above, 1.1), this connection between the gift and the presence and power of the giver is precisely what one would expect.

184. "Justification and Salvation History," pp. 74-75 ("Rechtfertigung und Heilsgeschichte," pp. 132-33).

185. E.g., "Gottesgerechtigkeit," p. 193.

186. "Paul and Israel," p. 185 ("Paulus und Israel," pp. 195-96).

187. "Paul and Israel," pp. 184-85 ("Paulus und Israel," p. 195).

icizes in Israel is representative of human sin in general (Paul's target is "the hidden Jew in all of us"),[188] but Israel's "boast" is not just a form of individual self-righteousness; it is a collective perversion of divine gifts into privileges, which as "demonstrable possessions" foster pride and "insubordination."[189] "What does the nomism against which Paul fought really represent? . . . It represents the community of 'pious' people which turns God's promises into their own privileges and God's commandments into the instruments of their own self-sanctification."[190]

Since grace is the embodiment of divine presence and power, it can never become a human property — a point of characteristically Lutheran anxiety (see above, 3.3.3). "Right and righteousness can only be ours insofar as God gives them to us anew every day — i.e. in faith. It is not that his gifts guarantee continuity, says 1 Cor 10.1-13: their importance is rather that they direct us back to the Giver."[191] Pauline anthropology reveals that no human is truly autonomous, and the gift of salvation entails a freedom that is paradoxically also enlistment for a new service: gift *(Gabe)* and task *(Aufgabe)*, grace *(Gnade)* and service *(Dienst)* coincide (see Rom 6:12-23). But the decision of obedience must be renewed each day, in a perpetual return to baptism (another Lutheran motif; see above, 3.3.3). It is not always clear how Käsemann understood the relation between divine and human agency in the believer's obedience. Although he spoke of powers that "determine" *(bestimmen)* our lives, he also spoke of a human decision that appropriates grace.[192] The divine gift is prior and enabling, and the believer cannot create but only authenticate or verify *(bewähren)* this gift. But the power of God does not replace or supersede the agency of the believer, who is called to active and responsible obedience, not passivity or mystical absorption into the divine.

According to Käsemann, believers' active partisanship should cross the borders of "religion," the false division between the "sacred" and the "profane," thus penetrating the whole of the world that has been reclaimed by God. This boundary-crossing exodus (or "pilgrimage") can take social and political expression. Especially in his popular writings and speeches, Käsemann took the

188. "Paul and Israel," p. 186 ("Paulus und Israel," p. 196: "In und mit Israel wird der verborgene Jude in uns allen getroffen"). The way that "the Jew" becomes here a type of sinfulness exposes a hugely problematic tendency in this tradition, whose roots may be traced all the way back to Augustine.

189. *Unbotmäßigkeit:* "Gottesgerechtigkeit," p. 192 ("Righteousness of God," p. 180).

190. "Justification and Salvation History," p. 72 (slightly altered) ("Rechtfertigung und Heilsgeschichte," pp. 127-28).

191. "Paul and Israel," p. 185 ("Paulus und Israel," p. 196).

192. E.g., "Ministry," p. 79 ("Amt," p. 122).

"justification of the ungodly" to imply the engagement of the church with the suffering, the lost, and the marginalized, elucidating the message of Paul with motifs from the ministry of Jesus (in which he revived scholarly interest). His impatience with conservative, middle-class Christianity became clear in such contexts, alongside his sympathy with revolutionary movements in Europe, South Africa, and South America.[193] In fact, it is precisely this connection between theology and politics that has kept Käsemann's legacy alive. He successfully mediated, and renewed, the Protestant emphasis on the justification of the ungodly and the incongruity of grace, in a generation that was losing confidence in Bultmann's existentialist reading of these motifs. Where the Lutheran tradition had typically traced the operation of incongruous grace in the life of the individual, Käsemann drew out its social and political significance and thus revitalized Pauline theology for a new, politically-conscious generation, both in America and in Germany. Like Luther and Bultmann, Käsemann showed no interest in perfecting the *singularity* of grace, since for him grace is always the paradoxical gift of the Lord and Judge. Also like Luther and Bultmann (but unlike Augustine and Calvin), he was disinclined to perfect the *efficacy* of grace, since his emphasis lay on the active submission of believers in service to their Lord. By restoring the mythological language of "powers," Käsemann emphasized the power and demand of the Giver of grace, resisting the tendency in the Lutheran tradition to a unilateral or non-circular perfection of this motif (see above, 3.3.4), with its dangerous tendency toward "cheap grace." Grace conveys not just the gift but also the demand of the Giver — or rather, the demand that is integral to the gift. But it does so only in transforming its recipients, turning the weak, the hopeless, and the outsider into the site of God's creative power. Where Käsemann resisted attempts to downplay justification (e.g., by Stendahl), this was not just out of loyalty to the Lutheran tradition, but because, in his reading, this Pauline theme (the justification of the *ungodly*) brought to its sharpest expression the capacity of God's grace to work in utterly incongruous and therefore socially subversive forms. If Pauline theology continues to burn with "revolutionary fire," this has much to do with the influence of Käsemann and his political reading of the incongruity of grace.[194]

193. See *On Being a Disciple* — for instance, his account of "The Righteousness of God in Paul," pp. 15-26. Käsemann's daughter, Elisabeth, was murdered in 1977 in an Argentinian prison for her opposition to the military junta.

194. Käsemann was committed to maintaining the heritage of the Reformation "in the face of a theology of history which has lost its past revolutionary fire and is now planting conservatively laid-out gardens on the petrified lava," "Justification and Salvation History," p. 90. Käsemann's vivid rhetoric, even where it creates imprecision, remains a significant factor in his capacity to inspire.

3.5.4. J. Louis Martyn

Martyn's analysis of Paul appeared in print largely after the publication of Sanders's *Paul and Palestinian Judaism* (1977), to be discussed in the next section (3.6.1); but the theological tradition that he develops is that of Barth and Käsemann. Barth's conviction that Paul's gospel announces the act of God in terms that are not continuous with human cognition or achievement (see above, 3.5.1) stands behind Martyn's insistence that the "apocalypse of Christ" (Gal 1:12, 16; 3:23) constitutes an invasive interruption of the world "from beyond," destroying the illusions and differentiations generated by human "religion."[195] At the same time, drawing on Käsemann's reading of Paul as an "apocalyptic" theologian, Martyn reacts strongly against readings of Paul focused on the individual, refuses to demythologize Paul's language of "powers," and emphasizes that the Christ-event and its aftermath are the enactment of divine power, not the opening of a human "possibility."[196]

For his part, Martyn develops the construal of Paul as an "apocalyptic" theologian in new and additional forms. Conscious that the term carries many different connotations, and drawing from a history-of-religions distinction between "forensic" and "cosmological" strands in Jewish apocalyptic thought, Martyn finds in Galatians a distinctively Pauline version of a cosmological apocalyptic theology.[197] The apocalyptic theme of contrasting "aeons" is fundamental to this reading. If Paul announces the novelty of the Christ-event by placing "the new creation" (Gal 6:15) in antithesis to "the present evil age" (Gal

195. For Martyn's Barthian use of the term "religion," see, e.g., J. L. Martyn, *Galatians: A New Translation with Introduction and Commentary* (Anchor Bible; New York: Doubleday, 1997), pp. 37, 163-64. In these terms, the difference between Paul and the "Teachers" in Galatia can be reduced to the difference between "apocalyptic" and "religion" (*Galatians*, p. 38). For God's "invasive movement from beyond," see J. L. Martyn, "The Apocalyptic Gospel in Galatians," *Interp* 54 (2000): 246-66, at p. 254.

196. For all these motifs, see, e.g., J. L. Martyn, "The Gospel Invades Philosophy," in D. Harink, ed., *Paul, Philosophy, and the Theopolitical Vision* (Eugene: Cascade, 2010), pp. 13-33. Martyn's long friendship with Käsemann began with a year's Fulbright scholarship in Göttingen; see his tribute, "A Personal Word about Ernst Käsemann," in B. Davis and D. Harink, eds., *Apocalyptic and the Future of Theology: With and Beyond J. Louis Martyn* (Eugene: Cascade, 2012), pp. xiii-xv.

197. The two "tracks" were identified and distinguished by M. C. de Boer, "Paul and Jewish Apocalyptic Theology," in J. Marcus and M. L. Soards, eds., *Apocalyptic and the New Testament: Essays in Honor of J. Louis Martyn* (Sheffield: Sheffield Academic Press, 1989), pp. 169-90, an essay frequently referenced by Martyn and in part dependent on his own organizing antithesis between human and divine agencies. For de Boer, "cosmological-apocalyptic eschatology" is dominated by the notion that the world is under the dominion of evil, angelic powers, and can be rescued not by human effort, only by divine intervention.

1:4), the critical question for the Galatians is "what time is it?"[198] In Pauline apocalyptic, what is new is not an "unveiling" of secrets but God's "invasion" of the cosmos in the Christ-event, a cosmos presently enslaved to anti-God powers such as sin and death (Gal 3:22).[199] Pauline apocalyptic is thus a three-actor drama: it involves not just God and humanity, but also the enslaving forces from which Christ liberates humanity and against which the believer is enlisted in the warfare newly engaged between the spirit and the flesh.[200]

Martyn's reconfiguration of "apocalyptic" shares Käsemann's emphasis on the cosmic scope of salvation, with the impetus to cross, or rather to obliterate, the traditional ("religious") divisions of reality that are no longer relevant in Christ (Gal 3:28). Martyn stresses the cognitive dimensions of this phenomenon — a complete reconfiguration of reality is entailed — and, on the basis of Galatians, reacts more strongly than Käsemann against a "salvation-historical" relation between the Christ-event and previous history.[201] Against the "narrative" readings offered by some representatives of the "new perspective on Paul" (see below, 3.6.2), Martyn displays a deep aversion to the attempt to locate the Christ-event on a context-forming trajectory that starts from the history of Israel.[202] More important, for our purposes, is the way that "apocalyptic" focuses, for Martyn, several related questions concerning divine and human *agency*. If "apocalyptic" signals the powerful invasion of grace in Christ, then at least two things must be said with great emphasis:

1. The line of movement in salvation is always *first* from God to humanity (not vice versa), in an act that changes reality. God does not offer the *pos-*

198. Martyn, *Galatians*, pp. 104-5; if it is the time after the apocalypse of Christ, the decisive war of liberation has begun. The imminence of the Parousia is not, as it was for Käsemann, a significant issue.

199. For Paul's use of the verb ἀποκαλύπτω to mean not "unveil" but "come on the scene" (Gal 3:23), see J. L. Martyn, "Apocalyptic Antinomies in Paul's Letter to the Galatians," *NTS* 31 (1989): 410-24 (at p. 424 n. 29).

200. For the importance of the three-actor drama, see Martyn, "Gospel Invades," pp. 26-29. For Martyn's construal of "apocalyptic," see esp. *Galatians*, pp. 97-105.

201. For the cognitive transformation, see the essay "Epistemology at the Turn of the Ages," reprinted in J. L. Martyn, *Theological Issues in the Letters of Paul* (Edinburgh: T&T Clark, 1997), pp. 89-110.

202. For Martyn's suspicion of "salvation-history," in reaction to Dunn, see "Events in Galatia: Modified Covenantal Nomism versus God's Invasion of the Cosmos in the Singular Gospel: A Response to J. D. G. Dunn and B. R. Gaventa," in J. M. Bassler, ed., *Pauline Theology*, vol. 1 (Minneapolis: Fortress Press, 1991), pp. 160-79. Against "salvific linearity," Martyn stresses Paul's "punctiliar" presentation of both Abraham and Christ in Galatians. His brief comments on Romans 9–11 in *Galatians*, pp. 29-34, show a partial modification of this antithesis, but only in relation to that later (and not necessarily superior) letter.

sibility of a human decision that will establish a circular exchange between humanity and God. That is what the Teachers were offering in Galatia (in their tradition-based, "religious" message), but it is the opposite of what Paul preaches. The "works of the law" being urged on the Galatians were for them (though not for Jews) a way to *transfer*, to gain entry into Israel, and thus a human act that is the necessary condition for God's response. But what Paul announces is the *prevenient* act of God, a liberating invasion of the cosmos *prior* to any human movement.[203]

2. After this first divine act, Paul does not call for a separable, autonomous human decision, as if humans were capable of responding independently to the salvific act. Divine agency is present *also* in the human response, which is "generated," "elicited," or "kindled" by grace. In other words, God's agency is not just past and future, but also *present* in the very willing and doing of the believing community.[204]

This construal of agency plays a decisive role in Martyn's advocacy for the subjective genitive reading of the ambiguous Pauline phrase πίστις Χριστοῦ (Gal 2:16; 3:22; etc.). Martyn is convinced that if the genitive is taken as objective ("faith in Christ"), Paul would merely be offering two human alternatives: either do the works of the law, or believe in Christ. But in Galatians, from start (1:1) to finish (6:15), "Paul draws contrasts not between two human alternatives, such as works and faith, but rather between acts done by human beings and acts carried out by God."[205] Therefore, it is of "monumental" significance that one read this phrase aright, as a subjective genitive ("the faithfulness of Christ").[206] Whatever may be said regarding human faith can only be secondary to the prior and generative faith or faithfulness of Christ. Human faith is "incited" and "ignited" by divine power, never an independent or autonomous decision.

203. On the importance of this prior "line of movement," against notions of "circular exchange," see "Apocalyptic Gospel," pp. 246-51. For the Teachers' requirement that the Galatians "transfer," as a "human enterprise," see *Galatians*, p. 269. Martyn is careful to indicate that this does not entail any judgment on Judaism as such, only on the Teachers' attempt to introduce it in the Galatian Gentile churches. But he elsewhere indicates that the Pauline "antinomy" between the apocalypse of Christ and "religion" is universal in scope, and would have to include Judaism in the latter category (*Galatians*, p. 38).

204. For this emphasis, ubiquitous in Martyn's most recent writing, see, e.g., "Apocalyptic Gospel," pp. 251-52; "Gospel Invades"; "Epilogue: An Essay in Pauline Meta-Ethics," in J. M. G. Barclay and S. J. Gathercole, eds., *Divine and Human Agency in Paul and His Cultural Environment* (London: T&T Clark, 2006), pp. 173-83.

205. Martyn, "Apocalyptic Gospel," p. 250.

206. "Apocalyptic Gospel," p. 250; cf. *Galatians*, pp. 263-75.

Thus, Martyn perfects the motif of grace in a number of distinctive ways. For him, as for Käsemann and others in the Reformation tradition, grace is essentially and emphatically *incongruous* to the condition of the recipient (in his terms, "presuppositionless" and "uncontingent").[207] Martyn's focus on agency, however, places particular stress both on the *priority* of grace and on its continuing *efficacy* in the agency of believers.[208] That God should be considered the prior and prime actor in the actions of believers, even in their faith, was, as we have seen, a distinctively Augustinian emphasis (see above, 3.2), and although Martyn focuses less than Augustine on the capacity of the "will" and the inner psychology of human motivation, he evidences the same concern to attribute the agency of believers to God. At several points, Martyn insists that this emphasis by no means renders believers "marionettes," but the relation between divine and human agency is left somewhat unclear, and he is chiefly concerned to deny the "autonomy" of human agents, even after their liberation by grace.[209] In this connection, Martyn's implicit target is the church (and certainly not Judaism).[210] While supportive of the emancipatory movements that have engaged the churches in America since the 1960s, Martyn is wary lest the church's social and political action becomes disengaged from its source, God's action in Christ. If it does, ethics takes the place of theology, and reliance is placed on human agency in a cosmos that is conflicted at a deeper and more intractable level than the church is apt to recognize. In the context of a church that he perceives to be weakened by a moralism neither founded in nor energized by the gospel, Martyn stresses both the *priority* and the *efficacy* of grace as a liberating vision that frees the church to act boldly without relying on itself, and also carries the hope that, despite setbacks, God's gracious power will triumph in the end.[211]

207. "Apocalyptic Gospel," pp. 248, 263.

208. Thus God's grace not only creates, transforms, and inspires believers: it is also in some sense "causative" of their behavior ("Gospel Invades," pp. 31, 33; "Epilogue," p. 182).

209. Not marionettes: J. L. Martyn, "De-apocalypticizing Paul: An Essay Focused on *Paul and the Stoics* by Troels Engberg-Pedersen," *JSNT* 86 (2002): 61-102, at p. 92. Martyn refers to the concept of "dual agency," developed by Hunsinger and Webster in interpretation of Barth ("Gospel Invades," pp. 28-31), but its meaning is not much elucidated.

210. Martyn's post-Holocaust sensitivities place him at this point at some remove from Käsemann; see Martyn, *Theological Issues*, pp. 77-84, insisting that Galatians is not an "anti-Judaic" text, since the horizon of Galatians is not Judaism but the Jerusalem-based mission established by Jewish Christians.

211. This "apocalyptic" reading of Paul has inspired several leading Pauline scholars (e.g., M. C. de Boer, B. R. Gaventa, S. Eastman, D. Campbell) and has attracted much interest from theologians who meld Martyn's exegesis with a form of Barthian theology responsive to theology's new pluralistic context in the West. See, e.g., the appreciative essays in Davis and Harink, eds., *Apocalyptic and the Future of Theology.*

3.6. Sanders and the New Perspective on Paul

3.6.1. E. P. Sanders

A significant shift in the history of the reception of Paul on grace was effected by Sanders in 1977 with the publication of *Paul and Palestinian Judaism.*[212] The goal of this book was in part negative, to refute the interpretation of rabbinic (and Palestinian) Judaism as a religion of "works-righteousness," and to expose this as a pejorative and theologically loaded construction of nineteenth- and twentieth-century scholarship. In the Weber-Bousset-Billerbeck tradition, which had strongly influenced Bultmann and his school, rabbinic Judaism was routinely represented as a narrow and formalistic religion in which salvation was acquired by good works. Fulfillment of the law's commands constituted a human achievement *(Leistung)* by which one might accumulate for oneself (or gain from others) the merit *(Verdienst)* necessary for salvation. Biblical notions of the prior, free grace of God were overshadowed by a system of recompense *(Vergeltung),* resulting in self-trust *(Selbstvertrauen)* or in anxious concern about the future judgment.[213] This reconstruction created a neat foil to Paul, but, as Sanders pointed out, it did so only by reproducing Reformation tropes. Where notions of grace were identified in Judaism, they were taken to be undermined by concepts of merit or synergism.[214]

Sanders's large-scale analysis of primary sources from Palestinian Judaism succeeded in overturning this prejudicial reading, at a time when post-Holocaust scholarship was especially critical of Christian misrepresentations of Judaism.[215] In its place, he represented the theology of Palestinian Judaism

212. E. P. Sanders, *Paul and Palestinian Judaism: A Comparison of Patterns of Religion* (London: SCM, 1977).

213. See the survey and critique in *Paul and Palestinian Judaism,* pp. 33-59, 164-65, 183-98, 212-16, 222-28, 394-97. Sanders's translation of *Vergeltung* as "retribution" (pp. 184, 234) misses the theological nuance of this term, which reflects the Lutheran antithesis between recompense *(quid pro quo)* and non-circular grace.

214. For the echoes of Reformation battles, see *Paul and Palestinian Judaism,* pp. 55, 57, 97, 183-85 (the merit of the fathers as "works of supererogation"). A citation from Thyen (in *Paul and Palestinian Judaism,* p. 53 n. 71) is particularly explicit in evoking the Lutheran tradition.

215. See, e.g., R. Radford Ruether, *Faith and Fratricide: The Theological Roots of Anti-Semitism* (New York: Seabury Press, 1974); C. Klein, *Theologie und Anti-Judaismus* (Munich: Chr. Kaiser Verlag, 1975; trans. E. Quinn, *Anti-Judaism and Christian Theology* [London: SPCK, 1978]). As Sanders acknowledges, his protest against misrepresentations of Judaism had precursors, not least the work of G. F. Moore in the 1920s. Moore had insisted that in rabbinic Judaism the election of Israel is by the "free grace" of God; it is not "wages earned by works, but is bestowed by God in pure goodness upon the members of his chosen people, as 'eternal

as explicitly founded on the grace of God, in the election of Israel and in the gift of the covenant. As we shall see, Sanders's analysis of the structure and content of Judaism emphasized primarily the *priority* of grace, the divine initiative that founded the people of Israel and contextualizes their observance of the Torah. He succeeded in demonstrating that, understood in these terms, grace is everywhere in Second Temple Judaism.[216] Whether other perfections of grace can also be found in all of the relevant sources is, as we shall see, a moot point.

In comparing "patterns" of religion, Sanders focused on "soteriology," which he crucially defined as a matter of *sequence.*[217] A pattern of religion is its "sequence from its starting point to its conclusion" (17), and this is best examined by enquiring "how getting in and staying in are understood" (17, 70), that is, how one "enters" and how one "remains in" the community of the saved (178, 212, 237, 424). In relation to Palestinian Judaism, "it was a major point of inquiry whether election was perceived to precede the requirement of obedience, and we concluded that it was. Here the relationship of the sequential steps to each other was crucial" (548).[218] This puts all the weight on the question of *priority:* it matters greatly what comes first, and thus that God's election or grace comes *before* the demands of the Torah. This is exemplified for Sanders by the primacy of the covenant. The notion of a covenant relationship with God is basic to all forms of Judaism (even if not everywhere explicit), and God's election of Israel is "the fundamental basis of religion" (177). God's love for Israel is foundational (104-5): he chose Israel and "only then" gave commands (87); he "acted before" the commandments were given (101). Thus, everything that is said about obedience, reward, repentance, and atonement is to be placed within the frame of an already existent covenant, which is the product of "prevenient grace" (178). Obedience is the fitting *response* to the God who chose Israel and instituted the covenant (81-83, 104, 106): it cannot

---

life' in Christianity is bestowed on the individuals whom he has chosen, or on the members of the church," G. F. Moore, *Judaism in the First Centuries of the Christian Era: The Age of the Tannaim,* vol. 2 (Cambridge, MA: Harvard University Press, 1927-30), p. 95.

216. What is said about Palestinian Judaism in *Paul and Palestinian Judaism* is also said elsewhere of other forms of Second Temple Judaism; see E. P. Sanders, "The Covenant as a Soteriological Category and the Nature of Salvation in Palestinian and Hellenistic Judaism," in R. Hammerton-Kelly and R. Scroggs, eds., *Jews, Greeks, and Christians: Studies in Honor of W. D. Davies* (Leiden: Brill, 1976), pp. 11-44; E. P. Sanders, *Judaism: Practice and Belief, 63 B.C.E.–66 C.E.* (London: SCM Press, 1992), pp. 262-78.

217. *Paul and Palestinian Judaism,* pp. 1-20; in what follows, numbers in parentheses in the main text are page references to this book.

218. Cf. the stress on sequence elsewhere: E. P. Sanders, "Jesus, Paul, and Judaism," in *ANRW* 2.25.1, pp. 390-450, at p. 397.

be said to "win," "achieve," or "earn" salvation, since it is not how one *gets into* the covenant, only how one *remains in.* The imperative follows the indicative (177-78); "the gift precedes the demand."[219]

Sanders dubbed this common pattern of religion "covenantal nomism," most fully defined as follows (422, cf. 75, 236-37):

> The "pattern" or "structure" of covenantal nomism is this: (1) God has chosen Israel and (2) given the law. The law implies both (3) God's promise to maintain the election and (4) the requirement to obey. (5) God rewards obedience and punishes transgression. (6) The law provides for means of atonement, and atonement results in (7) maintenance or re-establishment of the covenantal relationship. (8) All those who are maintained in the covenant by obedience, atonement, and God's mercy belong to the group which will be saved. An important interpretation of the first and last points is that election and ultimately salvation are considered to be by God's mercy rather than human achievement.

As this definition makes clear, obedience to the law, together with reward for obedience and punishment for transgression, are integral to this pattern of religion, but it is crucial to identify where they stand within the overall pattern. "Obedience maintains one's position in the covenant, but it does not earn God's grace as such. It simply keeps an individual in the group which is the recipient of God's grace" (420). In terms of the structure of religion, obedience is the condition for *remaining in* the covenant, but not the means for *getting in:* "Obedience, especially the intention to obey ('confessing') is the *conditio sine qua non* of salvation, but it does not *earn* it" (141; cf. 146-47, 178-80, 189-90, etc.). Perfect obedience is not required: what is crucial is intention. One's covenant status is put in jeopardy not by transgressions but by a fundamental denial of the covenant or a principled repudiation of God (147, 157, 168). Repentance for transgressions is always possible, although this is not a "status-achieving" activity by which one wins the mercy of God, but a "status-maintaining" or "status-restoring" attitude, signaling one's intention to remain in the covenant (158-80). Thus "obedience . . . is the *condition* of salvation (when it is coupled with repentance for transgression), but not its cause" (371).

219. E. P. Sanders, "Patterns of Religion in Paul and Rabbinic Judaism: A Holistic Method of Comparison," *HTR* 66 (1973): 455-78, at p. 461. Thus, Sanders makes "the priority of grace" the feature that characterizes ancient Judaism as "a religion of grace," *Judaism: Practice and Belief*, pp. 275-78.

Sanders concluded that "grace and works were not considered alternative roads to salvation. Salvation (except in IV Ezra) is always by the grace of God, embodied in the covenant. The terms of the covenant, however, require obedience" (297). This makes perfect sense, so long as grace is here perfected only in terms of its *priority.* What is less clear is whether one may also speak here of other perfections, and particularly of the *incongruity* of grace. Because he does not distinguish between these different perfections of the motif, Sanders is inclined to use language that evokes perfections of grace other than priority, including those characteristic of the Augustinian and Reformation traditions. Thus, in relation to rabbinic texts, Sanders insists that election, being prior to the promulgation of the law, is also "totally gratuitous" (87). God chose Israel out of "sheer mercy" (99), and since God is reliably faithful to his promises, the covenant itself is not conditional on Israel's obedience, even though it implies the obligation to obey (96-97, 177, 204-5). Grace may be glossed, simply, as "unmerited election" (328), and the Dead Sea Scrolls provide evidence of the "eternal and irresistible grace of God" (261), a form of "predestining grace" (269, 312). Indeed, Sanders was anxious to insist that salvation is not *ultimately* conditioned by human behavior. Thus, the definition of "covenantal nomism" cited above ends with an antithesis ("by God's mercy rather than human achievement"), whose force is clarified elsewhere:

> The theme of mercy . . . serves to assure that election and ultimately salvation cannot be earned, but depend on God's grace. One can never be righteous enough to be worthy in God's sight of the ultimate gifts, which depend *only* on mercy. The theme of God's mercy as being the *final reliance* even of the righteous appears in all the literature surveyed except IV Ezra. (422, italics added)

This seems to suggest that God's grace is ultimately *incongruous* as well as *prior,* and although Sanders allowed for some differences between texts (e.g., special features in the Dead Sea Scrolls), it is this double understanding of grace that he took to be common to all the literature discussed, with the single named exception.

At two notable points, Sanders ran up against textual features that suggest some *congruity* between divine grace and human worth. It is characteristic of his honesty that he acknowledged this phenomenon, but equally characteristic of his general concern that he insisted even here on the ultimate incongruity of grace. The first case is the rabbinic theology of election (84-107). Here Sanders first gathered texts which stress "gratuity," emphasizing the "priority" of grace ("sheer mercy," 99), according to which commandments are "preceded" by acts of mercy; election is "totally gratuitous, without prior cause in those being elected" (87). He then noted a number of texts which explain the election of Israel, many of which refer to the worth or "merit" of the recipients of this grace: either Israel as a whole was worthy (since it alone accepted the covenant), or there was some "merit" in the patriarchs, in the exodus generation, or in future generations who were predicted to obey the commandments (87-101). Sanders insisted that the language of "merit" does not correspond to the (Protestant) notion of earning salvation (cf. 183-98 on "the merits of the fathers"), but he acknowledged that "grace and merit did not seem to [the Rabbis] to be in contradiction to each other" (100).[220] "In attempting to give a rationale for the election, the Rabbis appealed to the free grace of God and sometimes to the concept of merit" (106). As he suggested, underlying the appeal to merit is the concern to show that God's grace in election was not capricious or arbitrary (91, 98; cf. 182, 234, 422): God's gifts are distributed justly, and justice and mercy are correlated to ensure that God's mercy does not appear unfair (127).

This issue could have been illuminated by a distinction between the priority and the incongruity of grace. The Rabbis strongly emphasized grace as God's prior gift, but they did not, for good reason, perfect this motif in the form of incongruity; on that they were fully in accord with the ancient assumption that a good gift is given discriminately to people of worth (see above, 1.4). Grace is not necessarily in this sense "totally gratuitous" and "without prior cause" (or at least, prior reason). Since he did not make this distinction, Sanders was forced to conclude that the Rabbis were not fully clear in their thinking. Merit is not a "systematic explanation" of God's election (99), and the juxtaposition of grace and "merit" (or justice) suggests that the Rabbis were not systematic (cf. 120, 124, 132); they were simply following the biblical juxtaposition (100), or attempting to explain a motif (election) that remains necessarily inexplicable (101). Ultimately, Sanders insisted, election is both prior and "unconditional" (96-97), and individual Israelites by no means earn their place within the covenant (101). There seems to operate here a hidden assumption that if grace were shown to be congruous with the worth of its recipient, it could not be considered grace at all. But, as we have seen (chapter 2), that is by no means a necessary perfection of grace.[221]

220. The fact that Sanders prefaced this statement with "one would have expected the Rabbis to develop a clear doctrine of prevenient grace" suggests that he equated or confused the *incongruity* of grace with its *priority*.

221. As Sanders indicated, the rabbis frequently spoke of the reward of the righteous as a *gift* (pp. 171-72, 176). For scrutiny of Sanders's discussion of rabbinic theology on this point, see S. Westerholm, *Perspectives Old and New: The "Lutheran" Paul and His Critics* (Grand Rapids: Eerdmans, 2004), pp. 343-50. As he rightly points out, Sanders correctly finds here the

The second case concerns the *Psalms of Solomon,* where divine mercy is repeatedly described as accorded to the "pious" or "righteous." Here Sanders confronts the reading of Braun, who in an essay on this text identified a contrast between two perspectives on mercy that were dialectically juxtaposed. On the one hand, the mercy of God is "freely and gratuitously bestowed" *(frei und umsonst zugewandte),* without preconditions; on the other, that same mercy is "earned by pious humanity" *(vom frommen Menschen verdiente).*[222] On Braun's reading, the text swings inconsistently between these two poles, between "faith in God and trust in oneself" *(Gottesglauben und Selbstvertrauen).* As Sanders points out (392-97), Braun here imposed a Lutheran frame of reference, contrasting (genuine) grace with human "achievement" *(Leistung).* But rather than questioning the foundation of this Lutheran frame — its assumption that "grace" and "worth" are by definition incompatible — Sanders seems at pains to downplay the significance of the motif of merit.[223] The fact that the righteous, even as the righteous, receive *mercy* is intended, he insisted, to deny that they gain anything by merit. References to God's mercy on the righteous do not detract from the "free unmerited grace bestowed by God in electing and preserving Israel" (396). This "original electing grace" (396) is not compromised by the characterization of God's beneficiaries as righteous, since "the salvation of the righteous is due not to their own merits but *purely* to the mercy of God, who chose them and who forgives them" (393; italics added). It seems that Sanders, like Braun, assumed that God's grace, if "free" and "pure," must be "unmerited" and "groundless" (394). This assumption — that incongruity is an essential characteristic of grace — reflects the influence of the Augustinian and Reformation traditions, but would have seemed peculiarly one-sided in ancient discussions of gift or grace.

Sanders found significant differences between Paul and Palestinian Judaism in their patterns of religion: in Paul, one is saved not by membership in God's covenant with Israel but by participation in Christ, the eschatological

---

language of grace, but overreaches the evidence in claiming that it is "totally gratuitous." In Westerholm's terms, if one is looking for "unmerited favour," "utter gratuity," or "sheer divine mercy" (i.e., in our terms, the incongruity of grace), the rabbinic material hardly supports *this* notion of grace. Westerholm thus finds Sanders to impose a "Lutheran" construction on the texts (p. 348). To put that another way, Sanders operates on the unnecessary assumption that grace is only grace if it is unmerited.

222. H. Braun, "Vom Erbarmen Gottes über den Gerechten: zur Theologie der Psalmen Salomos," in *Gesammelte Studien zum Neuen Testament und seiner Umwelt,* 2nd ed. (Tübingen: Mohr Siebeck, 1967), pp. 8-69.

223. Sanders effectively questions Braun's assumptions about sin, but not, it seems, the related assumptions about grace (pp. 396-97).

Lord of the world (431-542). But at a deep level, in their understanding of grace and works, there is no difference at all. This assertion, strongly opposing the Reformation tradition and especially its Bultmannian expression, follows from the fact that Sanders's *main* emphasis had fallen on the *priority* of grace:

> On the point on which many have found the decisive contrast between Paul and Judaism — grace and works — Paul is in agreement with Palestinian Judaism . . . *salvation is by grace but judgment is according to works; works are the condition of remaining 'in,' but they do not earn salvation.* . . . The point is that God *saves* by grace, but that *within* the framework established by grace he rewards good deeds and punishes transgression. (543; italics original)

Although Paul's theology is not fundamentally structured by the notion of covenant (511-15), he does affirm both grace and judgment by works (515-18), and that combination precisely matches what is found in other Jewish texts. Because Paul, like other Jews, affirms the priority of grace, he cannot be at odds with them on that topic, even in the antithesis between faith and works of the law. "What is wrong with Judaism is not that Jews seek to save themselves and become self-righteous about it, but that their seeking is not directed towards the right goal" (550). "The basis for Paul's polemic against the law, and consequently against doing the law, was his exclusivist soteriology. Since salvation is only by Christ, the following of *any* other path is wrong" (550; italics original). The fact that Christ has come to save everyone renders Jewish covenantal nomism obsolete *a posteriori;* Paul has no critique of an inherent fault in the Jewish concept of grace.[224]

Sanders performed an enormous service to students of ancient Judaism and of Paul. His challenge to the then-prevalent caricatures of Judaism has altered all subsequent discussion of Second Temple Judaism, and his insistence on the ubiquity of grace in Second Temple literature has been widely influential. Nonetheless, at the heart of his project is a lack of clarity concerning the very definition of grace. As we have seen, his structural analysis of "getting in" and "staying in" laid emphasis on the *priority* of grace, but there is a tendency for other perfections of grace, and in particular its *incongruity,* to be assumed as part and parcel of the same idea. Against the negative characterizations of Judaism, Sanders declared his positive appreciation of what he had found: "by consistently maintaining the basic framework of covenantal nomism, the gift and the demand of God were kept in a healthy relationship with each other"

224. Hence the famous conclusion: "this is what Paul finds wrong in Judaism: it is not Christianity" (p. 552).

(427).[225] He acclaimed a rabbinic prayer that "seems to imply a doctrine of prevenient grace and which clearly puts the indicative and the imperative in what even Bultmannians would concede to be the correct relationship" (178). But a Bultmannian, of course, is interested in far more than the priority of grace (see above, 3.5.2), and by failing to distinguish between this and other perfections of grace, Sanders leaves unclear to what extent Jewish texts from this period do, or do not, *also* perfect the incongruity of grace.

As we shall see, this lack of clarity on the meaning of "grace" has caused considerable confusion in the reaction to Sanders by both Pauline scholars and scholars of ancient Judaism. It also led Sanders to homogenize Second Temple texts that arguably advance *differing* conceptions of divine mercy or grace. Although Sanders recognized some differences among the texts he discussed, and in particular the unique stress on predestination in the Qumran *Hodayot* (1QH[a]), he chiefly emphasized the "uniformity" of Judaism on this subject (421), with the single exception of *4 Ezra*. The concern to counter images of Judaism in which the concept of grace was lacking or corrupt led Sanders to emphasize its ubiquity, its "healthiness," and its uniformity, not to attempt differentiation between distinct construals of this theme. Finding grace everywhere, he gave the impression that grace is everywhere the same, and that one perfection (priority) necessarily entails another (incongruity). In our analysis of Second Temple texts (in Part II), our task will be to examine if this is indeed the case; we can then reassess where Paul stands on this topic in relation to his fellow Jews (Parts III and IV).

225. Elsewhere he asserts that the rabbis "kept the indicative and imperative well-balanced and in the right order" (p. 97) and that "the Judaism of before 70 kept grace and works in the right perspective" (p. 427). This acclamation may lie behind Neusner's complaint that Sanders has done no more than address to the Jewish material questions derived from "Pauline-Lutheran scholarship," so as to "impose the pattern of one religious expression, Paul's, upon the description of another," J. Neusner, "The Use of Later Rabbinic Evidence for the Study of Paul," in W. S. Green, ed., *Approaches to Ancient Judaism II* (Chico: Scholars Press, 1980), pp. 43-63, at pp. 50-51. But the notion that God's gifts are prior to, and even the source of, human action, is hardly unique to Paul or to Luther. For discussion of the "covert Protestantism" in Sanders's framework, see R. B. Matlock, "Almost Cultural Studies? Reflections on the 'New Perspective' on Paul," in J. C. Exum and S. D. Moore, eds., *Biblical Studies/Cultural Studies: The Third Sheffield Colloquium* (Sheffield: Sheffield Academic Press, 1998), pp. 433-59, at pp. 444-47. Alexander's plea that "the superiority of grace over law is not self-evident," and his claim that "Tannaitic Judaism can be seen as fundamentally a religion of works-righteousness, and it is none the worse for that" helpfully alerts us to hidden ideological assumptions in scholarship, but fails to scrutinize the central concepts themselves; see P. S. Alexander, "Torah and Salvation in Tannaitic Literature," in D. A. Carson, P. T. O'Brien, and M. A. Seifrid, eds., *Justification and Variegated Nomism*, vol. 1: *The Complexities of Second Temple Judaism* (Tübingen: Mohr Siebeck, 2001), pp. 261-302, at p. 300; cf. his review of Sanders's *Jesus and Judaism* in *JJS* 37 (1986): 103-6.

3.6.2. The New Perspective on Paul

In the wake of Sanders's *Paul and Palestinian Judaism,* it has become problematic to identify "grace" as a matter of dispute between Paul and any of his fellow Jews. Because Sanders's thesis homogenized the Second Temple texts as representatives of a common "covenantal nomism," and tended to essentialize ancient Judaism as "a religion of grace," Paul's theology of grace could no longer be taken as a point of difference between himself and any other Jews — unless one wanted to return to now-discredited representations of Judaism as a grace-deficient religion of legalism and works-righteousness. The "new perspective" on Paul (so dubbed by J. D. G. Dunn) takes as its starting point that Paul and other Jews of the Second Temple period *agreed* on this theme. As Dunn puts the matter: "The Judaism of what Sanders christened as 'covenantal nomism' can now be seen to preach good Protestant doctrine: that grace is always prior; that human effort is ever the response to divine initiative; that good works are the fruit and not the root of salvation."[226] It is noticeable that what Dunn picks out here is the *priority* of grace, and that he assumes that this (alone?) is the essence of "good Protestant doctrine" regarding grace. In fact, as we have seen (3.2–3.4), neither for Augustine nor for the Reformers was it sufficient to say that "grace is always prior" and that "human effort is the response to divine initiative." They insisted on adding other perfections, not least the incongruity of grace. Like Sanders, Dunn appears to take one perfection of grace (priority) to include the rest. On this assumption, grace is a matter of complete agreement between Paul and all other Jews. "But," as Dunn adds, "if that is so, where does that leave Paul? And where does it leave justification by faith?"

Dunn's answer to his question is that the Pauline antithesis between justification by faith and justification by works of the law means *not* that "every individual must cease from his own efforts and simply trust in God's acceptance," *but* that "justification is not confined to Jews as marked out by their distinctive works; it is open to all, to Gentile as well as Jew, through faith."[227]

226. J. D. G. Dunn, *The New Perspective on Paul: Collected Essays* (Tübingen: Mohr Siebeck, 2005), p. 193 (from a 1991 essay, "The Justice of God"). At the root of the new perspective on Paul, indeed a major influence on Dunn, was the early work of N. T. Wright; in a seminal 1978 essay he hails Sanders for showing that "Judaism, so far from being a religion of works, is based on a clear understanding of grace, the grace that chose Israel in the first place to be a special people. Good works are simply gratitude, and demonstrate that one is faithful to the covenant," "The Paul of History and the Apostle of Faith," *TynBul* 29 (1978): 61-88 (at p. 80); reprinted in *Pauline Perspectives: Essays on Paul, 1978-2013* (London: SPCK, 2013), pp. 3-20 (at p. 15).

227. Dunn, *New Perspective,* p. 199 (from the same essay cited in the preceding note).

This formulation of the matter, which summarizes both the negative and the positive thrust of the new perspective on Paul, draws on a deep-seated shift in Pauline studies that took place outside of Germany during the 1960s and 1970s. This shift is best represented in the work of Stendahl and has three significant components:[228]

(i) There is a strong emphasis on the *historical specificity* of Paul's theology, against the assumption that what Paul says is universally relevant across all time. For both historical and hermeneutical reasons, Stendahl demanded a clear distinction between "then" and "now," combining a historical anxiety about "modernizing" Paul with a deep suspicion of the Bultmannian presumption of the continuity and universality of the human condition. In this vein, proponents of the new perspective insist that Paul's theology of justification was articulated not just *in the context* of his mission to the Gentiles (as if the inclusion of both Gentiles and Jews were simply an example illustrating a broader point), but *for the purpose* of defending and promoting that mission.[229] The emphasis fell on the irreducible historical particularity of Paul's first-century concerns, joined to a widespread suspicion of "theological" (e.g., Bultmannian) interpretation as insufficiently attentive to first-century realities. Paul's theology cannot be presumed to be timeless and generalizable, at least not in the usual soteriological terms.[230]

(ii) The second characteristic of this shift is its criticism of a "Western" obsession with sin, guilt, and *the individual's relation to God;* in place of that,

228. Stendahl's 1963 essay, "The Apostle Paul and the Introspective Conscience of the West," is collected with other essays in K. Stendahl, *Paul among Jews and Gentiles* (London: SCM, 1977); cf. his later lectures on Romans published as *Final Account: Paul's Letter to the Romans* (Minneapolis: Fortress Press, 1995). Other contemporary representatives of this trend include M. Barth, "Jews and Gentiles: The Social Character of Justification," *JES* 5 (1968): 241-61; N. A. Dahl, "The Doctrine of Justification: Its Social Function and Effects," in *Studies in Paul* (Minneapolis: Fortress Press, 1977), pp. 95-120 (originally published in Norwegian in 1964); G. Howard, *Paul: Crisis in Galatia* (Cambridge: Cambridge University Press, 1979).

229. In Stendahl's terms, "the centre of gravity in Paul's theological work is related to the fact that he knew himself to be called to be the Apostle to the Gentiles" (*Paul among Jews and Gentiles,* p. 15); the recovery of this original *Sitz im Leben* allows the Pauline texts to be (again) the critic of the tradition that bears them (*Final Account,* pp. 35, 40). A theology designed not just *in* but *for* the Gentile mission can also be described, in functionalist terms, as its legitimating ideology; cf. F. Watson, *Paul, Judaism, and the Gentiles: Beyond the New Perspective,* 2nd ed. (Grand Rapids: Eerdmans, 2007), pp. 21, 51.

230. Stendahl's insistence that Romans concerns "missiology, not soteriology" (*Final Account,* p. 41) was intended to undermine the Augustinian tradition with its focus on sin as the common human plight and grace as its divine solution. Stendahl and others in the new perspective were ready to find contemporary relevance in Pauline theology, but in different terms (see below).

the primary emphasis rests on the *social relations between groups.* Stendahl's sharp distinction between Paul and the "introspective conscience of the West" was directed most explicitly against the Lutheran focus on interiority, but also against the Augustinian tradition lying behind it: "Paul's thoughts about justification were triggered by the issues of divisions and identities in a pluralistic and torn world, not primarily by the inner tensions of individual souls and consciences."[231] The topic of grace had typically been framed in individualistic terms ("How can I, a sinner, find a gracious God?").[232] Thus, the new reading of Pauline theology, by pulling away from an individualistic focus, decentered the motif of grace. With new social and political interests, interpreters of Paul identified Jew-Gentile issues as central to both Galatians and Romans: there, Paul's discussion of "works of the law" concerns not an inner attitude to one's works (so Luther; see above, 3.3.2) but the social praxis of a cultural tradition. For Stendahl, "the doctrine of justification by faith was hammered out by Paul for the very specific and limited purpose of defending the rights of Gentile converts to be full and genuine heirs to the promises of God to Israel."[233] The language of "rights," like the references to "equality" and "inclusion," matched the altered horizons of theology in and after the 1960s.[234]

(iii) Thirdly, the mood-shift demanded much more sensitive articulation of *the relationship between Paul and Judaism.* For Stendahl, the false notion that Paul was dissatisfied with Judaism and attacked it as a legalistic religion was at the root of Christian anti-Judaism: Jewish-Christian relations were a priority of Stendahl's life, and, increasingly, a pluralistic theology of religions free of Christian "imperialism."[235] Paul's justification theology, he insisted, was not polemical but apologetic: he was not attacking Judaism but defending the terms of his mission to Gentiles.[236] Taking Romans 9–11 as the climax of the letter, Stendahl noted that Paul does not describe the salvation of "all Israel" in explicitly Christological terms, but leaves this matter a mystery, warning against Gentile Christian anti-Semitism.[237] In Stendahl's wake, a number of

231. Stendahl, *Paul among Jews and Gentiles,* p. 40.

232. Stendahl regards this question as typical of Western concerns, not Paul's; it is the question of a "plagued conscience" (*Paul among Jews and Gentiles,* pp. 83, 131; *Final Account,* p. 14).

233. Stendahl, *Paul among Jews and Gentiles,* p. 2.

234. Gentile "rights": Stendahl, *Paul among Jews and Gentiles,* pp. 2, 130-31; "equality": pp. 29, 81; "inclusion": p. 28. For "the rights of Gentiles," cf. Barth, "Jews and Gentiles," p. 246.

235. Stendahl, *Paul among Jews and Gentiles,* pp. 126-27, 132.

236. Stendahl, *Paul among Jews and Gentiles,* p. 130.

237. Stendahl, *Paul among Jews and Gentiles,* p. 85 (cf. p. 29: Romans 1–8 is merely the preface to the climax in Romans 9–11). In *Final Account,* p. 7 (cf. pp. x-xi), Stendahl maintains

scholars have argued that Paul's discussions of the law were concerned solely with Gentile believers (and not with Jews or Jewish believers), and that Paul not only has nothing at all negative to say about Jews or Judaism, but is confident that their salvation lies in a covenant relationship to God quite distinct from the Gentile relationship to Christ.[238] Others have found Paul critical of certain aspects of Judaism, but only of a Judaism that had lost or misunderstood its own traditions.[239] What everyone wishes to avoid is the continuation of the old stereotypes of the Jew as the archetypical "religious," "pious," or "legalistic" person — stereotypes associated, via Bultmann and Käsemann, with the Lutheran tradition.

This threefold break with the Augustinian and Reformation traditions altered the analysis of the place and the significance of "grace" in Pauline theology for those who promoted the new perspective, but in different ways. For some, the central issue in Paul's debate with Judaism concerned the inclusion of the Gentiles, but not the understanding of grace. Sanders, finding agreement between Paul and Judaism on grace and works (see above), identified the key points of difference in the exclusivism of Paul's soteriology (if salvation is in Christ, it cannot be in anything else, including the Torah) and in Paul's conviction that, in faith, salvation is open to all, both Jews and Gentiles, without distinction.[240] By a "principle of equality," Paul insists that Gentile and Jew stand on an "equal footing" with an "equal status": if Paul has a criticism of Judaism, it is not for an attitudinal sin of self-righteousness but for an "assumption of Jewish privilege."[241]

In similar terms, N. T. Wright speaks of the "equal terms" on which Jew and Gentile enter the people of God, and Paul's determination that Gentiles

---

that he did not mean to advocate that Paul envisaged a *Sonderweg* for Israel, just a mystery left in the hands of God.

238. See, e.g., L. Gaston, *Paul and the Torah* (Vancouver: University of British Columbia, 1987); S. Stowers, *A Rereading of Romans: Justice, Jews, and Gentiles* (New Haven: Yale University Press, 1994); J. Gager, *Reinventing Paul* (Oxford: Oxford University Press, 2000); C. Johnson Hodge, *If Sons, Then Heirs: A Study of Kinship and Ethnicity in the Letters of Paul* (Oxford: Oxford University Press, 2007).

239. See below on Dunn and Wright. Other symptoms of this shift include Martyn's argument that Galatians does not have Jews or Judaism in its critical purview (see above, 3.5.4) and Watson's insistence, following Sanders, that for Paul there was simply an irreducible difference between Torah-observance and Christ-faith (as between the Jewish synagogue and the Christian community), not a problem in one that is solved in the other (*Paul, Judaism, and the Gentiles*, pp. 12-26).

240. Sanders, *Paul and Palestinian Judaism*, pp. 489-90, 497; idem, *Paul, the Law, and the Jewish People* (Philadelphia: Fortress Press, 1983), pp. 5, 18, 27.

241. *Paul, the Law*, pp. 30-34, 38, etc.

should not have "second class" status.[242] Placing this commitment in a wider theological frame, Wright takes Paul to announce the renewal and fulfillment of the Abrahamic covenant in which God's plans for a single, united, multiethnic family are fulfilled in Christ, who, as Messiah, offered to God the obedience that Israel had failed to perform. Part of Israel's failure (its "meta-sin") was the determination to hold on to ethnic or national privilege.[243] On this reading, Paul's reference to "their own righteousness" (Rom 10:3; cf. Phil 3:9), fundamental to Bultmann's antithesis between a human-achieved and a God-given salvation (see above, 3.5.2), is taken in a quite different sense: what Paul protests against here is a "national righteousness," in antithesis to a righteousness available to *all* the nations.[244] Although Wright has sometimes articulated this antithesis as a difference between "grace" and "race,"[245] he has generally not made grace a central issue in Pauline theology. Since the Christ-event reaffirms election, it brings the fulfillment of the covenant, not a new or differently nuanced understanding of salvation. While describing grace as "free" and "unmerited," Wright differs from the figures discussed above (see 3.5) in declining to make this construal of grace the core feature in Paul's understanding of faith or in his definition of membership in the people of God in Christ.[246] In this respect, as in the emphasis on the universality of Paul's mission (beyond the "restrictions" of the Jewish tradition), the new perspective echoes Baur's configuration of Pauline theology, which was also directed against a Lutheran reading of Romans.[247]

242. N. T. Wright, *Paul: Fresh Perspectives* (London: SPCK, 2005), pp. 30, 38; idem, "The Letter to the Galatians: Exegesis and Theology," in J. B. Green and M. Turner, eds., *Between Two Horizons: Spanning New Testament Studies and Systematic Theology* (Grand Rapids: Eerdmans, 2000), pp. 205-36 (at p. 222); reprinted in *Pauline Perspectives*, pp. 191-215 (at p. 205).

243. "Meta-sin": N. T. Wright, *The Climax of the Covenant* (Edinburgh: T&T Clark, 1991), p. 240; exclusive privilege as a "second-order form of idolatry," *Fresh Perspectives*, p. 36.

244. Wright, "Paul of History," pp. 82-83 (reprint, *Pauline Perspectives*, pp. 16-17).

245. E.g., *Climax of the Covenant*, pp. 168, 240.

246. For grace in Paul as "free," "sheer," "pure gift," and "unmerited," see N. T. Wright, "Romans," in *The New Interpreter's Bible*, vol. 10 (Nashville: Abingdon, 2002), pp. 471, 492-93, 495. This clearly highlights the incongruity of grace, but Wright seems at pains to insist that while "faith, grace and promise are vital" to Romans 4, "they are not its main subjects" (p. 497; cf. p. 485).

247. Baur took Romans to do away with "Jewish exclusiveness" and "particularism," in promoting the Christian universalism that extends to all nations. "Its great significance lies not so much in its doctrinal statements about sin and grace, as in its practical bearing on the most important controversy of these times, the relation between Jew and Gentile," F. C. Baur, *The Church History of the First Three Centuries*, vol. 1 (Edinburgh: Williams and Norgate, 1875), p. 72. For the resonance between the new perspective and Baur's post-Enlightenment thematics, see Watson, *Paul, Judaism, and the Gentiles*, pp. 40-47, and D. Boyarin, *A Radical Jew: Paul and the Politics of Identity* (Berkeley: University of California Press, 1994).

The theme of grace *is* significant to Dunn's reading of Pauline theology, but he is careful to avoid creating a simple antithesis to Judaism. Speaking of Paul's "conversion," Dunn writes:

> It did not teach him of God's grace, as though for a Jew he was learning of it for the first time. It did, however, bring home to him that his own typically Jewish attitude had obscured that grace and to a serious degree perverted it. But, once again, not by prompting him to think he had a claim upon God by virtue of his own merits. The error which came home to him on the Damascus road was much more that Israel's claim to a special relationship with God was perverting the more basic insight of God's grace, that as a free grace it was open to all and not restricted in effect to Jews alone and their proselytes. In this way and in this sense Paul rediscovered justification by grace on the Damascus road.[248]

Here, Dunn encapsulates an apparently paradoxical phenomenon. On the one hand, Paul fully agreed with his Jewish tradition, and merely "rediscovered" what was already there.[249] On the other hand, he reacted against a "typically Jewish attitude" that had "obscured" and "perverted" this grace, interpreting it as "restricted," not "free" and "open to all." This language reflects the way Dunn often characterizes the object of Paul's critique: Paul's opponents want to "restrict" the membership of the covenant on ethnic or national lines, they have a "narrow" understanding of God's plan, their mission is "exclusive" of Gentiles as Gentiles, and they want to impose practices (such as circumcision and food-rules) that function as "boundary-markers" between Jews and Gentiles. This amounts to a policy of "separation," "distinction," "confinement," and "division," particularly egregious as it reflects "fleshly" lines of descent, ethnicity, and racial identity.[250]

248. Dunn, *New Perspective,* p. 369 (from a 1997 article).

249. Elsewhere Dunn speaks of justification as "acceptance into a relationship with God characterized by the grace of Israel's covenant," *The Theology of Paul the Apostle* (Grand Rapids: Eerdmans, 1998), p. 388. Paul's insistence on the "initiative of divine grace" was "simply a restatement of the first principles of his own ancestral faith," p. 345. For Dunn's grounding in Reformed theology, with its emphasis on a single covenant of grace ("one and the same under various dispensations"), see *New Perspective,* p. 18.

250. The spatial metaphors are already prominent in Dunn's earliest essay on this theme ("The New Perspective on Paul," reprinted in *New Perspective,* pp. 89-110) and remained dominant thereafter. On Dunn's reading, Paul objects to a "narrowing of divine grace" (*New Perspective,* p. 69). Dunn's controversial reading of "the works of the law," as only (or primarily) a reference to specific "boundary markers" between Jews and Gentiles, is discussed one last time in *New Perspective,* pp. 22-26. Dunn finds many points of contemporary relevance in

How this policy became "typical" of Judaism at the same time that "covenantal nomism" preached "good Protestant doctrine" on grace (see above) is a question Dunn grapples with throughout. As with Sanders, the issue might be clarified if a distinction were made between the *priority* of grace and its *incongruity*. The former, grace given before demand, is what Dunn means by works being "the fruit and not the root" (see above, p. 159). The latter, grace given without regard to worth, is apparently what he has in mind when he speaks of grace as "free" and "open."[251] According to Dunn, Paul's protest was against "the assumption that ethnic origin and identity is a factor in determining the grace of God and its expression . . . a different way of assessing human worth, but one more fundamental than the question of ability to perform good works."[252] This, like his description of "the unconditional character of grace expressed in the gospel," suggests that Dunn finds Paul to perfect also the incongruity of grace; in this respect he stands in continuity with the Lutheran tradition.[253]

If Paul disagreed with his fellow Jews on the "openness" of God's grace, but not on the fact that works are the product of grace, one could use the analytical tool offered above (chapter 2) to pinpoint more precisely why, in Dunn's reading, Paul's relationship to Judaism seems so paradoxical. It would not be a case of anyone "obscuring" or "perverting" the grace of God. The difference lies in different perfections of grace, and the issue could be simply put: Paul and his fellow Jews agreed on the *priority* of grace, but disagreed on its *incongruity*, at least in relation to ethnic worth. That, at least, appears to be Dunn's reading of the matter. One would clearly need to reexamine the texts to see if this was so, but, on this reading, what needs to be clarified is not *whether* grace is perfected by Paul and by other Jewish authors, but *how*.

---

his reading of Pauline theology, in relation both to inner-ecclesial divisions and to racial and ethnic conflicts across the globe (e.g., *New Perspective*, p. 199).

251. Cf. *New Perspective*, p. 105: "What Jesus has done by his death and resurrection, in Paul's understanding, is to free the grace of God in justifying from its nationalistically restrictive clamps for a broader experience (beyond the circumcised Jew) and a fuller expression (beyond concern for ritual purity)."

252. J. D. G. Dunn, *The Theology of Paul's Letter to the Galatians* (Cambridge: Cambridge University Press, 1993), p. 142.

253. J. D. G. Dunn, *The Epistle to the Galatians* (London: A & C Black, 1993), p. 265; cf. p. 269. Dunn himself would accept this connection with the Lutheran tradition, since he regards himself not as contradicting central Lutheran emphases, but as extending them into the social sphere, their original Pauline home; see *New Perspective*, pp. 17-22, 54, 87-88; *Theology of Galatians*, pp. 140-43. On the Lutheran shape of Dunn's reading of Paul, see R. B. Matlock, "Sins of the Flesh and Suspicious Minds: Dunn's New *Theology of Paul*," *JSNT* 72 (1998): 67-90 (at pp. 82-86), and Westerholm, *Perspectives Old and New on Paul*, pp. 184-89.

3.7. Recent Discussions of Paul and Grace

In recent years, Paul's theology of grace has featured in three, largely unconnected, contexts of debate: in convoluted discussions of the "new perspective," in the radically new reading of Paul by the French philosopher, Alain Badiou, and in new studies of the Pauline language of *charis* in relation to its Greco-Roman context. We will here survey each of these, as all three provide an important context for the reading of Paul that follows in Parts Two and Three of this book, and because each can be illumined (and attendant confusions clarified) by applying the analytical tool of the six perfections that was developed above in chapter 2.

3.7.1. After the New Perspective

The new perspective on Paul has had a mixed reception. The wide variety of reactions reflects not only the normal diversity of scholarly viewpoints, but also the fact that the new perspective itself has different ingredients and diverse representatives.[254] On the topic of Paul and grace, a double dissatisfaction has frequently been expressed. First, the new perspective has seemed to limit the horizon and import of Pauline soteriology: while Paul is clearly discussing the unity and equality of Jew and Gentile, the grounds for his discussion are still felt by many to lie in a generalizable theology of grace and faith. Secondly, there has been resistance to Sanders's argument that on the subject of grace and works there is no discernible difference between Paul and his fellow Jews. Sanders, we may recall (see above, 3.6.1), emphasized the priority of grace in covenantal election, and sometimes associated that with its incongruity; but many scholars have found his analysis of "covenantal nomism" unconvincing or lacking the essential (Pauline) hallmarks of "grace." Where Dunn hailed Sanders's Judaism for preaching "good Protestant doctrine" (3.6.2), others have insisted that on *their* understanding of "grace" that is by no means the case.

Thus, Carson, surveying Second Temple texts in reaction to Sanders, found evidence for a "merit theology," with a general tendency "to view human merit and worth as the rationale for the divine choice, instead of understand-

254. See the diverse reactions, representing both English- and German-speaking scholarship, in P. Stuhlmacher, *Revisiting Paul's Doctrine of Justification: A Challenge to the New Perspective* (with an essay by D. A. Hagner; Downers Grove: InterVarsity, 2001); M. Bachmann and J. Woyke, eds., *Lutherische und Neue Paulusperspektive: Beiträge zu einem Schlüsselproblem der gegenwärtigen exegetischen Diskussion* (Tübingen: Mohr Siebeck, 2005).

ing that choice to be in defiance of human demerit and unworthiness."[255] "Human merit," "earned reward," and "mechanical retribution" are to be contrasted with "sheer grace," which is, by definition, "out of nothing other than [God's] own free, sovereign, electing love."[256] Carson finds in Second Temple texts evidence for "the diluted value of 'grace' and 'mercy.' God may be 'gracious' to his people, but it is no longer grace in defiance of demerit and rooted in the sovereign goodness of God. Rather, it is a kind of response to merit."[257] Subsequently, in his conclusion to a set of essays reviewing Second Temple texts, Carson puts emphasis on the fact that, in Sanders's scheme, human obedience is a necessary condition for "remaining in" the covenant. In his view, this amounts to a "meritorious righteousness" and a soteriology that operates by "tit-for-tat reciprocity." "Over against merit theology stands grace."[258]

The necessity within "covenantal nomism" for Torah observance and its salvific significance at the eschatological judgment are the focus of studies by Gathercole and Eskola.[259] For Gathercole, if obedience is given this "instrumental" role (118) as the means for final salvation (248), God's "gracious election" of Israel cannot be the all-encompassing principle of soteriology in the way that Sanders had suggested. Instead, we find the dual principles of

255. D. A. Carson, *Divine Sovereignty and Human Responsibility* (Atlanta: John Knox Press, 1981), p. 44.

256. Carson, *Divine Sovereignty*, p. 33; cf. pp. 50, 104.

257. Carson, *Divine Sovereignty*, p. 69; cf. pp. 108-9. Cf. R. H. Gundry, "Grace, Works, and Staying Saved in Paul," *Biblica* 66 (1985): 1-38, reprinted with different title and additional conclusion in idem, *The Old Is Better: New Testament Essays in Support of Traditional Interpretations* (Tübingen: Mohr Siebeck, 2005), pp. 195-224. On Gundry's reading, Paul attacks "a corruption of grace and faith" (p. 12); in no sense has "synergism" "watered down [Paul's] doctrine of grace" (p. 35).

258. D. A. Carson, P. T. O'Brien, and M. A. Seifrid, eds., *Justification and Variegated Nomism*, vol. 1: *The Complexities of Second Temple Judaism* (Tübingen: Mohr Siebeck, 2001), pp. 544-45. Cf. the conclusion of Enns earlier in this volume, that, since obedience is necessary in maintaining covenantal status, "it might be less confusing to say that election is by grace, but salvation is by obedience" (p. 98). Many contributors to this volume speak of grace as "unmerited," "undeserved" (pp. 14, 27, 37, 353), and "free" (pp. 324, 353), operating in principle "alone," where salvation is "purely" and "entirely" God's action (pp. 37, 69, 95, 413). The essays also regularly contrast "grace" with "merit" (pp. 16, 43, 156, 238, etc.), with "legalism" (pp. 396, 411), with "works-righteousness" (pp. 72, 97, 272, etc.), and with "earning salvation" (pp. 32, 38, 51, 105, 378, etc.).

259. S. J. Gathercole, *Where Is Boasting? Early Jewish Soteriology and Paul's Response in Romans 1–5* (Grand Rapids: Eerdmans, 2002); in what follows, numbers in parentheses are page references to this work. T. Eskola, *Theodicy and Predestination in Pauline Soteriology* (Tübingen: Mohr Siebeck, 1998), esp. pp. 52-60, 267-75 (on covenantal nomism as a kind of "synergistic nomism").

"election" and "works" (48-49, 67, 261-64, etc.), which stand alongside one another in unresolved tension (151-56, 264). One principle concerns "grace" (God's "free choice," 71; in Paul's case, "sheer grace," 244), the other, "just recompense" (64) in a reward theology that operates by "commutative justice" (249), "symmetrical judgment" (66), or "tit for tat" (245).[260] Gathercole wishes to distinguish this "double-sided soteriology" (71) from that of Paul. Although in his case obedience also plays a decisive role in the final vindication of believers, here the Spirit as "indwelling divine grace" enables and empowers obedience; there is no possibility of "synergism" in Paul (16, 132-35, 223-24).

Approaching Sanders's thesis from a parallel perspective, Laato highlights the significance of "human achievement" in Second Temple Judaism: in his view, confidence in human ability to keep the Law is what accounts for a soteriology marked by "synergism."[261] Given Jewish belief in human freedom, and thus in the capacity to obey (or to repent in the aftermath of transgression), obedience to the Law becomes a matter of human responsibility alone, without the necessity of grace. By contrast, Paul's pessimism places human actors under the power of sin, unless they are transformed and empowered through the Spirit. In this sense, even believers' achievements are a matter of grace: "Christ does the good works of Christians" *(Christus tut die guten Werke der Christen).*[262] In a similar fashion, other scholars argue that, although Paul's talk of judgment by works may appear to make salvation conditional on human actions, in fact, grace transforms believers to be agents of God's activity; moreover, for some, "they cannot be otherwise than practically righteous" thanks to the indwelling of the Spirit.[263]

260. Cf. Condra, for whom any both-and combination of "divine grace" and "human good works" is sufficient to prove that we can no longer speak logically of grace: "divine grace mixed with a human responsibility to keep the Law falls outside the realm of a gracious soteriology," E. Condra, *Salvation for the Righteous Revealed: Jesus amid Covenantal and Messianic Expectations in Second Temple Judaism* (Leiden: Brill, 2002), p. 49; cf. pp. 47, 53-54, 196.

261. T. Laato, *Paulus und das Judentum* (Åbo: Åbo Akademis Förlag, 1991); translated as *Paul and Judaism: An Anthropological Approach,* trans. T. McElwain (Atlanta: Scholars Press, 1995), pp. 73-82, 185-211.

262. Laato, *Paulus,* p. 203.

263. B. D. Smith, *What Must I Do to Be Saved? Paul Parts Company with His Jewish Heritage* (Sheffield: Phoenix Press, 2007), p. 3; cf. pp. 226, 239. For similar, though less predestinarian, statements, see C. H. Talbert, "Paul, Judaism, and the Revisionists," *CBQ* 63 (2001): 1-22 (divine enablement and empowerment ensure that Paul is not synergistic but upholds a kind of monergism, pp. 16-17, 20-22). Like Gundry ("Grace, Works, and Staying Saved"), O'Brien speaks of the good works of believers as evidence of, not grounds for, their salvation, echoing Calvin (see above, 3.4.3): "Was Paul a Covenantal Nomist?" in D. A. Carson, P. T. O'Brien, and M. A. Seifrid, eds., *Justification and Variegated Nomism,* vol. 2: *The Paradoxes of Paul* (Tübingen: Mohr Siebeck, 2004), pp. 249-96 (at pp. 265-70).

It is notable that these reactions to Sanders and to the new perspective generally use the terminology of the Reformation tradition (works-righteousness, legalism, synergism, merit, *sola gratia*) or make at least implicit appeal to Augustine's debates with Pelagius. They therefore perfect the theme of grace in ways that reflect those traditions. If salvation is "by grace alone" (without human cooperation, and in utter dependence on God), it is not sufficient that it is merely *prior:* it must also be *incongruous* with the worth of the recipient (even at the final judgment) and *efficacious* in one form or another (through the work of the Spirit). On these readings, Paul has every form of the perfections of grace that one or both of the leading Reformers were looking for, while other forms of grace identifiable in Second Temple Judaism are judged to lack the proper constituents of "grace." Jewish texts may be said to have marginalized grace,[264] to have "diluted it" (Carson), or to have combined it with its opposite in an "unsystematic" mixture of contrary principles, "grace" and "recompense."[265] What is not considered is whether grace and recompense may be a perfectly normal combination in antiquity (gift to the worthy, gift as reward).[266] As we have seen, this is not a self-contradiction; it simply entails that grace is not perfected *as an incongruous gift,* as espoused by Augustine and in the Protestant tradition. In the readings mentioned here, a particular definition of "grace" is taken for granted, and little attempt is made to distinguish between different meanings of the term or (in our terms) different perfections of this motif.[267]

Other contributions to the debate can also be seen to foreground certain perfections of grace in their discussions of Paul, though here an effort is made to go "beyond the new perspective" without reverting to the categories and

264. E.g., R. Bauckham, "Apocalypses," in Carson et al., eds., *Variegated Nomism,* pp. 1.135-87, on cases where "the emphasis is overwhelmingly on meriting salvation by works of obedience to the Law, with the result that human achievement takes center-stage and God's grace, while presupposed, is effectively marginalized" (p. 174).

265. This thesis was advanced by F. Avemarie, who argued that rabbinic literature shows two incompatible principles, of elective grace *(Gnadenwahl)* and recompense *(Vergeltung);* see *Tora und Leben: Untersuchungen zur Heilsbedeutung der Tora in der frühen rabbinischen Literatur* (Tübingen: Mohr Siebeck, 1996); idem, "Erwählung und Vergeltung: Zur optionalen Struktur rabbinischer Soteriologie," *NTS* 45 (1999): 108-26.

266. Gathercole, however, notes that it is possible to imagine a gift being the prize for work, *Where Is Boasting?,* p. 115.

267. Seifrid recognizes that Paul's construal of grace may be different from that in Second Temple texts ("One of the amazing things about grace is that it is an exceedingly elastic concept"), but he does not follow this with any analysis of the differences; M. A. Seifrid, "Unrighteous by Faith: Apostolic Proclamation in Romans 1:18–3:20," in Carson et al., eds., *Variegated Nomism,* vol. 2, pp. 105-45 (at p. 144). The most thoughtful discussion of this matter remains Westerholm, *Perspectives Old and New,* pp. 341-51.

structures of the Reformation antitheses. Watson, whose work reflects aspects of the post-Stendahl ethos (see above, 3.6.2) but is also distinct from the new perspective on Paul, maintains that Paul's differences from his fellow Jews rest not on general, abstract soteriological principles (against Lutheran readers, such as Bultmann and Käsemann) but on a concrete, incommensurable difference between a community that lives by faith in Christ and a community whose life is focused on observance of the Torah. This particularity resists reduction to generalizable principles of "grace" and "works." Sanders's conviction that Paul reasons from the Christ-event backwards (if Christ, then not Torah) is fundamentally right: Paul has no theoretical disagreement with Judaism on the grounds of its soteriological system.[268] On the other hand, at a secondary and subordinate level, Paul does use the term "grace" in antithetical contexts, which suggests that in Pauline terms (not necessarily those of Judaism as a whole), the Christ-event evidences grace in a special form. This is explained by Watson partly in sociological terms and partly in terms of Paul's scriptural hermeneutics.

Sociologically, Paul evidences the contrast between a "static" form of grace (common to those born into a religion) and a "dynamic" form (common in conversionist movements); in the latter, the experience of divine agency is immediate and transformative.[269] Hermeneutically, Paul detects within the Scriptures a contrast between faith (as human acknowledgement of divine initiative) and Torah observance (the product of human agency), a contrast evident in Galatians 3:11-12 and Romans 10:5-8.[270] This highlights the special way in which Paul reads the Abrahamic promises; they are not only "prior," but also "unconditional," "irreversible," and "unilateral," in contrast to the way other Pentateuchal texts (e.g., Lev 18:5; Deut 30:19-20) present salvation as "conditional" and "contingent," dependent on the success of human agency in keeping the Torah.[271] Watson thus foregrounds the question of agency in a way parallel to the work of Martyn (3.5.4), although he is careful to clarify that Paul urges no absolute contrast between divine and human agencies (the believer is by no means rendered passive).[272] As with Martyn, the grace-perfections

268. This emphasis is preserved in *Paul, Judaism, and the Gentiles*, 2nd ed. (Grand Rapids: Eerdmans, 2007).

269. This motif is also taken over from the first into the revised version of *Paul, Judaism, and the Gentiles* (pp. 15-16, 126, 149-50, 265).

270. See Watson, *Paul, Judaism, and the Gentiles*, pp. 129-30, and idem, *Paul and the Hermeneutics of Faith* (Grand Rapids: Eerdmans, 2004), especially pp. 314-53.

271. *Paul and the Hermeneutics of Faith*, pp. 8, 183-208, 464-73.

272. *Paul and the Hermeneutics of Faith*, pp. 69 n. 79, 218, 464. For other explorations of the theme of grace in relation to divine and human agency, see J. M. G. Barclay and S. J.

of *incongruity* (God's gracious promise irrespective of human obedience) and *efficacy* ("God assumes total responsibility")[273] appear to be at work, together with a gesture toward *non-circularity,* if "unilateral" grace means that it requires no return.

This last motif becomes a significant theme in the work of Campbell. In his analysis of differing readings of Paul, Campbell posits a structural distinction between *conditional* (contractual) and *unconditional* salvation, a distinction that requires a "clear" definition of "grace."[274] A conditional scheme of salvation may *begin* with an unmerited act of God (in our terms, grace may be prior and incongruous), but it is revealed to be "contractual" if some human response is deemed *necessary* for salvation to be effective or complete (if there is, in fact, any necessary condition or criterion to be fulfilled on the human side).[275] An unconditional soteriology, on the other hand, is not simply "undeserved" but *requires no matching response.* According to Campbell, "the language of 'grace' commonly refers to *unconditional* actions by God that deliver salvation to a given constituency with no strings attached, as pure gift."[276] A human response may be appropriate, but it is *not necessary* or of any salvific significance: God's action has saving efficacy "in its own right" and leaves no element of uncertainty.[277] This places all the emphasis on divine agency (in exclusionary antithesis to human agency);[278] thus, Campbell insists that Paul's phrase πίστις Χριστοῦ (Gal 2:16; 3:22, etc.) be read not as "faith in Christ" (in his view, an "anthropocentric" reading that makes faith a human criterion for salvation) but as "the faith/faithfulness of

Gathercole, eds., *Divine and Human Agency in Paul and His Cultural Environment* (London: Continuum, 2006) (especially the essays by Westerholm, Watson, and Barclay); J. Maston, *Divine and Human Agency in Second Temple Judaism and Paul* (Tübingen: Mohr Siebeck, 2010).

273. *Paul and the Hermeneutics of Faith,* p. 199; it is not clear, however, whether this principle, relevant to the Abrahamic promise, would be applied by Watson to the operation of grace in believers' lives.

274. D. A. Campbell, *The Deliverance of God: An Apocalyptic Reading of Justification in Paul* (Grand Rapids: Eerdmans, 2009), pp. 100-105, 955 n. 14.

275. Thus, Campbell judges Sanders's model of covenantal nomism (in which Torah-observance is necessary to stay in the covenant) to be a form of conditional soteriology, not theoretically distinguishable from "legalism" and not inappropriately described as an "earning" of salvation (*Deliverance,* pp. 101-22).

276. Campbell, *Deliverance,* p. 100. From our discussion of the anthropology of gift (see chapter 1), we recognize the peculiarly modern notion of gift operating here. Cf. *Deliverance,* p. 27: if grace is merely undeserved and not also unconditional, "one wonders whether it really is 'grace' in the way that that signifier is usually defined theologically." No sources are cited for this "usual" definition.

277. Campbell, *Deliverance,* p. 101, with pp. 955-56 n. 14; cf. pp. 161, 956-57 n. 24.

278. Campbell, *Deliverance,* pp. 64-65, 185, 212.

Christ" (according to which the believer participates in the prior and effective faith of Christ).[279]

On the basis of this conceptual schema, Campbell contrasts an "apocalyptic," participatory reading of Pauline soteriology with "Justification Theory," a constellation of assumptions (contractual, conditional, voluntarist, and individualistic) which he finds to infect most readers of Paul, including the Reformers. Exegetically, he considers, the latter has its roots in a reading of Romans 1–4, with its "forensic" language of judgment and justification, and here another distinction emerges, between two "fundamentally different notions of God." In the justification model, God is viewed as "just," exercising punitive, retributive, and coercive justice; in the "apocalyptic" model (of Romans 5–8), God is characterized fundamentally by benevolence, not justice.[280] Campbell insists that Paul's gospel can be recovered only if one recognizes that the apocalyptic, benevolent God is the God advocated by the real Paul, while the "just" God of "Justification Theory" represents the view that Paul *opposes* in Romans. The material in Romans 1–4 that represents this view is to be heard as the voice of an opposing "teacher," or as Paul drawing out the illogicality of his opponent's position.[281]

Campbell's conceptual schema derives from an inner-Calvinist debate about different forms of "covenantal" theology.[282] It forms an extension of Reformation debates, and addresses a number of perceived dangers in contemporary Western theology.[283] In fact, it constitutes a particularly fine example of the "perfectionist" tendencies in theological discourse on grace. The motif of grace is drawn out on all fronts to logical conclusions and end-of-the line

279. Campbell, *Deliverance*, pp. 25-27, 256, 756. Campbell has written extensively on this topic elsewhere, e.g., *The Rhetoric of Righteousness in Romans 3:21-26* (Sheffield: JSOT Press, 1992); "Romans 1:17 — A *Crux Interpretum* for the ΠΙΣΤΙΣ ΧΡΙΣΤΟΥ Dispute," *JBL* 113 (1994): 265-85.

280. Campbell, *Deliverance of God*, pp. 15-16, 75-76; cf. 184, 192, 1110 n. 72 (Paul's God is "best not characterized by justice at all, in any sense").

281. Campbell, *Deliverance of God*, pp. 469-761.

282. See Campbell, *Deliverance*, pp. xxiv, 14-15, 212, 939-40 n. 10, with reference to the analysis of "Federal Calvinism" by J. B. Torrance. At times, Campbell seems aware that his conditional versus unconditional schema is distinctly "Western" (*Deliverance*, p. 465).

283. The modern issues are surveyed in *Deliverance*, pp. 284-309. Campbell sees himself as offering a more coherent version of Lutheran/Protestant insights (*Deliverance*, p. 934); for his critique of Luther and Calvin, see pp. 250-76. In our terms, where Luther tended toward the perfection of non-circularity (see 3.3.4) and Calvin perfected the efficacy of grace (but not its non-circularity: God *requires* the believer's Spirit-generated obedience; see 3.4.3), Campbell adopts both perfections of grace: there is *no* required response to grace, and in any case the constitutive agency in the Christian life is that of God.

extremes that rhetorically disqualify alternative construals as inadequate or misleading definitions of the term. Indeed, of all the authors we have surveyed in this chapter, Campbell is the only one to insist on *all six* possible perfections of grace (as analyzed in chapter 2): for him, grace is not only *superabundant* and *prior* (originating), and not only *incongruous* (undeserved) and *efficacious* (God's agency being all-sufficient), but also *singular* (God is benevolent and not just) and *non-circular* (there is no necessary human response, no "strings attached"). In perfecting the singularity of grace, Campbell sounds most like Marcion (deploying some of the same vocabulary; see above, 3.1); in perfecting its non-circularity, he develops a Lutheran motif into the characteristically modern form of the "pure gift." All the other interpreters we have surveyed have considered Paul an excellent theologian of grace without finding all six possible perfections, since they do not consider them all to be necessary constituents of its meaning. On Campbell's view, grace is only grace if perfected in all six possible dimensions, and Paul is taken to be the perfect exemplar of this phenomenon.

An equal and opposite approach is also possible: to take just one perfection as *the* definition of grace and to find it lacking not only in Second Temple Judaism but also (ultimately) in Paul. This is the thesis of VanLandingham, who starts from a modern dictionary definition of the grace of God as "the free and unmerited favor of God as manifested in the salvation of sinners and the bestowing of blessings."[284] This definition rests solely on the perfection of *incongruity,* the mismatch between the gift and the worth of the recipient. In VanLandingham's view, adjectives such as "pure," "free," and "unmerited" "stress the typical meaning of the terms, derived primarily from the letters of Paul, as God's favor given without respect to human merit, favor credited solely to God's initiative." Crucially, then, "God can never confer 'grace' as a recompense; for, indeed, the opposite of grace is reward for good behavior."[285] On the basis of this antithesis between grace and recompense (or grace and *quid pro quo*),[286] VanLandingham proceeds to investigate the structures of election and salvation in Second Temple Judaism and in Paul, in dialogue with Sanders's model of "covenantal nomism" (see 3.6.1). Everywhere in post-

284. *The Oxford English Dictionary,* vol. 4 (Oxford: Clarendon Press, 1961), p. 326, cited (along with other dictionaries and modern discussions of grace) in C. VanLandingham, *Judgment and Justification in Early Judaism and the Apostle Paul* (Peabody, MA: Hendrickson, 2006), p. 20 n. 8; cf. p. 116, where reference is made to grace "as defined by conventional canons."

285. Both citations are from VanLandingham, *Judgment,* p. 20.

286. *Quid pro quo* covers all forms of reward, merit, desert, and human "earning" (*Judgment,* p. 2 n. 1).

biblical Judaism, he finds evidence that the election of Israel, and even of the patriarchs, is "*not* a gift of God's grace, but a reward for good behavior."[287] Philo's presentation of Abraham's call as a reward for his search for God is a case in point: "considering . . . what 'grace' means, Philo's portrayal of Abraham's election cannot be characterized as such."[288] Since obedience to the Torah is necessary for final salvation, "salvation is earned, at least in the sense that there is a *quid pro quo* or cause and effect relationship between obedience to God in this age and eternal life in the next."[289] What is more, VanLandingham finds the same to be true of the final judgment according to works in Paul. Even if Paul speaks of forgiveness (justification) as undeserved grace at the *start* of the believer's life, *in the end* salvation is decided on the basis of obedience (not justification by faith), and is thus a matter of justice and reward, not grace.[290] Of course, the passages in Paul's letters that depict "judgment by works" (e.g., Rom 2:6-16) have long been a matter of controversy, and not only since the Reformation.[291] What VanLandingham adds to the debate is the thesis that these texts rule out any possibility of speaking of "grace" in Paul, if that term is defined according to a single and essential perfection.

What may we conclude from these heated and often confused debates in the wake of Sanders? In large measure, they revolve around unexamined assumptions and predetermined decisions concerning the meaning of the term "grace." Even when a definition is provided, its historical and cultural roots are generally left unexamined, as if the concept had some essential meaning across all times and cultures. That Sanders meant by "grace" the *priority* of God's initiative in election, but sometimes added the language of "unmerited" (that is, *incongruous*) grace, is one cause of the subsequent confusion. But it is also often the case that a particular definition, accorded a structural role in the thesis to be argued, is taken for granted as obvious, "typical," or "common."

287. VanLandingham, *Judgment*, p. 18 (italics original); cf. p. 333.

288. VanLandingham, *Judgment*, p. 27.

289. VanLandingham, *Judgment*, p. 333. Here and elsewhere (cf. pp. 64-65), VanLandingham takes exception to Sanders's use of the terms "free" and "unmerited" in relation to grace, i.e., those places where Sanders perfected grace in Judaism as not only prior, but also incongruous (see above, 3.6.1).

290. VanLandingham, *Judgment*, pp. 175-335.

291. For other recent discussion of these texts, see K. L. Yinger, *Paul, Judaism, and Judgment according to Deeds* (Cambridge: Cambridge University Press, 1999); K. Kim, *God Will Judge Each One according to Works: Judgment According to Works and Psalm 62 in Early Judaism and the New Testament* (Berlin: de Gruyter, 2010). I have offered a solution to some of the current dilemmas in J. M. G. Barclay, "Believers and the 'Last Judgment' in Paul: Rethinking Grace and Recompense," in H.-J. Eckstein, C. Landmesser, and H. Lichtenberger, eds., *Eschatologie — Eschatology* (Tübingen: Mohr Siebeck, 2011), pp. 195-208.

Many of the terms in this debate also turn out to be ambiguous: does "free" (as in "free grace") mean free from prior conditions in the recipient, unobliged, or unobliging, or some combination of these three? Does "unconditional" mean without prior conditions, without subsequent obligations, or both? Our analytical work in chapters 1 and 2 allows us to clarify the different assumptions at work in this scholarly maelstrom and to understand what is going on in straightforward terms: *different scholars are assuming different perfections of grace.* The resulting controversies are partly, but not only, due to assumptions inherited from the Reformation. More profoundly, they result from a lack of analytical clarity concerning grace, the most significant concept in this whole post-Sanders debate. By providing such clarity, I hope to be able to move decisively beyond this debate in the analysis of Paul, and of Paul's relationship to Judaism, offered below.

3.7.2. Alain Badiou

Among the European philosophers who have recently shown keen interest in Paul, Alain Badiou has offered the most comprehensive engagement with Pauline theology, including his theology of grace.[292] Since he has no religious commitment, and distances himself clearly from the "fable" at the heart of Paul's theology, Badiou's reactivation of Paul as a "contemporary" is derived from the *formal* features of Paul's thought rather than their religious content (4-15). In particular, he acclaims Paul as a seminal figure in the way he configures truth as founded in an *incalculable and unconditioned event* from which arises a radically new "militant" subjectivity, which is faithful to the event and (crucially) unconfined by cultural particularity. Reacting against both the false "universalism" of globalized capitalism and divisive forms of identity politics (based on ethnicity, nationality, or gender), Badiou explores how Paul conceives a form of universalism that is not limited by any com-

292. A. Badiou, *Saint Paul: La Fondation de l'universalisme* (Paris: Presses Universitaires de France, 1997); translated as *Saint Paul: The Foundation of Universalism,* trans. R. Brassier (Stanford: Stanford University Press, 2003). In what follows, citations and page numbers are from the French edition, with the equivalents in the English translation (ET) in parentheses. Other philosophers who have contributed to this new wave of engagement with Paul include: G. Agamben, *The Time That Remains: A Commentary on the Letter to the Romans,* trans. P. Dailey (Stanford: Stanford University Press, 2005 [original 2000]); S. Breton, *A Radical Philosophy of Saint Paul,* trans. J. N. Ballan, with introduction by W. Blanton (New York: Columbia University Press, 2011 [original 1998]). For a response to Badiou's reading of Paul by another philosopher, see S. Žižek, *The Ticklish Subject* (London: Verso, 1999), pp. 127-70.

munitarian aggregate ("ensemble"), either in its origin or in its horizon; it is addressed to all, traversing, but not erasing, all social and cultural differences. To render Paul useful in this context, Badiou offers a "secularized" version of his theology, including an interpretation of "grace" shorn of reference to God.[293] Nonetheless, his acute observations on the structure of Paul's theology have been acclaimed by many Pauline scholars, including those with theological investments in Paul.[294]

At the heart of Badiou's philosophy (and of his reading of Paul) is the notion of an event that ruptures history with a radical novelty, one which cannot be explained or even named within pre-existing categories of thought and practice.[295] For Paul, that event is the resurrection of Christ (which Badiou foregrounds and separates from the crucifixion): it constitutes a radical new beginning whose effect is the formation of a new human subject ("It is no longer I who live, but Christ who lives in me," Gal. 2:20). Badiou wishes to mark a clear distinction between the *site* of an event (the historical and cultural context in which it takes place; for Paul, the Jewish traditions through which the Christian message was expressed) and the *event itself*.[296] The reality-fracturing event takes place *in* a specific cultural and historical context, but is not constituted *by* it: it occurs without prior cause or assignable reason, and is therefore unconfined by the context in which it takes place. Readers of Badiou will notice how often the verb *surgir* is used in connection with the event, together with its cognates *surgissant* and *surgissement* (the verb rendered variously in translation as "erupt" or "suddenly emerge").[297] The event is not just a new departure in the ongoing flow of history; it is an interruption that breaks away from pre-existing structures of sense and legality. It is neither accounted for, nor structured by, any general truth or pre-formed community,

293. Badiou's aim is to "secularize" grace and "arracher le lexique de la grâce et de la rencontre à son enfermement religieux" ("to tear the lexicon of grace and of encounter from its religious confinement"), *Saint Paul*, p. 70 (ET: 66).

294. See, e.g., the partly critical but also strongly appreciative reception of Badiou by D. Martin and D. Boyarin in J. D. Caputo and L. M. Alcoff, eds., *St. Paul among the Philosophers* (Indianapolis: Indiana University Press, 2009); and by S. Fowl and others in D. Harink, ed., *Paul, Philosophy, and the Theopolitical Vision* (Eugene: Cascade Books, 2010).

295. See A. Badiou, *L'être et événement* (Paris: Seuill, 1990); translated as *Being and Event*, trans. O. Feltham (New York: Continuum, 2005). A short and accessible account of Badiou's thought can be found in A. Badiou, *Ethics: An Essay on the Understanding of Evil*, trans. P. Hallward (London: Verso, 2001). Among the many critical evaluations of Badiou's philosophy, see P. Hallward, *Badiou: A Subject to Truth* (Minneapolis: University of Minnesota Press, 2003).

296. See, e.g., *Saint Paul*, pp. 23-24, 26, 74-75 (ET: 22-23, 25, 70-71). Badiou returns to this difficult issue in his *Logiques des Mondes* (Paris: Seuill, 2006).

297. See, e.g., *Saint Paul*, pp. 12, 19, 28, 29, 38 (ET: 11, 18, 27, 28, 36).

but is "absolutely new," "pure event, opening of an epoch, transformation of the relations between the possible and the impossible."[298] Because it is not limited by previously existent conditions or qualifications the event is of completely universal significance: it is both utterly singular ("one") and "for all." Thus, for Paul, the discourse arising from the Christ-event does not arise from nor conform to either Jewish or Greek discourses (1 Cor 1:18-25). It is borne by a presently small community of those who are faithful to this event, but the message they carry is destined for all and true for all, and is not intended to form a new, exclusive identity.[299] Because the event itself is "subtracted" from all pre-constituted communities, it is detached from every particularism: because it comes from nowhere, it goes everywhere. "The sudden emergence of the Christian subject is unconditioned."[300]

Badiou thus traces in Paul a form of universalism that is not simply another hegemonic particularism masquerading as "universal" (and thus vulnerable to postmodern critiques of "universalism"). Neither does it erase differences in imposing a uniform "sameness." In this connection, Badiou employs the metaphor of the "diagonal." The truth declared by those reconstituted by the event neither affirms nor rejects cultural and historical particularity: it crosses them "at a diagonal."[301] It operates in and across social and cultural differences, but is indifferent to them, because it recognizes nothing "real" in the distinctions they maintain. Hence Paul can be "all things to all people" (1 Cor 9:22), and his converts can be faithful to the truth, remaining within, but not beholden to, their various cultural traditions and social positions. Indeed, they themselves have no singular or stable identity, since their own subjectivity is divided by the "truth-process" of which they are part. They live in a perpetual state of "becoming," being both in the flesh and in the spirit, a state of "not . . . but" that is continually activated in their persisting conviction and in their labor of love.[302]

Paul's theology of grace plays a central role within this structure of thought. "Grace" is, in fact, one way of naming the event, and everything that is said about grace has the character of the event ("la grâce événementielle," 67; "evental grace," 63). For Badiou, grace as "pure givenness" is characterized

298. *Saint Paul,* pp. 46, 47: "absolument nouveau," "événement pur, ouverture d'une époque, changement des rapports entre le possible et l'impossible" (ET: 43, 45).

299. Badiou thus views the Pauline churches not as exclusive sects, a sub-group with their own particular truth, but as carriers of a universal truth, like the French resistance movement during World War II, *Saint Paul,* p. 21 (ET: 20).

300. *Saint Paul,* p. 19: "Le surgissement du sujet chrétien est inconditionné" (ET: 18).

301. *Saint Paul,* pp. 15, 29, 46, 105-7 (ET: 14, 28, 43, 98-100).

302. *Saint Paul,* pp. 59-68, 91-103 (ET: 55-64, 86-97).

by an "excess" or "superabundance," which is not the plenitude of something that can be known or calculated, but is "incalculable," beyond the categories and forms of thought that go into counting.[303] It is thus in a strong sense "supernumerary": it escapes the structures (and strictures) of law and convention, and thus the rites and restrictions of the Jewish law ("you are not under law but under grace," Rom 6:14). Understood in non-religious terms, Paul is speaking of the kind of chance or contingency that happens to someone but is immediately recognizable as the truth that henceforth structures their existence (e.g., falling in love, or a new scientific intuition, or the sudden eruption of revolutionary politics, as in 1968).[304] In Paul's own terms, he is speaking of the grace that breaks out of the particularities and predications of law (its necessarily limiting role in defining and partitioning what it controls). Indeed, it is "translegal" in another sense, in that it comes "without being due," as Romans 4:4-5 makes clear. "This is a profound insight of Paul's, which, through its universal and illegal understanding of the One, undoes every particular or communitarian incorporation of the subject. . . . *That which founds a subject cannot be what is due to it.*"[305] Because the subject is founded on grace, as a "pure gift" irrespective of what is due, and without assignable qualification or cause, Paul's message is addressed to *everyone* without any social, ethnic, cultural, or psychological condition. "There is for Paul an essential link between the 'for all' of the universal and the 'without cause.' There is an address for all only according to that which is without cause. Only what is absolutely gratuitous can be addressed to all. Only charisma and grace measure up to a universal problem."[306]

Badiou thus finds central to Paul the perfections we have named as *superabundance* and *incongruity.* Whereas superabundance is normally assumed without special notice in the history of reception of Paul, Badiou makes special play of this motif because it signifies for him a notion of "excess" that breaks with the normal rules of thought and convention. Superabundant grace is not just more of what we know, but something we do not and cannot know

303. *Saint Paul,* pp. 60, 67-69, 82, 85 (ET: 57, 63-65, 78, 81).

304. *Saint Paul,* pp. 102, 113 (ET: 96, 106); on the four spheres of event (science, love, art, politics), see *Saint Paul,* pp. 12-14 (ET: 12-13).

305. *Saint Paul,* p. 81: "Il y a là une intuition profonde de Paul, qui défait, par sa compréhension universelle et illégalle de l'Un, toute incorporation particulière, ou communautaire, du sujet. . . . *Ce qui fonde un subject ne peut être ce que lui est dû*" (italics original; ET: 77).

306. *Saint Paul,* p. 81: "Entre le 'pour tous' de l'universel and le 'sans cause,' il y a pour Paul un lien essentiel. Il n'y a d'adresse à tous qu'au régime du sans cause. N'est addressable à tous que ce qui et absolument gratuit. Seul le charisma, la grâce, sont à la mesure d'un problème universel" (ET: 77).

in advance, and thus something that crosses the prefigured boundaries and particularities that divide one human being from another. Indeed, as excess, as the exceptional "but," it has a nomadic, de-centered existence that cannot be confined in any community, including the community of the faithful.[307] Thus understood, the notion of superabundance is connected closely to the incongruity of grace, its misfit with expectations of what is necessary, proper, possible, or due. Grace therefore becomes the key to Paul's universalism, his mission to all, Gentiles as well as Jews, because it is unconditioned by qualification or worth; it is the dynamic that creates his freedom from the limiting conditions of ethnic or cultural particularity. "Pure gift" or "absolute gratuity" means for Badiou this liberating incongruity, offering an alternative to the current alliance between global capitalism and closed identities. In his interpretation of grace as event and rupture, there are clearly parallels between Badiou's configuration of Pauline theology and those of Barth, Bultmann, and Martyn; indeed, here, and in his reading of Paul as anti-philosopher, there are strong resonances between this non-theological reading of Paul and the Lutheran tradition of interpretation. What is striking is the way that Badiou (like Käsemann) traces the significance of *incongruous grace* beyond the individual domain, finding here the root of Paul's universal mission and the resource that enables him to reconfigure reality in the social and political domains. At a time when theological readings of Paul oriented to the individual have largely lost their cultural salience, Badiou, as a political philosopher standing outside the theological tradition, offers a reading of Paul's theology of grace that attracts attention not least because of its relevance to the social and political dilemmas of the contemporary world.

3.7.3. New Research on Grace and Benefaction in the Roman World

Finally, we may note the recent flurry of research that has positioned Paul's theology of grace within the context of the ancient systems of benefaction and patronage that we surveyed in chapter 1 (1.2). Building on earlier research by Wetter,[308] which examined the use of χάρις in its Hellenistic and "oriental" contexts, scholars have shown a new interest in the ways in which this and related terms were used in the inscriptions honoring Greek or Roman bene-

307. *Saint Paul,* p. 82, speaks of the "nomadisme de la gratuité" (ET: the "nomadism of gratuitousness," 78).

308. G. P. Wetter, *Charis: Ein Beitrag zur Geschichte des ältesten Christentums* (Leipzig: Hinrichs Buchhandlung, 1913), pp. 6-200.

factors, and whether, or in what respects, Paul's configuration of this motif was distinctive.[309] Thus Joubert, using the interpretative framework of benefit exchange, highlights the religious dimensions of the collection for Jerusalem: by including God in this transaction, Paul establishes a three-way reciprocal dynamic that shifts attention from the normal desire for return or reward.[310] In Joubert's view, Paul emphasizes the inner disposition of the giver and promotes a form of "selfless giving," "irrespective of the reaction on the side of the recipient," a kind of non-circular gift.[311] In parallel terms, Peterman urges that divine reward for the human giver (in his view, a uniquely Jewish notion) removes the sense of debt or obligation typically imposed on the recipient of a gift. Paul thus modifies the normal rules of reciprocity at a highly significant point.[312]

Harrison has offered the fullest analysis of Pauline theology in the ancient context of gift-reciprocity.[313] He documents in detail how the term χάρις constituted a leitmotif of Greco-Roman systems of benefaction, with a pool of associations on which Paul drew in both his theology and his ethics. Nonetheless, according to Harrison, Paul wished to "up-end" the reciprocity ideologies of antiquity; in the context of the Greco-Roman world, his construal of grace constituted a social and not just a theological *novum*.[314] Paul's theology of grace (dubbed "unilateral," "free," "sovereign," and "unmerited") constituted a "radical alternative to the Graeco-Roman benefaction system," quite different from typical notions of a "reciprocal contract."[315] The contrast is not always simple: Paul sometimes "moves cautiously, affirming many of the traditional

309. Seminal in this regard was F. W. Danker, *Benefactor: Epigraphic Study of a Greco-Roman and New Testament Semantic Field* (St. Louis: Clayton Publishing House, 1982). For a wider cultural survey of the language of χάρις, see D. Zeller, *Charis bei Philon und Paulus* (Stuttgart: Verlag Katholisches Bibelwerk, 1990), pp. 13-32.

310. S. Joubert, *Paul as Benefactor: Reciprocity, Strategy, and Theological Reflection in Paul's Collection* (Tübingen: Mohr Siebeck, 2000), pp. 149-50, 201-3, 216.

311. Joubert, *Paul as Benefactor,* pp. 7, 217. Cf. D. J. Downs, *The Offering of the Gentiles: Paul's Collection for Jerusalem in Its Chronological, Cultural, and Cultic Contexts* (Tübingen: Mohr Siebeck, 2008), emphasizing the theological dimensions of the collection (in the Pauline metaphors of "worship" and "harvest") such that the return for the gift goes mainly to God, and not to the human beneficiaries (pp. 132-34, 158, 163-65).

312. G. W. Peterman, *Paul's Gift from Philippi: Conventions of Gift Exchange and Christian Giving* (Cambridge: Cambridge University Press, 1997), pp. 157-60, 194, 199.

313. J. R. Harrison, *Paul's Language of Grace in its Graeco-Roman Context* (Tübingen: Mohr Siebeck, 2003). In what follows, numbers in parentheses in the main text represent page numbers in this book.

314. *Paul's Language of Grace,* pp. 287-88; cf. 20-21, 343, 350. Harrison speaks in this connection of the "darker side" of ancient benefaction practices (pp. 166, 347).

315. *Paul's Language of Grace,* pp. 287, 35; for the epithets, see, e.g., pp. 18, 35 (unilateral), 322 (free), 124 (sovereign), 346 (unmerited).

reciprocity conventions of the household" (e.g., in relation to Philemon, 349), yet "where the apostle does countenance reciprocity rituals, it is usually in a highly qualified way" (343). The matter clearly requires a nuanced treatment.

In relation to divine gift-giving, Harrison's conclusion is strong: "Only the grace of Christ — in sharp contrast to the beneficence of the gods and human beings — is unilateral, not reciprocal" (288). "Not reciprocal" here means, primarily, non-obliged, God's giving being neither solicited nor required by human piety or gift. Harrison represents religious gifts and sacrifices in the ancient world as a way of putting the gods under obligation (56-57, 87, 191, 211), a "contractual" system by which the gods are "manipulated" into giving to humans (245, 284, 350). On this system, God rewards merit, and justification comes by works (113, 123, 346). By contrast, Paul's God, the God of "unilateral" covenant grace (100-101, 345-46), extends his giving to the ungrateful and unworthy (219, 225, 267, 351). Such "unconditioned generosity" (165) is here dubbed "unilateral." Does this also mean that God's giving requires no return? At one point, following Käsemann, Harrison notes that "according to Paul, the acceptance of divine beneficence imposes an obligation to live worthily of the Benefactor" (247; cf. 287). But elsewhere, "Paul spotlights the fact that the grace of Christ expected no requital. The humiliation and self-sacrifice of the incarnation is totally other-centred" (266). It seems that several different perfections (priority, incongruity, and non-circularity) are at play in Harrison's analysis of divine gift, but are not clearly articulated or distinguished. As he insists, whatever humans return to God is in no way commensurate with God's giving (271, 284-85, 321), but this does not itself establish whether God's gifts are, or are not, intended to elicit some return.

In relation to human gift-giving, Harrison finds Paul to emphasize "grace rather than obligation" (331). Giving should be voluntary, joyful, and spontaneous, not wrung out of givers by the "shameful and bitter obligation" of reciprocity (347; cf. 246, 271) — although this, as we have noted (see above, 1.1-2), was common to all gifts in antiquity, where notions of "freedom" and "obligation" were hardly antithetical. More significantly, Harrison suggests that the grace exercised by the human giver "neither demands nor expects commensurate return" (299). Even so, there are texts that suggest otherwise: Harrison finds in Paul a "struggle . . . to achieve the fine balance between the freedom of grace and the obligation it imposes: that is, between the freedom to serve without the expectation of recompense and the obligation of continuously reciprocating the debt of love" (331).

Once again, these complexities (or confusions) could have been clarified by distinguishing between different perfections of gift. In particular, Harrison's pervasive antithesis between "grace" and "reciprocity" seems to conflate two kinds of perfection. It is one thing to say that God's grace is *incongruous,* unconditioned by the prior worth of the recipient; it is quite another to construe it as (in our sense) *non-circular,* putting the recipient under no obligation or demand. Like "unconditional," the term "unilateral" seems ambiguous: it may refer either to the absence of *previous conditions* or to the absence of *subsequent expectations,* or both. Here as elsewhere, there is much to be gained by applying the kind of analytical differentiations suggested in chapter 2; then we will know more precisely what we do, or do not, mean by "grace."

CHAPTER 4

Summary and Conclusions to Part I

The three interrelated chapters of this Part have laid the foundations for the following parts of this book by establishing a new frame in which to analyze "grace." We have located this topic within the anthropology of gift (1.1), a terrain whose scope embraces many forms of benefaction, favor, and service beyond what most Western cultures label as "gifts." Paul, like his contemporaries, described both human and divine gifts in the same terms, drawing from a broad lexical pool of related vocabulary (see Appendix: The Lexicon of Gift). The anthropology of gift encompasses that breadth in a way that includes, but is not limited by, theological discourse on "grace." This anthropological point of entry also gives us perspective on the special connotations that have become attached to "grace," while simultaneously providing some analytical distance from the cultural assumptions of the modern, Western world.

Anthropology offers no model of "the gift" and provides no single definition, but it alerts us to the dynamics of reciprocity, power, and obligation that have been common in gift-relations, but are easily missed or misconstrued. Studies of gift-giving in pre-modern societies are of particular heuristic value in raising questions worth testing against ancient sources. In particular, we have noted that:

(i) gifts are generally given in order to create or reproduce social bonds; they foster mutuality, and for this reason are typically neither unilateral nor anonymous;

(ii) the rules of reciprocity raise the expectation of return, even in unequal social relations and even if the return is generally different from the gift in quantity and kind;

(iii) the recipient of the gift is under a strong though non-legal obligation to reciprocate;

(iv) the gift is often associated with the person of the giver, and is therefore, to some degree, "inalienable";
(v) reflecting this personal investment, gifts are usually construed as voluntary and expressive of goodwill, even if they arise from pre-existing bonds of obligation;
(vi) thus, gifts and counter-gifts may be both voluntary and obligatory at the same time, and similarly both "interested" and "disinterested." The scrambling of these categories does not cohere with modern concepts of "altruism," "the pure gift," and "the gift without strings."

These observations do not constitute "results" that can be universalized or a timeless essence of the gift, but they do suggest dynamics that may be present in our sources. If nothing else, they suggest that modern, Western assumptions about gifts serve us poorly in analyzing the language and practice of antiquity. To gain further precision, we have sketched the practices and ideologies of gift-reciprocity in the Greco-Roman world (1.2), a domain that we have taken to include ancient Judaism, despite its special emphasis on the certainty of return *from God* (1.2.4). We have traced some of the social relations inflected by gift and gift-reciprocity, from small-scale practices of neighborly support to lavish civic euergetism and Roman senatorial or imperial patronage. Relations between humans and gods have evidenced similar patterns of gift-exchange. In particular, we have emphasized that in the Greco-Roman world:

(i) gifts were assumed to create social ties and were not generally designed as one-way, unreciprocated donations;
(ii) the rules of reciprocity placed the recipient under obligation to offer a return, a debt that could clash with other social responsibilities (creating, in our terms, the problem of the "bribe");
(iii) gift-relations were generally distinguished from loan, sale, and pay, while sharing some vocabulary and much of the reciprocal structure of *quid pro quo*. Gifts were taken to be characterized by personal, enduring, and voluntary relations of goodwill, escaping calculation and legal enforcement;
(iv) because gifts created ties and expected returns, donors generally ensured that gifts were distributed discriminately, to fitting or worthy recipients; "worth" could be variously defined, but even (or especially) for the gods/God, the proper distribution of significant gifts required careful selection;
(v) philosophical reflection on the gift, of which Seneca's *De Beneficiis* was our prime examplar (1.2.5), recognized multiple difficulties in the practice of benefaction but did not remove gift-giving from the sphere of circular exchange. Stoic focus on the spirit of the giver (and recipient)

de-emphasized the material value of the gift and the utility of the return; but it was designed to foster mutually beneficial relations and did not regard a return as sullying or annulling the gift.

Within such parameters, there was considerable latitude in definition, perception, and practice. Many forms of exchange were sufficiently ambiguous to be construed either as gift or as some other form of transaction. Either party in human relations (and in relations between humans and gods) might wish to *negotiate* their relationship as "gift." Accordingly, our survey has attempted not to *delimit* what Paul or his contemporaries could consider gifts, but to clarify the vocabularies, social repertoires, and ideological assumptions available to them. How they spoke and acted within this domain could be traditional or creative, conservative or revolutionary. Only the study of individual examples can reveal how each navigated this terrain.

Our attempts to comprehend ancient conceptions of the gift have resulted in relativizing modern assumptions, especially the Western notion of the "pure gift" (1.3). We have suggested in outline the gradual transformations that have shaped the distinctively modern ideal of a gift-without-return. In this sketch, large-scale social, political, and economic changes were connected to the emergence of the preference for the one-way gift. This latter may have roots in Lutheran theology, but was universalized in Kantian ethics with its resistance to externally imposed obligation. We have thus become wary of the protestations of Derrida and others that a gift is truly such only if it entails no reciprocity or return. That peculiarly modern presumption does *not* correspond to the assumptions of antiquity and should not be allowed to determine what Paul or his fellow Jews might have understood by the grace or gifts of God.

A second feature of this Part has been the construction of a taxonomy that classified different possible "perfections" of grace (chapter 2). We have noted the tendency to draw the theme of gift/grace to an end-of-the-line extreme, especially for polemical purposes and in relation to God; and we have observed the variety of forms that this "perfecting" tendency can take. Since gift-giving is a complex social relation, it is possible to "perfect" grace (to define its essence in some "pure" or "ultimate" form) in a number of ways. We have identified six possible perfections:

(i) *superabundance:* the supreme scale, lavishness, or permanence of the gift;
(ii) *singularity:* the attitude of the giver as marked solely and purely by benevolence;
(iii) *priority:* the timing of the gift before the recipient's initiative;

(iv) *incongruity:* the distribution of the gift without regard to the worth of the recipient;
(v) *efficacy:* the impact of the gift on the nature or agency of the recipient;
(vi) *non-circularity:* the escape of the gift from an ongoing cycle of reciprocity.

These perfections are all evidenced in antiquity or in the history of ideas concerning gift or grace, and their variety has ensured that grace has acquired multiple connotations. Importantly, the perfection of one facet of grace does not require or imply the perfection of all (or any) of the others: they do not constitute a "package." Theologians, including interpreters of Paul, have often perfected grace in one or another of these forms, and sometimes in a cluster, but not always in the same ways. Thus, differences between interpreters frequently amount not to greater or lesser *degrees of emphasis* on grace but to *the perfection of different facets* of this motif. However, interpreters may regard their particular construal of grace as its essential, defining characteristic, and so disqualify others. This phenomenon may help to account for long-running disputes about the meaning of grace. When two authors speak of grace, but disagree on its meaning and its implications, this may be not because one "believes in" or "emphasizes" grace more than the other, but because each is concerned to draw out a different perfection of this multifaceted concept.

Our long third chapter has illustrated this phenomenon by tracing shifting patterns in the perfection of grace among interpreters of Paul, from Marcion to the present day. Through in-depth analysis of select, but pivotal, figures in the history of the reception of Paul, we have achieved several goals:

(i) Reaching into the past has clarified a number of current debates, whose historical roots are not always articulated or understood. Augustine and Luther stand behind the most recent discussions of Paul, even (in fact, especially) in the case of those who reject that heritage. Thus, both Sanders and his critics are generally dependent on pre-formed assumptions about the meaning of grace, while Martyn can be understood only by appreciating his inheritance from Barth and Käsemann, and his reaction against Bultmann. Without a long perspective, one can hardly comprehend, let alone contribute to, contemporary debates on such historically charged topics.
(ii) Using the taxonomy developed in chapter 2, we have attempted to disentangle the varied ways in which "grace" has been perfected in the history of interpretation. Interpreters have essentialized "grace" in different ways, not because χάρις and *gratia* are polysemous terms, but because divine gift-giving can be perfected in any of the six ways described. We

have thus gained the capacity to scrutinize what is meant when grace is hailed as "free," "pure," "unconditional," "gratuitous," "alone," or the like. Disagreements can be illumined: as we have noted, both Augustine and Pelagius were theologians of grace, but they perfected this concept in different ways. The differences between the Reformers and their Catholic contemporaries, between Luther and Calvin, and between Sanders and his critics, can all be clarified by this analytical tool, which explains not only *that* they are different, but also *why.* Our survey has shown that it is neither necessary nor common to perfect grace in all six dimensions; in fact, only Campbell appears to have made this attempt.

(iii) We are thus equipped to ask different questions concerning Second Temple Judaism. The issue is not whether Judaism is a "religion of grace," or whether Jewish constructions of grace are "watered down." Our question becomes at once more complex and less loaded: where Jewish texts speak of the grace or mercy of God, do they perfect this concept, and if so, how? We can now observe *different* Jewish perfections of grace without presuming that any one is necessary or proper, or that all will be the same.

(iv) Paul's relation to Second Temple Judaism should not be confined to two current but overly simplistic options: either Paul advocated grace against a grace-less and "legalistic" Judaism, or Paul was in full agreement with all his fellow Jews on the character of grace. We may start with a simpler question: *how do Paul's perfections of grace compare with those of his fellow Jews?* If there is diversity on this matter among Second Temple Jews, Paul needs to be placed neither *over against* his fellow Jews, nor in *total agreement* with them. Without presuming any essential or superior definition of this motif, our task is simply to locate Paul's position on a complex and variegated map.

(v) Since no perfection of grace can be regarded as its core characteristic, or its *sine qua non,* we are under no pressure to prove or to disprove that Paul is the bearer of some "essential" meaning. Nor can we assume that the more perfections of grace, the better. In fact, we may be wary of the tendency to pile perfections on top of each other, or to extend single perfections to a greater and greater extreme. Such tendencies may serve ideological interests, but there is no reason to think that the greater the number of perfections, the better the concept of grace.

(vi) History teaches hermeneutical self-consciousness. Our studies have revealed how historical and polemical contexts have fostered varied perfections of grace. Equipped to relativize every definition (even those in dictionaries), we are also made aware of our own contexts and interests in interpreting the texts. No reading is completely disinterested; every reading, including the one advanced here, reflects contemporary concerns and responsibilities. The present book makes no attempt to pretend otherwise (see Prologue).

It is time to get to the texts themselves, armed with the analytical resources and the hermeneutical self-consciousness provided in Part I. Freed from some of the assumptions that frame current debates, we explore first some texts from Second Temple Judaism (Part II). Thereafter, we will turn to Paul's own letters, examining his theology of grace first in Galatians (Part III) and then in Romans (Part III).

PART II

Divine Gift in Second Temple Judaism

At the start of the Abraham narrative, God issues a command and a striking promise of blessing: "Go from your country and your kindred and your father's house to the land that I will show you. I will make of you a great nation, and I will bless you, and make your name great, so that you will be a blessing" (Gen 12:1-2). From this beginning, and from Abraham's obedience to this command, spring the covenant promises of innumerable and eternal "seed" and of the land they are to be given — ancestral "oaths" that form the foundation of the relationship between God and Israel thereafter. How should one understand this divine act of favor? Was the initiative wholly God's, or did it reflect the fact that Abraham's family had made a prior pilgrimage (Gen 11:31-32)? Why did God make these stupendous promises to Abraham? Was the choice completely indiscriminate, without regard to his quality, or was it a fitting election of a man worthy of the call, like righteous Noah who found favor in God's eyes (Gen 6:8-9)? Should one presume from Gen 17:1 that Abraham's character was blameless, or on the way to becoming so? And did the promises spring from his obedience to God, as Gen 22:15-18 might suggest ("because you have done this . . .")? Or was the promise unconditioned, without regard to Abraham's work or worth?

The opening chapters of Deuteronomy, which look back to the "covenant with your ancestors" (Deut 4:31; 7:8; 9:5), place heavy emphasis on the divine initiative in "love." Addressing a community with a history of disloyalty to God, Moses enquires why God had "set his heart" on them and would give them victory on entering the land: not because of their size (7:7-8), nor due to their strength (8:17), nor because of their own righteousness (9:4-6), but only because of God's covenant promises, and because of the wickedness of the nations they will supplant (7:8; 8:18; 9:5-7). So, does God's action in history take account of the worthlessness of other nations but not the worthlessness of Israel? Is God's election of Israel therefore arbitrary, or does it have some deep rationale? Does the repeated reference to the ancestors who received the covenant promises suggest that they, at least, were a worthy foundation?

That God's actions follow some moral order, enshrined in his law, is suggested by the fact that his election of Israel requires a return. Moses' appeal in these chapters is for Israel to keep God's laws, setting before them both blessing and curse: blessing if they obey the commandments of God, curse if they do not (Deut 11:26-27). The God of love is also the God of "jealousy" and anger, the God who "maintains the covenant and steadfast love (חסד; ἔλεος) to those who love him and keep his commandments to a thousand generations, and who repays in their own person those who reject him" (Deut 7:9-10). This double image of God, who both punishes the wicked and is faithful to those who obey him, is enshrined in the Decalogue itself (Deut 5:9-10: cf. Exod 20:5-6). Indeed, it is dramatically acted out in the immediate aftermath of the giving of the law at Sinai, where the idolatry of the Golden Calf leads to judgment (Exod 32), but also to the revelation of God's nature as:

> a God merciful and gracious, slow to anger and abounding in steadfast love and faithfulness, keeping steadfast love for the thousandth generation, forgiving iniquity and transgression and sin, yet by no means clearing the guilty, but visiting the iniquity of the parents upon the children and the children's children to the third and fourth generation. (Exod 34:6-7)

Should the two halves of this double image be given equal weight, or does the prior and expansive list of gracious attributes suggest that benefaction and mercy are God's primary and abiding characteristics?[1]

With a set of narratives and a pool of texts as rich, complex, and open-ended as these, there is clearly space for deep and diverse reflection in subsequent Jewish tradition on the goodness and benevolence of God. Our task is to explore how Jewish writings handle such texts and associated questions during the Second Temple period.[2] Do they "perfect" divine benevolence in any of the ways we have classified in chapter 2, and if so, how? Is there a difference between the language-pools of "gift/benefaction" and "mercy/compassion," and between texts written in Greek or in Hebrew? Do they perfect divine benevolence in the same way, or is there significant diversity at this point? Do

1. Cf. the echoes of this text in Psalm 86:5; 103:8-10; 145:8-9; Joel 2:13; Jonah 4:2.

2. The "Second Temple" period is here defined flexibly, stretching beyond 70 CE to the end of the first century. The texts here chosen all date from the last two centuries of this period (100 BCE to 100 CE).

they all consider God's "grace" to be *prior,* and is this priority rooted in history, or in a previous, pre-creational decision of divine predetermination? Is God's goodness perfected in its *singularity* (as his sole characteristic), or is it balanced with an equal emphasis on his punishment of evildoers? Does God give "with no strings attached" (as a *non-circular gift*), or do his gifts carry obligations and the responsibility to respond in obedience? Is God's goodness *efficacious,* transforming the agency of those it affects? Are God's gifts and mercies *superabundant,* and if so with what scope? Finally, is God's benevolence given without regard to worth (an *incongruous* gift), or is it distributed discriminately, to people who, on one ground or another, are deemed fitting recipients?

As we shall discover, Second Temple Jewish texts discuss all these questions, rarely in abstract form, but in relation to the politically turbulent and intellectually fertile circumstances in which they were written. Historical experience and philosophical education both questioned the rationale for God's election of Israel, and whether or why his choice was irrevocable. It was important to determine whether God's "steadfast love" to Israel was finally without condition, or whether it made sense within a universalizable order of reason and morality. How were God's justice and his mercy to be correlated, and was it problematic to speak of his anger and his punishment of sin, which cause evil to humans? In a time of political disappointment, not least after 70 CE, it was natural to ask whether God's "steadfast love" to Israel had failed, or would be restored, and if so, to whom. Was God's benevolence restricted to the righteous in Israel, and did such a category exist? Had he selected a remnant, an Israel-within-Israel, and if so, was that choice conditioned by this group's worth, or was it an act of incongruous mercy, justified by nothing other than his gracious will?

The depth and complexity of these questions resist reduction to a simple matrix of analysis. Sanders's model of "covenantal nomism," for all its benefit in banishing a pejorative representation of Judaism, proves too flat to be useful in this regard. In our analysis of his work (see above, 3.6.1), we have shown how his emphasis on sequence (distinguishing the stages of "getting in" and "staying in") gave primary attention to the *priority* of grace/mercy, and was largely content to identify this as the common denominator of Palestinian Judaism. But the resulting homogeneity of the texts, when analyzed on these terms, does less than justice to their diversity and complexity. In our terms, a common emphasis on the priority of God's benevolence captures only one of the six possible perfections of grace. If prior grace is (arguably) everywhere, this does not make grace everywhere the same: there is ample room for diversity in relation to the singularity, efficacy, or incongruity of this grace. In fact, as we saw, Sanders tends to assume that the grace of the covenant is also incongruous ("unmerited"), on the basis of a deep (but unexamined) assumption that grace and desert are incompatible in principle. But, as our anthropological and historical studies have shown, there is no reason to assume that divine gifts of grace must be unmerited and unconditioned, placed in principled antithesis to reward, recompense, or worth. If we resist these (modern dictionary) definitions of grace, we are free to observe where texts differ on this point, some perfecting the incongruity of grace, but most for good reason declining to do so.

As we have seen (3.7.1), Sanders's treatment of "grace" has led to considerable confusion in subsequent debates on the nature of Second Temple Judaism. Some have taken the priority of grace to define Judaism as a "religion of grace" (as opposed to a religion of "works-righteousness"); others have detected aspects of reward and conditioned gift, and thereby deduced a deficiency in the Jewish understanding of "grace" or an irreducible tension between irreconcilable perspectives. Hidden Christian presumptions often emerge in this debate via the deployment of loaded categories ("grace alone," "synergism," "Pelagianism"), making more urgent the need for a different form of analysis. We are now able to provide an alternative analytical frame that departs from Sanders's model of "covenantal nomism." Building on the anthropological and historical studies of chapter 1, we have offered a taxonomy of the possible "perfections" of grace (chapter 2), which allows for a less loaded and more complex mode of investigation. Making no presumptions about the "essence" of grace, or its superior or inferior forms, our task is to assess in what ways our texts perfect this theme, and to analyze why.

I have chosen five texts (or authors) for analysis in this part, representing five different voices from Second Temple Judaism. I make no claim that these are representative of the whole gamut of Second Temple viewpoints, and one could certainly add other texts that make our topic a central theme.[3] I have selected texts from both Palestine and the Diaspora, originally written in both Hebrew and Greek, conscious of how different cultural and linguistic environments can affect Jewish theology on this topic (for the linguistics, see the Appendix). Our texts range from the first century BCE (the Qumran *Hodayot* and, perhaps, *The Wisdom of Solomon*) to c. 100 CE *(4 Ezra)*, though I have chosen to treat our two Diaspora authors first (*The Wisdom of Solomon* and Philo), before three from the homeland (Pseudo-Philo's *Liber Antiquitatum*

3. For instance, *Psalms of Solomon, Sirach, Letter of Aristeas,* and *2 Baruch.* From a later period, the rabbinic texts offer rich examples of further debate on this theme (see F. Avemarie, *Tora und Leben: Untersuchungen zur Heilsbedeutung der Tora in der frühen rabbinischen Literatur* [Tübingen: Mohr Siebeck, 1996]).

Biblicarum, the Qumran *Hodayot*, and *4 Ezra*). We will conclude this Part (chapter 10) by drawing our findings together. By then, I hope, the value of our taxonomy of perfections of grace will have become clear.

CHAPTER 5

The Wisdom of Solomon

The Wisdom of Solomon is a skillful amalgam of Jewish traditions and genres, whose stylistic and thematic consistency encourages us to read the text as a coherent whole, whatever the origin of its various parts.[4] The variety in focus leads most interpreters to posit a three-part structure, although the author's careful stitching of the seams makes precise definition of units difficult, and perhaps unhelpful.[5] The opening address to rulers exposes and refutes a world-view that espouses the futility and injustice of life (1:1–6:25). The central section personifies and eulogizes the Wisdom that regulates the cosmos, offering saving instruction to those, like Solomon, who earnestly desire her (6:12–10:21). A final section retells the story of the Exodus, matching the plagues with the means of salvation in a sevenfold comparison designed to illustrate the equitable structure of God's merciful justice (10:15–19:22). References at the end to Egyptian "hatred of strangers" (19:15) and the revocation of shared "rights" (19:16) have led most interpreters to locate this text near the start of Roman rule over Egypt (from 30 BCE), when disputes about civic rights and taxable status created hostility between Jews and other ethnic groups in Alexandria.[6]

4. For the trend away from source criticism to a presumption of unity and coherence, see D. Winston, "A Century of Research on the Book of Wisdom," in A. Passaro and G. Bellia, eds., *The Book of Wisdom in Modern Research: Studies on Tradition, Redaction, and Theology* (Berlin: de Gruyter, 2005), pp. 1-18.

5. For discussion of the structure, see D. Winston, *The Wisdom of Solomon* (New York: Doubleday, 1979), pp. 9-12; M. Kolarcik, *The Ambiguity of Death in the Book of Wisdom 1–6* (Rome: Pontifical Biblical Institute, 1991), pp. 1-28; L. L. Grabbe, *Wisdom of Solomon* (Sheffield: Sheffield Academic Press, 1997), pp. 18-23; M. Gilbert, "The Literary Structure of the Book of Wisdom: A Study of Various Views," in Passaro and Bellia, eds., *Book of Wisdom*, pp. 19-32, with bibliography. In what follows, I allow for overlaps between the sections, since the author seems intent on managing transitions in a way that defies neat lines of division.

6. On the history of Alexandrian Jews in the period, see J. M. G. Barclay, *Jews in the*

The cultured sophistication of the author's Greek, and parallels with philosophical motifs and polemical tropes in Philo, also suggest an Alexandrian point of origin, sometime in the period between c. 20 BCE and 70 CE.[7] The sense of threat to which the first and third sections of the work respond sets the rhetorical tone of the whole. *Wisdom* is designed to reassure its readers of God's just governance of history, and it is within that framework and for that purpose that it also discusses the goodness, the generosity, and the mercy of God.

5.1. Death and the Question of Justice (1:1–6:11)

The opening chapters of *Wisdom* are addressed to "the rulers of the earth" (1:1-11; 6:1-11) to signal that the issues under discussion are of universal import and concern the value of aligning human power with the governing principles of the cosmos. *Wisdom* grapples with a problem present in all theistic traditions of the Hellenistic age (including Jewish wisdom literature): is it possible to believe in God's providential ordering of a world that is haunted by death, where good people suffer injustice, and the fragility of human life too often renders virtue fruitless?[8] Combining the twin problems of mortality and injustice, the text vividly portrays the unjust death of the righteous at the hands of immoral people of power (2:1–5:14), but maintains, against the empirical evidence, that God's justice will prevail: "the righteous will live for ever" (5:15) and God, armed with the powers of creation, will defeat his enemies and establish justice (5:17-23).[9] The text opens with a heavy emphasis on the *goodness* of God,

Mediterranean Diaspora from Alexander to Trajan (323 BCE–117 CE) (Edinburgh: T&T Clark, 1996), pp. 48-71; E. Gruen, *Diaspora* (Berkeley: University of California Press, 2002), pp. 54-83. A precise dating to the crisis of 39-41 CE does not seem justified by the text (*pace* Winston, *Wisdom of Solomon,* pp. 20-25), and most interpreters now suggest a more general connection to the Alexandrian disputes over Jewish rights in the early Roman period; see, e.g., M.-F. Baslez, "The Author of Wisdom and the Cultural Environment of Alexandria," and L. Mazzinghi, "Wis 19.13-17 and the Civil Rights of the Jews of Alexandria," in Passaro and Bellia (eds.), *Book of Wisdom,* pp. 33-52 and pp. 53-82, respectively.

7. Cf. J. J. Collins, *Jewish Wisdom in the Hellenistic Age* (Louisville: Westminster John Knox Press, 1997), p. 195.

8. For the centrality of the question of justice in Wisdom, see M. F. Kolarcik, "Universalism and Justice in the Wisdom of Solomon," and F. Raurell, "From ΔΙΚΑΙΟΣΥΝΗ to ΑΘΑΝΑΣΙΑ," in N. Calduch-Benages and J. Vermeylen, eds., *Treasures of Wisdom: Studies in Ben Sira and the Book of Wisdom* (Tübingen: Mohr Siebeck, 2010), pp. 289-301 and pp. 331-56, respectively.

9. For the use here of apocalyptic motifs in the service of the wisdom tradition, see J. J.

whose will is life, not death. God did not create death and takes no pleasure in the destruction of living things (1:13). He created all things to live (not to die; 1:14), and the generative powers of the cosmos are salvific (not destructive; σωτήριοι αἱ γενέσεις τοῦ κόσμου, 1:14). Thus, despite appearances and despite the self-destructive instincts of humanity (1:12, 16; or the devil, 2:24), the basic design of the universe is for life and justice.[10] God created humanity for incorruption (2:23), and the wisdom that permeates the universe is a "human-friendly spirit" (φιλάνθρωπον πνεῦμα, 1:6). With a duality similar to Exodus 34:6-7, that "kindliness" is juxtaposed with, and connected to, the judgment of evil: Wisdom scrutinizes the words and inmost feelings of humanity and "will not free blasphemers from the guilt of their words" (1:6). God's goodness to humanity is not indulgence; it is articulated precisely in the justice by which wrongdoing is detected and judged.

This claim to the victory of justice is maintained despite the ubiquity of death, including untimely and unjust death, against the cynicism that claims that might is right (2:11). The death of the righteous forms the test case (2:17-20), which must prove whether the righteous will be vindicated, even if they die violently, early, and childless. *Wisdom* famously insists that this will be so: "the souls of the righteous are in the hand of God, and no torment will ever touch them" (3:1). The prospect of life with God *beyond death* demonstrates the good ordering of the universe, within which reasons can be given for premature death (e.g., to preserve the righteous from corruption, 4:10-15), and compensation can be offered for those who die without offspring (3:13–4.9). *Wisdom* constructs an imaginary scenario to showcase alternative readings of the world. The unrighteous are given two long speeches (2:1-20; 5:2-14), first to articulate their vision of chaos, and then to ponder their self-fulfilling commitment to futility.[11] Sandwiched between these speeches (3:1–5:1), and at the conclusion to the whole (5:15–6:11), our author offers assurance that the world makes sense according to a moral and natural order guaranteed by God.[12]

Collins, "The Reinterpretation of Apocalyptic Traditions in the Wisdom of Solomon," in Passaro and Bellia, *Book of Wisdom*, pp. 143-57.

10. The devil makes only this one, fleeting, appearance in *Wisdom* ("Through the devil's envy death entered the world"); cf. *Vita Adae* 12-17. Dodson suggests a concern to clear God of blame for bringing death into the world: see J. R. Dodson, *The "Powers" of Personification: Rhetorical Purpose in the* Book of Wisdom *and the Letter to the Romans* (Berlin: de Gruyter, 2008), pp. 56-68.

11. On the creative reuse of Jeremiah and Isaiah in the second speech, see S. Manfredi, "The Trial of the Righteous in Wis 5:1-14 (1-7) and in the Prophetic Traditions," in Passaro and Bellia, eds., *Book of Wisdom*, pp. 159-78.

12. For excellent recent analysis of this section, drawing parallels with the *Epistle of Enoch*,

At stake here is the question of true or false perception (2:1, 21; 3:10; 4:14, 17): to see the world aright is to see it structured by divine justice and moral symmetry. The "wicked" or "ungodly" ultimately receive exactly what they deserve. They draw upon themselves the death with which they form their pact (συνθήκη, 1:16), being "fit" or "worthy" (ἄξιοι) to belong to death's company (1:16; cf. 2:24). They will be punished exactly in accordance with their own reasoning (3:10-11): if they thought death made life futile (2:1-5), their deaths will be as meaningless as they imagined (5:9-14). The righteous, by contrast, will get "the reward of holiness" (μισθὸς ὁσιότητος, 2:22; cf. 5:15). μισθός here means not "pay" (the relationship is not one of contract or wage), but fitting recompense or reward.[13] It is crucial to the whole ideology of this text that the proper people get the appropriate treatment by God. The suffering of the righteous was *not* their punishment: it was their discipline, minor in comparison with God's bounty (3:4-6: ὀλίγα παιδευθέντες μεγάλα εὐεργετηθήσονται), designed as the means for God to prove them "worthy of himself" (εὗρεν αὐτοὺς ἀξίους ἑαυτοῦ, 3:5).

The outcome of life, then, is not the product of chance (2:2) or ultimately unfair: in accordance with what is morally, socially, or rationally fitting, the ungodly will meet their end in death (1:16) while the godly can anticipate immortality (3:4). The latter "will shine forth in the time of their visitation" (3:7), when they will receive the right to rule, under the authority of God (3:8). Thus "the faithful will abide with [God] in love, for favor/grace and mercy will be on his elect" (χάρις καὶ ἔλεος τοῖς ἐκλεκτοῖς αὐτοῦ, 3:9; cf. 4:15, with the expansion, "he watches over his holy ones").[14] Election here is no arbitrary choice by God, but corresponds to a moral and rational order. "Grace and mercy" are the effects of the generosity and goodness of God, but they are, and must be, distributed with discrimination. Likewise, it is fitting that the eunuch who has done no evil, nor even thought it, should be given "special favor" (χάρις ἐκλεκτή) with regard to his faithfulness (πίστις, 3:14).[15] "Grace"

---

see J. A. Linebaugh, *God, Grace, and Righteousness in Wisdom of Solomon and Paul's Letter to the Romans: Texts in Conversation* (Leiden: Brill, 2013), pp. 25-42.

13. Even in 10:17, where μισθός rewards κόποι, "payment" may be an overloaded translation. On the changing sense of words for "reward," as transactions shift over time from relations of gift-exchange to relations of commerce and pay, see E. Benveniste, *Le vocabulaire des institutions indo-européennes: 1. Économie, Parenté, Société* (Paris: Minuit, 1969), pp. 163-70.

14. The manuscripts of 3:9 variously add or omit the expansion.

15. Cf. Isa 56:4-5, the biblical source for this motif. In the same vein, *Wisdom* refers to the "lot" (κλῆρος) of the righteous (3:14; 5:5) as the product not of chance but of justice, the "fruit" of good labors (3:13, 15).

and "recompense" are here entirely compatible: the fitting distribution of the gift is what makes it good.[16]

This moral order is what *Wisdom* is concerned to trace on a cosmic scale: Wisdom permeates and polices the universe, including the plans of monarchs (1:1-11), and God will use creation itself in punishment of the wicked (5:17-23). Thus, God's power and justice guarantee the original design of the universe. His providence extends to all by ensuring that the mighty are made answerable to a moral and cosmic regime — a law (6:4), a plan (6:4), and a truth (5:6) — more powerful than themselves (6:1-11). *Wisdom*'s commitment to stability, to equity, and to symmetry serves to reassure the righteous in the face of evidence that suggests an arbitrary, unfair, or chaotic universe. In such a context, God's goodness and mercy may operate as a means of his justice, but can hardly be expected to create incongruities in the structure of the cosmos.

5.2. Wisdom, the Ultimate Gift (6:12–10:21)

The central section of *Wisdom* offers an extended meditation on Wisdom, her character, her accessibility, and her salvific operation in the history of the world. The canvas here is as broad as before: while the central character is highly particular (by allusion, the king Solomon, 9:7-8) the Wisdom that he requests and celebrates is the governing principle of all existence. As the fashioner of creation (8:6), Wisdom knows the laws of nature and the physical structures of the cosmos (7:17-21; 8:5-6), but also the secrets of history, past and present (8:8). She is also the principle of divine law and justice (6:18; 9:5, 9), and thereby the template for the proper ordering of politics (8:9–15) and virtue (8:7). In other words, Wisdom is the architect of the sacred order that governs the universe, in which the natural, social, and moral orders cohere. She orders and works all things (8:1, 5), and is thus, in theistic terms, the mind of God (9:13–17).[17] Being divine, she arranges everything in a kindly manner (χρηστῶς, 8:1) and is both beneficent and humane (εὐεργετικόν, φιλάνθρωπον,

16. Thus M.-J. Lagrange properly speaks of "récompense gracieuse," "Le Livre de Sagesse, sa doctrine des fines dernières," *RevB* 4 (1907): 85-104, at p. 95 (cited by Linebaugh, *God, Grace*, pp. 38-39). To identify here a "tension" and a "double-sided soteriology" would be to presuppose that "grace" ought to be unconditioned and incongruous: see S. J. Gathercole, *Where Is Boasting? Early Jewish Soteriology and Paul's Response in Romans 1–5* (Grand Rapids: Eerdmans, 2002), p. 71. See above, 3.7.1.

17. For the dependence of *Wisdom* on middle-Platonic notions of an intermediary figure, see R. Cox, *By the Same Word: Creation and Salvation in Hellenistic Judaism and Early Christianity* (Berlin: de Gruyter, 2007), pp. 56-87.

7:23), offering to humanity both the ability to understand the universe and the means to navigate through it safely and well.

These central chapters of *Wisdom* emphasize that Wisdom is a *gift*, not integral to humanity's constitution from birth, but readily accessible to those who ask. The gift is freely available: "she is easily discerned by those who love her, and is found by those who seek her. She anticipates those who desire her in making herself known" (6:12-13). It is necessary to make sense of the fact that some receive this gift and others, apparently, do not. Wisdom is given to those who ask for her in prayer (7:7; 8:21; 9:1-18), to those who desire her and seek for her (6:11-13, 17, 20; 8:2, 18), to those who love her (6:12, 17; 8:2) and honor her (6:21), and determine to make her their friend (8:9). There seems no special concern to claim who has *priority* in agency. Normally, the request is made before the gift is given (7:7; 8:21), but it can also be said that Wisdom *anticipates* (φθάνει, 6:13) her recipients in making herself known.[18] More important than priority is the fittingness of the gift: "in every generation she passes into holy souls and makes them friends of God" (7:27). Once again, we find the term ἄξιος, which means here not only "worthy" in a moral sense, but also fitting, suitable, or appropriate. Wisdom goes about seeking (note her initiative) those who are ἄξιοι αὐτῆς (6:16), who form a suitable home. *Wisdom*'s interest here is not causality or priority, but *affinity*. Like any responsible benefactor in the ancient world, God gives gifts to those able and willing to receive them, and this proper "fit" between gift and recipient does not make the gift any less a gift (it is entirely that), but ensures it is a *good* gift, not wasted, ineffective, or inappropriate.

Solomon's prayer (9:1-18) exemplifies this dynamic. Having properly recognized the unique and superior benefits of wisdom over every other form of symbolic capital (7:8-14), Solomon is conscious of his *need* for wisdom. In a development of its biblical source (1 Kings 3:7-9), *Wisdom* portrays Solomon praying to God, in recognition that he is weak and limited, worth nothing without this single gift "from you" (ἀπὸ σοῦ, 9:5-6; cf. 7:7). This strong statement of human inadequacy makes clear that the gift is needed, and is entirely and fully a *gift from God*, whom Solomon addresses as "God of the ancestors and Lord of mercy" (9:1). But the preface to the prayer also makes clear the fittingness of the request. Solomon speaks of himself as naturally gifted: "a good soul fell to my lot, or rather, being good, I entered an undefiled body"

18. Goering emphasizes human initiative in seeking the gift, but the point seems less emphatic than he suggests: see G. S. Goering, "Election and Knowledge in the Wisdom of Solomon," in G. G. Xeravits and J. Zsengéller, eds., *Studies in the Book of Wisdom* (Leiden: Brill, 2010), pp. 163-82, at pp. 166-68.

(8:19-20).[19] The quality of this pre-formed "good soul" (ἀγαθὴ ψυχή) appears to be one reason why Solomon's prayer was answered, and the very fact that he prayed was a sign of his insight (φρόνησις, 8:21). His status as king, chosen to rule over God's "sons and daughters" (9:7-8), seems to be another aspect of his suitability to be a recipient of the gift. It was a sign of Solomon's insight that he knew that wisdom was a gift (χάρις) and whose gift it was (8:21), but its giving was by no means arbitrary or unfair. After all, the purpose of Wisdom is to create an order governed by "holiness and justice" (9:2-3).[20]

This affinity between Wisdom and her beneficiaries is a dominant principle in the survey of early biblical (world) history in *Wisdom* 10.[21] In line with the earlier statement on God's salvific designs (1:14), Wisdom here acts always to save, preserve, and prosper her beneficiaries (cf. 9:18), in a pattern of benevolence stretching from Adam to the Exodus. Seven examples are chosen: Adam (10:1-2; saved from his own transgression); Noah (10:3-4; saved from the flood, caused by Cain's sin); Abraham (10:5; saved from the Babel-generation, and strengthened against his own compassion for Isaac); Lot (10:6-9; saved from the sins of the Pentapolis inhabitants); Jacob (10:10-12; saved from his brother, his oppressors, and his enemies); Joseph (10:13-14; saved from sin and from his false accusers); and Israel (10:15–21/11:1; saved from her persecutors and enemies).[22] It is important to note how her beneficiaries are described.[23] In the first case, Adam, we are apt to miss the criterion involved: "she preserved the first-formed father of the world, when he alone had been created;

19. Cf. 7:27-28 on Wisdom's entering "holy souls." There is good reason to find in 8:19-20 the notion of a pre-existent soul: see C. Larcher, *Études sur le Livre de la Sagesse* (Paris: Gabalda), pp. 270-79; Winston, *Wisdom of Solomon*, pp. 25-32, 198-99.

20. Cf. Linebaugh, *God, Grace*, p. 60: "The logic behind the fitting destinies of the righteous and the ungodly (*Wis* 1–6) is therefore mirrored in the discerning distribution of the divine χάρις of Wisdom. The gift of divine Wisdom, as a *gift*, is necessarily unearned, but it is also, as a *good* gift, necessarily explainable. Human worth and divine χάρις are coordinated to ensure a proper fit between the divine benefit and the human recipient" (italics original).

21. The agency of Wisdom in this chapter places it within the central section of the book, but its historical focus, climaxing in the Exodus, provides a neat transition to the final section. On the starting point of this section (arguably 9:18) and conclusion (arguably 11:1 or 11:4), see A. Schmitt, "Struktur, Herkunft und Bedeutung der Beispielreihe in Weish 10," *BZ* 21 (1977): 1-22.

22. As is often noted, the internal structure of this passage is revealed by the repeated αὕτη. Commentators normally miss, however, that this includes the phrase ἀποστὰς ἀπ' αὐτῆς (10:3); see, however, M. McGlynn, *Divine Judgement and Divine Benevolence in the Book of Wisdom* (Tübingen: Mohr Siebeck, 2001), p. 130 n. 114. This gives a complete sevenfold usage, mirroring the seven examples of salvific action.

23. See Linebaugh, *God, Grace*, p. 48 n. 23: "*Wisdom*'s interest is not so much in *how* humans contribute to their salvation (i.e. causality), but rather *whom* Wisdom saves (i.e. the worthy)."

she delivered him from his own transgression and gave him strength to rule all things" (10:1-2). Adam certainly cannot be credited with righteousness, unlike those to follow, but Wisdom's benevolence is not without rationale: his status as "the father of the world" is enough to justify her intervention on his behalf.[24] After Adam, all five individuals saved by Wisdom (Noah, Abraham, Lot, Jacob, and Joseph) are accorded moral, and not just social, worth. During the flood, Wisdom saved the world, "steering the righteous man (ὁ δίκαιος) by a paltry piece of wood" (10:4). After Babel, she recognized the righteous man [Abraham] and preserved him blameless before God (10:5). Again she rescued a righteous man [Lot] from the fire that destroyed the Pentapolis (10:6-8). The pattern continues in the case of Jacob (a righteous man who fled his brother's wrath, 10:10-12) and Joseph (another righteous man delivered, 10:13-14). As the foil to this catalogue of the rescued righteous, the text mentions in each case the unrighteous who deserted Wisdom (10:3), engaged in wickedness (10:5, 6-8), or oppressed the righteous (10:11-12, 14); in many cases, the judgment they deserved and received is detailed. The stage is set for the rescue of the "holy people and blameless race" (10:15) from the hands of their oppressors, a stage divided neatly between opposing groups of actors.

The principle that governs chapter 10 is thematized at its center: "wisdom rescued from troubles those who served her" (10:9).[25] To draw out such a principle requires the careful negotiation of the biblical source. Following his biblical designation, Noah is described as "righteous" (Gen 6:9), and *Wisdom* quite reasonably appears to assume that this fact, and this alone, justifies his rescue from the flood. It also deduces from Abraham's prayer for Sodom that Lot and his family were the righteous few in cities otherwise characterized by wickedness (Gen 18:22-33). One could also find good reason in the Genesis source to regard God's favor toward Abraham as befitting his worth. If God speaks to Abraham about his "reward" (Gen 15:1; LXX: μισθός), one may presume that there was something worth rewarding, while a Genesis-derived epithet, "blameless" (Gen 17:1), is found in *Wisdom* 10:5. Once on this track,

24. It is not necessary to find here an implied act of repentance, despite the parallels cited in this connection by F. Watson, *Paul and the Hermeneutics of Faith* (Grand Rapids: Eerdmans, 2004), pp. 388-89 n. 53. As the firstborn of humanity (cf. 7:1) and "father" of the cosmos, Adam has a unique status quite elevated enough to justify Wisdom's aid (cf. Philo, *Virt.* 203 on Adam, "who for nobility [εὐγένεια] stands beyond comparison with any other mortal"). Since, in the pattern of the chapter, Adam has to be rescued from *something*, it is natural to mention the only threat, his own sin.

25. On the place of this verse at the midpoint of the chapter, see U. Schwenk-Bressler, *Sapientia Salomonis als ein Beispiel frühjüdischer Textauslegung* (Frankfurt am Main: Peter Lang, 1993), pp. 58-59, 77-78.

our author continues the sequence, moralizing the stories of Jacob and Joseph, whose details he obviously knows well. The moral ambiguities of those tales make interpretation notoriously difficult, or remarkably open, and one can trace in *Wisdom* 10 the press of an interpretative paradigm onto awkward or recalcitrant material. What is paramount is the effort to make clear that the sacred order articulated in the earlier chapters is the blueprint of history: there is always a reason why some perish and some are rescued from destruction, and discerning that moral or social principle makes history both comprehensible and hopeful.

5.3. Divine Equity in the Exodus Events (10:15–19:22)

The last and longest section of *Wisdom* is structured by seven diptychs, where the punishments of the ungodly (the plagues of Egypt) are contrasted with the rescue or discipline of the righteous (the wilderness experiences of Israel).[26] As we shall see, much more is involved here than a simple rearrangement of the biblical narrative: to make their point, many of the stories have to be expanded, altered, and adapted. Since the case our author wishes to make is as much theological as moral, it is no surprise to find him stepping aside early in the sequence to discuss God's *modus operandi,* and in particular the relation between God's mercy and justice (11:21–12:22). Thus, after summarizing the symmetries that govern the articulation of the diptychs, we will focus especially on this formative passage of reflection.[27]

For the author of *Wisdom,* it is critically important to show that history operates according to moral and rational norms, and that the biblical plagues and wilderness trials were neither random nor unfair. The most basic symmetry is between punishment and crime (11:16): omitting all reference to God's hardening of Pharaoh's heart, our author allows no dilution of Egyptian guilt, and attempts to show how each of the plagues matches particular Egyptian crimes. Thus, the fouling of the Nile is punishment for the cruel decree ordering the slaughter of the Israelite children (11:6-7); so also is the death of

26. For recent discussion, see Schwenk-Bressler, *Sapientia;* McGlynn, *Divine Judgement,* pp. 170-219; Watson, *Paul and the Hermeneutics of Faith,* pp. 380-411; Linebaugh, *God, Grace,* pp. 61-80; S. Cheon, *The Exodus Story in the Wisdom of Solomon* (Sheffield: Sheffield Academic Press, 1997). Cf. Exodus 15:25-26, where God is described as bringing diseases to some and healing to others.

27. As Linebaugh notes (*God, Grace,* pp. 63-69), the traditional designation of this passage, and of the long discussion of idolatry (13:1–15:17), as "digressions" does not do justice to their significance within the text.

the Egyptian firstborn (18:5). The animal plagues are amalgamated and generalized, as fitting punishment for the Egyptians' senseless worship of animal deities (11:15-16; 15:18–16:4; 16:5-14). The plague of darkness is revenge for the imprisonment of God's children, who are the channel of light to the world (17:1–18:4). Death at the Red Sea is punishment for inhospitality (19:13-17). At many such points the author goes beyond the text of Exodus, inventing reasons for plagues that impress on his readers the justice of God's acts.[28] God, he insists, would hardly condemn anyone who did not *deserve* such punishment (12:15, 20).

But the diptychs also fashion a more elaborate symmetry: the ungodly are punished *by the very means* by which the righteous gain benefit (11:5). Such applies, for instance, to the motifs of water (the fouling of the Nile matches the provision of water in the desert, 11:1-14), of fire (the plague of fire in hail matches the blessing of fire-resistant manna, 16:15-29) and of night (a time of terror for Egyptians, and of Passover rescue for Israel, 18:6-19). It seems important to our author that these symmetries are observed not just in hindsight, but by the participants themselves (however unrealistic this may be in chronological terms). The ungodly must *know* that their punishment corresponds exactly to their crime (e.g., 11:12, 16; 16:18; 18:18-19), and must *recognize* the action of God in what they experience (11:13; 12:27; 16:8; 18:13); at the same time, the godly must *understand* the rationale for the benefits or the discipline that they receive (e.g., 11:8-9; 16:4, 21-23, 26; 18:21-22).[29] In other words, justice must not only be done but must be *seen to be done* on all sides, and we the readers (for whose sake all these educative comments are made) must be given the satisfaction of watching a coherent universe regulated by fully comprehensible standards of justice.

Wisdom does not name the parties involved in this drama as "Egyptians" and "Israelites," but the multiple and dense allusions to the biblical text, and the frequent references to "your children" (e.g., 12:7, 19; 16:10, 21, 26; 18:13) or "your people" (e.g., 12:19; 15:14; 16:20) make the identification clear enough.[30] The lack of ethnic labels does not render *Wisdom*'s categories universal, or the people of

28. In many cases, the author may draw on preexistent exegetical expansions of the biblical text; see P. Enns, *Exodus Retold: Ancient Exegesis of the Departure from Egypt in Wis 10.15-21 and 19.1-19* (Atlanta: Scholars Press, 1997). Philo has a different way of matching punishment to crime (e.g., *Mos.* 1.98).

29. This educative motif is already present in the biblical account of the plagues (e.g., for the Egyptians, Exod 7:5, 17; 8:10, 19, 22; 9:14-16; for the Israelites, Exod 10:1–2; regarding the wilderness experiences, cf. Deut 8:2-10).

30. Here, as in chapter 10, the text is sufficiently rich in allusion to make it well-nigh incomprehensible for anyone who did not know the biblical tradition; the technique may owe something to Alexandrian literary fashion (see Winston, *Wisdom of Solomon*, p. 139).

Israel "paradigmatic" of others, as if the particularism of the Exodus account could be masked and the tale made relevant to "righteous" persons anywhere.[31] Rather, the use of moral/religious epithets instead of ethnic designations seems designed to indicate that God's people are saved, and their enemies punished, not on the grounds of their ethnicity (i.e., not *qua* Israelites or Egyptians), but because in moral or rational terms they *deserved* their respective fates.[32] The plagues fall on the "ungodly" precisely because they *are* ungodly (ἀσεβεῖς): they are stupid enough to worship utterly worthless animals and cruel enough to victimize innocent guests. Similarly, the blessing or testing of the "righteous" has a proper rationale. Alongside references to the "oaths" and "promises" made to their fathers (12:21; 18:6, 22), our author takes time to point out that they are the only people on the stage with the good sense to recognize the Artificer of creation and to avoid the folly of idolatry; they are in principle, and for that very reason, a people who practice righteousness (13:1–15:17).[33]

One might think that these claims would be hard to sustain when interpreting the narratives of the wilderness experience of Israel, narratives that contain such incidents as the Golden Calf (Exodus 32) and the plague (Numbers 16). It is here, in fact, that the author makes his most strenuous efforts to reshape his biblical source. The Golden Calf episode is completely omitted (except for the remotest hint at 15:1-4; see below), and all the incidents in the desert, however biblically portrayed, are reconfigured as moments of blessing or (at worst) warning or discipline. Thus, the provision of water at Marah (Exodus 15; Numbers 20) is recounted without reference to Israelite "grumbling" or testing of God. It is given only to test, discipline, and warn the righteous (11:9-

31. It is frequently suggested that *Wisdom* is creating types of "the righteous" and "the godless" that constitute universalizable paradigms, not limited to the biblical figures or the people of Israel; see, e.g., Schmitt, "Struktur," pp. 18-19; J. J. Collins, "Cosmos and Salvation: Jewish Wisdom and Apocalyptic in the Hellenistic Age," *HR* 17 (1977): 121-42, at p. 127. But the specificity of reference is inescapable (the narrative is tied to a very particular narrative), and the anonymity does not dehistoricize or departicularize the biblical stories, but clarifies the rationale for God's actions. See Linebaugh, *God, Grace*, pp. 78-79, 82-83.

32. Thus the use of moral/religious labels, rather than proper names, indicates the didactic intent to show that history accords with the moral and religious structures of the universe. The theology of *Wisdom* is thus "universalistic" in the sense that the truths it portrays are true at a cosmic/universal level (and thus applicable to "God's children," Israel, in the author's own day). But, *pace* Goering ("Election and Knowledge"), this does not imply that what is said of Israel could be said with equal validity of other nations. It is hard to imagine who could fit the criteria for piety laid out in chapters 13–15 (aniconic worship of a single creation-transcendent deity) except Jews and proselytes.

33. The connection between intellectual error (false reasoning) and moral failure (wickedness) is correspondingly close: see, e.g., 11:15; 14:12-27, 30-31; 15:14; 19:3. This alignment of rational with moral structures is integral to the author's vision of the coherence of the universe.

10; cf. 3:5-6), and so that they should know how much worse was the thirst of their enemies (11:8, 14). The quail are given without hint of Israelite complaint or divine wrath (Exodus 16; Numbers 11), merely to show how their enemies were "tortured" (16:4). The serpents of Numbers 21 become a pedagogical event without reference to Israel's sin and subsequent confession. God is said to be angry (16:5), but it is not said why, and in any case his anger was short-lived and incomplete; the whole episode is merely a "reminder" of God's laws (16:6, 11) and a good experience of his mercy (16:10). Even "the destroyer" in the desert (the plague of Numbers 16) becomes a "test" (18:20, 25), a danger quelled by Aaron without reference to the preceding rebellion; there are references to wrath, but these are rendered impersonal (not attributed to God), and in any case the wrath did not last long (18:20).[34] To be sure, this whitewashing of the wilderness experience has some precedent in the Bible itself (e.g., tendencies in Deuteronomy and Psalm 105), but it is clearly crucial to the structure of our treatise. It would hardly be satisfactory to have Israel blessed *despite* her sinfulness, while the Egyptians are punished for their sins. There must be excellent and evident reasons why one category of people (the unrighteous, the ungodly, and the theologically dim-witted) is ultimately "punished" (11:5, 8, 13, etc.), "whipped" (16:16), "tortured" (11:9; 12:23, etc.) and "condemned" (11:10), while the other (the righteous, the godly, and the people of God) is "benefited" (11:5, 13; 16:2, etc.) or "warned" (11:10; 16:6) — or, in the worst cases, "tested" (11:10), "disciplined" (11:9; 12:22), and "taught" (12:19).

If the beneficiaries of God's mercy and fatherly discipline are dubbed "children of God" (9:7; 12:7, 19-21; 16:10; 18:4, etc.) or "your people" (12:19; 15:14; 16:2, 20, etc.), and if reference is made to the "oaths" and "covenants" contracted with their ancestors (12:21; 18:6, 22), the structure of the discourse makes clear that this special status does not derive from some arbitrary elective choice, but corresponds to their superior religious and moral alignment with God. The long analysis of godlessness in 13:1–15:17 includes many forms of "ignorance" of God (13:1), philosophical mistake and plain stupidity, but it boils down to a twofold indictment: thinking wrongly about God and (accordingly) adopting an amoral or immoral lifestyle (14:12, 30). It is on this basis that the penalties that overtake such people will be seen to be "just" (14:30). Conversely, chapter 15 begins with a notable echo of the depiction of God's mercy in Exodus 34:6-7: "You, our God, are kind and true, patient and ruling all things

34. See the penetrating analysis of *Wisdom*'s strategy in these episodes in Watson, *Paul and the Hermeneutics of Faith*, pp. 398-404, demonstrating also the displacement of biblical themes from one party to the other. For the personifications of Logos and Wrath, which distance God from the action, see Dodson, *"Powers,"* pp. 82-100.

in mercy' (Σὺ δέ, ὁ θεὸς ἡμῶν, χρηστὸς καὶ ἀληθής, μακρόθυμος καὶ ἐλέει διοικῶν τὰ πάντα, 15:1).[35] The following verse, with its repeated designation of "us" as "yours" (σοί ἐσμεν) and "accounted yours" (σοὶ λελογίσμεθα) also echoes Exodus 34:9 (LXX: ἐσόμεθα σοί, 34:9):[36]

> For even if we sin, we are yours, knowing your power;
> But we will not sin, knowing that we are accounted yours.
> For to know you is complete righteousness,
> And to know your power is the root of immortality.
> For neither has the malicious intent of men led us astray,
> Nor the fruitless labor of illusion-painters . . . (*Wis* 15:2-4)

There is the slightest hint here ("even if we sin") of a reference to the Golden Calf, but our author could not spell out this allusion to the context of Exodus 34 without ruining the neat antithesis he is creating.[37] The point is rather that "we" do *not* worship idols, because "we" know God and recognize his power (*Wis* 15:2-3).[38] Being the elect people of God and knowing God's power (i.e., refraining from idolatry) are mutually implicative: to be elect is to know God's power, and to know God's power is to be God's people. In other words, it is crucial for our author that his biblical traditions of covenant and election correspond to the moral and intellectual structure of the universe. When God allocates punishments or benefits, these follow not some random choice or arbitrary preference, but a beautifully patterned design.

5.4. The Correlation of Mercy and Justice (11:21–12:22)

The first diptych sets out the equity of God's treatment of humanity in a programmatic form: when the righteous were being tried (by thirst), that

35. It is notable that the description is particular to Israel ("our God"), while God's mercy is hailed as universal ("ruling *all things* in mercy." Cf. the discussion of 11:21–12:22, below). The echoes of Exodus 34 are noted by C. Larcher, *Le Livre de la Sagesse, ou, La Sagesse de Salomon*, 3 vols. (Paris: Gabalda, 1983), vol. 3, pp. 847-49; cf. H. Hübner, *Die Weisheit Salomons* (Göttingen: Vandenhoeck & Ruprecht, 1999), pp. 183-84.

36. On the echo and the possible meanings of σοί, see Larcher, *Livre*, vol. 3, pp. 849-50.

37. For further discussion, see J. M. G. Barclay, "'I Will Have Mercy on Whom I Have Mercy': The Golden Calf and Divine Mercy in Romans 9–11 and Second Temple Judaism," *Early Christianity* 1 (2010): 82-106.

38. So, rightly, Winston, *Wisdom of Solomon*, pp. 281-82; Gathercole, *Where Is Boasting?* pp. 166-68.

is, being "disciplined in mercy" (ἐν ἐλέει παιδευόμενοι), they learned how the ungodly were being tormented in wrath (by the turning of the Nile into blood): "for you tested them as a parent does in warning, but you scrutinized the others like a stern king in condemnation" (11:9-10). The second begins with another example of "measure for measure": the ungodly worshipped irrational and worthless animals, and so were punished by the same (11:15-16). But there is a problem here: God did not seem to act very like a "stern king" in this matter, as the punishment was by a variety of *insects,* and not by powerful animals that could have instantly demonstrated God's powerful condemnation (11:17-20). Already in the Exodus account of the plagues there is reflection on why God did not simply wipe out the Egyptians with a single blow: "For by now I could have stretched out my hand and struck you and your people with pestilence, and you would have been cut off from the earth. But this is why I have let you live: to show you my power and to make my name resound through all the earth" (Exod 9:15-16). But how do the insects demonstrate God's power?

This enigma provides the opportunity for the author to reflect at some length on the power, the mercy, and the justice of God (*Wis* 11:21–12:21), in a highly revealing fashion.[39] There is no question about the extent and capacity of God's "all-powerful hand" (11:17): "for it is always in your power to show great strength" (11:21). But that power is immediately defined as *the power to have mercy.* "You are merciful to all, *because* you can do all things" (ἐλεεῖς δὲ πάντας, ὅτι πάντα δύνασαι, 11:23; cf. 12:16). *Wisdom* here echoes a motif discussed elsewhere in Second Temple Judaism that was also familiar in Hellenistic and early Roman discussions of kingship: that a ruler's sovereignty is displayed not so much in the naked application of power, but in his control of anger and his merciful patience toward wrongdoers.[40] Thus, the text places

39. The position of this "excursus" has puzzled commentators, since it appears to interrupt the sequence of seven diptychs at a very early point. But, as we have seen, the diptychs serve a strong didactic purpose concerning the mechanisms of divine justice and mercy, and the start of the second diptych, relating the punishment by comparatively paltry animals, raises the question of why God's justice was so drawn out and initially so limited. That the same question occurs to Philo in relation to the same topic (the plague of gnats, *Mos* 1.109-12) indicates that our author is following, and expanding, a traditional topic of debate in Jewish philosophy. The opening of the excursus (οὐ γάρ, 11:17) suggests that he is taking up a debating point.

40. See, for instance, *Letter of Aristeas,* 188–215 and 254: God governs the universe in kindliness and without anger, and so should the king. There are repeated references here to God's justice, mildness (ἐπιείκεια), and mercy, not least in allowing time for repentance (188); see the discussion in G. Boccaccini, *Middle Judaism: Jewish Thought 300 B.C.E. to 200 C.E.* (Minneapolis: Fortress Press, 1991), pp. 169-74. On the relation of this passage to Hellenistic kingship-treatises, see O. Murray, "Aristeas and Ptolemaic Kingship," *JTS* 18 (1967): 337-71. The

heavy stress on the universality of God's love and mercy: "you love all things that exist, and hate none of the things that you have made" (11:24); "you spare all things, for they are yours, Lord, you who love the living. For your immortal spirit is in all things" (11:26–12:1). Despite the impression of 11:9-10, with its duality of mercy on some and wrath on others, our author also wants to stress the *universality* of mercy.[41]

The purpose of God's use of paltry animals in judgment of Egypt is thus made clear. God corrects those who sin "little by little" (κατ' ὀλίγον), reminding them of the essence of their sin (animal worship), "so that they might change from their evil and put their trust in you, Lord" (ἵνα ἀπαλλαγέντες τῆς κακίας πιστεύσωσιν ἐπὶ σέ, κύριε, 12:2).[42] This principle can be illustrated from God's treatment of the Canaanites (12:3-11). The LXX (Exod 23:28) represents God as promising that he would send "wasps" before the invading Israelites, and one might ask why God would use this somewhat bizarre form of punishment. The purpose was to give them time and opportunity to repent (*Wis* 12:10; cf. 12:19-20): a slow form of destruction ("little by little," 12:8, 10) is also a form of "sparing" (12:8). Our author speaks at length of the wickedness of the Canaanites, who were guilty of the crimes most universally abhorred, cannibalism and child-sacrifice (12:3-7). Moreover, God knew that their wickedness was inborn and ineradicable; they were an accursed race from the beginning (12:10-11). *Even so,* God spared them, and that he should be merciful in this extreme case shows the lengths to which he will go on behalf of humanity.[43] Out of his love for all God overlooks sins, for the sake of repentance (11:23).

Divine sovereignty thus has a double expression: it operates in unimpeachable justice and generous mercy, and the two are found to be mutually reinforcing. Switching back to a discussion of divine power (surely God did not leave the Canaanites unpunished for so long out of deference to someone

---

ruler's control of anger and exercise of *clementia* is further extended in application to the emperor in Seneca, *De Ira* and *De Clementia.*

41. Words from the πας-root are used five times in 11:21–12:1, and four times in 12:13-16.

42. The motif of "little by little" is transferred here from the biblical account of God's treatment of the Canaanites (Exod 23:30; Deut 7:22, κατὰ μικρὸν μικρόν), to which our author will immediately turn for further illustration (12:2-11). He seems sensitive to the philosophical discussion concerning delays in the exercise of God's justice, a matter of importance for all who maintained that God's providence was real and active. As Plutarch's tractate on this matter makes clear, one explanation for the lack of instant judgment of evil is that God is kind and merciful and, if there is the slightest possibility of repentance, allows time for evildoers to change (*Mor.* 550d–551c).

43. There is some cost to the logic: if God knew in advance that they could not change, it makes little sense for him to give them time to do so. That our author risks this logical incoherence is a sign of the stress he wishes to lay on God's superabundant mercy.

else?, 12:11b),[44] a climactic paragraph correlates God's power with both his justice and his mercy (12:12-18). By a series of rhetorical questions ("Who will say, 'What have you done?'" 12:12), *Wisdom* asserts that God is answerable to no one, while his justice is absolutely fair (12:13). God is just *in the exercise of his mercy,* because through it he allows full time for repentance, and thus examines who is truly and incorrigibly evil. The point is that God, who uniquely cares for all people (12:13), rules all things righteously, "deeming it alien to your power to condemn anyone who does not deserve to be punished" (12:15). His mercy thus delays but also *proves* his justice, while his unimpeachable justice must surely follow and complete his mercy: eventually, for the unrepentant, the "utmost condemnation" (τὸ τέρμα τῆς καταδίκης) will be exacted (12:27). The point of this reflection on God's goodness and mercy is not to undermine but precisely to confirm God's just judgment of the guilty: "those who have not heeded the warning of mild rebukes will experience the fitting judgment (ἀξία κρίσις) of God" (12:26).[45] Rather than let God's justice and God's mercy fall into an irreconcilable tension, our author takes pains to *correlate* them, understanding both as expressing the fitting order of the cosmos.

A number of moral lessons are drawn from this fascinating discussion of mercy and justice (12:19-22). God's people learn to judge kindly (12:19) but also to look to God for mercy when chastened or judged: "so that when we judge we might remember your goodness, and when we are judged we might expect mercy" (12:22).[46] There is no judgment without mercy, and also no mercy without judgment. Having established the moral principles of the universe, and while proceeding to illustrate them further in the diptychs to follow, our author can hardly take mercy to *exclude* or *overrule* judgment: it modifies, delays, extenuates, and finally justifies its operation. At the end of the day God

44. The switch in focus at 12:11b is rightly recognized by A. Schmitt, *Das Buch der Weisheit* (Würzburg: Echter Verlag, 1986), p. 107.

45. The term ἄξιος recurs later, in the meting out of punishment: 15:6; 16:1, 9; 18:4; 19:4 (cf. 19:13). Cf. the righteous as a "fitting" (ἀξία) colony of God's holy land, 12:7.

46. A difficult textual question arises at 12:22a. The text reads ἡμᾶς οὖν παιδεύων τοὺς ἔχθρους ἡμῶν ἐν μυριότητι μαστιγοῖς. If this statement relates to its immediate context, this "ten thousandfold" scourging seems out of place after such emphasis on divine mercy, and it hardly leads to the conclusion of 12:22b; besides, μυριότης is a *hapax legomenon* in Greek. A. Vanhoye (following G. Kuhn) suggested the emendation μετριότητι ("Mesure ou démesure en Sap. 12.22," *RSR* 50 [1962]: 530-37), yielding the sense, "by the measuredness of your scourging." For the positive reception of this conjecture by J. Ziegler (the editor of the LXX-text), see Winston, *Wisdom of Solomon,* p. 244; for further argumentation in support, see Larcher, *Le Livre de la Sagesse,* vol. 3, p. 736. However, if one takes the larger context into account, the extreme punishment of the truly deserving does not seem wholly out of place (cf. 11:9-10; 12:23-27).

has to punish those "*deserving of* death" (ὀφειλόμενοι θανάτῳ), even if he does so with great care and indulgence (12:20). As the matter is put in the preface to the reflection, "you [God] have arranged all things by measure and number and weight" (πάντα μέτρῳ καὶ ἀριθμῷ καὶ σταθμῷ διέταξας, 11:20).[47] There is proportionality, measure, and control in God's governance of the cosmos, a justice made equitable by the operations of mercy; but there is also, and by the same token, a proper return for human evil and a proper reward of the godly. The universally merciful God is also, necessarily, just: the structures of the universe would buckle if it were any other way.

This profound reflection on God's mercy and justice indicates clearly that Second Temple Jews with a philosophical interest did not merely assert the goodness and the mercy of God; they also reflected deeply on the meaning of these divine attributes and worked hard to relate them positively to the justice of God. It was intolerable to limit either the range or the depth of God's mercy, but equally unacceptable to configure God's mercy in a way that compromised God's ability and right to judge and destroy what is evil. Our author shows how God's power can be connected as much to God's mercy as to God's justice, and strives to chart a path whereby mercy and justice can inform each other without ending in self-contradiction.

On this basis, our text perfects the theme of divine mercy or grace in a set of distinctive ways. As we have seen, the text is replete with references to divine goodness and benevolence, whose *superabundance* is evident in the cosmic and the human sphere. Wisdom is given freely and fully to those who seek her; God is loving and sparing to *everything and everyone* that he has made, as a function of his universal power. Reference can be made to the *priority* of grace in Wisdom's anticipation of those who seek her (6:13), but this hardly seems a dominant motif; similarly, while Wisdom is responsible for the saving of humanity, little is said to indicate her *efficacy* in the formation or direction of the human will. It would clearly be impossible for our author to perfect the *singularity* of grace, since the simultaneous operation of God's judgment of evil is precisely what makes the operation of the universe good.[48] And it is this

47. This philosophical tag expresses both a physical and an ethical proportionality, on the assumption that the material ordering of the cosmos contains clear moral lessons (see Winston, *Wisdom of Solomon*, pp. 234-35; McGlynn, *Divine Judgement*, pp. 39-42). Its political and moral consequences are most fully drawn out in Plato, *Laws* 756e–758a, where it is argued that indiscriminate equality (all having the same) is really a form of injustice; justice is only served if the better people get more (as they deserve) and the poorly educated (!) less.

48. Although God's love explicitly excludes hatred (11:24; but cf. 12:4), it does not and cannot exclude the exercise of judgment and condemnation (as Marcion and others have considered necessary).

commitment to the fair and non-arbitrary governance of the cosmos (together with a need to reassure a community under pressure) that sets a definite limit to the *incongruity* of God's mercy or grace. As the Canaanite example shows, God's mercy goes to extreme lengths to spare sinners, delaying and limiting God's judgment for an unreasonable length of time (12:3-11). But our author cannot in the end allow an incongruous mercy to govern his configuration of the cosmos, and for very good reason. It is because God is supremely and abundantly good that he guarantees a system of moral and rational symmetries, whereby the foolish and unrepentant wicked get what they deserve, and the gifts of God reach their proper and fitting beneficiaries. If we can distance ourselves from the prejudice that "grace" means *by definition* a gift to the unworthy, we can see that this Second Temple text has a strong theology of grace, perfected in its superabundance, but it does not and cannot perfect its incongruity without undermining its sense of moral and rational equity. This "fittingness" of punishment and reward does not signal the *absence* of grace, or its dilution by "works-righteousness," but expresses a basic theistic presumption that the universe is fitly and morally ordered. If the universe did not operate by such symmetry and proportionality, it would certainly look arbitrary, chaotic, or grossly unfair.[49] The author of *Wisdom* assures us that it is not, and he aligns the biblical tradition with that assurance; he knows that otherwise life would be either intolerably senseless or unbearably sad.

49. In his discussion of divine patience, Plutarch insists that the order of the cosmos teaches a moral lesson. At all costs, we must avoid behavior that is random or arbitrary (τὸ εἰκῆ καὶ ὡς ἔτυχεν), which is the source of vice and error (*Mor* 550d); cf. the influential statement of Plato to the same effect (*Tim* 47a-c).

CHAPTER 6

Philo of Alexandria

Philo, the Jewish philosopher from Alexandria (c. 20 BCE–c. 50 CE), makes divine generosity one of the central themes in his philosophical interpretation of Scripture, but the richness and range of his comments on this topic create a number of difficulties in interpretation. Philo writes in several modes, approaching the biblical text (in Greek) with diverse exegetical methods and varying interests; the different kinds of treatise may also have differing audiences in view.[1] Since his philosophy is normally conducted through exegesis and adopts the vocabulary of the scriptural source, his ideas can take diverse linguistic forms. What is more, Philo is philosophically eclectic, utilizing Platonic or Stoic motifs as suits his purpose.[2] Although Philo is the most philosophically informed and intellectually rigorous of our Second Temple authors, his coherence lies not in precise propositions, consistently expressed, but in

1. Philo's works are usually classified in five groups: "Questions," "Allegorical Commentary," "Exposition of the Law," "Apologetic and Historical Works," and "Philosophical Works"; see J. R. Royse, "The Works of Philo," in A. Kamesar, ed., *The Cambridge Companion to Philo* (Cambridge: Cambridge University Press, 2009), pp. 32-64. It is generally accepted that the "Quaestiones" and "Allegorical Commentary" were directed to an elite circle of philosophically educated Jews, while some of the others could have envisaged a more "exoteric," even Gentile, audience. For discussion of this matter, see V. Nikiprowetzky, *Le commentaire de l'Écriture chez Philon d'Alexandrie: Son charactère et sa portée* (Leiden: Brill, 1977), pp. 192-202; E. Birnbaum, *The Place of Judaism in Philo's Thought* (Atlanta: Scholars Press, 1996), pp. 17-20; C. Noack, *Gottesbewußtsein: Exegetische Studien zur Soteriologie und Mystik bei Philo von Alexandria* (Tübingen: Mohr Siebeck, 2000), pp. 18-26, 216-48, with further bibliography.

2. Philo's philosophical commitments defy easy categorization. See J. Dillon, *The Middle Platonists: A Study of Platonism 80 B.C. to A.D. 220* (London: Duckworth, 1977), p. 182: Philo was "essentially adapting contemporary Alexandrian Platonism, which was itself heavily influenced by Stoicism and Pythagoreanism, to his own exegetical purposes." Cf. G. Sterling, "Platonizing Moses: Philo and Middle Platonism," *Studia Philonica Annual* 5 (1993): 96-111.

the ground rules, or "grammar," of his theology. Thus, our analysis needs to trace, amidst Philo's diverse and even contradictory expressions, the signs of maximum emphasis, greatest caution, and consistent principle in his theology of gift. These will help reveal the regular patterns and non-negotiable boundaries of Philo's abundant discourse on divine benefaction.[3]

All of Philo's works, despite offering minimal biographical information, bear the trace of his historical and social context.[4] Even when abstract and universalized, Philo's thinking serves the interests of the Jewish community in Alexandria, to which he gave intellectual and political leadership, not least in a delegation to Gaius Caligula at a time of acute political crisis (39-41 CE). Philo's brother, Alexander, was a fabulously wealthy trading magnate, with strong connections to Rome,[5] and everything Philo writes (and the leisure he had to write it) suggests a large cushion of wealth; he was clearly far removed from the needs of the "common herd," for whom he expresses both social and moral disdain.[6] Building on extensive training in the "*encyclia*" and in the Greek philosophical tradition, Philo brought the Jewish Alexandrian history of cultural conflation to its climax: he succeeded in creating a "Jewish philosophy" textually rooted in the Greek Pentateuch, as impressive in its architectonic structure as in its handling of textual minutiae.[7] Philo is convinced that *the Jewish tradition* is not just on a par with Greek philosophy, but is superior to it, either as its source or as a higher, more consistent, or better practiced form of the truths and values that the best Greek philosophers had only im-

3. What follows expands and reframes some of my earlier work on Philo. See J. M. G. Barclay, *Jews in the Mediterranean Diaspora from Alexander to Trajan (323 BCE–117 CE)* (Edinburgh: T&T Clark, 1996), pp. 158-80; idem, "'By the Grace of God I Am What I Am': Grace and Agency in Philo and Paul," in J. M. G. Barclay and S. J. Gathercole, eds., *Divine and Human Agency in Paul and His Cultural Environment* (London: T&T Clark, 2006), pp. 140-57; idem, "Grace Within and Beyond Reason: Philo and Paul in Dialogue," in P. Middleton, A. Paddison, and K. Wenell, eds., *Paul, Grace and Freedom* (London: T&T Clark, 2009), pp. 9-21.

4. For recent analysis, see D. R. Schwartz, "Philo, His Family, and His Times," in Kamesar, ed., *Cambridge Companion to Philo*, pp. 9-31.

5. See Josephus, *War* 5.205; *Ant.* 18.159; 19.276.

6. For the lesser abilities of οἱ πολλοί, see, e.g., *Abr.* 147; for his desire to escape from the hubbub and cess-pit of the city, see *Decal.* 2-13. While Philo struggles to control his appetite at massively indulgent banquets (*Leg.* 3.156), he assumes that food, water, and shelter are easily obtainable by all (*Praem.* 99) and that it would be beneath God's dignity to concern himself with a matter as trivial as a beggar's cloak (*Somn.* 1.92-101, on Exod 22:26-27).

7. On Philo's education, see A. Mendelson, *Secular Education in Philo of Alexandria* (Cincinnati: Hebrew Union College Press, 1982); for the Jewish Alexandrian tradition of engagement with Greek culture, see Barclay, *Jews in the Mediterranean Diaspora*, pp. 19-228. For traces of Roman influence on Philo, see M. Niehoff, *Philo on Jewish Identity and Culture* (Tübingen: Mohr Siebeck, 2001).

perfectly expressed (see below, 6.4). With Moses as the perfect sage, Judaism was blessed with a text and a cultural practice that instantiated a superior piety and a more excellent path to virtue, both of which it exercised on behalf of the whole world. But if Philo is in these ways unapologetically a Jew, he is also *a philosopher,* displaying the social assumptions congruent with that intellectual role. As a philosopher, he puts a premium on the worth of education and the life of the mind; he shares the ancient philosophical assumption that reason is superior to the passions, the soul to the body, and the inner good of the mind to the external "goods" of embodied life.[8] From his privileged position, Philo's value system reproduces the typical hierarchies of the social elite, elevating the rational, the active, and the socially powerful (and therefore the male) over the irrational, the passive, and the subordinate (and therefore the female).[9] As we shall see, both Philo's assumptions regarding Jewish superiority and his hierarchical categories of worth influence his discourse on divine gift in significant ways.

6.1. Ground Rules in the Interpretation of Divine Gift

The term χάρις is only one of the words used by Philo in relation to divine gift, but a useful point of entry to our subject is provided by his comments in *Deus* 86-110 on Genesis 6:8, the first use of χάρις in the Septuagint ("Noah found favor [εὗρε χάριν] with the Lord God"). Unfamiliar with the Hebrew idiom and focusing first on the verb "to find" (*Deus* 86-103), Philo analyzes both the "rediscovery" of divine gifts exemplified in the Great Vow (Num 6:2-12) and the "discovery" of unknown and unexpected divine benefits, illustrated by the gift to Israel of cities and houses in the land (Deut 6:10-11). In both cases, Philo emphasizes that God is the sole and single *Cause* of such gifts: the Great Vow recognizes that God himself and by himself, without co-worker (μηδενὸς συνεργοῦντος), is the Cause of good things (τὸ αἴτιον ἀγαθῶν), including the productivity of the earth, human health, and human offspring (87); the "cities" and "houses" represent virtues (generic and specific) that spring up, without human toil or effort, when God gives his wisdom (91-96). But the fact that God gives so many and such diverse gifts to humanity raises a difficulty: why does the text (Gen 6:8) single out Noah as "finding favor" (104)?[10] This can

8. Cf. F. Siegert, "Philo and the New Testament" in Kamesar, ed., *Cambridge Companion,* pp. 175-209, at p. 207: "Philo writes for pure minds, that is, for readers without an abdomen."

9. For the ways Philo's elite assumptions map onto his depiction of male and female, see D. Sly, *Philo's Perception of Women* (Atlanta: Scholars Press, 1990).

10. The same question elsewhere leads Philo in a different direction: Noah found χάρις

hardly mean that he alone obtained (ἔτυχεν) favor (or grace) (χάρις), since this has been given (δεδώρηται) to practically all creatures, even those composed of simple elements: all have been counted worthy (ἠξιωμένα) of divine favor (104). But was Noah judged to be uniquely worthy of favor (χάριτος ἄξιος ἐνομίσθη)? Philo considers it not unreasonable that the Cause (τὸ αἴτιον) should judge those to be worthy of his gifts (δωρεῶν ἄξιοι) who do not "deface" by disgraceful practices the sacred mind, the internal "coin" that bears the impress of God (105). Yet he tentatively (ἴσως) dismisses this solution as well: how great must someone be to be considered worthy of divine favor? Even the whole world, the first, the greatest, and the most perfect of God's works (cf. Plato, *Tim.* 92c) could hardly claim this status (106). Philo thus advances his third explanation, fitting the wider context of his discourse: Noah represents the cultivated individual (ὁ ἀστεῖος) who in his zealous enquiry "finds grace" in the sense that he finds, as the supreme truth, that all things are the grace or gift of God. God needs nothing but has given the world to itself, not because it is worthy of gift, but out of his sole goodness: it is God's blessed nature to be beneficent (εὐεργετεῖν, 107-8). Thus if anyone asks what is the reason (αἰτία) for the creation of the world, he will find it purely in the goodness (ἀγαθότης) of God (108).

Before moving on, Philo notes one more detail in his text: Noah found χάρις before "the Lord God." These titles are identified here, as elsewhere, with the two Powers of the Existent One (τὸ ὄν), and a contrast can be drawn with Moses, who is said to have found χάρις with God without mention of such titles (Exod 33:17). Thus Noah, as a secondary wisdom, is treated only to the Powers, while "He Who Is" (ὁ ὤν) through his own agency judged the supreme wisdom in Moses worthy of grace or favor (ἀξιοῖ χάριτος, 109-10).

This multifaceted text reveals several central elements of Philo's theology of gift.[11] In the first place, there is a notably heavy emphasis on God as *the sole cause* of the world and of all that is good: God is titled τὸ αἴτιον ("the Cause") and accorded the unique causative role in the creation of the world and in stamping the mind on human nature, even in the formation of human virtue. What Philo most wants to emphasize about Noah is his discovery, after eager enquiry, that God's goodness is the sole cause of all there is (107). This goodness can be described with a plethora of terms: χάρις is here closely associated

because he alone was grateful to God (εὐχάριστος), although the entire human race enjoyed God's beneficence. And in a special sense he was worthy of favor as his household was the seed of a new humanity, and thus both the end and the beginning of humankind (QG 1.96).

11. See the commentary on this passage in D. Winston and J. Dillon, *Two Treatises of Philo of Alexandria: A Commentary on* De Gigantibus *and* Quod Deus Sit Immutabilis (Chico: Scholars Press, 1983), pp. 320-35.

with other terms for gift, goodness, and benefaction. These divine gifts can be traced in various domains: in the creation of the cosmos, the formation of the human being, and the development of human virtue. The scope can be as universal as the inanimate cosmos or as particular as an individual's wisdom. Secondly, we may note how the language of "worth" (ἄξιος, ἀξιόω) accompanies that of gift: it is so routine in Philo's discourse that he uses it repeatedly even in a context where he questions its appropriateness. The questions he raises are designed to fend off two misunderstandings of such language. First, if "worth" suggests some equivalence between the gift and its recipient, it must be clear that God as Creator is wholly *incommensurate* with the recipient of his gifts, even with his first, his greatest, and his most perfect gift, the world itself (106). Secondly, "worth" can never be used to *explain* a divine gift in a causative sense. God gave the world not because it was "worthy" but purely because of his goodness (108); nothing can be allowed to compromise the conviction that *God alone is the Cause.* Within these boundaries, and despite the hesitations they induce, Philo employs the terminology of "worth" in relation to the world (104), to Noah as a reason-fostering man (at least as a reasonable suggestion, 105), and to Moses, the exemplar of supreme wisdom (110). So long as it is clear that the worth of the recipient does not reduce the infinite distance between God and his creation, and is not a *cause* of divine gifts, only a *condition* for their specific distribution, Philo finds it appropriate, even necessary, to speak of God's gifts as distributed to fitting or worthy recipients.

Three further details in this text signal important themes in Philo's discourse of grace. In describing the creation of the world, Philo speaks of the "abundance" of good things (ἄφθονα τὰ ἀγαθά, 108) that God has given; that is a perfection of grace which we will certainly find prominent elsewhere. He also speaks of the source of this gift in God's goodness (ἀγαθότης), the essence of God's "happy and blessed nature" (108); this hints at another perfection, the singularity of divine beneficence, which can be traced in other texts. Finally, the references to differences of value, to the world as God's "greatest" gift (106), and to wisdom existing in "supreme" or "secondary" forms (108), hint at a hierarchy of gifts and statuses which may prove significant in Philo's configuration of divine benefaction.

In what follows, we will pursue these leads across the Philonic corpus.[12] We will focus first on Philo's central theme, the divine causation of good, exploring also its singularity and abundance (6.2). We will then scrutinize

12. For parallel treatments of this theme in Philo, see D. Zeller, *Charis bei Philon und Paulus* (Stuttgart: Verlag Katholisches Bibelwerk, 1990), pp. 33-128; O. McFarland, *The God Who Gives: Philo and Paul in Conversation* (PhD thesis, Durham University, 2013).

more closely the language of "worth," its rationale, and its limits (6.3), before exploring how Abraham and Israel represent the piously wise and virtuous, who are fittingly rewarded for their correspondence with God's design of the cosmos and of humanity (6.4). On this basis we will be able to clarify what "perfections" of grace Philo does or does not promote, and why (6.5).

6.2. God as the Sole and Singular Cause of Abundant Good

Our impression from *Deus* 86–110, that God's sole causation of good is a ground rule of Philo's philosophy, is amply borne out by wider study. Philo's sensitivity on this matter is well illustrated by his discussion of the proper use of prepositions, and their implications for agency. In discussing Genesis 4:1-2, he criticizes Adam for saying he had acquired his son Cain "through God" (διὰ θεοῦ; *Cher.* 125–30). The preposition διά would suggest that God was merely an instrument (ὄργανον) for the birth, not the cause (αἴτιον); but Philo insists by appeal to (a version of) the Aristotelian causes that all things were created *by* God (ὑπὸ θεοῦ), not through him (God being the efficient, not formal or instrumental, cause), while their final αἰτία is the goodness of the Creator (125–27).[13] The theological grammar is more important than its precise wording: following the Greek text of the Pentateuch, Philo finds the same lesson to be just as clear in Moses' exhortation to Israel to stand fast and see salvation "from the Lord" (παρὰ τοῦ κυρίου, Exod 14:13; *Cher.* 130). However worded, this is the non-negotiable principle for those who follow an unerring philosophy (ἀψευδὴς φιλοσοφία, 129): in the cosmos, in "salvation," even in human mental activity (128), God is the Creator, the Craftsman, and the Cause.[14]

A parallel passage in *Ebr.* 105–10 (on Abraham's refusal to accept gifts in Gen 14:22-23) shows that Philo's concern here is no philosophical nicety but goes to the heart of his piety. In this episode, Abraham rightly accepted nothing as originating from (ἀπό) the world, or from any part of it, even from his own physical capacities; the true source is the only wise Being, who extends his beneficent powers (χαριστήριοι δύναμεις) everywhere, and through them

13. On the Aristotelian scheme, adapted to the Platonic note of divine goodness, see the note by Colson in the LCL edition, ad loc. For the "prepositional metaphysics" on which Philo draws, see Dillon, *Middle Platonists,* pp. 137-50; D. Runia, *Philo of Alexandria and the Timaeus of Plato* (Leiden: Brill, 1986), pp. 171-74; G. Sterling, "Prepositional Metaphysics in Jewish Wisdom Speculation and Early Christological Hymns," *SPA* 9 (1997): 219-38.

14. It is common for Philo to describe God as the "primal" (πρῶτον), the "most original" (πρεσβύτατον), and the sole (μόνον) cause of the world; e.g., *Conf.* 123; *Ebr.* 73, 75; *Leg.* 3.32-35.

renders help (106). "So he who has the vision of the Existent One knows the Cause" (107) — in contrast to the "blind," who think that the sense-perceptible world is the cause of everything. Such people create material "gods" and fill the world with idols; their polytheism constitutes a kind of atheism in its refusal to honor the true, but invisible, Cause (108–110). This theme is developed at length in Philo's commentary on the first two commandments (*Decal.* 52–81) where, in a schema parallel to *Wisdom* 13–15, he runs through a spectrum of false religion, from the deification of the cosmos to Egyptian animal cults. Common to these all is a failure to perceive the "invisible and conceptual Cause" (ἀόρατον καὶ νοητὸν αἴτιον), a fault parallel to, and as basic as, the failure to recognize the soul within the body (*Decal.* 59–60). Whether they deify the elements, or worship the stars, or construct images of gods, or pay homage to sacred animals, all such forms of religion (in practice, all non-Jewish religion) miss the basic fact of nature: "they have no knowledge of Him who truly is, Who is the primal and most perfect good (τὸ πρῶτον ἀγαθὸν καὶ τελεώτατον), from Whom is showered, as from a spring, each particular good upon the world and those in it" (*Decal.* 81).

The first two commandments are foundational for Philo: just as the source/head (ἀρχή) of all that exists is God, so piety (εὐσέβεια) is the source/head of the virtues (*Decal.* 52). That piety should certainly be expressed in proper cultic practice, but, for Philo, mental attitudes are crucial as well. The key task is to "refer all things to God": to think that events happen by some automatic process, or that we ourselves, by the power of our minds, create events, skills, or cultures, is to turn our backs on God (*Leg.* 3.29). Human pride, the apportioning of causation to ourselves, is a constant target for Philo, who considers Protagoras's dictum that "humanity is the measure of all things" the epitome of the foolish opinion that the human mind is the cause of its own powers (*Post.* 33-39). Human disaster is invariably the result of self-centered conceit (φιλαυτία), "which cannot bear to acknowledge the gift-loving and perfecting God as the Cause of good things" (*Agr.* 173, on Deut 8:18: "God who gives strength to enact power").

Scriptural narratives of miraculous births give Philo ample occasion to reinforce this point, since they signal a divine role in conception (God "opens the womb" of the barren). Philo considers it true at a literal level that every human birth has its origin not in the human parents but in the Cause of all that comes into being (*Spec.* 1.10, one of the truths signified by circumcision). But when the texts are interpreted allegorically, this principle is also applied to the "birth" of virtue, thought, or happiness within the human soul: such is demonstrated, for instance, by an allegorical reading of the stories of Rachel and Leah (Gen 29–30; *Leg.* 2.46-48), Hannah (1 Sam 1–2; *Deus* 5–15), and Sarah (e.g., *Leg.* 3.217–19; *Migr.* 139–42).[15] Philo recognizes that to speak of God "begetting" runs the risk of an over-literal understanding (it is language to be used only among "initiates," *Cher.* 40–47), but the Allegorical Commentaries are a safe enough environment for such daring language. In fact, the stories of divinely sown offspring are perfect vehicles for the leitmotif of God as generous Cause: "it is he then who sows, but the fruit which he sowed, his own, he gives as a gift" (δωρεῖται, *Cher.* 44).[16]

If a ground rule of Philo's theology is that God is Cause, even of apparently human achievements, he is anxious to express a limitation, or refinement, of this notion: God is the cause *only of what is good,* not of evil. This principle applies as much to God's will as to its effects: although God *could* do anything, what he wills to do is only what is excellent (*Abr.* 268; *Spec.* 4.187). One may trace here the influence of Plato, who insisted that God, being purely good, did only what was beautiful and good (*Tim.* 29b-d; *Resp.* 379b-d). Thus, Philo insists on a clear distinction: God is not the Cause of all things indiscriminately, but of good things only (μόνων τῶν ἀγαθῶν, *Agr.* 129; cf. *Post.* 80).[17] Reacting strongly to Deut 8:2, which describes God as having "afflicted" (ἐκάκωσε) Israel in the wilderness, Philo insists that it would be sheer impiety to consider God the cause of evil, since he is good, the Cause of good things, the Benefactor, the Savior, and the bountiful Giver: the text has to be read allegorically and the verb given the sense of "discipline" or "admonish" (*Congr.* 170–74). And it is for this reason (again following Plato, *Tim.* 42d) that Philo places a gap between God and the creation of such a morally mixed phenomenon as the human race. Exploiting the peculiar plural in Genesis 1:26 ("let us make humanity"), Philo finds a clue that God used fellow-workers in his creation of humanity. Thus, when humans think and act aright, that is attributed to God, but when they do the opposite, his subordinates are held responsible: "for the Father could not be the cause of evil to his offspring" (*Opif.* 72–75; cf. *Fug.* 68–70; *Mut.* 30–31).[18]

15. *Praem.* 158-60 discovers the same theme in Isaiah 54:1, a text of importance also to Paul (Gal 4:26-27).

16. See further Zeller, *Charis,* pp. 79-83.

17. For a parallel point, Philo cites Plato's *Theaet.* 176c, that God is never or in any way unrighteous (ἄδικος) but the most righteous entity there can possibly be (*Fug.* 82). Cf. *Spec.* 4.187: God and his beneficent Powers always transform the faultiness of the worse and make them better.

18. See C. Termini, *Le Potenze di Dio: Studio su δύναμις in Filone di Alessandria* (Rome: Institutum Patristicum Augustinianum, 2000), pp. 139-52; D. Winston, *The Ancestral Philosophy: Hellenistic Philosophy in Second Temple Judaism* (Providence: Brown Judaic Studies, 2001), pp. 128-34.

These "subordinates" are his "potencies" or "powers" (δύναμεις), often identified as the beneficent or creative power "God" (θεός) and the ruling or punishing power "Lord" (κύριος).[19] Thus, biblical punishments and penalties are generally attributed not to "the Existent One" himself, but to one of his powers (e.g., *Conf.* 168–82 on divine reaction to the Tower of Babel). The language varies, as determined by the texts discussed, but the same concern is evident throughout: it is fitting that the Existent One "is present to give good gifts through his own agency, but should leave the operation of the opposite purely in the hands of his powers acting in his service, so that he might be considered the Cause of good things, but not primarily (προηγουμένως) of anything evil" (*Abr.* 143).[20] The issue is clearly awkward for Philo, who cannot allow any "power" to operate independently or in opposition to God without compromising his monotheism, yet cannot dilute to any degree the sense of God's pure goodness. If a source of evil is to be identified, it lies in the mortality of the created world and the related moral corruption of the human race (*Congr.* 84; *Plant.* 53; *Fug.* 79–80).[21] Whether or not that explanation is philosophically adequate, Philo's discourse is governed by the unbending rule that "the fountains of God's eternal gifts (χάριτες) should be kept free from not only what is, but also from what is thought to be, evil" (*Conf.* 182).

Philo's references to the two "powers" are another indication of reflection in Second Temple Judaism on the relation between God's justice and his goodness/mercy. Philo's approach to this topic is different to that we have traced in the discussion of mercy and justice in *Wisdom of Solomon* (see above, 5.4), but the issues are similar. As (or in) his power as κύριος, God rules the world in justice, a role that necessarily involves judgment and the punishment of sin. The language of divine "anger" has to be carefully handled, lest God appear human and subject to emotion,[22] but it is not possible to imagine God's governance of the cosmos without his exercise of justice, as the biblical text reveals. At the same time, Philo puts maximum emphasis on the beneficence of God,

19. The topic is complex and Philo's language somewhat fluid; see Zeller, *Charis,* pp. 43-48, with further literature; C. Termini, "Philo's Thought within the Context of Middle Platonism," in Kamesar, ed., *Cambridge Companion,* pp. 95-123, at pp. 100-101; F. Calabi, *God's Acting, Man's Acting: Tradition and Philosophy in Philo of Alexandria* (Leiden: Brill, 2008), pp. 73-109. For variations according to the text discussed, see, e.g., *Plant.* 85–88; *Cher.* 27–29; *Sacr.* 59–60; *Fug.* 94–95.

20. The adverb προηγουμένως is nicely ambiguous: other possible translations are "principally" or "directly."

21. Cf. *Mos.* 2.147: sin is endemic (συμφυές) to created beings, just because they are created. On the problem of evil in the theology of Philo, see R. Radice, "Philo's Theology and Theory of Creation," in Kamesar, ed., *Cambridge Companion,* pp. 124-45, at pp. 130-31.

22. See Dillon in Winston and Dillon, *Two Treatises,* pp. 222-26.

and the language of goodness, gift, and mercy is far easier to integrate into his theology than the punitive elements of justice.[23] God's mercy tempers his judgment of sinners, and necessarily so, otherwise all would be condemned. In this sense, God shows beneficence even to the unworthy, and mercy is never secondary to justice; rather, mercy is the primary characteristic of God's stance toward the world, "older" than justice (*Deus* 74–76).

The semantic field of God's beneficence is correspondingly rich. The language of gift (χάρις, δωρεά, and cognates) is freely mixed with reference to God's goodness (ἀγαθότης), benevolence (εὐεργεσία), wealth (πλοῦτος), care (ἐπιφροσύνη), kindness (χρηστότης), and providence (πρόνοια). Where the biblical text suggests, this is supplemented with reference to divine mercy (ἔλεος), pity (οἶκτος), or compassion (God as ἵλεως), terms especially associated with the divine response to human suffering, weakness, or sin.[24] But "mercy" is not for Philo the central or most significant motif; it is perhaps too limited in range and too emotion-laden (and philosophically strange) in comparison with the language of "gift" and "benefaction." In fact, Philo accords God the unusual adjective φιλόδωρος ("lover of gifts") no less than twenty-five times. As we have seen, the scope of this gift-giving extends from the world itself, with all its components (*Deus* 108; *Mos.* 2.148), to the whole range of human capacities. Since God and nature (φύσις) can be readily identified, all the natural gifts of life, birth, and fruitfulness are attributable ultimately, and in their completion, to God (not to the human farmer or parent, *Her.* 114–22).[25] Within the human sphere, the primary gift is reason (for a philosopher such as Philo, the mark of human "kinship" to God, *Opif.* 77), but Philo can consider as gifts all the movements of the soul, including the use of the senses, so long as one places "first in value" all virtues and virtuous acts (*Sacr.* 72–73; *Ebr.* 119–20). God's grace is thus a store of treasure, poured out for all (*Leg.* 3.163-64) from his "boundless and illimitable wealth" (ἀπεριόριστος καὶ ἀπερίγραφος πλοῦτος, *Sacr.* 124), or, to use Philo's favorite metaphors of fluidity, it is showered down like rain, or poured out from a spring, in a continuous and inexhaustible flow (e.g., *Post.* 32, 127–28; *Her.* 31–32; *Decal.* 81; *Det.* 55; *Plant.* 89). In this connection, Philo frequently uses the language of excess, abundance, and unstinting generosity (περιττός, ὑπερβάλλω, ἀφθονία; e.g.,

23. Cf. *Legat.* 6–7, where the punitive power is carefully placed under the category of the beneficial (since punishment has a corrective purpose and potential).

24. See, e.g., *Det.* 93, 146; *Deus* 74; *Conf.* 166. In *Fug.* 95 mercy is one of five powers operated by God.

25. On Philo's somewhat ambivalent attitude to the created world, see C. A. Anderson, *Philo of Alexandria's Views of the Physical World* (Tübingen: Mohr Siebeck, 2011); the terms φύσις and κόσμος are generally given a positive nuance.

Leg. 1.34; *Virt.* 6; *Legat.* 118) and piles up comprehensive adverbs, adjectives, and nouns: "God supplies richly and ungrudgingly all the good things of peace to all people everywhere and always" (*Decal.* 178). It would be hard to find a stronger, a more consistent, or a more eloquent emphasis on the superabundance of divine generosity.

If the world is constituted by gift, the greatest human obligation is to offer thanksgiving (εὐχαριστία) to God, the return of χάρις for χάρις (*Her.* 104). God of course needs nothing himself, and we can only give back to God what is already his (*Deus* 4–7). Indeed, at one point, in rhetorically contrasting God as Giver with the human benefactors who, like hucksters, sell their munificence for a return, Philo suggests that God is no salesman "but a giver of all things, pouring forth eternal fountains of gifts, not seeking a return (ἀμοιβή). For he has no needs himself and no created thing is able to pay him back a gift (δωρεά)" (*Cher.* 122–23). But so long as one recognizes that there is no commensurable gift-exchange, it is entirely proper to figure thankfulness as the one thing creation *can* return to the Creator, its most appropriate work (οἰκειότατον, *Plant.* 130), in fact, itself a gift of God (*Leg.* 1.82).[26] This is for Philo the proper meaning of all offerings, but especially of "first-fruits," which he interprets as the return of thanks to the source of all good things (e.g., *Sacr.* 72–75; *Somn.* 2.75-77). Commenting on God's instruction to Abraham to "take for me" (λαβέ μοι, Gen 15:9; *Her.* 102–24), Philo points out that every good thing we have is not our own, but provided by Another (*Her.* 103), and that what we take (from God) we take not for ourselves but for God, that is, not for our own selfish use, but as trusts from God to be returned to him in thanks. Finding a similar expression elsewhere (Exod 25:1-2), Philo can expand the point: what we "take for God" are the first-fruits (ἀπαρχαί), recognizing that God is the beginning or source (ἀρχή), as also the completion, of every gift of nature and every human virtue (*Her.* 113–24).[27] Once again, divine causation emerges as the basic principle of Philo's theology; it is matched by the chief expression of piety, the giving of thanks to God.[28]

26. Thus hymns, sacrifices, prayers, and other expressions of gratitude are forms of "return" (ἀμείβεσθαι) to God (*Spec.* 1.224).

27. See the careful analysis of this passage in C. Noack, "Haben oder Empfangen: Antithetische Charakterisierungen von Torheit und Weisheit bei Philo und bei Paulus," in R. Deines and K.-W. Niebuhr, eds., *Philo und das Neue Testament: Wechselseitige Wahrnehmungen* (Tübingen: Mohr Siebeck, 2004), pp. 283-307.

28. On the significance of this theme, see J. LaPorte, *Eucharistia in Philo* (New York: Edwin Mellen Press, 1983); J. Leonhardt, *Jewish Worship in Philo of Alexandria* (Tübingen: Mohr Siebeck, 2001).

6.3. The Fitting Gift

As we saw above (6.1), it is characteristic of Philo to associate divine gifts with some reference to the "worth" of their recipients, though this language must be constrained or questioned in at least two respects: whatever is said in this vein must not imply commensurability between God and the recipients of his gifts (in that sense, nothing is "worthy"); neither must it slip from condition to cause, since God is always the one and only Cause. The topic clearly requires further investigation.[29]

In a notable passage (*Leg.* 3.65-106), Philo examines a series of cases that appear to challenge the rationality and justice of the cosmos. The exegetical occasion is a puzzle in Genesis 3. In the case of Eve, a charge (αἰτία) was laid against her and an opportunity given for defense, as seems just; but in the case of the serpent, God simply pronounces a curse (Gen 3:14). The reason must be that the serpent — the symbol of pleasure — is intrinsically evil (ἐξ ἑαυτῆς μοχθηρά), without a trace of virtue; thus, outright judgment is entirely fitting (65–68). A parallel can be found in the case of Er (Gen 38:7), whom the text pronounces "wicked" without explanation, and whom God summarily kills without evident charge/reason (χωρὶς αἰτίας περιφανοῦς, 69–76). But his name means "leathery" and he represents the body, a thing wicked by nature (πονηρὸν φύσει) and a corpse even before it dies. Philo concludes that God has made in the soul some natures (φύσεις) intrinsically faulty and blameworthy, and others in all respects excellent and worthy of praise, just as he has made some plants and animals harmful, and others useful (75–76). Since his interpretative mode is allegorical, and the figures in the text stand for soul-qualities, not historical individuals, Philo is not quite asserting that God has created good and evil people, but the phenomena he is describing seem to be divinely caused characteristics witnessed in real souls.

The argument calls for examples of divine *blessing* similarly "without apparent reason/cause" (αἰτία), and Philo offers a catalogue of examples where Scripture pronounces a divine blessing without any indication of achievement or work (ἔργον, 77–103). The seven figures in this catalogue — Noah, Melchizedek, Abram, Isaac, Jacob, Ephraim, and Bezalel — vary a little in detail, but are united by the fact that some blessing or promise was given to them before any record of work, and in two cases (Isaac and Jacob) even before they were born. But it is unthinkable that such stupendous divine judgments could have been made without any reason at all, and Philo fixes on the one factor that

29. See the careful nuancing of this subject in Zeller, *Charis,* pp. 65-72 and McFarland, *God Who Gives.*

might reveal the divine rationale: their names. Following the Pentateuch's own interest in the meaning of names, Philo finds allegorically symbolized in each name some innate characteristic or quality that indicates what was worthy of blessing. Thus Noah, who is said to have found favor (χάρις) with God (Gen 6:8) before any indication of deeds (even before he is called "righteous," Gen 6:9), is shown to represent a praiseworthy constitution and nature (σύστασις καὶ γένεσις) because his *name* means rest (from wickedness) or righteous (77). It turns out to be "necessary" (ἀνάγκη) that such a character finds favor with God (77), although this "finding" of χάρις means not only that he is well-pleasing to God, but also that he finds that all things in the world, and the world itself, are a gift of divine grace (δωρεὰ καὶ εὐεργεσία καὶ χάρισμα, 78). Similarly, Melchizedek is found to be worthy (ἄξιος) of priesthood before any indication of his work, as his name itself ("righteous king") indicates noble characteristics (79–82).

In each subsequent case, Philo shows himself alert to the sequence of material in the text. Abram is given a promise by God *before* anything is said about his achievements (Gen 12:1-3), but his character was "worthy of esteem" (σπουδῆς ἄξιον) since his name means "high-soaring father" (a praiseworthy label, 83). Promises were made concerning Isaac and Jacob even before they were born. In the case of Isaac (Gen 17:19), God rightly forms, arranges, and chooses (προῄρηται) him for a good lot before birth, since his name, which was given before birth, means "joy," a condition of the soul that operates as much in anticipation as in the expected event (85–87). In the case of Jacob, where a different argument is required, the explanation lies in God's foreknowledge (88–89): even at the earliest stages of their formation, God knew the respective capacities, works, and passions of Jacob and Esau. Even the slightest whiff of virtue or vice is detected by God and reflected in his prenatal verdict (89; cf. Gen 25:23).

In each of these examples, where "works" are absent from the record, Philo presses behind the work, via the name, to the soul-character or "nature" that is recognized by God and accounted worthy of benefit or grace. The adjective ἄξιος and the cognate verb ἀξιόω occur repeatedly in this discussion (79, 83, 87, 93, 94, 106). Philo is concerned to avoid any hint of arbitrariness in God's interactions with the world: God makes no random choices and issues no groundless judgments. The "worth"-language serves to safeguard the fairness and rationality of God's blessings, which could hardly be given at random or without some discrimination. At the same time, this element of condition by no means encroaches on the prerogative of God as *cause*, since Philo makes clear enough that whatever it is that constitutes their worth is already the effect of the work of God: even the good natures God rewards are the product of his own making (77). This strong statement of causation could lead to a problem in theodicy: if God causes good natures, does he also cause the bad? In his conclusions to this section (104–6), Philo acknowledges that God "molds" (πλάττω) two kinds of nature, those intrinsically (ἐξ ἑαυτῆς) harmful and those intrinsically useful. By pointing to the "nature" (φύσις) that was present before any works, and in some cases before birth, Philo makes it impossible to attribute such characteristics to human agency; the responsibility must lie with the molder, God. Philo seems aware of the theological danger he courts at this point, but he concludes the discussion on a hopeful note. He urges his readers to pray that "God may open to us his own treasury" (cf. Deut 28:12) and close up the treasuries of evil things (cf. Deut 32:34-35). The biblical text indicates *both* kinds of divine causation, but since the latter treasury is "sealed up" (Deut 32:34), the final emphasis rests on the goodness of God (105): God gives good things so quickly that he anticipates the recipient, but inflicts evil things slowly, "giving time for repentance and for the healing and setting on his feet again of the one who had slipped" (106).

That Philo gets so close to acknowledging that God is the cause of evil natures is a sign of the strength and significance of his principle that God is always the Cause. For this reason, the language of worth, which explains the rationale of God's gift-distribution, never encroaches on the terrain of causation: whatever makes humans worthy of divine benefaction is itself the result of the prior act of God. Even in the sphere of human virtue, which is, as we shall see, among the criteria of worth, Philo will not allow a human to take the credit: while virtue is certainly the result of human effort, especially (for the philosopher Philo) the ascetic effort to suppress the appetites of the body and to maximize the rule of the mind, virtues too, and even the effort toward them, must be attributed to God: "it is necessary that the soul should not ascribe to itself its toil for virtue, but that it should take it away from itself and refer it to God, confessing that not its own strength or power acquired nobility, but He who gave also the love of it" (*Leg.* 3.136). Indeed, in one fragment Philo insists that on a *proper* reading of Moses (one not divulged to the uninitiated), God speaks only in human terms when he exhorts us to act, since by a "first and better principle" Moses "ascribes the powers and causes of all things to God, leaving no work for a created being but showing it to be inactive and passive."[30] That even in this passage Philo continues to speak of the "worth" of the recipient indicates clearly that the principle of worth constitutes the fittingness of the gift, not its ground in any causative sense.

Why should its fittingness matter to Philo? In essence, because God nec-

30. For the text, from the lost *Leg.* 4, see Barclay, "By the Grace of God," pp. 145-46.

essarily exercises discrimination and rewards value. Philo regularly uses the phrase ἄξιον (ἐστιν) to indicate what it is right, proper, fitting, or worthwhile to do (e.g., *Post.* 22, 91; *Mut.* 236), while the verb ἀξιόω means to "see fit" or "decide," discerning what is appropriate, or proper. The adjective ἄξιος thus implies an evaluation or judgment (it is frequently associated with the verb κρίνω or νομίζω, e.g., *Congr.* 5; *Somn.* 1.212) according to some criterion of significance, quality, value, or worth. It evokes a set of evaluative norms, assumed standards of quality. If divine gifts are given to those who are ἄξιοι, they represent and uphold the values that matter to God.

Philo's configuration of quality often reflects a hierarchy of *status,* which is properly recognized by the unequal distribution of gifts. As we have noted, Philo considers that nothing could be more worthy than the world itself, "the first, the greatest, and the most perfect of the divine works" (*Deus* 106; cf. *Cher.* 112). Some such measure of rank, in which priority is given to the first, the most significant, and the most complete, pervades Philo's use of ἄξιος and its cognates. As the first man and the only world citizen, Adam was held worthy (ἀξιωθείς) of the governance of the world, God deeming him worthy (ἠξίου) of rank second only to himself (*Opif.* 142, 148). The elder is worthy (ἐπάξιος) of honor, privilege, and higher rank (*Sacr.* 77), unless, as with Jacob, the younger is for special reason judged worthy of the elder's rank (*Sacr.* 42; cf. *Sobr.* 22). Old age is judged worthy of preeminence (ἀξιόω προνομίας, *Spec.* 2.238), while in a strict sense God alone is worthy of honor (ἄξιος τιμῆς, *Somn.* 1.246). Certain numbers are naturally worthy of preeminence (*Opif.* 54, on the number four), while the immortal mind, the repository of reason, is judged worthy of freedom by the Father who begat it (*Deus* 47; cf. *Sacr.* 29 on the soul).

The worth of status is not far removed from the worth linked to *condition, character,* or *achievement.* It was Moses' superior wisdom that qualified him to be worthy of God's self-revelation (*Deus* 109), and it is wisdom or reason that is (for Philo, quite obviously) worthy of life or reward (*Plant.* 44, 69; *Ebr.* 72). Deuteronomy 4:6-7 describes Israel as a "wise and understanding nation" to whom God draws near; reasonably so, remarks Philo, since it is lovers of wisdom and knowledge who are "worthy of (divine) aid" (ἄξιοι ὠφελεῖσθαι, *Migr.* 56–58). And wisdom is, for Philo, integral to virtue: wise action is "worthy of praise" and Moses is judged worthy of (divine) favor (ἀξιοῦται τῆς χάριτος) for waging a campaign on behalf of virtue against the passions (= the Egyptians, *Leg.* 3.14-15). Just as wrongdoing is worthy (ἄξιος) of dishonor, punishment, divine anger, and death (e.g., *Opif.* 156; *Fug.* 74, 84; *Deus* 171; *Decal.* 141), so there are those judged worthy (ἀξιόω) of rewards and gifts (μισθοὶ καὶ δωρεαί) because they have worked to acquire virtue (*Ebr.* 94) or have kept their gifted nature uncontaminated by evil (*Abr.* 37). Thus Noah, a righteous man dear to

God, was deemed worthy to be the last of the old race of humanity and the first of the new (*Abr.* 46), while God, the lover of the good, bestowed on Moses his fitting reward (γέρας ἄξιον αὐτῷ) on account of his virtue and civilized values (ἀρετῆς ἕνεκα καὶ καλοκαγαθίας, *Mos.* 1.148). In such cases, the notion of "worth" comes close to the meaning of "desert," but this by no means undermines or qualifies the gift-character of what the worthy receive. Gifts, like "prizes," are given to those who deserve them; the modern antithesis between gift and recompense does not apply. On the contrary, the worthiness of the recipient clarifies the rationale and justifies the appropriateness of the gift.[31]

The necessary fittingness of the gift makes the language of "worth" ubiquitous in Philo's discourse. Faith believes that in both present and future the gifts of God (χάριτες τοῦ θεοῦ) are lavishly distributed to people of worth (ἄξιοι, *Leg.* 3.164). God loves to give when the recipients are worthy of gift (ἄξιοι χάριτος): those who live a laudable life gladden him, just as virtuous children please their parents (*Somn.* 2.176). God gives Isaac (laughter) to Abraham, since he does not begrudge joy to people of worth (ἄξιοι), who follow God's will and turn from passion and vice (*Abr.* 200-204). By the same token, when (as always) Philo interprets the "covenants" as "gifts," he assumes that "covenants are drawn up for those who are worthy of gift" (*Mut.* 52, cf. 58, on Gen 17:2). When considering Abraham's offspring, one naturally asks who is the "fitting/worthy heir" (ἄξιος κληρόνομος) of divine blessings (*Her.* 33). Those who bring sacrifices in intercession should ensure that they are worthy of the blessing for which they pray (*Spec.* 1.283-84). Since the soul can be inhabited by God, it must be beautiful, a lodging worthy (ἀξιόχρεων) of God (*Cher.* 98–100; cf. *Leg.* 3.27). In a comment on the divine self-revelation of Exodus 33:17-23, God's response to Moses ("I will be gracious to whom I will be gracious") is taken to mean, "I give (χάριζομαι) what is fitting (τὰ οἰκεῖα) to the recipient, so to one who is worthy of gift (τῷ χάριτος ἀξίῳ) I extend all that he is capable of receiving" (*Spec.* 1.43). Capacity to receive can thus be associated with, or part of, the notion of worth (cf. *Post.* 139; *Deus* 80), but this hardly exhausts its meaning.[32] The ἄξιος-language evokes a value system, an index of quality, in accordance with which divine gifts are differentially and thus properly distributed.

As we saw from *Deus* (above, 6.1), the principle of worth is not absolute, and where it threatens to clash with other fundamental principles in

31. For the ancient conceptions of gift, and their modern Western transformations, see above, chapter 1.

32. Cf. Dillon in Winston and Dillon, *Two Treatises,* p. 223, drawing parallels with the Neoplatonic notion of "suitability for reception."

Philo's philosophy, such as divine incommensurability or divine causation, it must give way. There is no comparison between God and the recipient of his gifts, and from that perspective humanity has no worth: as sacrificers sprinkle themselves with ashes, so, paradoxically, the only person worthy of offering sacrifices is the one who knows he is worth nothing (μηδενὸς ἄξιος, *Somn.* 1.210-12).[33] There are three kinds of vanity: those who forget that what they have comes from God (illustrated by Deut 8:12-14), those who proudly think that they themselves are the cause (αἴτιον) of good events (rebuked by Deut 8:17-18), and those who know that God is the cause of the good but consider that they have obtained it "reasonably" (εἰκότως), as their virtues make them worthy of God's favor (*Sacr.* 54–57). Against this third category Philo cites a significant text, the denial of Israelite virtue as a reason for divine election (Deut 9:4-5): it was not for its righteousness or virtue that God chose Israel, but to "establish the covenant which he swore to our fathers." "Covenant" signifies God's χάριτες, and these are whole and complete: one cannot attribute virtues partly to human actors and partly to God, but must accord them wholly and purely to the divine Giver.[34] In other words, the notion of "worth" is dangerous if it challenges God's sole causation of the good, including his causation of human virtue. But within that boundary, it is acceptable, indeed integral, to Philo's discourse.

There are additional limits on the notion of worth that safeguard other principles of Philo's theology. Since no boundary can be placed around God's bounty, at least some of God's gifts will pass to the unworthy as well as the worthy, the insignificant as well as the important (*Sacr.* 124; *Leg.* 1.33-34; *Migr.* 186). At the same time, since humans are inevitably sinful, God's benevolence extends to the unworthy, otherwise no one would receive anything other than condemnation (*Deus* 70–76). Thus, in certain respects, and at certain levels, God does give to the unworthy, but Philo is generally anxious to justify this anomaly. As the Sodom episode indicates (God's being willing to save the city for the sake of ten righteous), God dispenses his wealth to the unworthy, but only on account of the worthy (διὰ τοὺς ἀξίους, *Sacr.* 121–25).[35] If gifts are given even to the imperfect, that is to encourage them to virtue (*Leg.* 1.33-34). There is a minimum of giftedness in all creatures who participate in the gift of the cosmos, and particularly for humans, endowed with reason (*Mos.*

33. On the principle that there is absolutely nothing like God, see *Leg.* 2.1; *Somn.* 1.73.

34. The logic here is not entirely clear, but the emphasis on wholeness makes best sense on this reading; see the note by Colson ad loc. and Birnbaum, *The Place of Judaism*, pp. 134-35.

35. The notion is Stoic: see Seneca, *Ben.* 4.28. Philo takes the blessing of the nations in Abraham (Gen 12:3) to mean that God bestows his gifts on those becoming perfect (Abraham) and because of them on others (*Migr.* 118–27).

2.61). But any gift that can be given with discrimination, and any that draws humans upward toward the vision of God, will be given in accord with worth. External goods are one thing, part of the endowment of the world (*Mos.* 2.53, 148; *Ebr.* 117–18); but the gifts that matter most in Philo's scheme of value, gifts of wisdom and virtue, are given discriminately to people of worth (*Ebr.* 119; cf. *QG* 2.75).

God's generosity is not morally indifferent; his gifts reflect the order he has built into the cosmos. If the world is governed by a set of values, hierarchically ordered in proportional equity, one can hardly expect God to flout this normative system in the generosity of his gifts.[36] The closer one comes to God, the greater the fit that God's gifts both recognize and create; if the goal of human perfection is "to become like God, as far as this is possible" (*Fug.* 63, citing Plato, *Theaet.* 176a-b), God will naturally reward those most like himself.[37] Thus, God graciously shows himself to those who yearn to see him (*Fug.* 141); the fountains of his grace are open to "suppliants," who love a virtuous life (*Virt.* 79). In cleansing themselves from voluntary sins and bodily passions, people become a dwelling worthy of God (*Cher.* 98–101), God's worthy "portion" (*Mut.* 25–26). More fitting gifts become available for those closer to God, undefiled and released from the body, on the upward trajectory to the vision of God (*Mut.* 219). Not surprisingly, the values rewarded on this path of ascent match Philo's social presumptions — the "natural" priority of the first, the older, the free, the masculine, and the active — combined with his philosophical preference for the educated, the rational, the soul, the moral, and the invisible. Both scales reflect Philo's elite status. Of course God gives to people of "quality": to think otherwise would be to expect the Cause to contradict himself and to flout his own nature.

6.4. Israel and the Reward of the Wise and Virtuous

Deuteronomy 10:12-15 contains an important statement about the election of Israel: although all the world, heaven and earth, belongs to the Lord, "yet

36. In line with Stoic discourse, the ἄξιος-language sometimes occurs in connection with justice: justice is distributed κατ' ἀξίαν just as gifts are given τοῖς ἀξίοις (*Mos.* 2.9; cf. *Leg.* 1.87; *Sobr.* 40; among Stoics, *SVF* 3.262). Following Plato (*Tim.* 30a), Philo finds in the creation of the world a divine ordering that creates perfect balance and harmony (*Opif.* 22; *Spec.* 4.187).

37. On Philo's use of the Platonic motif of "assimilation to God," see G. van Kooten, *Paul's Anthropology in Context: The Image of God, Assimilation to God, and Tripartite Man in Ancient Judaism, Ancient Philosophy, and Early Christianity* (Tübingen: Mohr Siebeck, 2008), pp. 181-98.

the LORD set his heart in love on your ancestors alone and chose you, their descendants after them, out of all the peoples, as it is today" (v. 15). Why? In a commentary on this passage, Philo explains: "out of the whole human race he chose as of special excellence (ἀριστίνδην) those who are truly human (τοὺς πρὸς ἀλήθειαν ἀνθρώπους), and judged them worthy (ἠξίωσε) of all providential care (προνοίας),[38] and called them to worship him, the eternal fountain of good things, from which he showers the other virtues" (*Spec.* 1.303). The comment encapsulates Philo's understanding of the status of his people: Israel is a special nation because it is the highest form of humanity, properly aligned to the truth of the cosmos (worshipping the one transcendent God) and supreme in its receipt and exercise of virtue.

Philo takes the Mosaic address to "Israel" (Deut 10:12) to apply to the mind (διάνοια, *Spec.* 1.299), and if Israel is "truly human," it is because it fulfills the vocation of the mind, the "truly human" and highest element in the human constitution (cf. *Plant.* 42; *Fug.* 71). Elsewhere Philo illustrates God's "providential care" for this people in the recent crisis in Alexandria, since God takes particular care for "the race of suppliants" (τὸ ἱκετικὸν γένος): their name "Israel" means "he who sees God," and to see God, to "soar above all created things" to the invisible and blessed God, is the most precious human possibility and the greatest foundation for virtue and civilized values (ἀρετὴ καὶ καλοκαγαθία, *Legat.* 3–5). Normally, Philo uses the label "Israel" only in the allegorical treatises (it is never used in the "Exposition of the Law"), where its reference to the vision of God enables him to discover in the biblical text the story of the soul's journey toward God, climaxing in the (Platonic) metaphor of sight. But its deployment here in a historical treatise reflects Philo's capacity to relate literal to allegorical meanings, which are neither identical nor wholly distinct: the people spoken of in the biblical text are special to God *both* as the soul-type of those who see God in the philosophical sense (τὸ ὁρατικὸν γένος in the sense of "the visionary genus," e.g., *Deus* 144) *and* as the forebears and exemplars of the contemporary Jewish people (τὸ ὁρατικὸν γένος in the sense of "the seeing people," e.g., *Mos.* 2.196).[39] This ambiguity allows the inclusion of proselytes, whose "nobility" (εὐγένεια, "good γένος") is defined by their quality of soul, not by ancestry alone (*Virt.* 187–227). But in *Legat.* 3–5, Philo is content for the allegorical sense of "Israel" to enrich his presentation of the Jews as a historical nation, because the Jews' (and proselytes') unique capacity

38. All MSS read προνοίας, and there seems no need to emend to προνομίας ("preeminence") with Colson (LCL ad loc.).

39. For the ambiguity of γένος and the allegorical sense of the phrase, see Birnbaum, *Place of Judaism*, pp. 52-58.

to "see" the truth about God (cf. *Mos.* 2.271; *Spec.* 1.54; *Virt.* 179, 221) is central to his understanding of their special status and role.[40]

As the first of the "ancestors," Abraham (Abram) provides the foundational paradigm for the special qualities of the Jews. His story is one of movement and change: from Ur (via Haran) to Canaan (Gen 11:31; 12:1-6); from Hagar to Sarah (Gen 16–18); from "Abram" to "Abraham" (Gen 17:5). At the climax, he is exhorted to be blameless, just when he receives a vision of God (Gen 17:1). For Philo, these are clues that Abraham's story is the story of human progress toward perfection, climaxing in the vision of God. Abraham was both a historical figure, the "founder" (ἀρχηγέτης, *Mos.* 1.7; *Praem.* 57) or "ethnarch" (*Her.* 279) of the Jewish nation, and, in allegorical terms, an archetype (ἀρχέτυπος, *Abr.* 54, 88), one of three soul-types, the teachable soul (alongside Isaac, the naturally virtuous, and Jacob, the practicer of virtue). What Abraham learns is therefore foundational for Judaism and exemplary for everyone: his story encapsulates the twin lessons of truth and virtue (*Praem.* 27).[41]

In the first place, Abraham's journey from Ur to Canaan is a migration toward the *truth* about the world and about God. This migration may be telescoped into a single move (from Chaldean astronomy to the worship of the Cause, *Somn.* 1.160-61; *Virt.* 211–19), or traced as a two-stage journey, from Ur (astronomy) to Haran (examination of the self/body), and from there to the truth about God (e.g., *Migr.* 176–95; *Abr.* 68–80). The Chaldean interest in the heavenly bodies is representative of a more general error: the belief that the world itself is the cause of events and thus that the Cause (αἴτιον) is immanent, created, and visible (*Migr.* 179). In attacking such theological materialism, Philo targets not just Stoicism but all forms of "polytheistic opinion" and idolatry (*Virt.* 214, 219), which fail the most basic test of piety: the ascription of honor to the uncreated, invisible Cause. Looking out on his religious environment, Philo sees a vast error, one that grips not just the masses but even philosophers, who reverence images of gods and speak in the polytheistic

40. Birnbaum's discussion *(Place of Judaism)* tends toward a disjuncture between the allegorical, universal "Israel" and the literal, particular "Jews" in a way that threatens to separate what Philo conjoins. Although Philo's allegorical method has the potential to "dejudaize" his text, the thrust of his work brings his philosophical and hermeneutical resources into the service of Judaism; see Barclay, *Jews in the Mediterranean Diaspora*, pp. 170-80. As D. Dawson remarks, Philonic allegory "is an effort to make Greek culture Jewish rather than to dissolve Jewish identity into Greek culture" (*Allegorical Readers and Cultural Revision in Ancient Alexandria* [Berkeley: University of California Press, 1992], p. 74).

41. I here draw together common threads in the various representations of Abraham in the different kinds of Philonic treatise. For an appeal to distinguish these, in view of their different modes of exegesis and probably different audiences, see M. Böhm, *Rezeption und Funktion der Vätererzählungen bei Philo von Alexandria* (Berlin: de Guyter, 2005).

discourse ubiquitous in the Roman world. Abraham is the founder of the Jewish nation as the archetypical migrant from this mist of delusion to the light of truth (*Abr.* 78).

Since "Haran" means "holes" and thus the bodily orifices that channel the senses, Philo takes Abraham's move thence as involving analysis of the human constitution, with the discovery that it is governed by the rational, immaterial, and invisible mind; from that one may deduce the existence of a governing Mind outside the world (*Migr.* 184–91; *Abr.* 72–76). Thus, everything points beyond itself to the Cause, with reason speeding upward toward the truth (*Abr.* 88). This movement, prompted by divine commands, is effected both by human perception (ἔννοια) and by divine inspiration (ἐπιθειασμός, *Virt.* 214). Philo here invokes both human and divine agencies without special emphasis on either: illumined by God (*Praem.* 25), the mind begins to see the beam of truth (*Abr.* 70), drawn to it as iron is drawn to a magnet (*Praem.* 58); the climax is the moment when God "is seen" (ὤφθη, that is, reveals himself, *Abr.* 77–80). Philo takes the vision of God, or at least of his Powers, as a privilege granted by special divine initiative ("light from light") when the mystic ascends to the ultimate level of truth (*Fug.* 166–76; *Deus* 77–79; *Praem.* 36–46).[42] But the first steps in this pilgrimage are readily accessible and concern the simplest facts about the world and its Cause: it is by journeying along this path that the Jewish people are uniquely in tune with reality and thus uniquely pious.

But Abraham's migration is, secondly, the progress of the soul toward *virtue*, and away from its imprisonment in the body and its desires. The instruction to Abraham to leave his land, his kindred, and his father's house (Gen 12:1) is, at an allegorical level, the bidding of the soul to leave body, sense, and speech (*Migr.* 1–6; *Det.* 159) — not a complete departure (which is impossible before the blessed release of death), but a refusal to give way to bodily pleasures or sense-impressions, an investment only in the life of the mind (*Migr.* 7–12). When Abram nears perfection (Gen 17:1), his name is changed (Gen 17:5), a sign of his improvement of character (*Mut.* 70). Abraham, the "elect father of sound," is elect because he is now a cultivated character (ἀστεῖος), "chosen out of all on the grounds of his excellence" (ἐπικριθεὶς ἐξ ἁπάντων ἀριστίνδην, *Abr.* 83). His progress to virtue coincides with the switch from Hagar to Sarah in Genesis 16–18, that is, from encyclical education to philosophy (*Congr.* passim). By this means, Abraham is able to "mate" satisfactorily

42. E. R. Goodenough's famous analysis of this mystical ascent in *By Light, Light: The Mystic Gospel of Hellenistic Judaism* (Amsterdam: Philo Press, 1969 [1935]) has now been supplemented and balanced by Noack, *Gottesbewußtsein*.

with virtue (the allegorical meaning of "Sarah") — that is, with piety, along with justice, courage, moderation, and wisdom, capped with a special virtue, faith (*Abr.* passim).[43]

Virtue and truth are intimately connected: movement from the body and from external "goods" toward the life of the mind is founded on the realization that an eternal Mind, the source of all good things, exists beyond this physical world. What is true and good is the truth and goodness of nature (φύσις), an eternal ordering of reality that is obscured by the bodily entrapment of the soul and the failure of human reason, yet is rooted in the reason and goodness of the invisible Cause. Abraham's faith (Gen 15:6; the first example of this virtue, *Virt.* 216) is his confidence in this firm and unwavering reality (*Leg.* 3.228; *Abr.* 262–72; *Her.* 90–93). It is because he "sees" correctly this natural state of affairs that Abraham's life is the archetypical pilgrimage to intellectual truth and moral virtue (*Abr.* 60–61).

An aspect of that pilgrimage was Abraham's obedience to divine commands, including God's statutes and laws (Gen 12:4; 22:18; 26:5). Philo took these biblical texts to indicate that Abraham (and the other patriarchs) conformed to, and embodied, the unwritten laws of nature, of which the written Mosaic law was a copy (*Abr.* 1–6, 276). This accorded with his analysis of the Pentateuch as consisting of three parts: cosmology, the lives of the patriarchs, and legislation. If the three cohere (as they must), it is because the written legislation encapsulates the law of the cosmos, which is built into the nature of reality and "ensouled" in the lives of the patriarchs (*Opif.* 1–3; *Mos.* 2.46-52). Although the relationship between the Mosaic law and "nature" can be expressed in a variety of ways, what is crucial is the basic principle: what Jews observe on a daily basis is not some ethnically particular legislation, still less some arbitrary collection of customs, but the tangible instantiation of the order of the cosmos.[44] To keep the law is to follow the grain of the universe: those who do so are obviously most pleasing to God and most worthy of his gifts.[45]

This is the conviction that makes Philo delight in the phenomenon of proselytism. On a migration patterned like Abraham's (*Virt.* 219), proselytes (ἐπήλυται) abandon theological error in coming to honor the truly Existent

43. See S. Sandmel, *Philo's Place in Judaism: A Study of Conceptions of Abraham in Jewish Literature* (Cincinnati: Hebrew Union College Press, 1971), pp. 96-212.

44. For the relation between the Mosaic law and the "law of nature," see H. Najman, "The Law of Nature and the Authority of Mosaic Law," *StPhA* 11 (1999): 55-73; eadem, "A Written Copy of the Law of Nature: An Unthinkable Paradox?," *StPhA* 15 (2003): 54-63.

45. For Philo's Jewish adaptation of Greek notions of a "higher law" (the unwritten law, the law of nature, or the "living law" of the king), see J. W. Martens, *One God, One Law: Philo of Alexandria on the Mosaic and Greco-Roman Law* (Leiden: Brill, 2003).

One. Such converts have a lot of folly to unlearn,[46] and while Philo knows that it is an enormous social wrench to abandon such ancestral "vanity" (*Spec.* 1.52; 4.178; *Virt.* 102), he celebrates this movement from "deep darkness" toward "a little ray of truth" (*Virt.* 221, of Tamar). For Philo, the adoption of Judaism is more fundamentally the embrace of reality (*Spec.* 1.51, 309; *Virt.* 178): proselytes adopt a better "constitution" because Judaism's "overseer" is truth (*Virt.* 219). In other words, Jewish theology is not superior because it is Jewish, or more ancient, or founded in divine oracles, but simply because it is true: it corresponds to the way the world is governed by the truly existent God (ὁ ὄντως ὢν θεός, *Virt.* 102), the one Cause and Father of all (*Virt.* 221; *QE* 2.2). Converts have "deserted to God" (*Praem.* 152) and thus "crossed over to piety" (*Spec.* 1.51, 309).

Truth-based piety is bound to have moral effects: just as ignorance is the root of vice, so correct knowledge of the Existent God will foster all the virtues (*Virt.* 180–82). Philo thus understands proselyte conversion as a grand "refitting of life," a transition from its present "misfit" (ἀναρμοστία, *Virt.* 183) into a "better order" (ἀμείνων τάξις, *Spec.* 1.51) that corresponds to reality. Such realignment with truth naturally wins its reward: as proper worshippers of God, converts fittingly (ἀξίως) receive divine providential care (*Spec.* 1.309), and among the "great prizes" is the reward of a place in heaven (*Praem.* 152). Interpreting Deuteronomy 30:11-14, Philo insists that this refitting is not hard to obtain, so long as mouth, heart, and hands are coordinated, with the convert becoming both God-beloved (θεοφιλής) and God-loving (φιλόθεος, *Virt.* 183–84). The double dynamic of this relationship — both attunement to God and welcome by God — is encapsulated in the statement of Deuteronomy 26:17-18: "you have today chosen God to be God for you, and God has chosen you today to be a people for him" (*Virt.* 184). Philo finds here a "glorious reciprocity of choice" (παγκάλη τῆς αἱρέσεως ἀντίδοσις): humanity hastens to worship the Existent One, and God without delay takes the suppliant to himself, anticipating (προαπαντᾶν) those who honestly and sincerely come to worship him (*Virt.* 185). God's eagerness, even priority, in giving is reasonably conditioned by the readiness and desire of the human soul.

On the same terms, God's election of Israel is both reasonable and fitting: God takes as his "portion" what is closest and most harmonious with himself. As Deuteronomy 4:6-7 says, Israel is a "wise and understanding nation": God accordingly listens to their sanctified prayers and draws near as they call upon him (*Migr.* 56–59; *Praem.* 82–84). It was not because they were numerous

46. For example, fables taught since childhood (*Spec.* 1.51, 309), a belief in many gods (πολυαρχία, *Spec.* 4.178; *QE* 2.2), the habit of honoring nonexistent gods (τοῖς οὐ θεοῖς, *Virt.* 179), and ridiculous customs with lifeless images (*Virt.* 102, 219-21).

(Deut 7:7): it is not the many, but the few, well-ordered and governed by reason, who are beloved by God (*Migr.* 60–63). God's choice was not because of their righteousness (Deut 9:4-5). To forestall pride, it is necessary to insist that election is based on the wickedness of others and the covenant with the fathers, and that covenant, a symbol of God's gifts, indicates that God alone is the source of virtue (*Sacr.* 54–57). In other words, it was not because of *Israel's* righteousness that it was chosen, but so long as God is recognized as the Source and Cause, comparative righteousness is clearly the determining condition. On the basis of its knowledge and virtue, Israel is the nation closest to God and "dearest to God" (θεοφιλέστατον); it "has obtained the role of priest and prophet on behalf of the whole human race" (*Abr.* 98). Two factors connected to the ceremony of the "Sheath" (*Spec.* 2.162-67) indicate that "what the priest is to the city-state, the nation of Jews is to the whole world" (162). First, Jews, like priests, keep themselves pure in the unusually strict control they put on the pleasures of the body and the impulses of the soul (163). Secondly (and given greater emphasis, 164-67), Jews have a special relationship to God based on their superior avoidance of polytheistic error. Passing over created things, the Jews chose the service (θεραπεία) only of the Uncreated and Eternal, the Ruler and the Maker. Jewish aniconic monotheism makes Jews the only authentic worshippers of God, offering to the truly Existent God (ὁ ὄντως ὢν θεός) the service that others also owe, but have reprehensively evaded.[47]

There is an apologetic tone to this passage (it answers accusations of Jewish "inhumanity," 167), but it represents a common and insistent claim by Philo, that Jews, and Jews alone, are rightly oriented to the truth of the cosmos, giving proper honor to the invisible Cause of all. The Hebrew nation has thus been "allotted" (προσκεκληρωμένοι) to the Maker and Father of all (and is hated for it, *Virt.* 34); they are no ordinary nation, but have the highest possible claim (ἐπάγγελμα) in supplication (ἱκεσία) of the Maker and Father of all (*Virt.* 64). Philo concedes that pupils of "the most excellent philosophy" may know about this uncreated primal Cause (*Praem.* 43–44; *Spec.* 2.44-48), but the Jews' superiority lies in the fact that this truth is embedded in their customs and laws (*Virt.* 65). Every Sabbath in their synagogue meetings they occupy themselves with "knowledge" and with the "truths of nature," becoming well schooled, week by week, in "prudence, courage, temperance and justice, and also piety, holiness and every virtue, by which duties human and divine are discerned and rightly directed" (*Mos.* 2.216; cf. *Decal.* 96–101; *Spec.* 2.61-63). Jewish isolation is explained by the fact that "they live under

47. On the significance of the aniconic dimension to Jewish monotheism, see Barclay, *Jews in the Mediterranean Diaspora*, pp. 429-34.

exceptional laws, which are necessarily severe, as they inculcate the highest standard of virtue" (πρὸς τὴν ἄκραν ἀρετήν, *Spec.* 4.179). Jewish difference, then, is not a matter of irreducible ethnic particularity, but the expression of greater stringency and higher quality on a common scale of "virtue." If this explains their unpopularity to "the pleasure-seeking mass of humanity," it also explains why they are specially cared for by the Ruler of the universe: out of all the human race they are a kind of "first-fruits" set apart for the Maker and Father (*Spec.* 2.180).[48] Bound together by wisdom (in the worship of God) and prudence (in the regulation of human life), they are drawn toward God (*Praem.* 64–65, 79–81).[49]

Philo is conscious of the blessings that the Jewish people draw from the piety and virtue of their "founders," notably Abraham, Isaac, and Jacob (*Praem.* 61–66). As the "ethnarch," Abraham is the root of the plant, the people that see and worship God (*Her.* 279), whose preciousness to God Philo traces to "the priceless righteousness and virtue of the founders of the nation," which "survive like imperishable plants bearing undecaying fruit for their descendants, salvific and beneficial in every way, even if they happen to sin in a curable fashion — but not if their sins are completely incurable" (*Spec.* 2.181).[50] The final qualification is important. "Nobility" (εὐγένεια) is a matter of the soul, not of ancestry (*Virt.* 187–27). That is why proselytes can share in the patriarchs' heritage, while Jews must be warned not to place confidence in the virtue of their ancestors (πεποίθησις προγονικῆς ἀρετῆς, *Virt.* 226). Committed to the moral structure of the universe, Philo could hardly allow that the ancestral benefits of the Jewish nation conferred a guaranteed reward. In fact, both curses and blessings (Lev 26; Deut 26–28) are applicable to the Jewish nation as it looks to the future (*Praem.* 79–172). Curses and penalties will be deserved (ἄξιον) by those who disregard the laws of righteousness and piety and are seduced by polytheistic myth (*Praem.* 162). On the other hand, all the biblical blessings, "external" as well as spiritual, will be poured out on those who cultivate virtue and the holy laws (*Praem.* 119), those who are pious, admirable (σπουδαῖος), frugal, and wise, worthy of blessing and salvation (ἄξιοι εὐλογίας/σωτηρίας, *Praem.* 87, 113).[51] As Philo concludes: "These are the blessings of good people

48. Cf. *Mos.* 1.278-79, with reference to the Jews' distinct customs that constitute them as specially righteous, their souls sprung from divine seeds, akin to God.

49. See further, McFarland, *God Who Gives*, pp. 102-104 on the fitting donation of divine gifts to "Israel," allegorical and literal. As he remarks, "Israel expresses the truism that God benefits the worthy" (p. 104).

50. For the root metaphor, cf. *Praem.* 172: if there is a "root" that survives through disaster, it operates like a tiny seed of virtue left in the soul, capable of producing great plants.

51. The exact contours of this future are not completely clear (cf. *Praem.* 162–72; *Mos.*

(ἀγαθοὶ ἄνθρωποι) who fulfill the law by their actions (ἔργα), blessings which it says will be completed by the grace (χάρις) of the gift-loving God who dignifies and rewards what is excellent because of its likeness to himself" (τὰ καλὰ διὰ τὴν πρὸς αὐτὸν ὁμοιότητα σεμνοποιοῦντος καὶ γεραίνοντος, *Praem.* 126).

6.5. Philo's Perfections of Grace

Philo's delight in the beneficence of God as Cause and Giver of all good things leads him to perfect divine grace in many of the dimensions we have categorized (see chapter 2). The constant overflow of divine gifts, poured incessantly into the cosmos, leads him to wax eloquent on the *superabundance* of divine generosity, as we have seen. Philosophical concern to keep God, the source of all goodness, free from the causation of evil in any sense (even punishment) leads Philo toward the *singularity* of grace, as far as the biblical text will allow. At the same time, a persistent and unyielding emphasis on God as Cause makes Philo emphasize the *priority* of grace; the same emphasis entails that, even while stressing the (ascetic) effort of virtuous persons, Philo, in certain remarks to the philosophically initiated, will press the divine causation of virtue into a form of *efficacy* that renders the human agent entirely passive, at least at the highest point of ascent to God. As we have seen, a desire to distinguish God's giving from the world of commerce can lead Philo to insist that God's benefits seek and require no gift in return, but he normally figures thanksgiving as the proper return to God and does not generally idealize the *non-reciprocal* gift in anything like its modern form. But, as has become clear throughout our study, God's gifts are generally and for good reason *congruous* with the quality of the recipient. Although there are limits to this rule, especially if "worth" suggests comparability with God or human causation of the gift, Philo is *not* generally concerned to perfect the *incongruity* of the gift.

It is important to be clear about what this entails. A *congruous* gift is still a gift: it has not been "debased" into a form of payment, "earned" by the good works of the recipient. Commentators on Philo who assume that divine grace is, in principle, unrelated to human value or worth have found Philo's combination of divine gift with human worth inconsistent (an arbitrary alternation between salvation by grace and self-salvation), a form of "synergism,"

2.44; *QE* 2.76). There are hints at a form of messianism (*Praem.* 95 on Num 24:7), but also the assurance that God will intervene and Israel's own virtue will be the cause of its universal respect. Cf. U. Fischer, *Eschatologie und Jenseitserwartung im hellenistischen Diasporajudentum* (Berlin: de Gruyter, 1978), pp. 187-213.

or simply bizarre.[52] But if we rid ourselves of the assumption that divine grace is, by definition, given to the *unworthy,* an assumption that (for ideological reasons) makes one perfection of grace its defining characteristic, it is perfectly possible to hail Philo as a profound theologian of grace, even though he does not perfect its incongruity.[53] As we have seen, there are good reasons why Philo finds God to give to the "worthy," reasons that have nothing to do with "synergism," "legalism," "works-righteousness," or other such categories. If the world is ordered by a system of values instituted by God himself, and if the superior values represent God's own nature and the virtues closest to himself, it is natural that God should reward what is most like himself with the gifts of his grace.[54] To do otherwise as a matter of principle would render God's generosity contradictory to his goodness, a random or self-defeating beneficence that would cut against the values of the cosmos. But God is no arbitrary giver. He rewards the values he has instituted himself, and thus ensures that rightly ordered humans can reach the perfection that he has graciously designed for them to attain.

52. So, respectively, H. Windisch, *Die Frömmigkeit Philos und ihre Bedeutung für das Christentum: Eine Religionsgeschichtliche Studie* (Leipzig: J. C. Hinrichs, 1909), pp. 10-23; W. Völker, *Fortschritt und Vollendung bei Philo von Alexandrien: Eine Studie zur Geschichte der Frömmigkeit* (Leipzig: J. C. Hinrichs, 1938), pp. 115-32; and D. Carson, who marks the Philonic phrase "worthy of grace" with an incredulous *sic,* and finds Philo's notion of election devoid of "sheer grace" ("Divine Sovereignty and Human Responsibility in Philo: Analysis and Method," *NovT* 23 [1981]: 148-64, at pp. 160-62). For discussion of this theme, in debate with Windisch and Völker, see Zeller, *Charis,* pp. 65-72, and McFarland, *God Who Gives.* Cf. J. R. Harrison, *Paul's Language of Grace in Its Graeco-Roman Context* (Tübingen: Mohr Siebeck, 2003), who surveys scholarly discussion of this topic (pp. 114-20) and emphasizes Philo's use of benefaction terminology, concluding that an "Old Testament understanding of covenantal grace" has been "distorted" by the introduction of a "Graeco-Roman understanding of merit" (p. 133). But as we have seen, to contrast "gift" and "merit" (Birnbaum, *Place of Judaism,* pp. 143, 183) or "human merit" and "divine grace" (Termini, "Philo's Thought," p. 123: they meet in "synergy") is to misconstrue the structure of Philo's thought.

53. Cf. H. A. A. Kennedy, *Philo's Contribution to Religion* (London: Hodder & Stoughton, 1919), pp. 142-57, though the conclusion that Philo's theology of grace is therefore identical to Paul's is unwarranted, as we shall see (Parts III and IV).

54. Philo thus gives a stronger and deeper *theological* (and philosophical) rationale for the principle of "worth" than does *The Wisdom of Solomon* (see chapter 5), although there is also much in common between them.

CHAPTER 7

The Qumran *Hodayot* (1QH[a])

The Thanksgiving Hymns from Qumran represent another striking articulation of divine benevolence, with the distinctive accents of a sectarian community. Effusive expressions of gratitude for divine goodness punctuate these hymns with extraordinary regularity: in multiple variations God is addressed with thanks for what has transpired "by your kindnesses" (בחסדיכה), "according to the abundance of your compassion" (כהמון רחמיכה), because of "your abundant goodness" (רוב טובכה), and through "forgiveness" (סליחות) (e.g., 1QH[a] XII.38; XV.33; XVII.34).[1] The language of "abundance" mirrors the almost obsessive articulation of this theme, which matches the fact that the signature tune of all these compositions is the attribution of knowledge, righteousness, power, and glory — indeed, every dimension of salvation — to God. At the same time, there is an equal emphasis on the worthlessness of the recipients of mercy, an insistent assertion that there is nothing in the material, social, or moral quality of the human object that could provide grounds for this outpouring of grace. The Qumran hymns thus place divine grace and hu-

1. In the wake of the now definitive DJD edition of 1QH[a] by H. Stegemann with E. Schuller (and translation by C. Newsom), *1QHodayot[a]* (DJD XL; Oxford: Clarendon Press, 2009), I cite all texts according to their column and line numbers, and use the accompanying translation by Newsom. Sukenik's numbering system, employed in the commentaries by S. Holm-Nielsen (*Hodayot: Psalms from Qumran* [Aarhus: Universitetsforlaget, 1960]) and M. Mansoor (*The Thanksgiving Hymns* [Leiden: Brill, 1961]) and in all scholarly work up to the 1990s, is now superseded. The translation by F. Garcia Martínez and E. J. C. Tigchelaar (*The Dead Sea Scrolls Study Edition*, 2 vols. [Leiden: Brill, 1997-98]) uses the Stegemann (and Puech) column numbers, but follows the older line-numbering, now rendered obsolete by the Stegemann and Schuller edition. For a bibliography of scholarship on the *Hodayot* up to 1989, see N. Lohfink, *Lobgesänge der Armen* (Stuttgart: Katholisches Bibelwerk, 1990), pp. 126-36; cf. E. M. Schuller and L. DiTommaso, "A Bibliography of the Hodayot, 1948-1996," *DSD* 4 (1997): 55-101; E. M. Schuller, "Recent Scholarship on the *Hodayot* 1993-2010," *CBR* 10 (2011): 119-62.

man worth in the starkest possible contrast (quite the opposite to Philo), and in this regard they create a polarity more extreme than can be found in any Second Temple text other than the letters of Paul. We must clearly attend to the logic by which this extreme polarity makes theological sense. After introducing the hymns and their conceptuality (7.1), we will contrast the worthlessness of humanity (7.2) with the goodness of God (7.3) before exploring the rationale by which the hymnists made sense of this anomaly (7.4).

7.1. Introduction

The Thanksgiving Hymns *(Hodayot)* of 1QH[a] are an anthology, a collection of hymns (or psalms) with many similarities in theme and emphasis, but some diversity in the self-positioning of the speaker. From Cave 4 we have fragments of six other versions of this anthology, which indicate that there was no fixity in content or order, though the individual hymns found in these various collections are almost entirely identical.[2] Since it is the fullest and the best preserved, our focus here will be on the *Hodayot* compiled in 1QH[a], probably in the first century BCE.[3] Within this anthology some hymns, which form the bulk of columns X-XVII, depict the speaker in a position of leadership; he is the gateway into the community and the medium of divine revelation, though beset by opposition. The special features of these *Hodayot* have led scholars to distinguish between "Leader Hymns" and "Community Hymns," and a long debate, from the 1960s to the present day, has raged around the possible iden-

2. See E. Schuller in E. Chazon et al., *Qumran Cave 4, XX: Poetical and Liturgical Works, Part 2* (Oxford: Clarendon Press, 1999), pp. 69-254, 421-32, with a chart of the relationships between the anthologies on pp. 72-73. This indicates that some followed the same order as 1QH[a] (e.g., 4QH[b]) and some not (4QH[a]), while one included only those hymns in 1QH[a] that scholars designate "Leader Hymns" (4QH[c]; see below). The fact that there are few variations in the verbal contents of the individual hymns suggests that they constituted a limited and authoritative repertoire, faithfully copied though variously selected and compiled. For a survey of the textual data, see Schuller, "Recent Scholarship," pp. 122-31, concluding that "there is virtually no evidence of sustained recensional activity that is theologically or ideologically motivated" (p. 131).

3. For the dating, see D. K. Falk, "Prayers and Psalms," in D. A. Carson, P. T. O'Brien, and M. A. Seifrid, eds., *Justification and Variegated Nomism*, vol. 1: *The Complexities of Second Temple Judaism* (Tübingen: Mohr Siebeck, 2001), pp. 7-56, at p. 27, and Schuller, "Recent Scholarship," p. 132 (1QH[a] is the latest of our copies of the hymns, and dates from the early Herodian period, 30–1 BCE). A. Lange (*Weisheit und Prädestination: Weisheitliche Urordnung und Prädestination in den Textfunden von Qumran* [Leiden: Brill, 1995], pp. 201-2) dates the earliest hymns to the second half of the second century BCE.

tification of this leader-figure with the "Teacher of Righteousness."[4] For our purposes, it is not necessary to enter this debate, since the two types of hymn do not differ significantly in the dynamics of divine mercy. The insertion of the Leader Hymns within a set of Community *Hodayot* in a single anthology, and the presence of worthlessness-confessions within the Leader Hymns identical to those found elsewhere (e.g., XII.31–XIII.6; XV.29-36), indicate that those who created and used this anthology saw no generic difference between these two types of hymn; whatever their origin, they served current purposes by being combined.[5]

It is another matter to determine what those purposes may have been. There is no doubt that these *Hodayot* reflect and inculcate a distinctive sectarian ideology of knowledge and truth.[6] Although they stand in the tradition of biblical psalmody, they adapt this and other scriptural language in highly idiosyncratic ways, through additions, qualifications, new collocations — indeed, the entire reframing of biblical motifs.[7] One has the impression that they comprise a carefully composed discursive repertoire, whose constant use would serve to shape the consciousness and sensibilities of the user. Given our sketchy knowledge of the *yaḥad* alluded to in these texts, it is difficult to say where

4. The thesis that these Leader Hymns were authored by (or represent the persona of) the founding figure known elsewhere as the "Teacher of Righteousness" was advanced by a series of dissertations in the 1960s (G. Jeremias, *Der Lehrer der Gerechtigkeit* [Göttingen: Vandenhoeck & Ruprecht, 1963]; J. Becker, *Das Heil Gottes: Heils- und Sundenbegriffe in den Qumrantexte und im Neuen Testament* [Göttingen: Vandenhoeck & Ruprecht, 1964]; H.-W. Kuhn, *Enderwartung und gegenwärtiges Heil* [Göttingen: Vandenhoeck & Ruprecht, 1966]) and, after a period of skepticism, has been revived with new argumentation by M. Douglas, "The Teacher-Hymn Hypothesis Revisited: New Data for an Old Crux," *DSD* 6 (1999): 239-66. The main contrary thesis is that the hymns represent a generic *mythos* of an oppressed leader, which was available for appropriation by different generations and various types of leader; their reception served to shape the *ethos* of the whole community, both leaders and led (see, e.g., Lohfink, *Lobgesänge;* C. Newsom, *The Self as Symbolic Space: Constructing Identity and Community at Qumran* [Leiden: Brill, 2004], pp. 287-346). For recent discussion, see S. Hultgren, *From the Damascus Covenant to the Covenant of the Community* (Leiden: Brill, 2007), pp. 410-16; A. K. Harkins, "Who Is the Teacher of the Teacher Hymns? Re-examining the Teacher Hymns Hypothesis Fifty Years Later," in E. Mason et al., eds., *A Teacher for All Generations: Essays in Honor of James C. VanderKam* (Leiden: Brill, 2012), pp. 449-67.

5. Although source-critical analysis has speculated that the above "worthlessness" passages are secondary insertions into the Leader Hymns (see Becker, *Heil Gottes,* pp. 54-55; Douglas, "Teacher-Hymn Hypothesis," pp. 245, 249), we are concerned here with the present form of the anthology, not its possible stages of redaction.

6. The epithet "sectarian" is not without its problems, but is here used to refer to the compositions constructed or adapted by the Qumran *yaḥad.*

7. On the relation of these texts to biblical subtexts, see, e.g., Holm-Nielsen, *Hodayot* and J. A. Hughes, *Scriptural Allusions and Exegesis in the Hodayot* (Leiden: Brill, 2006).

this usage would have occurred. An earlier thesis regarding the "liturgical" use of these texts has been brought into question with the publication of prayers from Qumran that clearly had a liturgical *Sitz im Leben,* and it is now common to locate these hymns within the vaguely defined category of "personal devotion."[8] The attribution of some of the Community Hymns to "the Maskil" (V.12; VII.21; XX.7; XXV.34), who himself speaks in XX.14, and the presence of a similar *hodayah* related to "the Maskil" at the end of some versions of the "Community Rule" (1QS X.1–XI.22), suggest that these hymns, despite their first-person-singular perspective, had more than a merely private function. If they were associated with the Maskil, and with other leaders, they may have served didactic purposes in shaping the ethos and self-understanding of the community.[9] Given the internal references to regular times of prayer (XX.7-12; cf. 1QS X.1-5), these may have been authorized prayers for the use of members of the community, whose oral (and surely overheard) repetition would shape the sectarian sense of privilege and destiny.[10] There was perhaps no practice more significant for the internal formation of members of the *yaḥad* than the forms and contents of their address to God. Those soaked in the language of these *Hodayot* would have learned to see themselves in distinctive ways that both explained and solidified their social location in the Qumran community.[11]

8. For the liturgical thesis, see Holm-Nielsen, *Hodayot,* pp. 332-48; for the contrast with more recognizably "cultic" or "liturgical" prayers from Qumran, see B. Nitzan, *Qumran Prayer and Religious Poetry,* trans. J. Chipman (Leiden: Brill, 1994), pp. 321-51. For the hypothesis of "personal devotion" see, e.g., J. J. Collins, "Amazing Grace: The Transformation of the Thanksgiving Hymn at Qumran," in H. Attridge and M. E. Fassler, eds., *Psalms in Community: Jewish and Christian Textual, Liturgical, and Artistic Traditions* (Atlanta: Society of Biblical Literature, 2003), pp. 75-85. Hughes provides a summary of the debate (*Scriptural Allusions,* pp. 12-34). The apparent call to worship at the end of 4Q427 (= 4QH[a]) fragment 7 has raised again the question of a "liturgical" setting. For recent discussion, see A. K. Harkins, "The Performative Reading of the Hodayot: The Arousal of Emotions and the Exegetical Generation of Texts," *JSP* 21 (2011): 55-71.

9. Evidence of the communal context of the hymns appears in various guises; note, e.g., the allusions to the (entrance) oaths of the speaker in VI.28-30.

10. For a comprehensive study of prayer at Qumran, see D. K. Falk, *Daily, Sabbath, and Festival Prayers in the Dead Sea Scrolls* (Leiden: Brill, 1998); as he notes (pp. 100-103), some hymns seem to combine the themes of worship and instruction (e.g., V.12-23). On the practice of "praying together," see 1QS 6.7-8.

11. My approach is generally indebted to Newsom *(Symbolic Space),* who probes with great effect the ways in which the *Hodayot* create and maintain the special subjectivity of those who used them. She recognizes, of course, that the "I" who speaks here is located within a community, and at certain points I will attempt to bring out further the social function of these prayers. For older but still valuable discussions of the theology of 1QH[a] see J. Licht, "The Doctrine of the Thanksgiving Scroll," *IEJ* 6 (1956): 1-13, 89-101, and Holm-Nielsen, *Hodayot,* pp. 273-300.

Our special focus on the discourse of divine benevolence gives us many possible points of entry into the *Hodayot,* since the theme is practically ubiquitous. We may begin with a representative hymn (in fact, a hymn about hymns) that introduces many of the topics we will here explore [XIX.6-17]:

> [6] I thank you, O my God, that you have acted wonderfully with dust, and with a creature of clay you have worked so very powerfully.
>
> What am I that [7] you have [inst]ructed me in the secret counsel of your truth, and that you have given me insight into your wondrous deeds, that you have put thanksgiving into my mouth, pr[ai]se upon my tongue, [8] and (made) the utterance of my lips as the foundation of jubilation, so that I may sing of your kindness and reflect on your strength all [9] the day? Continually I bless your name, and I will recount your glory in the midst of humankind. In your great goodness [10] my soul delights.
>
> I know that your command is truth, that in your hand is righteousness, in your thoughts [11] all knowledge, in your strength all power, and that all glory is with you. In your anger are all punishing judgments, [12] but in your goodness is abundant forgiveness, and your compassion is for all the children of your good favor.
>
> For you have made known to them the secret counsel of your truth, [13] and given them insight into your wonderful mysteries. For the sake of your glory you have purified a mortal from sin so that he may sanctify himself [14] for you from all impure abominations and from faithless guilt, so that he may be united with the children of your truth and in the lot with [15] your holy ones, so that a corpse-infesting maggot may be raised up from the dust to the council of [your] t[ruth], and from a spirit of perversion to the understanding which comes from you, [16] and so that he may take (his) place before you with the everlasting host and the [eternal] spirit[s], and so that he may be renewed together with all that i[s] [17] and will be and with those who have knowledge in a common rejoicing.[12]

As one would expect, this thanksgiving hymn resounds with praises of God's "wonderful deeds" and recounts his acts of salvation on behalf of the speaker; but the special fingerprint of the community is immediately recognizable. The speaker is characterized as "dust" (עפר) and "a creature of clay" (יצר חמר, 6),

12. Translation by Newsom, from Stegemann and Schuller, *1QHodayot^a*, pp. 247-48; for an analysis of the structure and poetry of this passage see Kuhn, *Enderwartung*, pp. 78-92; B. Kittel, *The Hymns of Qumran: Translation and Commentary* (Chico: Scholars Press, 1981), pp. 109-19. This may be the beginning of a longer *hodayah* (Stegemann and Schuller, *1QHodayot^a*, pp. 242-43).

two stock items from the language of self-denigration which peppers the *Hodayot.* The "wonderful deeds" are thus rendered spectacular precisely by their incongruity — the extraordinary treatment of inert, low-grade materials, such that a "corpse-infesting maggot" is elevated from the dust to stand before God with the angelic "host" and "the eternal spirits" (15-16). The cognitive content of this dramatic elevation is also a special feature of the *Hodayot:* the first and most important dimension of God's "deeds" is "instruction" in "the secret counsel of [God's] truth" (7, 12), the "insight" (שכל), "knowledge" (דעה), and "understanding" (בינה) that are a gift from God (7, 12, 15). This epistemological privilege is both the core content of salvation and the capacity to appreciate it: it is because *he knows* that he knows the secrets of God that the sectarian is equipped to praise the one who reveals them (7-10).

The central section of this passage attributes to God the controlling design of the universe (10-12): his command is "truth" (אמת), a proper ordering of reality,[13] and in his hand is "righteousness" (צדקה), the correct enactment of that truth; in his "thoughts" (or better, "plans," מחשבת) is all knowledge (10-11). God's power is thus directed toward, and his glory reflected in, the fulfillment of a universal design that entails, in dualistic pattern, both his wrath and his goodness — the one in "punishing judgments," the other in "abundant forgiveness" (רוב סליחות, 11-12). These binary effects of God's power mirror, of course, a biblical pattern (e.g., Exod 34:6-7; Ps 145:20, both texts of importance to the *Hodayot* authors), but the distinctive twist at Qumran is apparent in the gloss added to the second category, "and your compassion is for all the children of your good favor" (ורחמיכה לכול בני רצונכה, 12). "Children of God's good favor" (or "preference," רצון; see below), like "children of truth" (בני אמת, 14), is a special sectarian self-label: their identity is defined in terms that are neither national ("Israel") nor ancestral ("children of Abraham"), but selective, and their selection represents a "preference" deep in the design of God.

The rest of our passage describes the outworking of that design: God grants knowledge of "secrets" and "wonderful mysteries," and an accompanying purification, whose effect, in social terms, is to be "united with the children of your truth" (להוחד עם בני אמתך, 14), and "in the lot with your holy ones" (בגורל עם קדושיכה, 14-15) — that is, to join the sectarian community.[14] The

13. For "truth" as correct ordering, see, e.g., XIV.28-29 (drawing off Isa 28:17) and XVIII.32; God's plans are "true" in the sense that a plumb line ensures that buildings are "true" (for the metaphor, see IX.30-31; XVI.22-23). As Newsom comments, "for the sect, truth is inseparable from right ordering" (*Symbolic Space,* p. 136).

14. For the meaning of "the holy ones" as the community itself, see Kuhn, *Enderwartung,* pp. 90-93.

language of "lot" suggests an election within a pre-determined divine plan, and as a rhetorical finale, the hymnist pulls back to view the full panorama of this extraordinary plan. The "holy ones" are destined to take their place alongside the heavenly and everlasting "spirits," with their "renewal" as part of the divine rectification of "all that is and will be" — a cosmos intended to be united in a chorus of eternal praise (16-17).[15]

Even from this brief extract it is clear that one cannot understand the special accentuation of divine beneficence in the *Hodayot* except in its juxtaposition with the extreme statements of self-humiliation that accompany it, and except by reference to the predetermined order of the cosmos. In fact, as we shall see, it is this latter that explains the anomaly of God's extraordinary mercy to the utterly worthless. But it is also clear that this striking theological complex is closely related to a peculiar social context. The person who "all the day" and "continually" (8-9) engages in such thanksgiving expresses, reinforces, and in a sense *manufactures* the kind of privileged knowledge of which he speaks. While at one level this experience is intensely individual, at another the preformed language and its stereotyped repertoire create for the sectarians a shared identity as "children of God's preference," uniting them in a "common rejoicing." We would be surprised if the extraordinary statements of divine mercy were not in some way connected to the unusual sectarian context in which they were expressed.

7.2. The Worthlessness of the Human

It is characteristic of the *Hodayot* that the praise of God is regularly interrupted by the self-analysis of the speaker, who pours doubt on his capacity and worth. "Pours" is an apposite verb: with lavish self-scorn, piling up numerous forms of negative self-evaluation, the speaker repeatedly diminishes himself before God. A stock vocabulary and a limited pool of formulae make up these numerous interjections of *"Niedrigkeitsdoxologie."*[16] The following is a typical sample (XX.27-38):

15. The notion of joining angelic hosts in cosmic praise is dramatically illustrated in the "Songs of the Sabbath Sacrifices"; see the discussion in B. Frennesson, *"In a Common Rejoicing": Liturgical Communion with Angels in Qumran* (Uppsala: Uppsala University Press, 1999); E. Chazon, "Liturgical Communion with the Angels at Qumran," in D. K. Falk et al., eds., *Sapiential, Liturgical, and Poetical Texts from Qumran* (Leiden: Brill, 2000), pp. 95-105.

16. The term was coined by Kuhn, *Enderwartung*, p. 27; for detailed analysis of the terminology of such passages, see H. Lichtenberger, *Studien zum Menschenbild in Texten der Qumrangemeinde* (Göttingen: Vandenhoeck & Ruprecht, 1980), pp. 73-98.

> [27] As for me, from dust [you] took [me, and from clay] I was [sh]aped [28] as a source of pollution and shameful dishonor, a heap of dust and thing kneaded [with water, a council of magg]ots, a dwelling of [29] darkness. And there is a return to dust for the creature of clay at the time of [your] anger [ ] dust returns [30] to that from which it was taken. What can dust and ashes reply [concerning your judgment? And ho]w can it understand [31] its [d]eeds? How can it stand before the one who reproves it? . . . [33] There is none who can reply [34] to your rebuke. For you are just, and there is none corresponding to you. What, then, is he who returns to his dust? [35] As for me, I remain silent. What could I say concerning this? According to my knowledge I have spoken, a creature mixed from clay. What [36] can I say unless you open my mouth? How can I understand unless you give me insight? What can I s[peak] [37] unless you reveal it to my mind? How should I walk the straight way unless you establ[ish my st]ep? [How shall] [38] [my] step stand [without your making it] firm in strength?

Here, as elsewhere, the sectarian describes himself in terms of the lowest elements of the cosmos: he is merely "dust" (עפר, 28),[17] a "creature of clay" (יצר חמר, 29), "kneaded with water" (מגבל במים, 28), or simply "flesh" (בשר, e.g., V.15 and over twenty-five times elsewhere). The "dust" designation places emphasis on human mortality: this is a transitory creature that is doomed to "return to his dust" (שב אל עפרו, 34), an insignificant speck in the cosmos. But there is more: he is also a "source of pollution" (or "impurity," מקור נדה, 28), a state associated here with "shame" (קלון, 28) and elsewhere with a "perverse spirit" (רוח נעוה, V.32; VIII.18, etc.), with "iniquity" (עוון, IX.24; XII.30, etc.) and "sin" (חטאה, XIX.23; IX.24, etc.).[18] Most of these terms are, of course, derived from the Hebrew Scriptures (e.g., Gen 2:7; 3:19; 6:3; Isa 29:19; Ps 51), and the declarations of insignificance are closest to the characterizations of humanity in Job (e.g., Job 4:17-21; 14:1-4; 15:14-16). But the way in which they are

17. The term occurs more than thirty times in 1QH[a], including in formulae such as "a creature of dust" (יצר עפר, XXI.25) and "dust and ashes" (עפר ואפר, cf. XVIII.7).

18. For a narrative account of sinfulness, see XV.37–XVI.4. The use of the phrase "spirit of flesh" (רוח בשר, IV.37; V.15, 30) indicates that there is no "flesh-spirit" anthropological dualism in the *Hodayot* (see H. Hübner, "Anthropologisher Dualismus in den Hodayoth?" *NTS* 18 [1971-72]: 268-84). רוח indicates the "character," "disposition," or driving force of a human, which can be either "perverted" or "holy" (the latter as granted by God). For the use of רוח at Qumran, see A. E. Sekki, *The Meaning of* Ruaḥ *at Qumran* (Atlanta: Scholars Press, 1989), and for בשר, see J. Frey, "Flesh and Spirit in the Palestinian Jewish Sapiential Tradition and in the Qumran Texts: An Inquiry into the Background of Pauline Usage," in C. Hempel et al., eds., *The Wisdom Texts from Qumran and the Development of Sapiential Thought* (Leuven: Leuven University Press, 2002), pp. 367-404.

here piled up and amplified, and the relentless return to this theme throughout the *Hodayot,* is unique in Second Temple literature.[19] Together they draw a portrait of human *misalignment* and *incapacity,* and underline the sectarian's *incongruent position* in the cosmic plan — three related aspects of the human condition that are worth examining in a little detail.

The motif of *misalignment,* or "perversity" and "faithless guilt" (אשמת מעל, XIX.14), depicts the human as twisted or lapsed from orientation to the will of God. If God's "righteousness" represents his proper ordering of the world, the wayward human is exposed to his "judgments" (משפטם), if not now, certainly at the *eschaton* (e.g., IX.25). This exposure constantly bears on the speaker of these hymns, who anticipates, as in our sample text (above), what it would be like to encounter God's "rebuke" or "reproof." The anticipation is terrifying because humans would be rendered utterly speechless — overawed by the majesty of the judge and unable to defend themselves in their guilt. A series of rhetorical questions underlines the hopelessness of this situation (e.g., XX.34-38, cited above): What can a human creature reply? How can I stand? How can I speak? This relentless questioning is frequently reinforced by the language of impurity; a polluted creature can have no dealings with the holiness of God.[20] Such misalignment seems integral to the human condition; there is no attempt to provide a theoretical explanation, although references to a "dwelling of darkness" (XX.28-29) and the "rule" of a "perverted spirit" (V.32) partially parallel the rationale offered in the "Treatise of the Two Spirits" (1QS III.13–IV.26). Strikingly, the rhetoric of repudiation is directed not only, as one would expect, against the "evildoers" and "people of deceit" outside the sectarian community, but also against the speaker himself. Thus, even the sectarian fits this wholly negative characterization, but for one critical factor: the agency of God. As our sample shows, the addition of the particle "unless" (כיא אם, XX.36-37) and a change in the subject of the verbs finally switches the self-doubting questions into a different mode: "How can I understand . . . *unless you give me* insight?" (XX.36). Misalignment remains the lifelong condition of human beings (cf. XII.30-31), *but for* a divine agent who recalibrates their cognitive and moral bearings.

19. For the distinctive linking of Genesis 2:7 with Genesis 3:19 in the *Hodayot,* see J. Maston, *Divine and Human Agency in Second Temple Judaism and Paul* (Tübingen: Mohr Siebeck, 2010), pp. 88-94. For the particular use of Job and the distinctive accenting of biblical material in this construction of human ontology, see N. A. Meyer, "Adam's Dust and Adam's Glory: Rethinking Anthropogony and Theology in the Hodayot and the Letters of Paul" (PhD thesis, McMaster University, 2013).

20. For sin as impurity at Qumran, see J. Klawans, *Impurity and Sin in Ancient Judaism* (Oxford: Oxford University Press, 2000), pp. 67-91.

This switch of subject is related to the second characteristic of human worthlessness, *incapacity* before God. To the rhetorical formula "Who/how . . . unless?" there corresponds the statement that "the way of humanity is not established except (כי אם) by the spirit God has fashioned for it" (XII.32). In the same context, the hymn deploys the contrastive formula, "not to humankind . . . to God": "As for me, I know that righteousness does not belong to humankind (לא לאנוש צדקה) nor perfection of way to a mortal. To God Most High (לאל עליון) belong all the works of righteousness" (XII.31-32). This denial of capacity covers a large range of human activities: without God, the "I" of these hymns cannot "speak" (in self-defense or praise), cannot "understand," cannot "walk," and cannot "stand" (remain stable, or take his place before God). This does not efface human agency, or render the sectarian passive or inactive: on the contrary, he now vigorously "holds fast to the covenant" (XII.40) and walks in the "perfection of way." The sectarians' agency is not autonomous, but it is active, and the point of these antithetical formulae is to trace the conditions under which it is possible for the human subject to "walk the straight way" (XX.37). If the hymns deny human capacity, in order to trace its source in God, the purpose is not to characterize the two agencies as mutually exclusive, but to hang every sectarian act on the will and initiative of God.[21]

Even so, this coordination of agents (or of divine agent and human agency)[22] leaves the distance between God and humanity as large as possible. In XVII.15-18, the author acknowledges that among human beings there are degrees of relative righteousness, wisdom, honor, and strength. But between God and humanity the difference is absolute: "one spirit may prove stronger than another. But compared with your [stren]gth there is none (equal) in power, and your glory has no [and] your wisdom no measure" (XVII.16-17). There remains an infinite difference between humanity and God, to which the hymns return time and again. After a further series of rhetorical self-debasements, another *hodayah* bursts out (XVIII.10-14):

> [10] Behold, you are the prince of gods, the king of the glorious ones, lord of every spirit, and ruler of every creature. [11] Apart from you nothing is done; nothing is known without your will; and except for you, there is nothing. [12] There is none beside you in strength, none comparable to your glory, and for your strength there is no price. Who [13] among all your

21. So rightly Maston, *Divine and Human Agency,* pp. 94-110. As he remarks, "the significance of the hymnist's action is not lessened because it is rooted in God's action, for it is precisely because God acted on behalf of the hymnist that he decides to act" (pp. 96-97).

22. On the speaker in the *Hodayot* as "not an agent but an agency through whom God works," see Newsom, *Symbolic Space,* p. 207.

wondrous great creatures can retain the strength to stand before your glory? [14] And what, then, is he who returns to his dust that he could summon such strength? For your glory alone you have done all these things.

The repeated negatives of lines 11-12 (לא . . . ולא . . . ואין . . . ואין. . . ואין . . . אין) could not be more emphatic: if the human can appear on this scene hereafter this will be only because of the universal reach and total efficacy of the divine "will" (רצון, 11).

Such contrasts throw into relief the third aspect of human *Niedrigkeit,* the *incongruity* of human participation in the plan of God. This feature is brought out most clearly when one puts such bursts of self-effacement within their larger literary context. For instance, in column IX (to which we will return), the standard denigration of the human (IX.23-25) immediately follows a sweeping description of the design of the cosmos (IX.9-22): the worthlessness of the speaker underscores his amazement that his "ears have been opened" to appreciate such "wondrous mysteries" (IX.23). In the same way, the question at the end of column V, "What is one born of woman amid all your [gre]at fearful acts?" (V.31), is the rhetorical foil to an extended (though sadly fragmentary) depiction of God's cosmic plan, which was established from before the creation of the world and encompasses all reality, from "the host of your spirits and the congregation of [the heavenly beings]" all the way down through the strata of the cosmos to "the seas and the deeps" (V.24-26). The enormity of scale is as impressive in time as it is in space: this plan has been "established from ages of old" and is for "all the eternal epochs and the everlasting visitation" (V.26-27). Against that backdrop how indeed is "the spirit of flesh" meant to "understand all these things," and what is one "born of woman" (V.30-31)? It seems ridiculously implausible that a "heap of dust" should be privy to the secrets of the universe, should be "glorified" and given "dominion with abundant delights together with eternal peace" (V.34-35), and should "take (his) place before you with the everlasting hosts and the [eternal] spirit[s]" (XIX.16). But such indeed is the claim of these hymns. Their sense of wonder is articulated through wild fluctuations of focus between cosmic eternity and the transient "person of nothingness" (XV.35) who is somehow granted a place in this eternal plan.

Thus, not only the immeasurable greatness of God, but also, and more especially, the mind-boggling scope of God's plans provide the literary and theological frame of these litanies of human worthlessness. The "thing constructed of dust and kneaded with water" (V.32) is placed into a cosmic drama whose script (God's word) "will not turn back" (V.35, 36). In this context, the preposition ל that attributes all agency to God ("to God [לאל] belong all the works of righteousness," XII.32) also expresses the alignment of all things to

God's purpose: "For yourself, O [my G]od, and not for the sake of humankind (לכה א[ל]י] ולא לאדם) is all that you have made, for you yourself created the righteous and the wicked" (XII.38-39). Aetiology and teleology are conjoined in this single letter, and the sectarian takes his place between beginning and end, cause and purpose, with a sense of exultant amazement that he is not only a positive part of this plan, but also privileged to understand it.

Carol Newsom has explored with great sensitivity how the self in the *Hodayot* "enacts its own nothingness in radical contrast to the being of God," such that at the moment it "vanishes into a human nullity" it simultaneously "elusively vanishes back into God."[23] This produces an unstable self at the intersection of two contrasting dynamics, whose extreme polarity leaves the sectarian suspended from the divine plenitude that alone can fill his lack. But Newsom also recognizes that these hymns (and not only the Leader Hymns) serve the *social* interests of the Qumran community. We may posit, in fact, that these confessions of human worthlessness helped the sectarian community to reinforce its boundaries.[24] By condemning himself as misaligned, humiliating himself in his weakness, and mocking his incongruous position in the cosmos, the sectarian nullifies all "worth" except that defined by the terms of the *yaḥad,* and thus bolts from the inside any exit route from the community. Outside the community there is no basis for worth: indeed, in several passages the value of wealth, an alternative source of symbolic capital, is strongly repudiated (e.g., VI.30-32; VII.35-37; XVIII.24-33). If the human being is nothing but dust kneaded with water, perverse and impure — nothing else *but for* the divine gifts endowed within the community — then there is nothing worth having outside the community. It appears from some passages in the *Hodayot* that apostasy is a threat to the community (see especially XIII.22-25 within XIII.20–XV.5), and from the strong curses that the sectarians pronounced at their entry to the covenant we may sense a special anxiety about inconsistent members who were liable to backslide (1QS II.16-18; cf. VII.15-25). Continual repetition of these hymns would help reduce that danger. By repudiating his ancestral and personal past (XII.35-36; cf. Lev 26:40), and by characterizing even his present condition as "a structure of clay" and "a spring of impurity," the sectarian rhetorically reinforces his total dependence on the power and

23. Newsom, *Symbolic Space,* pp. 220-21; cf. pp. 172-74, where she speaks of the cultivation of the "masochistic sublime" (an adaptation of Peter Berger's "masochistic theodicy").

24. Cf. Newsom, *Symbolic Space,* pp. 193-94, 269, 275, 349-50. As she comments, "by nurturing a distinctive discourse of the self, one is progressively alienated from a socially dominant language of the self or from a previous sense of self. The content and structure of this new subjectivity serves as a condensed critique of the dominant culture" (p. 294).

the mercy of God. His only worth lies in belonging to the "children of [God's] preference."

7.3. The Goodness of God

In their genre, their diction, and their distinctive syntax, the *Hodayot* are consistently oriented to the goodness or mercy of God. Most hymns begin with the formula, "I thank you, O Lord" (אודכה אדוני, e.g., XV.9), usually followed by an explanatory כי ("for"), while others (and many subsections) address God with an opening, "Blessed are you . . ." (ברוך אתה, e.g., VII.21; VIII.26).[25] Placing himself in a mode of gratitude, the speaker lifts his eyes to the source of all good things, using multiple syntactical forms (verbs of agency; the *hiphil;* prepositional phrases, etc.) to emphasize divine agency. Thus in 1QH VI.19-27, it is God who "gives" or "places" (הנותן) understanding "in the heart of your servant" (VI.19), and who has "caused your servant to have insight" (תשכל עבדך) regarding the lots of humankind (VI.22). Where the speaker says "I know," this is consciously qualified: "I know from the understanding that comes from you" (ידעתי מבינתך, VI.23). His closeness to God is expressed in his zeal against evil in faithfulness to God's commands, but this is possible only because "you draw him closer to your understanding" (תגישנו לבינתך, VI.24-25). At every point, and by every means, the speaker wishes to place his agency within the frame of a larger causative dynamic.[26]

At the root of this dynamic lies not just God's power, but more particularly God's "goodness" (טוב), "kindness" (חסד), and "mercies" (רחמים). These near synonyms recur throughout the *Hodayot* with remarkable frequency; often they are piled up on top of one another or joined to qualifiers adding size and abundance: "your great kindnesses" (גדול חסדיך); "your plentiful goodness" (רוב טובך); "your abundant mercies" (or "compassion," המון רחמיך).[27] It is occasionally possible to trace the influence of specific biblical sources for such language: God's חסד for those who love him and keep his commandments (Exod 20:6; Deut 5:10) is invoked in some contexts (e.g., VIII.31, 35), while the list of divine gracious attributes in Exodus 34:6-7 has strongly shaped

25. The division of the psalms has been a long-running matter of uncertainty and debate; I here follow the conclusions of Stegemann and Schuller, *1QHodayot^a^*.

26. See Newsom, *Symbolic Space*, pp. 204-21.

27. These three terms are by far the most frequent labels for the divine benevolence experienced within human lives (רחמים and חסד each occur thirty-five times in the extant text; טוב, fourteen times); by comparison, words from the root חנן are rare (noun and adjective once each; verb only six times).

other texts (e.g., VI.34-36; VIII.34-35).[28] But what is striking in the *Hodayot* is not only the ubiquity and prominence of such language, but its "perfecting" through its juxtaposition with the worthlessness of the objects of mercy.[29]

One of the smallest hymns in the anthology provides a good example of this rhetoric of thanks for the goodness of God (XV.29-36):

> [29] I thank yo[u, O Lor]d, that you have instructed me in your truth, [30] and made known to me your wondrous mysteries, and (made known) both your kindness toward a [sinful] person and your abundant compassion for the one whose heart is perverted. [31] For who is like you among the gods, O Lord? Who has truth like yours? Who can be righteous before you when he is judged? There is no [32] utterance of the breath to offer in reply to your rebuke, and none is able to stand before your wrath.
>
> But all the children of [33] your truth you bring before you in forgiveness to cleanse them from their transgressions through your great goodness, and through your overflowing compassion [34] to station them before you for ever and ever.
>
> For you are the eternal God, and all your ways are established from age to [35] age, and there is none apart from you. And so, what is a person of nothingness and a possessor of vanity that he should contemplate your wondrous [36] great works?

The opening and closing of this hymn identify the preeminent possession of the sectarian community: knowledge. Instruction in "truth" is the first of the blessings for which God is thanked (29), and the hymn finishes with the sectarian in knowledgeable contemplation of God's wonderful works (35-36). Indeed, knowledge or understanding is not just one of the benefits of salvation, it is the *foundation* and *frame* for the rest: the sectarian is given knowledge such that he understands what salvation entails and how that salvation fits the designs of God. It is no accident that the sectarians describe themselves here as "the children of truth" (32-33): they are first and foremost a cognitive community. As the Leader Hymns (in columns X–XVII) make clear, there are certain figures especially responsible for imparting and interpreting this "truth," and for examining and grading the knowledge of the community (e.g., X.15-16). This knowledge, graciously endowed, opens up God's "wondrous mysteries"

28. See Holm-Nielsen, *Hodayot*, pp. 225, 239-40; Stegemann and Schuller, *1QHodayot*^{a}, p. 69 (on IV.24).

29. The notion of "perfecting" (drawn from K. Burke) is used in this context by Newsom, *Symbolic Space*, pp. 266-67.

(רזי פלאכה, XV.30) such that the sectarian knows the secret operations of the cosmos to a unique and stunning degree.[30]

Among those wonders are God's "kindness" toward and "compassion" on utterly undeserving humans: God's "abundant compassion" is shown to those whose heart is "perverted" and who have absolutely no defense before the inexorable judgment of God (XV.30-32). Integral to that compassion is God's "forgiveness" (סליחות, 33) of sin, the "cleansing" of transgression that rids humans of their disqualifying impurity. Elsewhere, this can be glossed as the "covering" (כפר) of guilt (XII.38; XXIII.33), but the *Hodayot* are less interested in the mechanism than in the extraordinary phenomenon that guilty persons, who cannot "stand" before the wrath of God (XV.32), are given grace such that God "stations them" (or "causes them to stand," העמידם) before him forever (XV.34). This "standing" has multiple senses in the *Hodayot.* At one level, "standing" means resolute commitment to the law and to the way of God, a "standing in perfection" (XIII.11) that holds fast to the covenant, "choosing truth and righteousness," loving God freely, and loving all that he loves (e.g., VI.34-40). At another, it evokes stability and endurance, the capacity to withstand testing and affliction, as in the Leader Hymns with their vivid metaphors of collapse and stability, dissolution and firmness (e.g., XI. 6-41). At yet another level, however, "standing" signifies the "station" enjoyed by the sectarian who, purified from guilt, takes his place (מעמד) with "the host of the holy ones," in fellowship with "the children of heaven" and "the spirits of knowledge" (XI.22-24). It is this elevated eternal destiny that strikes the speaker of these hymns as the most extraordinary outcome of the abundant divine compassion.

How does it come about that a God whose wrath is turned against all sin has compassion on "a person of nothingness," such that one will be stationed before him forever and ever (XV.32-35)? Or, to sharpen the question, how is it that "by your abundant compassion to me, you pardon iniquity and thus clean[se] a person from guilt" precisely "through your righteousness" (בצדקתכה, XII.38)? Since righteousness is the quality by which we may expect God to judge and condemn the sinful human (e.g., IX.32), how is it here invoked as the means by which he pardons and cleanses? It does not seem sufficient to say that the term "righteousness" simply varies in meaning from distributive justice to "graciousness," without offering some explanation for this striking variance.[31] If it is by God's "righteousness" that some people are

30. For knowledge as the essential core of salvation in the *Hodayot,* see Kuhn, *Enderwartung,* pp. 139-75; E. P. Sanders, *Paul and Palestinian Judaism* (London: SCM Press, 1977), pp. 260-61; Maston, *Divine and Human Agency,* pp. 113-17.

31. See Newsom, *Symbolic Space,* pp. 267-68, with reference to Sanders, *Paul and Palestinian Judaism,* pp. 310-11. For discussion of the root צדק in 1QH^a, see Becker, *Heil Gottes,*

condemned to "the day of slaughter" while other equally undeserving humans are made to "stand" before him, has the term changed its meaning, or does it reflect a logic other than an abstract notion of "justice"? In the passage cited above (XV.29-36) we are given a hint of that logic by the reference to God's "ways," which "are established (יכונו) from age to age" (XV.34-35). This suggests that God's compassion on sinful persons is not an arbitrary decision based on a random alternation between "justice" and "compassion," but corresponds to a plan and a purpose eternally laid down. In other words, "righteousness" in the *Hodayot* is not a system of distributive justice, to which God is answerable by a code of fairness more foundational than himself. Rather, his "correctness" is defined by the rules of his own making. He is "righteous" in keeping fully to the script that he himself has written.[32] "Righteousness" is thus a relative and not an absolute quality: it is a correct or proper alignment to God's own rules, commitments, or decisions. And these rules, or eternal "ways," have established in advance that humanity falls into different "lots" (cf. XV.37), such that it is entirely "correct" for God to have compassion on some, sinful as they are, while condemning others to merciless wrath.

This predestinarian backdrop protrudes in almost every context where the hymnist celebrates the kindness and mercy of God. In a passage rich with reference to God's compassion and graciousness (VIII.22-36), the sectarian confesses that it is "by your goodwill (better: "preference," ברצונ[ך]) toward a person that you have multiplied his inheritance in [your] righteous deeds" (VIII.22); "because I know that you have recorded the spirit of the righteous, I myself have chosen to cleanse my hands according to your wil[l]" (כרצו[נ]ך, VIII.28). The key term רצון can be variously translated as "will," "goodwill," or "favor"; it signifies what God wills (i.e. desires) or his willing it (his preference or selection), and thus gestures to the deep patterning structures of the world.[33]

---

pp. 149-55; O. Betz, "Rechtfertigung in Qumran," in J. Friedrich, W. Pöhlmann, and P. Stuhlmacher, eds., *Rechtfertigung. Festschrift für E. Käsemann* (Tübingen: Mohr Siebeck, 1976), pp. 17-36; E. Zurli, "La Giustificazione 'solo per grazia' in *1QS* X,9–XI e *1QH*^{a}," *Revue de Qumran* 79 (2002): 445-77.

32. For the close relationship between "correctness/truth" (אמת) and "righteousness" (צדקה), see, e.g., VI.26, 36-37; IX.28-29, 32; XIX.10; 1QS 4.24; 9.17; 11.14; cf. "judgment of your truth" (משפט אמתכה, 1QH^a XXV.12). Truth is "set" (נכון, XVII.32), just as a measuring line or plumb line ensures that a building is "true" (see IX.30-31; XI.28; XVI.22-23). Hultgren, *Damascus Covenant*, pp. 431-43, argues for a connection in the *Hodayot* between God's "righteousness" and his faithfulness to the covenant.

33. The word occurs twenty-six times in 1QH^a, sometimes in the sense of what God wills or desires (i.e. the objects of God's will; e.g., IV.35; VI.21; VIII.28), and sometimes of God's willing or desiring (i.e. as a verbal noun, God's willing of those objects; e.g., VI.24, 38; IX.17, 22). The term designates not "will" in an abstract sense but "selective preference," God's positive

The hymnist appeals "by the spirit that you have given to me" that God make his kindness complete,

> cleansing me by your holy spirit and drawing me nearer by your good favor ("preference," ברצונך), according to your great kindness (כגדול חסדיך) [wh]ich you have shown to me, and causing [my feet] to sta[nd in] the whole station of [your] good fa[vor] ([רצו[נך), which you have cho[sen] (בח[ר]תה) for those who love you and for those who keep your commandments. (VIII.30-31)

Here, the classic scriptural statement of God's חסד for "those who love him and keep his commandments" (Exod 20:6; Deut 5:10; 7:9) is prefaced, interrupted, and amplified by a series of clauses signaling election, choice, and "preference."[34] These amplifications undergird and ultimately explain the operation of God's kindness. In other words, God's mercy on the sectarian is the historical expression of his prior, eternal election. That previously established "preference" (רצון) is a decision of God's will, preformed from eternity but now enacted through his compassion.

7.4. Predetermination and the Design of the Cosmos

The determinism by which God's mercy is directed to worthless humanity is given fullest expression in a number of remarkable passages. Most striking is a hymn that describes a form of "double predestination," dividing humanity into two contrasting groups (VII.21-39); the key passage is as follows (VII.25-33):

> [25] And as for me, I know, by the understanding that comes from you, that it is not through the power of flesh [that] an individual [may perfect] [26] his way, nor is a person able to direct his steps. And I know that in

---

selection and thus favor. For brief discussion see N. Walker, "Critical Note: The Renderings of *RASON*," *JBL* 81 (1962): 182-84; E. H. Merrill, *Qumran and Predestination: A Theological Study of the Thanksgiving Hymns* (Leiden: Brill, 1975), pp. 17-18.

34. See Holm-Nielsen, *Hodayot,* p. 240. The familiar scriptural phrase is incorporated but amplified thus (scriptural source in italics): "drawing me nearer by your good favor, according to your great *kindness* [wh]ich you have *shown* to me, and causing [my feet] to sta[nd in] the whole station of [your] good fa[vor], which you have cho[sen] *for those who love you and for those who keep your commandments.*" The amplifications signal that God's "kindness" is placed within the frame of his elective "preference."

> your hand is the inclination of every spirit, [and all] its [activi]ty [27] you determined before you created it. How could anyone change your words?
>
> You alone [crea]ted [28] the righteous, and from the womb you prepared him for the time of favor, to be attentive to your covenant and to walk in all (your way,) and to advance (him) upon it [29] in your abundant compassion, and to relieve all the distress of his soul for eternal salvation and for everlasting peace, without lack. And so you raise [30] his honor higher than flesh.
>
> But the wicked you created for the [pur]pose of your wrath, and from the womb you dedicated them for the day of slaughter. [31] For they walk in the way that is not good, and they despise yo[ur] covenant, [and] their soul abhors your [statutes]. They do not take pleasure in anything that [32] you have commanded, but they choose what you hate. For you have determined them for the a[ges of] your [wra]th in order to execute great judgments upon them [33] in the sight of all your creatures, and to be a sign and a por[tent for] everlasting [generations], so that all may know your glory and your great strength.

After an introduction that traces back to God the "inclination" (יצר) of "every spirit," irrevocably "determined" (כון) before it was created (25-27), the hymn describes in parallel the predetermination of first "the righteous" (27-30) and then "the wicked" (30-33), signaling a fixed division of humanity, one part destined for "eternal salvation," the other for "the day of slaughter" (cf. VI.22-23; XII.39).[35] Each group has a distinguishing pattern of willed behavior. The righteous attend to God's covenant and "walk" in his way (28), while the wicked despise God's covenant and choose what he hates (31-32): the language of "walking" and "choice" (בחר, 32; cf. VI.21; XII.18) indicates that the human actors are neither passive nor automata. Yet these inclinations and patterns of "step" are themselves already "determined": the verb כון, one of the most common in the *Hodayot* (appearing more than fifty times), recurs with extraordinary frequency in this passage (VII.26, 27, 28, 32, 34, 35), signifying a fixity of human destiny and corresponding behavior that is the work of God. What is more, this "determination" of the human spirit took place *before* it was created (27): the two types of humanity were allotted their destiny "from the womb" (28, 30). It is thus made clear that however much their choice of behavior might *display* their destiny, it could neither determine nor alter it. The humanity here portrayed is a willing player acting out

35. For close analysis of the structure and poetry of this text, see Hughes, *Scriptural Allusions*, pp. 63-95.

an already scripted drama, whose beginning, continuation, and conclusion are irrevocably laid down by the design of the Author; for "how could anyone change your words?" (27).[36]

The marks of this determinism can be found everywhere across the text of the *Hodayot.* Although humans may be said to "choose," at a deeper level God has already "chosen" his own from among humankind, his "elect of righteousness" (בחירי צדק, X.15; cf. IV.33; VI.13, 26; XVIII.28). These elect appear to have degrees of "inheritance" (נחלה, VI.30; VIII.22; XVIII.30), but it is clear that their "lot" (גורל) has been cast in one direction and not in another — not with the "vile" or the "assembly of fraud" (XI.26; XV.37) but with "the spirits of knowledge" and the "angels of God's presence" (XI.23; XIV.16; XIX.14).[37] We have already noted the determining effect of God's "will" or "preference" (רצון), a notion reflected again in our text, in the claim that the righteous have been prepared from the womb for "the time of preference" (למועד רצון, VII.28), that is, for the time when God's pre-established preference will take effect.[38] Although this "preference" takes historical form in the lives of the sectarians, they recognize that its origin lies in a design established beyond and before their own contingent lives.

It is important to note here that the language of "mercy" (רחמים), "kindness" (חסד), and "goodness" (טוב), frequent as it is, is never used in connection with the pre-temporal (or pre-birth) determination of human destiny: "election" and the "determination" of humanity into "lots" is characterized not by God's "compassion" or "goodness," but by his "preference" (רצון). We may thus distinguish two pools of vocabulary that depict different dimensions of God's benevolence. The authors of the *Hodayot* employ mercy/kindness terminology to describe God's rescue of humanity from its plight of worthlessness, weakness, and sin; but where they speak of God's favor in connection with the pre-fixed destiny of "the sons of truth," they speak not of God's "mercy" but of his "preference." God's mercy is experienced "at the time of his preference"

36. Discussions of determinism in Qumran (e.g., Merrill, *Qumran and Predestination*) typically pit predestination against "free will" (in something like the modern sense of autonomy). Sanders (*Paul and Palestinian Judaism*, pp. 257-70) rightly sensed that this was not an issue in the Scrolls, but still considered their theology inconsistent. Maston (*Divine and Human Agency*, pp. 110-13) is correct to insist that the problem derives from modern assumptions about "free will" that do not apply to the *Hodayot*.

37. For the language of "lot" (גורל) alongside other predestinarian vocabulary in the Scrolls, see F. Nötscher, *Zur theologischen Terminologie der Qumran-Texte* (Bonn: Hanstein Verlag, 1956), pp. 169-73.

38. Cf. the parallel expression קץ רצונכה ("time of your favor") at XXIV.13. For this time as present, and not merely future, see Kuhn, *Enderwartung*, pp. 103-11.

(VII.28; cf. Isa 49:8), but that "preference" was not itself an act of "mercy"; it represents the selectivity exercised by the preformed will of God.[39]

If this differentiated vocabulary places the "mercy" of God in the larger frame of his eternal "preference," that preference is itself integral to a universal design that orders all space and time. There is evidence to suggest that the sectarians were enormously impressed by the regularities of the cosmos, which they took to represent a comprehensive ordering of reality; their own destiny was just one tiny element in a vast web of interconnected structures.[40] This creational matrix is especially clear in the hymn of column IX. Although the opening lines are badly damaged, from line 10 onward it becomes clear that the formation and determination of every human spirit are here placed on a comprehensive map of the cosmos, where God's will/preference (רצון, 10, 12, 17, 22) has equally determined (כון, 11, 12, 16, 19, 21, 30) the forces that rule the heavens and the earth. In the heavens, the "powerful spirits" are governed by divine "laws," while the "holy angels" and "eternal spirits" are determined in their "dominions," and the luminaries, the stars, the winds, and the storehouses are arranged according to their "mysteries" and "tasks" (11-15). On the lower levels, the earth, the seas, and the depths are designed, ordered, and established according to God's will (15-17). Such ordering of space is complemented by a patterning of historical "times" and "seasons," according to which God's design moves inexorably toward its conclusion (17-21). The language of "design" (מחשבה, 15, 16) is prominent here, as elsewhere (e.g., V.17, 26; XVIII.3; XIX.10-11; XXI.8). The blueprint of space and time, every detail of the cosmos and every moment in its development, is laid down from before the beginning: "in the wisdom of your knowledge you determ[i]ned their des[t]iny before they existed. According to your wi[ll] everything [comes] to pass; and without you nothing is done" (IX.21-22).[41]

The language of this hymn echoes Genesis 1, but in such a way as to sug-

39. Thus, God's compassion is exercised on "the children of his preference" (בני רצונו, XII.33-34; XIX.12), but this preference is already pre-established: "For your forgiveness I wait hopefully, for you yourself have formed the spi[rit of your servant, and according to] your [wil]l you have determined me" ([וכרצ]ונכה הכינותני, XVIII.23-24); cf. VI.24; VIII.22, 30; IX.21-22; XIV.9; XVII.14.

40. The calendrial texts from Cave 4 (e.g., 4QPhases of the Moon [4Q 317]; 4QCalendrical Document E [4Q 326-27] and 4QMishmarot [4Q 320-325, 328-30]) are especially revealing; see S. Talmon et al., *Qumran Cave 4: XVI, Calendrical Texts* (Oxford: Clarendon Press, 2001). For links between astrology and physiognomy see M. Popović, *Reading the Human Body: Physiognomics and Astrology in the Dead Sea Scrolls and Hellenistic–Early Roman Period Judaism* (Leiden: Brill, 2007). As Newsom comments, "calendrical time can become a potent symbol of harmony, of being 'in sync' with the cosmos — or not" (*Symbolic Space*, p. 181).

41. For close analysis of this text, see Lange, *Weisheit und Prädestination*, pp. 204-29; as

gest that a primordial blueprint lies *behind* the creation of visible phenomena: the visible structures of sequence and governance are the material imprint of a pre-programmed design.[42] The sectarians' own election, and the divided destinies of humanity, are particular manifestations of this cosmic plan, and since there is no going behind this blueprint, one is not required to explain the determining preference of God for his elect any more than one need explain why the sun shines in the day or the moon in the night.[43] It seems the *yaḥad* sectarians understood themselves to have been brought by divine mercy into harmony with this macro-design: their routines of prayer are synchronized with the daily patterns of light and darkness, just as the seasons and "the cycles of the festivals" "are fixed by their signs, for all their dominion in proper order, reliably, at the command of God" (XX.7-12). As Newsom comments, "What marks the created world as the expression of the divine plan is its obedient and rule-ordered activity. . . . Creator and creation are symmetrically arranged."[44] Awed by the predictable regularity of the natural world, the sectarians submitted themselves to that "proper order," following the (correct interpretation of) "the command of God"; they thus aligned themselves to this universal symmetry, with the thrill of understanding, and fitting, the ordered beauty of all things.

When the *Hodayot* refer to the creational design of "what is and what will be" (XX.12), which is determined by "the wisdom of your knowledge" (IX.21), we sense their congruence with the cosmic interests of the sapiential materials found at Qumran.[45] There are close parallels with the deterministic theology of creation found in 4QInstruction,[46] and with the predestined

---

he points out, the pre-existent wisdom is here described as "engraved" onto the material of the universe (IX.25-26).

42. Cf. Newsom, *Symbolic Space*, pp. 86-87 on 1QS III-IV establishing itself as a "pre-text for Genesis 1."

43. The many references to "wonderful mysteries" in the *Hodayot* signal not that the sectarians cannot understand this design, but precisely that, uniquely, they *do* understand it, across all levels of reality and all "periods" of time; it is knowable precisely because it was pre-ordained (IX.23). Since the election of the "sons of righteousness" is part of the cosmic design, it does not need an explanation such as would be required if God first made humanity and then chose from among them. His will constitutes and brings into existence "the sons of his preference" in distinction from "the lot of the vile," just as he constituted "day" and "night" by separating light from darkness (Gen 1:14-19).

44. Newsom, *Symbolic Space*, p. 224. Cf. her discussion of the time-notices in the Maskil's prayer in 1QS X-XI (pp. 174-186).

45. For recent discussion of this sapiential material, see, e.g., M. J. Goff, *Discerning Wisdom: The Sapiential Literature of the Dead Sea Scrolls* (Leiden: Brill, 2007).

46. For suggestions that 1QH^a actually cites from 4QInstruction (e.g., 1QH^a XVIII.29-30 from 4Q418 55.10), see Lange, *Weisheit und Prädestination*, pp. 46, 226. The phrase רצי נהיה,

design articulated in the "Treatise on the Two Spirits" (1QS III.13–IV.26), a text that may have been inserted into (and adapted for) one version of the Community Rule (1QS) from a non-sectarian source.[47] The incorporation of this "Treatise" into 1QS indicates its value to the *yaḥad* as a construal of the cosmos, and its introduction bears a striking resemblance to the theological assumptions of the hymns: "From the God of knowledge stems all there is and all there shall be. Before they existed he established their entire design (ולפני היותם הכין כול מחשבתם). And when they have come into being, at their appointed time, they will execute all their works according to his glorious design (כמחשבת כבודו), without altering anything" (1QS III.15-16).[48] Although the antagonism between "the Prince of Lights" and "the Angel of Darkness" is not evidenced in the *Hodayot,* the comprehensive division of humanity, with its corresponding paths, into antithetical "lots" (גורלות) bears some similarities to the anthropological dualities of the hymns.[49] At the least, both texts bear testimony to the sectarians' sense of preordained destiny, their special role in the cosmos, and their unique "time," according to a divine "will/preference" established from all eternity.[50]

This eternal "preference" explains how the hymns can extol the mercy and

---

which is characteristic of 4QInstruction, is not found in 1QH^a^. For the deterministic theology of the former, see Lange, *Weisheit und Prädestination,* pp. 45-92 and E. J. C. Tigchelaar, *To Increase Learning for the Understanding Ones: Reading and Reconstructing the Fragmentary Early Jewish Sapiential Text 4QInstruction* (Leiden: Brill, 2001) (suggesting links to the *Hodayot,* pp. 194-207).

47. Following the discovery of the Cave 4 version of the *Serekh,* and the suggestions of S. Metso (*The Textual Development of the Qumran Community Rule* [Leiden: Brill, 1997] and *The Serekh Texts* [London: T&T Clark, 2007]), many scholars consider this section of 1QS a late insertion into the Rule (for an alternative view, see P. Alexander, "The Redaction-history of the Serekh ha-Yaḥad: A Proposal," *RevQ* 65-68 [1996]: 437-53), and it is possible that the whole text (in at least some of its strata) has a pre- or non-sectarian origin (see Lange, *Weisheit und Prädestination,* pp. 121-70). For the possible redaction of the text by those who incorporated it into 1QS, see C. Hempel, "The *Treatise on the Two Spirits* and the Literary History of the *Rule of the Community,*" in G. G. Xeravits, ed., *Dualism in Qumran* (London: T&T Clark, 2010), pp. 102-20.

48. Translation by García Martínez and Tigchelaar, *Dead Sea Scrolls,* 1.75.

49. For contrasting "lots" and "inheritances" (נחלת), see 1QS IV.15-16, 24-26; on its deterministic theology, see P. Alexander, "Predestination and Free Will in the Theology of the Dead Sea Scrolls," in J. M. G. Barclay and S. J. Gathercole, eds., *Divine and Human Agency in Paul and His Cultural Environment* (London: T&T Clark, 2006), pp. 27-49. For connections between 1QH V and the Treatise, see Stegemann and Schuller, *1QHodayot^a^,* p. 78. On dualism in Qumran, especially in 1QS III–IV, see G. G. Xeravits, *Dualism in Qumran* (London: T&T Clark, 2010).

50. Cf. 1QS IV.1 for the verb רצה (of God's "delighting" in the Spirit of light).

kindness of God at the same time as they place an extreme emphasis on the unworthiness and insignificance of its recipients. That God should be generous to the unworthy is not, as we have seen, a necessary or a common construal of divine "grace"; in fact, it raises urgent questions regarding the rationale for divine kindness. If those of no ontological or moral worth have been accorded God's kindness, has he distributed it recklessly, with an arbitrary disregard for the unfittingness of the recipients? Only our assumption that God's grace is *by definition* "unmerited" can cause us to miss the sense of wonder, even shock, that the sectarians express in the fact that such mean, worthless matter has been given such unimaginable privileges. The more they stress their worthlessness, the greater the degree of shock, but the matter is not left without explanation. It makes sense for God to show mercy on precisely *these* worthless specimens of humanity because he has written their special status into the rubric of the universe; they have always been predestined to enjoy this privileged role. Thus, the sectarians render themselves not an anomaly but the manifestation of a remarkable design feature in the architecture of the cosmos. The predestinarianism of the *Hodayot* is no isolated or superfluous motif, but the structure within which the rest of their theological convictions make sense.

7.5. Conclusions

As Newsom has argued, the *Hodayot* are not simply texts to be read (or heard); they are hymns to be performed, and the performance itself constitutes a good measure of their rhetorical power. In taking up these words (perhaps on a regular basis), the sectarians not only absorbed much distinctive theology, but they also joined themselves, as speakers, with the "I" of the hymns, and thus constituted themselves the worthless but graced creatures of whom the hymns speak. It is impossible to speak such words, repeatedly and sincerely, without *becoming* a "creature of clay" marvelously corrected, forgiven, and elevated by the immense kindness of God. What is more, to speak such words is no trivial matter, since the articulation of praise is precisely the highest calling of a sectarian, the fulfillment of his destiny to join the cosmic chorus of "common rejoicing." "Monotonous" as such hymns may seem to modern ears,[51] their careful composition suggests an investment of effort in making such worship just right; there is even a suggestion that the words themselves follow a calculus or poetic "measure" that matches the ordering of all things (IX.29-33). This is no random collection of phrases: the *Hodayot* represent

51. Cf. Licht, "Thanksgiving Scroll," p. 2.

one of the most carefully articulated theologies of Second Temple Judaism, even if in a genre and an intellectual idiom very different from our academic conception of "theology."

The construal of divine "grace" in these hymns is, as we have seen, subtly contoured. Not only are the traditional biblical themes of divine "mercy" and "kindness" reiterated with an unusual density and emphasis, but they are "perfected" in a number of distinctive ways.[52] The *abundance* of God's goodness and mercy has been apparent in many forms. But it is clear that it serves as the foil to, not the substitute for, God's anger and "punishing judgments"; there is no move toward perfecting the *singularity* of divine benevolence, such as we have found in Philo (and Marcion). What *is* distinctive and central in 1QH[a], however, is the *incongruity* of divine mercy, its pointed contrast with its human object, which is defined with relentless negativity as weak, mortal, polluted, and mean. This extreme polarity fuels the "wonder" with which the hymns are suffused, but there is good reason to think that this is not just a poetic or pious stance in prayer before God, but the consciously foundational doctrine of these hymns.[53] Yet it is important to be clear what is and is not implied by this incongruity. The implication is not that the sectarian has no further obligations toward God (divine grace is not *non-circular*): forgiveness, purification, and insight are provided precisely so that their beneficiaries may be "renewed" and walk in faithfulness and purity in a Torah-observant community and in company with God's "holy ones." If the worthless are thereby made worthwhile, the *Hodayot* are replete with comments on the *efficacy* of God's benevolence, through the strength, or knowledge, or spirit which he imparts. As we have seen, this powerful divine agency is not articulated in a form that excludes or even competes with the agency of the purified sectarian;

52. Sanders comments: "Few documents from Judaism or Christianity emphasize the grace of God as does 1QH" (*Paul and Palestinian Judaism*, p. 298). But as we have seen in Part I, the crucial issue in analyzing grace is not relative degrees of emphasis but differentiated forms of perfection.

53. Sanders suggests a partial explanation of the emphasis in the *Hodayot* on divine grace as a function of the hymnic genre (as address to God and self-comparison with God), in contrast to the more optimistic assumptions about human capacity in exhortation or *halaka* (*Paul and Palestininian Judaism*, pp. 288-89, 292, 297, 328); his suggestion has been adopted and extended by C. VanLandingham, *Judgment and Justification in Early Judaism and the Apostle Paul* (Peabody: Hendrickson, 2006), pp. 131-35. But many features of these hymns are also didactic (cf. V.12-14), and the utter dependence of abject humanity on the mercy of God seems to be part of the "insight" gained by the speaker. There are many prayers among the Qumran scrolls that do not exhibit this polarity (see Nitzan, *Qumran Prayer*, and Maston, *Divine and Human Agency*, p. 80, citing 4Q504-506 as a rare parallel). For comparison with the prayer language of the biblical psalms, see Newsom, *Symbolic Space*, pp. 269-73.

God's enabling energy does not suppress but rather activates the willed obedience of its recipients. There is no necessary contradiction between divine grace and human agency, between incongruous divine mercy and strenuous human observance of the Law.[54]

If the *Hodayot* thematize and celebrate the incongruity of divine mercy, they do not leave it as an inexplicable mystery from which the human mind must simply recoil. On the contrary, the understanding of this mystery, the knowledge that fathoms God's purpose, is a dominant motif in most of these hymns, since the sectarians have uniquely privileged access to God's knowledge through his Spirit. What is revealed in such "instruction" is the primordial design of the cosmos, including the decision of God to create — from worthless human material — knowledgeable participants in the heavenly praise. It is this predestinarian framework that bridges the gulf between divine goodness and valueless humanity, since God's remarkable mercy fits the cosmic design. As we have seen, one effect is a distinction in vocabulary itself: God may be said to determine the lots of humanity according to his "preference" (רצון), but this phenomenon is not attributed to his "mercy" or "kindness." These latter terms are reserved for a secondary phenomenon, God's intervention in the lives of the sectarians. To apply the term "grace" indistinguishably to these two dimensions of divine benevolence would be to miss the distinctive contours of the *Hodayot.*

The peculiar accents of this theology mirror the unusual social location of its authors. Formed as "children of truth" not by ethnicity or ancestry but by divine "preference," they cultivated a strong sense of differentiation from other "wicked" Jews, with boundaries that, though permeable, required clear definition.[55] As has often been noted, the idea of a pre-scripted destiny undergirds this "sectarian" ethos.[56] This idea is also integral, I have suggested, to the extreme expressions of human worthlessness and divine mercy, which serve to maintain sectarian identity as a uniquely privileged status, and to guard against apostasy. The articulation of this theology in the form of thanksgiving prayers is peculiarly appropriate: a theology composed from this perspective is best

54. Sanders (*Paul and Palestinian Judaism,* pp. 261-70) recognizes that this combination does not seem to be problematic in the *Hodayot,* but still feels the need to excuse their authors as "not systematic theologians" (p. 265). The issue is handled more effectively in Maston, *Divine and Human Agency,* pp. 94-122.

55. Cf. D. Dombrowski Hopkins, "The Qumran Community and 1QHodayot: A Reassessment," *RevQ* 10 (1981): 323-64, who wrongly concludes from the permeability of the boundaries (allowing outsiders in, and insiders out) that the community saw itself as partially overlapping with the terrain of evildoers. For the strong sense of guarded boundaries see, e.g., XVI.5-16.

56. See Sanders, *Paul and Palestinian Judaism,* pp. 257-70.

articulated in such a form. It was as a special coterie of pious Jews, destined to enjoy unique insight into the secret purposes of the cosmos, that the authors of these hymns developed this uniquely contoured discourse of "grace," in accents quite different from those of other Second Temple Jews.

To shoehorn this distinctive combination of perfections (grace that is abundant, prior, efficacious, and incongruous) into a commonly shared "pattern" of "covenantal nomism" (Sanders) would flatten the contours of the *Hodayot*. Sanders, concerned to clarify sequence (the "stages" of salvation; see above, 3.6.1), aimed to prove, first and foremost, the priority of divine grace and thus the elective and covenantal context of "gratuity" in which even the heightened emphasis on Torah-observance at Qumran is properly to be placed.[57] While noting the peculiar accent on predestination at Qumran, and its sectarian affirmation of mercy on the elect (not the nation as a whole), Sanders was chiefly concerned to locate Torah-obedience as the *consequence* of being in the covenant and the *requirement for remaining in it*, but not itself a means to "salvation." To identify this "religious pattern," shared with the Rabbis, required only the identification of "grace" as *prior to* human obedience.[58] But this is to miss the distinctive flavor of the *Hodayot* and to render "grace" a generalized concept too loose to permit serious analytical work. Little is gained, in response to Sanders, by redescribing the relation between divine grace and human works in equally general terms.[59] Besides acknowledging the construals and terminologies of "grace" particular to each text, what is needed is a form of analysis that recognizes the differing dimensions of this multifaceted concept and its special accents and functions in each text or author. As we have suggested, a richer and deeper analysis is made possible by disaggregating the various perfections of grace. *Priority*, we have seen, is only one dimension of "grace," and rarely its sole or most significant feature. Even in this regard the

57. See Sanders, *Paul and Palestinian Judaism*, pp. 287-98, 316-21.

58. As we have seen (see above, 3.6.1), Sanders assumed that grace is also "unmerited" (of the Scrolls, see *Paul and Palestinian Judaism*, p. 328), so that the remarkable perfection of the incongruity of grace in the *Hodayot* seemed only an exaggerated expression of what could be generally assumed.

59. See, e.g., S. J. Gathercole, *Where Is Boasting? Early Jewish Soteriology and Paul's Response in Romans 1–5* (Grand Rapids: Eerdmans, 2002), pp. 91-111; C. VanLandingham, *Judgment and Justification*, pp. 102-35; P. M. Sprinkle, *Paul and Judaism Revisited: A Study of Divine and Human Agency in Salvation* (Downers Grove: InterVarsity Press, 2013), pp. 125-44. On Qumran soteriology in general, cf. M. A. Seifrid, *Justification by Faith: The Origin and Development of a Central Pauline Theme* (Leiden: Brill, 1992), pp. 81-99, 255-57; Falk, "Prayers and Psalms," pp. 31-34. For an earlier discussion of grace in the *Hodayot*, applying Pauline and/or Lutheran categories of analysis, see S. Schulz, "Zur Rechtfertigung aus Gnaden in Qumran und bei Paulus," *ZTK* 56 (1959): 155-85.

Hodayot articulate a distinctive perspective: God acts first not in the calling of the patriarchs, nor in the establishment of a covenant with Israel — indeed, not in history at all — but in his eternally determined design of the universe. This construal of priority is most significant in undergirding and explaining the really striking feature of the *Hodayot,* their maximized articulation of the *incongruity* between divine goodness/mercy and the impoverished and filthy condition of its elect recipients. Such an emphasis on "unmerited" divine benevolence would have shocked the author of *The Wisdom of Solomon,* whose moral universe is sustainable only if God's grace is accommodated within the equitable operation of fitting recompense. Philo would have found much to appreciate in the *Hodayot,* not least their stress on divine causation and the gift of insight; but his philosophical rendering of divine causation, which creates the worth suitable for the giving of gifts, would have made him balk at the extreme polarity between divine benevolence and the worthlessness of the elect.[60] All three texts/authors place considerable emphasis on "grace," but each in a distinctive way. There is limited benefit in a one-dimensional focus on the sequential relation between "grace" and "works." Much more can be revealed by distinguishing the perfections of grace, and thereby identifying the diversity of voices in Second Temple Judaism in their varied articulation of this central *theologoumenon.* By perfecting its incongruity, the *Hodayot* do not have a "higher," "purer," or more emphatic construal of grace. But they articulate this motif differently from many other Second Temple Jews, while providing a theological rationale for what would otherwise make God seem arbitrary or unfair.

60. The personal (or mythological) language of "preference" (רצון) would also have sounded suspiciously arbitrary to a philosopher such as Philo, who was trained to identify rational reasons for the actions of God.

CHAPTER 8

Pseudo-Philo, *Liber Antiquitatum Biblicarum*

The text traditionally labeled *Liber Antiquitatum Biblicarum* (henceforth, *LAB*), and once wrongly attributed to Philo, consists of an interpretative recasting of the biblical narrative from Adam to the death of Saul.[1] Many linguistic features suggest that our (fourth century?) Latin text is derived from a Hebrew original (probably through an intermediary stage in Greek),[2] and comparison with other Palestinian Jewish texts points to a date of composition around the first century CE. Multiple references to the expectation that Israel would pass through repeated cycles of sin, abandonment by God, and restoration by divine mercy (e.g., 9.4; 12.6, 9-10; 13.10; 30.1-7), and the unusual prominence given to the period of judges, have suggested to many scholars

1. The text, noted in the sixteenth century, was rediscovered by L. Cohn at the end of the nineteenth century and has only recently received the attention it deserves. For a critical edition of the Latin text (by D. J. Harrington), with French translation and commentary, see C. Perrot and P.-M. Bogaert, *Pseudo-Philon: Les Antiquités Bibliques* (SC 229, 230; Paris: Gabalda, 1976). Jacobson has reprinted this text, but his English translation reflects his own reconstruction of the original Hebrew, as explained in his very extensive commentary; see H. Jacobson, *A Commentary on Pseudo-Philo's* Liber Antiquitatum Biblicarum, 2 vols. (Leiden: Brill, 1996). There is a German translation and commentary in C. Dietzfelbinger, *Pseudo-Philo: Antiquitates Biblicae (Liber Antiquitatum Biblicarum)* (JSHRZ II/2; Güterloh: Gerd Mohn, 1975). Whether the work originally ended where it currently does continues to be a matter of dispute; see L. H. Feldman, "Prolegomenon," in M. R. James, *The Biblical Antiquities of Philo* (New York: Ktav, 1971 [1917]), pp. ix-clxix, at lxxvii; Jacobson, *Commentary*, pp. 253-54 (arguing from 26.12-15 that the author locates himself chronologically before the construction of Solomon's temple).

2. Originally proposed by L. Cohn, "An Apocryphal Work Ascribed to Philo of Alexandria," *JQR* 10 (1898): 277-332, at pp. 307-13; endorsed with additional argumentation in Jacobson, *Commentary*, pp. 215-24. Jacobson attempts to reconstruct the Hebrew underlying our sometimes garbled or cloudy Latin text, though at some points even he is defeated; this problematic linguistic situation makes our reconstruction of the meaning of *LAB* sometimes uncertain.

that *LAB* was written in a context of disappointment, and perhaps domination by a foreign power; but the few tantalizing references to the Temple have left scholarly opinion divided regarding its relation to the 70 CE watershed.[3] The constant reiteration of the conviction that God's covenant promises to Israel are *eternal,* and his anger only "for a time" (see below), suggests that the work was intended to encourage a demoralized nation inclined to doubt that it would ever again encounter the favor of God.[4] In this context, using the biblical language of "mercy,"[5] *LAB* offers the most emphatic assertion of God's unfailing mercy to be found in Second Temple Judaism.

However one characterizes the genre of *LAB,* which is replete with explanations and supplementations of the biblical text, there is a notable concern to *connect* apparently disparate episodes and unconnected motifs in the jumble of traditions collected in the Bible. Where Philo presses for the philosophical sense that underlies and unites such diverse sagas, *LAB* finds literary echoes, parallels, forecasts, and fulfillments that synthesize and unify the biblical texts at a narrative level. Moses' lifespan of 120 years is found to be predicted in God's limiting of the life of humanity after the flood (9.8; connecting Deut 34:7 with Gen 6:3); the selection of Aaron's rod (Num 17) is reminiscent of the

3. The temple to be destroyed in 12.4 is the Solomonic temple (but there may be echoes of more contemporary history); the date of the breaching and encircling of the "place" on the "seventeenth day of the fourth month" (19.7) has been connected with rabbinic datings of the destruction of the second temple by Titus (so Cohn, strongly supported by Jacobson, *Commentary,* pp. 199-210). Otherwise the relative lack of interest in the temple, and the probable ending of the text before the construction of Solomon's temple, may suggest a point (after 70 CE) when Palestinian Judaism was learning to focus instead on synagogue worship (cf. 11.8, for the purpose of the Sabbath). Others argue for a pre-70 date: see D. J. Harrington, "Pseudo-Philo," in J. Charlesworth, ed., *Old Testament Pseudepigrapha,* 2 vols. (London: Darton, Longman & Todd, 1985), vol. 2, p. 299; Perrot and Bogaert, *Pseudo-Philon,* pp. 68-74. Still others remain undecided: so E. Reinmuth, *Pseudo-Philo und Lukas: Studien zum Liber Antiquitatum Biblicarum und seiner Bedeutung für die Interpretation des lukanischen Doppelwerks* (Tübingen: Mohr Siebeck, 1994), pp. 17-26; B. Fisk, *Do You Not Remember? Scripture, Story. and Exegesis in the Rewritten Bible of Pseudo-Philo* (Sheffield: Sheffield Academic Press, 2001), pp. 34-45.

4. On the purposes of *LAB,* see Fisk, *Do You Not Remember?* pp. 327-31; Jacobson, *Commentary,* p. 253; F. J. Murphy, "The Eternal Covenant in Pseudo-Philo," *JSP* 3 (1988): 43-57, at p. 54. Nickelsburg suggests that the emphatically negative version of God's promises (God will *not* let Israel be utterly destroyed) indicates that the text "is spoken to people who suppose that they may have been totally rejected by God," "in fear for their existence as a nation"; see G. W. E. Nickelsburg, "Good and Bad Leaders in Pseudo-Philo's *Liber Antiquitatum Biblicarum,*" in J. J. Collins and G. W. E. Nickelsburg, eds., *Ideal Figures in Ancient Judaism: Profiles and Paradigms* (Chico: Scholars Press, 1980), pp. 49-65, at p. 62.

5. For the relation between the language of "mercy" and that of "gift," see the Appendix at the end of this book.

rods displayed by Jacob to his sheep (Gen 30) (*LAB* 17.3).[6] This is not just a literary technique, intended to delight the reader. It illustrates and cements a strong motif running through the text, that God has a plan for the course of history, a plan unfailingly fulfilled and a purpose never ultimately "in vain." Whereas human intentions are often thwarted, God's words (his predictions, his oaths, and his promises) are utterly dependable: even in the details of the story (such as God's strange prediction that Jephthah would sacrifice his first-born child), God ordains events "in order that my word be fulfilled and my plan that I thought out not be foiled" (40.4; cf. 39.11).[7] Central to this intricate tapestry of prediction and event are the covenant promises of God and his indestructible commitment to Israel, the themes that will form the focus of our discussion here.

8.1. Covenant Promises That Cannot Fail

The recurring pattern that unites the scriptural narrative for the author of *LAB* is the theme of covenant — a divine commitment that is utterly reliable and will never be found to fail. The motif begins with the most general covenantal relation, God's promises to Noah and to humanity in the wake of the flood.[8] After lists of "generations" and genealogical links, the flood story is the first proper narrative in *LAB*, recounting God's covenant with the "righteous and

6. For the hermeneutical significance of the deployment of "secondary Scripture" throughout *LAB*, see Fisk, *Do You Not Remember?* Reinmuth has demonstrated at length how the interweaving of the Scriptures creates the vision of a single, interconnected story (*Pseudo-Philo*, pp. 27-127).

7. For similar general notices on the fulfillment of what God predicts, cf. 18.3; 27.13; 46.1; 47.2; 51.6. That none of God's purposes can be "in vain" *(in vano* or *in vanum)* is repeatedly emphasized: see, e.g., 9.4; 12.4, 9; 15.5; 18.11; 23.13. For discussion of this striking motif in *LAB*, see F. J. Murphy, "Divine Plan, Human Plan: A Structuring Theme in Pseudo-Philo," *JQR* 77 (1986): 5-14; idem, "God in Pseudo-Philo," *JJS* 19 (1988): 1-18; E. Reinmuth, "'Nicht vergeblich' bei Paulus und Pseudo-Philo, *Liber Antiquitatum Biblicarum*," *NovT* 33 (1991): 97-123. As Fisk notes, "there is an observable symmetry between Pseudo-Philo's *explicit* statements about God's faithfulness throughout Israel's history, and his *implicit* claims — advanced by deploying secondary Scripture — that Israel's story is self-explanatory, self-glossing, and internally consistent," *Do You Not Remember?* p. 327.

8. The mysterious vision of Cenaz in 28.6-9 might suggest an even more basic prediction of the extent of human history (7,000 years), issued before the flood. For the unity of the various covenants in *LAB*, see J. R. Levison, "Torah and Covenant in Pseudo-Philo's *Liber Antiquitatum Biblicarum*," in F. Avemarie and H. Lichtenberger, eds., *Bund und Tora: Zur theologischen Begriffsgeschichte in alttestamentlicher, frühjüdischer und urchristlicher Tradition* (Tübingen: Mohr Siebeck, 1996), pp. 111-27.

blameless" Noah (3.4; cf. 3.11, 14): after the destruction of the world by flood, God commits himself never again to "curse the earth" and "destroy all living creatures" (3.9). In an important addition to the biblical text (Gen 8:21-22), *LAB* makes a significant distinction between *judgment* and *destruction:* humanity will indeed sin, and will necessarily be judged (by famine, sword, fire, disease, and exile), but the earth will not be destroyed by flood.[9] The covenant sign is, of course, the rainbow (3.11-12), whose importance is shown by repeated reference later in the narrative (4.5, "the memorial of the covenant"; 13.7-8). Particularly significant is the parallel our author draws between Noah's rainbow and Moses' staff (19.11); each is a reminder that when people sin, and are necessarily judged, God's commitment outlasts his judgment: "I will recall your staff and spare them in accord with my mercy" (19.11). The Noahic and Mosaic covenants are similarly shaped: they expect (indeed, predict) human sin and divine judgment, but guarantee divine mercy *beyond* the inevitable cycle of transgression and punishment.

The covenant promises to Abraham are similarly inviolable. Abraham is picked out as early as 4.11 as "perfect and blameless" (cf. Gen 17:1), and the long narrative of his refusal to compromise with the idolatrous construction of the Tower (6.1-18) serves not only to connect Genesis 12 to Genesis 11 but to highlight the quality of the founding "fathers" and the particular virtue of *trust* in God (6.11). From the beginning it is clear that the covenant is indestructible: Abraham's "covenant will not be broken, and his seed will be multiplied forever" (4.11).[10] With subtle alteration of the biblical text, Abraham is promised via Sarah an "eternal seed" (*sempiternum semen,* 8.3),[11] and this is strongly affirmed in the vivid expansion of Scripture in the story of Amran, the father of Moses (9.1-16). Appealing to the covenant established with Abraham, Amran insists that "sooner will the world be destroyed for ever or the universe sink into the immeasurable or the heart of the deep touch the stars than that the race of the sons of Israel will be destroyed" (9.3). His insistence on having children, despite Egyptian threats, is honored by God with his fathering of the uniquely privileged Moses (9.7). His action is founded on the confidence that

9. Jacobson, *Commentary,* p. 322, notes the rabbinic discussions of God's means of punishment, but the distinction in *LAB* is as much about the difference in severity between judgment and destruction.

10. Cf. 7.4: "I will establish my covenant with him and will bless his seed and be called by him the eternal God" (here and elsewhere translations are taken from Jacobson, *Commentary*).

11. See Jacobson, *Commentary,* pp. 387-88, on the adaptation of Genesis 17:16; cf. the references in Genesis 17:7, 13 to an "everlasting covenant." For the delicate handling in *LAB* of the promise of the *land,* see B. Halpern-Amaru, *Rewriting the Bible: Land and Covenant in Postbiblical Jewish Literature* (Valley Forge: Trinity Press International, 1994), pp. 69-94.

"God will not continue in his anger, nor will he forget his people forever, nor will he cast forth the race of Israel into nothingness upon the earth; nor did he emptily *(in vanum)* establish a covenant with our fathers" (9.4).

This covenant is further defined through the revelation of the law on Sinai, the "law of the eternal covenant," which consists of "everlasting commandments that will not pass away" (11.5). Thereafter, *LAB* repeatedly emphasizes, through recurrent patterns in the narrative and through constant direct expression, the *double* truth of Israelite sin, which elicits divine abandonment and judgment, *and* God's promise not to forsake his people or forget his promises forever. This doubleness is not without precedent in the biblical text (e.g., Exod 32–34; Deut 31–32), but its centrality to the narrative of *LAB* is nonetheless remarkable. Practically all the speakers in this narrative bear witness to this pattern. God himself wearily notes Israelite sin and predicts his abandonment of them, while promising that he will "turn again and be reconciled to them" (12.6; see below). While instructing Moses on Israel's potential to flourish if they walk in his ways, he predicts their failure *and* his faithfulness: "But I surely know that they will corrupt their ways and I will abandon them, and they will forget the covenants that I have established with their fathers; but nevertheless I will not forget them forever" (13.10).[12] Even disobedient Israelites draw attention to this pattern of history, either by explicitly casting doubt on God's commitment to his promises just before he fulfills his word (10.2-3; 15.4), or by wishing that he did not constantly punish and restore, but would finish them off once and for all (35.2; 49.6). But the main spokespeople for the message that God will punish sin but will not cast off his people forever are the leaders that emerge in the history of Israel, some in biblical roles amplified by our author, some created wholesale by him or by the traditions he uses. Thus, Joshua recalls the covenant promises of God, duly fulfilled ("The Lord has done everything that he said to us") and prays that "the covenant of the Lord remain with you and not be ruined" (21.9-10). Interestingly, he recognizes that the fulfillment of God's promises may not be witnessed in every generation: God's time span is not confined to a human lifetime, and "though we will be in the underworld, you will fulfill your words" (21.4).[13] As a result, the confirmation of God's word (which must be fulfilled

12. The speech closes with a reference to God's faithfulness ("I am faithful to what I say"), but this comes in the wake of a further prediction of sin and abandonment, and its precise reference is not clear (see Jacobson, *Commentary,* p. 525). For further statements by God of his commitment to his promises, see 14.2 ("I will diminish nothing of what I have said to their fathers"), 23.11 ("I fulfilled my covenant that I spoke to your fathers"), and 15.5 ("behold now the plan that issues from me will not be in vain [*in vano*]"), though the latter is focused more on God's plans to *punish* a wayward nation.

13. The reference here to "preferring one generation to another" is somewhat obscure,

and seen to be fulfilled) may have to be conveyed to the fathers after their deaths, when their souls are stored ready for the new world ("They will know that I have not chosen you to no purpose [*in vanum*]," 23.13). However, it is clear that God *will* fulfill his promises and his "toil," despite and beyond Israel's sin, as is affirmed by Cenaz: "Will the shepherd destroy his flock for no reason, unless it has sinned against him? But now he is the one who will spare us according to the abundance of his mercy *(iuxta abundantiam misericordiae suae)*, because he has toiled so much over us" (28.5).

It is Moses and Deborah who are accorded the most elaborate explications of this recurrent motif, not least in their farewell discourses to the nation. Moses begins with a restatement of the cyclical pattern: "I know that you will rise up and forsake the words established for you through me, and God will be angry at you and abandon you and depart from your land. And he will bring upon you your enemies, and they will rule over you — but not forever, because he will remember the covenant that he established with your fathers" (19.2). This prediction is confirmed by God: "this people will rise up and not seek me, and they will forget my Law, by which I have enlightened them, and I will abandon their seed for a time" (19.6). The qualification — "for a time" — is confirmed by the assurance symbolized by Moses' rod: "When they sin, I will be angry with them, but I will recall your staff and spare them in accord with my mercy. Your staff will be before me as a reminder for ever, and it will be like the bow with which I established my covenant with Noah" (19.11). Remarkably little weight is given here or elsewhere to the Deuteronomic theme of repentance: what ultimately counts is not human remorse but God's unbreakable commitment.[14] Thus, Deborah insists that "the Lord will be favorably disposed to you today, not because of you but because of the covenant that he established with your fathers and the oath that he swore not to abandon them forever" (30.7; cf. 35.3). In her survey of Israel's history, focusing on the Abrahamic covenant and the covenant established at Sinai (32.1-9), she reiterates the theme of divine memory ("God has remembered both his new and his old promises and displayed his deliverance to us," 32.12) and instructs the creation and the angels to inform the fathers in their soul-chambers that "God has not forgotten the least of the promises that he established with us" (32.13). Like all the other leaders, she is cynical about Israel's ability to keep

but the stress on the eternity of God ("you who are before the world and after the world live on") seems designed to refute those who conclude, on the basis of their lifetime's experience, that "God destroys the people whom he has chosen for himself" (21.4); see Jacobson, *Commentary,* pp. 681-82.

14. See Murphy, "The Eternal Covenant." There are, however, some references to repentance (e.g., 21.6).

the law (30.7), but is nonetheless confident about the future. Expanding the biblical reference to the military assistance of the stars (Judg 5:20), Deborah imagines the stars forming an embassy to God on Israel's behalf when the nation is in distress: "and he will remember that day and send the redemption of his covenant" (32.14).

God's faithfulness to his word, the utter impossibility that God, who knows the future, would predict something that does not come true (cf. 18.4; 50.4), and the dismissal of the impious thought that God's "toil" should come to nothing, are all factors in our author's confidence that *despite Israel's disobedience* God will fulfill his covenant promises. As a further factor, he enhances the biblical motif that God should protect his own reputation (Exod 32:12; Num 14:13-16; Deut 9:28); God must watch what others might say (*LAB* 20.4; 22.5; 23.12; 36.4) and take care for his own "name" (10.4; 28.4; 49.7). But something more basic remains that we have yet to explore. Why has God made such covenant promises to *this particular people?* Why is Israel special and chosen from all the nations? Is God's commitment to this people arbitrary, or is there a rationale for such an irrevocable election of one people by the God who made all nations and all the world? This is the question that we must now address.

8.2. Why Israel Is Special

The thread that links the varied episodes of *LAB,* like the biblical stories which it amplifies and connects, is the special status of Israel. As in Numbers, the mysterious story of Balak and Balaam serves to articulate this status: "It is easier to take away the heavens and all their expanse and to extinguish the light of the sun and to darken the light of the moon than for one who so wished to uproot the planting of the Most Powerful or to destroy his vine" (18.10). The metaphor of the vine (adopted from the Bible; e.g., Isa 5; Ps 80; Ezek 17:5-10; cf. 1QH[a] VI.15) is a favorite of our author (cf. 12.8-9; 18.11; 23.11-12; 28.4; 30.4; 39.7), sometimes with special emphasis on the choice of this one vine, named after God (28.4). Another common metaphor figures Israel as a flock (e.g., 17.3; 28.5; 30.5; cf. Jer 13:17; Ezek 34), or as the ram chosen to lead the flock: "when you [God] distributed all the peoples and nations of the earth, did you not choose Israel alone and liken it to no animal except to the ram that goes before and leads the flock?" (31.5). The fact that Israel is chosen above all others, the "one people from all the nations of the earth" (30.2) is repeatedly emphasized; they are God's chosen nation "because you loved them beyond all others" (19.8; cf. 35.2). But why is Israel God's "portion" (*hereditas,* 12.9; 19.8; cf. Deut 9:26, 29), and this forever (28.4), even when (as so often) the nation goes astray?

Deborah's statement that God will be favorably disposed to his wayward people "not because of you but because of the covenant that he established with your fathers" (30.7) directs our attention to the origins of the nation. This is reinforced by the angel's message to Gideon that God "will have mercy, as no one else has mercy, on the people of Israel, though not on your account but on account of those who are asleep" (35.3), apparently spotlighting the earliest generations. We have noted Abraham's designation as "perfect and blameless" (4.11); his unique trust in God during the Babel-brick episode (6.1-18) is remarked upon more than once in the subsequent narrative (23.5; 32.1). The covenants of land and seed are specifically connected to Abraham (7.4; 8.3; 9.3), and his offering of Isaac is once said to be foundational to the election of Israel: "his offering was acceptable to me, and in return for his blood I chose them" (18.5). But it is doubtful whether this reflects more than the *confirmation* of the covenant promises in Genesis 22:15-18,[15] and when the text coordinates the choice of Abraham with the choice of the nation (32.1), this probably signifies only that Abraham was well suited to be the foundation and figurehead of the elect nation, not that the nation was elect *because of* him.[16] In the same way, Moses is singled out as an exceptional servant of God, from before his birth (9.6) to the moment of his death (19.16). Beloved of the Lord (24.3; 25.3, etc.) and glorious above all men (9.16), he was accorded many unique powers and privileges (9.8), but his role was to mediate God's law and redemption to a nation already chosen above others.[17] What has to be explained is why God should choose to elect a nation (through Abraham) and to redeem that nation (through Moses), despite their failure to obey him even during Moses' lifetime, and repeatedly thereafter. If the election of Israel *qua the righteous* made evident sense in *The Wisdom of Solomon* as the affirmation of the moral structures of the universe (see above, chapter 5), how can *LAB* account for God's faithfulness to Israel *qua Israel,* despite her repeated rounds of idolatry and disobedience?

The best entry to our query is to be found in *LAB* 12, the author's account of the Golden Calf. It is notable that, unlike *The Wisdom of Solomon,* which glides over this incident in silence, the Golden Calf narrative is here recounted at length, with later back-references (19.7; 22.5; 25.9), and regarded

15. See Jacobson, *Commentary,* pp. 583-84.

16. Similarly, the statement that God loved Jacob and hated Esau "because of his deeds" (32.5) indicates that God's choice is fitting (and not arbitrary) but does not explain why God should choose this people in the first place.

17. Certain privileges are given to Israel "on account of" Miriam, Aaron, and Moses (20.8); these seem to be examples of fitting gifts, but not the reason why gifts should be given to this particular nation.

not as an isolated sin but as the start of a recurrent pattern of Israelite failure. Although an effort is made to exonerate Aaron (12.3) and those of the people who acted out of fear (12.7),[18] Israel's sin in making the calf (12.3) and flouting the second commandment (11.6) is described in full.[19] Adapting God's speech in Exodus 32:7-10, *LAB* has God complain about the people's "corruption," predicting that if such corruption has already occurred *before* they enter the land promised to their fathers, it will be even worse once they do so (12.4).[20] This representation of God's reaction is telling, both because it avoids the biblical suggestion that God might wholly replace the Abrahamic nation with another[21] and because it predicts that Israel's sinful behavior will continue, and worsen, once they are in the land. This will take the form of repeated crises in which gross Israelite sin leads to divine abandonment of Israel, followed by divine reconciliation: "Now I in turn will abandon them, but I will turn again and be reconciled with them so that a house may be built for me among them, a house that in turn will be destroyed because they will sin against me" (12.4). God can thus predict the future not only of Israel's sin but also of his reaction to that sin: he seems reconciled to this pattern of sin, temporary abandonment, and restoration, although his final remark on the nugatory value of all humanity ("the race of men will be to me like a drop from a pitcher and will be counted as spittle"; cf. 7.3-4; Isa 40:15)

18. On the intertextual echo of the drinking ordeal of Numbers 5, see Fisk, *Do You Not Remember?* pp. 176-90. As Fisk notes, this motif to some degree limits the scope of Israelite culpability and the resulting punishment, but the surrounding speeches (by God and Moses) make clear that Israel as a people is responsible and in serious jeopardy.

19. The explicit cross-reference to the Tower of Babel (12.3; cf. 7.2) and Israel's desire to "be like other nations" (12.2) suggest that the idolatry identifies Israel fully with the Tower-idolaters; see Reinmuth, *Pseudo-Philo und Lukas,* pp. 52-53; Fisk, *Do You Not Remember?* pp. 145-52 ("For Pseudo-Philo, the Sinai act was a *de facto* repudiation of her elect status as Abraham's seed," p. 151).

20. For this construal of the Latin, see (against Harrington) Jacobson, *Commentary,* pp. 487-88, and Dietzfelbinger, *Pseudo-Philo,* p. 134. There seems to be an assumption that temptations to idolatry will be far greater once Israel is settled in the land.

21. As Fisk demonstrates, Pseudo-Philo subtly replaces the Exodus threat that God would transfer the Abrahamic promise to Moses (Exod 32:10; cf. Gen 12:2) with God's ongoing commitment to the promise of the land (Gen 12:7): "Having suppressed the scandalous message of Exod 32:10, including its echo of antecedent Scripture, Pseudo-Philo has given voice to the larger covenantal context to which that text alluded, in order to protect, rather than undermine, Israel's secure status as chosen heir to the land" (*Do You Not Remember?* p. 161). For God to suggest breaking his own covenant promises is apparently too scandalous for Pseudo-Philo to contemplate. See C. Begg, "The Golden Calf Episode According to Pseudo-Philo," in M. Vervenne, ed., *Studies in the Book of Exodus: Redaction — Reception — Interpretation* (Leuven: Leuven University Press, 1996), pp. 577-94, at pp. 581-84.

suggests that Israel by its disobedience would relegate itself to the status of the worthless nations.[22]

Moses is devastated by the sight of the calf (12.5), but is encouraged by God's words to intercede on Israel's behalf: as he reasons, "even if they have sinned, what was declared to me on high will not be in vain *(in vano)*" (12.6). His intercession in 12.8-9 is an expansion of elements of Exodus 32:11-13, with multiple supplements:[23]

> Behold now, O God, you who have planted this vine and set its roots in the deep and stretched out its shoots to your lofty seat, look upon it at this moment, because that vine has put forth its fruit[24] but does not recognize its cultivator. And now, if you will be angry at your vine and uproot it from the deep and dry up its shoots from your lofty and eternal seat, no longer will the deep come to nourish it, nor will your throne come to cool that vine of yours that you have destroyed.
>
> And you are he who are all light, and you have adorned your house with precious stones and gold; and you have sprinkled your house with perfumes and spikenard and balsam wood and cinnamon and roots of myrrh and costum; and you have filled it with various foods and the sweetness of various drinks. Therefore, if you do not have mercy on your vine, all things, Lord, have been done in vain *(in vano),* and you will have no one to glorify you. And even if you plant another vine, it will not trust you, because you destroyed the former one. For if you indeed abandon the world, then who will do for you that which you spoke as God? And now let your anger be kept from your vine. Rather, let that which was said previously by you and what remains to be said be done, and let not your labor be in vain *(in vanum),* and let not your portion be sold cheaply. (12.8-9)

God's response to this remarkable set of arguments is positive ("behold I am made merciful *(misericors factus sum)* in accordance with your words," 12.10) and it is worth attending closely to their logic. In the first place, Moses suggests that Israel, as the vine, is integral to the fabric and meaning of the cosmos. With its roots "in the deep" and its topmost shoots at God's throne, the vine

22. See F. J. Murphy, *Pseudo-Philo: Rewriting the Bible* (Oxford: Oxford University Press, 1993), p. 71; Fisk, *Do You Not Remember?* pp. 164-74.

23. Elements from Exodus 32:11-14 echoed here are: that God has made promises he must keep; that God has labored over Israel already; and that God's honor is at stake. Significantly, the content of the covenant promises has already been mentioned by God himself (12.4).

24. So Jacobson, following Δ *(emisit);* most other editors follow the alternative reading (*amisit,* "has lost"; cf. 28.4); see Jacobson, *Commentary,* pp. 497-98.

stretches across the universe from bottom to top and constitutes a central structuring feature of the created world. God has adorned this cosmos with all kinds of splendor — precious stones, spices, food and drink.[25] All of this would come to nothing if God has no mercy on his vine — presumably because the vine is what gives meaning and purpose to all the richness of the created world. That this is the logic of Moses' speech is reinforced by what is said of the relation between Israel and the cosmos elsewhere. As we have already noted, both Amran (9.3) and Balaam (18.10) indicate that the world would sooner collapse in on itself than that "the race of Israel" or "the planting of the Most Powerful" be destroyed. Now we can see that this is not just a figure of speech indicating the impossibility of such a disaster, but an indication of the centrality of Israel to the structure of the cosmos: if God's plant were destroyed, the cosmos would truly buckle with the loss of its *raison d'être.* Elsewhere we learn that God had planned the vineyard of humanity and chosen Israel, the plant, in "the time that was before the world, the time when man did not exist and there was no wickedness in it" (28.4): Israel is no post-Babel afterthought, but was central to God's purposes from before the creation of humanity.[26] When God took a rib from Adam, he knew "that from his rib Israel would be born" (32.15): it was not just humanity in general, but Israel in particular that was already in view in the Genesis account of creation. It is not surprising that the elements of the cosmos are present in force at the giving of the law (11.1, 5; 23.10; 32.7-8), just as creation worked wonders for Israel both in the Exodus and on many occasions since (15.5; 30.5; 32.9-10, 14-15). Israel is, in truth, the nation for whom the world was made, its goal and purpose. We are not therefore surprised to hear the people pray: "Lord, pay attention to the people you have chosen, and do not destroy the vine that you have planted, in order that this nation, which *you have had from the beginning* and always preferred, and *for whose sake you make the habitable world,* and which you brought into the land you promised them, should be before you as a portion" (39.7).[27] God's promises to Israel are irrevocable because Israel constitutes the rationale for the cosmos as a whole: to abandon Israel forever would be to "abandon the world" (12.9).[28]

25. Although these elements are sometimes connected with the temple or with Paradise, it is better to take the *domus* ("house") here as the whole world; so Harrington, "Pseudo-Philo," ad loc. and Jacobson, *Commentary,* pp. 499-502.

26. Likewise, the law is described as "the foundation of understanding that [God] had prepared from the creation of the world" (32.7).

27. Italics mine; for rabbinic parallels to the notion that God made the world for the sake of Israel, see Jacobson, *Commentary,* p. 953.

28. Conversely, the flourishing of Israel is accompanied by the flourishing of the cosmos (13.10; 23.10-13).

Moses' second main, and related, argument in 12.8-9 concerns Israel's unique place in the service of God. If God were to destroy Israel, there would be no one left to glorify him; no other nation would take its place (who would trust him, if he reneged on his promise to Israel?) and "who would do for you that which you spoke as God?" (12.9). Israel is unique as the bearer of God's glory: it is this nation among whom God will place his glory and proclaim his ways (9.7) and whom God will "glorify above all nations" when he issues through them a "light to the world," the illumination of his laws (11.1).[29] If God's glory resides particularly in the tabernacle (11.15; cf. 15.6; 21.6), it more generally rests upon his people: "I chose one people from all the nations of the earth, that my glory should abide in this world with it" (30.2).[30] It is in Israel that he has placed his "majesty" and among them that he has kindled his eternal light (19.4); this is a people that bears his name (28.4; 49.7). If Israel were to disappear forever, there would be no trace remaining of God's presence, God's glory, and God's law. Israel is the irreplaceable representative of God on earth, and if all that is left is the other, useless nations (as valueless as spit, 7.3; 12.4), God might as well "uproot" creation, such is his abhorrence of human sin (44.6, 8). Thus, even if Israel is judged, and particular generations destroyed, God *must* restore this nation in mercy; without it, creation would no longer be worthwhile.

At several points, to be sure, *LAB* looks beyond creation to a new world that will be created "when the years of the world will be complete" (3.10). This eschatological vision includes a final judgment, when God will render to each according to their works (3.10), and when everyone, it seems, will be responsible for themselves and unable to rely on the merits of others (33.1-6). There is some hope that those who are sinful in this life, if properly contrite, might be given mercy when God resurrects the dead (25.7), but unless one presses hard on the vague statement that "the lot of each of you will be in eternal life" (23.13), it is not clear that "all Israel" will have a share in this future world. The lack of clarity on this matter indicates that for *LAB* (unlike *4 Ezra,* to be discussed in the next chapter), the present world remains important, and Israel's future on earth remains a pressing concern. Whatever the miseries and disappointments of the present, our author cannot accept that God's judgment of Israel would last forever. His covenant promise must hold; his plan cannot be ultimately "in vain." On this rests not only God's reputation, his consistency, and his faithfulness to his word; on it rests also the purpose and value of the cosmos

29. Cf. 20.4, where the fact that God has not chosen other nations is balanced by the fact that he is not indulgent to Israel (and does not "regard persons"), since he punishes them for their sin.

30. The language of election *(eligere; electio)* of Abraham (7.4) and of Israel, from all the nations (18.5, 6, 11; 21.4; 23.13; 28.4; 30.2; 31.5; 32.1; 35.2), is notably frequent.

that God has toiled to make. If God were not to exercise mercy when Israel goes astray, he might as well abandon the whole of creation.

8.3. The Mercy of God

On numerous occasions we have found "mercy" to be the central characteristic of God, in his commitment to restore and sustain Israel. The repeated references to "mercy" (*misericordia, misereor,* etc.) probably go back to an original Hebrew חסד or רחמים;[31] they are occasionally supplemented by *longanimitas,* as a near synonym (19.8, 9; 39.5; 49.3).[32] This mercy is often described as *abundant* (19.14; 21.4; 28.5), as it "fills the earth" (39.6), but it is clearly not a *singular* characteristic of God: it is frequently juxtaposed with, or is the aftermath to, the anger or judgment of God (e.g., 11.6; 25.3; 28.2; 43.10). In many examples we have noted, divine mercy is obviously *incongruous* with the worth of the recipient. It is when Israel has sinned and been justly abandoned by God that God has mercy on the nation (e.g., 12.10, 19.9), and without that undeserved mercy Israel would have no future at all (12.9). But this is not always the case: despite what we might expect (from the connotations of the English term "mercy" and the Latin *misericordia*), God's mercy is often, in fact, quite fitting. Thus, in an echo of Exodus 20:5-6, God jealously visits the sins of ancestors on their children but "acts mercifully for a thousand generations to those who love me and keep my commandments" (11.6). A similarly broad sense of "mercy" as faithful love (cf. Hebrew חסד, generally translated into Greek as ἔλεος) pervades other texts: "If they will walk in my ways," declares God, "I will not abandon them but will have mercy on them always" (13.10; cf. 3.4, of Noah; 50.4, of Hannah). In a programmatic statement, the God who kills and makes alive is said to kill the unjust with righteous judgment, but to bring the just to life with mercy (51.5). In other words, "mercy" does not always imply grace to the undeserving; it takes its particular nuance from the context of use, not from the independent associations of the term itself. There are a number of occasions when "mercy" is exercised both *in spite of* Israel's sin and *because of* some other, countervailing, factor, such as the assurance that God "will have mercy, as no one else has mercy, on the people of Israel, though not on your account but on account of those who are asleep" (35.3; cf. 30.7; 35.4).

31. The most common related terms in our Latin text are: *miseratio* (19.8; 21.4); *misereor* (12.9; 13.10; 15.7; 19.9; 22.7; 25.7; 31.2; 35.3); *misericordia* (3.4; 11.6; 13.6; 15.7; 19.8, 11, 14; 21.4; 22.5; 24.3; 28.5; 39.6; 51.5; 59.4); *misericors* (12.10; 22.6).

32. Cf. *pietas* in 15.7 and references to God as one who gives (53.13) and forgives (35.4; 62.6). *Gratia* is practically confined to the translation of the Hebrew idiom "to find favor" (3.4; 6.10; 42.8).

Our text does not, therefore, celebrate incongruity as the essential, or even the proper, characteristic of mercy. Nonetheless, it does demonstrate, time and again, that God has had, and will have, mercy on a disobedient and wayward nation, as promised by God himself and as predicted by Israel's leaders. In response to Moses, God has mercy on Israel after the idolatry of the Golden Calf (12.10; cf. 22.5; Num 14:20); later, even when they sin and he is justly angry, he will recall Moses' staff and spare them in accord with his mercy (19.11; cf. 19.14). Acutely aware of the waywardness of humanity, Moses appeals to God: "Who is the man who has not sinned against you? And unless your patience abides, how will your portion be secure, unless you are merciful to them?" (19.9; cf. 15.7). Although God's mercy might be more likely if sins are committed in ignorance (22.6) or are confessed before death (25.7), in many cases mercy is simply juxtaposed to sin, as in God's assurance that "though my people have sinned, nevertheless I have will have mercy on them" (31.2; cf. 39.6). This extension of mercy beyond God's kindness to the faithful so as to entail his restorative forgiveness of the sinful is necessary, we have seen, if Israel is to be sustained, and if the world is therefore to retain its value and its purpose. In other words, incongruity is not the essence of God's mercy, but it is essential for the fulfillment of his irrevocable promises and indefeasible plans. As in 1QH[a] (see the previous chapter), the incongruity of grace can be celebrated and proclaimed, but it is not a self-evident phenomenon, and it requires a deep rationale. That God should have mercy *even* on sinful Israel is an indication that God, unlike humans, can restrain himself, in long-suffering patience (39.4-5); more profoundly, it is a necessary phenomenon if the purposes of the cosmos are to be fulfilled *through Israel,* as God has determined them to be.

Thus, it is the irreplaceability of Israel in the design of the universe that is here the most basic justification for the incongruity of divine mercy. This mythological basis is parallel in certain respects to the creation-rationale of God's choice in 1QH[a], though here its recipient is the nation of Israel, not an elect contingent within it. Unlike *The Wisdom of Solomon,* which strenuously maintains the *congruity* of divine favor in order to preserve the moral order of history, the *Liber Antiquitatum Biblicarum* posits no moral or rational structuring of the cosmos. In fact, its universe is skewed toward Israel *qua Israel,* mythologically justified by Israel's structuring role in creation and its unique relationship to God. Within this framework, mercy can be perfected in being exercised on the sinful. If this text was written in consciousness of Israel's failure and directed to readers whose woes constituted not the persecution of the righteous but the judgment of God, there was every reason to offer comfort by maximizing the biblical motif that God will have mercy on Israel, even or especially when it does not deserve such lenient treatment.

CHAPTER 9

4 Ezra

4 Ezra (2 Esdras 3–14) is one of the most profound theological reflections on the history and hope of Israel from the Second Temple era (*stricto sensu,* just after its end). Dating from the end of the first century CE, the text reflects the crisis of faith precipitated by the destruction of Jerusalem (70 CE), voicing deep laments that question the integrity of God's promises to Israel and the validity of God's purposes for creation.[1] These questions are eloquently aired by the respected figure of "Ezra," and they come to their climax in a long and subtle debate about the mercy and justice of God. It is significant that Ezra's doubts are treated with sympathy, but equally significant that (as I shall argue) they are eventually resolved with clarity and consistency. As a work of theology, *4 Ezra* is an intellectual achievement within Jewish apocalypticism as impressive as anything achieved, with Greek resources, by Philo or in *The Wisdom of Solomon.*

A number of factors make the interpretation of this text problematic. All extant versions stand at two removes from its original, probably Hebrew, text,[2]

1. The dating of *4 Ezra* relies less on the opening notice of "the thirtieth year after the destruction of Jerusalem" (3.1, echoing Ezek 1:1) than on the "three heads" of the (Roman) eagle, the last precise feature of the eagle vision (11.29-35; 12.22-28), probably a reference to the three Flavian emperors; see J. M. Myers, *I and II Esdras,* AB 42 (Garden City: Doubleday, 1974), pp. 129-31, 299-302; J. Schreiner, *Das 4. Buch Esra,* JSHRZ 5/4 (Güterloh: Mohn, 1981), pp. 291-306; M. E. Stone, *Fourth Ezra,* Hermeneia (Minneapolis: Fortress Press, 1990), pp. 9-10, 363-65.

2. It is generally agreed that all the versions (Latin, Syriac, Georgian, Ethiopic, Armenian, etc.) derive from (a number of) Greek versions, which probably themselves derive from a Hebrew original; see Stone, *Fourth Ezra,* pp. 1-11. The Latin text cited here is that reconstructed in A. F. J. Klijn, *Der lateinische Text der Apokalypse des Esra* (Berlin: Akademie-Verlag, 1983); cf. also A. F. J. Klijn, *Die Esra-Apokalypse (IV. Esra)* (Berlin: Akademie Verlag, 1992), with German translation. Readers of recent translations (e.g., in NRSV [English] or Schreiner, *4. Buch Esra* [German]), should also consult the translation in Stone, *Fourth Ezra,* which draws from all the versions and is supported by textual notes.

and although textual studies of *4 Ezra* have reached a high level of sophistication, there are residual uncertainties about the content of the original text at a number of points. There are also persistent questions about the coherence of the text, not least in its various eschatological expectations. Radical source-critical hypotheses have now been replaced, rightly, by attempts to trace the essential unity of the text,[3] although opinions differ on whether the vision of the "end," described both as messianic kingdom and as final judgment, is fundamentally coherent or represents a loose amalgam of national "this-worldly" and individualistic "other-worldly" perspectives.[4] But the text poses challenges for readers at other levels, too. How are we to take the dialogues of episodes 1 to 3 (3.1–9.25), where two apparently authoritative figures, Ezra and Uriel (a spokesman for God), argue about God's treatment of Israel and the world from fundamentally different perspectives? Is the reader meant to sympathize with one or the other — or both? Does the text then flip into a different mode in episodes 4 to 6 (9.26–13.58), leaving the issues raised in the dialogues unresolved? Or does Ezra undertake a journey in comprehension, with its turning point at episode 4 (9.26–10.59), moving from initial complaint against God (3.6-36) to eventual praise (13.57-58)? Should we trace here Ezra's increasing recognition of his own worthiness (6.32-34; 7.76-77; 8.47-48; 10.39; 12.35-36), until he is himself an agent of revelation on a par with Moses (14.1-50)?

In general, my reading of these issues is congruent with their careful reso-

3. The source-critical hypotheses of earlier generations (Volkmar, Kabisch, Box, Oesterley) have been largely superseded by readings that trace a unified progression of thought through the seven episodes of the text. This trend is most fully exemplified in E. Brandenburger, *Die Verborgenheit Gottes im Weltgeschehen: Das literarische und theologische Problem des 4. Esrabuches* (Zürich: Theologischer Verlag, 1981) and Stone, *Fourth Ezra* (cf. B. W. Longenecker, *2 Esdras* [Sheffield: Sheffield Academic Press, 1995]). For a survey of scholarship, see Stone, *Fourth Ezra*, pp. 11-23, who concludes that the book is a sophisticated literary unity, though it incorporates pre-existing materials (such as the vision of the Man from the Sea, 13.1-50); for a more recent survey, see K. M. Hogan, *Theologies in Conflict in 4 Ezra: Wisdom Debate and Apocalyptic Solution* (Leiden: Brill, 2008), pp. 9-35.

4. Stone's work on this topic has moved beyond the simple and misconstrued dichotomies prevalent in previous scholarship; see, for instance, his response to Kabisch and Keulers in M. E. Stone, "Coherence and Inconsistency in the Apocalyses: The Case of 'The End' in 4 Ezra," *JBL* 102 (1983): 229-43; idem, *Features of the Eschatology of IV Esra* (Atlanta: Scholars Press, 1989); and *Fourth Ezra*, pp. 204-7. Such dichotomies lurk in A. L. Thompson, *Responsibility for Evil in the Theodicy of IV Ezra* (Missoula: Scholars Press, 1977) and B. W. Longenecker, *Eschatology and the Covenant. A Comparison of 4 Ezra and Romans 1–11* (Sheffield: JSOT Press, 1991), in the latter case compounded by the contrast between a traditional Jewish "ethnocentric" covenantalism and an individualistic "legalism." Longenecker, *2 Esdras*, represents a partial retreat from this antithesis, recognizing in the text the redefinition rather than the abandonment of Jewish covenantal traditions.

lution by Stone. Since it is unwise to identify the authorial viewpoint, in a simple sense, with either Ezra or Uriel, Stone analyzes how the two perspectives in the dialogues develop in reaction to each other, clarifying what is at stake in two different views of the world.[5] It is not satisfactory to treat Ezra's views in these dialogues as representative of a *Gegenpartei,* or of a consistently skeptical, dualistic viewpoint.[6] Rather, we should trace the ways in which his bewildered accusations against God turn into impassioned laments, as he comes to understand, and then to share, Uriel's perspective, and how these laments, increasingly resigned, are then superseded by the visions in episodes 4 to 6 until Ezra himself articulates an exhortation that matches Uriel's view in the dialogues (14.28-36).[7] As we shall see, both viewpoints in the climactic third dialogue (episode 3: 6.26–9.35) are accorded equal seriousness, but not equal finality: while talk of Ezra's subsequent "conversion" may be overdramatic, it is Uriel's two-world perspective that eventually prevails in both the mouth of Ezra and the text.[8] However, because the two voices in the dialogues must

5. See, e.g., Stone, *Fourth Ezra,* p. 231.

6. *Pace* W. Harnisch, who built on the suggestions of E. Brandenburger, *Adam und Christus: Exegetisch-religionsgeschichtliche Untersuchung zu Röm. 5,12-21* (Neukirchen: Neukirchen-Vluyn, 1962) and detected in Ezra's complaints a contemporary skeptical, fatalistic, and dualistic (in some respects Gnostic-like) stream of thought, with which the author was in polemical dialogue (through Uriel; *Verhängnis und Verheissung der Geschichte: Untersuchungen zum Zeit- und Geschichtsverständnis im 4. Buch Esra und in der syr. Baruchapokalypse* [Göttingen: Vandenhoeck & Ruprecht, 1969], pp. 19-60). Although Brandenburger subsequently distanced himself from some elements in this reconstruction and its misrepresentation by others (*Die Verborgenheit Gottes,* pp. 42-50, 159-60), both he and Harnisch took the "Ezra" of the text to represent a theological error, rather than a limited vision requiring the depth of perspective offered by Uriel's ability to see both worlds at once. For criticism of Harnisch, see A. P. Hayman, "The Problem of Pseudonymity in the Ezra Apocalypse," *JSJ* 6 (1975): 47-56 and K. Koch, "Esras erste Vision. Weltzeiten und Weg des Höchsten," *BZ* 22 (1978): 46-75, at pp. 55-58 (rightly seeing in Ezra not a *"Gegenpartei"* but a debating partner requiring better information). Since the "Ezra" of the text is a literary creation, it seems precarious to reconstruct extra-textual currents of thought from this evidence (a difficulty only partially acknowledged by Brandenburger, *Die Verborgenheit Gottes,* p. 161). Hogan finds evidence of current wisdom debates in the dialogues between Ezra and Uriel (*Theologies in Conflict,* pp. 101-57), but her identification of a third kind of theology in the last three episodes underestimates the continuities with Uriel's eschatological hopes outlined in the earlier episodes.

7. This progression, partially articulated by E. Breech, "These Fragments I Have Shored against My Ruins: The Form and Function of 4 Ezra," *JBL* 92 (1973): 267-74, was explored in detail by Stone, *Fourth Ezra.* E. P. Sanders's treatment of *4 Ezra* (*Paul and Palestinian Judaism* [London: SCM Press, 1977], pp. 409-18) is shaped by now outdated source-theories and applies an ill-fitting Protestant dichotomy between covenant grace and "legalistic" works-righteousness; see above, 3.6.1.

8. H. Gunkel, impressed by the weight given to both sides in the dialogues, took them to

be distinguished, and because the text traces a progression both within and between episodes, it is especially dangerous in this case to take isolated texts as "the viewpoint" of the author. Rather, we must trace the dialectical patterns of the text in sequence, from episode 1 through to episode 7.[9]

9.1. The Desolation of Zion and the World to Come (Episode 1): 3.1–5.20

The first dialogue sets a pattern that is repeated in the second and adapted in the third. After an opening complaint from Ezra that questions God's dealings with Israel (3.4-36), Uriel starts a disputatious dialogue with Ezra (4.1-25), resulting in a prediction of the future (4.26-32). Ezra responds to this prediction with comparatively innocuous questions regarding the eschatological timetable (4.33-52), and the dialogue is wrapped up with Uriel's depiction of the signs of the last days (5.1-13).[10] Ezra's long initial complaint offers an analysis of history from the creation, through key stages in Israel's history (election,

represent the inner conflict of the author ("eine zerrissene Natur": "Das vierte Buch Esra," in E. Kautsch. ed., *Die Apokryphen und Pseudepigraphen des Alten Testaments* [Tübingen: Mohr Siebeck, 1900], vol. 2, pp. 331-401, at p. 343), and much recent English-language scholarship has similarly traced in the text the author's personal tensions or developments. Thus, Stone finds in episode 4 traces of the author's personal conversion-like experience (*Fourth Ezra*, pp. 28-33, 326-27; cf. J. J. Collins, *The Apocalyptic Imagination: An Introduction to Jewish Apocalyptic Literature*, 2nd ed. [Grand Rapids: Eerdmans, 1998], pp. 205-6, 211; Hogan, *Theologies in Conflict*, pp. 38-40). But it seems naïve to trace the tensions and progressions in the text to the author's psycho-religious conflicts or developments, as if the text were a coded autobiography; for criticism of the Gunkel heritage see Brandenburger, *Die Verborgenheit Gottes*, pp. 37-52, and of Stone, see P. F. Esler, "The Social Function of *4 Ezra*," *JSNT* 53 (1994): 99-123, at pp. 110-13. F. Watson's fine reading of episode 3 (*Paul and the Hermeneutics of Faith* [London: T&T Clark, 2004], pp. 475-503) rightly resists talk of Ezra's "conversion" (pp. 477-78), but wrongly concludes that the text leaves the clash between the views of Ezra and of Uriel unresolved (pp. 502-3). Ezra's farewell address (14.28-36, unmentioned by Watson, but rightly stressed by Brandenburger, *Die Verborgenheit Gottes*), in appealing to the final judgment of the "just judge," indicates clearly enough that he has adopted Uriel's vision of reality. And since Uriel speaks not only for, but often *as* God (e.g., 6.1-6; 9.17-22), this is precisely what we would expect.

9. I follow the normal division into seven episodes (which I name as such, not as "visions," since the first three and the seventh have minimal visionary elements): 1 (Dialogue One, 3.1–5.20); 2 (Dialogue Two, 5.21–6.35); 3 (Dialogue Three, 6.36–9.25); 4 (Vision of the Mother/Zion, 9.26–10.59); 5 (Vision of the Eagle, 11.1–12.51); 6 (Vision of the Man from the Sea, 13.1-58); 7 (Ezra as Agent of Revelation, 14.1-50). For fuller structural analysis, see Stone, *Fourth Ezra*, pp. 50-51, together with his introductions to each main section.

10. See Stone, *Fourth Ezra*, pp. 60-61, 80-81, 91-92, 107-8, distinguishing between disputatious and informative phases in the dialogue, either side of the key prediction in 4.26-

Sinai, construction of Jerusalem), up to the exile (3.4-36). This complaint takes its bearings from "the desolation of Zion" (3.2) and the anomaly that God's own people are in exile, at the mercy of a triumphant and prosperous Babylon whose sins weigh heavier than those of Israel (3.28-36). The climactic section of the complaint (3.28-36) raises significant questions about the integrity of God's justice, according to which reward or punishment should be meted out in proportion to virtue or vice;[11] but this issue is combined with a deeper set of questions about God's oversight of history as a whole. Ezra traces the divine effort expended in the creation of world and the revelation at Sinai (3.4-6, 17-19), only to show that it was fruitless. Adam's sin (3.7), replicated in the flood generation (3.8-10), and in Israel's history post-Sinai (3.20-22) and post-Jerusalem (3.25-27), has brought only death and suffering. The whole of history, including the history of Israel, is vitiated by an "evil heart" *(cor malignum),* which has obliterated human goodness (3.20-22), and which, Ezra implies, God has been neglectful enough neither to counter nor to remove (3.8, 20).[12] Ezra here identifies a problem deeper and broader than the horrors of the exile: the whole of humanity is infected with a "sickness" (*infirmitas,* 3.22) that appears to doom all human history to the futility of suffering and death. It is because he has diagnosed the human plight in such terms, later corroborated by Uriel (in terms of an "evil seed," 4.27-31), that the solution Ezra seeks needs to be more radical than a straightforward rectification of Israel's political downfall. Current hopes for the restoration of Jerusalem and the rebuilding of the Temple are here subtly undermined.[13]

---

32. For a fine analysis of this episode, stressing its focus on "the way of the Most High," see Koch, "Esras erste Vision."

11. The justice that Ezra seeks in history operates by comparative recompense. Although Israel has certainly sinned (3.25-27, 34), other nations are comparatively worse in their iniquity and neglect of God (3.29, 33-36), while Israel's "labor" has produced no "fruit" or "reward" (*merces,* 3.33). Uriel will pick up these terms but will apply them not to history but to the final judgment (4.35).

12. This charge, unlike that in 3.28-38, does not question God's justice (*pace* Stone, *Fourth Ezra,* pp. 60, 61), since Ezra acknowledges that transgression of God's commandments, by humanity in general or Israel in particular, leads rightly to judgment (3.7-10, 25-27). But the two statements of God's non-action (*non prohibuisti,* 3.8; *non abstulisti,* 3.20) imply that God could have intervened but did not. There is no suggestion that God is the cause of the "evil heart," whose origin remains a mystery (4.4).

13. Josephus, writing at about the same time, seems to assume that the Temple would be restored; see *Ant.* 4.314; *Apion* 2.193 (with J. M. G. Barclay, *Flavius Josephus, Translation and Commentary.* Volume 10: *Against Apion* [Leiden: Brill, 2007], ad loc.); cf. *Sib. Or.* 5.418-33 and in Christian circles *Barn.* 16.3-4. On attitudes toward the destruction of the Temple, see J. Hahn, with the assistance of C. Ronning, *Zerstörungen des Jerusalemer Tempels: Geschehen — Wahrnehmungen — Bewältigungen* (Tübingen: Mohr Siebeck, 2002).

Uriel's reply in the dialogue-dispute (4.1-25) offers an epistemological shock: Ezra simply cannot understand the world from within its own terms — not in scientific fact, still less in its deeper rationale ("the way of the Most High," 4.4, 11, 21; cf. 3.31). This stress on Ezra's ignorance is designed not to "mystify" history but to insist that it can be understood only from a different, eschatological perspective. When Uriel speaks of a distinction between an earthbound and a heavenly perspective (4.21), Ezra understands this in spatial terms and continues to press his questions about Israel's historical woes (4.22-25). But Uriel's distinction is really between the *unifocal perspective* of "this age" and a *bifocal view* in which the present sad age is seen alongside, and with the added perspective of, the world to come (4.26-32). Uriel thus blocks off hopes of a resolution to Israel's plight within ordinary history: this age is simply too weak and tragic to bring to pass the fulfillment of God's promises (4.27). Significantly, the recipients of those promises are described as "the righteous" (*iusti*, 4.27; cf. 4.35, 39): it is of reward *(merces)* for the righteous (4.35) that Uriel speaks, from a perspective beyond the present passing age (4.26). It is not yet clear how these "righteous" relate to the "Israel" that concerns Ezra, but the difference in discourse seems significant. While Ezra asks about Israel and the nations within the ordinary course of history, Uriel answers by speaking of ultimate justice for "the righteous." As we shall see, this does not mean that Uriel has no concern for Israel, but it suggests that, from his bifocal view of reality, Israel's future must be described in carefully chosen terms. For the moment, however, beyond the vision of the righteous waiting in their "treasuries" (4.35-37), Uriel can predict only that history, as bad as it is, will get worse (5.1-12). By exploring so fully the injustices and futilities of history, the first Dialogue has confirmed that *ordinary history* can produce nothing except *Unheilsgeschichte*. It is only if Ezra can be shaken out of his false expectations for a promising future in this sphere that he will be able to glimpse "the way of the Most High."[14]

9.2. Election and Future Judgment (Episode 2): 5.21–6.35

The reference at the end of episode 1 to hearing "greater things" (5.13) indicates that this new episode will build on the last, even if it seems to begin at a similar

14. For the author's "two-age" perspective, and his loss of hope for salvation within ordinary history, see Harnisch, *Verhängnis und Verheissung*, pp. 89-178. The intervention of Phaltiel at the end of this episode (5.16-19) reminds the reader that Israel-concerns have not gone away; but Ezra's dismissal of Phaltiel indicates that he has more to learn before he can "shepherd the flock" entrusted to him. The final episode will show him doing exactly that.

point: like a spiral, each of the three Dialogues reverts to common themes, but in a cumulative momentum that takes the reader on from one episode to the next. This second Dialogue is structured much like the first: after Ezra's complaint (5.23-30), Uriel highlights Ezra's ignorance within a dialogue-dispute (5.31-40) that leads into questions concerning the end (5.41–6.10), climaxing in a recital of "signs" (6.11-28). In content, however, this Dialogue takes us beyond the first. A new theme is introduced — the divine judgment — and the "signs" go beyond the final woes to describe this definitive judgment and conditions beyond "the end of my world."[15]

Ezra's complaint focuses on the enigma of election (5.23-30). Developing motifs from 4.22-25 (on God's love for and covenants with his people), he uses multiple metaphors to stress the divine selection of Israel, a fact that contrasts with their present degraded condition. It is important that here, as in the earlier references to election (3.13-16; 4.23-25), no explanation is given for this divine choice. Neither the virtues of the fathers nor divine mercy has been invoked, but simply the fact of God's love (4.23; 5.27). This significant lacuna leaves the status of Israel open to varying interpretations. Is God unconditionally committed to the whole of Israel beyond and despite its sin, or does his love for Israel operate within a rubric of justice, by which he rewards the righteous? Uriel is quite clear that God loves Israel (more than Ezra, 5.33) and he envisages a goal *(finis)* for that love that he has promised to his people (5.40): the author's interest in Israel (or Zion, 6.19) has not been superseded by some "universalistic" eschatology.[16] But we are already aware that that "goal" will not be fulfilled within the conditions of ordinary history ("this age"). What it will mean is not yet accessible to Ezra's understanding (5.35-40).

One clue to the proper frame of comprehension, however, is supplied by the new emphasis on "judgment." Ezra's concern to comprehend "the way of the Most High" (5.34; cf. 4.1-4) is now combined with a desire to "search out some part of his judgment" (*iudicium,* 5.34). This term recurs in Uriel's reply (5.40) and is the focus of the informational dialogue that begins in 5.41 (e.g., 5.42-43). Divine judgment is the key feature of "the end" here discussed, with Uriel's circular metaphor ("my judgment is like a crown," 5.42) suggesting that although this end is in one sense a temporal endpoint, it is also the focal point of every human life, its significance being "equidistant" to every moment in history.[17] Using a different mode of explanation, Uriel asserts that this "end"

15. The new theme of judgment is rightly identified by Koch, "Esras erste Vision," pp. 70-72.

16. So, rightly, Longenecker, *Eschatology and the Covenant,* pp. 73-74.

17. *Pace* Stone, *Fourth Ezra,* p. 151, the point is not that a circle has no beginning or end, but that every point on a circle is equidistant from its center (here, its central point of signifi-

has been pre-planned and pre-ordained even before the creation of the world (6.1-6): it is the climactic and definitive fact about God's dealings with the world, from whose standpoint the sadness of human history, including the "travail of Jacob" (5.35), appears merely a prelude. Thus, once again, Uriel requires Ezra to view the present "in retrospect": from the perspective of the future, the "present years" (6.5), with their mixture of sin and faith, constitute the "former times" (6.34).

This two-age vision is now made increasingly explicit ("when will be the end of the first age and the beginning of the age that follows?", 6.7). The "end" (6.6) or "visitation" (5.56; 6.18) that will mark the hinge between the two is described in a mixture of metaphors that will only be unraveled in the succeeding episodes. Some elements suggest the survival of a remnant (5.41; 6.25), who will see God's salvation in the vindication of Zion (6.19, 25; cf. 6.8-10, if "Jacob" represents Israel and "Esau" Rome). Others suggest a complete refashioning of the cosmos (5.45; 6.14-16), in which time will stand still and human hearts will be remade (6.24-26). In either case, the essential fact about this "end" is that justice will finally be done in a publicly visible judgment (6.20), with the punishment of sin, the complete eradication of evil, and the full vindication of truth (6.19-20, 27-28).[18] Without this endpoint, which is also the meaning of reality, history remains incomprehensible; but from the present confusion of faithlessness and faith (6.5, 28) will emerge a clarity that displays the unambiguous triumph of truth and justice, adjudicated by God. Ezra is capable of a deeper appreciation of this truth because he is himself the kind of righteous person who will be vindicated (6.31-33; cf. 6.5). But he has to cease his "vain thinking" regarding "former times" (6.34), a process that will continue through the next dialogue until his perspective shifts definitively in episode 4.

---

cance); cf. the (inconclusive) discussion by Harnisch, *Verhängnis und Verheissung,* pp. 293-94. The context makes clear that this judgment is eschatological, not also this-worldly (*pace* Stone, *Fourth Ezra,* pp. 131, 150).

18. For the different senses of "the end" in *4 Ezra,* see Stone, "Coherence and Inconsistency"; *Features of the Eschatology,* pp. 83-97; and *Fourth Ezra,* pp. 103-4. For the form and content of the lapidary statements in 6.27-28, see Stone, *Fourth Ezra,* pp. 115. The two scenarios sketched here — the survival of a remnant and the remaking of the cosmos — both form a climactic vindication of justice; they are fused at this point in the text because their essential function is to move Ezra (and the readers of this text) from expectations of a historical vindication of Israel to trust in an ultimate justice. Their difference and temporal sequence will become clear only later. For the eschatological hopes of this text, see J. A. Moo, *Creation, Nature, and Hope in 4 Ezra* (Göttingen: Vandenhoeck & Ruprecht, 2011), pp. 105-59.

9.3. Mercy and Justice in a Two-Age Framework (Episode 3): 6.36–9.25

The third dialogue is by far the longest, and a comparison with the first two indicates where this elongation has taken place. After the familiar opening complaint by Ezra (6.38-59) and an initial reply by Uriel (7.1-16), the expected dialogue-dispute, which begins at 7.17, continues right through the huge chapter 7 to 8.62, before closing with the normal indication of "signs" (9.1-13). Although there is one passage of informational dialogue in the midst of this dispute (7.75-101), this is slotted into the disputation between Ezra and Uriel (just before its second half, 7.102–8.62); and as a further indication that dispute is the predominant mood in this dialogue, a final coda (9.14-22) repeats one of its major themes, the tiny number of the saved.[19] This last and longest dialogue is thus climactic: we may expect here in the engagement between Ezra and Uriel the clarification of the author's central concerns.

Ezra's complaint (6.38-59) and Uriel's reply (7.1-16) indeed solidify the key structural thesis of *4 Ezra:* "the world" must be viewed as a dual entity, comprising both "this world" and "the greater world" beyond (7.12-13; cf. 7.50).[20] Ezra rehearses God's care in the six-day construction of the world for the sake of humanity (6.38-54), and the divine promise that "the world" was created for Israel (6.55-59), in order to contrast this promise with the present reality of Israel's political subordination: "If the world has indeed been created for us, why do we not possess our world *(nostrum saeculum)* as an inheritance?" (6.59). Uriel insists that the promise still holds (7.10): an inheritance will take place (7.9), but the term "the world" has to be interpreted on two levels. "This world" has been corrupted by Adam's sin and condemned to sorrow, evil, and hardship (7.11-12; cf. Gen 3:14-19): it forms the difficult entrance into "the greater world," where the things "reserved" *(reposita)* are

19. I thus propose the following structure: Ezra's complaint (6.38-59); Uriel's reply on the two worlds (7.1-16); three speeches from Ezra eliciting Uriel's replies on the operation of God's eschatological justice (7.17-74, see detail below); informational dialogue on the immediate postmortem state (7.75-101); six speeches from Ezra exploring the possibility of final mercy, evoking emphatic denials from Uriel (7.102–8.62; see detail below); signs of the end (8.63–9.13); final coda (9.14-22). For alternative structural analyses see, e.g., Stone, *Fourth Ezra,* pp. 50-51, and at relevant points in his commentary; Longenecker, *Eschatology and the Covenant,* pp. 75-76. The analysis of episode 3 in W. Harnisch, "Der Prophet als Widerpart und Zeuge der Offenbarung: Erwägungen zur Interdependenz von Form und Sache in IV. Buch Esra," in D. Hellholm, ed., *Apocalypticism in the Mediterranean World and the Near East* (Tübingen: Mohr Siebeck, 1983), pp. 460-93, nearly exactly matches my own.

20. On the meaning of "world" or "age" *(saeculum)* in this text, see Stone, *Features of the Eschatology,* pp. 54-56; idem, *Fourth Ezra,* pp. 218-19; Moo, *Creation, Nature, and Hope,* pp. 97-99.

truly to be received (7.13-14; cf. 7.1-9). This insistence on a bifocal vision is foundational for the rest of this dialogue (cf. 7.50; 8.1-3; 9.17-22). Ezra will understand God's rationale in both present and future only if he adheres to this perspective and gives his prior attention to "what is to come" rather than "what is present now" (7.16).

In the section that follows (7.17-74), Ezra adopts Uriel's two-world view (7.18, 47, 66) but refuses his advice on focusing his mind, instead asking searching questions about the many ungodly in the present world who will never benefit from the world to come. In three speeches he considers their plight, and in each case he evokes statements from Uriel about the operation of God's justice (7.17-18, evoking 7.19-44; 7.45-48, evoking 7.49-61; and 7.62-69, evoking 7.70-74). In the first, Ezra recognizes that the law is inexorable: the righteous will inherit the good things promised, but the ungodly will perish (7.17; cf. Deut 30:15-17). But this leaves the ungodly suffering the evils of the present age without seeing the "more spacious things" to come (7.18). Uriel immediately appeals to the superior justice of the divine judge ("You are not a better judge than the Lord, or wiser than the Most High," 7.19). The justice enshrined in the divine law is indeed the supreme rule of the universe: "Let many perish who are now living than that the law of God that is set before them be disregarded" (7.20). Uriel insists that God's commands were accessible to those who "came into the world" (7.21; cf. 3.7-8). The Deuteronomic choice of life or punishment (Deut 30:16-18) is addressed to everyone, since God's fair judgment of the world requires that all are equally accountable before him: it is the deliberate, conscious rejection of God's laws by "the many" that brings about their deserved punishment.[21] The world is thus governed by a principle of equity: empty things for the empty and full things for the full (*vacua vacuis et plena plenis,* 7.25). Anything else would flout the requirements of justice.

In Uriel's subsequent predictions of the final things (7.26-44), it is made clear for the first time that a messianic kingdom, involving city and land, will precede the final "end" (see below on episodes 5 and 6). But the emphasis falls on the absoluteness of justice in the final judgment scene. When the Most High appears on the seat of justice, "compassion shall pass away *(misericordiae pertransibant),* mercy shall be made distant, and patience *(longanimitas)* shall be withdrawn" (7.33).[22] The language of "passing away" *(transire)* recalls the

21. *4 Ezra* presumes that the law is accessible to, but rejected by, humanity as a whole; see K. M. Hogan, "The Meanings of tôrâ in 4 Ezra," *JSJ* 38 (2007): 530-52; Moo, *Creation, Nature and Hope*, pp. 71-82.

22. On the reconstructed text and translation, see Stone, *Fourth Ezra*, p. 202. This sen-

"passing away" of the present world (e.g., 6.20): compassion is a feature of the present age that cannot endure into the next. "Only judgment (or: justice [*iudicium*]) shall remain, truth shall stand, and faithfulness shall grow strong" (7.34). The purity of this justice will finally ensure the distribution of reward *(merces)* and recompense (7.35), and the wicked will understand exactly the reasons for their torment (7.36-38). Indeed, this definitive justice will illumine the day of judgment with nothing less than the full glory of God (7.38-44). For what indeed could be more splendid than justice finally being done and finally being seen to be done?

Ezra's second speech in this section raises the objection that this glorious judgment will result in the condemnation of "almost all" (7.45-48). Building on the earlier diagnosis of the *cor malignum* (7.48; cf. 3.20-26; 4.28-31), he contemplates the universality of sin: "the world to come will bring delight to few but torments to many" (7.47). Uriel considers that exactly right (both correct and just): if we remember that God has made not one world but two (7.50), we can understand why the present mixed world of righteous and ungodly must be superseded by another, peopled only by those of quality and worth (7.52-61). Their rarity is an index of their quality: who would choose common, base materials over silver and gold (7.54-57)? One cannot expect God's eye for quality to do other than rejoice over the precious few who are saved at the final judgment (6.60): no one grieves over the burning of rubbish (6.61). Uriel thus refutes Ezra's concern about *quantity* with a counter-emphasis on *quality;* it is hard to see how a just judge can do other than recognize and reward the latter.

Ezra's third speech (7.62-69) is his most emotional so far: he laments the fate of the mass of humanity who will perish but (unlike animals) have minds able to recognize that this is their destiny (7.64-66). Uriel's reply is devastatingly on target (7.70-74), turning Ezra's objection against himself (7.71). It is precisely because humans have minds that they are accountable for their sin: "For this reason those who live on earth shall be tormented, because though they had understanding they committed iniquity" (7.72). Against the hint in Ezra's lament that sin is a matter of fate (7.68), Uriel insists that it is willful, informed, and entirely culpable. The day of judgment is therefore not some unfortunate disaster that God kindly delays as long as possible: "patience" has been prolonged only because the times are pre-determined (7.74), since the judgment day is in fact the *telos* to which all history is moving. As Uriel states: "When the Most High made the world and Adam and all who have

---

tence anticipates the major theme of the second half of this dialogue, the incompatibility of mercy with justice in the final judgment (7.102–8.62).

come from him, he first prepared the judgment (day) and the things that pertain to the judgment/justice" (7.70). This makes absolutely clear that the enactment of God's justice is the supreme point of orientation for history and for the cosmos; it is here that God will finally and definitively bring the world to its appointed goal.[23]

Commentators on *4 Ezra* frequently side with Ezra in this dialogue, and complain that Uriel's answers are uncompromising, callous, or harsh. Ezra's objections are certainly presented with sympathy (not dismissed as "heresy"); they convey all the passion that a plaintiff can muster in defense of the admittedly guilty.[24] But our distaste for Uriel's responses is more a product of our modern instincts than a fair assessment of his tone.[25] In each case, as we have seen, he gives carefully reasoned justification for his "harsh" judgments, and Ezra raises no complaint that his viewpoint is unfair. In fact, fairness, or justice, is precisely the core motif in Uriel's vision, and if he fails to win our assent it is only because we do not share his fundamental passion for justice. It is hard to see how justice can be enacted without the condemnation of those who willfully disobey the law, and if such sin defies the divine/cosmic law, it is difficult to imagine how it can have less than catastrophic consequences. That such punishment affects the (vast) majority of humanity may be shocking; but on Uriel's terms it can hardly be thought unfair.

The following segment, containing an informational dialogue about the post-mortem state of souls (7.75-101), probably draws on preformed material, but it is hardly out of place.[26] In Uriel's account, all souls after death get a seven-day foretaste of the torments or pleasures in store at the end,[27] and the carefully matched descriptions of the two categories of souls (who have scorned or kept the way of the Most High, 7.79-87, 88-99) indicate the justice meted out at the final judgment. The ungodly will get precisely what they deserve, while the righteous will receive their reward, and both parties will see

23. Stone's interpretation of God's predetermination of this day is thus too weak (*Fourth Ezra*, pp. 229, 234): the function of such language is not just to declare this day "foreseen," but to place it at the center of God's design of the cosmos.

24. Ezra consistently places himself among sinners (see the use of "we" in 7.48, 67-69, 75) and will continue to do so even after he is rebuked for this tactic (7.76-77; repeated in milder terms in 8.47-49). He thus represents the counsel for the defense, while Uriel articulates the perspective of the judge. But in this case the counsel cannot plead other than "guilty," and his rhetoric seems designed to elicit fuller and clearer statements of the laws of justice due to operate on the day of judgment.

25. The point is partially recognized by Thompson, *Responsibility for Evil*, pp. 137, 143.

26. See Stone, *Fourth Ezra*, pp. 238-39.

27. In that sense, judgment is equally near to all human beings, at whatever stage they live in the course of history; cf. the "crown" metaphor in 5.42.

and understand exactly what is going on. The neatness of this pattern signals the precision of the justice that has been Uriel's chief theme thus far. Although this final settling of accounts is not to take place before the last judgment, it is seen at least in anticipation by all souls as soon as they quit the body at death.

At this point the dialogue takes a new turn as Ezra asks about intercession at the last judgment (7.102-3), and thus opens up a long debate with Uriel on the possibility of mercy in that context (in six segments continuing through to 8.62).[28] The length of this section, and the eloquence and strength of Ezra's pleas, form a climax in the clash between Ezra and Uriel and dramatize a central theological issue, the relationship between divine mercy and divine justice (cf. *The Wisdom of Solomon* 11:21–12:22, discussed in 5.4, above). By attending to both sides of this debate, we will be able to trace the shift that Uriel requires of Ezra if he is to see the world aright.

Ezra's initial question, whether the righteous can intercede for the ungodly on the day of judgment (7.102-3), receives a brusque but revealing reply: each must bear his own burden of righteousness or unrighteousness (7.104-5).[29] This is not a generic preference for individualism over social or ethnic solidarity, but a function of Uriel's legal framework; he cites parallels from other individualized spheres (7.103), but his insistence on individual accountability is exactly what we would expect if the dominant metaphor is a courtroom judgment. Moreover, this is no ordinary judgment but the final, decisive, and definitive settling of justice: "the day of judgment is decisive (Latin: *audax*) and displays to all the seal of truth" (7.104). If the full facts are finally revealed, as justice requires (cf. 7.34), there can be no hiding under the cover of another's virtues. Intercession would not reveal but cover the truth, brushing unrighteousness under the carpet. If Uriel's response is "harsh," it represents the harshness of reality fully revealed.

The next interchange demonstrates the significance of Uriel's two-world perspective. Ezra appeals to numerous biblical instances of intercession by

28. 7.102-3 evokes Uriel's reply in 7.104-5 (no intercession is appropriate); 7.106-11 evokes 7.112-15 (intercession/mercy fits this world, not the next); 7.116-26 evokes 7.127-31 (this life is not a tragedy but a contest and an opportunity to choose life); 7.132-40 evokes 8.1-3 (God's image as merciful on the many fits this world, not the world to come); 8.4-36 evokes 8.37-41 (pleas for mercy on the many are not appropriate to the next world, fitted for the righteous few); and 8.42-45 evokes 8.46-62 (a final plea for mercy is deflected by indicating the justice in God's decision). For parallels to the themes of this section in literature closely related to it, see R. J. Bauckham, *The Fate of the Dead: Studies on the Jewish and Christian Apocalypses* (Leiden: Brill, 1998), pp. 132-48.

29. Cf. Deborah's insistence in Pseudo-Philo, *LAB* 33.4-5, that she cannot pray for anyone after death.

the righteous, from Abraham through to Hezekiah, and asks why this is permissible now *(modo)*, when corruption is so great, but not then *(tunc)*, on the day of judgment (7.106-11). His distinction between "now" and "then" already invites the answer (cf. *tunc* in 7.115). Uriel does not deny the propriety of intercession (or mercy) *within the conditions of the present world:* the present corrupt world, lacking the full glory of God, is the appropriate arena in which the strong may pray for the weak (7.112). "But the present world is not the end" (7.112). As the hinge between "this age" and "the immortal age to come," the day of judgment cannot permit any trace of sin to contaminate the fully glorious future. As a day of absolute justice and truth (7.114), it cannot allow any modification of judgment in either direction: there can be no mercy on those justly condemned, and no penalty for those properly judged in the right ("victorious," 7.115). The logic is clear and impeccable. *Mercy would represent a compromise with sin. Such a compromise is necessary in this imperfect world, but it can have no place in a future world where justice and truth take maximal effect.* If the judgment is truly *final,* no one can tinker with its results.[30]

It is because he understands and even accepts this analysis that Ezra opens a lament (7.116-26, parallel to 7.62-69), regretting the earth's production of sinful humanity, and bemoaning the agony of knowing about eternal bliss while "we" will never attain it. Looking at the whole of reality from the perspective of the present, Ezra sees only a mass of sin, an unattainable future, a threatening judgment, and thus unrelieved grief. Uriel's reply (7.127-31) offers a quite different perspective, from the standpoint of the future and the rewarded righteous. From that vantage point, this earthly life appears as a contest *(certamen),* into which every person is enlisted at birth:[31] losers will certainly suffer what Ezra has catalogued, but Uriel wants to focus on the victorious, who will receive what *he* has depicted (7.127-28). Against Ezra's pessimistic near-fatalism (7.116-17), Uriel insists that humans have choice, and cites Moses' parting instruction to Israel: "Choose life for yourself, so that you may live" (Deut 30:15).[32] From this perspective, while Ezra sees only grief, Uriel emphasizes "joy over the life of those who did believe" (7.131).[33]

We might have expected these three interchanges (since 7.102) to persuade Ezra to abandon his hopes for mercy at the last judgment, but in fact he returns to this theme in each of his next three speeches (7.132-40; 8.4-36; 8.42-45),

30. For this reason, while repentance is always possible in this life (7.133; 9.11), it is impossible after death (7.82).

31. For the "contest" and "victory" metaphors, see also 3.21; 7.92, 115.

32. Cf. Watson, *Paul and the Hermeneutics of Faith,* pp. 475-503, who rightly emphasizes the influence of this Deuteronomic passage throughout this third Dialogue (cf. 7.17-21).

33. Stone, *Fourth Ezra,* p. 253, following versions other than the Latin.

which all appeal in various ways to God's own character and thus constitute the most intense *theo*logical moment in the text. The first speech (7.132-40) is an exposition of the depiction of God in Exodus 34:6-7, a text often employed in the Jewish tradition to define the character of God.[34] Ezra selects, highlights, supplements, and glosses key terms from the biblical text:

> I know that the Most High is now called merciful *(misericors)*, because he has mercy on those who have not come into the world; and gracious *(miserator)*, because he is gracious to those who turn in repentance to his law; and patient *(longanimis)*, because he shows patience to those who have sinned, since they are his own creatures; and bountiful *(munificus)*, because he would rather give than take away; and abundant in compassion *(multae misericordiae)* . . . ; and he is called the giver *(donator)*, because if he did not give out of his goodness so that those who have committed iniquities might be relieved of them, not one ten thousandth of humankind could have life; and the judge *(iudex)*, because if he did not pardon those who were created by his word and blot out the multitude of their sins, there would probably be left very few of the innumerable multitude. (7.132-40)

The language of "mercy" and "compassion" is notably here mixed with the language of "gift," and both are taken to be the quintessential characteristics of God in this subtle exposition of Exodus 34. Ezra relentlessly emphasizes the proper and necessary *incongruity* of God's mercy/gift, stressing the sinfulness of its recipients. He even manages to turn the final statement about God's justice in Exodus 34:6-7 ("yet by no means clearing the guilty . . .") into yet another mark of the mercy of God, who pardons the sinful precisely as "judge"! God's scripturally endorsed character of mercy is here celebrated precisely *in the face of human sin;* it is the only means by which the sin-ridden world has been and can be sustained.

However, as far as Uriel is concerned, Ezra has conceded everything in his very first sentence: "I know that the Most High is now *(nunc)* called merciful . . ." (7.132). "Now" is one thing, "then" is another (cf. above on 7.111-15): "The Most High made *this world* for the sake of the many, but *the world to come* for the sake of only a few" (8.1). To be sure, *this world* is sustained by

34. Biblical echoes include Psalm 86:5, 15; 103:8; 145:8-9; Joel 2:13; Jonah 4:2; Nahum 1:3; Nehemiah 9:17; we have noted above (pp. 205-6) an echo in *Wisdom* 15:1-2. For 7.132-40 as commentary on Exodus 34:6-7, see D. Simonsen, "Ein Midrasch 4. Buch Ezra," in M. Brann and J. Elbogen, eds., *Festschrift zum Israel Lewy's 70. Geburtstag* (Breslau: Marcus, 1911), pp. 270-78; Stone, *Fourth Ezra*, p. 256; Watson, *Paul and the Hermeneutics of Faith*, pp. 500-502; for its connection with Jewish liturgy, see D. Boyarin, "Penitential Liturgy in 4 Ezra," *JSJ* 3 (1972): 30-34.

God's mercy: its multitude of sinners is permitted to live only because within these conditions God is as gracious as Ezra insists. But *the world to come* operates under different conditions, in which quality (like gold-dust) counts for everything (8.2). "Many have been created [and graciously allowed to continue in the compromised present world], but only a few [whom God's justice evaluates as righteous] shall be saved" (8.3). Uriel grants everything Ezra wants to claim in 7.132-40 about the incongruous graciousness of God — so long as it is confined to this world. But in the world to come, divine justice, with its necessary selection of quality, requires that mercy — in the sense of a gift to the *unworthy* — must be left behind.

The following interchanges (from 8.4 to 8.62) explore this antithesis (mercy in the present creation, justice in the world to come) in greater depth. Ezra's long speech (8.4-36) highlights the care that has gone into the creation of humanity (8.4-14) and God's investment in Israel, his people, and his inheritance (8.15-19). In the light of what he has heard about the judgment, will all this really come to nothing? The prospect propels him to prayer (8.20-36) and a powerful appeal to mercy. No less than five times (8.26-30), Ezra asks God not to "look on" the sinful (whose failings are described in ever more heinous forms) but to "remember" or have regard for the righteous who have served God and kept his commandments; surely for *their sake,* he suggests, the rest of the people could be saved. Switching tack, he then appeals to the reputation of God as the God of *mercy:* "If you have desired to have pity on us, who have no good works, then you will be called merciful. . . . In this, O Lord, your goodness will be declared, when you are merciful to those who have no store of good works" (8.32, 36).[35] Three times here (8.31, 32, 36), Ezra appeals to the mercy of God, and to the text (Exod 34:6-7) that he had earlier exegeted (7.132-40). In each case, mercy is perfected with full incongruity as *mercy on the sinful,* in contrast to the way God deals with the righteous, who have a store of good deeds and will receive their fitting "reward" (*merces,* 8.33). This climactic prayer is Ezra's last throw of the theological dice, appealing to God's mercy precisely in the *absence* of human worth.

Uriel's reply is by now predictable, and certainly consistent. Looking at

35. Reading *bonitas tua* without *iustitia tua* (with Stone, *Fourth Ezra,* p. 270). Ezra is pressing God's goodness and mercy: he should know by now that "justice" is on the other side. Ezra's arguments are often judged to be inconsistent since his statements about the universality of sin (e.g., 8.35) seem incompatible with his talk about the righteous (e.g., 8.33); see Stone, *Fourth Ezra,* pp. 271-72. But his claims that sin is universal are always rhetorical exaggerations, since from the start he acknowledges the presence of a righteous few (e.g., 3.11; 7.45-48). As Uriel points out, such rhetoric is a commendable sign of humility, but is not to be taken literally (8.47-49).

reality through the prism of the future, he does not concern himself with the sinners and their destruction,[36] because all that matters is the righteous, "their pilgrimage, their salvation, and their receiving their reward *(merces)*" (8.39). The farmer is concerned with the crop, not with every seed that has gone to waste (8.41). If the *telos* of the cosmos is indeed the harvest of the righteous (few though they be), God cannot be expected to fret about unfruitful elements that fail along the way.

Ezra's sixth address is his most feisty. Seed is one thing, but humans, made in God's image, are quite another — and so, *a fortiori,* is Israel, "your people" and "your inheritance": surely God will have mercy on his own creation (8.42-45). And since God is the Creator (not the farmer), is the failure of the seed partly attributable to him ("if it has not received *your rain* in due season . . . ," 8.43)? Uriel's extended reply (8.46-62) quashes any suggestion of divine callousness or unfairness. If Ezra is consumed by love for creation, "you come far short of being able to love my creation more than I love it" (8.47). The divine perspective from the future *telos* represents not a disregard of this world, which is still emphatically *God's* creation, but an investment in what has always been planned and prepared, a perfection and glory reserved for the righteous (8.51-54). The "wastage" from the present world is entirely the responsibility of the sinners themselves: Uriel stresses here their freedom to choose (*libertas,* 8.56; cf. 7.129), and their informed decision against God (8.58, *pace* Ezra's claims in 7.126). It was never God's intention that any be destroyed, but human creatures have themselves ruined God's purposes of life (8.59-60). Here, forced onto the defensive, Uriel explicitly clears God of any blame in the sad fate of "the many." If God will not grieve over their destruction, it is because they have only themselves to blame.[37]

In the course of this speech, which opens by insisting once more on the difference between the present and the future (8.46), Uriel twice urges Ezra to shift his perspective. Instead of viewing the future from the standpoint of the present (where the picture is dominated by the multitude of sinners, and future judgment induces dread), he should view the present from the standpoint of the future (where the focus lies on the righteous few, who are rewarded for

36. Uriel gives a subtle twist to Ezra's words: God will not indeed "look on" people's sins, but not in Ezra's sense (that he will ignore the sin) but in another (he will not be troubled by their judgment). The closeness of the verbal interchange here (and in the following passage, 8.41-44) indicates the fine crafting of this text, matching its theological sophistication.

37. Human culpability, admitted by Ezra in 7.118, is a repeated theme in Uriel's speeches (cf. 7.19-25, 37, 70-74, 78-87, 127-31) but is made most emphatic here (and in the following 9.9-13, where the *libertas* motif recurs, 9.11). Harnisch rightly emphasizes that for our author sin is *Schuld* not *Schicksal* (*Verhängnis und Verheissung,* pp. 142-98).

victory in the present contest). "Think of your own case and inquire concerning the glory of those who are like yourself" (8.51) and "do not ask any more questions about the great number of those who perish" (8.55). This instruction continues in the final description of the signs of the end (9.1-13), where Ezra is told, "do not be curious about how the ungodly will be punished, but inquire how the righteous will be saved, those to whom the age belongs and for whose sake the age was made" (9.13). These instructions prepare the way for the great change in perspective that takes place in the course of episode 4 (from viewing the Jerusalem of the present to viewing the Jerusalem of the future/above); they represent the fundamental shift to which Ezra is now called. There are only some who can be granted this perspective (7.44; 8.62), and it is because he is (emphatically) among the righteous (8.47-51) that it is fitting for him to view reality from a future designed for such as him (8.51-55).

For the present, Ezra's transition to Uriel's viewpoint is not complete. While he has learned to see not one world but two, and has apparently accepted that God's impeccable justice at the judgment day rules out the possibility of mercy, he still sees the world from the viewpoint of the many to a great enough extent that he rues once more the small number of the saved (9.14-16).[38] The comment elicits a final, compressed statement of Uriel's position (9.17-22): God prepared a good creation, but humans have spoiled it (9.18-19); the earth is now irretrievably doomed (*perditum,* 9.20); justice works by recompense (what you sow, you reap, 9.17); and with his eye on the future age, God has spared some with great effort, "one grape out of a cluster, and one plant out of a great forest" (9.21). "So let the multitude perish that has been born in vain, but

38. The fact that Ezra prefaces this comment with "I said before, I say now, and will say it again" (9.15) has led many interpreters to conclude that Ezra's position has not shifted at all, so that the dialogue breaks off with all issues unresolved; the next episode will show Ezra simply giving up the effort of logical thought (9.39; 10.5) and allowing himself to be persuaded by visionary experience (Esler, "The Social Function of *4 Ezra,*" pp. 110-13; Watson, *Paul and the Hermeneutics of Faith,* pp. 498, 502-3; Collins, *The Apocalyptic Imagination,* pp. 203-4, 209-11; Hogan, *Theologies in Conflict,* pp. 42, 234-35). But: (1) This would dismiss all the careful argumentation, in which Uriel has engaged Ezra point by point, as a fruitless cul-de-sac — an odd conclusion in relation to a thinker as careful as our author has proved to be. (2) The tone of 9.14-16 is resigned grief, not complaint or plea: after six questions concerning mercy, it is notable that that subject has been dropped. Thus, although 9.14-16 in part echoes 7.45-48, it is not as though *nothing* has changed. (3) Ezra will repeat once more this sort of rueful comment (9.29-37, as an expression of his still "troubled" heart, 9.27; 10.10) but this last vestige of his present-rooted perspective is about to disappear in the course of episode 4. Ezra's transformation is thus subtle and gradual: if it is a mistake to identify a single point of total change, it is also mistaken to conclude from some elements of continuity at this point that nothing is changing at all.

let my grape and my plant be saved, because with much labor I have perfected them" (9.22). God himself thus looks away from the disaster of the present to the quality harvest of the future; Ezra is bidden to follow suit.

Before we move to the next episode, a number of conclusions may be drawn on the basis of this crucial Dialogue.

(1) In the progression of Dialogues, Uriel has now articulated a vision that requires two things of Ezra: (a) he must take account of not one world but two: instead of thinking only of this world, he must reckon also with the world to come, inaugurated by, and founded on, the judgment; (b) the whole of reality must be viewed from the perspective of its future *telos* (with a focus on the reward of the righteous few), not from the perspective of the present (with a focus on the doomed mass of sinners). Although Ezra finishes this Dialogue in grief, articulating the residue of a present-based perspective, it is now clear in what direction he has to move, and why.[39]

(2) Ezra's long and powerful pleas still play a crucial role. Not only do they elicit and clarify Uriel's position, constantly pressing him to justify his stance, but they articulate a common, and commonsense, view of the world, which the author exposes in full in order to demonstrate why it must be supplemented or changed. The expectation of divine mercy and of the restoration of prosperity for Israel appears to have been widespread, even after 70 CE. As will emerge by the end (14.29-37), by urging Israel to focus rather on the future world, and the final day of judgment, the author of *4 Ezra* seeks to redirect his readers' attention to their present task, the careful observance of the Torah.[40]

(3) Uriel's future-based view of the world requires that the anchor-point of the cosmos is the justice of God. This justice entails the reward of the righteous (3.33; 4.35; 7.33-35, 83, 98; 8.33, 39), a recompense in which God's benefaction (salvation and inheritance of the world to come) matches the fittingness of its recipients. With great difficulty, God has "spared" *(peperci)* one grape out of a cluster (9.21-22), and that effort has been expended on the worthy, who have

39. Although Ezra and Uriel are not yet reconciled in perspective, Ezra has moved deeply into and finally away from his appeal to mercy. The text is not static or stalled, and the tension that remains propels the text forward into the following episodes.

40. Cf. R. J. Bauckham, "Apocalypses," in D. A. Carson, P. T. O'Brien, and M. A. Seifrid, eds., *Justification and Variegated Nomism*, vol. 1: *The Complexities of Second Temple Judaism* (Tübingen: Mohr Siebeck, 2001), pp. 135-87, at p. 164: Ezra's inclusive view of God's covenant mercy on Israel "is presented so sympathetically, even persuasively, that it must be part of the book's rhetorical strategy to allow this view its full weight. Not that the book is in the least equivocal about which view it finally endorses. But the unconverted Ezra's position must be given its full due, which is considerable, if the need for it to be superseded is to be presented convincingly to those whose response to the fall of Jerusalem Ezra voices."

honored him (7.60), have trusted his covenants (7.83), and have lived a pure life (7.122). The reward is not "pay," but is the prize for those who have emerged victorious in the contest (3.21; 7.92, 115), who are "worthy of mercy" (4.24) in the sense of a fitting gift (cf. 14.34). This is a perfectly natural and common construal of divine benefaction, as we have seen (Part I), especially when that benefaction is framed by the demands of justice. It is "gift," but without the perfection of incongruity.[41]

In this third Dialogue, however, Ezra has pressed the claims for another view of "mercy" and "benefaction" (the language is mixed in 7.132-40) — one in which mercy is perfected as *incongruous.* As we have seen, he has appealed to biblical precedents (7.106-11), and to the biblical presentation of the character of God (7.132-40), in order to justify this view of mercy. Indeed, he has gone so far as to insist that God's goodness and mercy are so called precisely when they are incongruous. In his view, mercy is *mercy* only if exercised on the sinful: "For in this, O Lord, your goodness will be declared, when you are merciful to those who have no store of good works" (8.36; cf. 8.31-32). It is only because of this sort of incongruous mercy, he insists, that those who inhabit the world have survived at all (7.137-38): if God did not blot out their sins, there would be precious few people left at all (7.140). Uriel accepts this claim fully *with respect to the present world.* But he insists that this incongruous mercy cannot be exercised at the final judgment, since it does not finally accord with the justice of God. There will indeed be precious few who survive that judgment — but that is what one would expect, and even hope for, from a fair and discriminating judge.[42]

(4) The shift in perspective required by Uriel entails that the question of Israel not be abandoned but be thoroughly reframed.[43] In his appeals on behalf of Israel in this Dialogue (6.55-59; 8.15-19, 26, 45), Ezra has placed Israel in the context of humanity as a whole, and its sinfulness makes treating it as a special case problematic. But Uriel's framework, which views present history

41. Longenecker protests that at the eschaton God's mercy is "available only to those who merit his favour by their works in accordance with the law (that is, grace is available to those who have no need of it!)" (*Eschatology and the Covenant,* p. 271). But this presumes that mercy/grace is by definition an incongruous gift to the unworthy — which, in Uriel's vision of the last judgment, it is precisely not. In other words, mercy (like the biblical *hesed*) can be construed as either congruous or incongruous (see Moo, *Creation, Nature, and Hope,* pp. 112-13).

42. *Pace* Watson, *Paul and the Hermeneutics of Faith,* pp. 502-3, who regards the debate as unresolved and evenly matched; he does not take into consideration Uriel's emphasis on the two worlds (e.g., 8.1-3), which accounts for why mercy is operative in this world but not in the next. The issue is not whether God is merciful *now,* but whether he will (and should) be *then.*

43. Stone, *Fourth Ezra,* p. 174, refers to "a wider, or a different, frame of reference," but does not fully explain the reason for the shift.

(including Israel's history) from the standpoint of the age to come, alters the categories of analysis, so that the decisive labels are, in his discourse, "the righteous" and "the ungodly." This does not mean that Israel is forgotten (7.10), or that the text shifts from national interests to the individualized plight of humanity as a whole.[44] Rather, what may be said concerning the salvation of Israel is said within the framework of the salvation of the righteous: if Israel is saved, it is *qua* "the righteous (few)," not *qua* "Israel."[45] This means that hopes may be articulated within this Dialogue (9.7-8) and more in the episodes to come (episodes 4 to 6) about the land, Zion, and the messianic kingdom; but these have now been reframed, so that the "remnant" are those who survive on account of their works and faith, not on account of their ethnic ancestry (9.7).[46]

9.4. Breakthrough to a Bifocal Vision (Episode 4): 9.26–10.59

Readers who acknowledge the literary unity of *4 Ezra* unanimously identify episode 4 as the hinge point in the narrative. This episode starts with a troubled speech from Ezra (9.27-37), before he encounters a mourning woman (9.38–10.4) and attempts to comfort her (10.5-25). He subsequently sees a remarkable vision in which the woman turns into a magnificent city (10.25-28), a scene interpreted by Uriel as a vision of Zion, built over no human foundation (10.30-59). The links both backwards (in form and content) and forwards (this vision leading into the following two, 10.55-59) mark this episode as transitional, but the exact nature of the transition remains a matter of dispute.[47]

44. *Pace* Sanders, *Paul and Palestinian Judaism*, pp. 409-18, and Longenecker, *Eschatology and the Covenant.*

45. Hence, *qua* the single grape (9.21), the righteous "few," not *qua* the vine (5.23), made up of the righteous and ungodly (5.30). M. A. Elliott, *The Survivors of Israel: A Reconsideration of the Theology of Pre-Christian Judaism* (Grand Rapids: Eerdmans, 2000), pp. 341-43, is right to interpret this "grape" as, in effect, the righteous remnant within Israel. But if there is here a redefinition and reduction of the referent "Israel," this arises from the author's theological vision of the future world, not simply from a reaction against "national" theologies of Israel.

46. In this sense, Longenecker, *2 Esdras*, is right to go beyond his own earlier work (1991) in seeing the ethnic and covenant categories "redefined" rather than abandoned (cf. Bauckham, "Apocalypses," pp. 166-75). But it is important to appreciate why *4 Ezra*'s vision (backwards from the future) requires this redefinition, by recategorizing reality. Thus, Ezra's view that the world was made for Israel (6.55-59; cf. Pseudo-Philo, *LAB* as discussed in 8.2, above) is first redefined in terms of the two worlds (7.1-16) and then reframed: in Uriel's terms, the world/age was made for the sake of *the righteous* (9.13).

47. See esp. Brandenburger, *Die Verborgenheit Gottes*, pp. 58-90; Longenecker, *Eschatology and the Covenant*, pp. 99-112; idem, *2 Esdras*, pp. 59-69 (a better reading); Stone, *Fourth Ezra*,

As is now widely recognized, the changes in Ezra's location, stance, and diet (9.23-25) are symbolic of other changes under way, and it is noticeable that his initial speech, though still troubled and pessimistic (9.27; cf. 3.3; 5.21), issues not in questions or complaints, but in acceptance of the human fate and in recognition of the eternity of the law (9.36-37; cf. Uriel in 7.20). Clearly, something is changing here, although it seems unwise to take 9.39 and 10.5 (where Ezra breaks off his reflections in his encounter with the woman) as *the* signal of a change of heart, since in his speeches to the woman he continues to view reality from the perspective of this world and its majority who are doomed (10.10, echoing 9.14-16); and although he exhorts the woman to trust in God (10.16, 24), he cannot yet offer her Uriel's vision of a future glorious world. Indeed, this vision is only granted to him in the transformation of the woman into a city (10.25-28), the centerpiece of this episode. It seems best to interpret the early parts of this episode as indicating Ezra's readiness for the change of vision granted in 10.25-28: as 10.38-39 suggests, it is because of the correct stance indicated by his mourning that he is in a proper condition to receive the vision.

The fact that Ezra is satisfied by his flower-diet (9.26) is a signal that, while he is deeply pessimistic on the condition of Israel (9.29-37), his mood is now resignation and acceptance. Unlike in earlier speeches, Ezra does not rail at the anomalies in Israel's position, nor issue questions or complaints. His mood is certainly grief, in solidarity with sinners: "we who have received the law and sinned will perish" (9.36). Indeed, his "consolation" of the bereaved mother consists largely of putting her grief in the context of the grief of Zion and the sorrow of the whole earth (10.5-17); regarding humanity, "almost all go to perdition, and a multitude of them will come to doom" (10.10). But this is a resigned grief that has moved beyond anger and frustration: the long and pained depiction of the destruction of Jerusalem and its Temple (10.20-23) does not end by asking when it will be restored. Ezra has accepted that hopes for the historical restoration of Jerusalem are definitively blocked off, and it is perhaps precisely for this feature of his mourning that he is commended by Uriel (10.39, 50).[48] Although there are references to trust in God's "decree" (10.16) and hope for a "respite from troubles" (10.24), Ezra cannot yet articulate a vision that looks from the future back to the present. His only anchor-point is the assurance that the law will survive in its glory, whatever may be its failure

---

pp. 311-12, 318-21, 377, whose discovery here of "deep psychological insight" (pp. 320-21, 326-27) is, however, open to question.

48. See H. Najman, "Between Heaven and Earth: Liminal Visions in 4 Ezra," in T. Nicklas et al., eds., *Other Worlds and Their Relation to This World: Early Jewish and Ancient Christian Traditions* (Leiden: Brill, 2010), pp. 151-67, at pp. 158-59.

to bear fruit in this world (9.34-37). The prominence here given to the law (cf. 7.17-20) indicates that there is a marker of God's justice already visible in this world, a fact that will become foundational for Ezra's paraenesis in the final episode (14.28-36).

By abandoning hopes for a resolution of Israel's plight within the ordinary course of history, Ezra is ready for the central event of this episode, where the woman turns into an enormous city before his very eyes (10.25-28). Uriel stresses the fact that this city appears in a field "where no house has been built" (9.24; cf. 10.51-52), "where there was no foundation of any building, because no work of human construction *(opus aedificii hominis)* could endure in a place where the city of the Most High was to be revealed" (10.53-54). In other words, this city is most emphatically *God's* creation, not the development or completion of a human project on the historical plane. Thus, *what Ezra attains in this episode is what Uriel has been nudging him toward all along,* a vision of reality that not only recognizes the existence of two worlds, but looks from the future world back to the present (or from the heavenly world down to the earth), rather than the other way around. It is when he sees the city, in place of the mourning woman (10.42), that he begins to see reality aright. This Zion, "the city of the Most High" (10.54), is, one may say, both the future and the present heavenly reality.[49] Because "the world to come" (8.1) is already planned, promised, prepared, and reserved (4.27; 7.14, 60, 83-84; 8.52 ["a city is built"], 59), it is not only a future reality yet to be revealed but also the truth behind all reality. The temporal (future) and spatial (heavenly) metaphors both designate a way of seeing reality that escapes the limitations of a commonsense empirical perspective, adopting a stance from which it is possible to grasp the truth of the cosmos. The "many secrets" revealed to Ezra (10.38) are a new way of seeing history, from a vantage point whose foundations lie deeper than history itself. It is this epistemological shift for which Ezra is finally ready (cf. 4.1-25): looking at the world from the future/above (i.e., looking at the story of Zion from this vision of a God-constructed Zion), it all now begins to make sense.[50]

Precisely what sense it makes has been indicated already by Uriel's earlier speeches and will be spelled out more in the episodes to come. It is important, however, to put the following two visions in perspective. As Uriel makes clear, the Vision of the Eagle (episode 5) and the Vision of the Man from the Sea

49. So, rightly, Stone, *Fourth Ezra*, p. 335.

50. This analysis of the *logic* in episode 4 thus resists interpretations which see here only the abandonment of argument and its replacement by "mysterious change" (Brandenburger) or by the power of "experience" or "pastoral necessity" (e.g., Collins, *The Apocalyptic Imagination*, pp. 210-11: "We believe because we need to believe. . . . If our problems cannot be solved, we must look away from them and contemplate what is positive," p. 211).

(episode 6) are visions not of the ultimate end (the final judgment and beyond) but of the penultimate end, "what the Most High will do to those who inhabit the earth in the last days" (10.59). It is from the perspective of the divine "Zion" that he can get a glimpse of those "last days" on earth, but they are not the full or the final reality that "Zion" represents. To some extent, beyond noting "the brilliance of her glory and the loveliness of her beauty" (10.50), there is not much that can be said (or at least revealed in writing) about the content of this "Zion." All that is revealed in this text is how the last days will take shape under messianic initiative (episodes 5 and 6) and what should be done in the present, in obedience to the law (episode 7).[51] What matters is less what Zion contains (there are limits to what can be taken in, 10.55-56) than that there is a "Zion" and that Ezra is now enabled, through this direct vision, to comprehend the world from the standpoint of divine perfection, rather than the confusion and ambiguity of the present.

9.5. The Messianic Future (Episodes 5 and 6): 11.1–13.58

The two visions of episodes 5 and 6 rework traditional Danielic materials (11.9; cf. Dan 2 and 7), and are selectively interpreted to highlight certain features of the "messianic kingdom" as the penultimate "end." Earlier episodes had dropped hints about the conditions of this pre-judgment era, in which "survivors" *(derelicti)* would endure woes to see the "signs" or "wonders" associated with a temporary messianic era in "the land," to be followed by the final judgment (6.25-28; 7.26-29; 9.7-9). These allusions are now filled out (with verbal connections, 11.46; 12.34; 13.16-20, 47-50) by means of visions of the Lion's condemnation of the oppressive eagle (episode 5) and the Man's destruction of the "innumerable multitudes" who wage war against him (episode 6). These "last events of the times" (12.9) represent "the end" of the earthly age, but they are explicitly the prequel to the ultimate "end," the day of judgment, which was discussed in earlier episodes (12.34; cf. 7.29-34).[52]

Both forms of "end" represent a divine intervention, a resolution of earthly anomalies not through the ordinary processes of history, but via an act of

51. *4 Ezra*'s sister text, *2 Baruch,* in this respect contains an illuminating contrast: there, while the ultimate Zion is a matter of the eschatological future (4.1-7), the author entertains very clear hopes for the historical restoration of the Temple (6.1-9; 32.1-7; 68.1-8) at a time of Israel's historical repentance and restoration.

52. On the messianic kingdom as the penultimate "end," see Stone, *Fourth Ezra,* pp. 204-10, 362-63, and on the varied (but contextually consistent) use of "end" language, see Stone, "Coherence and Inconsistency"; idem, *Fourth Ezra,* pp. 103-5.

judgment which, at a stroke, reestablishes divine justice. The Lion is a Davidic Messiah, but he has been "kept" by God for many ages until the end (12.32; 13.26). His main work is condemnation and judgment (11.37-46; 12.33) as a penultimate statement of the final universal judgment. There is no role here for political or military action by historical Israel, although his rule will include the "remnant" *(residuum)* of God's people, a last generation kept joyful until the final end (12.34). The Man emerges from a mysterious source (13.3, 51-52) and carves out a mountain of unknown origin (13.7), identified as "Zion," already prepared and built "without hands" (13.36) — an echo of the "Zion" of episode 4 that is the product of divine, not human, construction (10. 51-54). Here, as in his emphasis on a "peaceable multitude" (13.12-13, 39, 47), our author seems at pains to distance this vision from normal political and military expectations.[53] The ingathering of a "remnant," including, remarkably, the ten tribes (13.39-50), indicates that this text has not abandoned its expectations for Israel and shifted to a "universal" or "individualistic" eschatology.[54] But the crucial characteristic of these "survivors" is their total commitment to the law (13.42): their "works and faith" toward God make them suitable recipients of divine protection (13.23; cf. 9.7). Thus, we do not need to play off against one another the text's hopes for "Israel" and its promises to "the righteous." Both the messianic events and the final day of judgment will operate by the canons of divine justice, such that "Israel" will be saved to the extent (and only to the extent) that it is counted among "the righteous."[55] As Ezra himself makes clear in 12.46-49, and as will be demonstrated in the final episode (14.27-36), what therefore matters is the full engagement of Israelites in the "struggle" (12.47), the necessary "contest" against evil in obedience to the law (cf. 7.92, 115, 127-31). God will be faithful to his promises to Abraham (3.15), but his justice requires that salvation is a reward to the righteous (7.83, 98; 8.33, 39, etc.), neither guaranteed by birth nor given without discrimination to the sinful.

53. See Bauckham, "Apocalypses," pp. 165-66.

54. *Pace* Longenecker, who then has to take Ezra's words to the people in 12.40-51 and 14.27-36 as "misleading" and "insincere," paying mere "lip service" to traditional expectations (*Eschatology and the Covenant*, pp. 119-21). Bauckham, "Apocalypses," pp. 166-69, rightly lays stress on the ten tribes as a sign of God's continuing commitment to Israel.

55. One might ask how Uriel's emphasis on the fewness of the righteous (e.g., 8.3, out of the many created) can be squared with the "multitude" mentioned in these visions (13.12-13). It is possible that this "multitude" is still only a "few" compared to the "innumerable multitudes" who are condemned (13.5; cf. Bauckham, "Apocalypses," p. 167); and in any case what matters to the author is less the numbers than the principle that final justice requires a divine selection of the righteous. On the remnant theology in these visions, see Elliott, *The Survivors of Israel*, pp. 502-14, 561-69.

9.6. Ezra as Agent of Revelation (Episode 7): 14.1-50

The close of episode 6 indicates that Ezra has journeyed the whole way from complaint (3.4-36) to worship (13.57-58): he is now recognized as having devoted himself to God's ways and wisdom, in searching out his law (13.53-56). It is therefore appropriate that in this final episode he no longer needs an angelic mediator, but is in direct contact with God, and operates not just as a recipient but as an agent of revelation.[56] In explicit parallel with Moses, Ezra now communicates God's wisdom, some parts taught openly to everyone, others reserved for the wise (14.1-6, 44-46; cf. Deut 29:29). At two points earlier in the narrative, we had sensed the press of Ezra's wider audience, in the person of Phaltiel (5.16-18) and in the concerns of "all the people" (12.40-50), so it is appropriate finally for Ezra to address them directly. Indeed, here we see the promised paraenetic outcome of the text (12.49; 14.13) with its revelation of the future divine justice, for it is here made explicit that this future justice impacts the present precisely in the demand to observe the Torah.[57] In response to the people's despair (12.40-45), Ezra recalls them to "the law of life" (14.30; cf. 7.129). It is the Torah (or Scripture as a whole, 14.45) that provides the path to life (14.21-22), because it is the standard of justice on the final day of judgment. The God who gave the "law of life" is also the "righteous judge" (14.30, 32) and his justice is the ultimate blueprint of the universe: "If you, then, will rule over your minds and discipline your hearts, you shall be kept alive and after death you shall obtain mercy. For after death, the judgment shall come, when we shall live again; and then the names of the righteous shall become manifest and the deeds of the ungodly shall be disclosed" (14.34-35). We are not surprised that in the final scenario of justice, "mercy" is not an incongruous gift, but a fitting benefaction to the righteous. With these final words, Ezra indicates how the whole of the present life can be governed by eschatological justice, through obedience to the law, its ultimate standard of judgment; at the same time, he indicates that the problem of the *cor malignum* is not, in fact, insoluble. Although "the wise" have another seventy books that perhaps explain how God's justice will take effect, their "wisdom" is a searching *into* the law, not *beyond* it (13.54). The ultimate triumph of God's justice is simultaneously the vindication of his law

56. See Stone, *Fourth Ezra*, pp. 408-12, rightly treating this final episode as the climax of the narrative and not just a legitimation of Ezra's authority.

57. The echo of Deuteronomy 29:29 in 14.6 also leads in this direction: what belongs in the public domain ("to us and to our children *for ever*") is "observing all the words of this law." On the centrality of the law, see M. P. Knowles, "Moses, the Law, and the Unity of 4 Ezra," *NovT* 31 (1989): 257-74.

(7.20): the most urgent practical appeal of this text is to leave history to the mysterious direction of God and to live in the light of the future judgment by keeping "the ways" commanded by God (14.31).

9.7. Conclusions

4 Ezra provides another example of the thematic discussion of God's goodness or mercy (the two semantic fields intertwined, 7.132-40), in ways that are comparable to what we have traced in other Second Temple texts but are also distinctive in important respects. Its vision of justice as the ultimate anchor-point of the cosmos requires that it concludes by configuring "mercy" as the congruous benefaction of God on the righteous, who keep God's ways and discipline their hearts (14.33-36). When Ezra prays for the judgment and mercy of God (11.46), the two will eventually be correlated in God's mercy on the remnant who have been faithful to the law (12.34). The principle of equity emerges as the dominant theme of the text: "empty things for the empty, and full things for the full" (7.25). At several points it was made clear that Ezra himself was an exemplar of this principle. The revelations that have been accorded to him are (despite his humble protestations of sinfulness) a fitting reward for his devotion to God's law: it is for this reason that his requests have been heard (12.7), and for this reason that he has been granted these visions (6.31-32; 8.62; 10.38-39, 50; 13.53-56).[58] He thus serves as a paradigm of the righteous who have a "treasury of works" (7.76-77; cf. 8.33); immediately at death they will see the reward stored up for them (7.76-101), when their faithfulness to God and their disciplined service in obedience to the law will reap their eventual reward. There is no reason to dub this fitting reward as a form of "legalism" or "works-righteousness"[59] — terminology that reflects distinctly Augustinian and Protestant theologies, and that presumes as natural or necessary a perfection of grace as an incongruous gift to the unworthy. The works of the righteous are the expression of their "faith(fulness)" and service to God (cf. 6.5; 9.7; 13.23),[60] and their "reward"

58. Cf. the frequent introduction to a request, "If I have found favor in your sight" (4.44; 5.56; 6.11; 7.75, 102; 8.42; 14.22), which 7.104 shows is not an empty formula.

59. *Pace* Sanders, *Paul and Palestinian Judaism*, pp. 409-18.

60. See W. Mundle, "Das religiöse Problem des IV. Esrabuches," *ZAW* n.f. 6 (1929): 222-49, at pp. 229-31. References to repentance (7.82; 9.11) indicate that "perfection" in law-keeping (7.89) need not be taken literally (so rightly Bauckham, "Apocalypses," pp. 171-72; J. A. Moo, "The Few Who Obtain Mercy: Soteriology in *4 Ezra*," in D. M. Gurtner, ed., *This World and the World to Come: Soteriology in Early Judaism* [London: T&T Clark, 2011], pp. 98-113, at p. 110; cf. Harnisch, *Verhängnis und Verheissung*, p. 155 n. 1).

(merces) represents the normal construal of benefaction that distributes benefits to the worthy (cf. 12.9, 36; 13.14).

At the same time, *4 Ezra* has dramatized, through Ezra's appeals in episode 3, an alternative construal of mercy, as incongruous benefaction to the undeserving. These appeals indicate the availability of this perfection of "grace" in the Second Temple period, and the sharp awareness that, when thus perfected, mercy is difficult to reconcile with the justice of God. As we have seen, Ezra's dialogue with Uriel constitutes a profound discussion of this problem, which emerges particularly in pleas and prayers to God. Ezra can appeal to biblical precedents and to key biblical depictions of God in service of his plea; indeed, from his perspective, with its pessimistic view of human sinfulness, it is only because God is merciful on sinners that *anyone* survives at all (7.137-40). Mercy in this sense, as God's gift to the unworthy, can be construed as the proper and necessary mode of God's dealings with humanity in this world, and it is important that Uriel goes a long way to concede Ezra's point, as far as concerns survival in the present age.

What Uriel will not concede is that such incongruous mercy can be God's *last word* in the ordering of the cosmos. In the judgment that ushers in and founds the world to come, that is, in the conditions of perfection that represent God's original and ultimate purpose for the world, God's just and congruent mercy *on the righteous* must be the operative principle. This judgment is the first thing God prepared (7.70), and it will restore the world to what he intended it to be. In the interim, under the present evil conditions, his incongruous mercy is a necessary means for the maintenance of that world; but it cannot represent God's final disposition of a cosmos properly ordered by equity and law. In the last resort, this righteousness must prevail, even if the righteous turn out to be as rare as gold-dust. It is the law that lasts forever, not the fallible human vessels in which it is implanted (9.31-37), and Ezra's final appeal to Israel to keep the law (14.27-38) represents the text's insistence that this is the eternal anchor-point in the cosmos. The perfection of mercy as God's benevolence to the undeserving is acknowledged to have strong emotional appeal. But in the final analysis, it must be hedged and limited by a prior and ultimate commitment to the just operation of God, in his congruous saving action.

4 Ezra thus adds to our increasingly complex map of Second Temple theology. In its pessimism regarding the sinfulness of humanity, it comes close to the abject denigration of humanity in the *Hodayot,* but it preserves the image of a righteous minority (even if a tiny minority) who are able to keep the law, despite the "evil heart." Its confidence in a cosmic order of justice, grounded in God's law, has parallels in *The Wisdom of Solomon* and in Philo, though in conceptual categories and in an eschatological framework very different from theirs. Like *Wisdom,* it probes deeply into the relationship between God's mercy and God's justice, though it depicts the relation between the two rather differently, with God's *incongruous* mercy in "this world" contrasted with his necessary and perfect justice in the next. Its insistence that, in the end, it must be *the righteous* who are rewarded places it close to *Wisdom,* but at some distance from the *Liber Antiquitatum Biblicarum,* whose expectation of God's renewed and renewable mercy on Israel *qua Israel* takes a different path in exploring the future salvation of "Israel." Of all our texts, *4 Ezra* displays most openly the theological problems associated with divine mercy or gift if they are perfected as incongruous benefits to the unworthy. It reminds us that "grace" is neither a simple nor an uncontroversial topic in the theology of Second Temple Judaism.

CHAPTER 10

The Diverse Dynamics of Grace in Second Temple Judaism

The five chapters of Part II have provided a sample of the diverse ways in which Second Temple Jews reflected on the beneficence of God. This is by no means a complete range of early Jewish perspectives, but it is enough to show the complexity of our topic and some of the diverse vocabularies, frameworks, and interests with which it was discussed. In drawing the threads together here, I will first summarize the main findings from each chapter (10.1), before noting the different kinds of diversity involved and the intra-Jewish debates in which these texts are engaged (10.2). This will allow us to identify how and why we have moved beyond Sanders's "covenantal nomism," the analytical frame that has dominated the last forty years of scholarship on the soteriology of Second Temple Judaism (10.3). Finally, I will outline Paul's location *within* this Jewish discussion of divine benevolence, distinctive in its own way just as *each* of our Jewish authors spoke from a distinct perspective (10.4).

10.1. Summary

Responding to political and social injustice in Alexandria, *The Wisdom of Solomon* counters the perception that good is futile and "might is right" with a vision of the cosmos rightly ordered by a universal Wisdom. God's generosity toward all humanity is celebrated throughout this text, but its emphasis on a just and non-arbitrary cosmos requires that God's gifts are fairly distributed to those "worthy" to receive them. Wisdom is a gift freely offered to those who desire and seek her and, like all good gifts, is fittingly given; the text traces the salvific role of Wisdom in regard to the "righteous," as "wisdom rescued from troubles those who served her" (10.9). To ground and illustrate this phenomenon, the biblical account of the exodus and wilderness experience is adapted to show the just operation of divine recompense in history: the wicked are punished very precisely for the evil that they do (even through the very means by which they sin), while God's righteous children are rewarded, with some "discipline" along the way. The people of Israel are here reframed as the "godly" and "righteous," since God's beneficence toward them reflects not some arbitrary preference but the fitting reward of those who are rightly aligned to truth and virtue, while they eschew the error of idolatry and the debasement of vice. Reflecting on the relation between divine mercy and justice (both manifestations of divine power), *Wisdom* shows how God's love for all humanity tempers and delays his justice to an extraordinary degree, although mercy cannot be extended to the undeserving to the point of undermining the justice that sustains the universe. God's "grace" (articulated sometimes as χάρις, sometimes as ἔλεος) is thus superabundant in scale and scope but not finally incongruous, and could not be so without endangering the equity of the cosmos and undercutting the hope of vindication to which the audience must hold. Although the priority of grace is sometimes stated, it is not especially perfected, and none of the other possible perfections of grace (efficacy, singularity, non-circularity) appear in this text.

Philo stands at the apex of the Jewish Alexandrian community and uses his advanced philosophical training to discover hidden depths in his Greek biblical texts. Central to his philosophical theology is the representation of God as the Cause of all good things. Divine gifts (χάριτες, δῶρα, etc.) flood the universe, in an excess of superabundance, and should be acknowledged with thanksgiving, with the recognition that God is the source of every good. Anxious to distance God from the causation of evil, Philo has God operate through his "powers," especially the ruling power of justice and the beneficent power of goodness. Nonetheless, he presses the efficacy of divine causation far into the realm of human agency by insisting that even human virtue should be attributed to God. Because God's gifts are neither random nor unjust, Philo presupposes that God will give to those who are "worthy" of his benefits. Worth is a condition of God's giving, but by no means its cause, and it is recognized by Philo as a dangerous notion if it encourages conceit or makes the recipient appear commensurate with God. However, God necessarily rewards what is rational and virtuous, because he celebrates the values by which he governs the cosmos. Thus Abraham, a pilgrim to truth and virtue, is rewarded with a covenant-gift, and Gentile proselytes who follow his path reap the same rewards. "Israel" represents those who "see" (the truth about) God and are oriented to that truth in their embrace of virtue and the suppression of bodily appetites. The "grace of the gift-loving God . . . dignifies and rewards what is excellent because of its likeness to himself" (*Praem.* 126). God's singular goodness or generosity thus upholds a hierarchy of values, reflecting Philo's own hierarchies of worth. Accordingly, Philo perfects the priority of grace (placing God as prior Cause), its singularity (God is good, and good alone), and its efficacy (God creates the virtue by which humans themselves act). He also perfects its superabundance in terms more effusive than any other Jew, but does not perfect the incongruity of grace, for the reasons here outlined. This does not render God's gifts a form of "pay." Philo exemplifies how gift and recompense, which to modern Western minds seem irreconcilable principles, are compatible in ancient constructions of the perfect gift.

The Qumran *Hodayot* (1QH[a]) articulate a theology designed to explain and maintain the existence of a "sectarian" community, an elect few in a generally foul and ignorant world. The hymns celebrate the goodness (טוב), loving-kindness (חסד), and mercy (רחמים) of God, in lavish terms. They also perfect the incongruity of this divine beneficence by constructing an extreme polarity between the perfectly righteous God and the physically and morally worthless humans who have been granted his grace. The author(s) articulate the wonder of God's grace, attributing to God, and God alone, the extraordinary transformation of those who are given insight into their salvation and the ability to reciprocate in obedience. Like Philo (but without his philosophical terminology), the *Hodayot* parade the efficacy of God's goodness, since God alone gives the speaker the capacity to walk in God's paths. Unlike Philo (and lacking his philosophical sensitivity on this score), there is no concern to protect the singularity of this goodness: God's mercy is all the more wonderful as the flipside of his ruthless punishment of sin. The incongruity of grace that the *Hodayot* celebrate would have seemed shocking to Philo and to the author of *Wisdom,* whose vision of a stable world depends on the congruity between God's gifts and their recipients. But such incongruity is not random or without rationale. God's "righteousness" (his script for the order of creation) has established a selective preference (רצון), whose roots go back to the foundation of creation. God has predetermined the distinctions of the cosmos, between light and darkness, day and night, the elect and the non-elect: his selective mercy on certain specimens of worthlessness is built into the rubric of the universe. The explanation is more "mythological" than philosophical, and might not have satisfied Philo, but it illustrates the necessity to provide some explanation if God's benevolence does not match the quality of its recipients. The *Hodayot* thus perfect "grace" differently from Philo and *Wisdom,* but they share with Philo a number of perfections (its superabundance, efficacy, and priority, though not its singularity).

The *Liber Antiquitatum Biblicarum* of Pseudo-Philo was apparently written in an atmosphere of national disappointment and self-criticism, around 70

CE. A central concern is to affirm God's irrevocable commitment to the nation of Israel, despite and beyond its repeated failure to remain faithful. Stressing the promise of an eternal covenant that outlasts God's anger and punishment of sin, the text makes frequent reference to the mercy *(misericordia)* of God, persisting beyond the cycles of sin and temporary abandonment. Unlike *Wisdom*, *LAB* makes no attempt to cover up Israel's idolatrous disobedience; if anything, it amplifies this motif in the history of Israel in order to profile, by contrast, God's principled determination that he will never finally or fully abandon his people. This story of "despite" and "nevertheless" perfects God's mercy as incongruous with the worth of its recipients, parallel to the incongruity we have traced in the *Hodayot,* though without the latter's extreme representation of human imperfection. Unlike in the *Hodayot,* God's abundant mercy is applied not to a select few within Israel but to the nation as a whole — not necessarily in every generation, but over the long course of history. Israel is the special recipient of this mercy not because of its righteousness (as in *Wisdom*), nor because of its proximity to God (as in Philo), but as the nation central to God's design for the world. As "the vine," Israel is integral to the structure of the universe — from top to bottom and from beginning to end — as the centerpiece of a cosmic plan that can be fulfilled through this nation alone. God can no more finally abandon Israel than he can abort the project of creation. Our author shares neither the predestinarian logic of the *Hodayot,* nor the philosophical training of Philo, but he nonetheless offers a theological explanation for what might otherwise seem the arbitrary application of God's incongruous grace. At times, "mercy" seems to fit the quality of its recipients, but Israel's larger story is permeated by a mercy incongruous with its persistent sin. This mercy is also perfected as prior to Israel's history (part of the purpose of creation), and superabundant in scale, but not in any other of our perfections (singularity, efficacy, or non-circularity).

4 Ezra reflects a mood of despair after the destruction of Jerusalem in 70 CE; its pessimism concerning the conditions of this world, and the flaws that spoil humanity (including Israel) is reminiscent of the *Hodayot,* though expressed in a different theological medium. Using the form of a dialogue between conflicting viewpoints, it articulates the need to view history alongside, and from the perspective of, the world to come — a bifocal vision that defers the fulfillment of the divine plan to a new world founded on the full and final reckoning of eschatological justice. In the dialogues, and especially in the climactic third, Uriel maintains that God will reward the righteous with congruous mercy, though they are as rare as gold-dust in a terrain of useless dirt. Ezra, by contrast, presses for the exercise of divine mercy as pity on the *undeserving,* appealing to Exodus 34 and to God's "merciful" character in this incongruous sense. Uriel accepts that this is a necessary and proper phenomenon in *this age*, but not at the final judgment, which ushers in *the age to come*. His apparently "harsh" viewpoint makes rational sense (in a properly just world there can be no compromise with sin). Through his mourning Ezra comes to share this two-age perspective, placing his hope in God's eventual vindication of the righteous, however few they might be. God's love for Israel remains intact, and will be displayed in the messianic kingdom and the age to come, but those who are saved will be saved *qua* the righteous and the Torah-observant, not on the grounds of sentiment or arbitrary preference. Truth and justice must exercise their discriminating power: *vacua vacuis et plena plenis* (7.25: "empty things for the empty, and full for the full"). God's benevolence is thus perfected in limited ways (only in its superabundance). The text shows the strong emotional appeal of an incongruous "grace," but it cannot allow this notion to have the final word if God is fittingly to reward the righteous minority and to punish the guilty majority of humankind.

10.2. Diversity and Debate

All of our texts participate in the shared discourse of a common cultural tradition. In various modes, they draw on the same scriptural resources: *Wisdom* adapts and interprets the stories of the patriarchs and the exodus; Philo makes the Greek Pentateuch the textual basis of his philosophy; the *Hodayot* are shot through with scriptural language, supplemented and redeployed; *LAB* offers a re-reading of biblical history; *4 Ezra* appeals to a central text on divine goodness (Exod 34:6-7) that is also important to the *Hodayot*. In each case, the beneficence of God forms a central theme, expressed in the language of "gift," "mercy," or "preference" (in Greek, Hebrew, or Latin). The differences between these texts do not lie in the *degree of emphasis* that they give to this theme; it is of central importance to them all, and one could hardly say that the *Hodayot* place greater emphasis on divine goodness than Philo, or vice versa. Nonetheless, our texts are irreducibly diverse; to characterize them all as products of a "religion of grace" would hardly be illuminating. That diversity lies partly, but only partly, in their different *vocabularies*, with "gift" language predominating in some and "mercy" vocabulary in others. But the same terms can also be variously construed, and there are significant differences also in the *frame* and *scope* of their respective theologies. As we have seen, some trace God's benevolence within the sphere of human history (Philo; *LAB*); others place this history in relation to an eschatological horizon, where its problems are finally resolved *(Wisdom; 4 Ezra)*; others again press before history to a pre-creational plan *(Hodayot)* that provides the rationale for divine preferences in history. In all of our texts, Israel (or a subset thereof) takes center stage in the display of divine benevolence, but this "Israel" is variously defined and variously related to the cosmos as a whole. In the *Hodayot,* the scope of God's benevolence is circumscribed by his predetermined choice: the rest of humanity falls outside its remit. For Philo, by contrast, the whole cosmos is, in a broad sense, the gift of God; Jews are uniquely attuned to the truth of the cosmos, and thus uniquely recipients of divine benevolence, but this special place is primarily predicated on their relationship to the truth, not on ancestral, covenant promises (as in *LAB*). For this reason, Philo can celebrate the inclusion of non-Jews (as proselytes) in the Abrahamic pilgrimage toward the truth; in *LAB* and *4 Ezra* non-Jews appear to fall outside the parameters of God's love.

These differing definitions of the scope of divine benevolence reflect deep differences in the authors' conceptual frames: some are indebted to the Greek philosophical tradition, others are content with the more "mythological" discourse of the Bible itself. On top of such differences, the texts' varying historical and social contexts influence their discussions of divine benevolence. An appeal to the mercy or goodness of God functions differently in the study of an Alexandrian philosopher, the worship of a Qumran "sectarian," the confidence of a successful Diaspora community, or the despair of homeland Jews in the wake of the Jewish War. Addressing different problems and concerns, God's generosity or mercy plays differing rhetorical and pragmatic roles in the strategies of the text.

But the diversity we have identified, importantly, extends also to the *meaning* of divine benevolence, a phenomenon we have charted by tracing the variety of ways in which this concept was "perfected." These perfections — the ways in which divine benevolence or grace was drawn into a pure or totalized form — represent not differing *degrees of emphasis* on their theme but the development of *different facets* of this multivalent concept into varying end-of-the-line extremes. Using the sixfold schema of perfections described in chapter 2, we have found that our texts agree at some points, and differ widely at others. *All of them* perfect the superabundance of divine "grace," stressing the excess of gifts poured into the world, or the "abundance" of divine mercy and goodness, extended in manifold ways. On the other hand, in another point of agreement, *none of them* perfect the non-circularity of grace, the notion that God gives without expectation of return. Although Philo can distinguish God from a salesman who operates by *quid pro quo,* even he presupposes that God's gifts are not unilateral; for him, as for others, "grace" elicits thanksgiving, worship, and obedience. Beyond these two points of agreement, however, the forms of perfection vary greatly. Some (e.g., Philo) tend toward the singularity of God's benevolence (God as the cause of good alone); others (e.g., the *Hodayot*) let God's mercy shine against the backdrop of his wrath and punishing judgment. Some (e.g., Philo and the *Hodayot*) suggest the efficacy of grace, attributing to God the human response that God's grace elicits; others (e.g., *Wisdom of Solomon*) show no interest in qualifying human agency in any such way. Some stress the priority of God's benevolence, whether in a pre-creational determination of human destiny (the *Hodayot*) or in God's prior causation of all human acts (Philo). Most strikingly, and most importantly for our study, some (e.g., the *Hodayot* and *LAB;* Ezra in *4 Ezra*) stress the incongruity of divine mercy, while others (e.g., Philo, *Wisdom,* Uriel in *4 Ezra*) do not. This is not because some have a "higher" or "purer" view of grace than others. This is only one of six possible perfections, and to decide that incongruity is the *sine qua non* of "grace" — as modern dictionary definitions (and the Christian tradition) tend to do — would be to skew our analysis from the beginning. It is just the case that our texts disagree on how they configure divine goodness in this regard, and it would be equally mistaken to regard the incongruity of grace as ubiquitous in Second Temple Judaism as to consider it absent from its repertoire of perfections.

In fact, there is reason to think that the congruity or incongruity of grace was one of several related issues that were *debated* among Second Temple Jews. In stressing the singularity of God's goodness, and warding off any suggestion that God was the cause of evil, Philo tiptoes around a difficult philosophical problem familiar to him from his training in the Greek tradition. The heavy emphasis in *Wisdom* on God's universal benevolence betrays a similar sensitivity, even if the text does not distance God from the punishment of the wicked as Philo seems constrained to do. The fact that this is not an issue in other texts (such as the *Hodayot*), which stress the greatness of God's goodness against the backcloth of his wrathful judgment, suggests that the problem was most likely to be felt in intellectual circles influenced by Greek philosophy. Philo alone uses the notion of God's "powers" to distance God from the causation of evil, but the topic was bound to concern other philosophically sensitive theologians and would be taken up in different forms and with different solutions in later rabbinic literature and in Marcion (see above, 3.1).

A contiguous issue is the relationship between justice and mercy. As we have seen (above, 5.4), *Wisdom* wrestles with this issue, seeking to coordinate divine justice and mercy in a way that gives space to both. Philo's "ruling" and "benevolent" powers perform something of the same function, while the debate between Ezra and Uriel in the third dialogue of *4 Ezra* signals how this topic became important in other Jewish circles. The ambiguity of foundational biblical texts such as Exodus 20:5-6 and Exodus 34:6-7 lends itself to discussion on this matter. Whether God's mercy has limits, set by the demands of justice, or whether it is divine precisely in its limitless range and endless scope, was clearly a complex but important matter for discussion. Jewish texts are united not by unanimity of viewpoint on this topic but by common wrestling with it as a theological problem.[1]

This discussion clearly impacted the question of the congruity of grace, an issue on which we have found our texts notably diverse: was God's mercy or favor accorded only (or chiefly, or at least ultimately) to fitting recipients who were in one sense or another worthy of their receipt? Or was it given incongruously, without regard to worth? The rationale for the congruent gift is obvious. Benefactors display their values by their distribution of gifts, and one cannot expect God to identify himself through gifts to the wicked: moral discrimination is what makes God's gifts good. Gifts should also be appropriate to their recipients; an ill-fitting gift is unseemly, and can even be cruel. Most of all, one would expect God to act in a way that is both reasonable and fair. Since what is random or arbitrary is erroneous or evil (cf. Plato, *Tim.* 47a-c), and since justice requires the good, and not the evil, to be rewarded, congruity between divine grace and the worth of its human recipients was the default assumption in antiquity (see chapter 1).

On the logic of the congruent gift, God's grace is not the opposite of recompense, but is *simultaneously* gift and reward. There is no antithesis here between gift and merit; grace and recompense stand in conjunction, not opposition. This is not to make the gift any less a gift or something akin to "pay." Those who deserve gifts are still the recipients of gifts, given voluntarily and without legal requirement. They do not *cause* the gift to be given (that is always a matter of the benefactor's will), but they prove themselves to be its suitable recipients and thus provide the *condition* for its proper distribution. We must insist, against our instincts, that the ancients knew, and had reason to celebrate, a form of divine grace that rewarded those who were fitting recipients of its free and lavish beneficence.

As Philo shows, to hold that God gives to the worthy could raise misgivings. Philo was anxious lest notions of worth give the impression that humans were commensurate with the divine benefactor or were somehow the cause of his gifts. He was also conscious that the discriminating distribution of gifts limited their range, and insisted that the more basic gifts of creation were

1. For discussion of this topic elsewhere in Palestinian Judaism, see E. Sjöberg, *Gott und Sünder im palästinischen Judentum* (Stuttgart: Kohlhammer, 1938). See also the overly formulaic treatment by B. D. Smith, *The Tension between God as Righteous Judge and as Merciful in Early Judaism* (Lanham: University Press of America, 2005), who decides rather too quickly that mercy and justice coexist "at best" in an uneasy compromise.

given in common to worthy and unworthy alike (see above, 6.3). The most vivid analysis of this problem occurs in *4 Ezra*, where it is recognized that only an *incongruous* mercy could cover the sins of unrighteous humanity (*4 Ezra* 8.26-36) — a critical issue since, as both parties agree, most of humanity (and most of Israel) is deeply unrighteous. To uphold the necessary congruity of divine grace (God's mercy exercised on the righteous alone) thus reduces its scope, perhaps drastically so. But Uriel in *4 Ezra*, among others, is prepared to pay this price, since the alternative, a compromise with sin, is ultimately more costly.

Those who figure divine gifts as necessarily congruent are as insistent as others on the generosity of God; they simply perfect that benevolence in other ways. No one (not even Paul) is as eloquent as Philo about the lavishness, extravagance, and superabundance of divine beneficence; and no one (certainly not Paul) insists with greater emphasis on divine causation of all that is good, including human virtue. But, for good reason, Philo does *not* press for the perfection of incongruity. There is no terminological distinction between the vocabulary he uses for this congruent divine generosity and that used by others who figure God's gifts as incongruent. Both Philo and Paul talk about the χάρις of God, just as *4 Ezra* uses the same term (in Latin, *misericordia*) both for God's incongruous mercy in this life and for his congruous mercy at the final judgment. We have no right to translate Paul's χάρις as "grace" and Philo's χάρις as something else, unless we have already decided, by ideological fiat, that "grace" means only what we take it to mean in Paul. *The difference between an incongruous and a congruous gift is a difference in one perfection of grace, not a categorical distinction between grace and non-grace.*

That God's grace can also be figured as incongruous has become clear not only in the *Hodayot*, but also in the covenant theology of *LAB*. *4 Ezra* acknowledges this as a feature of God's mercy in the conditions of the present world, though Uriel insists that it cannot apply in the final judgment. Thus, the notion of a divine incongruous gift ("grace in defiance of demerit") is certainly a possible perfection of grace in Second Temple Judaism and *not* uniquely Pauline. But it requires a strong rationale to protect this notion from the implication of arbitrariness or injustice. In the *Hodayot*, God's extraordinary kindness is explained by appeal to divine predetermination: built into the design of the cosmos is the selection of God's "children of preference." In *LAB*, God's repeated acts of mercy on his worthless people represent his faithfulness to the covenant promises given to the patriarchs, promises that make God's world-plan unalterable: sooner will the world implode than Israel perish. In this way, the incongruous manifestation of God's grace can be justified, but it is noticeable that in both these cases the justification requires an appeal to something beyond the gift itself, a rationale that ensures that a seemingly arbitrary action of God matches a deeper rationality on a cosmic scale.

Irrationality and injustice are the double problematic of incongruous grace, the reason why congruous grace makes the most sense. This is especially so if, as befits God's special gifts, the distribution of the gift is not universal but selective. If the recipients of such gifts are no more fitting than others, why should God give to them in particular? The ancient aversion to randomness and the fierce desire to preserve the fairness of the universe made it necessary to place examples of incongruous divine gifts into some larger frame of reason; otherwise, one could hardly speak of justice or providence. Uriel's conviction that the world must *ultimately* be just leads him to posit that, whatever the indulgence of the present age, justice must prevail at the final judgment, without special pleading for the unrighteous or unrepentant. Thus, there are strong grounds for excluding incongruous grace as an ultimate rationale, or at least a standalone explanation, for God's dealings with the world. That God should, in principle, give his greatest gifts to those who are entirely unfitting is, on the face of it, bizarre — and not only bizarre but theologically dangerous. It is by no means obvious that this is the best or the most perfect form of grace; since it threatens to undermine the goodness of the Giver, it is often specifically excluded or treated as an unusual phenomenon. Without a deeper rationale, the notion is inherently subversive of theism itself. There were plenty of ways in which one could perfect the beneficence of God without venturing onto this dangerous path.

10.3. Beyond Covenantal Nomism

We may now clarify how we have moved beyond the analysis of Jewish soteriology offered by E. P. Sanders's model of "covenantal nomism," and beyond the debates that have raged around this model during the last forty years. As we saw above (3.6.1), Sanders performed an outstanding service in refuting the caricatures of Second Temple Judaism that had utilized Reformation categories to denigrate Judaism as a religion of works-righteousness. He rightly insisted that divine grace was central, indeed foundational, to most expressions of Judaism in this era. Yet Sanders's analysis of soteriology as *stages in a sequence* (first "getting in," then "staying in") meant that his focus rested on the *priority* of grace: grace precedes and grounds the subsequent demand for Torah-obedience, which is a means of staying in the covenant, not of earning or achieving salvation. Because priority constitutes the defining characteristic of "covenantal nomism," Sanders found this pattern of salvation to be everywhere the same (with the exception of *4 Ezra*): within this "uniformity," the differences between texts represent only different *degrees of emphasis* (e.g., a "special emphasis" and "heightened sense" of grace in the Dead Sea Scrolls).[2] As we noted earlier (3.6.1, above), Sanders also stated or implied that grace is by definition "free," in the sense of "unmerited." Where merit or reward features in the texts, he took their juxtaposition with grace to signify "unsystematic" thinking. At a deep (and often hidden) level, Sanders assumed that grace is, at least in some respect, *incongruous,* and that this incongruity is integral to the definition of the concept.

Following our analysis of five Jewish texts/authors (chapters 5-9), and using the analytical frame of our six "perfections" of grace (chapter 2), we can now move *beyond* Sanders's "covenantal nomism." His observations on the *priority* of grace are valid, but this constitutes *only one* of the six possible perfections of grace, and, crucially, does not entail all, or indeed any, of the other perfections. *If grace is prior, it is not necessarily also incongruous.*[3] To identify a "common pattern" in Second Temple Judaism based on the priority of grace (the covenantal foundation) is to offer a *one-dimensional* analysis that discovers uniformity only by downplaying every other form of difference. Sanders is right that grace is everywhere; but this does not mean that grace is everywhere the same. Once we scrutinize the meaning of this concept, and disaggregate its various perfections, we find that our Jewish texts differ *not (primarily) in degrees of emphasis* on grace, but *in the forms of perfection* with which they articulate it. Of the five texts we have studied, some perfect grace as incongruous, and others (for good reason) do not. Again, this is not because some "believe in grace" and others do not. We should resist the assumption that grace is *by definition* incongruous, and that the concept has become "diluted" or "corrupted" when it is not perfected in this form. That assumption is built into modern dictionary definitions of "grace" for historical reasons: it has become integral to *Christian* views of grace at least since Augustine, under inspiration from Paul. But incongruity is only one possible perfection of grace, and not necessarily present whenever grace-language is employed.

When we disaggregate the possible perfections of grace, we can comprehend the diversity in Second Temple Judaism on this topic, a diversity that "covenantal nomism" not only masks but is conceptually incapable of grasping. As we have seen, this diversity is not between texts that emphasize grace

2. E. P. Sanders, *Paul and Palestinian Judaism* (London: SCM Press, 1977), pp. 296-98, comparing the Dead Sea Scrolls with rabbinic texts; for the "uniformity" of Judaism regarding its covenantal foundation, see p. 421.

3. Besides our Jewish texts (e.g., Philo), Augustine's disputes with Pelagius illustrate this clearly enough; see above, 3.2.3.

and those that marginalize or deny this concept: it is rather between different construals of grace and different perfections of this motif. The discovery of these differences internal to Second Temple Judaism makes its characterization as "a religion of grace" of limited use: the label refutes outdated caricatures of a grace-less religion, but has little analytical power. More positively, the discovery enables us to ask afresh where to place Paul *within the diversity of Second Temple Judaism.* Freed from the old antitheses, it becomes senseless to ask whether Paul represents "real" grace, as opposed to its "diluted" forms in Judaism. Nor is it accurate to declare that on the subject of grace and works "Paul is in agreement with Palestinian Judaism,"[4] as if the latter were an unvariegated unity. The question now becomes more interesting: how does Paul perfect the theme of divine beneficence and how does his voice compare with others in his diverse Jewish context?

Those who criticize Sanders's work (see 3.7.1) tend to assume that if salvation is contingent on human works or worth, either in initial election or in final salvation, one cannot speak of "grace" in its proper form as "free," "sheer," or "pure," on the assumption that *one* perfection of grace, its incongruity, is its defining characteristic. Where recompense, reward, or any form of *quid pro quo* accompanies the language of gift or mercy in Second Temple texts, it is often assumed that the theology is inconsistent or riddled with tensions. On this reasoning, Sanders's insistence that grace is everywhere is supposedly countered by evidence that God's grace is conditioned by the worth of the recipient — and thus not "grace" at all. We can now see why these debates misfire. Taking one perfection of grace (its priority) as its defining characteristic, Sanders found it everywhere, but assumed, sometimes against the evidence, that another perfection (incongruity) was wrapped up in the definition of the term. Taking this other perfection (incongruity) as its very essence, his critics highlighted Jewish texts that spoke of a congruous grace, and concluded that such texts were not speaking consistently of grace at all. Neither side scrutinized carefully enough what they meant by "grace" and why they defined it as they did. To define grace as "unmerited favor" is a historically specific, not a timeless, definition of the term. Our survey in chapter 3 has indicated some of the sources for this definition, what alternative construals it combated, and why it has carried such weight. This historical perspective has proved vital in gaining some analytical distance from a presumption that continues to influence, in unrecognized form, practically all contemporary debates around the topic of grace in Paul and Second Temple Judaism.

Freed from this presumption about the meaning of grace, we can recog-

4. *Paul and Palestinian Judaism,* p. 543, cited above, 3.6.1.

nize in Second Temple Judaism many construals of this motif. Paul emerges as one participant in an ongoing Jewish dialogue in which the motif of grace was perfected in various ways, with no single or predominant form. Paul thus regains his historical place, neither against Judaism nor in undifferentiated agreement with all his fellow Jews.

10.4. Placing Paul in the Mix

A preliminary indication of Paul's place within the Second Temple conversation on divine grace may be provided by setting the main themes of Romans 9–11 in comparison with each of the texts we have studied in Part II. We will return to this climactic portion of Romans below (chapter 17), but a brief overview here will serve to indicate the extent to which Paul debates the same questions we have found to be significant in other Second Temple texts. It will also reveal some of his distinctive emphases and special concerns. As we have found, *every* Second Temple text is different in its own way, and to identify certain distinctive traits in Paul is not to place him *outside* the Jewish conversation, but merely as one of the varied voices within it.[5] In these chapters of Romans, Paul stands on terrain that is recognizably the same as our other authors. He speaks self-consciously as an "Israelite" (Rom 11:1), even — or rather, especially — while he "speak[s] . . . in Christ" (9:1), and he strongly identifies with other Israelites, "my brothers, my kinsmen according to the flesh" (9:3; cf. 11:14). He is concerned throughout with the future of Israel, and draws heavily on the Jewish Scriptures, in ways closely comparable to our other five authors. Standing within this cultural matrix, he inflects the theme of divine grace — variously articulated as "mercy" (Rom 9:15-18; 11:28-32), "gift/favor" (Rom 11:5-6; 11:29), "election/calling" (Rom 9:6-12; 11:28), and "love" (Rom 9:13, 25) — in forms recognizably similar to those of other Jews, but also in a distinctive and characteristically Pauline pattern. We may trace some of the chief similarities and differences through comparisons between key themes in Romans 9–11 and each of our five texts.

Romans 9–11 is pervaded by a sense of crisis, perplexity, and (finally) hope

5. Cf. the display of inner-Jewish diversities, and of Paul's place within them, offered by F. Watson, *Paul and the Hermeneutics of Faith* (London: T&T Clark, 2004). It is only if we assume, unjustifiably, that Judaism is monolithic (or reducible to a "lowest common denominator") that we need take Paul's disagreements with fellow Jews on certain points as indicating that he stands somehow "outside" Judaism. The same error leads to the equal and opposite presumption that, since Paul speaks as a Jew, he cannot be imagined to say anything different, atypical, or controversial in Second Temple Judaism.

regarding the fate of Israel, and at this point it runs parallel to the mood of *4 Ezra*.[6] As we have seen (above, chapter 9), the crisis in *4 Ezra* is occasioned by "the desolation of Zion" (3.2) and the destruction of the Temple (10.19-23), but this is the product of a deeper problem, the "evil heart" that persistently causes Israel to disobey God (3.4-36). Paul also begins with lament for Israel, expressing "great sorrow and unceasing anguish" for his "kinsfolk" (Rom 9:2-3); like Ezra, he prays for the salvation of Israel (Rom 10:1) and is equally pessimistic about the capacity of sin to frustrate obedience to the law (Rom 3:9-20; 5:12-21; 7:7-25). However, for Paul the event that occasions the crisis is not the destruction of Jerusalem but, paradoxically, the arrival of Israel's Messiah, a "stumbling-stone" for Israel (Rom 9:30-33).

Just as Ezra appeals to the special status of Israel (*4 Ezra* 5.23-30; 6.55-59), Paul clings to the fact that his kinsfolk are "Israelites, and to them belong the sonship, the glory, the covenants, the giving of the law, the (temple) worship and the promises: theirs are the patriarchs, and from them springs the Messiah, according to the flesh" (Rom 9:4-5). As in *4 Ezra,* the question is not the validity of the promise entailed by these privileges, but how it will be realized beyond the present crisis. Just as Uriel assures Ezra that God has not abandoned his love for his people (*4 Ezra* 5.33), so Paul considers it impossible that God's promise could fail (Rom 9:6). Ezra-like, he asks whether God has rejected his people (11:1); Uriel-like, he replies, "No way!" (11:1).

In *4 Ezra,* God's faithfulness to Israel will be fulfilled through God's fitting mercy on a righteous remnant (*4 Ezra* 7.26-29; 9.7-8), "one grape out of a cluster" (9.21). It transpires that this includes the ten missing tribes, but the criterion for inclusion in all cases is faithfulness to the Torah (7.17-20, 127-31; 14.28-36). Paul also speaks of a "remnant" (Rom 9:27-29): like the 4,000 at the time of Elijah, "so too at the present time there is a remnant" (11:5). But two things stand out in Paul's depiction of this scenario. Paul emphasizes that the remnant are chosen "by grace, not by works" (11:6), a definitional gesture at odds with *4 Ezra*'s redemption of the remnant in accord with their "works and faith" (*4 Ezra* 9.7-8; 13.23; 14.28-35). Secondly, for Paul, the salvation of the remnant is *not* the end of the story. At the present time, Israel has failed to obtain what it was seeking (Rom 11:6), but God's purpose reaches beyond this "stumbling" to restoration (11:11-15), beyond the part to the whole (11:12): "a hardening has come upon Israel in part until the full number of the Gentiles comes in, and so all Israel will be saved" (11:25-26). Where *4 Ezra* sees God's love for Israel necessarily (because justly) fulfilled in the salvation of the righ-

6. For a full-length comparison, see B. W. Longenecker, *Eschatology and the Covenant: A Comparison of 4 Ezra and Romans 1–11* (Sheffield: JSOT Press, 1991).

teous few, Paul traces a paradoxical plan whereby God "has consigned all to disobedience, in order that he may have mercy on all" (Rom 11:32). *4 Ezra* (in the voice of Uriel) sees the fulfillment of God's purpose when justice disallows any merciful compromise with sin; Paul imagines the future as the triumph of an incongruous mercy (11:15-28).

In a related point of contrast, *4 Ezra*'s concern for Israel contains no hope for the rest of the world: the "one vine" has been chosen "from all the multitude of peoples" (*4 Ezra* 5.21-27), who are "nothing" before God and "like spittle" (6.56-57). In a post–70 CE context, those nations are figured as "domineering" and "devouring" Israel (3.28-36; 6.57-59). For Paul, however, the future of Israel is inclusive of "the nations"; the one "olive tree" can have Gentiles (unnaturally) grafted in (Rom 11:17-24). Paul's context is the success of his Gentile mission (Rom 10:9-18; 11:13-15), which is not at the expense of Israel's restoration, but the means by which it will come about (11:11-16). Both Gentiles and Jews are to be embraced by God's incongruous mercy (9:24-26). The task of the messianic Redeemer from Zion (Rom 11:26-27) will not be to destroy the oppressive nations (cf. *4 Ezra* 11–13), but to ensure that Israel is included in God's purpose of mercy on all the disobedient, even the Gentiles.

Philo's construal of divine grace provides different points of comparison and contrast with Paul.[7] We noted as paradigmatic the way he handles the apparently arbitrary distribution of divine favor to a number of scriptural figures, including the patriarchs (*Leg.* 3.65-106; see above, 6.3). For Philo, God's rationale can be detected in the names of the recipients, since names betoken character, and God's gifts are fittingly given to people who are or will be people of quality. Philo thus maintains both the priority of the grace of God (who "molds" the natures that he rewards with grace) and the congruity between the gift and the recipient. Paul shows interest in the same patriarchal stories (Rom 9:6-18), which were of foundational significance for the identity of Israel, and is drawn to the fact that God's verdict is in one case pronounced even before birth (Rom 9:11; cf. Philo, *Leg.* 3.85-89). Like Philo, Paul concludes that God's choice operates without regard to work; unlike Philo, he does not appeal to God's foreknowledge of the "capacities, works, and passions" of Esau or Jacob, nor to the traces of virtue or vice formed in their characters before birth. Paul's

7. For a full comparison of Paul and Philo on this topic, see O. McFarland, "The God Who Gives: Philo and Paul in Comparison" (PhD thesis; Durham University, 2013). I have written two essays on this theme: "'By the Grace of God I Am What I Am': Grace and Agency in Philo and Paul," in J. M. G. Barclay and S. J. Gathercole, eds., *Divine and Human Agency in Paul and His Cultural Environment* (London: T&T Clark, 2006), pp. 140-57; "Grace within and beyond Reason: Philo and Paul in Dialogue," in P. Middleton, A. Paddison, and K. Wenell, eds., *Paul, Grace, and Freedom: Essays in Honour of John K. Riches* (London: T&T Clark, 2009), pp. 9-21.

emphasis lies entirely, and by Philo's lights dangerously, on the *inexplicable* initiative of God, on God's choice and predetermination without regard to a corresponding condition of worth (9:11-12). In fact, Paul rules out numerous qualifying criteria for divine selection: birth (natural rights of descent), status (comparative "greatness"), and action ("works"). Where Philo, on examination of the text, found traces of "worth," Paul has declined to find any, and has paraded, by contrast, the independence and autonomy of divine choice. Hence his question: "is there injustice (ἀδικία) with God" (9:14)? His answer, which we will consider below (17.2), suggests that the only factor conditioning God's mercy is God's mercy itself (9:15-18).

In comparison with Philo, what stands out is Paul's refusal to trace any line of congruence between God's mercy and its recipients, even if this risks making God seem arbitrary or unfair. Paul also shows little concern to deny that God could cause harm: where Philo was at pains to show that God's "treasury of evil" was "sealed up" (as in Deut 32:34), Paul shows no embarrassment in depicting God as "hating" and "hardening" (Rom 9:13, 17-18). Of the various perfections, Paul's primary concern is with the *incongruity* of grace; he shows little interest in perfecting its *singularity*.

Like Philo (but unlike *4 Ezra*), Paul is enthusiastic about the addition of Gentiles into the "commonwealth" of Israel (Philo) or "the root" (11:17-24). The "calling" traced in 9:6-18 applies to "both Jews and Gentiles" (9:24) in a process that turns those who are "not my people" into "my people" (9:25-26). Philo welcomed Gentile proselytes as migrants to the truth, since they recognized, with Israel, the universal truth of the one, invisible, cosmic Creator. But Paul doubts that Israel "sees" the truth about God without reference to Christ (10:2-3). While he speaks of the one God (of Jews and Gentiles, cf. Rom 3:29), he reinterprets Joel's reference to "calling on the name of the Lord" in Christological terms, as gesturing to the "Lord Jesus" who is confessed in faith (10:9-13). The Gentiles thus recognize the truth not of nature, but of an event, the event in which God raised Jesus from the dead and designated him "Lord" (10:9; cf. 1:3-4).

Paul's remarkable emphasis on the incongruity of God's grace, while shocking to Philo, would not have shocked the authors of the Qumran *Hodayot*.[8] As we have seen, the juxtaposition of human worthlessness (material, social, and moral) with the glory and righteousness of God is one of the hall-

8. Recent comparisons of Paul and the *Hodayot* include J. Maston, *Divine and Human Agency in Second Temple Judaism and Paul* (Tübingen: Mohr Siebeck, 2010); N. A. Meyer, "Adam's Dust and Adam's Glory: Rethinking Anthropogony and Theology in the *Hodayot* and the Letters of Paul" (PhD thesis; McMaster University, 2013).

marks of those hymns. Although Paul does not wallow in the worthlessness of the human in quite the same terms (cf. Rom 3:10-18; 5:12-21; 7:7-25), like the *Hodayot* he figures humanity as "flesh" (9:8) and "clay" (9:20-21) and attributes salvation solely to the mercy of God (cf. 11:36). Even the antithetical style is reminiscent of the hymns, whose authors would surely have endorsed Paul's comment that "it is not of the one who wills, or of the one who runs, but of God who has mercy" (9:16).

As in the *Hodayot,* the attribution of saving power to God *alone* leads Paul toward a divine determinism that traces the destinies of human beings to God's own action. The double predestination of the *Hodayot* has God creating both the righteous and the wicked, preparing the one for "the time of favor," the other for "the day of slaughter," "so that all may know your glory and your great strength" (1QH[a] VII.25-33). In similar fashion Paul, adapting Exodus, has God raise up Pharaoh "so that I might show my power in you and so that my name may be proclaimed in all the earth" (Rom 9:17). Without reference to Pharaoh's own conduct, Paul speaks of God hardening whom he wills, as he has mercy on whom he wills (9:18). Against possible objections, he declines to modify such strong statements of divine agency, and refutes the very notion of answering back to God (9:20). In the end, however, what God will do with the "vessels of wrath" is left tantalizingly unclear (9:22); characteristically, Paul's eye seems drawn not to the completion of two opposite destinies, but to God's display of "the wealth of his glory" in the calling of both Gentiles and Jews.

Indeed, at this point of similarity, a structural difference emerges. Qumran predestinarianism articulated a cosmic plan, rooted in creation as part of its design: God's mercy on the "sectarians" was the expression of an eternally established "preference" (רצון). In Romans 9–11 Paul also speaks of God's "election" (ἐκλόγη, 9:11; 11:5, 28), of his "purpose" (πρόθεσις, 9:11), and "pre-preparation" (προετοιμάζω) of the "vessels of mercy" (9:23; cf. 8:29-30). But election is not here traced to the structures of nature, nor coordinated with the divisions and alternations of the cosmos. Rather, the purpose of God seems shaped by its *telos,* actualized in the present. Paul's contemporary experience of the Christ-event and of the Gentile mission has convinced him that the central dynamic of God's plan is constituted not by nature, but by an event, not by primordial cosmic design, but by the enactment of God's "glory" in the worldwide reach of the gospel (cf. 10:14-21). God's calling of Jews and Gentiles is certainly the realization of his promise (9:8), but the line of direction in Paul's theological reasoning is not from the eternal past to the present, but from the present backwards to its anticipation — and forwards to its completion. Rom 9:30–10:21, like the earlier chapters of the letter, indicates that, for Paul, the present defining moment is the Christ-event, specifically the death and resurrection of Christ together with their proclamation throughout the world.

Like *The Wisdom of Solomon,* Paul speaks in Romans 9–11 of righteousness and knowledge in a world full of paradox (Rom 9:30–10:21).[9] *Wisdom* assures its readers of a just moral order, a wisdom whose righteous rule permeates nature and governs history, rewarding the worthy and punishing the impious. Paul also speaks of a reality that embraces all humanity (Jews and non-Jews, 10:12), its writ spreading across the entire world (10:18). But the focus of his attention is the *re-ordering* of history brought about by the event of Christ. Where *Wisdom* is confident in Israel's knowledge of God (*Wisdom* 15:1-4), Paul denies that Israel "knows God" (10:2-3) unless and until it knows the righteousness of God enacted in Christ's life, death, and resurrection (10:5-13; cf. 3:21-31). The righteousness of God is here redefined by reference to Christ (10:4) and faith (10:6, 10). A crucial biblical text on the accessibility of the Torah (Deut 30:12-14) is so thoroughly re-read that Christ is made the object of the putative quests (10:6-7), while the "word" that is near is "the word of faith" being preached (10:8). Even the title κύριος is given new definition by reference to the "Lord Jesus" (10:9). Paul has reframed his tradition: he reconfigures what he shares with *Wisdom* in Christological terms.

Like *Wisdom,* Paul's vision is universal and comprehensive, but on a very different basis. *Wisdom* appeals to the universal truth of a regulative cosmic order, a pre-existing reality to which all things conform. Paul appeals to an event — the resurrection of Jesus and his installation as "Lord" — that makes a claim on all (10:12). This event embraces Jew and Gentile "without distinction" (10:12) as an unconditioned gift of "wealth" (10:12), given without regard to ethnic or other forms of worth. The incongruity of this gift, comparable to the configuration of mercy in the *Hodayot* and *LAB,* contrasts with *Wisdom*'s concern to demonstrate symmetry in God's governance of the world. In Paul's scenario, Gentiles who were not pursuing righteousness have attained it (Rom 9:30), while Torah-pursuing Israel turns out to be ignorant and disobedient (Rom 9:31; 10:3, 21). God is found not by those who seek him (cf. *Wisdom* 6:11-13) but by those who do not (Rom 10:20). Citing Isaiah 65, Paul presents Israel as a disobedient and contrary nation (10:21), quite unlike *Wisdom*'s chastened but righteous children of God. Thus, if Israel is eventually to be saved, it will be saved not *qua* the righteous or pious, but (paradoxically) *qua* the disobedient

9. For a recent comprehensive comparison, see J. A. Linebaugh, *God, Grace, and Righteousness in Wisdom of Solomon and Paul's Letter to the Romans: Texts in Conversation* (Leiden: Brill, 2013).

(11:25-32). In place of *Wisdom*'s structured moral universe, Paul appears to hang every hope on a single thread, the mercy of God.

In its stubborn hope for Israel's future, and associated emphasis on the mercy of God, Romans 9–11 stands particularly close to the theology of *Liber Antiquitatum Biblicarum.* As we have seen, Pseudo-Philo charts a recurrent pattern of sin, divine abandonment in punishment, and divine restoration in mercy: despite Israel's repeated disobedience, God's covenant promises are irrevocable and his labor will not be "in vain." Paul also finds elements of a pattern: there is a parallel between the time of Elijah and his own (Rom 11:5-6), while Scripture announces a hardening like that of the present (11:8-10). Like *LAB,* Paul is confident that, ultimately, God will have mercy, and supports that confidence with appeal to the "covenant" (11:27), "the patriarchs" (11:28), and "election" (11:5, 28); in words that could have come from *LAB,* "the gifts and the calling of God are irrevocable" (11:29). Parallel to the "vine" in *LAB,* Paul has an "olive tree" as a central metaphor for the work of God in history (11:17-24).

In *LAB,* Israel as a vine stands apart from the other nations, who are considered of nugatory value before God ("like a drop from a pitcher . . . counted as spittle," *LAB* 7.3-4; 12.4). Paul's parallel metaphor, however, is developed to speak of the process by which non-Jews, from a "wild olive tree," are grafted into the succulent stock of the olive tree, while hope remains for the natural branches (11:17-24). Indeed, Paul's Gentile mission constitutes an integral part of the divine plan. Israel's sin has been instrumental in the salvation of the Gentiles, as the enrichment of the world (11:11-12); conversely, Paul's Gentile mission is instrumental in the salvation of Jews, provoking them to jealousy (11:11, 14). Paul's vision for the future of Israel thus includes the salvation of "the full number" of the Gentiles (11:25); God's mercy on Israel takes place by means of his mercy on the nations (11:28-32). Paul's hope for Israel is thus here disaggregated from the promise of the land, which took a central place in Pseudo-Philo's theology.

In *LAB,* Israel is integral to the purpose of creation, and the function of God's mercy is to *restore* the nation to its proper place in this plan. Paul's construal of the calling of the patriarchs (9:6-13) suggests a subtle difference: mercy goes all the way down to the origin and the root, as the very source of Israel's history. In this sense, mercy is for Paul not just restorative, but *creative:* it brings into being what was otherwise impossible, creating not just "reconciliation" but "life from the dead" (11:15). As in *LAB,* God's mercy is incongruous with the worth of its recipients; Romans 9–11 suggests that this is so not only because it has to be (in the face of universal disobedience) but because it was ever so even in the formation of Israel, and will remain so in the salvation of both Gentile and Jew.

As these five comparisons suggest, Paul participates in a number of Jewish conversations concerning God's beneficence toward Israel and the world, such that his themes, his questions, and many of his answers stand in close proximity to those of other Second Temple Jews. It would make little sense to say that he emphasizes grace *more* than other Jews of his time, but it is also clear that his views are not identical to those of the others surveyed, just as they disagree among themselves. If Paul's voice is consistently distinctive, that difference concerns the Christ-event and the Gentile mission, and the relation of both to the incongruous mercy of God. Such, at least, is the impression gained from our rapid comparative surveys, based on Romans 9–11. Our task is now to offer a deeper analysis of Paul's theology of grace, with a more complete reading of both Galatians and Romans. Conscious of the different ways grace can be construed — its various possible perfections, its varied deployment in Second Temple Judaism, and the freighted significance of certain perfections in the history of reception of Paul — we now attempt a new reading of key Pauline texts to ask if and how he perfected this theme, within what context, and to what end. A narrow focus on a single term would obviously yield too limited results, and in the search for a rounded understanding of Pauline theology we must commit ourselves to the study of these two letters as wholes. Wary of preconceptions about the meaning of "grace," and freed from the terms of analysis provided by Sanders and the post-Sanders debate, we can approach Paul's letters by asking afresh: what did *Paul* mean by grace?

PART III

Galatians: The Christ-Gift and the Recalibration of Worth

CHAPTER 11

Configuring Galatians

11.1. Gift in Galatians

Paul's explosive letter to the Galatians is replete with the language of gift. In the epistolary prescript, the greeting formula opens with the word χάρις (χάρις ὑμῖν καὶ εἰρήνη ἀπὸ θεοῦ πατρὸς ἡμῶν καὶ κυρίου Ἰησοῦ Χριστοῦ; "grace to you and peace from God our Father and the Lord Jesus Christ," 1:3). At the end, Paul signs off with a matching benediction, ἡ χάρις τοῦ κυρίου ἡμῶν Ἰησοῦ Χριστοῦ μετὰ τοῦ πνεύματος ὑμῶν, ἀδελφοί ("the grace of our Lord Jesus Christ be with your spirit, brothers," 6:18). Bracketing his letter in this way, Paul situates its contents within a movement of grace from God (and Christ) to the Galatians: all its arguments and appeals are intended not just to inform its recipients about this grace, but to place them within its transformative dynamic.[1] The opening greeting identifies this χάρις with the act of Jesus' self-giving (τοῦ δόντος ἑαυτὸν ὑπὲρ τῶν ἁμαρτιῶν ἡμῶν; "who gave himself for our sins," 1:4), a phrase possibly derived from early Christian tradition but clearly important to Paul; he later adapts it when speaking of "the Son of God who loved me and gave himself for me" (τοῦ ἀγαπήσαντός με καὶ παραδόντος ἑαυτὸν ὑπὲρ ἐμοῦ, 2:20). This self-giving of Christ, "the Christ-gift," is an event (note the aorist tenses), and refers here specifically to his self-donation in death. To the statement of 2:20 Paul immediately adds: "I do not repudiate the grace of God (οὐκ ἀθετῶ τὴν χάριν τοῦ θεοῦ); for if righteousness were through the

1. Galatians is, in this respect, typical of Paul's epistolary style (cf., for example, 1 Cor 1:3; 16:23; Phil 1:2; 4:23; Phlm 3, 25), but the phenomenon is nonetheless striking and, among ancient authors, uniquely Pauline. On the greeting formula of 1:3, see 12.1, below. On the letter to the Galatians (including its oral performance) as a gospel-event, see J. L. Martyn, *Galatians: A New Translation with Introduction and Commentary,* Anchor Bible 33A (New York: Doubleday, 1997), p. 23.

Law, Christ died for nothing" (2:21).[2] The self-giving death of Christ, here identified with (or as) "the grace of God," rules out an alternative, "righteousness through the Law." The same antithetical structure appears when Paul urges the Galatians against adopting circumcision, which entails commitment to the whole Law: "you have been invalidated, in disjunction from Christ, you who are justified in the Law; you have fallen out of grace" (κατηργήθητε ἀπὸ Χριστοῦ οἵτινες ἐν νόμῳ δικαιοῦσθε, τῆς χάριτος ἐξεπέσατε, 5:4). "Christ" and "grace" (associated by assonance in Greek: Χριστός and χάρις) are rhetorically and logically merged: to lose one is to lose the other.[3] In combination, they exclude "righteousness/justification in the Law" and thus forge one of the central polarities of the letter.

The language of gift is also prominent in the depiction of believers' experience. Paul rebukes the Galatians for deserting the one who "called you in the grace of Christ" (τοῦ καλέσαντος ὑμᾶς ἐν χάριτι Χριστοῦ, 1:6).[4] A few verses later, he describes his own experience as one set apart before birth whom God "called through his grace" (καλέσας διὰ τῆς χάριτος αὐτοῦ, 1:15). In both cases, theirs and his (Gentile and Jewish), the "calling" is an act of divine gift or favor, enacted in the announcement or the revelation of Christ. The promised Spirit (3:14) is also received by believers as a gift (ἵνα . . . δοθῇ τοῖς πιστεύουσιν, 3:22), the beginning of an inheritance once gifted to Abraham through a promise (τῷ Αβραὰμ δι' ἐπαγγελίας κεχάρισται ὁ θεός, 3:18); conversely, the Law is described not as "gifted" but "added" (3:19).[5] Finally, in an isolated use of the term "mercy" (ἔλεος), Paul wishes "mercy" on "the Israel of God" (6:16), a sentence whose construal remains hotly disputed (see below,

2. "For nothing" (δωρεάν) is another word from the gift-domain; the adverb had developed this meaning from the recognition that a gift could not guarantee a return, and thus might be characterized as "to nil effect." It would be a travesty of God's gift if the Galatians were to make it, in this sense, δωρεάν by refusing its transformative effects. For Paul's normal use of the adverb in the simpler sense "as a gift," see Rom 3:24; 2 Cor 11:7.

3. The assonance creates a chiastic relation between the flanking clauses of 5:4: κατηργήθητε ἀπὸ Χριστοῦ . . . τῆς χάριτος ἐξεπέσατε.

4. In some texts (P^{46vid}, G, H^{vid} and some Western Fathers) τοῦ Χριστοῦ is lacking, perhaps omitted by scribes to match the language of 1:16. Stronger external evidence supports the inclusion of the genitive, with the sense "enacted in Christ," or (in apposition) "which is Christ"; see M. C. de Boer, *Galatians: A Commentary,* New Testament Library (Louisville: Westminster John Knox Press, 2011), pp. 96-97.

5. In 3:21, Paul considers a hypothetical scenario: "if a law had been given that could make alive" (εἰ γὰρ ἐδόθη νόμος ὁ δυνάμενος ζῳοποιῆσαι), then indeed righteousness would come via the Law. But this was not the case, and "gift" is thus associated only with "promise" and "faith" (ἐδόθη, 3:21, echoed in δοθῇ, 3:22). The only divine benefits on the stage, as far as this letter is concerned, are the promises given to Abraham, their fulfillment in the Christ-event, and the transformative effects of that event in the work of the Spirit.

13.3.3). Thus, the main vocabulary for divine beneficence in Galatians is the normal Greek terminology for "gift" or "favor," with the sole exception of the biblically resonant phraseology of 6:16.[6]

The Christological configuration of the gift of God is clear from the very first sentences of Galatians. Paul reworks Jewish tradition throughout this letter, whose central chapters are thick with scriptural citations and allusions, but he interprets the divine beneficence celebrated in Judaism through the prism of the Christ-event. How does he use this motif — what we may call the "Christ-gift" — and what role does it play in the logic of the letter? Does Paul "perfect" grace in any of the ways we have identified (see chapter 2), and if so, how and why? Does the polarity between "grace" and "righteousness through/in the Law" in 2:21 and 5:4 represent a structuring principle of this letter, and if so, what does it mean? If Paul associates "grace" with his own calling and with the calling of the Gentiles, can it explain why he conducts his Gentile mission on apparently scandalous terms, and forms communities that are beholden not to the Torah but to "the law of Christ" (6:2)?

The following chapters (12-14) pursue these questions through a new reading of Galatians, following the argument of the letter more or less in sequence. The terrain is, of course, heavily contested and cluttered with exegetical argument, only some of which can be treated here. To set the scene, we must first determine the nature of Paul's conflict in Galatia (11.2). We may then collate the polarities that dominate Paul's configuration of the conflict (11.3), the antithetical formulations whose interpretation is decisive in any reading of the letter. We will finish this chapter by mapping four significant readings of Galatians (by Luther, Dunn, Martyn, and Kahl) whose differences serve to sharpen and deepen our questions concerning the meaning and effects of Paul's theology of grace (11.4).

11.2. The Conflict in Galatia

Paul writes to the Galatians in desperation (4:20), frustrated at his distance from the assemblies of believers who are receptive to a version of the "good news" different from his own (1:6). Our only certain source of information is this emotional letter, and much of the Galatian situation remains for us unknown and unknowable; nonetheless, we have just enough clues for a partial reconstruction.[7] The Galatian believers, largely of non-Jewish background

6. See the Appendix on the Lexicon of Gift.

7. On the problems and possibilities of "mirror-reading," see J. M. G. Barclay, "Mirror-

(4:8), are being persuaded to adopt key elements of the Jewish cultural tradition — most dramatically (for the menfolk), circumcision (5:2-6; 6:12-13; cf. 5:12).[8] Paul warns them of the implications of this move: a commitment to observe the whole Law (5:3). But it seems that Torah-observance is precisely what many of them want (4:21).[9] Naming this trend in general terms, Paul speaks of people being "considered righteous in the Law" (5:4), a phrase that implies their assessment that the Torah defines God's criteria of value (see below, 12.5). There is a hint in 4:10 ("you observe days, months, seasons, and years") that some are inclined to observe the Jewish calendar, embracing the Torah in its alignment with the structures of nature.[10]

This trend is influenced ("compelled," 6:12) by people Paul labels "your troublers" (1:7; cf. 5:10). It is not clear how they themselves viewed Paul, and it may be only from his perspective that they were his "opponents."[11] There are indications that these other missionaries in Galatia were also believers in Christ. Paul refers to their message as "another good news" (ἕτερον

Reading a Polemical Letter: Galatians as a Test Case," *JSNT* 31 (1987): 73-93; cf. J. L. Sumney, *Identifying Paul's Opponents: The Question of Method in 2 Corinthians* (Sheffield: JSOT Press, 1990) and idem, *"Servants of Satan," "False Brothers," and Other Opponents of Paul* (Sheffield: Sheffield Academic Press, 1999). A consensus of current scholarship supports the following reconstruction of the Galatian conflict, but the letter is often unclear (e.g., on the relationship between Jerusalem and Galatia), and many are tempted to go beyond the clearest evidence into overly speculative results.

8. See J. M. G. Barclay, *Obeying the Truth: A Study of Paul's Ethics in Galatians* (Edinburgh: T&T Clark, 1988), pp. 45-60 with further literature.

9. Ambiguous texts such as 5:3 and 6:13 have led some to challenge this reconstruction, but Paul's persistent argumentation against the regulative authority of the Torah is strong evidence in its favor; see Barclay, *Obeying the Truth,* pp. 60-72.

10. The terms used in 4:10 are non-specific (contrast Col 2:16) and could apply to almost any religious calendar. J. Hardin, *Galatians and the Imperial Cult,* WUNT 2.237 (Tübingen: Mohr Siebeck, 2008), pp. 116-47 (following T. Witulski, *Die Adressaten des Galaterbriefes: Untersuchungen zur Gemeinde von Antiochia ad Pisidiam* [Göttingen: Vandenhoeck & Ruprecht, 2000]) finds an allusion to the calendar of "the imperial cult." But the general terminology does not point clearly in that direction and seems designed to fit Paul's rhetorical charge: by adopting the Jewish calendar, the Galatians are reinstating a pattern of calendrical ritual like the one they followed, as pagans, before. They are thus *returning* to "slavery" to the "elements of the cosmos" (4:8-9); see M. C. de Boer, "The Meaning of the Phrase τὰ στοιχεῖα τοῦ κόσμου in Galatians," *NTS* 53 (2007): 204-24.

11. The question hangs on the extent to which Paul's narrative in Galatians 1–2 is read as apologetic in tone. He clearly rebuts an alternative version of his story (1:20), but it is not clear if that was hostile to Paul. On the problem of nomenclature, see M. D. Nanos, *The Irony of Galatians: Paul's Letter in First-Century Context* (Minneapolis: Fortress, 2002), pp. 115-31, proposing the neutral term "influencers." Martyn *(Galatians)* has popularized a different, unweighted label, "the Teachers."

εὐαγγέλιον, 1:6), a label he was unlikely to employ unless these others were at least speaking of Christ. Moreover, Paul's discussions and disputes with Jewish believers in 2:1-14 were probably recounted because of their parallels to the dispute in Galatia (see 2:5).[12] It is uncertain whether the other missionaries originated from, or were influenced by, the church in Jerusalem; it is possible that they followed Paul from Antioch (2:11-14), or were local believers of Jewish origin, or were newly circumcised themselves (6:13).[13] What is most significant for our purposes is that they saw no reason why the Christ-event should reduce or relativize the authority of the Torah. If they too appealed to Abraham, the patriarch could have modeled for them, as for Philo (see above, 6.4), the "migration" from idolatry to piety, and from vice to virtue (later given written articulation in the Mosaic Torah). From this perspective, there was every reason for Gentiles, once converted to the worship of the true and only God, to adopt the Abrahamic mark of circumcision and to obey the commands of God integral to the Abrahamic-Mosaic covenant.[14] The Christ-event constituted the climax of the covenant, the final chapter in God's plan

12. Nanos holds that "the influencers" were local *non-believing* Jews, thus judging the narrative in Galatians 1–2 only remotely parallel to the situation in Galatia (*Irony of Galatians*, pp. 62-72; on 2:5, see pp. 147-52). As Nanos insists, there is irony in Paul's reference to "another good news" (1:6), but εὐαγγέλιον denotes an announcement of news, not simply a "good message" as envisaged in Nanos's reconstruction (*Irony of Galatians*, pp. 11, 51-53, 141-42). An attempt to "distort (μεταστρέψαι) the good news concerning Christ" (1:7) sounds as if it was launched from some shared Christian premises (*contra* Nanos, *Irony of Galatians*, pp. 52-59, 285-316).

13. The present (passive or middle) participle, οἱ περιτεμνόμενοι, in 6:13 has led some to conclude that the leaders of the circumcision movement in the Galatian churches were themselves newly circumcised (J. Munck, *Paul and the Salvation of Mankind*, trans. F. Clarke [London: SCM, 1959], pp. 87-89), a thesis now revived by Nanos, *Irony of Galatians*, pp. 234-42, 277-82. But the evidence is extremely unclear: besides the textual uncertainty, there are numerous ways of reading the participle and the relationship of this clause to those before and after it; for details, see Barclay, *Obeying the Truth*, pp. 42-43. The connection between the Galatian missionaries and Jerusalem was foundational for F. C. Baur's interpretation of early Christianity, and is central to the reconstructions of the Galatian conflict by Martyn *(Galatians)*, F. Watson (*Paul, Judaism, and the Gentiles: Beyond the New Perspective* [Grand Rapids: Eerdmans, 2007]), and many others. But Paul seems slightly uncertain about their identity (3:1; 5:10) and does not draw the geographical or personal connections with Jerusalem that one might expect. Hardin argues for a local origin (*Imperial Cult*, pp. 92-94).

14. For the significance of Abraham in the Galatian conflict, see Barclay, *Obeying the Truth*, pp. 52-55; G. W. Hansen, *Abraham in Galatians: Epistolary and Rhetorical Contexts* (Sheffield: Sheffield Academic Press, 1989); N. Calvert-Koyzis, *Paul, Monotheism, and the People of God: The Significance of Abraham Traditions for Early Judaism and Christianity* (London: T&T Clark, 2004).

to redeem the world. The Galatian converts had begun well, but Paul had left them half-converted (3:3).[15]

Attempts to place this debate within the social and cultural context of Galatia are handicapped by uncertainty about the "Galatia" in question and by the paucity of evidence about the Galatian converts and their social and religious context. Several recent audience-related interpretations have sought to explain the attraction of the missionaries' persuasion by appeal to the Galatian context.[16] The antiquity, social recognition, and comprehensiveness of the Jewish "constitution" may certainly have given weight to their message.[17] It is doubtful whether religious honors given to the emperors had any special role in the crisis, either for the missionaries or for Paul's converts.[18] But Gentile believers who had abandoned their traditional religious practices were certainly vulnerable to social pressure, and one may imagine the Galatian be-

15. The Galatian debates thus run partly parallel to the disputes in the court of Adiabene regarding the circumcision of Izates (Josephus, *Ant.* 20.17-96); cf. Barclay, *Obeying the Truth,* pp. 55-56. P. Fredriksen appeals to biblical traditions on the eschatological inclusion of Gentiles that do not specify circumcision or Torah-observance ("Judaism, the Circumcision of Gentiles, and Apocalyptic Hope: Another Look at Galatians 1–2," *JTS* 42 [1991]: 532-64); but she is then hard pressed to explain why Paul's rivals in Galatia should make such demands.

16. See, e.g., S. Elliott, *Cutting Too Close for Comfort: Paul's Letter to the Galatians in Its Anatolian Cultic Context* (London: T&T Clark, 2003) on Anatolian Mother-cults, with convincing critique by Hardin, *Imperial Cult,* pp. 5-11.

17. For examples of Jewish self-presentation in the Diaspora, see Barclay, *Obeying the Truth,* pp. 56-60, 70-72, and idem, *Flavius Josephus: Translation and Commentary,* vol. 10: *Against Apion* (Leiden: Brill, 2007).

18. B. W. Winter (*Seek the Welfare of the City: Christians as Benefactors and Citizens* [Grand Rapids: Eerdmans, 1994], pp. 123-44; idem, "The Imperial Cult and Early Christians in Pisidian Antioch [Acts XIII 13-50 and Gal VI 11-18]," in T. Drew-Bear et al., eds., *Actes du Ier Congrès International sur Antioche de Pisidie* [Lyon: Kocaeli, 2002], pp. 67-75) and Hardin (*Imperial Cult,* pp. 85-115) have argued that the missionaries' attempt to avoid persecution and to "display a good face" (6:12-13) reflects pressure from civic authorities, shocked by their association with Gentiles who had deserted "the imperial cult" (cf. B. Kahl, *Galatians Reimagined: Reading with the Eyes of the Vanquished* [Minneapolis: Fortress Press, 2010], pp. 81-82, 226-27). But the letter attests to "persecution" only from Jewish sources (1:13, 23; 4:29; 5:11): like Peter in Antioch (2:12), the missionaries were probably under pressure from fellow Jews to dissociate from Gentile believers (4:17). The Galatian Gentiles would hardly reduce pagan pressure on themselves or their teachers by "judaizing" to the point of circumcision: proselytes were the object of heavy criticism for abandoning ancestral traditions and betraying their ethnicity (Juvenal, *Sat.* 14.96-106; Tacitus, *Hist.* 5.5.2; Josephus, *Ant.* 20.17-96; cf. Dio 67.14.1-2). The worship of the emperors was clearly a powerful social force *within the context of the larger pagan religious system* (see J. M. G. Barclay, *Pauline Churches and Diaspora Jews* [Tübingen: Mohr Siebeck, 2011], pp. 345-62). But there is no evidence in Galatians that it formed a distinct threat to Paul's converts.

lievers struggling to create, regulate, and defend a communal lifestyle that took its bearings from the Christ-event but had no precedent or social analogue. Their reception of Paul's message had disrupted their previous *habitus*, with its traditional customs and dispositions, but they had yet to develop a robust alternative. In this liminal and uncertain state, it was attractive to place their new convictions about Jesus, and their new experience of the Spirit, within the established matrix of the Jewish tradition.[19]

11.3. Pauline Polarities

Galatians is characterized by a starkly *antithetical* rhetoric: Paul typically sets before its hearers two, and only two, alternatives. The letter is riven by polarities, and the greatest challenge to interpreters is to work out how they are connected, and what they mean. In the very first verse, an antithesis emerges between "humans" and Christ/God: "Paul, an apostle, not from human beings or through a human agent, but through Jesus Christ and God the Father" (1:1). A few verses later, Paul insists that he serves not human beings but Christ: the good news he preaches does not match human criteria, and was received not through human agency but through a revelation of Christ (1:10-12). The "God-humanity" antithesis is here configured in Christological terms, in the light of a Christological "apocalypse" (1:13, 16). But this is not the only duality in the letter, and others pile up to complicate the picture. Paul narrates his story in a disjunctive, antithetical shape (1:11-17): once, in his former life "in Judaism," he persecuted "the assembly of God" (1:13); now he preaches "the faith" he attempted to destroy (1:23). There is no place for neutrality or indifference: there are two positions, and he has moved from one to the other. In Jerusalem, an agreement can be made on two missions representing the one (and only one, 1:6-7) good news (2:1-10), but there emerges here also a conflict between "freedom" and "slavery" (2:4-5), a polarity that will reverberate through chapter 4 (4:1-7, 9, 21-31) to reach its climactic expression in 5:1: "For freedom Christ has set you free; stand therefore and do not submit again to the yoke of slavery." For the Galatians, also, there is no middle position and no intermediate state: to "progress" to the Law (3:3) would be to *regress* to "slavery."

19. For the under-defined and therefore vulnerable ethos of early Christianity, cf. the analysis of the church in Corinth in S. Chester, *Conversion at Corinth: Perspectives on Conversion in Paul's Theology and the Corinthian Church* (Edinburgh: T&T Clark, 2003). As M. Murray, *Playing a Jewish Game: Gentile Christian Judaizing in the First and Second Centuries* C.E. (Waterloo, Ont.: Wilfrid Laurier University Press, 2004) has shown, many Gentile believers of the first two centuries found that "judaizing" made excellent social and religious sense.

In the context of the Antioch dispute, Paul introduces another antithesis: justification is either ἐξ ἔργων νόμου or ἐκ (or διὰ) πίστεως Ἰησοῦ Χριστοῦ (2:16; disputed phrases I leave untranslated for now). In various forms, this antithesis recurs throughout the letter, setting "Law" or "works of the Law" in antithetical relation to faith, Christ, or grace (2:19-21; 3:2, 5, 11-12, 23-25; 5:2-6). Apparently associated is the polarity between "flesh" and "Spirit" (3:3; 4:23, 29), which structures the paraenesis from 5:13 to 6:10. The climactic postscript (6:11-18) introduces yet more. Some take pride in "your flesh," but Paul takes pride only in the cross (6:13-14; cf. 5:11). "The world is crucified to me and I to the world" (6:14); in contrast to "the world," there emerges for the first time talk of a "new creation" (6:15).

God–humanity, Spirit–flesh, freedom–slavery, Christ–Law, πίστις Χριστοῦ–ἔργα νόμου, new creation–world: these dualities reverberate through Galatians and rhetorically polarize the Galatian options. Meanwhile, other apparent dualities are reduced to insignificance. The distinction between circumcision and uncircumcision, so important to Paul's rivals, is boldly declared irrelevant (5:6; 6:15), while the baptismal formula of 3:28 asserts that other kinds of duality are insignificant in Christ ("there is neither Jew nor Greek, neither slave nor free, no male and female"). Ethnic, status, and gender differentials are here considered unimportant for those who have "put on Christ," as if the new polarities created by the "good news" have rendered invalid the social binaries and hierarchies normally taken for granted.

Paul's letter to the Galatians thus remaps reality with a cartography capable of blurring traditional categories by means of newly minted distinctions.[20] These polarities take their bearings from the Christ-event: general terms such as "freedom," "Spirit," and "grace" (even "God") are here related to a Christological referent. The challenge for interpreters lies in the fact that these varied polarities are not always connected and do not self-evidently resolve into a single macro-contrast. How should we correlate and integrate what is merely juxtaposed? Does one polarity embrace and organize the others, and if so, which? Galatians has spawned a rich history of interpretation *and every reading is determined by the way it construes and organizes the polarities of the letter.*[21] This phenomenon will become clear as we survey four paradigmatic

20. See J. L. Martyn, "Apocalyptic Antinomies in Paul's Letter to the Galatians," *NTS* 31 (1985): 410-24: what Martyn terms "antinomies" are not just rhetorical constructs, but categories of reality by which Paul redescribes what is actually the case.

21. For an enthralling survey, see J. K. Riches, *Galatians through the Centuries* (Oxford: Blackwell, 2008). A compilation of patristic readings is provided by M. Meiser, *Galater* (Göttingen: Vandenhoeck & Ruprecht, 2007); for a selection from the medieval period, see I. C. Levy, *The Letter to the Galatians* (Grand Rapids: Eerdmans, 2011).

interpretations of Galatians (11.4) before offering our own reading of its organizing themes (chapters 12-14).

11.4. Four Readings of Galatians

What is Galatians most fundamentally about? We here survey four different answers to this question, each of which will form, to varying degrees, a dialogue partner for the reading that follows.

11.4.1. Luther

Martin Luther's interpretation of Galatians has exercised an enormous influence on Protestant readings of Paul, and remains influential today, not least through the neo-Lutheran revival of the early twentieth century.[22] We have already analyzed and contextualized Luther's reading of Paul (above, 3.3); drawing on that analysis, we focus here on his 1531 lectures on Galatians (published in 1535).[23] Luther's special affinity with this letter derives from his resonance with its antithetical style: the sharpness of Paul's polarities matched Luther's concern to make clear distinctions between matters that had become, in his view, disastrously confused.

Luther's introduction defines a polarity he considers basic to the argument of the letter, between "active" and "passive" righteousness. The former, righteousness in obedience to laws (human and divine) is not itself wrong, but is "clean contrary" to the righteousness spoken of in the gospel, a "passive righteousness" that we simply receive, since it is freely given by God through Christ.[24]

22. For analysis of Bultmann and Käsemann, see above, 3.5. Commentaries in the Lutheran/Bultmannian tradition include those by H. D. Betz (*Galatians,* Hermeneia [Philadelphia: Fortress Press, 1979]) and H. Schlier (*Der Brief an die Galater,* KEK [Göttingen: Vandenhoeck & Ruprecht, 1971]). Others drawing consciously on the Lutheran tradition include R. N. Longenecker (*Galatians,* Word Biblical Commentaries [Dallas: Word, 1990]), S. Westerholm (*Perspectives Old and New on Paul: The "Lutheran" Paul and His Critics* [Grand Rapids: Eerdmans, 2004]), and M. Silva ("Faith versus Works of Law in Galatians," in D. A. Carson, P. T. O'Brien, and M. A. Seifrid, eds., *Justification and Variegated Nomism,* vol. 2: *The Paradoxes of Paul* [Tübingen: Mohr Siebeck, 2004], pp. 217-48). The latter two add elements from "the new perspective" but resist its self-distancing from the "Lutheran" Paul.

23. English translation in *LW* 26–27; original in *WA* 40.1 and 40.2. An earlier series of lectures on Galatians (in 1516-17) was published by Luther in 1519 and revised in 1523 (see *LW* 27).

24. *LW* 26.4-12; "here we work nothing, render nothing to God; we only receive and permit someone to work in us, namely God" (5; *WA* 40.1 41.4-5).

Here, Luther articulates his configuration of the gospel as *the incongruous gift of God* in Christ: in the gospel Christ is neither Judge nor Lawgiver, but Savior, freely bestowing *his* righteousness on (permanently) unworthy sinners.

Luther thus highlights the theme of "righteousness" (justification) and organizes his reading of Galatians around the Pauline polarity between "works of the Law" and "faith in Christ" (2:16; 3:2, 5; 3:11-12; 5:4-6); the repetition of this antithesis in 2:16 occasions strong criticism of the forms of soteriology that Luther opposed.[25] Luther is well aware that Paul speaks in this letter about circumcision (and other *Jewish* practices), but he cannot agree with Jerome that the only issue is whether believers observe the "ceremonies" of the Jews.[26] For Luther, the issue is not the content of the law (which is good and right, in its proper place), but the construal of works *as the means to elicit God's grace.* Paul speaks here of the divine law (all of it, including the Decalogue), but what he says is applicable by extension to any "law" (even laws made by the church), inasmuch as they require obedience as a necessary means of salvation. Paul "shuts out the Jews, and all such as will work for their salvation" *(operarii).* Since he attacks a universal error, Paul's theology is directed against anyone ("whether he be a papist, a Jew, a Turk, or a sectarian") who "observes any rule, tradition, or ceremony with the opinion that thereby he will obtain the forgiveness of sins, righteousness, and eternal life."[27] As we noted above (3.3.2), it is the self-understanding of the person who does such works (the faulty understanding, corrupt motivation, and anxious or arrogant attitude that attends the working) that Luther contrasts with the proper understanding of salvation, *given* wholly, completely, and once for all in Christ.

"Faith in Christ," the phrase that Paul sets in contrast to "works of the Law," is significant not because of "faith" — for Luther, everyone has faith in (trusts in) something — but because of what faith grasps and receives, Christ. "Faith therefore justifies because it takes hold of and possesses this treasure, the present Christ. . . . Therefore the Christ who is grasped by faith and lives in the heart is the true Christian righteousness, on account of which God counts us righteous and grants us eternal life."[28] This "alien" righteousness, imputed not achieved, springs from the union with Christ effected by faith, such that Paul can say "it is no longer I who live, but Christ who lives in me" (Gal 2:20).

25. *LW* 26.122-41; *WA* 40.1 217-47.

26. *LW* 26.122-23; *WA* 40.1 218-19.

27. *LW* 27.9; *WA* 40.2 17-21.

28. *LW* 26.130; *WA* 40.1 229.22-30. For a recent exposition clarifying Luther's understanding of the "objective genitive," see J. A. Linebaugh, "The Christo-Centrism of Faith in Christ: Martin Luther's Reading of Galatians 2.16, 19-20," *NTS* 59 (2013): 535-44.

Paul's violent reaction against his rivals in Galatia matches Luther's own reaction to the "destruction" of the gospel: in both cases, the all-sufficient work of Christ as Savior has been usurped by an arrogant (or desperate) confidence in works.[29] There is a place for good works, as the fruit of justification, the effect of faith.[30] But everything hangs on making clear that justification (salvation) itself is not dependent on human works, but is complete by "faith alone" *(sola fide)* because it is effected by Christ alone *(solus Christus)*. In this sense, faith must be distinguished from love, since "this faith justifies without love and before love" *(haec fides sine et ante charitatem iustificat)*.[31]

Luther correlates the other antitheses in Galatians with this central polarity. "New creation" (6:15) signifies the "new creature" formed by union with Christ in faith: grace effects a "new man" whose standing before God is secure. This "new man" still lives "in the flesh" (2:19-20) and needs the discipline of the law to control the body for as long as he lives; "flesh" and "Spirit" are both realities of the Christian life (5:17). In fact, "flesh" can mean different things in different places, but at its most general means "the highest righteousness, wisdom, worship, religion, understanding, and will of which the world is capable."[32] All of this is fine in its proper place, but it must not be confused with the righteousness and wisdom of the gospel, in which the conscience is secure in Christ. Luther thus reads several Pauline antitheses as dialectical expressions of a twin, simultaneous reality. In their own persons, as embodied men and women, believers are sinners, necessarily subject to laws, and residents of the "old world"; but inasmuch as they are joined to Christ, they are justified, free from the law, and inwardly secure. This had dramatic consequences on the practical level: among other things, it undercut the rationale for celibacy. But the prime target of this gospel is "the conscience" or the "inner man." This is where Galatians locates freedom: "Christ has set us free, not for a political freedom or a freedom of the flesh but for a theological or spiritual freedom, that is, to make our conscience free and joyful, unafraid of the wrath to come."[33] It is here, first and foremost in the individual conscience, that Paul's theology of grace should be experienced as liberating good news.

29. "Therefore he who has strayed away from this Christian righteousness will necessarily relapse into the active righteousness; that is, when he has lost Christ, he must fall into a trust in his own works *(fiducia operum)*," *LW* 26.9; *WA* 40.1 48.31-33.

30. Luther thus responds to the criticism that his doctrine led to indifference regarding good works; for the common metaphor of the tree and its fruit, see, e.g., *LW* 26.155; *WA* 40.1 265.32.

31. *LW* 26.137; *WA* 40.1 239.16.

32. *LW* 26.140; *WA* 40.1 244.21-22.

33. *LW* 27.4; *WA* 40.2 3.22-24.

11.4.2. Dunn

James Dunn's reading of Galatians, a classic expression of "the new perspective" on Paul, is characterized by its concern to identify the ethnic dynamics in the historical situation of the letter: what Paul faced was "the attempt to enforce a uniform *Jewish* understanding of the gospel" by requiring Gentile converts to adopt specifically Jewish markers of identity (28).[34] The question raised by the rival missions in Galatia concerns how "Gentiles could come to share in the heritage of Abraham" and enter "the story of Israel" (65). Paul's theology differs from that of his rivals, but not because he was "anti-Jewish." His "call" is his commission to preach to Gentiles, not a "conversion" from Judaism (40-41), and he understands the story of Jesus to be "superimposed on the story of Israel to bring that story to its climax and focus" (44). Even Paul's emphasis on "justification by faith" represents no break with the assumptions of his opponents or of Jews in general: since all Jews believed in the "prevenience of grace" in their covenantal relationship with God, "we can recognize Paul's doctrine of 'justification by faith' to be a thoroughly Jewish doctrine. The Christian specific, 'by faith in Christ Jesus,' did not mark any fundamental shift in the thinking of Paul the Jew or Peter the Jew" (76).[35]

The difference between Paul and the other missionaries concerned the cultural practices to be required of Gentile converts. Since circumcision "embodied and expressed Jewish identity," its adoption by Gentile converts would require the "complete assimilation and absorption of distinctively Gentile identity into the status of Jewish proselyte," a form of "Jewish ideological and nationalistic imperialism."[36] When Paul contrasts "faith in Christ" with "works of the Law," the latter represents not the soteriology of self-achieved salvation, but the observance of Jewish covenantal obligations. In context (Gal 2:11-16) the phrase evokes the maintenance of *distinction* from non-Jews, especially through food laws, circumcision, and Sabbath-observance. Paul was not opposed in principle to the Jewish Law, which had a "continuing role" in the life

34. Dunn's readings of Galatians are multiple but coherent (e.g., "The New Perspective on Paul," *BJRL* 65 [1983]: 95-122; *The Theology of Paul's Letter to the Galatians* [Cambridge: Cambridge University Press, 1993]; *The Epistle to the Galatians,* Black's New Testament Commentaries [London: A&C Black, 1993]). The chief variations have been in his reading of "the works of the law," on which see Dunn, *The New Perspective on Paul: Collected Essays* (Tübingen: Mohr Siebeck, 2005), pp. 22-26. For the characteristics of the "new perspective," see above, 3.6.2. All references in parentheses are to Dunn, *Theology of Paul's Letter.*

35. On Dunn's dependence on Sanders, whose "covenantal nomism" emphasized the priority of grace, see above, 3.6.

36. Dunn, *Galatians,* pp. 265, 267.

of believers (45, 114-16 on Gal 5:14). What he objected to was the continuation of its boundary-preserving practices after the time of Christ, and the "over-evaluation" of such identity markers among his fellow Jews (95). This "over-evaluation" represents a "misunderstanding" of the Law, imposing a "narrow," "restrictive," and "exclusive" definition of the people of God, requiring "separation," "distinction," and "divisiveness."[37] Paul's antithesis between "flesh" and "Spirit" represents the contrast between an external, ethnic, or racial definition of membership in God's people and the inner transformation of a person's character (112-14, 130).[38]

The theological logic of Galatians is driven by two factors: Paul's scriptural reading (that the promise to Abraham was for *all the nations*, 3:8), and his conviction that Christ has introduced the era when the promise has reached fulfillment.[39] The cross marks this transition, as Christ was there "cursed" and placed among outsiders, like the Gentiles (86-87).[40] Of course, the other missionaries also spoke of Abraham and of the cross of Christ, but Paul considers the coming of Christ a more radical change on the basis of his *experience of the Spirit:* "a realized eschatology of such existential power was bound to relativize whatever had come before" (95). Paul's appeals to experience — his own (1:13-17) and that of his converts (3:1-5) — thus contribute crucially to the argumentative force of the letter.

It is characteristic of Dunn's "new perspective" reading that Galatians is placed in a historically specific context, that the focus rests not on the individual but on group (here, ethnic) relations, and that care is taken not to distance Paul from "Judaism" (see above, 3.6.2). The polarities of the letter resolve to a single question: is it necessary for Gentiles to "judaize" in order to belong to the people of God (2:14)? Although the "new perspective" generally pits itself against the "Lutheran" tradition, Dunn finds some common ground: he iden-

37. Cf. Dunn, "New Perspective," *passim; The Theology of Paul the Apostle* (Grand Rapids: Eerdmans, 1998), pp. 119, 147, etc. For the spatial metaphors in Dunn's "new perspective" and their relation to the social-political concerns of the 1960s and 1970s, see above, 3.6.2. While Dunn sometimes takes boundary-maintenance to be the "social function" of the Law (e.g., *New Perspective*, pp. 112-15), and thus a sociological necessity, he generally considers it a Jewish "misunderstanding." It is important for Dunn that, as an attitudinal mistake, this clears the Law itself, and Judaism in general, of any inherent fault; see R. B. Matlock, "Sins of the Flesh and Suspicious Minds: Dunn's New Theology of Paul," *JSNT* 72 (1998): 78-86.

38. Thus, the "freedom" to which Paul refers is the freedom "to express [the gospel] differently, with different emphases in different contexts" (*Theology of Paul's Letter*, p. 28).

39. Dunn refers to this transformation as an "apocalyptic transition" (*Theology of Paul's Letter*, pp. 61, 97), but his use of the adjective "apocalyptic" lacks the distinctive resonances to be found in Martyn (see below, 11.4.3).

40. Cf. Dunn, *New Perspective*, pp. 112-30.

tifies a shared emphasis on "the sufficiency of faith" (140-43) and makes appeal to "the unconditional character of the grace expressed in the gospel."[41] But, for Dunn, Paul's argument was directed not against a generalizable hermeneutic of works, as a means to salvation (Luther), but against "the assumption that ethnic origin and identity is a factor in determining the grace of God" (142). This is not a specific application of the Lutheran critique of "works"; it locates the focus of Paul's theology not in existential issues of conscience, trust, and motivation but in social attitudes toward ethnicity, community, and boundaries. On the basis of his historical construal of the Galatian conflict, Dunn insists that these were Paul's issues; that they have contemporary relevance is clearly also significant.[42]

11.4.3. Martyn

J. Louis Martyn's reading of Galatians is also founded on a precise historical reconstruction of the conflict between Paul and his rivals in Galatia ("the Teachers").[43] This is important in at least two ways. First, Martyn identifies many places where Paul echoes the Teachers' language or thought, and such reconstructions play a significant role in configuring the issues at stake.[44] Sec-

41. Dunn, *Galatians,* p. 265. Summarizing his work, Dunn insisted that he was not fundamentally at odds with Protestant concerns (*New Perspective,* pp. 17-22, 87-88); for analysis and evaluation, see Matlock, "Dunn's New Theology," pp. 82-86, and Westerholm, *Perspectives,* pp. 183-89. Those reading Paul from a Lutheran perspective (e.g., P. Stuhlmacher, *Revisiting Paul's Doctrine of Justification: A Challenge to the New Perspective* [Downers Grove: InterVarsity, 2001]) generally dispute Dunn's claim.

42. For the contemporary application of the "new perspective" see, e.g., Dunn, *New Perspective,* pp. 16-17, 34-36, 95-96, 196-97. The targets for criticism include Christian anti-Semitism, apartheid, and internal divisions within the church.

43. Martyn's interpretation of Galatians is best evidenced *in nuce* in J. L. Martyn, "Events in Galatia: Modified Covenantal Nomism versus God's Invasion of the Cosmos in the Singular Gospel: A Response to J. D. G. Dunn and B. R. Gaventa," in J. M. Bassler, ed., *Pauline Theology,* vol. 1: *Thessalonians, Philippians, Galatians, Philemon* (Minneapolis: Fortress Press, 1991), pp. 160-79, and Martyn, "The Apocalyptic Gospel in Galatians," *Interp* 54 (2000): 246-66; it is found in full in Martyn, *Galatians.* His work has influenced many recent readings of the letter, including R. B. Hays, "Galatians," in *New Interpreter's Bible,* vol. 11 (Abingdon: Nashville, 2000), pp. 181-348; S. Eastman, *Recovering Paul's Mother Tongue: Language and Theology in Galatians* (Grand Rapids: Eerdmans, 2007); and de Boer, *Galatians.*

44. For Martyn's reconstructions of the Teachers' message, see *Galatians,* pp. 117-27, 302-6, 399-40; at several points, his "disciplined freedom" stretches the evidence further than many would allow. The reconstructions serve to show that Paul "marches clean off the theological map of the Teachers, refusing their frame of reference altogether" ("Events in Galatia," p. 175).

ondly, in identifying the dispute as an intra-church conflict, Martyn limits the horizon of the letter: Paul targets Jewish-Christian missionaries, not Jews or Judaism, and his polemics must not be read as in any sense "anti-Judaic."[45]

On Martyn's reading, the central polarity in Galatians is that between divine and human agency (1:1, 10-12), encapsulated in the antithesis between "works of the Law" and "the faithfulness of Christ" (Martyn's translation of πίστις Χριστοῦ, 2:16; 3:2, 5, 22). Underlying this antithesis is the antinomy between "apocalypse" and "religion,"[46] two terms charged by Martyn with a special meaning. An "apocalypse" (the noun in 1:16; 2:2; its cognate verb in 3:23) is not so much an "unveiling" as a newly creative event — for Paul, God's powerful "invasion" of the world in the sending of Christ. Paul's "apocalyptic" theology thus maps a change in the cosmos effected by the coming of Christ, the outbreak of God's warfare against malignant and enslaving "powers," such as sin and flesh.[47] Its opposite is "religion," a term designating "human enterprise," and in particular the human attempt "to come to know God and to influence God."[48] In Galatians, Paul announces the liberating movement of God toward the world in Christ. What he opposes is the Teachers' requirement that Gentile believers *transfer* through Law-observance into the people of Israel, a human movement toward God that responds to God's *conditional* offer of a new possibility.[49]

These alternatives are encapsulated in Galatians 2:16, where Paul speaks of God's "rectifying" (δικαιόω) not ἐξ ἔργων νόμου but ἐκ πίστεως Χριστοῦ. ἔργα

45. Martyn thus shares the sensitivity of Dunn and Kahl (see below) in seeking to clear Paul of Christian hostility to Judaism: "the subject of church and synagogue lies beyond the letter's horizon" (*Galatians,* p. 40).

46. "To a great extent, the cosmic antinomy between religion and apocalypse is *the* issue of Galatians" (*Galatians,* p. 38). On Martyn's use of the term "antinomy," see *Galatians,* pp. 23, 570-74.

47. Martyn's definition of "apocalyptic" places emphasis not on an imminent future but on the present eschatological "turn" and the warfare it initiates; see Martyn, *Galatians,* pp. 97-105, and the analysis of Martyn offered above, 3.5.4.

48. Martyn, *Galatians,* pp. 37 n. 67, 38-41, 163-64; cf. idem, "Apocalyptic Gospel," p. 248 n. 4: "I use the terms 'religious' and 'religion' to speak of the various communal, cultic means — always involving the distinction of sacred and profane — by which human beings seek to know and to be happily related to the gods or God . . . religion is a human enterprise and thus the polar opposite of God's apocalyptic act in Christ." For Martyn's use of this term, and its Barthian origin, see above, 3.5.1 and 3.5.4.

49. This line of movement, for Martyn, characterizes not the Law as such (as practiced by Jews), but what is demanded of *Gentiles:* the Teachers hold that "Gentiles *can move,* by Law observance, *into* the covenant community" ("Events in Galatia," p. 167; italics original). Cf. *Galatians,* p. 100 n. 57: "At numerous points, the line of movement shows clearly the basic differences between the theology of Paul and that of the Teachers."

νόμου (Law-observances) are ruled out because they here represent "a merely human act," which is given salvific significance.[50] The contrasting phrase, πίστις Χριστοῦ, cannot signify an alternative human act, as traditionally understood (faith in Christ): it signifies, rather, the "faith (or faithfulness) of Christ," specifically his death on the cross (2:21).[51] "It is not by means of something the human being does — observe the Law — that God has elected to carry out his rectification, his making the human being right. God's means of rectification is solely the divine act of Christ's faith."[52] Paul can also speak of human faith (even in 2:16), but this is not a human initiative (to which God responds) but a human response elicited and kindled by the act of God in Christ.[53]

The other "antinomies" in Galatians cluster around this central polarity. The battle between the Spirit and the flesh (5:17) reflects the cosmic warfare; it would be a mistake to interpret Galatians 5–6 as offering a human choice between "two ways." The postscript announces in apocalyptic terms the end of the "cosmos" and the dawn of a new creation (Gal 6:14-15); at the hinge-point, the cross marks the singular and "punctiliar" interruption of time, not the climax of a "linear" story (of Israel) beginning before Christ.[54] Since the new creation is God's intervention "from outside,"[55] "grace" is "presuppositionless" and "without prior conditions."[56] The gospel announces this prevenient and generative movement of God toward humanity in the coming of Christ; it banishes the false expectation that humans can act competently or independently in movement toward God.[57]

Martyn pays close attention to the particulars of the Galatian crisis, but this specificity does not limit the message of Galatians: although the "works of the Law" are the specific Torah-observances required of Gentiles, they *represent* a more general failure to read the human situation in the wake of Christ.[58] The

50. Martyn, "Events in Galatia," p. 165; *Galatians*, p. 251.

51. Martyn, "Apocalyptic Gospel," p. 250: "From the epistle's beginning to its end, Paul draws contrasts not between two human alternatives, such as works and faith, but rather between acts done by human beings and acts carried out by God (1:1; 6:15)."

52. Martyn, *Galatians*, p. 252.

53. Martyn, *Galatians*, pp. 271, 276, 289.

54. Martyn, "Events in Galatia," pp. 166-76.

55. Martyn, *Galatians*, p. 39.

56. Martyn, "Events in Galatia," p. 177; *Galatians*, pp. 164, 271. Cf. *Galatians*, pp. 87-88: "The gospel is God's grace because it is the good news that, quite apart from human activity, and specifically in spite of the development of religion, God has acted in Christ to bring people into the 'space' of the new creation . . . not a single thing that humans can do could possibly serve as the fountainhead of their redemption."

57. For further analysis of Martyn's theology of grace, see above, 3.5.4.

58. Thus, for Martyn, the central question of the letter is not (as for Dunn) "how do

divine-human polarity concerns opposing *points of origin* (lines of movement from God or from humanity), rather than, as for Luther, alternative *objects of trust.* The question of agency, especially the generative locus of human agency, bears the primary weight. The difference between the traditional reading of πίστις Χριστοῦ as "faith in Christ" and Martyn's (and others') "subjective genitive" reading ("the faithfulness of Christ") is considered "monumental,"[59] since the whole theology of the letter is here at stake. On one side of Paul's polarity stands a singular event, God's intervention in history in the coming of Christ; on the other is *any initiative toward God* that represents a "merely human activity."[60] Unlike Luther, Martyn does not focus on individuals' understanding of themselves and their work, or the freedom or captivity of their consciences. But he takes Paul to address the *general structure of relations between humanity and God* in the wake of an act that has changed the objective structures of the cosmos — and thus any action "on the human side of the divine-human antinomy."[61] Such a reading of Galatians is readily universalized.

11.4.4. Kahl

Brigitte Kahl's "contextual re-imagination" of Galatians[62] starts from the premise that the name "Galatia" evokes a set of cultural tropes in Paul's Roman environment: "Galatia" represents the threat to "civilization" from "barbarous lawlessness," a threat symbolically subdued in visual representations of dying Gauls/Galatians, and in the victory of the gods over the giants, as displayed on the Great Altar of Pergamon. Having described this loaded visual culture, Kahl reads Paul's "good news" as a theo-political intervention. Here the world is viewed from the underside, from the viewpoint of the vanquished "Galatians," as a challenge to the imperial order. What unites Paul's various polarities is, for Kahl, a macro-contrast between the imperial "combat order," characterized by competition, violence, and conquest, and a communal vision of love, inclusivity, and solidarity with "the other."[63]

Gentiles enter the people of God?" but "What time is it?" or "In what cosmos do we actually live?" (*Galatians,* p. 23). For his response to Dunn's reading of the letter, see esp. Martyn, "Events in Galatia."

59. Martyn, "Apocalyptic Gospel," p. 250.

60. Martyn, "Events in Galatia," p. 165.

61. Martyn, "Events in Galatia," p. 165.

62. Kahl, *Galatians Reimagined,* p. 75; numbers in parentheses refer to pages in Kahl, *Galatians Reimagined.*

63. For a similar reading of Paul as "apostle to the conquered," see D. C. Lopez, *Apostle*

In reaction to common readings of Galatians, which pit Paul against some form of Judaism, Kahl interprets the conflict in Galatia to concern complicity with, or opposition to, the *Roman* order. The other missionaries are advocating circumcision and Torah-observance, but not for genuinely Jewish reasons: under pressure from Roman or civic authorities, they are encouraging Paul's Galatian converts, who have boycotted the imperial cult, to regularize their position by becoming proper Jews.[64] At base, therefore, Paul's issue is not with Torah-observance but with a compromised Judaism operating under Roman control. When Paul disqualifies "works of the law," he is attacking first and foremost "works of the (imperial) law" (205), "the law of empire" (207), and the "good works" of Roman euergetism, which manipulate beneficiaries into political compliance (10, 196). "The law Paul confronts is not Jewish law as such, but Jewish law in enforced servitude to Roman law" (227).[65]

Thus Paul's real battle in Galatians is against Rome, or more precisely against Rome *qua* "imperial order." Liberally applying the adjective "imperial," Kahl reads Paul's target not as one historical empire, but as any system of "imperial" power that perpetrates violence, competition, hierarchy, and exclusion. Paul's allegiance to the One God of the Jewish tradition ("the nonimperial God of Abraham and Sarah," 223) draws him into opposition to all forms of "idolatry," and specifically the imperial cult: this "idolatry" constitutes an "ideology" (245) making global and exclusive claims for an "imperial monotheism" (130), and offering a "gospel of imperial salvation" (225) in the interests of "imperial

---

to the Conquered (Minneapolis: Fortress Press, 2008). For a sample of political readings of Paul that draw on postcolonial theory, see C. Stanley, ed., *The Colonized Apostle: Paul through Postcolonial Eyes* (Minneapolis: Fortress Press, 2011).

64. This reading of 6:12-13 (Kahl, *Galatians Reimagined,* pp. 81-82, 226-27) is dependent on Hardin, *Imperial Cult,* pp. 85-115; for critique, see above, note 18.

65. Like Hardin, *Imperial Cult,* Kahl takes Galatians 4:10-11 to depict a return to the imperial cult (pp. 220-21, 225). Since Rome is nowhere mentioned in Galatians, Kahl appeals to Scott's notion of "the hidden transcript" (a message the oppressed cannot afford to air in public; see J. C. Scott, *The Weapons of the Weak: Everyday Forms of Peasant Resistance* [New Haven: Yale University Press, 1985] and *Domination and the Arts of Resistance: Hidden Transcripts* [New Haven: Yale University Press, 1990]; Kahl, *Galatians Reimagined,* pp. 48, 82, 250-52). This requires the supposition that Paul's letters were subject to scrutiny by spies and informers (pp. 251-52, 257), such that we nowhere see what Paul really thought about the political implications of his gospel. As I have argued elsewhere (Barclay, *Pauline Churches,* pp. 382-83), Scott's model does not fit letters written to insiders, and there is no reason to suspect that Paul's letters mask what he truly thought (or said in private). Kahl's thesis hypothesizes that Paul attacks a target he never names, which requires a further hypothesis as to why he never names it. The strain this puts on exegesis is evident in her reading of the "mediator" of Galatians 3:19 as "Caesar or any other imperial ruler" (*Galatians Reimagined,* pp. 227, 238, 283); this seems exegetically unsupportable, since the law here mediated is dated 430 years after Abraham (3:17).

law and order" (224). Paul's allegiance to the vanquished Christ, scandalously raised by God, sets him in opposition to "the imperial battle order and its law of conquest and subjugation" (259). "Rome" thus embodies for Kahl every "imperial law of segregation, competition, and combat" (302), in particular the "Western aggressive self" (6) and the "occidental semiotics of combat" (15), which she finds replicated in "Constantinian" Christianity and lurking at the roots of conquest, colonialism, and every form of "othering" (6-17).

On this reading, Galatians expresses a clash of socio-political ideologies. Paul's vision of community (articulated in Galatians 5–6) represents peace-making and border-crossing inclusion, in which competitive "boasting" is outlawed and the self is fulfilled in self-giving for the other.[66] In line with recent trends to give due weight to Galatians 5–6, Kahl acclaims this passage as "the climax of the letter" (269); she thus corrects an "abstract" and "non-political" tradition of interpretation (6-7, 20-21) that fosters a "disembodied" (27) or "otherworldly" theology (256). Recovering Paul's vision of "an alternative community and commonality" (246), Kahl takes Paul's theology to legitimate a self-giving, non-violent solidarity with the poor, the victim, and the excluded.

Here are four contrasting readings of Galatians, each with significant insights into the letter, but clearly incompatible in multiple ways. They differ not just in the degrees of emphasis they give to the original context of the letter, but in the ways they read that context, and the connections they draw between it and the contemporary concerns of the interpreter. They integrate the polarities of the letter in very different ways, and even where they agree on its central polarity, they interpret this differently. It is not hard to detect the *constructive* work of the interpreter as each attempts to correlate the varied themes of the letter; the reading of Galatians that now follows (chapters 12-14) is unashamedly also a constructive labor of interpretation. We are forced to ask ourselves again what Galatians is truly about, with specific interest in how the divine gift in Christ structures the theology of the whole. Was Luther right to conclude that Paul here perfects the incongruity of grace, and if so, did he draw from this the right deductions? Is Dunn correct in making ethnic division the focal point of the letter, and has he identified a way to connect Paul's resistance to Gentile "judaizing" with the impact of the gift of Christ? What does Paul imply by the polarity between God and humans, and is Martyn right to make agency and "line of movement" the central issue of the letter? How does Paul shape

66. See especially the diagram of "the Messianic Order of One-an(d)-Other" (*Galatians Reimagined*, p. 268), which stands in contrast to the "combat squares" used elsewhere to diagram the opposition of imperial order to the "otherness" of lawlessness.

a communal ethos in this letter, and has Kahl correctly grasped its social and political dimensions?

In what follows I will argue that Paul's theology in Galatians is significantly shaped by his conviction, and experience, of the Christ-gift, as the definitive act of divine beneficence, given *without regard to worth*. By its misfit with human criteria of value, including the "righteousness" defined by the Torah, the Christ-event has recalibrated all systems of worth, creating communities that operate in ways significantly at odds with both Jewish and non-Jewish traditions of value. This incongruous gift has subverted previous measurements of symbolic capital, establishing its own criteria of value and honor that are no longer beholden to the authority of the Torah. The Christ-event *as gift* is thus the foundation of Paul's Gentile mission, in which Paul resists attempts to reinstitute preconstituted hierarchies of ethnic or social worth, and forms alternative communities that take their bearings from this singular event. This reading of the letter will overlap in varying degrees with each of the four outlined above, while differing also from them all. It is required to be exegetically robust, historically plausible, and successful in integrating the various polarities of the letter. But it is also proper to ask whether the reading thus produced is coherent and productive in our own contemporary context, and capable of replicating, at least in part, the explosive power of this letter.

CHAPTER 12

The Christ-Gift and the Recalibration of Norms (Galatians 1–2)

12.1. Greeting in Grace (1:1-5)

The epistolary prescript of Galatians (1:1-5) follows a standard pattern and is replete with stock Christian phraseology, but Paul has shaped it into an expression of the dynamic that characterizes his "good news."[1] He immediately defines the source of his apostleship: "not from human beings nor through a human agent, but through Jesus Christ and God the Father . . ." (1:1). Besides perhaps countering alternative accounts of his disputed apostleship,[2] this expression aligns himself — and the "good news" of which he is an apostle — with the divine initiative announced in 1:3-4, an initiative of "grace" (χάρις) and "peace" (εἰρήνη) "from God the Father and the Lord Jesus Christ. . . ." This formula may be read simply as a wish (or blessing) bestowed on the Galatians (cf. the matching closure in 6:18). But the fact that it here, uniquely, prefaces a statement of the Christ-event (1:4), with a closing doxology (1:5), suggests that Paul wishes to place himself and the churches in Galatia within a narrative line and an experiential relationship: the grace that issues from "God-and-Christ" has decisively altered the cosmos, effecting a "rescue from the present evil age" that elicits, in return, a human ascription of glory to God. Placing himself

1. Early Christian formulae here probably include "God who raised [Jesus] from the dead" (1:1); "grace and peace" (1:3); "who gave himself" (1:4; cf. 2:20); "for our sins" (1:4); "to whom be glory for ever and ever" (1:5). I translate εὐαγγέλιον (1:6, 11, etc.) as "good news" to preserve the force of the Greek, which suggests the announcement of an *event*, not of a general truth.

2. An alternative and perhaps hostile opinion, that his apostleship derived from Antioch or Jerusalem, is imaginable (see M. C. de Boer, *Galatians: A Commentary*, New Testament Library [Louisville: Westminster John Knox Press, 2011], pp. 67-71). The denials of 1:10 and 1:20 may also have apologetic purpose (cf. H. D. Betz, *Galatians*, Hermeneia [Philadelphia: Fortress Press, 1979], ad loc.).

and the Galatians jointly ("us") as the beneficiaries of this movement of gift or favor, Paul prompts a communal "Amen" (1:5) as an affirmation that together they owe their existence to this transformative event.[3]

The formula χάρις καὶ εἰρήνη (1:3) is uniquely Pauline as an epistolary salutation, and it is here loaded with semantic content specific to the Christ-story.[4] Paul wishes (or proclaims) "χάρις and εἰρήνη from God the Father and the Lord Jesus Christ," the one preposition (ἀπό) serving for both persons (cf. 1:1), such that the source of favor-and-peace is simultaneously God and Jesus.[5] Moreover, this gift is given Christological content (Christ "gave himself for our sins," 1:4), just as God was earlier associated with Jesus, as the Father "who raised him [Jesus] from the dead" (1:1). The gift is thus identified as a gift-event, focalized in the specific story of Jesus' death and resurrection. This event is emphatically both a God-event (God raised Jesus, 1:1; Jesus' rescue-mission was "according to the will of God our Father," 1:4) and a Jesus-event (it takes place in his death and resurrection), such that Christ is here "integral to the identity and the activity of God."[6] This Christological specification amounts to a highly particular and, in Jewish terms, unprecedented interpretation of "grace." God's beneficence is here traced not in the gifts of nature (Philo), nor in the covenant history of Israel (*LAB;* or of the righteous: *The Wisdom of Solomon*), nor even in the gift of the Torah *(4 Ezra):* it took place in a specific but world-changing event, the death and resurrection of Christ.[7]

3. Cf. J. L. Martyn, *Galatians: A New Translation with Introduction and Commentary,* Anchor Bible 33A (New York: Doubleday, 1997), pp. 92, 106. Since this letter lacks the normal expression of "thanksgiving" to God (1 Thess 1:2, etc.), the doxology also articulates a return movement in the "circle of grace" (from God, among humans, back to God in thanks or praise): giving glory to God is the equivalent of giving God thanks (Rom 1:21). If the Galatians now "reject" the grace of God (2:21), they will fall out of this gift-cycle (5:4) and return to a condition of impoverishment, dislocated from God (4:8-11).

4. The closest parallel is "mercy and peace be to you" in *2 Baruch* 78.2 (whose Greek source probably read ἔλεος καὶ εἰρήνη). See the definitive treatment in L. Doering, *Ancient Jewish Letters and the Beginnings of Christian Epistolography* (Tübingen: Mohr Siebeck, 2012), pp. 406-15, canvassing all the possibilities for the source of Paul's language, and highlighting Paul's choice of the gift-term χάρις and his Christological modifications of a Jewish tradition of salutation. See further J. M. Lieu, " 'Grace to You and Peace: The Apostolic Greeting,' " *BJRL* 68 (1985-86): 161-78; F. Schnider and W. Stenger, *Studien zum neutestamentlichen Briefformular* (Leiden: Brill, 1987), pp. 28-33.

5. The terms may be arranged as a chiasm, with χάρις and Χριστός as the outer pair (connected by assonance; cf. 5:4), containing the inner pair of "peace" and "God" (cf. Rom 5:1-2). But the unity is emphatic, with the same preposition governing both God and Christ.

6. De Boer, *Galatians,* p. 78.

7. Paul's use of rhetorical shorthand or synecdoche (see M. M. Mitchell, "Rhetorical Shorthand in Pauline Argumentation: The Function of 'the Gospel' in the Corinthian Cor-

A singular gift here embraces both Jews (Paul) and non-Jews (the Galatians), redeeming them from the grip of "the present evil age" (cf. 6:14). By what rationale? Why should the Christ-gift be directed to these hapless beneficiaries? Paul's pessimism regarding "the present evil age" is parallel to that of *4 Ezra* (see above, chapter 9), and might have left room for a tiny minority of righteous individuals. On that basis, Christ would have rescued "one grape out of a cluster, and one plant out of a great forest" (*4 Ezra* 9.21). But this opening statement of Paul's "good news" does not signal any such selection of the righteous, and nothing in the rest of the letter will indicate that the recipients of the Christ-gift were qualified to receive it. Is there a hidden pre-constituted rationale for God's benevolence toward these trapped and sinful beneficiaries? Or is it precisely the absence of that rationale that makes Paul's good news so creative?

12.2. The Good News and the Disjunction of Divine from Human Norms (1:6-12)[8]

Paul's opening rebuke, charging "defection" from "the one who called you in the grace of Christ" (1:6-7), makes clear that in his view there is one, and only one, "good news," the "good news of Christ" (1:7). This news announces an event that is incomparable and singular in its effect. The anathemas of 1:8-9 indicate that Paul is concerned with the content rather than the mediator of this news: counterfeit news is excoriated even if Paul, or an angel, were to be the messenger (1:8). The critical issue is the source of this news, since source determines content and establishes its norms. Even if encountered via a human agent, the good news of Christ (1:7) derives from a revelation of Christ (1:12; cf. 1:1, 16): it therefore constitutes its recipients as beholden to Christ (as "slaves of

respondence," in L. A. Jervis and P. Richardson, eds., *Gospel in Paul: Studies on Corinthians, Galatians, and Romans for Richard N. Longenecker* [Sheffield: Sheffield Academic Press, 1994], pp. 63-88) enables him to refer to the whole story of Christ (his "sending," birth, life, death, and resurrection) by any one of these items, or by the dynamic (self-giving) that permeates them all. Galatians is marked by a special emphasis on the crucifixion (2:19-20; 3:1, 13; 5:24; 6:14), which signals the disjuncture created by the Christ-event. The resurrection (1:1) is presupposed throughout as the source of the "life" (cf. 2:19-20; 3:21; 5:25; 6:8) or "new creation" (6:15) generated therein.

8. Rhetorical analysis might suggest that a new section of the letter begins at 1:11 ("I make known to you"), which opens an account of Paul's life running into chapter 2. But 1:11-12, like 1:10, has a transitional function and shares the divine-human polarity of 1:10. Commentators remain divided over where to place breaks in Paul's argumentative flow (see Betz, *Galatians*, pp. 44-46; de Boer, *Galatians*, pp. 63-65, 76).

Christ," 1:10) and countermands other values defined in merely human terms (1:10). Paul bears witness not to general truths about the nature of God or the constitution of the cosmos, but to a "singular universal," a particular historical event that has redefined and re-divided the whole of reality.[9]

In wavering from their alignment to this event, the Galatians are deserting not Paul but "the one who called you in the grace of Christ" (1:6).[10] Such "calling" is issued by God (cf. 1:15; 5:8; 1 Thess 5:24; 1 Cor 1:9; 7:17-24). Indeed, "calling" (καλέω, κλῆσις) is Paul's favorite terminology for the saving initiative of God, which creates new realities without regard to conditions of capacity, status, or moral worth (cf. Rom 4:17; 9:6-12; 1 Cor 1:26-28; 7:17-24).[11] That incongruous dynamic is evident in the case of the Galatians. Before their "calling," they were ignorant of God, enslaved to "no-gods" (4:8-9); as Gentiles, they were "sinners," without relation to the Law (2:15). They have now come to know God, but not on the basis of their epistemological capacity. In 4:9, Paul makes a point of correcting himself when describing their history: "having come to know God, or rather having been known by God" (γνόντες θεόν, μᾶλλον δὲ γνωσθέντες ὑπὸ θεοῦ). He thus parades a divine initiative that bears no relation to human progress toward the truth.[12] They have received God's Spirit, though not because of prior (even partial) alignment to "righteousness" through practice of the Torah (3:2, 5). God's calling is qualified only and simply by the phrase ἐν χάριτι Χριστοῦ. In Pauline discourse, χάρις appears to have acquired a particular perfection: it functions without regard to the worth of its recipients.

9. On the "universalism" created by an unconditioned event, see A. Badiou, *Saint Paul: La Fondation de l'Universalisme* (Paris: Presses Universitaires de France, 1997; E.T. *Saint Paul: The Foundation of Universalism*, trans. R. Brassier [Stanford: Stanford University Press, 2003]) (discussed in 3.7.2 above). For Paul's redefinition and re-division of reality, see J. L. Martyn, "Apocalyptic Antinomies in Paul's Letter to the Galatians," *NTS* 31 (1985): 410-24.

10. On the text, which should include τοῦ Χριστοῦ, see above, page 332, n. 4. The preposition ἐν may be instrumental ("through grace"; cf. 1:15: διὰ τῆς χάριτος), or locative ("in the sphere of the Christ-gift"). For the first alternative, see R. N. Longenecker, *Galatians*, Word Biblical Commentaries (Dallas: Word, 1990), p. 15; for the second, Betz, *Galatians*, p. 48; de Boer, *Galatians*, p. 100, with reference to 1 Corinthans 7:15; 1 Thessalonians 4:7.

11. On Paul's "calling" language, see S. Chester, *Conversion at Corinth: Perspectives on Conversion in Paul's Theology and the Corinthian Church* (Edinburgh: T&T Clark, 2003), pp. 59-112; on its use in Romans 9–11, see B. R. Gaventa, "On the Calling-into-Being of Israel: Romans 9:6-29," in F. Wilk and J. R. Wagner, eds., *Between Gospel and Election: Explorations in the Interpretation of Romans 9–11* (Tübingen: Mohr Siebeck, 2010), pp. 255-69.

12. By contrast, Philo portrays the proselyte as one who (like Abraham) migrates toward the truth, and is properly rewarded by God (see above, 6.4). For *Wisdom*'s confidence that Gentiles should be able to deduce the nature of God from observation of the cosmos, see *Wisdom* 13.1-10.

The Galatians' experience thus suggests the counterintuitive character of the Christ-gift. In issuing accusations and anathemas (1:6-9), Paul consciously disregards the criteria that carry persuasive force in normal human discourse: "am I now persuading human beings, or God?" (1:10). Like every practitioner of rhetoric, Paul knew that "persuasion" is effective only when it deploys the normative criteria cherished by one's audience (cf. 1 Cor 1:18–2:16). Philosophers criticized rhetoric on just such grounds, charging "sophistic" discourse with appealing to popular and degraded norms.[13] Like them, Paul eschews crowd-pleasing, but the "crowd" whose opinion he dismisses is not the uneducated populace, but humanity as a whole: his arguments do not count for much among human beings, but they count before God.[14] In his rhetoric, as in his practice, Paul's allegiance is to Christ: "if I were still pleasing human beings, I would not be a slave of Christ" (1:10). Although Paul will celebrate "the freedom which we have in Christ Jesus" (2:5; 5:1), it is clear from this early declaration of "slavery" that what he means by freedom is the consequence of an allegiance to norms newly constituted in Christ.

The "good news" thus realigns and recalibrates Paul's loyalties: announcing the incongruous gift enacted in Christ, he is at odds with the normative conventions that govern human systems of value. Hence the emphatic statement of 1:11: "I want you to know that the good news announced by me is not in accord with human norms" (οὐκ ἔστιν κατὰ ἄνθρωπον).[15] This negation is of central significance to the theology of the letter.[16] It signals a relation of misfit, even contradiction, between the "good news" and the typical structures

13. For discussion in relation to 1 Corinthians 1–2, see B. Winter, *Paul and Philo among the Sophists: Alexandrian and Corinthian Responses to a Julio-Claudian Movement*, 2nd ed. (Grand Rapids: Eerdmans, 2002), and D. Litfin, *St. Paul's Theology of Proclamation: 1 Corinthians 1–4 and Greco-Roman Rhetoric* (Cambridge: Cambridge University Press, 2004).

14. That Paul *is* committed to "persuading" (or pleasing) God (i.e., that the "or" in 1:10a is truly disjunctive) is evident from the antithesis that immediately follows, between pleasing humans or serving Christ, and from the God–humanity polarity of 1:1, 11-12; cf. 1 Thess 2:4-6. See Martyn, *Galatians*, pp. 137-40; de Boer, *Galatians*, pp. 139-41; B. G. Lyons, *Pauline Autobiography: Towards a New Understanding* (Atlanta: Scholars Press, 1985), pp. 136-46 (*pace* Betz, *Galatians*, pp. 54-55; J. D. G. Dunn, *The Epistle to the Galatians*, Black's New Testament Commentaries [London: A&C Black, 1993], pp. 48-50).

15. NRSV unaccountably translates this phrase "not of human origin," assimilating it to παρὰ ἀνθρώπου in the following verse (1:12); many commentators follow suit (e.g., de Boer, *Galatians*, p. 162).

16. Paul elsewhere uses κατὰ ἄνθρωπον with reference to human patterns of speech (Gal 3:15; Rom 3:5; 1 Cor 15:32) or human behavior (1 Cor 3:3; 9:8; Rom 7:22). Martyn's paraphrase ("this is not what human beings normally have in mind when they speak of 'good news' ") unnecessarily limits the interpretation to the conceptual oddity of Paul's message (*Galatians*, pp. 136, 142; cf. 146-48).

of human thought and behavior.[17] The good news stands askance to human norms because its origin lies outside the human sphere: it was not received from human authority, nor delivered by human instruction, but came "through a revelation of Jesus Christ" (1:12). Paul's message is not the result of human ratiocination; it is not a cultural product in the way of every human idea. Its origin as "other" founds the "otherness" of its cognitive and behavioral norms. Paul's οὐ κατὰ ἄνθρωπον signals the capacity of the good news to challenge every value-system and every pre-formed tradition, including Paul's own.

Denying that he *still* pleases human beings (1:10), Paul implies that he had previously done just that, in the "former" life he is about to describe.[18] Since the good news distinguishes divine from human norms, the narrative that follows takes a surprising shape: loyalty to God proved to be unexpectedly at odds with Paul's upbringing and tradition (1:13, 14). Because Paul places a Christologically defined polarity between "God" and "the human" as the heading to his life story, we may expect that this narrative will contain striking abnormalities by the standards of his fellow Jews.

12.3. Paul's Call as the Drama of an Incongruous Gift (1:13-24)

The narrative that begins in 1:13 (and continues until 2:21) undoubtedly contains apologetic elements (cf. 1:20), reflecting the fact that Paul's story was variously narrated (1:23; cf. Acts 8–26). But Paul also offers a paradigm — not that the Galatians could imitate his story as a Jew or as an apostle, but because Paul's biography and the pattern of his ministry model the reorientation effected by an encounter with Christ.[19] Since the reported reaction to Paul's

17. This principle *includes* Paul's capacity to critique the hegemonic systems of the Roman Empire, but is not restricted to that domain; Kahl's reading of Galatians (see above, 11.4.4) thus unwittingly limits the range of Paul's critical perspective.

18. There may be an additional apologetic tone, if Paul rebuts criticism that he tailors his lifestyle to suit his cultural context; see Dunn, *Galatians*, pp. 48-49. But the parallels in Romans 2:29, where a "Jew" is (re)defined as one whose praise comes from God, not humans, indicates that Paul is thinking broadly of the transformation in his own system of values.

19. The paradigmatic purpose is recognized by Lyons, *Pauline Autobiography*, though he wrongly suggests that Paul offers himself as an ideal for imitation. For a better reading, see J. H. Schütz, *Paul and the Anatomy of Apostolic Authority* (Cambridge: Cambridge University Press, 1975), pp. 114-58; B. R. Gaventa, "Galatians 1 and 2: Autobiography as Paradigm," *NTS* 28 (1986): 309-26; and B. Lategan, "Is Paul Defending His Apostleship in Galatians?" *NTS* 34 (1988): 411-30. For an earlier treatment of this passage, see J. M. G. Barclay, "Paul's Story: Theology as Testimony," in B. W. Longenecker, ed., *Narrative Dynamics in Paul* (Louisville: Westminster John Knox Press, 2002), pp. 136-46.

story is praise *to God* (1:24), and since its turning point is effected by the decision and the call *of God* (1:15), the tenor of this account is testimony rather than self-praise. It bears witness both to the extrinsic origin of the gospel, "not from a human source" (οὐ παρὰ ἀνθρώπου, 1:12), and to its independence of human systems of value, "not in accord with human norms" (οὐ κατὰ ἄνθρωπον, 1:11). If Paul is no longer beholden to the traditions of his erstwhile "Judaism," and if he seeks no legitimation from human authorities or traditional seats of power, this is because God's "calling in grace" has transformed his identity and redefined his criteria of value. He walks to a different drumbeat, on a path now oriented to "the truth of the good news" (2:5, 14).

Paul's description of his "former conduct" (ἀναστροφή) offers us two strong images, of opposition to "the assembly of God" (1:13) and of progress in "zeal" (1:14), both correlated with Ἰουδαϊσμός ("Judaism"). Paul's persecution of the "assembly of God" is not explained (except by implication, 1:14; cf. Phil 3:6). The accent lies on a striking juxtaposition of two facts: that this conduct took place "in Judaism" and that it *opposed* (the assembly of) God. It was not Paul's "Judaism" that qualified him for the divine call; his conduct "in Judaism" set him directly *against,* not for, God. His previous advance in zeal (1:14) evokes his excellence in terms of his former cultural capital (cf. Phil 3:2-11). That capital was invested "in Judaism" (ἐν Ἰουδαϊσμῷ):[20] the label

20. The term Ἰουδαϊσμός is found only here in Paul, and is otherwise attested only in the Maccabean literature (2 Macc 2:21; 8:1; 14:38; 4 Macc 4:26) and in a late Roman inscription (see Y. Amir, "The Term Ἰουδαϊσμός: A Study in Jewish-Hellenistic Self-Definition," *Immanuel* 14 [1984]: 34-41). In all cases, it places the Jewish cultural tradition in juxtaposition with others — in the Maccabean case (but not in the Roman), in exclusive relation to "Hellenism." The term thus betokens an "etic" perspective on Jewish faithfulness to God, an ability to view the Jewish tradition from an outsider's frame of reference and thus relative to others. The term here refers to "the Jewish way of life" (cf. 2:14 for the related notion of "living Jewishly"), which Paul relativizes from the perspective of an event that has placed all human "traditions" under a new and critical light. Since nothing is said here about Jewish attitudes to Gentiles, there is no reason to regard the term as signaling a "fiercely nationalistic" attitude (*pace* Dunn, *Galatians*, p. 56). Of course, what *we* mean by "Judaism" only partially overlaps with Paul's usage of the term, which will be kept in quotation marks throughout. Paul speaks of his "*former* life in Judaism" (1:13); by *our* definition of the term, he remains in many respects within it. I translate Ἰουδαῖος and Ἰουδαϊσμός as "Jew" and "Judaism," although a strong case has been made for "Judean" and "Judeanism" (S. Mason, *Josephus, Judea, and Christian Origins* [Peabody: Hendrickson, 2009], pp. 141-84; cf. however D. R. Schwartz, "'Judean' or 'Jew'? How Should We Translate *ioudaios* in Josephus?" in J. Frey, D. R. Schwartz, and S. Gripentrog, eds., *Jewish Identity in the Greco-Roman World* [Leiden: Brill, 2007], pp. 3-28). No English translation is fully adequate, and different texts nuance these terms differently. Although "Judean" seems suitable in the case of Josephus (see J. M. G. Barclay, *Flavius Josephus, Translation, and Commentary,* vol. 10: *Against Apion* [Leiden: Brill, 2007], p. lxi), it appears less so in relation to Paul, for whom a

evokes an ethnic tradition of Ἰουδαῖοι, a people (γένος) whose continuity was articulated in the maintenance of "ancestral traditions" (πατρικαὶ παραδόσεις, 1:14).[21] These traditions established standards of value, according to which Paul surpassed his contemporaries. History, community, ethnicity, and moral excellence combine as cultural assets that, in their own terms, are of outstanding value. We might presume that, despite his error of judgment in persecuting "God's assembly" (1:13), such capital would constitute Paul's worthiness to receive the divine call.

Quite the contrary. On Paul's account, what happened next was an event that bore no relation to the worth of his Jewish identity or to his former conduct "in Judaism." Three features of his "calling," as described in 1:15-16, indicate this rupture. First, what happened next (ὅτε δέ) was *not* another stage in his development within "Judaism," a further step in his progress of zeal. Rather, it was the effect of a divine decision (εὐδόκησεν [ὁ θεός] . . . ἀποκαλύψαι, "[God] was pleased . . . to reveal"). The change of subject interrupts a string of verbs depicting Paul's agency in 1:13-14 and 1:17ff., and calls attention to the fact that this event originated from outside Paul's initiative or control. Secondly, this revelation resulted from "[God] who set me aside from my mother's womb" (ὁ ἀφορίσας με ἐκ κοιλίας μητρός μου). The phrase echoes the prophetic call narratives (Jer 1:4-5; Isa 49:1-6) and places Paul's mission "to the nations," like theirs, within the eschatological hopes of Israel.[22] But it also undercuts the positive capital described in 1:14 (Paul's progress) — and overturns the negative capital described in 1:13 (Paul's persecution) — by placing God's decision before Paul's birth, and thus outside the frame of his "former conduct in Judaism." As we shall see in relation to Romans 9:6-13 (below, 17.2), Paul is particularly interested in what God says or does before the birth of a person, because this circumvents definitions of worth given by birth or accumulated thereafter. Thirdly, Paul describes God as "the one who . . . called [me] through his grace" (ὁ . . . καλέσας διὰ τῆς χάριτος αὐτοῦ) — match-

---

geographical connection to Ἰουδαία does not seem integral to the term Ἰουδαῖοι (for "Judaea," see Gal 1:22; 1 Thess 2:14; Rom 15:31).

21. The reference is not to Pharisaic "oral traditions" additional to the written law (*pace* Dunn, *Galatians*, p. 60), but to the Torah and its pattern of life, using phraseology employed by both Jews and non-Jews in a Greek-speaking environment (e.g., Josephus, *Ant.* 14.235, 258; see B. Schröder, *Die 'väterlichen Gesetze': Flavius Josephus als Vermittler von Halachah an Griechen und Römer* [Tübingen: Mohr Siebeck, 1996]). But that Paul fails to identify God as the source of such traditions is strongly suggestive of the novel perspective from which he now views his former life.

22. See K. O. Sandnes, *Paul — One of the Prophets? A Contribution to the Apostle's Self-Understanding* (Tübingen: Mohr Siebeck, 1991).

ing the "calling" language previously used of his non-Jewish converts (1:6).[23] Whatever may be unique in Paul's call (which included his commission as an apostle) is founded on a "calling in χάρις" shared by Torah-observant Jews and non-Jewish "sinners" (cf. 2:15-16). Whether Paul's "call" also took place before birth (as the common definite article in the phrase ὁ ἀφορίσας . . . καὶ καλέσας might suggest), or in the "revelation of Christ" (1:16), it was only the latter that transformed his life. God's "calling" was thus, for Paul, inseparably conjoined with his experience of Jesus Christ.[24]

These three features of 1:15-16, in combination and as the sequel to 1:13-14, indicate that what has reconstituted Paul's life is a divine act of grace without regard to his ethnicity, tradition, and excellence, and without regard to his former opposition to God. The fact that Paul speaks of his "former conduct in Judaism" (τὴν ἐμὴν ἀναστροφήν ποτε ἐν τῷ Ἰουδαϊσμῷ, 1:13)[25] indicates that the "revelation of God's Son" (1:16) has undercut his loyalty to the cultural norms he once considered authoritative. However *we* might characterize his practice as a believer (perhaps as an anomalous form of "Judaism"), *Paul* took his life in Christ to be governed no longer by the traditions of (what *he* calls) "Judaism," even though he continues to call himself a "Jew" (2:15), identifies with his "people" (1:14; cf. 13.3, below), and finds the "Jewish" Scriptures resonant with echoes of the good news (3:6-13; 4:21-31).[26] As a believer, Paul is

23. See O. McFarland, "'The One Who Calls in Grace': Paul's Rhetorical and Theological Identification with the Galatians," *HBT* 35 (2013): 151-65.

24. Dunn occludes this Christological specificity by referring to Paul's call as "a recall to a proper understanding of the grace-character of Israel's calling" (*Galatians*, p. 63). How this Christ-call may be correlated with the calling of Israel will become evident only in Romans 9–11 (see chapter 17). Paul traces no progress in grace in the story of his life (his "advance" only pitted him against "the assembly of God"). God's revelation of Christ was thus fully congruous with God's earlier decision regarding Paul, but not with Paul's conduct or worth; cf. Barclay, "Paul's Story," p. 140; S. Eastman, *Recovering Paul's Mother Tongue: Language and Theology in Galatians* (Grand Rapids: Eerdmans, 2007), p. 41.

25. The phrase is a unit and does not imply that he now has a different mode of "conduct in Judaism" (*pace* M. D. Nanos, "Paul and Judaism: Why Not Paul's Judaism?" in M. D. Given, ed., *Paul Unbound: Other Perspectives on the Apostle* [Peabody: Hendrickson, 2010], pp. 141-44; J. D. G. Dunn, *The New Perspective on Paul: Collected Essays* [Tübingen: Mohr Siebeck, 2005], p. 181, on Gal 2:15). Cf. the ποτε . . . νῦν contrast of 1:23. Paul's present mode of life in Christ is not placed on a trajectory continuing from his past, and is nowhere described as being "in Judaism" (cf. 1 Cor 9:19-23).

26. The current debate about Paul's continuing "Judaism" regularly but wrongly takes Paul's continuing identity as a Jew and his commitment to the future of his people Israel to signal a continuing allegiance to the authoritative norms of the "Jewish" way of life. For recent examples, see C. Johnson Hodge, *If Sons, Then Heirs: A Study of Kinship and Ethnicity in the Letters of Paul* (Oxford: Oxford University Press, 2007); P. Eisenbaum, *Paul Was Not a Chris-*

a "Jew" who (in his terms) no longer remains "in Judaism": his ethnicity has not been renounced but subsumed within an identity and an allegiance governed by the event of Christ (cf. 2:19-21). His "ancestral traditions" no longer constitute his salient currency of worth.

Paul thus emphasizes God's agency and priority in grace in order to clarify the *incongruity* of God's intervention in his life. His transformation was neither occasioned by his own action nor conditioned by his previous worth; it resulted from the unconditioned gift of God-in-Christ. Paul does not frame his former life as blasphemously reliant on himself in his pursuit of righteousness; nor did it constitute a form of "religion," a humanly-propelled initiative toward God.[27] Paul's super-zealous commitment to his ancestral traditions is not associated with a "narrow" interpretation of God's covenant with Israel.[28] Rather, the contrast between 1:13-14 and 1:15-16 bespeaks the incongruity of God's action and its dramatic effect on the "objective" value of cultural norms. Paul had lived enthusiastically in accordance with the well-established norms of "Judaism," but God's "calling in grace" had nothing to do with his success in those terms. As in 1:6, χάρις signals the fact that God's call is unconditioned by the social worth of the recipient — without regard to superior ethnicity, status, or cultural prestige, or to negative worth in sinfulness, ignorance, and tooth-and-nail opposition to God. As a result, previously self-evident norms are suspended, relativized, or recalibrated: in the newly generated life in Christ, they are subordinated to a superior norm, "the truth of the good news" (2:5, 14).

Paul's call endows him with a new task: "that I might preach him [Christ] as good news among the Gentiles" (ἵνα εὐαγγελίζωμαι αὐτὸν ἐν τοῖς ἔθνεσιν, 1:16). Whether this mission began immediately, and on what initial terms, cannot be known, but Paul now associates this revelation and call with a mission that is not only directed to "the Gentiles" (lit., "the nations," with the meaning "the non-Jewish nations") but also resists attempts to make them "judaize" (2:14). This

---

tian (New York: HarperCollins Press, 2009); and Nanos, "Paul and Judaism." *Being a Jew* but *not living Jewishly* is the anomalous policy Paul commends in Antioch (2:14). No doubt Paul (sometimes), like other Jewish believers (generally), observed the Torah, in honor of the Lord (1 Cor 7:17-24; 9:20-21; Rom 14:1-12). But circumcision no longer defined his worth (Gal 5:6; 6:15), and allegiance to Christ took priority over allegiance to the Torah (Gal 2:14-21; 1 Cor 9:20-21). Paul proclaims freedom from the authority of the Torah (Gal 2:19; 5:1, 13, 18), while integrating features of the Torah that are "fulfilled" in a life directed by the Spirit (5:13-14).

27. Martyn turns to the category of "religion": Paul "saw that Judaism was now revealed to be a religion," since "the advent of Christ is the end of religion" (*Galatians*, p. 164). For the Barthian category and its influence on Martyn, see above, 3.5.1; 3.5.4; 11.4.3.

28. *Pace* Dunn, *Galatians*, pp. 60-62. Although "zeal" in defense of the Law was often associated with the preservation of Jewish integrity, there is no indication in Paul's text (here or in Phil 3:6) that his zeal was specifically concerned with threats to the boundaries of Judaism.

norm-breaking mission is integral to Paul's theology, as "the new perspective on Paul" correctly insists, but we can now identify from Galatians 1:15-16 its radical rationale. Paul's "calling in grace," unconditioned by his worth, undermined his previous confidence in the defining values of his former "Judaism." There is now for him no stable Jewish tradition whose boundaries might be enlarged to embrace outsiders. On the contrary, he announces an event that reformulates the identity of both Jew and non-Jew.[29] Paul's radical policy in his Gentile mission is not a protest against "nationalism": it is the disruptive aftershock of the incongruous gift of Christ. Because Paul experiences this event as a divine intervention, which neither continues nor completes his progress in "Judaism," it cannot be contained within the ethnic frame of his "ancestral traditions." As a singular, particular, but unconditioned event it belongs to no subset of humanity, but is destined for all. Since no one is granted this gift on the grounds of their ethnic worth, no one of any ethnicity is excluded from its reach.

It is unlikely that this interpretation of the Christ-gift came to Paul fully formed in his Damascus-experience: he reconstructs this connection after many years alongside Gentile converts, whom he found gifted with the Spirit despite their failure to observe the Torah (cf. Gal 3:2-5). Paul's experience, scriptural re-reading, reflection on the story of Christ, and extended interaction with "un-judaized" believers combined to forge his theology of incongruous gift. It is hard to imagine how Paul's theology could have taken this shape had his mission been limited to Jewish communities in the homeland or the Diaspora: his Gentile mission not only embodied but also shaped his thought. Theology and practice reinforced one another in a protracted dialectical relationship that made his apostolic calling *to the Gentiles* central to his version of the "good news."

The years following Paul's call are sketched in the barest of outlines, but with enough detail to signal the significance of experience, including location. Paul's distance from Jerusalem, and his single visit there within a span of fourteen (or seventeen) years (1:18; 2:1), are cited in support of his contention that he "did not consult with flesh and blood" (i.e., any human being, 1:16).[30] Because

29. Johnson Hodge, *If Sons, Then Heirs,* rightly insists that Paul's Gentile converts acquire a new "kinship" to Abraham without becoming "Jews." But as Paul will indicate in Galatians 3–4, the relationship of Jews to Abraham is also refounded, in an act of divine "adoption" that is possible only in Christ (4:1-6). Paul's narrative in 1:10-16 thus suggests the reformulation of his identity as a Jew, in a way he makes paradigmatic of others in 2:19-21. There is no reason to take his Antioch policy (2:11-14) as applying only to Jewish "teachers" of Gentiles (*pace* Johnson Hodge, *If Sons, Then Heirs,* pp. 58, 123-25).

30. The use of the biblical expression "flesh and blood" (1:16), meaning "human being," introduces the significant term "flesh" (σάρξ), whose antithetical pairing with "Spirit"

his message was unaligned to human norms (οὐ κατὰ ἄνθρωπον, 1:11), it did not need to be checked for compliance to preexisting criteria. Paul remains independent of human authorization because he is answerable to the authority of the Christ-event, which establishes anew his norms of judgment and behavior. For many years, his *habitus* was shaped outside Jerusalem, at a distance from "the assemblies of Judea" (1:22). Whatever he was doing in Arabia, Damascus, Syria, and Cilicia (1:17, 21), what matters is that he was *there* and not in Jerusalem. Although it constituted the central locus of authority within Paul's "ancestral tradition," Jerusalem was no longer Paul's primary point of reference. As a "slave of Christ" (1:10) Paul is no free spirit, but Jerusalem is now important only in recognizing an authority derived from elsewhere (2:7-9). His mother-city is now "the Jerusalem above" (4:26): by his "calling in grace," Paul's life is suspended from a reality distinct from every human institution.

12.4. Jerusalem and the Relativization of Previous Cultural Capital (2:1-10)

Paul's partial account of the agreement in Jerusalem focuses on the recognition from all sides that the good news could either incorporate or ignore the practice of circumcision. He is delighted to report that Titus, a Greek, was "not compelled to be circumcised" (2:3; contrast 6:12), although there was pressure to compromise "the freedom which we have in Christ Jesus" (2:4). We should not underestimate the significance of this agreement, given the value accorded to circumcision within the Jewish tradition. As a mark of ethnicity and a sign of difference, male circumcision was a critical component of Jewish identity, then as now. It was also integral to Jewish masculinity and, through its relevance to sex and procreation, it safeguarded the practice of endogamy that kept Jewish descent "pure."[31] Paul acknowledges that God is active in Peter for his "apostleship of circumcision" (or "to the circumcised," 2:8, 9). The Christ-event

---

will continue in subsequent chapters (3:3; 4:29; 5:13; 6:8, 12-13) as a new form of the polarity "human–divine."

31. Recent literature on circumcision is abundant: see, e.g., H. Eilberg-Schwartz, *The Savage in Judaism: An Anthropology of Israelite Religion and Ancient Judaism* (Bloomington: Indiana University Press, 1990); L. Hoffmann, *Covenant of Blood: Circumcision and Gender in Rabbinic Judaism* (Chicago: University of Chicago Press, 1996); A. Blaschke, *Beschneidung: Zeugnisse der Bibel und verwandter Texte* (Tübingen: Francke Verlag, 1998); M. Thiessen, *Contesting Conversion* (Oxford: Oxford University Press, 2011). For its relevance to procreation and descent, see J. M. G. Barclay, *Jews in the Mediterranean Diaspora from Alexander to Trajan (323 BCE–117 CE)* (Edinburgh: T&T Clark, 1996), pp. 411-12, 438-40.

renders this cultural marker no longer a sign of superior status (cf. 5:6; 6:15), but precisely because this Jewish practice is a matter of indifference, there is nothing to prevent its maintenance among Jews (cf. 1 Cor 7:17-20). But the Christ-event also grounds an apostleship to the nations (2:8), and this entails "the good news of the foreskin" (or "to the foreskinned," τὸ εὐαγγέλιον τῆς ἀκροβυστίας, 2:7). Modern Gentile readers, who have never been socialized to consider the foreskin a sign of inferior otherness or repulsive disgrace, generally fail to register the shock of this oxymoronic expression: the "good news of the foreskin" constitutes a stunning challenge to the system of valuation operative in Jewish culture.[32] A central token of cultural capital within the Jewish tradition is here acknowledged to be disposable in the mission to Gentiles — certainly not because that mission is of less significance, or the status of Gentile converts lower than that of Jews, but because *God is at work* as much in one form of mission as in the other (2:8). The Jerusalem apostles are required to recognize the validity of the "foreskin mission" of Paul and Barnabas, because they are required to acknowledge (not to authorize) a divine evaluation of worth. According to Paul, it was acknowledged that God was "at work" in both forms of mission (2:8), since "the pillars" recognized the "grace of God given to me" (2:9). Both missions were beyond their participants' control, following terms of reference outside of their choice. Again Paul emphasizes divine agency in the origin and dynamic of the good news, not to diminish human agency but to subvert the human criteria of value carried by its agents.

Paul gives full recognition to the God-energized mission to "the circumcised" and to the commissioning of "the pillars" for that task (2:9). Indeed, he admits that he presented to them his version of the good news "lest I was running or had run in vain" (2:2). Paul hardly needed approval for the terms of his gospel (cf. 1:17), but he desired their recognition of its fruit, his largely Gentile assemblies.[33] Without this recognition, his work would be "in vain," not because it might be invalid before God (cf. 2:7-9), but because it could be complete only when Jewish and Gentile assemblies recognized the validity of each other, and thereby relativized their differences through their common allegiance to Christ. It matters greatly to Paul that there is a successful mission to Jews. What he desires is not the formation of a Gentile church, independent of Jewish believers, but an interdependent fellowship of Jews and non-Jews in

32. Kahl rightly identifies this locution as "an astonishingly bold phrase" (*Galatians Re-imagined: Reading with the Eyes of the Vanquished* [Minneapolis: Fortress Press, 2010], p. 275). It is the Galatians equivalent to "the justification of the ungodly" (Rom 4:5).

33. See Martyn, *Galatians*, pp. 190-93. That he went to Jerusalem κατὰ ἀποκάλυψιν ("according to a revelation," 2:2) indicates that his visit was not prompted by a Jerusalem summons or an Antioch commission; see Martyn, *Galatians*, p. 190, and de Boer, *Galatians*, pp. 216-18.

Christ. The "right hand of fellowship" (2:9) is the recognition that the mission to Gentiles can proceed beyond the limits of the Jewish tradition, *but also* that the Jewish mission can proceed within them. If Paul's promise to "remember the poor" (2:10) relates specifically to "the poor" in Jerusalem, his commitment to Jewish believers, and to the Jewish mission, remains the final impression of the conference.[34] Such a commitment, I shall suggest, finds an echo at the end of the letter, in Paul's prayer for mercy on "the Israel of God" (6:16; see below, 13.3.3), and is prominent in his hopes and prayers for Israel in Romans 9–11.

The equal acknowledgement of the mission-with-circumcision and the mission-with-foreskin entails that neither condition has superior value as an essential component of the good news. Paul does not disparage either practice, but he relativizes the value of both, and gives this relativization the emotive label "freedom" (2:4). The context suggests that this "freedom" is not an inner "spiritual" condition, but "liberation" from the constraints and parameters of any single cultural tradition.[35] As we know from Josephus, the cultural authority of the Torah could be represented, pejoratively, as a kind of "tyranny" resented by the "free." When Josephus imagines the motivation of Zambrias (Zimri), he pictures a renegade Jew deploring the "tyranny" of Moses — although in Josephus's evaluation the bid for "freedom" was merely a disguise for self-authorized license (*Ant.* 4.145-49). Paul uses similar terminology in this letter, but loads the rhetorical dice otherwise: he celebrates the "freedom" that "we" (both Jews and non-Jews) enjoy "in Christ," and resists all efforts to "compel," to "enslave," or to enforce "subjection" (2:3-5). This freighted vocabulary will recur in later paragraphs, in a variety of forms (3:23–4:7; 4:21–5:1; 5:13-14). Here the freedom "which we have in Christ Jesus" (2:4) is the freedom to transgress cultural limits, to challenge "ancestral traditions" (1:14), and to resist the claims of final authority advanced by the Torah, or by any other cultural norm. It is located "in Christ Jesus" because it is the Christ-event, unconditioned by those constraints, that founds a new form of life and effects a new life-orientation. The result is not absolute freedom (cf. 1:10; 5:13, 18, 25), because it is not conceived in abstract terms: freedom "in Christ Jesus" entails "obeying the truth" (5:7). But to insist on Gentiles' conformity to the Torah-tradition, or to any pre-constituted cultural norm, would be to deny the truth of the good news (2:5) by denying its essential character as incongruous gift.

34. This is the normal reading of 2:10, suggested by the Jerusalem context and the reference to "the poor among the saints in Jerusalem" in Romans 15:26; for additional arguments, see de Boer, *Galatians*, pp. 243-46.

35. See the discussion of background and Pauline usage in S. Vollenweider, *Freiheit als neue Schöpfung: Eine Untersuchung zur Eleutheria bei Paulus und in seiner Umwelt* (Göttingen: Vandenhoeck & Ruprecht, 1989).

The scope of this "freedom" is already suggested by Paul's boldness in challenging the accepted attribution of status. Four times he refers to the Jerusalem leaders as "those with a reputation" (οἱ δοκοῦντες, 2:2, 6 [x2], 9), ironically distancing himself from the honor associated with their status. Despite their credentials ("whatever they were makes no difference to me," 2:6),[36] the essential fact is that "God takes no account of human, external status" (πρόσωπον [ὁ] θεὸς ἀνθρώπου οὐ λαμβάνει, 2:6). Once again Paul makes clear that God's criteria are "not in accordance with human norms" (οὐ κατὰ ἄνθρωπον, 1:11): God pays no attention to entitlement or symbolic capital measured in human terms. This dissolution of the normal systems of honor has enormous significance in the construction of community, as will become clear in 5:13–6:10 (where words from the δοκ-root are prominent, 5:26; 6:3-4). Where honor and worth are recalibrated by the truth of the gospel, communities can disregard traditional hierarchies of status, and the ("worthless") poor can be accorded countercultural attention (2:10).[37]

12.5. The Antioch Incident and the Suspension of the Torah as Norm (2:11-21)

12.5.1. The Antioch Incident

Paul's account of his clash with Cephas/Peter includes a speech that begins in 2:14 and continues in "we"-form until 2:17, before shifting to the first person singular in 2:18-21. Although by the end Paul's discourse seems less imme-

36. Dunn's suggestion (*Galatians*, pp. 102-3, following Klein) that ποτε (2:6) indicates Paul's *previous* recognition of their honor is not convincing: Paul probably alludes to the status derived from their previous connections to Jesus, by ties of family or discipleship. Cf. Schütz, *Apostolic Authority*, p. 142: "For him . . . their position depends on their submission to the truth of the gospel and nothing else." The fact that Barnabas followed Peter's example in Antioch, after the arrival of "people from James" (2:12-13), indicates the authority exercised by these "pillars," even outside Jerusalem; on the label, see C. K. Barrett, "Paul and the 'Pillar' Apostles," in J. N. Sevenster and W. C. van Unnik, eds., *Studia Paulina* (Haarlem: De Ervem F. Bohn, 1953), pp. 1-19.

37. For a reading of 2:10 as indicating concern for the poor in general (not just "the poor among the saints" in Jerusalem), see B. W. Longenecker, *Remember the Poor: Paul, Poverty, and the Greco-Roman World* (Grand Rapids: Eerdmans, 2010), pp. 157-219. However one reads the referent in 2:10, Longenecker rightly highlights the peculiarity of a community where poverty elicits not disdain but generous attention; cf. L. L. Welborn, "'That There May Be Equality': The Contexts and Consequences of a Pauline Ideal," *NTS* 57 (2012): 73-90, on "equality" in 2 Corinthians 8:13-14.

diately directed to Peter, the whole passage explains his challenge to Peter and unfolds "the truth of the good news" to which he appeals (2:14). Our uncertainty about how much (if any) of 2:14-21 Paul actually spoke to Peter should not obscure the fact that 2:11-21 is a single literary-rhetorical unit.[38] The Antioch dispute is important for Paul not merely as a historical datum, but because it allows him to explicate "the good news" in precisely these terms.

Paul's narrative is reduced to the minimum necessary, leaving many details uncertain. Why was Peter in Antioch? Why was he followed by "certain people from James" (2:12)? Who were these people, and what pressure did they exert? Are they or others the ones whom Peter feared ("people from circumcision," οἱ ἐκ περιτομῆς)?[39] The questions are largely unanswerable, since all that matters for Paul is that Peter was in the habit of eating with non-Jews in Antioch (συνήσθιεν suggests a habitual practice, 2:12), but that afterwards, under pressure (in "fear"), he "drew back" and "separated himself," drawing the "other Jews" and "even Barnabas" into his "hypocrisy" (2:12-13).

We cannot be sure on what terms Peter ate with non-Jews. Scholars speculate concerning who played host, for what sort of meals, and with what degree of conformity or non-conformity with the Jewish tradition.[40] What matters for Paul's argument is what he claims in his rebuke (2:14): "If you, although a Jew (Ἰουδαῖος ὑπάρχων), live in a Gentile and not in a Jewish fashion (ἐθνικῶς καὶ οὐχὶ Ἰουδαϊκῶς ζῇς), how is it that you are compelling Gentiles to live like Jews (πῶς τὰ ἔθνη ἀναγκάζεις ἰουδαΐζειν)?" The rebuke charges Peter with "hypocrisy" (2:13): he is pressuring Gentiles to adopt a Jewish way of life that

38. Of course, 2:15-21 also introduces terminology to be deployed in the following chapters, such that Betz identifies these verses as the rhetorical *propositio* (*Galatians*, pp. 113-14). In fact, Paul has an eye on the Galatian situation throughout the opening two chapters (cf. 2:5).

39. Those labeled οἱ ἐκ περιτομῆς are apparently Jews (whether Christ-believers or not). The phrase suggests a point of cultural origin or self-definition, and will be contrasted with οἱ ἐκ πίστεως ("those defined from faith") below (3:9); for parallel examples of Pauline shorthand, cf. Gal 3:10; Rom 4:12, 14, 16; Col 4:11; Titus 1:10. There is no reason to translate the phrase "those *for* circumcision" (*pace* M. D. Nanos, *The Irony of Galatians: Paul's Letter in First-Century Context* [Minneapolis: Fortress, 2002], pp. 287-92).

40. The recent wave of debate was sparked by J. D. G. Dunn, *Jesus, Paul, and the Law: Studies in Mark and Galatians* (London: SPCK, 1990), pp. 129-82 (first published in 1983). Does "eating with" Gentiles imply that the latter were hosts? Did the meals include "the Lord's Supper"? Were such meals clearly in defiance of the Torah, or were they to some degree observant of Jewish tradition? That the Torah was in the main still observed has been argued, in varying forms, by Dunn, "The New Perspective on Paul," *BJRL* 65 (1983): 95-122; M. D. Nanos, "What Was at Stake in Peter's 'Eating with Gentiles' at Antioch?" in M. D. Nanos, ed., *The Galatians Debate* (Peabody: Hendrickson, 2002), pp. 282-318; and M. Zetterholm, *The Formation of Christianity in Antioch: A Social-Scientific Approach to the Separation between Judaism and Christianity* (London: Routledge, 2003), pp. 129-66.

he does not consistently practice himself. We do not know how far this pressure extended:[41] what Paul objects to is the requirement that Gentiles adopt specifically "Jewish" norms. Similarly, it is not clear in what respects Peter's meal-practice constituted "living in a Gentile and not in a Jewish fashion":[42] all that matters is that something other than his ethnic identity has come to determine his behavioral norms. Whether Peter's break with tradition concerned the food eaten or his repeated meal-intimacy with non-Jews, Paul notes and applauds his capacity to challenge his inherited structure of values.[43] It was when he reneged on this policy, withdrawing from Gentile company and thus requiring them to adopt the Jewish tradition, that he and others could be charged with "not walking straight in line with the truth of the good news" (οὐκ ὀρθοποδοῦσιν πρὸς τὴν ἀλήθειαν τοῦ εὐαγγελίου, 2:14).[44]

Paul thus frames the issue in Antioch as a clash between two regulative

41. Whether this includes or excludes male circumcision turns on the nuance of the rare verb ἰουδαΐζειν, which elsewhere indicates conformity to the Jewish tradition, but to varying degrees and not always to the extent of male circumcision (see the debate in Dunn, *Jesus, Paul, and the Law,* pp. 149-50; P. F. Esler, *Galatians* [London: Routledge, 1998], pp. 137-40; S. J. D. Cohen, *The Beginnings of Jewishness: Boundaries, Varieties, Uncertainties* [Berkeley: University of California Press, 1999], pp. 179-97; and Nanos, "What Was at Stake," pp. 306-10). If circumcision was clearly demanded, Paul could have accused Peter of reneging on the Jerusalem agreement.

42. Dunn doubted that Peter's commensality with Gentiles completely disregarded the dietary laws; he suggested that it was held on "Noachide" terms but lacked Pharisaic standards of purity and tithing, and on these grounds shocked the "people from James" (*Jesus, Paul, and the Law,* pp. 156, 158, 179). In reply, Sanders rightly questioned whether Pharisaic rules on purity and tithing were relevant in the Diaspora ("Jewish Association with Gentiles and Galatians 2.1-14," in R. T. Fortna and B. R. Gaventa, eds., *The Conversation Continues: Studies in Paul and John in Honor of J. Louis Martyn* [Nashville: Abingdon Press, 1990], pp. 170-88). Nanos has recently argued that no Torah-rules were broken, but that James's people were shocked that Gentiles were treated not as guests but as proselytes ("What Was at Stake," pp. 300-311); but there is no evidence that Jewish meal-practice accorded different status to proselyte and non-proselyte Gentiles. For other attempts to minimize the cultural deviance in Peter's initial meals with Gentiles, see Zetterholm (*Formation of Christianity,* pp. 129-66, omitting mention of the clause "not in a Jewish fashion") and Johnson Hodge (*If Sons, Then Heirs,* pp. 121-25).

43. The statement ("you live [present tense] in a Gentile and not in a Jewish fashion") represents not James's objection to Peter (*pace* Dunn, *Galatians,* p. 128), but Paul's portrayal of Peter's normal policy (which was temporarily masked by his "hypocrisy").

44. The verb ὀρθοποδεῖν, combined with the preposition πρός, evokes the notion of proper alignment to a goal or norm; Paul later speaks of "lining up" (στοιχεῖν) in accord with a "standard" (κανών, 6:16; cf. 5:25). See BAGD ad loc. and G. Kilpatrick, "Gal 2.14 ὀρθοποδοῦσιν," in W. Eltester, ed., *Neutestamentliche Studien für R. Bultmann,* 2nd ed. (Berlin: A. Töpelmann, 1957), pp. 269-74; for the metaphor, cf. 1QH[a] XV.17 ("directing my steps toward the paths of righteousness").

structures, one defined by the norms of the Jewish tradition, the other oriented to "the truth of the good news." By withdrawing from meals with Gentile believers, Peter has reinstituted the Jewish tradition as the supreme normative framework, with the effect of requiring other believers to adopt his Jewish rule of life. But in Paul's view, he thereby proves unfaithful to "the truth of the good news," which as a *superior norm* bears the capacity to countermand others. For those aligned to the Christ-event, "the Jewish way of life" is no longer an unqualified standard of righteous behavior, *even for Jews.* Peter and Paul do not cease to be Jews (2:14-15), but the normative claim of the Jewish way of life has been subordinated to the higher, and in this case clashing, demand that their lives be oriented to "the good news."[45]

It is no accident that the superordinate authority of the Christ-event becomes clear in the context of communal activity. Peter's alignment to this "truth" is tested in commensality, the conditions of possibility for community, and reciprocity, in Christ. The construction of reciprocal social relations, freed from prevalent criteria of differential worth, is integral to Paul's vision in Galatians, as will become clear in 5:13–6:10. But it is impossible to create a community beholden to "the law of Christ" in "bearing one another's burdens" (6:2) if the members of the community cannot eat together. As Paul sees the matter, Peter's withdrawal implies that community can be restored only within the normative terms of the Jewish tradition (by the Gentiles "judaizing," 2:14). His separation thus expresses and imposes a distinctively Jewish tradition that made meals a site of social differentiation. In the contemporary Diaspora, Jews could associate freely with non-Jews in many spheres of life, but were known to set limits to this association in certain sensitive spheres, such as cultic practice, marriage, and meals.[46] The limits around commensality, regarding the food

45. The superior authority of "the good news" might require, in other circumstances, that Gentile believers adapt their behavior to that of Jewish believers, if this is necessary for the latter to retain their allegiance to Christ (Rom 14:1–15:13). But this is only the case if *both parties* recognize that Jewish practice is a non-necessary expression of faith in Christ (14:1-11) — and the stronger their faith, the deeper this recognition goes; see 16.4 below, and J. M. G. Barclay, "Faith and Self-Detachment from Cultural Norms: A Study of Romans 14–15," *ZNW* 104 (2013): 192-208. Thus, Paul by no means prevents Jews on principle from practicing the Jewish tradition; but he renders that tradition subordinate to the demands of a higher allegiance, which is always potentially, and sometimes actually, at odds with the requirements of the Torah (cf. Gal 2:19-20, on Paul's paradigmatic "death to the Law").

46. For a summary of the evidence regarding meals, see Barclay, *Jews in the Mediterranean Diaspora*, pp. 434-37. P. Esler's survey (*Community and Gospel in Luke-Acts* [Cambridge: Cambridge University Press, 1987], pp. 73-86) suffers from over-generalization, but the critique by Sanders, "Jewish Association," fails to distinguish between general social interaction and the intimacy of meal-sharing. For the distinction, noted by B. Holmberg, "Jewish *versus* Christian

consumed or the company kept, were not always strictly observed; and, if observed, sometimes special measures could ensure that, when eating in Gentile company, Jewish scruples were nonetheless maintained.[47] But there is good evidence that Jews, in faithfulness to their "ancestral traditions," commonly abstained from certain foodstuffs (including, in Antioch, oil from Gentile sources) and ate separately from Gentiles.[48] Both pagan and Jewish sources note Jewish separatism in this connection, though of course they evaluate this practice very differently.[49]

Paul does not critique Peter's withdrawal on the grounds that Jews were antisocial or misanthropic;[50] the issue is not the "narrowness" of a national tradition (Dunn). Peter's policy is found wanting only by reference to "the truth of the good news" (2:14), which suspends every judgment of worth that is based on criteria extrinsic to the Christ-event. Both Jews and non-Jews are "called" by an incongruous grace into common belonging to Christ. Their previous evaluations of one another and of their traditions, based on the cultural norms of ethnic distinction, are subverted by an event that has paid no regard to pre-constituted criteria of value. They are therefore drawn into an association of mutual recognition that is blind to ethnic evaluations, as to other differentials of worth (3:28). To reinstate a Jewish rule of sociality would be to condition this association by a differentiating norm that is not derivable

---

Identity in the Early Church?" *Revue Biblique* 105 (1998): 397-425, see especially Josephus, *C. Ap.* 2.209-10, with commentary in Barclay, *Flavius Josephus.*

47. For laxity in the Diaspora (sometimes judged as apostasy) see, e.g., 3 Macc 7:10-11 and J. M. G. Barclay, "Who Was Considered an Apostate in the Jewish Diaspora?" in G. N. Stanton and G. Stroumsa, eds., *Tolerance and Intolerance in Early Judaism and Christianity* (Cambridge: Cambridge University Press, 1996), pp. 80-98; for practical arrangements that preserved Jewish distinction at meals, see, e.g., Josephus, *Vita* 14; *Let. Aris.* 184-85, and Barclay, *Jews in the Mediterranean Diaspora,* p. 435.

48. For Gentile oil in Syria, see Josephus, *Vita* 74; *B.J.* 2.591, and M. Goodman, "Kosher Olive Oil in Antiquity," in P. R. Davies and R. T. White, eds., *A Tribute to Geza Vermes* (Sheffield: JSOT Press, 1990), pp. 227-45.

49. Pagan sources include Diodorus 34.1.2; Tacitus, *Hist.* 5.5.2; Philostratus, *Vit. Apoll.* 33. Diaspora Jews sometimes celebrated this differentiation as a mark of their distinction (e.g., *Let. Aris.* 139-42; 3 Macc 3:4; Josephus, *C. Ap.* 2.173-74, 209-10, 234, in response to the critique of Apollonius Molon; see Barclay, *Flavius Josephus,* ad loc.). To conclude from such evidence that Jews were generally inhibited from eating with non-Jews is not at all to succumb to "the traditional stereotypes of Jewish exclusiveness" (*pace* Nanos, "What Was at Stake," p. 297).

50. For critique of Jews on these grounds, see K. Berthelot, *Philanthrôpia Judaica: Le débat autour de la "misanthropie" des lois juives dans l'Antiquité* (Leiden: Brill, 2003), pp. 79-184; 1 Thessalonians 2:15 (if Pauline) is the only example of such a line of criticism in Paul. On the cultural sources of hostility to Jews in antiquity, see J. M. G. Barclay, *Pauline Churches and Diaspora Jews* (Tübingen: Mohr Siebeck, 2011), pp. 157-77.

from the "truth of the good news." In fact, the good news is good precisely in its disregard of former criteria of worth, both Jewish and Gentile: the gospel stands or falls with the incongruity of grace. This is the logic that 2:15-21 proceeds to expound.

12.5.2. The Logic of 2:15-21

The statements of 2:15-21 are extremely compressed, but they are likely to make sense best in relation to the scenario at Antioch, however much they may also receive explication in the rest of the letter.[51] There is no break in address between 2:14 and 2:15, which seamlessly discuss "Jew" and "Gentile." Moreover, since the first-person plural ("we") continues as subject from 2:15 to 2:17, we should assume that Paul's statements relate to the Antioch dispute, even if they are also framed in terms relevant to Galatia.[52] The many verbal and thematic links between 2:14 and 2:15-17 indicate that the latter expound the issues at Antioch. σὺ Ἰουδαῖος ὑπάρχων ("although you are a Jew," 2:14) is echoed in the plural ἡμεῖς φύσει Ἰουδαῖοι καὶ οὐκ ἐξ ἐθνῶν ἁμαρτωλοί ("we who are Jews by birth, and not sinners from the Gentiles," 2:15). The term ἐθνικῶς ("in a Gentile fashion," 2:14) is echoed in ἐξ ἐθνῶν ἁμαρτωλοί ("sinners from the Gentiles," 2:15), and both illuminate the statement that "we also were found to be sinners" (εὑρέθημεν καὶ αὐτοὶ ἁμαρτωλοί, 2:17). The connection suggests that "we" were found to be classifiable as "sinners" precisely by living "in a Gentile fashion." That Peter has been living οὐχὶ Ἰουδαϊκῶς ("not in a Jewish fashion," 2:14) is therefore most likely to be what is in view in the (thrice repeated) οὐκ . . . ἐξ ἔργων νόμου ("not from works of the Law," 2:16). Even the reference to "living" (ζῇς, 2:14) finds an echo in the redefinition of "life" (ζάω) in 2:19-20 (x5).

51. It is striking that the two fullest, and in many ways illuminating, discussions of these verses in recent German scholarship both *begin* their analysis at 2:15. See M. Bachmann, *Sünder oder Übertreter: Studien zur Argumentation in Gal 2,15ff* (Tübingen: Mohr Siebeck, 1992), and H.-J. Eckstein, *Verheissung und Gesetz: Eine exegetische Untersuchung zu Galater 2,15–4,7* (Tübingen: Mohr Siebeck, 1996).

52. The general recognition that this paragraph has a double reference (back to Antioch, forward to Galatia) has encouraged some to think that the "we" in 2:15-17 includes reference to the other missionaries in Galatia, or is even "primarily directed" to them (de Boer, *Galatians*, p. 267). But the letter is nowhere else addressed to these figures, and there is no indication here of a shift in addressee. In addressing Peter, Paul's statements embrace all Jewish believers in Christ, but there is no warrant for finding here traces of the theology, and even vocabulary, of Paul's rivals in Galatia (*pace* M. C. de Boer, "Paul's Use and Interpretation of a Justification Tradition in Galatians 2.15-21," *JSNT* 28 [2005]: 189-216).

Such threads encourage us to read 2:15-21 as Paul's explanation of his rebuke of Peter, in which he appeals to shared knowledge in Christ (the "truth of the good news") as the grounds for continuing unconditioned commensality with Gentile believers. In summary, 2:15-21 may be paraphrased as follows:

> You and I, Peter, are Jews, used to thinking of ourselves as categorically distinct from "Gentile sinners." But we know (through conviction and experience) that a person (whether Gentile or Jew) is not considered of worth ("righteous") by God through Torah-observance ("living Jewishly"), but through faith in (what God has done in) Christ. We look to God to consider us valuable ("righteous") in Christ, not through obeying the Torah, and this is so even if (in situations like Antioch's) our resulting behavior makes us look like "sinners" ("living in a Gentile fashion"). Does that mean that Christ has led us into sin? No way! Only if one were to reinstate the Torah as the arbiter of worth ("righteousness") would "living like a Gentile" in Christ be classified as "transgression." In fact (taking myself as a paradigm), I have died to the Torah — it is no longer what constitutes my standard of value — because I have been reconstituted in Christ. My old existence came to an end with the crucified Christ; my new life has arisen from the Christ-event and is therefore shaped by faith in the death of Christ, who loved me and gave himself for me. This divine gift I will by no means reject: if "righteousness" were measured by the Torah, the death of Christ would be without effect.

The numerous exegetical decisions that go into this reading can be defended here only in outline. Several problems cluster around 2:16, but by no means only there. In fact, the weight placed on 2:16 in the interpretative tradition has improperly isolated that verse from its argumentative context: in recent years, everything has come to hang on the interpretation of "the works of the law" and the ambiguous πίστις Χριστοῦ (2:16 x2). But the exegetical difficulties of 2:16 are resolvable if we trace the argumentative flow of 2:14-21 along the lines just given.

12.5.3. Galatians 2:15-16

Paul's first step is to increase the shock implicit in the claim that Peter, though a Jew, was right to enjoy table-fellowship with Gentile believers "in a Gentile fashion" (2:14). Identifying himself with Peter to include him in the direction of his argument, Paul evokes a standard form of Jewish self-differentiation: "We,

Jews by birth and not sinners from the Gentiles . . ." (οὐκ ἐξ ἐθνῶν ἁμαρτωλοί, 2:15).[53] This serves to raise the stakes. If Jewish believers are required to live like Gentiles, for the purposes of table-fellowship in Christ, they are crossing the line from Jewish "righteousness" into Gentile "sin," with the result that "we also were found to be sinners" (εὑρέθημεν καὶ αὐτοὶ ἁμαρτωλοί, 2:17). The incident at Antioch thus brings to the surface a critical question concerning the identity and allegiance of Jewish believers. Should they maintain their Jewish self-differentiation (following a Torah-based definition of "sin"), and thus withdraw from the meal-company of Gentile believers? Or should they eat with non-Jews, out of loyalty to "the good news," even if that results in being labeled "sinners"? In this situation, Torah-loyalty will preserve their "righteousness"; Christ-loyalty will convict them of "sin." There is a clear choice: either they abandon their allegiance to "the truth of the good news," or they let the Christ-event itself define "righteousness," regardless of the definition determined by the Torah.[54]

In 2:16, Paul summarizes what he and Peter "know" (εἰδότες): from a new epistemological standpoint, they recognize that a person is considered "righteous" not by ἔργα νόμου but by πίστις Χριστοῦ (translations below).[55] This knowledge reflects their experience both in Jerusalem and in Antioch: it is the acknowledgement that God's action in Christ has defined what constitutes

53. For "sinners" as standard terminology for non-Jews, see, e.g., *4 Ezra* 3.28-36 and the assumptions and vocabulary of *Wisdom of Solomon* analyzed above (chapter 5); other texts are collected in Dunn, *Jesus, Paul, and the Law,* pp. 150-51.

54. Such a reconfiguration of "righteousness" will not erase the label Ἰουδαῖοι ("Jews," 2:15), but it will give it a different connotation. Qualified here by φύσει ("by nature" = "by birth"), the label remains in place, but the reconstitution of the self effected by execution with Christ and by the new life of "Christ in me" (2:19-20) means that Jewish ethnicity is no longer the primary form of self-identification, or the ultimate determinant of norms. Jewishness is not obliterated, but relativized in its normative significance by the superior status of belonging to Christ, an alteration effected in baptism (3:26-28). Sechrest is wrong to dub Paul "a former Jew," but she rightly insists that Paul's ethnic identity has been radically reconceptualized in Christ (L. L. Sechrest, *A Former Jew: Paul and the Dialectics of Race* [London: T&T Clark, 2009]). Thus, whether or not δέ is read in 2:16a (it is absent in P^{46} and A, but read in ℵ, B, C, D*, etc.), the content of 2:16 modifies the typical construal of Jewish identity that is evoked in 2:15.

55. For the structure of this sentence, see especially R. B. Matlock, "The Rhetoric of πίστις in Paul: Galatians 2.16, 3.22, Romans 3.22, and Philippians 3.9," *JSNT* 30 (2007): 173-203, at pp. 197-99. He suggests that an initial general antithesis ("a person is not considered righteous on the basis of works of the Law, but by faith in Christ") is then made personal and concrete ("we have believed in Christ Jesus"). Then, inverting this sequence, the personal confession is articulated in an antithetical form ("in order that we might be considered righteous by faith in Christ and not by works of the Law") before the sentence ends with a general statement matching its start ("because by works of the Law will no one be considered righteous").

worth in terms different from the canons of the Jewish tradition.[56] What they know is that a person (ἄνθρωπος, any person, Jew or Gentile) is not considered "righteous" on the basis of Torah-observance, but on the basis of faith directed toward (and arising from) what has happened in Christ.[57] Jewish believers ("we") have demonstrated this alternative construal of "righteousness" in putting their faith in Christ: they know they are considered "righteous" by God not on the basis of Torah-observance, but on the basis of their faith in Christ — that is, on the basis of their new existence created by the Christ-event (2:19-20). In fact, no one will be considered "righteous" by Torah-observance (a general fact whose grounds become clear in 3:10-12 and 3:22).

At least three interpretative decisions are interwoven in this reading of 2:16: (a) the referent of ἔργα νόμου; (b) the meaning of δικαιοῦσθαι; and (c) the meaning of πίστις Χριστοῦ. We will take each in turn:

(a) ἔργα νόμου. The context suggests that ἔργα νόμου here refers to *the practice of the Jewish Law (the Torah).* The phrase explicates the earlier comment about whether or not Peter "lives Jewishly" (2:14), Jewish life-practices being understood by Paul, and by his contemporaries, as a matter of regulation by the Torah.[58] "Works of the law" is Pauline shorthand and not precisely paralleled in Greek-speaking Judaism, but it echoes the many scriptural commands

56. This knowledge is therefore derived at least in part from practice (Matlock, "Rhetoric," p. 199 n. 26). There is no reason to find here the echo of a formula propounded by the other missionaries in Galatia (*pace* de Boer, "Paul's Use"); only Paul is known to have put matters in such antithetical terms. Cf. the discussions in Martyn, *Galatians,* p. 264 n. 158; D. Campbell, *The Deliverance of God* (Grand Rapids: Eerdmans, 2009), pp. 842-47.

57. Paul's wording, "a person is not justified on the basis of works of the Law except (ἐὰν μή) through faith in Christ" (2:16), has prompted considerable discussion. Does he initially allow "works of the Law" and "faith in Christ" to be conjoined grounds for justification, before he sets them in an antithesis? If so, is this initial allowance a rhetorical move, or does it reflect a shared Jewish-Christian formula? See the debate in Dunn, *Jesus, Paul, and the Law,* pp. 195-98; de Boer, "Paul's Use"; A. A. Das, "Another Look at ἐὰν μή in Galatians 2:16," *JBL* 119 (2000): 529-39. There are a number of possible readings that do not require that Paul radically alter his viewpoint mid-sentence: ἐὰν μή could be used with the sense "but," or, if it does express an exception, it could be construed with the opening clause ("a person is not considered righteous . . . except through faith in Christ") with the intervening phrase ("on the basis of works of the Law") prematurely canvassing the alternative (see H. Räisänen, "Galatians 2.16 and Paul's Break with Judaism," *NTS* 31 [1985]: 543-53; Longenecker, *Galatians,* pp. 83-84). The polarity between Torah-practice and faith in Christ is eventually, at least, quite clear.

58. Although the adverb ἰουδαϊκῶς (2:14) is rare (cf. Josephus, *B.J.* 6.17), it is not uncommon for Josephus and Philo to refer to "Jewish laws" (ἰουδαϊκοὶ νόμοι/ἰουδαϊκὰ νόμιμα, Josephus, *Ant.* 14.258; 18.55; Philo, *Legat.* 159, 170, 256). "To live Jewishly" was readily understood in antiquity as meaning "to observe the Jewish laws."

to "do" or "practice" the Torah (e.g., LXX Exod 18:20, with the noun ἔργα).[59] There is no material difference in this letter between "works of the Law" and "the Law": δικαιοῦσθαι ἐξ ἔργων νόμου (2:16), διὰ νόμου δικαιοσύνη (2:21), and ἐν νόμῳ δικαιοῦσθαι (5:4) seem to mean much the same thing.[60] The term ἔργα reflects the fact that the Law requires observance in practice, but what is significant is not the bare fact of practices (and thus not "works" as such) but that they derive from, and are oriented to, the Torah. Although the Gentile mission threw certain of these practices into special relief (e.g., circumcision and dietary laws), there is no reason to restrict the referent of ἔργα νόμου "primarily" or "in practice" to those rules that created boundaries between Jews and Gentiles (*pace* Dunn).[61] Rather, Paul uses the Antioch incident to speak about Torah-observance in general: the issue is the validity of the Torah in grounding and defining "righteousness." When read in this context, it becomes clear that the issue is *not* the subjective value of "works" as a misconstrued means of eliciting God's favor (Luther), nor "human enterprise" that depends on human rather than divine initiative (Martyn), but the practice of the Torah as though it were the authoritative cultural frame of the good news. The qualifier νόμου (which generally in this letter means the Jewish Torah)[62] gives ἔργα in Galatians their problematic connotations (cf. 3:2, 5, 10), because the Torah is no longer the definitive measurement of "righteousness" (value) that counts before God.[63] Although Paul's theology in Galatians has wide im-

59. For full discussion of this evidence, see de Boer, *Galatians*, pp. 273-78. Philo, *Praem.* 126, speaks of good people who accomplish the laws by works (τοὺς νόμους ἔργοις ἐπιτελούντων).

60. Similarly ἐξ ἔργων νόμου (3:2, 5, 10) seems to be identical to the simpler formulation ἐκ νόμου (3:18, 21).

61. Following his 1983 essay on the "New Perspective," Dunn has expressed in a variety of forms his conviction that this phrase has as its primary referent certain practices that constitute "boundary-markers" between Jews and non-Jews. While acknowledging that, at one level, the phrase denotes Torah-observance in general, Dunn has insisted that Paul's particular target is the practice (or function) of the Torah in dividing Jew from non-Jew: "in practice" Paul has these Torah-practices "primarily" or "particularly" in view (see Dunn, *Jesus, Paul, and the Law*, pp. 194-95, 223; *Galatians*, pp. 135-37; *The Theology of Paul the Apostle* [Grand Rapids: Eerdmans, 1998], pp. 354-59; *New Perspective*, pp. 213-15; for his latest statement, see *New Perspective*, pp. 23-28). For a critique of Dunn's treatment of this matter, see F. Watson, *Paul and the Hermeneutics of Faith* (London: T&T Clark, 2004), pp. 334-35 n. 41 and R. B. Matlock, "Sins of the Flesh and Suspicious Minds: Dunn's New Theology of Paul," *JSNT* 72 (1998): 78-80.

62. This is unambiguously clear in 3:17, if not already from the connection between 2:14 and 2:16. To find reference here to Roman political euergetism (Kahl, *Galatians Reimagined*, pp. 196, 199) lacks both philological and contextual support. Galatians 5:23 and 6:2 are the only cases in this letter where νόμος could mean something other than "Mosaic Law" or "Torah."

63. The noun and verb from the ἐργ-root are valued positively in the Spirit (5:6; 6:4, 9-10).

plications (3:28; 6:14-15), this breadth does not arise from the fact that "works" or "working" signifies a faulty soteriology. "Not by works of the Law" means, quite concretely, "not by the practice of the Torah."[64]

(b) δικαιοῦσθαι/δικαιοσύνη. The knowledge shared by Christ-believing Jews is that a person is not "considered righteous" (δικαιοῦσθαι) on the basis of the practice of the Torah. As we have seen, terms for "sin" (ἁμαρτωλοί, ἁμαρτία, 2:15, 17) cluster around this verb from the δικαι-root, "sin" and "righteousness" being common antonyms in Pauline discourse (cf. Rom 5:12–6:21). Elsewhere in Galatians, the verb δικαιοῦσθαι is placed in parallel to the noun δικαιοσύνη (3:6-8; 5:4-5) and the adjective δίκαιος (3:11), such that all three require to be interpreted together. The issue in 2:16 is the basis on which people are properly categorized with labels from the δικαι-root. The verb δικαιοῦται (its first occurrence in 2:16) is probably in the passive voice.[65] Although the passive could be impersonal ("is considered δίκαιος") it probably implies *the assessment of God;* the phrase δικαιοῦται παρὰ τῷ θεῷ in 3:11 (cf. Rom 2:13) suggests that God's verdict is in view (cf. 3:8). Thus, the question discussed in 2:16 is the basis on which someone is considered δίκαιος by God.

The verb δικαιοῦσθαι both in Hellenistic Greek and in the LXX has a fairly consistent meaning: to be thought, or adjudged, "righteous" (in the sense of "in the right," "proper," or "innocent").[66] Since the label "righteous" is socially

64. The discovery of an equivalent Hebrew phrase in 4QMMT (= 4Q398, frag. 14-17, col. II) has led to varying evaluations of whether and how it stands parallel to Paul (e.g., Dunn, *New Perspective,* pp. 333-39). As Bachmann observes, the exact phrase in 4QMMT (C 27) might be better translated "the regulations of the Torah" (M. Bachmann, *Anti-Judaism in Galatians? Exegetical Studies on a Polemical Letter and on Paul's Theology,* trans. R. L. Brawley [Grand Rapids: Eerdmans, 2008], pp. 19-31). But it is not clear how this translation could fit Galatians 2:16, where the Greek phrase suggests the practice of such regulations; in any case, it is doubtful that this rare Hebrew expression can determine the meaning of Paul's Greek. Nonetheless, Bachmann (pp. 1-18) is right that the emphasis in Paul lies not on the "doing" as such but on the Torah as the normative structure of life. For further analysis of the issue, see J. de Roo, *Works of Law in Qumran and in Paul* (Sheffield: Sheffield Phoenix Press, 2007); M. Bachmann, "Was für Praktiken? Zur jüngsten Diskussion um die ἔργα νόμου," *NTS* 55 (2009): 35-54.

65. The verb is clearly passive in its two other occurrences in 2:16, as in 2:17. The verb can occur in the middle (e.g., Sir 7.5), and may do so in Galatians 5:4, which would thus mean "you who consider yourselves 'righteous' in the terms of the Torah"; it is less likely that this latter constitutes a "conative" passive ("you who try to be considered 'righteous,'" *pace* de Boer, *Galatians,* p. 270 n. 204).

66. For recent literature on this topic see, e.g., Esler, *Galatians,* pp. 159-69, and Westerholm, *Perspectives Old and New,* pp. 261-84; for older literature on Septuagintal usage, see J. A. Ziesler, *The Meaning of Righteousness in Paul: A Linguistic and Theological Enquiry* (Cambridge: Cambridge University Press, 1972), pp. 47-85; N. Watson, "Some Observations on the Use of

attributed (i.e., dependent on the opinion of others), this verb is used for the recognition, in legal or non-legal contexts, that someone is properly to be considered "righteous" or "in good standing" — in a general sense, "vindicated," or in the specific context of a criminal lawsuit, "acquitted" (innocent of the charge).[67] In our context, the future δικαιωθήσεται in 2:16c might evoke a "final judgment" (cf. 5:5, the "hope of righteousness"), but the present tenses in 2:16 (cf. 3:8, 11; 5:4) suggest that what matters is not only who *will be* considered "righteous" at the end of history, but also who *is* considered such (by God) already now.[68]

In 2:16, Paul appeals to the recognition common among Jewish believers that a person is considered "righteous" by God not on the basis of Torah-observance, but on the basis of πίστις Χριστοῦ (on which, see below).[69] As

---

ΔΙΚΑΙΟΩ in the Septuagint," *JBL* 79 (1960): 255-66. The normal meaning of the verb, as all agree, is to recognize or declare someone to be "righteous" — generally, someone who already is so, but whose status was under challenge or doubt. One thus needs very strong warrant to find here a quite different meaning, "to rectify," "to set things right" (Martyn), or to "make righteous" (de Boer, *Galatians,* p. 291). As we shall see, one can make good sense of Paul's argument in Galatians without departing from the normal meaning of the verb: in the case of a believer, God recognizes as "righteous" a person who has been reconstituted in Christ. That reconstitution is articulated in other terms (2:19-20), not conveyed by the verb δικαιοῦσθαι. This verb describes the recognition by God of the worth of a person who has already been transformed by participation in Christ.

67. Thus in the LXX the verb means in a general sense to be regarded, declared, or proved to be "righteous" or "in the right" (e.g., LXX Ps 18:9; 72:13; Mic 6:11; Isa 45:26; Ezek 16:51-52; Sir 1:21; 9:12; 34:5). Since this often takes place in the face of suspicion or opprobrium, it has the additional sense "to be vindicated." In the impersonal third person, it can mean simply that something is thought right or proper (Tob 6:11; 12:4; parallel to ἀξιοῦται, cf. LSJ s.v.). In a legal context, where a judge makes this decision, the verb in the passive voice means (in a civil case) to receive a decision in one's favor (to be declared in court to be "in the right"), or (in a criminal case) to be acquitted (cleared of an accusation); see, e.g., LXX Exod 23:7; Deut 25:1; 1 Kgs 8:32; Mic 7:9. But it is important to note that acquittal here means that one is shown to be in the right, not that one is forgiven or absolved of guilt. The verb thus has, as Ziesler insists, "declaratory force" (*Meaning of Righteousness,* p. 48). If there is forgiveness or absolution involved, it is described in other terms.

68. Bultmann, following Luther, took the connection of the term with God's future and final judgment (1 Cor 4:3-5; Rom 2:13) to indicate a fixed meaning: "to be justified" means to be declared "just" by God in the eschatological courtroom (a verdict, however, already anticipated for those who are in Christ; Bultmann, *Theology of the New Testament,* 2 vols. [London: SCM Press, 1952], vol. 1, pp. 270-85). But one could equally read the evidence the other way around: those considered "righteous" (by God) are those who believe in Christ, as will be fully evident and finally confirmed at the last judgment; for a critique of Bultmann on this point, see E. P. Sanders, *Paul and Palestinian Judaism* (London: SCM Press, 1977), pp. 493-95.

69. Paul is unusual in attaching to the verb δικαιοῦσθαι the prepositions ἐκ and διά: the two appear to be interchangeable in 2:16. The former may be influenced by the wording of Habakkuk (see Gal 3:11), but parallel expressions with ἐν (3:11; 5:4; cf. 1 Cor 4:4) suggest that

we saw in Part II, the label "righteous" is commonly applied in Jewish texts to those who are fitting candidates for God's saving beneficence. In *Wisdom* 10, it is the "righteous" (δίκαιοι) who are qualified to be beneficiaries of the salvation granted by "Wisdom" (10:4, 5, 6, etc.): to be "righteous" does not mean to be "saved," but it means to be worthy of the divine gift of salvation (see above, 5.2). Similarly, in *4 Ezra*, the "righteous" *(justi)*, who are proved to be such at the final judgment, will be those on whom God will "have mercy," as he ushers them into the glorious age to come (e.g., 7.88-99; 14.28-35). "Righteous" is thus a standard label for those who are fit for salvation — understandably so, since God would naturally give gifts to those worthy of them. Paul is no doubt conscious of the common Jewish assumption that the people to whom this label belongs are those who keep the Torah; but he here specifically denies that anyone is considered "righteous" (by God) on the basis of Torah-observance. Peter and he realize that God reckons as "righteous" those whose lives are marked by faith in Christ — those whose faith displays that they derive their new mode of existence from the death and resurrection of Christ (2:19-21).[70] If "righteousness" is defined in such terms, the most important task is to stay loyal to "the truth of the good news." Believers can stray over the Torah-line (living "in a Gentile fashion" like Peter in Antioch), because the Torah is not in fact the norm of "righteousness" recognized by God.

Since "to be recognized as righteous" is *to be considered a worthy recipient of salvation,* but not itself to be saved, there is no implication that Jews outside of Christ thought that they could *achieve salvation* by Torah-observance, earning it by their efforts rather than receiving it from God.[71] As we have seen,

---

the prepositions do not have distinct connotations (*pace* C. H. Cosgrove, "Justification in Paul: A Linguistic and Theological Reflection," *JBL* 106 [1987]: 653-70). In all cases, the reference is to the evidential basis for God's verdict that a person's status is "righteous." The question is, what is God looking for when he pronounces someone "in the right"? Is it practice of the Torah, or faith directed toward what has happened in Christ?

70. Wright properly resists the tendency in the theological tradition to treat "justification" as a summary label for every feature of "salvation." But he transmutes the language of "righteousness" into quite other terms (the verb means "to be reckoned by God a true member of his family," N. T. Wright, *Justification: God's Plan and Paul's Vision* [London: SPCK, 2009], pp. 96-101) and thus blunts the sharp point in Paul's denial that the Torah is the normative standard for "righteousness" and "sin." If God acknowledges as "righteousness" the effects of the Christ-event, believers who live in faith, and thus on the basis of that event, can brush off charges of "sin" that will arise from others using the Torah as the basis of judgment.

71. Two interpretative misjudgments lead to this erroneous reading: (1) that δικαιοῦσθαι means "to be *made righteous*" (a causative meaning impossible to justify from Greek usage, Jewish or non-Jewish, *pace* Martyn, *Galatians,* p. 265); and (2) that "to be righteous" means *in itself* to be saved. In combination, on this reading, Paul is denying that a person can get oneself saved by keeping the Law. Even Bultmann, who tends to make "being justified" synonymous

it is everywhere recognized in Second Temple Judaism that salvation is a gift of God. But it is also common (though not universal) to insist that God gives this supreme gift to fit and worthy beneficiaries (see above, 10.2). What Paul here denies is that Torah-observance makes a person a fitting beneficiary of divine gift, since no one is (or will be) considered "righteous" on that basis.[72] What Jewish believers have come to realize, through their "calling" in grace and their experience in Christ, is that *the saving gift has already been given in Christ, without regard to worth, and that God considers "righteous" those whose new lives, evidenced in faith, have been generated from the Christ-event* (2:19-20).[73] To be "considered righteous by faith in Christ" is thus the result of the Christ-gift, not the condition for it.[74] But with "righteousness" thus redefined, a key definition of worth — the main currency of the old symbolic capital — has been recalibrated by "the truth of the good news."

(c) πίστις Χριστοῦ. I interpret this phrase as "faith in Christ," and the positive statements of 2:16 can be taken to mean, "we know that a person is considered righteous by God on the evidence of faith in Christ." As the following verses make clear, "to be considered righteous by faith in Christ" (2:16) is "to be con-

---

with "being saved," recognizes that in Paul, "strictly speaking, righteousness is the condition for receiving salvation or 'life' " (*Theology*, vol. 1, p. 270). As Philo would insist, there is a distinction between a *cause* and a *condition:* salvation is a gift from God (cause), but (on his view) it is properly given only to those who are fitting (condition); see above, 6.3.

72. The categorical statement of 2:16c ("by works of the Law will no flesh be considered righteous") may hint at a further reason for Paul's discounting of Torah-practice: it is doomed to failure and could never win recognition in God's eyes as "righteousness." If so, the reason for this failure is not spelled out (as it is in Romans), but similar hints to the failure of the Torah may be given in 3:10-12 and 3:21-22. Paul's reasoning would thus draw on a double logic: "righteousness" in terms of the Law is not only excluded by the Christ-event, but also impossible on its own terms. As 3:21-22 suggests, the "life" that counts as "righteous" before God cannot be given by the Law (since its sphere of operation is under the power of sin). But it is given in Christ (2:20), and its presence, marked by faith in Christ, is what God reckons as "righteousness."

73. We should therefore resist the suggestion that the verb δικαιοῦσθαι takes on a new meaning in Paul, becoming a *transfer term* for "getting into the body of the saved" (Sanders, *Paul and Palestinian Judaism*, pp. 470-72, 544-46). Westerholm rightly notes that the application of this term in Paul is extraordinary (*Perspectives Old and New*, pp. 273-84) but this is not because its meaning shifts, but because people are regarded as "righteous" on the basis of an extraordinary, incongruous gift. The verb does not change in meaning from "consider righteous" to "make righteous"; it applies to people who have been changed.

74. Those now considered "righteous" in Christ are accordingly worthy to be heirs of the future inheritance (3:29; 4:7), that is, of "the kingdom of God" (5:21) or "eternal life" (6:8). But their worth is derived from incorporation in the effects of the Christ-gift, which was given without regard to worth.

sidered righteous in Christ" (2:17): faith is the evidence that one's life is incorporated into the saving, transformative dynamic of the Christ-event, which is nothing less than the death of the self (2:19) and the emergence of a new life more properly described as "Christ in me" (2:20). "Torah-practice" and "faith in Christ" are in one sense parallel: they are both evidenced in human lives and could be taken as grounds for being considered "righteous." But "faith in Christ" is not just an alternative orientation or a different pattern of life: it is the mode of a new life, suspended from an event that has *created what is humanly impossible,* life out of death (2:19-20). God considers this "righteous" not because faith is a superior disposition, but because faith in Christ is the expression of a life derived from the Christ-event, a new creation (6:15) that has been released from the power of "the present evil age" (1:4). We do not have to imagine here a "transfer" of "the righteousness of Christ," effected through a believer's union with Christ.[75] It is enough to say that God recognizes as "righteous" those who indicate, by faith in Christ, that the Christ-event has become the ground of their being.

This recognition is accorded on the basis of "faith in Christ," not because this faith in itself establishes a kind of "worth," but because it is directed to the event in which was created, without regard to worth, a new source and mode of life in relation to God (2:19). Just as the emphasis in the first of the two antithetical phrases, "works of the Law" (ἔργα νόμου), falls on the second term (the practice of the *Torah,* cf. the shortening in 2:21 and 5:4), so in the second, "faith in Christ" (πίστις Χριστοῦ), the emphasis falls not on "faith" but on the *Christ* on whom this faith is founded (cf. the shortening in 2:17). For Paul, what is essential about faith is only that one is "seeking to be considered righteous *in Christ*" (2:17).[76] The "faith" terminology is valuable because it echoes what was "pre-announced" regarding Abraham (3:6) and what was prophesied in Habakkuk (3:11): both scriptural sources connect "righteousness" to "faith." "Faith" had also already become early Christian shorthand for "the good news" and for its effect on human lives (cf. 1:23; 3:23). But Paul has no interest in "faith" as such, as a special cognitive mode or subjective experience, only in *faith in Christ,* which is the mark of those whose lives have been reconstituted and reordered by the death and life of Christ.[77]

75. For Luther's reading, which combines concepts of "justification" and "participation," see S. Chester, "It Is No Longer I Who Live: Justification by Faith and Participation in Christ in Martin Luther's Exegesis of Galatians," *NTS* 55 (2009): 315-37.

76. Cf. F. Neugebauer, *In Christus: Eine Untersuchung zum paulinischen Glaubensverständnis* (Göttingen: Vandenhoeck & Ruprecht, 1961), pp. 156-72, for the close relationship between ἐκ πίστεως and ἐν Χριστῷ.

77. On this reading, the *content* of "faith in Christ" is given in the confessional statements

There are several reasons for reading the phrase πίστις Χριστοῦ as an "objective genitive" ("faith in Christ") or, better, a "genitive of quality" ("Christ-faith"), referring to the faith exercised by believers that signals their dependence on and reconstitution by Christ.[78] The phrase is helpfully disambiguated by Paul himself in the center of 2:16 by the appearance of the verb, used not of Christ but of believers: "we have believed in Christ Jesus" (εἰς Χριστὸν Ἰησοῦν ἐπιστεύσαμεν). Similarly, in the subsequent chapter, the expression ἐκ πίστεως appears three times following the foundational text about Abraham's faith ("he believed in God," ἐπίστευσεν τῷ θεῷ, 3:6-9).[79] The early Greek readers of Paul interpreted the πίστις Χριστοῦ phrase in this way, even though the faithfulness or obedience of Christ (expressed in different terminology) was for many an important theological motif.[80] Paul does not mean, of course, that people are "saved" by doing one thing (believing) rather than doing another (practising the Law). The salvific divine initiative took place in the Christ-event (1:4; 2:20) and takes its grip on human lives in the "calling" of God through grace (1:6, 15). What Paul is discussing in 2:16 are not complete soteriological systems, but the evidential basis on which God can consider someone "righteous" (or worthy) in his sight. "Christ-faith" (or "faith in Christ") is the sign of a prior, transformative event: it is the mode of life generated by the self-gift of Christ (2:20).[81]

---

of 2:19-20. These make clear that faith is no subjective achievement, but the self-involving recognition that what God has given in Christ is the death of the "I" and the creation of a new life dependent on the life of Christ.

78. If the term "objective" reduces the Christ-event to an objective fact external to the believer (rather than the ground and source of one's new being), the label may be misleading. An alternative label (an "adjectival" genitive or "genitive of quality") or a different translation ("Christ-faith") might avoid this implication. But the relation between the two nouns can be determined only on wider contextual grounds (here, Gal 2:11-21), not by disputes over grammatical labels. See M. Wolter, *Paulus: Ein Grundriss seiner Theologie* (Neukirchen: Neukirchen-Vluyn, 2011), pp. 76-78, suggesting that the genitive functions like the not-yet-invented adjective "Christian," and "bringt die exklusive Bestimmtheit des Glaubens durch seiner Ausrichtung auf Jesus Christus zum Ausdruck" (p. 77).

79. See Matlock, "Rhetoric," explicating this equivalence. Campbell's response (*Deliverance*, pp. 840-41, 1145-46) fails to blunt the force of Matlock's structural analysis and depends on an implausible reading of πιστεύειν ἵνα (2:16) as "believe that."

80. See M. Silva, "Faith versus Works of Law in Galatians," in D. A. Carson, P. T. O'Brien, and M. A. Seifrid, eds., *Justification and Variegated Nomism*, vol. 2: *The Paradoxes of Paul* (Tübingen: Mohr Siebeck, 2004), pp. 226-34, and R. Harrisville, "ΠΙΣΤΙΣ ΧΡΙΣΤΟΥ: Witness of the Fathers," *NovT* 36 (1994): 233-41; the counter-examples since adduced have proved unconvincing, or at best uncertain. Ephesians 2:8-10 and James 2:14-26 show early interpreters of Paul reading his references to πίστις as believers' faith (R. B. Matlock, "Even the Demons Believe: Paul and πίστις Χρίστου," *CBQ* 64 [2002]: 300-318, at pp. 306-7).

81. Cf. F. Watson, "By Faith (of Christ): An Exegetical Dilemma and Its Scriptural Solu-

The alternative reading, the "subjective" (or "authorial") genitive ("the faithfulness of Christ"), plays a central role in Martyn's reading of Galatians (see above, 11.4.3). Building on linguistic arguments advanced by Hays and others, Martyn suggests that Paul here adapts a Jewish-Christian formula that connected "righteousness" to the work of Christ (e.g., Rom 3:25; 4:25; 1 Cor 6:11). He also finds in 2:21 an indication that "the faithfulness of Christ" alludes to the death of Christ (both being placed in antithesis to "righteousness" through "Law"). He concludes that "*pistis Christou* is an expression by which Paul speaks of Christ's atoning faithfulness as, on the cross, he died faithfully for human beings while looking faithfully to God."[82] In the extended discussion of this conundrum over recent years, linguistic and grammatical arguments have proved to be indecisive. If the objective genitive reading creates "redundancy" (e.g., at Gal 2:16; 3:22), that is hardly a substantial objection: on any account, 2:16 is full of repeated or redundant expressions.[83] The relevant genitival phrases in Galatians are all accompanied by verbs that unambiguously speak of human "believing" (2:16; 3:6, 22), while nowhere in this letter is the verb πιστεύειν or the adjective πιστός used of Christ.[84]

Martyn's reading of this phrase (like the parallel readings by Hays and Campbell) seems influenced by his reaction to certain Protestant construals of "faith," and by the polarity between divine and human initiative that he finds to dominate the letter (see above, 11.4.3).[85] Against the Bultmannian language

tion," in M. Bird and P. M. Sprinkle, eds., *The Faith of Jesus Christ: Exegetical, Biblical, and Theological Studies* (Milton Keynes: Paternoster Press, 2009), p. 159: "faith constitutes the righteousness of the generic individual only insofar as it is oriented towards and grounded in Christ and the saving divine action enacted in him."

82. Martyn, *Galatians,* p. 271; cf. pp. 249-53, 263-75.

83. For a classic statement of the arguments on both sides, see R. B. Hays, *The Faith of Jesus Christ: The Narrative Substructure of Galatians 3:1–4:11,* 2nd ed. (Grand Rapids: Eerdmans, 2002), pp. 249-97. It is clear that ambiguous genitives such as this should be interpreted from their immediate context, not from "parallels" adduced elsewhere (e.g., Rom 3:3; 4:16) or from general observations about genitival expressions.

84. The adjective is used of Abraham in 3:9. Elsewhere in Paul's letters, 2 Corinthians 4:13 is the only possible candidate for the application of the verb to Christ, but even that is disputable. Christ's obedience (ὑπακοή) is a motif of importance in Romans 5:19 (cf. Phil 2:8), but this is never glossed by Paul as his faithfulness to God (or to his calling). In fact, the relationship between Christ and God (e.g., "looking faithfully to God") is nowhere the subject of attention in Galatians, and it is not clear why Paul should speak of his death by metonomy in this roundabout way. For a critique of the semantic confusion caused by loose glosses of the term πίστις as faith/faithfulness/obedience, which create a "hyper-concept" encompassing practically every aspect of the Christ-event, see R. B. Matlock, "Detheologizing the ΠΙΣΤΙΣ ΧΡΙΣΤΟΥ Debate: Cautionary Remarks from a Lexical Semantic Perspective," *NovT* 42 (2000): 1-23.

85. As Matlock points out, if a contrast is intended with the agency of humans, why did

of "decision," where faith is a human act made "possible" by the act of God in Christ, Martyn insists that "for Paul faith does not lie in the realm of human possibility": God's prior act in Christ both elicits and causes human faith.[86] With parallel concerns, Hays argues that the objective genitive reading would place emphasis on a human "religious disposition," a "cognitive disposition or confessional orthodoxy"; indeed, to interpret our phrase as "faith in Christ," he suggests, "verges on blasphemous absorption in our own religious subjectivity."[87] But Paul has no interest here in faith as a religious disposition, only as belief (or better, *trust*) in the generative event of the death and resurrection of Christ. What matters is not the subjectivity of belief, but the focus and basis of that faith: the unconditioned gift of God in Christ. To describe the choice as between an "anthropological" and a "Christological" alternative is (as Watson has remarked) "disingenuous": "the reference to Christ is absolutely fundamental in both cases."[88]

As we have seen (above, 11.4.3), Martyn takes the antinomy between "works of the Law" and "the faithfulness of Christ" to express *in nuce* the divine-human polarity that he finds central to the letter. "Law-observance is a merely human act, whereas the faith of Christ is the deed of God."[89] To make human "faith in Christ" the basis for "rectification" would reverse the sequence in Pauline soteriology: "God's rectifying act . . . is no more God's response to

---

Paul not speak more clearly about the ἔργον Χριστοῦ ("Detheologizing," pp. 11-13)? Martyn's other arguments appear less than decisive: none of the cited Jewish-Christian formulae contain the word πίστις; on 2:21, see below.

86. Martyn, *Galatians,* pp. 275-77. Martyn's strong reaction to the notion of "autonomous wills" (p. 276) is characteristic of his theological concerns; his acknowledgement that Paul also speaks of human believing is hedged about by concerns to show that God's act ("the faithfulness of Christ") is both prior to and causative of human faith (p. 276). For these "perfections" of grace in Martyn's theology, see above, 3.5.4. For the Bultmannian language, see Bultmann, *Theology,* pp. 274-75, 284, 314-30, and the analysis above in 3.5.2.

87. Hays, *Faith of Jesus Christ,* pp. 171, 184-85, 283, 293. For a collection of statements by Hays and others expressing this anxiety, see Matlock, "Even the Demons Believe," pp. 309-11.

88. Watson, "By Faith (of Christ)," p. 159, in reaction to Hays, *Faith of Jesus Christ,* p. 277, who contrasts "the salvific efficacy of Jesus Christ's faith(fulness)" with "the salvific efficacy of the human act of faith directed toward Christ." No one (not even Bultmann) would claim that human faith has "salvific efficacy." Campbell's claim that the objective genitive leaves faith "anthropocentric" ("Romans 1.17 — A Crux Interpretum for the *Pistis Christou* Debate," *JBL* 113 (1994): 265-85, at p. 273) and Keck's assertion that the objective genitive "separates Christ from justification, which now depends solely on human believing" (L. E. Keck, "'Jesus' in Romans," *JBL* 108 (1989): 443-60, at p. 454) both misrepresent what they oppose. For a reminder of the original Lutheran reading, see J. A. Linebaugh, "The Christo-Centrism of Faith in Christ: Martin Luther's Reading of Galatians 2.16, 19-20," *NTS* 59 (2013): 535-44.

89. Martyn, *Galatians,* p. 251.

human faith than it is God's response to human observance of the Law. God's rectification is not God's response at all. It is the *first* move; it is God's initiative carried out by him in Christ's faithful death . . . Christ's faith is not only prior to ours but also causative of it."[90] Besides the questionable reading of δικαιοῦσθαι (which, as already noted, does not mean "to be rectified" but "to be considered righteous"), what we may observe here is the concern to amplify the *priority* and *efficacy* of grace (Martyn's characteristic concerns; see above, 3.5.4), with the additional support of "the faithfulness of Christ."[91] But this is unnecessary (as well as exegetically unproven): Paul is absolutely clear that the saving event in Christ, and its impact in "calling" both Jews and Gentiles, is a divine initiative, incongruous with any worth (including any "initiative") by human agents. Faith in Christ, as we have seen, does not compromise this in any way: it is the mark of one who is incorporated into that transformative event.

We may sum up our reading using the anthropologists' metaphor of symbolic "capital" (and the Pauline language of accounting, λογίζεσθαι; Gal 3:6; 2 Cor 5:19). To consider "the works of the Law" the criterion of worth (i.e., "righteousness") is to assume the validity of a symbolic capital that has been shown to count for nothing before God. To make the Gentiles "Judaize" is to invest in that symbolic capital, but "we know" in Christ that this is not what God considers valuable. To take "the works of the Law" as the measure of value is to bank on an outdated currency — like collecting sixpences in the UK, when the country no longer uses shillings and pence. That is dead currency, because the Christ-gift has rendered it no longer of value; in fact, as Scripture shows, it was never the currency some have taken it to be (cf. Gal 3:10-12, 21). So, what is the new currency? Hardly some other human capacity or some inherent token of worth, but "faith in Christ" — the acknowledgement that the only thing of value is Christ himself. Faith is not an alternative human achievement nor a refined human spirituality, but a declaration of bankruptcy, a radical and shattering recognition that the only capital in God's economy is the gift of Christ

90. Martyn, *Galatians*, pp. 271, 276. In parallel fashion, Hays takes the subjective genitive as crucial for the theological interpretation of the letter: "this unrelenting emphasis on the priority of Christ's (or God's) willing and doing over any human will or action is the theological keynote of the whole letter"; "we are justified not by anything we do but by Jesus Christ" (*Faith of Jesus Christ*, pp. 155, 211; cf. pp. 275 and xlvii). He differs from Martyn in interpreting the faithfulness of Christ as "representative" of human faith, such that believers participate in Christ's faith(fulness); cf. M. D. Hooker, *From Adam to Christ* (Cambridge: Cambridge University Press, 1990), pp. 165-86. Hays's reading is supported by finding reference to Christ in the figure of the "righteous one by faith" (Gal 3:11; cf. Rom 1:17) — a thesis decisively undermined by Watson, "By Faith (of Christ)."

91. Cf. Matlock, "Even the Demons Believe," pp. 309-13, for a parallel critique of the "hyper-Protestantism" operative in this reading.

crucified and risen. Faith directed to, and centered on, Christ recognizes, under the impact of the good news, that there is no element of value locatable in the human being. It invests everything in the only capital that counts: Christ.

12.5.4. Galatians 2:17-21

We may now rejoin the flow of the argument, reading on from 2:17 to 2:21. Jewish believers, Paul claims, have come to see that "righteousness" is not defined by Torah-observance. What God recognizes as "righteous" is a life marked by faith in Christ, a life created by, and oriented to, the Christ-event. Thus "righteousness" (and its antonym, "sin") have been recalibrated by the Christ-event. It is very important that Jewish believers themselves have come to realize and to practice this in Antioch, at least before the arrival of the people from James, since that creates the environment in which Gentile believers regulate their lives not by "living Jewishly" but by faith in Christ. The implications are clarified by the objection of 2:17: if we (that is, "we Jews," 2:15), who seek to be considered "righteous" in Christ, have been found to be "sinners" (by living in a "Gentile fashion," 2:14), does this mean that Christ promotes sin?[92] Here the context for reading is crucial: in the wake of the Antioch dispute, this sentence reflects not a general discovery that all humanity is sinful (cf. 3:22), but those specific occasions (such as in Antioch) when living "in a Gentile fashion" out of loyalty to the good news causes believers to be labeled "sinners" (as defined by the Torah).[93] Paul constructs an absurd image of Christ as an agent of sin in order to force the choice with which he confronted Peter: either abandon Christ in reinstating the authority of the Torah, or challenge the Torah's definition of "sin." This latter option is depicted in 2:18-20 as the route undertaken by a paradigmatic "I." Since it is absurd to imagine that Christ could sanction sin, Paul gives the rationale for the alternative, the subversion of the Torah as an ultimate authority.

92. The following μὴ γένοιτο suggests that ἀρα (however accented) introduces a question (see J. M. G. Barclay, *Obeying the Truth: A Study of Paul's Ethics in Galatians* [Edinburgh: T&T Clark, 1988], p. 79 n. 11). Christ would promote sin (as a διάκονος ἁμαρτίας) if out of allegiance to Christ they had indeed committed "sin" (e.g., in commensality with Gentiles at Antioch).

93. For the passive of εὑρίσκω as "be identified" or (in a negative sense) "be found out," see 1 Cor 4:2; Phil 3:9; 1 Cor 15:15. I retain this reading of 2:17-18 (cf. Barclay, *Obeying the Truth,* pp. 78-80) despite the iteration of alternatives (e.g., J. Lambrecht, *Pauline Studies: Collected Essays* [Leuven: Peeters, 1994], pp. 205-36), which diminish or deny the connection to the Antioch incident: Lambrecht finds Paul "forgetting" the Antioch incident in 2:14b-17 only to return to it abruptly in 2:18. Eckstein, *Verheissung,* pp. 30-41, follows the traditional reading that Jewish believers here discover in Christ that they too are sinners — because everyone is.

That the Antioch dispute is the context for this line of argument indicates the importance of social experience in radicalizing attitudes toward the Torah. In eating with Gentiles out of loyalty to "the truth of the good news," Jewish believers have found themselves looking like "sinners" in the eyes of the Torah, and that experience has brought to a head a clash of authority that Paul finds inherent in the Christ-event itself. That Paul is more ready than Peter to recognize this clash is a symptom of his greater exposure to the company of Gentile believers and the modified *habitus* thus formed. Although a Jew, he has lengthy experience of communities whose social intimacy and shared meals were apt to disregard Jewish customs and thus to suspend the authority of the Torah. His experience has created a disjunction in his cultural allegiance, matching and arising from the disjunctive effect of the Christ-event.[94] As he expresses the matter here, because his incorporation into the Christ-event has executed his former self, his previously total allegiance to the Torah has been broken; a new identity has emerged, solely grounded in and oriented to Christ.

Using himself as a paradigm, Paul contends that if he were to reconstruct what he has demolished (that is, the authority of the Torah), he would constitute himself a "transgressor" in Torah-terms, by repeated Gentile-like behavior (2:18).[95] But the authority of the Torah *has been demolished:* he has "died to the Law through the Law in order to live to God" (2:19). What is announced here is not the cessation of the Torah itself, but the end of its claim of ultimate authority in the life of Paul (*qua* believer). Believers are no longer "under the law" (3:25; 5:18): it has ceased to exercise a definitive or normative role. That this break has come about "through the Torah" (διὰ νόμου, 2:19) is highly ironic. Paul may allude here to his own experience (where loyalty to the Torah led him to oppose God's "assembly," 1:13) or to the dilemmas of his mission, where the clash between the demands of the Torah and allegiance to Christ undermined his former allegiance.[96] On any account, in comparison with all we know of Second Temple Judaism, Paul's statement in 2:19 is absolutely

94. This dialectical relationship between experience and theology is noted by Holmberg, "Jewish *versus* Christian Identity"; cf. B. Holmberg, "Understanding the First Hundred Years of Christian Identity," in B. Holmberg, ed., *Exploring Early Christian Identity* (Tübingen: Mohr Siebeck, 2008), pp. 1-32, on the "feedback" effect of social experience.

95. Paul would make himself a παραβάτης (a transgressor of a rule), not because it is impossible to live under the Torah without sin, but because, by reinstating the authority of the Torah, he would condemn as sinful his previous failure to live in accord with its rules ("living in a Gentile fashion"). For literature and further argumentation in support of this reading, see Barclay, *Obeying the Truth,* p. 80.

96. Other readings of the Torah's role in its own demise are possible: that the Torah had a hand in the cursing of Christ (3:13) or that it reveals or incites sin (Rom 7:7-25).

breathtaking: his break with the Torah, he says, is *in order to live (in faithfulness) to God* (ἵνα θεῷ ζήσω). The capacity to make such a statement signals a profound dislocation: like all other Jews, he desires to "live to God," but the Torah no longer defines what this entails.

The language of "death" and "life" (2:19) already hints at the cause of this dislocation, which is immediately made explicit: "I have been crucified with Christ"; "it is Christ who lives in me" (2:19-20). Paul has broken with the authority of the Torah not because of a willful decision on his part, but under the impact of the Christ-event, which has wholly reconstituted his existence. The crucifixion of Christ — not just a death, but a cursed and scandalous execution (3:13; 5:11) — marks a radical disjunction. The reference to the "Christ who lives in me" gestures to the resurrection (1:1), which founds a radically new existence. For believers, these are not past events contemplated from a distance: they are imprinted onto their very existence ("I have been crucified with Christ") in a way that collapses the distance between past and present.[97] "Living to God" is not just a reorientation of the self, but a mode of existence founded on, and shaped by, the life of another, the life of "Christ in me." The Christ-event therefore founds not only a change of vision and value, but a change of "self." Out of that newness, every value is newly evaluated and every norm reassessed.

Since it is "Christ who lives in me," "the life I now live in the flesh I live by faith in the Son of God who loved me and gave himself for me" (2:20). With characteristic subtlety, Paul depicts the believer's agency as both replaced ("it is no longer I who live . . .") and remade ("the life I now live . . .").[98] Because a new self has been created in Christ, everything that may later be said regarding the agency of believers has reference back to that generative foundation. But because Paul is untroubled by later Christian controversies over the causative roots of the believer's agency, he will address his hearers, without hesitation, as responsible agents (e.g., Gal 6:7-10). What is important in our context is the orientation of this new life, in faith. If the Torah is no longer the final authority on how to "live to God," a new criterion is formed by the narrative of "the Son of God who loved me and gave himself for me" (2:20). This incongruous gift has subverted the normal definitions of worth and instituted, in their place, new norms, motivations, and practices, whose central value is love (cf. 5:6, 13; 6:2).

97. See Barclay, "Paul's Story," pp. 142-46.

98. On Paul's ability to alter and reverse expressions of agency, see J. M. G. Barclay, "'By the Grace of God I Am What I Am': Grace and Agency in Philo and Paul," in J. M. G. Barclay and S. J. Gathercole, eds., *Divine and Human Agency in Paul and His Cultural Environment* (London: T&T Clark, 2006), pp. 140-57. For later reflections of this same complexity, see Gal 4:19; 5:25.

Paul's discourse thus reaches its climax in the theme of gift, the Son's self-giving (2:20) and the χάρις of God (2:21). There emerges here a perfect homology between the narrative shape of the Christ-event and its character as incongruous gift. In narrative terms, the good news describes a radical disjunction, a death from which arises a miraculous new life. Faith is the sign that believers recognize this disjunctive story as the truth about themselves, as they share in the narrative of Christ. But Christ's death is also a gift given without regard to the worth of the recipients. Because it is incongruous, this gift bypasses and subverts preexisting norms; it does not fit any pre-constituted system of value. Thus, both in content and character, the Christ-event shatters every human paradigm of congruity and connection: it grounds a life that is "not in accord with human norms" (οὐ κατὰ ἄνθρωπον, 1:11), not beholden to schemata of value derived from human history or culture.

2:21 clinches the argument that has run from 2:14. Paul will not refuse the gift of God (οὐκ ἀθετῶ τὴν χάριν τοῦ θεοῦ), which has been enacted in the self-gift of Christ in death.[99] For "if righteousness were by the Torah" (that is, if "righteousness" were defined by the standard of the Torah), "Christ died to nil effect." To continue as if believers were obliged to live "Jewishly," in accordance with the Torah's definition of value, would be to refuse the transformative impact of the Christ-event. The death of Christ entails death to the Torah (2:19): to continue to live under its authority would be to nullify the impact of the cross (2:21; cf. 5:11). Paul evokes the death of Christ not to exclude an alternative soteriological mechanism (salvation by works), but to counteract an appeal to the Torah as the normative definition of "righteousness" — the appeal advanced both in Antioch and in Galatia. The Christ-event has revolutionized the believers' existence, recalculating their norms. If they think that "righteousness" is Torah-defined, or act as if it were, they are no longer true to the good news. The gift enacted in the death of Christ has fundamentally reshaped every system of values, and to reestablish the Torah as the ultimate norm would be to refuse God's gift. That event is either reflected in the norm-breaking practice of communal life or is in danger of being altogether denied. The good news stands or falls with the realization, in thought and practice, of the incongruous Gift.

99. It is overly speculative to take this sentence as response to an accusation that Paul rejects the grace of God embodied in the Law (Martyn, *Galatians*, p. 259). But the implication is that the Galatians' subordination to the Torah would entail a rejection of the gift of God in Christ (1:6; 5:4).

CHAPTER 13

The Christ-Gift, the Law, and the Promise (Galatians 3:1–5:12, with 6:11-18)

The first two chapters of Galatians have made clear that Paul identifies God's "gift" specifically with what was enacted in Christ. The multiple manifestations of this gift — the call of believers, the creation of new "life," and, as we shall see, the gift of the Spirit — refer back to its definitive instantiation in the death (the self-gift) of Christ (1:4; 2:20). Because this gift was given to both Jews and non-Jews without regard to preexisting criteria of worth, its recipients are "free" from the conventional assessments of cultural capital. The gift effects, in Pauline terms, a "co-crucifixion" with Christ (2:19), bringing a former mode of existence to an end; as the source of a new life, it reorders the identity and allegiance of believers. The Antioch incident revealed that loyalty to "the truth of the good news" may conflict with the standards of the Torah. In Paul's view, the capacity of the good news to override cultural constraints is confirmed or denied in such diagnostic events: to reinstate the Torah as the ultimate authority would be to deny the essence of the Christ-event as an unconditioned gift. This gift is thus evidenced in the formation of new communities whose patterns of social life challenge the regnant systems of value.

The middle chapters of Galatians, with their intricate discussion of Law and promise and their complex weave of Scriptures, appear at first sight removed from this practical agenda. However, Paul makes clear at the beginning (3:1-5), the middle (4:8-20), and the end (5:2-12) of this section that the pressing issues in the Galatian churches remain uppermost in his mind. Against the other missionaries' persuasive demands that the Galatians align their faith in Christ to the practice of the Torah, Paul insists that the Christ-event is the fulfillment of God's promise but does *not* confirm the Torah as the authoritative framework for life. In this chapter, I will plot the way in which Paul coordinates the Christ-gift with "promise" but not with "Law," creating a narrative characterized by continuity and consistency *at the level of divine purpose,* but by discontinuity and incongruity *at the level of human history*, reflecting the incongruous relation between the divine gift and its recipients. First, however, we will survey a number of passages that frame this discussion and ground it in the Galatian realities. These passages demonstrate the misfit between the Christ-gift and the systems of value influencing the Galatians, and therefore clarify the socially creative dynamic of the gift.[1]

13.1. The Christ-Gift and the Refusal of Pre-constituted Systems of Worth

13.1.1. Galatians 3:1-5

Paul's direct address to the Galatians (3:1) goes to the heart of the issue: "this only is what I want to learn from you" (3:2).[2] The event "displayed" in Paul's announcement of the good news was the crucifixion of Jesus (3:1), that is, the χάρις of God (2:21) and the self-gift of Christ (2:20). As far as Paul is concerned, every dimension of the Galatians' life in Christ grows out of, and revolves around, this gift-event, but the current risk of losing this incomparable benefit makes him wonder what envious "evil eye" has been cast upon them.[3] The new life arising from this gift (2:20) has been active and powerful among them in the form of the Spirit (3:2, 5). This, too, is a gift "received" (λαμβάνειν, 3:2, 14), the gift of the promise to those who believe (ἵνα . . . δοθῇ τοῖς πιστεύουσιν, 3:22) — not a second gift given after, and independent of,

1. The following discussion presupposes a structural analysis of the letter in which 3:1 begins a new section that runs with minor variations of focus and rhetoric through to 5:12; for recent discussion, see M. C. de Boer, *Galatians: A Commentary*, New Testament Library (Louisville; Westminster John Knox Press, 2011), pp. 11-15 (who finds here two major sections, 3:1–4:7 and 4:8–5:12). What is striking is the constant interruption of the "theoretical" train of argument by paragraphs concerning the Galatians' experience and their current social options (3:1-5; 3:26-28; 4:8-20; 5:2-12).

2. C. H. Cosgrove, *The Cross and the Spirit: A Study in the Argument and Theology of Galatians* (Macon: Mercer University Press, 1988), rightly highlights the importance of this section in revealing the current issue in Galatia; but he downplays the extent to which Paul has already framed the crisis in the opening two chapters.

3. Paul asks, "Who has bewitched you (or, cast on you the evil eye)?" The verb βασκαίνω is associated with envy (an envious glance causing damage to others), and thus presupposes that the Galatians have a benefit of which others are jealous (cf. 4:17). For discussion (with additional, but less certain, suggestions), see J. H. Neyrey, "Bewitched in Galatia: Paul and Cultural Anthropology," *CBQ* 50 (1988): 72-100; B. W. Longenecker, *The Triumph of Abraham's God: The Transformation of Identity in Galatians* (Edinburgh: T&T Clark, 1998), pp. 150-55; and S. Eastman, "The Evil Eye and the Curse of the Law: Galatians 3.1 Revisited," *JSNT* 83 (2001): 69-87.

the Christ-gift, but the presence of the divine gift in Christ at the existential level (the Spirit of God's Son "in the heart," 4:6). Paul wants to know what the conditions were in which, having "seen" the good news of this gift (Christ crucified, 3:1), they experienced it in the form of the Spirit. Did (and does) God distribute this gift according to the criteria of worth expressed in the practice of the Torah (ἐξ ἔργων νόμου, 3:2, 5), or in accordance with the message that was received in faith (ἐξ ἀκοῆς πίστεως)?[4] If the gift of the Spirit did not, and does not, require Torah-practice as the necessary qualification for receipt, it cannot be embedded within the system of worth ("righteousness") defined by the Torah (2:21; 3:6). What Paul wants the Galatians to remember is that there was nothing that made them worthy of the gift. All they did was receive the message in faith, that is, in the declaration of bankruptcy that recognizes in Christ's unconditioned love the sole source of their worth (2:20).[5]

This appeal to experience therefore establishes a logic no different from what has already been argued in 2:15-21 and will be demonstrated from Scripture (3:6ff.). The Christ-gift was not a Torah-event: it was not enacted, distributed, or experienced within the criteria of value established by the Torah. The initial and continuing gift of Christ's Spirit to Gentiles who do not practice the Torah is the phenomenological evidence that the Christ-gift is not located within the framework of "living Jewishly" (2:14). As in Acts (see

4. The expression ἐξ ἀκοῆς πίστεως is capable of many translations, as both nouns and the genitive relation between them can be variously interpreted; for a summary of options, see H. Schlier, *Der Brief an die Galater,* KEK (Göttingen: Vandenhoeck & Ruprecht, 1971), pp. 121-22; R. B. Hays, *The Faith of Jesus Christ: The Narrative Substructure of Galatians 3:1–4:11,* 2nd ed. (Grand Rapids: Eerdmans, 2002), pp. 124-32; de Boer, *Galatians,* pp. 174-75. Given its usage elsewhere in Paul (1 Thess 2:13; Rom 10:16-17), the first noun probably means "the message" (rather than the act of hearing). In relation to πίστις (probably "faith" as the act of believing, rather than "the faith" believed, cf. 1:23), the phrase could mean either "the message received in faith" or "the message that elicited faith."

5. Martyn's paraphrase of ἐξ ἀκοῆς πίστεως ("the proclamation that has the power to elicit faith") and his discussion of 3:2 (*Galatians: A New Translation with Introduction and Commentary,* Anchor Bible 33A [New York: Doubleday, 1997], pp. 286-89) evidence the same anxiety about the role of human agency that we noted in his reading of 2:16 (see above, 12.5.3). He finds here the same antithesis between a *human* act (observance of the Law) and the *divine* act (the message from God that elicits faith). De Boer takes this polarity even further, finding in πίστις a reference not to human faith but to the faithful death of Christ (*Galatians,* pp. 175-77). But the fact that Paul does not disambiguate his expression suggests that he does not share this concern, and the immediately following reference to Abraham's faith (3:6) puts de Boer's reading into doubt. Of course the faith of believers refers to and arises from the Christ-event, but Paul does not need to marginalize human faith, or to specify its cause, because faith in Christ is not a human achievement or a condition for God's granting of the gift, only the recognition that the gift has already been given in "Christ crucified" (3:1).

Acts 10:44-48; 11:17-18; 15:8-11), it is when they witness the scandalous gift of the Spirit to Gentiles that Jewish observers are shocked into recognition that the Christ-event cannot be confined within the parameters of their tradition. For Paul, this is the confirmation of (and also the grounds for) his conviction that the Christ-event is an incongruous gift.[6] What shocks him about the Galatian believers is not that they are trusting in their own good works, as a subjective fault in self-understanding, which puts the self in the place of the sufficient work of Christ (Luther), but that, by adopting the socially ratified standards of value embodied in the Torah, they are confining the gift within pre-established systems of worth. The Spirit is given where the good news is received in faith — that is, where its recipients have been reconstituted by, and reoriented to, an event that occurred without regard to worth. To repackage this gift as given in alignment with Torah-practice would be to transform it into a gift of "Judaism" (1:13, 14). For Paul, the cross cannot be thus contained without being nullified (5:10; 6:12). The Spirit cannot be thus confined without being lost (3:4). A Torah-conditioned Spirit is no Spirit at all, only flesh (3:3).[7]

13.1.2. Galatians 5:2-6

Framing the discussion of Law and promise at its other end is a paragraph written with pointed directness (5:2): "Look, I Paul say to you. . . ." Here circumcision, the key feature of Torah-practice being urged on Galatian male converts, comes into focus (cf. 6:12-13), and, as before, Paul presents the options as all or nothing. To take on circumcision would not be an addition to their faith in Christ: they would lose thereby all the benefits of Christ (5:2). Circumcision, Paul insists, would be for them a sign of submission to the

6. Gal 3:1-5 gives credence to Dunn's claim (noted above, 11.4.2) that a good part of Paul's argument rests on *experience* (his own and that of the Galatians; cf. 1:12-17; 4:12-20). But it was not simply the "existential power" of the experience of the Spirit that "relativize[d] whatever had come before" (*The Theology of Paul's Letter to the Galatians* [Cambridge: Cambridge University Press, 1993], p. 95). This experience was interpreted by Paul with reference to the character of the Christ-gift (and vice versa). The unconditioned grace of the Christ-event was correlated with the experience of God's unconditioned action in the lives of believers.

7. The appearance of the potent term σάρξ, in unqualified form and in antithesis to πνεῦμα, is significant. The word is already associated with human existence (1:16), but acquires additional connotations in its polarity with the newly arrived Spirit (cf. 4:6). For discussion, see below, 14.1.1. Paul's reference to "perfecting in the flesh" is ironic, reflecting his claim that to move "forwards" into Torah-observance is a disastrous move "backwards" to the Galatians' pre-believing past (cf. 4:8-11).

entirety of the Law (5:3). It would represent the acceptance of the Torah as the criterion of righteousness ("you who would be considered righteous in terms of the Law," οἵτινες ἐν νόμῳ δικαιοῦσθε), framing the Christ-event as a Torah-conditioned gift (5:4). From Paul's perspective, this does not just qualify or limit the Christ-gift: precisely in this qualification and limitation it annuls it altogether — or rather, annuls their benefit from the gift: "you have been invalidated, in disjunction from Christ (κατηργήθητε ἀπὸ Χριστοῦ), you who would be considered righteous in terms of the Law; you have fallen out of the gift (τῆς χάριτος ἐξεπέσατε)" (5:4). We note again the identification of "Christ" and "gift" (aided by the assonance between Χριστός and χάρις/χάριτος), such that "gift" is no free-standing category but is defined by its relation to Christ. To set this gift, the Christ-gift, within a commitment to the regulative authority of the Torah is not to enhance or protect it, but to lose it altogether.

Why so? The logic of exclusion is first affirmed in 5:5 and then explained in 5:6 (each opening with γάρ). It is by the Spirit, Paul maintains, that we await the hoped-for righteousness by faith (5:5) — a compressed summary of Galatians 3–4, stressing that righteousness is associated not with Torah-practice but with the Spirit-given status of heir, granted to those who believe in Christ (3:8, 14, 22). But why is this gift incompatible with the requirement that Gentile believers get circumcised? Paul has nothing against circumcision as a rite, or as a physical mark of Jewish ethnicity. He does not reverse his own circumcision, nor does he expect other Jews to do so (cf. 1 Cor 7:17-19). But to require circumcision of Gentile believers is to place the Christ-event within the parameters of worth defined by the Jewish tradition, and that would make the Christ-gift conditioned by something outside and before itself, in this case the values of Jewish ethnicity and Torah. It is not that Paul thinks *uncircumcision* — the unmarked state of the male — is in any sense superior. While Jews regarded male circumcision as a sign of Jewish distinction, non-Jews in a Hellenistic and Roman environment were apt to consider circumcision a barbaric disfigurement of the male body.[8] But because the Christ-gift was given without regard to this (or any other) physical distinction — because it was given to circumcised Jews *and* uncircumcised non-Jews — it is indifferent to both states of the male body and would be wholly misconstrued if either were made a necessary condition for its receipt or continuing effect. "In Christ Jesus," Paul insists, "neither circumcision is worth anything (τι ἰσχύει) nor uncircumcision" (5:6). The Greek τι ἰσχύει is derived from the world of finance, and means, "is worth

8. For Hellenistic critique of circumcision and Jewish response, see Josephus, *C. Ap.* 2.137; Philo, *Spec. Leg.* 1.1-3. The Jewish custom was often the butt of jokes in Rome (e.g., Petronius, *Sat.* 102.14; Martial 7.82; 11.94).

something."[9] Both conditions are denied differential value (neither is worth more than the other) because the gift was given in Christ without regard to either. Paul is not advocating some third state beyond this pair, but insisting that neither of these particular configurations of the male body determines the distribution of the gift. To insist on one or the other (in the Galatian context, to insist on circumcision as a superior condition) would be to pervert the good news, which stands or falls by its status as an *unconditioned* gift.

If the issue here were the gaining of salvation by self-reliant works (Luther) it is hard to see why Paul would discount *both* circumcision *and* uncircumcision. Circumcision could be figured as a work aimed to elicit God's favor, but it is not clear how leaving oneself uncircumcised is a "work" in this or any other sense.[10] Yet Paul equally discounts *both* circumcision *and* uncircumcision. Similarly if the issue were "nationalistic imperialism" or the "restriction" of the covenant to Jews alone (Dunn), why is uncircumcision also here devalued?[11] It seems Paul's target is neither ethnocentrism nor the false opinion that good works can gain benefit from God. He subverts *any* form of symbolic capital that operates independently of Christ. In this case, the Christ-gift has no regard to either circumcision or uncircumcision because both are irrelevant to the giving of the gift. What matters now is "faith working through love" (5:6), because the gift evokes faith in an act of unconditioned

9. When ἰσχύει governs a direct accusative, as here, its sense is either legal (to validate something; cf. the intransitive in Heb 9:17) or financial (to be worth something; e.g. Josephus, *Ant.* 14.106; see *BDAG* 4; *LSJ* ἴσχω 3.2; Moulton-Milligan *ad loc.*). Martyn is incorrect to find here connotations of power ("neither circumcision nor uncircumcision accomplishes anything," *Galatians*, pp. 472-73), which are not applicable when the verb, as here, has a direct object (τι); cf. H. D. Betz, *Galatians*, Hermeneia (Philadelphia: Fortress Press, 1979), p. 263. The connotation of "worth" is correctly identified by F. Mussner, *Der Galaterbrief*, HTK (Freiburg/Basel/Vienna: Herder, 1974), p. 352, as already by Marius Victorinus (see S. A. Cooper, *Marius Victorinus' Commentary on Galatians: Introduction, Translation, and Notes* [Oxford: Oxford University Press, 2005], p. 330).

10. Luther takes Paul to critique circumcision on the basis that it represents *trust in* circumcision (*qui confidit circumcisione, WA* 40.2 11.31). He interprets Paul to "exclude the Jews and the work-righteous *(operarii)*; for he says, 'In Christ no circumcision, that is no works or worship or kind of life are of any avail, but faith alone, without any trust in works *(fiducia operum)*' " (*LW* 27:30; *WA* 40.2 37.18-21). He offers no explanation for Paul's equal discounting of uncircumcision.

11. Dunn takes circumcision to symbolize "distinctively Jewish identity": its adoption by Gentiles would require the "complete assimilation and absorption of distinctively Gentile identity into the status of Jewish proselyte," representing "a means of Jewish ideological and nationalistic imperialism" (*The Epistle to the Galatians*, Black's New Testament Commentaries [London: A&C Black, 1993], pp. 265, 267). He does not explain why uncircumcision also loses its symbolic value.

love (2:20), whose creative energy is continued in love-regulated patterns of behavior (5:14; 6:2).

13.1.3. Galatians 6:11-16

The final paragraph of the letter sums up its challenge by again presenting the Christ-event as subversive of normative systems of worth. With personal emphasis (6:11), Paul warns the Galatians against those whose only motives (in his view) are to "make a good showing in the flesh" (εὐπροσωπῆσαι ἐν σαρκί, 6:12) or to "take pride in your flesh" (ἵνα ἐν τῇ ὑμετέρᾳ σαρκὶ καυχήσωνται, 6:13). This terminology highlights the system of honor by which tokens of superiority are made the object of public pride.[12] "Taking pride" (or "boasting") is not problematic in itself (Paul is about to "boast," 6:14; cf. 6:4): what matters is the ground or source of pride. According to Paul, the other missionaries take pride in circumcision, a symbol of worth that in the "good news" system of values is "neither here nor there." Since "circumcision" and "flesh" are readily associated (circumcision is called "the covenant in your flesh," Gen 17:13), Paul trades on the negative connotations of the term σάρξ developed earlier in this letter (3:3; 4:23; 5:13–6:10). But he displays no negativity toward the body as such, and his conceptual map is not recognizably influenced by a bias toward the inner or the invisible. What relegates *both* circumcision *and* uncircumcision to the status of secondary phenomena (6:15) is that there is one, and only one, Archimedean point from which everything else is judged: "For me, there is no way I can take pride in anything except the cross of Christ, through whom the world has been crucified to me and I to the world" (6:14).

This extraordinary statement echoes and amplifies the death announcement of 2:19-20. There Paul pronounced his break with the ultimate authority of the Torah ("I have died to the Law," 2:19); here the caesura has even wider implications. The cross of Christ shatters every ordered system of norms, however embedded in the seemingly "natural" order of "the world" (cf. 4:3).[13] In

12. The reference to "having a good face" (εὐπροσωπῆσαι; cf. God's disregard of the πρόσωπον, 2:6) gestures to the public sphere in which honor-claims are made. There is no reason to find a specifically *legal* sense here (*pace* B. W. Winter, "The Imperial Cult and Early Christians in Pisidian Antioch [Acts XIII 13-50 and Gal VI 11-18]," in T. Drew-Bear et al., eds., *Actes du Ier Congrès International sur Antioche de Pisidie* [Lyon: Kocaeli, 2002], pp. 67-75, followed by J. Hardin, *Galatians and the Imperial Cult* [Tübingen: Mohr Siebeck, 2008], pp. 86-91).

13. Among the connotations of the term κόσμος there belong notions of order, design, and a "natural" structure of values; see E. Adams, *Constructing the World: A Study in Paul's Cosmological Language* (Edinburgh: T&T Clark, 2000).

form (as unconditioned gift), in *content* (as death), and in *mode* (the shame of crucifixion), the cross of Christ breaks believers' allegiance to pre-constituted notions of the honorable, the superior, and the right. Whereas Philo took "the world" (ὁ κόσμος) to be the properly ordered gift of God, whose stable values were reinforced by gifts to worthy beneficiaries, Paul parades the cross as the standard by which every norm is judged and every value relativized. This single and particular event is of universal significance not because it reveals some timeless and universal principle of the cosmos, but because it is beholden to no pre-calculated system of distinction, and privileges no subset of humanity. It is the original radically unconditioned event.[14]

The enormous creativity made possible by this vision of reality is immediately obvious: "For neither circumcision counts for anything, nor uncircumcision, but new creation (καινὴ κτίσις)" (6:15). As in 5:6, Paul announces the irrelevance of taxonomic systems by which society had been divided in subtly hierarchical terms: old "antinomies" are here discounted in the wake of a new reality that has completely reordered the world.[15] The connotations of the phrase "new creation" stretch well beyond individual conversion, gesturing to a cosmic refashioning awaited in the future (cf. 1:4).[16] But in context the primary focus is the *social* novelty of communities that disregard former boundaries by discounting old systems of worth. The "new creation" is indifferent to traditional regulative norms and generates new patterns of social practice: it is instantiated among "those who walk by this κανών" (6:16). In this context, circumcision is neither valued nor denigrated: the circumcised are neither superior nor inferior by being so marked. Precisely by discounting (i.e., not counting) this potentially potent marker of identity, refusing a valuation *either way*, newly formed communities chart a course "at a diagonal" to normal and normative evaluations. Their new identity and allegiance can encompass both states without according ultimate significance to either. To

14. The point is well grasped by A. Badiou, *Saint Paul: La Fondation de l'universalisme* (Paris: Presses Universitaires de France, 1997; translated as *Saint Paul: The Foundation of Universalism*, trans. R. Brassier [Stanford: Stanford University Press, 2003]), though he wrongly identifies the event exclusively with the resurrection (see above, 3.7.2). Badiou finds in the Pauline articulation of the event "the ruin of every attempt to assign the discourse of truth to preconstituted historical aggregates" (p. 6).

15. See Martyn, "Apocalyptic Antinomies in Paul's Letter to the Galatians," *NTS* 31 (1985): 410-24, for whom "antinomy" refers to a pair of opposites foundational to the cosmos.

16. M. V. Hubbard's thesis (*New Creation in Paul's Letters and Thought* [Cambridge: Cambridge University Press, 2002]) that "new creation" refers primarily to the refashioning of the individual (cf. 2 Cor 5:17) overly limits the scope of this concept; for the latest discussion, see T. R. Jackson, *New Creation in Paul's Letters: A Study of the Historical and Social Setting of a Pauline Concept* (Tübingen: Mohr Siebeck, 2010).

mark *indifference* at this point is as strategically important as the dispute over meal-company at Antioch. It indicates that for those created by and beholden to the "new creation," the finally authoritative norm is not the Torah but "the truth of the good news" (2:14), the Christ-event itself (6:14).

13.1.4. Galatians 3:26-28

The framing paragraphs just discussed give us perspective on a key set of sentences, directed to the Galatians ("you"), in the middle of the argument on Law and promise (3:26-28). Here, citing baptismal formulae, Paul celebrates the reconstitution of those who, through baptism, have become identified with Christ: "those who were baptized into Christ have put on Christ" (3:27). Amplifying his earlier statements on the paradigmatic "I" (2:19-20), Paul uses multiple expressions to indicate the creation, in baptism, of a new subjectivity generated by, and dependent on, the Christ-event: believers are "baptized into Christ," have "put on Christ," constitute one person "in Christ," and henceforth "belong to Christ" (3:27-29). This new "location" scrambles previously hegemonic systems of social classification: "there is neither Jew nor Greek, neither slave nor free, no male and female: for you are all one in Christ Jesus" (3:28). The first and last pairings are most relevant to the Galatian crisis, in which both Jewish privilege and male distinction (as the bearer of circumcision) are at issue.[17] But the breadth of scope is comparable to the statement regarding "the world" in 6:14: even apparently "natural" taxonomic distinctions are denuded of their significance in communities united by their overriding identification with Christ.

Paul's baptismal declaration may bear traces of a mythical "oneness" at the origins of history (3:28).[18] However, the unity that Paul here evokes is no original or natural sameness that underlies "superficial" differences of gender, race, and status, but solidarity in identification with an event that deprives con-

17. The pairing "neither Jew nor Greek" counters the higher evaluation of Jewish identity at Antioch, which created a prejudicial withdrawal from non-Jewish company (2:11-15). Kahl rightly observes a scrambling of traditional male roles in Galatians ("No Longer Male: Masculinity Struggles Behind Galatians 3.28?" *JSNT* 79 [2000]: 37-49), not only in relation to circumcision.

18. See W. Meeks, "The Image of the Androgyne: Some Uses of a Symbol in Earliest Christianity," *HR* 13 (1974): 165-208. The denial of the pairing "male and female" is particularly intriguing in its contradiction of Genesis 1:26: it may relate to Paul's preference for celibacy as a better condition for both genders (1 Cor 7). Neither gender requires "completion" or "expression" through marriage (or sex), as each is independently valued and fulfilled in Christ.

tinuing differences of their normal valuation. All the pairings cited by Paul are strongly endowed with hierarchical assumptions. For Jews, to be Jewish is not just "different" from being "Greek," but self-evidently superior to it — and vice versa for "Greeks."[19] The status of "slave" is in everyone's eyes inferior to that of "free," while "male" is on multiple grounds a condition superior to "female."[20] The differences between these categories are not eradicated. Neither ethnic nor gender identity could be simply removed, and in the eyes of the law everyone counted as either "free" or "slave" (or "freed").[21] Paul and Peter remained Jews (2:15; cf. Titus, a "Greek," 2:3), and Paul was still identifiably masculine and free. What is altered, however, is the *evaluative freight* carried by these labels, the encoded distinctions of superiority and inferiority. In common solidarity with Christ, baptized believers are enabled and required to view each other without regard to these influential classifications of worth. Jewish believers should not withdraw from shared meals with non-Jews on the basis of their different, "inferior," ethnicity (2:11-14). Slaves should not be disdained as "mere slaves," since their worth as "siblings" is established in Christ (Phlm 16). What now counts for worth is only one's status in Christ, and the consistency of one's allegiance to him. Paul is free, but *more importantly* a slave of Christ (1:10; cf. 1 Cor 7:17-24); his body is masculine and circumcised, but *more importantly* marked by scars that signal his commitment to the cross (6:17; cf. 5:11).[22] All forms of symbolic capital not derived from "belonging to Christ" now lose their ultimacy. Baptism "into Christ" provides a radically new foundation for communities freed from hierarchical systems of distinction, not because of some generalized commitment to "equality" but because of the unconditioned gift of Christ, which undercuts all other reckoning of worth.[23]

19. The Jewish sense of superiority is evident in Galatians 2:15 and is given a rational grounding in the philosophy of Philo (see above, 6.4). For ancient ethnic claims to superiority, see B. Isaac, *The Invention of Racism in Classical Antiquity* (Princeton: Princeton University Press, 2004).

20. This hierarchical assumption is still partly operative elsewhere in Paul's letters (e.g., 1 Cor 11:2-16). For the many dimensions of female inferiority in antiquity, see A. Carson, "Putting Her in Her Place: Women, Dirt and Desire," in D. Halperin et al., eds., *Before Sexuality* (Princeton: Princeton University Press, 1990), pp. 135-64.

21. The third category, "freed" (1 Cor 7:22), is elided here for rhetorical reasons, but would make no material difference to Paul's claim.

22. For the στίγματα τοῦ Ἰησοῦ (Gal 6:17), see Martyn, *Galatians*, pp. 568-69.

23. Boyarin's powerful critique of Pauline "universalism" (*A Radical Jew: Paul and the Politics of Identity* [Berkeley: University of California Press, 1994]) takes the baptismal formula to express a politics of "coercive sameness" under the guise of an ontological equality. But if unity is derived from common allegiance to an unconditioned event (the Christ-gift), there is no devaluation of particularity in principle, only an insistence that every difference is shorn of

13.1.5. Galatians 4:12-20

In this poignant paragraph Paul again reminds the Galatians of the conditions in which they first received the good news (4:13; cf. 3:1-5), this time emphasizing their astonishing freedom from standard assessments of worth. His preaching was accompanied by some "weakness of the flesh" (4:13), which would normally have led to disdain and rejection. In an over-compressed expression, Paul speaks of their "test" (πειρασμός) in his flesh (4:14): his condition was diagnostic, revealing the extent to which the good news was taking hold among them.[24] Surprisingly, they did not despise him (οὐκ ἐξουθενήσατε, 4:14) in his weakened condition, nor "spit" (ἐξεπτύσατε) — an expression of disdain (and/or fear) in the face of physical deformity.[25] Against normal expectations, they did him no harm (4:12) but, on the contrary, showed a depth of welcome, even friendship, such that they would gladly have donated their very eyes (4:15). Paul's explanation for this counterintuitive and countercultural reaction is simple: they welcomed him as an angel of God, as Christ Jesus himself (4:14). Their reception of this dishonorable preacher "as Christ Jesus" signaled the fact that the good news had revolutionized their assessment of worth.

Friendship entails reciprocity, to which Paul appeals: "become like me, since I (have become) like you" (γίνεσθε ὡς ἐγώ, ὅτι κἀγὼ ὡς ὑμεῖς, 4:12). Although it is not entirely clear what this appeal implies, it is likely that Paul alludes to earlier statements in the letter. As a missionary among Gentiles, he has allowed the truth of the good news to override his previous commitment to the Torah: he has become like them, "living in a Gentile fashion" (2:14), because his allegiance is now exclusively to Christ, the source of his new life in faith (2:19-20).[26] He can

---

prior connotations of worth. If any difference is subsequently reassigned some value, that will be only on the grounds of its worth to Christ (cf. Rom 14–15, discussed below, 16.4). Against Boyarin, Hansen rightly argues that "Paul has demoted all cultural indices apart from those based on participation in Christ and refuses not their preservation but their use as bases of exclusion and judgement" (*"All of You Are One": The Social Vision of Gal 3.28, 1 Cor 12.13, and Col 3.11* [London: T&T Clark, 2010], p. 105).

24. I follow the *lectio difficilior* (τὸν πειρασμὸν ὑμῶν, 4:14) with א*, A, B, and D*, among others. For the meaning, see de Boer, *Galatians,* pp. 279-81.

25. See *BDAG* s.v. The spitting may express insult, revulsion, or the warding off of evil spirits. It is possible that Paul's condition was caused by persecution (A. J. Goddard and S. A. Cummins, "Ill or Ill-Treated? Conflict and Persecution as the Context of Paul's Original Ministry in Galatia [Galatians 4.12-20]," *JSNT* 52 [1993]: 93-126), thus making their welcome of Paul an even stronger indication of their social nonconformity, but this inference is uncertain.

26. Note the similar prominence of the pronoun ἐγώ in 2:19-20; for the general principle, cf. 1 Cor 9:19-21; for this reading see, e.g., R. N. Longenecker, *Galatians,* Word Biblical Commentaries (Dallas: Word, 1990), p. 189; Dunn, *Galatians,* p. 232.

surely expect them to reciprocate as friends, becoming like him in allowing their selves, and thus their values, to be refashioned by the Christ-event. Hence his appeal for imitation of himself (4:12) turns into a yearning that they be shaped not by him but by Christ: "my children, with whom I am again in labor until Christ be formed within you" (μέχρις οὗ μορφωθῇ Χριστὸς ἐν ὑμῖν, 4:19). The echo of 2:19-20 is especially strong ("it is no longer I who live, but Christ who lives in me," ζῇ δὲ ἐν ἐμοὶ Χριστός, 2:20). As Paul diagnoses the Galatian condition, they need to be "rebirthed" such that Christ becomes both the source and the measure of their lives.[27] Their reconstitution by the good news once revolutionized their honor code and its associated system of values; the same freedom from cultural constraints needs to be employed in refusing the demand to submit to the Torah (4:21; 5:1). Those in whom Christ "takes shape" live in accordance with a structure of commitments regulated by the authority of the Christ-event itself, a norm (6:16) to which every other norm must bend. As 5:13–6:10 will show, Paul is conscious that the new communities fashioned around Christ need to be as free from the quest for honor as they are free, in the Spirit, from the dominance of the Torah (5:1, 13, 18). In both respects, this freedom is founded on the capacity of the Christ-gift to remold existence around a cosmos-shattering event (6:14).

The last three passages (6:11-16; 3:26-28; 4:12-20) indicate the breadth of the canvas on which Paul paints the Galatian crisis. At issue is not simply the adoption of this or that Jewish practice, but the capacity of the Christ-gift to re-found and reorient life by a logic that challenges every other attribution of value. To identify, by faith, with the Christ-event is to allow the "new creation" to shatter the taxonomic structures of "the world." Paul views the issues that arise in Galatia as both highly particular (specific demands for male circumcision and Torah-observance) and widely generalizable, since they represent one example of the universal disruption created by the good news. For Paul, the Christ-event changes the story of the cosmos (6:14) and, when creatively embedded in human relationships, it challenges the default setting of every classificatory system (3:28). He announces an unconditioned event that recognizes no cultural or historical pre-conditions and thus reaches into, and challenges, every cultural-historical context. Preexistent systems of distinction, whether derived from the Torah or from a culture of honor, yield to a higher authority established by a truth-event that is beholden to no criteria beyond itself (1:11). For this reason, Paul's world is divided into two, and only two do-

27. For the Christomorphic transformation operative in both Paul and the Galatians, see S. Eastman, *Recovering Paul's Mother Tongue: Language and Theology in Galatians* (Grand Rapids: Eerdmans, 2007), pp. 25-61; B. R. Gaventa, *Our Mother Saint Paul* (Louisville: Westminster John Knox Press, 2007), pp. 29-39.

mains, differentiated not by abstract, eternal truths, nor by cultural traditions embedded in ethnic or social differentiation, but by a unique, unrepeatable, and unconditioned event. This new map of the world — distinguishing what is of God and what is merely human (1:10-12), what is Spirit and what is flesh (3:3), what is "new creation" and what is "the world" (6:14-15) — reconfigures every other map by orientation to a single point of reference, the gift of God in Christ. We must now observe how Paul places the Torah and the Abrahamic promise on that map in the course of Galatians 3–4, and how the narrative of Israel and the witness of the Scriptures are themselves reconfigured by reference to Christ.

13.2. The Christ-event and the Story of the Law

The Christ-event did not come out of the blue. Since it was, for Paul, an unconditioned gift, it did not fit the prior preparedness or worthiness of its recipients; but it did fit God's prior promises and plans. It is crucial for him to identify, however, which features of God's prior acts and purposes correspond to the gift, since these will clarify its quality and character. It is likely that his rivals in Galatia placed the Christ-gift on a narrative line that featured the Torah as the supreme expression of God's will, confirmed by the Messiah Jesus and fulfilled in the Torah-observance of believers.[28] This is precisely what one would expect in any expression of Judaism in Paul's day. In the rich tapestry of Second Temple Judaism, it is hard to find any strands that do not identify the Torah as the definition of virtue or righteousness: in both the homeland and the Diaspora, to be Jewish entailed commitment to the Torah, however diversely justified and variously interpreted. From the texts we have studied (Part II), *4 Ezra* identifies the gift of the Torah at Sinai as the climactic moment in the history of the covenant (*4 Ezra* 3.12-19), such that "law" and "covenant" are practically interchangeable (cf. 7.23-24). Whatever else may falter in the course of history, the Torah cannot be abandoned: "Let many perish who are now living, rather than that the Law of God that is set before them be disregarded" (7.20). Thus, the righteous few who will inherit the age to come are identified by their loyalty to "the Law of life" (14.30). Within a different intellectual frame, but to the same end, Philo took the Torah to express the unwritten law of nature (*Abr.* 1-6, 276), such that the covenant with Abraham already embodied the

28. See above, 11.2. For their possible lines of argument, including arguments from Scripture, see J. M. G. Barclay, *Obeying the Truth: A Study of Paul's Ethics in Galatians* (Edinburgh: T&T Clark, 1988), pp. 65-68.

Torah; observance of the Torah by Jews and proselytes aligns them with the truth of the universe and its moral order. The future blessings of God are for "good people who have fulfilled the Laws by their actions (ἔργα), blessings that [Scripture] says will be completed by the favor (χάρις) of the gift-loving God who dignifies and rewards what is excellent because of its likeness to himself" (*Praem.* 126). The missionaries in Galatia could draw on the Scriptures and on any number of strands in the Jewish tradition to take pride in the Torah as the center-piece of God's engagement with Israel and the world. It was entirely natural that they should place the Christ event within this Torah-configured frame. It seemed obvious that God's gift of Christ (and the Spirit) should be understood in accordance with the Torah, the blueprint of the cosmos and the definitive expression of God's will.

What was entirely *unnatural* for anyone reared in the Jewish tradition was to decenter the Torah, to limit its role in history to an interlude, and to distinguish it categorically from "covenant" and "promise." But this is precisely what Paul does in Galatians 3–4, a narrative account of the purposes of God whose interpretative center is the Christ-event itself. In this section (13.2), we will trace the ways in which Paul subordinates the Torah to the promise(s), and declares its incapacity to provide any worth for God to reward. In the next (13.3), we will survey how Paul connects the Christ-event to "the promises," and in the process redefines their meaning.

13.2.1. The Distinction between Torah and Promise

The crucial narrative arc in Galatians 3–4 is from the Abrahamic promise(s) to the Christ-event (and Spirit), a line in which the Torah plays a subsidiary and time-limited role. Paul first traces this arc in 3:6-14, connecting the Abrahamic promise to faith and to the blessing of the Gentiles (3:6-9), a promise/blessing fulfilled in Christ Jesus and in the receipt of the Spirit (3:14).[29] Along this arc, the blessing is *not* associated with those "who have fulfilled the Law by their actions" (Philo; see above). On the contrary, "those who take their bearings from the practice of the Torah" are associated with *curse* (3:10), while the Torah is strongly *distinguished from* the life "that takes its bearings from faith" (3:11-12; see below). The Torah is thus neither integral to, nor a means toward, the fulfillment of the Abrahamic blessing.

29. 3:14 constitutes the first conclusion to the argument of chapters 3–4 (see de Boer, *Galatians*, p. 167), identifying the Spirit, experienced by the Galatians, with the scriptural promises given to Abraham; this verse ties together many of the key terms from 3:6-9.

This astonishing marginalization of the Torah is given a narrative rationale in 3:15-25. Here, trading on the standard meaning of διαθήκη as "testament" or "will," Paul insists that the original διαθήκη given to Abraham could be neither revoked nor supplemented by the Mosaic Torah, which came 430 years later (3:15-17). This time interval is taken to represent a categorical distinction: inheritance comes either through "promise" or through "Law" (3:18), not through a promise clarified, specified, or otherwise qualified by the Law. It is notable that, having introduced his testamentary analogy (real or contrived),[30] Paul reclassifies the Abrahamic "covenant" as "promise" (ἐπαγγελία): this noun and its cognate verb are found no less than eight times within 3:14-22. The term "covenant" was perhaps employed too loosely in contemporary Judaism with reference to *both* the patriarchal promises *and* the Sinai Torah to serve Paul's purposes in distinguishing between them.[31] "Promise" for Paul points forward to the Christ-event, the new center of his narrative. "Covenant" would do so only ambiguously (cf. 4:24), and "Law" not at all.

If the Law is time-limited at one end (it came *after* the patriarchal covenant), it is also, for Paul, time-limited at the other: its period of office lasts only until the "promise" is fulfilled, that is, only until Christ (3:24). In this connection, Paul uses the metaphor of the παιδαγωγός, the child-minding slave whose job was to protect and discipline children *until such time* as they became adults.[32] Scholarly debate has raged over whether the "confining" role of the παιδαγωγός (expressed in the preposition ὑπό and the verbs φρουρέω and συγκλείω, 3:23) entails some "positive" role (protective, even educational)

30. In most ancient legal systems, it was entirely possible for the testator to change his own will; for recent discussion, see Longenecker, *Galatians*, pp. 128-30. If Paul thinks of the final "ratification" of the will that takes place at the testator's death (so Augustine; see E. Plumer, *Augustine's Commentary on Galatians: Introduction, Text, Translation, and Notes* [Oxford: Oxford University Press, 2003], p. 162), the analogy with God's διαθήκη is rather weak. If he means that no one *other than the testator* can alter or add to the will (so de Boer, *Galatians*, pp. 219-21), he presupposes that the Torah is not of divine origin; but this is more than 3:19-20 expressly states (see below).

31. After 3:17, Paul drops the term διαθήκη, until it is used in relation to *two* "covenants," represented by Sarah and Hagar (4:24, the latter associated with Sinai and thus with Torah). This indicates that (whatever one may say of the *concept*) the *term* "covenant" has neither a significant nor a stable place within Paul's discourse in Galatians. If the concept is made central to Pauline theology (e.g., N. T. Wright, *The Climax of the Covenant: Christ and Law in Pauline Theology* [Edinburgh: T&T Clark, 1991]), this has to be justified on other grounds, and requires a careful differentiation from Torah, and thus from other "covenantal" theologies in Second Temple Judaism.

32. For the role, see *PW* 18.2375-85; N. H. Young, "*Paidagogos:* The Social Setting of a Pauline Metaphor," *NovT* 29 (1987): 150-76.

for the Torah, or only a "negative" (restrictive) one.[33] Whatever one decides, the central point of Paul's metaphor is that "with the coming of faith we are no longer under a παιδαγωγός" (3:25). From the perspective of the Christ-event, Paul sees the Torah as *temporary* and *past:* he is alone among extant Second Temple authors in applying to the Torah the metaphor of the temporary παιδαγωγός, just as he alone articulates the notion of "dying to the Torah" in order to live to God (2:19). Like the guardians and overseers of children in their minority (4:1-2), the role of the Torah comes to an end at the time set by the Father (ἡ προθεσμία τοῦ πατρός, 4:2). The Torah is an interlude in the history of the promise: it is neither the rubric for, nor the centerpiece of, God's ordering of the world.

In its subsidiary, temporary role, Paul accords to the Torah some function in revealing (or perhaps limiting) "transgression" (3:19),[34] but he also distances it, somewhat obliquely, from God (3:19-20). Boldly redeploying a traditional motif regarding the presence of angels at Sinai, Paul says that the law was "arranged" (διαταγείς) through angels (δι' ἀγγέλων, 3:19).[35] It is notable that Paul does not use here the language of gift, which he had employed, just before, for the inheritance promised to Abraham (κεχάρισται, 3:18). Unlike that promise, the Torah is not directly connected to the Christ-gift, and thus, for Paul, falls out of the domain of "gift." Angelic mediation and "the hand of a mediator" (Moses) here place some distance (though not a polarity) between God and

33. For different sides of this debate, see, e.g., D. J. Lull, "'The Law Was Our Pedagogue': A Study in Galatians 3.19-25," *JBL* 105 (1986): 481-96 and D. Sänger, "'Das Gesetz ist unser παιδαγωγός geworden bis zu Christus' (Gal 3,24)," in D. Sänger and M. Konradt, eds., *Das Gesetz im frühen Judentum und im Neuen Testament* (Göttingen: Vandenhoeck & Ruprecht, 2006), pp. 236-60.

34. The expression τῶν παραβάσεων χάριν (3:19) is ambiguous, and interpretations necessarily draw on readings of the surrounding context and of other letters. Those for whom Paul accords the Torah a largely negative role are apt to find here the Torah's function in revealing or even producing transgression (cf. Rom 3:20; 5:14, 20; 7:7; e.g., Schlier, *Galater,* pp. 152-54; de Boer, *Galatians,* pp. 230-31). Those who emphasize the disciplinary or protective role of the παιδαγωγός posit a role in limiting, punishing (or even atoning for) transgression (e.g., Dunn, *Galatians,* pp. 188-90).

35. For angels at Sinai, see LXX Deut 33:2; Acts 7:38, 53; Heb 2:2; Josephus, *Ant.* 15.136; *LAB* 11.5. The participle διαταγείς, in echoing ἐπιδιατάσσεται (3:15), reinforces the sense that the Torah stands outside the covenant/promise trajectory; but the use of the preposition διά rather than ὑπό suggests that the angels are the agents but not the authors of the Torah (*pace* H. Hübner, *Law in Paul's Thought,* trans. J. Greig [Edinburgh: T&T Clark, 1994], pp. 26-27; K. Kuula, *The Law, the Covenant, and God's Plan,* vol. 1: *Paul's Polemical Treatment of the Law in Galatians* [Göttingen: Vandenhoeck & Ruprecht, 1999], pp. 96-133; de Boer, *Galatians,* p. 229, "angels acting independently of God"). Paul's argument requires a *distance* between God and the Torah, not a *complete dissociation.*

the Torah.[36] The strategy is similar to that used by Philo to distance (but not wholly dissociate) God from the creation of fallible humanity. Concerned to maintain God's reputation as the giver of unmixed blessings, Philo found it convenient to use the plural pronoun in Genesis 1:26 ("let us make") to place a gap between God and the creation of humanity, a morally ambiguous creature, with the plural pointing to his intermediary powers (*Opif.* 72–75). By a parallel device, Paul, in re-plotting God's purposes on a trajectory from Abraham to Christ, uses the presence of angels at Sinai to make God's relation to the Torah less immediate and less direct than his relation to the promise. There is no outright denial of a divine role behind the promulgation of the Torah, and no suggestion that the Torah was unworthy of the God of Jesus Christ (an extrapolation easily drawn by Marcion). But because the Torah was neither integral to the story of the promise, nor effective in securing its fulfillment, it is portrayed as standing in an indirect relation to the "one God," whose singular purpose for history was carried by the gift of the promise, anticipating Christ (3:16, 18).[37] This relegation of the Torah arises not from the singularity of the gift, such that gift is in principle dissociated from punishment and law (so Marcion), nor from its perfection as a non-circular donation, free from the demands of law (so Luther). Rather, it reflects Paul's Christological definition of the divine gift, whose anticipation can be traced in the Abrahamic promise, but not in the Sinaitic Law.

13.2.2. The Incapacity of the Torah to Create Worth

Alongside his arguments for the temporary and marginal location of the Torah in the history of the promise, Paul issues a set of statements that indicate its incapacity to produce blessing or life and thus to provide the conditions for the progress or fulfillment of the promise. None of these are fully explained:

36. The mediator is clearly Moses (cf. Philo, *Somn.* 1.143), *pace* Kahl, *Galatians Reimagined*, p. 227 ("an allowance from Caesar or any other imperial ruler"). For the phrase "by the hand of," commonly used in this connection, see, e.g., Lev 26:46 (de Boer, *Galatians*, p. 227 n. 327).

37. Paul takes Moses' role as mediator to suggest that the Torah came through a plurality (the angels) rather than directly from "the one," that is, God (3:20). This implies that God stands at one remove from the "addition" of the Torah, but not that he had nothing to do with it, or that the angels were "tampering with God's promise" (de Boer, *Galatians*, pp. 228-31; cf. Martyn, *Galatians*, pp. 355-58, 364-70). Wright's reading of 3:20a as "mediator of the one family" is unconvincing (*Climax*, pp. 157-74). It posits a close parallel with 3:16, where "the seed," however, is Christ, and not a "single family," and forges an association between monotheism and "a single united family" that has no obvious warrant in this passage.

they gesture to submerged assumptions, or undeveloped ideas, that lie beyond the parameters of this letter. It seems more important to Paul to state *that* the Torah was unable to produce positive conditions of worth than to explain *why.* Such gaps have invited numerous interpretative solutions, some of which invoke the fuller discourse of Romans. For our purposes, however, it is sufficient to note simply how Paul marks the inadequacy of the Torah. His remarks not only reinforce the marginalization of the Torah in relation to the promise, but also establish the character of the Christ-gift as an *incongruous* gift, which neither completes nor rewards any worthiness established through the Torah.

The first indication of this incongruity is Paul's association of the Torah not with blessing (linked to promise, 3:8-9, 14) but with *curse.* Citing Deuteronomy 27:26, Paul rehearses the covenant curse on "everyone who does not remain within everything written in the book of the Law, to do it" (3:10). One might expect this text to be a useful tool in encouraging obedience to the Torah (and perhaps it *was* so used by Paul's rivals), but Paul takes it for granted that the curse is in fact operative on those who live within the Torah, such that "we" require redemption by Christ from "the curse of the Law" (3:13). The interweaving of further scriptural texts in 3:11-12 (echoing Deuteronomy's ποιεῖν ["to do"]) has led some to suggest that the curse rests on the very attempt to "do" the law.[38] But it seems better to follow the surface claim of the citation in 3:10 (a curse on those who do *not* abide by the Law) and to trace Paul's logic to an assumed pessimism about the capacity of those governed by the Torah to remain faithful to it. We have found good evidence for such pessimism in other Second Temple texts — Pseudo-Philo's sad prediction that Israel will sin again and again, *4 Ezra*'s diagnosis of the *cor malignum* ("evil heart") that corrupted Israel from the beginning, and the extreme denigration of the human condition in the Qumran *Hodayot.* Paul's logic (more explicit in Romans 1–3) may overlap with one or more of these, but he seems to take it for granted that the salient condition of those whose lives take their bearings from practice of the Torah (ὅσοι ἐξ ἔργων νόμου) is curse rather than blessing.[39] The compressed argument in 3:11-12, contrasting Habakkuk 2:4 with

38. Schlier, *Galater,* pp. 132-35, deploying the Lutheran interpretation of "works of the law" as presumptuous trust in one's own righteousness (see Luther's lectures on Galatians ad loc.). Dunn suggests that the curse rests on those "who put too much emphasis on the distinctiveness of Jews from Gentiles, and on the special laws which formed the boundary markers between them," *Galatians,* p. 172; cf. Dunn, *Jesus, Paul, and the Law: Studies in Mark and Galatians* [London: SPCK, 1990], pp. 215-41), but this depends on his special reading of "the works of the law." On the weaknesses in both readings of this phrase, see above, 12.5.3.

39. Paul's logic does not assume that blessing would require individuals to be perfect in Torah-observance, but simply that Israel's history proved her collective and persistent inca-

Leviticus 18:5, reinforces the incapacity of the Torah. Because no one is found "righteous" in the sight of God within the terms of the Torah, righteousness is promised (in Habakkuk) on the basis of faith; and the Torah concerns not faith but the practice of its own commands.[40] Thus, the Torah cannot produce the conditions (faith) in which the promise can be fulfilled, and in which it would be fulfilled when "faith arrived" at the coming of Christ (3:14, 25). All that Torah can effect is curse: thus, the arrival of Christ will not be the completion of one blessing with another, but the miraculous creation of *blessing out of curse* (3:13-14), by the counterintuitive mechanism of Christ's becoming "accursed" (3:13). Although the logic of this method is not spelled out, what

---

pacity to be obedient. Understood in this sense, some Jewish texts consider that Israel stood under the covenant curses of Deuteronomy 27–30, some (though by no means all) specifying this curse as "exile." This construal of the curse as "exile" has been assumed to be prevalent in more cases than may be justified in the otherwise helpful analyses of Wright, *Climax*, pp. 137-56, and J. M. Scott, "'For as Many as Are of Works of the Law Are Under a Curse' (Galatians 3:10)," in C. A. Evans and J. A. Sanders, eds., *Paul and the Scriptures of Israel* (Sheffield: Sheffield Academic Press, 1993), pp. 187-221. It is corrected, with new insights, in R. Morales, *The Spirit and the Restoration of Israel: New Exodus and New Creation Motifs in Galatians* (Tübingen: Mohr Siebeck, 2010), pp. 78-114.

40. With a growing number of interpreters, I punctuate 3:11 as "Because (ὅτι) no one is justified before God within the terms of the Torah [as just shown in 3:10; cf. 2:16c], it is clear that (δῆλον ὅτι) 'the righteous person will live from faith'" (cf. F. Thielman, *From Plight to Solution: A Jewish Framework for Understanding Paul's View of the Law in Romans and Galatians* [Leiden: Brill, 1989], pp. 127-28; B. Witherington III, *Grace in Galatia: A Commentary on St. Paul's Letter to the Galatians* [Edinburgh: T&T Clark, 1998], p. 234; A. H. Wakefield, *Where to Live: The Hermeneutical Significance of Paul's Citations from Scripture in Galatians 3:1-14* [Atlanta: Society of Biblical Literature, 2003], pp. 162-67, 207-14; de Boer, *Galatians*, pp. 202-3). In the usual reading (and normal text punctuation), there is an unnaturally long gap between the first ὅτι and the δῆλον that is taken to govern it, and the Habakkuk quote is taken somehow to *prove* the impossibility of righteousness in the Law (although that was already indicated in 3:10). The Leviticus citation, because it matches Deuteronomy 27:26 (sharing the terms ποιεῖν, αὐτά, and ἐν) and stands in contrast to Habakkuk 2:4 (they share the term ζήσεται but describe two different kinds of "life"), cements the conclusion that the way of the Torah is clearly distinguishable from that of righteousness and faith, and does not contribute toward them. There is no reason to find here a generalized contrast between the conditional Torah (which demands "doing") and the promise (which requires only "faith" in God's unconditional saving act; so F. Watson, *Paul and the Hermeneutics of Faith* [London: T&T Clark, 2004], pp. 162-63, 276-77; developed in P. M. Sprinkle, *Law and Life: The Interpretation of Leviticus 18:5 in Early Judaism and in Paul* [Tübingen: Mohr Siebeck, 2008], pp. 133-64). Paul makes it clear that faith also involves action (5:6), arising from and made possible by the Christ-gift (2:20), and that in such action eternal life remains at stake (5:21; 6:8). The Torah is problematic for Paul, not for setting conditions, or for demanding human action prior to God's, but because it stands apart from the promise fulfilled in Christ and is incapable of producing either the righteousness or the faith to which the promise points.

is clear is that history is transformed by the Christ-event, and specifically by the death of Christ, which constitutes not a reward to the previously righteous but a fully incongruous gift.[41]

Further signs of this structure of thought are evident later in Galatians 3–4. Having removed the Torah from the trajectory of the promise, and after making the relation between God and the Torah ambiguous and indirect (3:15-20), Paul asks whether the Torah is actually opposed to the promises of God (3:21). He will certainly not allow such a straightforward antithesis, but in any case, none is necessary, because the Torah and the promises are not two possible means to the same goal. One is simply impossible: the Torah can do nothing to match the efficacy of the promise (3:21-22). If a Law had been given which was able to "make alive" (ζῳοποιῆσαι) — that indeed would have been a gift in Pauline terms — then righteousness would have been attainable and definable within the terms of the Torah (3:21). Paul assumes here that this was not possible, giving as his explanation (γάρ) only that "Scripture enclosed all things under sin" (3:22). We seem to strike here on a submerged assumption parallel to that just noted in 3:10 — and previously evident both in 1:4 ("the present evil age") and in the last clause of 2:16 ("no one will be considered righteous on the basis of Torah-practice"). The assumption is that a dominant power, sin (singular), enjoys hegemony over everything, reducing it to a condition that requires not only release but also the creation of life (ζῳοποιέω). This latter implies that the condition of humanity before Christ is not only slavery to sin but also death: something as miraculous as "making-alive" is required, that is, life from the dead. The logical connections are not brought to the surface of the discourse (a similar iceberg-tip can be sighted in 1 Corinthians 15:56), but they seem to be explicated in Romans (3:10-17; 5:12-21; 7:7-25). What is clear (and all that is necessary for Galatians) is that the Torah was incapable of producing the necessary solution: it could neither liberate people from the dominance of sin, nor give life to the dead. It is not in itself evil or opposed to God's promises, but it is trapped in the same negative condition as "all things." It is precisely from such a disastrous scene of sin and death that the gift of God has erupted as the "new creation" (6:15).

One further dimension of the incapacity of the Torah, neither justified nor explained, leads to the most shocking conclusion of all. As we have seen, Paul associates the παιδαγωγός metaphor with the preposition "under" (ὑπό, 3:25), and this is one of a set of statements in which the Torah is directly or

41. On the logic of redemption from the curse of the Torah through the accursed death of Christ, see M. D. Hooker, *From Adam to Christ* (Cambridge: Cambridge University Press, 1990) (though it is unnecessary to contrast Christ's representative and substitutionary roles).

indirectly linked to this potent preposition (cf. 3:23; 4:2, 3, 5, 21; 5:18). If Paul here uses a Jewish motif to articulate the authority of the Torah,[42] he turns this in a negative direction, representing submission to this authority as a form of "slavery." When an heir, as a minor, is under guardians and household managers (a further metaphor for the Torah), his condition is no different from that of a slave (4:1). Such language entails that when "in the fullness of time" (4:4) the heir acquires his heritage, he does so not by some natural progression of maturation but as a dramatic alteration of existence — a "liberation" from slavery under the law (4:5) and a grant of adoption (ἵνα τὴν υἱοθεσίαν ἀπολάβωμεν).[43] It may seem bizarre than someone already designated an heir (4:1), inhibited simply by age, should be said to require *adoption.* We shall return below (13.3.3) to the indication that the "we" in this passage enjoy a special status as heirs but, even so, Paul's emphasis here lies on an alteration in status, a change from the status of *slave* (4:1, 3, 7) to the altogether different status of *son* (4:5-7). The Torah not only is unable to effect this change but is also implicated in the former slavery; only the Christ-event (the sending of *the Son,* 4:4) can alter this negative condition and create from it a positive result. On every front, it appears, Paul is concerned to frame the Christ-event not as the completion of a Torah-narrative, nor even as a surprising turn within its progression. It is the reversal of the previous human condition and is inexplicable when viewed from the preceding human state, including the state of those under the authority of the Torah.

The most remarkable aspect of Torah-"enslavement" appears in 4:3, where Paul asserts that "we" were enslaved under (again ὑπὸ) τὰ στοιχεῖα τοῦ κόσμου. The meaning of this phrase, which is echoed in "the weak and destitute στοιχεῖα" of 4:9, is heavily disputed; at the same time, that these στοιχεῖα are apparently associated *both* with the Galatians' former pagan worship *and* with their adoption of a Jewish calendar (4:9-10) has seemed to many either

42. Cf. Josephus, *C. Ap.* 2.174: ὑπὸ πατρὶ τουτῷ καὶ δεσπότῃ (the same preposition with a different case); see further J. Marcus, "'Under the Law': The Background of a Pauline Expression," *CBQ* 44 (2001): 606-21.

43. For the association of λαμβάνειν with gift, cf. 3:14, 22; ἐξαγοράζειν (4:5) is associated with buying out of slavery. It is generally agreed that the term υἱοθεσία means here not "sonship" but "adoption," that is, a change of status (here, from slave to son, 4:7); see B. Byrne, *"Sons of God" — "Seed of Abraham": A Study of the Idea of the Sonship of God of All Christians in Paul* (Rome: Biblical Institute, 1979) and J. M. Scott, *Adoption as Sons of God: An Exegetical Investigation into the Background of ΥΙΟΘΕΣΙΑ in the Pauline Corpus* (Tübingen: Mohr Siebeck, 1992). This new status depends not on ancestry but on the sending of *the* Son (4:4) and the receipt of his Spirit (4:6); for the "we" of 4:1-3, it is only this event that enables them to attain their intended identity. For the development of this line of thought in Romans 9–11, see chapter 17.

impossible or nonsensical.[44] But it is hard to deny that Paul makes these associations in both directions. If the Galatians are accused of turning *back* to the "weak and destitute στοιχεῖα" to whom they want to be enslaved *again* (4:9), it is clear that their former "enslavement" to "beings that are non-Gods" (4:8) falls into the category of enslavement to στοιχεῖα. Equally, if the "we" who were heirs while under the guardianship of the Torah can be described as "enslaved under τὰ στοιχεῖα τοῦ κόσμου" (4:3), and if the Galatians' *reversion* to these στοιχεῖα takes place not in a renewal of pagan worship but in the adoption of Jewish calendrical practice (4:10), it appears that life under the Torah can also be characterized as enslavement to στοιχεῖα. It is important to observe the force and the limits of Paul's rhetoric. He is not claiming that pagan worship and Torah-observance are substantially identical; nor does he *identify* the στοιχεῖα either with the "non-Gods" of the pagan pantheon or with the Torah itself. He is simply stating (though this "simply" is shocking enough) that, from his perspective, pagan religious practice and life under the rule of the Torah may be classified in the *same* category of subjection to the στοιχεῖα of the world.

After decades of debate, recent research has confirmed that τὰ στοιχεῖα τοῦ κόσμου most likely refers to the physical elements of the world (not to "rudimentary teaching" or "elemental spirits").[45] Paul's remarkable statements are not explained here (nor in Colossians 2:8-20), but the best available explanation is that Paul represents both Torah-observance and pagan religious practice — hugely different though they were — as beholden to the natural order of the cosmos through alignment to its elemental, physical components.

44. The general terminology of 4:10 ("days," "months," "seasons," "years"; contrast Col 2:16) has led a number of scholars to doubt that Paul is speaking of specifically Jewish practice: alternatives range from "Gnostic" or "syncretistic" practices to the observance of the imperial cult (for the former, see literature cited in Barclay, *Obeying the Truth*, pp. 39 n. 6 and 61 n. 72; for the latter, T. Witulski, *Die Adressaten des Galaterbriefes: Untersuchungen zur Gemeinde von Antiochia ad Pisidiam* [Göttingen: Vandenhoeck & Ruprecht, 2000], pp. 152-68; for pagan timekeeping in general, see T. W. Martin, "Pagan and Judeo-Christian Time-Keeping Schemes in Gal 4.10 and Col 2.16," *NTS* 42 [1996]: 105-19). But there was good reason for Paul to refer to specifically Jewish practices (cf. 4:21) in such general terms. By using terminology that covered both Jewish and pagan timekeeping, he signals the *similarity* with the Galatians' religious past, which is precisely his polemical point in this context (4:8-10); see Barclay, *Obeying the Truth*, pp. 63-64; Martyn, *Galatians*, pp. 416-17; M. C. de Boer, "The Meaning of the Phrase τὰ στοιχεῖα τοῦ κόσμου in Galatians," *NTS* 53 (2007): 204-24, at pp. 216-17.

45. See the fine analysis of de Boer, "Meaning," rightly concluding from the research of Blinzler, Schweizer, and Rusam that "the phrase is a technical expression referring in the first instance to the four elements of the physical universe: earth, water, air, fire" (p. 207); see, e.g., Philo, *Aet.* 107. For a full survey of scholarly views, see Witulski, *Adressaten des Galaterbriefes*, pp. 83-152.

Redeploying the Jewish critique of pagan religiosity as unable to penetrate beyond the physical cosmos to its invisible Creator,[46] Paul characterizes the Jewish calendar, in its alignment to the physics of the cosmos, as *another* symptom of entrapment within the domain of the cosmic elements.[47] Judging by the lack of explication, what seems important to Paul is not *why* (this aspect of) Torah-observance comes under this negative umbrella, only *that* it does. The rhetorical effect is the suggestion that far from moving *forwards* in adopting the Torah, they are moving *backwards* to where they began (4:8-10; cf. 3:3). The Torah is therefore no advantage or aid, no positive framework for "living to God" (2:19). To come under its authority would entail becoming entrapped once more in networks of association that will bring no benefit at all. The στοιχεῖα provide no power to alleviate the human condition: they are weak (ἀσθενῆ). They bring no benefit or gift: they are utterly destitute (πτωχά, 4:9).

As the reference to calendrical observance makes clear (4:10), Paul's discussion of the Torah throughout Galatians 3–4 is directed to a practical end. In marginalizing the Torah in the narrative of promise-to-fulfillment, and in stating in multiple ways its inability to effect that fulfillment, he has more than theoretical purposes in view. The Galatians are being urged by the other missionaries to put their faith in Christ under the authority of the Torah, taking the Jewish way of life as their definitive framework of value (righteousness). Their day-to-day practice is already being shaped in that direction. For Paul, this would not simply turn the clock back to an era pre-Christ. It would place them outside of the trajectory of divine gift, promised and fulfilled (3:15-29). It would not fulfill but nullify their allegiance to Christ (5:4). And it would submit them to a regime wholly unable to resolve the human crisis (4:9). Unlike almost all of his fellow Jews, Paul finds in the Torah an impasse from which only the gift of Christ can provide an exit; and that exit is opened not by God's blessing the fittingly righteous (there are none), but by God's creating life out of death and granting blessing out of curse.

46. *Wisdom of Solomon* 13 critiques those who cannot go beyond the cosmos to the Maker and Lord of all, focusing especially on their supposition that the four elements are themselves "gods" (13:1-4; see de Boer, "Meaning," pp. 218-20). As T. Engberg-Pedersen notes, this looks like a critique of Stoic philosophy in particular (*Cosmology and Self in the Apostle Paul: The Material Spirit* [Oxford: Oxford University Press, 2010], pp. 90-92), though it could be broadened to indict all pagan religiosity for its confusion of the divine with the natural components of the cosmos.

47. This made perfect sense to ancient commentators such as Marius Victorinus, who associated the physical elements with the stars, the calendar, and the force of necessity in the cosmos (see Cooper, *Victorinus' Commentary*, pp. 302-3, 311-14).

13.3. The Christ-event as the Fulfillment of the Promise

13.3.1. Divine Promise and Human History: Narrative Trajectory and Radical Caesura

Although the Christ-gift cannot be situated within the narrative of the Torah, it *is* related to a divine plan articulated in promises first given to Abraham. It is likely that the Abraham narratives featured strongly in the persuasion of the other missionaries in Galatia, but Paul's appeal to such scriptural testimonies does not arise only from the need to counter his rivals.[48] The weight of emphasis in Galatians rests on the Christ-event itself, but this is not comprehensible without reference to "the Father" (1:1-3; 4:1-4), who is unconfined by time (1:5), or to the Scriptures, whose authority is taken for granted (3:8, 22; 4:30). As we have seen, the Abraham story is, for Paul, above all a story of *promise.* The scriptural address to Abraham *looks forward* to the justification of the Gentiles (3:8), who receive the *promise* when they receive the Spirit (3:14). The "covenant" with Abraham consists of *promises* spoken to him and his seed (3:16); the subsequent Torah cannot annul the *promise* (3:17). From this point onwards, ἐπαγγελία (singular and plural) and its cognate verb reverberate through the rest of chapters 3–4 (after 3:14, 16, 17, see 3:18, 19, 21, 22, 29; 4:23, 28), while the divine purpose (see the ἵνα-clauses of 3:22, 24; 4:5) is said to climax in a divinely appointed "time" (ἡ προθεσμία τοῦ πατρός, 4:2). This pattern of language has a double effect. It throws the spotlight onto the Christ-event as *the* moment to which the divine promise was pointing, at the "fullness of time" (τὸ πλήρωμα τοῦ χρόνου, 4:4). And it places this moment within a purposeful trajectory: it occurs neither at random nor by the intervention of an alien God (Marcion), but in accordance with a promise given initially to Abraham and witnessed in the Scriptures.[49]

48. For the place of Abraham in their message, see C. K. Barrett, "The Allegory of Abraham, Sarah, and Hagar in the Argument of Galatians," in J. Friedrich, W. Pöhlmann, and P. Stuhlmacher, eds., *Rechtfertigung: Festschrift für Ernst Käsemann* (Tübingen: Mohr Siebeck, 1976), pp. 1-16; Barclay, *Obeying the Truth,* pp. 52-54 (with reference to earlier literature); Martyn, *Galatians,* pp. 302-6. Martyn suggests that "had the Teachers not had such extraordinary success with their Abraham sermons, we would probably know nothing of Paul's interpretation of the patriarch, for Romans 4 is a reworking of Galatians 3" ("Events in Galatia: Modified Covenantal Nomism versus God's Invasion of the Cosmos in the Singular Gospel: A Response to J. D. G. Dunn and B. R. Gaventa," in J. M. Bassler, ed., *Pauline Theology,* vol. 1: *Thessalonians, Philippians, Galatians, Philemon* [Minneapolis: Fortress Press, 1991], p. 166 n. 15). But Paul's interest in the Abraham stories seems more than merely reactive; for a balanced assessment, see Watson, *Paul and the Hermeneutics of Faith,* pp. 167-219.

49. From Tertullian's response, it appears that Marcion omitted all reference to Abraham

It is crucial to observe, however, that this trajectory represents the history of the promise of *God,* not the continuity or development of the history of *humanity.* The only event recounted between the giving of the promise and its fulfillment in Christ is the "arrangement" of the Torah (3:17-19), but that, as we have seen, is not part of the history of the promise and contributes nothing to blessing or redemption. *At the human level,* the Christ-event is a matter of *discontinuity* and reversal; it is God's counter-movement to the human condition, moving believers from ignorance to knowledge (4:9), from curse to blessing (3:13-14), from slavery to adoption (4:1-7). What arrives at "the fullness of time" is not a development from preceding epochs of human history, but the *reversal* of previous human conditions. On both an individual (1:12-17; 2:19-20) and a global level (3:15–4:11), it represents not continuity, but interruption, transformation, caesura, and miracle. It is not a "shock" at the end of a "many-staged" plan,[50] but God's counter-statement to the previous conditions of the possible, a new creation in the midst of the present evil age (1:4; 6:14-15).

Thus, the Christ-event completes a narrative line projected by the divine promise, but not a narrative progression in human history. By a slanted reading of the promise to Abraham's "seed," Paul finds reference not to multiple generations of Israelite history, but to a single seed, Christ (3:16), and only after and in Christ to a plurality (3:29).[51] In between, there is no development in the story of Israel, no progress or preparation for the future. In relation to the promise, even Israel's history before Christ is represented as an undifferentiated era of unfulfilled anticipation. Where other Second Temple texts (such as Pseudo-Philo, *LAB,* and *The Wisdom of Solomon*) traced in Israel's history

---

in Galatians 3 (Gal 3:6-9, 14a, 15-20, 29) and extensively revised 4:21-31 — no doubt claiming that these passages had been inserted or corrupted after Paul had written the letter; see E. Evans, ed. and trans., *Tertullian: Adversus Marcionem,* 2 vols. (Oxford: Clarendon Press, 1972), vol. 2, pp. 644-45.

50. See N. T. Wright, *Paul: Fresh Perspectives* (London: SPCK, 2005), pp. 53-54. He summarizes his view: "We cannot expound Paul's covenant theology in such a way as to make it a smooth, steady progress of historical fulfilment; but nor can we propose a kind of 'apocalyptic' view in which nothing that happened before Jesus is of any value even as preparation" (p. 54). In Galatians, however, it is not clear that anything has happened *on the human level* as valuable "preparation" for the Christ-event; the divine promise given to Abraham is not preparation but pre-announcement.

51. Paul's insistence on the singular σπέρμα in Genesis 17:8 (Gal 3:16) may be influenced by 2 Samuel 7:12 (for a Messianic reading, see 4Q174 1.10-11), but its singular Christological interpretation has the effect of implying that "between the promise and Christ . . . there were no offspring of Abraham, no heirs of the promise that God made to Abraham" (de Boer, *Galatians,* p. 223).

God's gracious fulfillment of his promises to the patriarchs, Paul glosses over such history as a period of waiting: there is no exodus, no entry into the land, no temple, no division of the kingdoms, no exile, and no return. All we have is an interval during which the heir waits for the time set by the Father (4:1-2). If this heir is Israel (see below, 13.3.3), it is accorded here no agency and no process of maturation. The relation of past human history to the present in Christ is not that of the partial to the complete, or the beginning to the end; it is the relation of potential to actual, anticipated to realized, frustrated to enacted. The "fullness of time" is not an additional chapter in a developing human story: it is that moment when what was promised and foreseen by God, but until then absent on the human stage, was made present in Christ.

If we maintain this distinction between the purpose of God and the development of human history, we can see that the Christ-gift is both entirely *congruous* with the promise of God and wholly *incongruous* with the prior conditions of human (including Israelite) history. The long debates on the place of "narrative" in Pauline theology, and the relative weight to be placed on "continuity" or "discontinuity," can thus be clarified.[52] Galatians certainly places the good news in the framework of a narrative: it announces not the timeless graciousness of God, but the intervention in history of the grace of God in Christ. At the human level, the good news narrates disjunction, not progress: what it reveals is precisely the reversal of conditions between "before" and "after." Martyn's emphasis on the *invasive* character of the Christ-event (his reading of its "apocalyptic" character) rightly stresses this incongruity with the human condition.[53] His aversion to *Heilsgeschichte* ("salvation-history") represents his distrust of human sagas of progress, and reflects the absence from Galatians of a "many-staged plan" on the human level.[54] Wright's notion that Paul "saw himself on a map, a grid, constructed . . . out of the controlling narratives of ancient Israel" hardly fits what we have found in Galatians, while Dunn's emphasis on "the continuity between the story of Israel and that of Christ" suggests a human-level line of progression that is precisely absent from

52. For recent debate on narrative in Paul, see, e.g., B. W. Longenecker, *Narrative Dynamics in Paul: A Critical Assessment* (Louisville: Westminster John Knox Press, 2002). For an earlier significant contribution, see U. Luz, *Das Geschichtsverständnis des Paulus* (Munich: Kaiser Verlag, 1968).

53. See above, 3.5.4 and 11.4.3.

54. See Martyn, "Events in Galatia," contrasting the invasive character of the Christ-event with a "pre-Christ linearity," a notion he considers essential to meaningful use of the term *Heilsgeschichte* ("Events in Galatians," p. 173). As he writes elsewhere, "there are no through-trains *from* the patriarchal traditions and their perceptive criteria . . . *to* the gospel of God's Son" ("Paul and His Jewish-Christian Interpreters," *USQR* 42 [1987-88]: 6, emphasis original).

this letter.[55] At the same time, Martyn's emphasis on the "punctiliar" character of the Christ-event fits only how Paul plots this event on the course of human history (and only in Galatians), *not* its location on the narrative arc from the Abrahamic promise to Christ.[56]

If human history is traced in patterns of cause-and-effect, the divine continuity of promise is apt to work despite, or against, the continuity of the human story: in this sense, "salvation-history" cannot be read out of normal accounts of "history."[57] This paradox is central to the "allegory" of Abraham's two sons in 4:21–5:1. The one (Ishmael) is born according to the normal conditions of human history, "according to the flesh" (κατὰ σάρκα, 4:23, 29); he stands correlative to "the present Jerusalem" (4:25), which may be located on a standard historical map. The other (Isaac) is born contrary to all conditions of the possible, the child of a barren mother (4:27): he comes into existence "through the promise" (δι' ἐπαγγελίας, 4:23) and "according to the Spirit" (κατὰ πνεῦμα, 4:29), a figure for the "children of promise" (4:28) birthed from no historical phenomenon, but from "the Jerusalem above" (4:26). At its foundation, the story of the promise thus "foresees" and "pre-preaches" the good news enacted in Christ (3:8). The Christological signature is traceable in the capacity of divine promise to create the humanly impossible, where reality is suspended from a truth "above" or beyond history, as normally understood. In this regard, Paul's language of "promise" entails the prediction that *God* would do what *only God* could do, defying human expectation.[58] The incongruity of the Christ-gift is the definitive vehicle of this divine commitment to achieve what cannot be imagined in human terms (cf. 1 Cor 2:9-12).

55. Wright, *Paul,* p. 162; Dunn, *Theology of Paul's Letter,* p. 121.

56. Martyn acknowledges that in Galatians Abraham is the recipient of God's promise, but insists that he is a "punctiliar," not a "linear" figure, "not at all the beginning of a line that can be traced through something properly called history" ("Events in Galatia," p. 173). But to describe the covenant promise during the time between Abraham and Christ as existing "in a sort of docetic state" (pp. 172-73) seems to deprive it of its substantial reality as a signpost to the future (Christ). However, my reading of Galatians is analogous to Martyn's view that "Paul's radical reading [of Genesis 16–21] is anthropologically discontinuous in order to be theologically continuous" (p. 176).

57. For the value and the problematics of "salvation-history," see E. Käsemann, *Perspectives on Paul,* trans. M. Kohl (London: SCM Press, 1971), pp. 60-78. He rightly emphasizes its difference from "a theology of history" and its inherently paradoxical character in Paul.

58. For the significance of the promise-motif in this regard, see T. Söding, "Verheißung und Erfüllung im Lichte paulinischer Theologie," *NTS* 47 (2001): 146-70. For the power of the promise as the power to *create* new believers, see M. Wolter, "Das Israelproblem nach Gal 4,21-31 und Röm 9–11," *ZTK* 107 (2010): 14-15, rightly finding a parallel in Philo, *QG* 3.18.

13.3.2. The Christological Re-reading of Scripture

Paul's narrative — both of divine continuity and of human discontinuity — has been shaped by the Christ-event itself. Even the Abraham stories are Christologically refashioned: Paul insists on the singularity of the seed (σπέρμα), identified as Christ (3:16), and equates the blessing promised to the Gentiles (3:8-9) with the Spirit (3:14), a feature entirely absent from the Abraham narrative. The scriptural story is thus reshaped — its texts selected, connected, filled out, and interpreted — by its fulfillment in Christ. Scripture "looks forward" (προοράω) to what unfurls in Christ (3:8), and the notable verb "pre-preach" (προευαγγελίζομαι, 3:8) is employed to identify the Abrahamic announcement as an anticipation of the good news concerning Christ. This indicates that, in hermeneutical terms, the Abrahamic stories are not the interpretative frame within which the Christ-story is to be understood, but the reverse: the good news about Christ is the frame in which "pre-announcements" may be identified and interpreted. Paul's carefully chosen verbs signal simultaneously the *historical* priority of the announcement to Abraham and the *hermeneutical* priority of the Christ-event.[59]

It would be a mistake, then, to suggest that the story of Christ is simply "superimposed upon the story of Israel," if that is understood to mean that the Christ-story is added to a pre-shaped narrative.[60] To the contrary, the narratives of Abraham and of Israel are refashioned around Christ. If the *characters* are shared with some of the varied narratives current in Second Temple Judaism, the *plot* is new; it is doubtful if it makes sense to speak of Paul's inhabiting the "same" story.

The degree to which Paul can reconfigure biblical resources in Christological terms is most visible in his redescription of Abraham's two sons (4:21–5:1). Although Paul names his reading of the Genesis stories "allegorical" (ἅτινά ἐστιν ἀλληγορούμενα, 4:24) he does not use allegory in Philonic fashion to

59. Cf. R. B. Hays, *Echoes of Scripture in the Letters of Paul* (New Haven: Yale University Press, 1989), pp. 105-11, on Gal 3:6-14, emphasizing the hermeneutical function of the experience of the Spirit in communities of Gentile believers: "The fulfilment precedes the promise, hermeneutically speaking: only because he sees in the Christian community the fulfilment of the promised blessings does Paul venture a retrospective interpretation of its latent sense" (p. 109). Watson, emphasizing that Scripture is not a "secondary confirmation of a Christ-event entire and complete in itself," rightly insists that Scripture is constitutive of this event (*Paul and the Hermeneutics of Faith*, pp. 16-17). But judging from Galatians, in the dialectical relation between Christ and Scripture, most weight rests on the capacity of the Christ-event to discover the meaning of Scripture.

60. Dunn, *Theology of Paul's Letter*, p. 41.

dehistoricize the text, that is, to transfer textual figures from historical particularity into universal truth.[61] Although Paul correlates almost all the figures in the Genesis stories with other realities, these equivalences do not remove them from their historical location in the past. "Just as *then* the one born according to the flesh persecuted the one born according to the Spirit, so it is *now*" (4:29): the figures in the text relate to their equivalents in Paul's time by moving not outside of time but across time, from τότε ("then") to νῦν ("now"). In other words, by taking the text to "speak otherwise," Paul expects its figures not to dissolve into signifiers of a timeless truth, but to reverberate in their own historical particularity with meanings now discovered from the perspective of another.[62]

The perspective is recognizably Christological even if Christ does not appear until the very end (5:1). The twin axes by which Paul interprets the Sarah-Hagar stories — freedom/slavery, miraculous/natural birth — reflect motifs already present in the Genesis stories, while other Scriptures (Isa 54:1) and further Jewish traditions (the Jerusalem above, 4:26; Ishmael's "persecution" of Isaac, 4:29) are woven into the tapestry of this passage.[63] But the central categories are filled with new meaning on the basis of the Christ-centered narrative sketched earlier in the letter. The slavery of Hagar, equivalent to the enslavement of the present Jerusalem, is the slavery of those under the authority of the Torah (4:21) or Sinai (4:24-25), which can be classified as "slavery" only from the perspective of the culture-relativizing "freedom" created by

61. On Philo's allegorical hermeneutic and its limits, see D. Dawson, *Allegorical Readers and Cultural Revision in Ancient Alexandria* (Berkeley: University of California Press, 1992), and J. M. G. Barclay, *Jews in the Mediterranean Diaspora from Alexander to Trajan (323 BCE–117 CE)* (Edinburgh: T&T Clark, 1996), pp. 165-70.

62. Martyn refers to the birth of Isaac in Galatians 4 as "a type of the birth of Gentile congregations" ("Events in Galatia," p. 176). But the type here remains "figural," since it retains its historical concreteness. Paul seems to claim here not just an interpretation of the past, but a *discovery* of its previous reality. On the resistance of "figural" reading to the allegorical dissolution of the historical and the concrete, see D. Dawson, *Christian Figural Reading and the Fashioning of Identity* (Berkeley: University of California Press, 2002). With reference to Origen, Dawson speaks of the way in which "the gospel as the arrival of the Word in the flesh makes former things gospel." He adds: "By making former things gospel, the gospel as the Word's arrival does not supply new content, but unveils a 'gospelness' already present in those former things; former things and events become more of what they already were, although in such a way that this becoming more themselves depended on the occurrence of the later event" (p. 134).

63. See G. Sellin, "Hagar und Sara: Religionsgeschichtliche Hintergründe der Schriftallegorese Gal 4,21-31," in U. Mell et al., eds., *Das Urchristentum in seiner literarischen Geschichte* (Berlin: de Gruyter, 1999), pp. 59-84.

God's gift in Christ (2:4; 5:1).[64] Likewise, Ishmael's natural birth is categorized as κατὰ σάρκα ("according to the flesh," 4:23, 29) in contrast to the birth of Isaac κατὰ πνεῦμα ("according to the Spirit," 4:29), a polarity made visible only since the gift of the Spirit of Christ (3:2-5, 14; 4:6).[65] To configure "the promise" as a generative power, capable of bearing "children" (4:23, 28) without regard to their "fleshly" identity, is to read the text as a prefigurement of the "new creation" (6:15), where groups of baptized, Spirit-formed believers are able to disregard inherited criteria of worth (2:15-17; 3:26-28; 5:13–6:10).[66] The familiar Abrahamic stories now make different sense in the light of Christ.

It is important to insist, against Boyarin, that discovery of this new mean-

64. I am not convinced by arguments that "the present Jerusalem" (4:25) refers only to the Jerusalem church, which Paul perceives to be sponsoring the alternative mission in Galatia (Mussner, *Galaterbrief,* p. 325; Martyn, *Galatians,* pp. 439, 457-66; idem, *Theological Issues in the Letters of Paul* [Edinburgh: T&T Clark, 1997], pp. 191-208; M. C. de Boer, "Paul's Quotation of Isa 54.1 in Gal 4.27," *NTS* 50 (2004): 370-89; idem, *Galatians,* pp. 300-301). Paul's commitment to the collection (2:10) suggests that he would hardly characterize this church in such negative terms, while the equivalence he draws with Sinai (4:24-25) indicates that "the present Jerusalem" includes *all* those under the "slavery" of the Torah (cf. 4:1-5). This is not to say, however, that the allegory "disinherits" Jews (*pace* Betz, *Galatians,* pp. 250-51, with a long line of Christian interpretation). The lines of distinction here are not between "Jews" and "(Gentile) Christians," but between those under the Torah (of whatever ethnicity) and those in "freedom" (including Jews such as Paul; see the "we" in 4:31). The birthing of the "free" has nothing to do with ethnicity (4:28-29; so rightly M. Bachmann, *Anti-Judaism in Galatians? Exegetical Studies on a Polemical Letter and on Paul's Theology,* trans. R. L. Brawley [Grand Rapids: Eerdmans, 2008], pp. 85-100, followed by R. L. Brawley, "Contextuality, Intertextuality, and the Hendiadic Relationship of Promise and Law in Galatians," *ZNW* 93 [2002]: 99-119). The "Jerusalem above" is "above," not a church (*pace* de Boer, *Galatians,* pp. 301-2) but a divine phenomenon beyond human creation. As other texts show, Paul is hopeful that God will have mercy on his fellow Jews, as God has had mercy on him (Gal 1:15; 6:16 — see below). If Torah-promoters must be expelled from the communities of Galatian believers (4:30), they are not expelled from God's mercy: the Son was sent precisely in order that the enslaved might be freed (4:4-5).

65. Philo was equally fascinated by the biblical stories of miraculous births, which he took to signal that God alone is the Cause of the good (see above, 6.2). Paul has linked this motif to the eschatological gift of the Spirit (Gal 3:14), and will return to this phenomenon in Romans 4, where Isaac's birth is again related to the Christ-event, but in a different way.

66. The citation from Isaiah 54 in 4:27 draws in resonances from the promises to Jerusalem/Zion in Deutero-Isaiah (Hays, *Echoes,* pp. 118-20; de Boer, "Paul's Quotation"). Its emphasis on birth from barrenness (parallel to the case of Sarah) identifies the birthing generated by promise (4:23, 28) as a miraculous phenomenon, beyond the conditions of normal birth and the categories of ethnicity and gender (2:15; 3:28); cf. Söding, "Verheißung und Erfüllung," p. 159. As in *4 Ezra* 10 (see above, 9.4), the heavenly Jerusalem jolts the reader beyond the horizon of human projections. Looking from the future that is already "above," one can refigure reality without the limitations of an empirical perspective, and thus dare to imagine (and even practice) what seems humanly impossible.

ing in the scriptural text is drawn from a historically particular event (the Christ-gift), not from an "onto-theology," in which Christ is merely the revelation of an already existent, "spiritual" reality.[67] The Christ-event does not disclose "the universally true meaning . . . that always subsisted within and above history."[68] Rather, Paul's figural readings find reverberations *in history* of the Christ-event, which reveals what that history (and not just those texts) were really about. Christ is the hermeneutical key to both Scripture and history, because all of reality takes its bearings from the unique and particular event of his death and resurrection. It is the good news of an event that Paul hears resonating backwards and forwards in history, and backwards and forwards in the text. To invert a well-known phrase, Paul finds *echoes of the gospel in the Scriptures of Israel.*[69]

13.3.3. A Unique Place for Israel?

This structure of thought throws up a number of paradoxes that Galatians itself is unable to resolve. A linear sense of chronology, climaxing in "the fullness of time" (4:4), spotlights an event in which God's promise is fulfilled in the gift of the promised Spirit (3:14; 4:6) and the arrival of faith (3:25). Yet in explicating the universal significance of this singular and particular event, Paul depicts Isaac as having been born "according to the Spirit" (4:29) — many centuries before the promised Spirit had been given! He portrays Abraham, to whom the good news was "pre-preached," as already exercising "faith" (before "faith arrived," 3:23); moreover, that faith "was considered as righteousness" (3:6) when everything was still "under sin" (3:22). In one sense, Abraham stands as a type for what was yet to happen in Christ; in another, he has his own standing as a believer, to whom believers can trace their ancestry in faith (3:7, 29). At one level, Abraham constitutes only the promise of what would come, the prologue to the story of salvation that *begins* with Christ; at another, he emerges, in the light of Christ, as the originating moment in a narrative arc created by God.

This ambiguity in the status of Abraham and Isaac is matched by a number of hints that suggest that the people of Israel play a role in the story of Christ that (to coin a paradox) is simultaneously *special* and *not at all unique.*

67. Boyarin's discussion of Galatians 4:21-31 (*A Radical Jew*, pp. 32-36) is paradigmatic of his thesis that Paul draws from a Hellenistic and dualistic distinction between the allegorical/spiritual/universal and the literal/physical/particular.

68. Boyarin, *A Radical Jew*, p. 35.

69. Inverting the title of Hays's fine monograph, *Echoes of Scripture in the Letters of Paul.*

Commentators have long puzzled over Paul's distinctions between "us" and "you," which appear at key points in this letter (3:13-14; 3:23-29; 4:1-7).[70] Christ has redeemed "us" from the curse of the Law in order that "the Gentiles" might receive the blessing of Abraham, so that "we" might receive the promise of the Spirit (3:13-14). Does this first "us" refer specifically to Jewish believers (for whom else were the Deuteronomic curses salient?), or is it a generic, "confessional" reference to all believers (as the final "we" might be)? Giving weight to a distinction between Jews and Gentiles in the apportionment of the first- and second-person pronouns is the fact that Paul earlier identified himself with other Jews as "we" (2:15-17). The "we" who were guarded by the Torah (3:23-25) are also more readily identifiable as Jews than as the whole of humanity. It makes sense for Paul to speak of Israel as the "heir" awaiting its inheritance (4:1-2), the "we" who were under the Torah and (in a distinctive way) under the στοιχεῖα (4:3-4).[71] In an important sense, this "we" is in a state no different from the rest of humanity. "All things" were under sin (3:22)

70. The earliest commentators already note this phenomenon (for Augustine, see Plumer, *Augustine's Commentary,* p. 177), and it was common in the Middle Ages to identify the "we" specifically with Jews/Jewish believers: see, e.g., on the "we" in Galatians 4:3, T. Aquinas, *Commentary on Saint Paul's Epistle to the Galatians,* trans. F. R. Larcher (Albany: Magi Books, 1966), pp. 108-11; "Bruno the Corinthian and Nicholas of Lyra," in I. C. Levy, *The Letter to the Galatians* (Grand Rapids: Eerdmans, 2011), pp. 160-62, 246. The modern debate on this matter has been stimulated especially by D. W. Robinson, "Distinction between Jewish and Gentile Believers in Galatians," *ABR* 13 (1965): 29-48, and T. L. Donaldson, "The 'Curse of the Law' and the Inclusion of the Gentiles: Galatians 3.13-14," *NTS* 32 (1986): 94-112.

71. For discussion of these texts, with extensive further literature, see Donaldson, "Inclusion of the Gentiles." His thesis, that Paul alludes here to a schema in which Israel's redemption is a necessary precursor to the salvation of all nations, has been adopted and expanded in much recent scholarship (though with minor variations on the reference of "we" in 3:14 and 4:5). See, e.g., M. Bachmann, *Sünder oder Übertreter: Studien zur Argumentation in Gal 2,15ff* (Tübingen: Mohr Siebeck, 1992), pp. 136-38; idem, *Anti-Judaism,* pp. 187-88 n. 52; Longenecker, *Triumph,* pp. 90-95; Morales, *Restoration of Israel,* pp. 78-130; and among the commentators, Longenecker, *Galatians;* F. J. Matera, *Galatians,* Sacra Pagina 9 (Collegeville: Liturgical Press, 1992); Witherington, *Grace in Galatia;* and R. B. Hays, "Galatians," in *New Interpreter's Bible,* vol. 11 (Abingdon: Nashville, 2000), pp. 181-348; cf. the discussion in Hays, *Faith of Jesus Christ,* pp. 73-117. For the contrary view, that the "we" statements are universal, since all humanity is under the στοιχεῖα and the curse of the law, see Martyn, *Galatians,* pp. 334-36; de Boer, *Galatians,* pp. 209, 236, 256-61. This latter view is hardest to maintain of the "we" of 3:23-25, since Paul takes his Gentile addressees to be not (yet) under the Torah (cf. 4:21), even if all humanity is under sin (3:22) and (in different forms) under the στοιχεῖα (4:3, 8-10). Of course, in a wider sense, Christ's death is "for all" (2 Cor 5:14; implied in Gal 3:1; 6:14). The only question is whether this is the immediate theme of Galatians 3:13 and 4:4-5. In favor of a universal "we" at these points, see D. Sänger, *Die Verkündigung des Gekreuzigten und Israel* (Tübingen: Mohr Siebeck, 1994), pp. 273-79, esp. p. 273 n. 466.

and this "heir" is in a condition of slavery, subject to the στοιχεῖα, just like the rest of humankind (4:3, 8-9). With regard to worth, salvation for Israel is as incongruous as for the whole of humanity: both Paul and his Gentile converts were "called through grace" (1:6, 15). Yet is it possible that Israel has a special place in the story, a role hinted at by these references to "we/us," but left tantalizingly unexplained?

That specialness arguably emerges in the final blessing of the letter, when peace is pronounced on all who walk by the "rule" of the new creation, "and mercy also on the Israel of God" (καὶ ἔλεος καὶ ἐπὶ τὸν Ἰσραὴλ τοῦ θεοῦ, 6:16). This construal of the Greek is only one of several options, and the majority of commentators take the "Israel of God" to refer to current believers in Christ.[72] But the echoes of traditional prayers for Israel, the special label "Israel *of God*," Paul's appreciation of the mission to "the circumcised" (2:7-9), and (crucially) the prayer for *mercy* — a motif rare in Paul but strongly associated with Israel in Romans 9–11 — have led some readers to find reference here to the nation of Israel.[73] If Israel has had a real, if unmarked, presence in the letter, it would be understandable if Paul prays at the end for mercy on a largely unbelieving but still special entity in the purposes of God. The double tones in which Paul thus speaks of Torah-beholden Jews — as enslaved yet heirs, as descendants

72. The Greek is ambiguous both as to the relation between the two elements of the blessing ("peace" and "mercy") and as to the relation between its objects ("on those who will walk by this rule," "on the Israel of God"). The final καί could be epexegetic (". . . and mercy, that is, upon the Israel of God") or additive ("and mercy also on the Israel of God"). For a careful presentation of the options, see de Boer, *Galatians,* pp. 404-8. Most readers have sided with N. A. Dahl ("Der Name Israel: Zur Auslegung von Gal 6.16," *Jud* 6 [1950]: 161-70) in his debate with Schrenk, taking "the Israel of God" as those who are already Christ-believers (both Jews and Gentiles), the object of the benediction of both "peace" and "mercy." For strong supporting arguments, see Martyn, *Galatians,* pp. 574-77. Some have argued that a second group is intended, e.g., Jewish Christians who already believe (G. Schrenk, "Was bedeutet 'Israel Gottes'?" *Jud* 5 [1949]: 81-94; idem, "Der Segenswunsch nach der Kampfepistel," *Jud* 6 [1950]: 170-90), or who currently oppose Paul and claim the designation "Israel of God" (de Boer, *Galatians,* pp. 407-8).

73. The strongest recent arguments for this view are in Bachmann, *Anti-Judaism,* pp. 101-23, and S. Eastman, "Israel and the Mercy of God: A Re-reading of Galatians 6.16 and Romans 9–11," *NTS* 56 (2010): 367-95; cf. earlier P. Richardson, *Israel in the Apostolic Church* (Cambridge: Cambridge University Press, 1969), pp. 74-84 (a prayer for a future Jewish remnant) and, among commentators, Mussner, *Galaterbrief,* p. 417; Dunn, *Galatians,* pp. 343-46. On this reading, the statement amounts to a *prayer,* the appeal for mercy presupposing that Israel, although it belongs to God, is currently in a precarious position. As Eastman writes, "At the end of this letter in which he has declared the obsolescence of the way of the law that his fellow Jews still follow, Paul prays for God's mercy on Israel, that Israel also will be saved only by grace" ("Israel and the Mercy of God," p. 389).

of Hagar yet objects of a prayer for mercy — preclude the designation of Galatians as boldly "supersessionist." On this reading, it would also be mistaken to claim that (unbelieving) Israel lies beyond the horizon of this letter.[74] In what sense and for what reason Israel's position might be considered special is not explained in this letter, but the hints that this is so are enough to suggest that Romans 9–11 is a development, not a reversal, of this aspect of Galatians.[75] As we shall see in Part IV, on this as on other fronts, Romans relates the Christ-event to time, to Israel, and to the total scope of the mercy of God in ways that are underdeveloped in the *Christological* frame of Galatians, but can be better clarified against a *theological* horizon.

13.4. Conclusions

Despite these ambiguities at the edge of its vision, Galatians represents a consistent attempt to remap God's dealings with humanity from the perspective of the Christ-event. What has emerged is the coherence of that event with the plan and promise of God, but its incongruity with the conditions and the potential of human history. From the perspective of the divine plan, the Christ-event is the fulfillment of an ancient promise; from the perspective of human affairs, including the history of Israel, it is a reversal, a disjunction, and an impossibility. Paul's chief concern is to demonstrate that the Torah is not to be integrated with the story of God's promise, and that it neither determined nor enabled the fulfillment of that promise in Christ. This means that faith in Christ (the faith that "arrived" with the coming of Christ, 3:23) is neither embedded within, nor conditioned by, the rubrics of Torah-practice. As an unconditioned gift, the Christ-event fits no preformed evaluative schema, not even the schema of the Torah. It crosses conventional taxonomies "at a diagonal," beholden to no preexistent measurements of symbolic capital, but only to its own, given in Christ. Throughout Galatians, Paul indicates what this means at the practical, communal level — in the freedom of common meals

74. Martyn's reading of 6:16 and of the "we/you" pronouns matches his insistence that Galatians is tightly focused on the dispute between two Christian missions, such that "no Jews are being spoken about in the letter" (*Galatians*, p. 40). For the place of this letter in Jewish-Christian dialogue, see his sensitive discussion in *Theological Issues*, pp. 191-208.

75. *Pace* Wolter, "Israelproblem," who reads Galatians 4:21-31 as distinguishing "Christian" from "Jewish" identity and implicitly disinheriting "non-Christian" Jews. My reading concurs with his in taking Paul to imply that Torah-observant Jews are "in slavery," but Galatians 4:21–5:1 is not directed against Jews as such (Paul has no counter-category, "Christian"), nor does it preclude hope for their future.

shared by Jews and non-Jews, in the creative operations of the Spirit, and in a communal ethos, grounded in baptism, that disregards normal criteria of honor and worth. Toward the end of the letter, he sketches what this means for patterns of community behavior, and it is with that passage (5:13–6:10) that we complete our reading of Galatians.

CHAPTER 14

The New Community as the Expression of the Gift (Galatians 5:13–6:10)

Because it is an incongruous gift, given without regard to worth, the Christ-gift neither reflects nor endorses the criteria of value operative in its context. Through "crucifixion to the world" (6:14), the community of the "new creation" has the freedom to follow its own system of values, unconstrained by the dominant systems of cultural capital: declaring that "neither circumcision nor uncircumcision counts for anything," it follows its own "rule" (κανών, 5:6; 6:15-16). As we have seen, the Christ-gift is experienced among believers in the form of "the Spirit" (3:2-5). Through the receipt of that gift, the Galatians were given proof of their status as "children of God" (4:5-6); in the Spirit's miraculous powers and in their "Abba"-prayers, believers have evidence of their calling in grace (3:5; 4:6). This novel endowment now governs the tenor of their life together. Baptismal identification with the Christ-event has rendered irrelevant their prior evaluations of worth (3:26-28). The new life generated by the Christ-gift is not beholden to the Torah, with its normative patterns of practice ("works of the Torah"), but to "the truth of the good news" (2:14), not least in the common meals that define the quality and limits of their community (2:11-17). As Paul summarizes the matter in 5:5-6, it is in the Spirit and on the basis of faith (in Christ) — and not on the basis of the Torah (5:4) — that believers anticipate that God will recognize their worth ("we await the hope of righteousness"). For in Christ Jesus, neither circumcision counts for anything, nor the "unblemished" male body, but faith operative through love (πίστις δι' ἀγάπης ἐνεργουμένη, 5:6). As this final phrase makes clear, in disregarding previous criteria of distinction the Christ-event has released a new creative energy, a quality of social commitment named "love."

All the main motifs of this summary (5:5-6) are developed in 5:13–6:10. Here, those in the "household of faith" (6:10) are instructed to "keep in step with the Spirit" (5:16, 25), no longer beholden to the Torah (5:18) but committed first and foremost to love (5:13, 22). Despite these (and other) connections with the main body of the letter,[1] interpreters have long struggled to integrate this "paraenetic" section with its epistolary context.[2] Once-influential hypotheses that these verses constitute general instructions without immediate relevance (Dibelius), or the opening of a "second front" against "libertinism" (Lütgert and Ropes), are now rightly discounted, and recent decades have seen varied efforts to relate 5:13–6:10 (or at least 5:13-26) to the argument of the letter and to the Galatian crisis.[3] Some have read this passage as primarily defensive, with Paul assuring his converts that they have adequate moral direction by the Spirit, even without the Torah.[4] Others, challenging the distinction between "theology" and "ethics," find here the norms integral to believer-identity, the topic of the letter as a whole.[5] The passage has been labeled the "culmination" or "climax of the whole letter,"[6] since it depicts "the form of life that Paul aims to present to his Galatian addressees as *the true, positive alternative* to the kind of life enjoined by his opponents."[7] In fact, most now maintain, although on many varied grounds, that the communal life here prescribed is integral to Paul's "good news."[8]

1. Others include the flesh-Spirit polarity (3:3; 4:29; 5:16-25; 6:7-8) and the motif of freedom (2:4; 5:1, 13).

2. "Paraenesis" itself is a difficult genre to define (see now J. Starr and T. Engberg-Pedersen, eds., *Early Christian Paraenesis in Context* [Berlin: de Gruyter, 2005]). The combination in our passage of declaration (5:18), description (5:22-23), warning (5:21; 6:7-8), prohibition (5:26), and instruction (6:1-6) makes its function difficult to classify. In structural terms, the turning point toward direct instruction of the Galatians has been variously placed at 4:12, 4:21, 5:1, 5:2, and 5:13. For older discussion, see O. Merk, "Der Beginn der Paränese im Galaterbrief," *ZNW* 60 (1969): 83-104, and J. M. G. Barclay, *Obeying the Truth: A Study of Paul's Ethics in Galatians* (Edinburgh: T&T Clark, 1988), pp. 24-26; the best recent analysis is by T. Engberg-Pedersen, *Paul and the Stoics* (Edinburgh: T&T Clark, 2000), pp. 132-36.

3. For a survey of opinions current up till the late 1980s, see Barclay, *Obeying the Truth*, pp. 9-23.

4. See H. D. Betz, *Galatians*, Hermeneia (Philadelphia: Fortress Press, 1979), pp. 8-9, 273-74, 295-96; Barclay, *Obeying the Truth*, pp. 68-72, 216-20.

5. See P. F. Esler, "Group Boundaries and Intergroup Conflict in Galatians: A New Reading of Gal. 5:13–6:10," in M. G. Brett, ed., *Ethnicity and the Bible* (Leiden: Brill, 1996), pp. 215-40; idem, *Galatians* (London: Routledge, 1998); B. O. Ukwuegbu, "Paraenesis, Identity-Defining Norms, or Both? Galatians 5:13–6:10 in the Light of Social Identity Theory," *CBQ* 70 (2008): 538-59.

6. So B. Kahl, *Galatians Reimagined: Reading with the Eyes of the Vanquished* (Minneapolis: Fortress Press, 2010), p. 269; cf. F. J. Matera, "The Culmination of Paul's Argument to the Galatians: Gal. 5.1–6.17," *JSNT* 32 (1988): 79-91.

7. Engberg-Pedersen, *Paul and the Stoics*, p. 136 (italics his); for a further statement of this case, see M. Konradt, "Die Christonomie der Freiheit: Zu Paulus' Entfaltung seines ethischen Ansatzes in Gal 5.13–6.10," *EC* 1 (2010): 60-81.

8. As T. Wilson comments, "the question now for students of Galatians is not *whether* 5.13–6.10 relates to the earlier parts of the letter, but *how* it does so" (*The Curse of the Law and*

The reading of Galatians offered thus far supplements this trend in a distinctive way. As the Antioch episode made clear, the dispute about the Law concerns the norms that govern communal interaction (2:11-21). The Spirit has already been identified as the chief characteristic of life in Christ (3:2-5), and it is the communal dynamics of that Spirit-directed life that are the topic of 5:13–6:10. Social practice is, for Paul, the necessary expression of the Christ-gift, and it will now become clear that non-competitive communities, ordered by a new calibration of worth, realize and help *define* the Christ-event as an unconditioned gift. "The truth of the good news" (2:14) is ineffective unless it "takes place" within communities whose behavior instantiates its novelty. Galatians 5:13–6:10 seems designed both to describe and to encourage that social expression of the good news.[9]

14.1. Freedom for the Spirit's Regime of Love

In 5:13 Paul configures the "freedom" depicted earlier in the letter (2:4; 4:21–5:1) with a new precision: "For you were called to freedom; only do not turn this freedom into an opportunity for the flesh (σάρξ), but through love be slaves of one another."[10] "Freedom" is here given a distinctive shape: opposed to (and threatened by) "the flesh," it entails a new allegiance (paradoxically, a form of "enslavement"), whose hallmark is love. Each of these features is explicated in the verses that follow (5:13-25).

14.1.1. Flesh and Spirit

The reference to "the flesh" in 5:13, followed by the list of "the works of the flesh" in 5:19-21, led older commentators to suggest that Paul here opens a

---

the Crisis in Galatia [Tübingen: Mohr Siebeck, 2007], p. 4). S. Schewe, *Die Galater zurückgewinnen: Paulinische Strategien in Galater 5 und 6* (Göttingen: Vandenhoeck & Ruprecht, 2005), pp. 16-59, analyzes three ways in which 5:13ff. has been found integral to the letter (dogmatic, rhetorical, and historical). Her text-immanent reading offers another option.

9. In comparison with my earlier work on this passage *(Obeying the Truth)*, I here connect communal life more adequately to the Christ-gift and to the articulation of the good news, while highlighting Paul's ethic of reciprocal support as the Christ-governed alternative to the competitive ethos of the Mediterranean world. I hope to meet thereby some of the valid criticisms leveled by Schewe, *Galater*, pp. 50-58, and Wilson, *Curse of the Law*, pp. 11-16.

10. For the verb to be supplied in the phrase μόνον μὴ τὴν ἐλευθερίαν εἰς ἀφορμὴν τῇ σαρκί, see M. C. de Boer, *Galatians: A Commentary*, New Testament Library (Louisville: Westminster John Knox Press, 2011), p. 335.

new topic, warning against a "libertine" danger quite different from the one confronted earlier in the letter.[11] But a closer reading indicates otherwise. The Spirit-flesh antithesis has already emerged as a structural frame for Paul's statements regarding the Torah (3:3; 4:29). Thus, at 5:13 the camera does not *pan across* to a different object: it *pulls back* to reveal the larger context in which the Torah-debate is sited. Like "the present evil age" (1:4), "the flesh" represents the environment of all human agency untransformed by the Spirit — including life under the Torah, which was incapable of "creating life" because of the power of sin (3:21-22). In one respect, the association of the Torah-regime with "flesh" is supported by the fact that circumcision is marked "in your flesh" (6:12-13; cf. Gen 17:9-14). In another, a link can be made between the Sinai covenant and ethnic heredity through birth "according to the flesh" (4:23, 29). These linguistic associations certainly bolster the rhetorical force of Paul's argument. But they also signal something else, a distinctive construal of reality. The Christ-gift, because it escapes and subverts the normal classifications of reality, has created a new taxonomy. In a novel structure of polar opposites, God's action in Christ stands over against a constellation of pre-established norms, which on any ordinary reading would appear categorically distinct.

In the previous chapter, we noted one startling example of Paul's capacity to remap the cosmos: although idolatry and Torah-allegiance appear in most respects entirely different, even mutually exclusive, from the perspective of the Christ-event they are variant forms of a common "slavery" to the "elements of the world" (4:3, 8-10; see above, 13.2.2). In that case, a single point in common (calendrical patterns of worship, 4:10) was taken by Paul as a token of a commonality deeper than their obvious difference. In a similar fashion, Paul takes the investment made "in the flesh" through the inscription of Jewish identity by circumcision as symptomatic of the fact that the regime of the Torah is located within a broad terrain that he labels "the flesh." In disregarding this central mark of Jewish difference, Paul has relativized a significant distinction between the Torah-tradition and its Gentile environment. The "new creation" in Christ subverts and replaces a "world" that invests such value in this marker, or in its absence (6:14-15). From the perspective of the Christ-gift, which is unconditioned and therefore unaligned to previous norms, everything is either beholden to God-in-Christ or beholden to human tradition (1:10-11), either

11. See, e.g., E. de Witt Burton, *A Critical and Exegetical Commentary on the Epistle to the Galatians* (Edinburgh: T&T Clark, 1921), pp. 290-91. When scholars characterized Paul's earlier target as "legalism" or "nomism," it was easy to form a neat antithesis: now he turns against its abstract opposite, "libertinism" or "antinomianism" (e.g., R. Jewett, "The Agitators and the Galatian Congregation," *NTS* 17 [1970-71]: 198). But if "the law" in Galatians is contextually specified as the Law of Moses, this modern polarity loses its value.

"new creation" or *passé* cosmos (6:14-15), either Spirit or flesh (3:3). The Torah is not itself responsible for what Paul labels "the works of the flesh" (5:19-21),[12] but life in the Spirit is still placed in contrast *both* to gratifying "the desire of the flesh" (5:16-17) *and* to life "under the regime of the Law" (5:18) — in contiguous sentences. On Paul's redrawn map of reality, both can be categorized as "flesh," inasmuch as both stand outside what has been created, co-opted, or transformed by the Christ-event.[13]

Compared to earlier and later uses in this letter (1:16; 3:3; 4:23, 29; 6:8, 12-13), a distinctive feature of "the flesh" in 5:13-25 is its active role in "desiring" and in "opposing" the Spirit (5:16-17, 24). Thus, personified as an agent, the "Flesh" has seemed to many an "apocalyptic" power, part of the cosmic "conflict" initiated by the "apocalypse" of Jesus Christ (cf. 1:16).[14] Some aspects of Paul's language might support this "military" reading (5:13, 17), but the total picture is neither precise nor consistent (cf. 5:19, 24).[15] The personification of "the flesh" seems to be a function of its role in Paul's discourse, where it stands in contrast to a personified "Spirit" (4:6). Its agency reflects the power of norms and values to structure human action in a way that transcends an individual's consciousness or will.[16] But it is precisely such norms that the Spirit is able to challenge, and the dominant note in these verses is the liberation and power granted by the Spirit to forge an alternative pattern of existence. "Walk in the Spirit and you will certainly not fulfill the desire of the flesh," Paul tells the

12. B. W. Longenecker, *The Triumph of Abraham's God: The Transformation of Identity in Galatians* (Edinburgh: T&T Clark, 1998), pp. 74-78, thinks that it is, finding a connection in the exclusionary "zeal" of the other missionaries (4:17) and in their desire to gain honor through circumcision (6:12-13). But such links seem tenuous, and Paul fails to make a polemical point on this score.

13. Like "the world" in 6:14, "the flesh" is a category defined by its opposite — in the one case, "new creation," in the other, "the Spirit." Neither is capable of a stand-alone definition, however expansive. For earlier discussion, see Barclay, *Obeying the Truth,* pp. 178-215, noting the rhetorical work performed by the strategic association of diverse phenomena through the use of a single term (see further, Schewe, *Galater,* pp. 86-95). Paul's rhetoric involves a conceptual cartography that maps reality by reference to a single event. Thus, "flesh" is most readily defined in negative terms (as "non-Spirit"): it represents what is neither aligned to, nor generated by, the Spirit.

14. See especially J. L. Martyn, *Galatians: A New Translation with Introduction and Commentary,* Anchor Bible 33A (New York: Doubleday, 1997), pp. 482-84; de Boer, *Galatians,* pp. 335-39. The latter recognizes that statements such as 6:8 are hard to fit into this mold (p. 338).

15. For doubts on the primacy of the military metaphor, see R. Morales, *The Spirit and the Restoration of Israel: New Exodus and New Creation Motifs in Galatians* (Tübingen: Mohr Siebeck, 2010), pp. 141-43.

16. Cf. Engberg-Pedersen, *Paul and the Stoics,* pp. 152-53: "the flesh" is described as an active power when it is given a normative role.

Galatians, in encouraging tones (5:16).[17] The opposition between "flesh" and "Spirit" leaves you neither helplessly torn nor morally uncertain, but directed by the Spirit ("so that you do not do whatever you want," 5:17).[18] Those who belong to Christ Jesus have "crucified" the flesh, with its passions and desires (5:24). While a relapse is always possible, and would be extremely serious (6:7-8), Paul's chief concern is to celebrate the fact that the Spirit creates a new mode of existence, exposing the multi-headed Hydra of "the flesh" (5:19-21) and slaying it by a superior power (5:16, 24). The new community is not fated to repeat the failures and dysfunctions of "the flesh." The creative power of the Spirit has fashioned a new alternative.

14.1.2. Freedom for Slavery

In 5:13 Paul reminds the Galatians of their calling (in grace, 1:6; 5:7) and their freedom. The two themes are connected because God's incongruous "call" paid no regard to their previous worth, liberating them from the pervasive systems of symbolic capital that previously determined their cultural norms. Since they are free to disregard such systems of worth, a wholly fresh pattern of existence is made possible. This, of course, has its own norms, with an alternative understanding of worth: what counts is allegiance to Christ and adherence to the Spirit. Paul's paradoxical interpretation of freedom as slavery ("for freedom you have been called . . . through love be slaves of one another," 5:13) recalls the opening statement of 1:10-11: Paul is free from human criteria of value ("seeking to please human beings") because he is a slave of Christ (1:10). For Paul, "freedom" is not autonomy but the product of an allegiance that breaks

17. The strong assurance of 5:16b (often mistranslated as a prohibition) is recognized by almost all modern commentators.

18. The interpretation of 5:17 continues to be disputed, since the identity of "what(ever) you want" in the final clause is unclear (for the history of reception, see J. K. Riches, *Galatians through the Centuries* [Oxford: Blackwell, 2008], pp. 264-83). But the context prohibits interpreting this clause as a prediction that the desires of the Spirit will be defeated. It should be read as an assurance that believers can escape their fleshly desires (cf. 5:24), or (as I have argued elsewhere) that they are enlisted on one side of the struggle, not given unstructured "freedom" to do whatever they wish (Barclay, *Obeying the Truth*, pp. 110-16). For a reprise of the reading (inspired by Romans 7:7-25) that "whatever you want" means the Spirit-inspired good desired by the believer, see J. Lambrecht, "The Right Things You Want to Do: A Note on Galatians 5,17d," *Biblica* 79 (1998): 515-24. As he admits, this leaves 5:17 as a hypothetical scenario, overruled by the verses that come before and after. For the latest discussion, see J.-N. Aletti, "Paul's Exhortations in Gal 5, 16-25: From the Apostle's Techniques to His Theology," *Biblica* 94 (2013): 395-414, at pp. 401-9.

the power of previously taken-for-granted (and now "alien") norms. He is dead to the regime of the Law, since his life is derived from and governed by the Christ-event: "it is no longer I who live, but Christ who lives in me" (2:19-20). All other criteria of value have been discounted by the superordinate worth of belonging to Christ.[19]

In 5:13–6:10, Paul clarifies how this allegiance to Christ takes place in the life of a community. Two pithy sentences in 5:24-25 sum up the break with "normality" that this entails: "Those who belong to Christ Jesus have crucified the flesh with its passions and desires. If our life derives from the Spirit, it is with the Spirit that we should keep in step."[20] Death to the old form of existence and life in the new bespeak both freedom and order; the decisive break with the past is effected and accompanied by a new orientation. The language of crucifixion ("have crucified," 5:24) signals that this break draws its efficacy from the Christ-event. It was when they were "co-crucified with Christ" (2:19) and baptized into Christ (3:27) that believers exited their former structures of existence (cf. 6:14). But the active voice indicates that this is no passive phenomenon: it is in their patterns of behavior that believers demonstrate and actualize the change that has taken place. It is difficult to imagine what it would mean to say that believers had been "crucified with Christ," if they still fulfill "the desires of the flesh." If they have not "crucified the flesh," in what sense do they belong to Christ? It is *in practice*, both individual and communal, that the reality of the Christ-event is either articulated or denied. Since the Spirit constitutes their new mode of existence (as "Christ in me," 2:20; 4:6), it is the Spirit that shapes their practice (5:25). There is little choice in this matter; the only alternative would be to deny one's identity (6:7-8). It would be a contradiction in terms for someone whose life depended on the Spirit to live in disregard of the Spirit's norms: that would be to say, "the Spirit is everything to me, but I do not care what the Spirit requires." Practice and behavior are not simply the consequence of this new "life": they are its expression. The

19. For "freedom" in Galatians as a form of "Christonomy," see Konradt, "Christonomie," pp. 66-70. Wolter notes parallels in Greek political discourse, where "freedom" means the right to live under one's own laws, not alien laws imposed from outside; by the same token, Paul figures the imposition of the authority of the Torah as a "slavery" interfering with the regulative system instituted by the Christ-event ("the law of Christ," 6:2); see M. Wolter, *Paulus: Ein Grundriss seiner Theologie* (Neukirchen: Neukirchen-Vluyn, 2011), pp. 372-76.

20. I take εἰ ζῶμεν πνεύματι (5:25a) to refer to the Spirit as a life-giving power (cf. the weighty references to "life" in 2:19-20; 3:21). Thus, 5:24-25 evidences the same "death-life" dynamic as 2:19-20 and 6:14-15 (cf. 1:1-4 of Christ); to interpret "live" here in a merely "ethical" sense would make the second half of the verse redundant. στοιχεῖν (5:25b; cf. 6:16) has connotations of order and alignment (de Boer, *Galatians*, p. 372), suggesting that the Spirit has a normative as well as a liberationist role.

indicative of "life" is a statement not of *status,* divorceable from practice, but of *existence,* whose reality is necessarily evidenced in practice.[21] That "life" is not humanly generated (it derives from the Spirit) but it is humanly expressed, and it can hardly be said to be real without such expression.

14.1.3. Love and the Law of Christ

The prime expression of this life is love (5:13-14, 22), the commitment to others that forms the foundation of community. We shall return below to its distinctively Pauline configuration as mutual slavery ("through love be slaves of one another," 5:13; see below, 14.2), but for now we note the social orientation of practically all of Paul's "virtues" (5:22-23). The highest goal of existence "in Christ" is not self-knowledge or self-mastery for the sake of individual perfection, but a pattern of pro-social behavior issuing in love, joy, peace, patience, kindness, goodness, faithfulness, gentleness, and self-control (5:22-23). It is striking how many of these qualities are given concrete form in the communal maxims that follow (5:26–6:10). When a member of the community goes astray, those who are "spiritual" (note the new definition of symbolic capital) should apply correction "in a spirit of *gentleness*" (6:1); all are to bear one another's burdens (6:2), the expression of mutual slavery in *love* (5:13); individuals should take care not to trumpet their work (6:3-4), applying *self-control* for the enhancement of the community; those who are taught should share "all good things" (6:6), an application of *goodness* generalizable as "doing good to all" (6:10); in so doing, they should not give up but look forward with *patience* (6:9-10). The "fruit" that springs from the Spirit's life is here identified in the delicate negotiation of communal relations, in behavioral qualities fostered over time. The love that stands at their head is inherently social; if faith is operative in love (5:6), it could never be reduced to an individual relationship to Christ.

A huge amount of scholarly attention has been paid to two phrases in which Paul connects love to "the law" (5:14; 6:2). After sidelining the Torah from the history of the promise (3:15–4:7), Paul's statement that "the whole law has been fulfilled in one word, 'You shall love your neighbor as yourself'" (5:14), has seemed perplexing to many. But Paul's earlier statement that he had "died to the Torah" (2:19) does not mean that all its contents are in principle disregarded, only that its absolute authority is undermined by a higher

21. For fresh discussion of (and beyond) the "indicative and imperative" in Pauline ethics, see F. Horn and R. Zimmermann, eds., *Jenseits von Indikativ und Imperativ* (Tübingen: Mohr Siebeck, 2009).

allegiance to "the truth of the gospel" (2:14). Accordingly, Paul here affirms that those who are led by the Spirit are not under the authority of the Torah (5:18), but it is no contradiction to say that the love that is generated by the Spirit brings to fulfillment what the Torah had envisaged.[22] Paul's statement in 5:14 is notably *not* a command to obey the law, nor a reinstatement of the Law in a "third use" (Calvin). Paul does not here *prescribe* observance of the Torah, but employs the rare language of "fulfillment" to *describe* what happens when the Christian command to love is carried out (it actually fulfills what the Torah envisaged, 5:13).[23] Besides the rhetorical gain (claiming the support of the Torah without submitting to its authority; cf. 4:21; 5:3), Paul here hints at a conviction, clearer in Romans, that there are echoes of the good news even in the Torah (cf. Rom 3:21, 31; 8:4; 10:5-13). Viewed in retrospect, and with love of "neighbor" broadly defined (6:10), "the Torah as a whole" finds fulfillment in the love unleashed in the Christ-event (cf. 2:20).

A parallel redefinition is evident in the statement that a mutual bearing of burdens will fulfill "the law of Christ" (ὁ νόμος τοῦ Χριστοῦ, 6:2). The echoes of 5:13-14 incline many to find an allusion to the Torah, reconfigured in Christ. Alternatively, the phrase represents Pauline wordplay, akin to his insistence in 1 Corinthians 9:20-21 that he is neither "under the law" (ὑπὸ νόμον) nor lawless in relation to God (ἄνομος θεοῦ), but "lawfully beholden to Christ" (ἔννομος Χριστοῦ).[24] Either way, what is unambiguous is the redefinition of obligation by reference to Christ. The Christ-event has reshaped the norms and values of "the household of faith." If one uses the language of νόμος ("law"), this must be qualified and redefined via a normative and paradigmatic event,

22. I am unpersuaded by Wilson's argument that ὑπὸ νόμον in 5:18 (and elsewhere in Galatians) means specifically "under the curse of the law" ("'Under Law' in Galatians: A Pauline Theological Abbreviation," *JTS* 56 [2005]: 362-92; *Curse of the Law*); the "under"-language seems contextually related to the motif of authority and "slavery."

23. For fuller discussion, see Barclay, *Obeying the Truth*, pp. 135-42. De Boer has mounted a strong argument that Paul understood Leviticus 19:18 (cited in Galatians 5:14) not as a command, but as a promise (the future tense could be construed that way): what the Torah predicted (that "you will love your neighbor as yourself") is fulfilled by those who walk in the Spirit (de Boer, *Galatians*, pp. 343-50). This makes much sense, although it blurs the distinction between "Law" and "promise(s)" that was important in 3:15ff.

24. For analysis, in debate with all the interpretive options, see Barclay, *Obeying the Truth*, pp. 126-35. See further R. B. Hays, "Christology and Ethics in Galatians: The Law of Christ," *CBQ* 49 (1987): 268-90, who finds reference to the life-pattern of Jesus, the paradigm for the community (2:20). M. Winger insists that no legal instruction is here in view, only "the way Christ exercises his lordship over those called by him" ("The Law of Christ," *NTS* 46 [2000]: 537-46, at p. 544). For a recent discussion of options, see Wilson, *Curse of the Law*, pp. 100-104. The rarity of the phrase makes interpretation exceptionally difficult.

by which love has been installed as the essence of a Christ-formed community (2:20; 4:19).[25]

14.2. From Rivalry to Reciprocal Support

14.2.1. The Competitive Quest for Honor

Paul's appeal for mutual love is no bland generality, but specifically targets habits of intra-communal rivalry that were characteristic of ancient Mediterranean society. After setting the norm of mutual slavery in love (5:13), Paul issues a dire warning against its dysfunctional alternative: "if you bite and devour one another, watch out lest you be consumed by one another" (5:15). Here, the polar opposite to love is not isolation or indifference, because it is assumed that individuals will interact in one form of reciprocity or another: the only question is whether that interaction will take the form of mutual support or mutual destruction. In the following "works of the flesh" (5:19-21), it is notable that the standard Jewish characterizations of the Gentile world (sexual immorality, impurity, idolatry, magical practice, 5:19-20) are filled out with an extensive catalogue of socially destructive behavior: "hostile acts, strife, jealousy, outbursts of anger, selfish actions, dissensions, factions, acts of envy, inebriated loutishness, and drinking parties" (5:20-21).[26] Although some such items often appear in ancient lists of "vices," including Paul's elsewhere (e.g., Rom 1:29-31; 2 Cor 12:20-21), commentators rightly note their heavy concentration here, as if the damage of social life was Paul's particular concern.[27] Matching this list is an exhortation not to be vain, provoking one another or envying one another (μὴ γινώμεθα κενόδοξοι, ἀλλήλους προκαλούμενοι, ἀλλήλοις φθονοῦντες, 5:26) — an exhortation that immediately follows and fills out the appeal to "keep in step with the Spirit" (5:25).

Many commentators would agree that the repetition of these warnings suggests actual or threatened disunity in Paul's churches, though the recon-

25. Thus, love is a "zuinnerst pneumatisch gewirkte Partizipation an der Proexistenz Jesu Christi" (T. Söding, *Das Liebesgebot bei Paulus: Die Mahnung zur Agape im Rahmen der paulinischen Ethik* [Münster: Aschendorff, 1995], p. 206).

26. I include the last two items (μέθαι and κῶμοι) because it was often noted in Roman society that excessive drink was the cause of lasting damage to social relations. An earlier item, φαρμακεία ("magical practice") was also a cause of conflict, since "magic" was widely suspected of intent to cause harm.

27. See Barclay, *Obeying the Truth*, pp. 153-54, with extensive reference to commentators; cf. F. J. Matera, *Galatians*, Sacra Pagina 9 (Collegeville: Liturgical Press, 1992), p. 210.

struction of specific scenarios to account for their prominence may be overly speculative.[28] Paul lived in a face-to-face society where self-advertisement, rivalry, and public competition were a perpetual cause of tension in everyday life. Part of the purpose of Galatians 5:13–6:10 is to present a vision of communal life in which the destructive features of this agonistic culture can be recognized and effectively repulsed. If so much hinges on the establishment of mutually constructive communities, strong measures must be taken to counter the operations of "the flesh" that continually threaten to undermine this critical embodiment of the good news.

As recent research has emphasized, almost all social relations in Paul's cultural context were both ordered and threatened by the competition for honor.[29] In the absence of "objective" measures of quality (such as educational qualifications), a person's worth was heavily dependent on his public reputation, a "dignity" energetically claimed and fiercely defended. The pursuit or defense of honor was, many ancient commentators claimed, the chief motivating force for action: "By nature we yearn and hunger for honor, and once we have glimpsed, as it were, some part of its radiance, there is nothing we are not prepared to bear and suffer in order to secure it" (Cicero, *Tusc.* 2.24.58). The multiple criteria for honor — wealth, ancestry, age, education, legal status, physique, character, and virtuous action — made the quest for honor ubiquitous across the social scale, while the very diversity of these marks of value ensured that strength in one dimension could be challenged by criticism of weakness in another.[30] And challenge was, indeed, the very essence of this culture. Honor was derived from comparison, from placing oneself (or being placed by others) higher on some hierarchical scale, in which one person's superiority means

28. See Barclay, *Obeying the Truth,* pp. 152-54, 156, 166-69; Morales, *Restoration of Israel,* pp. 152-53; de Boer, *Galatians,* pp. 360, 368. It is often suggested that these social malfunctions relate to the disturbance caused by the other missionaries (5:10, 12). 4:16-18 might hint at some connection, but Paul does not elaborate; for skepticism on this point, see F. Vouga, *An die Galater,* HNT 10 (Tübingen: Mohr Siebeck, 1998), pp. 144-45.

29. The point was rightly stressed by Esler (e.g., "Group Boundaries"; *Galatians*), following the work of B. J. Malina (e.g., *The New Testament World: Insights from Cultural Anthropology,* rev. ed.[Louisville: Westminster/John Knox Press, 1993]), and others, who drew on the anthropology of Mediterranean society (e.g., J. G. Peristiany, ed., *Honour and Shame: The Values of Mediterranean Society* [London: Weidenfeld and Nicolson, 1966]). Major recent studies of the honor-dynamics specific to the Roman world include J. E. Lendon, *Empire of Honour: The Art of Government in the Roman World* (Oxford: Oxford University Press, 1997), and C. A. Barton, *Roman Honor: The Fire in the Bones* (Berkeley: University of California Press, 2001).

30. Although competition among the upper strata of society is most visible in our sources, there is good evidence that it was characteristic of all social levels in the Greco-Roman world; see Barton, *Roman Honor,* pp. 11-13, 75.

that another is comparatively demeaned. This made honor ever the subject of contest: indeed, the ordeal or test was the very arena in which honor was proved. In this environment, every claim to honor was a real or potential provocation, and every challenge required an active riposte.[31] Honor was a precious but unstable commodity, requiring active promotion and persistent demonstration in a court of opinion that continually looked on with a critical eye.[32] Precisely because glory needed to "shine," it was the object of perpetual surveillance. It was under the spotlight of communal attention that individuals would either display or damage their worth.[33]

Within strongly bonded communities, such honor contests could encourage great feats of heroism and even self-sacrifice.[34] But the intensely competitive spirit could also foster pride, hostility, and revenge. With the slightest breakdown in mutual respect, the contest for honor becomes a socially destructive force, and Greek and Roman authors often note the danger that ambition will turn to arrogance, comparison to insult, and rivalry to aggression.[35] The desire for honor provokes the strongest emotions — pride, envy, resentment — and can spawn the most destructive acts of insult and retaliation. As Barton comments, there is a tendency to "insistent inflation." "Every tiff is a tumult, every wrangle a war."[36] The brazenness with which honor was advertised and the ferocity with which it was attacked are liable to surprise only those, in the modern world, whose honor is protected from competition. Paul's warning against vendettas (5:15) is neither empty nor unusual: the lust for honor could as easily destroy as enhance a community.

31. Cf. Cicero, *Sull.* 46: "You will compel me to give thought to my own dignity: no one ever brought the tiniest suspicion on me whom I did not overturn and wreck."

32. See Barton, *Roman Honor,* p. 62: "The honor, the fullness of one's being in ancient Rome was never safely or permanently earned."

33. On the importance of visibility, see Dio Chrysostom 31.22: "You could not get a single man out of a multitude to do what he deems a noble deed for himself alone, if no one else shall know of it." Cf. Barton on the necessary glitter and audibility of honor (*Roman Honor,* pp. 58-64). On the public dimension of the acknowledgement of honor, note Lendon, *Empire of Honour,* pp. 54: "honor is a public thing; it is not a consequence of opinion merely, but of opinion publicly expressed."

34. For an analysis of such phenomena in the Roman Republic, in which the quest for honor, being more important than life itself, encouraged self-sacrifice for the public good, see Barton, *Roman Honor,* pp. 29-88.

35. Sallust notes that whole cities are internally destroyed "when men will defeat other men by any means whatsoever, and when the defeated are bitterly intent on vengeance" (*Bell. Jug.* 42.4). Cf. Barton's analysis of "the bad contest" turned brutal, when "the rules of the game were arbitrary or unknown, where there were no limits to the scope or intensity of the contest, or where the contestants were too unequally matched" (*Roman Honor,* pp. 89-90).

36. Barton, *Roman Honor,* p. 66.

14.2.2. Paul's Counter-Strategy

Paul's strategy to overcome these destructive forces of "the flesh" is double-pronged. On the one hand, the people reconstituted by the Christ-gift have discounted the value placed on forms of honor over which their contemporaries compete. Since ethnicity, status, and gender are no longer criteria of superior worth (Gal 3:28), and since God pays no regard to the "face" (Gal 2:6) but distributes his grace without regard to worth, the normal grounds for competition have lost their former significance. The assembly of believers forms a new community of opinion, constituted by the gift to the unworthy. Within this community there arises, of course, an alternative system of worth, a new form of "symbolic capital": here, some are to be honored as teachers of the word (6:6) and others given responsibility as "spiritual people" (οἱ πνευματικοί, 6:1), insofar as they are attuned to the Spirit. But — and this is the second characteristic of Paul's social strategy — the hallmark of this alternative system of value is that it is specifically directed against rivalry: the greatest honor is for those who work *against* the competitive spirit of honor itself. As we have seen, nearly all of the characteristics catalogued as "the fruit of the Spirit" (5:22-23) are directed toward the construction of community, from love downwards. "Spirit-people" are so designated because they work with sensitivity to repair the community (6:1-2). What counts among believers, according to Paul, is precisely the antithesis to arrogance and competition.

The rubric that governs the ethos of this community is a formula of reciprocity as creative as it is paradoxical. The Galatian freedom will not become an opportunity for "the flesh" inasmuch as they are "*slaves to one another* through love" (διὰ τῆς ἀγάπης δουλεύετε ἀλλήλοις, 5:13). This is a remarkable expression, since it adjusts an inherently hierarchical relationship (slavery) not by canceling it, in the name of "equality," but by making it reciprocal, a hierarchy that turns both ways. The simple but powerful word ἀλλήλοις turns a one-way relationship of power and superiority into a mutual relationship of reciprocal deference, where *each* seeks to promote the interests of the other. The same structure of relations is outlined in the matching phrase in 6:2: "bear one another's burdens (ἀλλήλων τὰ βάρη βαστάζετε) and you will fulfill the law of Christ." Burden-bearing, the work of slaves, is again made a task for all in relation to all. Submission to the interests of others is saved from becoming a charter for the crushing of the weak by being turned also into reverse, such that service and honor are continually exchanged. This reciprocity of relations, which does not eradicate but continually inverts a hierarchical order, is a hallmark of Pauline social ethics, not only with respect to the church as a "body" (1 Cor 12:12-31; Rom 12:3-8), but also in marriage (1 Cor 7:3-4) and in the continual competition to be the first not to receive honor but to give it to others (Rom 12:10).[37] This policy turns competition on its head. What matters is not to gain superiority but to cede it, and in ceding it to be honored in return. To this extent, Kahl is right to point to Galatians 5–6 as evidence that Paul strongly resists the combative ethos ever present in Romanized culture — though Paul's policy is less the eradication of hierarchy than its continual inversion.[38]

Paul's redefinition of honor thus gives prestige to those traits that promote social cohesion and mutual construction. The finely crafted collection of maxims in Gal 6:1-6 offers a good example of this social policy in practice.[39] After warning against the insidious tendency to provocation and envy (5:26), Paul turns to the sort of occasion when a community is likely to splinter in the competitive quest for honor: when someone has transgressed a communal norm, and is vulnerable to public disgrace, others naturally seize the opportunity for competitive advantage. Paul clearly recognizes this danger and counters it by appeal to the ethos of the Spirit (6:1). When someone has been overtaken (or found out) in such trespass, it is necessary for the community to act for the sake of its integrity. But the purpose is less judgment than restoration (καταρτίζετε τὸν τοιοῦτον), which is to be administered by those who are "spiritual" in a "spirit of gentleness" (ἐν πνεύματι πραΰτητος, 6:1), that is, without the opprobrium that brings irremediable dishonor for the offender. Meanwhile, the restorers must themselves guard against the temptation of pride, the tendency to honor themselves in comparison with others: "look to yourself," says Paul (addressing each individual concerned), "lest you too be tempted" (6:1). "Gentleness" is thus allied to humility, the modesty that recognizes its own vulnerability and restrains the urge to advance a provocative claim to excellence.

In 6:3-5, Paul presses further this demand for modesty, as a crucial preservative of community and a necessary antidote to the "hunger for honor."[40]

37. On this remarkable policy of "reciprocal asymmetry," "making universalising egalitarianism pass through the reversibility of an inegalitarian rule," see A. Badiou, *Saint Paul: The Foundation of Universalism*, trans. R. Brassier (Stanford: Stanford University Press, 2003), pp. 98-106 (at 104); cf. J. M. G. Barclay, "Manna and the Circulation of Grace: A Study of 2 Corinthians 8:1-15," in J. R. Wagner, C. Kavin Rowe, and A. K. Grieb, eds., *The Word Leaps the Gap: Essays on Scripture and Theology in Honor of Richard B. Hays* (Grand Rapids: Eerdmans, 2008), pp. 409-26, with reference to the reciprocity in gift anticipated in 2 Corinthians 8–9.

38. See Kahl, *Galatians Reimagined*, pp. 261-71, with the redrafting of the "combat squares" she considers typical of Roman imperialism.

39. For an earlier analysis of these maxims, see Barclay, *Obeying the Truth*, pp. 155-70. Like many previous commentators, Betz, *Galatians*, p. 291, considered these verses no more than a loose collection of *sententiae*.

40. For a fine analysis of the coherence of these verses, showing how Paul's attention to the individual is for the sake of the harmony of the community, see D. W. Kuck, "'Each Will

His first move is to counter the tendency to an inflated self-opinion, which he had already highlighted in the exhortation not to be κενόδοξοι ("vain," 5:26): "If anyone thinks he is something, when he is nothing, he deceives himself" (6:3). This is not an assertion of universal worthlessness: if believers can say that "the Son of God loved me and gave himself for me" (2:20), who could have greater worth? Rather, Paul warns against the arrogance that delights in its own self-appraisal, or in a reputation granted by others that really counts for nothing; the echoes of Paul's comments on the Jerusalem pillars, ironically dubbed οἱ δοκοῦντες (2:6, 9), are loud. The social value of the moderate measure of oneself — the virtue of "shame" (Latin, *pudor*) — was well recognized in antiquity, though it was constantly overruled by the equal requirement to advertise one's virtues in an inflated form.[41] That tendency to display is directly countered in 6:4: "let each person test his own work and then keep his boast to himself alone, and not direct it toward others" (καὶ τότε εἰς ἑαυτὸν μόνον τὸ καύχημα ἕξει καὶ οὐκ εἰς τὸν ἕτερον, 6:4).[42] The importance of self-scrutiny, the splitting of oneself into both subject and object of assessment, is that this does *not* take part in the game of public self-advertisement, with its tendency to exaggeration and deceit. It is notable that Paul does not deny all grounds for "boasting" and thus all forms of honor. Believers take pride ("boast") in the cross, disavowing every form of capital operative in "the world" (6:14-15). But they have grounds for honor in their "work," within the criteria of value established by the Christ-event: on the right basis, and within the right limits, it is proper for honor to be offered and received (4:18).[43] However, its public

---

Bear His Own Burden': Paul's Creative Use of an Apocalyptic Motif," *NTS* 40 (1994): 289-97. As S. K. Williams points out, "an unrealistic assessment of one's own capacities can make a person aloof to the ideal of mutuality" just outlined in 6:2 (*Galatians* [Nashville: Abingdon Press, 1997], p. 155).

41. See Barton, *Roman Honor*, pp. 210-15.

42. I continue to think that this is the best translation (see Barclay, *Obeying the Truth*, p. 160; supported by Martyn, *Galatians*, p. 550), despite arguments advanced to the contrary (de Boer, *Galatians*, pp. 382-83, translating, "then he will have a boast in himself alone and not in the other"; cf. J. Lambrecht, "Paul's Coherent Admonition in Galatians 6,1-6: Mutual Help and Individual Attentiveness," *Bib* 78 (1997): 33-56, at pp. 48-49, who discounts the excellent parallels in 2 Corinthians 8:24 and Romans 4:2.

43. See H. Hübner, *Law in Paul's Thought*, trans. J. Greig (Edinburgh: T&T Clark, 1994), pp. 101-8: "Paul does recognise a genuine claim on the part of the Christian to 'glory' on the basis of his life's work" (p. 108). The contrary argument of G. Klein, "Werkruhm und Christusruhm im Galaterbrief und die Frage nach einer Entwicklung des Paulus," in W. Schrage, ed., *Studien zum Text und zur Ethik des Neuen Testaments* (Berlin: de Gruyter, 1986), pp. 196-211, is well critiqued in Lambrecht, "Paul's Coherent Admonition"; cf. Schewe, *Galater*, pp. 160-65. Since he sees Paul's target in Galatians as the human attempt at self-sufficient achievement, W. Harnisch is forced to take the positive language about "boasting" in 6:3-4 as an ironic

display is dangerous, most especially when it becomes promotion by oneself: by telling the justly "proud" person to keep one's boast to oneself, Paul effectively neuters a crucial impulse of his contest-culture.

The reason why the "boast" does *not* need to be broadcast is that its essential "audience" is not human but divine (cf. Rom 2:29; 1 Cor 4:1-5): the reminder that "each person will bear his own load" (6:5) is a gesture to the eschatological judgment, where the decisive arbiter of value will be God.[44] The fact that "each will bear his own load" does not prioritize the individual over the community. Paul has urged everyone to bear one another's burdens (6:2), and the purpose of this statement in 6:5 is to protect the community from the competitive boasting that threatens to unravel its bonds. That each is finally accountable before God removes from the community the necessity, or temptation, to adjudicate the value of one another. Precisely because it is responsible to God, the community can be rid of envious comparisons and liberated for mutual construction in love.

That mutuality "in all good things" is given one further illustration, in the instruction to support those who "teach the word." Again, there is no need to invoke particular local circumstances.[45] At this early stage of formation, one of the few differentia between members of the community was that between those capable of offering instruction and those to whom it was given (cf. 1 Thess 5:12-14). Paul frames this mutual relationship as a form of "sharing" (κοινωνείτω, 6:6; cf. 2:9), since the relationship of exchange between members is not self-generated (as self-authored gift and return), but arises from common dependence on the good news itself: within that context, the good things exchanged are "shared" benefits, derived from God (cf. 2 Corinthians 8–9).[46] But it is crucially important for Paul that there *is* a pattern of exchange, that differing tasks are understood as mutuality in gift and receipt. This whole paragraph stands under the rubric of "bearing one another's burdens" (6:2), an

---

self-contradiction ("Einübung des neuen Seins: Paulinische Paränese am Beispiel des Galaterbriefs," *ZTK* 84 [1987]: 294-95).

44. In context (cf. 5:10, 21; 6:7-8), the future tense is best taken in an eschatological sense (Vouga, *Galater*, p. 148; de Boer, *Galatians*, pp. 383-84; *pace* Lambrecht, "Paul's Coherent Admonition," p. 50); the sense runs closely parallel to *4 Ezra* 7.105. For convincing arguments for this eschatological reading, with additional Pauline parallels, see Kuck, "Each Will Bear." As he notes, "the symbolic language of future judgment helps to resolve the tension between the desire for individual status and the need to sublimate that desire for the sake of the unity of the church" (p. 296).

45. *Pace* Martyn, *Galatians*, pp. 551-52, who posits the threat in Galatia to the teachers whom Paul had installed.

46. On κοινωνία in 6:6, see J. Hainz, *Koinonia: "Kirche" als Gemeinschaft bei Paulus* (Regensburg: Pustet, 1982), pp. 62-89.

ethos of mutually supportive relations that represents "the law of Christ." It is as they participate in long-lasting relationships of mutual enrichment that the community is created and enhanced, and it is the capacity of that community to flout the normal tendencies to aggressive competition that demonstrates what it means to live in accordance with the "new creation" (6:15-16).

14.3. Social Practice as the Realization of the Gift

The gift of God in Christ is articulated as an unconditioned gift in its creation of a community that neither mirrors nor endorses the regnant systems of value. The incongruous gift is defined *as incongruous* in the formation of a community that marches to a different step — and it is only in practice that that difference can be effected and evidenced. By its strategic indifference to preconstituted evaluations of worth — ethnic, social, sexual, or other — the community declares and enacts its freedom. By its "crucifixion of the flesh" — its break with the dispositions and habits that stand contrary to the values of the Spirit — it demonstrates an alternative allegiance derived from an alternative source of meaning and "life." Through resisting the tendencies to intra-communal rivalry, it affirms its special identity as a community beholden to "the law of Christ."

Both sociology and theology point to the *necessity* of social practice as the realization of the Christ-gift. To express and embody its alternative form of "capital" — a gift given without regard to excellence in other forms of capital, symbolic, social, or cultural — there has to be not an abstract idea but a community, which recognizes a distinctive form of "wealth." In theological terms, the new creation in Christ presses toward the formation and flourishing of a community in which the truth of God's self-giving in Christ is expressed in loving relations, strongly resistant to the normal contest for honor. As in the Antioch dispute, so at the end of the letter Paul makes clear that the truth of the good news is entirely lost if it is not enacted in creative social relations that are apt to challenge central features of their cultural environment. The relationship between "theology" and "social practice" is thus mutually constitutive: it is the Christ-event that gives meaning and shape to communal practice, while it is in social practice that the nature of the Christ-event is, or is not, realized. For Paul's Galatian communities to adopt Jewish circumcision as a condition of entry, or to revert to the aggressive competition that bespeaks a "fleshly" code of honor, would be to deny the truth of the unconditioned gift in Christ — indeed, to annul it altogether as a reality in Galatia. The truth of Paul's gospel has to be both recognized and enacted — in fact, recognized in its enactment. It is only as communities are remolded in exclusive allegiance to "the law of Christ" that they may be said to affirm the baptismal confession, "Jesus is Lord" (Rom 10:9). Social practice is not, for Paul, an addition to belief, a sequel to a status realizable in other terms: it is the *expression* of belief in Christ, the enactment of a "life" that can otherwise make no claim to be "alive."[47]

This dialectical relationship between the Christ-gift and social practice undermines the categorical distinction between "theology" and "ethics," without in the least reducing theology to ethics. Paul's "good news" is composed of the announcement of an event, the death and resurrection of Jesus as the gift of God. But the meaning of that event, and its quality as unconditioned gift, is discovered only in its social embodiment, in social experience and practice. If, as we have seen, justification by faith means God's recognition of worth solely on the basis of the Christ-event, the continuation of ethnic distinctions at meals in Antioch is not just a communal malfunction, but an outright denial of justification by faith. In this sense, justification *sola fide* cannot be "before and without works" (Luther), since it is in the practice of communities, which in the name of Christ disregard other criteria of worth, that *sola fide* comes to necessary expression. Of course, as Luther rightly insisted, such social practice does not create or elicit the gift, either past or present; but it is so much integral to the gift that without it the Christ-gift simply ceases to have existential reality.

It is for this reason that Paul is so anxious lest the Galatians "fall out of grace" (5:4). The letter is full of warnings. If they come under the authority of the Torah, they will be cut off from Christ (5:3-4); if they bite and devour one another, they will be altogether consumed (5:15); if they practice the works of the flesh, they will fail to inherit the kingdom of God (5:21); if they sow to their flesh, they will reap corruption (6:8). Since these warnings are directed to the believing community, it is clearly possible to lose all the benefits of the Christ-gift. A community that fails to live in accord with the gift has lost contact with its saving power. Thus, Paul makes clear that the gift that was given without regard to preexisting worth nonetheless requires its recipients to live "worthily" of its own quality of rule (cf. 1 Thess 2:12). The *incongruity* between the gift and the recipients' previous worth is designed to bring about a deep and lasting *congruity* between the character of the gift and the ethos of its recipients. The one who "sows to the Spirit" is the one who will "reap eternal life" (6:8): already in the present, though most fully at the eschaton, there will

47. Cf. Konradt, "Christonomie," p. 72: "Das neue Leben gehört insofern *samt seinen sozialen Bezügen* selbst zu dem dem Glaubenden zugeeigneten Heil. Christliches Handeln erhält von daher Zeugnischarakter: Es verweist auf die geschenkte Teilhabe an der Christuswirklichkeit in der Kraft des Geistes" (italics original).

be a "fit" between the gift and the quality of life evidenced by those who have received it (cf. 1 Thess 3:13).

It is important to be clear. The life in which believers "sow to the Spirit" is itself generated by the Christ-event through the Spirit (2:19-20; 5:25). The "eternal life" promised as their "inheritance" (cf. 3:29; 4:7) is *not a new gift* conditional on a self-generated life of obedience, but *the completion of the gift* by which they were granted status as heirs (4:1-6). Since the Spirit is the source and energy of their lives, the life of Christ within (2:20; 4:19), there remains to the end a permanent incongruity between the "natural" existence of the believers and their existence as "children of the promise" (4:23, 28). Indeed, as Romans 5–8 will make more explicit, Paul regards the very existence of believers as a counterintuitive miracle, drawn from a source outside of themselves, the resurrected life of Christ. But within that constitutive and permanent incongruity of existence, Paul expects the gift to find expression in the practice of believers — and he is not embarrassed to warn them that God will be the judge of that (6:5, 7). Seen within this frame, the final judgment of believers does not at all contradict the good news of the unconditioned gift.[48]

The fact that the believer's life is best described as "Christ living in me" (2:20; 4:19) complicates notions of agency in Pauline thought. The presence of Christ within as "the Spirit" means that believer-agency is by no means self-generated or independent, let alone autonomous. Paul's instruction to "walk by the Spirit" (5:16, 25b) gestures to the fact that the Spirit is not only the rule of life but also its source and energy (5:25a), generating "the fruit of the Spirit" (5:22). At the same time, Paul has no hesitation in speaking of believers as agents. As we have seen, they are importantly the subject of the verb "to crucify" in 5:24, just as they are urged to work the good (6:9-10), with "work" by no means an inappropriate term. Indeed, each person is to test *his or her own* work (τὸ ἔργον ἑαυτοῦ, 6:4), whose quality may be the object of a (limited) boast (6:4); it is clearly possible to consider that work the product of the believer *as well as* the product of the Spirit. On the one hand, the Spirit is the source of the fruit (5:22); on the other, one can (or can fail to) "sow to the Spirit" (note the subject of the verb, 6:7-8). The alternation of agencies in 2:20 ("It is no longer I who live, but Christ who lives in me; and the life I now

48. As we have noted before, in this volume "unconditioned" is to be distinguished from "unconditional," if the latter means "without subsequent expectations and demands." For an earlier attempt to grapple with this topic, see J. M. G. Barclay, "Believers and the 'Last Judgement' in Paul: Rethinking Grace and Recompense," in H.-J. Eckstein, C. Landmesser, and H. Lichtenberger, eds., *Eschatologie — Eschatology* (Tübingen: Mohr Siebeck, 2011), pp. 195-208. The sense in which the gift remains incongruous in the life of a believer will be clarified below (chapter 16).

live . . .") should have alerted us to the fact that agency is no simple matter for Paul: neither monergism nor the synergism of independent actors will do justice to his varying expressions. Despite the (understandable) concerns of some of his interpreters, Paul does not seem anxious to preface every reference to believer-agency with mention of its prior grounding in grace. There is no doubt that "life in Christ" is sourced and constituted in the Christ-event, but the believer is thereby created, not diminished, as an actor. Paul's language requires us to banish "zero-sum" calculations of agency (the more God, the less the human), it seems better to speak of a pattern of "energism" in Pauline agency. His paraenesis points simultaneously to divine- and believer-agency, as the expression and realization of the good news.[49]

This duality reflects the dialectical relationship between "the truth of the good news" and the practice of believers. The good news is first and foremost the act of God-in-Christ, but if it is not enacted in the social practice of believers, it ceases to be existentially real. Paul did not possess the philosophical training of some of his contemporaries (e.g., Philo) and some of his interpreters, who might wish to refine his expressions of agency; but there is also little indication that this was his chief concern. The most important question was not how believer-agency could be correlated with or derived from the prior agency of God, but whether the life of his churches was grounded in and reflective of the incongruous gift of God, or whether they were beholden to systems of worth outside of that gift. The Christ-gift could not take effect in the Galatian churches if it did not enjoy sole and supreme authority to shape their lives. To the extent that it found expression in innovative communities, which maintained a critical distance from both Jewish and non-Jewish traditions of value, it was constituted in their midst as the unconditioned gift.

14.4. Conclusions to Part III

By tracing through Galatians the content and ramifications of the Christ-event as gift, I have offered a reading that integrates the letter and joins motifs in

49. For further discussion, in debate with Martyn and Engberg-Pedersen, see J. M. G. Barclay, "'By the Grace of God I Am What I Am': Grace and Agency in Philo and Paul," in J. M. G. Barclay and S. J. Gathercole, eds., *Divine and Human Agency in Paul and His Cultural Environment* (London: T&T Clark, 2006), pp. 140-57; idem, "Grace and the Transformation of Agency in Christ," in F. E. Udoh, ed., *Redefining First-Century Jewish and Christian Identities* (Notre Dame: University of Notre Dame Press, 2008), pp. 372-89. My position lies closest to Barth; see J. Webster, *Barth's Ethics of Reconciliation* (Cambridge: Cambridge University Press, 1995).

ways previously unexplored or underdeveloped. The key features of this reading may be summarized here, in dialogue with the four paradigmatic readings outlined above in 11.4.

(1) As my reading of the Antioch dispute and Paul's "paraenesis" has shown, the theology of Galatians drives toward *the formation of innovative communities,* which not only span the boundary dividing Gentiles and Jews, but practice a communal ethos significantly at odds with the contest-culture of the Mediterranean world. The close correlation between Pauline theology and the Gentile mission was one of the strongest features of the "new perspective" readings of Galatians (Dunn), and we have seen good reason to endorse and develop Kahl's emphasis on Paul's social vision as a radical alternative to prevailing cultural norms. But I have sought to ground this radicality in the Pauline construal of grace, in a form under-explored by either Dunn or Kahl. What shapes Paul's vision, I have argued, is not merely the wording of the Abrahamic promises, nor a principled resistance to national "exclusivity" (Dunn) or "imperial" violence (Kahl), but the radical implications of the Christ-gift, which was given without regard to worth (ethnic, social, or other) and therefore challenges pre-established conventions of value and distinction. By placing this Christological conviction at the heart of Galatians, and by tracing the dialectical relation between theology and social practice, I have tried to do justice to Paul's repeated appeals to the death of Christ, without reducing his horizon to the individual conscience or private belief.

(2) Throughout, I have emphasized *the incongruity* (and not just the priority) *of grace* enacted in the Christ-event and experienced in the Spirit, since this contributes powerfully to the reconfiguration of reality on the Pauline map. Because the Christ-gift neither recognized nor rewarded the worth of Paul's life "in Judaism," and equally was given irrespective of the worth (or worthlessness) of Gentiles, it jolts its recipients into a new construal of the cosmos. At this point, this reading of Galatians resonates deeply with those of Luther and Martyn: it shares with them both their Christological focus and their captivation by the notion of a radical break with "the world" (6:14). In distinguishing between "divine-level" continuity and "human-level" disjunction, I have attempted to nuance Martyn's emphasis on the "punctiliar" character of the Christ-event; I share with him the conviction that Galatians shows no effort to trace linear connections through the history of Israel to Christ (on Romans, see Part IV). Much of what Martyn wishes to emphasize in deploying the category of "apocalyptic," and much of what Luther asserted with the slogan *sola gratia,* I have attempted to explore in different terms through the motif of the incongruity of grace. In each case, what is at stake is the denial that God's action in Christ is the recognition or reinforcement

of a human narrative of worth — whether that narrative concerns Israel or anyone else. Whereas Luther explored this dynamic primarily at the level of the individual (who no longer looks to himself or herself to elicit the grace of God) and Martyn at the level of the cosmos (through the invasive "apocalypse" of Christ), my goal was to draw out the original social ramifications of a gift that disregards and therefore subverts the normative schemas at the core of cultural systems of worth.

(3) The above reading has attempted to give weight both to *the contextual specificity* of the letter, in disputes about circumcision and Torah in the Gentile mission, and to *the breadth of the canvas* on which Paul depicts these issues. With the "new perspective" (Dunn), it has offered an interpretation of Galatians attuned to the historical realities of the early Jesus-movement and of Second Temple Judaism. It has accordingly emphasized that by "works of the Law" Paul means Jewish practices beholden to the Torah, not "works" or "law" in a generalized sense. At this point, my difference from the Lutheran reading runs quite deep. If Paul is not attacking a life-hermeneutic that looks to works to secure the favor of God, he is not countering an erroneous soteriology dependent on the good works of the devout. Thus, his foil in this letter is not works-righteousness (either Jewish or other), and his purpose is not to rescue the proud (or anxious) conscience in its pursuit of this goal. On the reading offered here, Paul's target is not working as such on the subjective motivation of the worker, but the "objective" (socially constructed) value systems that make works, and other forms of cultural or symbolic capital, accounted worthwhile or good. What Paul objects to is the enclosure of the Christ-event within the value-system of the Torah, because for those whose lives are reconstituted in Christ, the supreme definition of worth is not the Torah but the truth of the good news. It is because the Christ-event has subverted every other regime of value that it cannot be repackaged within the taxonomies of the Torah without losing its character as incongruous gift. And neither does it conform to the quest for honor or the definitions of capital that are regnant in the "world" (6:14) on human terms (1:10-11).

(4) If the issue of the Law in Galatians is not law-as-demand or law-as-means-to-salvation, we are able to appreciate in a new way how *communal practice is integral to the expression of the good news*. Luther's careful placement of justification by faith "before and without love" created a dichotomy that, understandable in its context, has made it harder to integrate "faith" with "ethics" in Pauline theology, and is liable to make faith only an interior, individual phenomenon. I have shown above how "faith in Christ" is the mark of those whose lives have begun anew in the death and resurrection of Christ, such that "living by faith" is necessarily expressed in new patterns of loyalty

and behavior. As the source of this life, the Spirit is also its director and norm: the new creation is evident precisely in (and not independently of) reordered patterns of social and personal behavior. I have questioned Martyn's concern to preface every statement of believer-agency with the causative agency of God (and thus his insistence on the subjective genitive, "faithfulness of Christ"). By reducing the Galatian polarities to a foundational antithesis between the initiative of God and the initiative of humans, Martyn threatens to make Paul's statements of believer-agency problematic, and to overload these with hidden reference to divine causality. Of course, for Paul, all believer-agency is founded on the Christ-event. But his chief concern in Galatians was not human agency per se, but the transformation in values effected by incorporation into the act of God in Christ. Thus, the responsible behavior of believers is crucial to him, although it is by no means self-generated or autonomous.

(5) Finally, we have offered a reading that requires *no denigration of Judaism,* while clarifying how Paul's allegiance to the truth of the good news necessarily questions *the ultimate authority of the Torah.* In line with most recent interpreters (e.g., Martyn and Kahl), I would repudiate those readings of Galatians that have resulted in the demonization of Jews and Judaism. I would also now distance myself from the tendency of the "new perspective" to characterize Paul's target as a form of "narrow" particularism (Dunn). But the horizon of the letter does extend to Jews outside the believing community (*pace* Martyn). I have noted traces of Paul's interest in Jews (as "we" or "us"), whose special status as "heirs" is unexplained beyond a cryptic reference to "the Israel of God" (6:16). This is enough to indicate a topic that is greatly developed in the letter to the Romans. Even in Galatians, Paul hopes that unbelieving Jews will encounter the good news (he supports the mission to "the circumcised"), and (arguably) prays for mercy upon them (6:16). However, his reaction to Peter at Antioch and his subsequent argument in 2:15-21 show that the demands of the good news surpass the authority of the Torah. Paul's paradigmatic "death to the Law" strips it of its ultimate authority, so that at moments critical for the enactment of the good news (such as common meals at Antioch), the Torah's rules may be suspended for the sake of Christ. Such strategic and situational dissidence, which he here expects of himself and of other Jews, is expected also of his Gentile converts. Since the Christ-event upstages every system of worth established on other grounds, its capacity to unsettle believers' cultural attachments is, in principle, unlimited.

Like other Jews of his day, Paul is a theologian of divine beneficence. As Galatians has shown, his interpretation of this gift is *Christological* in focus, and therefore centered not on a general truth about divine benevolence but on an *event* — the death and resurrection of Christ — that has effected a transformation of reality. This divine gift is here coordinated neither with creation nor with Torah, but with a particular event endowed with universal significance. Paul puts no particular stress in this letter on the *superabundance* of grace, nor does he perfect this motif by taking God's beneficence to be *singular*, excluding the possibility of divine judgment or curse. The emphasis, I have argued, lies on the *incongruity* of grace — its shocking lack of match with the worth of its beneficiaries, in ethnic, cognitive, moral, or other terms. I have identified here the primary root of the creativity of this letter — its ability to define new taxonomies of reality, new configurations of history, and new patterns of social life. It is important to Paul that this new creation has already been enacted by God in the form of the Christ-gift; it is not a goal yet to be attained or a favor yet to be gained from God. In that sense, the *priority* of grace is presupposed behind the "call" of believers, though this is not developed in the language of "predestination." He does not perfect the *efficacy* of grace, its causative role in believers' response, to the degree expected by some of his interpreters. As depicted in this letter, the grace of God in Christ is "unconditioned" (without prior considerations of worth) but not non-circular or "unconditional," if that means without expectation of return. To the contrary, practice arising from and aligned to the truth of the good news is integral to what Paul means by "faith." Thus, not every perfection of grace developed through the history of interpretation of Paul can be convincingly identified in this letter. But if we place Paul in his own context, we find that what has become familiar to us was unusual, if not shocking, to his contemporaries, and radical in its effects: the gift of Christ did not correspond to the worth of its recipients, nor to any previously established system of worth. As Galatians shows, to recognize that fact was a warrant for theological and social innovation on a remarkable scale.

PART IV

Romans: Israel, the Gentiles, and God's Creative Gift

CHAPTER 15

The Creative Gift and Its Fitting Result (Romans 1:1–5:11)

15.1. Gift and Mercy in Romans

To turn from Galatians to Romans is to find ourselves in part on familiar ground, but in part taken onwards into a new and differently landscaped terrain of grace. This is so even on the level of Paul's lexicon. As in other letters, Paul brackets his whole discourse with a pronouncement of divine χάρις, closely associated with Christ (1:7; 16:20), but the opening two chapters of this letter make sparse reference to divine favor beyond that accorded to Paul himself in regard to his apostleship (1:5; cf. 12:3; 15:15), and beyond reference to God's goodness (χρηστότης; τὸ χρηστόν) and patience (μακροθυμία, 2:4).[1] However, at the point where Paul first describes the operation of the righteousness of God in the Christ-event (3:21-26), he strongly underscores the gift-character of God's action (δικαιούμενοι δωρεὰν τῇ αὐτοῦ χάριτι, 3:24). He then repeats this motif in his analysis of the Abraham story (4:4, 16) and uses it to summarize the locus of believers: through Christ "we have access to this χάρις in which we stand" (5:2). Here (5:1-11), and in the matching summary of 8:18-39, Paul explicates this gift/favor with the vocabulary of "love." It is the "love of God" (ἀγάπη τοῦ θεοῦ) that has been "poured into our hearts through the Holy Spirit given to us" (5:5; cf. 5:8), just as God's handing over (παραδίδωμι) of the Son, the ground of hope for all future gifts ("how will he not also give us [χαρίσεται] all things with him?," 8:32) is glossed as the "love of God/Christ" (8:35, 37, 39). As in Galatians 2:20 ("the Son of God who loved

1. The former terms, used only here and in 11:22 (three times) in the undisputed Paulines (cf. Eph 2:7; Titus 3:4), echo the address to God in *Wisdom of Solomon* 15:1 (χρηστὸς καὶ ἀληθής, μακρόθυμος . . .). The assonance between χρηστός and Χριστός may have been significant in the choice of this vocabulary, at least in 11:22.

me and gave himself for me"), the Christ-gift is to be understood not as an impersonal or random distribution of divine benefaction, but as the expression of love (to the ἀγαπητοί, Rom 1:7; 11:28; cf. 9:25), a willed and personal commitment from which God will not withdraw.[2]

The contrast between Adam and Christ (5:12-21) that introduces the second section of Romans (5:12–8:39) piles the gift-language into an overflowing heap: within the space of three verses (5:15-17) Paul uses near-synonymous gift terminology no less than eight times (χάρις x3; χάρισμα x2; δωρεά x2; δώρημα x1), a rhetorical abundance matching his elucidation of the "superabundance" of divine gift/favor (5:15, 17, 20).[3] The theme continues into the next chapter, where the believers' existence is characterized as "under grace" (ὑπὸ χάριν, 6:14, 15). As in 5:2, salvation itself takes the form of gift: "the χάρισμα of God is eternal life in Christ Jesus our Lord" (6:23).

The gift-language continues in Romans 9–11, but is supplemented here by reference to the mercy of God (ἔλεος, ἐλεέω; cf. Gal 6:16). The remnant of Elijah's day, like the present-day remnant of Israel, came into being "according to the election of χάρις" (11:5-6); in fact, Israel's future depends on the irrevocable χαρίσματα and calling of God (11:29). But there is intertwined now the language of "mercy," which springs first from a citation of Exodus 33:19 (in Rom 9:15) and echoes through these chapters (9:16, 18, 23; 11:30-32) into the summary statement of 15:8-9.[4] The semantic fields of "gift" and "mercy" are not identical, but we have found them mixed elsewhere in Jewish literature of this period (e.g., *Wis* 3:9; 4:15; *4 Ezra* 7.132-40), and their intermingling in Romans 9–11 suggests that they are mutually interpretative. It is not a surprise when we find the celebration of God's mercy in Romans 11 completed in speaking of God as the Giver of gifts (11:35, citing Job 41:11).[5]

As in Galatians, the language of gift can be positioned within a rhetorical contrast; here, in Romans, it is placed in antithesis to the payment owed to a

2. For emphasis on the personal and emotional dimensions of God's χάρις in Romans, see T. Engberg-Pedersen, "Gift-Giving and Friendship: Seneca and Paul in Romans 1–8 on the Logic of God's Χάρις and Its Human Response," *HTR* 101 (2008): 15-44; cf. idem, "Gift-Giving and God's Charis: Bourdieu, Seneca, and Paul in Romans 1–8," in U. Schnelle, ed., *The Letter to the Romans* (Leuven: Peeters, 2009), pp. 95-110.

3. Cf. the language of "wealth" in 9:23; 10:12; 11:12, 33, in each case evoking not the storage but the distribution of this wealth in divine generosity.

4. Cf. 12:1, whose οἰκτιρμοί echoes the οἰκτιρέω of Exodus 33:19, cited in Romans 9:15.

5. Cf. the proximity of the language of gift (ὁ μεταδιδούς) and mercy (ὁ ἐλεῶν) in relation to human generosity in Romans 12:8. For these semantic fields, and their cultural resonances, see the Appendix: The Lexicon of Gift. Cf. the discussion of these terms in C. Breytenbach, *Grace, Reconciliation, Concord: The Death of Christ in Graeco-Roman Metaphors* (Leiden: Brill, 2010), pp. 207-38.

worker (4:4), to the law (6:14-15), to the "wages" (ὀψώνια) of sin (6:23), and to "works" (11:6). Only the context can determine the meaning of such antitheses, but these contrasts are likely to evoke one or another "perfection" (see chapter 2), whether by Paul or by his interpreters. One perfection of grace is immediately clear from Romans 5:12-21: Paul here delights in the *superabundance* of grace, using the language of excess (περισσεία) that is also common in Philo (see above, 6.1). This, we may note, was not evident in Galatians, where this facet of grace was not clearly perfected. Romans is not a restatement of Galatians, and we must not be surprised if it limits, expands, or refocuses the perfections we have traced in the earlier letter. Although Romans is rich in the language of mercy and gift, only careful scrutiny can decide how Paul here does or does not perfect this motif.

One shift in focus may be noted at the outset. As we saw in Part III, the gift-language in Galatians is focalized in the event of Christ: "the χάρις of God" (Gal 2:21; cf. 1:15) is more or less identified with the Christ-gift, in promise (Gal 3:16-18) and event (Gal 2:20; cf. 1:6; 5:4). In Romans, the emphasis lies the other way around: the Christ-gift represents *the gift of God.*[6] In neither case can a wedge be inserted between the Christ-event and God, but the development of a fuller *theo*logical frame has significant implications. In Galatians, the Christ-event was the action of God (Gal 1:1; 4:4-6), and in accord with God's will (Gal 1:4), but it was "the good news of *Christ*" (Gal 1:7) that Paul was eager to foreground. In Romans, he seems concerned to demonstrate that this is, after all, "the good news of *God*" (Rom 1:1; 15:16), without it being any less "the good news of Christ" (1:9; 15:19). The gospel is "the power of *God* for salvation" (1:16); in it is revealed "the righteousness of *God*" (1:17; 3:21, 26). Christ became a servant of the circumcised "on behalf of the integrity of *God*" (15:8), and the gospel thus establishes *God's* faithfulness (3:3). In a recurrent pattern, Paul talks of God's acting "through" (διά) Christ, whether in salvation (3:22, 24; 5:1, 17, 21; 7:25) or judgment (2:16); justification takes place by God's grace "*through* the redemption in Christ Jesus" (3:24). Elsewhere Paul speaks of divine gift "*in* the grace of the one man Jesus Christ" (5:15), and of "the gift of God" (or "the love of God") "*in* Christ Jesus our Lord" (6:23; 8:39). In all these cases, there is the closest possible identification between God and the Christ-event, but the source of the action is consistently

6. B. Gaventa speaks of "a dramatic difference between the christocentrism of Galatians and the theocentrism of Romans" ("The Singularity of the Gospel: A Reading of Galatians," in J. M. Bassler, ed., *Pauline Theology,* vol. 1 [Minneapolis: Fortress Press, 1991], pp. 147-59, at p. 150); cf. J. P. Sampley, "Romans and Galatians: Comparison and Contrast," in J. T. Butler et al., eds., *Understanding the Word: Essays in Honor of Bernhard W. Anderson* (Sheffield: JSOT Press, 1985), pp. 315-39.

God.[7] The fact that in Romans 9–11 the gifts and the mercy of God are traced back to the origins ("the root") of Israel will require us to consider how the Christ-event relates to this *theo*logical narrative and its scriptural expressions (see chapter 17).

15.2. From Galatians to Romans

It was argued above (Part III) that Paul's emphasis in Galatians on the incongruity of the Christ-gift — its disregard of the worth of its recipients — entailed a recalibration of worth that rendered the Torah no longer the definitive expression of "life for God" (Gal 2:19). For believers to submit to the Torah was not simply to revert to an era superseded by the coming of Christ, but to reinstall a norm of "righteousness" incompatible with "the truth of the good news" (Gal 2:11-18). Because the Christ-gift was given to both Torah-observant Jews and Torah-ignorant Gentiles, without regard to Torah-defined worth, its recipients stand at a critical distance to the Torah, "freed" from its authority (Gal 5:1, 13, 18). As we noted (above, 14.1.3), Paul identifies the love generated by the Spirit as the fulfillment of the Torah (Gal 5:14), since "death to the Torah" (Gal 2:19) entails the end of its authoritative regime, not the disregard of all its ingredients. Nonetheless, Paul's stress in Galatians on how the good news subverts the normative status of the Torah leaves unclear how one might also identify points of resonance between them.

In parallel fashion, Galatians relativizes the status of Jews without clarifying if or how their role is also special. If the Christ-gift was given without regard to ethnic worth, it founds a social sphere of existence in which "there is neither Jew nor Greek" (Gal 3:28). Galatians depicts a universal slavery from which *all* require adoption (Gal 4:1-11), and in the stories of Abraham Paul finds a prediction of Gentile believers and of the Christ-seed (Gal 3:6-9, 16), of children born of the Spirit not of the flesh (Gal 4:21-31), in which Jewish ethnicity retains no obvious value. On the other hand, we noted hints that Israel's status may be in some sense special: the "we" statements at strategic locations (Gal 3:13; 4:1-4) and the final prayer for mercy on "the Israel of God"

7. In Galatians, Christ is twice depicted as giving himself (Gal 1:4; 2:20); in Romans, the giver is God (Rom 8:32; cf. 5:8). Similar rhetorical shifts take place elsewhere: compare 2 Corinthians 8:9 ("the grace of our Lord Jesus Christ") with 2 Corinthians 9:15 ("thanks be to God for his inexpressible gift"). On the language of God in Romans, see H. Moxnes, *Theology in Conflict: Studies in Paul's Understanding of God in Romans* (Leiden: Brill, 1980); J. Flebbe, *Solus Deus: Untersuchungen zur Rede von Gott im Brief des Paulus an die Römer* (Berlin: de Gruyter, 2008).

(Gal 6:16) could be taken to point in that direction (see 13.3.3, above). The fact that these hints (if such they are) receive no explanation in Galatians is a token of its polarizing rhetoric. God's plan for humanity matches no developments or capacities at a human level; it corresponds to no fittingness on the part of anyone, including Jews. In transgressing standard taxonomic systems, God's grace founds a community in which ethnicity was counted neither an advantage nor a disadvantage in belonging to Christ (Gal 2:6-9; 5:6; 6:15).

In respect to both these topics — the Torah and the status of Jews/Israel — Romans displays a notable development beyond Galatians, expanding, adding, modifying, and even apparently reversing aspects of the earlier letter.[8] In relation to the Torah, Paul still insists that believers are "dead to the Torah" (Rom 7:4, 6), are not justified though its works (3:20), and no longer stand "under" it (6:14). The discussion of food and days in Romans 14–15 indicates that Torah-observance, while not incompatible with faith in Christ, is not its only or essential expression (14:5-6, 14). However, Romans explains *why* the Torah is incapable of "bearing fruit for God" (Rom 7:5): the cryptic notices of Galatians 3:19 and 3:21 are now filled out with discussion of the powerlessness of the Torah in relation to sin, and its role in the knowledge and even the expansion of sin (Rom 3:20; 4:15; 5:20; 7:7-25). More strikingly, Paul here emphasizes that the Torah cannot itself be considered sin (7:7), and lauds it as holy, righteous, good, and even spiritual (7:12, 14). In the same vein, besides describing the effect of the Spirit as the fulfillment of the Torah (Rom 8:4; 13:8-10; cf. Gal 5:14), he sets great store on "doing" or "keeping" the Torah (2:13-14, 25-27) and maintains that his emphasis on faith does not abolish the Torah but "establishes" it (3:31; cf. 10:4). Several of these statements arise in the context of rhetorical questions that elicit an emphatic "by no means" (μὴ γένοιτο, 3:31; 7:7, 13; cf. Gal 3:21), as if Paul were anxious to head off misreadings of his theology. Paul has not backtracked on Galatians by positioning the Christ-event within the normative frame of the Torah, but the positive connections he traces between the Torah and Spirit-led behavior suggest a concern to show that the

8. The tendency in recent Anglophone scholarship to produce synthetic theologies of Paul (e.g., J. D. G. Dunn, *The Theology of Paul the Apostle* [Grand Rapids: Eerdmans, 1998]; N. T. Wright, *Paul: Fresh Perspectives* [London: SPCK, 2005]; idem, *Paul and the Faithfulness of God* [London: SPCK, 2013]) may be a reaction to atomizing tendencies in previous scholarship, but it is in danger of downplaying important differences between Galatians and Romans. German scholarship is generally more inclined to recognize diversity and development in Pauline theology (see, e.g., U. Schnelle, *Paulus: Leben und Denken* [Berlin: de Gruyter, 2003]). Even in his thematic discussion of Pauline theology, M. Wolter notes differences between Galatians and Romans on our topics (*Paulus. Ein Grundriss seiner Theologie* [Neukirchen-Vluyn: Neukirchener, 2011]).

results of the Christ-gift are not an arbitrary novelty but correspond, at some level, to the intent or meaning of the Torah.

In similar fashion, statements in Romans about "Jews" and "Israel" take on a different complexion from their appearance in Galatians. The same equalization of Jew and Gentile under the power of sin is evident throughout Romans (3:9, 19-20, 23; 5:12-21), and both are called by grace in Christ without regard to ethnic worth (9:24; 10:11-13). Circumcision and uncircumcision continue to be relativized in similar ways (3:29-30; 4:9-12). Nonetheless, a notable modification takes places at the heart of this equalizing moment: the good news is the power of God for salvation for everyone who believes, "to both the Jew — *first* — and the Greek" (1:16; cf. 2:9-10).[9] This priority, like the claim of advantage for the Jew ("much in every way," 3:1-2), receives its explanation in Romans 9–11. There, Paul seems anxious to emphasize his grief regarding his fellow Jews and his heartfelt prayer for their salvation (9:1-3; 10:1). He insists that God's word has not failed (9:6), and that God has not rejected his people (11:1; cf. 11:14), using the same, strong μὴ γένοιτο denials that we noted in relation to the Torah (3:4; 11:1, 13). Paul also claims that, even as "the apostle to the Gentiles," his work is instrumental in the salvation of "my kin," an outcome that he confidently expects (11:13-14, 26-27). In all these ways, Romans makes a scriptural case for the specialness of Israel, even while positioning Jews and Gentiles as common recipients of mercy (10:10-12; 11:28-32). Has Paul found some hidden, preexistent element of worth in Israel that justifies its special place? Or is Israel's specialness itself the product of the incongruity (and therefore the universality) of grace?[10]

Thus, in respect to both Torah and Israel, Romans develops the theology of Galatians, adding dialectical counterpoints that alter the impact of the whole.[11] I shall argue that these changes reflect not the weakening but the expansion of Paul's central perfection of grace — its incongruity with the worth of its recipients. By placing this incongruous grace within a wider frame, Paul demonstrates its centrality to the promises to Israel, and thus to the identity and history of the Abrahamic family. The communities created by the Christ-gift are the fulfillment of a scriptural promise whose effects have always taken

9. Paul's awkward Greek (Ἰουδαίῳ τε πρῶτον καὶ Ἕλληνι) inserts a distinguishing πρῶτον *in the middle of* the binding τε καί, and thus dramatizes a tension that I try to reproduce by describing Israel as special but not unique. Cf. N. T. Wright's translation, "for the Jew first and also, equally, for the Greek" ("Romans and the Theology of Paul," in D. M. Hay and E. E. Johnson, eds., *Pauline Theology,* vol. 3: *Romans* [Minneapolis: Fortress Press, 1995], p. 35).

10. Cf. J. L. Martyn, *Galatians* (New York: Doubleday, 1997), pp. 32-34.

11. For a wider discussion of this phenomenon, see T. Tobin, *Paul's Rhetoric in Its Context: The Argument of Romans* (Peabody: Hendrickson, 2004), pp. 58-78, 98-103.

paradoxical form, now manifested as Jews and Gentiles are equally suspended from the unconditioned mercy of God. The eschatological horizon of this story is the fitting judgment of God, but those found there to accord with the inner purpose of the Torah are people whose obedience arises from their receipt of life from death. If Galatians showed how believers' allegiances are recalibrated by the gift given without regard to worth, Romans, which partially repeats this theme (Romans 12–15), traces their very existence to the creative mercy of God and to a life created for them, and beyond them, by the resurrection of Jesus. Faith is the expression of this eccentric existence, marking a self and a community created by the miraculous power of God.[12] Incongruous grace is thus the mark of the God who creates *ex nihilo.* It is the root of Israel's existence and the reality that grounds the identities and the loyalties of Jews and Gentiles in Christ.

15.3. The Occasion of Romans

The long-running debate on the "reasons for Romans" shows no signs of abating, however confidently it is claimed to have been "solved."[13] The modern presumption that Romans should have as specific an occasion as any other of the authentic letters has questioned previous assessments of the letter as a general summary of Pauline theology; at the same time, the acknowledgment that the greetings in chapter 16 are original to the letter to Rome, and the majority reading of Romans 14–15 as addressed to live issues among Roman believers, have directed attention to Rome as the target of this letter.[14] None-

12. For the notion of "eccentric existence" see D. Kelsey, *Eccentric Existence: A Theological Anthropology* (Louisville: Westminster John Knox, 2009).

13. The main alternatives in the modern form of the debate were gathered in K. P. Donfried, *The Romans Debate: Revised and Expanded Edition* (Edinburgh: T&T Clark, 1991); cf. the summaries and negotiations of the options in A. J. M. Wedderburn, *The Reasons for Romans* (Edinburgh: T&T Clark, 1988); L. A. Jervis, *The Purpose of Romans* (Sheffield: JSNT Press, 1991); M. Theobald, *Studien zum Römerbrief* (Tübingen: Mohr Siebeck, 2001), pp. 2-14. Four recent and incompatible attempts to solve this problem may be found in M. D. Nanos, *The Mystery of Romans: The Jewish Context of Paul's Letter* (Minneapolis: Fortress Press, 1996); R. Jewett, *Romans* (Minneapolis: Fortress Press, 2007), pp. 46-91; A. A. Das, *Solving the Romans Debate* (Minneapolis: Fortress Press, 2007); and D. A. Campbell, *The Deliverance of God: An Apocalyptic Rereading of Justification in Paul* (Grand Rapids: Eerdmans, 2009), pp. 469-518.

14. On the reintegration of Romans 16, see H. Gamble, *The Textual History of the Letter to the Romans* (Grand Rapids: Eerdmans, 1977). On Romans 14–15 as addressing Torah-issues (food and Sabbaths), disputed by diverse types of believer in Rome, see (among many recent works) J. M. G. Barclay, "'Do We Undermine the Law?' A Study of Romans 14.1–15.6," in

theless, the mixed and meager information that Paul offers regarding his reasons for writing (1:8-15; 15:14-33) has spawned considerable uncertainty about his intentions, and it remains the case that large tracts of this letter lack overtly *specific* reference to Rome, to the Roman believers, or to the particular issues behind Romans 12–15.[15] Resort to external evidence introduces a speculative element, which only reduces confidence. Many recent reconstructions of the Roman churches' historical context place inordinate weight on the opaque notice of Suetonius that Claudius expelled Jews from Rome (in 49 CE?) *impulsore Chresto* (*Claud.* 25.4). That this notice reflects clashes between believing and non-believing Jews in Roman synagogues, that Jewish believers were for the most part expelled, and that their return (after 54 CE) to a predominantly Gentile church spawned the tensions evidenced in Romans 14–15 constitutes a train of uncertain inferences that cannot bear the weight they are often required to carry.[16] It seems that we must look to the *letter itself* to find a specific reason for Paul to write a letter of such length and such general content, which nonetheless covers not the whole of his theology but only those particular themes discussed.

In fact, Paul gives us just enough information to be able to meet this requirement. He is explicit about writing to churches that he has neither founded nor visited, but that will be the most important context for his work in the foreseeable future (after his visit to Jerusalem; 1:8-15; 15:22-33). He hopes for a mutually beneficial visit to Rome, and for their support as he moves on west to Spain (1:11-12; 15:24, 28). But neither of these outcomes is possible unless

---

J. D. G. Dunn, ed., *Paul and the Mosaic Law* (Tübingen: Mohr Siebeck, 1996), pp. 287-308; reprinted in J. M. G. Barclay, *Pauline Churches and Diaspora Jews* (Tübingen: Mohr Siebeck, 2011), pp. 37-59.

15. On the current fashion to read "Rome" (or Caesar, the imperial cult, or "empire" in general) as the hidden target of this letter, see my essay, "Why the Roman Empire Was Insignificant for Paul," in *Pauline Churches,* pp. 363-87. Many of the questions there addressed to Wright apply to N. Elliott, *The Arrogance of Nations: Reading Romans in the Shadow of Empire* (Minneapolis: Fortress Press, 2008). Wright's reply (*Paul and the Faithfulness of God,* pp. 1271-319, modifying some of his earlier arguments) does not reduce my skepticism. Whereas Josephus, writing partly for a Roman audience, had good reason to use allusive language, Wright has yet to offer a convincing explanation for Paul's supposedly coded criticisms of Rome in letters directed to Christian believers.

16. I have discussed the expulsion in J. M. G. Barclay, *Jews in the Mediterranean Diaspora from Alexander to Trajan (323 BCE–117 CE)* (Edinburgh: T&T Clark, 1996), pp. 303-6. For my skepticism regarding the use of such data in reconstructing the reasons for Romans, see my review of Jewett, *Romans* in *JSNT* 31 (2008): 89-111. For similar methodological caution, see T. Engberg-Pedersen, *Paul and the Stoics* (Edinburgh: T&T Clark, 2000), pp. 180-86. The best exemplar of this reconstruction of the occasion of the letter is F. Watson, *Paul, Judaism, and the Gentiles: Beyond the New Perspective,* 2nd ed. (Grand Rapids: Eerdmans, 2007), pp. 163-91.

the Roman believers recognize Paul as the recipient of a unique calling, as the apostle to the Gentiles and thus the apostle to *them.* It is notable how emphatically Paul presents himself to the Roman believers as "apostle to the Gentiles" in the introductory greeting (1:1, 5; cf. 1:13-14), in a critical part of his argument (11:13), and in the letter's closing (15:16-21). Because he did not found the believer-communities in Rome, his approach toward them is delicately nonintrusive (1:11-12; 15:14-15); and because he has not visited, he can hardly comment in detail on what he knows only at second hand. There is a more basic necessity: the Roman believers must first understand and embrace him as *their* apostle.[17] The most important exigency that Paul addresses in this letter is the one that he himself will create: his imminent arrival in Rome as "apostle to the Gentiles."[18]

This *specific* reason for writing explains why Paul here elucidates certain themes in his theology, but not all. Theological topics addressed elsewhere in treatment of others' problems (e.g., the resurrection body; the Lord's Supper) are not relevant here. What is relevant is the calling of the Gentiles alongside (and on the basis of) the calling of Israel, and the purpose of Paul's ministry, to bring about the obedience of the Gentiles as an "acceptable offering" to God (1:5; 15:16-18). Because he writes as "apostle to the Gentiles" and thus as *their* apostle (the *only* basis on which he can address them), he writes about the rationale, the basis, and the goal of the worldwide spread of the gospel. His impending visit to Jerusalem, with the collection from Gentile churches for the Jerusalem "poor," may have sharpened Paul's perspective; and, some knowledge of tensions in Rome, over Torah-stipulations regarding food and Sabbaths, may have increased his awareness of the delicacy and relevance of these topics. But the subject matter of the letter, and its length and generality, are dictated by the fact that Paul is here required to explain what his whole ministry is about — whence it arises (from the Christ-event as God's answer

17. As Byrne notes, "Paul cannot pass through Rome a 'private citizen,' so to speak, just another fellow believer. He must come as 'apostle to the Gentiles' or not at all" (B. Byrne, "'Rather Boldly' (Rom 15,15): Paul's Prophetic Bid to Win the Allegiance of the Christians in Rome," *Biblica* 74 [1993]: 83-96, at 89).

18. Failure to recognize this as the primary occasion of the letter, despite what Paul himself says in the letter frame, may arise from disbelief that Paul could consider himself, and his understanding of the good news, a matter of such importance for Gentile believers, even those he has neither converted nor visited. He articulates — he believes — not just one way of viewing reality, but *the* way in which Gentile believers should understand their identity, because he writes as their divinely appointed apostle (1:1-7). They did not require an apostolic foundation (*pace* G. Klein, "Paul's Purpose in Writing the Epistle to the Romans," in Donfried, ed., *Romans Debate*, pp. 29-43), but they did need instruction from the person uniquely capable of describing who they were.

to human sin), on what basis it operates (through God's grace without regard to ethnic or moral worth), and how it completes God's purposes (as found in Scripture and the history of Israel) in the context of God's mercy and judgment.[19] He is reluctant to deliver paraenesis at length, as he does in other letters (15:14). But he has set out what is most fundamental both about him and about them, as Gentile believers (15:15-16): that they are part of God's promised plan to have mercy on the world, a purpose fulfilled in Christ for Jews and Gentiles alike (15:7-13).

Thus, Paul's presentation of his good news is *both* enormously broad in scope *and* wholly relevant to the believers in Rome: as their apostle, Paul sees it as his duty to "remind" them of their identity and of their expected "obedience" (15:15-18). As recent scholarship has shown, Paul writes to these believers *as Gentiles* (as the "implied audience"; 1:5-6, 13; 11:13), even if the diatribe conversations with a Jewish interlocutor (in Rom 2–3) enable him also to address topics specifically relevant to Jews.[20] Paul's special sensitivities regarding Torah and Israel, which we noted above, may reflect anxieties about his own reputation (suggested by 3:8 and 9:1-2). His controversial stance on circumcision and on the authority of the Torah made it easy for Gentile believers to hail him (and for Jewish believers to distrust or hate him) as leading the Jesus-movement away from its Jewish roots.[21] But it was important to Paul for theological, and not just for apologetic reasons, to explain that, even as

19. Campbell's argument that Romans 16:17-20 reveals the real purpose of the letter (to counter an impending visit by opponents, *Deliverance of God,* pp. 495-518) is implausible: it is unlikely that Paul would hold off giving his reason for writing till this point, and then describe the threat in terms which do not match the earlier arguments. The similarities between Galatians and Romans arise not from a similar situation, but because two different situations required a partially overlapping response: in the one case, Paul had to justify his mission to Gentiles on terms that did not require their observance of the Law; in the other, he needed the Gentile believers in Rome to place themselves (on his terms) on the map of God's purposes for Israel and the world.

20. For the implied audience as Gentile, see S. K. Stowers, *A Rereading of Romans: Justice, Jews, and Gentiles* (New Haven: Yale University Press, 1994); cf. Das, *Solving,* pp. 53-114. As Stowers points out, the diatribe conversations with a Jewish interlocutor do not imply Jewish addressees of the letter or Jewish opponents behind it. But it would be rare for such diatribe to be utterly irrelevant to the actual audience of the letter (which Paul knows will include Jews, 16:3-16).

21. For "apologetic" elements in this letter, see P. Stuhlmacher, "The Purpose of Romans," in Donfried, ed., *The Romans Debate,* pp. 231-42; Wedderburn, *Reasons for Romans,* pp. 104-39; R. N. Longenecker, *Introducing Romans: Critical Issues in Paul's Most Famous Letter* (Grand Rapids: Eerdmans, 2011), pp. 123-26, 153-54. Unfortunately, our evidence for Paul's reputation is very patchy (cf. Acts 21:21), and it would be a mistake to give the defensive moments in Romans 3:8 and 9:1-2 a dominant role in explaining the letter.

"apostle to the Gentiles," he understood his work to derive from the scriptural promises, and to be compatible, at a deep level, with "the law and the prophets" (1:2; 3:21; 15:7-13).

Whether Gentile believers in Rome boasted over taking the place of Jews is unclear (the "you" in 11:17-24 is singular, addressed in diatribe style). But the impression of "supersession" could arise wherever the good news received a better reception among Gentiles than Jews, and from Paul's own insistent self-presentation as "apostle to the Gentiles." Paul rejects this impression for scriptural reasons, and the depth of his commitment to uniting Gentile converts with Jewish believers is evident both in his risky collection for Jerusalem (15:30-32) and in his efforts to accommodate Torah-observant believers (14:1–15:6). His ultimate vision is of Gentile believers joining with Jews in worship to hail the universal mercy of God (15:7-13); his pointed presentation of the Christ-gift in Galatians had omitted this larger picture, with perhaps disastrous results.[22] The Romans needed to see the whole picture as he saw it, both for their sakes and for his. The careful restatement of his vision on a large scale, dealing with Gentile and Jewish salvation (Rom 1–4), with "the obedience of faith" that characterizes believers (5–8), with the foundational calling of Israel (9–11), and with the formation of communities in a Christ-shaped *habitus* (12–15), fits exactly this occasion and this purpose.[23]

15.4. The Framework of the Good News (1:1-7; 15:7-13)

The verses generally taken as stating the theme of the letter (1:16-17) are already framed by a careful introduction (1:3-4), which, in important respects, matches the concluding paragraph of the body of the letter (15:7-13). Paul makes it immediately clear that "the good news of God," to which he is set aside as apostle, is rooted in scriptural (and specifically prophetic) promises (1:2); we are alerted

22. Does the absence of Galatia from the contributors to the collection (Rom 15:26; cf. 1 Cor 16:1) indicate that Paul lost his authority over the Galatian churches? And was this loss caused by the one-sidedness of his arguments in his letter? Neither of these questions can be answered with certainty, but this scenario is certainly possible.

23. This analysis renders unnecessary the strained efforts to find covert relevance in every paragraph to specific problems in the Roman churches. While we may wonder at his self-importance, Paul apparently judged that what the Romans needed most was the benefit of his vision of their place and purpose, their benefits and their responsibilities, within the plans of God. Since they are (figured as) Gentiles, and he is their apostle, he is uniquely placed to impart this vision; since they have not gained this from him before, they need it, and better to have it now, in advance, before he arrives. Thus, the letter is written very specifically for Rome, but is only partially directed to *problems* in the Roman congregations.

at once to the long historical and deep scriptural grounding of what follows. The good news concerns God's Son, "born of the seed of David according to the flesh" (1:3). The messianic identity of Jesus, underlined in 9:5 (cf. 15:12), provides a specifically Jewish context for the Christ-event, as reiterated in 15:8-9: Christ is there figured as a "servant of the circumcision on behalf of the integrity (ἀλήθεια) of God, to realize the promises given to the patriarchs" (15:8). This pithy statement, summarizing much of Romans 9–11 (cf. 3:1-7), suggests a double truth: that Paul views the Christ-event from the perspective of the promises issued at the start of Israel's story, and views this story from the perspective of its "realization," an event that clarifies the meaning of the whole.[24] The dialectic is comparable to that between Christ and promise in Galatians (see above, 13.3), but the references to David, the patriarchs (plural), and the circumcision make explicit, as Galatians had not, that these promises are the special heritage of Israel.

Nonetheless, these framing passages also indicate that the actualization of those promises embraces the Gentiles, who are called to "the obedience of faith" (1:5); although the syntax is difficult, the purpose of the "servant of the circumcision" appears to include the Gentiles' "glorifying God for his mercy" (15:9).[25] The following catena of citations (15:9-12) depicts the unity of Gentiles and Jews in worship and hope under the rule of the root of Jesse. The whole passage ties threads from earlier chapters (3–4, 9–11) tightly together and suggests what the awkward expression in 1:16 points toward: that Paul will place Jew and Gentile on a par, but on a distinctly Jewish foundation, interpreted in the light of Christ and through the prism of the mercy of God. Any reading of Romans is required to do justice to all the features that are integrated in these summary statements.

The Christological fulfillment of God's promises is related in 1:3-4 specifically to the event of the resurrection: there, Jesus is "designated Son of God in power according to the Spirit of holiness by resurrection from the dead." Even if the formula is traditional, its relevance is acute, for the related themes of power, Spirit, and resurrection signal the creative divine agency that forms a

24. To "confirm" a promise (βεβαιόω) means to prove its reliability, and thus to realize it or bring it to pass; see *BDAG* s.v. and E. Käsemann, *An die Römer* (Tübingen: Mohr Siebeck, 1980), p. 385 ("Bestätigung und Erfüllung").

25. Commentators differ on how to connect the first clause of 15:9 with what precedes, but it seems best to take τὰ δὲ ἔθνη κτλ. as a second purpose of Christ's "service" to the circumcision (so, e.g., Jewett, *Romans*, pp. 892-93). The variant interpretation offered by J. R. Wagner, "The Christ, Servant of Jew and Gentile: A Fresh Approach to Romans 15:8-9," *JBL* 116 (1997): 473-85 ("Christ is servant . . . also with respect to Gentiles on behalf of the mercy of God") seems strained: see the critique by Engberg-Pedersen, *Paul and the Stoics*, pp. 356-57 n. 29.

leitmotif of the letter.[26] The power set loose in the good news (1:16) is the divine power (cf. 1:20) to bring life out of death (4:17, 21), to graft or re-graft into the root of mercy (11:23). The Spirit, responsible for the circumcision of the heart that constitutes the identity of "the Jew" (2:29), is the gift in the heart (5:5) that mediates the newness of life (7:6), grounding the identity, and forming the obedience, of the children of God (8:1-39; 15:13, 19). And the resurrection of Jesus is that explosive moment when the power of the Spirit was unleashed, creating the life from death on which the believers' faith is pinned (4:24-25) and out of which their identity is formed (6:1-12; 8:9-11).[27] This trio — power, Spirit, resurrection — constitutes the mode by which the Christ-gift takes transformative effect in the human sphere. Unlike Galatians, the prescript of Romans does not foreground the theme of divine gift (cf. Gal 1:3-4), except in relation to Paul himself (1:5). But by highlighting the resurrection and the power of the Spirit, it identifies what will constitute the hallmark of gift and mercy in Romans: its capacity to create *ex nihilo* as the incongruous power of God.

15.5. Human Sin and the Creative Power of God (1:16–3:20)

Paul's good news announces the *power of God* for salvation — a power that disregards the distinction between "Jew" and "Greek," yet also respects the priority of the Jew ("to the Jew first," 1:16). This power is linked to the revelation of God's righteousness (δικαιοσύνη θεοῦ), which elicits faith (1:17): the meaning of these terms and the relationship between them will emerge in 3:21–4:25, where the Habakkuk citation ("the righteous will live by faith") will be interpreted by the Christ-event and the story of Abraham.[28] But it is clear that

26. The citation of traditional material in 1:3-4 is widely recognized; see J. D. G. Dunn, *Romans 1–8* (Waco: Word, 1988), pp. 11-16.

27. For the significance of the resurrection in Romans, and its programmatic role in 1:1-7, see J. R. D. Kirk, *Unlocking Romans: Resurrection and the Justification of God* (Grand Rapids: Eerdmans, 2008).

28. Since all the terms of 1:17 are bare of contextual explanation, and "from faith to faith" notoriously cryptic, it seems best to let their interpretation arise from the later context where they are echoed and deployed (3:21ff.). The Christological reading of 1:17 (Jesus as the "righteous one who will live by faith"), championed by (among others) Hays and Campbell, is tied to a "subjective genitive" reading of πίστις Ἰησοῦ Χριστοῦ in 3:22-26, which there is reason to doubt (see above, 12.5.3, on Gal 2:15-16, and below on Rom 3:21-26). See R. B. Hays, *The Conversion of the Imagination* (Grand Rapids: Eerdmans, 2005), pp. 119-42; D. Campbell, "Romans 1:17 — A *Crux Interpretum* for the Πίστις Χριστοῦ Debate," *JBL* 113 (1994): 265-85. See the response by F. Watson, *Paul and the Hermeneutics of Faith* (London: T&T Clark, 2004), pp. 43-53; idem, "By Faith (of Christ): An Exegetical Dilemma and Its Scriptural Solution," in

whatever is subsequently said about salvation or "life" will be traceable to an act of divine power: unless we have strong grounds for thinking otherwise, we should assume that, in the passage to follow (1:18–3:31), depictions of human righteousness, obedience, or "eternal life," however variously expressed (2:7, 10, 14-15, 26-29), will presume the operation of a creative power sourced in God.

Alongside the righteousness of God is revealed "the wrath of God against all ungodliness and unrighteousness of human beings who in unrighteousness suppress the truth" (1:18).[29] The double use of "unrighteousness" (ἀδικία) stands in the sharpest possible contrast to the "righteousness" (δικαιοσύνη) of God: if God's righteousness is to prevail, it will be not *because of* but *despite* the condition of human beings. As we shall see, this mismatch is the theme of 3:1-8: in the midst of human faithlessness, unrighteousness, and falsity, God's faithfulness, righteousness, and integrity are displayed (3:3-7). The contrast between 3:9-20 and 3:21-26 will underscore the same point: where all (both Jew and Gentile) are "under sin" (3:9), and when the scriptural witness to the desperate human condition (3:10-18) has shown the whole world to stand under the judgment of God (3:19), the saving righteousness of God is revealed in Christ (3:21-26). Thus, the act of God in Christ is emphatically not the vindication or the reward of the righteous, but the justification of sinners (3:23-24; 4:4-8; 5:6-8, 12-21). That incongruity gives the χάρις manifested in Christ its characteristically Pauline shape (3:24).

The foundational analysis of human unrighteousness is given in 1:18-32; the charge issued in that passage is noted in 3:9 and given scriptural corroboration in 3:10-18.[30] Given the parallels in Jewish indictments of the Gentile world, and given the similarities in theme and content with *The Wisdom of Solomon,* interpreters have often assumed that 1:18-32 catalogues only the sins of non-Jews, and that Paul's universal conclusions (3:9, 19-20, 23) arise from a *subsequent* charge against Jews, somewhere between 2:1 and 3:18.[31] But Paul

---

M. Bird and P. M. Sprinkle, eds., *The Faith of Jesus Christ: Exegetical, Biblical, and Theological Studies* (Milton Keynes: Paternoster, 2009), pp. 147-63.

29. The particle γάρ in 1:18 links this revelation to the preceding announcement of the good news; on the relation, see C. E. B. Cranfield, *A Critical and Exegetical Commentary on the Epistle to the Romans,* 2 vols. (Edinburgh: T&T Clark, 1975), vol. 1, pp. 106-8. Campbell's thesis (*The Deliverance of God,* pp. 469-600) that 1:18-32 represents the views of an opponent, not of Paul, runs counter to the signals of the text. For fresh observations on the link between 1:17-18 and much else in 1:18–3:20, see M. A. Seifrid, "Unrighteous by Faith: Apostolic Proclamation in Romans 1:18–3:20," in D. A. Carson, P. T. O'Brien, and M. A. Seifrid, eds., *Justification and Variegated Nomism,* vol. 2: *The Paradoxes of Paul* (Grand Rapids: Baker Academic, 2004), pp. 105-45.

30. For the role of this scriptural catena, see Watson, *Hermeneutics of Faith,* pp. 57-66.

31. The parallels between Romans 1–2 and *Wisdom* 13–15 have been noted and discussed

makes clear in 2:1-3 that he considers no one exempt from the charges in 1:18-32: any person (ἄνθρωπος) who criticizes such sins as if he were exempt is, in the *truthful* judgment of God (2:2), guilty of the same (2:1, 3).[32] A close reading of 1:18-32 suggests that there are echoes here of a biblical rebuke of Israelite idolatry (LXX Ps 105:20 in Rom 1:23), and as we know from Pseudo-Philo and *4 Ezra,* even substantial distinctions between Jews and Gentiles can be accompanied by a general critique of Israel's waywardness and corruption.[33] Paul's inclusion of Jews within a pessimistic portrayal of the human condition is not unparalleled among Second Temple authors.

In fact, Paul's discussion of God's justice intersects closely with two of the texts we have considered above (Part II). The connections with *The Wisdom of Solomon* extend into Romans 2, for in 2:1-5 Paul turns against a form of exceptionalism evidenced in that text. *Wisdom* had used the exodus from Egypt to parade the protection of "the righteous" and the destruction of "the ungodly," demonstrating thereby God's just governance of the cosmos, which was tempered but not overruled by mercy (see chapter 5, above). Interrupting the historical comparison with a contemporary demonstration of this contrast, *Wisdom* included a lengthy diatribe against Gentile idolatry (*Wisdom* 13–15), while indicating that "we" know better (15:1-4). Here, echoing Exodus 34:6-7, the author expressed trust in God's kindness, patience, and reliability, and was confident that, knowing God's power, "we" will not indulge in the appalling idolatry characteristic of others. As many scholars have shown, Paul attacks this line of thought (perhaps precisely this passage) in Romans 2:1-5.[34] He will allow neither such exceptionalism nor any easy appeal to the "kindness" of God, even one drawn from Exodus 34. A "kind" God still requires repentance (cf. *Wisdom* 11:21-26), but Paul has diagnosed the human heart as senseless

---

at least since 1892 (Grafe); for a history of research, see J. R. Dodson, *The "Powers" of Personification: Rhetorical Purpose in the* Book of Wisdom *and the Letter to the Romans* (Berlin: de Gruyter, 2008), pp. 4-13; for analysis of the similarities and differences, see Watson, *Hermeneutics of Faith,* pp. 405-11. For 1:18-32 as directed against the Gentile world, and 2:1–3:20 against Jews, see, e.g., Käsemann, *Römer,* pp. 32, 48.

32. These verses thus frame what precedes as directed against *humans* as such; see J. A. Linebaugh, "Announcing the Human: Rethinking the Relationship between Wisdom of Solomon 13–15 and Romans 1.18–2.11," *NTS* 37 (2011): 214-37.

33. In Romans 11:1-6, Paul alludes to a major instance of Israelite idolatry, involving all but four thousand of the people. As Pseudo-Philo shows, it was easy to read Israel's history as punctuated by repeated episodes of "impiety."

34. The shared descriptions of God's kindness and forbearance (*Wisdom* 15:1; Rom 2:4) and the references to repentance (*Wisdom* 11:23; Rom 2:4, terminology very rare in Paul) are telling; for discussion, see Watson, *Hermeneutics of Faith,* pp. 409-11; D. Moo, *The Epistle to the Romans* (Grand Rapids: Eerdmans, 1996), p. 133.

(1:21), hardened, and completely incapable of repentance (2:5). Because the "we" of *Wisdom* was not explicitly identified as Jewish (only as "the righteous"), Paul directs his attack in 2:1-5 not at "Jews," but at self-confident critics in general. But his close engagement with this Jewish debate shows that Jewish exceptionalism is here at least partly in view.[35] Indeed, Paul finishes this paragraph with a double repetition of the motif of 1:16, emphasizing the common position of Jew and Greek, and the priority of the Jew in both salvation and judgment (2:9, 10). He thereby destabilizes an assumption that the distinction between Jew and non-Jew is liable to count favorably for the former in the "just judgment" (δικαιοκρισία) of God (2:5).

The seriousness with which Paul treats this future judgment is reminiscent of *4 Ezra*. There, the debates between Ezra and Uriel showed up the corruption of this age and the importance of the final judgment as the portal to the age to come. As we saw (chapter 9), Uriel envisages a rigorous application of justice in that judgment: against Ezra's plea for clemency, including his appeal to Exodus 34:6-7, Uriel insists that at the final judgment God can exercise nothing but justice (*4 Ezra* 7.102-40). Paul also resists an appeal to God's "kindness" that would justify his tolerance of evil, and he describes an eschatological judgment, scrupulous in its impartiality, which looks closer to Uriel's perspective than to Ezra's.[36] God's recompense (Rom 2:6) recognizes and rewards the patient conduct of good works with eternal life; for evil workers the opposite result ensues (2:7-10). We seem to be exactly in Uriel's scenario of reward and punishment (*4 Ezra* 7.75-101), while the pessimism of both our authors regarding human corruption raises the urgent question: who is eligible to be counted in the positive category? For *4 Ezra*, it emerged, there is a tiny cohort of righteous Jews — as rare as gold-dust — who will justly inherit the world to come (*4 Ezra* 8.1-3). But who are those in Romans 2:7-10 who can be fairly described as "doing good"?

We encounter here a famous conundrum in the interpretation of Romans, which has led some interpreters to the desperate conclusion that the bulk of this chapter cannot be attributed to Paul.[37] For most others, the problems are

35. The identity of the figure addressed in 2:1ff. has become hotly contested, since Stowers revived the argument that this was not to be taken as a Jew (*Rereading*, pp. 101-4; the target is a literary figure, the "pretentious person"). The echoes of *Wisdom* 15, and the interlocutor's appeal to the kindness of God (2:4), have convinced most readers that he has Jewish characteristics, but I here attempt to explain why the text in echoing *Wisdom* 15 does *not* address its target explicitly as a "Jew."

36. For the motif of divine impartiality (2:11), see J. M. Bassler, *Divine Impartiality: Paul and a Theological Axiom* (Atlanta: Scholars Press, 1982).

37. Campbell takes most of 2:1-16 to be spoken by Paul's opponent (with occasional

acute: if one reads Romans 1:18–3:20 as a single block, displaying the human plight outside, or before, Christ, it seems anomalous to find *anyone* in this context described as "patiently doing good," especially in the case of Gentiles keeping the Law (2:14, 26-27). If this textual unit (1:18–3:20) describes conditions before Christ, these can only be "righteous Gentiles" of a pre-Christian era, whose existence confounds claims for Jewish superiority but flagrantly contradicts Paul's thesis on the universal depth and range of sin.[38] If it depicts the situation of "wrath" apart from the righteousness of God, they can only be a hypothetical entity, which the rest of the argument proves to be non-existent.[39] That Paul describes this judgment scene at all, and (worse) in terms that suggest recompense *according to works* (2:6-10), is all the more difficult for those who perfect grace in Lutheran terms as the polar opposite to any notion of divine *quid pro quo* (see above, 3.3).[40] If Christ is to be considered only as Savior and not as Judge, what is he doing, with reference to good news, in Romans 2:16? If one perfects the singularity of grace (God is nothing but gracious), the notion of God's just punishment of sin must on principle be considered non-Pauline.[41]

This is a good moment to remember what we noted in chapter 2: a perfection of grace in one facet does not mean its perfection in all the rest. If there is evidence to believe that Romans, like Galatians, is structured around the *incongruity* of grace, there is no reason to assume that it also perfects its *singularity* (which would rule out the just condemnation of sin) or its *non-circularity* (which would rule out the significance of the believers' works as the necessary response to grace).[42] If Paul devotes such attention to the "good

---

additions by Paul); see his revised translation in *Deliverance of God*, pp. 588-89. E. P. Sanders considered Romans 2 a synagogue sermon that had little if anything to do with Pauline theology (*Paul, the Law, and the Jewish People* [Minneapolis: Fortress, 1983], pp. 123-35).

38. See, e.g., G. N. Davies, *Faith and Obedience in Romans: A Study in Romans 1–4* (Sheffield: Sheffield Academic, 1990), pp. 53-71.

39. See R. H. Bell, *No One Seeks for God: An Exegetical and Theological Study of Romans 1.18–3.20* (Tübingen: Mohr Siebeck, 1998), p. 253: "On reading 3.9-20 one must conclude that the pious Jews and pious Gentiles of Romans 2 . . . *do not exist*" (italics his).

40. Bell finishes *No One Seeks* with a clear expression of this Lutheran perfection: if justification is *sola fide* and *sola gratia*, there can be no judgment for believers; and "if works are required for justification, faith is insufficient, and by implication God's grace is also insufficient" (p. 273). An Augustinian or Calvinist perfection of grace has less difficulty in integrating *believers'* works with the operation of grace.

41. Campbell's claim that the language of divine wrath and divine deliverance represent "fundamentally different conceptions of God" — the one a "retributively just" God, the other, "the God of Jesus Christ" (*Deliverance*, p. 543) — is a product of his perfection of grace as "singular." At such points his viewpoint is strongly reminiscent of Marcion (see above, 3.1 and 3.7.1).

42. For the definition of these terms, see above, 2.2.

work" of 2:7 and 2:10, noting the righteousness of Gentiles (2:14-15, 26-27) and the heart-circumcision of Jews (2:28-29), it is unlikely that he considers these purely hypothetical. In fact, there is growing recognition that the description in 2:28-29 of "the Jew," circumcised in the heart by the Spirit, alludes to a specifically "Christian" phenomenon.[43] All that is necessary is to break the assumption that 1:18–3:20 is a unit whose *single theme* is the sinfulness of all humanity. Once this presumption falls, the way is open to find Paul *also* describing here the eschatological horizon of the good news, when "eternal life" will be accorded to those obedient to God from the heart (2:15, 29; cf. 6:15-23), that is, to Jews and Gentiles whose existence has been radically reconstituted by God. If we can show that this eternal life is, for Paul, *both* an incongruous gift (6:23) *and* the fitting completion of a life of good work (2:6-7), we will have solved a conundrum that renders the early chapters of Romans the greatest stumbling block for interpreters of Paul.[44]

The first step is to observe that there is more going on in 1:18–3:20 than simply the indictment of humanity. Quite apart from the paragraph about the faithfulness of God (3:1-8, typically considered a "digression"), there is too much here about Gentiles and Jews who *do* "the just requirements of the law" for this regular assumption to hold.[45] To be sure, 3:21-26 depicts the revelation of the righteousness of God that was first mentioned in 1:17, but that does not mean that the intervening material is devoted only to one extended topic. On the contrary, several tasks are here interwoven. After issuing an indictment of human sin (1:18-32), Paul wards off claims to exemption from this judgment by invoking the impartial justice of God, which is anchored and revealed in the final judgment (2:1-11). In imagining and portraying that ultimate, *future* horizon, Paul expects there to be some, both Jews and Gentiles, who will

43. The verbal link to Romans 7:6, not to mention the parallel in 2 Corinthians 3:6, makes this conclusion almost inescapable. Even those who doubt the "Christian" identity of the Gentiles in 2:14-15 are now apt to concede that the Jew of 2:28-29 is described in terms that can fit only a believer; see, e.g., Käsemann, *Römer*, pp. 70-72; Engberg-Pedersen, *Paul and the Stoics*, p. 359 n. 41.

44. The fact that Galatians, whose center is the incongruous gift of Christ, nonetheless expects the "reaping" of eternal life by those who "sow to the Spirit," through patiently "working the good" (6:8-10; cf. Rom 2:7), should give us pause before we consider the eschatological scenario of Romans 2 incompatible with the strongest emphasis on the incongruity of grace. For a preliminary discussion of this issue, see J. M. G. Barclay, "Believers and the 'Last Judgment' in Paul: Rethinking Grace and Recompense," in H.-J. Eckstein, C. Landmesser, and H. Lichtenberger, eds., *Eschatologie — Eschatology* (Tübingen: Mohr Siebeck, 2011), pp. 195-208.

45. As rightly noted by N. T. Wright, "The Law in Romans 2," in Dunn, *Paul and Mosaic Law*, pp. 131-50 (reprinted in N. T. Wright, *Pauline Perspectives: Essays on Paul, 1978-2013* [London: SPCK, 2013], pp. 134-51).

come out on the right side. The future judgment is a fixed part of his mental furniture (cf. 3:6), and his good news requires that there will be *some* at least who will escape from wrath (cf. 8:31-34; 14:10-12; 1 Cor 4:1-5). In extrapolating (like *4 Ezra*) from present sin to future judgment, Paul anticipates the eschatological resolution, but everything he says in Romans 2–3 presupposes the good news that he has already outlined (1:3-4, 16-17) and will soon describe in detail. His mission to the Gentiles is designed to ensure that, surprisingly, there will be *Gentiles* on the right side of judgment (cf. 15:15-18): that result is briefly described in 2:14-15 and 2:26-27 and attributed to an inscription of the Law on Gentile hearts (2:15). Since what God will judge is not ethnicity but obedience, what is justly required of Jews is not just ancestry, circumcision, or even the knowledge contained in the Law, but a heart transformation effected by the Spirit (2:17-29). For both Gentiles and Jews, it is the act of God that produces the necessary human obedience, and in that act the God of Israel will display his righteousness in spite of human sin (3:1-8). Like *4 Ezra,* Paul uses the final judgment to show what counts before God, what is ultimate in every sense (see chapter 9). Unlike *4 Ezra,* what he finds there is not a tiny quota of righteous Jews, but an unspecified number of Jews *and Gentiles* who, despite being equally corrupted by sin, have been *transformed* in their inmost being ("the hidden things" of "the heart") by divine power. This power is *incongruous* in its impact on sinful human material, but its transformative results are finally *congruous* with the just judgment of God.

The argument for this reading can be presented here only in its essentials. Romans 2:12-16 explains the surprising claim that the final judgment will take no account of the ethnic difference between Jew and Greek (2:6-11). Paul insists that mere possession of the Law makes no difference. Sin is counted as sin whether you have the Law or not (2:12-13); what counts as righteousness *before God* (cf. 2:29; 4:2) is not hearing the Law but doing it (2:13). But surely only Jews can do the Law? Not so, says Paul, because he knows of Gentiles who do not have the Law by birth (φύσει), but nonetheless do what it requires; they can even be said to be a "law to themselves" (2:14). There is good reason to take φύσει (2:14) with the clause that precedes ("Gentiles who do not have the Law by birth") rather than with the clause that follows ("they do the things of the Law"): this is a natural word order, and the sense accords with Paul's statements elsewhere that draw attention to Jewish difference φύσει (Gal 2:15) or to Gentile difference ἐκ φύσεως (Rom 2:27).[46] What is more, 2:15 indicates

46. For persuasive arguments on this critical point, see S. J. Gathercole, "A Law unto Themselves: The Gentiles in Romans 2.14-15 Revisited," *JSNT* 85 (2002): 27-49, strengthening points earlier advanced by Barth, Flückiger, Cranfield, and others. In 2000, Engberg-Pedersen

how they do what the Law expects — not by nature, but because "the work of the Law" has been "written on their hearts" (γραπτὸν ἐν ταῖς καρδίαις αὐτῶν). Considering what Paul had said earlier about the futility of human thinking (1:21, 28), the darkening of senseless hearts (1:21), and the sinful passions of human hearts (1:24), this inscription of the Law on Gentile hearts is no natural phenomenon, an exception that somehow evaded Paul's analysis of sin. In fact, the echo of Jeremiah 31 (LXX 38):33 — a text deeply influential on Paul — is loud and clear.[47] The inscription of a moral consciousness on obtuse hearts can only be the transformative work of God, and it is such secret things (τὰ κρυπτὰ τῶν ἀνθρώπων) that will ultimately count on the day when God judges every person through the agency of Jesus Christ (2:16).[48]

Paul is able to parade these heart-obedient Gentiles on the basis of years of experience in founding Gentile churches. He has found "sinful Gentiles" (Gal 2:15) miraculously endowed with a moral consciousness, a capacity to discern and obey God's will (cf. Gal 3:2-5; 5:22-23), a fact that gives hope for their future destiny "on the day of Christ" (Phil 1:9-11). What he describes here is "the obedience of the Gentiles" (15:18), which is the product of his mission and a result attributed to divine activity, to "what Christ has done through me" (15:17), or

---

could declare that the old question on the identity of these Gentiles — believers or non-believers — had been settled in favor of the second option (*Paul and the Stoics,* p. 358 n. 39; cf. pp. 202-5 and 359 n. 42; he appeals among others to Bassler, *Divine Impartiality,* pp. 141-45). I sense, at least in British scholarship, a turn to the other option (believers): besides Gathercole, see Wright, "Law in Romans 2," pp. 143-48 and Watson, *Paul, Judaism, and the Gentiles,* pp. 205-16, with further argumentation. Of course, Paul may *also* evoke a philosophical trope about the wise being a law unto themselves, but he applies this here to believers (as also, perhaps, in Gal 5:23).

47. So Cranfield, *Romans,* vol. 1, pp. 158-59; for other allusions to Jeremiah 31, see 1 Corinthians 11:25 and especially 2 Corinthians 3:2-6. That this new covenant promise should apply as much to Gentiles as to Jews is Paul's remarkable experience and claim.

48. The conflicting λογισμοί (2:15) are better taken as thoughts than arguments (cf. 1:21, *pace* Watson, *Paul, Judaism, and the Gentiles,* pp. 208-9); see, e.g., U. Wilckens, *Der Brief an die Römer,* 3 vols. (Zürich/Neukirchen-Vluyn: Benziger/Neukirchener Verlag, 1978-1982), vol. 1, p. 136. Engberg-Pedersen finds the conflict of thoughts, and the presence of accusations, a sign of incomplete directedness toward God (*Paul and the Stoics,* pp. 202-5). But Paul is impressed by the fact that Gentiles have any kind of moral conscience. Their internal accusations may be directed against their former or their present sins (cf. Gal 6:1 for the latter possibility), and it is this internal awareness of right and wrong that Paul finds remarkable, given his expectation of futile thinking and darkened minds (1:21). Such a change is attributable only to the internal inscription of the Law — that is, the teaching effected by God (1 Thess 4:9). For the emphasis on interiority, cf. 2:29, 14:22, and 1 Cor 4:1-5, a text closely parallel in many respects. Because Paul looks "deeper" than ethnicity, to the resurrection-life already present in mortal bodies, he prioritizes what is evident only to God, in the "secrets" of the heart (cf. 1 Cor 14:24-25).

to the sanctifying work of the Spirit (15:16).[49] Once again, Paul's theology is a reflex of his practice (and his practice a reflex of his theology). It is impossible to imagine a Jew making this strong assertion of Gentile Law-observance, and thereby relativizing Jewish privilege, unless, like Paul, he regularly encountered the transformation of Gentile lives and interpreted this phenomenon as the miraculous work of the Spirit.[50]

Paul's address to "the Jew" (2:17-29) also climaxes in describing the hidden work of God in the heart (2:29), a transformation so profound that it reconstitutes Jewish identity.[51] Paul by no means wishes to exclude Jews in favor of Gentiles, and there is no reason to think that he here applies the label "Jew" to all believers, Gentiles as well as Jews.[52] Rather, he is asking how, in the sight of God, Jewish identity is received and recognized. The critique in 2:17-24 is carefully measured: there is no faulting of Jewish possession of the Law, and no criticism of boasting in self-generated or self-reliant achievement. On the contrary, Paul recognizes the superior value of the Law, which might qualify Jews to be instructors of Gentiles (2:17-20). The "boasting" mentioned in this context is not boasting in the self, but "boasting in God" (2:17) through "boasting in the Law" (2:23). As we saw in Galatians (6:12-14), to "boast" in something means to accord it value, to recognize its worth, to treat it as superior "symbolic capital" (Bourdieu): if Jews boast in the Law, they value it as of supreme importance. The problem for Paul is that what they take pride in turns out to produce not glory but shame (shame *on God,* 2:23-24) — and that not because the Law is

49. Although God is not named in 2:15 as the inscriber, it is hard to imagine who else can inscribe the Law on the heart and so alter the default condition of Gentiles (cf. 2 Cor 3:2-3); 2:29 will describe the same phenomenon, with reference to the Spirit. It is no objection that Paul omits mention here of faith: what counts in this context is *the work* of the believer, which is also discussed without reference to faith in 6:12-23 and 15:16-19 (cf. Gal 6:6-7). If, as we have argued regarding Galatians (above, chapters 11–14), a distinctive pattern of life is integral to the faith that signals God's saving activity, Paul can describe the work of Gentile believers without having to mention, at the same time, the faith that it represents.

50. Watson's fine reading of this chapter finds it directly relevant to Gentile and Jewish believers in the churches of Rome (*Paul, Judaism, and the Gentiles,* pp. 192-216). But the Gentiles are described only in third-person terms, and it seems more likely that, in establishing his special role as the apostle to the Gentiles, Paul here traces the general effects of the Gentile mission (cf. 15:14-20).

51. The opening of this diatribe, "If you call yourself a Jew," does not indicate that it is really addressed to a Gentile who merely claims to be a Jew (*pace* R. M. Thorsteinsson, *Paul's Interlocutor in Romans 2* [Stockholm: Almqvist & Wicksell, 2003]). Rather, it directs attention to the question of what constitutes Jewish identity, which is answered in 2:28-29.

52. *Pace* Wright who speaks of "the Gentile in 2:29" ("Law in Romans 2," p. 134). The discussion of Gentile Law-observance in 2:26-27 pinpoints what counts before God, which raises the question of what constitutes a "Jew," but does not fill that category.

faulty but because they have themselves been unable to keep it. The accusatory questions in 2:21-22 do not imply that every Jew has committed the sins here listed; they are simply a charge that Jewish Torah-observance has been persistently poor.[53] Making the Law the object of pride ends up, tragically, in the worst possible sin — bringing disgrace to the name of God (2:23-24).[54]

The distinctive mark of Jewish difference — male circumcision — is thus strongly relativized: if it does not issue in Law-observance, it is no better than Gentile uncircumcision (2:25). The following arguments (2:26-29) radically subvert the reasonable assumption of Jewish superior worth, and make best sense in the context of Paul's Gentile mission and the experience of the Spirit. Mirroring 2:14-15, Paul speaks of "the uncircumcision" who observe the just requirements of the Law (2:26), such that one could count them "circumcised" and reckon them superior to the circumcised, but Law-breaking, Jew (2:27). This is not a hypothetical category of "righteous Gentiles" (whose non-reality would carry no argumentative force): Paul is speaking of real Gentiles, believers whom he has witnessed loving one another and thus fulfilling the Law (Gal 5:14; Rom 8:3-4; 13:8-10). These obedient Gentile believers can now be used to interrogate the meaning of Jewish identity. If God has shown what counts without regard to physical circumcision, this does not imply that "the Jew" means nothing, but it does indicate that his value before God is calculable in other terms. Paul thus dares to perfect the biblical motif of "the circumcision of the heart." This inner heart-circumcision is not here a supplement to the outer profile of Jews; rather, it is identified as the *only* essential definition of a Jew.[55] If what is valued by God is a transformation of the heart, performed by

53. Echoes of a famous incident in Rome itself (the defrauding of a proselyte by Jewish instructors, Josephus, *Ant.* 18.81-84) are possible, but hardly necessary for the argument. Paul shares with Pseudo-Philo and *4 Ezra* a lachrymose perspective on Jewish history — but offers a significantly different solution.

54. The Bultmannian reading of "boasting," as taking pride in one's self as the ground for achievement, has rightly been criticized as an imposition on this text (see S. J. Gathercole, *Where Is Boasting? Early Jewish Soteriology and Paul's Response in Romans 1–5* [Grand Rapids: Eerdmans, 2002]). What distinguishes Paul's boast in God (5:2; 15:17-18) from the boasting of this Jew in God-and-the-Law (2:17, 23) is that the former has renounced every form of symbolic capital (pride in every kind of distinction) except for the transformative and creative work of God: it looks for praise from God and not from humans (2:29). Paradoxically, for that reason, it is better equipped to fulfill the Law than the Jew who boasts in it (cf. 9:30–10:4).

55. For the progressive logic in 2:25-29, see T. W. Berkley, *From a Broken Covenant to Circumcision of the Heart: Pauline Intertextual Exegesis in Romans 2:17-29* (Atlanta: SBL, 2000), pp. 141-54. He highlights the echoes of Deuteronomy 30:6 (God's circumcision of the heart) and Deuteronomy 29:29 ("the secret things belong to the Lord our God, the public things to us and our children").

the Spirit (2:29), Jewish identity is not inherited but received. It is created not by birth or custom, but by God.

A comparison with Philo will enable us to appreciate the radical implications of Paul's statement.[56] Philo can imagine the complete spiritualization of circumcision both in theory and in practice — and he recoils in horror at a move that would dissolve the traditions of the Jewish community, where maintenance of ancestral customs is the basis of communal honor (*Migr.* 89–93). Paul recognizes that using the motif of "the circumcision of the heart" to relativize physical circumcision will win "praise" (i.e., honor) not from humans, but only from God (2:29); his disregard for this rite in his Gentile mission has proven deeply unpopular in the Jewish community. But his concern is what ultimately counts before God, at the judgment that scrutinizes the "secrets of people's hearts" (2:16). Accordingly, heart circumcision "in secret" is far more important than whatever is evidenced "in public" (2:28-29). Paul thus stakes all on an inner reality. This is not out of Hellenistic preference for the soul over the body (for the invisible and rational over the visible and sub-rational), but because the only thing of ultimate significance is the work of God in the power of the Spirit (1:4; 7:6; 8:1-17; 15:13), and that is operative *at this moment* in the inner creation of the person, and *only later* in bodily transformation (8:11, 23). "The Jew" is not here allegorized into a purely "spiritual" reality, but his identity is reconceived as hanging by a single thread from the creative work of the Spirit.[57] This phenomenon — that Israel's identity and very existence are received from the creative work of God — is later to be traced to the very beginning of its story: both for Abraham (4:16-22) and for the subsequent patriarchs and Moses (9:6-18), the essential truth about Israel is that it was generated solely by divine promise, through the incongruous action of God.

Romans 3:1-8 indicates that the Jewish people are characterized by dependence on this unconditioned act of God, and that this is the hope for humanity as a whole. In rapid brush strokes, to be filled in later (Romans 9–11), Paul insists that by relativizing physical circumcision he is not denying that the Jewish people carry a certain privilege — but it rests, however, not

56. See further, J. M. G. Barclay, "Paul and Philo on Circumcision: Romans 2.25-29 in Social and Cultural Context," *NTS* 44 (1998): 536-56, reprinted in Barclay, *Pauline Churches*, pp. 61-79.

57. As indicated in Barclay, "Paul and Philo," I here disagree with D. Boyarin, *A Radical Jew: Paul and the Politics of Identity* (Berkeley: University of California, 1994). For πνεῦμα as indicating not an eternal transcendent truth, but the re-creative work of God, cf. 1:4; 7:6; 8:9-11; 15:16. For the concrete ways in which Paul thinks about its operation, see T. Engberg-Pedersen, *Cosmology and Self in the Apostle Paul: The Material Spirit* (Oxford: Oxford University Press, 2010).

in themselves but in bearing the Scriptures (τὰ λόγια, 3:2), including their promises (cf. 1:2; 9:6-13). The fact that some have not believed (cf. 11:17-24) by no means negates the faithfulness of God (3:3). In fact (by a logic in which Paul delights, cf. 5:12-21), the greater the failure on the human side, the greater the demonstration of God's opposite qualities: human unbelief (or faithlessness) evokes divine faithfulness (3:3); human falsity, divine integrity (3:4, 7); human unrighteousness, divine righteousness (3:5). The camera pans out here from Israel to every human being (3:4) and to the world (3:6). That is not because for Paul the promises to Israel are secondary to a larger and more universal frame of reference, but because the unconditioned mercy of God to Israel is the root of his merciful righteousness to the whole world. As Romans 9–11 will show, it is only when they are grafted into *this* root of God's incongruous mercy to Israel that non-Jews will encounter the faithfulness of God.[58]

Paul here accentuates the mismatch between human worth and divine salvific action: the consistency of God has "overflowed in my falsity to his glory" (3:7).[59] This is the ideology of the *superabundant* and *incongruous* gift, but Paul knows well the problems inherent in this notion, which we have remarked on from the beginning (see above, 2.2). If a giver gives without regard to worth, has he abandoned his values? Can a gift be incongruous and still retain its goodness, or has it become indiscriminate, immoral, and unjust? Paul faces precisely that question: if our unrighteousness serves to establish God's righteousness, can God still fairly apply his wrath (3:5)? "If the consistency of God has overflowed to his glory in my falsity, why am I still judged as a sinner?" (3:7). These are not artificial questions, created to help Paul score cheap rhetorical points.[60] They go to the heart of the problem of the incongruous gift, of the magnificent giver who might win superficial praise for his giving irrespective of merit, only to find his values questioned

58. At this critical juncture, Käsemann reads Paul's theological focus as shifting from Israel to the world, making the Jewish covenant subordinate to a covenant directed to all creation (*Römer*, pp. 75-79). This is foundational to his reading of Romans 9–11, in which Israel becomes merely the paradigm of "the religious person" (see above, 3.5.3). But it is not the case that Paul "am Sonderfall Israel Gottes Verhalten mit aller Welt exemplifiziert" (*Römer*, p. 77); rather, he locates in Israel's Scriptures (2:2) and in the promises to the patriarchs (1:2; 15:8) the ground for hope for the world as a whole.

59. Watson offers a very different reading of these verses, taking God's righteousness to signify not his salvation but his judgment, his faithfulness to the scriptural indictment of humanity (*Paul, Judaism, and the Gentiles*, pp. 222-27); but this makes the question of 3:7 and the charge of 3:8 much harder to understand.

60. Because they fail to recognize the moral problem in the incongruity of God's action, commentators often struggle to make sense of the question in 3:7 (see, e.g., Cranfield, *Romans*, vol. 1, p. 185; Wilckens, *Römer*, vol. 1, pp. 166-67).

by his failure to attend to the worth of the recipients.[61] As we saw in discussion of *The Wisdom of Solomon* and *4 Ezra*, it was for precisely this reason that some Jews were unwilling to perfect the incongruity of grace. Paul clearly *does* perfect that facet of grace, but he has to face the obvious objection: does God's incongruous giving subvert the moral order of the cosmos? Does a God who gives like this retain the moral authority to judge the sinner (3:7) and the world (3:6)?

Paul's emphasis on the incongruity of the grace of God was apparently well known, and was easily taken to undermine morality; some represented him as suggesting, perversely, "let us do evil that [God's salvific] good may come" (3:8; cf. 6:1). Paul swiftly dismisses this notion, because it remains axiomatic that God is just and will judge the world (3:6). But the questions have put their finger on a central problem in Pauline theology. Can Paul perfect the incongruity of grace — God's gift to the *ungodly* — while also maintaining that God cares about ungodliness, and is resolutely set to condemn it with all necessary judgment? Romans 2, with its affirmation of the ultimate δικαιοκρισία of God (2:5), indicates that Paul *is* concerned to maintain the justice of the cosmos: when it comes to the final judgment, God will neither condone sin nor ignore its effects. Like *4 Ezra*, he insists that there *will* be a distinction between good and evil, a fit between the praise of God and the "good work" that it acknowledges (2:6-11). But — and this is the crucial Pauline point — *the basis for that fit, the foundation and frame of the patient good work that leads to eternal life, is an act of divine power, an incongruous gift to sinful humanity whose transformative effects will be evident at the judgment.* This incongruity (God's faithfulness to the faithless) is the ground for Paul's hope, in a world he considers corrupted by the universal effects of sin; it is also what gives him confidence, backed by experience, that God pays no regard to ethnic background, moral upbringing, or access to the Law. But *the purpose of the unfitting gift is to create a fit,* to turn lawless Gentiles into those who do the Law (2:12-15), and trespassing Jews into Spirit-circumcised servants who bear fruit for God (2:29; 7:5-6). God's dramatic act of righteousness in the face of human unrighteousness is designed to create not moral chaos but justified and purified creatures. As the letter proceeds, it will become clear that these persons are not old selves morally improved, but new creatures forged *ex nihilo* from the resurrection life of Christ, by an act of "calling into being" basic to the story of Abraham and of Israel as a whole. But it is clear

61. Cf. N. Zemon Davis's discussion of the French king's right to give without regard to merit, and the objections that raised (*The Gift in Sixteenth-Century France* [Oxford: Oxford University Press, 2000], pp. 159-66).

already that this creation is *an incongruous gift,* given without regard to prior worth, that founds an existence whose lived practice is *congruous* with the righteous judgment of God.

15.6. The Christ-Gift (3:21-26; 5:1-11)

As in Galatians, the good news announces not the general character of God but an *event* of divine χάρις enacted in Jesus Christ. It is no accident that the language of gift suddenly clusters at the point where Paul describes this event (3:21-26): "For all sinned and lack the glory of God, being considered righteous (δικαιούμενοι) as a gift (δωρεάν) by his [God's] favor (τῇ αὐτοῦ χάριτι), through the redemption that is in Christ Jesus" (3:23-24). The doubling of gift terms (echoed by further multiplication in 5:15-17) matches the stark incongruity between the two parts of this sentence: "all sinned . . . being considered righteous." What was already indicated in 3:1-8 is manifest here. God's action in Christ is no calibrated reward for the godly, or merciful protection of the faithful few, but a gift of utter incongruity, showing no correspondence with the worth of its recipients. As we saw, this was the hallmark of the Christ-event also in Galatians, but whereas there the negative condition of humanity as a whole was mentioned only in passing (Gal 1:4; 3:10, 22), here the statements of 1:18–2:5 and 3:10-18 have given the incongruity of the Christ-gift an "empirical" and scriptural base. That Paul dares to assert the universality of the human plight without exception — without *4 Ezra*'s "one grape out of a cluster and one plant out of a great forest" (*4 Ezra* 9.21) — matches the fact that he figures God's saving action as a completely incongruous gift.[62] Like the *Hodayot,* he

62. That in this sense Paul's theology has discovered through the "solution" the depth of the "plight" seems undeniable. Even if Paul shares with some contemporary Jews a general sense of human sinfulness, including Israel's unsatisfactory condition, his radical refusal to recognize exceptions is a mirror of his conviction that both Jews and Gentiles have been rescued in Christ through an undeserved gift. On this issue, raised by E. P. Sanders, see F. Thielman, *From Plight to Solution: A Jewish Framework for Understanding Paul's View of the Law in Galatians and Romans* (Leiden: Brill, 1989); S. Westerholm, "Paul's Anthropological 'Pessimism' in Its Jewish Context," in J. M. G. Barclay and S. J. Gathercole, eds., *Divine and Human Agency in Paul and His Cultural Environment* (London: T&T Clark, 2006), pp. 71-98. Despite the surface impression that Paul's reasoning in Romans 1–3 runs from plight to solution, there are several indications even here that his analysis of the plight *in such terms* arises from the good news itself: the wrath of 1:18ff. is revealed in the wake of the revelation of the good news (the γάρ of 1:18 pointing backwards); the character of the final judgment is known from this same good news (2:16); and the "faithlessness" of Jews (3:3) is recognized fully in their reaction to its preaching (cf. 10:19–11:10). Campbell's claim that only his own (to my mind implausible)

finds *nothing* in the state of humanity that could explain the miracle of salvation (see above, chapter 7); but whereas the authors of the *Hodayot* find an explanation in the predestined blueprint of creation, Paul points to an event in history that has altered the conditions of the world.

A gift — even a divine gift — given without regard to worth requires some explanation. Such a gift is likely to appear either unjust (disregarding proper values) or trivial (too insignificant to register on the moral scale). One could imagine a powerful ruler distributing largesse without regard to merit, but one could hardly praise him for fairness. One could recognize lesser gifts — the emperor's distribution of dole, or the gods' gifts of sun and rain — as general distributions to people of differing worth, but these could carry little emotional or moral weight: they were benefactions that made no one feel valued or special. For Paul, the Christ-gift was given without regard to worth, but it was *also* just — an expression of "the righteousness of God" — and far from trivial — an expression of God's "love." The justice of the Christ-gift is claimed in 3:21-26, its costly significance in 5:1-11.

The tightly packed depiction of the Christ-event in 3:21-26 is punctuated by references to "the righteousness of God" (3:21, 25, 26), the third expanded by the statement that God himself is "righteous" in "considering righteous" the person who lives ἐκ πίστεως Ἰησοῦ (3:26).[63] The deep disagreements that divide scholars in their interpretation of "the righteousness of God" (δικαιοσύνη θεοῦ) cannot be unraveled here.[64] For our purposes, it is necessary only to note three aspects of this phrase in this context. First, Paul stresses that God's righteousness is revealed "now" (3:21), "at the present time" (3:26), in the Christ-event itself. Whatever the previous connotations of this motif, and however "the law and the prophets" bear witness to it (3:21), its meaning emerges only

reading of Romans 1–4 maintains Paul's *a posteriori* discovery of the human plight is exaggerated (*Deliverance of God*, passim).

63. With most commentators, I take the καί that joins δίκαιον to δικαιοῦντα as explicative (see Jewett, *Romans*, p. 292).

64. The modern debate on the meaning of δικαιοσύνη θεοῦ demonstrates the entanglement of exegesis with wider judgments on the shape of Pauline theology: scholars place this phrase within such diverse conceptual frames (e.g., gift, power, promise, covenant, or apocalypse) as to make agreement impossible. After the debate between Bultmann and Käsemann, developed in the work of Kertelge, Stuhlmacher, and others (see the summary by M. T. Brauch in E. P. Sanders, *Paul and Palestinian Judaism* (London: SCM, 1977), pp. 523-42), recent scholarship has stressed the biblical associations of the phrase with covenant faithfulness or the salvific victory of God; see, e.g., S. K. Williams, "The 'Righteousness of God' in Romans," *JBL* 99 (1980): 241-90; N. T. Wright, *Justification* (London: SPCK, 2009). It is unclear whether this polyvalent phrase, used by Paul in varying contexts, can be given a single meaning or fitted into any one conceptual matrix.

in the good news itself.[65] Secondly, Paul points to the death of Christ as the enactment of this righteousness, a moment of atonement (ἱλαστήριον) that no longer passes over previous sins but dispenses with them in a decisive form (3:25-26; cf. 4:25; 8:3).[66] What seems to matter here is the claim that this is a *just* reckoning with sins, one which does not bypass justice but enacts it. And thirdly, Paul connects this "righteousness" closely to the verb δικαιοῦν (to "consider righteous"), which is used twice in this paragraph (3:24, 26) and repeatedly thereafter (3:28, 30; 4:5 etc.). If this "considering righteous" is no mere pretense that sinners are righteous, it represents either a performative statement (making people "in the right" when it announces them so) or the declaration of a new reality, which is true of lives now generated from the Christ-event.[67] In the latter case, God justly considers such sinners "in the right" because they are reconciled to God through the erasure of sin (5:1, 10-11), and now live from a new reality created through the death and resurrection of Christ (cf. 4:25).

This new reality is characterized by "faith," specifically defined by its reference to Jesus Christ (πίστις Ἰησοῦ Χριστοῦ). The sudden prominence of πίστις in this paragraph is striking (noun in 3:22, 25, 26; verb in 3:22); thereafter it is shown to be central to the Abrahamic story from its very beginning (4:1-25). Here, as with the identical phenomenon in Galatians (see above, 12.5.3), interpretations that take the ambiguous expression πίστις Ἰησοῦ Χριστοῦ as a "subjective" genitive ("the faithfulness of Jesus Christ") are supported by diverse arguments: behind a variety of linguistic and literary arguments, there often lurks a theological anxiety that the faith of believers might become itself the focus of attention or some anthropocentric condition of salvation.[68]

65. Paul later claims that Jews (as familiar as he with the law and the prophets) do not know the righteousness of God, unless and until they see it enacted in Christ (10:3-4). This suggests that the meaning of this phrase *for Paul* can hardly be determined by its contextual sense in biblical or Second Temple texts.

66. The meaning of all the key words in 3:25-26 is strongly contested; see D. A. Campbell, *The Rhetoric of Righteousness in Romans 3.21-26* (Sheffield: Sheffield Academic Press, 1992).

67. For the meaning of δικαιόω (not to rectify but to declare someone "righteous" or "in the right"), see above, 12.5.3.

68. On the debate, see above, 12.5.3. In relation to this passage in Romans, the strongest arguments for the "subjective genitive" are those offered by Campbell and Johnson; see Campbell, *Rhetoric of Righteousness,* and L. T. Johnson, "Rom. 3.21-26 and the Faith of Jesus," *CBQ* 44 (1982): 77-90. Wright constructs the issue differently from most, figuring Jesus as the faithful Jew who fulfills Israel's duty of faithfulness to God ("Romans," p. 470). But there is no indication in Jewish sources that "God's plan of salvation had always required a faithful Israelite to fulfill it," and such a schema is nowhere else evident in Pauline theology. The texts often cited as parallel (Rom 5:12-21 and Phil 2:5-11) use the language of "obedience," which could readily

However, since nowhere else in this letter does Paul refer to Jesus as "faithful," since (as in Gal 2:16) he clarifies the meaning of his shorthand as soon as he uses it (3:22: "for all who believe"),[69] and since the following chapter offers Abraham (not Christ) as the foundational and paradigmatic person of faith (not faithfulness), the πίστις of 3:21-26 is better understood as that of believers, signaling their participation in, and derivation from, the Christ-event.[70] God's righteousness has effected a new kind of being, whose faith is the signal that their life is constructed not in the normal configuration of human existence, but from Christ. The fact that this mode of dependence is evidenced in both Jew and Gentile, among *all* who believe despite their common condition of sin (3:22-23), is a sign that the gift on which it hangs was given without discrimination and without regard to worth.

Romans 5:1-11 (we shall return below to Romans 4) celebrates "this χάρις in which we stand," where the grounds for confidence or pride ("boasting") lie entirely in God, who has created a new reality in Christ and guarantees the future of what he has created (5:2, 11). Despite suffering, hope is secure, because the heart, transformed by the gift of the Spirit (cf. 2:15, 29), has been filled with the love of God (5:5). Paul goes out of his way here to underline the total absence of worth on the human side: it was while we were weak (ἀσθενεῖς) that Christ died, on behalf of the ungodly (ἀσεβεῖς, 5:6); God proves (συνίστησιν, cf. 3:5) his love, in that "while we were still sinners" (ἁμαρτωλοί), Christ died for us (5:8); it was when we were enemies (ἐχθροί) that we were reconciled to God (5:10). The variety of terms, portraying the absence of value from multiple perspectives, seems designed to underline as emphatically as possible that the conditions for the gift were anything but positive. This is not the giving of covenants to the worthy (Philo; see above, 6.3); no fitting features can be traced in the recipients of God's love, not even in their hidden potential.

Paul himself comments on the rarity of such an incongruous gift: "rarely will anyone die for a righteous person; though perhaps for a good person someone might be courageous enough to die" (5:7).[71] His statement reflects

---

have been used here if such was Paul's meaning. Israel's ἀπιστία (Rom 3:3) is never brought into contrast with Jesus' πίστις.

69. See R. B. Matlock, "The Rhetoric of πίστις in Paul: Galatians 2.16, 3.22, Romans 3.22, and Philippians 3.9," *JSNT* 30 (2007): 173-203.

70. For cogent arguments in this direction, see Watson, *Paul, Judaism, and the Gentiles*, pp. 231-45. As he notes, the genitive "functions almost adjectively, to delimit the scope of πίστις, but leaves the relationship between 'faith' and 'Jesus [Christ]' relatively undefined" (p. 244); he later speaks of "the faith that pertains to God's saving action in Christ — originating in it, participating in it, and oriented towards it" (p. 255).

71. It is not clear what, if any, is the distinction between the two categories; the labels

the general ancient presumption that good gifts are given to the worthy, and the costlier the gift the more discriminatingly it is given. The gift of one's life — the costliest gift imaginable — would hardly be given to an undeserving cause: as Seneca comments, if a person is worthy *(dignus)*, I shall defend him even at the cost of my own life; if he is unworthy *(indignus)*, I will do what I can to aid him, but not at such a cost (*Ben.* 1.10.5).[72] Yet Christ died in those inconceivable conditions — a gift that, Paul seems anxious to insist, is no mere throwing away of life, but an expression of love, the deepest personal commitment. This love is figured as God's rather than Christ's (5:5, 8; contrast Gal 2:20), since the death of Christ is God's handing over of his only Son (8:32); but the difference is not great (cf. 8:39: the love of God in Christ). This gift is neither a trivial token, tossed to whomever it might reach, nor a costly gift carefully targeted at the highly deserving. It is the costliest gift, given with the deepest sentiment and the highest commitment to those who, at the time of its giving, had nothing to render them fitting recipients. It is this strange and nonsensical phenomenon that Paul parades in 5:5-11 (cf. 9:6-18). On the basis of this extraordinary gift, Paul can take confidence: if enemies have been reconciled in such a fashion, how much more will the reconciled be saved (5:10)!

In this presentation of the death of Christ as gift, Paul joins elements of the ancient conception of gift in a unique and rhetorically powerful combination. Like other ancient thinkers, he can speak of a divine generosity that reaches to *all:* as we have seen, the universality of divine gift could evoke the perfection of incongruity, since the gifts of nature (rain and sun, light and heat) are given to all, both good and bad.[73] But an undiscriminating gift could be considered morally questionable, and careful reflection on the general gifts of God might qualify them as gifts of lesser significance, or gifts given only for the sake of the good.[74] For Paul, however, there are no good people to constitute the special target of the gift. Moreover, since he identifies the gift of God not with the benefactions of nature but with the death of Christ, this gift could never

---

appear to be general, and there is no good reason to take the second as a benefactor, even if benefactors, among others, can sometimes be termed "good" (*pace* Cranfield, *Romans,* vol. 1, pp. 264-65). Paul doubles the positive scenario to underline the point: it is just conceivable that such a gift could be given to a person of value — but only just. Dying for the worthless is off the scale of what is imaginable.

72. Cf. Philo, *Spec.* 3.154-55, insisting that fathers should not die for sons who are deserving of punishment, out of misplaced or excessive affection, since "it is right to show friendship to those whose actions are worthy of friendship, but no evil-doer is a true friend" (155). To die for the unworthy is thus morally reprehensible. I am grateful to Orrey McFarland for drawing this passage to my attention.

73. See Seneca, *Ben.* 1.1.9-10; on this perfection in ancient discourse, see above, 2.2.

74. See Seneca, *Ben.* 4.28; Philo, *Sacr.* 121–25.

be diminished as random or trivial; it expresses God's *love,* a movement of personal and individualized commitment — toward the unworthy. Indeed, since this gift takes place in *the death of Christ,* Paul can evoke, and overturn, ancient sensibilities concerning the proper distribution of the gift.[75] Human beings do not give the costliest gifts to worthless people; the death of Christ for the ungodly confounds the normal expectation of the congruous gift. Thus, *as a divine gift, given to all in the death of Christ, an act of love for the wholly unworthy, Paul figures the Christ-gift as the ultimate incongruous gift.* He was not the first to imagine that divine gifts could be incongruous with the worth of their recipients, but he has gone out of his way to depict the Christ-gift as a gift that breaks the mold.

15.7. The Abrahamic Family Trait

The extended commentary on Genesis 15:6 that forms the frame of Romans 4 highlights both the *scope* of the Abrahamic family and its *characteristic family trait.* Paul had used Abraham texts in Galatians both to support his Gentile mission (Gal 3:6-29) and to showcase the miraculous creation of the Abrahamic offspring (Gal 4:21–5:1; see chapter 13). Romans 4 unites and develops these themes while signaling the presence of Jewish believers among the co-heirs of Abraham, as was never explicit in Galatians. Paul here traces not only the *breadth* of the Abrahamic promise for the construction of a Jew-and-Gentile family, but also the distinctive character of its *means* — as evidenced in an Abrahamic narrative shot through with the incongruous action of God.

Differing readings of this chapter reveal alternative construals of the letter as a whole.[76] In reaction against Bultmannian individualism, Käsemann took

75. It seems important for this discourse that the gift is figured in human terms, as the death of Christ, even if it is also, at the same time, the gift of God (8:32; even here, the gift is given an anthropomorphic depiction, as the handing over of God's "only Son"). That a human should give his life for the worthless is a much more striking contradiction of norms than that God should distribute largesse to good and bad alike.

76. At an earlier stage in German scholarship, a radical Bultmannian reading of Romans 4 by Klein (portraying Abraham as an isolated, individual precursor of Christian faith) was countered by interpretations of the patriarch as the origin of the history of salvation (or election); see G. Klein, "Römer 4 und die Idee der Heilsgeschichte," *EvTheol* 23 (1963): 424-47; U. Wilckens, "Die Rechtfertigung Abrahams nach Römer 4," in *Rechtfertigung als Freiheit: Paulusstudien* (Neukirchen: Neukirchener Verlag, 1974), pp. 33-49; cf. U. Luz, *Das Geschichtsverständnis des Paulus* (Munich: Kaiser Verlag, 1968), pp. 168-86. For a recent discussion, including surveys of scholarship, see B. Schliesser, *Abraham's Faith in Romans 4* (Tübingen: Mohr Siebeck, 2007).

Paul's account of Abraham and his seed to justify speaking of a (humanly discontinuous) "salvation history,"[77] but his emphasis lay on the scriptural story as "proof" of the doctrine of justification by faith.[78] For Käsemann, the heart of the chapter is 4:1-8, climaxing in the statement of "the justification of the ungodly" (4:5; *Römer,* 100-107); throughout this chapter Paul counters Jewish opponents, who used Abraham to justify a soteriology of works (99-100).[79] As an "example" of faith (99), this story disqualifies "the boasting of the pious person" who seeks security before God by works (of the law; 97, 106-7). The topic of circumcision is raised (4:9-12) only in order to respond to a possible "objection" (108); it stands for a generalized tendency to "make salvation a privilege of the religious" (98). Indeed, Romans 4 represents Paul's rejection of every tendency to turn God's Law perversely into "a principle of achievement" (*Leistungsprinzip;* 99). Abraham is cited here as the model of the opposing "principle" (the justification of the ungodly, by faith alone), which constitutes the heart of Paul's good news.[80]

The main alternative reading of the chapter, which has taken shape in "the new perspective on Paul," interprets Abraham not as the scriptural proof of a theological concept but as the founding progenitor of a historical family.[81] For Wright, the main topic of this chapter is the "covenant family of Abraham," which includes both Gentiles and Jews (Wright, 487): "faith, grace and promise . . . are vital to this chapter, but they are not its main subjects" (497). With the center of gravity located in 4:9-17, Abraham's significance lies in his role as "father" of a single multiethnic family, the subject of a past promise now fulfilled in Christ.[82] Paul here contrasts not two opposing soteriologies,

77. See E. Käsemann, "Justification and Salvation History in the Epistle to the Romans," and "The Faith of Abraham in Romans 4," in *Perspectives on Paul* (Philadelphia: Fortress Press, 1971), pp. 60-78 and 79-101; cf. his *Römer,* 110-11.

78. See his title for 4:1-25: "Der Schriftbeweis aus der Geschichte Abrahams," *Römer,* p. 99; what it proves is the thesis of 3:21-26 or "die Glaubensgerechtigkeit," p. 110. Page numbers in parentheses in the main text refer to Käsemann, *Römer.*

79. Crucially, for Käsemann, "ἐργάζεσθαι meint nicht mehr 'arbeiten,' sondern 'mit Werken umgehen'" (104). It is this "concern for works" that signals, in Lutheran terms, the antithesis to faith; see above, 3.3.

80. For the tendency in the Lutheran tradition to read Paul as a conceptual theologian, and to take the term "Jew" as a cipher for "the religious/pious person," see above, 3.5.

81. E,g., N. T. Wright, "The Letter to the Romans," in *The New Interpreter's Bible,* vol. 10 (Nashville: Abingdon Press, 2002), pp. 395-770, at pp. 487-507. Romans 4 is "a chapter about the scope and nature of Abraham's family, rather than a chapter about 'justification by faith'" (489); Paul is "not . . . using Abraham primarily as an example" (495). Page numbers in parentheses refer to this commentary.

82. "The overall subject of the larger section is . . . the revelation of God's covenant faithfulness and the creation of a Jew-plus-Gentile family" (497).

abstractly conceived, but two competing construals of the Abrahamic family: one in which membership is based on ethnicity ("fleshly descent"), the other not based on ethnicity, for Jew and Gentile alike.[83]

The reading offered below attempts to give equal weight to every section of this chapter, relegating none to the status of "answers to objections" or "metaphorical expansions."[84] Our task is to integrate Paul's dual portrayal of Abraham, as both *believer* in God and *father* of a multinational family.[85] It will be argued here that the calling of both Gentiles and Jews into the Abrahamic family is central to Paul's argument, not an illustration or a polemical addition. This is the critical feature of the good news that characterizes Paul's work as apostle to the Gentiles; since Paul's theology is developed from and for the Gentile mission, the breadth of the patriarchal promise is at the heart of this chapter, and of the letter as a whole (cf. 15:7-13, 16-21). But the *mode* of Abraham's relationship to God (faith), and the *means* by which his seed has come into being (by creation *ex nihilo*), are also objects of central attention (4:2-8, 16-22). What integrates these concerns is the fact that the Abrahamic family is marked by a peculiar trait. Its inclusion of Jews and Gentiles, united in faith, is the reflection of the fact that the Abrahamic family, from the beginning, has been created by the grace and the calling of God, who has never paid regard to human criteria of capacity or worth. This incongruity between divine action and human status is the unifying theme of Paul's argument: it is the *theological rationale* for the calling of Gentiles, and also the calling of Jews, into the single Abrahamic family.[86]

83. For a significant earlier statement of this reading of the chapter, see R. B. Hays, "'Have We Found Abraham to Be Our Forefather according to the Flesh?' A Reconsideration of Rom 4:1," *NovT* 27 (1985): 76-98, reprinted in *The Conversion of the Imagination: Paul as Interpreter of Israel's Scripture* (Grand Rapids: Eerdmans, 2005), pp. 61-84. For the distinctive interpretation of Romans 4:1 in this reading, see below.

84. The first represents Käsemann's treatment of 4:9-12; for the second, see Wright on 4:2-8: these verses are "much better understood as a further metaphorical expansion, rather than the inner substance, of Paul's point" ("The Letter to the Romans," p. 490). Wright offers a fuller and stronger reading of 4:1-8 in "Paul and the Patriarch" (in his *Pauline Perspectives: Essays on Paul, 1978-2013* (London: SPCK, 2013), pp. 554-92, though even here 4:4 is characterized as "embroidery" that "carries no weight in the passage as a whole" (p. 563; cf. p. 586). Wright finds the main topic of chapter 4, "the unity and equality of believing Jews and believing Gentiles," to be completed by the end of 4:17; the rest of the chapter (4:18-25) relates to everything from 1:18 onwards, but less specifically to 4:1-17 ("The Letter to the Romans," p. 499).

85. For a similarly integrative reading, see Schliesser, *Abraham's Faith*, pp. 221-390.

86. Watson's reading of Romans 4 in relation to the Genesis narratives (*Hermeneutics of Faith*, pp. 167-219) is structured by the polarity between God's *unconditional* promise and the *conditionality* of a narrative contingent on human obedience or human initiative; this works less well with Romans 4:17-22, where God's act is contrasted not with human initiative but

As for many other Jews, the Abraham story defines for Paul both the origin and the shape of the narrative of Israel. Of the authors studied in Part II, Philo particularly highlights the significance of Abraham in characterizing the election of Israel, and thus the purpose of God for the world. As we saw above (6.4), Abraham represented for Philo the primordial journey toward the truth about God, and the paradigmatic migration to virtue. As the teachable soul, he learned that God is the invisible Cause of the cosmos, while traveling from bodily vices to the virtues of the mind (*Migr.* 1–6, 176–95). This twin movement, intellectual and moral, made Abraham the father of Israel and the paradigm for proselytes: he is both founding father and model, because he begins the story with the precise characteristics in which it will continue (*Abr.* 78). Paul's configuration of Abraham is very different, but here, too, there is no need to choose between his originating and his exemplary functions: Abraham is the father of both Jews and Gentiles exactly in the way in which he and his offspring were constituted as bearers of the promise.

Taking 3:27-31 as the thematic introduction to the Abraham chapter, we sense how the scope and the means of justification are interlinked.[87] Because all human capital is disregarded ("boasting is excluded," 3:27), including that defined by works (of the Law), it becomes clear that a person is justified through faith (3:27-28). Accordingly, ethnic difference is irrelevant, and the one God justifies Jews and Gentiles alike, through faith (3:29-30). As in Galatians, the discussion of justification serves a practical purpose, grounding a mission to Gentiles that does not require a "Judaizing" frame: justification by faith marks both the goal (the inclusion of Gentiles with Jews) and the means (the disregard of the normal tokens of value). The programmatic Abraham story encapsulates both this means (through faith, 4:1-8) and this goal (Jew and Gentile alike, 4:9-12). The fact that Paul begins with the means (4:1-8) signals not that Abraham is an illustration of a theological concept, but that the social goal is attainable only through God's distinctive method. The non-

---

with human capacity. But Watson is right to see that Paul is interested in the *pattern* of the Abrahamic narratives. By expressing this pattern as the "incongruity" between divine action and human capacity or worth, I hope to capture the core dynamic of the whole of the chapter.

87. There are close verbal links between 3:27-28 and 4:1-8: καύχησις (3:27) is matched by καύχημα (4:2), and χωρὶς ἔργων (3:28) echoed in 4:6. Similarly, "circumcision" and "uncircumcision" (3:29-30) are taken up in 4:9-12. One may thus read the first two paragraphs of chapter 4 (4:1-8, 9-12) as unpacking and grounding the claims of 3:27-30; cf. Campbell, *Deliverance of God*, pp. 725-27 (arguing also for a link between 3:31 and 4:13-16). These ties across the chapter division suggest that Paul's claim to "confirm" the Law (3:31) represents his understanding that the good news fulfills the Abrahamic narrative (for this sense of νόμος in precisely this context, cf. Gal 4:21). For discussion, see C. Rhyne, *Faith Establishes the Law* (Chico: Scholars Press, 1981), and Wilckens, *Römer*, vol. 1, pp. 249-50.

distinction between Jew and Gentile in faith makes sense for Paul not by a political principle of "equal access," nor merely by reference to the "many nations" promised in the Abrahamic texts (cited later, in 4:17-18). It is explicable because the Abrahamic story is fulfilled as it began: in faith-dependence upon a divine decision irrespective of inherent human worth.

Despite an intriguing suggestion to the contrary, it is best to read Romans 4:1 as it is usually translated: "What then shall we say that Abraham, our forefather according to the flesh, has discovered?"[88] For the purposes of debate, Paul starts from the standard recognition of Abraham as the physical progenitor of Jews:[89] as the chapter continues, he will redefine this fatherhood (4:11, 16-18), after redefining the character of Abraham himself.[90] What Abraham "discovered"[91] is what Scripture itself says (Gen 15:6), and what Paul has also

88. For a challenge to this reading, see Hays, " 'Have We Found?' " Hays rightly points out that the extension of the usual rhetorical question ("What shall we say?") is unusual, and that the description of Abraham as "our forefather according to the flesh" will be modified by the new definition of his lineage in the verses that follow. But his own reading ("What shall we say? Have we found Abraham to be our forefather according to the flesh?") is fatally flawed: if it were a predicate, "forefather" would have no definite article, which it has in Paul's Greek (for this and other objections, see Engberg-Pedersen, *Stoics*, p. 363 n. 3; there is no evidence that "the forefather" was a well-known title for Abraham). Wright's adaptation of Hays's proposal (taking "we" to be believers, not Jews) is no more convincing: it imagines Gentile believers (and proselytes) asking themselves whether they were descended from Abraham "according to the flesh" (members of Abraham's "fleshly family," "Romans," p. 490). But as far as we know, no one in Paul's day considered that Gentiles, even proselytes, could claim *physical ancestry* from Abraham (see "Romans," pp. 487, 490); circumcision would not mean discovering Abraham to be their "physical father" (p. 494); cf. Wright, "Paul and the Patriarch," pp. 579-84.

89. As Stowers has shown, the question-and-answer style of 3:27–4:2 has similarities with the "diatribe" exchange of ancient school-rhetoric (*The Diatribe and Paul's Letter to the Romans* [Chico: Scholars Press, 1981], pp. 155-74). But it is not clear that this continues the engagement with the Jewish interlocutor of 2:17-24: instead of a "you" address, 3:27–4:2 has several "we" statements, which, on Stowers's allocation of voices, are spoken by both "parties" (3:28, 31; 4:1) — an "atypical formal feature" in diatribe, as Stowers admits (p. 165). This signals that the dialogue remains internal to Paul's own thought processes, and has not been externalized to the degree asserted by Stowers (and Campbell, *Deliverance of God*, pp. 715-25, with a different allocation of questions and answers), sufficient to yield the profile of a Jewish interlocutor.

90. For a parallel use of κατὰ σάρκα, relativized but not rejected, see Rom 1:3; 9:3, 5. The rest of Romans 4 will argue what is summarized in 9:8, that the form of descent from Abraham that counts before God is that created by God: physical ancestry is not excluded by this unconditioned act, but it cannot demarcate the limits of the descendants whom God is creating from nothing (4:17). Philo also both recognizes and relativizes the Jewish claim of patriarchal ancestry, but on very different grounds: such nobility, he insists, is ultimately a matter of virtue (*Virt.* 206–27).

91. The verb (εὑρίσκω) may allude to the common Diaspora tradition that Abraham was the discoverer or inventor (εὑρέτης) of very significant truths; for examples, see J. M. G.

discovered in the wake of the Christ-event: that what counts before God has nothing to do with works, whether of the Law or of any other sort.[92] There is no reason to think that here, or anywhere else in Romans, Paul targets a Jewish (or any other) presumption that one could "earn" salvation by good works. He neither charges nor assumes that Law-keepers boast in their achievements, in the sense of looking to themselves, *rather than to God,* as the ground of their salvation.[93] If we remove this ideological freight from the language of "works," Paul's point is far simpler: nothing Abraham did made him worthy of the favor of God.[94] In Genesis 15:1, Abraham is told that his "reward" (LXX: μισθός) would be very great, and it was natural to assume that a divine reward must correspond to the value of Abraham's progress.[95] Such reward from God would be understood, of course, as gift, not pay, but God would hardly issue rewards without good reason. Thus, in spelling out the means of God's indiscriminate justification of Jew and Gentile, Paul's first task is to insist on an *absence* in

---

Barclay, *Jews in the Mediterranean Diaspora from Alexander to Trajan (323 BCE–117 CE)* (Edinburgh: T&T Clark, 1996), pp. 127-32 (Artapanus), and Watson, *Hermeneutics of Faith,* pp. 257-67 (Josephus, Eupolemus, and others).

92. In overreaction against the Lutheran reading of "works" as signaling a soteriology of self-justification ("works-righteousness"), "new perspective" readings of this passage are at pains to insist that even where ἔργα is mentioned without qualifier (in 4:2, as in 3:27; 4:6; 9:32; 11:6) it is limited in meaning to Torah-practice ("works of the Law"), most notably those works that distinguish Jews from Gentiles (see, e.g., Dunn, *Romans 1–8,* pp. 192, 200; Wright, "Paul and the Patriarch," pp. 584-85). But there are good reasons why Paul could not speak of "works of the Law" in the case of Abraham (whom he dates before the arrival of the Law, 5:13-14). His point is to exclude from God's reckoning not only one but *any* form of symbolic capital that might be taken to constitute a source of worth before God (cf. 9:6-13).

93. It is a common mistake to read 4:4-5 as the mirror-image of Paul's contemporary Judaism, which on this reasoning advocated salvation by due and not by grace (see Gathercole, *Where Is Boasting?* pp. 244-46). But Paul does not attribute this view to anyone; 4:4-5 serves an exegetical but not a polemical purpose. As we have seen (e.g., in *Wisdom of Solomon* and Philo, chapters 5-6 above), where the language of "due reward" occurs in Jewish texts, this is not a denial of God's gifts but a celebration of their fair distribution.

94. Abraham's imagined "boast" (4:2) would not be the substitute but the grounds for God's reward; for *Jubilees'* emphasis on Abraham's obedience, tested, and rewarded, see Watson, *Hermeneutics of Faith,* pp. 222-36. Paul rejects "works (of the Law)" as a ground of "boasting" not because they might form a basis for salvation *alternative to* grace, but because they would figure God's grace as *fitting* to the recipient's worth. Because the Christ-gift was unfitting, Paul redefines "grace" as an incongruous gift and thus creates the antithesis of 4:4-5 (see below). But nothing here suggests that other Jews, or Jews in general, thought that "working" was a sufficient route to salvation, without the need for grace.

95. Philo, for instance, figures "faith" as Abraham's reward (ἆθλον) for virtue, in a treatise that emphasizes the match between divine reward and the character or actions of the person rewarded (*Praem.* 27).

the text: there was nothing in Abraham's conduct that made God's crediting of "righteousness" a matter of congruous reward.

Paul underlines this negative point — this absence — in 4:4-8, by a special adaptation of a familiar ancient theme. His strategy is two-fold. First, he takes the term μισθός, derived from Genesis 15:1, in the sense of "pay," rather than reward, and figures God's gift as standing in contrast to pay, as voluntary gift not obligatory remuneration. As we noted above in 1.2, the realm of gift operated in the Greco-Roman world alongside, and partly in contrast to, the realm of pay. Pay was contractual, calculable, and generally impersonal; gift, by contrast, was surrounded by sentiment, not subject to law, and unpredictable in its quantity and timing. Romans 4:4 presumes this common ancient contrast between pay and gift, using μισθός in the sense of "pay":[96] for a worker, pay is not a matter of gift but obligation (τῷ ἐργαζομένῳ ὁ μισθὸς οὐ λογίζεται κατὰ χάριν ἀλλὰ κατὰ ὀφείλημα).[97] However, both pay and gift were characterized in antiquity by correspondence, pay as a recompense for work, gift (generally) as fitting the recipient's worth (see above, 1.1 and 1.2). But Paul takes here a second step, configuring χάρις as an *undeserved* gift. He could have contrasted pay, the recompense of labor characteristic of people at lower social levels, with gift, an ennobling act of friendship, marking the value of the recipient:[98] on these terms, it would have been possible to represent Abraham as not (demeaningly) "paid," but (nobly) "rewarded," his virtues fittingly recognized by divine gift. Instead, Paul "perfects" the notion of gift in what we have come to see as his typical fashion. The term χάρις is perfected as an *incongruous gift*, so that the opposite to pay-for-work is here not gift-to-the-worthy but a startling expression of non-correspondence: "for the one who does not work, but believes in him who justifies the ungodly, his faith is reckoned as righteousness" (4:5). We encounter again the Pauline presumption that to talk of God in relation to gift is to speak of divine action wholly at odds with worth, drastically

96. For the ambiguity of μισθός, whose semantic field covers both "reward" and "pay," see above, 1.2.1, with literature referenced in note 80. Paul uses the term in both senses (reward: 1 Cor 9:17-18; pay: here and 1 Cor 3:8; both: 1 Cor 3:14?). The term designates "pay" when recompense for work is understood as a contractual obligation.

97. As noted in chapter 1, gifts are assumed to evoke obligations or debts, and in this sense a *return*-gift might be construed as a matter of debt/obligation (e.g., Rom 15:26-27). But the emphasis on the voluntary character of gift made it preferable to distinguish gifts from the payment of debts. Thus, Thucydides contrasts a gift that puts others under obligation with a return-gift that feels more like obligation than gift (οὐκ ἐς χάριν, ἀλλ' ἐς ὀφείλημα τὴν ἀρετὴν ἀποδώσων, 2.40.4). Certainly, in the realm of pay, as Paul says, contractual obligations are not a matter of χάρις but of ὀφείλημα; on pay as "owed," see Xenophon, *Hell.* 6.2.16.

98. See above, 1.2.1, on the different social values of gift and pay, and the possibility for polemical representation of gifts as a form of demeaning "pay."

contrary to all conditions of fit: to "justify the ungodly" is the very opposite of "just reward."[99] The best explanation for this perfection of χάρις, and this dramatic contradiction of biblical norms, is the fact that Paul views the gift of God through the prism of the event of Christ, who "at the appropriate time died for the ungodly" (5:6). The absence of worth that Paul finds to be foundational to the Abraham story, and thus to the justification of his multiethnic offspring, is in narrative terms the beginning, but in conceptual terms the reflection, of the startling incongruity that believers have experienced in the gift of Christ.[100]

Abraham's faith thus marks not the fit but the *misfit* between Abraham and the righteousness accredited to him by God. In the first of a series of steps that signify why the Abrahamic family is justified *by faith* (cf. 4:16-18, 19-22), Paul clarifies his citation of Genesis 15:6 by showing that to speak of πίστις or πιστεύειν is to register a state of bankruptcy by every measure of symbolic capital. The citation of David (Ps 32:1-2) hammers home this point (4:6-8): blessing is here pronounced not on those with accredited worth, but on the person to whom God credits righteousness "without works" (4:6).[101] Both Abraham and David thus witness to the foundational characteristic of the narrative of Israel (cf. 3:3-7): God acts in the absence of human worth. As the following verses make clear, the formation of a family of Jewish and Gentile believers is the goal and climax of that story, but such a phenomenon cannot be explained without bringing to light its means of creation.

God's counterintuitive blessing indicates its disregard for worth by its chronological placement in the Abraham story (4:9-12). Here, the spotlight

99. For the biblical (but also universal) definition of the just judge as the one who does *not* declare the guilty righteous, see Exodus 23:7; Proverbs 17:15; Isaiah 5:23.

100. As we have noted, Ezra's plea in *4 Ezra* 8.31-36 contrasts divine "mercy" with "the reward of the righteous in consequence of their deeds" (8.33); see above, section 9.3. Paul is not alone among Jews in imagining that God might act without regard to the worth of works, only in using this notion to define divine "gift," and in identifying here the definitive mark of God's action, under the impress of the Christ-event. To suggest that Paul's contrast "flew in the face of the dominant Jewish theology of the day, which joined faith and works closely together, resulting in a kind of synergism with respect to salvation" (D. Moo, *The Epistle to the Romans* [Grand Rapids: Eerdmans, 1996], p. 263) is to repeat an old representation of Judaism using loaded Augustinian terms.

101. The breadth of the category "works" signals that God's act of justification takes place in the absence of any form of "righteousness": thus to "credit righteousness" (4:6) is equivalent to "not crediting sin" (4:8). Later, Paul will broaden the categories still further (9:6-12, 16) in order to rule out every conceivable form of human capital. That the wholly incongruous divine gift ("without works") forms the foundation and frame for human works that fit God's judgment (2:6-10) is contradictory only if the unconditioned gift is taken to be also unconditional (in the sense of seeking no return). We shall return to this phenomenon in the following chapter.

falls on the token of worth — circumcision — that was of central importance in Paul's mission to the Gentiles, but Paul makes sure to indicate also the application to Jewish believers. Whereas Galatians had relativized the Torah by noting its appearance long after the promise to Abraham (Gal 3:15-18), Paul here relativizes circumcision by a parallel argument: the circumcision of Abraham took place *after* the blessing of Genesis 15:6, which thus was operative without regard to that distinctive mark (4:9-10). To be sure, Abraham was circumcised, but that is now to be understood as a "sign," the "seal" of something more basic, "the righteousness of faith" (4:10-11).[102]

Galatians emphasized the significance of this fact for Gentiles (3:6-9, 29), but here Paul puts equal emphasis on Abraham's fatherhood of Jews ("those from circumcision").[103] As in 2:25-29, the phenomenon of uncircumcised believers is not designed to replace Jews, but it clarifies who really counts before God as a Jew (2:28-29) or as a child of Abraham (4:12). In both cases, it is probably the experience of the Gentile mission that has made Paul rethink his categories, including the most basic categories of Jewish identity; in both cases, Jewish difference is recognized at the same time as Paul points to a fundamental similarity between Gentile and Jew, both here characterized by Abrahamic faith. It seems that, for Paul, even the most basic constituents of Jewish identity take on a new definition in the light of God's action in Christ. In 3:29-30, the basic Jewish confession, that "God is one," acquires a new and richer meaning when the one God is found to justify both Jews and Gentiles in the very same way.[104] Now drilling deep into the Abrahamic story, Paul rethinks the foundational narrative of the Jewish tradition in a form that relativizes the difference between Jews and non-Jews. The rationale for this reading is provided neither by logic nor by exegesis alone: it resides in the Christ-generated discovery that, from the beginning, the Abrahamic blessing was blind to every token of differential worth.

If 4:1-8 has described the characteristic trait of the Abrahamic family as

102. Noting that Genesis 17:11 refers to circumcision as "the sign of the covenant," Wright takes the primary meaning of "righteousness" in Paul to be "covenant membership" ("Romans," p. 494). But one could equally argue the other way around: the primary meaning of "covenant" for Paul was divine promise (Gal 3:15-22; Rom 15:8) and its anthropological correlate, "righteousness from faith."

103. For the construal of the two clauses of 4:12 as referring to the same group (believers who are circumcised but also walk in Abraham's steps of faith), see L. L. Sechrest, *A Former Jew: Paul and the Dialectics of Race* (London: Continuum, 2009), pp. 120-23, adducing multiple parallels.

104. For a classic treatment of Romans 3:29, and its relation to parallel Jewish expressions of belief in the "oneness" of God, see N. A. Dahl, *Studies in Paul* (Minneapolis: Augsburg, 1977), pp. 178-91.

faith despite the absence of worth, and 4:9-12 its intended inclusion of Gentile and Jewish believers, the following section of this chapter, 4:13-18, joins these themes together, interpreting the promise to Abraham and his offspring as the impossible creation of a multiethnic family.[105] Paul offers both negative and positive arguments: this promise cannot come through the Law (4:13-15), but it does come through faith, in accordance with grace (4:16-18). The promise that Abraham and his offspring would inherit the world (4:13) would be impossible "from the Law" (ἐκ νόμου), not because "from the Law" would instantiate an antithetical "principle of achievement" (Paul uses the same phrase in describing some who *are* included among the offspring, 4:16), nor because the Law would confine the offspring to one nation, while the promise was to many.[106] Rather, as Paul explains in 4:15, to channel the promise through the Law would lead to a dead end, not to the eschatological inheritance of the world. The Law leads only via transgression to wrath (4:15; cf. 3:10-20); it cannot provide the glorious future envisaged in the promise. Thus, a trajectory of promise that ran through the Law would bring the promise to a shuddering halt (κατήργηται ἡ ἐπαγγελία, 4:14). It would also "empty" faith (4:14) in its distinctively Abrahamic form (cf. 4:1-8), since it would introduce a criterion of positive worth, whereas Abrahamic faith is the mark of those who have none.

In fact, however, the promise runs through faith, "in accordance with χάρις" (echoing 4:4-5), "to secure the promise for all his seed" (4:16). Why so? Paul now introduces the language of "all" (4:16) and "many" (4:17-18, citing Gen 17:5), as if "faith" and "grace" provide the key to the fertility or universality of the promise-made-secure (4:16). From all we have seen thus far, the reason is not hard to identify. Because God acts in incongruous grace, and thus without regard to worth, there is no possible limit on the membership of this

105. My analysis is thus designed to unite what Hays takes to be competing options: "The crucial issue in the chapter is not how Abraham got himself justified but rather whose father he is and in what way his children are related to him" (*Conversion*, p. 83). In fact, Romans 4 shows that Abraham is father of both Jews and Gentiles only because of the way in which he was justified: by sole dependence on the unconditioned grace and power of God. The internal structure of 4:13-22 is difficult, but I think it best to take 4:13-15 as explaining "not through the Law," and 4:16-18 as expounding "from faith" in relation to "the father of many nations," with 4:19-22 unpacking the narratives that show Abraham's faith in the God of 4:17. Placing a division at the beginning, middle, or end of 4:17 would violate the grammatical flow of Paul's sentence (*pace*, e.g., Cranfield, *Romans*, vol. 1, pp. 224-25; Byrne, *Romans*, p. 153). Moo notes the coherence of 4:13-22 around the theme of promise (*Romans*, p. 272).

106. The first option represents the interpretation of Käsemann, the second of Wright. It was quite possible for Philo and others to imagine many nations attaining salvation precisely by keeping the Law (*Mos.* 2.44), since the Torah itself was by no means exclusively accessible to Jews.

people, no ethnic frontier that would keep some nations out. That Abraham's seed will inherit the world (4:13) is thus a truly multiethnic phenomenon, because no one is either qualified or disqualified by his or her birth. At the same time, this family will be marked by faith because faith is the Abrahamic response to God, who operates from the null point, in the absence of worth. The significance of this trait is now spelled out in traditional phraseology in 4:17: "before the God in whom Abraham believed, who gives life to the dead and calls into existence the things that do not exist."[107]

Paul is acutely conscious of the context of Genesis 15:6, the statement about Abraham's faith: Abraham trusted in the promise of an offspring *at a time when bearing children was impossible* (4:18-21, citing Gen 15:5). The promise to Abraham was secure only because it was given by the God who does the impossible: human worthlessness, nothingness, even death are no obstacle to this promise, which operates precisely in this incongruous form. Abraham's hope against all reasonable expectations (4:18) is a mirror of his faith in the absence of works (4:4-5): Paul traces a deep homology between the incongruity of divine grace and the incongruity of divine power. That God operates in the fashion here described is Paul's justification for his conduct of the Gentile mission, requiring neither circumcision nor submission to the Law. But it also grounds Paul's hope for the future of the world (Rom 8:18-39) and for the salvation of Israel (11:11-32). By tracing God's *creatio ex nihilo* in the story of Abraham, the starting point of election, Paul can place Israel, believers, and the world on a common trajectory, since nothing is impossible for the mercy of God (11:28-36).[108]

Romans 4:19-22 expounds the character of Abraham's faith in "the God who gives life to the dead": since Abraham's age and Sarah's barrenness approximate to "death" (4:19), faith amounts to the declaration of incompetence, or total dependence on the competence of God (4:20-22). This depiction of Abraham and Sarah allows Paul to draw a parallel between the faith of Abraham and the faith of believers in the resurrection of "Jesus our Lord" (4:23-24; cf. 10:9): both entail faith in "resurrection from the dead." But this surface simi-

107. On the traditional Jewish phraseology, see Dunn, *Romans 1–8*, pp. 217-18. Here and in the verses that follow there are close conceptual parallels to the celebration of the "barren woman" and the children birthed from "the Jerusalem above" in Galatians 4:26-27.

108. Stowers's reading of this chapter turns Abraham's πίστις (translated by Stowers as "faithfulness" or "trusting loyalty") into a condition for God's grace, which was given "in response to human faithfulness" (*A Rereading of Romans*, pp. 241-44). This requires key additions to the text ("Abraham's act of faithfulness was, first, simply to trust in the promise and then to have sexual relations with Sarah," p. 230), and misconstrues 4:4-8 and 4:17-22, which emphasize not the congruity but the incongruity between the action of God and human capacity.

larity accompanies a significant difference: in the one case, Abraham believed that God *would create something from his and Sarah's deadness,* while in the other, believers believe that God *has raised Jesus from the dead.* Faith in what God will do for oneself is here paralleled with faith in what God has done for another. Is Paul content with this limited parallel, or does the believers' faith regarding Christ also, like Abraham's, concern "life out of death" *in relation to themselves?* Later chapters will show that the parallel does indeed extend this far: to believe in the resurrection of Jesus is to believe not only in a past event about someone else, but in the present and future basis for "life" regarding oneself (6:1-11; 8:11).[109] In fact, 4:25 already indicates that belief about Christ is self-involving, and in no sense *only* about Christ. The story of "Jesus our Lord" relates his death "because of our trespasses," and his resurrection "for the sake of our justification" (4:25). The fate of believers is entangled in these events.[110] What was written for Abraham was written also "for us" (4:23-24), because believers live by an identical faith that the God who does the impossible and raises the dead has created *their* "newness of life" in and by the resurrection of Jesus (6:1-6).

15.8. Conclusions

The opening chapters of Romans confirm that here, as in Galatians, Paul figures God's gift or favor as incongruous with the worth of its recipients, and consciously develops this perfection of the motif. The righteousness of God is revealed in Christ in the justification of sinners (3:21-26); Christ died not for the good but for the ungodly (5:6-8). Paul parades not the match but the mismatch between the act of God and the value or condition of its human beneficiaries: divine faithfulness is displayed in human faithlessness (3:1-8), life is created out of human death (4:16-22). Such non-correspondence shapes Paul's development of the ancient contrast between pay and gift (4:4-5): the term χάρις is here endowed with the perfected meaning of an *incongruous* gift. As 3:5-8 makes clear, this theology carries risks: it could be heard to undermine

109. See Byrne, *Romans,* p. 155, who locates the parallel, however, in "belief in the future capacity and faithfulness of God" to do for believers' mortal bodies what he did for Christ. But the present "life" of believers is already a miraculous product, derived from the resurrection of Christ (6:1-11).

110. This by no means suggests that Abraham be read as a type of the faithfulness of Christ, as argued by Campbell, *Deliverance of God,* pp. 750-54. Romans 4:23-24 makes clear where the parallel lies, between Abraham and believers, and to insert "by participation in the faithfulness of Christ" is to foist something extraneous onto the text.

the moral order of the cosmos. But it is also an ideology especially suited to innovation and change. If God operates outside the categories of the normal and the fitting, if he "calls into existence the things that do not exist" (4:17), boundaries can be crossed and social experiments dared. As in Galatians, Paul's theology of incongruous grace is at the service of the Gentile mission. It legitimates a social practice in which the traditional distinctions between "Jew" and "Greek" are no longer of definitive significance. This new evaluation of Gentiles is not an "illustration" or "application" of a theology first developed in the form of abstract or generalized doctrines. Paul's missionary theology is fundamentally *about* the place of Gentiles in the Abrahamic family, who are more than "examples" of a theological principle. But this mission has a distinctive rationale, which is deeper than a social commitment to inclusive equality. Paul's Gentile mission reflects his reading of the Christ-event as God's fulfillment of the Abrahamic promises in the mode of incongruous grace.

There is no reason to think that Paul hereby sets himself in principled opposition to Second Temple Judaism. Although he criticizes a Jewish pride in the Law that is not matched by practice (2:17-29) and is no doubt aware of alternative construals of the Abraham story (4:1-2), he does not here present the Jewish tradition, or his fellow Jews, as wedded to a soteriology of "works" in contradistinction to "grace." One can well imagine why many Jews (and not just Jews) would have found Paul's perfection of divine incongruous gift theologically dangerous; Paul knows himself that this is so (3:8; 6:1). But there is nothing inherently "un-Jewish" about Paul's theology on this matter: as we saw in Part II, he is part of a contemporary Jewish *debate* about the operation of divine mercy and gift. Within this debate, what is distinctive about Paul is not that he believed in the possibility of God's incongruous grace, but that (a) he identified this phenomenon with a very specific event (the love of God *in Christ*), that (b) he developed this perfection for the sake of his Gentile mission (founding Jew-Gentile unity on novel terms), and that (c) he thereby rethought Jewish identity itself, tracing from Abraham onwards a narrative trajectory of the power of God that creates *ex nihilo* and acts in gift or mercy without regard to worth.

Far more than in Galatians, Romans figures the mismatch between divine act and human worth as integral to the scriptural story and to the core identity of "the Jew." It is here much clearer that the Abrahamic story is, from the start, a story of the non-correspondence between human worth and divine gift, between human capacity and divine power — and that this story is continued into the present, both in the addition of Gentiles and in the reconstitution of Jews. Romans 3:1-8 gives hints that this non-correspondence is integral to the experience of Israel — hints that await development in Romans 9–11 — and

4:1-22 takes care to name among Abraham's children both Gentile *and Jewish* believers. When the narrative of the Abrahamic family is told in this incongruous shape, it emerges that all people, Jew and Gentile, derive their identity, in faith, from the God who gives life to the dead and has now raised Jesus as the source of new life. Here the Jesus-event seems to parallel, to manifest, but also even to shape the pattern of the Abrahamic story; how this is so is a matter to which we will return in our study of Romans 9–11 (see chapter 17, below).[111]

Finally, in attending to Paul's depictions of judgment (Romans 2), we have noted that on the eschatological horizon of the gift of Christ there is the fitting outcome of a life of "good work." This scenario, we have argued, is neither hypothetical nor un-Pauline, because the incongruous and unconditioned gift in Christ is not also unconditional, in the sense of expecting no alteration in the recipients of the gift. God's grace is designed to produce obedience, lives that perform, by heart-inscription, the intent of the Law. God's righteousness is displayed in the midst of human unrighteousness, not because God is morally indifferent (that would undermine his capacity to judge the world, 3:6), but because he intends to *transform* the human condition. As apostle to the Gentiles, Paul is perpetually conscious of the incongruity of grace as gift to the ungodly and disobedient; but his goal is not their continuing disobedience, but "the obedience of faith" (1:5). Deriving from *faith,* this obedience is the product of a life created through God's incongruous gift; as *obedience,* it is committed to patterns of behavior that befit its new allegiance. That the life of a believer thus remains an incongruous gift *at the same time* as it conforms to the holiness of God is a paradox we shall carry into the study of Romans 5–8.

111. Cf. H. Boers's discussion of Romans 4 in *Theology out of the Ghetto* (Leiden: Brill, 1971), pp. 74-104. We shall have reason to disagree with his assessment that Paul, in exploring a structural parallel between the faith of Abraham and faith in Christ, transcended (or "pierced") his own Christological system of thought. But how the story of Abraham, and of Israel up to Paul's day, is conceived by Paul as both chronologically prior to Christ and historically shaped by a Christological meaning is a question to which we will return at the end of chapter 17.

CHAPTER 16

New Life in Dying Bodies: Grace and the Construction of a Christian *Habitus* (Romans 5:12–8:39; 12:1–15:13)

In the early chapters of Romans we have traced a double and initially puzzling phenomenon. On the one hand, Paul has emphasized in multiple ways the incongruity of the divine gift in Christ, which operates neither by the reward of the righteous, nor by the selection of the worthy: Christ died for the utterly unworthy (5:6-8), so that the ungodly are justified (3:22-23; 4:4-5). Tracing this creative incongruity to the beginnings of the Abrahamic family (4:13-22), Paul has redefined χάρις to mean not simply gift instead of pay, but an incongruous gift that bears no relation to the moral or social worth of its beneficiaries (4:1-11). On the other hand, at the eschatological horizon, Paul envisages the just distribution of "wrath" or "eternal life" according to works (2:1-16). On this horizon, he portrays Gentiles who fulfill the essence of the Law written on their hearts (2:14-15, 26-27), and in the process redefines the Jew as one heart-circumcised by the Spirit, able not just to teach but to practice the Law (2:17-29). In his eschatological scenario, Paul describes *congruity* rather than *incongruity:* he foresees a final judgment in which the righteous are rewarded and the unrighteous are condemned.

An attentive reading of Galatians might have prepared us for this apparent paradox. There, both Paul and the Galatians are recipients of divine grace without regard to their worth (Gal 1:6, 15-16); as we have seen, the theology of the entire letter is premised on the incongruity of the divine gift. Yet Paul is clear that those who do the works of the flesh will not inherit the kingdom of God (Gal 5:21), and only those who sow to the Spirit will reap eternal life (Gal 6:7-8). What begins as an *unfitting* gift founds the *fit* between the lives of believers and the final outcome of salvation. Does this mean that grace is operative as incongruous gift only at the *start* of the believer's life? Does it disappear thereafter or turn into something else?

In Romans 5–8, Paul parades both the incongruity of grace in a world dominated by sin and death (5:12-21) and its powerful effect in forming heart-obedience and holiness, whose fruit is eternal life (6:15-23). The length at which Paul here describes this double-sided phenomenon, and the event of baptism that stands at its core (6:1-14), enables us to see how the incongruous grace of life in Christ in an important sense *remains incongruous* with the condition of believers even while they "bear fruit for God" (7:4) and please God through the Spirit (8:1-13). In exploring this phenomenon, we will discover the importance of the body as the site of believers' obedience, and the significance of practice as the expression of the gift of life. Since the "presentation" of the body links chapter 6 (6:12-14, 19) with the opening of chapter 12 (12:1-2), we will follow the thread of Paul's thought from the chapters that outline the new disposition of believers (6:1–8:13) into those that spell out what this means in practice, in communal life (12:1–15:6). Here we will find that, as in Galatians, the life of the community is shaped by its foundational experience of the grace (or "mercy," 12:1) of God. Tracing the outlines of this new social practice, we will see how the reconfiguration of worth established by God's "welcome" in Christ fosters a communal life of reciprocal enhancement despite, indeed within, significant differences in cultural heritage and practice.

16.1. Under the Reign of Grace (Romans 5–6)

Placing the Christ-event into comparison and contrast with the effects of Adam's sin (5:12-21) enables Paul to highlight the extraordinary incongruity of a gift that neither matches the worth of its recipients, nor simply passes over their unworthiness: it positively reverses their condition.[1] After establishing

1. While the paragraph 5:12-21 clearly expands some themes from 5:1-11, it also places the Christ-event on a cosmic map whose implications are unraveled in the subsequent chapters. The close verbal links between 5:1-11 and 8:18-39 were noted by Dahl, but could lead to more than one structural analysis: that 5:1-11 is the start of a new section whose themes are echoed by *inclusio* in chapter 8, or that 5:1-11 forms an initial conclusion to the earlier chapters, echoed in expanded form in a second conclusion in 8:18-39. See N. Dahl, *Studies on Paul* (Minneapolis: Fortress Press, 1977), pp. 88-91, following his earlier article, "Two Notes on Romans 5," *ST* 5 (1951): 37-48. Since on any reading 5:12-21 constitutes a *bridge* between material before and after, it is probably futile to expend energy arguing whether it belongs more one way or the other; see T. Engberg-Pedersen, "Galatians in Romans 5–8 and Paul's Construction of the Identity of Christian Believers," in T. Fornberg and D. Hellholm, eds., *Texts and Contexts: Essays in Honor of Lars Hartman* (Oslo: Scandinavian University Press, 1995), pp. 477-505 (at 479-82). As Dahl notes, "the problem of whether a main line of division should be drawn between chapters 4 and 5 or between 5 and 6 or, possibly, between 5:11 and 5:12 becomes acute only if we ask for some systematic outline and fail to follow Paul's vivid argumentation" (*Studies*, p. 91).

the Adam-Christ comparison (5:12-14), Paul characterizes the Christ-event with a variety of gift terms. What is initially described as τὸ χάρισμα (5:15) is spelled out as ἡ χάρις τοῦ θεοῦ καὶ ἡ δωρεὰ ἐν χάριτι τῇ τοῦ ἑνὸς ἀνθρώπου Ἰησοῦ Χριστοῦ (5:15). Immediately thereafter, the same event is described as τὸ δώρημα and (again) as τὸ χάρισμα (5:16), whose effect is the human receipt of the abundance of χάρις and δωρεά (οἱ τὴν περισσείαν τῆς χάριτος καὶ τῆς δωρεᾶς τῆς δικαιοσύνης λαμβάνοντες, 5:17). Where sin abounded, χάρις abounded still more (5:20) such that, in summary, the reign of sin is overpowered by the reign of χάρις (5:21). We find here an extraordinary concentration of gift-terminology, whose variation seems to be more rhetorical than substantial (the -μα endings creating neat verbal antitheses); within 5:15-21 words from the χαρ- and δωρ- roots occur no fewer than ten times, eight within verses 15-17 alone. Moreover, in almost every case (verse 17 is the exception), this "gift" is the subject of verbs, or otherwise forms the main theme of the sentence. Divine gift is the focus of this paragraph like nowhere else in Paul's letters.

The grace Paul speaks about here is not a general characteristic of God, but is tied to a specific event. The aorist tenses of 5:15, 20 (χάρις "abounded" or "hyper-abounded") indicate Paul's focus on a specific historical moment, and it is clear from the double expression of 5:15 ("the grace of God and the gift in the grace of the one man Jesus Christ") that the event of Jesus is that moment (cf. "through Jesus Christ" in 5:17, 21). The language of "abundance" is very prominent here, in the verb περισσεύω (5:15), the noun περισσεία (5:17), and the striking, rare verb ὑπερπερισσεύω (5:20; cf. 2 Cor 7:4). We are reminded of the language of abundance in Philo's descriptions of the overflowing bounties of creation,[2] but the rhetorical context in Romans 5 gives this perfection of grace a different function. Whereas Philo celebrates the hyper-generosity of the divine Giver who showers good things on all his creatures (cf. 2 Cor 9:8-10), Paul's focus in Romans 5 is on the overcoming of a negative condition by the more-than-matching surplus of its opposite: "where sin increased, grace hyper-abounded" (5:20). In other words, the perfection of abundance is here at the service of another perfection, the one we have already noted as the Pauline hallmark: God's grace through Christ is marked as extravagant precisely in its *incongruity* with the human condition.

The mismatch between the divine grace and the Adamic condition of sin and death is strongly underlined by the contrasts that dominate the comparisons in 5:15-17. Despite some good arguments to the contrary, the opening sentences of 5:15 and 5:16 are probably best taken as statements (not questions), awkwardly phrased to bring out the contrast between the sin and the gift:

2. See above, 6.2.

"but *not* like the sin, such is the gift" (5:15).[3] Paul seems to presuppose that a comparison can be drawn between the event of Adam and the event of Christ (5:14; cf. 1 Cor 15:21-22), but before he draws out the similarities (5:18-21), he puts emphasis on the mismatch between them. If sin has led to the death of "many," "how much more" has the grace of God in Christ abounded for many — the second not just an equal but a far greater force, since it is not merely the action of "one man," but the action of *God* in "one man" (5:15; cf. the same phrase in 5:17).[4] But the difference is not just that between the lesser and the greater; it is also, and more strikingly, a matter of *reversal.* If judgment from one man's sin led to condemnation, the gift, out of many sins, leads to . . . justification (5:16). The gift does not start from a point of equilibrium, nor does it return matters to the status quo: it takes place in the context of multiplied sin to enable the very opposite of what is deserved. The relentless momentum of sin, with its inexorable consequence of condemnation and death, is here not just stopped in its tracks, but reversed by the establishment of a counter-momentum leading out of sin into life (5:17). This re-creative dynamic is again the hallmark of χάρις (cf. 4:17), creating life out of its opposite, death (5:21).[5]

It is because of this counterintuitive incongruity that the question of 6:1 can arise: if grace abounds in the context of *sin,* should we maximize this incongruity by remaining in sin? It is impossible to imagine that question arising in contexts where the divine gift is (reasonably) figured as the fitting reward of the worthy. It is only because Paul perfects the misalliance between χάρις and the condition of its recipients that his theology appears to threaten the order of the cosmos (cf. 3:7-8). If grace (on Paul's definition) is not reward, and sin, under such conditions, is not destined for punishment, the question raised in 6:1 is by no means "risible" (Jewett); a gift that is given without regard to the worth of its recipients certainly threatens to undercut the moral order. To press

3. For the construal of these sentences as questions ("Is it not the case that just as the sin, so also the gift?"), which shifts emphasis to the *similarity* between Adam and Christ, see C. Caragounis, "Romans 5.15-16 in the Context of 5.12-21: Contrast or Comparison?" *NTS* 31 (1985): 142-48, supported by (among others) R. Jewett, *Romans* (Minneapolis: Fortress Press, 2007), pp. 379-82. Although this reading does solve some exegetical and grammatical problems, it is not clear how the readers could be expected to recognize a positive answer to this question as obvious, and it is odd that the implied assertion of similarity in 5:16a should be followed and explained immediately by a statement that emphasizes only dissimilarity (5:16b).

4. The "how much more" presumes a point of similarity (as in 1 Cor 15:21-22), but indicates the outweighing of the first by the second, which represents the redemptive power of God (see E. Käsemann, *An die Römer* [Tübingen: Mohr Siebeck, 1980], pp. 145-47).

5. Cf. N. T. Wright, "The Letter to the Romans," in *The New Interpreter's Bible,* vol. 10 (Nashville: Abingdon Press, 2002), pp. 395-770, at p. 528: "the gift of grace is nothing short of new creation, creation not merely out of nothing but out of anti-creation, out of death itself."

this incongruity, and to celebrate the growth of the gift in the expansion of sin (5:20), looks like a recipe for moral chaos.

Already in 5:12-21 there are indications that the Christ-gift is *not* morally vacuous, an unconditional gift that winks at human sin: it contains transformative power. The recipients of this grace are said to receive the gift of righteousness (5:17) and to be constituted righteous (5:19): where sin once reigned, now grace reigns "through righteousness" to bring about eternal life (5:21). The language of "reigning" (βασιλεύω) figures grace as a counteracting power whose authority replaces that of sin; far from offering a license for sin, the Christ-gift establishes an alternative regime of power.[6] As we shall see, Paul locates the content of that power in the resurrection life of Christ (6:1-14), but he also draws on the ancient assumption that gifts are vehicles of power, creating obligations and allegiances through their very character as gift (see above, chapter 1). The "reign" of χάρις in 5:21 already hints in this direction, but this phenomenon becomes explicit in chapter 6, where those miraculously reconstituted through the resurrection of Jesus operate in a "newness of life" (6:4), which has a new structure of allegiance. They are not to let sin reign in their mortal bodies, to obey its desires (6:12). From the echo of 5:21, we know why not: there is an alternative power structure now at work in their lives, the power of χάρις. That implication is confirmed by 6:14, where, using variant language for the same phenomenon, Paul says that "sin will not lord it over you (ὑμῶν οὐ κυριεύσει), because you are not under the Law but under grace" (ὑπὸ χάριν). Once again, grace is described as a power, this time more explicitly as a "power over." Accordingly, the subsequent verses (6:15-23) are replete with the language of "slavery" and "obedience": everyone is subject to one power or another, sin or righteousness, and Paul pointedly thanks God that they have been freed from one in order to be enslaved to the other (6:18, 22). There is no neutral zone in Paul's cosmos, no pocket of absolute freedom, no no-man's land between the two fronts. The gift of God in Jesus Christ has established not liberation from authority, but a new allegiance, a new responsibility, a new "slavery" under the rule of grace.

Although the phrase ὑπὸ χάριν may have been coined by Paul (to match his regular expression, ὑπὸ νόμον), the idea that gift establishes a relation of obligation is very common in ancient sources. When the historian Manetho noted that the king of Ethiopia was beholden to Amenophis, king of Egypt, out of gratitude (χάριτι ἦν αὐτῷ ὑποχείριος, *apud* Josephus, *C. Ap.* 1.246), he

6. For the language of power in this passage, see M. C. de Boer, *The Defeat of Death: Apocalyptic Eschatology in 1 Corinthians 15 and Romans 5* (Sheffield: Sheffield Academic Press, 1988), pp. 157-69.

expressed the common assumption that gifts or favors create obligations and expect a return. As we have seen (chapter 1), the presumption of reciprocity was ubiquitous in antiquity, in both pagan and Jewish worlds. In the continuous cycle of gift, the recipient is obliged to make a return, in one form or another: if not in a counter-gift, at least in honor or gratitude. This expectation might make potential recipients reluctant to accept a gift, especially if it was large and difficult to return or from a person to whom one would not wish to be beholden (see Seneca, *Ben.* 2.18-21). But the notion of a gift "with no strings attached" was practically unimaginable in antiquity; it is a product of the modern era (see above, 1.3.3). None of Paul's hearers would have been surprised to learn that as recipients of the divine gift they were placed under obligation to God.[7]

That Paul develops the motif of gift-obligation under the figure of slavery (6:16-23) is somewhat striking, and is perhaps a result of the way he has figured the Adamic condition as slavery to sin (6:6; cf. Gal 3:22; 4:1-7). When in 6:19 he steps aside to comment that he speaks "in a human fashion, because of the weakness of your flesh" (ἀνθρώπινον λέγω διὰ τὴν ἀσθένειαν τῆς σαρκὸς ὑμῶν), some commentators take this as a kind of apology not only for the metaphor of slavery but even for the sense of obligation here implied. On this reading, Paul really expects believers to act for God willingly, "from the heart" (6:17), without external pressure or demand; but he speaks in this "human fashion" to make a point in an unfortunately exaggerated fashion (cf. 8:15).[8] But, as we noted in chapter 1, the sphere of the gift is apt to mix obligation with voluntariness: the gift and its return must certainly be willing and not coerced, but they can also arise, at the same time, from a strong sense of obligation. The metaphor of slavery is repeated with such force in this passage, both before

7. Paul naturally figures his Gentile converts as under obligation (ὀφειλέται εἰσίν) to the Jerusalem church for the spiritual goods they have shared (Rom 15:27; cf. 1:14 of his own obligation to preach). It is probably because he did not want to be seen as the donor of the gospel (putting its recipients under obligation *to him,* rather than *to God*) that he refused to take fees while founding a church; see D. E. Briones, *Paul's Financial Policy: A Socio-Theological Approach* (London: T&T Clark, 2013).

8. See, e.g., T. Engberg-Pedersen, *Paul and the Stoics* (Edinburgh: T&T Clark, 2000), pp. 235-37: they should want to do God's will of themselves (like Stoics), not because they have to. Jewett, *Romans,* pp. 419-20, takes the slavery motif as an insult to Paul's readers, although Paul unfortunately continues in this vein even after this apology. Contrast C. E. B. Cranfield, *The Epistle to the Romans,* 2 vols. (Edinburgh: T&T Clark, 1975, 1979), vol. 1, pp. 325-26, who takes the phrase as an apology only for the figure of slavery, not for the sense of "total obligation, total commitment" that characterizes the life under grace; cf. U. Wilckens, *Der Brief an die Römer,* 3 vols. (Zürich: Benziger; Neukirchen-Vluyn: Neukirchener, 1978-82), vol. 2, pp. 37-38: slavery is not a perfect image, but not a wholly inappropriate one.

and after 6:19, and is used unapologetically elsewhere in Romans both for Paul's (1:1) and for the Roman believers' relationship to God (12:11; 14:4), that it would be hard to conclude that Paul thought the metaphor fundamentally inappropriate (though see 8:15 for qualifications). He may be excusing the presentation of gift-obligation in such extreme terms, or the rather odd expression "slavery to righteousness" (6:18; cf. 6:22: enslaved to God); or he may be not excusing himself at all, but explaining why he insists on this figure, lest they be tempted by pride (in "fleshly weakness") to think themselves above any kind of enslavement (cf. 12:3).[9] In any case, the sense of submission and obligation runs strongly through 6:11-23, and Paul has no difficulty in describing the "newness of life" as a life lived under the rule of grace.

Ernst Käsemann has been the Pauline scholar most insistent on this *Gnadenherrschaft,* linking "grace" very closely to the Lordship of Christ.[10] In Käsemann's view, a one-sided emphasis on "gift" (which he detected in Bultmann) fails to appreciate the sense of power and competing power structures that dominates Paul's theology: what grace conveys is not just gift but also the power of the Giver:

> The gift which is being bestowed here [in salvation] is never at any time separable from its Giver. It partakes of the character of power, in so far as God himself enters the arena and remains in the arena with it. Thus personal address *(Anspruch),* obligation *(Verpflichtung)* and service *(Dienst)* are indissolubly bound up with the gift. When God enters the arena, our experience is that he maintains his lordship even in his giving; indeed it is his gifts which are the very means by which he subordinates us to his lordship and makes us responsible beings.[11]

What we have found from the anthropology of gift (see above, 1.1) clarifies and corroborates this configuration of gift. Gifts, as we have seen, convey the power and even the presence of the giver; some are "inalienable" in the sense that they continue to belong to the giver even when given. Obligation thus arises not just from the authority of the giver (in Paul's case, the Lordship of Christ) but from the structure of gift-giving itself. Gifts convey power *as gifts;* attention to

9. Käsemann, *An die Römer,* pp. 174-5, insisting that δουλεία is the "Stichwort" of this paragraph.

10. For the term, see *An die Römer,* p. 175; for the theme, see especially his essay "Gottesgerechtigkeit bei Paulus," *ZThK* 58 (1961): 367-78, translated with additional footnotes in "The Righteousness of God in Paul," *New Testament Questions of Today* (London: SCM Press, 1969), pp. 168-82. For a summary of Käsemann's theology of grace, see above, 3.5.3.

11. "Gottesgerechtigkeit," p. 371; "The Righteousness of God," p. 174.

the ancient dynamics of gift would indicate that "cheap grace" (gifts expecting nothing in return) was not an option in ancient thought.

Paul thus combines two features that appear paradoxical only to us. On the one hand, he perfects the incongruity of the gift, its donation to those unfitting to be its recipients; on the other, he presumes its strongly obliging character, reorienting the allegiances of those to whom it is given. Here it is crucial to remind ourselves that a perfection of gift in one dimension does not entail the perfection of every other: Paul perfects the incongruity of the gift (given to the unworthy) but he does *not* perfect its non-circularity (expecting nothing in return). The divine gift in Christ was *unconditioned* (based on no prior conditions) but it is not *unconditional* (carrying no subsequent demands). Paul can contrast the χάρισμα of God with the ὀψώνια of sin (6:23): unlike "wages" (or soldiers' rations), the Christ-gift does not correspond to the worth of the recipient. At the same time, he can insist that the gift (of eternal life) is the τέλος of a life lived in righteousness and holiness (6:22). Paul does not figure this holiness as a gift given back to God, eliciting a further, second, gift from God at the last judgment. Nor does he figure the incongruous gift as merely the starting point of the believer's life, which is superseded by a new relationship with God, characterized by something other than gift. The incongruous gift that is strongly obliging, and that bears as its "fruit" obedience to God, remains, in fact, *incongruous.* How so? Because the very life that offers this obedience is a miraculous and incongruous phenomenon, the resurrection life of Christ, which is not just the beginning but the continuing reality of the Christian life. To understand this notion, we must study Paul's depiction of baptism and the "newness of life" created therein (6:1-10).

16.2. Newness of Life: An "Eccentric" Existence in Christ

Paul's distinctive anthropology maps the life of the believer onto the death and resurrection of Jesus. Reconciled by his death, the believer is confident of being saved "in/by his life" (ἐν τῇ ζωῇ αὐτοῦ, 5:10). Where sin has led to death, grace effects a new reality, the reigning of believers "in life" through Jesus Christ (5:17; cf. 5:18: δικαίωσις ζωῆς). This incorporation is enacted in baptism, which constitutes simultaneously death and life — the death of the "old humanity" (6:6) and a "newness of life" (6:4). In both cases, Paul imagines not just an imitation of Christ, but a form of participation, such that the believers' new life is no ordinary existence, but the product of an impossibility, the resurrection of Christ. Because Paul associates the word "resurrection" (ἀνάστασις) with the reconstitution of *bodies* (cf. 8:23) and because this new life is present within still mortal bodies (6:12), conformity to "resurrection" in the fullest sense is left in the future tense (6:5; contrast Eph 2:5-6). But this does not lessen the sense in which everything that may be said about the believers' new mode of existence — their new allegiances, dispositions, emotions, and actions — is attributable to the miraculous life of Christ himself. Believers are to consider themselves "dead to sin and alive to God," in both respects like Christ (6:10) and in Christ (6:11). They present themselves "as those alive from the dead" (6:13) because they draw upon a reality extrinsic to themselves, true of them because it is true first of all of Christ. If "the Spirit of the One who raised Jesus from the dead" already inhabits them (8:11), not only *will* he raise their mortal bodies, but he *already* constitutes their new and humanly impossible mode of existence (8:10-11).

It is crucial to Paul's theology that this new life is not in the first place an *anthropological* phenomenon: it is experienced by human beings only inasmuch as they share in, and draw from, a life whose source lies outside of themselves, the life of the risen Christ. Paul repeatedly draws attention to the resurrection of Jesus throughout Romans 6–8 (6:4, 5, 8, 9; 7:4; 8:11) because this "newness of life" (6:4; cf. 7:6) is not some reformation of the self, or some newly discovered technique in self-mastery; it is an "eccentric" phenomenon, drawing on the "life from the dead" that was inaugurated by Jesus' resurrection.[12] Believers "live to God" (6:11) as walking miracles, all the more evidently miraculous because this new creation life begins, in their case, not on the other side, but on this side of death. It is not for nothing that Paul emphasizes several times in these chapters the mortality of the body: "let sin not reign in your mortal bodies" (ἐν τῷ θνητῷ ὑμῶν σώματι, 6:12); the Spirit will finally vivify "your mortal bodies" (τὰ θνητὰ σώματα, 8:11); the present body is "a corpse on account of sin" (νεκρὸν διὰ ἁμαρτίαν, 8:10); it is in fact a "body of death" (τὸ σῶμα τοῦ θανάτου, 7:24). Whereas Christ has finished with death (6:9), believers have not: they are dead to sin (6:11), but not to death. This puts their lives in a state of permanent incongruity: in one respect they are bound to death ("on account of sin," that is, as a residue of their Adamic heritage, 8:10); in another they are alive, in an eternal "life from the dead" that in its source and character is the life of Christ.

As we saw above (3.3), Luther attempted in several ways to express the permanent, and structurally basic, incongruity of grace in the life of a believer, most famously in the phrase *simul justus et peccator.*[13] The strongest

12. On the notion of "eccentric existence," see D. H. Kelsey, *Eccentric Existence: A Theological Anthropology,* 2 vols. (Louisville: Westminster John Knox Press, 2009). In the light of Romans 8, one may equally describe this as a form of "pneumatic" existence.

13. E.g., in the 1535 Galatians lectures, *WA* 40.1 366.26; *LW* 26.232; in discussing Romans, at *LW* 25.63.

exegetical base for that notion comes from Romans 6–8, but it draws on what now seems to most a faulty reading of Romans 7–8 as a dialectical depiction of two dimensions of the Christian life.[14] If, to the contrary, 7:7-25 describes life "in the flesh" before becoming a believer (cf. 7:5), not a continuing aspect of the believer's life, Luther's *simul . . . peccator* looks less convincing. Yet Romans 6–8 does express the permanent paradox of grace in the life of the believer, only in a different form. The believer is here described as both mortal and eternally alive, *simul mortuus et vivens*. On the one hand doomed to death, in a body that is bound by mortality, believers are also and at the same time the site of an impossible new life, whose origin lies in the resurrection of Jesus and whose goal is their own future resurrection (8:11). "If Christ is in you" (the self newly centered "from outside"), "the body is defunct because of sin, but the Spirit is life, because of righteousness" (τὸ μὲν σῶμα νεκρὸν διὰ ἁμαρτίαν, τὸ δὲ πνεῦμα ζωὴ διὰ δικαιοσύνην, 8:10).[15] The believer is thus at the same time dead and alive, and this life is operative only from Christ and through the Spirit, which is another way of saying that this "newness of life" is established, sustained, and governed not by believers themselves, but

14. The later Augustinian view, shared by the Reformers, that Romans 7:7-25 expresses in certain respects the continuing experience of the believer, is carried forward in the Romans commentaries of Cranfield and Dunn. This derives some weight from Christian experience, but the antithesis of 7:5-6 (whose terminology corresponds to the contrast between 7:7-25 and 8:1ff.) and the language of enslaved captivity under sin (7:14) identify 7:7-25 as a description (from a believer-viewpoint) of life "when we were in the flesh" (7:5). This post-Kümmel near-consensus among scholars is ably discussed and developed in S. J. Chester, *Conversion at Corinth* (Edinburgh: T&T Clark, 2003), pp. 183-95.

15. I take the first clause as concessive (the deadness of the body is the case in spite of being in Christ, not because of it); see, e.g., D. Moo, *The Epistle to the Romans* (Grand Rapids: Eerdmans, 1996), pp. 491-92. I also take ἁμαρτία here to be not the believers' own present sin (*pace* Cranfield, *Romans*, vol. 1, p. 389), but the sin of Adam and of their past, in a cosmos infected by sin and thereby doomed to death (5:11-21; 7:5, 7-11). That this cannot mean their sinfulness as believers is indicated by the fact that they are now "dead to sin" (6:11) and "freed from sin" (6:19) in being enslaved to God. Others find reference to the believers' death to sin in baptism (6:11: the expression is tellingly different) or to the condemnation of sin at the cross (8:3); see Wilckens, *Brief*, vol. 2, p. 132. In the second phrase, commentators now agree that πνεῦμα refers to the Spirit of God (cf. 8:11; 1 Cor 15:45), but the meaning of δικαιοσύνη ("justification"; "righteousness") and its relation to "life" is much disputed. Protestant anxieties lest righteousness be taken as a condition of eternal life lead many to interpret the phrase as "life because of justification" (or "imputed righteousness"), or (with a different meaning of διά) "life for the sake of righteousness"; for the former, see Cranfield, *Romans*, vol. 1, p. 390; Moo, *Romans*, p. 492; for the latter, Käsemann, *An die Römer*, p. 216; Wilckens, *Brief*, vol. 2, p. 133. But if righteousness is itself the product of the miraculous new life, there is no difficulty in seeing it also as the means to the continuation and perfection of that life in the Spirit (cf. 5:21; 6:22-23; Gal 6:8); cf. B. Byrne, *Romans* (Collegeville: Liturgical Press, 1996), p. 245.

by God.[16] This paradox is the sign that God's grace is permanently at odds with the natural (post-Adamic) condition of the human being, however much believers may (and should) grow in holiness.[17]

This permanent *incongruity* of new life in dying bodies is expressed in the *congruity* or fit between the new human obedience and the purpose or will of God. The contrast between the normal human condition and the new existence in Christ is dramatized in Romans 7–8 by the contrast between life "in the flesh" and life "in the Spirit," the one unable to keep the Law despite the best intentions (7:7-25), the other enabled to "fulfill the just requirement of the Law" (8:1-4). As we know from Romans 2, it is not knowing but doing the Law that counts before God; as in Romans 2 (2:14-15, 28-29), this capacity depends on a transformation of the self or, better, a *new* self, derived from the risen Christ. The more this new self is pleasing to God, the more it is visibly out of kilter with the default human condition (8:1-11): the incongruity of grace, wholly contradictory to Adamic existence, has rendered human lives in tune with the Spirit of God. When Paul turns from description to exhortation (6:11-13; 8:12-13), what he expects from believers is not that they create a new existence, but that they express what has already been created by and in Christ. Whatever may be said in the indicative is true of them only because it is true already of Christ; that primary reality can be neither created nor revoked. The secondary reality, their derivation from Christ, exists in a form that is contrary to its surrounding habitat: life in the midst of death. And such a life only subsists to the extent that it is active. To "present yourselves as alive from the dead" (6:13) and to "put to death the deeds of the body" (8:13) are the positive and negative poles of a demand to practice or exercise the new life that has been given. That new life cannot be said to be active *within* believers unless it is demonstrably acted out *by* them.

16. See de Boer, *Defeat of Death*, pp. 175-76: "The significance of this dialectical interplay between the reality of the old age and the reality of the new age is that justification/righteousness/life is present now *only and always as a gift of God's own rectifying, life-giving power,* i.e. of His grace (5:21)" (italics original).

17. Byrne, following Lyonnet, emphasizes the gratuitousness of salvation while also underlining the significance of moral righteousness in Romans 6–8 by insisting that "the moral life of the Christian is entirely the product of the indwelling Spirit" (B. Byrne, "Living Out the Righteousness of God: The Contribution of Rom 6.1–6.13 to an Understanding of Paul's Ethical Presuppositions," *CBQ* 43 [1981]: 557-81, at p. 577 n. 59). My argument here is slightly different. Paul's theology of grace is coherent with emphasis on the necessity of human obedience not so much via the *efficacy* of grace (with God as the acting agent in believers' action) as via its *incongruity* (with human righteousness as the product of a divinely created life that is wholly at odds with the normal human condition). In the latter reading, one does not have to play down human agency (to make way for the divine agent), since the new agent who acts is itself newly created and derived from an external reality.

16.3. The Body and the Construction of a Christian *Habitus*

We should note the importance of the body as the site of this paradoxical co-existence of mortality and life. After insisting that the σῶμα τῆς ἁμαρτίας ("body of sin") is rendered inoperative (καταργεῖσθαι) in baptism (6:6), Paul urges the Roman believers to consider themselves "dead to sin and alive to God in Christ Jesus" (6:11) and explicates what this "considering" (λογίζεσθαι) looks like in the following imperatives (6:12-13). These verses are made up of four clauses, two negative (A) and two positive (B):

> A[1] So, do not let sin rule *in your mortal body* to make you obey its desires,
> A[2] nor present *your organs* as weapons of unrighteousness to sin,
> B[1] but present yourselves to God, as people alive from the dead,
> B[2] and *your organs* as weapons of righteousness to God.

It is striking that in three of these four clauses what is ruled or presented is *the body* or *the organs* (τὸ σῶμα or τὰ μέλη, the second a particularization of the first). That the first positive command (B[1]) concerns "yourselves" (ἑαυτούς) should not be read in an idealist or dualist fashion, as if "the self" is something anterior to, or separable from, the body. To the contrary, the fact that "yourselves" is embedded here in statements about the body suggests that the self can be "ruled" or "presented" only as the body is "ruled" or "presented." It accords with this that Paul puts stress on the "organs" as slaves of either uncleanness or righteousness again in 6:19, and identifies the power of sin (which goes so far as to co-opt the Law) as operative in the "organs" no less than three times in chapter 7 (7:5, 23, 25). The body, unambiguously identified in its physicality by this term "organs" (μέλη), is thus the site where "the self" is identified and defined.[18]

Bultmann's famous discussion of σῶμα as an anthropological term rightly noted how "the body" in Paul can be synonymous with the person ("man does not have a *soma;* he is *soma*"). He then wrongly took this to mean that in most places, including Romans 6:12-13, we can empty the term of any overtones of materiality or physicality, since σῶμα means "the self," as the object of human

18. The traditional translation of μέλη as "limbs" is too restrictive: Paul imagines under this category ears, eyes, and sexual organs, as well as feet and hands (1 Cor 12:12-26). There is a danger that the term becomes detached from its corporeality if taken to mean something as vague as "natural capacities" (e.g., Cranfield, *Romans,* vol. 1, pp. 317-18). For proper emphasis on its physicality, see R. Jewett, *Romans,* pp. 410-11, following his earlier book, *Paul's Anthropological Terms: A Study of Their Use in Conflict Situations* (Leiden: Brill, 1971).

action or reflection.[19] Käsemann rightly objected that this made nonsense of most of Paul's uses of the term σῶμα, and that *Leiblichkeit* (corporeality or physicality) was an essential component of Paul's anthropology, which could not be conjured away by Bultmann's existentialist wand. Käsemann himself put stress on the body as the sign of human "creatureliness," and as the signal of our participation in, and solidarity with, entities much larger than the individual; in particular he stressed the condition of belonging to "powers," since the body is a part of the world that is always beholden to a sphere of sovereignty *(Herrschaftsbereich),* either divine or anti-divine.[20] He thus insisted that in our Romans texts the body language is crucial to Paul's theology: "that part of the world that we are in our bodies" ("das Stück Welt, das wir in unserm Leibe sind") is what God lays claim to, wresting it from its enslavement to sin for obedience to righteousness. Moreover, as he adds, "bodily obedience is necessary as an anticipation of the reality of bodily resurrection. Otherwise it would not be clear that we are engaged in the eschatological struggle for power."[21]

We can sharpen this further. The body is, for Paul, the site where the "I" is expressed and enacted; Paul's commitment to the notion of the "resurrected body" (8:11; cf. 1 Cor 15:42-44) suggests that the self cannot be operative or communicative in any other way. If so, the body is the place where the resurrection life of Jesus (the new self) becomes visible and active in human lives. The renewal of the mind that Paul speaks of in Romans 12:2 cannot take effect, in fact cannot be real in any meaningful sense, unless it is expressed in "the presentation of your bodies" as a living sacrifice (of which he had spoken *first* in 12:1). This means that the body is the site of that fundamental incongruity that we noted just now: it is in the body that the believer is both visibly on the path to death and is required, visibly and demonstrably, to display the presence of the resurrection of Christ, in the service of righteousness and holiness. It is precisely in his/her corporeality that the believer is *simul mortuus et vivens* (cf. 2 Cor 4:10-11). It is not for nothing that Paul here uses military language ("weapons," 6:13, 19; cf. 13:14), since the body is the critical site of resistance. Once appropriated by sin, the body is re-appropriated by Christ. The very location where sin once had most visible sway, and where its grip still draws believers' bodily selves towards death, is now the location where the "newness

19. R. Bultmann, *Theology of the New Testament,* 2 vols. (London: SCM Press, 1952), vol. 1, pp. 192-203 (citation, p. 194).

20. See esp. E. Käsemann, "On Paul's Anthropology," in *Perspectives on Paul,* trans. M. Kohl (London: SCM Press, 1971), pp. 1-31; for Käsemann's reading of Paul in general, see also above, 3.5.3. For further critique of Bultmann on this point, see R. Gundry, *Sōma in Biblical Theology, with Emphasis on Pauline Anthropology* (Cambridge: Cambridge University Press, 1976).

21. Käsemann, *An die Römer,* pp. 169-70; *Romans,* pp. 177-78.

of life" breaks through into action, displaying in counterintuitive patterns of behavior the miraculous Christ-life that draws their embodied selves toward the "vivification" (8:11) or "redemption" (8:23) of the body. In this tug-of-war between death and life, Christian obedience *in the body,* the former stronghold of Sin, displays the fact that a miraculous counterforce is already at work. By "putting to death the deeds of the body" (8:13) — that is, by killing the killer at the site of the crime (see 8:13 with 7:24) — the obedience to righteousness demonstrates that the believer is on a trajectory toward a victory whose finale will be the resurrection of the body and the redemption of the cosmos (8:18-39).

Paul encroaches on what we call "ethics" in Romans 6–8 in a way that seems to anticipate Romans 12–15 (there are verbal links between Romans 6:12-21 and 12:1-2), yet without the specificity of ethical instruction or example that is given in those later chapters.[22] There are imperatives or exhortations here (6:11-13; 8:12-13), but the chapters are concerned not so much with norms or practices as with ethic-structuring orientations, allegiances, and dispositions. Even when speaking of the body, Paul is talking about a system of loyalties and alignments that appears to go "deeper" than any particular practice. At issue is what he calls τὸ φρόνημα ("the mindset") — either of the flesh or of the Spirit (8:6-8) — which governs the body while being expressed not outside or behind it, but precisely in the physical deployment of its "organs." What is he talking about here? Can we interpret this in terms that make sense to us?

One of the best analysts of this kind of "structuring structure" is the anthropological theorist Pierre Bourdieu, who developed the much-discussed and still useful concept of the *habitus.*[23] In an effort to go beyond the sterile dualisms of "structure" and "free agency," of "objective" and "subjective" forces in human action, Bourdieu suggested that, at a level deeper than articulated norms and specified rules, cultures operate by a *habitus,*

> a system of lasting, transposable dispositions which, integrating past experiences, functions at every moment as a *matrix of perceptions, appreciations, and actions* and makes possible the achievement of infinitely diversified tasks.[24]

22. See the shared emphasis on the "ethical" character of 6:1–8:13 (together with agreement on 8:13 as the end of this sub-unit) in Byrne, "Living Out the Righteousness of God," and Engberg-Pedersen, "Galatians in Romans 5–8."

23. See P. Bourdieu, *Outline of a Theory of Practice,* trans. R. Nice (Cambridge: Cambridge University Press, 1977), pp. 72-95; idem, *The Logic of Practice,* trans. R. Nice (Stanford: Stanford University Press, 1980), pp. 52-79. For discussion and criticisms, see e.g., R. Jenkins, *Pierre Bourdieu* (London: Routledge, 1993), pp. 74-84; A. King, "Thinking with Bourdieu against Bourdieu: A 'Practical' Critique of the Habitus," *Sociological Theory* 18 (2000): 417-33.

24. Bourdieu, *Outline,* pp. 82-83, italics original.

These dispositions concern the unspoken, and often unconscious, systems of classification by which we order reality, as well as the taken-for-granted limits of the possible, the sensible, the proper, and the imaginable, which limit our action without articulation in rules of behavior. In an unending circularity, these dispositions and conceptual schemas are produced by practices, but they also, in turn, govern practices, at a level so deep that they are very hard to change unless (Bourdieu thought) there are major shifts in physical or economic conditions.[25] They represent what we take to be necessary and self-evident, "what goes without saying because it comes without saying." The *habitus* defines the sense of reality, of responsibility, of beauty, of value, and of the sacred and profane.

For Bourdieu, it is crucial that the *habitus* is *embodied,* inscribed in all manner of bodily habits and expectations:

> nothing seems more ineffable, more incommunicable, more inimitable, and, therefore, more precious, than the values given body, made body by the transubstantiation achieved by the hidden persuasion of an implicit pedagogy, capable of instilling a whole cosmology, an ethic, a metaphysic, a political philosophy, through injunctions as insignificant as "stand up straight" or "don't hold your knife in your left hand."[26]

In this respect, "what is 'learned by body' is not something that one has . . . but something that one is" — a nice complement to Bultmann's famous statement about σῶμα in Paul ("man does not have a *soma;* he is *soma*"), but this time much nearer to Paul's conception of the physical body. It is at this level of the "structuring structures" of thought and action that Bourdieu places the body not as a medium of some prior, purely mental, activity but as a constitutive ingredient of how we perceive, order, and practice reality itself.[27]

When Paul talks about "the body of sin" (Rom 6:6), it would be unwise

25. The ultimate causality attributed to material, physical, and economic conditions indicates the pull of Marxist determinism in Bourdieu's work; critics often note that he finds it hard to explain how the *habitus* can be altered. For this reason, we may need to go beyond Bourdieu to explain the change in *habitus* envisaged in Romans 6, while utilizing his thought to illuminate how the *habitus* functions through the medium of the body.

26. Bourdieu, *Outline,* p. 94.

27. The point is well expounded by T. Engberg-Pedersen, *Cosmology and the Self in the Apostle Paul* (Oxford: Oxford University Press, 2010), esp. pp. 141-42 and p. 185: "ideas should in principle *always* be seen as part of practices. Together with all other less articulated types of cognition, they enter into the bodily habitus that is expressed in practices" (italics his). This represents a shift from his earlier discussion of Romans 6, which suggested that the cognitive "I" was logically separate from and prior to the body (*Paul and the Stoics,* pp. 228, 238).

either to "spiritualize" this phrase as signifying something vague such as "the sinful person," or to limit its range of meaning to certain physical acts (for instance, the μέθαι and κοίται of 13:13). He seems to have a sense that the body has been commandeered by sin, such that its dispositions, emotions, speech-patterns, and habitual gestures are bound to systems of honor, self-aggrandizement, and license that are fundamentally at odds with the will of God. Thus even the Law, good and holy as it is (7:12), ends up "bearing fruit for death" (7:5). When received by a body "inhabited" by Sin (7:17, 20) — endued with a deeply inculcated *habitus* of sin — it cannot achieve what it promises. The "law" that is at work in the organs (7:23) is a set of predispositions and orientations too deep to be altered by the instructions of the Torah, however much the mind may approve of them. What is needed is "rescue from this body of death" (7:24) — a new φρόνημα of cognitive and practical schemas operative in physical deportment, corporeal practice, and bodily appetites.

One could hardly imagine a more effective demonstration of this "rescue" than the physical rite of baptism, which Paul interprets as a transition from death to life *performed on and with the body.* Henceforth, believers give themselves over to this new life ("as alive from the dead," 6:13), inasmuch as they "present their organs as weapons of righteousness to God" (6:13; cf. 12:1) — in other words, they are committed to instantiate a new embodied *habitus.* This commitment could never be a solo affair: while the body is individual, it is also shaped in and by its social interaction. The attempt to break with the old schematizations (μὴ συσχηματίζεσθε τῷ αἰῶνι τούτῳ, 12:2) and to express a new, transformed νοῦς (12:2) will require collective practices that challenge the old taxonomic systems (the structuring "antinomies" of the present age) and embody new apperceptions and goals. That is why the bodily reorientation described in Romans 6 is given some exemplification in Romans 12–15, which concerns the formation of a community structured by and oriented to the good news.

16.4. A Community Constructed by Unconditioned Welcome (Romans 12:1–15:13)

When Paul renews his appeal for a new embodied *habitus,* it is not surprising that its foundation is located in "the mercy (lit. "mercies") of God" (12:1). The plural echoes the Hebrew רחמים (cf. 2 Cor 1:3; Phil 2:1), while the content is supplied by the preceding chapters, which had mixed the language of "gift/ favor" (11:5-6, 29) with that of "mercy" (9:15-18; 11:28-32; see chapter 17, below). Like the gift, the mercy of God bears no relation to the preceding status, achievement, or worth of its recipients (9:6-18; 11:32). Paul thus calls for a way of life recalibrated in disregard of whatever ethnic, social, or individual characteristics had previously constituted the believers' cultural or symbolic capital, whatever had formed their grounds for distinctive or superior value. On the basis of this act of divine mercy, believers are to present their bodies in exclusive orientation to God (12:1; cf. 6:12-23), a mode of "reasonable worship" (λογικὴ λατρεία) whose criteria of "reason" are newly defined by the act of God in Christ.[28] The "transformation" Paul expects of believers in the "renewal of the mind" (12:2) will not clash at every point with the modes of behavior common in their surroundings: there will be some overlap in the recognition of what is "good" and "bad" (12:17; 13:3) and no *inevitable* clash with the interests of the governing authorities (13:1-7).[29] But the new orientation to the Lord (12:11) will involve a mindset whose assumptions, priorities, and dispositions are newly configured, in differentiation from "this age" (12:2). Given Paul's close correlation between "mind" and "bodily practice," we should expect to find in these chapters the outlines of routine communal behavior that embodies this altered cognition.

As in Galatians (see above, 14.2), a high premium is here placed on a communal spirit that counters the competitive quest for honor. When he turns specifically against "the works of darkness" and the "desires of the flesh," Paul thinks not just of the excessive indulgence of physical passions (for food, drink, and sex) but also of the rivalry and jealousy (ἔρις καὶ ζῆλος) that threaten communal coexistence (13:13). The renewal of the mind entails the ability to perceive oneself and others in such a way that the desire to establish and promote one's honor is not merely muted but specifically counteracted. If the only legitimate "boast," the only ground of worth, is in the work of God in Christ (5:11; cf. 3:27), those who reconceptualize themselves "in Christ" are divested of every claim to superiority, attributed or acquired.[30] Thus, the very first "ethical" instruction Paul offers, pointedly directed at *every* hearer (12:3), is not to inflate

28. To translate this phrase "spiritual worship" is in danger of elevating spirit over matter, which is clearly ruled out by the reference to the presentation of "bodies"; see Dunn, *Romans*, pp. 711-12. Although the adjective is reminiscent of the Stoic prioritization of "reason," it is clear from the following verse that the logic controlling the Christian *habitus* is self-consciously at odds with the prevailing logics of contemporary society.

29. For agreements between Romans 12–13 and current Stoic attitudes in Rome, see R. M. Thorsteinsson, *Roman Christianity and Roman Stoicism: A Comparative Study of Ancient Morality* (Oxford: Oxford University Press, 2010).

30. For a pioneering exploration of this theme, connecting Romans 12–15 with the earlier chapters of the letter around the theme of honor/boasting, see H. Moxnes, "Honor and Righteousness in Romans," *JSNT* 32 (1999): 61-77.

their opinion of themselves (μὴ ὑπερφρονεῖν παρ' ὃ δεῖ φρονεῖν) but to think of themselves moderately or modestly (ἀλλὰ φρονεῖν εἰς τὸ σωφρονεῖν, 12:3). The language recalls the Greek virtue of σωφροσύνη (moderation or modesty), but its grounding is specifically Pauline.[31] As the echoes of 11:18-20, 25 make clear (μὴ ὑψηλὰ φρόνει . . . ἵνα μὴ ἦτε ἐν ἑαυτοῖς φρόνιμοι), every believer is to reckon himself or herself dependent upon the single gift of divine mercy: believers cannot boast as if there were *something about themselves* that rendered them worthy of the divine call. Thus, re-grounded in "the mercy of God," they are able to perceive their differential roles within the believer-community as divinely distributed *gifts* (12:3-8). Just as Paul's authority to instruct is a product of χάρις (12:3; cf. 1:5; 15:15), so each of them has a χάρισμα by the χάρις given to them (12:6); each is apportioned a measured role of communal responsibility (μέτρον πίστεως, 12:3).[32] Within this community, honor does not have to be sought: all the honor that counts has already been given, or will be given, by God (cf. 2:29; 1 Cor 4:1-5). Freed from the need to establish their honor, in competition or retaliation (12:14, 17-21), believers can afford to grant it to others: in loving one another, they *strive to be first in being last,* bidding to take the lead not in claiming honor but in giving it to one another (τῇ τιμῇ ἀλλήλους προηγούμενοι, 12:10).[33]

As in Galatians 5–6 ("be slaves to one another," Gal 5:13), Paul articulates a paradoxical pattern of reciprocal asymmetry, with each believer serving the interests of the other, in oscillating relations of disequilibrium. Developing the body-motif from its earlier use in 1 Corinthians 12:12-31, Paul imagines a community so interdependent that all are figured, individually, as *organs of*

31. As H. Moxnes notes, Paul draws on the Greek critique of *hybris,* and his exhortation "is directed not to an individual character trait, but to a total system of relations between individuals of unequal status," "The Quest for Honor and the Unity of the Community in Romans 12 and in the Orations of Dio Chrysostom," in T. Engberg-Pedersen, ed., *Paul in His Hellenistic Context* (Edinburgh: T&T Clark, 1994), pp. 203-20, at p. 222. Cf. H. North, *Sophrosune: Self-knowledge and Self-restraint in Greek Literature* (Leiden: Brill, 1972).

32. This puzzling phrase has been illuminated by Goodrich, who has illustrated the contemporary use of the term πίστις in the sense of "trusteeship" or "entrusted responsibility," and has shown how rendering this phrase "to each as God assigned a measure, namely a trusteeship" fits both the immediate context and the parallels in other Pauline letters; see J. K. Goodrich, "'Standard of Faith' or 'Measure of a Trusteeship'? A Study in Romans 12:3," *CBQ* 74 (2012): 753-72.

33. As Jewett notes (*Romans,* pp. 761-62), the participle is best translated "taking the lead," which entails the paradoxical notion of being the leader not in receiving honor but in giving it (cf. Phil 2:3-4). Instead of losing honor by thus giving it to others, the ethic of reciprocity means that believers are bound together in relationships where everyone's responsibility is to give honor to everyone else.

one another (12:5): everyone is essential to everyone else. In practical terms, such a *habitus* inculcates (and is itself shaped by) practices of mutual service. Sharing the needs of the saints (12:13), they give each other financial as well as moral and spiritual support (12:7-8). In "brotherly love" they "weep with those who weep and rejoice with those who rejoice" (12:15), their new emotional attachments and vulnerabilities cementing their social solidarity. In hospitality (12:13), commensality (14:1-2), and the "holy kiss" (16:16), they practice new social attachments across now-insignificant differences of ethnicity and status. The socially superior are required to shed their snobbery in associating, on a level, with "the humble" (12:16): the deep commonality they find across social divisions is the evidence of a new *habitus* that disregards the taxonomies and "schemas" of "this age" (12:2). By fostering this new communal life, oriented to God through Christ in service and worship (12:11; 15:6-13), bodily practice is reoriented and newly regulated in its post-baptismal form. "Putting on the Lord Jesus Christ" (13:14) enlists every organ of the moribund body for a new allegiance, whose social shape reflects the capacity of the Christ-gift to question every norm.

The instructions about meals in 14:1–15:6 provide the fullest and most illuminating description of a community formed by this recalibration of value. There is good reason to think that Paul here addresses real (not hypothetical) problems in the Roman congregations, as he reapplies principles from 1 Corinthians to circumstances in which the common meals of the Roman believers — core expressions of their communal life — are being fractured by disputes over the observance of *kashrut*.[34] The divisions did not fall neatly along ethnic lines between Jewish and Gentile believers (Paul associates himself with "the strong," 15:1), but Paul's terminology regarding "clean" food (κοινός, καθαρός, 14:14, 20) and his discussion of "days" (14:5-6) best fit a social context in which the observance of Jewish food laws and Sabbaths caused a strong difference of opinion. There were good rhetorical reasons for Paul *not* to spell out the entanglement of these issues with "the Law" or with ethnic affiliations and at-

34. I have discussed the social context of these chapters in an essay that has cemented and developed a now widespread consensus regarding the cultural issues at stake: see J. M. G. Barclay, "'Do We Undermine the Law?' A Study of Romans 14:1–15.6," in J. D. G. Dunn, ed., *Paul and the Mosaic Law* (Tübingen: Mohr Siebeck, 1996), pp. 287-308, reprinted in J. M. G. Barclay, *Pauline Churches and Diaspora Jews* (Tübingen: Mohr Siebeck, 2011), pp. 37-59 (hereafter cited from the latter location). Nanos's suggestion that "the weak in faith" were non-believing Jews has been refuted by many, including M. Reasoner, *The Strong and the Weak: Romans 14.1–15.13 in Context* (Cambridge: Cambridge University Press, 1999), pp. 131-36. Reasoner's suggestion that the labels represent differing social levels among the Roman believers is possible, but not well supported from the text of Romans itself.

tractions.[35] But the terms of his discourse are also chosen to reflect the framework that he considers most salient, ignoring norms or identities extraneous to the good news. Paul addresses the Romans not *qua* Jews or Gentiles but *qua* believers, welcomed by Christ and servants of a common Master, since it is on this basis alone that their varying behavior might be justifiable, and on this basis that the dispute can also be resolved (14:1-12; 15:7).[36]

A careful reading of the evidence suggests that those whom Paul calls "weak in faith" are inclined to refuse all meat at the Christian common meals, lest it be tainted by uncleanness in one way or another (they eat only vegetables, 14:2), while "the strong" believe (like Paul) that anything can be eaten, as nothing is unclean in itself (14:14, 20; 15:1). The "weak" thus condemn the "strong" for their laxity, while the "strong" despise the "weak" for their scruples (14:3). Rather than adjudicate immediately on the status of the food, Paul begins by re-presenting the believers to each other, according to their "welcome" by God. To judge or despise a fellow believer is to impose a valuation of worth wholly contrary to that person's evaluation by God. Using the language of "welcome" (προσλαμβάνεσθαι) appropriate to the discussion of hospitality, Paul insists that God has welcomed them, with an attribution of worth that no human valuation can overturn (14:3; 15:7). What is at stake here is what God has created ("the work of God," 14:20), a person whose value is grounded in the fact that Christ has died for him or her (14:15). They are to be welcomed to meals not just *in the same way* as Christ has welcomed them, but also *because* they stand before God on the basis of Christ's welcome alone (15:7). If there are echoes here of the earlier warning against applying human judgments (2:1-5), there are also echoes of "the grace in which we stand" (5:2; cf. 14:4).[37] To recognize one another in that light is already to dissolve the presumption that old norms and traditional criteria of judgment can be transferred without ado into the community of believers.

35. Supporting previous observations that Paul could not afford to be overly explicit regarding issues in churches he had neither founded nor visited, Sampley has suggested that he deliberately adopted a rhetorical pose of indirectness (see J. P. Sampley, "The Weak and the Strong: Paul's Careful and Crafty Rhetorical Strategy in Romans 14.:1–15:13," in L. M. White and O. L. Yarbrough, eds., *The Social World of the First Christians: Essays in Honor of Wayne A. Meeks* (Minneapolis: Augsburg Fortress, 1995), pp. 40-52. *Pace* Sampley, this does not mean that anyone could apply whatever label they thought fitted them; the different positions are defined in sufficient detail to make quite clear whom Paul considers "the weak" and "the strong."

36. For a fuller analysis of this passage, expanding the following few pages, see J. M. G. Barclay, "Faith and Self-Detachment from Cultural Norms: A Study of Romans 14–15," *ZNW* 104 (2013): 192-208.

37. See W. A. Meeks, "Judgment and the Brother: Romans 14:1–15:13," in his *In Search of the Early Christians* (New Haven: Yale University Press, 2002), pp. 153-66. The core values of "righteousness, peace, and joy in the holy Spirit" (14:17) take up the themes of Romans 5:1-5.

With the new status comes a new allegiance: welcomed by Christ, each believer is also beholden to Christ, as a house-slave is beholden to no one other than his/her Master (14:4-12). The space Paul allots to establishing this point indicates how seriously he wants to bring all moral decisions into the sphere of orientation to Christ. Whatever the decision — eating or not eating, observing or not observing special days — it is justifiable only if it is done "to the Lord" and "with thanks to God" (14:6-9). What is or is not according to the Torah is not the final criterion; even if the believers' "obedience of faith" is *also* in important respects the fulfillment of the Torah (8:4; 13:8-10), their allegiance is ultimately to Christ, not to the Torah. If, as Paul allows, the "weak in faith" keep *kashrut* and observe Sabbaths, this is not here described as "keeping the Law" but as "serving Christ"; there may be various means of expressing that allegiance, but all must spring from faith (14:22-23). This "faith" is none other than what was spoken of earlier in the letter. Newly grounded and centered in the death and resurrection of Christ, believers are to "live by faith," giving honor and service to Christ, in whom they find their identity and worth.[38]

Recent analysis of the "weak" and "strong" groups in the Roman churches has focused on their practices and cultural traditions, with little attention to Paul's understanding of these labels. Whether he borrowed or invented the terms "weak" and "strong," his comments on faith in Romans 14:22-23 indicate careful reflection on the different self-understandings of the two types of believer.[39] So what did Paul take to be the difference in faith between the "weak" and the "strong"? That the "weak in faith" are to be welcomed (14:1), within the welcome of Christ (15:7), shows that their faith is to be accepted as genuine: Paul assumes that their refusal to eat non-kosher is integral to their desire to honor Christ as Lord (14:6). That orientation is crucial, and the last thing he wants is for them to act outside of that conviction (14:5), since to act without assurance that one is honoring Christ is to behave outside the realm of faith, and "whatever does not arise from faith is sin" (14:23).[40] What makes

38. The tag ἐκ πίστεως (twice in 14:23) recalls the heavy use of this phrase in earlier chapters (1:17; 3:30; 4:16; 5:1). *Pace* Cranfield (*Romans,* vol. 2, pp. 697-98) and Fitzmyer (J. A. Fitzmyer, *Romans* [New York: Doubleday, 1992], pp. 688-89, 698-700), πίστις is not here used in a different sense ("confidence" or "conviction").

39. For an argument that the terms were current already in Rome, see J. Marcus, "The Circumcision and Uncircumcision in Rome," *NTS* 35 (1989): 67-81; Reasoner, *Strong and Weak,* pp. 55-58. As is often noted, there are many echoes here of Paul's discussion of Abraham's faith in 4:19-22. For arguments that Paul himself devised these terms, see V. Gäckle, *Die Starken und die Schwachen in Korinth und in Rom* (Tübingen: Mohr Siebeck, 2005), pp. 437-49, 515-18, and Barclay, "Faith and Self-Detachment."

40. 14:22-23 make clear that "weakness" in faith in this context is not a matter of doubt, or lack of confidence: Paul expects the weak to act fully and solely from faith, and refuses to

their faith "weak" is that a set of cultural traditions remain integrally attached to their faith in Christ. These are not an alternative or additional ground of salvation, but they are so closely interwoven with their faith response to the Christ-event that to depart from them would be, for them, an abrogation of that faith.[41] The Christ-event is for them of supreme and definitive importance, but kosher- and Sabbath-traditions remain intrinsic ingredients of their response to that event, a constituent element of their faith. Paul recognizes this as a valid form of faith (he has met plenty of Jewish believers who think likewise), and he is extremely anxious lest pressure exerted by the "strong" cause these weak believers to act against their faith — and thus to abandon altogether their commitment to Christ. As his references to "destruction" show (14:15, 20), Paul is concerned here not with causing "offence" to the "weak" but with undermining their allegiance to Christ. The one thing Paul does demand from the "weak" is the recognition that *other* believers can act otherwise (e.g., eating "unclean" food), also in honor of Christ (14:6); they are not to be "judged" for doing so (14:3-4, 13). That is a considerable concession, since it undermines in principle a necessary connection between "honoring the Lord" and "keeping kosher."[42] But Paul accepts that, *in their own perception of their own behavior,* these cultural traditions are inseparable from their sense of service to Christ and gratitude to God.

The "strong" are also expected to act at all times from faith: if they eat "everything" and "observe every day" alike, this is permissible on no other grounds than that they do so in honor of God (14:5-7). Paul also expects them not to criticize believers (the "weak") who think and act differently in these

allow them to be pressurized into behavior for which they might "judge themselves" as acting contrary to their faith.

41. *Pace* Barrett, their weakness is not a failure to recognize that people are justified by faith in Christ alone, rather than by vegetarianism or sabbatarianism (C. K. Barrett, *A Commentary on the Epistle to the Romans* [London: A&C Black, 1971], pp. 256-57). That Paul recognizes them as living "from faith" (14:23) indicates that the Christ-event is the ground of their identity. They do not believe in Christ *and* in certain practices, but they believe in Christ *through* the practice of customs that they cannot dissociate from what it means to serve and believe in Christ. Paul confirms elsewhere that there are degrees of strength or growth in faith (Rom 4:20; 1 Thess 3:10; 2 Cor 10:15).

42. This concession is what Peter did not allow in Antioch, where his withdrawal from table-fellowship with Gentiles signaled to Paul that Peter could not accept their integrity in Christ unless they also adopted Jewish food laws (he "compelled them to judaize," Gal 2:14). By thus framing faith in Christ within the norms of the Torah, Peter failed to "walk in accordance with the truth of the good news" (Gal 2:14). For the deep concession that Paul expects from the "weak," while protecting their right to apply their convictions to themselves, and while expecting the "strong" to accommodate and even adopt their practices, see Barclay, "'Do We Undermine?'" pp. 54-59.

matters (14:1, 3, 13). More than that, he requires here that the "strong" accommodate their behavior at communal meals to the scruples of the "weak." Since their priority is to walk in love, nothing they do must end up causing harm (14:15); they are committed to peace and to the task of mutual construction, so they must eschew disputes and any form of behavior that would cause others to be destroyed (14:19-20). They must thus refrain from any food or drink that would cause the "weak" to stumble, even if that means adopting kosher practices that they consider unnecessary for themselves (14:21).

Paul can urge this behavior on the "strong" because he reckons them able to live both kosher and non-kosher lifestyles in honor of Christ. They are "strong" in their faith precisely because such customs are *not* integral to their faith — neither positively integral nor negatively incompatible. The strength in their faith is the degree to which they have been able to disassociate their faith in Christ from *every* norm and value that is not derived from the good news itself. By this dissociation, other norms are relativized, rendered not just *less important* but *unimportant.* To eat kosher or to eat non-kosher is not a constituent element of their faith: they can adopt either pattern of behavior because each is *only* of instrumental value to the service of Christ, contingent upon particular circumstances and social conditions.

Paul's structure of thought here runs parallel to the Stoic notion of *adiaphora.*[43] Like the Stoics, he has constructed an alternative system of value or worth (ἀξία) in which a single good (for Paul: serving Christ; for the Stoics: virtue) puts all other "goods" into a different category: these are now fundamentally unimportant even if they may be contingently preferable or non-preferable according to their instrumental usefulness for the only true good. For Paul, the gift (or "welcome") of Christ, because it neither matched nor reinforced preexistent norms or values, has put all other value systems into question. The only salient values for believers are those that arise from the good news, what is true "in the Lord Jesus" (14:14) and what accords with "the kingdom of God" (14:17). Because love, peace, and self-denying service to others *are* integral to this good news, Paul insists that "the strong" imitate Christ by "bearing the burdens of the weak" (15:1-3); "walking in love" is a non-negotiable "good" that must be practiced at all times (14:15; cf. 13:8-10). If this

43. For an exploration of such parallels in general, see J. J. Jaquette, *Discerning What Counts: The Function of the* Adiaphora Topos *in Paul's Letters* (Atlanta: Scholars Press, 1995). For close application to Romans 14–15, see T. Engberg-Pedersen. "'Everything Is Clean' and 'Everything That Is Not of Faith Is Sin': The Logic of Pauline Casuistry in Romans 14.1–15.13," in P. Middleton, A. Paddison, and K. Wenell, eds., *Paul, Grace, and Freedom: Essays in Honor of John K. Riches* (London: T&T Clark, 2009), pp. 22-38. Paul places this topos within a different symbolic matrix, formed by a gift-event that reevaluates every value.

requires the "strong" to adopt kosher food customs for the sake of the "weak," that is unproblematic: it is precisely because such customs are *unimportant* that the "strong" can adopt them as the demands of love require, without fearing that they will thereby cease acting out of faith (14:22-23). It is because food *does not matter* (14:17) that they can adjust their eating habits one way or another, attending to the one thing that *does matter,* the brother for whom Christ died (14:14-15). The "strong" thus have a greater capacity for cultural flexibility to the extent that their faith has been divested of non-gospel values. They have deeply internalized the fact that the unconditioned gift of God in Christ paid no regard to their previous systems of value: henceforth, the *only* salient criterion of value for faith is the good news of Jesus Christ itself. Because different eating habits are neither demanded by the good news, nor excluded by it, they can do whatever is required for the sake of love, in service of Christ (cf. 1 Cor 9:19-23).[44]

16.5. Conclusions

Paul's careful handling of the Roman disputes over food indicates how important it is that the "newness of life" arising from the Christ-event is expressed in practices that are reframed and reoriented in allegiance to Christ. In one sense, food and drink do not matter, because they are not integral to faith (14:17). In another sense, how believers handle these routine concerns matters greatly, because through them they show if and how their values have been reconfigured in Christ. The "kingdom of God" is not a purely "spiritual" affair, if by that is meant something detached from bodily practice. In their eating habits, as in every other dimension of life, believers are to utilize their bodies for the service of Christ (12:2). The new *habitus* of the believer — the new perceptions, goals, dispositions, and values — can become effective only in practice. Outside of bodily practice, it is not clear that "newness of life" would mean anything at all.

The fact that the one extended discussion of practice in Romans 12–15 concerns communal meals is no accident. As at Antioch (Gal 2:11-14), Paul is acutely aware of the importance of meals in the formation of early Christian

44. As Horrell suggests, "perhaps Paul's conviction that the basis for solidarity and identity is Christ, so firmly asserted in Galatians, provides the grounds for Paul's 'tolerance' in Romans, where different customs with regard to food, no longer defining of identity and belonging, are in themselves indifferent and so can be treated with a Christ-like generosity" (D. G. Horrell, "Solidarity and Difference: Pauline Morality in Romans 14:1–15:13," *Studies in Christian Ethics* 15.2 [2002]: 60-78, at p. 73; cf. his *Solidarity and Difference: A Contemporary Reading of Paul's Ethics* [London: T&T Clark, 2005], pp. 182-89, 193-95).

communities, and it is in communal practice that the newly formed *habitus* of life in Christ will, or will not, be displayed. There are moments in these chapters where Paul's theological focus is strongly individuated: *each* believer has a responsibility and a *charisma* within the body (12:3-8), and *each* is answerable to Christ for the practice of his/her faith (14:12, 22). But this individuation is always in the context of, and for the sake of, the community as a whole. As in Galatians 6:1-5, Paul underscores the individual's relationship to God (14:22) precisely to rein in the potentially destructive desire to seek affirmation or agreement from others. He recognizes and allows individual differences of perception in order to protect and enhance the life of the community. It is as they form a community in Christ, Jew with non-Jew (15:7-13), the superior with the inferior (12:16), the "weak" with the "strong," that they reveal their distance from the prevailing social norms. As they recognize and embed in practice the worth of others who are "welcomed" by Christ (15:7), they demonstrate how this welcome undercuts the normal systems of differentiation, and thus enact the unconditionality of the gift. The community where each is committed to honor the other (12:10), and to build up the other in mutual construction (14:19), creates a context in which an alternative set of values is brought to expression, whose meaning is evident only in this social form.

That life "under grace" (6:14) has its own structure of allegiance and obligation is clear in the way Paul figures believers as "slaves" both in Romans 6 and in Romans 14. Their obligations to one another (15:1) arise out of their common responsibility to "the Master" (14:6-12). However, their belonging to Christ is the product of their "welcome" by Christ (14:3; 15:7): everything in Romans 12–15 arises from "the mercy of God" (12:1). Christian "obedience" thus responds to the prior, incongruous gift of God in Christ; it is symptomatic of a new life that runs clean contrary to the death-doomed life of the "natural" human being. That incongruity is evident in the fact that this life is present precisely in the *mortal* human body, as is dramatized and ritualized in the baptismal break with the past. Christian life is an impossible newness given as an unfitting gift, such that everything in this new life refers back to its source and foundation in the Christ-gift, and forward to its eschatological fulfillment as eternal life. Everything that can be said about Christian action, obedience, and obligation arises from this generative basis, because the very life that believers now live is created and sustained by the resurrection life of Christ. To live from faith is to "put on the Lord Christ Jesus" (13:14), whose presence in power motivates, enables, and shapes their patterns of behavior (15:1-3).

Hence, the obligation now incumbent on believers is not to "gain" grace (or salvation), nor to win another installment of grace. There is a single χάρισμα of eternal life (6:23) that runs from the Christ-event to eternity (cf.

8:32), not a series of "graces" won by increases in sanctification. Paul certainly expects that the *moral* incongruity at the start of the Christian life will be reduced over time, as the believers' slavery to righteousness draws them toward holiness (6:19). In that sense, what began as a morally incongruous gift will be completed as a morally congruous gift. When believers come before the judgment seat of God and give an account of themselves (14:10-12), Paul expects that they will be able to evidence a life lived in light, not darkness (13:12; cf. 2:6-16). But this does not reduce the essential incongruity of grace, since the very life from which this holiness emerges is not the believers' own life (which is doomed to death) but the resurrection life of Christ. Right up to the moment of resurrection a believer remains *simul mortuus et vivens*. What is given to them is not a new set of competencies added to their previous capacities, nor an enhancement of their previous selves: what is given is a death and the emergence from that death of a new self, essentially "eccentric" in its dependence on the resurrection life of Christ.

Because the life of the believer is thus *derived* from Christ, Paul does not have to play the agency of the believer off against the agency of Christ/the Spirit; he does not need to insist that the *real* agent is the Spirit. He can certainly speak of the presence of Christ (or the Spirit) within believers (8:9-11), and he can talk of Christian behavior taking place generically in the Spirit (πνεύματι, 8:13-14; cf. 12:11). But he does not need to articulate this on each occasion when he speaks of believers as agents. He gives genuine exhortations to genuinely freed agents who are urged to more than passive acquiescence in the work of another. In other words, Paul does not perfect the efficacy of grace as a form of monergism, because it is clear for him from the baptismal event that the very life in which the believer acts and decides is a life sourced, established, and upheld by Christ (a "life from the dead").[45] Within this frame, and on this basis, plenty of statements can be made regarding believers as responsible agents who are required to present their bodies in one direction rather than another. Christian obedience is thus vital, but only ever in a responsive mode: it arises in conjunction with faith and gratitude as the answer to a prior gift. The gift is entirely undeserved but strongly obliging: it creates agents who are newly alive, required to live the life they have been given. This obedience is not instrumental (it does not acquire the gift of Christ, nor any additional gift from God), but it is integral to the gift itself, as God wills newly

45. For further reflections on grace and agency in Paul, as a non-competitive relation between divine life and human action, see J. M. G. Barclay, "Introduction" and "'By the Grace of God I Am What I Am': Grace and Agency in Philo and Paul," in J. M. G. Barclay and S. J. Gathercole, eds., *Divine and Human Agency in Paul and His Cultural Environment* (London: T&T Clark, 2006), pp. 1-8, 140-57.

competent agents who express in practice their freedom from sin and slavery to righteousness. God's grace does not exclude, deny, or displace believing agents; they are not reduced to passivity or pure receptivity. Rather, it generates and grounds an active, willed conformity to the Christ-life, in which believers become, like Christ, truly human, as obedient agents (5:19).[46] Without this obedience, grace is ineffective and unfulfilled.

46. For a careful analysis of this theme in Barth, see J. Webster, *Barth's Ethics of Reconciliation* (Cambridge: Cambridge University Press, 1995).

CHAPTER 17

Israel, Christ, and the Creative Mercy of God (Romans 9–11)

Recent discussion of Romans 9–11 has reached consensus on at least two matters: that these chapters are an integral component of the letter (not an appendix to its main argument) and that their subject matter is God's dealings with Israel (not election or predestination in abstract).[1] Within that consensus, plenty of issues remain disputed, but it is clear that Paul's presentation of the good news in Romans includes the election of Israel as God's people (Rom 11:2) and as the bearer of God's promises for the world (15:8-12). In Romans 9–11, Paul speaks as an "Israelite" (11:1), closely identified with other Israelites, "my brothers, my kinsmen according to the flesh" (9:3; cf. 11:14). It is not until 11:13 that he addresses "you Gentiles." Up to that point, he has been speaking in the company of fellow Jews (though not directly to them) regarding a shared tradition and a common inheritance ("our father, Isaac," 9:10). As we noted in outline above (10.4), Paul's discourse here intersects particularly thickly with the other Second Temple texts discussed in Part II, and other connections could be traced all over contemporary Jewish literature. Like other Jews, Paul does theology by thinking about Israel, both because Israel's Scriptures constitute a primary resource for Jewish theology, and because he takes the story of Israel to be central to all God's dealings with humanity. Here, Paul is simultaneously most Jewish and most theologically creative, and in that creativity, induced by the paradox of the Christ-event, he rethinks the identity of Israel. In this chapter, we shall examine how Paul traces throughout Scripture

1. The literature on these chapters is unmanageably immense. For analysis of recent trends in German- and English-language scholarship, see the essays by K. Haacker ("Das Thema von Römer 9–11 als Problem der Auslegungsgeschichte") and M. Reasoner ("Romans 9–11 Moves from Margin to Center, from Rejection to Salvation: Four Grids for Recent English-Language Exegesis") in F. Wilk and J. R. Wagner, eds., *Between Gospel and Election: Explorations in the Interpretation of Romans 9–11* (Tübingen: Mohr Siebeck, 2010), pp. 55-72 and 73-89, respectively.

the pattern of incongruity that is basic to God's calling of Israel; on this basis, he can make sense of the strange reversals currently experienced (Israelite unbelief and Gentile belief) while signaling hope for the future of Israel. What gives theological coherence to these chapters (though they are often regarded as hopelessly inconsistent) is the fact that God's mercy (or grace) is given without regard to worth, and thus forms the creative root of God's purposes for the world. Within this vision, the Christ-event takes its place as the definitive expression of God's unconditioned gift of "wealth." It thus confirms the promises to Israel while clarifying Israel's identity as a people utterly dependent on God's incongruous call — a people for this reason special, though also for this same reason no longer unique, since the creative mercy of God in Christ has spread without condition to all the nations of the world.

17.1. The Crisis of Israel

As its opening verses make clear, Romans 9–11 is the product of grief and shock. Paul's deep sorrow (9:1-2) and his earnest prayer for Israel's salvation (10:1) arise from his strong identification with his fellow Israelites (9:3-4; 11:1), whom he perceives as standing in an alarming moment of crisis. The cause of that crisis is already clear from 3:3: the failure of "some" (in fact, most) to "believe" (ἀπιστέω; ἀπιστία; cf. 9:32-33; 11:20, 23). Paul's unreal wish that he could for their sake be "anathema from Christ" (9:3) indicates the seriousness of this crisis. This unbelief jeopardizes their salvation (10:1, 9-13) by severing their connection to the "root" that sustains Israel's very being (11:17, 20); Paul contemplates discarding *his* salvation (his connection to Christ) for the sake of theirs.[2] As commentators note, Paul's wish echoes that of Moses to be "blot-

2. The reading of Romans 9–11 as portraying two paths of salvation (Israel's via the Torah; the Gentiles' via Christ) is implausible on many grounds, but especially in its failure to take seriously Paul's conviction that Israel's salvation is at stake in its response to the good news about Christ (9:30–10:4). For critiques of this *Sonderweg*-hypothesis (associated especially with Stendahl, Gaston, and Gager), see, e.g., H. Räisänen, "Paul, God, and Israel: Romans 9–11 in Recent Research," in J. Neusner et al., eds., *The Social World of Formative Christianity and Judaism* (Philadelphia: Fortress Press, 1988), pp. 178-208; E. E. Johnson, *The Function of Apocalyptic and Wisdom Traditions in Romans 9–11* (Atlanta: Scholars Press, 1989), pp. 176-205; R. Hvalvik, "A 'Sonderweg' for Israel: A Critical Examination of a Current Interpretation of Romans 11.25-27," *JSNT* 38 (1990): 87-107. As F. Watson notes, "While such a reading can exploit the lack of explicit Christology in the latter part of Romans 11, it can offer no coherent explanation of Romans 10:1-13 in its relation to Paul's prayer for Jewish salvation in v. 1. Indeed, it becomes incomprehensible how Paul could ever have prayed such a prayer" (*Paul, Judaism and the Gentiles: Beyond the New Perspective* [Grand Rapids: Eerdmans, 2007], p. 329 n. 45).

ted out" of God's book on behalf of Israel (Exod 32:32),[3] and his subsequent citation of Exodus 33:19 ("I will have mercy on whom I have mercy," Rom 9:15) suggests that he sees parallels between Israel's disastrous unbelief in Christ and the near-termination of Israel's story in the construction of the Golden Calf.[4] What makes the present crisis especially shocking is that Israel's unbelief concerns the Messiah (9:5), who has become, paradoxically, a stumbling block (9:32-33): to come up short here is to miss the very goal of Israel's history (10:4). Just as *4 Ezra* laments the crisis of Israel's following "the desolation of Zion" (3:2), and struggles through grief, despair, and prayer to a more hopeful vision (see above, chapter 9), Paul grapples deeply with Israel's traditions in the light of his confusing experience. Each offers a profound reconfiguration of Israel's identity, *4 Ezra* in its celebration of a righteous remnant, Paul in his recognition that Israel, like believers from the Gentiles, is constituted by the incongruous mercy of God.

Like *4 Ezra,* Paul's immediate response to the crisis is to recount God's promises and Israel's privileges. Just as "Ezra" appeals to the covenants and to the special status of Israel among the nations (*4 Ezra* 5.23-30; 6.55-59), Paul reasserts the fact that his kinsmen are "Israelites, and to them belong the adoption, the glory, the covenants, the giving of the law, the (temple) worship and the promises; theirs are the patriarchs, and from them springs the Messiah, according to the flesh" (Rom 9:4-5). These are for Paul, as in *4 Ezra,* nonnegotiable privileges: the only question is how their promise will be realized. Paul considers it impossible that God's promise could fail: "It is certainly not that the word of God has fallen" (Rom 9:6; cf. *4 Ezra* 5.33). When he asks if God has rejected his people, the resounding reply is, "No way!" (Rom 11:1-2).

This conviction is foundational to Paul's theology. God's faithfulness to Israel does not just *support* Paul's independent assurance that "nothing can separate us from the love of God in Christ" (8:31-39) but *grounds* that assurance. Gentile believers are to find in God's dealings with Israel not a *parallel* story of divine reliability, but the *root* of their own experience of God's grace (11:17-24).[5] Paul's good news is the fulfillment of the scriptural promises (1:2),

3. C. E. B. Cranfield, *The Epistle to the Romans* (Edinburgh: T&T Clark, 1979), vol. 2, pp. 454-56; U. Wilckens, *Der Brief an die Römer,* 3 vols. (Zürich: Benziger Verlag; Neukirchen-Vluyn: Neukirchener Verlag, 1980), vol. 2, p. 187; R. Jewett, *Romans* (Minneapolis: Fortress Press, 2007), pp. 560-61; otherwise E. Käsemann, *An die Römer* (Tübingen: J. C. B. Mohr [Paul Siebeck], 1973), p. 248.

4. For discussion of Paul's use of this text, see J. M. G. Barclay, "'I Will Have Mercy on Whom I Have Mercy': The Golden Calf and Divine Mercy in Romans 9–11 and Second Temple Judaism," *Early Christianity* 1 (2010): 82-106.

5. In this respect, it is misleading to suggest that Paul defends God's faithfulness to Is-

which are here cited in their thickest concentration. Romans 9–11 spells out the means by which those promises are fulfilled, both for Israel and for the Gentiles, and in both cases in Christ (cf. 15:7-13). Throughout Romans, Paul has made clear that the Christ-event can be properly understood only with reference to Israel: the priority of the Jews has been repeatedly affirmed (1:16; 2:9-10; 3:1-8), while the current dynamics of faith have been traced to the foundational story of Abraham (4:1-25).[6] If our reading of Galatians is correct, there are hints even in that letter that the Jewish "we" is of special significance in the unfolding of redemption (Gal 4:1-6), which remains incomplete without mercy on "the Israel of God" (Gal 6:16; see above, 13.3.3). In Romans 9–11, such hints become statements, and structural features of Pauline theology become fully evident for the first time. Paul's discussion of Israel is not the residue of an ethnic bias, nor an illustration of a "doctrine" of justification independently deduced.[7] If Paul cannot make sense of what is happening to Israel through the Christ-event, he cannot make sense of history, Scripture, or Christ at all.

That all this should matter to Paul in Romans fits his purpose in writing (see above, 15.3). Preparing for his arrival in Rome, Paul needs to portray his message and his role as "apostle to the Gentiles" on a large canvas: the Roman believers need to know the purpose of his ministry and its place within the total design of God. His presentation of himself as both an Israelite (11:1) and an apostle to the Gentiles (11:13) is of a piece with the fact that his good news is the power of God for salvation "for both the Jew, first, and the Greek" (1:16). In fact, it is just here, where Paul places the Christ-event on the widest historical horizon, that he speaks most intensely of *himself* (9:1-3; 10:1-2; 11:1, 13-14).

---

rael in order to support the confident assertions of Romans 8 (Cranfield, *Romans*, vol. 2, pp. 446-47). Wolter rightly insists that Paul is concerned with Israel's relationship to God for its own sake, and not just to confirm God's faithfulness to his promises for the sake of Christian believers (M. Wolter, "Das Israelproblem nach Gal 4,21-31 und Röm 9–11," *ZTK* 107 [2010]: 1-30, at pp. 20-21). Romans 9–11 does not merely supplement what is said elsewhere about Christ, but provides the explanatory frame without which God's incongruous grace in Christ appears arbitrary.

6. On the thick verbal and thematic links between Romans 9–11 and the rest of Romans, see C. Stenschke, "Römer 9–11 als Teil des Römerbriefes," in Wilk and Wagner, eds., *Between Gospel and Election*, pp. 197-225.

7. For the older psychological explanation of these chapters as the product of Paul's patriotism, see the citation of A. von Harnack (1911), in Haacker, "Thema," pp. 70-71. Käsemann displays the tendency in twentieth-century Lutheranism to treat Romans 9–11 as an illustration of the doctrine of justification, with Israel representing the faults of "the religious man": see Käsemann, *Römer*, pp. 250, 256, 272, etc. Cf. his "Paul and Israel," in *New Testament Questions of Today* (London: SCM, 1969), pp. 183-87 ("in and with Israel he strikes at the hidden Jew in all of us," p. 186); see further above, 3.5.3.

This may reflect apologetic concerns — Paul's oath in 9:1-2 may counter the impression that he no longer cares about Israel[8] — but there is also a positive reason: he understands his own work as integral to God's purposes both for Gentiles and for Jews (11:11-15). His ambition to provoke his fellow Jews to jealousy (11:14) may seem unrealistic in hindsight, but it is clear that Paul could make sense of his life only in the context of God's promises to Israel. The temptation to regard Israel as a relic of the past, now supplanted by the Gentile church (11:17-24), may have been acute among Gentile believers in Rome (cf. 14:1–15:13), but the phenomenon was probably common wherever the Gentile mission was accompanied by (and itself evoked) the self-distancing of Jews.[9] That Paul combats this tendency and, against the evidence, insists that the future will include the salvation of Israel (11:25-32) reflects more than merely his disgust at Gentile "anti-Judaism." It demonstrates his conviction that without the salvation of Israel the history of the world would make no sense at all.

The burden of this chapter is to show that Paul makes sense of Scripture, of Israel, of the present crisis, of the Gentile mission, and of God's purposes for the future *by finding in all these interlinked phenomena the paradoxical operation of God's incongruent grace.* As these chapters unfold, Paul indicates that, from the start, Israel has been constituted by the purposes of a divine election that pays no regard to criteria of fittingness or worth (9:6-29). God's "calling" has never been coterminous with, or limited to, the physical descendants of Abraham, and God's sole prerogative to "have mercy on whom he has mercy" has ensured the survival of Israel by rendering it radically dependent on God's selective will. In a second step (9:30–10:21), Paul indicates how the present conditions in the wake of the Christ-event are characterized by a similar pattern of incongruity. In the role reversals between Gentiles and Jews, the expected criteria of correspondence between human worth and divine reward do not apply. In fact, Christ creates a stumbling block for anything other than radical dependence, in faith, on the righteousness and power of God. Finally, in projecting his vision to the future (11:1-32), Paul finds in the success of the Gentile mission evidence of God's unrestricted "wealth," and thus the grounds for confidence that God's mercy on Israel will not be limited to the selection of a remnant, while hardening the rest. Rather, the incongruous grace that has sustained Israel from the start will effect the

8. As Watson suggests, it is possible that Paul was accused of responsibility for the current crisis for Israel, since the success of his Gentile mission generally forfeited Jewish goodwill (*Paul, Judaism, and the Gentiles*, pp. 306-7).

9. From a time only shortly after Romans, the Gospel of Mark (12:1-11) appears to suggest that the legacy of salvation has passed from Israel to Gentile believers; Ephesians 2:11-22 may be designed to counter this already widespread impression.

reconstitution of Israel as a whole, since God's mercy on the *disobedient* has the capacity to encompass all.

By tracing through each section of these chapters the paradoxical working of an unconditioned grace, I will attempt to show the consistency of a textual unit that scholars are liable to consider fundamentally incoherent. Interpreters as diverse as H. Räisänen, J. Lambrecht, and T. Donaldson fragment these chapters into a series of mutually incompatible theses, with Paul trying out one explanation after another without logical or sequential coherence.[10] "Tensions" are discovered here between divine determinism and human free will, and between God's impartiality and his faithfulness to Israel; but the chief flaw in the coherence of these chapters is taken to be an unanticipated turn in Romans 11 (at either 11:1 or 11:11). As Donaldson summarizes the matter, "while in 9:1–11:10 the thrust of the argument is that the present situation is in no way inconsistent with God's promises to Israel, the argument from 11:11 proceeds on the assumption that the present situation has to be overcome if God is to be proved faithful."[11] The following analysis is intended to show that Paul's hope for Israel in 11:11-32 is not the product of a sudden change of heart from a previously settled opinion that God's promises to "Israel" are limited in scope to a believing remnant, but the development of the same pattern of reasoning that had characterized 9:1–11:10. Both before and after 11:11, Paul traces the incongruity of the mercy of God: the root on which Israel's existence depends is currently revealed in the paradoxical conditions of belief and unbelief, and its purpose will be fulfilled when the momentum of God's "wealth," extended to the Gentiles, incorporates the disobedient in the salvation of all Israel.

The incongruity of grace finds expression in these chapters in multiple rhetorical forms. The mismatch between divine call and human condition is sometimes expressed through rhetorical exclusion, a "not . . . but" that rules out a possible configuration of fit between God's merciful action and the worth

10. Räisänen, "Paul, God, and Israel"; cf. idem, "Römer 9–11: Analyse eines geistigen Ringes," *ANRW* 2.25.4, pp. 2891-2939; J. Lambrecht, "Israel's Future according to Romans 9–11: An Exegetical and Hermeneutical Approach," in *Pauline Studies* (Leuven: Peeters, 1994), pp. 34-54; T. Donaldson, "'Riches for the Gentiles' (Rom 11:12): Israel's Rejection and Paul's Gentile Mission," *JBL* 12 (1993): 81-98. Those who maintain the consistency of Romans 9–11 are sometimes dependent on implausible exegesis. For example, Wright defends their coherence by taking "all Israel" (11:26) to mean all Jewish *and Gentile* believers; see N. T. Wright, *The Climax of the Covenant* (Edinburgh: T&T Clark, 1991), pp. 231-57; idem, "The Letter to the Romans," in *The New Interpreter's Bible*, vol. 10 (Nashville: Abingdon Press, 2002), pp. 620-99. This has not won wide acceptance since it gives little substance to the "fullness" and "acceptance" of Israel mentioned in 11:12, 15, or to the contrast between the hardening of the part of Israel and the salvation of the whole in 11:25-26 (where "Israel" can hardly have two different referents).

11. Donaldson, "Riches for the Gentiles," p. 89.

of the recipient.[12] This is the dominant feature of 9:6-18 (e.g., 9:8, 12, 16), but it occurs also later in 10:6-8 ("do not say . . . but what does it say?") and 11:5-6. A second and associated rhetorical pattern is the denial of difference, as in statements that emphasize "all" (10:11-13) or disregard normal differentiation by insisting on a "not only . . . but also" (9:24). Thirdly, these chapters are replete with rhetorical reversals, where the lesser, the few, the disqualified, and the "unnatural" are the object of God's incongruous action (e.g., 9:12, 24-26, 30; 11:17-24), while the greater, the many, and the "natural" are excluded, disqualified, or cut off (e.g., 9:27, 31-33; 10:21; 11:17-24). This rhetoric of reversal is particularly powerful where symmetry creates a neat inversion: the non-competitors reach the goal, while the runners fail (9:30-32); the wild olive branches are grafted in while natural olive branches are cut off (11:17-24).[13] All these devices serve to point up the incongruity between the mercy or grace of God and the status or worth of its recipients. The achievement of Romans 9–11 is to demonstrate that this incongruity has all along been basic to the identity of Israel, that it is presently at work in the puzzling impact of the good news, and that it will finally determine the future of Israel and of the world.

17.2. The Creation of Israel by the Incongruity of Grace (Romans 9:6-29)

As is generally agreed, Romans 9:6-29 constitutes the first step in the argument of Romans 9–11, and its headline statement is given at its start: "it is certainly not that the word of God has fallen" (9:6a).[14] But the interpretation of what follows hinges on identifying the logical connection between this statement and the second half of this verse, "for it is not the case that all who are descended from Israel are Israel" (9:6b), which leads into the subsequent discussion of election. In recent years, 9:6-29 has come to be read as a demonstration that

12. On this form of Pauline argumentation, see F. Siegert, *Argumentation bei Paulus, gezeigt an Röm 9–11* (Tübingen: Mohr Siebeck, 1985), pp. 182-85.

13. The motif of reversal that permeates these chapters is well noted by S. Grindheim, *The Crux of Election: Paul's Critique of the Jewish Confidence in the Election of Israel* (Tübingen: Mohr Siebeck, 2005), pp. 136-68.

14. The Greek οὐχ οἷον gives particular emphasis to the following denial ("it is certainly not"). Paul does not raise this topic in a form of a rhetorical question (cf. 11:1): his first task is not to answer questions (real or imagined) but to lay down non-negotiable foundations for the discussion to follow. On the internal structure of Romans 9–11, see F. Wilk, "Rahmen und Aufbau von Römer 9–11," in Wilk and Wagner, eds., *Between Gospel and Election*, pp. 227-53. Wilk's conclusions slightly modify the typical three-part division of Paul's argument (9:6-29; 9:30–10:21; 11:1-32), which I follow here.

God's "word" concerns, and has only ever concerned, a selective portion of "Israelites"; thus, the present situation, where only a small number of Jews believe, does not disconfirm God's faithfulness to his word. On this reading, 9:6b supports 9:6a by indicating the limited scope of God's word, which concerns only an "Israel" within "Israel." The following scriptural examples offer typological correspondences with the present division between believing and unbelieving Jews: just as God distinguished between Isaac and Ishmael, Jacob and Esau, Moses and Pharaoh, so he calls some (believing Jews) and rejects others (unbelieving Jews).[15] According to this reading, Paul can affirm that God's word has not failed because God's promises were never directed to more than a remnant; a present reduction of "Israel" to Christ-believers alone is not the denial but the fulfillment of his "word."[16] So long as some Jews believe, that is enough for God and (at this point in the argument) enough for Paul.

Despite its popularity, this reading is beset with problems. For a start, it makes incomprehensible the continuation of Paul's argument in the rest of Romans 9–11, Paul's prayer for the salvation of his (supposedly non-elect) kinsmen (10:1-2), and his hope for the salvation of all Israel in 11:11-32. If the present reduction of Israel is all that God's word intended, why should Paul expect more in the future?[17] It is striking that the terms Paul uses in this opening argument reappear later, but on the reading just summarized with wholly

15. See, e.g., N. Dahl, "The Future of Israel," in *Studies in Paul* (Minneapolis: Fortress Press, 1977), pp. 137-58, at pp. 144-45; H. Hübner, *Gottes Ich und Israel: Zum Schriftgebrauch des Paulus in Römer 9–11* (Göttingen: Vandenhoeck & Ruprecht, 1984), p. 45; D. Moo, "The Theology of Romans 9–11," in D. M. Hay and E. E. Johnson, eds., *Pauline Theology*, vol. 3: *Romans* (Minneapolis: Fortress Press, 1995), pp. 240-58, at pp. 252-53. The wide currency of this reading is indicated by its adoption by readers as diverse as H. Räisänen and R. B. Hays: both take Paul to imply an equation between the unbelieving majority of Israel and Ishmael, Esau, and Pharaoh: see Räisänen, "Paul, God, and Israel," pp. 181-84; R. B. Hays, *Echoes of Scripture in the Letters of Paul* (New Haven: Yale University Press, 1989), p. 67.

16. Räisänen takes Paul's logic thus: "Because the majority of Israel never belonged to the elect, God's promise is not affected by the unbelief of empirical Israel" ("Paul, God, and Israel," p. 182); he thus takes Paul's later expectation of the salvation of "all Israel" as a self-contradiction. Hays adopts a very similar position, though he prefers to present Paul's logic as "dialectical" rather than contradictory: "if in Romans 9–10 Paul deconstructs Scripture's witness to Israel's favored status, Romans 11 dialectically deconstructs the deconstructive reading" (*Echoes of Scripture*, p. 67).

17. With characteristic attention to logic, Räisänen insists that (on his reading of Romans) there was no need for Paul to carry on after 9:29 ("Paul, God, and Israel," pp. 184-85). When Paul offers hope for all Israel in 11:11-32, he introduces something new: "God has not rejected his people. . . . Instead, Paul has rejected the thrust of his argument begun in 9.6" (p. 189). Finding a similar mismatch between the start and the end of Paul's discourse (which is united only by a single pragmatic intent), Watson suggests that "Paul himself does not know exactly

different reference. In Romans 9:6-29, God's "elect" (9:12) are (on this reading) current Jewish believers, whom he "calls" (9:7, 24) and "loves" (9:13), and upon whom he exercises mercy (9:15). But in 11:11-32, these same terms are applied to "all Israel," whose call is irrevocable (11:29), who are loved because of the patriarchs (11:28), and who are and will be the objects of God's mercy (11:31-32). In one case, God calls a select few within Israel, and that is enough to satisfy God's fidelity; in the other, this is by no means enough, and Paul looks *beyond* the partial hardening of Israel to the salvation of all (11:25-26). In 9:6 (on this reading), "Israel" is defined in a restricted sense, while in the rest of Romans 9–11 (9:3, 27, 31; 10:21; 11:1, 2, 7, 25, 26), "Israel" is used for Israel as a whole, and "Israelite" has no restricted meaning.[18] To find typological correspondence between the scriptural characters of Romans 9 and the present division within Israel is also problematic: nothing in Romans suggests that unbelieving Jews are to be considered equivalent to Ishmael, Esau, or Pharaoh. The distinctions that Paul recounts in 9:6-18 occur during moments in the *creation of Israel;* they do not represent distinctions within Israel's ranks. Moreover, on the one occasion when a scriptural citation in 9:6-29 is related to the present, the text is taken to refer not (or not only) to Jews, but to Gentiles (9:24-26).

Since following this interpretative path creates so many anomalies, we should ask if we have started in the right direction. It seems better to read 9:6b and the following verses as intended not to justify God's selection *within Israel* but to clarify *the grounds on which Israel as a nation was created and selected.*[19] Paul's confidence that God's word has not fallen is supported by the fact that God has created Israel, from the beginning, by a unique process of election, selection, and unconditioned mercy. That "not all who are descended from Israel are Israel" (9:6b) indicates that Israel has been constituted, at base, not by ethnic descent but by divine election. An Israel so formed, without regard to human qualification, will hardly be abandoned, because God has created it through his own promise and according to his own purpose. Paul's purpose in these verses is not to justify the status quo (the division within Israel be-

---

where his argument will take him" (*Paul, Judaism, and the Gentiles,* p. 322; cf. pp. 334-35 on the shift in Romans 11).

18. For the reading of "Israel" in 9:6 as Jewish believers, see, e.g., Hübner, *Gottes Ich,* pp. 17, 27-28; J. A. Fitzmyer, *Romans* (New York: Doubleday, 1993), p. 560. It is notable, however, that 9:6-29 is devoid of references to faith.

19. See H.-M. Lübking, *Paulus und Israel in Römerbrief* (Frankfurt: Peter Lang, 1986), pp. 61-66, rightly insisting that the weight of emphasis in 9:6-13 lies on the character of God's election (vv. 11-12), establishing "Gottes Verheissung und freie Erwählung als exklusiven Grund für die Teilhabe am wahren Israel" (p. 61). Cf. M. Rese, "Israel und Kirche in Römer 9," *NTS* 34 (1988): 208-17, at p. 212.

tween those who do and those who do not believe in Christ), but to trace the pattern of God's creative grace in the formation and history of Israel, and thus to establish the scriptural grounds for confidence regarding Israel in the wake of the Christ-event and the Gentile mission. If Paul can show that Israel was formed through an unconditioned mercy attributable to God and God alone, he can look beyond the present divinely created hardening to a future divinely established mercy. On this understanding, the repetition of key terms in 11:28-32, noted above, represents not a blatant contradiction but a confirmation of Israel's original constitution in the final resolution of Israel's plight.

Recent structural analysis of Romans 9:6-29 has highlighted its careful arrangement.[20] First, 9:6-18 contains three examples of selection (Isaac as a child of promise; Jacob over Esau; mercy for Moses, hardening for Pharaoh), with a repeated "not . . . but" refrain (9:6, 7, 12, 16). The third example is then expanded by the potter-analogy to clarify that the responsibility in selection is God's alone (9:19-23), before a return to scriptural texts indicates that God's purpose of unconditioned choice is capable of creating a people from "no-people" Gentiles (9:24-26) and to select in Israel a remnant, as a two-sided symbol of judgment and hope (9:27-29). Whether one identifies in this passage the flow of a historical sequence from Abraham to the exile, or a collection of witnesses from "the law and the prophets" (cf. 3:21), the artful construction of this passage requires that we pay attention both to the texts cited (and adjusted) and to the patterns of divine activity that they express.[21]

The crucial issue in 9:6-18 is not *whom* God has chosen (and whom he has left out), nor simply *that* he has exercised his choice. The emphasis lies on *how* God has chosen Israel, with repeated antitheses ("not . . . but") designed to exclude from the reckoning multiple criteria that might have influenced God's choice.[22] That "not all who are descended from Israel are Israel" (9:6b)

20. See, for example, J.-N. Aletti, "L'argumentation paulinienne en Rm 9," *Biblica* 68 (1987): 41-56; Watson, *Paul, Judaism, and the Gentiles*, pp. 308-22.

21. Wright suggests that Paul here tells the story of Israel from Abraham to the exile, with Israel progressively narrowed down until it forms only a remnant ("Romans," p. 634). This serves his thesis that Israel was finally represented by a single figure, the Messiah (p. 645), but the presence of Gentile believers in 9:24-26 does not fit this trajectory well. Watson suggests that the texts in 9:6-29 follow first a narrative and then a prophetic sequence (*Paul, Judaism, and the Gentiles*, pp. 317-19); cf. Aletti, "L'argumentation," p. 44, tracing a historical sequence from Abraham to Paul's present.

22. So, rightly, J. D. G. Dunn, *Romans 9–16* (Waco: Word, 1988), p. 543: "the issue is how God's purpose of election comes into effect." This is also underlined by Piper, whose emphasis on God's "sovereign freedom" is characteristic of the Calvinist tradition (see above, 3.4.4); see J. Piper, *The Justification of God: An Exegetical and Theological Study of Romans 9:1-23*, 2nd ed. (Grand Rapids: Baker Academic, 1993).

is explicated in 9:7: not all Abraham's children qualify as his "seed," but "in Isaac shall your seed be called" (9:7; Gen 21:12).[23] "Calling" here means neither "naming" nor "summons"; as we have seen (4:17), it is Paul's weighty term for God's creative word, which fashions what it promises (cf. 9:12, 24, 25, 26; 11:29).[24] Paul draws a lesson from the text with an antithetical contrast (οὐ . . . ἀλλά): "that is, it is not the children of the flesh who are the children of God, but the children of the promise are reckoned as seed" (9:8; cf. Gal 4:21-31). This rules out one means of construing the mechanism of election: it does not operate by natural descent (by lineage, genealogy, ethnicity, or biological connection). As biblically literate readers would know, Ishmael was also a son of Abraham, but he was not thereby qualified for election. Standing in contrast to "children of the flesh" is the perplexing locution "children of the promise." The importance of this phrase is underlined when Paul introduces the promise to Sarah (Gen 18:10, 14) by "this word is (a word) of promise" (9:9; λόγος echoes 9:6). What constitutes Isaac as the "seed" (or the "child of God," 9:8) is simply that God has promised him to be such. This is a divine decision alone ("I will return and there will be . . ."), corresponding to no intrinsic endowment in Isaac or in his parents. It projects a forthcoming reality (note the future tenses in 9:7, 9), recognizing not what has already been established, but what will be, in a future created by God. Isaac's status thus represents what is ascribed (λογίζεται, 9:8) by God, in a form and time frame that elude correspondence with inherent or pre-existing criteria.

Paul's second example, the choice of Jacob over Esau (9:10-13), tightens the analysis by removing factors that might have skewed God's choice in the first. In this case, the choice is made between two sons who were born of the same mother as well as the same father, and were even conceived at the same moment, thus ruling out *every* differential in their conditions of birth (9:10). But here Paul notes what he could have noted in the case of Isaac, that the de-

23. The Greek οὐδέ at the start of 9:7 suggests a close match between 9:6b and 9:7; the discussion of birth in the latter makes clear that ἐξ Ἰσραήλ in 9:6 means not "from within Israel" but "descended from Israel." The preposition ἐκ in the context of ethnicity signals descent elsewhere, in 9:5, 10; 11:1 (cf. Phil 3:5); only when governed by a verb does it have a partitive sense (e.g., Rom 9:24; Rev 7:4-8). Thus, 9:6b is not to be taken as a denial that all *within* (the present) Israel are (truly) Israel, but as a denial that Israel has been constituted by ethnic descent: from the beginning, God selected among the patriarchs' "children of the flesh" (9:8). The examples that Paul chooses indicate the selection of the Israelite lineage from a wider pool of patriarchal children ("not all descended from Israel constitute Israel"). The choice of Jacob over Esau was not a choice among "Israelites" but the determination of who would form the Israelite line.

24. See B. R. Gaventa, "On the Calling-into-Being of Israel: Romans 9.6-29," in Wilk and Wagner, eds., *Between Gospel and Election*, pp. 255-69. Cf. the discussion of Galatians 1:6, 15, above (12.2 and 12.3).

cision of election was made by God before birth and thus before the children could have done anything — good or bad — that might qualify or disqualify them for election (9:11). The antithesis expressed within this example (another οὐ . . . ἀλλά) is "not from works (οὐκ ἐξ ἔργων) but from the one who calls" (ἀλλ' ἐκ τοῦ καλοῦντος, 9:12), placing emphasis again on the creative initiative of God.[25] That initiative is also underlined in the purpose clause awkwardly embedded in 9:11: ἵνα ἡ κατ' ἐκλογὴν πρόθεσις τοῦ θεοῦ μένῃ ("in order that the pre-choice of God, in accordance with election, might stand firm"). All the emphasis lies on God's choice and predetermination (the προ- prefix signals divine priority), and what is noticeably absent is any corresponding condition in the humans concerned. As if to exclude yet one more option, Paul cites the divine pronouncement that "the greater shall serve the lesser" (Gen 25:23); in context, the terms designate age, but differentials of status of many sorts are also included, and declared irrelevant to God's choice. Hammering home his point, Paul finishes this step in the argument with the brutal statement of Malachi: "Jacob I loved, but Esau I hated" (9:13; Mal 1:2-3). Just that: no explanation, no rationale, nothing to indicate why one and not the other.[26]

Thus, Paul has ruled out numerous qualifying criteria for divine selection: birth (natural rights of descent), status (comparative "greatness"), and practice ("works"), all forms of symbolic capital humanly ascribed or achieved. The radicality of this emphasis is best appreciated by its contrast with Philo's treatment of the same or similar cases, which we analyzed in detail above (see 6.3). Puzzled by cases in which God appears to distribute rewards without reason, or even before birth, Philo is at pains to insist that there *is* always a reason for divine selection, even if only in God's foreknowledge of character, as evidenced in his attribution of names (*Leg.* 3.65-100).[27] Philo's anxiety on this point is characteristic: his aim is not to *dilute* the gifts and the grace of God, but to *explain* them, to offer a rationale that prevents God's choice from appearing arbitrary or unfair. For Philo there must be something about the

25. It seems unconvincing to restrict "works" here to "works of the Law" (*pace* Dunn, *Romans 9–16*, p. 543); the preceding reference to "doing anything, good or bad" (9:11) and the examples chosen (before the arrival of the Law, Rom 5:13-14) indicate that Paul is ruling out the significance of *any* human activity, in virtue or vice, as qualifications for divine election.

26. As Jewett notes, "The quotation fulfils a vital rhetorical function of sharpening to an excruciating degree the focus on the selectivity of God's word" (R. Jewett, *Romans* [Minneapolis: Fortress Press, 2007], p. 508).

27. For fuller comparison between Paul and Philo at this point, see J. M. G. Barclay, "Grace within and beyond Reason: Philo and Paul in Dialogue," in P. Middleton, A. Paddison, and K. Wenell, eds., *Paul, Grace, and Freedom: Essays in Honour of John K. Riches* (London: T&T Clark, 2009), pp. 9-21.

objects of God's choice that fits them to be chosen, even if that quality is itself created by God.[28] To assert otherwise is to bring into question the justice of God — which is exactly the question Paul raises in 9:14 ("is there injustice with God?"). Here, as in 3:1-8, Paul is consciously walking a risky path. That he nonetheless continues on this track is a sign that his understanding of Israel is staked on the outrageous claim that its election is justified by nothing outside of the will of God himself.

In the following verses (9:15-18), Paul advances a third example of divine selection, and cites God's programmatic promise in the aftermath of the Golden Calf: "I will have mercy on whom I have mercy, and I will have compassion on whom I have compassion" (9:15; Exod 33:19). The citation is simultaneously hopeful — if God will be merciful, as he was to Israel at Sinai, there is a path beyond deserved judgment — and strangely disorientating.[29] The text pointedly refuses to specify *to whom* God will be merciful (thus removing the possibility of identifying who is suited to such mercy), and it is phrased, like those in 9:7-9, in the divine first person singular and the future tense, directing the reader to a divine will that is unknown and in principle unknowable. That this disorientation is intended is indicated by another οὐ . . . ἀλλά antithesis, which draws the lesson from 9:15: οὐ τοῦ θέλοντος οὐδὲ τοῦ τρέχοντος, ἀλλὰ τοῦ ἐλεῶντος θεοῦ ("it is not of the one who wills, nor of the one who runs, but of the God who has mercy," 9:16). Two other possible elements in human worth are here ruled out: human will (motivation or disposition) and human success ("running"; cf. 1 Cor 9:24, 27; Phil 2:16). The only factor at work in God's mercy is God's mercy itself. Conversely — and here Paul indicates that his shock tactics are not over — there is God's word to Pharaoh, that God has raised him up to show God's power, so that God's name may be announced throughout the world (9:17; Exod 9:16 adapted). How those purposes will be achieved (and where and how that power will be salvific, cf. Rom 1:16) is not here specified. What strikes us as extraordinary is that the accent falls entirely on God's "I" and God's purpose, with no reference to Pharaoh's history of oppression, his character, or his disposition. That silence leads to Paul's truly scandalous conclusion: "So he has mercy on whom he wills (θέλει), and hardens whom he wills (θέλει)" (9:18).

By removing every element of correspondence between human worth and divine choice, Paul has placed all the emphasis on the divine will; and this,

28. A similar concern is evident in other Jewish texts that explain the choice of Jacob over Esau, the younger over the older: see, e.g., *Jubilees* 19.13-16; Pseudo-Philo, *LAB* 33.5 ("God loved Jacob, but he hated Esau because of his deeds").

29. For discussion of Paul's use of this Exodus text, in comparison with that of other Second Temple Jews, see Barclay, " 'I Will Have Mercy.' "

while shocking to Philo, would not have shocked the authors of the Qumran *Hodayot.* As we have seen (chapter 7), the juxtaposition of the material or moral worthlessness of the human being with the glory and righteousness of God is one of the hallmarks of those hymns. Although Paul does not here wallow in human worthlessness (cf. Rom 3:10-18; 5:12-21; 7:7-25), like the *Hodayot* he figures humanity as "flesh" (9:8) and "clay" (9:20-21), and attributes salvation solely to the mercy of God; his hymn-like conclusion to Romans 9–11 (11:33-36) would have fitted well in the *Hodayot.* As at Qumran, the attribution of saving power to God alone leads Paul toward a form of determinism that traces the dual destinies of human beings to God's action alone. The double predestination depicted in the *Hodayot* had God creating both the righteous and the wicked, preparing the one for "the time of favor," the other for "the day of slaughter"; in both cases this was "so that all may know your glory and your great strength" (1QH^{a} VII.25-33). Paul uses very similar terms in 9:22-23.

Before expounding this duality (9:21-23), Paul interrupts himself, imagining an objector who raises questions about human accountability in the face of the irresistible will of God (9:19). But like the Qumran hymnists, Paul declines to modify his strong statements of divine agency. Rather, he ridicules the very notion of answering back to God (9:20), highlighting the gulf between creature and Creator (the clay and the Potter).[30] Like the authors of the *Hodayot,* Paul raises rhetorical questions that challenge the very possibility of speaking in the presence of God, although his emphasis lies less on the guilt of the human speaker than on the inappropriateness of challenging the will of the Maker. As far as Paul is concerned, the Potter has the right (ἐξουσία) to use his clay as he wills (9:21).

The duality that Paul draws out in these verses is stark but strikingly incomplete. A potter makes one vessel "for honor" and another "for dishonor" (9:21); on the one hand, there are "vessels of wrath prepared for destruction" (σκεύη ὀργῆς κατηρτισμένα εἰς ἀπώλειαν), on the other, "vessels of mercy that [God] has prepared beforehand for glory" (σκεύη ἐλέους, ἃ προητοίμασεν εἰς δόξαν, 9:22-23). The dualism appears quite as stark and as predetermined as at Qumran, with twin fates fixed beforehand by the will of an all-powerful Creator. Yet the fulfillment of these destinies appears curiously unresolved. Of the "vessels of wrath," it is suggested that God wills to "display his wrath and make known his power" (9:22, echoing 9:17, of Pharaoh). Rather than portraying or even anticipating their destruction, Paul is content to say that God

30. As biblical and other Jewish texts indicate, the potter-clay metaphor could be put to varying use (e.g., Isa 29:16; Jer 18:1-6; Sir 33:13; *Wis* 15:7); it is not clear that Paul has any one of these texts particularly in mind.

"has endured them with much patience" (9:22) — a motif one associates more with mercy than with wrath (cf. 2:4). And, notoriously, the whole sentence is syntactically incomplete, lacking an apodosis that would clarify exactly what God will do in relation to these two kinds of "vessel."[31] The sentence tails off in the identification of the "vessels of mercy," the objects of God's calling "not only from the Jews, but also from the Gentiles" (9:24). Paul's eye is drawn not to a double resolution in the destruction of some and the salvation of others, but to God's display of "the wealth of his glory" (ὁ πλοῦτος τῆς δόξης αὐτοῦ, 9:23) in the contemporary and universal reach of the good news, calling Gentiles as much as Jews.

At precisely this point of similarity to the *Hodayot,* a deep structural difference emerges. The Qumran predestinarianism, we may recall, expressed a cosmic plan rooted in the very structures of creation: the twin fates of humanity were a design feature of the universe, and God's mercy on the sectarians represented the outworking of his "selective preference" (רצון), eternally established (see above, 7.4). In Romans 9–11 Paul also speaks of God's "election" (ἐκλογή, 9:11; 11:5, 28), of his "purpose" (πρόθεσις) that "remains" (9:11), and of his "pre-preparation" (προετοιμάζω) of the "vessels of mercy" (9:23; cf. 8:29-30, προορίζω). But this is not here linked with the structures of nature, nor coordinated with the divisions of the cosmos. Rather, the purpose of God is shaped by its *telos,* and the sudden introduction of the Gentiles indicates the importance for Paul of his own experience. Here is a hint, to be later confirmed, that for Paul the structure of God's plan is to be found not in some primordial cosmic design, but in the display of God's "wealth" and "glory" in the worldwide reach of the good news (cf. 10:14-21). God's plan is not a blueprint, but a promise. Those whom God calls are the product not of a pre-determined past, but of a purpose and promise. Because he sees that promise reaching fulfillment in the present, in the event of Christ and in the Gentile mission, Paul's theology of election is *teleological,* shaped by a sense of purpose.[32] What is more, the "wealth" of the present provides Paul with a pointer to the direction intended by the will of God.

The appearance of the Gentiles in 9:24-26 is good evidence that the topic of 9:6-29 is not the selection of Israelites within Israel, nor the narrowing of Israel to a tiny remnant. The adaptation of verses from Hosea regarding the

31. For contrasting attempts to resolve this incompleteness, see Wilckens, *Brief an die Römer,* vol. 2, pp. 202-5; J. R. Wagner, *Heralds of the Good News: Isaiah and Paul in Concert in the Letter to the Romans* (Leiden: Brill, 2002), pp. 71-78.

32. For Paul's "shift from symmetry to teleology," inspired by the purpose clause in the scriptural statement about Pharaoh (9:17), see Watson, *Paul, Judaism, and the Gentiles,* pp. 315-17. This teleology is what shapes the final movement of Paul's discourse in Romans 11.

creation ("calling") of a people from those who were "not my people" is the first example of that pattern of reversal that, as we noted above, is characteristic of God's incongruous call. That this calling makes something out of nothing, a "people" out of its opposite, is a sign of its creative ability to turn *any* circumstance to good (cf. 4:17). That the people concerned were not loved or loveable (9:25) indicates that God's calling gives no regard to the worth of its objects. It is no accident that Paul should signal this reversal first in relation to *Gentiles,* reading Hosea in a new referential sense.[33] As we have noted on several occasions, it is the Gentile mission that gives clarity and impetus to Paul's theology of incongruous grace. If Paul's theology legitimates his mission, it is also the case that his mission sharpens and defines his theology, and here confirms that God's call is both creative and unconditioned. Paul's adaptation of Hosea (changing the language of "mercy" to "calling" and "love") creates verbal links back to 9:12-13, but also points forward beyond a fixed binary of "loved"/"hated." If God here calls those who are *not loved,* there is hope beyond the present crisis. As we shall see, it is precisely the "wealth" of mercy that Paul experiences in the Gentile mission that gives him reason to look beyond the present distinction between "the remnant" and "the rest" (11:1-10) and to imagine a future in which even the excluded can be integrated again (11:11-32).

The two Isaiah citations concerning the remnant that conclude this section (9:27-29) speak of both selection and hope. Although the force of the first citation (combining Hos 1:10 with Isa 10:22-23) is open to dispute, its primary theme seems to be the reduction of "the sons of Israel" to a remnant (Rom 9:27-28). However, the second (from Isa 1:9) seems to lean in the opposite direction, with the remnant a sign of God's faithfulness to his people (9:29).[34] This ambiguity, characteristic of the remnant motif in the biblical tradition, fits Paul's purpose in this opening section.[35] What he has traced through 9:6-

33. For close analysis of Paul's adaptations of the Hosea citations, see Wagner, *Heralds of the Good News,* pp. 78-89.

34. See the detailed study in Wagner, *Heralds of the Good News,* pp. 92-116. Wagner argues that both citations from Isaiah are taken by Paul (in the context of 9:24) to promise hope, not condemnation: "Paul invokes Isaiah, not in order to establish the fact that Israel is suffering under God's wrath, but to claim that by calling 'us . . . from among the Jews,' God is faithfully preserving a remnant of Israel and bringing his people's chastisement to an end" (p. 107); cf. E. Seitz, "λογὸν συντελῶν eine Gerichtsankündigung? (Zu Röm 9,27/28)," *BN* 105 (2001): 61-76. For the opposite conclusion, see Grindheim, *The Crux of Election,* pp. 150-56 (with support from many commentators).

35. For the remnant motif as sign of both judgment and hope, see R. Clements, " 'A Remnant Chosen by Grace' (Romans 11:5): The Old Testament Background and Origin of the Remnant Concept," in D. A. Hagner and M. J. Harris, eds., *Pauline Studies* (Grand Rapids: Eerdmans, 1980), pp. 106-21.

29 is not an elaborate typological prefigurement of the present, but a multi-stranded pattern that lays bare the characteristics of Israel's election. This is a people created by divine choice alone, without regard to birth, achievement, disposition, or any other criterion of worth. Their existence dangles solely from the thread of God's purpose, which can exclude or include, jettison or preserve, hate or love — and also love those not loved — calling "children of God" into being by the word of his promise (9:8, 26). Everything is designed to put Israel's past, present, and future into the hands of God, so that when Paul analyzes his present (9:30–10:21) and looks to the future (11:1-32), the primary question is not "what will Israel do?" but "what is God capable of doing?" All these motifs are foundational for the sections that follow, and nothing in the rest of Romans 9–11 will *subtract* from this opening argument on the inexplicable promise of God. The "calling" and the "election" of God are the bedrock of Paul's confidence (11:29), while the motifs of "hardening" (10:19; 11:7-10, 25), "remnant" (11:1-6), works-blind election (11:5-6), and divine embrace of Gentile and Jew (10:12; 11:12, 33) will reverberate throughout the arguments to follow. What Paul sees happening to Israel in his present plays out features of Israel's formation. What he anticipates in its future is the fulfillment of a promise traceable to the very beginning of the Abrahamic family, an election whose momentum he sees reaching its positive *telos* in the wake of the Christ-event.

17.3. God's Incongruous Act in Christ (Romans 9:30–10:21)

The central section of Romans 9–11 (9:30–10:21) is the most difficult to comprehend. Its reference to the contemporary paradox of Gentile faith and Jewish unbelief is clear enough, but Paul's allusions to Christ, the cause of this paradox, are so brief and so heavily encased in scriptural citation that it is easy to lose the line of thought. The traditional reading, according to which Paul underlines the responsibility of Israel to balance his statements about predestination, seems overly beholden to the concerns of Christian dogmatics.[36] But it is also insufficient to suggest that Paul here "pauses in midcourse to describe how Israel has temporarily swerved off the track during an anomalous interval preceding the consummation of God's plan."[37] The Christ-event,

36. Following a "common view," Barrett relates this section to 9:6-29 in the following terms: "The unbelief of Israel may be looked at from two points of view, that of divine election and that of human choice, and Paul looks at it first from the one and then from the other" (C. K. Barrett, "Romans 9.30–10.21: Fall and Responsibility of Israel," in *Essays on Paul* [London: SPCK, 1982], pp. 132-53, at p. 136).

37. *Pace* Hays, *Echoes of Scripture*, p. 75. Moo similarly considers this section "something

the centerpiece of this section (9:33–10:12), is hardly an "anomalous interval." To the contrary, Paul points here to Christ, God's definitive and definitively unconditioned act (his "righteousness" or "wealth," 10:3, 12; cf. 3:21-31; 5:12-21), as the climax of God's purposes for Israel. Puzzling reversals abound: Gentiles succeed without trying, while zealous Israel misses the goal (9:30–10:4); God is found by those who do not seek him, provoking Israel with a "foolish nation" (10:19-21). The single explanation is Christ. Because his wealth is given to all, and requires no condition of worth, he is found by Gentiles who had not started to look; and because this incongruous gift subverts the system of value founded on the Law, it is apt to cause Law-committed Israel to stumble. The good news announces the coming and the resurrection of Christ, whose definitive significance is acknowledged in faith (10:6-10). Since no one was able (and none was required) to trigger this saving event, its wealth is distributed without condition to *all* whose confidence is placed in Christ, both Gentiles and Jews (10:11-12).

A foot-race metaphor dominates the opening of this section (9:30-32; cf. 9:16; Phil 3:12-16); it may continue till 10:4, where "the τέλος of the Law" is perhaps best interpreted as its "goal" or "fulfillment."[38] But the only runners in this race (Israel) have been impeded by a "stone of stumbling" (9:33), and the race has reached a paradoxical moment: the non-competitors (Gentiles), who were not "pursuing righteousness" (9:30), have reached the goal, but the runners (Israel), while pursuing "the Law of righteousness," have not attained to the Law (9:31).[39] Instead, they have stumbled on the stone that God has "laid in

of an excursus from Paul's main argument in chaps. 9–11" (D. Moo, *The Epistle to the Romans* [Grand Rapids: Eerdmans, 1996], p. 618).

38. See the full treatment of this term in R. Badenas, *Christ the End of the Law: Romans 10.4 in Pauline Perspective* (Sheffield: Sheffield Academic Press, 1985); for τέλος as a continuation of the race metaphor, see F. Flückiger, "Christus, des Gesetzes τέλος," *TZ* 11 (1955): 153-57, at p. 154. The meanings of the term may be multiple (just as "end" can mean both termination and goal) and continue to be heavily disputed; many interpreters still insist on the sense "termination," e.g., Dunn, *Romans 9–16*, pp. 589-91; E. Lohse, *Der Brief an die Römer* (Göttingen: Vandenhoeck & Ruprecht, 2003), pp. 291-93. For a recent treatment, supporting the meaning "Ziel" (goal), see F. Avemarie, "Israels rätselhafter Ungehorsam: Römer 10 als Anatomie eines von Gott provozierten Unglaubens," in Wilk and Wagner, eds., *Between Gospel and Election*, pp. 299-320, at pp. 306-15. In a rich essay on this passage, Meyer paraphrases 10:4 as "For the intent and goal of the law, to lead to righteousness for everyone who believes, is (nothing different from) Christ" (P. W. Meyer, "Romans 10:4 and the 'End' of the Law," in *The Word in This World* [Louisville: Westminster John Knox Press, 2004], pp. 78-94, at p. 89).

39. It is striking that Paul makes their goal not "righteousness" but "the Law of righteousness," although the sense of the genitive in the latter phrase is by no means clear. He could not deny that they had attained a certain righteousness, but it was not the real intent of the Law (cf. 3:31; 8:4-5; 10:4, 6-8).

Zion" (9:33), a stone whose composite Isaianic features, echoed in 10:11, point to Christ as the "rock of offense" (cf. Gal 5:11; 1 Cor 1:23).[40] The double effect of the Christ-event — welcomed by Gentiles but offensive to Jews — mirrors Paul's mission experience. But what counts in this context is not their relation to Paul, but their relation to God.

Israel's stumbling is here described in three forms. First, while their zeal is commendable, there is a failure of knowledge or recognition (οὐ κατ' ἐπίγνωσιν, 10:2); they are "ignorant" (ἀγνοοῦντες) of the righteousness of God (10:3). Second, in "seeking to validate their own" righteousness (τὴν ἰδίαν ζητοῦντες στῆσαι), they have not "submitted" to the righteousness of God (10:3).[41] And third, their pursuit of "the Law of righteousness" is conducted not on the basis of faith, but "as if from works" (ὡς ἐξ ἔργων, 9:32). How we interpret these somewhat cryptic remarks is bound to encompass much broader construals of the theology of Paul. A traditional interpretation identifies Paul's target as a religious disposition that seeks to acquire salvation through the performance of good works. Standing in the Lutheran tradition (analyzed above, see 3.3 and 3.5), Käsemann describes Jews as misunderstanding the Law as a "summons to achievement"; in this "perversion of God's will by pious achievement *(Leistungsfrömmigkeit)*" Paul has in mind "the typically Jewish offense."[42] On this reading, "works" refers in general to meritorious good works, and the fundamental sin of Israel (as of humans in general) is the attempt to establish a claim on God that is based on one's own achievements: such presumptuous self-assertion is nothing less than rebellion against God.[43] By contrast, the reading advanced in the "new per-

40. For the Isaianic amalgam here, see Wagner, *Heralds of the Good News,* pp. 126-55. Although the "stone" has been variously interpreted as the Law, the good news, God, or Christ, the last is the most likely reading with hindsight from 10:11.

41. For στῆσαι in the sense of "validate" or "confirm," cf. Romans 14:4; for Paul's use of the verb elsewhere in this sense, see Romans 3:31; 2 Corinthians 13:1. Paul is speaking not of the *achievement* or *creation* of a righteousness of their own, but of the *validation* of what is already in existence, its confirmation as constituting the criterion of worth (cf. *BDAG* s.v.; Jewett, *Romans,* p. 617).

42. Käsemann, *Romans,* pp. 277, 281-82. From a parallel (Reformed) perspective, Cranfield speaks of "their stubborn determination to establish their own righteousness, that is, a righteous status of their own earning" (*Romans,* vol. 2, p. 515); elsewhere he speaks of "works" as "their own meritorious achievement" (p. 547).

43. This interpretation is by no means confined to Protestant interpreters, since its roots lie deep in the theology of Augustine (see above, 3.2). Thus, Byrne writes of 10:3: "The essential contrast lies between God's offer of salvation and human beings' trying to achieve something out of their own resources apart from the Creator" (B. Byrne, *Romans* [Collegeville: Liturgical Press, 1996], pp. 311-12).

spective" takes the "works" here as "works of the Law," with specific reference to the "boundary-markers" that differentiate Jews from Gentiles (see above, 3.6.2). Israel's "own righteousness" is not its self-wrought achievement but its differentiation from others — Israel's "national privilege" in exclusion of Gentiles. On this reading, what Paul critiques is not works-righteousness, but the "national righteousness" that regards the Torah as a "charter of racial privilege."[44]

On any reading, this passage contains multiple echoes of Romans 3–4, and the interpretation here offered will develop our discussion of those chapters (see above, 15.6 and 15.7). We should first note Paul's starting point (9:30): the surprising attainment of righteousness by Gentiles. As evidenced in the Gentile mission, God has considered Gentiles "in the right" (they have "attained righteousness") inasmuch as their identity depends on Christ in faith ("the righteousness by faith"). Although they lacked Jewish descent and the Jewish credentials of righteousness (Torah-observance), God has considered them righteous without regard to such deficiencies; their faith is the evidence that their only basis of worth — their only ground of "boasting" — is what God has done in Christ. To recognize that all that counts is Christ is to "believe in him" (9:33); to discount every other form of symbolic capital is to "submit to the righteousness of God" (10:3). And here, Paul insists, is the challenge of the Christ-event for Jews: it requires the recognition that God pays no regard to their preexisting capital. Paul recognizes this truth in his own life, as he was "called" without regard to his former worth (Gal 1:12-16; Phil 3:3-11). In this letter, he has identified reliance on the gift and power of God as the defining characteristic of the Abrahamic story (Rom 4:1-23). Indeed, from the start, Israel was formed and preserved by the unconditioned grace of God (Rom 9:6-29). What is happening in the Gentile mission reveals a truth that is foundational to the existence and identity of Israel.

When Paul has spoken and acted in such terms, he has been well received by Gentiles. But this "good news" has not been welcomed by the majority of Jews, who have insisted, understandably, that Torah-defined righteousness constitutes a valid criterion of worth for the receipt of God's gifts. To unravel the meaning of 9:30–10:4, we may imagine a dialogue between Paul and non-believing Jews in the following terms:

44. Citations from Wright, *The Climax of the Covenant*, pp. 241-42; cf. Wright, "Romans," pp. 654-55 ("a covenant membership for Jews and Jews alone"); Dunn, *Romans 9–16*, p. 595 ("Israel's claim to a righteousness which was theirs exclusively, shared by no other people, possessed by them alone"); Jewett, *Romans*, p. 618 ("the sense of ethnic or sectarian righteousness claimed by Jewish groups as well as by various other groups in the Mediterranean world").

Paul: "God has acted in Christ with a grace that is wholly unconditioned, without regard to any prior definition of worth. The fact that Gentiles are blessed by God simply as they believe in Christ is the clearest evidence that God's righteousness is operative irrespective of the things we have previously considered of value." [Galatians; Romans 1–5; all of this implied in 9:30]

Unbelieving Jews: "That is scandalous. Surely God takes note of the fact that Gentiles do not observe the Torah, but we do. Such behavior ('works') must be a criterion for the generosity of God: he would hardly give gifts without regard to the worth of his beneficiaries." [9:32]

Paul: "No, it is not on the basis of our actions that God's favor is given: what we have done (or not done) has been shown to be irrelevant. You are impressively zealous for God, but you fail to recognize the righteousness of God enacted in Christ. What God has given in Christ was given irrespective of Torah-observance, and therefore given to all. Our only worth — for Jew and Gentile — is found in Christ. This is the fulfillment of what was envisaged by the Torah. 'He who believes in him will not be put to shame.'" [Rom 9:31-33; 10:2-4]

Unbelieving Jews: "But we insist: God's righteousness surely recognizes that only the righteous are fitted to receive his gifts!"

Paul: "No, to insist on that would be to validate your own righteousness in defiance of the righteousness of God." [Rom 10:3]

What this imagined dialogue intends to bring out is the specificity of Paul's critique of Israel, as well as its far-reaching consequences. Paul's comments do not constitute a general critique of Jewish religiosity, but arise from a specific but momentous juncture in history: he is addressing their reaction to the Christ-event. The runners have tripped because of the "stone of stumbling" (9:32-33), and it is the Christ-event that constitutes this obstacle. Their failure to "submit to the righteousness of God" (10:3) represents not a generic self-confidence in "pious achievement" but a specific failure to recognize that the righteousness of God has been enacted in Christ (10:4). It is *in this context* that the alternative arises between "validating their own righteousness" and "submitting to the righteousness of God." To validate their own righteousness would not be to *substitute* their righteousness for the righteousness of God; it would be to insist that God's righteousness should recognize, as its fitting object, the righteousness defined in their own, Torah-based terms. The Jews here criticized hold to the reasonable assumption that God's righteousness is not indiscriminate. But Paul insists that it has been displayed in Christ without regard to worth (3:21-26), and in this context to validate one's own righteousness (as a proper qualification for the receipt of divine gifts) constitutes a refusal to submit to the righteousness of God. In God's blessing and transformation of Gentile believers, it is obvious that the righteousness of God pays no regard to Torah-obedience. Torah-observance is not wrong; it is simply irrelevant to the righteousness of God in Christ.

Once again, it is the Gentile mission that both catalyzes and clarifies Paul's theology; the "new perspective" is correct to locate Paul's theology of Law and righteousness in this social and historical context. However, "their own righteousness" is criticized by Paul not for its restriction to "Jews and Jews alone" (Wright); in 10:3, its opposite is not a "non-Jewish righteousness" but "the righteousness of God" (cf. Phil 3:9).[45] Because God has acted in Christ in unconditioned grace, the value of "their own righteousness" must be discounted as the Gentile mission makes unmistakably clear. If Paul disregards ethnic distinctions, this is because God's righteousness recognizes *no* preexistent criteria of worth.

Thus, the foil to Paul's theology is not a human self-righteousness that attempts to earn salvation, but the natural assumption that when God acts in saving benevolence, he distributes his gifts to those we consider fitting or worthy. In the previous section (Rom 9:6-29), Paul had done his best to clarify that this is *not* how Israel was created and called. Here he draws on motifs from that earlier passage ("not of works" and "not of the one who runs," 9:12, 16), singling out the practice of the Law ("works"), since it was in its praxis that the superiority of the Jewish tradition seemed most evident.[46] As we have seen, the assumption that God's mercy or benevolence would be exercised on the

45. Paul's phraseology may echo the contrast in Deuteronomy 9:4-6 between "your righteousness" and the faithfulness of God (cf. Deut 8:17-18), especially since Deuteronomy 9:4 has influenced the wording of the citation from Deuteronomy 30 in 10:6 ("Do you say in your heart . . .").

46. The connection with 9:12 is noted by Westerholm, who rightly underlines Paul's insistence that the free operation of grace is "independent of" and "apart from" human performance; see S. Westerholm, "Paul and the Law in Romans 9–11," in J. D. G. Dunn, ed., *Paul and the Mosaic Law* (Tübingen: Mohr Siebeck, 1996), pp. 215-37. Westerholm takes this contrast between "grace" and "works" to represent a larger antithesis between the sovereignty of God and human initiative ("God is the only effective Actor," p. 235). On my reading, "works" represent not human initiative but the display of human worth as defined by criteria other than God's. Thus, the central question is not "do we trust in God or in our own efforts?" but "is God's saving action given to those we define as worthy, or without regard to worth?" Then, it is not Israel's "effort" that is the object of critique ("Israel's efforts at securing good standing with God," p. 233), but Israel's assumption that Torah-observers are the fitting recipients of the beneficence of God. Paul's target is not the achievement of worth in working, but the criteria by which worth is defined.

"righteous" was core to several (though not all) of our Second Temple texts (Part II). *4 Ezra* wrestles with the extent and character of the mercy of God, but finally concludes that only the righteous can receive the merciful judgement of God: as Uriel says (on God's behalf), "I will not concern myself about the fashioning of those who have sinned, or about their death, their judgment, or their destruction, but I will rejoice over the creation of the righteous, over their pilgrimage also, and their salvation, and their receiving their reward" (8.38-39). As the final scene of *4 Ezra* makes clear, it is those who have proved themselves righteous in obedience to the Torah who "after death shall obtain mercy" (14.27-35), since God's just governance of the cosmos requires that his Torah be vindicated and confirmed. Philo similarly upholds the moral structure of the cosmos and is at pains to point out that the gifts of God are given to the worthy, those who follow God, turning from passion and vice to the pursuit of virtue (*Abr.* 200–204). This is not a soteriology of "pious achievement," but simply the assumption that God's saving benevolence will be congruent with the worth of its recipients. As Philo sums up the scriptural rewards, "these are the blessings invoked upon good men, who fulfill the laws by their works (τοὺς νόμους ἔργοις ἐπιτελούντων) — which blessings will be accomplished by the grace of the gift-loving God (χάριτι τοῦ φιλοδώρου θεοῦ), who glorifies and rewards what is noble because of its likeness to himself" (*Praem.* 126).

Paul opposes this reasonable construal of divine gift because he thinks that God has acted in Christ in a way that draws no distinction between "the righteous" and "the unrighteous": "works" are irrelevant to the elective purposes of God (cf. 9:12). The extraordinary effects of preaching Christ in the Gentile world have convinced Paul that "the righteousness from faith" in Christ is not the same as "the righteousness from the Torah." The latter is straightforward in its assumption that Torah-practice is the pre-condition for "life" (10:5; cf. Gal 3:12); the former (which is actually the "goal" of the Torah, 10:4) arises from the announcement that life has already been given in God's raising of Jesus from the dead (10:6-8).[47] In Paul's remarkable reconfiguration of Deuteronomy 30:12-14, a statement about the ease of Torah-practice becomes a ban on imagining that the Christ-event is dependent on a human condition.[48]

47. With many commentators (e.g., Wilckens, *Brief an die Römer*, vol. 2, p. 224), I read 10:5-6 to express a contrast between righteousness ἐκ τοῦ νόμου and righteousness ἐκ πίστεως (cf. 4:14-16; Gal 3:11-12), despite the eloquent pleas to the contrary by Hays, *Echoes of Scripture*, pp. 75-77. A strong case for reading an antithesis between the text of Moses and "the word of faith" is advanced by F. Watson, *Paul and the Hermeneutics of Faith* (London: T&T Clark, 2004), pp. 315-41.

48. For Paul's adaptation of his source, see Wagner, *Heralds of the Good News*, pp. 159-66. Although the imagined ascents and descents are sometimes represented as a "quest," their ob-

The Deuteronomic statement ("it is not . . .") is turned into a prohibited idea ("Do not think in your heart . . ."), to sharpen another "not . . . but" antithesis (10:6, 8; cf. 9:7-8, 12, 16). What is to be resisted is the notion that the Christ-gift requires some precondition to enable his presence ("to bring him down") or to effect his resurrection ("to bring him up from the dead").[49] The gift has, in fact, already been given (Rom 8:32), and in the resurrection of Jesus ("for our justification," 4:25), the saving power of God has already been enacted.

Paul's preaching elicits faith (10:8, 16-17) because it evokes the recognition that God has taken the definitive, unconditioned initiative in Christ. In confessing that "Jesus is Lord" and believing that God has raised him from the dead (10:9) believers stake their all on this saving event, and recognize that they are henceforth wholly dependent on the resurrection life of Christ (cf. 6:1-13). In "calling on the name of the Lord" (10:13; i.e., in making this self-involving confession of faith), they recognize and experience God's saving "wealth" in Christ (10:12).[50] This wealth, because it depends on no human condition and matches no human qualification, is distributed without discrimination to Jew and Gentile alike (10:12-13). In the paradoxical circumstances of the present, where God is found by those who never sought him (10:20) and Israel denies God's saving embrace (10:21), Paul finds an anomaly predicted by both Moses and Isaiah (Deut 32:21; Isa 65:1-2). But these reversals take their current, climactic form in the wake of Christ, since the good news involves the recognition that the only source of value is the unconditioned gift of Christ. Offensive as this is to the value system suggested by the Law, this is the only righteousness, the only honor, that can count before God (cf. Rom 4:2); and "*everyone* who believes on him will not be put to shame" (10:11).[51]

Thus, the Christ-gift both confirms and deepens the pattern of incongruity traced through 9:6-29. As from the beginning of Israel's story, God has belied expectations of appropriateness or fit: his wealth is given to all who believe,

---

ject is not to *find* Christ, but to assist in his saving work (*bringing him* down or up). Paul takes the text to dismiss such a notion, since in the case of Christ no human assistance is needed and no human conditions apply.

49. To "bring him down" probably alludes to God's "sending" of the Son (so, e.g., Cranfield, *Romans*, vol. 2, pp. 524-25) rather than to attempts to bring the risen Lord back from on high (thus Dunn, *Romans 9–16*, p. 605) or to hasten the Messiah's arrival (so Jewett, *Romans*, pp. 626-27).

50. Paul interprets "calling on the name of the Lord" (Joel 2:32) to mean a confession of faith in Christ; see C. K. Rowe, "Romans 10:13: What Is the Name of the Lord?" *HBT* 22 (2000): 135-73.

51. For the notable addition of "everyone" (πᾶς) to the Isaiah citation in 10:11 (influenced by the following citation from Joel in 10:13), see J. W. Aageson, "Scripture and Structure in the Development of the Argument in Romans 9–11," *CBQ* 48 (1986): 265-89, at p. 276.

regardless of their ethnicity, their righteousness, or their previous quest. The strange inversions of the present time (9:30-33) — the fact that some Gentiles believe in Christ and the majority of Jews do not — confirm the incongruity of this gift. In these subversions, stumbles, and reversals, God brings the ever-paradoxical story of Israel to its climax in Christ. But does the Christ-event thereby solidify the current reduction of Israel to a grace-chosen remnant, or is it rather a signal of hope? Romans 10:21 concludes with an image of a disobedient people — and God's still-outstretched hands. In what follows, it emerges that there is more to come.

17.4. The Momentum of Mercy and the Salvation of Israel (Romans 11:1-36)

Romans 11 confirms God's commitment to Israel, and in multiple echoes of 9:6-29 underscores God's choice of Israel through "election" (11:5, 28; cf. 9:11), via a "remnant" (11:5; cf. 9:27, 29), by the power of God's "call" (11:29; cf. 9:7, 12, 25-26), and in the exercise of "mercy" (11:30-32; cf. 9:15-18). Paul's strong insistence that God has not rejected his "inheritance" or his "people" (11:1-2) reiterates the assurance of 9:6 ("it is certainly not that the word of God has fallen"). But there is a movement internal to this chapter that demands attention. Its opening verses (11:1-10) appear content to affirm God's faithfulness through the election of a remnant (11:1-6), with the hardening of "the rest" (11:7-10). But from 11:11 onwards, Paul looks beyond this division, offering hope for mercy on the presently excluded. The new rhetorical question, "Have they stumbled so as to fall?", is met by a confident reply, "No way!" (11:11); by the end, we are told of a mystery and the means by which "all Israel will be saved" (11:25-26). From Romans 9, we knew that mercy eludes calculation and reverses the status quo, but in Romans 11, we witness a growing confidence for Israel as a whole, rising to a pitch beyond anything indicated before. Although this movement is often regarded as an illogical shift, I shall argue that Paul has *grounds* for believing that God's promises to Israel will be completed in full: the evidence lies, oddly enough, in the overflow of "wealth" to the *Gentile* world.

The first ground of hope for the future of Israel is Paul himself (11:1). Where 9:30–10:21 had spoken of Israel only in negative terms, at least here is one "Israelite" who *has* submitted to the righteousness of God, and one who (by analogy with Elijah) finds himself in the company of others (11:2-4).[52] In the present

52. Paul's point extends beyond claiming to speak from "an authentically Jewish viewpoint" (*pace* Dunn, *Romans 9–16*, p. 635). He self-consciously belongs to the "Israelites" whose

climactic moment (11:5: "in the now time," cf. 3:26; 5:6), these constitute "a remnant according to the selection of grace" (λεῖμμα κατ' ἐκλογὴν χάριτος, 11:5). The analogy with the seven thousand Israelites who did not participate in the worship of Baal required careful handling by Paul, since it could be taken to indicate that God's choice of a remnant was made in accordance with their loyalty. Unlike in the cases of Isaac and Jacob (9:8-13), there would then be grounds to detect some *correspondence* between selection by God and the worth of those selected. So has the remnant been chosen, both then and now, in response to their loyalty to God? It is striking how urgently Paul *denies* this reading. The citation from 1 Kings 19 is subtly augmented ("I have left *for myself* seven thousand men, who have not bowed the knee to Baal") to highlight that the important choice in this case is that of God.[53] But the heaviest emphasis falls on χάρις (used four times within 11:5-6), which not only qualifies "selection" (11:5) but is programmatically defined in 11:6: "If it is by grace (χάριτι), it is not on the basis of works, otherwise grace would not be grace (ἐπεὶ ἡ χάρις οὐκέτι γίνεται χάρις)."[54] This is the only use of χάρις in Romans 9–11 (cf. χαρίσματα in 11:29), and it bears the trademark Pauline perfection, of *incongruous* favor or gift.

In his earlier discussion of Abraham's faith (4:1-8), Paul had extended the meaning of χάρις, perfecting its sense beyond the normal antithesis between gift and pay, such that it signaled an *incongruous* gift, a gift that takes no account of worth (see above, 15.7). Similarly, in his reading of the calling of Israel, Paul was at pains to highlight the absence of worth in the selection of the patriarchs (9:6-18; see above, 17.2). In both cases, the mismatch was evident, since God's grace or call took effect where there were no "works" (4:4-5; 9:12). In the case of the Elijah-remnant, however, "works" were obviously present in the Israelites' refusal to comply with the cult of Baal. Here, Paul cannot display the operation of grace in the *absence* of works. He insists, nonetheless, on the incongruity of grace, and secures this perfection by maintaining the *irrelevance* of "works": whatever the human activity may have been, it was *not* the reason for choice by God. His purpose is not to pit divine action ("grace") against

privileges were listed in 9:3-5 (cf. 2 Cor 11:22), and thus stands as a sample of God's faithfulness to his promises. As an "Israelite" he is a representative of Israel, and not just of the present Israel-remnant (11:1-6); as "apostle of the Gentiles" (11:13) he is witness to, and agent of, the wealth of God's mercy to the non-Jewish world. For this double role, see K.-W. Niebuhr, *Heidenapostel aus Israel: Die jüdische Identität des Paulus nach ihrer Darstellung in seinen Briefen* (Tübingen: Mohr Siebeck, 1992), pp. 158-78 (esp. pp. 169-71 on 11:1).

53. See Cranfield, *Romans*, vol. 2, p. 547.

54. With almost every commentator, I take both uses of οὐκέτι here in a logical, not a temporal sense (cf. Rom 7:17; 14:15); Wilckens, *Brief an die Römer*, vol. 2, p. 238, is a rare exception.

human activity ("works") in direct antithesis, as if they were, in principle, mutually exclusive attributions of agency. Nor is the grace of God here made the cause of the works, as might have been emphasized if agency were Paul's chief concern. What matters is that the election of God *pays no regard* to the worth of works: the favor of God that constitutes his people does not *correspond* to human worth, not even what worth might be identified in their practice.

Despite the fact that Paul is speaking of Israelites, in Elijah's day and in his own, the "works" here mentioned are not culturally specific ("works of the Law").[55] In this general definition of the character of χάρις, *every practice* is equally insignificant as a criterion for the favor of God. That God's χάρις can be χάρις only in this way is a conviction Paul has reached under the impact of Christ.[56] But since the Christ-event defines his understanding of God, this rule can hardly be limited by culture or time.[57] Although this verse might seem to us a straightforward definition of χάρις, it is actually nothing of the sort: the normal presumption in antiquity (as today) is that gifts, including God's, correspond to the worth of their beneficiaries. It is Paul who insists on this striking perfection of grace, which he deploys here in order to clarify an example that might otherwise weaken his argument. In so doing, he bequeathed to his interpreters a definitional perfection of "grace" (as an incongruous gift to the unworthy) that was readily taken up in later Christian theology (and polemics) and was easily supplemented by additional perfections (see chapter 3).

Paul's emphasis on grace-beyond-worth has thus explained the existence

55. Dunn's insistence that the phrase is shorthand for "works of the Law," and his interpretation of the latter as the demarcation of difference, requires that he takes Paul's target to be a "limitation" of election (*Romans 9–16*, p. 639). But limitation to Jews is not the issue in this context (the remnant of Israel could hardly include Gentiles), only the grounds for God's choice of this remnant. Although resistance to idolatry is part of Torah-practice, Paul proposes a definition of χάρις that is capable of broad generalization.

56. So also Jewett, *Romans*, p. 660, although he wrongly insists that the article (ἡ χάρις) must refer to a "definite grace." As he rightly notes, following Harrison, in the ancient world "grace was granted to the deserving and honorable and thus provided no antithesis to works." That Paul has perfected it as incongruous gift/favor is due to the Christ-event and Paul's experience of it. What is crucial for the history of reception is the generalization about the nature of χάρις that Paul makes in the wake of this event.

57. In this regard, the subsequent Pauline tradition (e.g., Eph 2:8-10; Titus 3:4-6) did not misinterpret Paul in its generalized statements that "works" are irrelevant for the operation of grace. 1 Clement has Paul precisely right in insisting that "we are not justified by our own wisdom or knowledge or piety or the works that we have performed in holiness of heart" (32:4). What changes is not that a specific Pauline rule ("works of the Law") becomes generalized as "works," but that Paul's critique of the *criteria* of worth being applied in the formation of the community becomes a critique of the *achievement* of worth whose criteria, in an established Christian tradition, are themselves unproblematic. See further, chapter 18.

of a chosen remnant (11:1-6), but it has not yet clarified the future of Israel as a whole. The remnant may stand as a symbol of hope for the future (cf. 9:29), but the discussion so far concerns only "the elect": "the rest" are another matter, and are subject to hardening by God (11:7-10). To be sure, Paul's definition of grace could provide a generalized ground for hope. If a remnant exists, it is only by a grace that pays no regard to its recipients' worth. In principle, therefore, there is nothing to inhibit the spread of God's mercy, and no human condition that could limit its range.[58] God *could* be merciful on the rest of Israel (cf. 9:18). But what makes Paul confident that he *will* be so?

The rhetorical question-and-answer of 11:11 ("Have they stumbled so as to fall? No way!") for the first time offers explicit hope for those in Israel who are outside the current remnant. Paul appeals now not to Scripture (there are no citations in 11:11-24) but to the Gentile mission, whose relationship to Israel is the chief topic of these verses.[59] His own role as "apostle of the Gentiles" features prominently, but there is more at stake here than self-promotion or an apologetic claim that his Gentile mission is oriented for, and not against, the salvation of Israel. We seem to strike here on a logic that finds in the success of the Gentile mission an indication that the momentum of mercy will finally enfold also Israel itself.

It is notable that it is the *trespass* (παράπτωμα) of Israel that is the occasion or mechanism for the salvation of the Gentiles (11:11). Paul does not elucidate this connection,[60] but the notion that *sin* could have such positive effects is explicable only through the paradoxical logic of Romans 5:12-21. "Where sin increased, grace super-abounded" (5:20): in the midst of sin and stumble, there emerges a positive dynamic of saving grace, crossing ethnic

58. To this extent Paul's remnant theology appears more hopeful than that of *4 Ezra*. As we noted above (chapter 9), Ezra finally accepts that God's faithfulness to Israel will be satisfactorily fulfilled through the preservation of a righteous remnant (*4 Ezra* 7.26-29; 9.7-8), the faithful few who form "one grape from a cluster" (9.21). In line with God's justice, the remnant consists of those who are faithful to Torah, who have loyally obeyed the "law of life" in the "contest" of the present difficult age (*4 Ezra* 7.17-20, 127-31; 14.28-36). Paul's remnant is not of such a kind, not least because he finds no one to have succeeded in the contest with sin (Rom 3:10-20, 23; 5:12-21; 7:7-25).

59. For the role of Gentiles in Romans 9–11 (elsewhere in 9:24-26, 30; 10:11-18, 19-20; 11:25), see D. Zeller, *Juden und Heiden in der Mission des Paulus: Studien zum Römerbrief* (Stuttgart: Verlag Katholisches Bibelwerk, 1976), pp. 202-68.

60. It is possible that this statement reflects the experience of mission, in which synagogue hostility propelled the mission to Gentiles (cf. Acts 13:45-48; 28:24-28), although 1 Thessalonians 2:14-16 suggests a different perception; see Watson, *Paul, Judaism, and the Gentiles*, pp. 69-86. For a survey of interpretive options, see R. H. Bell, *The Irrevocable Call of God* (Tübingen: Mohr Siebeck, 2005), pp. 244-49.

boundaries in an overflow that bears all the marks of a Christological event.[61] The effect of the trespass in this regime of grace is the "wealth of the world" (11:12) or "the wealth of the Gentiles" (11:12). The term "wealth" (πλοῦτος), another gift-word, was associated earlier with God (9:23; cf. 11:33), and the cognate verb was loaded with Christological connotations in its extension to *all* (10:12). If trespass leads to wealth, and loss to the "reconciliation of the world" (11:15), there is clearly here at work an incongruous counter-dynamic of extraordinary power.[62] If Paul extols his ministry among Gentiles (11:13), it is not his own achievement he is pointing toward, but what *Christ* is doing through him for the obedience of the nations (15:15-19). The power let loose for the salvation of Gentiles is remarkable enough (cf. 1:16); that this power is operative in the worst of conditions, in or through the unbelief of Israel, is a sign of its invincible strength.

Here lies a clue to Paul's confidence that the strange reversals of the present time (Gentile "wealth" and the "defeat" or "diminution" of Israel, 11:12) represent not the replacement of Israel by Gentiles, but a precursor to Israel's own "fullness" (11:12) and "acceptance" (11:15). In a subtle reuse of an earlier motif (10:19), Paul holds out the hope that the wealth of Gentiles will provoke Israel to jealousy (11:12, 14), as they recognize that what Gentiles are gaining belongs by origin to Israel.[63] Paul presumes throughout this letter that the salvation of Gentiles is anomalous, the miraculous extension of a promise whose origin and home is Israel itself (11:17-24). Thus, his imagination is fired by a logic of "greater and lesser" that he had also deployed elsewhere (cf. 5:9-10; 8:11, 30). If God's grace spills over into the Gentile world, how much more must it rebound on Israel (cf. 11:24)? And if Israel's trespass is the occasion

61. For the echoes of Romans 5:12-21, see Wright, "Romans," p. 681; for παράπτωμα, see 5:15, 16, 17, 18, 20. Paul's use of the text on Pharaoh (9:17-23) laid a foundation of expectation that even hardening could have a positive effect "in all the world." But the definitive turn from sin-and-death to life-and-righteousness is located by Paul in the Christ-event (5:15-18).

62. For a careful argument that "loss" and "acceptance" in 11:15 both refer to God's action toward Israel (cf. 11:28-29; against the protests of Fitzmyer, Jewett, and others), see J. R. D. Kirk, *Unlocking Romans: Resurrection and the Justification of God* (Grand Rapids: Eerdmans, 2008), pp. 182-84. On philological grounds, ἀποβολή (11:15) is more likely to mean "loss" *(Verlust)* than "rejection" *(Verwerfung),* but in this context the genitive is more likely to be objective (God "loses" Israel) than subjective. For the debate in German scholarship, see K. Haacker, "Die Geschichtstheologie von Röm 9–11 im Lichte philonischer Schriftauslegung," *NTS* 43 (1997): 209-22, at pp. 218-19.

63. For the motif, see R. H. Bell, *Provoked to Jealousy: The Origin and Purpose of the Jealousy Motif in Romans 9–11* (Tübingen: Mohr Siebeck, 1994). As is often noted, the list of Israel's privileges in Romans 9:3-5 includes many items that had earlier been said to belong to believers, both Gentiles and Jews.

of "wealth," what more must follow when that wealth overcomes the trespass itself (11:12, 15)?[64]

Here, as elsewhere (10:11-18), the remarkable success of the Gentile mission is evidence for Paul of an eschatological flood, a spreading dynamic of mercy that will surely track back to its origin and core. The reconciliation that is embracing the world (11:15) is overcoming every obstacle of Gentile impiety through the incongruous gift of the death of Christ (5:6-10). Israel's trespass can be similarly overcome, by an easier (more "natural") process of reintegration (11:24, 26). In the final "acceptance" of Israel, Paul anticipates the consummation of the purposes of God, the "life from the dead" that overcomes every last enemy (11:15; cf. 1 Cor 15:26).[65] This "life from death" is already at work following the resurrection of Jesus (4:23-25; 5:9-10; 6:1-10) and is present to believers in the life-giving power of the Spirit (8:2, 9-11). The presence of that life in the Gentile world convinces Paul that an invincible, non-reversible momentum is sweeping the world: the "firstfruits" (ἀπαρχή) are visible, and the rest will follow (11:16).[66] Everything Paul has said about Israel in 9:6-29 has secured the fact that *Israel* is the object of the promises of God; what gives him confidence that the process of fulfillment is now definitively under way is the victory of God's mercy on the most difficult (Gentile) terrain.[67] That Israel's trespass is the occasion of this victory only deepens its wonder: in fact, Israel now stands "in the exact right position" for a similar operation of incongruent grace (11:31-32).[68] The richness evidenced in the Gentile mission, whose power and wealth derive from the death and resurrection of Christ, confirms to Paul that nothing will separate Israel from the love of God in Christ (8:39; cf. 11:28; 15:7-9).

64. In each case, a greater *result* will follow a lesser, but the *achievement* of the first task is itself the greater (the harder or less expected), and the future therefore easier to predict (cf. 5:9-10).

65. That "life from the dead" here means the eschatological "harvest" (cf. 1 Cor 15:20-26) is recognized by nearly all commentators (see Moo, *Romans*, pp. 694-96). To interpret it as a metaphor or figure of speech ("like a kind of resurrection," Wright, "Romans," p. 683) is to limit the resonance of a phrase that evokes the resurrection of Jesus as the harbinger of the final resurrection (see 6:5; 8:10-11, 18-23). The parallel with "the reconciliation of the world" (11:15) indicates the cosmic scope of Paul's vision.

66. The referential meaning of "firstfruits" (for the image, see Num 15:20-21) is not entirely clear: Jesus, Jewish believers, or the patriarchs have been suggested (see, e.g., Cranfield, *Romans*, vol. 2, p. 564; Dunn, *Romans 9–16*, p. 659). In context, Gentile converts made "holy" by becoming God's people (1:7; 9:24-26) may also be in view, signaling the reconciliation of humanity as a whole (cf. 11:32).

67. For the Pauline logic here, see Zeller, *Juden und Heiden*, pp. 243-44.

68. So Grindheim, *Crux of Election*, p. 161.

In the middle of 11:16, Paul switches metaphor, from "firstfruits" (and the lump they represent) to "root" (and the branches it supports); he thus opens a new approach to his topic through the metaphor of the wild and the cultivated olive tree (11:17-24). The depiction of Israel as a plant or tree (normally a vine) is common enough in the Hebrew Bible and in Second Temple Judaism,[69] but Paul puts unusual emphasis on the *root* as the source of nourishment ("the root of fatness," 11:17) and as the support of the branches ("you do not support the root, but the root supports you," 11:18). It is therefore important to clarify the identity of this root. The suggestion that it represents Israel as a whole is hardly plausible:[70] it is clear from 11:17-24 that Israelites are the branches that *belong to this root,* and can be cut off from it and re-grafted in (11:17, 24), but they are *not the root-stock itself.*[71] It is commonly held that "the root" refers to the patriarchs, or to Abraham in particular: the reference to "the fathers" in 11:28, the focus on the early patriarchal generations in Romans 9:6-13, and Jewish precedent all give weight to this view.[72] But everywhere Paul discusses the patriarchs he is concerned to elucidate not *that* they were the origin of Israel, but *how* this was the case (Gal 3:6-18; 4:21-31; Rom 4:1-23; 9:6-13). If Israel is "beloved on account of the fathers" (11:28), this is because (γάρ) "the gifts and the calling of God are irrevocable" (11:29). As Romans 4:1-8 and 9:6-13 make clear, what matters about the patriarchs is that they were rendered significant by a grace and a calling that bore no relation to their intrinsic worth. In other words, the "root of fatness" that sustains the olive tree is not *the patriarchs themselves,* but *the calling or election of God* that constituted them as patriarchs, and thereby constituted Israel as a whole. The root is the unconditioned favor of God on which Israel's existence depends.[73]

69. From the texts studied in Part II, see, e.g., *4 Ezra* 5.21; 9.21; Pseudo-Philo, *LAB* 12.6-10; 18.10-11; 23.12; 28.4; 30.4; 39.7; 1QH[a] VI.15. For Israel as olive tree, see Jer 11:16; Hos 14:6.

70. *Pace* F. Mussner, *Traktat über die Juden* (Munich: Kösel Verlag, 1979), pp. 68-74. Many of those who take the "root" to refer to the patriarchs thereafter slip into identifying it as the people of Israel in general; thus, Käsemann suggests that "Gentile Christianity has its root in the Old Testament people of God" and speaks of "the people of God growing out of the root of Israel" ("aus der Wurzel Israels," *An die Römer,* pp. 299-300; cf. Wilckens, *Brief an die Römer,* vol. 2, pp. 246-47).

71. It is no more plausible to identify this root as Jewish believers: *pace* Barrett, it is hard to see how Paul could identify them as the source of "fatness" and support; see C. K. Barrett, *A Commentary on the Epistle to the Romans* (London: A&C Black, 1971), p. 216.

72. For identification with the patriarchs in general, see, e.g., Dunn, *Romans 9–16,* pp. 659-60; Dahl, "The Future of Israel," p. 151; with Abraham in particular (paralleled in *1 Enoch* 93.5, 8; cf. *Jub* 16.26), see W. Krauss, *Das Volk Gottes: Zur Grundlegung der Ekklesiologie bei Paulus* (Tübingen: Mohr Siebeck, 1996), pp. 315, 317, with reference to many others.

73. Cranfield rightly suggests that "the patriarchs are a holy root, not because of any innate

Many features of the olive tree allegory make better sense on this reading. If the root were simply the patriarchs (or Abraham in particular), and the branches were connected by physical descent (despite 9:6-8!), it is hard to see on what grounds they could be cut off (how is *ancestry* annulled?), or how they could be grafted in again (how is *ancestry* restored?).[74] But Paul makes clear that the determinative factor is not ancestry but whether or not they "remain in the kindness of God" (11:22). Connection to the root represents participation in the generative mercy of God, and it is certainly conceivable that "branches" could be cut off from this and later reconnected. Thus, the olive tree image does not contradict Paul's careful definition of the identity of "Israel" in 9:6-29 by reverting to a definition by "flesh" that was explicitly refuted there (9:6-8). On the contrary, Romans 9 described and defines the character of the "root," whose significance and "fatness" (πιότης; its nutritious value) is here made evident. Because Israel has been constituted by the calling of God, without regard to worth, it has survived all this time by drawing on this extrinsic source of life. Now, and for the same reason, Israel's calling can be supplemented by the calling of Gentiles (9:24-26), who as "wild olive" branches are *grafted into this grace* (11:17-18, 22). The root is "natural" to Israel since it is the means by which Israel was constituted from the beginning. But it is accessible also for "unnatural" additions, because the nutrition that supports this tree is a grace unlimited by ethnic differences or by any other criterion of worth.[75]

---

worth or merit of their own, but by virtue of God's election of grace," *Romans*, vol. 2, p. 565; cf. Moo, *Romans*, p. 700. Despite the use of the same term later for Christ (15:12), there is no good reason to see the root as a reference to Christ in this context. Walter rightly emphasizes divine election and promise as the sustaining root of Israel and of all who believe, but underplays the fact that it is specifically the election of *Israel* that remains foundational for Jew and Gentile alike (cf. 15:8-13); see N. Walter, "Zur Interpretation von Römer 9–11," *ZTK* 81 (1984): 172-95, at pp. 178-86; cf. Niebuhr, *Heidenapostel*, p. 152 n. 71.

74. For the logical problems here, see Krauss, *Volk Gottes*, pp. 315-16: like most, he considers that Paul's metaphor involves him in self-contradiction. Indeed, it is precisely at this point that the inconsistency most detect in Romans 9–11 comes most clearly to the fore: see, e.g., J. Lambrecht, "Israel's Future," pp. 48-49.

75. I here differ from the thesis of C. Johnson Hodge, *If Sons, Then Heirs: A Study of Kinship and Ethnicity in the Letters of Paul* (Oxford: Oxford University Press, 2007). Johnson Hodge maintains that Gentiles are saved by "affiliation" with Israel, a form of "aggregation" that creates "a hierarchical relationship between *Ioudaioi* and gentiles as distinct peoples of the God of Israel" (p. 143). But God is grafting Gentiles not into the *tree* (Israel) but into the *root*, whose richness sustains both natural and unnatural branches, both Jews and Gentiles. Thus, for Paul, heritage is *created* by grace: offspring are born by promise to be *children of God* (9:8). It is because Israel was formed in this way from the beginning that it is first in time, with a "natural" affiliation to divine mercy. Gentiles are brought into relation not to an ethnic deity ("the God of Israel," pp. 130-31) but to the God of whom Israel is a product and a witness.

As we saw in discussion of Pseudo-Philo, depictions of Israel as a plant or tree can have rich and multiple evocations. There, Israel's life as a "vine" is the organic structure that integrates the cosmos (*LAB* 12.4-10), and it is simply inconceivable that this magnificent entity could come to nothing and render God's plan "in vain" (see above, 8.2). Pseudo-Philo shows no special interest in the "root" (see *LAB* 12.8; 44.8; 49.6), because his focus lies less on the reason for God's promises to Israel, and more on the fact that the promises have been made and must be fulfilled. Paul's stress on the root, and on the rationale of election, is a sign that he presses to explain how Israel came to be, and in that explanation desires to understand its present crisis, its future hope, and the extraordinary supplementation to the stock of God's "inheritance" in the form of believing Gentiles. If its source of life (its "root") is the creative call that "raises the dead and calls into existence the things that do not exist" (4:17), one can readily explain both the in-grafting of Gentiles and the hope that, by the power of God (11:23), Israel will be reconstituted and complete again.

In the olive tree allegory (11:17-24), Paul's focus rests initially on the wild olive branches (Gentile believers), who are grafted in, against nature, just when some of the natural branches are lopped off (11:17-21). His metaphor, unconstrained by contemporary arboriculture, is intended to counter a Gentile tendency to pride, whether in Rome or elsewhere (the "you"-singular addressed in 11:17ff. is a rhetorical persona). He reminds Gentiles of their alien origin: they are "wild," inferior in origin to those who belong "by nature" (cf. 11:24). But the weight of emphasis lies on their dependence on the "root of fatness" — the *common* dependence (συγκοινωνός) of Jew and Gentile on the goodness of God. To boast over the cut-off branches is, at a deep level, to forget one's place before God: the warning against pride in 11:20 is simultaneously an instruction to "fear" God. Nothing makes Gentiles superior to unbelieving Jews, because no worth of theirs has established their connection to the root. The critique of human "boasting" that permeates this letter (cf. 2:17-20, 27; 4:2; 11:25; 12:3, 16) is here applied to Gentile arrogance. As always, the antidote is a reminder of their total dependence on the grace of God: "it is not you that supports the root, but the root you" (11:18).

This unnerving dependence on grace is the originating and primary characteristic of Israel. If its very existence derives from God's grace (the root), failure to "remain" in the goodness of God (11:22) constitutes a loss of connection to the source of life. To deny that goodness is to experience instead the "severity" (ἀποτομία, the "cutting off") of God (11:21-22). Paul here reintroduces the language of "faith" (πίστις) and "unbelief" (ἀπιστία; 11:20, 23; cf. 3:3) and thereby matches precisely the line of thought in 9:30–10:13. To "stand in faith" (11:20) is to live entirely from the gift of God (cf. 4:4-6; 14:4, 22-23), to "call on the name of the Lord" (10:13) in utter dependence on God's action in Christ (10:5-10), and thus to draw from "the root of fatness."[76] Unbelief, by contrast, constitutes a disconnection from this source of life. There is every reason to take "faith" in this context as the faith described in 9:30–10:17, the faith that confesses Christ and lives by participation in his resurrection life. Paul is not creating some arbitrary addition to the identity of Israel: to draw on Christ, the definitive expression of the "goodness of God," is to live by the grace that has constituted and sustained the people of Israel from its beginning.

To believe in Christ is nothing other than to live from "the root." If Israel's identity was always derivative and "eccentric," created and sustained by the calling of God, its nature is neither erased nor altered by its response in faith to God's calling in Christ. The olive tree allegory renders impossible the claim that Israel has been superseded by Gentiles or absorbed into a non-Jewish realm known as "the church." To the contrary, it is Gentiles who are "grafted in," but what they join is a people and a mode of existence utterly dependent on "the gifts and the calling of God" (11:29). On Paul's reading, by believing in Christ Israel draws again — in consummate fashion — on the sustenance of grace, thereby becoming *not less but more like itself.* Faith is a mode of eccentric existence, a life dependent on the gift of God. Since this is the essence of Israel's identity from Abraham onwards, what Paul expects is not the eradication but the realization of everything that Israel was destined to be, precisely by faith in the risen Christ.

We can now identify the source of that paradox in Paul whereby Israel is *special* in important respects, but also *no longer unique.* The good news concerns God's power of salvation for all who believe, "both to the Jew — first — and to the Greek" (1:16; 2:9-10). "To the Jew first," since the grace of God has its historical origins in the story of Israel, is attested in its Scriptures, and has constituted Israel as the bearer and exemplar of the creative promise of God (3:1-3; 9:6-29). In all these respects, for a Jew to believe is for a branch to be joined to its "natural" source (11:24; cf. 9:4-5). But also, at the same time, "both to the Jew and to the Greek," since the grace of God is not bounded by worth, ethnic or other, and the dynamic of unconditioned favor by which Israel was formed is reaching now to unworthy Gentiles (9:24-26; 10:1-13). In fact, *Israel is now no longer unique for the very same reason that it has always been special.* As Gentiles share in common dependence on the life-giving root,

76. If it was not clear already from Romans 4, it should be evident in Romans 9–11 that faith is a mode of dependence on an external source of saving grace, not itself a *ground* for salvation; see O. Hofius, "Das Evangelium und Israel: Erwägungen zu Römer 9–11," in *Paulusstudien* (Tübingen: Mohr Siebeck, 1989), pp. 175-202, at p. 182.

they come to experience what has made Israel "Israel" from the very beginning (9:6-13). Paul does not here revert to a default "ethnocentrism," nor create an irresolvable "tension" between privilege and impartiality, ethnic particularism and non-ethnic universalism.[77] Since the privilege of Israel is its dependence on incongruous grace, it is precisely its privilege that now undergirds the indiscriminate spread of good news. Gentiles are drawn into the election of *Israel,* but that election in principle, and now in actuality, knows no ethnic constraints.

That Israel is itself the product of grace is vividly illustrated by the condition of the "branches." Those that in "unbelief" (ἀπιστία) no longer draw from the root of God's unconditioned call are cut off from their life-giving source (11:17, 20). But it is altogether possible for God to graft them in again (11:23) — an exercise of power that would reproduce the pattern of reversal typical of grace. It is just like Israel to draw from the root in faith, and just like God to exercise mercy without regard to worth.[78] In fact, for God to restore Israel to its natural condition is easier to imagine than the current in-grafting of Gentile branches: "how much more will those that naturally belong be grafted back to their own olive tree" (11:24). The future passive (*"will be grafted,"* that is, by God) is remarkably confident. The miracle of Gentile faith is a pointer to God's superabundant power that will surely rehabilitate Israel (cf. 11:11-15).

This confidence undergirds the "mystery" articulated in 11:25-27. The Gentile mission is the sign of a momentum that has a definite end: "a hardening in part has come upon Israel until the fullness of Gentiles comes in, and so all Israel will be saved" (11:25-26). The present split within Israel between the elect and the hardened rest (11:7) will be resolved in the salvation of the whole, and it is the world-enriching spread of God's mercy that signals this singular

77. *Pace* Longenecker, who finds Paul's vision blind to ethnicity in the present but ultimately determined by his placement of salvation-history "within the confines of Jewish ethnocentrism" (B. W. Longenecker, "Different Answers to Different Issues: Israel, the Gentiles, and Salvation History in Romans 9–11," *JSNT* 36 [1989]: 95-123). But as Romans 9:6-29 made clear, Israel's (ethnic) identity is the product of God's calling in grace. Johnson finds a "dynamic tension" between "God's impartiality and faithfulness to Israel," *Function of Apocalyptic,* p. 120; cf. pp. 174-75. Cf. C. Cosgrove, who wrestles mightily with a supposed contradiction between "divine impartiality" and "the notion of a special election of the Jewish people" (*Elusive Israel: The Puzzle of Election in Romans* [Louisville: Westminster John Knox Press, 1997], p. 37; cf. pp. 76-90). His conclusion that "each people turns out to be like Israel, God's favorite child" (p. 96) is reached by way of the notion of rights ("the right to be Israel"), which completely contradicts the conceptual framework of Romans 9:6-29.

78. Thus, *pace* Käsemann, the olive tree allegory makes clear that what Paul regards as typical of Israel is not unbelief (in Käsemann's terms, the self-righteousness of "the devout Jew," as an exemplar of "the religious man," "Paul and Israel," p. 184), but faith.

goal.[79] The coming Redeemer (11:26-27), who is almost certainly to be identified with Christ (cf. 1 Thess 1:10),[80] will banish "impiety" and forgive Jacob's sins — an act of grace that mirrors Paul's earlier depiction of the "justification" of Abraham (4:5-8). Israel's Abrahamic identity will thus be re-grounded and restored in Christ, just as its covenant relation to God will be confirmed (11:27; cf. 9:4; 15:8).

Thus God's election, his gifts (χαρίσματα), and his call will not be revoked (11:28-29) but will reach their fulfillment in their original form, in a mercy that acts regardless of worth. The incongruity evident in the formation of Israel (9:6-29), and visible now in the paradoxical relations of Gentiles and Jews (9:30–10:21), will also shape God's final goal. Just as disobedient Gentiles have received mercy from God (in the course of Israel's own disobedience), so Israel, which is now disobedient (in the course of God's mercy on Gentiles), will itself receive mercy from God (11:30-31). The current reversals in the relations between Gentiles and Jews are a sign for Paul of the power of mercy, to which disobedience is no ultimate block. Because he witnesses the life-giving power that springs from the resurrection to reconcile and transform the Gentile world, Paul is confident that the God who promised "to have mercy on whom he has mercy" (9:15) has "shut up all in disobedience in order that he may have mercy on all" (11:32).

The paradoxes in this pattern of grace evoke Paul's final acclamation (11:33-36), which celebrates the depth of God's wealth, wisdom, and knowledge (11:33). The strange inversions that have been traced in these chapters indicate God's inscrutable judgments and untraceable ways (11:33-34). The

79. With most scholars, I take "all Israel" to refer to the whole people of Israel (in distinction from the hardening of part, 11:25); for a discussion of the options, see C. Zoccali, "And So All Israel Will Be Saved: Competing Interpretations of Romans 11.26 in Pauline Scholarship," *JSNT* 30 (2008): 289-318. Although it is grammatically possible to read καὶ οὕτως (11:26) in the sense "and then" (see P. W. van der Horst, "'Only Then Will Israel Be Saved': A Short Note on the Meaning of καὶ οὕτως in Romans 11.26," *JBL* 119 [2000]: 521-25), it is probably best to preserve its modal sense ("and in this way"). This again indicates that the Gentile story is essentially entwined with the story of Israel (cf. 11:11-15). Since Paul does not spell out the "mystery" more precisely, it seems unwise to fill its silences with speculation on the means of this salvation or the exact connotations of its reference to "all" (*pace* Hofius, "Evangelium," pp. 189-98); see Wolter, "Israelproblem," p. 26. The hope for the salvation of Israel, and the ambiguity about what precisely this means, are paralleled in the contemporary Pseudo-Philo, *LAB;* see above, chapter 8.

80. For discussion, see Cranfield, *Romans,* vol. 2, pp. 577-78; cf. the expectations of a coming Messiah in *4 Ezra* 11–13. That the Redeemer is here said to come "from Zion" (instead of "on its behalf") may show the influence of the Psalms (LXX Ps. 13:7; 52:7), but may also reflect Paul's insistence that salvation in Christ is not alien but integral to Israel's identity (cf. 1:3; 9:5; 15:8).

"wealth" of his mercy is underscored by the insistence (in a citation from Job) that God is never the second or the return giver: "who has given to him, that he should be recompensed in return?" (11:35). As elsewhere in these chapters, Paul assumes the *priority* of God's giving (see the προ- prefixes in 9:11, 23, and 11:2; cf. 8:28-29), but this is significant chiefly in underlining its *incongruity.* God does not give in return, to match a prior gift: there is no correspondence in this or any other respect. It is that absence of correspondence that makes God's mercy so unnerving, and at the same time pregnant with such promise for the future (cf. 15:13).[81]

17.5. Conclusions

This reading of Romans 9–11 renders Paul's line of thought consistent; it does not require that he veer between incompatible definitions of "Israel," nor resort at the end to an irrational hope based on an ethnic prejudice or a mysterious "revelation" in favor of Israel.[82] To be sure, there is a *development* to be traced through these chapters, which move from grief to praise, and from the prospect of a double predestination to the hope of a singular mercy upon all. But the consistent theme that holds this development together is the incongruity of divine election — the lack of correspondence between the mercy of God and the worth of its recipients. Because Israel has been chosen in this way (9:6-29), its identity and its future hinge not on ethnic origin or worthy praxis, but on the merciful will of God. Because the Christ-event is the climactic and definitive enactment of this life-giving grace, God has been found by Gentiles who had no worth, while Jews who insist on the worth of their Torah-praxis are apt to stumble over an event they fail to recognize (9:30–10:4). But the success of the Gentile mission signals for Paul the spreading impact of divine "wealth," which will return to its home when Israel is restored by faith in Christ to the "root" of God's unconditioned mercy (11:1-36). From start (9:6-8) to finish (11:30-32), Israel is constituted by a calling that bears no relation to its

81. Siegert, *Argumentation,* p. 127, speaks of God in Romans 9 as "konstant unberechenbar." For reflections on the paradoxes of these chapters, see W. Meeks, "On Trusting an Unpredictable God: A Hermeneutical Meditation on Romans 9–11," in *In Search of the Early Christians* (New Haven: Yale University Press, 2002), pp. 210-29. As he comments, Paul "reserves God's freedom to act, yet again, in an unexpected way" (p. 225).

82. Wolter re-articulates with admirable clarity the common opinion that the ending of Romans 9–11 (esp. 11:25-27) remains fundamentally inconsistent with its beginning at 9:6ff. and runs aground in an unsolved aporia ("Israelproblem," pp. 25-29); cf. M. Wolter, *Paulus: Ein Grundriss seiner Theologie* (Neukirchen-Vluyn: Neukirchener Verlag, 2011), pp. 424-36.

worth — and into this distinctively Israelite privilege, Gentiles also are drawn by an indiscriminate grace.

The central thread of these chapters, the radically incongruous grace of God, not only ties the beginning of this discourse to its end; it also sews many of its individual motifs into a common pattern. By tracing its operations in Scripture and in the calling and history of Israel, Paul matches the Christ-event with the identity of Israel, while bringing the language of gift/favor (χάρις) and mercy (ἔλεος) into conceptual accord. When God's *modus operandi* is understood in these terms, many aspects of the present become intelligible to Paul: the remnant of Jewish believers (chosen by grace), Jewish unbelief (stumbling on a "stone" that disqualifies the value of Torah-observance), God's purpose in laying this stumbling-stone (to elicit faith, a mode of dependence on God's wealth in Christ), and the paradox of Gentile believers (who attain a goal they were not pursuing through God's indiscriminate mercy). All of these oddities derive from the mismatch between divine favor and human worth, which is also Paul's antidote to Gentile (or any other) "boasting," since no one has anything except by connection to God's unconditioned call. At the same time, the incongruity of grace gives Paul confidence to look beyond the "disobedience" of Israel, since the God who called this people without regard to their desert wills to overcome their "impiety" by his world-embracing mercy. Whence did Paul derive this integrating theme? From his reading of Scripture, from the impact of the Christ-event, or from the experience of the Gentile mission? All of these could be, and were, interpreted otherwise by his contemporaries. In a powerful but complex dialectic, all three played their part in creating a textual and narrative grid by which Paul could make sense of his God, his Scriptures, his people, his allegiance to Christ, and his experience of the Gentile mission.

If incongruity is, once again, the chief perfection of grace in these chapters, do other perfections also cluster here? As we have seen, the motif of "wealth" evokes the *superabundance* thematized in Romans 5:12-21, and there are statements here that emphasize the *priority* of God's call or gift (9:11; 11:2, 35) in a way that supports its lack of correspondence to human worth. If Paul traces here a final *singularity* in the purpose of God's mercy (11:32), this is far from a principled insistence that God can only be benevolent: as we have seen, there are multiple references to God's hardening, wrath, and severity, alongside God's grace, both in relation to Israel (11:7-10) and in relation to Gentile believers (11:20-22). Paul's threat that branches may be cut off if they do not remain in God's goodness (11:17-24) calls into question any dogmatic, Augustinian commitment to "the perseverance of the saints." There is a general sense here of the *efficacy* of grace, in the fact that the Christ-event, and its preaching, elicit faith, but no reflection on the mechanism or means of that efficacy as many have developed this perfection (by appeal to "monergism" etc.; see above, chapter 3). Finally, as the preceding and following chapters make clear (e.g., Rom 6:1-23; 12:1-3), Paul's radical emphasis on the incongruity of grace by no means implies its *non-circularity:* the following appeal "by the mercies of God" (12:1) may be taken to indicate that grace has "strings attached." But the absence or lesser significance of these other perfections does not in the least diminish the radicality of the one perfection that *is* central to these chapters; as we have noted, the various perfections of grace are not a "package deal" (see above, chapter 2). What matters in Romans 9–11, as throughout this letter, is that God's grace or mercy is operative without regard to worth. It is because *this* is the core of Israel's identity and history that it is also the hope for the salvation of the world.

This raises one final question: what is the relationship between the grace that was operative in the calling of Israel and the grace enacted in the Christ-event? There is an appreciable difference here between Romans and Galatians. As we noted, the *Christological* focus of Galatians placed emphasis on the novelty of the Christ-event, with no reference to Israelite generations between Abraham and Christ. In Galatians, Christ is not added to a prior human narrative, but is the hermeneutical center of a scriptural witness that "pre-preached" the good news (Gal 3:8; see above, 13.3). This created some anomalies that Galatians was unable to explain on its own terms, such as the birth of Isaac (in history, "then") according to the Spirit (Gal 4:29) and the occurrence of Abraham's faith before "faith came" (Gal 3:25). The *theological* focus of Romans enables Paul to place the Christ-event on a historical line, with a past as well as a future: the origins of the Abrahamic family (Rom 4) and the means by which Israel was formed and preserved (Rom 9:6-29; 11:1-5) are here significant in themselves, and not merely as types of the present.[83] Although the Christ-event is still associated with newness (Rom 6:4; 7:6), Paul offers in Romans 9–11 something approximating to a history of divine mercy, whose origins go back to the "irrevocable call" of the patriarchs and whose power can be traced through many generations. The hints in Galatians regarding the special status of Israel are here developed into clear statements, and although Israel's story is full of contractions, reversals, and paradoxes, there is a persisting narrative of election, calling, and grace.

So, is the Christ-event in Romans simply one instance of a recurrent

83. Luz is right to insist that even here Paul is not interested in history for its own sake; see U. Luz, *Das Geschichtsverständnis des Paulus* (Munich: Kaiser Verlag, 1968). However, Luz's treatment of these chapters is in danger of reducing Israel's history to an illustration of the righteousness or faithfulness of God: it is the fact that God is righteous and faithful toward *Israel* that matters to Paul.

divine interaction with the world, another example of grace that calls forth generic faith in God before Christ and apart from Christ?[84] Is the Christ-event therefore to be interpreted *within* a larger historical frame, deriving its meaning from a story that has an independent meaning? And is the story of Christ in Romans "superimposed upon the story of Israel"?[85]

There are several reasons to conclude that even in Romans the Pauline picture is more complex than this. At the very least, the Christ-event is for Paul the *definitive* enactment of incongruous grace, in several senses. As the Messianic event, the Christ-event has an eschatological *finality* that places it in a category of its own: the "now time" (ὁ νῦν καιρός, 3:26; 11:5; cf. 1 Cor 10:11) is not just any time, but a climactic moment that gives meaning to all other times.[86] This is, for Paul, a moment of *completeness*, a τέλος (10:4) when the promises to Israel are "confirmed" (15:8) — both secured and fulfilled.[87] As the realization of the promise on which Israel's identity depends, the Christ-event thus has a unique status within the "history" of God's mercy. This event is also *decisive*, the historical turning point from sin and death to righteousness and life (3:21-26; 5:12-21), so that whatever may be said about God's grace in the past cannot be compared in its effect to the grace-event in Christ. Israel's connection to its root now depends on its faith or unbelief (11:17-24), and in the light of 9:30–10:13 there is every reason to understand these as faith or unbelief in Christ. Christ thus proves to be the ultimate crisis for Israel, and its ultimate source of unconditioned grace; he also enacts its *comprehensive* expression, embracing both Gentile and Jew. Definitive in all these respects (final, complete, decisive, and comprehensive), the Christ-event is not just the latest episode in a story of grace.

We can and must go further. If Paul cannot here make sense of the Christ-event without reference to Israel's creation and sustenance by God's elective call, neither can he make sense of Israel without reference to Christ. Christ and Israel are mutually interpretative. The Christ-event does not come "out of the

84. This is the reading developed by Boers on the basis of Romans 4, and by Stendahl and others on the basis of the fact that "faith" and "unbelief" in Romans 11 are not given explicit Christological reference; see H. Boers, *Theology out of the Ghetto: A New Testament Exegetical Study concerning Religious Exclusiveness* (Leiden: Brill, 1971); K. Stendahl, *Final Account: Paul's Letter to the Romans* (Minneapolis: Fortress, 1995).

85. So Dunn, regarding Galatians: J. D. G. Dunn, *The Theology of Paul's Letter to the Galatians* (Cambridge: Cambridge University Press, 1993), p. 41.

86. For reflection on this Pauline motif, see G. Agamben, *The Time That Remains: A Commentary on the Letter to the Romans,* trans. P. Dailey (Stanford: Stanford University Press, 2005), pp. 59-87.

87. On the meaning of βεβαιόω (15:8), see *BDAG,* s.v. ("prove the promises reliable, fulfill them").

blue" and is not self-interpreting: it constitutes the completion of the promise to Israel, whose identity and existence depend on the mercy of God. The Messiah is from Israel (9:5), and the Redeemer will come from Zion (11:26): placed in this context, the strange workings of grace in the Christ-event, including the salvation of Gentiles, can be seen as the climax of God's purposes for Israel, and thus the climax of history. But at the same time, the story of Israel — in fact, the identity of Israel — is interpreted in Romans 9–11 in the light of the Christ-event. This retroactive hermeneutic is more subtle than in Galatians, but no less significant. Paul does not retroject Christ-specific language onto the early history of Israel (as in Gal 4:21–5:1), but in his representation of that story he picks out scriptural features that resonate with the shape and character of the Christ-event. It was neither necessary nor obvious that one should highlight the apparent arbitrariness of God's elective choice (Rom 9:6-18). Paul dares to offer a reading of these texts that would have shocked many of his contemporary Jews, but that matches the shocking incongruity of grace in Christ. Right through Romans 9–11, in his selection, arrangement, adaptation, and interpolation of the Scriptures, Paul brings out how the Law and the prophets "bear witness" to the righteousness of God in Christ (3:21). Texts are read with reference to Christ (9:32-33; 10:6-8, 11-13) or to the Gentile mission (9:24-26; 10:19-20), mirroring Paul's conviction that the Scriptures make their fullest sense in his present day (4:23-24; 15:3-4). Even the story of Elijah is read as a narrative of grace that bears the Christological shape of the unconditioned gift (11:1-6). Thus, if Christ is read in the context of Israel, Israel is also, already, Christologically defined.[88]

To state the matter dialectically: the incongruity of grace is the hallmark of the Christ-event because it is characteristic of God's dealings with Israel; conversely, the incongruous pattern of God's dealings with Israel is Christologically determined. The connections and constellations of grace-shaped events traced in Romans 9–11 are hermeneutical products, the effect of Paul's interpretative work.[89] But in Paul's eyes, the identity of Israel and the shape of

88. This is in one sense no different from the efforts of other Second Temple Jews to define "Israel" in the light of their values and perceptions, a phenomenon particularly clear in Philo, in *4 Ezra,* and in the Dead Sea Scrolls.

89. For the possibility of history-telling as "grasping the constellations which [the historian's] own era has formed with a definite earlier one," see W. Benjamin, "Theses on the Philosophy of History," in *Illuminations,* ed. H. Arendt, trans. H. Zorn (London: Pimlico, 1999), thesis A. Benjamin goes on to speak of establishing "a conception of the present as 'the time of the now' which is shot through with chips [splinters] of Messianic time" — one of the features of his thought that has inspired Agamben *(The Time That Remains)* to find in Benjamin a close companion of Paul.

its history are not thereby created, but discovered.[90] Thus, the Christ-event is not simply a stage in Israel's history, even its final stage; it is the moment that gives meaning to the whole.[91]

In this way Romans resolves some of the anomalies of Galatians, while raising fresh questions of its own, not least regarding the relation between the Christ-event and time. Taking up hints from his letters (e.g., 1 Cor 8:6; 10:4, 9, reading Χριστόν), the subsequent Pauline tradition would address this question, placing Christ before all creation (Col 1:15-20), as the one in whom believers were chosen "before the foundation of the world" (Eph 1:3-10). In Romans, Paul's focus is elsewhere, relating Christ to the story of Israel, not to time itself nor to the story of the world. His achievement here is to integrate the scriptural witness to Israel's call with the good news concerning Christ, and with the strange success of the Gentile mission. A single frame of explanation unites them all: incongruous grace.

90. In interpreting later Christian "figural reading," Dawson speaks of "a strange retroactive power in which a present occurrence makes possible the reality of the event which prefigures it" (D. Dawson, *Christian Figural Reading and the Fashioning of Identity* [Berkeley: University of California Press, 2002], p. 136).

91. See Luz, *Geschichtsverständnis*, p. 82: "Im Lichte der eschatologischen Gnade Gottes wird für Paulus die Einheit des Heilshandelns Gottes durch die Geschichte hindurch sichtbar."

CHAPTER 18

Conclusions

This book has offered a new approach to the concept of "grace," a new analysis of Second Temple Jewish theologies of divine beneficence, and a new reading of Galatians and Romans through the lens of Paul's theology of grace. We may summarize its distinctive contributions under five headings.

18.1. Grace as Gift

Since both Paul and his contemporaries used the normal vocabulary of gift, favor, and benefaction in speaking of (what we call) "grace," we have located their discourse on this topic within the social domain that anthropologists label "gift." This conceptual frame has provided no templates, but it has alerted us to features of ancient gift-giving that modern Western eyes are apt to miss or to misconstrue. It has also afforded some analytical distance from the special connotations that have become attached to the term "grace."

Several significant themes emerged from our study of the Greco-Roman (including the Jewish) practices and ideologies of "gift." Against modern notions of "altruism," we found that benefits were generally intended to foster mutuality, by creating or maintaining social bonds. This expectation of reciprocity, with its (non-legal) obligations, created cyclical patterns of gift-and-return, even where there were large differentials in power between givers and recipients. Thus, throughout this book, we have been suspicious of the modern (Western) ideal of the "pure" gift, which is supposedly given without strings attached. We have been able to make sense of the fact that a gift can be *unconditioned* (free of prior conditions regarding the recipient) without also being *unconditional* (free of expectations that the recipient will offer some "return"). Paul has provided a parade example of this phenomenon, since he simultaneously emphasizes the incongruity of grace and the expectation that those who are "under grace" (and wholly refashioned by it) will be reoriented in the "obedience of faith." What has seemed in the modern world a paradoxical phenomenon — that a "free" gift can also be obliging — is entirely comprehensible in ancient terms.

But the study of "gift" highlighted another important issue. We noted that benefits, because they expected a return, were normally given discriminately (even if lavishly) to people considered on some grounds fitting or worthy recipients of the gift. The adequacy or fit of the recipient might be variously judged, according to the value-system of the benefactor, but it was normal that gifts — especially rare or significant gifts — should be distributed with discrimination, and were *good* gifts only if so disbursed. Under these conditions, "gift" could be associated with "reward": although gifts could be distinguished from calculable pay or legally actionable loans, there was no inherent conflict between gift and recompense, between the language of "grace" and the language of worth. It was certainly possible for some gifts to be construed as "unmerited" (as we have found both in Paul and in some other Jewish literature), but this was not a normal, and certainly not a necessary, connotation of the terms we generally translate as "grace." In fact, an unmerited gift from God was theologically problematic, and could threaten the justice and the rationality of the universe. Although Christian theologians (and modern dictionaries) regard it as self-evident that "grace" means a benefit to the unworthy, in ancient terms this was a striking and theologically dangerous construal of the concept.

18.2. Distinct Perfections of Grace

Crucial to the analytical work of this book have been the notion of "perfection" (the drawing out of a concept to an end-of-line extreme) and the distinction between different perfections of grace. Grace, we have found, is no simple or single-faceted idea: the various aspects of gift-giving can each be perfected in separable forms. In chapter 2, we identified six possible perfections of grace, which we labeled *superabundance, singularity, priority, incongruity, efficacy,* and *non-circularity.* Each of these perfections configure gift in some maximal form, but none are necessary features of the concept, and, crucially, none requires or even implies another. They are distinguishable perfections and do not constitute a "package deal."

This theoretical analysis has proved useful in understanding the different ways in which our texts, both Jewish and Christian, discuss this common concept, using identical vocabulary with very different connotations. It has suggested a new way to understand disputes about grace: what was for some the very definition of grace was for others an unnecessary or even unwelcome assumption. In analyzing the configurations of grace in the history of reception of Paul's letters (chapter 3), we traced the differing perfections of this motif in the varied historical and theological contexts of key interpreters. This clarified the differences among our interpreters (e.g., between Marcion and Augustine, between Luther and Calvin, between Martyn and Dunn), who all variously emphasized grace. It also revealed the tendency to add one perfection to another, and the temptation to attribute to Paul our own perfections of this motif.

Accordingly, we could ask afresh what was meant by "grace" (in its varied lexical expressions) in Second Temple Jewish texts, including the letters of Paul. An immediate gain was the capacity to clarify a confusion arising from the work of Sanders on Second Temple Judaism. Sanders's model of "covenantal nomism" laid stress on the *priority* of grace, while implying that grace is also *incongruous* with the worth of its recipients (see above, 3.6.1). He thus found Paul's theology of grace indistinguishable from a uniform Jewish view, a thesis that continues to be disputed among interpreters who spotlight different perfections of grace (see 3.6.2 and 3.7.2). By disaggregating perfections, we insisted that *priority* does not imply *incongruity:* a common Jewish commitment to the priority of grace in election did not imply uniformity on a separable matter, whether God distributes grace without regard to worth. Thus, the aspect of Sanders's "covenantal nomism" that has proved most theologically potent was found to be conceptually confused. By clarifying this matter, we have been able to understand both how Sanders unwittingly created a spurious uniformity within Judaism, and why interpreters have been variously satisfied or dissatisfied with his conclusions.

The analytical distinction between various perfections has, in fact, opened new ways of construing the theologies of grace in Second Temple Judaism. Each of the texts analyzed in Part II made divine grace (God's goodness, mercy, or beneficence) a central theme, but in notably diverse ways. Alongside differences in frame, horizon, and historical circumstance, we identified various perfections of this motif. In particular, we highlighted the difference between texts that emphasized the congruity between God's beneficence and the worth of its recipients (e.g., *The Wisdom of Solomon* and Philo) and those that represented God's grace as given without regard for worth (e.g., the Qumran *Hodayot* and *LAB;* see summary in 10.2)

This disaggregation of perfections made it possible to ask afresh what Paul meant by "grace" and whether or in what ways he perfected this motif. Against the tendency to trace in Paul a traditional set of perfections, or as many perfections as possible, we have approached Paul with as few pre-formed assumptions as possible, open to the possibility that he may perfect this motif in certain respects, and not at all in others. What this means for our reading of Paul, and for its relation to the history of interpretation, will be clarified below.

18.3. Paul among Jewish Theologians of Grace

Our theme has long been significant in attempts to place Paul among, or against, his fellow Jews. A theological reading of Paul's antithetical expressions has produced an image of Judaism as a religion of "works-righteousness," with the conviction that Paul, and Paul alone, grasped the meaning of "grace." On this reading, fostered by Reformation interpretations of "works" (see above, 3.3; 3.4; 3.5), other contemporary Jewish configurations of grace were judged self-contradictory, mixing grace with soteriologies of recompense or achievement. In reaction, Sanders's "covenantal nomism" represented Second Temple Judaism as a uniform "religion of grace," with Paul on this point indistinguishable from all his fellow Jews (see above, 3.6.1). Our analysis of selected texts has suggested a different conclusion: grace is everywhere in the theology of Second Temple Judaism, but not everywhere the same. On the critical question of the congruity of grace, we have found not unanimity but *diversity.* Some of our texts correlate God's mercy with his justice, such that God's beneficence is generally, or at least finally, accorded as a reward to fitting recipients (e.g., *Wisdom of Solomon;* Uriel in *4 Ezra*). Others perfect the incongruity of grace, tracing the mismatch between the goodness of God and the worthlessness of the human (1QH[a]) or the sinfulness of Israel *(LAB).* The dialogues of *4 Ezra* suggest that this subject was a matter of debate in Second Temple Judaism. It would be a mistake to regard the incongruity of grace as ubiquitous in Judaism, but equally wrong to consider this notion uniquely Pauline. Paul's is one Jewish voice in a chorus of divergent opinions, distinctive in certain respects, but not qualitatively or quantitatively *more distinct* than the voices of other Jews. Paul stands *among* fellow Jews in his discussion of divine grace, not *apart from* them in a unique or antithetical position. At the same time, he stands in the midst of a *debate,* and none of our Jewish authors can be taken as spokesmen for a single, simple, or uncontested notion of grace.

Paul's letters (notably, Rom 9–11) indicate his engagement with common themes in the Jewish discussion of our topic, but they also display the distinctive configuration of his thought. Paul, we have found, explores the *incongruity* of grace, which he relates to *the Christ-event* as the definitive enactment of God's love for the unlovely, and to *the Gentile mission,* where the gifts of

God ignore ethnic differentials of worth and Torah-based definitions of value ("righteousness"). In fact, this theology of grace, Christologically defined and articulated both for and from the Gentile mission, reshaped Paul's understanding of *the identity of Israel.* Paul's distinctive retelling of the Abrahamic and patriarchal origins of Israel (Rom 4 and 9) is patterned by the incongruous gift, which he finds integral to Israel's existence and destiny. Paul's theology is not directed *against* Judaism; neither does he consider assemblies of Jewish and Gentile believers as the *replacement* of Israel. On his reading, Israel is most truly itself when it is solely dependent on the root of God's unconditioned mercy; and that is fully and definitively the case when it draws on the "wealth" poured out to Jew and Gentile in Christ.

The way Paul radicalizes the incongruity of grace, and the distinctive way he connects that grace to the Christ-event and practices it in his Gentile mission, relativizes the authority of the Torah in a fashion unparalleled among his Jewish peers. His claim to have "died to the law in order to live to God" (Gal 2:19) signals a shocking devaluation of Jewish symbolic capital (cf. Phil 3:2-11) just when he embraces the Jewish ideal of "living to God." Paul is neither anti-Jewish nor post-Jewish, but his configuration of the grace of God in Christ alters his Jewish identity and makes him question his former allegiance to the Torah. Our reading of Paul has provided a new angle of vision on this perennially fascinating and controversial phenomenon.

18.4. Paul's Theology of Grace in Its Original Social Context

Paul's notion of the incongruous Christ-gift was originally part of his *missionary theology,* developed for and from the Gentile mission at the pioneering stage of community formation. Since God's incongruous grace dissolves former criteria of worth, it forms the basis for innovative groups of converts, by loosening their ties to pre-constituted norms and uniting them in their common faith in Christ. The starting point is the framing of the *Christ-event as gift.* Christ's death "for our sins" (e.g., 1 Cor 15:3-4) is interpreted by Paul in the language of gift (God's gift of his Son, or Christ's gift of himself). The life, death, and resurrection of Jesus are thus, for Paul, the focal point of divine beneficence: the witness of Scripture and the history and identity of Israel are interpreted in this light. Grace is discovered in an *event,* not in the general benevolence of God, and its focal expression lies not in creation nor in any other divine gift, but in the gift of Christ, which constitutes for Paul *the Gift.*

This Gift is experienced and interpreted as an *incongruous gift.* The Gentile mission is formative: non-Jews, wholly unqualified for divine beneficence, are found to be "called in grace" when they receive the good news of Christ, and are gifted with the Spirit. Paul's own experience matches this disregard of worth, since he too was "called in grace" irrespective of his Jewish privileges and despite his persecution of the church. Paul thus identifies a divine initiative in the Christ-event that disregards taken-for-granted criteria of ethnicity, status, knowledge, virtue, or gender. In a dialectical fashion, Paul's theology justifies the formation of norm-violating communities, while his missionary practice clarifies and radicalizes the incongruity of the gift of Christ.

Paul understands the *single* event of Christ to bring into question *every* pre-existent classification of worth. In figuring believers as "dead to the world" and as expressions of a "new creation" (Gal 6:14-15), he articulates the birth of dissident communities that are capable of disregarding distinctions between Jew and Greek, slave and free, male and female (Gal 3:28). Such social identities continue to exist, but they are declared insignificant as markers of worth in a community that is beholden to Christ and operates "at a diagonal" to the normal taxonomies of value (Gal 1:10-11). Ancestry, education, and social power are subordinated to a common "calling" that disregards previous assumptions of worth (1 Cor 1:26-31). Novel communities are encouraged to relativize their differences in culture, welcoming one another on the unconditioned terms by which each was welcomed in Christ (Rom 14–15).

Paul's discussion of "justification" and his antithesis between "works of the Law" and "faith in Christ" are formulated in and for the Gentile mission. Paul declares that the ethnic distinction between Jew and Gentile, which was foundational to his "ancestral traditions," has been dissolved by the incongruous gift of Christ. His mission experience, his controversies with other Jewish believers, and his own calling as apostle to the Gentiles make these themes central to Galatians and Romans. Here "works of the Law" means Jewish practices; the "Law" in question is the Torah. In declaring that God counts worth ("righteousness") by reference not to Torah-observance but to faith in Christ, Paul subverts the normative authority of the Torah, which is no longer to shape ("enslave") the common life of believers. Jewish believers are by no means prohibited from observing the Torah, but even for them its authority is subordinate to "the truth of the good news." They are required to acknowledge that it is not the common cultural framework of believers, and thus not to be imposed on Gentile converts. Although aspects of the Torah are "fulfilled" in Spirit-led conduct, it is not the believers' ultimate norm; to accept it as such would be to deny the grace of God in Christ. Believers are united by faith in Christ — the mark of their orientation to the event of Christ, which is the source of their "newness of life." Paul opposes those who think Torah-observance is the essential expression of faith not because "law" or "works" are problematic principles of soteriology, but because the Torah — like every other pre-constituted norm — has been dethroned as a criterion of worth by the unconditioned gift of Christ.

Two intersecting features of Pauline theology place this gift in a wider theological context — his theology of calling (his version of covenant-theology or "salvation-history") and his theology of sin (his anthropology). The Christ-gift is interpreted as the fulfillment of the promises to Abraham, but at the same time clearly distinguished from the Torah-covenant. In accord with this peculiar disjunction, Paul reinterprets the whole of Scripture, which grounds his theology inasmuch as it contains echoes of the good news. In Galatians, Israel's history is accorded no positive significance; the emphasis in that letter on curse and enslavement underlines, rather, the *incongruity* of grace. Romans does recount elements of Israel's story, but only where they bear the distinctively Pauline marks of disjunction: right from the start, and up to the present (and projected into the future), Paul traces the pattern of life from the dead, the justification of the ungodly, and mercy without regard to worth. The scope of this narrative is significant to Paul, since the new assemblies of believers have come into existence only by being grafted onto the root that has created and sustained Israel from its beginning. Paul is not citing scriptural episodes to illustrate abstract principles of soteriology. But the story he tells is not a common Second Temple narrative with a Christological conclusion: it has a newly discovered plot-line, shaped by the incongruity of grace.

The other context for the gift is Paul's theology of sin. Paul's pessimism regarding "the present evil age" (Gal 1:4) is radicalized by the conviction that the Christ-gift is given in the absence of worth, to the "ungodly" and the "weak." There are no exceptions: *all* (Jew and Gentile) are under the rule of sin, which holds the cosmos in subjection. Even the Torah is frustrated by this enslaving power (Rom 7), a further reason why there can be no justification within its terms. This grim anthropology forms the foil to Paul's news of freedom and reconciliation in Christ; his contrasts between before and after, outside and inside, reflect the experience of his converts. The drama of their movement from death to life, from flesh to Spirit, and from sin to righteousness is encapsulated in baptism, whose "newness of life," derived from Christ, is experienced in new social relations and in the reconstitution of each individual self (Gal 2:19-20).

The Christ-gift thus provides the basic soteriological shape for Paul's theology of calling and of sin — his configuration of the story of Israel and his representation of the plight of humanity. The integration of these theological matrices is Paul's distinctive achievement. Together they contextualize the Christ-gift, identifying its significance on a map that encompasses all of history and the whole of the cosmos. But because their focal point is the gift of Christ, each bears the mark of the incongruity of grace.

The goal of Paul's mission is the formation of communities whose distinct patterns of life bear witness to an event that has broken with normal criteria of worth. Paul expects baptism to create new life-orientations, including forms of bodily *habitus* that express the reality of resurrection-life in the midst of human mortality. The gift needs to be realized in unconventional practice or it ceases to have meaning as an incongruous gift. It creates new modes of obedience to God, which arise from the gift as "return" to God, but without instrumental purpose in eliciting further divine gifts. The transformative power of grace thus creates a fit between believers and God, which will be evident at the eschaton. Judgment "according to works" does not entail a new and incompatible principle of soteriology; it indicates that the incongruous gift has had its intended effect in embedding new standards of worth in the practice of those it transforms.

The *incongruity* of grace does not imply, for Paul, its *singularity* (since God's act of grace in Christ is predicated on his judgment of sin) or its *non-circularity* (since the gift carries expectations of obedience). Because it is incongruous, the *priority* of the gift is everywhere presupposed, but Paul rarely draws out predestinarian conclusions, as in the *Hodayot* or in the theologies of Augustine and Calvin. The *superabundance* of grace is also presupposed and sometimes explicit, but its *efficacy* is given less attention than the Augustinian tradition might suggest. While some Pauline texts suggest the efficacy of grace in the will and work of believers (1 Cor 15:9-10; Phil 2:12-13), this perfection receives no special profile in Galatians and Romans. Everything that may be said about the believer is predicated on the resurrection life of Christ, as the source of new life in the Spirit: no one can "walk in line with the Spirit" unless they "live by the Spirit" (Gal 5:25). But the efficacy of grace (in the sense of the present, causative agency of God within the agency of believers) is not of central concern in either Galatians or Romans, and is not a necessary entailment of their primary perfection, the *incongruity of the gift of Christ.*

18.5. New Contexts and New Meanings of Grace

Paul's theology of grace has been influential only because it has proved fertile in historical and social conditions beyond its original context. Its meaning has necessarily been altered in the process. Originally, as we have seen, it was integral to Paul's mission at the start of the Christian movement: it served to disjoin converts from their previous criteria of worth, scoring a line between their past and their present, between insiders and outsiders. After this initial generation, in a post-missional context and within Christian communities whose boundaries were already established, this same theology played a different role and acquired a different focus. Even where the incongruity of grace was re-emphasized, it served not to establish but to refine the Christian tradition, drawing lines of demarcation not *around* the Christian community but *within* it, and even within the subjectivity of believers.

This change of focus is related to the fact that the originating context of Paul's theology — the Gentile mission that dissolved the distinction between Jews and non-Jews and relativized the Torah — became a matter of merely historical interest to later theologians, who sought more contemporary relevance in the Pauline language of "works" and "law." But a more fundamental shift was at play: the language of grace that had once served to detach new communities from their previous cultural allegiances was now applied to believers with little or no consciousness of a break with their past (since their primary socialization was as Christians), and to communities whose external boundaries were either non-existent (in a solidly Christian culture) or already obvious. Their criteria of worth (what counted as honorable or righteous) were already strongly "Christianized." In such contexts Paul's theology of grace became a tool for the inner reform of the Christian tradition, its critical edge turned against believers, undermining not their pre-Christian criteria of worth but their pride or purpose in achieving Christian worth. Grace remained the means of access to the community, but the critical dissolution of pre-constituted norms ("what accords with human values," Gal 1:11) became an attack on the believer's confidence or independence in adhering to Christian norms. In a context where "the law," once passed through Christian filters, was granted full authority as divine law, it was impossible to imagine that the believer should challenge its authority as Paul had challenged the normative role of the Torah. Paul had placed "grace" and faith in contrast to righteousness in the Law, but it was inconceivable that he should have questioned the Law's normative criteria, and more likely that he intended to criticize a deficiency in the believer, either in measuring up to the Law or in construing its intention. The shift that takes place here is not from the particular to the universal (Paul himself covers both, working from the particularity of the Christ-event to its universal implications), nor from the specific to the abstract (like Paul, his interpreters have specific targets for their theology), nor from the communal to the individual (Paul's own theology of grace has both communal and individual dimensions). What changes, rather, is the social context. The critical theology of a new social movement, by which it formulated its identity and clarified its boundaries, becomes the self-critical theology of an established tradition: its missionary theology is turned inwards.

The first signs of this contextual shift may be traced in the deutero-Pauline letters, where "works" are refocused as moral achievements (Eph 2:8-10; 2 Tim 1:9; Tit 3:5) and "boasting" indicates not the cultural confidence of the Jew in the Torah (or of the Greek in wisdom), but pride in achievement (Eph 2:9). Grace is a marker of the divine source of worth ("not from you, but the gift of God," Eph 2:8). Augustine, as we saw (3.2, above), interpreted "boasting" as the pride of believers who attribute merit to themselves, and not to God. He took Paul's theology of grace to subvert not the standard human *criteria of worth,* but the human tendency to self-congratulation in the *attainment of worth.* The critical edge of Paul's theology is thus directed against Christian construals of virtue-acquisition. The incongruity of grace, which Augustine perfected together with its priority and efficacy, is taken to represent the axiomatic principle that God's healing aid is the necessary and effective source of all moral or spiritual achievement. The distinction between life "in the flesh" and new life "in the Spirit" (Rom 7–8) — a contrast for Paul between the former and the present life of a convert — is taken to represent the inner duality of the believer. To speak of grace is to speak of the believer's dependence on the agency of God.

The achievement of Luther (see above, 3.3) was to translate Paul's missionary theology of grace into an urgent and perpetual *inward mission,* directed to the church, but especially to the heart of each believer. Luther recaptured both the incongruity of grace in Paul and its origin in the *event* of Jesus Christ; the challenge was to make this significant in communities of believers long socialized in the Christian tradition. The subversive dynamic of Paul's theology is directed against a different target — not the old normative systems that believers are struggling to shed, but a faulty understanding of their own good works as necessary to gain God's favor. Paul's theology of gift is re-preached to effect the *perpetual conversion* of believers, who need to learn over and again to receive the gift of God and to banish the false opinion that their works will merit salvation. The gospel constitutes a mission to the self and a daily return to baptism, since the old nature persists in its tendency to arrogant self-sufficiency and must be countered by reminders that Christ has already given all. Thus, grace here scores a line through the life of the Christian, who is *simul justus et peccator,* both a believer and a sinful human being, and a believer only as he or she becomes one repeatedly in faith. Paul's polemics against "works of the law" are taken to be directed not against an external (and no longer valid) definition of worth (Torah-practice) but against the subjective evaluation of one's own good works as effective for salvation. This change in focus fostered a regrettable tendency to figure "Jews" as exemplars of human self-righteousness, but it constituted a brilliant re-contextualization of Pauline theology in the conditions of the sixteenth-century church.

As we have seen, the twentieth century saw several notable developments in the reading of grace as a rebuke to the church or a judgment on the self-understanding of every individual (3.5, above). For all their differences, these have generally continued the tradition in which "works" are the target of Paul's polemic against "works of the law." In this tradition, Paul's theology is taken to expose the human incapacity to fulfill the law's demands (Augustine; Calvin), or the "religious" movement toward God that is no more than a "human enterprise" (Barth; Martyn), or the false and subtly idolatrous presumption that one can rely upon oneself for salvation (Luther; Bultmann; Käsemann). In all cases, the object of Paul's critique is not the content of the works but the "doing" of them, not the criteria by which worth is measured, but the purported achievement of worth.

Viewed from this angle, the "new perspective" constitutes a break in the mainstream history of reception. Locating Paul's letters within first-generation conflicts over the Mosaic Torah, it construes the issue to lie not in the believers' performance of good works, but in the differentiation of the community of believers from (some of) the Jewish rules of Torah-observance (see above, 3.6). In agreement with the "new perspective," we have found the context for Paul's theology of justification to be the Gentile mission and the construction of communities that crossed ethnic (as well as social) boundaries. Moreover, these social effects are not just the context of Paul's theology, mere illustrations of soteriological principles, but its goal, since the calling of Jew and Gentile in Christ is the fulfillment of Israel's calling in mercy, and thus at the center of God's purposes in history. However, I depart from the "new perspective" in identifying the theological root of this Pauline mission. It is Paul's theology of the Christ-gift that shapes his appeals to the Abrahamic promises, to the experience of the Spirit, and to the oneness of God. This is certainly not to return to theologically pernicious contrasts between Pauline grace and Jewish works-righteousness; by contrast, we have demonstrated the significance of divine beneficence in a wide range of Jewish texts. Grace is everywhere in Second Temple Judaism. But it is the incongruous grace that Paul traces in the Christ-event and experiences in the Gentile mission that is the explosive force that demolishes old criteria of worth and clears space for innovative communities that inaugurate new patterns of social existence. It is because grace belongs to no one that it goes to everyone — and not because of a political or philosophical preference for the broad over the narrow, or the universal over the particular. Paul's ecclesiology has its roots in his soteriology of grace, which also shapes his understanding of the human plight at both a cosmic and an individual level and has theological significance and social implications far beyond its original context.

Thus, the reading of Paul offered in this book may be interpreted *either* as a re-contextualization of the Augustinian-Lutheran tradition, returning the dynamic of the incongruity of grace to its original mission environment where it accompanied the formation of new communities, *or* as a reconfiguration of the "new perspective," placing its best historical and exegetical insights within the frame of Paul's theology of grace. I have disagreed in significant ways with interpreters on both sides of this divide, and the reading offered here does not harmonize the two interpretative traditions but reshapes them both. Thus, it opens a path beyond current dichotomies, placing their respective strengths within a frame that is responsible both to Paul's historical conditions and to the theological structures of his thought.

This reading of Paul may also create resonances today. Because the Christological event of grace is both highly particular and impacts on *any* criteria of worth that are not derived from the good news itself, Paul's theology does not remain encased within its first-century context. One does not have to find "timeless principles" by extracting general truths from particular historical debates: Paul himself saw the general relevance of a theology of grace that reconfigured the map of reality. As we have seen, that theology fitted its original context of an inaugural mission, and is necessarily refocused when used in the reform of an established Christian tradition. Today, however, the Christian tradition is anything but stable and established. In fact, one might be struck by the *similarities* between Paul's missional context and the social context of many churches today. Not only in pioneer mission, but even (in fact, especially) in a pluralist or secularizing context, churches now find themselves needing to rediscover their social, political, and cultural identity. Taken-for-granted criteria of value regarding age, ethnicity, social status, education, gender, health, or wealth become in such circumstances the object of critical reevaluation, and churches identify anew what it is about the good news that makes them socially and ideologically distinctive. This new missional context makes Paul's theology of grace relevant not only in the re-contextualized forms in which it has become familiar (as an individualized theology of "amazing grace"), but also in its *original* dynamic accompanying the creation of innovative, countercultural communities of faith. By starting from the Christ-event, and by clarifying with radical sharpness the unconditioned grace that was given in Christ, Paul provides resources for the dissolution of pre-formed assumptions and for the construction of boundary-erasing communities. These resources could prove vital for churches as they renegotiate their identities in cultures where what it means to be "church" has become radically uncertain.

We have focused here on the divine gift of grace, *the gift* in its theological sense. As we have noted, this understanding of gift has its necessary embodiment in the life of transformed communities, but we have not had space to explore in its wider dimensions the significance of gift in Paul's configuration of human relations. The construction of community through the reciprocity of gift, the extension of gift-relations beyond the normal range of social relationships, the renegotiations of power and obligation that accompany the giving and receiving of gifts *in Christ* — all these remain Pauline topics barely touched upon here. Other Pauline letters beyond those addressed here (e.g., 1 and 2 Corinthians; Philippians; Philemon) would need to be added to the discussion. It may be that in these matters, as well, Paul's thought and practice, once contextualized in the economic conditions of the first century, have significant implications for a contemporary social and political ethic. But that will be the agenda for another book.

APPENDIX

The Lexicon of Gift: Greek, Hebrew, Latin, and English

"Gift" denotes the sphere of *voluntary, personal relations, characterized by goodwill in the giving of benefit or favor, and eliciting some form of reciprocal return that is both voluntary and necessary for the continuation of the relationship.* In accord with the anthropology of gift, its scope includes various forms of kindness, favor, generosity, or compassion enacted in diverse services and benefits, with the expectation of some reciprocating gratitude or counter-gift. Ancient languages articulate this field of relations in a rich variety of terms, which often overlap in meaning but may also contain subtly different connotations. As often in lexical semantics, we find fluidity and fuzzy boundaries, and should avoid the temptation of over-precise definitions. But in a social sphere where euphemism was necessary, nuance could be highly significant. A single transaction could be differently described — just like in English, where a monetary gift could be figured as a donation, an honorarium, a prize, or a bribe.

The prominence of the term χάρις in Hellenistic discourse on benefaction and in Pauline theology should not be taken to suggest that χάρις was *the* term for the gift in Greek-speaking antiquity. Still less should we confuse words with concepts so as to speak (as some do) of "the concept of χάρις." Studies of Paul's theology of grace have often limited themselves to this single lexeme, but Paul speaks of divine and human gift (favor, generosity, and benefit) with a wide range of terms.[1] In fact, the vocabulary employed in this field of social

1. Thus, regarding divine gift in Romans 9–11, alongside χάρις (11:5-6) and χαρίσματα (11:29), Paul's speaks of God's ἐκλογή (9:11; 11:5, 7, 28) and χρηστότης (11:22), and describes God's actions in verbs such as ἀγαπάω (9:13, 25; cf. 11:28), πλουτέω (10:12; cf. 9:23; 11:12, 33), ἐλεέω (9:15, 16, 18; 11:30-32; cf. 9:23), and οἰκτείρω (9:15). Of divine and human gifts in 2 Corinthians 8–9, besides χάρις (8:1, 4, 6, 7, 9, 19; 9:8), he speaks of ἁπλότης (8:2; 9:11, 13), ἁδρότης (8:20), κοινωνία (8:4; 9:13), and διακονία (8:4; 9:1, 12, 13; cf. 8:19, 20), and employs a range of verbs and nouns related to δίδωμι (8:1, 5, 10, 16; 9:7, 9, 15). χάρις is the primary, and almost sole,

relations is vast; we will limit our attention to the terms employed by the texts discussed in this book. After mapping the Greek lexemes, we will chart the "gift" language in our Hebrew texts, noting also the special connotations of Greek terms in texts that translate (or draw on translations of) a Hebrew source. We will then survey the Latin terminology, before noting the special problems of some English terms.[2]

1. "Gift" in Greek

(a) Although χάρις is only one of several terms for divine and human gifts, and in some texts is of marginal significance, it is convenient to start with this term, whose varied senses reflect different moments in the circular movement of gifts. The Greeks themselves were aware of this fact (one kind of χάρις generating another, Sophocles, *Ajax* 552; cf. *Oed. Col.* 779), which was portrayed in the circle-dance of the three Χάριτες (cf. Seneca, *Ben.* 1.3.2-5).[3] There are three interrelated meanings:[4]

(i) of the object of favor, *the quality of charm or agreeableness.* This is the most common meaning in older and poetic Greek, where χάρις can mean "charm" or "delight" (with cognate adjectives εὔχαρις, εὐχάριστος, χαρίεις, "charming" or "delightful"), the quality that elicits favor or is the object of it.[5] χάρις was employed in this sense by those who translated the Hebrew Bible into Greek (e.g., LXX Ps 44:2; Prov 10:32), not least in the idiom εὑρίσκειν χάριν ἐναντίον ("to find favor in the eyes of," Gen 6:8; 18:3, etc.), in all these

focus of attention in, e.g., J. Wobbe, *Die Charis-Gedanke bei Paulus: Ein Beitrag zur neutestamentlichen Theologie* (Münster: Aschendorff, 1932); J. R. Harrison, *Paul's Language of Grace in Its Graeco-Roman Context* (Tübingen: Mohr Siebeck, 2003).

2. For broader comments on the linguistics of gift and exchange, see E. Benveniste, *Problems in General Linguistics,* trans. M. E. Meek (Coral Gables: University of Miami Press, 1971), pp. 271-80. For older discussions of the key terms surveyed here, see, e.g., J. Moffatt, *Grace in the New Testament* (London: Hodder and Stoughton, 1931), pp. 21-43, 99-127; T. F. Torrance, *The Doctrine of Grace in the Apostolic Fathers* (Edinburgh: Oliver and Boyd, 1948), pp. 1-20.

3. Cf. K. Deichgräber, *Charis und Chariten: Grazie und Grazien* (Munich: Heimeran, 1971); cf. O. Loew, *ΧΑΡΙΣ* (Diss. Marburg, 1908; *non vidi*).

4. Cf. *LSJ* s.v. (using a different schema for the same differences in meaning) and E. A. Nida and J. P. Louw, *Lexical Semantics of the Greek New Testament* (Atlanta: Scholars Press, 1992), pp. 62-68 (finding six class meanings in New Testament Greek, but declining to map them onto the social domain of gift-relations).

5. See *LSJ* s.v. and the collection of examples in C. Spicq, *Theological Lexicon of the New Testament,* 3 vols. (Peabody, Mass.: Hendrickson, 1994), vol. 3, pp. 500-501. On the use of this important term in Pindar, see L. Kurke, *The Traffic in Praise: Pindar and the Poetics of Social Economy* (Ithaca: Cornell University Press, 1991).

cases translating חן (see below). It is found occasionally in this sense in the New Testament (e.g., Luke 1:30; 2:52; Acts 7:46; 1 Pet 2:19-20), though not in the undisputed letters of Paul (cf. Col 4:6).

(ii) of the giver or the gift, *the attitude of benevolence, or the favor or benefit given.* The attitude and the gift may be distinguishable or may shade into one another, since benevolence is often expressed in particular benefits. This is a common set of meanings in Greek literature (e.g., Thucydides 2.40.4) and is ubiquitous in the inscriptions that honor Greek and Roman benefactors, where the fuzzy boundary between attitude and action allows benefits to be celebrated as expressions of their donors' benevolence.[6] These meanings (for both singular χάρις and plural χάριτες) appear in the later Greek translations of the Hebrew Bible (e.g., Zech 12:10; Esth 6:3; cf. Sir 7:33; 19:25; 20:13), are ubiquitous in Philo (see chapter 6), and are common in the New Testament (e.g., Acts 4:33; 11:23), especially in Paul (who uses only the singular, χάρις). In late Hellenistic Greek, they can be expressed in verbal form as χαριτόω (e.g., Eph 1:6) and χαρίζομαι (e.g., Phil 1:29), the latter acquiring special meanings, such as "forgive" (e.g., 2 Cor 12:13). Paul can speak of God acting ἐν χάριτι (Gal 1:6), διὰ χάριτος (Gal 1:15) or simply χάριτι (Rom 3:24; cf. Eph 2:8-9), with reference to the *quality* of God's action toward his beneficiaries. But he also uses χάρις (and χάρισμα) for God's *act* of beneficence toward the world in Christ (Rom 5:15-21; Gal 2:21; 2 Cor 6:1) or that of Christ himself (2 Cor 8:9; Gal 5:4). And these senses overlap with another, the *gift itself* (2 Cor 4:15; 8:1; 9:8). In this last sense, χάρις is also used for human gifts (1 Cor 16:3; 2 Cor 8:6, 7, 19).

It is important to observe that neither here nor in other Greek usage does the lexeme χάρις itself have the specific sense of an undeserved or incongruous gift. Whether χάρις is "perfected" as an incongruous gift (see chapter 2) or given to worthy beneficiaries is determined not by the term itself but by the nature of the relationship between the benefactor and the recipient(s), as revealed by the literary or social context.

(iii) of the return of favor, *gratitude* or *thanksgiving.* Once again, this meaning of χάρις (in both singular and plural) is common in Hellenistic Greek, and is ubiquitous in papyri and inscriptions, together with its synonym, εὐχαριστία.[7] Both are found in Jewish texts of the Hellenistic/Roman period (Sir 12:1; 3 Macc 1:9; Philo *passim*), as in the New Testament (e.g., Heb 12:28; Rev 4:9), including Paul. Paul uses χάρις and εὐχαριστία in the sense of "thanks" (e.g., 1 Cor 10:30; 2 Cor 9:11-12, 15), and connects divine χάρις (in

6. For the best recent survey, see Harrison, *Language of Grace*, pp. 26-63.

7. See Spicq, *Lexicon*, vol. 3, pp. 503-4, with representative examples; for the papyri, Harrison, *Language of Grace*, pp. 64-96.

the sense of favor/gift) with human εὐχαριστία, an indication of the circle of reciprocity that these terms evoke (e.g., 1 Cor 1:4; 2 Cor 1:11; 4:15; 9:11-12).

(b) There are many other terms that express beneficence or the benefits given. Terms for divine beneficence in the Pauline corpus include χρηστότης (e.g., Rom 2:4; 11:22; "kindness"), ἔλεος (e.g., Rom 15:29, "favor" or "compassion" [see below, section 2]), εὐλογία (Rom 15:29; "blessing"), and φιλανθρωπία (e.g., Titus 3:4, "kindness to humans"). Philo likes to label God φιλόδωρος (e.g., *Leg.* 1.34; "loving to give"). The same terms can apply to human beneficence, with the addition of words such as μεγαλοψυχία ("magnanimity") and ἁπλότης ("generosity," e.g., 2 Cor 8:2). Paul uses ἀγάπη and ἀγαπάω ("love," both human and divine) in proximity with χάρις and δίδωμι (e.g., Rom 5:2-5; Gal 2:20-21; 2 Cor 8:19-24), evoking the personal and emotional dimensions of the gift relationship.

Verbs for beneficent action include many cognate to the nouns just noted. Of course, δίδωμι (and its numerous compounds) is extremely common in this sense (where it does not mean simply "convey"). Paul, like Philo, uses this verb in combination with χάρις (e.g., Rom 12:3; 2 Cor 8:1), indicating the semantic overlap of these terms. εὐεργετέω and its cognates are common in literature and inscriptions (but rare in the New Testament), while Paul employs verbs for God's benevolent selection nuanced by his Jewish tradition, such as εὐδοκέω (Gal 1:15), ἐκλέγομαι (1 Cor 1:27-28), and ἐλεέω (Rom 9:15; see below, section 2).

For the benefits themselves, there is a set of nouns related to the verb δίδωμι (δόσις, δόμα, δώρημα, δωρεά, δῶρον); on occasion these overlap largely if not completely with nouns from the χαρ- root (e.g., in Rom 5:15-17). A number of other terms (e.g., εὐλογία, κοινωνία, 2 Cor 9:5, 13) connote additional elements regarding the spirit of the gift or the relationship it creates. Since gifts carry social power, including the power to oblige (see chapter 1), they can function as "bribes." The "receipt of gifts" (δωροδοκία) is the nearest Greek comes to a technical term for this phenomenon in a political or judicial context (see above, 1.2.1). A gift that functions as a return can acquire a number of names, including μισθός, whose meaning shifts over time, from "reward" to "pay," mirroring structural shifts toward more formal and contractual forms of remuneration.[8] In the New Testament, μισθός can have either sense, or hovers on the border between them (e.g., 1 Cor 3:8, 14; 9:17-18). The adverb δωρεάν can mean "as a gift" (Rom 3:24) or "for free" (i.e., "not in return for payment";

8. See E. Benveniste, *Le vocabulaire des institutions indo-européens: 1. Économie, Parenté, Société* (Paris: Minuit, 1969), pp. 163-70, and discussion in S. von Reden, *Exchange in Ancient Greece* (London: Routledge, 1995), pp. 89-92.

e.g., 2 Cor 11:7; cf. 2 Thess 3:8). It can also mean "for no reason" (i.e., without causal factors, John 15:25 = LXX Ps 68:5) or "to nil effect" (i.e., not eliciting a response, Gal 2:21; cf. LXX Job 1:9?). Each indicates a possible "perfection" of the gift (see above, chapter 2).

The return of the gift is often (but not always) marked by the use of prepositional prefixes, for instance, ἀποδίδωμι or ἀνταποδίδωμι. Since what is returned can vary enormously (from a counter-gift to loyalty, obedience, or honor), the vocabulary is highly diverse: in relation to God what is due, alongside gratitude, is generally honor, sacrifice, or worship (e.g., Rom 1:21; 12:1).

2. "Gift" in Hebrew (and in Greek Influenced by Hebrew)

Our broad definition of gift (see above) captures a number of terms in biblical Hebrew (beyond the standard נתן, "give"). The noun חן means "charm" or "agreeableness" (much like the first sense of χάρις, noted above), as in the phrase "to give/have חן in the eyes of someone" (e.g., Gen 33:8); only occasionally, and in later texts, does it mean favor or gift. However, the cognate adjective חנון and verb חנן convey the meaning of favor or generosity toward someone (e.g., Gen 33:5).[9] In the revelation of the character of God in Exodus 34:6-7, the adjective חנון is accompanied by its near synonym רחום and the noun חסד; these three, together with the noun רחמים, are regularly grouped in biblical descriptions of God's nature and acts (e.g., Num 14:18; Neh 9:17-18; Ps 103:8-13). The noun חסד has a complex range of meanings, varying somewhat over time. It generally represents a personal, voluntary, and non-legal relationship, where the beneficence of a superior party sets up an expectation of return (or itself arises from a previous relationship). The term evokes loyalty or faithfulness in acts that provide an essential service to the beneficiary (such as protection or rescue; later, forgiveness).[10] Used both of human relations and of relations between God and humanity, it becomes one of the central terms for God's committed acts of kindness toward his people, not easily translated into English. Its associate, רחמים, has connotations of compassion or pity, with a more emotional tone. This constellation of terms is very common in the Qumran hymns (see above, chapter 7), where another term, רצון, signals God's favorable decision or selection.

9. On this root, see K. W. Neubauer, *Der Stamm* Chnn *im Sprachgebrauch des Alten Testaments* (Berlin: Ernst Reute Gesellschaft, 1964).

10. For discussion of this much-debated term, see K. Doob Sakenfeld, *The Meaning of* Hesed *in the Hebrew Bible* (Missoula: Scholars Press, 1978); G. R. Clark, *The Word* "Hesed" *in the Hebrew Bible* (Sheffield: JSOT Press, 1993).

In the Greek translation of the Hebrew Bible, Greek terms sometimes acquire unusual connotations, and this recalibration influences later Jewish authors writing in Greek. χάρις is a natural translation of חן (in the sense of something agreeable or charming), but the adjective חנון is normally translated by ἐλεήμων (sometimes οἰκτίρμων) and the verb חנן by ἐλέεω (sometimes οἰκτείρω). The noun חסד becomes ἔλεος (in Proverbs sometimes ἐλεημοσύνη). רחמים (when it does not mean "womb") is translated by οἰκτιρμός (or οἰκτιρμοί), the adjective רחום by οἰκτίρμων and the verb רחם by ἐλεέω, οἰκτείρω, or occasionally ἀγαπάω.

This pattern indicates extensive overlap between the verbs ἐλεέω and οἰκτείρω and between their respective nouns and adjectives (cf. Rom 9:15; 11:32; 12:1). In the process of translation, ἔλεος and its cognate verb ἐλεέω acquired new connotations. In normal Greek, they conveyed "pity" in the sense of compassion on the unfortunate (an emotion only fitting, in Aristotle's view, if the sufferer's misfortune is undeserved, *Rhet.* 1385b13-14). In a judicial context, pity implied clemency, a moderation of justice that defendants sought to evoke and philosophers criticized as a corruption of justice.[11] But in translating the Hebrew terms noted above, and thus in Greek texts written by Jews (and Christians), the connotations might be different. Thus, ἔλεος and ἐλέεω can refer to assistance or deliverance without suggesting clemency or compassion. The psalms frequently celebrate God's kindness or help with the use of such terms (ἔλεος is parallel to χρηστότης, σωτηρία, εὐλογία, βοήθεια, etc.), the sense of deliverance being derived from חסד (e.g., LXX Ps 5:8; 12:6; 24:7; 29:11; cf. Sir 2:7, 9; 4:7; 18:5-6; *Ps Sol* 4.25; 5.14-15). Where the recipient of this ἔλεος is weak, poor, or in trouble, compassion is also implied (e.g., LXX Ps 6:3; 9:14; cf. Sir 34:24; *Ps Sol* 5.2, 12; 10.6), and the noun ἐλεημοσύνη acquired a specific meaning, "almsgiving," an act of compassion on the poor (e.g., Sir 3:30; 7:10; 17:22). Where the context is judicial, or the recipient is guilty of transgression, ἔλεος and ἐλεέω indicate clemency (e.g., LXX Ps 24:6-7; 50:3; 102:8-12; Sir 2:11; 18:11-14; *Ps Sol* 8.27). However, outside such contexts, one cannot assume that ἔλεος is an incongruous gift. The *Psalms of Solomon* declare God's ἔλεος on the righteous, and on those who love him and call upon him (*Ps Sol* 2.35-36; 4.25; 6.6), echoing Exodus 20:6, an important root for Jewish uses of ἔλεος and חסד.

Thus, in the New Testament, ἔλεος and ἐλεέω may mean "pity" (in the sense of compassion or clemency), but often simply "kindness." As in other New Testament texts (e.g., Luke 1:72; 1 Pet 2:10), Paul's use of ἐλεέω is derived from the Greek version of the Bible (Rom 9:15) — while χάρις shows no sign

11. See D. Konstan, *Pity Transformed* (London: Duckworth, 2001); cf. Spicq, *Theological Lexicon*, vol. 1, pp. 471-79.

of such influence. Paul often uses ἔλεος/ἐλεέω for divine acts of deliverance or kindness (Rom 9:15-18, 23; 15:9; 1 Cor 7:25; cf. Jas 3:17; 1 Pet 1:3), without any connotation of compassion. Sometimes this terminology does imply compassion (on the suffering or needy; Phil 2:27; Rom 12:8; cf. οἰκτιρμοί in 2 Cor 1:3), or clemency (on the sinful; Rom 11:30-32; cf. 1 Tim 1:13; Jas 2:13). Which of these nuances is at play can be determined only from the context, not from the terms themselves.[12]

3. "Gift" in Latin

The Latin vocabulary for gift is rich. Givers are praised for their *liberalitas, magnanimitas,* or *humanitas:*[13] the gift itself may be labeled *donum, donatio, munus,* or *beneficium* (cf. Seneca, *De Beneficiis*). This is sometimes interchangeable with *officium* (cf. Cicero, *De Officiis*), although the latter encroaches on the sphere of legal obligation, whereas *beneficium* is always voluntary (even if morally obliged) and can be figured as "beyond the call of duty" (cf. Seneca, *Ben.* 3.18-28).[14] Giving *(do, dono, praesto, tribuo, confero)* places the recipient in debt: *obligor* and *debeo* are regularly used to acknowledge the gift, which is returned *(redo, refero)* in a variety of forms, not least in gratitude *(gratias ago; gratiam habeo).*

The uses of *gratia* match the three-fold pattern of χάρις (see above).[15] *Gratia* can mean (a) the state of being favored or esteemed, and thus charm, agreeableness (or political credit); *gratus* and *gratiosus* follow suit, in the sense of pleasing, dear, or agreeable; (b) favor, benevolence, and benefit or gift; *gratuitus* and the adverb *gratis* mean "as a favor" or "free," in the sense of not constituting a return or reward; (c) thanks, in the phrase *gratias ago* or *gratiam habeo* (cf. *gratus,* "thankful"). Translating χάρις in early Christian discourse, *gratia* became the chief Latin term for the divine gift in Christ. Augustine considered it equivalent to *beneficium,* but delighted in the wordplay with

12. *Pace* C. Breytenbach, who argues that Paul uses the benefactor language of χάρις as a metaphor "in which [he] wraps the Jewish notion of ἔλεος," since the latter suggests the merciful treatment of sin (*Grace, Reconciliation, Concord: The Death of Christ in Graeco-Roman Metaphors* [Leiden: Brill, 2010], pp. 207-238, at p. 226). But in Jewish discourse in Greek, ἔλεος can have a range of senses, and in many contexts may be exercised on fitting, rather than unworthy, recipients.

13. For *magnanimitas,* see R. A. Gauthier, *Magnanimité, l'idéal de grandeur dans la philosophie païenne et dans la théologie chrétienne* (Paris: Vrin, 1951).

14. See M. Griffin, "*De Beneficiis* and Roman Society," *JRS* 93 (2003): 92-113, at p. 98.

15. C. Moussy, *Gratia et sa famille* (Paris: Presses Universitaires de France, 1966).

gratuitus and *gratis* that clarified the incongruity of the divine gift (see above, 3.2). This was not without danger. *Gratia* commonly meant "favor" in the sense of partiality, and judges were forbidden to act *pretio aut gratia* (beholden to bribery or favoritism); affirming God's election by *gratia* could make God seem arbitrary or unjust.

For Augustine, divine *gratia* could be glossed as *misericordia* (compassion) or *clementia* (clemency or pity). Philosophers might draw fine distinctions between these terms (Seneca, *Clem.* 2.4.4; 5.4), but they generally overlapped. In the Latin translation of Jewish texts (e.g., *LAB; 4 Ezra*), *misericordia* and *misericors* probably translate ἔλεος or חסד, and stretch the Latin terms into new meanings.

4. "Gift" in English

I use the term "gift" in a broad anthropological sense (see above) not because "gift" is a fully satisfactory or even the best translation of any of the terms here mentioned. "Gift" captures only one possible nuance of χάρις; "favor" or "benefit" sometimes renders the sense more adequately. "Grace" (derived from *gratia*) may seem a more useful term: with its cognates, it covers all the moments in the circle of the gift, the graciousness of the giver, the grace conveyed, and the gratitude returned. Unfortunately, it comes to us over-determined by Christian assumptions and may import Christian nuances into non-Christian texts. But it would be misleading to reserve it for Christian texts alone, since the words it translates are hardly peculiar to Christianity. "Grace" is often taken to imply an "unmerited" or "undeserved" gift, but this connotation, we have argued, is only one possible perfection of the concept of gift, and is not implicit in χάρις or *gratia* themselves. Thus, I use "gift" and "grace" interchangeably, but often avoid the latter where it may prove misleading.

Similarly, as we have seen, "mercy" is not always the best translation of ἔλεος (see section 2). No single English term covers the full range of חסד and its Greek equivalents in Jewish discourse.

Bibliography

Aageson, J. W. "Scripture and Structure in the Development of the Argument in Romans 9–11." *Catholic Biblical Quarterly* 48 (1986): 265-89.

Adams, E. *Constructing the World: A Study in Paul's Cosmological Language*. Edinburgh: T&T Clark, 2000.

Agamben, G. *The Time That Remains: A Commentary on the Letter to the Romans*. Translated by P. Dailey. Stanford: Stanford University Press, 2005.

Aland, B. "Marcion/Marcioniten." *Theologische Realenzyklopädie* 22 (1992): 89-101.

Aletti, J.-N. "L'argumentation paulinienne en Rm 9." *Biblica* 68 (1987): 41-56.

———. "Paul's Exhortations in Gal 5,16-25: From the Apostle's Techniques to His Theology." *Biblica* 94 (2013): 395-414.

Alexander, P. S. "The Redaction-history of the Serekh ha-Yaḥad: A Proposal." *Revue de Qumran* 65-68 (1996): 437-53.

———. "Torah and Salvation in Tannaitic Literature." Pages 261-302 in *Justification and Variegated Nomism*. Volume 1: *The Complexities of Second Temple Judaism*. Edited by D. A. Carson, P. T. O'Brien, and M. A. Seifrid. Tübingen: Mohr Siebeck, 2001.

———. "Predestination and Free Will in the Theology of the Dead Sea Scrolls." Pages 27-49 in *Divine and Human Agency in Paul and His Cultural Environment*. Edited by J. M. G. Barclay and S. J. Gathercole. London: T&T Clark, 2006.

———. "Review of E. P. Sanders, *Jesus and Judaism*." *Journal of Jewish Studies* 37 (1986): 103-6.

Algazi, G., V. Groebner, and B. Jussen, eds. *Negotiating the Gift: Pre-Modern Figurations of Exchange*. Göttingen: Vandenhoeck & Ruprecht, 2003.

Amir, Y. "The Term Ἰουδαϊσμός: A Study in Jewish-Hellenistic Self-Definition." *Immanuel* 14 (1984): 34-41.

Anderson, C. A. *Philo of Alexandria's Views of the Physical World*. Tübingen: Mohr Siebeck, 2011.

Anderson, G. A. *Charity: The Place of the Poor in the Biblical Tradition*. New Haven: Yale University Press, 2013.

Appadurai, A., ed. *The Social Life of Things: Commodities in Cultural Perspective*. Cambridge: Cambridge University Press, 1986.

Aquinas, T. *Commentary on Saint Paul's Epistle to the Galatians.* Translated by F. R. Larcher; Albany: Magi Books, 1966.

Atkins, M., and R. Osborne, eds. *Poverty in the Roman World.* Cambridge: Cambridge University Press, 2006.

Avemarie, F. *Tora und Leben: Untersuchungen zur Heilsbedeutung der Tora in der frühen rabbinischen Literatur.* Tübingen: Mohr Siebeck, 1996.

———. "Erwählung und Vergeltung: Zur optionalen Struktur rabbinischer Soteriologie." *New Testament Studies* 45 (1999): 108-26.

———. "Israels rätselhafter Ungehorsam: Römer 10 als Anatomie eines von Gott provozierten Unglaubens." Pages 299-320 in *Between Gospel and Election: Explorations in the Interpretation of Romans 9–11.* Edited by F. Wilk and J. R. Wagner. Tübingen: Mohr Siebeck, 2010.

Babcock, W. S. "Augustine's Interpretation of Romans (A.D. 394–396)." *Augustinian Studies* 10 (1979): 55-74.

———. "Comment: Augustine, Paul, and the Question of Moral Evil." Pages 251-61 in *Paul and the Legacies of Paul.* Edited by W. S. Babcock. Dallas: Southern Methodist University Press, 1990.

Bachmann, M. *Sünder oder Übertreter: Studien zur Argumentation in Gal 2,15ff.* Tübingen: Mohr Siebeck, 1992.

———. *Anti-Judaism in Galatians? Exegetical Studies on a Polemical Letter and on Paul's Theology.* Translated by R. L. Brawley. Grand Rapids: Eerdmans, 2008.

———. "Was für Praktiken? Zur jüngsten Diskussion um die ἔργα νόμου." *New Testament Studies* 55 (2009): 35-54.

Bachmann, M., and J. Woyke, eds. *Lutherische und Neue Paulusperspektive: Beiträge zu einem Schlüsselproblem der gegenwärtigen exegetischen Diskussion.* Tübingen: Mohr Siebeck, 2005.

Badenas, R. *Christ the End of the Law: Romans 10.4 in Pauline Perspective.* Sheffield: Sheffield Academic Press, 1985.

Badian, E. *Foreign Clientelae (264–70 BC).* Oxford: Oxford University Press, 1958.

Badiou, A. *L'être et événement.* Paris; Seuill, 1990. Translated by O. Feltham as *Being and Event.* New York: Continuum, 2005.

———. *Saint Paul: La Fondation de l'universalisme.* Paris: Presses Universitaires de France, 1997. Translated by R. Brassier as *Saint Paul: The Foundation of Universalism.* Stanford: Stanford University Press, 2003.

———. *Ethics: An Essay on the Understanding of Evil.* Translated by P. Hallward. London: Verso, 2001.

———. *Logiques des Mondes.* Paris: Seuill, 2006.

Barclay, J. M. G. "Mirror-Reading a Polemical Letter: Galatians as a Test Case." *Journal for the Study of the New Testament* 31 (1987): 73-93.

———. *Obeying the Truth: A Study of Paul's Ethics in Galatians.* Edinburgh: T&T Clark, 1988.

———. *Jews in the Mediterranean Diaspora from Alexander to Trajan (323 BCE–117 CE).* Edinburgh: T&T Clark, 1996.

———. "'Do We Undermine the Law?' A Study of Romans 14.1–15.6." Pages 287-308 in *Paul and the Mosaic Law.* Edited by J. D. G. Dunn. Tübingen: Mohr Siebeck, 1996.

———. "Who Was Considered an Apostate in the Jewish Diaspora?" Pages 80-98 in *Tolerance and Intolerance in Early Judaism and Christianity.* Edited by G. N. Stanton and G. Stroumsa. Cambridge: Cambridge University Press, 1996.

———. "Paul and Philo on Circumcision: Romans 2.25-29 in Social and Cultural Context." *New Testament Studies* 44 (1998): 536-56.

———. "Paul's Story: Theology as Testimony." Pages 133-56 in *Narrative Dynamics in Paul.* Edited by B. W. Longenecker. Louisville: Westminster John Knox Press, 2002.

———. " 'By the Grace of God I Am What I Am': Grace and Agency in Paul and Philo." Pages 140-57 in *Divine and Human Agency in Paul and His Cultural Environment.* Edited by J. M. G. Barclay and S. J. Gathercole. London: T&T Clark, 2006.

———. *Flavius Josephus: Translation and Commentary.* Volume 10: *Against Apion.* Leiden: Brill, 2007.

———. "Manna and the Circulation of Grace: A Study of 2 Corinthians 8:1-15." Pages 409-26 in *The Word Leaps the Gap: Essays on Scripture and Theology in Honor of Richard B. Hays.* Edited by J. R. Wagner, C. Kavin Rowe, and A. K. Grieb. Grand Rapids: Eerdmans, 2008.

———. "Grace and the Transformation of Agency in Christ." Pages 372-89 in *Redefining First-Century Jewish and Christian Identities.* Edited by F. E. Udoh. Notre Dame: University of Notre Dame Press, 2008.

———. Review of R. Jewett, *Romans, Journal for the Study of the New Testament* 31 (2008): 89-111.

———. "Grace within and beyond Reason: Philo and Paul in Dialogue." Pages 9-21 in *Paul, Grace, and Freedom.* Edited by P. Middleton, A. Paddison, and K. Wenell. London: T&T Clark, 2009.

———. " 'I Will Have Mercy on Whom I Have Mercy': The Golden Calf and Divine Mercy in Romans 9–11 and Second Temple Judaism." *Early Christianity* 1 (2010): 82-106.

———. "Believers and the 'Last Judgment' in Paul: Rethinking Grace and Recompense." Pages 195-208 in *Eschatologie — Eschatology.* Edited by H.-J. Eckstein, C. Landmesser, and H. Lichtenberger. Tübingen: Mohr Siebeck, 2011.

———. *Pauline Churches and Diaspora Jews.* Tübingen: Mohr Siebeck, 2011.

———. "Faith and Self-Detachment from Cultural Norms: A Study of Romans 14–15." *Zeitschrift für die neutestamentliche Wissenschaft und die Kunde der älteren Kirche* 104 (2013): 192-208.

———. "Humanity under Faith." Pages 79-99 in *Beyond Bultmann: Reckoning a New Testament Theology.* Edited by B. W. Longenecker and M. C. Parsons. Waco: Baylor University Press, 2014.

Barclay, J. M. G., and S. J. Gathercole, eds. *Divine and Human Agency in Paul and His Cultural Environment.* London: Continuum, 2006.

Barrett, C. K. "Paul and the 'Pillar' Apostles." Pages 1-19 in *Studia Paulina.* Edited by J. N. Sevenster and W. C. van Unnik. Haarlem: De Ervem F. Bohn, 1953.

———. *A Commentary on the Epistle to the Romans.* London: A&C Black, 1971.

———. "The Allegory of Abraham, Sarah and Hagar in the Argument of Galatians." Pages 1-16 in *Rechtfertigung: Festschrift für Ernst Käsemann.* Edited by J. Friedrich, W. Pöhlmann, and P. Stuhlmacher. Tübingen: Mohr Siebeck, 1976.

———. "Romans 9.30–10.21: Fall and Responsibility of Israel." Pages 132-53 in *Essays on Paul.* London: SPCK, 1982.

Barth, K. *Der Römerbrief.* Reprinted, Zürich: Theologischer Verlag, 1954. Translated by E. C. Hoskyns as *The Epistle to the Romans.* 6th edition. London: Oxford University Press, 1933.

———. *Die Auferstehung der Toten.* Munich: Chr. Kaiser Verlag, 1924. Translated by H. J. Stenning as *The Resurrection of the Dead.* New York: Hodder and Revell, 1933.

Barth, M. "Jews and Gentiles: The Social Character of Justification." *Journal of Ecumenical Studies* 5 (1968): 241-61.

Barton, C. *Roman Honor: The Fire in the Bones.* Berkeley: University of California Press, 2001.

Baslez, M. F. "The Author of Wisdom and the Cultural Environment of Alexandria." Pages 33-52 in *The Book of Wisdom in Modern Research: Studies on Tradition, Redaction, and Theology.* Edited by A. Passaro and G. Bellia. Berlin: de Gruyter, 2005.

Bassler, J. M. *Divine Impartiality: Paul and a Theological Axiom.* Atlanta: Scholars Press, 1982.

Batten, A. "God in the Letter of James: Patron or Benefactor?" *New Testament Studies* 50 (2004): 257-72.

Bauckham, R. J. *The Fate of the Dead: Studies on the Jewish and Christian Apocalypses.* Leiden: Brill, 1998.

———. "Apocalypses." Pages 135-87 in *Justification and Variegated Nomism.* Volume 1: *The Complexities of Second Temple Judaism.* Edited by D. A. Carson, P. T. O'Brien, and M. A. Seifrid. Tübingen: Mohr Siebeck, 2001.

Baur, F. C. *The Church History of the First Three Centuries.* Edinburgh: Williams and Norgate, 1875.

Bayer, O. *Promissio: Geschichte der reformatorischen Wende in Luthers Theologie.* 2nd edition. Darmstadt: Wissenschaftliche Buchgesellschaft, 1989.

———. *Martin Luther's Theology. A Contemporary Interpretation.* Translated by T. H. Trapp. Grand Rapids: Eerdmans, 2003.

———. "The Ethics of Gift." *Lutheran Quarterly* 24 (2010): 447-68.

Beard, M., J. North, and S. Price. *Religions of Rome.* 2 volumes. Cambridge: Cambridge University Press, 1998.

Becker, J. *Das Heil Gottes: Heils- und Sundenbegriffe in den Qumrantexte und im Neuen Testament.* Göttingen: Vandenhoeck & Ruprecht, 1964.

Beeke, J. R. "Calvin on Piety." Pages 125-52 in *The Cambridge Companion to John Calvin.* Edited by D. K. McKim. Cambridge: Cambridge University Press.

Begg, C. "The Golden Calf Episode according to Pseudo-Philo." Pages 577-94 in *Studies in the Book of Exodus: Redaction — Reception — Interpretation.* Edited by M. Vervenne. Leuven: Leuven University Press, 1996.

Beintker, M. "Krisis und Gnade: Zur theologischen Deutung der Dialektik beim frühen Barth." *Evangelische Theologie* 46 (1986): 442-56.

Bell, R. H. *Provoked to Jealousy: The Origin and Purpose of the Jealousy Motif in Romans 9–11.* Tübingen: Mohr Siebeck, 1994.

———. *No One Seeks for God: An Exegetical and Theological Study of Romans 1.18–3.20.* Tübingen: Mohr Siebeck, 1998.

———. *The Irrevocable Call of God.* Tübingen: Mohr Siebeck, 2005.

Ben-Amos, I. K. *The Culture of Giving: Informal Support and Gift-Exchange in Early Modern England.* Cambridge: Cambridge University Press, 2008.

Benjamin, W. "Theses on the Philosophy of History." In *Illuminations.* Edited by H. Arendt; translated by H. Zorn. London: Pimlico, 1999.

Benveniste, E. *Le vocabulaire des institutions indo-européennes.* Volume 1: *Économie, Parenté, Société.* Paris: Minuit, 1969.

———. *Problems in General Linguistics.* Translated by M. E. Meek. Coral Gables: University of Miami Press, 1971.

Berkley, T. W. *From a Broken Covenant to Circumcision of the Heart: Pauline Intertextual Exegesis in Romans 2:17-29.* Atlanta: Society of Biblical Literature, 2000.

Berthelot, K. *Philanthrōpia Judaica: Le débat autour de la "misanthropie" des lois juives dans l'Antiquité.* Leiden: Brill, 2003.

Betz, H. D. *Galatians.* Hermeneia; Philadelphia: Fortress Press, 1979.

Betz, O. "Rechtfertigung in Qumran." Pages 17-36 in *Rechtfertigung: Festschrift für E. Käsemann.* Edited by J. Friedrich, W. Pöhlmann, and P. Stuhlmacher. Tübingen: Mohr Siebeck, 1976.

Billings, J. T. *Calvin, Participation, and the Gift: The Activity of Believers in Union with Christ.* Oxford: Oxford University Press, 2007.

Birnbaum, E. *The Place of Judaism in Philo's Thought.* Atlanta: Scholars Press, 1996.

Blaschke, A. *Beschneidung: Zeugnisse der Bibel und verwandter Texte.* Tübingen: Francke Verlag, 1998.

Boccaccini, G. *Middle Judaism: Jewish Thought 300 B.C.E. to 200 C.E.* Minneapolis: Fortress Press, 1991.

Boers, H. *Theology out of the Ghetto.* Leiden: Brill, 1971.

Böhm, M. *Rezeption und Funktion der Vätererzählungen bei Philo von Alexandria.* Berlin: de Guyter, 2005.

Bolkestein, H. *Wohltätigkeit und Armenpflege im vorchristlichen Altertum.* Utrecht: A. Oosthoek Verlag, 1939.

Bonner, G. *St. Augustine of Hippo: Life and Controversies.* Norwich: Canterbury Press, 1963.

Bourdieu, P. *Outline of a Theory of Practice.* Translated by R. Nice. Cambridge: Cambridge University Press, 1977.

———. *The Logic of Practice.* Translated by R. Nice. Stanford: Stanford University Press, 1990.

———. "Marginalia — Some Additional Notes on the Gift." Translated by R. Nice. Pages 231-41 in *The Logic of the Gift.* Edited by A. D. Schrift. London: Routledge, 1997.

Bouwsma, W. J. *John Calvin: A Sixteenth-Century Portrait.* Oxford: Oxford University Press, 1988.

Boyarin, D. "Penitential Liturgy in 4 Ezra." *Journal for the Study of Judaism* 3 (1972): 30-34.

———. *A Radical Jew: Paul and the Politics of Identity.* Berkeley: University of California Press, 1994.

Braaten, C. E., and R. W. Jenson, eds. *Union with Christ: The New Finnish Interpretation of Luther.* Grand Rapids: Eerdmans, 1998.

Brandenburger, E. *Adam und Christus: Exegetisch-religionsgeschichtliche Untersuchung zu Röm. 5,12-21*. Neukirchen: Neukirchen-Vluyn, 1962.

———. *Die Verborgenheit Gottes im Weltgeschehen: Das literarische und theologische Problem des 4. Esrabuches*. Zürich: Theologischer Verlag, 1981.

Braun, H. "Vom Erbarmen Gottes über den Gerechten: zur Theologie der Psalmen Salomos." Pages 8-69 in *Gesammelte Studien zum Neuen Testament und seiner Umwelt*. Tübingen: Mohr Siebeck, 1967.

Braund, D. "Function and Dysfunction: Personal Patronage in Roman Imperialism." Pages 137-52 in *Patronage in Ancient Society*. Edited by A. Wallace-Hadrill. London: Routledge, 1989.

Brawley, R. L. "Contextuality, Intertextuality, and the Hendiadic Relationship of Promise and Law in Galatians." *Zeitschrift für die neutestamentliche Wissenschaft und die Kunde der älteren Kirche* 93 (2002): 99-119.

Breech, E. "These Fragments I Have Shored against My Ruins: The Form and Function of 4 Ezra." *Journal of Biblical Literature* 92 (1973): 267-74.

Bremmer, J.-M. "The Reciprocity of Giving and Thanksgiving in Greek Worship." Pages 127-37 in *Reciprocity in Ancient Greece*. Edited by C. Gill, N. Postlethwaite, and R. Seaford. Oxford: Oxford University Press, 1998.

Breton, S. *A Radical Philosophy of Saint Paul*. Translated by J. N. Ballan; with introduction by W. Blanton. New York: Columbia University Press, 2011.

Breytenbach, C. *Grace, Reconciliation, Concord: The Death of Christ in Graeco-Roman Metaphors*. Leiden: Brill, 2010.

Briones, D. E. *Paul's Financial Policy: A Socio-Theological Approach*. London: T&T Clark, 2013.

Brown, P. *Augustine of Hippo*. New York: Dorset Press, 1967.

———. *Religion and Society in the Age of Saint Augustine*. London: Faber and Faber, 1972.

Bultmann, R. "Zur Geschichte der Paulus-Forschung." *Theologische Rundschau* n.f. 1 (1929): 26-59.

———. "Paulus." *Religion in Geschichte und Gegenwart* 4 (1930): 1019-45. Translated as "Paul." Pages 111-45 in *Existence and Faith: Shorter Writings of Rudolf Bultmann*. Edited by S. M. Ogden. London: Hodder and Stoughton, 1961.

———. "Römer 7 und die Anthropologie des Paulus." Pages 53-62 in *Imago Dei*. Edited by W. Schneemelcher. Giessen, 1932. Translated as pages 147-57 in *Existence and Faith: Shorter Writings of Rudolf Bultmann*. Edited by S. M. Ogden. London: Hodder and Stoughton, 1961.

———. *Glaube und Verstehen: Gesammelte Aufsätze*. Volume 1. Tübingen: Mohr Siebeck, 1933. Translated by L. Pettibone Smith as *Faith and Understanding*. Edited by R. W. Funk. London: SCM Press, 1969.

———. *Theologie des Neuen Testaments*. 2 volumes. Tübingen: Mohr Siebeck, 1948. Translated by K. Grobel as *Theology of the New Testament*. 2 volumes. London: SCM Press, 1952.

———. "Grace and Freedom." Pages 168-81 in *Essays Philosophical and Theological*. Translated by J. C. Greig. London: SCM Press, 1955.

———. "Christ the End of the Law." Pages 36-66 in *Essays Philosophical and Theological*. Translated by J. C. Greig. London: SCM Press, 1955.

———. *Primitive Christianity in Its Contemporary Setting.* London: Thames and Hudson, 1956.

———. "Karl Barth's *Römerbrief* in zweiter Auflage." Reprinted as pages 119-42 in *Anfänge der dialektischen Theologie,* volume 1. Edited by J. Moltmann. Munich: C. Kaiser, 1962. Translated as "Karl Barth's *Epistle to the Romans* in Its Second Edition." Pages 100-120 in *The Beginnings of Dialectical Theology.* Edited by J. M. Robinson. Richmond: John Knox Press, 1968.

———. "The New Testament and Mythology." Pages 1-43 in *The New Testament and Mythology and Other Basic Writings.* Translated and edited by S. Ogden. London: SCM Press, 1985.

Burke, K. *Permanence and Change: An Anatomy of Purpose.* Berkeley: University of California Press, 1954.

———. *Language as Symbolic Action: Essays on Life, Literature, and Method.* Berkeley: University of California Press, 1966.

Burton, E. de Witt. *A Critical and Exegetical Commentary on the Epistle to the Galatians.* Edinburgh: T&T Clark, 1921.

Byrne, B. *"Sons of God" — "Seed of Abraham." A Study of the Idea of the Sonship of God of All Christians in Paul.* Rome: Pontifical Biblical Institute, 1979.

———. "Living Out the Righteousness of God: The Contribution of Rom 6.1–6.13 to an Understanding of Paul's Ethical Presuppositions." *Catholic Biblical Quarterly* 43 (1981): 557-81.

———. "'Rather Boldly' (Rom 15,15): Paul's Prophetic Bid to Win the Allegiance of the Christians in Rome." *Biblica* 74 (1993): 83-96.

———. *Romans.* Collegeville: Liturgical Press, 1996.

Caillé, A. *Don, intérêt et désintéressement.* Paris: La Découverte, 1994.

Calabi, F. *God's Acting, Man's Acting: Tradition and Philosophy in Philo of Alexandria.* Leiden: Brill, 2008.

Calvert-Koyzis, N. *Paul, Monotheism, and the People of God: The Significance of Abraham Traditions for Early Judaism and Christianity.* London: T&T Clark, 2004.

Calvin, J. *Institutes of the Christian Religion.* 2 volumes. Translated by F. Lewis Battles; edited by J. T. McNeill. Philadelphia: Westminster Press, 1960.

Campbell, D. A. *The Rhetoric of Righteousness in Romans 3:21-26.* Sheffield: JSOT Press, 1992.

———. "Rom. 1:17 — A *Crux Interpretum* for the ΠΙΣΤΙΣ ΧΡΙΣΤΟΥ Dispute." *Journal of Biblical Literature* 113 (1994): 265-85.

———. *The Deliverance of God: An Apocalyptic Reading of Justification in Paul.* Grand Rapids: Eerdmans, 2009.

Caputo, J., ed. *Deconstruction in a Nutshell: A Conversation with Jacques Derrida.* New York: Fordham University Press, 1997.

Caputo, J. D., and M. J. Scanlon. *God, the Gift, and Postmodernism.* Bloomington: Indiana University Press, 1999.

Caputo, J. D., and L. M. Alcoff, eds. *St. Paul among the Philosophers.* Bloomington: Indiana University Press, 2009.

Caragounis, C. "Romans 5.15-16 in the Context of 5.12-21: Contrast or Comparison?" *New Testament Studies* 31 (1985): 142-48.

Carrier, J. G. *Gifts and Commodities: Exchange and Western Capitalism since 1700*. London: Routledge, 1995.

Carson, A. "Putting Her in Her Place: Women, Dirt, and Desire." Pages 135-64 in *Before Sexuality*. Edited by D. Halperin et al. Princeton: Princeton University Press, 1990.

Carson, D. A. *Divine Sovereignty and Human Responsibility*. Atlanta: John Knox Press, 1981.

———. "Divine Sovereignty and Human Responsibility in Philo: Analysis and Method." *Novum Testamentum* 23 (1981): 148-64.

Carson, D. A., P. T. O'Brien, and M. A. Seifrid, eds. *Justification and Variegated Nomism*. Volume 1: *The Complexities of Second Temple Judaism*. Tübingen: Mohr Siebeck, 2001.

Chadwick, O. *John Cassian*. 2nd edition. Cambridge: Cambridge University Press, 1968.

Chazon, E. "Liturgical Communion with the Angels at Qumran." Pages 95-105 in *Sapiential, Liturgical, and Poetical Texts from Qumran*. Edited by D. K. Falk et al. Leiden: Brill, 2000.

Chazon, E., et al. *Qumran Cave 4*. Volume 20: *Poetical and Liturgical Works, Part 2*. Oxford: Clarendon Press, 1999.

Cheal, D. J. *The Gift Economy*. London: Routledge, 1988.

Cheon, S. *The Exodus Story in the Wisdom of Solomon*. Sheffield: Sheffield Academic Press, 1997.

Chester, S. *Conversion at Corinth: Perspectives on Conversion in Paul's Theology and the Corinthian Church*. Edinburgh: T&T Clark, 2003.

———. "It Is No Longer I Who Live: Justification by Faith and Participation in Christ in Martin Luther's Exegesis of Galatians." *New Testament Studies* 55 (2009): 315-37.

Chow, J. K. *Patronage and Power: A Study of Social Networks in Corinth*. Sheffield: JSOT Press, 1992.

Clark, G. R. *The Word* "Hesed" *in the Hebrew Bible*. Sheffield: JSOT Press, 1993.

Clements, R. " 'A Remnant Chosen by Grace' (Romans 11:5): The Old Testament Background and Origin of the Remnant Concept." Pages 106-21 in *Pauline Studies*. Edited by D. A. Hagner and M. J. Harris. Grand Rapids: Eerdmans, 1980.

Cohen, S. J. D. *The Beginnings of Jewishness: Boundaries, Varieties, Uncertainties*. Berkeley: University of California Press, 1999.

Cohn, L. "An Apocryphal Work Ascribed to Philo of Alexandria." *Jewish Quarterly Review* 10 (1898): 277-332.

Collins, J. J. "Cosmos and Salvation: Jewish Wisdom and Apocalyptic in the Hellenistic Age." *History of Religions* 17 (1977): 121-42.

———. *Jewish Wisdom in the Hellenistic Age*. Louisville: Westminster John Knox Press, 1997.

———. *The Apocalyptic Imagination. An Introduction to Jewish Apocalyptic Literature*. 2nd edition. Grand Rapids: Eerdmans, 1998.

———. "Amazing Grace: The Transformation of the Thanksgiving Hymn at Qumran." Pages 75-85 in *Psalms in Community: Jewish and Christian Textual, Liturgical, and Artistic Traditions*. Edited by H. Attridge and M. E. Fassler. Atlanta: Society of Biblical Literature, 2003.

———. "The Reinterpretation of Apocalyptic Traditions in the Wisdom of Solomon."

Pages 143-57 in *The Book of Wisdom in Modern Research: Studies on Tradition, Redaction, and Theology.* Edited by A. Passaro and G. Bellia. Berlin: de Gruyter, 2005.

Condra, E. *Salvation for the Righteous Revealed: Jesus amid Covenantal and Messianic Expectations in Second Temple Judaism.* Leiden: Brill, 2002.

Cooper, S. A. *Marius Victorinus' Commentary on Galatians: Introduction, Translation, and Notes.* Oxford: Oxford University Press, 2005.

Cosgrove, C. H. "Justification in Paul: A Linguistic and Theological Reflection." *Journal of Biblical Literature* 106 (1987): 653-70.

———. *The Cross and the Spirit: A Study in the Argument and Theology of Galatians.* Macon: Mercer University Press, 1988.

———. *Elusive Israel: The Puzzle of Election in Romans.* Louisville: Westminster John Knox Press, 1997.

Cox, R. *By the Same Word: Creation and Salvation in Hellenistic Judaism and Early Christianity.* Berlin: de Gruyter, 2007.

Cranfield, C. E. B. *A Critical and Exegetical Commentary on the Epistle to the Romans.* 2 volumes. International Critical Commentary. Edinburgh: T&T Clark, 1975, 1979.

Crook, Z. A. *Reconceptualising Conversion: Patronage, Loyalty, and Conversion in the Religions of the Ancient Mediterranean.* Berlin: de Gruyter, 2004.

———. "Reflections on Culture and Social-Scientific Models." *Journal of Biblical Literature* 124 (2005): 515-32.

Dahl, N. A. "Der Name Israel: Zur Auslegung von Gal 6.16." *Judaica* 6 (1950): 161-70.

———. "Two Notes on Romans 5." *Studia Theologica* 5 (1951): 37-48.

———. *Studies in Paul.* Minneapolis: Augsburg Fortress Press, 1977.

———. "The Doctrine of Justification: Its Social Function and Effects." Pages 95-120 in *Studies in Paul.* Minneapolis: Augsburg Fortress Press, 1977.

Danker, F. W. *Benefactor: Epigraphic Study of a Graeco-Roman and New Testament Semantic Field.* St. Louis: Clayton, 1982.

Das, A. A. "Another Look at ἐὰν μή in Galatians 2:16." *Journal of Biblical Literature* 119 (2000): 529-39.

———. *Solving the Romans Debate.* Minneapolis: Fortress Press, 2007.

Davies, G. N. *Faith and Obedience in Romans: A Study in Romans 1–4.* Sheffield: Sheffield Academic, 1990.

Davies, W., and P. Fouracre, eds. *The Languages of Gift in the Early Middle Ages.* Cambridge: Cambridge University Press, 2010.

Davis, N. Z. *The Gift in Sixteenth-Century France.* Oxford: Oxford University Press, 2000.

Dawson, D. *Allegorical Readers and Cultural Revision in Ancient Alexandria.* Berkeley: University of California Press, 1992.

———. *Christian Figural Reading and the Fashioning of Identity.* Berkeley: University of California Press, 2002.

de Boer, M. C. *The Defeat of Death: Apocalyptic Eschatology in 1 Corinthians 15 and Romans 5.* Sheffield: Sheffield Academic Press, 1988.

———. "Paul and Jewish Apocalyptic Theology." Pages 169-90 in *Apocalyptic and the New Testament: Essays in Honor of J. Louis Martyn.* Edited by J. Marcus and M. L. Soards. Sheffield: Sheffield Academic Press, 1989.

———. "Paul's Quotation of Isa 54.1 in Gal 4.27." *New Testament Studies* 50 (2004): 370-89.

———. "Paul's Use and Interpretation of a Justification Tradition in Galatians 2.15-21." *Journal for the Study of the New Testament* 28 (2005): 189-216.

———. "The Meaning of the Phrase τὰ στοιχεῖα τοῦ κόσμου in Galatians." *New Testament Studies* 53 (2007): 204-224.

———. *Galatians: A Commentary.* New Testament Library. Louisville: Westminster John Knox Press, 2011.

de Bruyn, T. *Pelagius' Commentary on St. Paul's Epistle to the Romans.* Oxford: Clarendon Press, 1993.

de Roo, J. *Works of Law in Qumran and in Paul.* Sheffield: Sheffield Phoenix Press, 2007.

Deichgräber, K. *Charis und Chariten: Grazie und Grazien.* Munich: Heimeran, 1971.

Derrida, J. *Given Time.* Volume 1: *Counterfeit Money.* Translated by P. Kamuf. Chicago: University of Chicago Press, 1992.

———. *The Gift of Death.* Translated by D. Wills. Chicago: University of Chicago Press, 1995.

deSilva, D. A. *Honor, Patronage, Kingship, and Purity: Unlocking New Testament Culture.* Downers Grove: InterVarsity Press, 2000.

di Noia, J. A. "Religion and the Religions." Pages 243-57 in *The Cambridge Companion to Karl Barth.* Edited by J. Webster. Cambridge: Cambridge University Press, 2000.

Dietzfelbinger, C. *Pseudo-Philo: Antiquitates Biblicae (Liber Antiquitatum Biblicarum).* Jüdische Schriften aus hellenistisch-römischer Zeit II/2. Gütersloh: Gerd Mohn, 1975.

Dillon, J. *The Middle Platonists. A Study of Platonism 80 B.C. to A.D. 220.* London: Duckworth, 1977.

Dodson, J. R. *The "Powers" of Personification: Rhetorical Purpose in the* Book of Wisdom *and the Letter to the Romans.* Berlin: de Gruyter, 2008.

Doering, L. *Ancient Jewish Letters and the Beginnings of Christian Epistolography.* Tübingen: Mohr Siebeck, 2012.

Dombrowski Hopkins, D. "The Qumran Community and 1QHodayot: A Reassessment." *Revue de Qumran* 10 (1981): 323-64.

Donaldson, T. L. "The 'Curse of the Law' and the Inclusion of the Gentiles: Galatians 3.13-14." *New Testament Studies* 32 (1986): 94-112.

———. "'Riches for the Gentiles' (Rom 11:12): Israel's Rejection and Paul's Gentile Mission." *Journal of Biblical Literature* 12 (1993): 81-98.

Donfried, K. P. *The Romans Debate: Revised and Expanded Edition.* Edinburgh: T&T Clark, 1991.

Douglas, M. "The Teacher-Hymn Hypothesis Revisited: New Data for an Old Crux." *Dead Sea Discoveries* 6 (1999): 239-66.

Downs, D. J. *The Offering of the Gentiles: Paul's Collection for Jerusalem in Its Chronological, Cultural, and Cultic Contexts.* Tübingen: Mohr Siebeck, 2008.

Duby, G. *The Chivalrous Society.* Translated by C. Posten. Berkeley: University of California Press, 1977.

Dunn, J. D. G. "The New Perspective on Paul." *Bulletin of the John Rylands Library* 65 (1983): 95-122.

———. *Romans 1–8.* Word Biblical Commentaries. Waco: Word, 1988.

———. *Romans 9–16.* Word Biblical Commentaries. Waco: Word, 1988.

———. *Jesus, Paul, and the Law: Studies in Mark and Galatians.* London: SPCK, 1990.

———. *The Theology of Paul's Letter to the Galatians*. Cambridge: Cambridge University Press, 1993.

———. *The Epistle to the Galatians*. London: A&C Black, 1993.

———. *The Theology of Paul the Apostle*. Grand Rapids: Eerdmans, 1998.

———. *The New Perspective on Paul: Collected Essays*. Tübingen: Mohr Siebeck, 2005.

Eastman, B. *The Significance of Grace in the Letters of Paul*. New York: Peter Lang, 1999.

Eastman, S. "The Evil Eye and the Curse of the Law: Galatians 3.1 Revisited." *Journal for the Study of the New Testament* 83 (2001): 69-87.

———. *Recovering Paul's Mother Tongue: Language and Theology in Galatians*. Grand Rapids: Eerdmans, 2007.

———. "Israel and the Mercy of God: A Re-reading of Galatians 6.16 and Romans 9–11." *New Testament Studies* 56 (2010): 367-95.

Ebeling, G. *Luther: An Introduction to His Thought*. Translated by R. A. Wilson. London: Collins, 1970.

Eckstein, H-J. *Verheissung und Gesetz: Eine exegetische Untersuchung zu Galater 2,15–4,7*. Tübingen: Mohr Siebeck, 1996.

Eilberg-Schwartz, H. *The Savage in Judaism: An Anthropology of Israelite Religion and Ancient Judaism*. Bloomington: Indiana University Press, 1990.

Eilers, C. *Roman Patrons of Greek Cities*. Oxford: Oxford University Press, 2002.

Eisenbaum, P. *Paul Was Not a Christian*. New York: HarperCollins Press, 2009.

Elliott, M. A. *The Survivors of Israel: A Reconsideration of the Theology of Pre-Christian Judaism*. Grand Rapids: Eerdmans, 2000.

Elliott, N. *The Arrogance of Nations: Reading Romans in the Shadow of Empire*. Minneapolis: Fortress Press, 2008.

Elliott, S. *Cutting Too Close for Comfort: Paul's Letter to the Galatians in Its Anatolian Cultic Context*. London: T&T Clark, 2003.

Engberg-Pedersen, T. "Galatians in Romans 5–8 and Paul's Construction of the Identity of Christian Believers." Pages 477-505 in *Texts and Contexts: Essays in Honor of Lars Hartman*. Edited by T. Fornberg and D. Hellholm. Oslo: Scandinavian University Press, 1995.

———. *Paul and the Stoics*. Edinburgh: T&T Clark, 2000.

———. "Gift-Giving and Friendship: Seneca and Paul in Romans 1–8 on the Logic of God's χάρις and Its Human Response." *Harvard Theological Review* 101 (2008): 15-44.

———. "Gift-Giving and God's Charis: Bourdieu, Seneca, and Paul in Romans 1–8." Pages 95-111 in *The Letter to the Romans*. Edited by U. Schnelle. Leuven: Peeters, 2009.

———. "'Everything Is Clean' and 'Everything That Is Not of Faith Is Sin': The Logic of Pauline Casuistry in Romans 14.1–15.13." Pages 22-38 in *Paul, Grace, and Freedom: Essays in Honour of John K. Riches*. Edited by P. Middleton, A. Paddison, and K. Wenell. London: T&T Clark, 2009.

———. *Cosmology and Self in the Apostle Paul: The Material Spirit*. Oxford: Oxford University Press, 2010.

Enns, P. *Exodus Retold: Ancient Exegesis of the Departure from Egypt in Wis 10.15-21 and 19.1-19*. Atlanta: Scholars Press, 1997.

Eskola, T. *Theodicy and Predestination in Pauline Soteriology.* Tübingen: Mohr Siebeck, 1998.
Esler, P. F. *Community and Gospel in Luke-Acts.* Cambridge: Cambridge University Press, 1987.
———. "The Social Function of *4 Ezra.*" *Journal for the Study of the New Testament* 53 (1994): 99-123.
———. "Group Boundaries and Intergroup Conflict in Galatians: A New Reading of Gal. 5:13–6:10." Pages 215-40 in *Ethnicity and the Bible.* Edited by M. G. Brett. Leiden: Brill, 1996.
———. *Galatians.* London: Routledge, 1998.
Evans, E., ed. and trans. *Tertullian: Adversus Marcionem.* 2 volumes. Oxford: Clarendon Press, 1972.
Falk, D. K. *Daily, Sabbath, and Festival Prayers in the Dead Sea Scrolls.* Leiden: Brill, 1998.
———. "Prayers and Psalms." Pages 7-56 in *Justification and Variegated Nomism.* Volume 1: *The Complexities of Second Temple Judaism.* Edited by D. A. Carson, P. T. O'Brien, and M. A. Seifrid. Tübingen: Mohr Siebeck, 2001.
Feeney, D. C. *Literature and Religion at Rome: Cultures, Contexts, and Beliefs.* Cambridge: Cambridge University Press, 1998.
Feldman, L. H. "Prolegomenon." Pages ix-clxix in M. R. James, *The Biblical Antiquities of Philo.* New York: Ktav, 1971 (1917).
Festugière, A. J. "Ἀνθ' ὧν. La formule 'en échange de quoi' dans la prière grecque hellénistique." *Revue des sciences philosophiques et théologiques* 60 (1976): 369-418.
Finley, M. *The World of Odysseus.* London: Chatto & Windus, 1956.
Firth, R. *Primitive Economics of the New Zealand Maori.* Wellington: A. R. Shearer, 1929.
Fischer, U. *Eschatologie und Jenseitserwartung im hellenistischen Diasporajudentum.* Berlin: de Gruyter, 1978.
Fisk, B. *Do You Not Remember? Scripture, Story, and Exegesis in the Rewritten Bible of Pseudo-Philo.* Sheffield: Sheffield Academic Press, 2001.
Fitzmyer, J. A. *Romans.* Anchor Bible 33. New York: Doubleday, 1992.
Flebbe, J. *Solus Deus: Untersuchungen zur Rede von Gott im Brief des Paulus an die Römer.* Berlin: de Gruyter, 2008.
Flückiger, F. "Christus, des Gesetzes τέλος." *Theologische Zeitschrift* 11 (1955): 153-57.
Forbis, E. *Municipal Virtues in the Roman Empire.* Stuttgart: B. G. Teubner, 1996.
Fournier, M. *Marcel Mauss.* Paris: Fayard, 1994.
Fredriksen Landes, P. *Augustine on Romans.* Chico: Scholars Press, 1982.
Fredriksen, P. "Beyond the Body/Soul Dichotomy: Augustine's Answer to Mani, Plotinus, and Julian." Pages 227-51 in *Paul and the Legacies of Paul.* Edited by W. S. Babcock. Dallas: Southern Methodist University Press, 1990.
———. "Judaism, the Circumcision of Gentiles, and Apocalyptic Hope: Another Look at Galatians 1–2." *Journal of Theological Studies* 42 (1991): 532-64.
Frennesson, B. *"In a Common Rejoicing": Liturgical Communion with Angels in Qumran.* Uppsala: Uppsala University Press, 1999.
Frey, J. "Flesh and Spirit in the Palestinian Jewish Sapiential Tradition and in the Qumran Texts: An Inquiry into the Background of Pauline Usage." Pages 367-404 in *The*

Wisdom Texts from Qumran and the Development of Sapiential Thought. Edited by C. Hempel et al. Leuven: Leuven University Press, 2002.

Gäckle, V. *Die Starken und die Schwachen in Korinth und in Rom.* Tübingen: Mohr Siebeck, 2005.

Gager, J. *Reinventing Paul.* Oxford: Oxford University Press, 2000.

Gamble, H. *The Textual History of the Letter to the Romans.* Grand Rapids: Eerdmans, 1977.

Ganoczy, A. "Calvin als paulinischer Theologe." Pages 39-69 in *Calvinus Theologus.* Edited by W. H. Neuser. Neukirchen-Vluyn: Neukirchener, 1976.

Garcia, M. A. *Life in Christ: Union with Christ and Twofold Grace in Calvin's Theology.* Milton Keynes: Paternoster Press, 2008.

Garcia Martínez, F., and E. J. C. Tigchelaar. *The Dead Sea Scrolls Study Edition.* 2 volumes. Leiden: Brill, 1997-98.

Gaston, L. *Paul and the Torah.* Vancouver: University of British Columbia, 1987.

Gathercole, S. J. *Where Is Boasting? Early Jewish Soteriology and Paul's Response in Romans 1–5.* Grand Rapids: Eerdmans, 2002.

———. "A Law unto Themselves: The Gentiles in Romans 2.14-15 Revisited." *Journal for the Study of the New Testament* 85 (2002): 27-49.

Gauthier, R. A. *Magnanimité, l'idéal de grandeur dans la philosophie païenne et dans la théologie chrétienne.* Paris: Vrin, 1951.

Gaventa, B. R. "Galatians 1 and 2: Autobiography as Paradigm." *New Testament Studies* 28 (1986): 309-26.

———. "The Singularity of the Gospel: A Reading of Galatians." Pages 147-59 in *Pauline Theology,* volume 1. Edited by J. M. Bassler. Minneapolis: Fortress Press, 1991.

———. *Our Mother Saint Paul.* Louisville: Westminster John Knox Press, 2007.

———. "On the Calling-Into-Being of Israel: Romans 9:6-29." Pages 255-69 in *Between Gospel and Election: Explorations in the Interpretation of Romans 9–11.* Edited by F. Wilk and J. R. Wagner. Tübingen: Mohr Siebeck, 2010.

Gerrish, B. *Grace and Reason: A Study in the Theology of Luther.* Oxford: Oxford University Press, 1962.

———. *Grace and Gratitude: The Eucharistic Theology of John Calvin.* Minneapolis: Fortress Press, 1993.

Gilbert, M. "The Literary Structure of the Book of Wisdom: A Study of Various Views." Pages 19-32 in *The Book of Wisdom in Modern Research: Studies on Tradition, Redaction, and Theology.* Edited by A. Passaro and G. Bellia. Berlin: de Gruyter, 2005.

Gill, C., N. Postlethwaite, and R. Seaford, eds. *Reciprocity in Ancient Greece.* Oxford: Oxford University Press, 1998.

Gill, C. "Altruism or Reciprocity in Greek Ethical Philosophy?" Pages 303-28 in *Reciprocity in Ancient Greece.* Edited by C. Gill, N. Postlethwaite, and R. Seaford. Oxford: Oxford University Press, 1998.

Godbout, J. T., with A. Caillé. *The World of the Gift.* Translated by D. Winkler. Montreal: McGill-Queen's University Press, 1998.

Goddard, A. J., and Cummins, S. A. "Ill or Ill-Treated? Conflict and Persecution as the Context of Paul's Original Ministry in Galatia (Galatians 4.12-20)." *Journal for the Study of the New Testament* 52 (1993): 93-126.

Godelier, M. *The Enigma of the Gift.* Translated by N. Scott. Chicago: University of Chicago Press, 1999.

Goering, G. S. "Election and Knowledge in the Wisdom of Solomon." Pages 163-82 in *Studies in the Book of Wisdom.* Edited by G. G. Xeravits and J. Zsengéller. Leiden: Brill, 2010.

Goff, M. J. *Discerning Wisdom: The Sapiential Literature of the Dead Sea Scrolls.* Leiden: Brill, 2007.

Gofman, A. "A Vague but Suggestive Concept: The 'Total Social Fact.'" Pages 63-70 in *Marcel Mauss: A Centenary Tribute.* Edited by W. James and N. J. Allen. New York: Berghahn Books, 1998.

Gold, B. K., ed. *Literary and Artistic Patronage in Ancient Rome.* Austin, TX: University of Texas Press, 1982.

Goldhill, S. D. *Reading Greek Tragedy.* Cambridge: Cambridge University Press, 1986.

Goodenough, E. R. *By Light, Light: The Mystic Gospel of Hellenistic Judaism.* Amsterdam: Philo Press, 1969.

Goodman, M. "Kosher Olive Oil in Antiquity." Pages 227-45 in *A Tribute to Geza Vermes.* Edited by P. R. Davies and R. T. White. Sheffield: JSOT Press, 1990.

Goodrich, J. K. "'Standard of Faith' or 'Measure of a Trusteeship'? A Study in Romans 12:3." *Catholic Biblical Quarterly* 74 (2012): 753-72.

Gould, J. "On Making Sense of Greek Religion." Pages 1-33 in *Greek Religion and Society.* Edited by P. E. Easterling. Cambridge: Cambridge University Press, 1985.

Grabbe, L. L. *Wisdom of Solomon.* Sheffield: Sheffield Academic Press, 1997.

Gregory, C. A. *Gifts and Commodities.* London: Academic Press, 1982.

Greschat, K., and Meiser, M., eds. *Gerhard May. Markion: Gesammelte Aufsätze.* Mainz: Philipp von Zabern, 2005.

Griffin, M. "Imago Suae Vitae." Pages 1-38 in *Seneca.* Edited by C. D. N. Costa. London: Routledge & Kegan Paul, 1974.

———. *Seneca: A Philosopher in Politics.* 2nd edition. Oxford: Clarendon Press, 1991.

———. "*De Beneficiis* and Roman Society." *Journal of Roman Studies* 93 (2003): 92-113.

———. "Seneca's Pedagogic Strategy: *Letters* and *De Beneficiis.*" Pages 89-113 in *Greek and Roman Philosophy 100 B.C.–200 A.D.* Edited by R. Sorabji and R. W. Sharples. London: Institute of Classical Studies, University of London, 2007.

Griffin, M., and B. Inwood, trans. *Seneca: On Benefits.* Chicago: University of Chicago Press, 2011.

Grindheim, S. *The Crux of Election: Paul's Critique of the Jewish Confidence in the Election of Israel.* Tübingen: Mohr Siebeck, 2005.

Gruen, E. S. *The Hellenistic World and the Coming of Rome.* 2 volumes. Berkeley: University of California Press, 1984.

———. *Diaspora.* Berkeley: University of California Press, 2002.

Gundry, R. *Sōma in Biblical Theology, with Emphasis on Pauline Anthropology.* Cambridge: Cambridge University Press, 1976.

———. "Grace, Works, and Staying Saved in Paul." *Biblica* 66 (1985): 1-38.

———. *The Old Is Better: New Testament Essays in Support of Traditional Interpretations.* Tübingen: Mohr Siebeck, 2005.

Gunkel, H. "Das vierte Buch Esra." Pages 331-401 in *Die Apokryphen und Pseudepigraphen des Alten Testaments,* volume 2. Edited by E. Kautsch. Tübingen: Mohr Siebeck, 1900.

Haacker, K. "Die Geschichtstheologie von Röm 9–11 im Lichte philonischer Schriftauslegung." *New Testament Studies* 43 (1997): 209-22.

———. "Das Thema von Römer 9–11 als Problem der Auslegungsgeschichte." Pages 55-72 in *Between Gospel and Election: Explorations in the Interpretation of Romans 9–11.* Edited by F. Wilk and J. R. Wagner. Tübingen: Mohr Siebeck, 2010.

Hahn, J. *Zerstörungen des Jerusalemer Tempels: Geschehen — Wahrnehmungen — Bewältigungen.* With the assistance of C. Ronning. Tübingen: Mohr Siebeck, 2002.

Hainz, J. *Koinonia. "Kirche" als Gemeinschaft bei Paulus.* Regensburg: Pustet, 1982.

Hallward, P. *Badiou: A Subject to Truth.* Minneapolis: University of Minnesota Press, 2003.

Halpern-Amaru, B. *Rewriting the Bible: Land and Covenant in Postbiblical Jewish Literature.* Valley Forge: Trinity Press International, 1994.

Hamel, G. *Poverty and Charity in Roman Palestine: First Three Centuries C.E.* Berkeley: University of California Press, 1990.

Hammann, K. *Rudolf Bultmann: Eine Biographie.* Tübingen: Mohr Siebeck, 2009.

Hampson, D. *Christian Contradictions: The Structures of Lutheran and Catholic Thought.* Cambridge: Cambridge University Press, 2001.

Hansen, B. *"All of You Are One": The Social Vision of Gal 3.28, 1 Cor 12.13 and Col 3.11.* London: T&T Clark, 2010.

Hansen, G. W. *Abraham in Galatians: Epistolary and Rhetorical Contexts.* Sheffield: Sheffield Academic Press, 1989.

Hardin, J. *Galatians and the Imperial Cult.* Tübingen: Mohr Siebeck, 2008.

Harink, D., ed. *Paul, Philosophy, and the Theopolitical Vision.* Eugene: Cascade Books, 2010.

Harkins, A. K. "The Performative Reading of the Hodayot: The Arousal of Emotions and the Exegetical Generation of Texts." *Journal for the Study of the Pseudepigrapha* 21 (2011): 55-71.

———. "Who Is the Teacher of the Teacher Hymns? Re-examining the Teacher Hymns Hypothesis Fifty Years Later." Pages 449-67 in *A Teacher for All Generations: Essays in Honor of James C. VanderKam.* Edited by E. Mason et al. Leiden: Brill, 2012.

Harnack, A. von. *Marcion: Das Evangelium von Fremden Gott.* 2nd edition. Leipzig: J. C. Hinrichs, 1924.

Harnisch, W. *Verhängnis und Verheissung der Geschichte: Untersuchungen zum Zeit- und Geschichtsverständnis im 4. Buch Esra und in der syr. Baruchapokalypse.* Göttingen: Vandenhoeck & Ruprecht, 1969.

———. "Der Prophet als Widerpart und Zeuge der Offenbarung: Erwägungen zur Interdependenz von Form und Sache in IV. Buch Esra." Pages 460-93 in *Apocalypticism in the Mediterranean World and the Near East.* Edited by D. Hellholm. Tübingen: Mohr Siebeck, 1983.

———. "Einübung des neuen Seins. Paulinische Paränese am Beispiel des Galaterbriefs." *Zeitschrift für Theologie und Kirche* 84 (1987): 279-96.

Harrington, D. J. "Pseudo-Philo." Pages 297-378 in *Old Testament Pseudepigrapha.* Edited by J. Charlesworth. 2 volumes. London: Darton, Longman & Todd, 1985.

Harris, J. R. *Fragments from Philo Judaeus*. Cambridge: Cambridge University Press, 1886.

Harris, W. V. "Trade." Pages 710-40 in *The Cambridge Ancient History*. Volume 11: *The High Empire*. Edited by A. Bowman et al. 2nd edition. Cambridge: Cambridge University Press, 2000.

Harrison, C. *Augustine: Christian Truth and Fractured Humanity*. Oxford: Oxford University, 2000.

———. *Rethinking Augustine's Early Theology: An Argument for Continuity*. Oxford: Oxford University, 2006.

Harrison, J. R. *Paul's Language of Grace in Its Graeco-Roman Context*. Tübingen: Mohr Siebeck, 2003.

Harrisville, R. "ΠΙΣΤΙΣ ΧΡΙΣΤΟΥ: Witness of the Fathers." *Novum Testamentum* 36 (1994): 233-41.

Hart, K. "Marcel Mauss: In Pursuit of the Whole. A Review Essay." *Comparative Studies in Society and History* 49 (2007): 473-85.

Hayman, A. P. "The Problem of Pseudonymity in the Ezra Apocalypse." *Journal for the Study of Judaism* 6 (1975): 47-56.

Hays, R. B. "'Have We Found Abraham to Be Our Forefather according to the Flesh?' A Reconsideration of Rom 4:1." *Novum Testamentum* 27 (1985): 76-98.

———. "Christology and Ethics in Galatians: The Law of Christ." *Catholic Biblical Quarterly* 49 (1987): 268-90.

———. *Echoes of Scripture in the Letters of Paul*. New Haven: Yale University Press, 1989.

———. "Galatians." Pages 181-348 in *New Interpreter's Bible*, volume 11. Abingdon: Nashville, 2000.

———. *The Faith of Jesus Christ: The Narrative Substructure of Galatians 3:1–4:11*. 2nd edition. Grand Rapids: Eerdmans, 2002.

———. *The Conversion of the Imagination*. Grand Rapids: Eerdmans, 2005.

Helm, P. *Calvin at the Centre*. Oxford: Oxford University Press, 2010.

Hempel, C. "The *Treatise on the Two Spirits* and the Literary History of the *Rule of the Community*." Pages 102-20 in *Dualism in Qumran*. Edited by G. G. Xeravits. London: T&T Clark, 2010.

Herman, G. *Ritualised Friendship and the Greek City*. Cambridge: Cambridge University Press, 1987.

Hill, W. "The Church as Israel and Israel as the Church: An Examination of Karl Barth's Exegesis of Romans 9:1-5 in *The Epistle to the Romans* and *Church Dogmatics* 2/2." *Journal of Theological Interpretation* 6 (2012): 139-58.

Hoffmann, L. *Covenant of Blood: Circumcision and Gender in Rabbinic Judaism*. Chicago: University of Chicago Press, 1996.

Hofius, O. "Das Evangelium und Israel: Erwägungen zu Römer 9–11." Pages 175-202 in *Paulusstudien*. Tübingen: Mohr Siebeck, 1989.

Hogan, K. M. "The Meanings of tôrâ in 4 Ezra." *Journal for the Study of Judaism* 38 (2007): pp. 530-52.

———. *Theologies in Conflict in 4 Ezra: Wisdom Debate and Apocalyptic Solution*. Leiden: Brill, 2008.

Holm, B. K. *Gabe und Geben bei Luther: Das Verhältnis zwischen Reziprozität und reformatorischer Rechtfertigungslehre*. Berlin: de Gruyter, 2006.

Holm-Nielsen, S. *Hodayot: Psalms from Qumran.* Aarhus: Universitetsforlaget, 1960.

Holmberg, B. "Jewish *versus* Christian Identity in the Early Church?" *Revue Biblique* 105 (1998): 397-425.

———. "Understanding the First Hundred Years of Christian Identity." Pages 1-32 in *Exploring Early Christian Identity.* Edited by B. Holmberg. Tübingen: Mohr Siebeck, 2008.

Hombert, P.-M. *Gloria Gratiae: Se glorifier en Dieu, principe et fin de la théologie augustinienne de la grâce.* Paris: Études Augustiniennes, 1996.

Hooker, M. D. *From Adam to Christ.* Cambridge: Cambridge University Press, 1990.

Horn, F., and R. Zimmermann, eds. *Jenseits von Indikativ und Imperativ.* Tübingen: Mohr Siebeck, 2009.

Horner, R. *Rethinking God as Gift: Marion, Derrida, and the Limits of Phenomenology.* New York: Fordham University Press, 2001.

Horrell, D. G. "Solidarity and Difference: Pauline Morality in Romans 14:1–15:13." *Studies in Christian Ethics* 15.2 (2002): 60-78.

———. *Solidarity and Difference: A Contemporary Reading of Paul's Ethics.* London: T&T Clark, 2005.

Howard, G. *Paul: Crisis in Galatia.* Cambridge: Cambridge University Press, 1979.

Hubbard, M. V. *New Creation in Paul's Letters and Thought.* Cambridge: Cambridge University Press, 2002.

Hübner, H. "Anthropologisher Dualismus in den Hodayoth?" *New Testament Studies* 18 (1971-72): 268-84.

———. *Gottes Ich und Israel: Zum Schriftgebrauch des Paulus in Römer 9–11.* Göttingen: Vandenhoeck & Ruprecht, 1984.

———. *Law in Paul's Thought.* Translated by J. Greig. Edinburgh: T&T Clark, 1994.

———. *Die Weisheit Salomons.* Göttingen: Vandenhoeck & Ruprecht, 1999.

Hughes, J. A. *Scriptural Allusions and Exegesis in the Hodayot.* Leiden: Brill, 2006.

Hultgren, S. *From the Damascus Covenant to the Covenant of the Community.* Leiden: Brill, 2007.

Hunsinger, G. *How to Read Karl Barth: The Shape of His Theology.* Oxford: Oxford University Press, 1991.

———. *Disruptive Grace: Studies in the Theology of Karl Barth.* Grand Rapids: Eerdmans, 2000.

Hvalvik, R. "A 'Sonderweg' for Israel: A Critical Examination of a Current Interpretation of Romans 11.25-27." *Journal for the Study of the New Testament* 38 (1990): 87-107.

Hyde, L. *The Gift: Imagination and the Erotic Life of Property.* New York: Vintage Books, 1979.

Inwood, B. "Politics and Paradox in Seneca's *De Beneficiis.*" Pages 241-65 in *Justice and Generosity: Studies in Hellenistic Social and Political Philosophy.* Edited by A. Laks and M. Schofield. Cambridge: Cambridge University Press, 1995.

Isaac, B. *The Invention of Racism in Classical Antiquity.* Princeton: Princeton University Press, 2004.

Jackson, T. R. *New Creation in Paul's Letters: A Study of the Historical and Social Setting of a Pauline Concept.* Tübingen: Mohr Siebeck, 2010.

Jacobson, H. *A Commentary on Pseudo-Philo's* Liber Antiquitatum Biblicarum. 2 volumes. Leiden: Brill, 1996.

James, W., and N. J. Allen, eds. *Marcel Mauss: A Centenary Tribute.* New York: Berghahn Books, 1998.

Jaquette, J. J. *Discerning What Counts: The Function of the* Adiaphora Topos *in Paul's Letters.* Atlanta: Scholars Press, 1995.

Jenkins, R. *Pierre Bourdieu.* London: Routledge, 1993.

Jeremias, G. *Der Lehrer der Gerechtigkeit.* Göttingen: Vandenhoeck & Ruprecht, 1963.

Jervis, L. A. *The Purpose of Romans.* Sheffield: JSNT Press, 1991.

Jewett, R. "The Agitators and the Galatian Congregation." *New Testament Studies* 17 (1970-71): 198-212.

———. *Paul's Anthropological Terms: A Study of Their Use in Conflict Situations.* Leiden: Brill, 1971.

———. *Romans.* Hermeneia. Minneapolis: Fortress Press, 2007.

Johansen, J. P. *The Maori and His Religion in Its Non-Ritualistic Aspects.* Copenhagen: Muksgaard, 1954.

Johnson, E. E. *The Function of Apocalyptic and Wisdom Traditions in Romans 9–11.* Atlanta: Scholars Press, 1989.

Johnson, L. T. "Rom. 3.21-26 and the Faith of Jesus." *Catholic Biblical Quarterly* 44 (1982): 77-90.

Johnson Hodge, C. *If Sons, Then Heirs: A Study of Kinship and Ethnicity in the Letters of Paul.* Oxford: Oxford University Press, 2007.

Joubert, S. *Paul as Benefactor: Reciprocity, Strategy, and Theological Reflection in Paul's Collection.* Tübingen: Mohr Siebeck, 2000.

Kahl. B. "No Longer Male: Masculinity Struggles Behind Galatians 3.28?" *Journal for the Study of the New Testament* 79 (2000): 37-49.

———. *Galatians Reimagined: Reading with the Eyes of the Vanquished.* Minneapolis: Fortress Press, 2010.

Kant, I. *The Metaphysics of Morals.* Translated by M. Gregor. New York: Cambridge University Press, 1996.

Käsemann, E. "Amt und Gemeinde im Neuen Testament." Pages 109-34 in *Exegetische Versuche und Besinnungen,* volume 1. Göttingen: Vandenhoeck & Ruprecht, 1965. Translated by W. J. Montague as "Ministry and Community in the New Testament." Pages 63-134 in *Essays on New Testament Themes.* London: SCM Press, 1964.

———. "Die Anfänge christlicher Theologie." Pages 82-104 in *Exegetische Versuche,* volume 2. Translated as "The Beginnings of Christian Theology." Pages 82-107 in *New Testament Questions of Today.* Philadelphia: Fortress Press, 1969.

———. "Zur Thema der urchristlichen Apokalyptik." Pages 105-131 in *Exegetische Versuche und Besinnungen,* volume 2. Göttingen: Vandenhoeck & Ruprecht, 1965. Translated by W. J. Montague as "On the Subject of Primitive Christian Apocalyptic." Pages 108-137 in *New Testament Questions of Today.* Philadelphia: Fortress Press, 1969.

———. "Gottesgerechtigkeit bei Paulus." Pages 181-94 in *Exegetische Versuche,* volume 2. Translated as "'The Righteousness of God' in Paul." Pages 168-82 in *New Testament Questions of Today.* Philadelphia: Fortress Press, 1969.

———. "Paulus und Israel." Pages 194-197 in *Exegetische Versuche*, volume 2. Translated as "Paul and Israel." Pages 183-187 in *New Testament Questions of Today*. Philadelphia: Fortress Press, 1969.

———. "Der Glaube Abrahams in Röm 4." Pages 140-77 in *Paulinische Perspektiven*. Tübingen: Mohr Siebeck, 1969. Translated by M. Kohl as "The Faith of Abraham in Romans 4." Pages 79-101 in *Perspectives on Paul*. Philadelphia: Fortress Press, 1971.

———. "Zur paulinischen Anthropologie." Pages 9-60 in *Paulinische Perspektiven*. Translated as "On Paul's Anthropology." Pages 1-31 in *Perspectives on Paul*. Philadelphia: Fortress Press, 1971.

———. "Rechtfertigung und Heilsgeschichte im Römerbrief." Pages 108-39 in *Paulinische Perspektiven*. Translated as "Justification and Salvation History in the Epistle to the Romans." Pages 60-78 in *Perspectives on Paul*. Philadelphia: Fortress Press, 1971.

———. *An die Römer*. 4th edition. Tübingen: Mohr Siebeck, 1980. Translated by G. W. Bromiley as *Commentary on Romans*. London: SCM Press, 1980.

———. *Kirchliche Konflikte*. Göttingen: Vandenhoeck & Ruprecht, 1982.

———. "A Theological Review." Pages xii-xxi in *On Being a Disciple of the Crucified Nazarene: Unpublished Lectures and Sermons*. Edited by R. Landau. Translated by R. A. Harrisville. Grand Rapids: Eerdmans, 2010.

Keck, L. E. "'Jesus' in Romans." *Journal of Biblical Literature* 108 (1989): 443-60.

Kelsey, D. *Eccentric Existence: A Theological Anthropology*. 2 volumes. Louisville: Westminster John Knox, 2009.

Kennedy, H. A. A. *Philo's Contribution to Religion*. London: Hodder & Stoughton, 1919.

Kilpatrick, G. "Gal 2.14 ὀρθοποδοῦσιν." Pages 269-74 in *Neutestamentliche Studien für R. Bultmann*. Edited by W. Eltester. 2nd edition. Berlin: A. Töpelmann, 1957.

Kim, K. *God Will Judge Each One according to Works: Judgment According to Works and Psalm 62 in Early Judaism and the New Testament*. Berlin: de Gruyter, 2010.

King, A. "Thinking with Bourdieu against Bourdieu: A 'Practical' Critique of the Habitus." *Sociological Theory* 18 (2000): 417-33.

Kirk, J. R. D. *Unlocking Romans: Resurrection and the Justification of God*. Grand Rapids: Eerdmans, 2008.

Kittel, B. *The Hymns of Qumran: Translation and Commentary*. Chico: Scholars Press, 1981.

Klawans, J. *Impurity and Sin in Ancient Judaism*. Oxford: Oxford University Press, 2000.

Klein, C. *Theologie und Anti-Judaismus*. Munich: Chr. Kaiser Verlag, 1975. Translated by E. Quinn as *Anti-Judaism and Christian Theology*. London: SPCK, 1978.

Klein, G. "Römer 4 und die Idee der Heilsgeschichte." *Evangelische Theologie* 23 (1963): 424-47.

———. "Werkruhm und Christusruhm im Galaterbrief und die Frage nach einer Entwicklung des Paulus." Pages 196-211 in *Studien zum Text und zur Ethik des Neuen Testaments*. Edited by W. Schrage. Berlin: de Gruyter, 1986.

———. "Paul's Purpose in Writing the Epistle to the Romans." Pages 29-43 in *The Romans Debate*. Revised and expanded edition. Edited by K. P. Donfried. Edinburgh: T&T Clark, 1991.

Klijn, A. F. J. *Der lateinische Text der Apokalypse des Esra*. Berlin: Akademie-Verlag, 1983.

———. *Die Esra-Apokalypse (IV. Esra)*. Berlin: Akademie Verlag, 1992.

Knowles, M. P. "Moses, the Law, and the Unity of 4 Ezra." *Novum Testamentum* 31 (1989): 257-74.

Koch, K. "Esras erste Vision. Weltzeiten und Weg des Höchsten." *Biblische Zeitschrift* 22 (1978): 46-75.

Kolarcik, M. *The Ambiguity of Death in the Book of Wisdom 1–6*. Rome: Pontifical Biblical Institute, 1991.

———. "Universalism and Justice in the Wisdom of Solomon." Pages 289-301 in *Treasures of Wisdom: Studies in Ben Sira and the Book of Wisdom*. Edited by N. Calduch-Benages and J. Vermeylen. Tübingen: Mohr Siebeck, 2010.

Komter, A. E. *Social Solidarity and the Gift*. Cambridge: Cambridge University Press, 2005.

Konradt, M. "Die Christonomie der Freiheit. Zu Paulus' Entfaltung seines ethischen Ansatzes in Gal 5,13–6,10." *Early Christianity* 1 (2010): 60-81.

Konstan, D. *Friendship in the Classical World*. Cambridge: Cambridge University Press, 1997.

———. "Reciprocity and Friendship." Pages 279-301 in *Reciprocity in Ancient Greece*. Edited by C. Gill, N. Postlethwaite, and R. Seaford. Oxford: Oxford University Press, 1998.

———. *Pity Transformed*. London: Duckworth, 2001.

Krauss, W. *Das Volk Gottes. Zur Grundlegung der Ekklesiologie bei Paulus*. Tübingen: Mohr Siebeck, 1996.

Kuck, D. W. "'Each Will Bear His Own Burden': Paul's Creative Use of an Apocalyptic Motif." *New Testament Studies* 40 (1994): 289-97.

Kuhn, H.-W. *Enderwartung und gegenwärtiges Heil*. Göttingen: Vandenhoeck & Ruprecht, 1966.

Kurke, L. *The Traffic in Praise: Pindar and the Poetics of Social Economy*. Ithaca: Cornell University Press, 1991.

Kuula, K. *The Law, the Covenant and God's Plan*. Volume 1: *Paul's Polemical Treatment of the Law in Galatians*. Göttingen: Vandenhoeck & Ruprecht, 1999.

Laato, T. *Paulus und das Judentum*. Åbo: Åbo Akademis Förlag, 1991. Translated by T. McElwain as *Paul and Judaism: An Anthropological Approach*. Atlanta: Scholars Press, 1995.

Lagrange, M. J. "Le Livre de Sagesse, sa doctrine des fins dernières." *Revue Biblique* 4 (1907): 85-104.

Lambrecht, J. *Pauline Studies: Collected Essays*. Leuven: Peeters, 1994.

———. "Paul's Coherent Admonition in Galatians 6,1-6: Mutual Help and Individual Attentiveness." *Biblica* 78 (1997): 33-56.

———. "The Right Things You Want to Do: A Note on Galatians 5,17d." *Biblica* 79 (1998): 515-24.

Lancel, S. *Saint Augustine*. Translated by A. Neville. London: SCM Press, 2002.

Landmesser, C. "Rudolf Bultmann als Paulusinterpret." *Zeitschrift für Theologie und Kirche* 110 (2013): 1-21.

Lange, A. *Weisheit und Prädestination. Weisheitliche Urordnung und Prädestination in den Textfunden von Qumran*. Leiden: Brill, 1995.

LaPorte, J. *Eucharistia in Philo*. New York: Edwin Mellen Press, 1983.

Larcher, C. *Études sur le Livre de la Sagesse.* Paris: Gabalda, 1969.

———. *Le Livre de la Sagesse, ou, La Sagesse de Salomon.* 3 volumes. Paris: Gabalda, 1983.

Lategan, B. "Is Paul Defending His Apostleship in Galatians?" *New Testament Studies* 34 (1988): 411-30.

Leithart, P. J. *Gratitude: An Intellectual History.* Waco: Baylor University Press, 2014.

Lendon, J. E. *Empire of Honour: The Art of Government in the Roman World.* Oxford: Oxford University Press, 1997.

Leonhardt, J. *Jewish Worship in Philo of Alexandria.* Tübingen: Mohr Siebeck, 2001.

Levison, J. R. "Torah and Covenant in Pseudo-Philo's *Liber Antiquitatum Biblicarum.*" Pages 111-27 in *Bund und Tora: Zur theologischen Begriffsgeschichte in alttestamentlicher, frühjüdischer und urchristlicher Tradition.* Edited by F. Avemarie and H. Lichtenberger. Tübingen: Mohr Siebeck, 1996.

Lévi-Strauss, C. *Introduction to the Work of Marcel Mauss.* Translated by F. Baker. London: Routledge & Kegan Paul, 1987.

Levy, I. C. *The Letter to the Galatians.* The Bible in Medieval Tradition. Grand Rapids: Eerdmans, 2011.

Licht, J. "The Doctrine of the Thanksgiving Scroll." *Israel Exploration Journal* 6 (1956): 1-13, 89-101.

Lichtenberger, H. *Studien zum Menschenbild in Texten der Qumrangemeinde.* Göttingen: Vandenhoeck & Ruprecht, 1980.

Lieu, J. M. "'Grace to You and Peace': The Apostolic Greeting." *Bulletin of the John Rylands Library* 68 (1985-86): 161-78.

———. "'As Much My Apostle as Christ Is Mine': The Dispute over Paul between Tertullian and Marcion." *Early Christianity* 1 (2010): 41-59.

———. *Marcion and the Making of a Heretic: God and Scripture in the Second Century.* Cambridge: Cambridge University Press, 2014.

Lindberg, C. *Beyond Charity: Reformation Initiatives for the Poor.* Minneapolis: Fortress Press, 1993.

Linebaugh, J. A. "Announcing the Human: Rethinking the Relationship between Wisdom of Solomon 13–15 and Romans 1.18–2.11." *New Testament Studies* 37 (2011): 214-37.

———. *God, Grace, and Righteousness in Wisdom of Solomon and Paul's Letter to the Romans: Texts in Conversation.* Leiden: Brill, 2013.

———. "The Christo-Centrism of Faith in Christ: Martin Luther's Reading of Galatians 2.16, 19-20." *New Testament Studies* 59 (2013): 535-44.

Litfin, D. *St. Paul's Theology of Proclamation: 1 Corinthians 1–4 and Greco-Roman Rhetoric.* Cambridge: Cambridge University Press, 1994.

Loew, O. *ΧΑΡΙΣ.* Diss. Marburg, 1908.

Lohfink, N. *Lobgesänge der Armen.* Stuttgart: Katholisches Bibelwerk, 1990.

Löhr, W. "Did Marcion Distinguish between a Just God and a Good God?" Pages 131-46 in *Marcion and seine kirchengeschichtliche Wirkung.* Edited by G. May and K. Greschat. Berlin: de Gruyter, 2002.

Lohse, B. *Martin Luther's Theology: Its Historical and Systematic Development.* Minneapolis: Fortress, 2006.

Lohse, E. *Der Brief an die Römer.* Göttingen: Vandenhoeck & Ruprecht, 2003.

Lonergan, B. *Grace and Freedom. Operative Grace in the Thought of Thomas Aquinas.* London: Darton, Longman and Todd, 1971.

Longenecker, B. W. "Different Answers to Different Issues: Israel, the Gentiles, and Salvation History in Romans 9–11." *Journal for the Study of the New Testament* 36 (1989): 95-123.

———. *Eschatology and the Covenant: A Comparison of 4 Ezra and Romans 1–11.* Sheffield: JSOT Press, 1991.

———. *2 Esdras.* Sheffield: Sheffield Academic Press, 1995.

———. *The Triumph of Abraham's God: The Transformation of Identity in Galatians.* Edinburgh: T&T Clark, 1998.

———. *Remember the Poor: Paul, Poverty, and the Graeco-Roman World.* Grand Rapids: Eerdmans, 2010.

Longenecker, B. W., ed. *Narrative Dynamics in Paul: A Critical Assessment.* Louisville: Westminster John Knox Press, 2002.

Longenecker, R. N. *Galatians.* Word Biblical Commentaries. Dallas: Word, 1990.

———. *Introducing Romans: Critical Issues in Paul's Most Famous Letter.* Grand Rapids: Eerdmans, 2011.

Lopez, D. C. *Apostle to the Conquered.* Minneapolis: Fortress Press, 2008.

Lübking, H.-M. *Paulus und Israel in Römerbrief.* Frankfurt: Peter Lang, 1986.

Lull, D. J. "'The Law Was Our Pedagogue': A Study in Galatians 3.19-25." *Journal of Biblical Literature* 105 (1986): 481-96.

Luz, U. *Das Geschichtsverständnis des Paulus.* Munich: Kaiser Verlag, 1968.

Lyons, B. G. *Pauline Autobiography: Towards a New Understanding.* Atlanta: Scholars Press, 1985.

MacDowell, D. M. "Athenian Laws about Bribery." *Revue Internationale des Droits de l'Antiquité* 30 (1983): 57-78.

MacLachlan, B. *The Age of Grace:* Charis *in Early Greek Poetry.* Princeton: Princeton University Press, 1993.

Malherbe, A. J. *Ancient Epistolary Theorists.* Atlanta: Scholars Press, 1988.

Malina, B. J. *The New Testament World: Insights from Cultural Anthropology.* Revised edition. Louisville: Westminster/John Knox Press, 1993.

Malinowski, B. *Argonauts of the Western Pacific.* London: Routledge, 1922.

———. *Crime and Custom in Savage Society.* London: Kegan Paul, 1926.

Malysz, P. "Exchange and Ecstasy: Luther's Eucharistic Theology in Light of Radical Orthodoxy's Critique of Gift and Sacrifice." *Scottish Journal of Theology* 60 (2007): 294-308.

Manfredi, S. "The Trial of the Righteous in Wis 5:1-14 (1-7) and in the Prophetic Traditions." Pages 159-78 in *The Book of Wisdom in Modern Research: Studies on Tradition, Redaction, and Theology.* Edited by A. Passaro and G. Bellia. Berlin: de Gruyter, 2005.

Mannermaa, T. *Christ Present in Faith: Luther's View of Justification.* Translated and edited by K. Stjerna. Minneapolis: Fortress Press, 2005.

———. *Two Kinds of Love: Martin Luther's Religious World.* Translated by K. Stjerna; Minneapolis: Fortress Press, 2010.

Mansoor, M. *The Thanksgiving Hymns.* Leiden: Brill, 1961.

Marcus, J. "The Circumcision and Uncircumcision in Rome." *New Testament Studies* 35 (1989): 67-81.

———. "'Under the Law': The Background of a Pauline Expression." *Catholic Biblical Quarterly* 44 (2001): 606-21.

Marion, J-L. *Étant donné: Essai d'une phénoménologie de la donation.* 2nd edition. Paris: Presses Universitaires de France, 1997. Translated by J. L. Kosky as *Being Given: Towards a Phenomenology of Givenness.* Stanford: Stanford University Press, 1997.

Marshall, L. "Sharing, Talking, and Giving: Relief of Social Tensions among !Kung Bushmen." *Africa* 31 (1961): 231-49.

Martens, J. W. *One God, One Law: Philo of Alexandria on the Mosaic and Greco-Roman Law.* Leiden: Brill, 2003.

Martin, D. B. *Inventing Superstition: From the Hippocratics to the Christians.* Cambridge, MA: Harvard University Press, 2004.

Martin, T. W. "Pagan and Judeo-Christian Time-Keeping Schemes in Gal 4.10 and Col 2.16." *New Testament Studies* 42 (1996): 105-19.

Martyn, J. L. "Apocalyptic Antinomies in Paul's Letter to the Galatians." *New Testament Studies* 31 (1985): 410-24.

———. "Paul and His Jewish-Christian Interpreters." *Union Seminary Quarterly Review* 42 (1987-88): 1-15.

———. "Events in Galatia: Modified Covenantal Nomism versus God's Invasion of the Cosmos in the Singular Gospel: A Response to J. D. G. Dunn and B. R. Gaventa." Pages 160-179 in *Pauline Theology,* volume 1. Edited by J. M. Bassler. Minneapolis: Fortress Press, 1991.

———. *Theological Issues in the Letters of Paul.* Edinburgh: T&T Clark, 1997.

———. "Epistemology at the Turn of the Ages." Pages 89-110 in *Theological Issues in the Letters of Paul.* Edinburgh: T&T Clark, 1997.

———. *Galatians: A New Translation with Introduction and Commentary.* Anchor Bible 33A. New York: Doubleday, 1997.

———. "The Apocalyptic Gospel in Galatians." *Interpretation* 54 (2000): 246-66.

———. "De-apocalypticizing Paul: An Essay Focused on *Paul and the Stoics* by Troels Engberg-Pedersen." *Journal for the Study of the New Testament* 86 (2002): 61-102.

———. "Epilogue: An Essay in Pauline Meta-Ethics." Pages 173-183 in *Divine and Human Agency in Paul and His Cultural Environment.* Edited by J. M. G. Barclay and S. J. Gathercole. London: T&T Clark, 2006.

———. "The Gospel Invades Philosophy." Pages 13-33 in *Paul, Philosophy, and the Theopolitical Vision.* Edited by D. Harink. Eugene: Cascade, 2010.

———. "A Personal Word about Ernst Käsemann." Pages xiii-xv in *Apocalyptic and the Future of Theology: With and Beyond J. Louis Martyn.* Edited by B. Davis and D. Harink. Eugene: Cascade, 2012.

Mason, S. *Josephus, Judea, and Christian Origins.* Peabody: Hendrickson, 2009.

Maston, J. *Divine and Human Agency in Second Temple Judaism and Paul.* Tübingen: Mohr Siebeck, 2010.

Matera, F. J. "The Culmination of Paul's Argument to the Galatians: Gal. 5.1–6.17." *Journal for the Study of the New Testament* 32 (1988): 79-91.

———. *Galatians.* Sacra Pagina 9. Collegeville: Liturgical Press, 1992.

Matlock, R. B. "Almost Cultural Studies? Reflections on the 'New Perspective' on Paul." Pages 433-59 in *Biblical Studies/Cultural Studies: The Third Sheffield Colloquium*. Edited by J. C. Exum and S. D. Moore. Sheffield: Sheffield Academic Press, 1998.

———. "Sins of the Flesh and Suspicious Minds: Dunn's New *Theology of Paul*." *Journal for the Study of the New Testament* 72 (1998): 67-90.

———. "Detheologizing the ΠΙΣΤΙΣ ΧΡΙΣΤΟΥ Debate: Cautionary Remarks from a Lexical Semantic Perspective." *Novum Testamentum* 42 (2000): 1-23.

———. "Even the Demons Believe: Paul and πίστις Χρίστου." *Catholic Biblical Quarterly* 64 (2002): 300-318.

———. "The Rhetoric of πίστις in Paul: Galatians 2.16, 3.22, Romans 3.22 and Philippians 3.9." *Journal for the Study of the New Testament* 30 (2007): 173-203.

Mauss, M. "Essai sur le Don: Forme et Raison de l'Échange dans les sociétés Archaïques." Pages 145-279 in *Sociologie et Anthropologie*. Paris: Presses Universitaires de France, 1950. Translated by W. D. Halls as *The Gift*. London: Routledge, 1990.

May, G., and Greschat, K., eds. *Marcion and seine kirchengeschichtliche Wirkung*. Berlin: de Gruyter, 2002.

Mazzinghi, L. "Wis 19.13-17 and the Civil Rights of the Jews of Alexandria." Pages 53-82 in *The Book of Wisdom in Modern Research: Studies on Tradition, Redaction, and Theology*. Edited by A. Passaro and G. Bellia. Berlin: de Gruyter, 2005.

McCormack, B. L. *Karl Barth's Critically Realistic Dialectical Theology: Its Genesis and Development 1909-1936*. Oxford: Clarendon Press, 1995.

———. "Grace and Being: The Role of God's Gracious Election in Karl Barth's Ontology." Pages 92-110 in *The Cambridge Companion to Karl Barth*. Edited by J. Webster. Cambridge: Cambridge University Press, 2000.

McFarland, O. *The God Who Gives: Philo and Paul in Conversation*. PhD Thesis, Durham University, 2013.

———. " 'The One Who Calls in Grace': Paul's Rhetorical and Theological Identification with the Galatians." *Horizons in Biblical Theology* 35 (2013): 151-65.

McGlynn, M. *Divine Judgement and Divine Benevolence in the Book of Wisdom*. Tübingen: Mohr Siebeck, 2001.

McGrath, A. E. *Iustitia Dei. A History of the Christian Doctrine of Justification*. 2 volumes. Cambridge: Cambridge University Press, 1986.

McKee, E. A. *John Calvin on the Diaconate and Liturgical Almsgiving*. Geneva: Librairie Droz, 1984.

Meeks, W. "The Image of the Androgyne: Some Uses of a Symbol in Earliest Christianity." *History of Religions* 13 (1974): 165-208.

———. *In Search of the Early Christians*. New Haven: Yale University Press, 2002.

Meiser, M. *Galater*. Novum Testamentum Patristicum. Göttingen: Vandenhoeck & Ruprecht, 2007.

Melanchthon, P. *Paul's Letter to the Colossians*. Translated by D. C. Parker. Sheffield: Almond Press, 1989.

Mendelson, A. *Secular Education in Philo of Alexandria*. Cincinnati: Hebrew Union College Press, 1982.

Merk, O. "Der Beginn der Paränese im Galaterbrief." *Zeitschrift für die neutestamentliche Wissenschaft und die Kunde der älteren Kirche* 60 (1969): 83-104.

Merrill, E. H. *Qumran and Predestination: A Theological Study of the Thanksgiving Hymns.* Leiden: Brill, 1975.

Metso, S. *The Textual Development of the Qumran Community Rule.* Leiden: Brill, 1997.

———. *The Serekh Texts.* London: T&T Clark, 2007.

Meyer, N. A. "Adam's Dust and Adam's Glory: Rethinking Anthropogony and Theology in the Hodayot and the Letters of Paul." PhD thesis, McMaster University, 2013.

Meyer, P. W. "Romans 10:4 and the 'End' of the Law." Pages 78-94 in *The Word in This World.* Louisville: Westminster John Knox Press, 2004.

Michel, J. *Gratuité en droit romain.* Brussels: Université libre de Bruxelles, 1962.

Milbank, J. "Can a Gift Be Given? Prolegomenon to a Future Trinitarian Metaphysic." *Modern Theology* 11 (1995): 119-61.

———. *Being Reconciled: Ontology and Pardon.* London: Routledge, 2003.

Millar, F. *The Emperor in the Roman World, 31 BC–AD 337.* London: Duckworth, 1977.

Millett, P. *Lending and Borrowing in Ancient Athens.* Cambridge: Cambridge University Press, 1991.

Mitchell, L. *Greeks Bearing Gifts: The Public Use of Private Relationships in the Greek World, 435-323 BC.* Cambridge: Cambridge University Press, 1997.

Mitchell, M. M. "Rhetorical Shorthand in Pauline Argumentation: The Function of 'the Gospel' in the Corinthian Correspondence." Pages 63-88 in *Gospel in Paul: Studies on Corinthians, Galatians and Romans for Richard N. Longenecker.* Edited by L. A. Jervis and P. Richardson. Sheffield: Sheffield Academic Press, 1994.

Moffatt, J. *Grace in the New Testament.* London: Hodder and Stoughton, 1931.

Moll, S. *The Arch-Heretic Marcion.* Tübingen: Mohr Siebeck, 2010.

Moo, D. "The Theology of Romans 9–11." Pages 240-58 in *Pauline Theology.* Volume 3: *Romans.* Edited by D. M. Hay and E. E. Johnson. Minneapolis: Fortress Press, 1995.

———. *The Epistle to the Romans.* Grand Rapids: Eerdmans, 1996.

Moo, J. A. *Creation, Nature, and Hope in 4 Ezra.* Göttingen: Vandenhoeck & Ruprecht, 2011.

———. "The Few Who Obtain Mercy: Soteriology in *4 Ezra.*" Pages 98-113 in *This World and the World to Come: Soteriology in Early Judaism.* Edited by D. M. Gurtner. London: T&T Clark, 2011.

Moore, G. F. *Judaism in the First Centuries of the Christian Era: The Age of the Tannaim.* 3 volumes. Cambridge, MA: Harvard University Press, 1927-30.

Morales, R. *The Spirit and the Restoration of Israel: New Exodus and New Creation Motifs in Galatians.* Tübingen: Mohr Siebeck, 2010.

Morgan, T. *Popular Morality in the Early Roman Empire.* Cambridge: Cambridge University Press, 2007.

Mott, S. C. "The Power of Giving and Receiving: Reciprocity in Hellenistic Benevolence." Pages 60-72 in *Current Issues in Biblical and Patristic Interpretation: Studies in Honor of Merrill C. Tenney.* Edited by G. F. Hawthorne. Grand Rapids: Eerdmans, 1975.

Moussy, C. *Gratia et sa famille.* Paris: Presses Universitaires de France, 1966.

Moxnes, H. *Theology in Conflict: Studies in Paul's Understanding of God in Romans.* Leiden: Brill, 1980.

———. "The Quest for Honor and the Unity of the Community in Romans 12 and in the Orations of Dio Chrysostom." Pages 203-20 in *Paul in His Hellenistic Context.* Edited by T. Engberg-Pedersen. Edinburgh: T&T Clark, 1994.

———. "Honor and Righteousness in Romans." *Journal for the Study of the New Testament* 32 (1999): 61-77.

Muller, R. A. *The Unaccommodated Calvin: Studies in the Foundation of a Theological Tradition.* Oxford: Oxford University Press, 2000.

Munck, J. *Paul and the Salvation of Mankind.* Translated by F. Clarke. London: SCM Press, 1959.

Mundle, W. "Das religiöse Problem des IV. Esrabuches." *Zeitschrift für die alttestamentliche Wissenschaft* n.s. 6 (1929): 222-49.

Murphy, F. J. "Divine Plan, Human Plan: A Structuring Theme in Pseudo-Philo." *Jewish Quarterly Review* 77 (1986): 5-14.

———. "The Eternal Covenant in Pseudo-Philo." *Journal for the Study of the Pseudepigrapha* 3 (1988): 43-57.

———. *Pseudo-Philo: Rewriting the Bible.* Oxford: Oxford University Press, 1993.

Murray, M. *Playing a Jewish Game: Gentile Christian Judaizing in the First and Second Centuries* C.E. Waterloo, Ont.: Wilfrid Laurier University Press, 2004.

Murray, O. "Aristeas and Ptolemaic Kingship." *Journal of Theological Studies* 18 (1967): 337-71.

Mussner, F. *Der Galaterbrief.* Herders theologischer Kommentar. Freiburg/Basel/Vienna: Herder, 1974.

———. *Traktat über die Juden.* Munich: Kösel Verlag, 1979.

Myers, J. M. *I and II Esdras.* Anchor Bible 42. Garden City: Doubleday, 1974.

Najman, H. "The Law of Nature and the Authority of Mosaic Law." *Studia Philonica Annual* 11 (1999): 55-73.

———. "A Written Copy of the Law of Nature: An Unthinkable Paradox?" *Studia Philonica Annual* 15 (2003): 54-63.

———. "Between Heaven and Earth: Liminal Visions in 4 Ezra." Pages 151-67 in *Other Worlds and Their Relation to This World: Early Jewish and Ancient Christian Traditions.* Edited by T. Nicklas et al. Leiden: Brill, 2010.

Nanos, M. D. *The Mystery of Romans: The Jewish Context of Paul's Letter.* Minneapolis: Fortress Press, 1996.

———. *The Irony of Galatians: Paul's Letter in First-Century Context.* Minneapolis: Fortress, 2002.

———. "What Was at Stake in Peter's 'Eating with Gentiles' at Antioch?" Pages 282-318 in *The Galatians Debate.* Edited by M. D. Nanos. Peabody: Hendrickson, 2002.

———. "Paul and Judaism: Why Not Paul's Judaism?" Pages 117-60 in *Paul Unbound: Other Perspectives on the Apostle.* Edited by M. D. Given. Peabody: Hendrickson, 2010.

Neubauer, K. W. *Der Stamm* Chnn *im Sprachgebrauch des Alten Testaments.* Berlin: Ernst Reute Gesellschaft, 1964.

Neugebauer, F. *In Christus: Eine Untersuchung zum paulinischen Glaubensverständnis.* Göttingen: Vandenhoeck & Ruprecht, 1961.

Neusner, J. "The Use of Later Rabbinic Evidence for the Study of Paul." Pages 43-64 in

Approaches to Ancient Judaism, volume 2. Edited by W. S. Green. Chico: Scholars Press, 1980.

Newsom, C. *The Self as Symbolic Space: Constructing Identity and Community at Qumran.* Leiden: Brill, 2004.

Neyrey, J. H. "Bewitched in Galatia: Paul and Cultural Anthropology." *Catholic Biblical Quarterly* 50 (1988): 72-100.

Nickelsburg, G. W. E. "Good and Bad Leaders in Pseudo-Philo's *Liber Antiquitatum Biblicarum.*" Pages 49-65 in *Ideal Figures in Ancient Judaism: Profiles and Paradigms.* Edited by J. J. Collins and G. W. E. Nickelsburg. Chico: Scholars Press, 1980.

Nida, E. A., and J. P. Louw. *Lexical Semantics of the Greek New Testament.* Atlanta: Scholars Press, 1992.

Niebuhr, K.-W. *Heidenapostel aus Israel: Die jüdische Identität des Paulus nach ihrer Darstellung in seinen Briefen.* Tübingen: Mohr Siebeck, 1992.

Niehoff, M. *Philo on Jewish Identity and Culture.* Tübingen: Mohr Siebeck, 2001.

Nikiprowetzky, V. *Le commentaire de l'Écriture chez Philon d'Alexandrie: son charactère et sa portée.* Leiden: Brill, 1977.

Nitzan, B. *Qumran Prayer and Religious Poetry.* Translated by J. Chipman. Leiden: Brill, 1994.

Noack, C. *Gottesbewußtsein: Exegetische Studien zur Soteriologie und Mystik bei Philo von Alexandria.* Tübingen: Mohr Siebeck, 2000.

———. "Haben oder Empfangen: Antithetische Charakterisierungen von Torheit und Weisheit bei Philo und bei Paulus." Pages 283-307 in *Philo und das Neue Testament Wechselseitige Wahrnehmungen.* Edited by R. Deines and K.-W. Niebuhr. Tübingen: Mohr Siebeck, 2004.

Noonan, J. T. *Bribes.* New York: Macmillan Press, 1984.

Norelli, E. "Marcion: Ein Philosoph oder ein Christ gegen Philosophie?" Pages 113-30 in *Marcion and seine kirchengeschichtliche Wirkung.* Edited by G. May and K. Greschat. Berlin: de Gruyter, 2002.

North, H. *Sophrosune: Self-knowledge and Self-restraint in Greek Literature.* Leiden: Brill, 1972.

Nötscher, F. *Zur theologischen Terminologie der Qumran-Texte.* Bonn: Hanstein Verlag, 1956.

Oberman, H. A. *The Harvest of Medieval Theology: Gabriel Biel and Late Medieval Nominalism.* Cambridge, MA: Harvard University Press, 1963.

———. *The Dawn of the Reformation: Essays in Late Medieval and Early Reformation Thought.* Edinburgh: T&T Clark, 1986.

———. *Luther: Man between God and the Devil.* New Haven: Yale University Press, 1986.

O'Brien, P. T. "Was Paul a Covenantal Nomist?" Pages 249-96 in *Justification and Variegated Nomism.* Volume 2: *The Paradoxes of Paul.* Edited by D. A. Carson, P. T. O'Brien, and M. A. Seifrid. Tübingen: Mohr Siebeck, 2004.

Olson, J. E. "Calvin on Social-ethical Issues." Pages 153-72 in *The Cambridge Companion to John Calvin.* Edited by D. K. McKim. Cambridge: Cambridge University Press, 2004.

Osborne, R. "Roman Poverty in Context." Pages 1-20 in *Poverty in the Roman World.* Edited by M. Atkins and R. Osborne. Cambridge: Cambridge University Press, 2006.

Panoff, M. "Marcel Mauss's *The Gift* Revisited." *Man* 5 (1970): 60-70.

Parker, R. "Pleasing Thighs: Reciprocity in Greek Religion." Pages 105-25 in *Reciprocity in Ancient Greece*. Edited by C. Gill, N. Postlethwaite, and R. Seaford. Oxford: Oxford University Press, 1998.

Parker, T. H. L. *Calvin's Preaching*. Edinburgh: T&T Clark, 1992.

Parkin, A. "'You Do Him No Service': An Exploration of Pagan Almsgiving." Pages 60-82 in *Poverty in the Roman World*. Edited by M. Atkins and R. Osborne. Cambridge: Cambridge University Press, 2006.

Parry, J. "*The Gift*, the Indian Gift, and the 'Indian Gift.'" *Man* 21 (1986): 453-73.

Patout Burns, J. *The Development of Augustine's Doctrine of Operative Grace*. Paris: Études Augustiniennes, 1980.

Pattison, B. L. *Poverty in the Theology of John Calvin*. Eugene: Pickwick Publications, 2006.

Peristiany, J. G., ed., *Honour and Shame: The Values of Mediterranean Society*. London: Weidenfeld and Nicolson, 1996.

Perrot, C., and P.-M. Bogaert. *Pseudo-Philon: Les Antiquités Bibliques*. Sources chrétiennes 229, 230; Paris: Gabalda, 1976.

Peterman, G. W. *Paul's Gift from Philippi: Conventions of Gift-exchange and Christian Giving*. Cambridge: Cambridge University Press, 1997.

Piper, J. *The Justification of God: An Exegetical and Theological Study of Romans 9:1-23*. 2nd edition. Grand Rapids: Baker Academic, 1993.

Pitt-Rivers, J. "Postscript: The Place of Grace in Anthropology." Pages 215-46 in *Honor and Grace in Anthropology*. Edited by J. G. Peristiany and J. Pitt-Rivers. Cambridge: Cambridge University Press, 1992.

Plezia, M. *Aristotelis Privatorum Scriptorum Fragmenta*. Leipzig: Teubner, 1977.

Plumer, E. *Augustine's Commentary on Galatians: Introduction, Text, Translation, and Notes*. Oxford: Oxford University Press, 2003.

Polanyi, K. *The Great Transformation: The Political and Economic Origins of Our Time*. Boston: Beacon Press, 1944.

Popović, M. *Reading the Human Body: Physiognomics and Astrology in the Dead Sea Scrolls and Hellenistic–Early Roman Period Judaism*. Leiden: Brill, 2007.

Price, S. R. F. *Rituals and Power: The Roman Imperial Cult in Asia Minor*. Cambridge: Cambridge University Press, 1984.

Radice, R. "Philo's Theology and Theory of Creation." Pages 124-45 in *The Cambridge Companion to Philo*. Edited by A. Kamesar. Cambridge: Cambridge University Press, 2009.

Räisänen, H. "Galatians 2.16 and Paul's Break with Judaism." *New Testament Studies* 31 (1985): 543-53.

———. "Römer 9–11: Analyse eines geistigen Ringes." *Aufstieg und Niedergang der römischen Welt* 2.25.4: 2891-939.

———. "Paul, God, and Israel: Romans 9–11 in Recent Research." Pages 127-208 in *The Social World of Formative Christianity and Judaism*. Edited by J. Neusner et al. Philadelphia: Fortress Press, 1988.

Rajak, T. *The Jewish Dialogue with Greece and Rome: Studies in Cultural and Social Interaction*. Leiden: Brill, 2001.

Raurell, F. "From ΔΙΚΑΙΟΣΥΝΗ to ΑΘΑΝΑΣΙΑ." Pages 331-56 in *Treasures of Wisdom:*

Studies in Ben Sira and the Book of Wisdom. Edited by N. Calduch-Benages and J. Vermeylen. Tübingen: Mohr Siebeck, 2010.

Reasoner, M. *The Strong and the Weak. Romans 14.1–15.13 in Context.* Cambridge: Cambridge University Press, 1999.

———. "Romans 9–11 Moves from Margin to Center, from Rejection to Salvation: Four Grids for Recent English-Language Exegesis." Pages 73-89 in *Between Gospel and Election: Explorations in the Interpretation of Romans 9–11.* Edited by F. Wilk and J. R. Wagner. Tübingen: Mohr Siebeck, 2010.

Reinmuth, E. "'Nicht vergeblich' bei Paulus und Pseudo-Philo, *Liber Antiquitatum Biblicarum.*" *Novum Testamentum* 33 (1991): 97-123.

———. *Pseudo-Philo und Lukas: Studien zum Liber Antiquitatum Biblicarum und seiner Bedeutung für die Interpretation des lukanischen Doppelwerks.* Tübingen: Mohr Siebeck, 1994.

Rese, M. "Israel und Kirche in Römer 9." *New Testament Studies* 34 (1988): 208-17.

Rey, A. et al., eds. *Dictionnaire historique de la langue française.* 2 volumes. Paris: Dictionnaire Le Robert, 1992.

Reynolds, J. M., and R. Tannenbaum. *Jews and Godfearers at Aphrodisias.* Cambridge: Cambridge Philological Society, 1987.

Rhodes, P. J. *A Commentary on the Aristotelian* Athenaion Politeia. Oxford: Oxford University Press, 1993.

Rhyne, C. *Faith Establishes the Law.* Chico: Scholars Press, 1981.

Rich, J. "Patronage and International Relations in the Roman Republic." Pages 117-35 in *Patronage in Ancient Society.* Edited by A. Wallace-Hadrill. London: Routledge, 1989.

Richardson, P. *Israel in the Apostolic Church.* Cambridge: Cambridge University Press, 1969.

Riches, J. K. *Galatians through the Centuries.* Oxford: Blackwell, 2008.

Robinson, D. W. "Distinction between Jewish and Gentile Believers in Galatians." *Australian Biblical Review* 13 (1965): 29-48.

Rowe, C. K. "Romans 10:13: What Is the Name of the Lord?" *Horizons in Biblical Theology* 22 (2000): 135-73.

Royse, J. R. "The Works of Philo." Pages 32-64 in *The Cambridge Companion to Philo.* Edited by A. Kamesar. Cambridge: Cambridge University Press, 2009.

Ruether, R. Radford. *Faith and Fratricide: The Theological Roots of Anti-Semitism.* New York: Seabury Press, 1974.

Runia, D. *Philo of Alexandria and the Timaeus of Plato.* Leiden: Brill, 1986.

Saak, E. L. *High Way to Heaven: The Augustinian Platform between Reform and Reformation 1292-1524.* Leiden: Brill, 2002.

Sahlins, M. *Stone Age Economics.* 2nd edition. London: Routledge, 2004.

Sakenfeld, K. D. *The Meaning of* Hesed *in the Hebrew Bible.* Missoula: Scholars Press, 1978.

Saller, R. P. *Personal Patronage under the Early Empire.* Cambridge: Cambridge University Press, 1982.

———. "Patronage and Friendship in Early Imperial Rome: Drawing the Distinction." Pages 49-62 in *Patronage in Ancient Society.* Edited by A. Wallace-Hadrill. London: Routledge, 1989.

———. "Status and Patronage." Pages 817-54 in *The Cambridge Ancient History.* Volume

11: *The High Empire.* Edited by A. Bowman et al. 2nd edition. Cambridge: Cambridge University Press, 2000.

Sampley, J. P. "Romans and Galatians: Comparison and Contrast." Pages 315-39 in *Understanding the Word: Essays in Honor of Bernhard W. Anderson.* Edited by J. T. Butler et al. Sheffield: JSOT Press, 1985.

———. "The Weak and the Strong: Paul's Careful and Crafty Rhetorical Strategy in Romans 14:1–15:13." Pages 40-52 in *The Social World of the First Christians: Essays in Honor of Wayne A. Meeks.* Edited by L. M. White and O. L. Yarbrough. Minneapolis: Augsburg Fortress, 1995.

Sanders, E. P. "Patterns of Religion in Paul and Rabbinic Judaism: A Holistic Method of Comparison." *Harvard Theological Review* 66 (1973): 455-78.

———. "The Covenant as a Soteriological Category and the Nature of Salvation in Palestinian and Hellenistic Judaism." Pages 11-44 in *Jews, Greeks, and Christians: Studies in Honor of W. D. Davies.* Edited by R. Hammerton-Kelly and R. Scroggs. Leiden: Brill, 1976.

———. *Paul and Palestinian Judaism.* London: SCM Press, 1977.

———. "Jewish Association with Gentiles and Galatians 2.1-14." Pages 170-88 in *The Conversation Continues: Studies in Paul and John in Honor of J. Louis Martyn.* Edited by R. T. Fortna and B. R. Gaventa. Nashville: Abingdon Press, 1990.

———. *Judaism: Practice and Belief, 63 B.C.E.–66 C.E.* London: SCM Press, 1992.

———. "Jesus, Paul and Judaism." *Aufstieg und Niedergang der römischen Welt* 2.25.1: 390-450.

———. *Paul, the Law, and the Jewish People.* Philadelphia: Fortress Press, 1983.

Sandmel, S. *Philo's Place in Judaism: A Study of Conceptions of Abraham in Jewish Literature.* Cincinnati: Hebrew Union College Press, 1971.

Sandnes, K. O. *Paul — One of the Prophets? A Contribution to the Apostle's Self-Understanding.* Tübingen: Mohr Siebeck, 1991.

Sänger, D. *Die Verkündigung des Gekreuzigten und Israel.* Tübingen: Mohr Siebeck, 1994.

———. " 'Das Gesetz ist unser παιδαγωγός geworden bis zu Christus' (Gal 3,24)." Pages 236-60 in *Das Gesetz im frühen Judentum und im Neuen Testament.* Edited by D. Sänger and M. Konradt. Göttingen: Vandenhoeck & Ruprecht, 2006.

Satlow, M. L., ed. *The Gift in Antiquity.* Chichester: Wiley-Blackwell, 2013.

Schäfer, R. "Melanchthon's Interpretation of Romans 5.15: His Departure from the Augustinian Concept of Grace Compared to Luther's." Pages 79-104 in *Philip Melanchthon (1497-1560) and the Commentary.* Edited by T. J. Wengert and M. P. Graham. Sheffield: Sheffield Academic Press, 1997.

Scheidel, W., and S. von Reden, eds. *The Ancient Economy.* Edinburgh: Edinburgh University Press, 2002.

Scheidel, W., I. Harris, and R. Saller, eds. *The Cambridge Economic History of the Greco-Roman World.* Cambridge: Cambridge University Press, 2007.

Schewe, S. *Die Galater zurückgewinnen: Paulinische Strategien in Galater 5 und 6.* Göttingen: Vandenhoeck & Ruprecht, 2005.

Schlier, H. *Der Brief an die Galater.* Kritisch-exegeticher Kommentar. Göttingen: Vandenhoeck & Ruprecht, 1971.

Schliesser, B. *Abraham's Faith in Romans 4.* Tübingen: Mohr Siebeck, 2007.

Schmid, U. *Marcion und sein Apostolos.* Berlin: de Gruyter, 1995.

Schmitt, A. "Struktur, Herkunft und Bedeutung der Beispielreihe in Weish 10." *Biblische Zeitschrift* 21 (1977): 1-22.

———. *Das Buch der Weisheit.* Würzburg. Echter Verlag, 1986.

Schnelle, U. *Paulus: Leben und Denken.* Berlin: de Gruyter, 2003.

Schnider, F., and W. Stenger. *Studien zum neutestamentlichen Briefformular.* Leiden: Brill, 1987.

Schreiner, J. *Das 4. Buch Esra.* Jüdische Schriften aus hellenistisch-römischer Zeit 5/4. Gütersloh: Mohn, 1981.

Schrenk, G. "Was bedeutet 'Israel Gottes'?" *Judaica* 5 (1949): 81-94.

———. "Der Segenswunsch nach der Kampfepistel." *Judaica* 6 (1950): 170-90.

Schrift, A. D., ed. *The Logic of the Gift: Toward an Ethic of Generosity.* London: Routledge, 1997.

Schröder, B. *Die "väterlichen Gesetze": Flavius Josephus als Vermittler von Halachah an Griechen und Römer.* Tübingen: Mohr Siebeck, 1996.

Schuller, E. M. "Recent Scholarship on the *Hodayot* 1993-2010." *Currents in Biblical Research* 10 (2011): 119-62.

Schuller, E. M., and L. DiTommaso. "A Bibliography of the Hodayot, 1948-1996." *Dead Sea Discoveries* 4 (1997): 55-101.

Schulz, S. "Zur Rechtfertigung aus Gnaden in Qumran und bei Paulus." *Zeitschrift für Theologie und Kirche* 56 (1959): 155-85.

Schütz, J. H. *Paul and the Anatomy of Apostolic Authority.* Cambridge: Cambridge University Press, 1975.

Schwartz, D. R. " 'Judean' or 'Jew'? How Should We Translate *ioudaios* in Josephus?" Pages 3-28 in *Jewish Identity in the Greco-Roman World.* Edited by J. Frey, D. R. Schwartz, and S. Gripentrog. Leiden: Brill, 2007.

———. "Philo, His Family, and His Times." Pages 9-31 in *The Cambridge Companion to Philo.* Edited by A. Kamesar. Cambridge: Cambridge University Press, 2009.

Schwartz, S. "Josephus in Galilee: Rural Patronage and Social Breakdown." Pages 290-308 in *Josephus and the History of the Graeco-Roman Period.* Edited by F. Parente and J. Sievers. Leiden: Brill, 2004.

———. *Were the Jews a Mediterranean Society?* Princeton: Princeton University Press, 2010.

Schwenk-Bressler, U. *Sapientia Salomonis als ein Beispiel frühjüdischer Textauslegung.* Frankfurt am Main: Peter Lang, 1993.

Scott, J. C. *The Weapons of the Weak: Everyday Forms of Peasant Resistance.* New Haven: Yale University Press, 1985.

———. *Domination and the Arts of Resistance: Hidden Transcripts.* New Haven: Yale University Press, 1990.

Scott, J. M. *Adoption as Sons of God: An Exegetical Investigation into the Background of 'ΥΙΟΘΕΣΙΑ in the Pauline Corpus.* Tübingen: Mohr Siebeck, 1992.

———. " 'For as Many as Are of Works of the Law Are under a Curse' (Galatians 3.10)." Pages 187-221 in *Paul and the Scriptures of Israel.* Edited by C. A. Evans and J. A. Sanders. Sheffield: Sheffield Academic Press, 1993.

Seaford, R. *Reciprocity and Ritual: Homer and Tragedy in the Developing City-State.* Oxford: Oxford University Press, 1994.

Sechrest, L. L. *A Former Jew: Paul and the Dialectics of Race.* London: T&T Clark, 2009.

Seifrid, M. A. *Justification by Faith: The Origin and Development of a Central Pauline Theme.* Leiden: Brill, 1992.

———. "Unrighteous by Faith: Apostolic Proclamation in Romans 1:18–3:20." Pages 105-45 in *Justification and Variegated Nomism.* Volume 2: *The Paradoxes of Paul.* Edited by D. A. Carson, P. T. O'Brien, and M. A. Seifrid. Tübingen: Mohr Siebeck, 2004.

Seitz, E. "λογὸν συντελῶν eine Gerichtsankündigung? (Zu Röm 9,27/28)." *Biblische Notizen* 105 (2001): 61-76.

Sekki, A. E. *The Meaning of* Ruaḥ *at Qumran.* Atlanta: Scholars Press, 1989.

Sellin, G. "Hagar und Sara: Religionsgeschichtliche Hintergründe der Schriftallegorese Gal 4, 21-31." Pages 59-84 in *Das Urchristentum in seiner literarischen Geschichte.* Edited by U. Mell et al. Berlin: de Gruyter, 1999.

Siegert, F. *Argumentation bei Paulus, gezeigt an Röm 9–11.* Tübingen: Mohr Siebeck, 1985.

———. "Philo and the New Testament." Pages 175-209 in *The Cambridge Companion to Philo.* Edited by A. Kamesar. Cambridge: Cambridge University Press, 2009.

Sigaud, L. "The Vicissitudes of *The Gift.*" *Social Anthropology* 10 (2002): 335-58.

Silber, I. "Modern Philanthropy: Reassessing the Viability of a Maussian Perspective." Pages 134-50 in *Marcel Mauss: A Centenary Tribute.* Edited by W. James and N. J. Allen. New York: Berghahn Books, 1998.

Silva, M. "Faith versus Works of Law in Galatians." Pages 217-48 in *Justification and Variegated Nomism.* Volume 2: *The Paradoxes of Paul.* Edited by D. A. Carson, P. T. O'Brien, and M. A. Seifrid. Tübingen: Mohr Siebeck, 2004.

Simonsen, D. "Ein Midrasch 4. Buch Ezra." Pages 270-78 in *Festschrift zum Israel Lewy's 70. Geburtstag.* Edited by M. Brann and J. Elbogen. Breslau: Marcus, 1911.

Sjöberg, E. *Gott und Sünder im palästinischen Judentum.* Stuttgart: Kohlhammer, 1938.

Skottene, R. *Grace and Gift: An Analysis of a Central Motif in Martin Luther's* Rationis Latomianae Confutatio. Frankfurt am Main: P. Lang, 2007.

Sly, D. *Philo's Perception of Women.* Scholars Press: Atlanta, 1990.

Smith, B. D. *The Tension between God as Righteous Judge and as Merciful in Early Judaism.* Lanham: University Press of America, 2005.

———. *What Must I Do to Be Saved? Paul Parts Company with His Jewish Heritage.* Sheffield: Phoenix Press, 2007.

Söding, T. *Das Liebesgebot bei Paulus. Die Mahnung zur Agape im Rahmen der paulinischen Ethik.* Münster: Aschendorff, 1995.

———. "Verheißung und Erfüllung im Lichte paulinischer Theologie." *New Testament Studies* 47 (2001): 146-70.

Spicq, C. *Theological Lexicon of the New Testament.* 3 volumes. Peabody: Hendrickson, 1994.

Sprinkle, P. M. *Law and Life: The Interpretation of Leviticus 18:5 in Early Judaism and in Paul.* Tübingen: Mohr Siebeck, 2008.

———. *Paul and Judaism Revisited: A Study of Divine and Human Agency in Salvation.* Downers Grove: InterVarsity Press, 2013.

Stanley, C., ed. *The Colonized Apostle: Paul through Postcolonial Eyes*. Minneapolis: Fortress Press, 2011.

Starr, J., and T. Engberg-Pedersen, eds. *Early Christian Paraenesis in Context*. Berlin: de Gruyter, 2005.

Stegemann, H., with E. Schuller (and translation by C. Newsom). *1QHodayot*[a]. Discoveries in the Judaean Desert XL. Oxford: Clarendon Press, 2009.

Steinmetz, D. C. *Luther and Staupitz: An Essay in the Intellectual Origins of the Protestant Reformation*. Durham, NC: Duke University Press, 1980.

Stendahl, K. *Paul among Jews and Gentiles*. London: SCM Press, 1977.

———. *Final Account: Paul's Letter to the Romans*. Minneapolis: Fortress Press, 1995.

Stenschke, C. "Römer 9–11 als Teil des Römerbriefes." Pages 197-225 in *Between Gospel and Election: Explorations in the Interpretation of Romans 9–11*. Edited by F. Wilk and J. R. Wagner. Tübingen: Mohr Siebeck, 2010.

Sterling, G. "Platonizing Moses: Philo and Middle Platonism." *Studia Philonica Annual* 5 (1993): 96-111.

———. "Prepositional Metaphysics in Jewish Wisdom Speculation and Early Christological Hymns." *Studia Philonica Annual* 9 (1997): 219-38.

Stone, M. E. "Coherence and Inconsistency in the Apocalypses: The Case of 'The End' in 4 Ezra." *Journal of Biblical Literature* 102 (1983): 229-43.

———. *Features of the Eschatology of IV Esra*. Atlanta: Scholars Press, 1989.

———. *Fourth Ezra*. Hermeneia. Minneapolis: Fortress Press, 1990.

Stowers, S. *The Diatribe and Paul's Letter to the Romans*. Chico: Scholars Press, 1981.

———. *A Rereading of Romans: Justice, Jews and Gentiles*. New Haven: Yale University Press, 1994.

Strathern, M. *The Gender of the Gift*. Berkeley: University of California Press, 1998.

Stuhlmacher, P. "The Purpose of Romans." Pages 231-42 in *The Romans Debate*. Revised and expanded edition. Edited by K. P. Donfried. Edinburgh: T&T Clark, 1991.

———. *Revisiting Paul's Doctrine of Justification: A Challenge to the New Perspective*. With an essay by D. A. Hagner. Downers Grove: InterVarsity, 2001.

Sumney, J. L. *Identifying Paul's Opponents: The Question of Method in 2 Corinthians*. Sheffield: JSOT Press, 1990.

———. *"Servants of Satan," "False Brothers" and Other Opponents of Paul*. Sheffield: Sheffield Academic Press, 1999.

Talbert, C. H. "Paul, Judaism, and the Revisionists." *Catholic Biblical Quarterly* 63 (2001): 1-22.

Talmon, S., et al. *Qumran Cave 4. XVI, Calendrical Texts*. Oxford: Clarendon Press, 2001.

Tanner, K. *Economy of Grace*. Minneapolis: Fortress Press, 2005.

Termini, C. *Le Potenze di Dio: Studio su δύναμις in Filone di Alessandria*. Rome: Institutum Patristicum Augustinianum, 2000.

———. "Philo's Thought within the Context of Middle Platonism." Pages 95-123 in *The Cambridge Companion to Philo*. Edited by A. Kamesar. Cambridge: Cambridge University Press, 2009.

Testart, A. "Uncertainties of the 'Obligation to Reciprocate': A Critique of Mauss." Pages 97-110 in *Marcel Mauss: A Centenary Tribute*. Edited by W. James and N. J. Allen. New York: Berghahn Books, 1998.

Theobald, M. *Studien zum Römerbrief.* Tübingen: Mohr Siebeck, 2001.

Thielman, F. *From Plight to Solution: A Jewish Framework for Understanding Paul's View of the Law in Romans and Galatians.* Leiden: Brill, 1989.

Thompson, A. L. *Responsibility for Evil in the Theodicy of IV Ezra.* Missoula: Scholars Press, 1977.

Thorsteinsson, R. M. *Paul's Interlocutor in Romans 2.* Stockholm: Almqvist & Wicksell, 2003.

———. *Roman Christianity and Roman Stoicism: A Comparative Study of Ancient Morality.* Oxford: Oxford University Press, 2010.

Tigchelaar, E. J. C. *To Increase Learning for the Understanding Ones: Reading and Reconstructing the Fragmentary Early Jewish Sapiential Text 4QInstruction.* Leiden: Brill, 2001.

Titmuss, R. M. *The Gift Relationship: From Human Blood to Social Policy.* London: George Allen & Unwin, 1970.

Tobin, T. *Paul's Rhetoric in Its Context: The Argument of Romans.* Peabody: Hendrickson, 2004.

Torrance, T. F. *The Doctrine of Grace in the Apostolic Fathers.* Edinburgh: Oliver and Boyd, 1948.

Trigg, J. D. *Baptism in the Theology of Martin Luther.* Leiden: Brill, 1994.

Ukwuegbu, B. O. "Paraenesis, Identity-Defining Norms, or Both? Galatians 5:13–6:10 in the Light of Social Identity Theory." *Catholic Biblical Quarterly* 70 (2008): 538-59.

van der Horst, P. W. "'Only Then Will Israel Be Saved': A Short Note on the Meaning of καὶ οὕτως in Romans 11.26." *Journal of Biblical Literature* 119 (2000): 521-25.

van Kooten, G. *Paul's Anthropology in Context: The Image of God, Assimilation to God, and Tripartite Man in Ancient Judaism, Ancient Philosophy, and Early Christianity.* Tübingen: Mohr Siebeck, 2008.

Vanhoye, A. "Mesure ou démesure en Sap. 12.22." *Recherches de science religieuse* 50 (1962): 530-37.

VanLandingham, C. *Judgment and Justification in Early Judaism and the Apostle Paul.* Peabody, MA: Hendrickson, 2006.

Veyne, P. *Bread and Circuses.* Abridged and translated by B. Pearce. London: Penguin, 1990.

Völker, W. *Fortschritt und Vollendung bei Philo von Alexandrien: Eine Studie zur Geschichte der Frömmigkeit.* Leipzig: J. C. Hinrichs, 1938.

Vollenweider, S. *Freiheit als neue Schöpfung: Eine Untersuching zur Eleutheria bei Paulus und in seiner Umwelt.* Göttingen: Vandenhoeck & Ruprecht, 1989.

von Reden, S. *Exchange in Ancient Greece.* London: Routledge, 1995.

Vouga, F. *An die Galater.* Handbuch zum Neuen Testament 10. Tübingen: Mohr Siebeck, 1998.

Wagner, J. R. "The Christ, Servant of Jew and Gentile: A Fresh Approach to Romans 15:8-9." *Journal of Biblical Literature* 116 (1997): 473-85.

———. *Heralds of the Good News: Isaiah and Paul in Concert in the Letter to the Romans.* Leiden: Brill, 2002.

Wakefield, A. H. *Where to Live: The Hermeneutical Significance of Paul's Citations from Scripture in Galatians 3:1-14.* Atlanta: Society of Biblical Literature, 2003.

Walker, N. "Critical Note: The Renderings of *RASON*." *Journal of Biblical Literature* 81 (1962): 182-84.
Wallace, R. S. *Calvin, Geneva, and the Reformation*. Edinburgh: Scottish Academic Press, 1988.
Wallace-Hadrill, A., ed. *Patronage in Ancient Society*. London: Routledge, 1989.
———. "Patronage in Roman Society: From Republic to Empire." Pages 63-87 in *Patronage in Ancient Society*. Edited by A. Wallace-Hadrill. London: Routledge, 1989.
Walter, N. "Zur Interpretation von Römer 9–11." *Zeitschrift für Theologie und Kirche* 81 (1984): 172-95.
Wannenwetsch, B. "Luther's Moral Theology." Pages 120-35 in *The Cambridge Companion to Martin Luther*. Edited by D. K. McKim. Cambridge: Cambridge University Press, 2003.
Watanabe, N. "Calvin's Second Catechism: Its Predecessors and Its Environment." Pages 224-32 in *Sacrae Scripturae Professor: Calvin as Confessor of Holy Scripture*. Edited by W. H. Neuser. Grand Rapids: Eerdmans, 1994.
Watson, F. *Paul and the Hermeneutics of Faith*. Grand Rapids: Eerdmans, 2004.
———. *Paul, Judaism and the Gentiles: Beyond the New Perspective*. 2nd edition. Grand Rapids: Eerdmans, 2007.
———. "By Faith (of Christ): An Exegetical Dilemma and Its Scriptural Solution." Pages 147-63 in *The Faith of Jesus Christ: Exegetical, Biblical and Theological Studies*. Edited by M. Bird and P. M. Sprinkle. Milton Keynes: Paternoster Press, 2009.
Watson, N. "Some Observations on the Use of ΔΙΚΑΙΟΩ in the Septuagint." *Journal of Biblical Literature* 79 (1960): 255-66.
Wawrykow, J. P. *God's Grace and Human Action: "Merit" in the Theology of Thomas Aquinas*. Notre Dame: University of Notre Dame, 1995.
Way, D. W. *The Lordship of Christ: Ernst Käsemann's Interpretation of Paul's Theology*. Oxford: Clarendon Press, 1991.
Weber, M. *Economy and Society: An Outline of Interpretative Sociology*. Translated by E. Fischoff et al. Berkeley: University of California Press, 1978.
Webster, J. *Barth's Ethics of Reconciliation*. Cambridge: Cambridge University Press, 1995.
———. *Barth's Moral Theology*. Edinburgh: T&T Clark, 1998.
Wedderburn, A. J. M. *The Reasons for Romans*. Edinburgh: T&T Clark, 1988.
Weiner, A. *Women of Value, Men of Renown: New Perspectives in Trobriand Exchange*. Austin: University of Texas Press, 1976.
———. *Inalienable Possessions: The Paradox of Keeping-while-Giving*. Berkeley: University of California Press, 1992.
Welborn, L. L. "'That There May Be Equality': The Contexts and Consequences of a Pauline Ideal." *New Testament Studies* 57 (2012): 73-90.
Westerholm, S. "Paul and the Law in Romans 9–11." Pages 215-37 in *Paul and the Mosaic Law*. Edited by J. D. G. Dunn. Tübingen: Mohr Siebeck, 1996.
———. *Perspectives Old and New on Paul: The "Lutheran" Paul and His Critics*. Grand Rapids: Eerdmans, 2004.
———. "Paul's Anthropological 'Pessimism' in Its Jewish Context." Pages 71-98 in *Divine and Human Agency in Paul and His Cultural Environment*. Edited by J. M. G. Barclay and S. J. Gathercole. London: T&T Clark, 2006.

Wetter, G. P. *Charis: Ein Beitrag zur Geschichte des ältesten Christentums.* Leipzig: Hinrichs Buchhandlung, 1913.

Wetzel, J. *Augustine and the Limits of Virtue.* Cambridge: Cambridge University Press, 1992.

———. "Snares of Truth: Augustine on Free Will and Predestination." Pages 124-41 in *Augustine and His Critics: Essays in Honour of Gerald Bonner.* Edited by R. Dodaro and G. Lawless. London: Routledge, 2000.

Wilckens, U. "Die Rechtfertigung Abrahams nach Römer 4." Pages 33-49 in *Rechtfertigung als Freiheit: Paulusstudien.* Neukirchen: Neukirchener Verlag, 1974.

———. *Der Brief an die Römer.* 3 volumes. Evangelisch-katholischer Kommentar 6. Zürich: Benziger; Neukirchen-Vluyn: Neukirchener Verlag, 1978-1982.

Wilk, F. "Rahmen und Aufbau von Römer 9–11." Pages 227-53 in *Between Gospel and Election: Explorations in the Interpretation of Romans 9–11.* Edited by F. Wilk and J. R. Wagner. Tübingen: Mohr Siebeck, 2010.

Williams, S. K. "The 'Righteousness of God' in Romans." *Journal of Biblical Literature* 99 (1980): 241-90.

———. *Galatians.* Nashville: Abingdon Press, 1997.

Williams, T. "The Curses of Bouzyges: New Evidence." *Mnemosyne* 15 (1962): 396-98.

Wilson, T. " 'Under Law' in Galatians: A Pauline Theological Abbreviation." *Journal of Theological Studies* 56 (2005): 362-92.

———. *The Curse of the Law and the Crisis in Galatia.* Tübingen: Mohr Siebeck, 2007.

Windisch, H. *Die Frömmigkeit Philos und ihre Bedeutung für das Christentum: Eine Religionsgeschichtliche Studie.* Leipzig: J. C. Hinrichs, 1909.

Winger, M. "The Law of Christ." *New Testament Studies* 46 (2000): 537-46.

Winston, D. *The Wisdom of Solomon.* Anchor Bible 43. New York: Doubleday, 1979.

———. *The Ancestral Philosophy: Hellenistic Philosophy in Second Temple Judaism.* Providence: Brown Judaic Studies, 2001.

———. "A Century of Research on the Book of Wisdom." Pages 1-18 in *The Book of Wisdom in Modern Research: Studies on Tradition, Redaction, and Theology.* Edited by A. Passaro and G. Bellia. Berlin: de Gruyter, 2005.

Winston, D., and J. Dillon. *Two Treatises of Philo of Alexandria: A Commentary on* De Gigantibus *and* Quod Deus Sit Immutabilis. Chico: Scholars Press, 1983.

Winter, B. W. *Seek the Welfare of the City: Christians as Benefactors and Citizens.* Grand Rapids: Eerdmans, 1994.

———. "The Imperial Cult and Early Christians in Pisidian Antioch (Acts XIII 13-50 and Gal VI 11-18)." Pages 65-75 in *Actes du Ier Congrès International sur Antioche de Pisidie.* Edited by T. Drew-Bear et al. Lyon: Kocaeli, 2002.

———. *Paul and Philo among the Sophists: Alexandrian and Corinthian Responses to a Julio-Claudian Movement.* 2nd edition. Grand Rapids: Eerdmans, 2002.

Witherington, B., III. *Grace in Galatia: A Commentary on St. Paul's Letter to the Galatians.* Edinburgh: T&T Clark, 1998.

Witulski, T. *Die Adressaten des Galaterbriefes: Untersuchungen zur Gemeinde von Antiochia ad Pisidiam.* Göttingen: Vandenhoeck & Ruprecht, 2000.

Wobbe, J. *Der Charis-Gedanke bei Paulus.* Münster: Aschendorff, 1932.

Wolter, M. "Das Israelproblem nach Gal 4,21-31 und Röm 9–11." *Zeitschrift für Theologie und Kirche* 107 (2010): 1-30.
———. *Paulus: Ein Grundriss seiner Theologie.* Neukirchen: Neukirchener Verlag, 2011.
Wright, D. "Calvin's Role in Church History." Pages 277-88 in *The Cambridge Companion to John Calvin.* Edited by D. K. McKim. Cambridge: Cambridge University Press, 2004.
Wright, N. T. "The Paul of History and the Apostle of Faith." *Tyndale Bulletin* 29 (1978): 61-88.
———. *The Climax of the Covenant.* Edinburgh: T&T Clark, 1991.
———. "Romans and the Theology of Paul." Pages 30-67 in *Pauline Theology.* Volume 3: *Romans.* Edited by D. M. Hay and E. E. Johnson. Minneapolis: Fortress Press, 1995.
———. "The Law in Romans 2." Pages 131-50 in *Paul and the Mosaic Law.* Edited by J. D. G. Dunn. Tübingen: Mohr Siebeck, 1996.
———. "The Letter to the Galatians: Exegesis and Theology." Pages 205-36 in *Between Two Horizons: Spanning New Testament Studies and Systematic Theology.* Edited by J. B. Green and M. Turner. Grand Rapids: Eerdmans, 2000.
———. "Romans." In *The New Interpreter's Bible,* volume 10. Nashville: Abingdon, 2002.
———. *Paul: Fresh Perspectives.* London: SPCK, 2005.
———. *Justification: God's Plan and Paul's Vision.* London: SPCK, 2009.
———. *Pauline Perspectives: Essays on Paul, 1978–2013.* London: SPCK, 2013.
———. *Paul and the Faithfulness of God.* London: SPCK, 2013.
Xeravits, G. G. *Dualism in Qumran.* London: T&T Clark, 2010.
Yinger, K. L. *Paul, Judaism, and Judgment according to Deeds.* Cambridge: Cambridge University Press, 1999.
Young, N. H. "*Paidagogos:* The Social Setting of a Pauline Metaphor." *Novum Testamentum* 29 (1987): 150-76.
Zahl, P. *Die Rechtfertigungslehre Ernst Käsemanns.* Stuttgart: Calver Verlag, 1996.
Zeller, D. *Juden und Heiden in der Mission des Paulus: Studien zum Römerbrief.* Stuttgart: Verlag Katholisches Bibelwerk, 1976.
———. *Charis bei Philon und Paulus.* Stuttgart: Verlag Katholisches Bibelwerk, 1990.
Zetterholm, M. *The Formation of Christianity in Antioch: A Social-Scientific Approach to the Separation between Judaism and Christianity.* London: Routledge, 2003.
Ziesler, J. A. *The Meaning of Righteousness in Paul: A Linguistic and Theological Enquiry.* Cambridge: Cambridge University Press, 1972.
Žižek, S. *The Ticklish Subject.* London: Verso, 1999.
Zoccali, C. "And So All Israel Will Be Saved: Competing Interpretations of Romans 11.26 in Pauline Scholarship." *Journal for the Study of the New Testament* 30 (2008): 289-318.
Zurli, E. "La Giustificazione 'solo per grazia' in *1QS* X,9–XI e *1QH^{a}*." *Revue de Qumran* 79 (2002): 445-77.

Index of Authors

Index of Subjects

Index of Ancient Sources

CLASSICAL GREEK AND LATIN AUTHORS

PAPYRI

INSCRIPTIONS